PSYCHOLOGY APPLIED TO MODERN LIFE

Adjustment in the 90s

Third Edition

About the Authors

Wayne Weiten is a graduate of Bradley University and earned his Ph.D. from the University of Illinois at Chicago in 1981. He is the author of *Psychology: Themes and Variations* (Brooks/Cole, 1989) and is Professor of Psychology at the College of DuPage. He has received distinguished teaching awards from Division 2 of the American Psychological Association and the College of DuPage. He has conducted research on a wide range of topics, including cerebral specialization, educational measurement, jury behavior, attribution theory, and pressure as a form of stress.

Margaret A. Lloyd is a graduate of the University of Denver and received her Ph.D. from the University of Arizona in 1973. She is the author of *Adolescence* (Harper & Row, 1985) and is currently Department Head and Professor of Psychology at Georgia Southern University. Her research interests lie in the areas of identity and gender roles.

Robin L. Lashley is a graduate of Allegheny College and earned her Ph.D. from the State University of New York at Albany in 1983. Since that time, she has taught a variety of courses at the Tuscarawas Campus of Kent State University, where she has won awards for outstanding teaching. She has conducted research on taste aversion and opponent-process theory.

PSYCHOLOGY APPLIED TO MODERN LIFE

Adjustment in the 90s

Third Edition

Wayne Weiten
College of DuPage

Margaret A. Lloyd
Georgia Southern University

Robin L. Lashley
Kent State University

Brooks/Cole Publishing Company
Pacific Grove, California

Consulting Editor: Lawrence S. Wrightsman, University of Kansas

Brooks/Cole Publishing Company
A Division of Wadsworth, Inc.

Printed in the United States of America

10 9 8 7 6 5 4 3 2

Library of Congress Cataloging-in-Publication Data

Weiten, Wayne, [date]
    Psychology applied to modern life: adjustment in the 90s / Wayne
Weiten, Margaret A. Lloyd, Robin L. Lashley. — 3rd ed.
        p. cm.
    Includes bibliographical references.
    ISBN 0-534-09708-1
    1. Adjustment (Psychology) 2. Interpersonal relations. 3. Adult-
hood—Psychological aspects. 4. Self-help techniques.
I. Lloyd, Margaret A. (Margaret Ann), [date]. II. Lashley, Robin L. III.
Title.
BF335.W423   1990
158—dC20   90-34952
                                                         CIP

Sponsoring Editor: Claire Verduin
Editorial Associate: Gay C. Bond
Production Coordinator: Fiorella Ljunggren
Production: Nancy Sjoberg, Del Mar Associates
Manuscript Editor: John Bergez
Interior and Cover Design: John Odam
Cover Illustration: Ellen Schuster/The Image Bank West
Chapter-Opening Art Direction: Tom Gould
Interior Illustration: John Odam Design Associates
Photo Researcher and Permissions Editor: Linda L. Rill
Digital Typography: John Odam Design Associates and Del Mar Associates
Imagesetting: Laser Express
Color Separations: Rainbow Graphic Arts, Thompson Type
Printing and Binding: Rand McNally & Company

(Credits continue on p. 539.)

To two pillars of stability in this era of turmoil—my parents
W.W.

For my mentors and my students
M.A.L.

To the most inspiring people I know—my students
R. L. L.

To the Instructor

Many students enter adjustment courses with great expectations. They've ambled through their local bookstores, and in the "Psychology" section they've seen numerous self-help books that offer highly touted recipes for achieving happiness for a mere $4.95. After paying far more money to enroll in a collegiate course that deals with the same issues as the self-help books, many students expect a revelatory experience. However, the majority of us with professional training in psychology or counseling take a rather dim view of self-help books and the pop psychology they represent. We tend to view this literature as oversimplified, intellectually dishonest, and opportunistic. Often we summarily dismiss the pop psychology that so many of our students have embraced. We then try to supplant it with our more sophisticated academic psychology, which is more complex and much less accessible.

In this textbook, we have tried to come to grips with this problem of differing expectations between student and teacher. Our goal has been to produce a comprehensive, serious, research-oriented treatment of the topic of adjustment that also acknowledges the existence of popular psychology and looks critically at its contributions. Our approach involves the following.

• In Chapter 1 we confront the phenomenon of popular self-help books. We try to take the student beneath the seductive surface of such books and analyze some of their typical flaws. Our goal is to make the student a more critical consumer of this type of literature.
• While encouraging a more critical attitude toward self-help books, we do not suggest that they should all be dismissed. Instead, we acknowledge that some of them offer authentic insights. With this in mind, we highlight some of the better books in Recommended Reading boxes sprinkled throughout the text. These recommended readings tie in with the adjacent topical coverage and show the student the interface between academic and popular psychology.
• We try to provide the student with a better appreciation of the merit of the empirical approach. This effort to clarify the role of research, which is rare for an adjustment text, appears in the first chapter.
• Recognizing that adjustment students want to leave the course with concrete, personally useful information, we have ended each chapter with an application section. The Applications are "how to" discussions that address everyday problems. While they focus on issues that are relevant to the content of the particular chapter, they contain more explicit advice than the text proper.

In summary, we have tried to make this book both rigorous and applied. We hope that our approach will help students to better appreciate the value of scientific psychology.

PHILOSOPHY

A certain philosophy is inherent in any systematic treatment of the topic of adjustment. Our philosophy can be summarized as follows:

• *We believe in theoretical eclecticism.* This book will not indoctrinate your students along the lines of any single theoretical orientation. The psychodynamic, behavioral, and humanistic schools of thought are all treated with respect, as are cognitive, biological, and other perspectives.
• *We believe that an adjustment text should be a resource book for students.* We have tried to design this book so that it encourages and facilitates the pursuit of additional information on adjustment-related topics. It should serve as a point of departure for more learning.
• *We believe that effective adjustment requires "taking charge" of one's own life.* Throughout the book we try to promote the notion that active coping efforts are generally superior to passivity and complacency.

CHANGES IN THE THIRD EDITION

One of the exciting things about psychology is that it is not a stagnant discipline. It continues to progress at what seems a faster and faster pace. A good textbook must evolve with the discipline. Although the professors and students who used the first two editions of this book did not clamor for change, there are some significant alterations.

New Authorship

First and foremost is the addition of two coauthors. Margaret (Marky) A. Lloyd and Robin L. Lashley, who each have extensive experience teaching the adjustment course, will help to shepherd this book into the 21st century. In this edition, Marky took responsibility for the revision of Chapters 5, 6, 8, and 10, while Robin revised Chapters 9, 11, and 12. Wayne Weiten revised the remaining chapters and coordinated everyone's efforts to ensure consistency in content and style.

New Content

To improve the book and keep up with new developments in psychology, we have made a variety of content changes—adding and deleting some topics, condensing and reorganizing others. The major alterations from the second edition include the following.

Chapter 1: Adjusting to Modern Life. Material on religious cults and the correlates of happiness has been dropped in favor of expanded coverage of research methods and (in the Application) improving memory.

Chapter 2: Theories of Personality. A discussion of biological perspectives on personality has been added to the coverage of psychodynamic, behavioral, and humanistic perspectives. There is also additional material on the theories of Adler, Skinner, and Bandura.

Chapter 3: Stress and Its Effects. The psychological effects of stress are discussed in more detail, and there is new coverage of optimism and sensation seeking as factors that moderate the impact of stress.

Chapter 4: Coping Processes. The material on self-control through behavior modification has been shortened, and a section on time management has been added. The chapter also includes a new taxonomy of coping strategies along with a revised analysis of the adaptive value of illusions.

Chapter 5: Person Perception. Attribution processes and stereotyping are discussed in more detail. New topics include identity and illusory correlation.

Chapter 6: Interpersonal Communication. The main addition to this chapter is a timely discussion of date rape, which serves as an example of how communication can go awry. The coverage of nonverbal communication includes new material on gender differences and the detection of deception.

Chapter 7: Group Dynamics and Social Influence. This is an entirely new chapter. It covers helping, productivity, and leadership in groups, as well as persuasion, conformity, and obedience.

Chapter 8: Friendship and Love. This chapter contains new material on the repulsion hypothesis, the rules of friendship, the triangular theory of love, and the theory that people relive their early attachment experiences in their romantic relationships.

Chapter 9: Marriage and Intimate Relationships. This chapter includes new data on marital adjustment and voluntary childlessness, as well as significant updates on gay relationships, cohabitation, and the effects of divorce.

Chapter 10: Gender and Behavior. The terminology in this chapter has been revised to reflect changes in the field, and the findings on gender differences in behavior have been extensively updated. The discussion of the relationship between biological factors and gender differences has been expanded, and new material has been added on gender-role transcendence.

Chapter 11: Development in Adolescence and Adulthood. Reflecting increased interest in adult development, we have expanded the coverage of this topic from half a chapter to an entire chapter. New material on adolescence has been inserted, the coverage of adulthood has been expanded, and a section on effective parenting has been included as an Application.

Chapter 12: Vocational Development and Work. The coverage of vocations and work has also been increased from a half chapter to a full chapter. There is new material on women in the workplace, motivation in the workplace, work-related stress, workaholics, and looking for a job.

Chapter 13: Development and Expression of Sexuality. New or expanded topics in our discussion of sexuality include the hormonal regulation of sexual behavior, media influences on sexuality, variations in sexual scripts, contraception, and sexually transmitted diseases.

Chapter 14: Psychology and Physical Health. As projected in the last edition of this book, health psychology is becoming a standard topic in adjustment texts. Our coverage includes new data on Type A behavior, smoking, obesity, exercise, and AIDS.

Chapter 15: Psychological Disorders. The terminology in this chapter has been revised to be consistent with DSM-III-R. The chapter presents expanded coverage of the epidemiology of mental illness and new insights regarding the etiology of anxiety disorders, mood disorders, and schizophrenic disorders.

Chapter 16: Psychotherapy. New or expanded topics in this chapter include cognitive therapy, the evaluation of insight therapy, social skills training, and biofeedback.

Other Changes

As you look through this edition, you will see many other changes besides the shifts in content. The experiential exercises that were formerly found in the workbook have been moved into the text. Thus, at the end of each chapter, you will find a Questionnaire and a Personal Probe. To simplify students' reading task, we have deleted the Sidelight Boxes and replaced the running glossary in the margin with a running glossary that is integrated into the flow of the text. You'll also notice that we have significantly upgraded the illustration program to increase its instructional value.

WRITING STYLE

This book has been written with the student reader in mind. We have tried to integrate the technical jargon of our discipline into a relatively informal and down-to-earth writing style. In this edition, we have attempted to streamline and simplify the writing. Most of the chapters are 10%–15% shorter than in the previous edition. Although we believe that readability formulas are overrated, in most chapters we have brought the reading level down about one grade level.

FEATURES

This text contains a number of features intended to stimulate interest and enhance students' learning. These special features include Applications, Recommended Reading boxes, a didactic illustration program, Questionnaires, and Personal Probes.

Applications

The Applications should be of special interest to most students. They are tied to chapter content in a way that should show students how practical applications emerge out of theory and research. Although some of the material covered in these sections shows up frequently in adjustment texts, much of it is unique. Some of the unusual Applications include the following:

- Monitoring Your Stress
- Seeing Through Social Influence Tactics
- Getting Ahead in the Job Game
- Building Self-Esteem
- Dealing with Conflict
- Understanding the Games Couples Play
- Enhancing Sexual Relationships
- Becoming an Effective Parent

Recommended Reading Boxes

Recognizing students' interest in self-help books, we have sifted through hundreds of them to identify some that may be especially useful. These are highlighted in boxes that briefly review the book and include a provocative excerpt or two. These Recommended Reading boxes are placed where they are germane to the material being covered in the text. Some of the recommended books are very well known, while others are obscure. Although we make it clear that we don't endorse every idea in every book, we think they all have something worthwhile to offer. This feature replaces the conventional suggested readings lists that usually appear at the ends of chapters, where they are almost universally ignored by students.

We consider these boxes to be an important element of this book, and we invite your participation in suggesting self-help books to recommend in the next edition. If you have a self-help book that you and your students find exceptionally useful, please write to us about it in care of Brooks/Cole Publishing Company, Pacific Grove, CA 93950.

Didactic Illustration Program

The illustration program is now in full color, and the number of photographs and figures has more than doubled in this edition. Although the illustrations are intended to make the book attractive and help maintain student interest, they are not merely decorative. They have been carefully selected for their didactic value to enhance the educational goals of the text.

Cartoons

Because a little comic relief usually helps keep a student interested, numerous cartoons are sprinkled throughout the book. Like the figures, most of these have been chosen to reinforce ideas in the text. Some of them do exceptional jobs of driving points home.

Questionnaires and Personal Probes

At the end of each chapter there are experiential exercises designed to aid your students in achieving personal insights. The Questionnaires are psychological tests or scales that your students can administer and score for themselves. The Personal Probes consist of questions intended to help students think about themselves relative to issues raised in the text. Most students find these exercises interesting. They can also be fruitful in stimulating class discussion.

LEARNING AIDS

Because this book is rigorous, substantive, and sizable, a number of learning aids have been incorporated into the text to help your students digest the wealth of material:

- The *outline* at the beginning of each chapter provides the student with a preview and overview of what will be covered.
- *Headings* are employed very frequently to keep material well organized.
- *Key terms* are identified with ***italicized boldface*** type to alert students that these are important vocabulary items that are part of psychology's technical language.
- An *integrated running glossary* provides an on-the-spot definition of each key term as it is introduced in the text. These formal definitions are printed in **boldface** type.
- An *alphabetical glossary* is found in the back of the book, since key terms are usually defined in the integrated running glossary only when they are first introduced.
- *Italics* are used liberally throughout the book to emphasize important points.
- *Chapter summaries* are provided to give the student a quick review of the chapter's major points.
- A *Chapter Review* is found at the end of each chapter. Each review includes a list of learning objectives for the chapter, a list of the key terms that were introduced in the chapter, and a list of important theorists and researchers who were discussed in the chapter.

SUPPLEMENTARY MATERIALS

A complete teaching/learning package has been developed to supplement *Psychology Applied to Modern Life*. These supplementary materials have been carefully coordinated to provide effective support for the text.

Instructor's Manual

An Instructor's Manual is available as a convenient aid for your educational endeavors. Written by Patrick Williams, it provides a brief overview of each chapter along with a list of relevant films. It also includes questions for class discussion and/or essay exams. Most important, it contains an extensive collection of multiple-choice questions for objective tests. We're confident that you will find this to be a dependable and usable test bank.

Study Guide
Written by Michael Sosulski, the Study Guide is designed to help students master the information contained in the text. For each chapter, it contains a brief overview, learning objectives, a programmed review, several other types of review exercises, and a self-test. We're confident that your students will find it very helpful in their study efforts.

ACKNOWLEDGMENTS
This book has been an enormous undertaking, and we want to express our gratitude to the innumerable people who have influenced its evolution. To begin with, we must cite the contribution of our students who have taken the adjustment course. It is trite to say that they have been a continuing inspiration—but they have.

The quality of a textbook depends greatly on the quality of the prepublication reviews by psychology professors around the country. The following persons have contributed to the development of this book by providing constructive reviews of various portions of the manuscript in this or earlier editions:

Marsha K. Beauchamp, Mount San Antonio College; John R. Blakemore, Monterey Peninsula College; Paul Bowers, Grayson County College; M. K. Clampit, Bentley College; Dennis Coon, Santa Barbara City College; Salvatore Cullari, Lebanon Valley College; Kenneth S. Davidson, Wayne State University; Richard Fuhrer, University of Wisconsin at Eau Claire; Lee Gillis, Georgia College; Robert Helm, Oklahoma State University; Robert Higgins, Central Missouri State University; Clara E. Hill, University of Maryland; Michael Hirt, Kent State University; Fred J. Hitti, Monroe Community College; Joseph Horvat, Weber State College; Walter Jones, College of DuPage; Wayne Joose, Calvin College; Susan Kupisch, Austin Peay State University; Barbara Hansen Lemme, College of DuPage; Harold List, Massachusetts Bay Community College; Louis A. Martone, Miami–Dade Community College; William T. McReynolds, University of Tampa; Frederick Meeker, California State Polytechnic University, Pomona; John Moritsugu, Pacific Lutheran University; Gary Oliver, College of DuPage; Joseph Philbrick, California State Polytechnic University, Pomona; James Prochaska, University of Rhode Island; Joan Royce, Riverside City College; Thomas K. Saville, Metropolitan State College at Denver; Norman R. Schultz, Clemson University; Dale Simmons, Oregon State University; Kenneth L. Thompson, Central Missouri State University; Robert Thompson, Metropolitan State College; David L. Watson, University of Hawaii; Deborah S. Weber, University of Akron; J. Oscar Williams, Diablo Valley College; Raymond Wolf, Moraine Park Technical Institute; Raymond Wolfe, State University of New York at Geneseo; and Norbert Yager, Henry Ford Community College.

Perceptive professional review has also been provided by Larry Wrightsman, the consulting editor on this project. Superlatives are in order for Claire Verduin, who has served as supervising editor through all three editions of this book. Claire has been a great source of encouragement and insight. Fiorella Ljunggren and Nancy Sjoberg have handled the production of the book with efficiency and enthusiasm. Manuscript editor John Bergez has done an excellent job helping us to sharpen our writing. John Odam deserves great credit for rising to the challenge of creating an attractive design for the book. Linda Rill (permissions and photo editor), Tom Gould (art coordinator for the chapter openings), and Susan Pendleton (proofreader) have also made significant contributions.

In addition, Wayne Weiten would like to thank his wife, Beth Traylor, who has been a steady source of emotional support while enduring the grueling demands of her medical career. Margaret Lloyd would like to thank Anne-Marie Buttimer-Gay and Cynthia McCormick, graduate assistants, and to acknowledge the support and encouragement of colleagues and friends. Robin Lashley would like to thank Karen VonKaenel-Swenn for her assistance with the library research for Chapters 9 and 11.

Wayne Weiten
Margaret A. Lloyd
Robin L. Lashley

Brief Contents

Contents

*1 Adjusting
    to Modern Life*

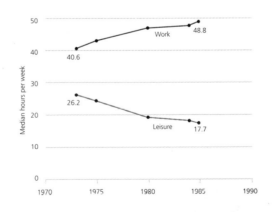

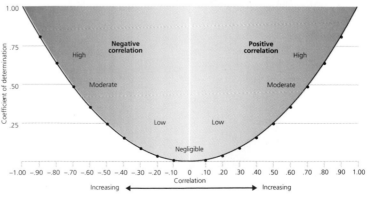

31 *Theories of Personality*

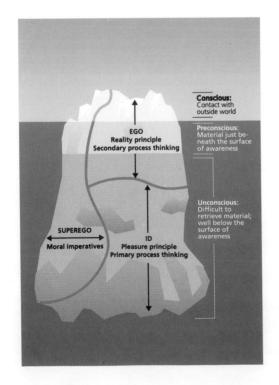

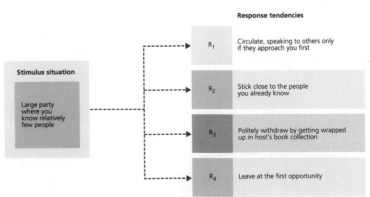

CHAPTER 3

63 *Stress and Its Effects*

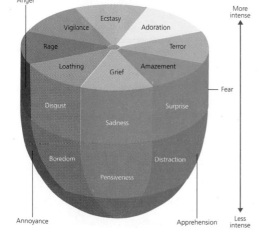

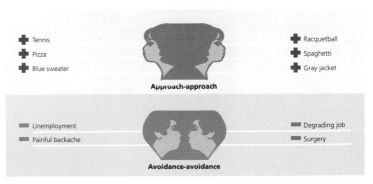

CHAPTER 4

95 *Coping Processes*

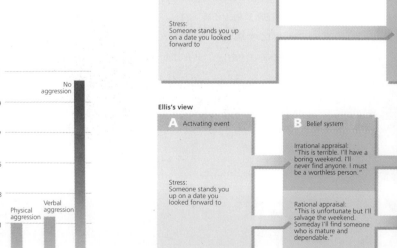

129 *Person Perception*

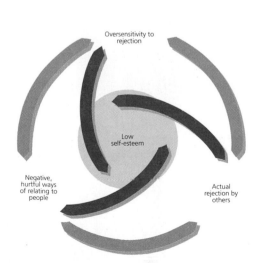

CHAPTER 6

157 *Interpersonal Communi-cation*

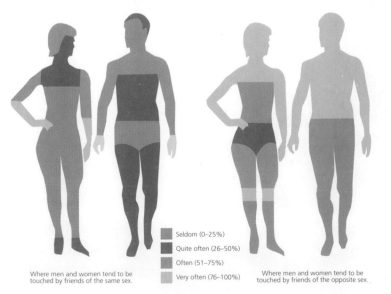

Seldom (0–25%)
Quite often (26–50%)
Often (51–75%)
Very often (76–100%)

Where men and women tend to be touched by friends of the same sex.

Where men and women tend to be touched by friends of the opposite sex.

185 *Group Dynamics and Social Influence*

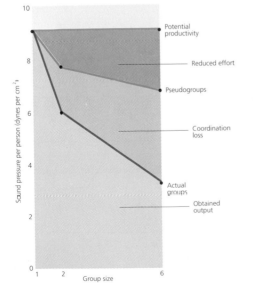

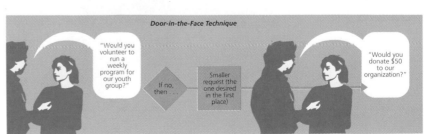

215 *Friendship and Love*

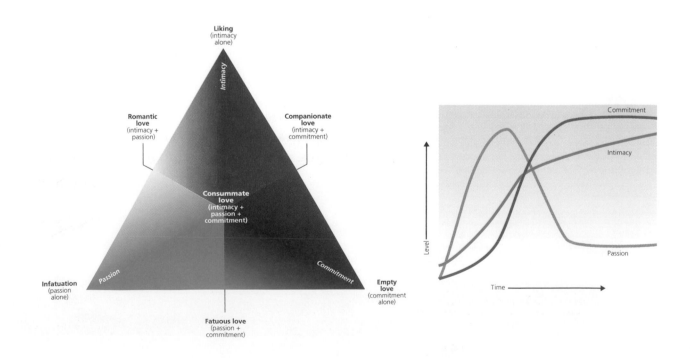

243 *Marriage and Intimate Relationships*

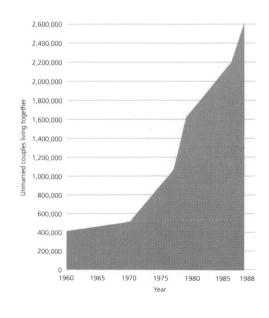

273 *Gender and Behavior*

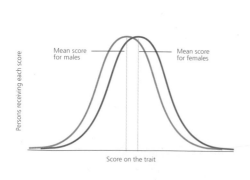

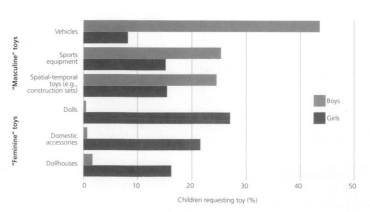

CHAPTER 11

303 *Development in Adolescence and Adulthood*

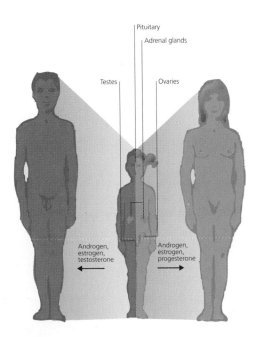

CHAPTER 12

333 *Vocational Development and Work*

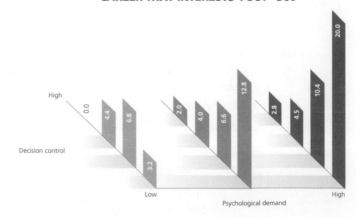

CHAPTER 13

361 *Development and Expression of Sexuality*

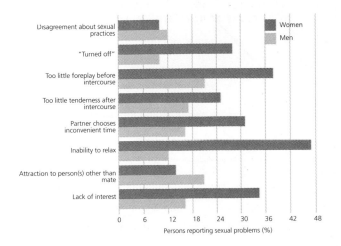

391 *Psychology and Physical Health*

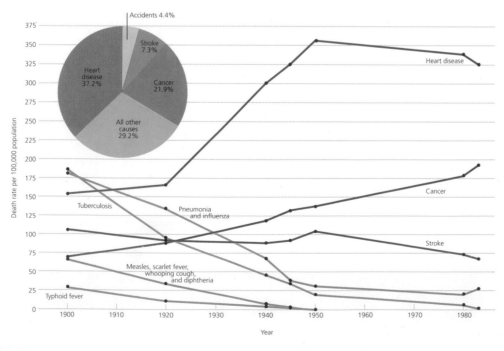

425 *Psychological Disorders*

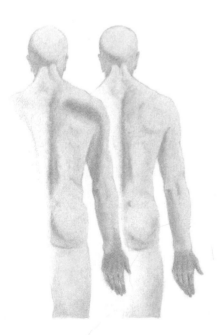

CHAPTER 16

457 *Psychotherapy*

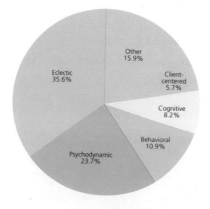

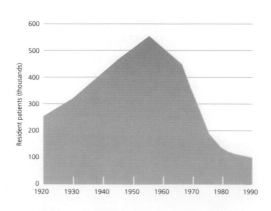

To the Student

In most college courses students spend more time with their textbooks than with their professors. Given this reality, it helps if you like your textbook. Making textbooks likable, however, is a tricky proposition. By its very nature, a textbook must introduce a great many new concepts, ideas, and theories. If it doesn't, it isn't much of a textbook, and instructors won't choose to use it—so you'll never see it anyway. Consequently, we have tried to make this book as likable as possible without compromising the academic content that your instructor demands. Thus, we have tried to make the book lively, informal, engaging, well organized, easy to read, practical, and occasionally humorous. Before you plunge into Chapter 1, let us explain some of the key features that can help you get the most out of the book.

LEARNING AIDS

Mastering the content of this text involves digesting a great deal of information. To facilitate this learning process, we've incorporated a number of instructional aids into the book.

- *Outlines* at the beginning of each chapter provide you with both a preview and overview of what will be covered.
- *Headings* are employed very frequently to keep material well organized.
- *Key terms* are identified with ***italicized boldface*** type to alert you that these are important vocabulary items that are part of psychology's technical language.
- An *integrated running glossary* provides an on-the-spot definition of each key term as it's introduced in the text. These formal definitions are printed in **boldface** type. It is often difficult for students to adapt to the jargon used by scientific disciplines. However, learning this terminology is an essential part of your educational experience. The integrated running glossary is meant to make this learning process as painless as possible.
- An *alphabetical glossary* is provided in the back of the book, since key terms are usually defined in the running glossary only when they are first introduced. If you run into a technical term that was introduced in an earlier chapter and you can't remember its meaning, you can look it up in the alphabetical glossary instead of backtracking to find the place where it first appeared. You can also use the Subject Index to locate references to important terms and concepts.

- *Italics* are used liberally throughout the book to emphasize important points.
- *Chapter summaries* are provided near the end of each chapter (before the chapter's Application) to help you quickly review the chapter's major points.
- A *Chapter Review* is found at the end of each chapter. Each review includes lists of learning objectives, key terms, and important theorists and researchers. Reading over these review materials can help you ensure that you've digested the key points in the chapter.

RECOMMENDED READING BOXES

This text should function as a resource book. To facilitate this goal, particularly interesting books on various topics are highlighted in boxes within the chapters. Each box provides a brief description of the book and a provocative excerpt. We do not agree with everything in these recommended books, but all of them are potentially useful or intriguing. The main purpose of this feature is to introduce you to some of the better self-help books that are available.

STUDY GUIDE

The Study Guide that accompanies this text is an excellent resource designed to assist you in mastering the information contained in the book. It includes a wealth of review exercises to help you organize information and a self-test for assessing your mastery. The Study Guide itself contains a much more detailed description of its features. You should be able to purchase it at your college bookstore. If it is not available there, you can obtain a copy by contacting the publisher (phone: 1-800-354-9706).

A CONCLUDING NOTE

We sincerely hope that you find this book enjoyable. If you have any comments or advice that might help us improve the next edition, please write to us in care of the publisher, Brooks/Cole Publishing Company, Pacific Grove, California 93950. There is a form in the back of the book that you can use to provide us with feedback. Finally, let us wish you good luck. We hope you enjoy your course and learn a great deal.

Wayne Weiten
Margaret A. Lloyd
Robin L. Lashley

PART I

**THE DYNAMICS OF
ADJUSTMENT**

1

Adjusting to
Modern Life

The immense Boeing 747 lumbers into position to accept its human cargo. The eager passengers-to-be scurry on board. In a tower a few hundred yards away, air traffic controllers diligently monitor radar screens, radio transmissions, and digital readouts of weather information. At the reservation desks in the airport terminal, clerks punch up the appropriate ticket information on their computer terminals and quickly process the steady stream of passengers. Mounted on the wall are video terminals displaying up-to-the-minute information on flight arrivals, departures, and delays. Back in the cockpit of the plane, the flight crew calmly scan the complex array of dials, meters, and lights to assess the aircraft's readiness for flight. In a few minutes, the airplane will slice into the cloudy, snow-laden skies above Chicago. In a mere three hours its passengers will be transported from the piercing cold of a Chicago winter to the balmy beaches of the Bahamas. Another everyday triumph for technology will have taken place.

THE PARADOX OF PROGRESS

We are the children of technology. We take for granted such impressive feats as transporting 300 people over 1500 miles in a matter of hours. After all, we live in the space age — a time of unparalleled progress. Our modern Western society has made extraordinary strides in transportation, energy, communication, agriculture, and medicine. Yet in spite of our technological progress, social problems and personal difficulties seem more prevalent and more prominent than ever before. This paradox is evident in many aspects of contemporary life, as seen in the following examples.

POINT. Modern technology has provided us with countless time-saving devices — automobiles, telephones, vacuum cleaners, dishwashers, photocopiers, fax machines. Today, cellular phones allow people to talk to friends or colleagues and battle rush hour at the same time. In a matter of seconds a personal computer can perform calculations that would take months if done by hand. COUNTERPOINT. Nonetheless, most of us complain about not having enough time. Our schedule books are overflowing with appointments, commitments, and plans. Surveys indicate that most of us spend more and more time working and have less and less time for ourselves (see Figure 1.1). As social critic Jeremy Rifkin (1987) notes, "It is ironic in a culture so committed to saving time we feel increasingly deprived of the very thing we value. The modern world of streamlined transportation, instantaneous communication, and time-saving technologies was supposed to free us from the dictates of the clock and provide us with increased leisure. Instead there seems never to be enough time.... Despite our alleged efficiency, as compared to almost every other period in history, we seem to have less time for ourselves and far less time for each other" (p. 19).

POINT. Thanks in large part to technological advances, we live in extraordinary affluence. Undeniably, there are pockets of genuine poverty, but Paul Wachtel (1989) argues convincingly that the middle and upper classes are larger and wealthier than ever before. Most of us take for granted things that were once considered luxuries, such as

Technology has enhanced our lives in uncountable ways—enabling us, for example, to fly across the American continent in a matter of hours. But this same technology has also complicated our lives in innumerable ways—consider the hassles involved in dealing with airports and air travel.

color television and air-conditioning. People spend vast amounts of money on expensive automobiles, stereo systems, video decks, clothing, and travel. Wachtel quotes a New York museum director who asserts that "shopping is the chief cultural activity in the United States" (p. 23). COUNTERPOINT. In spite of this economic abundance, Wachtel notes that a "sense of economic decline is widespread nowadays.... [We feel] that declining productivity has pinched our pocketbooks, that inflation has eaten up our buying power, that we can't catch up, much less get ahead" (p. 9). According to Wachtel, our economic system's commitment to growth, coupled with the effects of mass media advertising, has created an insatiable thirst for consumption. Although our standard of living has improved, most of us feel like we still need more goods and services. Rich by any previous standard, we are nevertheless subjectively distressed about our economic plight.

POINT. In recent years, our ability to process, store, and communicate information has improved dramatically. Using satellites, we can beam live telecasts around the globe almost instantaneously. We can access on-line computerized databases to track the stock market or to check airline schedules. Even more impressive, we can store the entire *Encyclopaedia Britannica* on a couple of compact disks.

COUNTERPOINT. Yet Richard Saul Wurman (1989) asserts that nearly everyone suffers from *information anxiety*—concern about the ever-widening gap between what we understand and what we think we *should* understand. The crux of the problem is the explosive growth of available information, which now doubles in amount about every five years. Wurman points out that a single weekday edition of the *New York Times* "contains more information than the average person was likely to come across in a lifetime in seventeenth-century England" (p. 32). According to Wurman, people exhibit symptoms of information anxiety when they complain about stacks of unread periodicals, when they bemoan their inability to keep up with what's going on, when they pretend that they are familiar with a book or artist that they've never heard of, when they feel overwhelmed by the 50 or 60 channels available on cable TV, and when they feel bewildered by the intricacies of their computers, VCRs, and digital watches.

POINT. Agricultural productivity has moved forward by leaps and bounds thanks to improvements in farm machinery, fertilizers, and pesticides. Since 1820, food output per farmer in the United States has increased eightfold. In 1983, the average farm worker produced enough food to feed 77 people (Miller, 1985).

Figure 1.1. Trends in the time devoted to work and leisure. Harris Survey respondents were asked to estimate how many hours per week they devoted to their job, school, housecleaning, and chores (work) as opposed to relaxation, hobbies, and entertainment (leisure). Since the early 1970s, the amount of time devoted to leisure has been declining, while the time devoted to work has been increasing.

COUNTERPOINT. In spite of these improvements in agricultural output, hunger and malnutrition continue to be problems in the United States. According to Patrick Quillin (1987), "While 10 percent of Americans are underfed, many of the remaining 90 percent are overfed or improperly fed" (p. 43). Nutritional deficiencies are found in all social classes. In one national survey discussed by Quillen, only 3% of the respondents in the best-fed nation in history were free of the 48 most common symptoms of malnutrition.

POINT. In the medical arena, we have made stunning advances. Doctors can reattach severed limbs, use lasers to correct microscopic defects in the eye, and even replace the human heart. Contagious diseases (those caused by infectious agents), such as tuberculosis, typhoid fever, smallpox, and cholera, are largely under control. Since the turn of the century, life expectancy in the United States has increased from 47 to 75 years.

COUNTERPOINT. Nonetheless, as noted in a *Time* magazine article, "Never have doctors been able to do so much for their patients, and rarely have patients seemed so ungrateful" (Gibbs, 1989, p. 49). The number of malpractice lawsuits doubled in the 1980s, and patients' confidence in the medical profession has declined noticeably. Moreover, the void left by contagious diseases has been filled all too quickly by chronic diseases that develop gradually, such as cancer, heart disease, hypertension, and ulcers. The increase in chronic diseases is attributable to stress and certain features of our modern lifestyle, such as our penchant for smoking and overeating, and our tendency to get little physical exercise.

The apparent contradictions just discussed all reflect the same theme: *The technological advances of the 20th century, impressive though they may be, have not led to perceptible improvement in our collective health and happiness.* Indeed, many social critics argue that the quality of our lives and our sense of personal fulfillment have declined rather than increased. This is the paradox of progress.

What is the cause of this paradox? There are many potential explanations. Let's turn now to the analyses of Erich Fromm, who offers some worthwhile insights about this perplexing question.

It seems trite and self-centered to carry on about how we live in "troubled times." Certainly, our ancestors had their share of problems, and it would be shortsighted to idealize the "good old days." However, in *Escape from Freedom*, Fromm (1963) has described how the character of personal problems has changed as we have evolved from a static, agricultural society into a modern, industrial world marked by instability.

Until a couple centuries ago, Fromm points out, people's lives tended to be clearly laid out for them. For instance, peasants in a feudal society typically knew that they were going to practice the same religion their parents practiced, pledge allegiance to the same feudal lord who ruled their parents, and plow the same fields that their parents worked. According to Fromm's analysis, *people had relatively little personal freedom in a static society.* Our prototype peasants may even have had their marriage arranged for them! They had few major decisions to make about their lifestyle and virtually no alternative pathways to ponder.

With the advent of the Renaissance, the Reformation, and the Industrial Revolution, the static quality of society began to erode. The yoke of economic, political, and

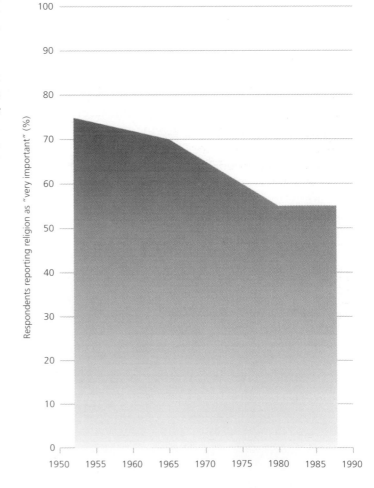

religious bondage was thrown off, and people gradually acquired more and more personal freedom. According to Fromm, this trend toward greater individual freedom has continued unabated, peaking in our present society.

Today we face a vast array of decisions about how to lead our lives. We must choose a career that we hope to find rewarding from a bewildering galaxy of options. We must decide where to live, whether to stay near our parents or move on to greener pastures. In the political arena, we must decide whether to be apathetic or concerned, liberal or conservative, Democrat, Republican, or Independent. In regard to religion and values, we must decide how we feel about changing sex roles, the new morality, and abortion. The list of decisions extends even to the details of everyday life. Every time we walk into a grocery store, we must choose from six brands of tuna fish, 20 brands of soda, and 40 brands of cereal. In all these ways we have more personal freedom than ever before.

Unfortunately, Fromm suggests, *while our personal freedom has been growing, our old sources of emotional sustenance and security have diminished in effectiveness.* Fromm notes that the church, the village, and the family used to provide people with a more solid base of security. In a static society people had a resolute faith in a single church, which told them exactly how to behave in order to gain eternal salvation. Today, we have a multiplicity of churches that provide a clear value system for fewer people (see Figure 1.2). Likewise, the residential stability of the old villages permitted solid friendship networks to develop over generations. Today, our tendency to repeatedly pick up and move leads us to live in ever-shifting communities where we may barely know our next-door neighbors The family, too, has declined as a source of security. In most segments of our society, the closely knit extended family—encompassing aunts, uncles, grandparents, and cousins—has become a relic of the past. Today, with our penchant for divorce and mobility, even the nuclear family is a less dependable source of emotional support.

This analysis leads Fromm to a rather startling conclu-

sion. He argues that as our old sources of security have declined we have found it more difficult to cope with our newfound freedom. He suggests that, *rather than embracing our increased freedom, many of us find it scary and threatening.* In fact, many of us find our freedom so aversive that we try to escape from it. This escape often takes the form of submitting passively to some authority figure, such as a political or religious leader.

Fromm pointed to Germany's ready submission to Hitler in the 1930s as a prime example of this tendency to abandon freedom. At the time of Hitler's ascendance to power, Germany was in a state of transition, chaos, and confusion. According to Fromm, it was this confusion and uncertainty that made the German populace surprisingly willing to give up its freedom to a dictator who offered simple solutions.

To summarize, Fromm's analysis suggests that the progress we value so much has undermined our sense of security, scrambled our value systems, and confronted us with difficult new problems of adjustment. *Hence, the basic challenge of life becomes the search for a sense of direction.* This search involves struggling with such problems as developing a solid sense of identity, a coherent philosophy of life, and a clear vision of a future that realistically promises fulfillment. Centuries ago, problems of this kind were probably much simpler. As we'll see in the next section, today it appears that many of us are floundering in a sea of confusion.

THE SEARCH FOR DIRECTION

There are many manifestations of our search for a sense of direction. Let's look at two striking expressions of this quest: the expanding popularity of "self-realization" programs and the spectacular success of best-selling "self-help" books. An examination of these phenomena can help us to better understand the modern struggle for a sense of direction and some of the ways in which it can go awry.

Figure 1.2. The importance of religion in people's lives. This graph shows the percentage of respondents to Gallup polls who report that religion is "very important" in their lives. Over 50% continue to view religion as very important, but this percentage has been declining since the 1950s.

Self-Realization Programs

Can people achieve enlightenment and fulfillment through workshops and seminars? Since the 1960s, many Americans have shown a willingness to bet on this possibility by investing large sums of money to enroll in "self-realization" programs. These are various kinds of training programs that are supposed to provide profound insights and turn one's life around, usually in a very brief period. They vary greatly in orientation, format, and themes, but most tend to promise participants spectacular benefits. Some of these training regimens have enjoyed enormous success, earning glowing testimonials from thousands of converts. We'll look at three programs (*est*, Scientology, and Silva Mind Control) that have attained a fair amount of popularity and evaluate their worth.

Forum/EST

Est stands for Erhard Seminars Training (in 1985 the name was changed to The Forum), an approach to personal growth developed by Werner Erhard (Bry, 1976). The training consists of intensive 16-hour-a-day seminars, usually conducted on two successive weekends, with about 250 people present. The goal of *est* is "getting it." The "it" is rather mysterious, and most *est* graduates have difficulty describing or explaining it. "It" allegedly involves some profound insight that revolutionizes the graduate's life.

The seminars are led by a trainer who is usually extremely articulate, with a commanding presence. The trainer lectures and leads discussion. The basic strategy is to break down the trainees' self-esteem and then gradually rebuild it. The trainees are told that they are bungling their way through life. They are often intimidated and made to feel foolish. After they have their self-esteem lowered, they are offered a variety of insights borrowed primarily from mainstream psychology. For example, much is made of Fritz Perls's (1969) idea that one should take responsibility for one's own life. *Est* emphasizes that it is useless to blame your problems on others; you can solve problems only if you accept responsibility for them.

Although many *est* graduates complain afterward that they don't feel any different, many others rave about the experience. Many prominent professionals claim that the training significantly changed their lives (Burg, 1974). The changes most commonly reported include improvements in self-image, accompanied by reductions in anxiety and in feelings of dependency.

Scientology

Scientology is a quasi-religious organization founded in the 1950s by L. Ron Hubbard. The goal in Scientology is to become "clear." Getting "clear" involves reaching a point where you are free of all programming in your mind that is not under your control. What exactly does that mean? Well, according to Hubbard (1989), people acquire automatic behavior patterns, called "engrams," which can be problematic. These engrams often involve nonadaptive emotional responses to situations. Hubbard asserts that you can rid yourself of a troublesome engram by consciously and completely reliving the original experience that created it, under the guidance of an "auditor." Scientology training may take a couple of years and can cost several thousand dollars.

Like *est*, Scientology borrows liberally from the mainstream of psychological theory. An engram is very similar to the conditioned response described by Russian physiologist Ivan Pavlov some 90 years ago. The idea that you can relive emotional experiences and thereby discharge the emotion was proposed by Sigmund Freud, the developer of psychoanalysis, over 100 years ago.

Silva Mind Control

Silva Mind Control courses have been available to the public since the mid-1960s. Developed by Jose Silva, the courses are supposed to train participants to control their brain activity (Silva & Miele, 1977). Silva maintains that it is optimal to operate at the lower rather than the higher brain-wave frequencies. Trainees are taught to use relaxation exercises and visual imagery in order to win conscious control over brain activity.

A glance at bookstore shelves verifies that the boom in self-help books continues unabated, fueled by people's ongoing need for guidance and direction in their personal lives.

As trainees acquire better mind control, behavioral self-control supposedly follows. Silva graduates supposedly can use their power of visualization to achieve great self-control. They can eat less, sleep less, work harder, or do whatever is necessary to achieve their goals in life. The mind-control training is also supposed to provide graduates with at least some extrasensory perception (ESP) capabilities.

The Silva Mind Control courses resemble *est* in cost and time commitment. The sequence of courses costs a few hundred dollars and requires about a week's time. Generally, the courses are conducted in small groups.

Critique

Although their teachings are very different, *est*, Scientology, and Silva Mind Control have much in common. First, they are, above all else, money-making propositions for their developers. None of them offers self-realization free; it costs, and the fees aren't cheap. All three organizations seem to be more interested in making money than in spreading enlightenment.

Second, the inventors of all three systems have little or no formal training in psychology. They all appear to have emerged from the ranks of hucksterism rather than science. Werner Erhard, for instance, was previously a door-to-door salesman whose real name was Jack Rosenberg. He has had a long history of involvement with questionable sales schemes (Brewer, 1975).

Third, to be blunt, all three systems are intellectual mush. Each system offers a few worthwhile insights, but these either are borrowed from mainstream psychology or are simple common sense. Most of their principles, however, are hopelessly vague or easily refuted by available scientific data.

While *est*, Scientology, and Silva Mind Control share the rather unsavory features just noted, they also have one other perplexing thing in common. All three have many disciples who claim that the training they received revolutionized their lives. If the systems have little real merit, how do we account for this puzzling reality? In all

probability, it is primarily a matter of placebo effects.

Placebo effects occur when people experience some change from an empty, fake, or ineffectual treatment because of their positive expectations about the treatment. Numerous studies show that if people believe a treatment or program will affect them in certain ways, then they are prone to see the expected effects. For instance, many a patient has been "cured" of a physical illness by the administration of "drugs" that were really sugar pills. Placebo effects can occur even when people are likely to observe themselves very objectively—and such objectivity generally is *not* present when people are seeking self-realization. People who take *est*, Scientology, or Silva training are clearly searching for something. They want, sometimes desperately, to see improvement in themselves. After investing time, money, and hope in some pathway to growth, they badly want to believe that it has paid off. Thus, they are exceedingly biased observers who are predisposed to see the effects that they have been led to expect. With this strong bias, it is not surprising that many participants offer glowing endorsements of *est*, Scientology, and Silva Mind Control. Unfortunately, most of their gains appear to be illusory and short-lived.

Self-Help Books

A second example of our search for a sense of direction is the popularity of "self-help books" that offer do-it-yourself treatments for common personal problems. A glance at the best-seller lists of recent years reveals that our nation has displayed a voracious appetite for self-help books such as *I'm OK—You're OK* (Harris, 1967), *Your Erroneous Zones* (Dyer, 1976), *How to Be Awake and Alive* (Newman & Berkowitz, 1976), *Winning through Intimidation* (Ringer, 1978), *Living, Loving & Learning* (Buscaglia, 1982), *The Art of Self-Fulfillment* (Litwack & Resnick, 1984), *Women Men Love—Women Men Leave* (Cowan & Kinder, 1987), *The Good News about Panic, Anxiety and Phobias* (Gold, 1989), *Willpower's Not Enough* (Watson & Boundy, 1989) and *Beyond Codependency* (Beattie, 1989). With their

simple recipes for achieving happiness, these books have generally not been timid about promising to change the quality of the reader's life. Consider the following excerpt from the back cover of a self-help book titled *Self Creation* (Weinberg, 1979):

More than any book ever written, *Self Creation* shows you who you are and reveals the secret to controlling your own life. It contains an action blueprint built around a clear-cut principle as basic and revolutionary as the law of gravity. With it you will discover how to conquer bad habits, solve sexual problems, overcome depression and shyness, deal with infuriating people, be decisive, enhance your career, increase creativity. And it will show you how to love and be loved. You created you. Now you can start to reap the boundless benefits of self-confidence, self-reliance, self-determination with *Self Creation*.

If only it were that easy! If only someone could hand you a book that would solve all your problems! Unfortunately, it is not that simple. Merely reading a book is not likely to turn your life around. If the consumption of these literary narcotics were even remotely as helpful as their publishers claim, we would be a nation of serene, happy, well-adjusted people. It is clear, however, that serenity is not the dominant national mood. The multitude of self-help books that crowd bookstore shelves represent just one more symptom of our collective distress and our search for the elusive secret of happiness.

Value of Self-Help Books

It is somewhat unfair to lump all self-help books together for a critique, because they vary widely in quality. There are some excellent books that offer authentic insights and sound advice. It would be foolish to dismiss all these books as shallow drivel (as many psychologists do). In fact, some of the better self-help books are highlighted in the Recommended Reading boxes that appear throughout this text. Unfortunately, however, the few gems are dwarfed

by the mountains of rubbish. Most self-help books offer little of real value to the reader. Generally, they have four fundamental shortcomings.

First, they are dominated by "psychobabble." The term *psychobabble*, coined by R. D. Rosen (1977), seems appropriate to describe the "hip" but hopelessly vague language used in many of these books. Statements such as "It's beautiful if you're unhappy," "You've got to get in touch with yourself," "You have to be up front," "You gotta be you 'cause you're you," and "You need a real high-energy experience" are typical examples of this new language. At best, such terminology is ill-defined; at worst, it is meaningless. Consider the following example, taken from a question/answer booklet promoting Werner Erhard's *est* training.

The EST training doesn't change the content of anyone's life, nor does it change what anyone knows. It deals with the context or the way we hold the content. . . . Transformation occurs as a recontextualization. . . .

"Getting it" means being able to discover when you have been maintaining (or are stuck with) a position which costs you more in aliveness than it is worth, realizing that you are the source of that position, and being able to choose to give up that position or hold it in a way that expands the quality of your life.

What exactly did those two paragraphs say? Who knows? The statements are so ambiguous and enigmatic that you can read virtually any meaning into them. Therein lies the problem with psychobabble; it is often so obscure that it is unintelligible. Clarity is sacrificed in favor of a hip jargon that prevents, rather than enhances, effective communication.

A second problem is that self-help books tend to place more emphasis on sales than on scientific soundness. The advice offered in these books is far too rarely based on solid, scientific research (Rosen, 1987). Instead, the ideas are frequently based on the authors' intuitive analyses,

I: THE DYNAMICS OF ADJUSTMENT

which may be highly speculative. Thus, Gerald Rosen (1987) concludes that "consumers increasingly risk the purchase of untested do-it-yourself programs" (p. 48). Moreover, even when responsible authors provide scientifically valid advice and are careful not to mislead their readers, sales-hungry publishers often slap outrageous, irresponsible promises on the books' covers (much to the dismay of some authors).

The third shortcoming is that self-help books usually don't provide explicit directions about how to change your behavior. These books tend to be smoothly written and "touchingly human" in tone. They often strike responsive chords in the reader by aptly describing a common problem that many of us experience. The reader says "Yes, that's me!" Unfortunately, when the book focuses on how to deal with the problem, it usually provides only a vague distillation of simple common sense, which often could be covered in two rather than two hundred pages. These books often fall back on inspirational cheerleading in the absence of sound, explicit advice.

Fourth, many of these books encourage a remarkably self-centered approach to life. Although there are plenty of exceptions, the basic message in many self-help books is "Do whatever you feel like doing, and don't worry about the consequences for other people." This "me first" philosophy emphasizes self-determined ethics and an exploitive approach to interpersonal relationships.

What to Look for in Self-Help Books

Since self-help books vary so widely in quality, it seems a good idea to provide you with some guidelines about what to look for in seeking genuinely helpful books. The following thoughts give you some criteria for judging books of this type.

1. Clarity in communication is essential. Advice won't do you much good if you can't understand it. Try to avoid drowning in the murky depths of psychobabble.

2. This may sound backward, but look for books that do not promise too much in the way of immediate change. The truly useful books tend to be appropriately cautious in their promises and realistic about the challenge of altering one's behavior.

3. Try to select books that mention, at least briefly, the theoretical or research basis for the program they advocate. It is understandable that you may not be interested in a detailed summary of research that supports a particular piece of advice. However, you should be interested in whether the advice is based on published research, widely accepted theory, or pure speculation by the author. Books that are based on more than speculation should have a list of references in the back (or at the end of each chapter).

4. Intellectually honest authors don't just talk about what we know—they also discuss what we do *not* know. There is much to be said for books that are candid about the limits of what the so-called experts really know.

5. Look for books that provide detailed, explicit directions about how to alter your behavior. Generally, these directions represent the crucial core of the book. If they are inadequate in detail, you have been shortchanged.

6. More often than not, books that focus on a particular kind of problem deliver more than those that promise to cure all of life's problems with a few simple ideas. Books that cover everything are usually superficial and disappointing. Books that devote a great deal of thought to a particular topic tend to be written by authors with genuine expertise on that topic. Such books are more likely to pay off for you. Figure 1.3 lists the ten self-help books that were recommended most frequently in a survey of thera-

RECOMMENDED READING

Psychobabble

by R. D. Rosen (Atheneum, 1977)

This book is a scathing indictment of the popular psychological jargon that permeates many of the best-selling self-help books. Rosen, a journalist, christens this hip terminology "psychobabble" and argues that it has muddled our thinking about ourselves and devitalized our communication. The book also contains penetrating (though one-sided) criticism of a number of modern approaches to psychotherapy.

> Psychobabble, as a style of speech (as opposed to the jargon of certain specific therapies . . .), is more than anything else a feature of contemporary decorum, a form of politesse, a signal to others that one is ready to talk turkey, to engage in real dialogue. Unfortunately, in the rush for revelation, real dialogue often turns out to be real monologue. When I asked a man to whom I had just been introduced at a party recently, "How are you?" (no doubt an early, but harmless, form of psychobabble!), he responded by describing, with an utter disrespect for brevity, his relationship with his wife. Confession, alas, is the new handshake.
> [p. 12]

pists (Stark, 1989). As you can see, they all focus on a specific topic.

THE APPROACH OF THIS TEXTBOOK

Clearly, in spite of our impressive technological progress, we are a people beset by a great variety of personal problems. Living in our complex, modern society is a formidable challenge. This book is about that challenge. It is about you. It is about life. Specifically, it summarizes for you the scientific research on human behavior that appears relevant to the challenge of living effectively in the 1990s. It will draw primarily, but not exclusively, from the science we call psychology.

This text deals with the same kinds of problems addressed by self-help books and self-realization programs: anxiety, frustration, loneliness, depression, self-control. However, it makes no boldly seductive promises about solving your personal problems, turning your life around, or helping you to achieve tranquillity. Such promises simply aren't realistic. Psychologists have long recognized that changing one's behavior is a difficult challenge, fraught with frustration and failure. Psychologists sometimes do intensive therapy with a person for years without solving the client's problem.

All this does not mean that you should be pessimistic about your potential for personal growth. You most certainly can change your behavior. Moreover, you can often change it on your own without consulting a professional psychologist. We would not be writing this text if we did not believe that some of our readers might experience some personal benefit from this literary encounter. But it is important that you have realistic expectations. Reading this book will not be a revelatory experience. There are no mysterious secrets about to be unveiled before you. All this book can do is give you some potentially useful information and point you in some potentially beneficial directions. The rest is up to you.

In view of our criticisms of many self-realization programs and self-help books, it seems essential that we lay out explicitly the philosophy that underlies the writing of this text. The following statements summarize the assumptions and goals of this book.

1. *This text is based on the premise that accurate knowledge about the principles of psychology is of value to you in everyday life.* It has been said that knowledge is power. Greater awareness of why people behave as they do should help you in interacting with others as well as in trying to understand yourself.

2. *This text should open doors.* The coverage in this book is very broad; we will tackle many topics. Therefore, there may be places where it lacks the depth or detail that you would like. However, you should think of it as a resource book that can introduce you to other books or techniques or therapies, which you can then pursue on your own.

3. *This text assumes that the key to effective adjustment is to "take charge" of your own life.* If you are dissatisfied with some aspect of your life, it does no good to sit around and mope about it. You have to take an active role in attempting to improve the quality of your life. This may involve learning a new skill or pursuing a particular kind of help. In any case, it is generally best to meet problems head-on rather than trying to avoid them.

THE PSYCHOLOGY OF ADJUSTMENT

Now that we have spelled out our approach in writing this text, it is time to turn to the task of introducing you to some basic concepts. In this section, we'll discuss the nature of psychology and the concept of adjustment.

What Is Psychology?

Psychology **is the science that studies behavior and the physiological and mental processes that underlie it and the profession that applies the accumulated knowledge of this science to practical problems.** Psychology leads a

Therapists' Top Ten Self-Help Selections	
1 *The Relaxation Response* by Herbert Benson and Miriam Z. Klipper (Avon)	**6** *What Color Is Your Parachute?* by Richard N. Bolles (Ten Speed Press)
2 *On Death and Dying* by Elisabeth Kübler-Ross (Macmillan)	**7** *When I Say No I Feel Guilty* by Manuel Smith (Bantam)
3 *Parent Effectiveness Training* by Thomas Gordon (McKay)	**8** *The Boys and Girls Book about Divorce* by Richard A. Gardner (Bantam)
4 *Between Parent and Child* by Haim G. Ginott (Avon)	**9** *Feeling Good: The New Mood Therapy* by David D. Burns (Morrow)
5 *Your Perfect Right: A Guide to Assertive Living* by Robert E. Alberti and Michael L. Emmons (Impact Publishers)	**10** *How to Survive the Loss of a Love* by Melba Colgrove, Harold Bloomfield, and Peter McWilliams (Bantam)

complex dual existence as both a *science* and a *profession*. Let's examine the science first.

Psychology is an area of scientific study, much like biology or physics. Whereas biology focuses on life processes, and physics on matter and energy, psychology focuses on *behavior and related processes*.

***Behavior* is any overt (observable) response or activity by an organism.** Psychology does *not* confine itself to the study of human behavior. Many psychologists believe that the principles of behavior are much the same for animals and humans. These psychologists often prefer to study animals—mainly because they can exert more control over the factors influencing the animals' behavior.

Psychology is also interested in the mental processes—the thoughts, feelings, and wishes—that accompany behavior. Mental processes are more difficult to study than behavior because they are private and not directly observable. However, they exert critical influence over human behavior, so psychologists have strived to improve their ability to "look inside the mind."

Finally, psychology includes the study of the physiological processes that underlie behavior. Thus, some psychologists try to figure out how bodily processes such as neural impulses, hormonal secretions, and genetic coding regulate behavior. Practically speaking, all this means that psychologists study a great variety of phenomena. Psychologists are interested in maze running in rats, salivation in dogs, and brain functioning in cats, as well as visual perception in humans, play in children, and social interaction in adults.

As you probably know, psychology is not all pure science. It has a highly practical side, represented by the many psychologists who provide a variety of professional services to the public. Although the profession of psychology is very prominent today, this aspect of psychology was actually slow to develop. Psychology emerged as an independent science back in the 19th century, but until the 1950s psychologists were found almost exclusively in the halls of academia, teaching and doing research. However, the demands of World War II (1942–1945) stimulated

rapid growth in psychology's first professional specialty—clinical psychology. ***Clinical psychology* is the branch of psychology concerned with the diagnosis and treatment of psychological problems and disorders.** During World War II, a multitude of academic psychologists were pressed into service as clinicians to screen military recruits and treat soldiers suffering from trauma. Frequently they found their clinical work interesting, and many of them returned from the war to set up training programs to meet the continued high demand for clinical services. Soon about half of the new Ph.D.'s in psychology were specializing in clinical work. Psychology had come of age as a profession.

Since then, the trend toward professionalization has continued. A variety of new professional specialties have emerged, including school psychology, industrial/organizational psychology, and counseling psychology. The growth of these professional arms of psychology, which concern themselves with practical problems, eventually led to increased interest in our topic—adjustment.

What Is Adjustment?

We have referred to the term *adjustment* several times without clarifying its exact meaning. The concept of adjustment was originally borrowed from biology. It was modeled after the biological term *adaptation*, which refers to efforts by a species to adjust to changes in its environment. Just as a field mouse has to adapt to an unusually brutal winter, a person has to adjust to changes in circumstances such as a new job, a financial setback, or the loss of a loved one. Thus, ***adjustment* refers to the psychological processes through which people manage or cope with the demands and challenges of everyday life.**

The demands of everyday life are diverse, so in studying the process of adjustment we will examine a broad variety of topics. In the first section of this book, The Dynamics of Adjustment, we discuss general issues, such as how personality affects our patterns of adjustment, how we are affected by stress, and how we use coping strategies

Figure 1.3. Therapists' top ten self-help books. Steven Sarker surveyed therapists about the self-help books they recommend to their patients. The ten most frequently recommended titles are listed here.

to deal with stress. In the second section, The Interpersonal Realm, we'll examine the adjustments that we make in our social relationships, exploring topics such as how we view others, communication, behavior in groups, friendship, and intimate relationships. In the third section, Developmental Transitions, we'll look at how we adjust to changing demands as we grow older. We'll discuss topics such as the development of gender roles, the emergence of sexuality, phases of adult development, and transitions in the world of work. Finally, in the fourth section, Mental and Physical Health, we'll discuss how the process of adjustment influences our psychological and physical wellness.

As you can see, the study of adjustment delves into nearly every corner of our lives, and we'll be discussing a diverse array of issues and topics. Before we begin considering these topics in earnest, however, we need to take a closer look at psychology's approach to investigating behavior—the scientific method.

THE SCIENTIFIC APPROACH TO BEHAVIOR

We all expend a great deal of effort in trying to understand our own behavior as well as the behavior of others. We wonder about any number of behavioral questions: Why am I so anxious when I interact with new people? Why is Sam always trying to be the center of attention at the office? Why does Joanna cheat on her wonderful husband? Are extroverts happier than introverts? Is depression more common during the Christmas holidays? Given that psychologists' principal goal is to explain behavior, how are their efforts different from everyone else's? The key difference is that psychology is a *science*, committed to *empiricism*.

Empiricism

Empiricism **is the premise that knowledge should be acquired through observation.** When we say that scientific psychology is empirical, we mean that its conclusions are based on systematic observation rather than on reasoning, speculation, traditional beliefs, or common sense. Scientists are not content with having ideas that sound plausible; they conduct research to *test* their ideas. Whereas our everyday speculations are informal, unsystematic, and highly subjective, scientists' investigations are formal, systematic, and objective. To gain more understanding of the empirical approach, let's look at how scientific studies are conducted.

Steps in a Scientific Investigation

Your best friend has been raving for weeks about a meditation group he has joined. He says it has turned his life around! He claims to be happier, more energetic, and

less anxious. You are skeptical. The only clear behavioral change you can see is that meditation is all he ever talks about. You wonder: Does meditation really have beneficial effects on one's mental health?

A question or problem like this one is the point of departure for any research endeavor. The question stimulates the scientist to seek information that may provide at least a partial answer.

A scientist, however, seeks information in a particular way. Scientific investigations are systematic. They follow an orderly pattern that can be broken up into a number of separate steps. Let's use our question about meditation to look at three key steps in scientific studies.

1. *Formulate a testable hypothesis.* The first step in a scientific study is to translate a general idea into a testable hypothesis. **A** *hypothesis* **is a tentative statement about the relationship between two or more variables.** *Variables* **in a study are any measurable conditions, events, characteristics, or behaviors that are controlled or observed.** Thus, in our imaginary study, you might hypothesize that learning to meditate (the first variable) will lead to reduced anxiety (the second variable).

To be testable, hypotheses must be formulated precisely, with clear definitions of the variables under study. To achieve this goal, researchers depend on operational definitions. **An** *operational definition* **describes the actions or operations that will be made to measure or control a variable.** For example, you might hypothesize that people who meditate four hours a week should score lower on the Taylor Manifest Anxiety Scale than comparable people who do not meditate. Thus, in the context of our study "learning to meditate" is defined as following a prescribed four-hour regimen of meditation, and "anxiety" is defined as a person's score on the Taylor Manifest Anxiety Scale (Taylor, 1953).

2. *Gather the appropriate data.* After you have clearly stated your hypothesis, the second step in a scientific investigation is to put it to a test. This involves selecting a research method and conducting the study. The research method chosen depends on the nature of the question under study. The various methods—experiments, case studies, surveys, and naturalistic observation—all have their advantages and disadvantages, some of which we'll discuss later.

To conduct your study, you will need to procure a sample of subjects. *Subjects* **are the persons or animals whose behavior is systematically observed in a study.** To gather data on our hypothesis about meditation, you would assemble two similar groups of subjects and require one of the groups to practice meditation four hours weekly for several months. You would then administer your measure of anxiety to see whether there was a substantial difference between the two groups, as predicted in our hypothesis.

3. *Report the findings.* Progress in understanding the world around us requires that scientists share their findings

with each other and the general public. The final step in a scientific investigation involves writing up a concise summary of the study and its findings. If our meditation study yielded interesting results, we would prepare a report that could be submitted to a technical journal for publication or presented at a scientific meeting (such as the annual convention of the American Psychological Association).

The process of publishing scientific studies allows other experts to evaluate and critique new research findings. Sometimes this process of critical evaluation discloses flaws in a study. If the flaws are serious enough, the results may be discounted or discarded. This evaluation process is intended to gradually weed out erroneous findings.

Advantages of the Scientific Approach

Science is certainly not the only method that we can use to draw conclusions about behavior. We all use logic, casual observation, and good old-fashioned common sense. Since the scientific method often requires painstaking effort, it seems reasonable to ask what the advantages of the empirical approach are.

The scientific approach offers two major advantages. The first is its clarity and precision. Commonsense notions about behavior tend to be vague and ambiguous. Consider the old truism "Spare the rod and spoil the child." What exactly does this generalization about child-rearing amount to? How severely should children be punished if we are not to "spare the rod"? How do we assess whether a child qualifies as "spoiled"? A fundamental problem is that statements like this mean different things to different people. When people disagree about this assertion, it may be because they are talking about entirely different things. In contrast, the scientific approach requires that we specify *exactly* what we are talking about when we formulate hypotheses. This clarity and precision enhance communication about important ideas.

The second advantage offered by the scientific approach is its relative intolerance of error. Scientists subject their ideas to empirical tests. They also scrutinize one another's findings with a critical eye. They demand objective data and thorough documentation before they accept ideas. When the findings of two studies conflict, they try to figure out why the studies reached different conclusions, usually by conducting additional research. In contrast, common sense and casual observation often tolerate contradictory generalizations, such as "Opposites attract" and "Birds of a feather flock together." Furthermore, commonsense analyses involve little effort to verify ideas or detect errors, so that many myths about behavior come to be widely believed.

All this is not to say that science has a copyright on truth. However, the scientific approach does tend to yield more accurate and dependable information than casual analyses and armchair speculation. Knowledge of empirical data can thus provide a useful benchmark against which to judge claims and information from other kinds of sources.

Now that we have an overview of how the scientific enterprise works, we can look at some of the specific research methods that psychologists depend on most. The two main types of research methods in psychology are *experimental research methods* and *correlational research methods*. We will discuss them separately because there is an important distinction between them.

Experimental Research: Looking for Causes

Does misery love company? This question intrigued social psychologist Stanley Schachter. How does anxiety affect our desire to be with others? When people feel anxious, do they want to be left alone, or do they prefer to have others around? Schachter's hypothesis was that increases in anxiety would cause increases in the desire to be with others, which psychologists call the *need for affiliation*. To test this hypothesis, Schachter (1959) designed a clever experiment. **The *experiment* is a research method in which the investigator manipulates an (independent) variable under carefully controlled conditions and observes whether there are changes in a second (dependent) variable as a result.** Psychologists depend on this method more than any other.

Independent and Dependent Variables

An experiment is designed to find out whether changes in one variable (let's call it x) cause changes in another variable (let's call it y). To put it more concisely, we want to know *how x affects y*. In this formulation, we refer to x as the independent variable, and we call y the dependent variable. **An *independent variable* is a condition or event that an experimenter varies in order to see its impact on another variable.** The independent variable is the variable that the experimenter controls or manipulates. It is hypothesized to have some effect on the dependent variable. The experiment is conducted to verify this effect. **The *dependent variable* is the variable that is thought to be affected by the manipulations of the independent variable.** In psychology studies, the dependent variable usually is a measurement of some aspect of the subjects' behavior.

In Schachter's experiment, *the independent variable was the subjects' anxiety level*, which he manipulated in the following way. Subjects assembled in his laboratory were told by a Dr. Zilstein that they would be participating in a study on the physiological effects of electric shock and that they would receive a series of electric shocks. Half of the subjects were warned that the shocks would be very painful. They made up the *high-anxiety* group. The other half of the subjects, assigned to the *low-anxiety* group, were told that the shocks would be mild and painless. These procedures were simply intended to evoke different levels of anxiety. In reality, no one was actually shocked at any time. Instead, the experimenter indicated that there would be a delay while he prepared the shock apparatus for use. The subjects were asked whether they would prefer to wait alone or in the company of others. *This measure of the subjects' desire to affiliate with others was the dependent variable.*

Experimental and Control Groups

To conduct an experiment, an investigator typically assembles two groups of subjects who are treated differently in regard to the independent variable. We call these groups the experimental and control groups. **The *experimental group* consists of the subjects who receive some special treatment in regard to the independent variable. The *control group* consists of similar subjects who do *not* receive the special treatment given to the experimental group.**

Let's return to the Schachter study to illustrate. In this study, the subjects in the high-anxiety condition were the experimental group. They received a special treatment designed to create an unusually high level of anxiety. The subjects in the low-anxiety condition were the control group.

It is crucial that the experimental and control groups be very similar, except for the different treatment they receive in regard to the independent variable. This stipulation brings us to the logic that underlies the experimental method. If the two groups are alike in all respects *except for the variation created by the manipulation of the independent variable*, then any differences between the two groups on the dependent variable *must be due to this manipulation of the independent variable*. In this way researchers isolate the effect of the independent variable on the dependent variable. Thus, Schachter isolated the impact of anxiety on need for affiliation. What did he find? As predicted, he found that increased anxiety led to increased affiliation. The percentage of subjects who wanted to wait with others was nearly twice as high in the high-anxiety group as in the low-anxiety group (see Figure 1.4).

The logic of the experimental method rests heavily on the assumption that the experimental and control groups are alike—except for their different treatment in regard to the independent variable. Any other differences between the two groups cloud the situation and make it difficult to draw solid conclusions about the relationship between the independent variable and the dependent variable. To summarize our discussion of the experimental method, Figure 1.5 provides an overview of the various elements in an experiment, using Schachter's study as an example.

Advantages and Disadvantages

The experiment is a powerful research method. Its principal advantage is that it allows us to draw conclusions about cause and effect relationships between variables. We can draw these conclusions about causation because the precise control available in the experiment permits us to isolate the relationship between the independent variable and the dependent variable. No other research method can duplicate this advantage.

For all its power, however, the experimental method has its limitations. One disadvantage is that we frequently are interested in the effects of variables that cannot be manipulated (as independent variables) because of ethical concerns or practical realities. For example, you might want to know whether being brought up in an urban area as opposed to a rural area affects people's values. A true experiment would require you to assign similar families to live in urban and rural areas, which obviously is impossible to do. To explore this question, you would have to use correlational research methods, which we turn to next.

Correlational Research: Looking for Links

As we just saw, in some situations psychologists cannot exert experimental control over the variables they want to study. In such situations, all a researcher can do is make systematic observations to see whether there is a link or association between the variables of interest. Such an

Figure 1.4. Results of Schachter's study of affiliation. The percentage of subjects wanting to wait with others was higher in the high-anxiety (experimental) group than in the low-anxiety (control) group. These results supported Schachter's hypothesis that anxiety would increase the desire for affiliation.

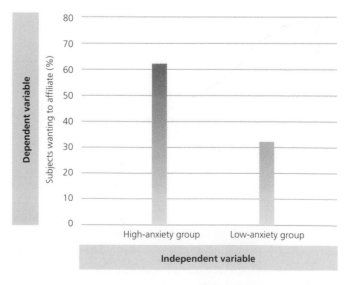

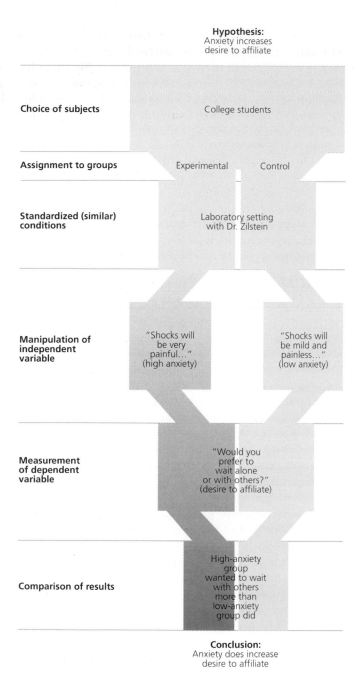

Hypothesis:
Anxiety increases
desire to affiliate

Choice of subjects — College students

Assignment to groups — Experimental   Control

Standardized (similar) conditions — Laboratory setting with Dr. Zilstein

Manipulation of independent variable — "Shocks will be very painful..." (high anxiety)   "Shocks will be mild and painless..." (low anxiety)

Measurement of dependent variable — "Would you prefer to wait alone or with others?" (desire to affiliate)

Comparison of results — High-anxiety group wanted to wait with others more than low-anxiety group did

Conclusion:
Anxiety does increase
desire to affiliate

Figure 1.5. The basic elements of an experiment. This diagram provides an overview of the key features of the experimental method, as illustrated by Schachter's study of anxiety and affiliation. The logic of the experiment rests on treating the experimental and control groups alike except for the manipulation of the independent variable.

association is called a correlation. **A *correlation* exists when two variables are related to one another.** The definitive aspect of correlational studies is that the researchers cannot control the variables under study.

Measuring Correlation

The results of correlational research are often summarized with a statistic called the *correlation coefficient*. This widely used statistic will be mentioned frequently as we discuss studies throughout the remainder of this text. **A *correlation coefficient* is a numerical index of the degree of relationship that exists between two variables.** A correlation coefficient tells us (1) how strongly related two variables are and (2) the direction (positive or negative) of the relationship.

There are two *kinds* of relationships that can be described by a correlation. A *positive* correlation indicates there is a *direct* relationship between two variables. This means that high scores on variable x are associated with high scores on variable y, and that low scores on variable x are associated with low scores on variable y. For example, there is a positive correlation between high school grade point average (GPA) and subsequent college GPA. That is, people who do well in high school tend to do well in college, and those who perform poorly in high school tend to perform poorly in college (see Figure 1.6).

In contrast, a *negative* correlation indicates that there is an *inverse* relationship between two variables. This means that people who score high on variable x tend to score low on variable y, whereas those who score low on x tend to score high on y. For example, in most college courses, there is a negative correlation between how frequently a student is absent and how well the student performs on exams. Students who have a high number of absences tend to earn low exam scores, while students who have a low number of absences tend to get higher exam scores (see Figure 1.6).

While the positive or negative sign indicates whether an association is direct or inverse, the *size* of the coefficient indicates the *strength* of the association between two vari-

Figure 1.6. Positive and negative correlations. Variables are positively correlated if they tend to increase and decrease together and negatively correlated if one variable tends to increase when the other decreases. Hence, the terms *positive correlation* and *negative correlation* refer to the *direction* of the relationship between two variables.

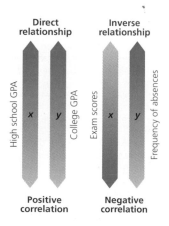

ables. This coefficient can vary between 0 and +1.00 (if positive) or between 0 and −1.00 (if negative). A coefficient near zero tells us there is no relationship between the variables. The closer the correlation is to either −1.00 or +1.00, the stronger the relationship is (see Figure 1.7). Thus, a correlation of +.90 represents a stronger tendency for variables to be associated than does a correlation of +.40. Likewise, a correlation of −.75 represents a stronger relationship than does a correlation of −.45. Keep in mind that the *strength* of a correlation depends only on the size of the coefficient. The positive or negative sign simply shows whether the correlation is direct or inverse. Therefore, a correlation of −.60 reflects a stronger relationship than a correlation of +.30.

There are a variety of correlational research methods, including naturalistic observation, case studies, and surveys. Let's examine each of these methods to see how researchers use them to detect associations between variables.

Naturalistic Observation

In *naturalistic observation* a researcher engages in careful observation of behavior without intervening directly with the subjects. This type of research is called *naturalistic* because behavior is allowed to unfold naturally (without interference) in its natural environment—that is, the setting in which it would normally occur.

As an example, consider a study by Stoffer, Davis, and Brown (1977), which sought to determine whether it is a good idea for students to reconsider and change answers on multiple-choice tests. The conventional wisdom is that "your first hunch is your best hunch," and it is widely believed that students should not go back and change their answers. To put this idea to an empirical test, Stoffer and his colleagues studied the answer changes made by college students on their regular exams in a psychology course. They simply examined students' answer sheets for evidence of response changes, such as erasures or crossing out of responses. As Figure 1.8 shows, they found that changes that went from a wrong answer to a right answer

outnumbered changes that went from a right answer to a wrong answer by a margin of nearly 3 to 1! The correlation between the number of changes students made and their net gain from answer changing was +.49, indicating that the more answer changing students engaged in, the more they improved their scores. These results, which have been replicated in a number of other studies (Benjamin, Cavell, & Shallenberger, 1984), show that popular beliefs about the harmful effects of answer changing are inaccurate.

Case Studies

A *case study* is an in-depth investigation of an individual subject. Psychologists typically assemble case studies in clinical settings where an effort is being made to diagnose and treat some psychological problem. To achieve an understanding of an individual, a clinician may use a variety of procedures, including interviewing the subject, interviewing others who know the subject, direct observation, examination of records, and psychological testing. Usually, a single case study does not provide much basis for deriving general laws of behavior. If researchers have a number of case studies available, however, they can look for threads of consistency among them, and they may be able to draw some general conclusions.

This was the strategy employed by a research team (Farina, Burns, Austad, Bugglin, & Fischer, 1986) that studied psychiatric patients' readjustment to their community after their release from a mental hospital. The researchers wanted to know whether the patients' physical attractiveness was related to their success in readjustment. As we'll discuss in upcoming chapters, good-looking people tend to be treated more nicely by others than homely people, suggesting that attractive patients may have an easier time adjusting to life outside the hospital. To find out, the research team compiled case history data (and ratings of physical attractiveness) for patients just before their discharge from a mental hospital and six months later. A modest positive correlation (+.38) was found between patients' attractiveness and their post-

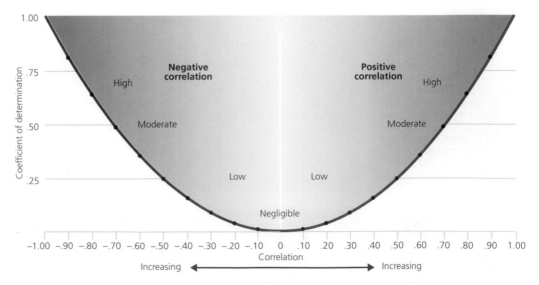

Figure 1.7. Interpreting correlation coefficients. The magnitude of a correlation coefficient indicates the strength of the relationship between two variables. The square of a correlation (called the coefficient of determination) is an index of the correlation's predictive power. The closer a correlation is to either +1.00 or −1.00, the stronger the relationship between the variables.

       I: THE DYNAMICS OF ADJUSTMENT

discharge social adjustment. Thus, the better-looking patients were better off, suggesting that physical attractiveness plays a role in psychiatric patients' readjustment to community living.

Surveys

Surveys are structured questionnaires designed to solicit information about specific aspects of subjects' behavior. They are sometimes used to measure dependent variables in experiments, but they are mainly used in correlational research. Surveys are frequently employed to gather data on subjects' attitudes and on aspects of behavior that are difficult to observe directly (marital interactions, for instance).

As an example, consider an influential study by Thomas Holmes and his colleagues (Wyler, Masuda, & Holmes, 1971) that explored the possible relationship between life stress and physical illness. They hypothesized that high stress would be associated with a relatively high frequency of physical illness. To test this hypothesis they gave 232 subjects a questionnaire that assessed the amount of stress the subjects had experienced in the past year and another questionnaire that assessed the amount of illness they had recently experienced. As predicted, there was a positive correlation (+.32) between subjects' level of stress and their amount of illness. This ground-breaking investigation inspired hundreds of follow-up studies that have enhanced our understanding of how stress is related to physical health (see Chapter 3).

Advantages and Disadvantages

Correlational research methods give us a way to explore questions that we could not examine with experimental procedures. Consider the study we just discussed on the association between life stress and health. Obviously, Holmes could not manipulate the life stress experienced by his subjects. Their divorces, retirements, pregnancies, and mortgages were far beyond his control. But correlational methods allowed him to gather useful information on whether there is a link between life stress and illness.

Thus, *correlational research broadens the scope of phenomena that psychologists can study.*

Unfortunately, correlational methods have one major disadvantage. The investigator does not have the opportunity to control events so as to isolate cause and effect. *Consequently, correlational research cannot demonstrate conclusively that two variables are causally related.* The crux of the problem is that correlation is no assurance of causation.

When we find that variables x and y are correlated, we can safely conclude only that x and y are related. We do not know *how* x and y are related. We do not know whether x causes y, or y causes x, or whether both are caused by a third variable. For example, survey studies show that there is a positive correlation between marital satisfaction and sexual satisfaction (Hunt, 1974; Tavris & Sadd, 1977). Although it's clear that good sex and a healthy marriage go hand in hand, it's hard to tell what's causing what. We don't know whether healthy marriages promote good sex, or whether good sex promotes healthy marriages. Moreover, we can't rule out the possibility that both are caused by a third variable. Perhaps sexual satisfaction and marital satisfaction are both caused by compatibility in values. The plausible causal relationships in this case are diagrammed for you in Figure 1.9, which illustrates the "third-variable problem" in interpreting correlations. This is a frequent problem in correlational research. Indeed, it will surface frequently in upcoming chapters.

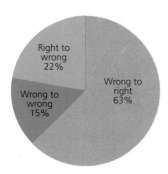

Figure 1.8. The effects of answer changing on multiple-choice exams. In a study of answer changes, Stoffer et al. (1977) found that wrong-to-right changes outnumbered right-to-wrong changes by a sizable margin. These results are very similar to those of other studies on this issue.

Right to wrong 22%

Wrong to right 63%

Wrong to wrong 15%

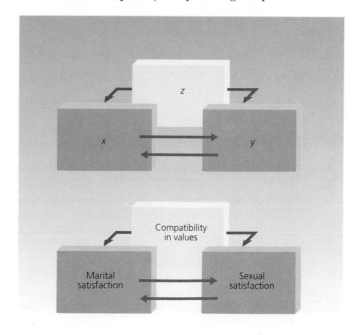

Figure 1.9. Possible causal relations between correlated variables. When two variables are correlated, there are several possible explanations. It could be that x causes y, or that y causes x, or that a third variable, z, causes changes in both x and y. As the correlation between marital satisfaction and sexual satisfaction illustrates, the correlation itself does not provide the answer.

SUMMARY

In spite of the great technological progress in our modern era, personal problems have not declined. In fact, theorists such as Fromm suggest that our progress brings new, and possibly more difficult, adjustment problems.

Self-help books and self-realization programs represent two interesting manifestations of our struggle to find a sense of direction in our confusing world. Unfortunately, self-realization programs have little real value, and their benefits are probably due to placebo effects. Some self-help books offer worthwhile advice, but most are dominated by psychobabble and are not based on scientific research. Many also lack explicit advice on how to change behavior, and some encourage a self-centered approach to interpersonal relations. Although this text deals with many of the same issues as self-realization programs and self-help books, its philosophy and approach are quite different.

Psychology is both a science and a profession that focuses on behavior and related mental and physiological processes. Adjustment is a broad area of study in psychology concerned with how people adapt effectively or ineffectively to the demands and pressures of everyday life.

The scientific approach to understanding behavior is empirical. Psychologists base their conclusions on formal, systematic, objective research rather than reasoning, speculation, or common sense. Scientific studies include three key steps: (1) formulating a testable hypothesis, (2) gathering the appropriate data to assess its validity, and (3) reporting the findings. The scientific approach is advantageous in that it puts a premium on clarity and has little tolerance for error.

Experimental research involves manipulating an independent variable to discover its effects on a dependent variable. The experimenter usually does this by comparing experimental and control groups, which must be alike except for the variation created by the manipulation of the independent variable. Experiments allow us to draw conclusions about cause-effect relationships between variables, but this method isn't usable for the study of many problems.

Psychologists conduct correlational research when they are unable to exert control over the variables they want to study. The correlation coefficient is a numerical index of the degree of relationship between two variables. Correlational research methods include naturalistic observation, case studies, and surveys. Correlational research allows us to investigate issues that may not be open to experimental study, but it cannot demonstrate that two variables are causally related.

We turn next to an example of how psychological research can be applied to everyday problems. In our first application section, we'll review evidence related to the challenge of being a successful student.

Improving Academic Performance

Answer the following true or false.

☐ **1.** It's a good idea to study in as many different locations (your bedroom or kitchen, the library, lounges around school, and so forth) as possible.

☐ **2.** If you have a professor who delivers chaotic, hard-to-follow lectures, there is little point in attending class.

☐ **3.** Cramming the night before an exam is an efficient way to study.

☐ **4.** In taking lecture notes, you should try to be a "human tape recorder" (that is, take down everything exactly as said by your professor).

☐ **5.** Outlining reading assignments is a waste of time.

As you will soon learn, all of the statements above are false. If you answered them all correctly, you may already have acquired the kinds of skills and habits that lead to academic success. If so, however, you are not typical. Today, a huge number of students enter college with remarkably poor study skills and habits—and it's not entirely their fault. Our educational system generally does not provide much in the way of formal instruction on good study techniques. In this first Application, we will try to remedy this oversight to some extent by sharing with you some insights that psychology can provide on how to improve your academic performance. We will discuss how to promote better study habits, how to enhance reading efforts, how to get more out of lectures, how to make your memory more effective, and how to improve your test-taking strategies.

DEVELOPING SOUND STUDY HABITS

Effective study is crucial to success in college. You may run into a few classmates who boast about getting good grades without studying. But you can be sure that if they perform well on exams—they study. Students who claim otherwise simply want to be viewed as extremely bright rather than studious.

Learning can be immensely gratifying, but studying usually involves hard work.

The first step toward effective study habits is to face this reality. You don't have to feel guilty if you don't look forward to studying. Most students don't. Once you accept the premise that studying doesn't come naturally, it should be clear that you need to set up an organized program to promote adequate study. Such a program should include the following steps.

1. *Set up a schedule for studying.* If you wait until the urge to study hits you, you may still be waiting when the exam rolls around. Thus, it is important to allocate definite times to studying. Review your time obligations (work, housekeeping, and so on) and figure out in advance when you can study. In allotting certain times to studying, keep in mind that you need to be wide awake and alert. It won't do you much good to plan on studying when you're likely to be very tired. Be realistic, too, about how long you can study at one time before you wear down from fatigue. Allow time for study breaks; they can revive sagging concentration.

It's important to write down your study schedule. Writing it down serves as a reminder and increases your commitment to the schedule. As shown in Figure 1.10, you should begin by setting up a general

Figure 1.10. Example of an activity schedule. One student's general activity schedule for a semester is shown here. Each week the student fills in the specific assignments to work on during the upcoming study sessions.

	Monday	Tuesday	Wednesday	Thursday	Friday	Saturday	Sunday
6 A.M.							
7 A.M.							
8 A.M.						Work	
9 A.M.	History	Study	History	Study	History	Work	
10 A.M.	Psychology	French	Psychology	French	Psychology	Work	
11 A.M.	Study		Study		Study	Work	
Noon	Math	Study	Math	Study	Math	Work	Study
1 P.M.							Study
2 P.M.	Study	English	Study	English	Study		Study
3 P.M.	Study		Study		Study		Study
4 P.M.							
5 P.M.							
6 P.M.	Work	Study	Study	Work			Study
7 P.M.	Work	Study	Study	Work			Study
8 P.M.	Work	Study	Study	Work			Study
9 P.M.	Work	Study	Study	Work			Study
10 P.M.	Work			Work			
11 P.M.							

schedule for the quarter or semester. Then, at the beginning of each week, plan the specific assignments that you intend to work on during each study session. This approach should help you to avoid cramming for exams at the last minute.

In planning your weekly schedule, try to avoid the tendency to put off working on major tasks such as term papers and reports. Time management experts, such as Alan Lakein (1973), point out that many of us tend to tackle simple, routine tasks first, while saving larger tasks for later, when we supposedly will have more time. This common tendency leads many of us to delay working on major assignments until it's too late to do a good job. You can avoid this trap by breaking major assignments into smaller component tasks that you schedule individually.

2. *Find a place to study where you can concentrate.* Where you study is also important. The key is to find a place where distractions are likely to be minimal. Most people cannot study effectively while watching TV, listening to the stereo, or overhearing conversations. Don't depend on willpower to carry you through these distractions. It's much easier to plan ahead and avoid the distractions altogether.

There is evidence that it helps to set up one or two specific places for study. If possible, use these places for nothing else. These places may become strongly associated with studying, so that they serve as cues that evoke good study behavior (Beneke & Harris, 1972). In contrast, places associated with other activities may serve as cues for these other activities. For example, studying in your kitchen may evoke more eating than reading.

3. *Reward your studying.* One of the reasons it is so difficult to motivate oneself to study regularly is that the payoffs for studying often lie in the distant future. The ultimate reward, a degree, may be years away. Even more short-term rewards, such as an A in the course, may be weeks or months away. To combat this problem, it helps to give yourself immediate rewards for studying. It is easier to motivate yourself to study if you reward yourself with a tangible payoff, such as a snack, TV show, or phone call to a friend, when you finish. Thus, you should set realistic study goals for yourself and then reward yourself when you meet them. This systematic manipulation of rewards involves harnessing the principles of *behavior modification*, which are described in some detail in the Chapter 4 Application.

IMPROVING YOUR READING

Much of your study time is spent reading and absorbing information. *These efforts must be active.* If you engage in passive reading, the information will pass right through you. Many students deceive themselves into thinking that they are studying by running a marker through a few sentences here and there in their book. If this isn't done with thoughtful selectivity, the student is simply turning a textbook into a coloring book. Underlining in your text can be useful, but you have to distinguish between important ideas and mere supportive material.

There are a number of ways of actively attacking your reading assignments. One of the more worthwhile strategies is Robinson's (1970) SQ3R method. **SQ3R is a study system designed to promote effective reading that includes five steps: survey, question, read, recite, and review.** Its name is an abbreviation for the five steps in the procedure:

• *Step 1: Survey.* Before you plunge into the actual reading, glance over the topic headings in the chapter and try to get an overview of the material. Try to understand how the various chapter segments are related. If there is a chapter outline or summary, consult it to get a feel for the chapter. If you know where the chapter is going, you can better appreciate and organize the information you are about to read.

• *Step 2: Question.* Once you have an overview of your reading assignment, proceed through it one section at a time. Take a look at the heading of the first section and convert it into a question. This is usually quite simple. If the heading is "Prenatal Risk Factors," your question should be "What are sources of risk during prenatal development?" If the heading is "Stereotyping," your question should be "What is stereotyping?" Asking these questions gets you actively involved in your reading and helps you to identify the main ideas.

• *Step 3: Read.* Only now, in the third step, are you ready to sink your teeth into the reading. Read only the specific section that you have decided to tackle. Read it with an eye toward answering the question that you just formulated. If necessary, reread the section until you can answer that question. Decide whether the segment addresses any other important questions and answer these as well.

• *Step 4: Recite.* Now that you can answer the key question for the section, recite it out loud to yourself in your own words. Use your own words because that requires understanding instead of simple memorization. Don't move on to the next section until you understand the main idea(s) of the present section. You may want to write down these ideas for review later. When you have fully digested the first section, go

on to the next. Repeat steps 2 through 4 with the next section. Once you have mastered the crucial points there, you can go on again. Keep repeating steps 2 through 4, section by section, until you finish the chapter.

• *Step 5: Review.* When you have read the chapter, test and refresh your memory by going back over the key points. Repeat your questions and try to answer them without consulting your book or notes. This review should fortify your retention of the main ideas and should alert you to any key ideas that you haven't mastered. It should also help you to see the relationships between the main ideas.

The SQ3R method does not have to be applied rigidly. For example, it is often wise to break your reading assignment down into smaller segments than those separated by section headings. In fact, you should probably apply SQ3R to many texts on a paragraph by paragraph basis. Obviously, this will require you to formulate some questions without the benefit of topic headings. However, the headings are not absolutely necessary to use this technique. If you don't have enough headings, you can simply reverse the order of steps 2 and 3. Read the paragraph first and then formulate a question that addresses the basic idea of the paragraph. The point is that you can be flexible in your use of the SQ3R technique. *What makes SQ3R effective is that it breaks a reading assignment down into manageable segments and requires understanding before you move on.* Any method that accomplishes these goals should enhance your reading.

It is easier to use the SQ3R method when your textbook has plenty of topic headings. This brings up another worthwhile point about improving your reading. It pays to take advantage of the various learning aids incorporated into many textbooks. If a book provides a chapter outline or chapter summary, don't ignore them. They can help you to recognize the important points in the chapter and to understand how the various parts of the chapter are interrelated. If your book furnishes learning objectives, use them. They tell you what you should get out of your reading.

DOONSBURY, © 1985 (1986) G. B. TRUDEAU. REPRINTED WITH PERMISSION OF UNIVERSAL PRESS SYNDICATE. ALL RIGHTS RESERVED.

GETTING MORE OUT OF LECTURES

Although lectures are sometimes boring and tedious, it is a simple fact that poor class attendance is associated with poor grades. For example, in one study, Lindgren (1969) found that absences from class were much more common among "unsuccessful" students (grade average: C– or below) than among "successful" students (grade average: B or above), as is shown in Figure 1.11. Even when you have an instructor who delivers hard-to-follow lectures from which you learn virtually nothing, it is still important to go to class. If nothing else, you'll get a feel for how the instructor thinks. This can help you to anticipate the content of

exams and to respond in the manner your professor expects.

Fortunately, most lectures are reasonably coherent. Research indicates that accurate note taking is related to better test performance (Palkovitz & Lore, 1980). Good note taking requires you to actively process lecture information in ways that should enhance both memory and understanding. Books on study skills (Pauk, 1984; Sotiriou, 1989) offer a number of suggestions on how to take good lecture notes. Some of these are summarized here.

• Extracting information from lectures requires *active listening procedures*, which are described in more detail in Chapter 6. Focus full attention on the speaker. Try to anticipate what's coming and search for deeper meanings. Pay attention to nonverbal signals that may serve to further clarify the lecturer's intent or meaning.
• When course material is especially complex and difficult, it is a good idea to prepare for the lecture by reading ahead on the scheduled subject in your text. Then you have less information to digest that is brand-new.
• You should not try to be a human tape recorder. Instead, try to write down the lecturer's thoughts in your own words. This forces you to organize the ideas in a way that makes sense to you. In taking notes, pay attention to clues about what is most important. Many instructors give subtle and not-so-subtle clues about what is important. These clues may range from simply repeating main points to saying things like "You'll run into this again."
• Asking questions during lectures can be very helpful. This keeps you actively involved in the lecture. It also allows you to clarify points you may have misunderstood. Many students are more bashful about asking questions than they should be. They don't realize that most professors welcome questions.

APPLYING THE PRINCIPLES OF MEMORY

Scientific investigation of memory processes dates back to 1885, when Hermann Ebbinghaus published a series of insightful studies. Thus, memory has been an important topic in psychology for over a century. As a result, a number of principles have been formulated that are relevant to effective study.

Engage in Adequate Practice

Practice makes perfect, or so you've heard. In reality, practice is not likely to guarantee perfection, but repeatedly reviewing information usually leads to improved retention. Studies show that retention improves with increased rehearsal. Continued rehearsal may also pay off by improving your *understanding* of assigned material (Bromage & Mayer, 1986). As you go over information again and again, your increased familiarity with the material may permit you to focus selectively on the most important points, thus enhancing your understanding.

There is evidence that it even pays to overlearn material. **Overlearning refers to continued rehearsal of material after you first appear to master it.** In one study, after subjects mastered a list of nouns (they recited the list without error), Krueger (1929) required them to continue rehearsing for 50% or 100% more trials. Measuring retention at intervals of up to 28 days, Kreuger found that overlearning led to better recall of the list. The implication of this finding is simple: you should not quit rehearsing material as soon as you appear to have mastered it.

Use Distributed Practice

Let's assume that you are going to study 9 hours for an exam. Is it better to "cram" all of your study into one 9-hour period (massed practice) or distribute it among, say, three 3-hour periods on successive days (distributed practice)? The evidence indicates that retention tends to be greater after distributed practice than massed practice, especially if the intervals between practice periods are fairly long, such as 24 hours (Zechmeister & Nyberg, 1982).

The inefficiency of massed practice means that cramming is an ill-advised study strategy for most students. Cramming will strain your memorization capabilities and tax your energy level. It may also stoke the fires of test anxiety.

Minimize Interference

Interference **occurs when people forget information because of competition from**

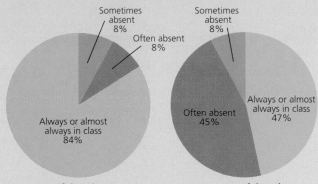

Successful students   **Unsuccessful students**

other learned material. Research suggests that interference is a major cause of forgetting, so you'll probably want to think about how you can minimize interference. This is especially important for students because memorizing information for one course can interfere with retaining information in another course. It may help to allocate study for specific courses to specific days. Thorndyke and Hayes-Roth (1979) found that similar material produced less interference when it was learned on different days. Thus, the day before an exam in a course, it is probably best to study for that course only. If demands in other courses make that impossible, study the test material last.

Of course, studying for other classes is not the only source of interference in a student's life. Other normal waking activities also produce interference. Therefore, it is a good idea to conduct one last, thorough review of material as close to exam time as possible (Anderson, 1980). This last-minute review helps you to avoid memory loss due to interference from intervening activities.

Organize Information

Retention tends to be greater when information is well organized. Gordon Bower (1970) has shown that hierarchical organization is particularly helpful. Hence, one of the most potent weapons in your arsenal of study techniques is to *outline* reading assignments. Outlining is probably too time-consuming to do for every class. However, it is worth the effort in particularly important or particularly difficult classes, as it can greatly improve retention.

Use Verbal Mnemonics

People retain information better when they make the information more mean-

Figure 1.11. Successful and unsuccessful students' class attendance. Lindgren (1969) found that attendance was much better among successful students than unsuccessful students.

Figure 1.12. The narrative method. Two examples of the narrative method for memorizing lists are shown here (Bower & Clark, 1969). The words to be memorized are listed on the left, and the stories constructed to remember them are shown on the right.

Word Lists to Be Memorized and Stories Constructed from Them	
Word Lists	**Stories**
Bird Costume Mailbox Head River Nurse Theater Wax Eyelid Furnace	A man dressed in a *Bird Costume* and wearing a *Mailbox* on his *Head* was seen leaping into the *River*. A *Nurse* ran out of a nearby *Theater* and applied *Wax* to his *Eyelids*, but her efforts were in vain. He died and was tossed into the *Furnace*.
Rustler Penthouse Mountain Sloth Tavern Fuzz Gland Antler Pencil Vitamin	A *Rustler* lived in a *Penthouse* on top of a *Mountain*. His specialty was the three-toed *Sloth*. He would take his captive animals to a *Tavern* where he would remove *Fuzz* from their *Glands*. Unfortunately, all this exposure to sloth fuzz caused him to grow *Antlers*. So he gave up his profession and went to work in a *Pencil* factory. As a precaution he also took a lot of *Vitamin* E.

ingful (Raugh & Atkinson, 1975). A very useful strategy is to make material *personally* meaningful. When you read your textbooks, try to relate information to your own life and experience. For example, if you're reading in your psychology text about the personality trait of assertiveness, you can think of someone you know who is very assertive.

Of course, it's not always easy to make something personally meaningful. When you study chemistry, you may have a hard time relating to polymers at a personal level. This problem has led to the development of many **mnemonic devices, or strategies for enhancing memory,** that are designed to make abstract material more meaningful.

ACROSTICS AND ACRONYMS. Acrostics are phrases (or poems) in which the first letter of each word (or line) functions as a cue to help you recall the abstract words that begin with the same letter. For instance, you may remember the order of musical notes with the saying "**E**very **g**ood **b**oy **d**oes **f**ine" (or "**d**eserves **f**avor"). A variation on acrostics is the *acronym*—a word formed out of the first letters of a series of words. Students memorizing the order of colors in the light spectrum often store the name "Roy G. Biv" to remember **r**ed, **o**range, **y**ellow, **g**reen, **b**lue, **i**ndigo, and **v**iolet.

NARRATIVE METHODS. Another useful way to remember a list of words is to create a story that includes each of the words in the right order. The narrative increases the meaningfulness of the words and links them in a specific order. Examples of this technique can be seen in Figure 1.12. Bower and Clark (1969) found that this procedure enhanced subjects' recall of lists of unrelated words.

Why—and how—would you use the narrative method? Let's assume that you always manage to forget to put one item in your gym bag on your way to the pool. Short of pasting a list on the inside of the bag, how can you remember everything you need? You could make up a story that includes the items you need.

> The wind and rain in COMBINATION LOCKED out the rescue efforts—nearly. CAP, the flying ace, TOWELed the SOAP from his eyes, pulled his GOGGLES from his SUIT pocket, and COMBED the BRUSH for survivors.

RHYMES. Another verbal mnemonic that we often rely on is rhyming. You've probably repeated, "I before E except after C" thousands of times. Perhaps you also remember the number of days in each month with the old standby, "Thirty days hath September . . ." Rhyming something to remember it is an old and very useful trick.

Use Visual Imagery

Memory can be improved through the use of visual imagery. One influential theory (Paivio, 1986) proposes that visual images create a second memory code and that two codes are better than one. Many popular mnemonic devices depend on visual imagery, including the following examples.

LINK METHOD. The *link method* involves forming a mental image of items to be remembered in a way that links them together. For instance, suppose that you are going to stop at the drugstore on the way home and you need to remember to pick up a news magazine, shaving cream, film, and pens. To remember these items, you might visualize a public figure likely to be in the magazine shaving with a pen while being photographed. There is evidence that the more bizarre you make your image, the more helpful it will be (McDaniel & Einstein, 1986).

LOCI METHOD. The *method of loci* involves taking an imaginary walk along a familiar path where you have associated images of items you want to remember with certain locations. The first step is to commit to memory a series of loci, or places along a path. Usually these loci are specific locations in your home or neighborhood. Then envision each thing you want to remember in one of these locations. Try to form distinctive, vivid images. When you need to remember the items, imagine yourself walking along the path. The various loci on your path should serve as retrieval cues for the images that you formed (see Figure 1.13). The method of loci assures that items are remembered in their correct order because the order is determined by the sequence of locations along the pathway. This method has demonstrated value for memorizing lists (Crovitz, 1971).

IMPROVING TEST-TAKING STRATEGIES

Let's face it: some students are better than others at taking tests. **Testwiseness is the ability to use the characteristics and formats of an exam to maximize one's score.** Students clearly vary in testwiseness, and these variations influence performance on exams (Fagley, 1987; Sarnacki, 1979). Testwiseness is not a substitute for knowledge of the subject matter. However, skill in taking tests can help you to show what you know when it is critical to do so.

General Tips

The principles of testwiseness were first described by Millman, Bishop, and Ebel (1965). Let's look at some of their general ideas.

• If efficient time use appears crucial, set up a mental schedule for progress through the test. Make a mental note to check whether you're one-third finished when one third of your time is gone. You may want to check again at the two-thirds time mark.
• On troublesome, difficult-to-answer

items, do not waste time by pondering them excessively. If you have no idea at all, just guess and go on. If you think you need to devote a good deal of time to the item, skip it and mark it so you can return to it later if time permits.
• If you complete all of the questions and still have some time remaining, review the test. Make sure that you have recorded your answers correctly. If you were unsure of some answers, go back and reconsider them.

Figure 1.13. The method of loci. In this example from Bower (1970), a person about to go shopping pairs items to be remembered with familiar places (loci) arranged in a natural sequence: (1) hot dogs/driveway; (2) cat food/garage; (3) tomatoes/front door; (4) bananas/coat closet; (5) whiskey/kitchen sink. As the last panel shows, the shopper recalls the items by mentally touring the loci associated with them.

RECOMMENDED READING
How to Take Tests
by Jason Millman & Walter Pauk (McGraw-Hill, 1969)

This is an excellent book on how to improve your test-taking skills. The first author has done extensive research on testwiseness, and the second has expertise in reading and study skills. Together, they have written a very thorough analysis of how to maximize performance on exams. If you're one of those people who have a hard time showing how much you know on exams, this is very worthwhile reading.

Students tend to place too little emphasis on the necessity for carefully reading directions and questions. A perfectly "correct" and well-written answer to a question not asked will receive no credit. Frequently, understanding what is wanted—understanding the question—may be more difficult than the idea or concept being tested for. Surely it makes good sense to look at the question before you leap into an answer. [p. 23]

- Adopt the appropriate level of sophistication for the test. Don't read things into questions. Sometimes, students make things more complex than they were intended to be. Often, simple-looking questions are just what they appear to be—simple.
- Unless it is explicitly forbidden, don't hesitate to ask the examiner to clarify a question when necessary. Many examiners will graciously provide a great deal of useful information.

Tips for Multiple-Choice Exams

Sound test-taking strategies are especially important on multiple-choice (and true-false) exams. These types of questions often include clues that may help you to converge on the correct answer (Mentzer, 1982; Weiten, 1984). You may be able to improve your performance on such tests by considering the following points.

- As you read the stem of each multiple-choice question, *anticipate* the answer if you can, before looking at the options. If the answer you anticipated is found among the options, there is a high probability that it is correct.
- Even if you find your anticipated answer among the options, you should always continue through and read all the options. There may be another option farther down the list that encompasses the one you anticipated. You should always read each question completely.
- Learn to quickly eliminate options that are highly implausible. Many questions have only two plausible options, accompanied by "throwaway" options for filler. You should work at spotting these implausible options so you can quickly discard them and narrow your search.

- Be alert to the fact that examiners sometimes "give away" information relevant to one question in another test item.
- On items that have "all of the above" as an option, if you know that just two of the options are correct, you should choose "all of the above." If you are confident that any one of the options is incorrect, you should eliminate both the incorrect option and "all of the above," and choose from the remaining options.
- Although there will always be exceptions, options that are more detailed than the others tend to be correct. Hence, it's a good idea to pay special attention to options that are extra-long or highly specific.
- Options that create broad, sweeping generalizations tend to be incorrect. Be vigilant for words such as *always, never, necessarily, only, must, completely, totally,* and so forth, that create improbable assertions.
- In contrast, options that create carefully qualified statements tend to be correct. Words such as *often, sometimes, perhaps, may,* and *generally* tend to show up in these well-qualified statements.

In summary, sound study skills and habits are crucial to academic success. Intelligence alone won't do the job (although it certainly helps). Good academic skills do not develop overnight. They are acquired gradually, so be patient with yourself. Fortunately, tasks such as reading textbooks, writing papers, and taking tests get easier with practice. Ultimately, you'll find that the rewards—knowledge, a sense of accomplishment, and progress toward a degree—are worth the effort.

1. Explain what is meant by the paradox of progress.

2. Summarize the theme of Fromm's book *Escape from Freedom*.

3. Summarize the text's critique of *est*, Scientology, and Silva Mind Control.

4. List four problems that are common in popular self-help books.

5. Summarize advice about what to look for in quality self-help books.

6. Describe the two key facets of psychology and explain the concept of adjustment.

7. Describe three major steps in a scientific investigation.

8. Explain two advantages of the scientific approach to understanding behavior.

9. Describe the experimental method, distinguishing between independent and dependent variables and between experimental and control groups.

10. Distinguish between positive and negative correlation and explain what the size of a correlation coefficient means.

11. Describe the three correlational methods discussed in the text.

12. Compare the advantages and disadvantages of experimental versus correlational research.

13. List three steps for developing sound study habits.

14. Describe the SQ3R method and what makes it effective.

15. Summarize advice on how to get more out of lectures.

16. Summarize how memory is influenced by practice, interference, and organization.

17. Describe several verbal and visual mnemonic devices.

18. Summarize advice on improving test-taking strategies.

KEY TERMS

Adjustment
Behavior
Case study
Clinical psychology
Control group
Correlation
Correlation coefficient
Dependent variable
Empiricism
Experiment
Experimental group
Hypothesis
Independent variable

Interference
Mnemonic devices
Naturalistic observation
Operational definition
Overlearning
Placebo effects
Psychology
SQ3R
Subjects
Surveys
Testwiseness
Variables

KEY PEOPLE

Erich Fromm

QUESTIONNAIRE

Testwiseness Scale

INSTRUCTIONS

Below you will find a series of 24 history questions for which you are *not* expected to know the answer based on your knowledge of history. However, you should be able to make a good guess on each of the questions if you can spot the flaws that exist in them. Each question is flawed in some way so as to permit solution by testwise examinees. Record your choice for each question by circling the letter for the correct alternative.

THE SCALE

1. The Locarno Pact
   a. is an international agreement for the maintenance of peace through the guarantee of national boundaries of France, Germany, Italy, Belgium, and other countries of Western Europe.
   b. allowed France to occupy the Ruhr Valley.
   c. provided for the dismemberment of Austria-Hungary.
   d. provided for the protection of Red Cross bases during wartime.

2. The disputed Hayes-Tilden election of 1876 was settled by an
   a. resolution of the House of Representatives.
   b. decision of the United States Supreme Court.
   c. Electoral Commission.
   d. joint resolution of Congress.

3. The Factory Act of 1833 made new provisions for the inspection of the mills. This new arrangement was important because
   a. the inspectors were not local men and therefore they had no local ties that might affect the carrying-out of their job; they were responsible to the national government rather than to the local authorities; and they were encouraged to develop a professional skill in handling their work.
   b. the inspectorate was recruited from the factory workers.
   c. the inspectors were asked to recommend new legislation.
   d. the establishment of the factory inspectorate gave employment to large numbers of the educated middle class.

4. The Ostend Manifesto aimed to
   a. discourage Southern expansionism.
   b. prevent expansion in the South.
   c. aid Southern expansionism.
   d. all of the above

5. The august character of the work of Pericles in Athens frequently causes his work to be likened to that in Rome of
   a. Augustus.
   b. Sulla.
   c. Pompey.
   d. Claudius.

6. The Webster-Ashburton Treaty settled a long-standing dispute between Great Britain and the United States over
   a. the Maine boundary.
   b. numerous contested claims to property as well as many other sources of ill will.
   c. damages growing out of the War of 1812 and subsequent events.
   d. fishing rights on the Great Lakes and in international waters.

7. Men who opposed the "Ten Hour Movement" in British factory history
   a. was a leader in the dominant political party.
   b. is convinced that shorter hours of work are bad for the morals of the laboring classes.
   c. is primarily motivated by concern for his own profits.
   d. were convinced that intervention would endanger the economic welfare of Britain.

8. The career of Marius (157–86 B.C.), the opponent of Sulla, is significant in Roman history because
   a. he gave many outstanding dinners and entertainments for royalty.
   b. he succeeded in arming the gladiators.
   c. he showed that the civil authority could be thrust aside by the military.
   d. he made it possible for the popular party to conduct party rallies outside the city of Rome.

9. The Locarno Pact
   a. was an agreement between Greece and Turkey.
   b. gave the Tyrol to Italy.
   c. was a conspiracy to blow up the League of Nations building at Locarno.
   d. guaranteed the boundary arrangements in Western Europe.

10. The first presidential election dispute in the United States to be settled by an appointed Electoral Commission was
    a. the Hayes-Tilden election.
    b. the Jefferson-Madison election.
    c. the John Quincy Adams-Henry Clay election.
    d. the Garfield-McKinley election.

11. The first of the alliances against the "Central Powers" that ended in World War I is to be found in
    a. the defensive treaty between China and Japan.
    b. the dual alliance of Mexico and the United States.
    c. the dual alliance of France and Russia.
    d. India's resentment against South Africa's attitude toward the Boer War, and her ensuing alliance with Japan.

12. The Proclamation of 1763
    a. forbade colonists to settle territory acquired in the French and Indian wars.
    b. encouraged colonists to settle territory acquired in the French and Indian wars.
    c. provided financial incentives for settlement of territory acquired in the French and Indian wars.
    d. all of the above

13. About what fraction of the 1920 population of the United States was foreign-born?
    a. less than 5%
    b. between 14% and 28%
    c. 25%
    d. between 30% and 50%

14. The Alabama claims were
    a. all settled completely and satisfactorily.
    b. claims against Jefferson Davis for seizure of all of the property in the state during wartime.
    c. claims of the United States against Great Britain.
    d. claims of every citizen of Alabama against every citizen of Georgia.

15. During the Italian Renaissance
    a. the papacy gained political power.
    b. there were frequent changes in government.
    c. the papacy became more important in Italian political affairs.
    d. all of the above

16. The 12th century was distinguished by a "real European patriotism" that expressed itself in
    a. the flowering of lyrical and epical poetry in the vernacular.
    b. great patriotic loyalty to the undivided unit of European Christendom.
    c. recurring attempts to form a world with a centralized administration.
    d. proposals to remove the custom barriers between the different countries of the time.

17. The dispute between Great Britain and the United States over the boundary of Maine was settled by

    a. the Treaty of Quebec.
    b. the Treaty of Niagara.
    c. the Webster-Ashburton Treaty.
    d. the Pendleton-Scott Treaty.

18. In the *Dartmouth College* case the United States Supreme Court held

    a. that the courts had no right under any circumstances ever to nullify an Act of Congress.
    b. that a state could not impair a contract.
    c. that all contracts must be agreeable to the state legislature.
    d. that all contracts must inevitably be certified.

19. The accession of Henry VII marked the close of the

    a. Crusades
    b. War of the Roses, between rival factions of the English nobility.
    c. Hundred Years' War.
    d. Peasants' Revolt.

20. The Magna Carta was signed

    a. before the Norman invasion.
    b. in 1215.
    c. after the opening of the 17th century.
    d. about the middle of the 14th century.

21. The Progressive Party in 1912

    a. favored complete protective tariffs.
    b. favored an appointed Congress.
    c. favored the creation of a nonpartisan tariff commission.
    d. favored restriction of the ballot to certain influential persons.

22. The first systematic attempt to establish the Alexandrian synthesis between Christian religious belief and Greek civilization was undertaken at

    a. Rome.
    b. Alexandria.
    c. Athens.
    d. Jerusalem.

23. The Bland-Allison Act

    a. made all forms of money redeemable in silver.
    b. standardized all gold dollars in terms of silver and copper.
    c. made none of the paper money redeemable in silver.
    d. directed the Treasury Department to purchase a certain amount of silver bullion each month.

24. The famed Bayeaux Tapestry is a

    a. enormous re-creation of the Magna Carta scene.
    b. extremely large impression of the Edict of Nantes.
    c. immense picture of the Battle of Tours.
    d. large representation of the Norman Conquest of England.

SCORING THE SCALE

There are eight item-writing flaws that appear on the Testwiseness Scale three times each. They are described below.

Flaw #1: The incorrect options are highly implausible.

Flaw #2: Equivalence and/or contradictions among options allow one to eliminate the incorrect options.

Flaw #3: Content information in other items provides the answer.

Flaw #4: The correct option is more detailed and/or specific than all the other options.

Flaw #5: The correct option is longer than all of the other options.

Flaw #6: There is grammatical inconsistency between the stem and the incorrect options but not the correct option.

Flaw #7: The incorrect options include certain key words that tend to appear in false statements (such as *always, must, never,* and so on).

Flaw #8: There is a resemblance between the stem and the correct option but not the incorrect options.

The scoring key is reproduced below. For each item it tells you the correct answer and indicates which flaw (as numbered above) you should have spotted to arrive at the answer. Circle those items that you got correct. Add up the number of correct items, and that is your score on the Testwiseness Scale. Record your score below.

1. A (5) **7.** D (6) **13.** C (4) **19.** B (5)
2. C (6) **8.** C (1) **14.** C (7) **20.** B (4)
3. A (5) **9.** D (3) **15.** D (2) **21.** C (1)
4. C (2) **10.** A (3) **16.** B (8) **22.** B (8)
5. A (8) **11.** C (1) **17.** C (3) **23.** D (7)
6. A (4) **12.** A (2) **18.** B (7) **24.** D (6)

MY SCORE _____

WHAT THE SCALE MEASURES

As its title indicates, this scale simply measures your ability to reason your way to answers on multiple-choice exams. The Testwiseness Scale (TWS) assesses test-taking skills. The scale you have just completed is an abbreviated version of a scale developed by Wayne Weiten (Weiten, Clery, & Bowbin, 1980). The full scale is a 40-item test with five items for each kind of flaw.

The TWS is built on some pioneering work by Gibb (1964). Through a series of revisions, reliability and validity have gradually been improved. The full-length version yields internal reliability coefficients in the .70s and .80s. Two lines of evidence currently provide support for the scale's validity. First, scores on the scale are very much affected (positively) by training in the principles of testwiseness. Second, as one would expect, the scale correlates positively (.40s) with classroom performance on multiple-choice tests. More important, this correlation between the TWS and classroom performance remains significant even when the influence of intelligence on both variables is factored out statistically.

INTERPRETING YOUR SCORE

Our norms are based on the performance of 76 undergraduates who took the most recent revision of the scale. These norms are for people who have *not* had any testwiseness training.

NORMS

High score:	17–24
Intermediate score:	9–16
Low score:	0–8

What Are Your Study Habits Like?

Do you usually complete your class assignments on time?	YES	NO
Do you usually find time to prepare adequately for your exams?	YES	NO
Do you frequently delay schoolwork until the last minute?	YES	NO

When do you usually study (mornings, evenings, weekends, etc.)?

Do you write out and follow a study schedule?	YES	NO
Are your study times planned for when you're likely to be alert?	YES	NO
Do you allow time for brief study breaks?	YES	NO

Where do you usually study (library, kitchen, bedroom, etc.)?

Do you have a special place set up for studying and nothing else?	YES	NO

What types of auditory, visual, and social distractions are present in your study areas?

Can you suggest any changes to reduce distractions in your study areas?

2

Theories of Personality

I
magine that you are hurtling upward in an elevator with three other persons when suddenly there is a power blackout and the elevator grinds to a halt 45 stories above the ground. Your three companions might adjust to this predicament differently. One might crack jokes to relieve tension. Another might make ominous predictions that "we'll never get out of here." The third person might calmly think about how to escape from the elevator. These varied ways of coping with the same stressful situation occur because each person has a different personality.

Personality differences significantly influence our patterns of adjustment. Thus, theories intended to explain personality can contribute to our effort to understand adjustment processes.

In this chapter, we will introduce you to various theories that attempt to explain the structure and development of personality. Our review of personality theory will also serve to acquaint you with four major theoretical perspectives in psychology: the psychodynamic, behavioral, humanistic, and biological perspectives. These theoretical approaches are conceptual models that help us explain behavior. Familiarity with them will help you understand many of the ideas that you will encounter in this book, as well as other books about psychology.

THE NATURE OF PERSONALITY

To discuss theories of personality effectively, we need to digress momentarily to examine a definition of personality and to discuss the concept of personality traits.

What Is Personality?

What does it mean if you say that a friend has an optimistic personality? Your assertion indicates that the person has a fairly *consistent tendency* to behave in a cheerful, hopeful, enthusiastic way, looking at the bright side of things, across a wide variety of situations. In a similar vein, if you note that a friend has an "outgoing" personality, you mean that she or he consistently behaves in a friendly, open, and extroverted manner in a variety of circumstances. Although none of us are entirely consistent in our behavior, this quality of *consistency across situations* lies at the core of the concept of personality.

Distinctiveness is also central to the concept of personality. We all have traits seen in other people, but we each have our own, distinctive *set* of personality traits. Each of us is unique. Thus, as illustrated by our chapter-opening scenario, we use the concept of personality to explain why we don't all act alike in the same situation.

In summary, we use personality to explain (1) the stability in a person's behavior over time and across situations (consistency) and (2) the behavioral differences among people reacting to the same situation (distinctiveness). We can combining these ideas into the following definition: **personality refers to an individual's unique constellation of consistent behavioral traits.** Let's look more closely at the concept of traits.

What Are Personality Traits?

We all make remarks like "Melanie is very *shrewd*" or "Doug is too *timid* to succeed in that job" or "I wish I could be as *self-assured* as Marlene." When we attempt to describe an individual's personality, we usually do so in terms of specific aspects of personality, called *traits*. **A personality trait is a durable disposition to behave in a particular way in a variety of situations.** Adjectives such as *honest, dependable, moody, impulsive, suspicious, anxious, excitable, domineering,* and *friendly* describe dispositions that represent personality traits.

Most approaches to personality assume that some traits are more basic than others. According to this notion, a small number of fundamental traits determine other, more superficial traits. For example, a person's tendency to be impulsive, restless, irritable, boisterous, and impatient might all derive from a more basic tendency to be excitable.

Figure 2.1. The five-factor model of personality. According to McCrae and Costa (1987), all personality traits are derived from the five basic traits described here.

Gordon Allport (1937, 1961) was one of the first theorists to make systematic distinctions between traits in terms of their importance. After sifting through an unabridged dictionary, Allport identified over 4500 personality traits. To impose some order on this chaos, he distinguished between three levels of traits. **A *cardinal trait* is a dominant trait that permeates nearly all of a person's behavior.** The influence of a cardinal trait is overwhelming. Mother Teresa's altruism, Machiavelli's manipulativeness, and William F. Buckley's arrogance are examples of cardinal traits. According to Allport, cardinal traits are rare; only a small minority of people display them.

In Allport's model, ***central traits* are prominent, general dispositions found in anyone.** They are the basic building blocks of personality. Central traits are very influential, but they do not rule our behavior in the way that cardinal traits do. How many central traits do we usually have? Allport's research led him to conclude that most of us have only five to ten central traits.

At the bottom of Allport's hierarchy are secondary traits. ***Secondary traits* are less consistent dispositions that surface in some situations, but not others.** For example, a person might be passive in most circumstances but highly aggressive in dealing with subordinates at work. This occasional aggressiveness would be a secondary trait.

Following Allport's lead, a number of psychologists have taken on the challenge of identifying the basic traits that form the core of personality. For example, Raymond Cattell (1950, 1966) has used complex statistical analyses to reduce Allport's list of traits to just 16 basic dimensions of personality, which he calls *source traits*. Cattell believes that all our other traits are derived from our source traits. He further asserts that we can thoroughly describe an individual's personality by measuring these 16 traits. Indeed, they are the 16 dimensions of personality measured by Cattell's widely used Sixteen Personality Factor Questionnaire (see Figure 2.17 in the Application).

More recently, Robert McCrae and Paul Costa (1985, 1987) have arrived at an even simpler *five-factor model of personality*. McCrae and Costa maintain that the vast majority of personality traits derive from just five critical traits: (1) neuroticism, (2) extraversion, (3) openness to experience, (4) agreeableness, and (5) conscientiousness. These dimensions of personality are described in Figure 2.1. Like Cattell, McCrae and Costa maintain that personality can be described adequately by measuring the basic traits they have identified. Their bold proposal to reduce the complexity of personality to just five fundamental dimensions is currently generating considerable debate.

The debate about how many dimensions are necessary to describe personality is likely to continue for many years to come. As you'll see throughout the chapter, the study of personality is an area in psychology that has a long history of "dueling theories." We'll begin our tour of these theories by examining the influential work of Sigmund Freud and his followers.

PSYCHODYNAMIC PERSPECTIVES

Psychodynamic theories **include all the diverse theories descended from the work of Sigmund Freud, which focus on unconscious mental forces.** Freud inspired many brilliant scholars who followed in his intellectual footsteps. Some of these followers simply refined and updated Freud's theory. Others veered off in new directions and established independent, albeit related, schools of thought. Today, the psychodynamic umbrella covers a large collection of related theories. In this section, we'll examine the ideas of Sigmund Freud in some detail and then take a brief look at the work of one of his most significant followers, Alfred Adler. Another psychodynamic theorist, Erik Erikson, is covered in a later chapter on adolescent and adult development (see Chapter 11).

McCrae and Costa's Five-Factor Model of Personality	
Factor	**Description**
Neuroticism	Anxious, insecure, guilt-prone, self-conscious
Extraversion	Talkative, sociable, fun-loving, affectionate
Openness to experience	Daring, nonconforming, showing unusually broad interests, imaginative
Agreeableness	Sympathetic, warm, trusting, cooperative
Conscientiousness	Ethical, dependable, productive, purposeful

Freud's Psychoanalytic Theory

Born in 1856, Sigmund Freud grew up in a middle-class Jewish home in Vienna, Austria. He showed an early interest in intellectual pursuits and became an intense, hard-working young man. He dreamed of achieving fame by making an important discovery. His determination was such that in medical school he dissected 400 male eels to prove for the first time that they had testes. His work with eels did not make him famous. However, his later work with people made him one of the most influential and controversial figures of modern times.

Freud was a physician specializing in neurology when he began his medical practice in Vienna toward the end of the 19th century. Like other neurologists in his era, he often treated people troubled by nervous problems such as irrational fears, obsessions, and anxieties. Eventually he devoted himself to the treatment of mental disorders using an innovative procedure he developed, called *psychoanalysis.*

Psychoanalysis required lengthy verbal interactions with patients in which Freud probed deeply into their lives. Decades of experience with his patients provided much of the inspiration for Freud's theory of personality. He also gathered material by looking inward and examining his own anxieties and conflicts. For over 40 years, Freud devoted the last half-hour of each workday to self-analysis.

Freud's theory attracted relatively little attention at first. It took eight years to sell the 600 copies of the first printing of his classic book, *The Interpretation of Dreams*—a humble beginning for a theorist who would greatly influence modern thought. After this slow beginning, Freud's ideas gradually gained prominence, but his success was not without its costs.

Most of Freud's contemporaries were uncomfortable with his theory for at least three reasons. First, he argued that unconscious forces govern our behavior. This idea was disturbing because it suggested that we are not masters of our own minds. Second, he claimed that childhood experiences strongly determine adult personality. This notion distressed people because it suggested that we are not masters of our own destinies. Third, he said that our personalities are shaped by how we cope with our sexual urges. This assertion offended the conservative, Victorian values of his time. Thus, Freud endured a great deal of criticism, condemnation, and outright ridicule, even after his work began to attract more favorable attention. Let's examine the ideas that generated so much controversy.

Structure of Personality

Freud (1901, 1924) divided personality structure into three components: the id, the ego, and the superego. He saw a person's behavior as the outcome of interactions among these three components.

The *id* **is the primitive, instinctive component of personality that operates according to the pleasure principle.** Freud referred to the id as the reservoir of psychic energy. By this he meant that the id housed the raw biological urges (to eat, sleep, defecate, copulate, and so on) that energize our behavior. The id operates according to the *pleasure principle,* **which demands immediate gratification of its urges.** The id engages in *primary process thinking,* which is primitive, illogical, irrational, and fantasy-oriented.

The *ego* **is the decision-making component of personality that operates according to the reality principle.** The ego mediates between the id, with its forceful desires for immediate satisfaction, and the external social world, with its expectations and norms regarding suitable behavior. The ego considers social realities—society's norms, etiquette, rules, and customs—in deciding how to behave. The ego is guided by the *reality principle,* **which seeks to delay gratification of the id's urges until appropriate outlets and situations can be found.** In short, to stay out of trouble, the ego often works to tame the unbridled desires of the id. As Freud put it, the ego is "like a man on horseback, who has to hold in check the superior strength of the horse" (Freud, 1923, p. 15).

Sigmund Freud maintained that underlying forces within us begin interacting early in life to shape our personalities.

In the long run, the ego wants to maximize gratification, just like the id. However, the ego engages in *secondary process thinking*, which is relatively rational, realistic, and oriented toward problem solving. Thus, the ego strives to avoid negative consequences from society and its representatives (for example, punishment by parents or teachers) by behaving "properly." It also attempts to achieve long-range goals that sometimes require putting off gratification.

While the ego concerns itself with practical realities, the *superego* **is the moral component of personality that incorporates social standards about what represents right and wrong.** Throughout our lives, but especially during childhood, we receive training about what is good and bad behavior. Eventually we internalize many of these social norms. This means that we truly *accept* certain moral principles, and then *we* put pressure on *ourselves* to live up to these standards. The superego emerges out of the ego at around 3 to 5 years of age. In some people, the superego can become irrationally demanding in its striving for moral perfection. Such people are plagued by excessive guilt.

According to Freud, the id, ego, and superego are distributed differently across three levels of awareness, which we describe next.

Levels of Awareness

Perhaps Freud's most enduring insight was his recognition of how unconscious forces can influence behavior. He contrasted the unconscious with the conscious and preconscious, creating three levels of awareness. **The *conscious* consists of whatever you are aware of at a particular point in time.** For example, at this moment your conscious may include the present train of thought in this text and a dim awareness in the back of your mind that your eyes are getting tired and you're beginning to get hungry. **The *preconscious* contains material just beneath the surface of awareness that can be easily retrieved.** Examples might include your middle name, what you had for supper last night, or an argument you had with a friend yesterday. **The *unconscious* contains thoughts, memories, and desires that are well below the surface of conscious awareness, but that nonetheless exert great influence on our behavior.** Examples of material that might be found in your unconscious would include a forgotten trauma from childhood or hidden feelings of hostility toward a parent.

Freud compared the mind to an iceberg that has most of its area hidden beneath the water's surface (see Figure 2.2). He believed that our unconscious (the area below the surface) is much larger than our conscious or preconscious. In his model, the ego and superego operate at all three levels of awareness. However, the id is entirely unconscious, expressing its urges at a conscious level through the ego. Of course, the id's desires for immediate satisfaction often trigger internal conflicts with the ego and superego. These conflicts play a key role in Freud's theory.

Conflict and Defense Mechanisms

Freud assumed that our behavior is the outcome of an ongoing series of internal conflicts. Internal battles between the id, ego, and superego are routine. Why? Because the id wants to gratify its urges immediately, but the norms of civilized society frequently dictate otherwise. For example, your id might feel an urge to clobber a coworker who constantly irritates you. However, society frowns on such behavior, so your ego would try to hold this urge in check, and you would find yourself in a conflict. You may be experiencing conflict at this very moment. In Freudian terms, your id may be secretly urging you to abandon reading this chapter so you can watch television. Your ego may be weighing this appealing

Conscious:
Contact with outside world

EGO
Reality principle
Secondary process thinking

Preconscious:
Material just beneath the surface of awareness

SUPEREGO
Moral imperatives

ID
Pleasure principle
Primary process thinking

Unconscious:
Difficult to retrieve material; well below the surface of awareness

Figure 2.2. Freud's model of personality structure. Freud theorized that we have three levels of awareness: the conscious, preconscious, and unconscious. To dramatize the size of the unconscious, he compared it to the portion of an iceberg that lies beneath the water's surface. Freud also divided personality structure into three components—id, ego, and superego—which operate according to different principles and exhibit different modes of thinking. In Freud's model, the id is entirely unconscious, but the ego and superego operate at all three levels of awareness.

option against your society-induced need to excel in school.

Freud believed that conflicts dominate our lives. He asserted that we career from one conflict to another. The following scenario provides a fanciful illustration of how the three components of personality interact to create constant conflicts.

Imagine your alarm clock ringing obnoxiously as you lurch across the bed to shut it off. It's 7 A.M. and time to get up for your history course. However, your id (operating according to the pleasure principle) urges you to return to the immediate gratification of additional sleep. Your ego (operating according to the reality principle) points out that you really *must* go to class since you haven't been able to decipher the stupid textbook on your own. Your id (in its typical unrealistic fashion) smugly assures you that you *will* get the "A" that you need. It suggests lying back to dream about how impressed your roommate will be. Just as you're relaxing, your superego jumps into the fray. It tries to make you feel guilty about the tuition your parents paid for the class that you're about to skip. You haven't even gotten out of bed yet—and there is already a pitched battle in your psyche.

Let's say your ego wins the battle. You pull yourself out of bed and head for class. On the way, you pass a donut shop and your id clamors for cinnamon rolls. Your ego reminds you that you're getting overweight and that you are supposed to be on a diet. Your id wins this time. After you've attended your history lecture, your ego reminds you that you need to do some library research for a paper in philosophy. However, your id insists on returning to your apartment to watch some sitcom reruns. As you reenter your apartment, you notice how messy it is. It's your roommates' mess and your id suggests that you tell them off. As you're about to lash out, however, your ego convinces you that diplomacy will be more effective. Three sitcoms later you find yourself in a debate about whether to go to the gym to work out, or to the student union to watch MTV. It's only midafternoon—and already you have been through a series of internal conflicts.

Freud believed that conflicts centering on sexual and aggressive impulses were especially likely to have far-reaching consequences. Why did he emphasize sex and aggression? Two reasons were prominent in his thinking. First, Freud thought that sex and aggression are subject to more complex and ambiguous social controls than other basic motives. The norms governing sexual and aggressive behavior are subtle, and we often get mixed messages about what is appropriate. Thus, he believed that these two drives are the source of much confusion.

Second, Freud noted that the sex and aggressive drives are thwarted more regularly than other basic biological urges. Think about it: If you get hungry or thirsty, you can simply head for a nearby vending machine or a drinking fountain. But if a department store clerk infuriates you, you aren't likely to slug the clerk, because this is socially unacceptable behavior. Likewise, when you see an attractive person who inspires lustful urges, you don't normally walk up and propose a tryst in a nearby broom closet. There is nothing comparable to vending machines or drinking fountains for the satisfaction of our sexual and aggressive urges. Thus, Freud ascribed great importance to these needs because social norms dictate that they are routinely frustrated.

Most of our conflicts are trivial and quickly resolved one way or the other. Occasionally, however, a conflict will linger on for days, months, and even years, creating internal tension. More often than not, these prolonged and troublesome conflicts involve sexual and aggressive impulses that society wants to tame. These conflicts are often played out entirely in the unconscious. Although you may not be aware of these unconscious battles, they can produce *anxiety* that slips to the surface of conscious awareness. This anxiety is attributable to your ego worrying about the id getting out of control and doing something terrible.

The arousal of anxiety is a crucial event in Freud's theory of personality functioning. Anxiety is distressing, so people try to rid themselves of this unpleasant emotion any way they can. This effort to ward off anxiety often involves the use of defense mechanisms. *Defense mechanisms* **are largely unconscious reactions that protect a**

Figure 2.3. Defense mechanisms. According to Freud, we use a variety of defense mechanisms to protect ourselves from painful emotions. Definitions of seven commonly used defense mechanisms are shown on the left, along with examples of each on the right. This list is not exhaustive, and other defense mechanisms are discussed in Chapter 4.

person from painful emotions such as anxiety and guilt. Typically, they are mental maneuvers that work through self-deception. Consider *rationalization,* **which involves creating false but plausible excuses to justify unacceptable behavior.** For example, after cheating someone in a business transaction you might reduce your guilt by rationalizing that "everyone does it."

According to Freud, the most basic and widely used defense mechanism is repression. *Repression* **involves keeping distressing thoughts and feelings buried in the unconscious.** We tend to repress desires that make us feel guilty, conflicts that make us anxious, and memories that are painful. Repression is "motivated forgetting." If you forget a dental appointment or the name of someone you don't like, repression may be at work.

Self-deception can also be seen in projection and displacement. *Projection* **involves attributing your own thoughts, feelings, or motives to another.** Usually, it's thoughts that would make us feel guilty that we use projection to defend against. For example, if your lust for a co-worker makes you feel guilty, you might attribute any latent sexual tension between the two of you to the *other person's* desire to seduce you. *Displacement* **involves diverting emotional feelings (usually anger) from their original source to a substitute target.** If your boss gives you a hard time at work and you come home and slam the door, kick the dog, and scream at your spouse, you are displacing your anger onto irrelevant targets. Unfortunately, social constraints often force us to hold back our anger until we end up lashing out at the people we love the most.

Other prominent defense mechanisms include reaction formation, regression, and identification. *Reaction formation* **involves behaving in a way that is exactly the opposite of one's true feelings.** Guilt about sexual desires often leads to reaction formation. Freud theorized that many males who ridicule homosexuals are defending against their own latent homosexual impulses. The telltale sign of reaction formation is the exaggerated quality of the opposite behavior. *Regression* **involves a reversion to immature patterns of behavior.** When anxious about

their self-worth, some adults respond with childish boasting and bragging (as opposed to subtle efforts to impress others). For example, a fired executive having difficulty finding a new job might start making ridiculous statements about his incomparable talents and achievements. Such bragging is regressive when it is marked by massive exaggerations that anyone can see through. *Identification* **involves bolstering self-esteem by forming an imaginary or real alliance with some person or group.** For example, youngsters often shore up precarious feelings of self-worth by identifying with rock-star heroes, movie stars, or famous athletes. Adults may join exclusive country clubs or civic organizations.

Additional examples of the defense mechanisms we've described can be found in Figure 2.3. If you see defensive maneuvers that you have employed, you shouldn't be surprised. According to Freud, we all use defense mechanisms to some extent. They become problematic only when we depend on them excessively. The seeds for psychological disorders are sown when our defenses lead to wholesale distortion of reality.

Various theorists have added to Freud's original list of defenses. We'll examine some of these additional defense mechanisms in Chapter 4 when we discuss the role of defenses in coping with stress. For now, however, let's turn our attention to Freud's ideas about the development of personality.

Development: Psychosexual Stages

Freud made the startling assertion that the foundation of an individual's personality is laid down by the tender age of 5! To shed light on these crucial early years, Freud formulated a stage theory of development. He emphasized how young children deal with their immature, but powerful, sexual urges (he used the term "sexual" in a general way to refer to many urges for physical pleasure, not just the urge to copulate). According to Freud, these sexual urges shift in focus as children progress from one stage to another. Indeed, the names for the stages (oral, anal, genital, and so on) are based on where children are

Defense Mechanisms, with Examples

Definition	Example
Repression involves keeping distressing thoughts and feelings buried in the unconscious.	A traumatized soldier has no recollection of the details of a close brush with death.
Projection involves attributing one's own thoughts, feelings, or motives to another.	A woman who dislikes her boss thinks she likes her boss but feels that the boss doesn't like her.
Displacement involves diverting emotional feelings (usually anger) from their original source to a substitute target.	After a parental scolding, a young girl takes her anger out on her little brother.
Reaction formation involves behaving in a way that is exactly the opposite of one's true feelings.	A parent who unconsciously resents a child spoils the child with outlandish gifts.
Regression involves a reversion to immature patterns of behavior.	An adult has a temper tantrum when he doesn't get his way.
Rationalization involves creating false but plausible excuses to justify unacceptable behavior.	A student watches TV instead of studying, saying that "additional study wouldn't do any good anyway."
Identification involves bolstering self-esteem by forming an imaginary or real alliance with some person or group.	An insecure young man joins a fraternity to boost his self-esteem.

focusing their erotic energy at the time. Thus, *psychosexual stages* **are developmental periods with a characteristic sexual focus that leave their mark on adult personality.**

Freud theorized that each psychosexual stage has its own unique developmental challenges or tasks, as outlined in Figure 2.4. The way these challenges are handled supposedly shapes personality. The notion of *fixation* plays an important role in this process. *Fixation* **involves a failure to move forward from one stage to another as expected.** Essentially, the child's development stalls for a while. Fixation is caused by *excessive gratification* of needs at a particular stage or by *excessive frustration* of those needs. Either way, fixations left over from childhood affect adult personality. Generally, fixation leads to an overemphasis on the psychosexual needs that were prominent during the fixated stage.

Freud described a series of five psychosexual stages. Let's examine some of the major features of this developmental sequence.

ORAL STAGE. This stage usually encompasses the first year of life. During this stage the main source of erotic stimulation is the mouth (in biting, sucking, chewing, and so on). How caretakers handle the child's feeding experiences is supposed to be crucial to subsequent development. Freud attributed considerable importance to the manner in which the child is weaned from the breast or the bottle. According to Freud, fixation at the oral stage could form the basis for obsessive eating or smoking later in life (among many other things).

ANAL STAGE. In their second year, children supposedly get their erotic pleasure from their bowel movements, through either the expulsion or retention of the feces. The crucial event at this time involves toilet training, which represents society's first systematic effort to regulate the child's biological urges. Severely punitive toilet training is thought to lead to a variety of possible outcomes. For example, excessive punishment might produce a latent feeling of hostility toward the "trainer," who

usually is the mother. This hostility might generalize to women in general. Another possibility is that heavy reliance on punitive measures might lead to an association between genital concerns and the anxiety that the punishment arouses. This genital anxiety derived from severe toilet training could evolve into anxiety about sexual activities later in life.

PHALLIC STAGE. In the third through fifth years, the genitals become the focus for the child's erotic energy, largely through self-stimulation. During this pivotal stage, the *Oedipal complex* emerges. Little boys develop an erotically tinged preference for their mother. They also feel hostility toward their father, whom they view as a competitor for mom's affection. Little girls develop a special attachment to their father. Around the same time, they learn that their genitals are very different from those of little boys, and they supposedly develop *penis envy.* According to Freud, the girls feel hostile toward their mother because they blame her for their anatomical "deficiency."

To summarize, **in the *Oedipal complex* children manifest erotically tinged desires for their opposite-sex parent, accompanied by feelings of hostility toward their same-sex parent.** The name for this syndrome was taken from a tragic myth from ancient Greece. In this myth, Oedipus is separated from his parents at birth. Not knowing the identity of his real parents, he inadvertently kills his father and marries his mother. (For many years, the term *Oedipal complex* referred to boys only, and the comparable syndrome in girls was called the *Electra complex.* However, use of a separate term for the female form of this syndrome has diminished in recent years.)

According to Freud, the way parents and children deal with the sexual and aggressive conflicts inherent in the Oedipal complex is of paramount importance. The child has to resolve the Oedipal dilemma by giving up the sexual longings for the opposite-sex parent and the hostility felt toward the same-sex parent. Healthy psychosexual development is supposed to hinge on the resolution of the Oedipal conflict. Why? Because continued hostile

Figure 2.4. Freud's stages of psychosexual development. Freud theorized that people evolve through the series of stages summarized here. The manner in which certain key tasks and experiences are handled during each stage is thought to leave a lasting imprint on one's adult personality.

Summary of Freud's Stages of Psychosexual Development			
Stage	Approximate ages	Erotic focus	Key tasks and experiences
Oral	0–1	Mouth (sucking, biting)	Weaning (from breast or bottle)
Anal	1–3	Anus (expelling or retaining feces)	Toilet training
Phallic	3–6	Genitals (masturbating)	Identifying with adult role models; coping with Oedipal crisis
Latency	6–12	None (sexually repressed)	Expanding social contacts
Genital	Puberty onward	Genitals (being sexually intimate)	Establishing intimate relationships; contributing to society through working

relations with the same-sex parent may prevent the child from identifying adequately with the same-sex parent. Without such identification, Freudian theory predicts that many aspects of the child's development won't progress as they should.

LATENCY AND GENITAL STAGES. Freud believed that from age 5 through puberty, the child's sexuality is suppressed—it becomes "latent." Important events during this *latency stage* center on expanding social contacts beyond the family. With the advent of puberty, the child evolves into the *genital stage*. Sexual urges reappear and focus on the genitals once again. At this point the sexual energy is normally channeled toward peers of the other sex, rather than toward oneself, as in the phallic stage.

In arguing that the early years shape personality, Freud did not mean that personality development comes to an abrupt halt in middle childhood. However, he did believe that the foundation for one's adult personality was solidly entrenched by this time. He maintained that future developments would be rooted in early, formative experiences and that significant conflicts in later years would be replays of crises from childhood.

In fact, Freud believed that unconscious sexual conflicts rooted in childhood experiences caused most personality disturbances. His steadfast belief in the sexual origins of disorders led to bitter theoretical disputes with his most brilliant colleagues—Carl Jung and Alfred Adler. Jung and Adler both argued that Freud overemphasized sexuality. Freud summarily rejected their ideas, and both theorists felt compelled to go their own way, developing their own psychodynamic theories of personality. Let's look at some of Adler's ideas.

Adler's Individual Psychology

Like Freud, Alfred Adler grew up in Vienna in a middle-class Jewish home. He was a sickly child who struggled to overcome rickets and an almost fatal case of pneumonia.

Nonetheless, he went on to earn his medical degree and practiced ophthalmology and general medicine before his interest turned to psychiatry. He was a charter member of Freud's inner circle—the Vienna Psychoanalytic Society. However, he soon began to develop his own theory of personality, which Freud denounced in 1911. Forced to resign from the Psychoanalytic Society, Adler took 9 of its 23 members with him to form his own organization. His new approach to personality was christened *individual psychology*.

According to Adler (1917, 1927), the foremost human drive is not sexuality, but a *striving for superiority*. For Adler, this striving did not necessarily translate into the pursuit of dominance or high status. Adler viewed striving for superiority as a universal drive to adapt, improve oneself, and master life's challenges. He noted that young children understandably feel weak and helpless in comparison to more competent older children and adults. These early inferiority feelings supposedly motivate us to acquire new skills and develop new talents.

Adler asserted that everyone has to work to overcome some feelings of inferiority. **Compensation involves efforts to overcome imagined or real inferiorities by developing one's abilities.** Adler believed that compensation was entirely normal. However, in some people inferiority feelings can become excessive, resulting in what is widely known today as an *inferiority complex*—exaggerated feelings of weakness and inadequacy. Adler thought that either parental pampering or parental neglect could cause an inferiority problem. Thus, he agreed with Freud on the importance of early childhood, although he focused on different aspects of parent-child relations.

According to Adler, "All neurotic symptoms are safeguards of persons who do not feel adequately equipped or prepared for the problems of life" (Adler, 1964, p. 95). Thus, he explained personality disturbances by noting that an inferiority complex can distort the normal process of striving for superiority. He maintained that some people engage in *overcompensation* in order to conceal, even from themselves, their feelings of inferiority. Instead

According to Freudian theory, toilet training is the first systematic social effort to control the child's biological urges.

of working to master life's challenges, people with an inferiority complex work to achieve status, gain power over others, and acquire the trappings of success (fancy clothes, impressive cars, or whatever looks important to them). They tend to flaunt their success in an effort to cover up their underlying inferiority complex. The problem is that such people engage in unconscious self-deception, worrying more about *appearances* than *reality*.

Adler's theory stressed the social context of personality development. For instance, it was Adler who first focused attention on the possible importance of birth order as a factor shaping personality. He noted that only children, firstborns, second-borns, and subsequent children enter very different social environments. Only children, he theorized, are often spoiled by excessive attention from parents. He thought that firstborns often were problem children because they are upset when they are "dethroned" by a second child. Second-born children would tend to be competitive because they have to struggle to catch up with an older sibling. Adler's hypotheses stimulated hundreds of studies on the effects of birth order. This research has proven very interesting. However, birth order effects have turned out to be weaker and less consistent than Adler expected (Schooler, 1972).

Adler's interest in birth order was just one manifestation of his emphasis on the importance of the social environment in shaping personality. The tragedies and heroism that he witnessed as a physician during World War I increased his appreciation of the social context in which we evolve. He concluded that human nature includes a unique *social interest*, an innate sense of kinship and belongingness with the human race. He saw this social interest as the source of humans' willingness to work together for the common good.

Evaluating Psychodynamic Perspectives

The psychodynamic approach has given us a number of far-reaching theories of personality. These theories yielded some bold new insights. Psychodynamic theory and re-search have demonstrated (1) that unconscious forces can influence behavior, (2) that internal conflict often plays a key role in generating psychological distress, and (3) that early childhood experiences can exert considerable influence over adult personality. Psychodynamic models have also been praised because they probe beneath the surface of personality and because they focus attention on how personality develops over time. Many widely used concepts in psychology emerged out of psychodynamic theories, including the unconscious, defense mechanisms, and the inferiority complex.

In a more negative vein, psychodynamic formulations have been criticized on several grounds, including the following.

1. *Poor testability.* Scientific investigations require testable hypotheses. Psychodynamic ideas have often been too vague to permit a clear scientific test. Concepts such as the superego, the preconscious, and social interest are difficult to measure.

2. *Inadequate evidence.* The empirical evidence on psychodynamic theories has often been characterized as inadequate. There has been too much dependence on case studies in which it is easy for clinicians to see what they expect to see based on their theory. Furthermore, the subjects observed in clinical situations are not particularly representative of the population at large. Insofar as researchers have accumulated evidence on psychodynamic theories, it has provided only modest support for the central hypotheses.

3. *Sexism.* Many critics have argued that psychodynamic theories are characterized by a bias against women. Freud believed that females' penis envy made them feel inferior to men. He also thought that females tended to develop weaker superegos and to be more prone to neurosis than men. He dismissed female patients' reports of sexual molestation during childhood as mere fantasies. Admittedly, sexism isn't unique to Freudian theories, and the sex bias in modern psychodynamic theories has been reduced to some degree. But the psychodynamic ap-

Figure 2.5. A behavioral view of personality. Behaviorists devote little attention to the structure of personality because it is unobservable, but they implicitly view personality as an individual's collection of response tendencies. A possible hierarchy of response tendencies for a specific stimulus situation is shown here.

proach has generally provided a rather male-centered viewpoint.

It's easy to ridicule Freud for concepts such as penis envy and to point to ideas that have turned out to be wrong. Remember, though, that Freud and Adler began to fashion their theories about a century ago. It is not entirely fair to compare these theories to other models that are only a decade old. That's like asking the Wright brothers to race the Concorde. Freud and his psychodynamic colleagues deserve great credit for breaking new ground. Standing at a distance a century later, one has to be impressed by the extraordinary impact that psychodynamic theory has had on modern thought. No other theoretical perspective in psychology has been as influential, except for the one we turn to next—behaviorism.

BEHAVIORAL PERSPECTIVES

Behaviorism **is a theoretical orientation based on the premise that scientific psychology should study observable behavior.** Behaviorism has been a major school of thought in psychology since 1913, when John B. Watson published an influential article. Watson argued that psychology should abandon its earlier focus on the mind and mental processes and focus exclusively on overt behavior. He contended that psychology could not study mental processes in a scientific manner because they are private and not accessible to public observation.

In completely rejecting mental processes as a suitable subject for scientific study, Watson took an extreme position that is no longer dominant among modern behaviorists. Nonetheless, his influence was enormous, as psychology did shift its primary focus from the study of the mind to the study of behavior.

The behaviorists have shown little interest in internal personality structures similar to Freud's id, ego, and superego, because such structures can't be observed. They prefer to think in terms of response tendencies, which can be observed. Thus, most behaviorists view an individual's personality as a *collection of response tendencies that are tied to various stimulus situations.* A specific situation may be associated with a number of response tendencies that vary in strength, depending on an individual's past experience (see Figure 2.5). As an example, consider the stimulus situation of a large party where you know few people. Your response tendencies in this situation, in order of strength, might be (1) to circulate, speaking to others only if they approach you first, (2) to stick close to the few guests you already know, making no effort to meet anyone new, (3) to politely withdraw by getting wrapped up in your host's book, record, or compact disc collection (or whatever is available), and (4) to leave as soon as you can.

Although behaviorists have shown relatively little interest in personality structure, they have focused extensively on personality *development.* They explain development the same way they explain everything else—through learning. In their scheme, the term *learning* is used very broadly to refer to any durable changes in behavior that are due to experience. Some behaviorists (for example, Dollard & Miller, 1950) agree with Freud on the importance of early childhood experiences, but most see personality development as a lifelong journey. They maintain that personality is shaped through a continual, evolutionary process. Hence, they see little value in proposing developmental stages. Instead, they focus on how our response tendencies are shaped through classical conditioning, operant conditioning, and observational learning. Let's look at these processes.

Pavlov's Classical Conditioning

Do you go weak in the knees when you get a note at work that tells you to go see your boss? Do you get anxious when you're around important people? When you're driving, does your heart skip a beat at the sight of a police car—even when you're driving under the speed limit? If so, you probably acquired these common responses through

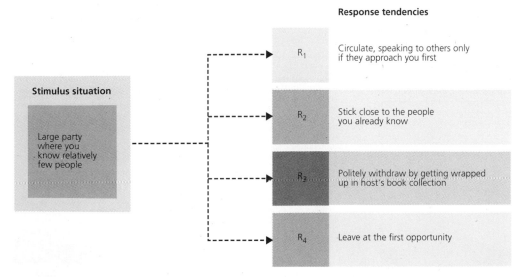

Response tendencies

R₁ — Circulate, speaking to others only if they approach you first

R₂ — Stick close to the people you already know

R₃ — Politely withdraw by getting wrapped up in host's book collection

R₄ — Leave at the first opportunity

Stimulus situation

Large party where you know relatively few people

classical conditioning. *Classical conditioning* **is a type of learning in which a neutral stimulus acquires the capacity to evoke a response that was originally evoked by another stimulus.** This process, which is also called *respondent conditioning,* was first described back in 1903 by Ivan Pavlov.

Pavlov was a prominent Russian physiologist who did Nobel Prize–winning research on digestion. He was a dedicated scientist who was obsessed with his research. Legend has it that Pavlov severely reprimanded an assistant who was late for an experiment because he was trying to avoid street fighting in the midst of the Russian Revolution. The assistant defended his tardiness, saying, "But Professor, there's a revolution going on, with shooting in the streets!" Pavlov supposedly replied, "Next time there's a revolution, get up earlier!" (Fancher, 1979; Gantt, 1975).

The Conditioned Reflex

Pavlov (1906) was studying digestive processes in dogs when he discovered that the dogs could be trained to salivate in response to the sound of a bell. What was so significant about a dog salivating when a bell was rung? The key was that the bell started out as a *neutral* stimulus; that is, originally it did not produce the response of salivation (after all, why should it?). However, Pavlov managed to change that by pairing the bell with a stimulus (meat powder) that did produce the salivation response. Through this process, the bell acquired the capacity to trigger the response of salivation. What Pavlov had demonstrated was *how learned reflexes are acquired.*

There is a special vocabulary associated with classical conditioning. In Pavlov's experiment the bond between the meat powder and salivation was a natural association that was not created through conditioning. In unconditioned bonds, **the *unconditioned stimulus (UCS)* is a stimulus that evokes an unconditioned response without previous conditioning. The *unconditioned response (UCR)* is an unlearned reaction to an unconditioned stimulus that occurs without previous conditioning.**

Figure 2.6. The process of classical conditioning. The sequence of events in classical conditioning is outlined here. As we encounter new examples of classical conditioning throughout the book, we will see diagrams like that shown in the fourth panel, which summarizes the process.

Ivan Pavlov

In contrast, the link between the bell and salivation was established through conditioning. In conditioned bonds, **the *conditioned stimulus (CS)* is a previously neutral stimulus that has acquired the capacity to evoke a conditioned response through conditioning. The *conditioned response (CR)* is a learned reaction to a conditioned stimulus that occurs because of previous conditioning.** Note that the unconditioned response and conditioned response often involve the same behavior (although there may be subtle differences). In Pavlov's initial demonstration, salivation was an unconditioned response when evoked by the UCS (meat powder), and a conditioned response when evoked by the CS (the bell). The procedures involved in classical conditioning are outlined in Figure 2.6.

Pavlov's discovery came to be called the *conditioned reflex.* Classically conditioned responses are viewed as reflexes because most of them are relatively involuntary. Responses that are a product of classical conditioning are said to be *elicited.* This word is meant to convey that these responses are triggered automatically.

Classical Conditioning in Everyday Life

What is the role of classical conditioning in shaping personality in everyday life? Classical conditioning contributes to the acquisition of emotional responses, such as fear and anxiety. This is a relatively small but very important class of responses, as maladaptive emotional reactions underlie many adjustment problems. For example, one middle-aged woman reported being troubled by a bridge phobia so severe that she couldn't drive on inter-

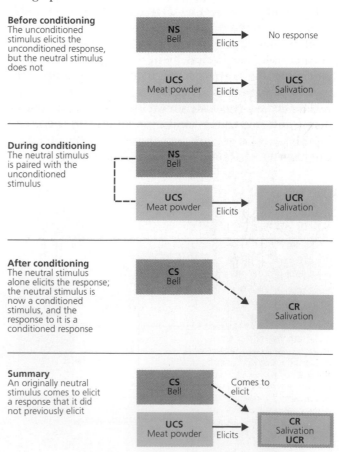

Before conditioning
The unconditioned stimulus elicits the unconditioned response, but the neutral stimulus does not

NS Bell — Elicits → No response

UCS Meat powder — Elicits → UCS Salivation

During conditioning
The neutral stimulus is paired with the unconditioned stimulus

NS Bell

UCS Meat powder — Elicits → UCR Salivation

After conditioning
The neutral stimulus alone elicits the response; the neutral stimulus is now a conditioned stimulus, and the response to it is a conditioned response

CS Bell → CR Salivation

Summary
An originally neutral stimulus comes to elicit a response that it did not previously elicit

CS Bell — Comes to elicit →

UCS Meat powder — Elicits → CR Salivation UCR

state highways because of all the viaducts she would have to cross. She was able to pinpoint the source of her phobia. Many years before, when her family would drive to visit her grandmother, they had to cross a little-used, rickety, dilapidated bridge out in the countryside. Her father, in a misguided attempt at humor, made a major production out of these crossings. He would stop short of the bridge and carry on about the enormous danger of the crossing. Obviously, he thought the bridge was safe, or he wouldn't have driven across it. However, the naive young girl was terrified by her father's scare tactics, and the bridge became a conditioned stimulus eliciting great fear (see Figure 2.7). Unfortunately, the fear spilled over to *all* bridges, and 40 years later she was still carrying the burden of this phobia. Although a number of processes can cause phobias (Marks, 1977), it is clear that classical conditioning is responsible for many of our irrational fears.

Classical conditioning also appears to account for more realistic and moderate anxiety. For example, imagine a news reporter in a high-pressure job where he consistently gets negative feedback about his work from his bosses. The negative comments from his supervisors function as a UCS eliciting anxiety. These reprimands are paired with the noise and sight of the newsroom, so that the newsroom becomes a CS triggering anxiety, even when his supervisors are absent (see Figure 2.8). Our poor reporter might even reach a point at which the mere *thought* of the newsroom elicits anxiety when he is elsewhere.

Fortunately, not every frightening experience leaves a conditioned fear in its wake. A variety of factors influence whether a conditioned response is acquired in a particular situation. Furthermore, a newly formed stimulus-response bond does not necessarily last indefinitely. The right circumstances can lead to *extinction*—**the gradual weakening and disappearance of a conditioned response tendency.** What leads to extinction in classical conditioning? The consistent presentation of the CS *alone*, without the UCS. For example, when Pavlov consistently presented

only the bell to a previously conditioned dog, the bell gradually stopped eliciting the response of salivation. How long it takes to extinguish a conditioned response depends on many factors. Foremost among them is the strength of the conditioned bond when extinction begins. Some conditioned responses extinguish very quickly, while others are very difficult to weaken.

Skinner's Operant Conditioning

Even Pavlov recognized that classical conditioning was not the only form of conditioning. Classical conditioning best explains reflexive responding controlled by stimuli that *precede* the response. However, both animals and humans make many responses that don't fit this description. Consider the response that you are engaging in right now—studying. It is definitely not a reflex (life might be easier if it was). The stimuli that govern it (exams and grades) do not precede it. Instead, your studying response is mainly influenced by events that follow it—specifically, its *consequences*.

This kind of learning is called *operant conditioning*. **Operant conditioning is a form of learning in which voluntary responses come to be controlled by their consequences.** Operant conditioning probably governs a larger share of human behavior than classical conditioning, since most of our responses are voluntary rather than reflexive. Because they are voluntary, operant responses are said to be *emitted* rather than *elicited*.

The study of operant conditioning was led by B. F. Skinner (1953, 1974), an American psychologist who spent most of his career at Harvard University. Skinner achieved renown for his research on learning in lower organisms, mostly rats and pigeons. Like Pavlov, Skinner never set out to develop a theory of personality. But both of them conducted deceptively simple research that became enormously influential, affecting thinking in all areas of psychology, including the explanation of personality.

The fundamental principle of operant conditioning is uncommonly simple. Skinner demonstrated that organ-

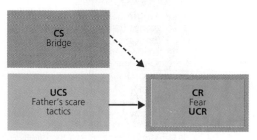

Figure 2.7. Classical conditioning of a phobia. Many emotional responses that would otherwise be puzzling can be explained as a result of classical conditioning. In the case of the woman's bridge phobia, the fear originally elicited by her father's scare tactics became a conditioned response to the stimulus of bridges.

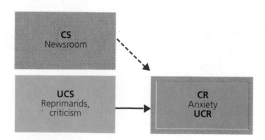

Figure 2.8. Classical conditioning of anxiety. A stimulus (in this case, a newsroom) that is frequently paired with anxiety-arousing events (reprimands and criticism) may come to elicit anxiety by itself, through classical conditioning.

isms tend to repeat those responses that are followed by favorable consequences, and that they tend not to repeat those responses that are followed by neutral or unfavorable consequences. In Skinner's scheme, favorable, neutral, and unfavorable consequences involve reinforcement, extinction, and punishment, respectively. We'll look at each of these in turn, and then discuss stimulus control of operant behavior.

The Power of Reinforcement

According to Skinner, reinforcement can occur in two different ways, which he called *positive reinforcement* and *negative reinforcement*. **Positive reinforcement occurs when a response is strengthened (increases in frequency) because it is followed by the arrival of a (presumably) pleasant stimulus.** Positive reinforcement is roughly synonymous with the concept of reward. Notice, however, that reinforcement is defined *after the fact*, in terms of its effect on behavior. Why? Because reinforcement is subjective. Something that serves as a reinforcer for one person may not function as a reinforcer for another person. For example, peer approval is a potent reinforcer for most people, but not all.

Positive reinforcement motivates much of our everyday behavior. You study hard because good grades are likely to follow as a result. You go to work because this behavior produces paychecks. Perhaps you work extra hard in the hopes of winning a promotion or a pay raise. In each of these examples, certain responses occur because they have led to positive outcomes in the past.

Positive reinforcement influences personality development in a straightforward way. Responses followed by pleasant outcomes are strengthened and tend to become habitual patterns of behavior. For example, a youngster might clown around in class and gain appreciative comments and smiles from schoolmates. This social approval will probably reinforce clowning-around behavior (see Figure 2.9). If such behavior is reinforced with some regularity, it will gradually become an integral element of the youth's personality. Similarly, whether or not a young-ster develops traits such as independence, assertiveness, or selfishness depends on whether the child is reinforced for such behaviors by parents and by other influential persons.

Negative reinforcement occurs when a response is strengthened (increases in frequency) because it is followed by the removal of a (presumably) unpleasant stimulus. Don't let the word *negative* here confuse you. Negative reinforcement *is* reinforcement. Like positive reinforcement, it strengthens a response. However, this strengthening occurs because the response gets rid of an aversive stimulus. Consider a few examples. You rush home in the winter to get out of the cold. You may clean your house to get rid of a mess. Parents often give in to their children's begging to halt the whining.

Negative reinforcement plays a major role in the development of avoidance tendencies. As you may have noticed, many people tend to avoid facing up to awkward situations and sticky personal problems. This personality trait typically develops because avoidance behavior gets rid of anxiety and is therefore negatively reinforced. Recall our imaginary newspaper reporter, whose work environment (the newsroom) elicits anxiety (due to classical conditioning). He might notice that on days when he calls in sick, his anxiety evaporates, so that this response is gradually strengthened— through negative reinforcement (see Figure 2.9). If his avoidance behavior continues to be successful in reducing his anxiety, it might carry over into other areas of his life and become a central aspect of his personality.

Extinction and Punishment

Like the effects of classical conditioning, the effects of operant conditioning may not last forever. In both types of conditioning, *extinction* refers to the gradual weakening and disappearance of a response. In operant conditioning, extinction begins when a previously reinforced response stops producing positive consequences. As extinction progresses, the response typically becomes less and less frequent and eventually disappears.

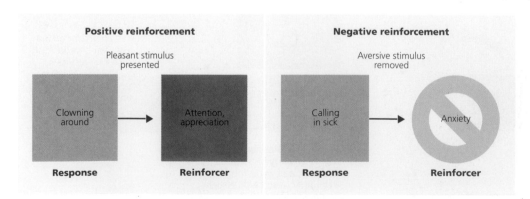

Figure 2.9. Positive and negative reinforcement in operant conditioning. Positive reinforcement occurs when a response is followed by a favorable outcome, so that the response is strengthened. In negative reinforcement, the removal (symbolized here by the "No" sign) of an aversive stimulus serves as a reinforcer. Negative reinforcement produces the same result as positive reinforcement: the person's tendency to emit the reinforced response is strengthened (the response becomes more frequent).

Thus, the response tendencies that make up one's personality are not necessarily permanent. For example, the youngster who found that his classmates reinforced clowning around in grade school might find that his attempts at comedy earn nothing but indifferent stares in high school. This termination of reinforcement would probably lead to the gradual extinction of the clowning-around behavior. How quickly an operant response extinguishes depends on many factors in the person's earlier reinforcement history.

Some responses may be weakened by punishment. In Skinner's scheme, *punishment* occurs when a response is **weakened (decreases in frequency) because it is followed by the arrival of a (presumably) unpleasant stimulus.** The concept of punishment in operant conditioning confuses many students on two counts. First, it is often mixed up with negative reinforcement because both involve aversive stimuli. Please note, however, that they are altogether different events with opposite outcomes! In negative reinforcement, a response leads to the removal of something aversive, and this response is strengthened. In punishment, a response leads to the arrival of something aversive, and this response tends to be weakened.

The second source of confusion involves viewing punishment as only a disciplinary procedure used by parents, teachers, and other authority figures. In the operant model, punishment occurs whenever a response leads to negative consequences. Defined in this way, the concept goes far beyond actions like parents spanking children or teachers handing out detentions. For example, if you wear a new outfit and your friends make fun of it and hurt your feelings, your behavior has been punished, and your tendency to to wear this clothing will decline. Similarly, if you go to a restaurant and have a horrible meal, in Skinner's terminology, your response has led to punishment.

The impact of punishment on personality development is just the opposite of reinforcement. Generally speaking, those patterns of behavior that lead to punishing (that is, negative) consequences tend to be weakened.

For instance, if your impulsive decisions always backfire, your tendency to be impulsive should decline.

Stimulus Control of Operant Behavior

Although operant behavior is ultimately controlled by its consequences, stimuli that *precede* a response can also influence operant behavior. If a response is consistently reinforced in the presence of a particular stimulus, that stimulus may come to serve as a signal indicating that the response is likely to lead to reinforcement. Once we pick up on these signals, we tend to respond accordingly. Thus, *discriminative stimuli* **are cues that influence operant behavior by indicating the probable consequences of a response.**

Social behavior is regulated extensively by discriminative stimuli. Consider the behavior of asking someone out for a date. Many people emit this behavior only very cautiously, after receiving many signals (eye contact, smiles, encouraging conversational exchanges) that reinforcement (an affirmative answer) is fairly likely. Learning to read subtle discriminative stimuli in social interaction is a significant part of developing adequate social skills.

According to Skinner (1987), conditioning in humans operates much as it does in the rats and pigeons that he has studied in his laboratory. Hence, he assumes that conditioning strengthens and weakens our response tendencies "mechanically," that is, without our conscious participation. Like John Watson (1913) before him, Skinner asserts that we can explain behavior without being concerned about individuals' mental processes.

Skinner's ideas continue to be very influential, but his mechanical view of conditioning has not gone unchallenged by other behaviorists. Theorists such as Albert Bandura have developed somewhat different behavioral models in which cognition plays a role. *Cognition* **refers to the thought processes involved in acquiring knowledge.** In other words, cognition is another name for the mental processes that behaviorists have traditionally shown little interest in.

B.F. Skinner

Skinner placed rats and other animal subjects in controlled environments where reinforcement could be regulated and responses accurately measured.

Bandura and Social Learning Theory

Albert Bandura is one of several behaviorists who have added a cognitive flavor to behaviorism since the 1960s. Bandura (1977), Walter Mischel (1973), and Julian Rotter (1982) take issue with Skinner's view. They point out that humans obviously are conscious, thinking, feeling beings. Moreover, they argue that in neglecting cognitive processes, Skinner ignores the most distinctive and important feature of human behavior. Bandura and like-minded theorists call their modified brand of behaviorism *social learning theory.*

Bandura (1977, 1986) agrees with the basic thrust of behaviorism in that he believes that personality is largely shaped through learning. However, he contends that conditioning is not a mechanical process in which we are passive participants. Instead, he maintains that we actively seek out and process information about our environment in order to maximize our favorable outcomes.

Observational Learning

Bandura's foremost theoretical contribution has been his description of observational learning. ***Observational learning* occurs when an organism's responding is influenced by the observation of others, who are called models.** Bandura does not view observational learning as entirely separate from classical and operant conditioning. Instead, he asserts that both classical and operant conditioning can take place indirectly when one person observes another's conditioning (see Figure 2.10).

To illustrate, suppose you observe a friend behaving assertively with a car salesman. Let's say that her assertiveness is reinforced by the exceptionally good buy she obtains on the car. Your own tendency to behave assertively with salespeople might well be strengthened as a result. Notice that the favorable consequence is experienced by your friend, not you. Your friend's tendency to bargain assertively should be reinforced directly. But your tendency to bargain assertively may also be reinforced indirectly.

The theories of Skinner and Pavlov make no allowance for this type of indirect learning. After all, this observational learning requires that you pay *attention* to your friend's behavior, that you *understand* its consequences, and that you store this *information* in *memory*. Obviously, attention, understanding, information, and memory involve cognition, which behaviorists used to ignore.

In recent decades, the potential influence of observational learning has been tragically demonstrated by the occurrence of "copycat crimes." One person hijacks an airliner, sticks a razor blade in Halloween candy, or slips cyanide into a few drug capsules, and before you know it, a half-dozen wretches are showing the power of observational learning. The power of models is often in evidence at rock concerts. Many fans try to emulate their favorite performers, leaving concert audiences choked with a surplus of Prince, Madonna, and David Byrne look-alikes.

Some models are more influential than others. Both children and adults tend to imitate people they like or respect more so than people they don't. We also are especially prone to imitate the behavior of people that we consider attractive or powerful (such as rock stars). In addition, imitation is more likely when we see similarity between the model and ourselves. Thus, children imitate same-sex role models somewhat more than opposite-sex models. Finally, as noted before, we are more likely to copy a model if we see the model's behavior leading to positive outcomes.

According to social learning theory, models have a great impact on personality development. Children learn to be assertive, conscientious, self-sufficient, dependable, easygoing, and so forth by observing others behaving in these ways. Parents, teachers, relatives, siblings, and peers serve as models for young children. Bandura and his colleagues have done extensive research showing how models influence the development of aggressiveness, sex roles, and moral standards in children (Bandura, 1973; Bussey & Bandura, 1984; Mischel & Mischel, 1976). Their research on modeling and aggression has been particularly influential.

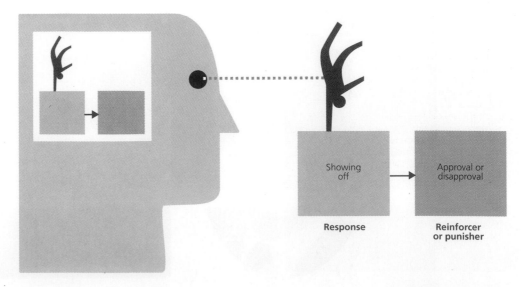

In a classic study, Bandura, Ross, and Ross (1963) showed how the observation of filmed models can influence the learning of aggressive behavior in children. They manipulated whether or not nursery school children saw an aggressive model on film and whether the aggressive models experienced positive or negative consequences. Soon after the manipulations, the children were taken to a toy room where their play was observed through a one-way mirror. Children who had seen the aggressive model rewarded engaged in more aggression than children in the other conditions. This landmark study was one of the earliest experimental demonstrations of a cause-effect relationship between media violence and aggressive behavior.

Self-Efficacy

Bandura believes that *self-efficacy* is a crucial element of personality. **Self-efficacy is our belief about our ability to perform behaviors that should lead to expected outcomes.** When self-efficacy is high, we feel confident that we can execute the responses necessary to earn reinforcers. When self-efficacy is low, we worry that the necessary responses may be beyond our abilities. Perceptions of self-efficacy are subjective and specific to different kinds of tasks. For instance, you might feel extremely confident about your ability to handle difficult social situations, but very doubtful about your ability to handle academic challenges. Perceptions of self-efficacy can influence which challenges we tackle and how well we perform.

Evaluating Behavioral Perpectives

Behavioral theories are firmly rooted in empirical research rather than clinical intuition. This commitment to research has kept the behavioral approach open to new findings and new ideas. Pavlov's model has shed light on how conditioning can account for our sometimes troublesome emotional responses. Skinner's work has demonstrated how our personalities are shaped by the consequences of our behavior. Bandura's social learning

Figure 2.10. Observational learning. In observational learning, an observer attends to and stores a mental representation of a model's behavior (for example, showing off by doing handstands) and its consequences (such as approval or disapproval from others). According to social learning theory, many of our characteristic responses are acquired through observation of others' behavior.

theory has shown how our observations mold our characteristic behavior.

The behaviorists have also provided the most thorough account of why people are only moderately consistent in their behavior. For example, a person who is shy in one context might be quite outgoing in another. Other models of personality largely ignore this inconsistency. The behaviorists have shown that this inconsistency occurs because we behave in ways that we think will lead to reinforcement in the situation at hand. In other words, situational factors play a significant role in controlling our behavior.

Of course, each theoretical approach has its shortcomings, and the behavioral approach is no exception. Major lines of criticism include the following.

1. *Overdependence on animal research.* Many principles in behavioral theories were discovered through research on animals. Some critics argue that behaviorists depend too much on animal research and that they indiscriminately generalize from the behavior of animals to the behavior of humans.

2. *Neglect of biological factors.* Most behaviorists would admit that biological factors influence our behavior. However, they have made little effort to integrate biological factors into their theories.

3. *Fragmentation of personality.* Behaviorists have also been criticized for providing a fragmented view of personality. The behavioral approach carves personality into stimulus-response associations. There are no unifying structural concepts (such as Freud's ego) that tie these pieces together. Humanistic theorists, whom we cover next, have been particularly vocal in criticizing this piecemeal analysis of personality.

HUMANISTIC PERSPECTIVES

Humanistic theory emerged in the 1950s as something of a backlash against the behavioral and psychodynamic theories that we have just discussed. The principal charge hurled at these two models was that they were dehumanizing. Freudian theory was criticized for its belief that primitive, animalistic drives dominate behavior. Behaviorism was criticized for its preoccupation with animal research and for its fragmented analysis of personality. Critics argued that both schools viewed people as helpless pawns controlled by their environment and their past, with little capacity for self-direction. Many of these critics blended into a loose alliance that was christened the "third force" in psychology because it surfaced as an alternative to the two dominant "forces" at the time (the psychodynamic and behavioral orientations).

This third force came to be known as humanism because of its exclusive interest in human behavior. *Humanism* **is a theoretical orientation that emphasizes the unique qualities of humans, especially their free will and their potential for personal growth.** Humanistic psychologists are interested only in issues important to human existence, such as love, creativity, loneliness, and personal growth. They do not believe that we can learn anything of any significance about the human condition from animal research.

Humanistic theorists take an optimistic view of human nature. In contrast to most psychodynamic and behavioral theorists, humanistic theorists believe (1) that human nature includes an innate drive toward personal growth, (2) that we have the freedom to chart our own courses of action and are not pawns of our environment, and (3) that we are largely conscious and rational beings who are not dominated by unconscious, irrational needs and conflicts. Humanistic theorists also maintain that one's subjective view of the world is more important than objective reality. According to this notion, if you *think* you are homely, or bright, or sociable, then these beliefs will influence your behavior more than the actual realities of how homely, bright, or sociable you are.

The humanistic approach clearly provides a different perspective on personality than either the psychodynamic or behavioral approaches. In this section we'll review the ideas of the two most influential humanistic theorists, Carl Rogers and Abraham Maslow.

Rogers's Person-Centered Theory

Carl Rogers (1951, 1961, 1980) was one of the fathers of the human potential movement, which emphasizes personal growth through sensitivity training, encounter groups, and other exercises intended to help people get in touch with their true selves. Working at the University of Chicago in the 1940s, Rogers devised a major new approach to psychotherapy. Like Freud, Rogers based his personality theory on his extensive therapeutic interactions with many clients. Because of his emphasis on a person's subjective point of view, Rogers calls his approach a *person-centered theory*.

The Self and Its Development

Rogers views personality structure in terms of just one construct. He called this construct the *self*, although it is more widely known today as the *self-concept*. **A *self-concept* is a collection of beliefs about one's own nature, unique qualities, and typical behavior.** Your self-concept is your mental picture of yourself. It is a collection of self-perceptions. For example, a self-concept might include beliefs such as "I am easygoing" or "I am pretty" or "I am hardworking."

Rogers stresses the subjective nature of the self-concept. Your self-concept may not be entirely consistent with your actual experiences. To put it more bluntly, your self-concept may be inaccurate. Most of us are prone to distort our experiences to some extent to promote a relatively favorable self-concept. For example, you may believe that you are quite bright academically, but your grade transcript might suggest otherwise. Rogers uses the term *incongruence* **to refer to the disparity between one's self-concept and one's actual experience.** In contrast, if a person's self-concept is reasonably accurate, it is said to be *congruent* with reality. Everyone experiences *some* incongruence; the crucial issue is how much (see Figure 2.11).

Carl Rogers

Rogers maintains that a great deal of incongruence undermines our psychological well-being.

In terms of personality development, Rogers was concerned with how childhood experiences promote congruence or incongruence. According to Rogers, we have a strong need for affection, love, and acceptance from others. Early in life, parents provide most of this affection. Rogers maintains that some parents make their affection very *conditional*. That is, they make it depend on the child's behaving well and living up to expectations. When parental love seems conditional, children often block out of their self-concept those experiences that make them feel unworthy of love. At the other end of the spectrum, Rogers asserts that some parents make their affection very *unconditional*. Their children have less need to block out unworthy experiences because they have been assured that they are worthy of affection, no matter what they do.

Rogers believes that unconditional love from parents fosters congruence and that conditional love fosters incongruence. He further theorizes that if we grow up believing that affection from others (besides our parents) is very conditional, we go on to distort more and more of our experiences to feel worthy of acceptance from a wider and wider array of people, so that incongruence continues to grow.

A person's self-concept evolves throughout childhood and adolescence. As our self-concept gradually stabilizes, we begin to feel comfortable with it and we usually are loyal to it. This loyalty produces two effects. First, our self-concept becomes a self-fulfilling prophecy in that we tend to behave in ways that are consistent with it. If you see yourself as an even-tempered, reflective person, you'll consciously work at behaving in these ways. If you happen to behave impulsively, you'll probably feel some discomfort because you're acting "out of character." Second, we become resistant to information that contradicts our self-concept. Contradictory information threatens our comfortable equilibrium. If your experiences begin to suggest that you are not as even-tempered as you thought, you will probably find ways to dismiss this evidence.

Anxiety and Defense

According to Rogers, experiences that threaten our personal views of ourselves are the principal cause of troublesome anxiety. The more inaccurate your self-concept is, the more likely you are to have experiences that clash with your self-perceptions. Thus, people with highly incongruent self-concepts are especially likely to be plagued by recurrent anxiety.

To ward off this anxiety, we often behave defensively. Thus, we ignore, deny, and twist reality to protect our self-concept. Consider a young woman who, like most of us, considers herself a "nice person." Let us suppose that in reality she is rather conceited and selfish, and she gets feedback from both boyfriends and girlfriends that she is a "self-centered, snotty brat." How might she react in order to protect her self-concept? She might ignore or block out those occasions when she behaves selfishly and then deny the accusations by her friends that she is self-centered. She might attribute her girlfriends' negative comments to their jealousy of her good looks and blame the boyfriends' negative remarks on their disappointment because she won't get more serious with them. Meanwhile, she might start doing some kind of charity work to show everyone (including herself) that she really is a nice person. As you can see, we often go to great lengths to defend our self-concept.

Rogers's theory can explain defensive behavior and personality disturbances, but he believes that it is also important to focus attention on psychological health. Rogers asserts that psychological health is rooted in a congruent self-concept. In turn, congruence is rooted in a sense of personal worth, which stems from a childhood saturated with unconditional affection from parents and others. These themes are similar to those that were emphasized by the other major humanistic theorist, Abraham Maslow.

Self-concept   Actual experience

Congruence
Self-concept meshes well with actual experience (some incongruence is probably unavoidable)

Self-concept   Actual experience

Incongruence
Self-concept does not mesh well with actual experience

Figure 2.11. Rogers's view of personality structure. In Rogers's model, the self-concept is the only important structural construct. However, Rogers acknowledges that one's self-concept may not jell with the realities of one's actual experience—a condition called incongruence. Different people have varied amounts of incongruence between their self-concept and reality.

Maslow's Theory of Self-Actualization

Abraham Maslow grew up in Brooklyn and spent much of his career at Brandeis University, where he provided crucial leadership for the fledgling humanistic movement. Like Rogers, Maslow (1968, 1970) argued that psychology should take a greater interest in the nature of the healthy personality, instead of dwelling on the causes of disorders. "To oversimplify the matter somewhat," he said, "it is as if Freud supplied to us the sick half of psychology and we must now fill it out with the healthy half" (Maslow, 1968, p. 5). Maslow's key contributions were his analysis of how motives are organized hierarchically and his description of the healthy personality.

Hierarchy of Needs

Maslow proposed that human motives are organized into a *hierarchy of needs*—**a systematic arrangement of needs, according to priority, in which basic needs must be met before less basic needs are aroused.** This hierarchical arrangement is usually portrayed as a pyramid (see Figure 2.12). The needs at the bottom of the pyramid are the most basic. They are fundamental physiological needs that are essential to survival, such as the need for oxygen, food, and water. These needs must be satisfied fairly well before we become concerned about needs at higher levels in the hierarchy. When we manage to satisfy a level of needs reasonably well (complete satisfaction is not necessary), *this satisfaction activates needs at the next level.*

The second tier in Maslow's pyramid is made up of safety and security needs. These needs reflect concern about *long-term* survival. People seek to live in a stable, safe world. Safety and security needs motivate adults to seek a secure job, buy insurance, and put money in their savings accounts. When safety and security needs are met adequately, needs for love and belongingness become more prominent. These needs lead people to seek affection—from family, from friends, and in intimate relationships. When these needs are gratified, esteem needs are activated. People then become more concerned about their achievements and the recognition, respect, and status they earn.

Like Rogers, Maslow argued that humans have an innate drive toward personal growth—that is, evolution toward a higher state of being. Thus, he described the needs in the uppermost reaches of his hierarchy as *growth needs*. These include the need for knowledge, understanding, order, and aesthetic beauty.

Foremost among them is the ***need for self-actualization, which is the need to fulfill one's potential; it is the highest need in Maslow's motivational hierarchy.*** Maslow summarized this concept with a simple statement: "What a man *can* be, he *must* be." According to Maslow, people will be frustrated if they are unable to fully utilize their talents or pursue their true interests. For example, if you have great musical talent but must work as an accountant, or if you have scholarly interests but must work as a sales clerk, your need for self-actualization will be thwarted. Maslow's own experiences may have influenced his emphasis on the need for self-actualization. He endured some frustration because his family pressured him to study law, but he soon managed to turn to his true interest, psychology.

Maslow theorized that the various levels of needs are ordered in the same way for nearly everyone. However, he recognized that some people might get their hierarchies scrambled because of unusual factors in their personal history. He speculated that the most common rearrangement of levels occurs when adults put higher priority on their esteem needs than on their love and belongingness needs. Such people often pour all their energy into their careers while their marriage or personal life deteriorates.

The Healthy Personality

Because of his interest in self-actualization, Maslow set out to discover the nature of the healthy personality. He tried to identify people of exceptional mental health, so that he could investigate their characteristics. In one case, he used psychological tests and interviews to sort out the healthiest 1% of a sizable population of college students. He also studied admired historical figures (such as Tho-

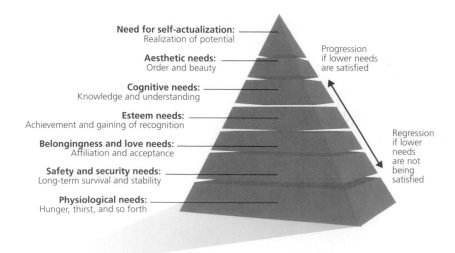

Need for self-actualization: Realization of potential

Aesthetic needs: Order and beauty

Cognitive needs: Knowledge and understanding

Esteem needs: Achievement and gaining of recognition

Belongingness and love needs: Affiliation and acceptance

Safety and security needs: Long-term survival and stability

Physiological needs: Hunger, thirst, and so forth

Progression if lower needs are satisfied

Regression if lower needs are not being satisfied

Figure 2.12. Maslow's hierarchy of needs. According to Maslow, our needs are arranged in a hierarchy, and we must satisfy our basic needs first, before we progress to higher needs. In the diagram, higher levels in the pyramid represent progressively less basic needs. We progress upward in the hierarchy when lower needs are satisfied reasonably well, but we may regress back to lower levels if basic needs cease to be satisfied.

© 1970 UNITED FEATURE SYNDICATE, INC REPRINTED BY PERMISSION.

mas Jefferson and psychologist-philosopher William James) and personal acquaintances characterized by superior adjustment. Over a period of years, he accumulated his case histories and gradually sketched, in broad strokes, a picture of ideal psychological health.

Maslow called people with exceptionally healthy personalities *self-actualizing persons* because of their commitment to continued personal growth. He identified various traits characteristic of self-actualizing people, which are listed in Figure 2.13. In brief, Maslow found that self-actualizers are accurately tuned in to reality and that they are at peace with themselves. He found that they are open and spontaneous and that they retain a fresh appreciation of the world around them. Socially, they are sensitive to others' needs and enjoy rewarding interpersonal relations. However, they are not dependent upon others for approval. Nor are they uncomfortable with solitude. They thrive on their work, and they enjoy their sense of humor. Maslow also noted that they enjoy "peak experiences" (profound emotional highs) more often than others. Finally, he found that they strike a nice balance between many polarities in personality, so that they can be both childlike and mature, rational and intuitive, conforming and rebellious.

Evaluating Humanistic Perspectives

The humanists added a refreshing perspective to the study of personality. Their argument that a person's subjective views may be more important than objective reality has proven compelling. Today, even behavioral theorists have begun to consider subjective personal factors such as beliefs and expectancies. The humanistic approach also deserves credit for making the self-concept an important construct in psychology. Finally, the humanists have often been applauded for focusing attention on the issue of what constitutes a healthy personality.

Of course, there is a negative side to the balance sheet as well. Critics have identified some weaknesses in the humanistic approach to personality, including the following.

1. *Poor testability.* Like psychodynamic theorists, the humanists have been criticized for proposing hypotheses that are very difficult to put to a scientific test. Humanistic concepts like personal growth and self-actualization are difficult to define and measure.

2. *Unrealistic view of human nature.* Critics also charge that the humanists have been overly optimistic in their assumptions about human nature and unrealistic in their descriptions of the healthy personality. For instance, Maslow's self-actualizing people sound *perfect*. In reality, Maslow had a very hard time finding self-actualizing persons. When he searched among the living, the results were so disappointing that he turned to the study of historical figures. Thus, humanistic portraits of psychological health are perhaps a bit unrealistic.

3. *Inadequate evidence.* Humanistic theories are based primarily on discerning but uncontrolled observations in clinical settings. Case studies can be valuable in generating ideas, but they are ill-suited for building a solid data base. More experimental research is needed to catch up

Figure 2.13. Characteristics of self-actualizing people.
Humanistic theorists emphasize psychological health instead of maladjustment. Maslow's sketch of the self-actualizing person provides a provocative picture of the healthy personality.

Characteristics of Self-Actualizing People

- Clear, efficient perception of reality and comfortable relations with it
- Spontaneity, simplicity, and naturalness
- Problem centering (having something outside themselves they "must" do as a mission)
- Detachment and need for privacy
- Autonomy, independence of culture and environment
- Continued freshness of appreciation
- Mystical and peak experiences

- Feelings of kinship and identification with the human race
- Strong friendships, but limited in number
- Democratic character structure
- Ethical discrimination between means and ends, between good and evil
- Philosophical, unhostile sense of humor
- Balance between polarities in personality

with the theorizing in the humanistic camp. This is precisely the opposite of the situation that we'll encounter in the next section, on biological perspectives, where more theorizing is needed to catch up with the research.

BIOLOGICAL PERSPECTIVES

Like many identical twins reared apart, Jim Lewis and Jim Springer found they had been leading eerily similar lives. Separated four weeks after birth in 1940, the Jim twins grew up 45 miles apart in Ohio and were reunited in 1979. Eventually, they discovered that both drove the same model blue Chevrolet, chain-smoked Salems, chewed their fingernails and owned dogs named Toy. Each had spent a good deal of time vacationing at the same three-block strip of beach in Florida. More important, when tested for such personality traits as flexibility, self-control and sociability, the twins responded almost exactly alike. [Leo, 1987, p. 63]

So began a *Time* magazine summary of a major twin study conducted at the University of Minnesota, where investigators have been exploring the hereditary roots of personality. The research team has managed to locate and complete testing on 44 rare pairs of identical twins separated early in life. Not all the twin pairs have been as similar as Jim Lewis and Jim Springer, but many of the parallels have been uncanny. Identical twins Oskar Stohr and Jack Yufe were separated soon after birth. Oskar was sent to a Nazi-run school in Czechoslovakia, while Jack was raised in a Jewish home on a Caribbean island. When they were reunited for the first time during middle age, they both showed up wearing similar mustaches, haircuts, shirts, and wire-rimmed glasses. A pair of previously separated female twins both arrived at the Minneapolis airport wearing seven rings on their fingers. One had a son named Richard Andrew, and the other had a son named Andrew Richard! Still another pair of separated twin sisters shared the same phobia of water. They even dealt with it in the same peculiar way— by backing into the ocean.

Could personality be largely inherited? These anecdotal reports of striking resemblances between identical twins reared apart certainly raise this possibility. In this section we'll discuss Hans Eysenck's theory, which emphasizes the influence of heredity, and look at recent research on the biological bases of personality.

Eysenck's Theory

Hans Eysenck was born in Germany, but fled to London during the era of Nazi rule. He went on to become one of Britain's most prominent psychologists. According to Eysenck (1967), "Personality is determined to a large extent by a person's genes" (p. 20). How is heredity linked to personality in Eysenck's model? In part, through conditioning concepts borrowed from behavioral theory. Eysenck (1967, 1982) theorizes that some people can be conditioned more readily than others because of inherited differences in their physiological functioning (specifically, their autonomic reactivity, which we'll discuss in Chapter 3). These variations in "conditionability" are assumed to influence the personality traits that people acquire through conditioning.

Like Gordon Allport and Raymond Cattell, Eysenck maintains that some traits are more important than others. Eysenck views personality structure as a hierarchy of traits. Numerous superficial traits are derived from a smaller number of more basic traits, which are derived from a handful of fundamental higher-order traits, as shown in Figure 2.14.

Eysenck has shown a special interest in explaining variations in *extraversion-introversion*, which is one of the fundamental personality traits in his model. He has proposed that people who become introverts have an inherited tendency to condition more easily than extraverts. According to Eysenck, people who condition easily acquire more conditioned inhibitions than others. These inhibitions make them more bashful, tentative, and uneasy in social situations. This social discomfort leads them to turn inward. Hence, they become introverted.

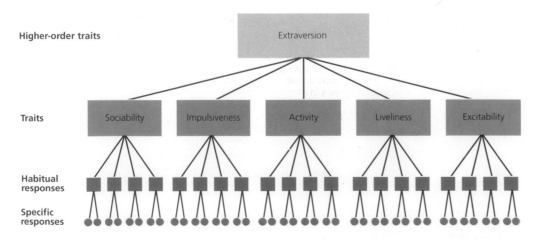

Higher-order traits

Traits

Habitual responses

Specific responses

Figure 2.14. Eysenck's model of personality structure. Eysenck describes personality structure as a hierarchy of traits. In this scheme, a few higher-order traits (such as extraversion) determine a host of lower-order traits (such as sociability), which determine our habitual responses (such as going to lots of parties). In turn, these determine our specific responses to situations.

Is there any empirical evidence to support Eysenck's theory? Yes. Eysenck and Levey (1972) found that introverts developed a classically conditioned eye blink response more easily than extraverts, as predicted. Additionally, there is some evidence that operant conditioning procedures (reinforcement) work more rapidly on introverts than extraverts (Eysenck, 1967).

Recent Research

Recent twin studies have also provided impressive support for Eysenck's hypothesis that personality is largely inherited. In **twin studies researchers assess hereditary influence by comparing the resemblance of identical twins and fraternal twins on a trait.** The logic underlying this comparison is as follows. *Identical twins* emerge from one egg that splits, so that their genetic makeup is exactly the same (100% overlap). *Fraternal twins* result when two eggs are fertilized simultaneously; their genetic overlap is only 50%. Both types of twins *usually* grow up in the same home, at the same time, exposed to the same relatives, neighbors, peers, teachers, events, and so forth. Thus, both kinds of twins normally develop under similar environmental conditions, but identical twins share more genetic kinship. Hence, if sets of identical twins exhibit more personality resemblance than sets of fraternal twins, this greater similarity is probably due to heredity rather than environment.

In one large study, 573 pairs of twins responded to five personality scales that measured altruism, empathy, nurturance, aggressiveness, and assertiveness (Rushton et al., 1986). Figure 2.15 shows the mean correlations observed on three of these traits. Higher correlations are indicative of greater similarity on a trait. On all five traits, identical twins were found to be much more similar to each other than fraternal twins. The investigators attribute the identical twins' greater personality resemblance to their greater genetic similarity. Based on the observed correlations, they *estimate* that genetic factors account for about 56% to 72% of the variation in the five traits studied.

Some skeptics still wonder whether identical twins might exhibit more personality resemblance than fraternal twins because they are raised more similarly. In other words, they wonder whether environmental factors (rather than heredity) could be responsible for identical twins' greater similarity. This nagging question can be answered only by studying identical twins who have been reared apart. This is why the twin study at the University of Minnesota is so important.

The Minnesota study (Tellegen et al., 1988) is the first to administer the same personality test to identical and fraternal twins reared together as well as apart. Most of the twins reared apart were separated quite early in life (median age of 2½months) and remained separated for a long time (median period of almost 34 years). Nonetheless, on all three of the higher-order traits examined, the identical twins reared apart displayed more personality resemblance than fraternal twins reared together. Based on the pattern of correlations observed, the researchers estimate that genetic inheritance accounts for at least 50% of the variation among people in personality.

Evaluating Biological Perspectives

Recent studies have provided convincing evidence that biological factors help to shape personality. Nonetheless, we must take note of some weaknesses in biological approaches to personality.

1. *Problems with estimates of hereditary influence.* Efforts to carve personality into genetic and environmental components with statistics are ultimately artificial. The effects of heredity and environment are twisted together in complicated interactions that can't be separated cleanly. Estimates of the genetic component in personality should be regarded as "ballpark" estimates that will vary somewhat depending on sampling procedures.

2. *Lack of adequate theory.* At present there is no comprehensive biological theory of personality. Eysenck's model does not provide a systematic overview of how biological

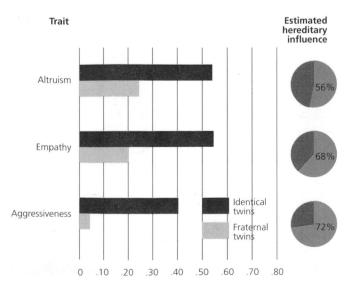

Figure 2.15. Heredity and personality. Selected results from the twin study of personality conducted by Rushton et al. (1986) are shown here. Identical twins showed stronger correlations in personality than fraternal twins, suggesting that personality is partly inherited. The correlational data yielded rather high estimates of hereditary influence for the personality traits examined in the study.

factors govern personality development (and was never intended to). Additional theoretical work is needed to catch up with recent empirical findings on the biological basis for personality.

AN EPILOGUE ON THEORETICAL DIVERSITY

Our review of perspectives on personality should have made one thing abundantly clear: Psychology is marked by theoretical diversity. Why do we have so many competing points of view? One reason is that no single theory can adequately explain everything that we know about personality. Sometimes different theories focus on different aspects of behavior.

Sometimes there is simply more than one way to look at something. Is the glass half empty or half full? Obviously, it is both. To take an example from another science, physicists wrestled for years with the nature of light. Is it a wave, or is it a particle? In the end, it proved useful to think of light sometimes as a wave, and sometimes as a particle. Similarly, if a business executive lashes out at her employees with stinging criticism, is she releasing pent-up aggressive urges (a psychoanalytic view)? Is she making a habitual response to the stimulus of incompetent work (a behavioral view)? Is she trying to act like a tough boss because that's a key aspect of her self-concept (a humanistic view)? Or is she exhibiting an inherited tendency to be aggressive (a biological view)? In some cases, all four of these explanations might have some validity.

In short, it is an oversimplification to expect that one view has to be right while all others are wrong. Life is rarely that simple. In view of the complexity of personality, it would be surprising if there were *not* a number of different theories.

It's probably best to think of the various theoretical orientations in psychology as complementary viewpoints, each with its own advantages and limitations. Indeed, modern psychologists increasingly recognize that theoretical diversity is a strength rather than a weakness (Wertheimer, 1970). As we proceed through this text, you will see how differing theoretical perspectives often inspire fruitful research and how they sometimes converge on a more complete understanding of behavior than could be achieved by any one perspective alone.

SUMMARY

The concept of personality explains the consistency in our behavior over time and situations while also explaining individuals' distinctiveness. Personality traits are dispositions to behave in certain ways. As Allport first noted, some traits are more basic than others.

Freud's psychoanalytic theory emphasizes the importance of the unconscious. Freud described personality structure in terms of three components that are involved in internal conflicts, which generate anxiety. According to Freud, we often ward off anxiety and other unpleasant emotions with defense mechanisms, which work through self-deception. Freud believed that the first five years of life are extremely influential in shaping adult personality. Adler's individual psychology emphasizes how we strive for superiority in order to compensate for our feelings of inferiority. Adler also emphasized the social context in which personality develops.

Psychodynamic theories have produced many groundbreaking insights about the unconscious, the role of conflict, and the importance of early, formative childhood experiences. However, they have been criticized for their poor testability, their inadequate base of empirical evidence, and their male-centered views of the human condition.

Behavioral theories view personality as a collection of response tendencies shaped through learning. Pavlov's classical conditioning can explain how we acquire emotional responses. Skinner's model of operant conditioning shows how consequences such as reinforcement, extinction, and punishment shape our habitual patterns of behavior. Bandura's social learning theory adds a cognitive flavor to behaviorism. It shows how we can be conditioned indirectly through observation.

Behavioral approaches to personality are based on rigorous research. They have provided ample insights about how situational factors and learning mold our personalities. However, the behaviorists have been criticized for their overdependence on animal research, their neglect of biological factors, and their fragmented analysis of personality.

Humanistic theories take an optimistic view of our conscious, rational ability to chart our own courses of action. Rogers focuses on the self-concept as the critical aspect of personality. He maintains that incongruence between one's self-concept and reality creates anxiety and leads to defensive behavior. Maslow theorized that our needs are arranged hierarchically. He asserted that psy-chological health depends on fulfilling our need for self-actualization.

Humanistic theories deserve credit for highlighting the importance of subjective views of oneself and for confronting the question of what makes for a healthy personality. However, they lack a firm base of research, are difficult to put to an empirical test, and may be overly optimistic about human nature.

Eysenck believes that individual differences in physiological functioning affect our conditioning and thus influence personality. Recent twin studies have provided impressive evidence that genetic factors shape personality. The biological approach has been criticized because there are problems with estimates of hereditary influence and because there is no comprehensive biological model of personality.

The study of personality illustrates how great the theoretical diversity in psychology is. This diversity is a strength in that it fuels research that helps us move toward a more complete understanding of behavior. The upcoming Application discusses how you can learn more about your personality (and abilities) through psychological testing. It describes the logic and limitations of such tests.

Assessing Your Personality

Answer the following true or false.

☐ **1.** Responses to personality tests are subject to unconscious distortion.

☐ **2.** The results of personality tests are often misunderstood.

☐ **3.** Personality test scores should be interpreted with caution.

☐ **4.** Personality tests may be quite useful in helping people to learn more about themselves.

If you answered "true" to all four questions, you earned a perfect score. Yes, personality tests are subject to distortion. Admittedly, test results are often misunderstood, and they should be interpreted cautiously. In spite of these problems, however, psychological tests can be very useful.

The value of psychological tests lies in their ability to help people form a realistic picture of their personal qualities. In light of this value, we have included a variety of personality tests in this book. As you may have noticed, you'll find a "Questionnaire" at the end of each chapter. Most of these questionnaires are widely used personality tests. We hope that you may gain some insights by responding to these scales. But it's important to understand the logic and limitations of such tests. To facilitate your use of these and other tests, this Application discusses some of the basics of psychological testing.

KEY CONCEPTS IN PSYCHOLOGICAL TESTING

A *psychological test* **is a standardized measure of a sample of a person's behavior.** Psychological tests are measurement instruments. They are used to measure abilities, aptitudes, and personality traits.

Note that your responses to a psychological test represent a *sample* of your behavior. This reality should alert you to one of the key limitations of psychological tests. It's always possible that a particular behavior sample is not representative of your characteristic behavior. We all have our bad days. A stomachache, a fight with a friend, a problem with your car—all might affect your responses to a particular

test on a particular day. The problem of getting a good sample is *not* unique to testing. It's a problem for any measurement technique. For example, someone taking your blood pressure might get an unrepresentative reading. Because of the limitations of the sampling process, test scores should always be interpreted *cautiously*. Most psychological tests are sound measurement devices, but test results should *not* be viewed as the "final word" on one's personality and abilities because of the ever-present sampling problem.

Most psychological tests can be placed in one of two broad categories: (1) mental ability tests, and (2) personality tests. *Mental ability tests*, such as intelligence tests, aptitude tests, and achievement tests, often serve as gateways to schooling, training programs, and jobs. *Personality tests* measure various aspects of personality, including motives, interests, values, and attitudes. Many psychologists prefer to call these tests personality *scales*, since the questions do not have right and wrong answers as do those on tests of mental abilities.

Standardization and Norms

Both personality scales and tests of mental abilities are *standardized* measures of behavior. *Standardization* **refers to the uniform procedures used to administer and score a test.** All subjects get the same instructions, the same questions, the same time limits, and so on, so that their scores can be compared meaningfully.

The standardization of a test's scoring system includes the development of test norms. *Test norms* **provide information about where a score on a psychological test ranks in relation to other scores on that test.** Why do we need test norms? Because in psychological testing, everything is relative. Psychological tests tell you how you score *relative to other people*. They tell you, for instance, that you are average in impulsiveness, or slightly above average in assertiveness, or far below average in anxiety. These interpretations are derived from the test norms.

The sample of people that the norms are based on is called a test's *standardization group*. Ideally, test norms are based on a large sample of people who were carefully selected to be representative of the broader population. In reality, the representativeness of standardization groups varies considerably from one test to another.

Reliability and Validity

Any kind of measuring device, whether it's a tire gauge, a stopwatch, or a psychological test, should be reasonably consistent. That is, repeated measurements should yield reasonably similar results. To appreciate the importance of reliability, think about how you would react if a tire pressure gauge gave you several very different readings for the same tire. You would probably conclude that the gauge was broken and toss it into the garbage because you know that consistency in measurement is essential to accuracy.

Reliability **refers to the measurement consistency of a test.** A reliable test is one that yields similar results for people upon repetition of the test (see Figure 2.16). Like most other types of measuring devices, psychological tests are not perfectly reliable. They usually do not yield the exact same score when repeated. A certain amount of inconsistency is unavoidable because human behavior is variable. Personality tests tend to have lower reliability than mental ability tests

because daily fluctuations in mood influence how we respond to such tests.

Even if a test is quite reliable, we still need to be concerned about its validity. *Validity* **refers to the ability of a test to measure what it was designed to measure.** If we develop a new test of assertiveness, we have to provide some evidence that it really measures assertiveness. Validity can be demonstrated in a variety of ways. Most of them involve correlating scores on a test with other measures of the same trait, or with related traits. Each of the tests that appear in this book will be accompanied by a brief discussion of the evidence for its validity.

PERSONALITY TESTING

We all engage in efforts to size up our own personality as well as that of others. When you think to yourself that "this salesman is untrustworthy," or when you remark to a friend that "Howard is too timid and submissive," you are making personality assessments. In a sense, then, personality assessment is part of daily life. However, psychological tests provide much more systematic assessments than our casual observations.

The vast majority of personality tests are self-report inventories. *Self-report inventories*

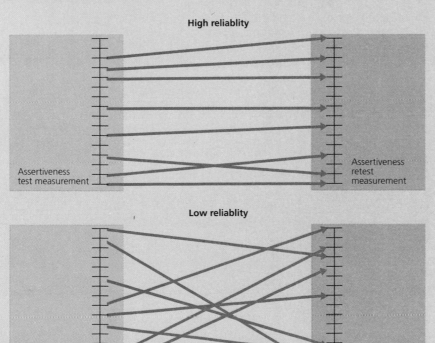

High reliablity

Assertiveness test measurement

Assertiveness retest measurement

Low reliablity

Assertiveness test measurement

Assertiveness retest measurement

Figure 2.16. Test reliability. Subjects' scores on the first administration of an assertiveness test are represented on the left, and their scores on a second administration (a few weeks later) are represented on the right. If subjects obtain similar scores on both administrations, the test measures assertiveness consistently and is said to have high reliability. If subjects get very different scores when they take the assertiveness test a second time, the test is said to have low reliability.

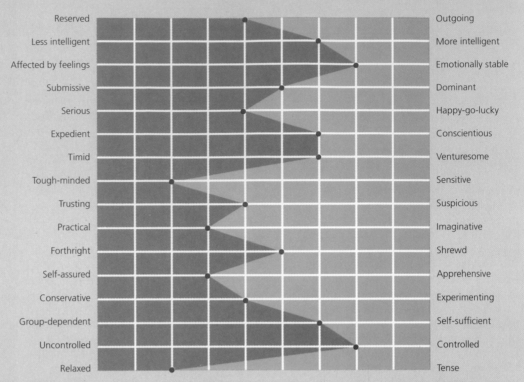

Figure 2.17. The Sixteen Personality Factor Questionnaire (16PF). Cattell's 16PF is designed to assess normal aspects of personality. The pairs of traits listed across from each other in the figure define the 16 factors measured by this self-report inventory. The profile shown is the average profile seen among a group of airline pilots who took the test.

Reserved		Outgoing
Less intelligent		More intelligent
Affected by feelings		Emotionally stable
Submissive		Dominant
Serious		Happy-go-lucky
Expedient		Conscientious
Timid		Venturesome
Tough-minded		Sensitive
Trusting		Suspicious
Practical		Imaginative
Forthright		Shrewd
Self-assured		Apprehensive
Conservative		Experimenting
Group-dependent		Self-sufficient
Uncontrolled		Controlled
Relaxed		Tense

ask individuals to answer a series of questions about their characteristic behavior. When you take a self-report personality scale, you endorse statements as true or false as applied to you, or indicate how often you behave in a particular way, or rate yourself with respect to certain qualities. For example, on the Minnesota Multiphasic Personality Inventory, people respond "true," "false," or "cannot say" to 550 statements such as the following.

I get a fair deal from most people.

I have the time of my life at parties.

I am glad that I am alive.

Several people are following me every-where.

The logic underlying this approach is very simple. Who knows you better than you do? Who has known you longer? Who has more access to your private feelings?

The entire range of personality traits can be measured with self-report inventories. Some scales measure just one trait, others simultaneously assess a multitude of traits. The Sixteen Personality Factor Questionnaire (16PF), developed by Raymond Cattell and his colleagues (Cattell, Eber, & Tatsuoka, 1970), is a representative example of a multitrait inventory. The 16PF is a 187-item scale that measures 16 basic dimensions of personality, called *source traits*, which are listed in Figure 2.17.

To appreciate the strengths of self-report inventories, consider how else you might assess your personality. For instance, how assertive are you? You probably have some vague idea, but can you accurately estimate how your assertiveness compares to others'? To do that, you need a great deal of comparative information about others' usual behavior—information that all of us lack. In contrast, a self-report inventory inquires about your typical behavior in a wide variety of circumstances requiring assertiveness and generates an exact comparison with the typical behavior reported by many other respondents for the same circumstances. Thus, self-report inventories are much more thorough and precise than our casual observations.

However, they are only as accurate as the information that we give them. In responding to self-report inventories, some people are unconsciously influenced by the social desirability or acceptability of the statements. Without realizing it, they endorse only those statements that make them look good. The problem of unconscious distortion provides another reason why personality test results should always be regarded as suggestive rather than definitive.

1. Explain the concepts of personality and traits and describe Allport's system for organizing traits.

2. Describe Freud's three components of personality and how these are distributed across levels of awareness.

3. Explain the importance of sexual and aggressive conflicts in Freud's theory and describe seven defense mechanisms.

4. Outline Freud's stages of psychosexual development and their theorized relations to adult personality.

5. Describe Adler's views on striving for superiority, inferiority feelings, and compensation.

6. Summarize the strengths and weaknesses of psychodynamic theories.

7. Describe Pavlov's classical conditioning and its contribution to personality.

8. Discuss how Skinner's principles of operant conditioning can be applied to personality development.

9. Describe Bandura's social learning theory and its relation to personality.

10. Summarize the strengths and weaknesses of behavioral theories.

11. Explain Rogers's views on self-concept, development, and defensive behavior.

12. Explain Maslow's hierarchy of needs and summarize his findings on self-actualizing persons.

13. Summarize the strengths and weaknesses of humanistic theories.

14. Describe Eysenck's biological theory of personality and recent twin studies that support it.

15. Summarize the strengths and weaknesses of biological theories of personality.

16. Discuss the value and the limitations of self-report inventories in personality assessment.

KEY TERMS

Behaviorism
Cardinal trait
Central trait
Classical conditioning
Cognition
Compensation
Conditioned response (CR)
Conditioned stimulus (CS)
Conscious
Defense mechanisms
Discriminative stimuli
Displacement
Ego
Extinction
Fixation
Hierarchy of needs
Humanism
Id
Identification
Incongruence
Need for self-actualization
Negative reinforcement
Observational learning
Oedipal complex
Operant conditioning

Personality
Personality trait
Pleasure principle
Positive reinforcement
Preconscious
Projection
Psychodynamic theories
Psychological test
Psychosexual stages
Punishment
Rationalization
Reaction formation
Reality principle
Regression
Reliability
Repression
Secondary trait
Self-concept
Self-efficacy
Standardization
Superego
Test norms
Twin studies
Unconditioned response (UCR)
Unconditioned stimulus (UCS)
Unconscious
Validity

KEY PEOPLE

Alfred Adler
Albert Bandura
Hans Eysenck
Sigmund Freud
Abraham Maslow
Ivan Pavlov
Carl Rogers
B. F. Skinner

Social Avoidance and Distress Scale

INSTRUCTIONS

The statements below inquire about your personal reactions to a variety of situations. Consider each statement carefully. Then indicate whether the statement is true or false in regard to your typical behavior. Record your responses (true or false) in the space provided on the left.

THE SCALE

_____ 1. I feel relaxed even in unfamiliar social situations.

_____ 2. I try to avoid situations which force me to be very sociable.

_____ 3. It is easy for me to relax when I am with strangers.

_____ 4. I have no particular desire to avoid people.

_____ 5. I often find social occasions upsetting.

_____ 6. I usually feel calm and comfortable at social occasions.

_____ 7. I am usually at ease when talking to someone of the opposite sex.

_____ 8. I try to avoid talking to people unless I know them well.

_____ 9. If the chance comes to meet new people, I often take it.

_____ 10. I often feel nervous or tense in casual get-togethers in which both sexes are present.

_____ 11. I am usually nervous with people unless I know them well.

_____ 12. I usually feel relaxed when I am with a group of people.

_____ 13. I often want to get away from people.

_____ 14. I usually feel uncomfortable when I am in a group of people I don't know.

_____ 15. I usually feel relaxed when I meet someone for the first time.

_____ 16. Being introduced to people makes me tense and nervous.

_____ 17. Even though a room is full of strangers, I may enter it anyway.

_____ 18. I would avoid walking up and joining a large group of people.

_____ 19. When my superiors want to talk with me, I talk willingly.

_____ 20. I often feel on edge when I am with a group of people.

_____ 21. I tend to withdraw from people.

_____ 22. I don't mind talking to people at parties or social gatherings.

_____ 23. I am seldom at ease in a large group of people.

_____ 24. I often think up excuses in order to avoid social engagements.

_____ 25. I sometimes take the responsibility for introducing people to each other.

_____ 26. I try to avoid formal social occasions.

_____ 27. I usually go to whatever social engagements I have.

_____ 28. I find it easy to relax with other people.

SCORING THE SCALE

The scoring key is reproduced below. You should circle your true or false response each time it corresponds to the keyed response below. Add up the number of responses you circle, and this total is your score on the Social Avoidance and Distress (SAD) Scale. Record your score below.

1. False	**8.** True	**15.** False	**22.** False
2. True	**9.** False	**16.** True	**23.** True
3. False	**10.** True	**17.** False	**24.** True
4. False	**11.** True	**18.** True	**25.** False
5. True	**12.** False	**19.** False	**26.** True
6. False	**13.** True	**20.** True	**27.** False
7. False	**14.** True	**21.** True	**28.** False

MY SCORE _____

WHAT THE SCALE MEASURES

As its name implies, this scale measures avoidance and distress in social interactions. David Watson and Ronald Friend (1969) developed the scale to assess the extent to which individuals experience discomfort, fear, and anxiety in social situations and the extent to which they therefore try to evade many kinds of social encounters. To check the validity of the scale, they used it to predict subjects' social behavior in experimentally contrived situations. As projected, they found that people who scored high on the SAD Scale were less willing than low scorers to participate in a group discussion. The high scorers also reported anticipating more anxiety about their participation in the discussion than the low scorers. Additionally, Watson and Friend found a strong negative correlation (–.76) between the SAD and a measure of affiliation drive (the need to seek the company of others).

INTERPRETING YOUR SCORE

Our norms are based on data collected by Watson and Friend (1969) on over 200 university students.

NORMS

High score:	16–28
Intermediate score:	6–15
Low score:	0–5

Who Are You?

1. Below you will find 75 personality-trait words taken from the list assembled by Anderson (1968). Try to select the 20 traits (20 only!) that describe you best. Check them.

sincere	headstrong	friendly	tactful
pessimistic	naive	gracious	loyal
open-minded	sloppy	shy	reliable
suspicious	grouchy	short-tempered	outgoing
patient	ethical	compulsive	dependable
tense	persuasive	sarcastic	persistent
cooperative	nervous	respectful	orderly
neat	clumsy	imaginative	energetic
logical	rebellious	impolite	modest
vain	studious	diligent	smart
sociable	understanding	prideful	kind
scornful	truthful	optimistic	good-humored
cheerful	mature	considerate	unselfish
honest	skeptical	courteous	cordial
reasonable	efficient	candid	wholesome
forgetful	resourceful	idealistic	generous
crafty	perceptive	warm	boastful
methodical	punctual	versatile	daring
sly	prejudiced	courageous	

2. Review the 20 traits that you chose. Overall, is it a favorable or unfavorable picture that you have sketched?

3. Considering Carl Rogers's point that we often distort reality and construct an overly favorable self-concept, do you feel that you were objective?

4. What characteristics make you unique?

5. What are your greatest strengths?

6. What are your greatest weaknesses?

3

Stress and Its Effects

You're in your car headed home from school with a classmate. Traffic is barely moving. A radio report indicates that the traffic jam is only going to get worse. You groan audibly as you fiddle impatiently with the radio dial. Another motorist nearly takes your fender off trying to cut into your lane. Your pulse quickens as you shout insults at the unknown driver, who cannot even hear you. You think about the term paper that you have to work on tonight. Your stomach knots up as you recall all the crumpled drafts you tossed into the wastebasket last night. If you don't finish the paper soon, you won't be able to find any time to study for your math test, not to mention your biology quiz. Suddenly you remember that you promised the person you're dating that the two of you would get together tonight. There's no way. Another fight looms on the horizon. Your classmate asks how you feel about the tuition increase the college announced yesterday. You've been trying not to think about it. You're already in debt up to your ears. Your parents are bugging you about changing schools, but you don't want to leave your friends. Your heartbeat quickens as you contemplate the debate you'll have to wage with your parents. You feel wired with tension as you realize that the stress in your life never seems to let up.

Many different circumstances can create stress in our lives. Stress comes in all sorts of packages: large and small, pretty and ugly, simple and complex. All too often, the package is a surprise. In this chapter, we'll try to sort out these packages. We'll analyze the nature of stress, outline the major types of stress, and discuss how people respond to stressful events at several levels.

In a sense, stress is what a course on adjustment is all about. Recall from Chapter 1 that adjustment essentially deals with how people manage to cope with various demands and pressures. These demands or pressures that require adjustment represent the core of stressful experience. Thus, the central theme in a course such as this is: How do people adjust to stress, and how might they adjust more effectively?

Interest in stress as a topic has intensified markedly in the last decade. The gradual realization that stress exerts considerable impact on our physical and psychological health has led to explosive growth in scientific research on stress. This expansion of research has been accompanied by a corresponding increase in the public's thirst for information on the subject. We'll begin our discussion by examining the nature of stress.

THE NATURE OF STRESS

The term *stress* has been used in different ways by different theorists. Some, such as Thomas Holmes (1979), define stress as a *stimulus* event that presents difficult demands (for instance, a divorce). Others, such as Hans Selye (1976), define stress as the *response* of physiological arousal elicited by troublesome events. A point of view that lies between these extremes is gradually taking hold in psychology. This viewpoint is the *transactional model of stress* advocated by Richard Lazarus and his colleagues, among others (Holroyd & Lazarus, 1982; Lazarus & Folkman, 1984).

Lazarus argues that stress is neither a stimulus nor a response, but a special stimulus-response transaction in which one feels threatened. Lazarus points out that the same event may be stressful for one person but not another. For example, getting up to talk in front of a speech class is a piece of cake for some people. For others, it can be a paralyzing experience. If specific events are stressful only for some people, then stress cannot lie entirely in the stimulus events. In a similar vein, Lazarus argues against equating stress with the response of physiological arousal, because we routinely experience such arousal in the absence of stress. For example, a beautiful sunset, lust, and a brisk walk can all cause physiological arousal.

Thus, Lazarus concludes that "stress resides neither in the situation nor in the person; it depends on a transaction between the two. It arises from how the person ap-

Richard Lazarus

praises an event and adapts to it" (Goleman, 1979, p. 52). In keeping with this theoretical perspective, we will define **stress as any circumstances that threaten or are perceived to threaten our well-being and thereby tax our coping abilities.** The threat may be to our immediate physical safety, to our long-range security, to our self-esteem, to our reputation, or to our peace of mind. This is a complex concept—so let's dig a little deeper.

Stress Is an Everyday Event

The term *stress* tends to spark images of overwhelming, traumatic crises. People think of hijackings, hurricanes, military combat, and nuclear accidents. Undeniably, these are extremely stressful events. However, these unusual events represent the tip of the iceberg. Many everyday events such as waiting in line, having car trouble, shopping for Christmas presents, misplacing your checkbook, and staring at bills you can't pay are also stressful. In recent years, researchers have found that everyday problems and the minor nuisances of life are also important forms of stress (Burks & Martin, 1985).

You might guess that minor stresses would produce minor effects, but that isn't necessarily true. Research shows that routine hassles may have significant negative effects on our mental and physical health (Delongis, Folkman, & Lazarus, 1988; Kanner, Coyne, Schaefer, &

Lazarus, 1981). Richard Lazarus and his colleagues have devised a scale to measure stress in the form of daily hassles. Their scale lists 117 everyday problems, such as misplacing things, struggling with rising prices, dealing with delays, and so forth. They compared their hassles scale against another scale that assessed stress in the form of major life events (Kanner et al., 1981). They found that scores on their hassles scale were more strongly related to subjects' mental health than scores on the scale that measured major stressful events.

Why would minor hassles be more strongly related to mental health than major stressful events? The answer isn't entirely clear yet, but it may be because of the *cumulative* nature of stress. Stress adds up. Routine stresses at home, at school, and at work might be fairly benign individually, but collectively they could create great strain.

The everyday nature of stress need not alarm you. Discussions of stress usually emphasize its negative effects, but stress isn't all bad. Some types of stress can be enjoyable challenges, and stress can sometimes lead to positive outcomes. Although you might find a new job highly stressful, you might also find it interesting and exciting. Moreover, this stress might force you to develop new skills and acquire new strengths. Hans Selye coined the term *eustress* to refer to "good stress" that has beneficial effects. He pointed out that life would be very dull indeed if it were altogether free of stress.

Stress Lies in the Eye of the Beholder

The experience of feeling threatened depends on what events we notice and how we choose to appraise or interpret them. Events that are stressful for one person may be "ho-hum" routine for another. For example, many people find

flying in an airplane somewhat stressful, but frequent fliers may not even raise an eyebrow. Some people enjoy the excitement of going out on a date with someone new; others find the uncertainty terrifying.

In discussing appraisals of stress, Lazarus and Folkman (1984) distinguish between primary and secondary appraisal. *Primary appraisal* **is an initial evaluation of whether an event is (1) irrelevant to you, (2) relevant, but not threatening, or (3) stressful.** When you view an event as stressful, you are likely to make a *secondary appraisal,* **which is an evaluation of your coping resources and options for dealing with the stress.** Thus, your primary appraisal would determine whether you saw an upcoming job interview as stressful. Your secondary appraisal would determine how stressful the interview appeared, in light of your assessment of your ability to deal with the event.

Often, we are not very objective in our appraisals of potentially stressful events. A study of hospitalized patients awaiting surgery showed that there was only a slight correlation between the objective seriousness of a person's upcoming surgery and the amount of fear the person experienced (Janis, 1958). Thus, stress lies in the eye (actually, the mind) of the beholder. Our appraisals of stressful events are highly subjective.

Stress May Be Self-Imposed

We tend to think of stress as something imposed on us from without by others and their demands. Surprisingly often, however, stress is self-imposed. For example, you might sign up for extra classes to get through school quickly. Or you might actively seek additional responsibilities at work to impress your boss. People frequently put pressure on themselves to get good grades or to climb the corporate ladder rapidly. Many people create stress by embracing unrealistic expectations for themselves.

Meyer Friedman and Ray Rosenman (1974) have described a personality syndrome, the Type A personality, that involves a great deal of self-imposed stress. **The** *Type A personality* **is characterized by competitive, aggres-** sive, impatient, hostile behavior. Type A people are highly motivated, and they have to "win" at everything they do. They usually are workaholics who have a hard-driving involvement in their jobs. They tend to take on too many projects and to drive themselves with many deadlines. They are exceedingly time-conscious and fidget frantically over the briefest delays. These intense individuals clearly subject themselves to unnecessary and avoidable stress. That's apparently why they have an elevated vulnerability to heart disease (Friedman & Booth-Kewley, 1988). We'll discuss the link between Type A behavior and heart disease in more detail in Chapter 14.

Because stress is often self-imposed, we have more control over our stress than many people realize. However, to exert this control, we need to be able to recognize the sources of stress in our lives. Hence, in the next section we'll discuss the major types of stress.

MAJOR TYPES OF STRESS

An enormous variety of events can be stressful for one person or another. To achieve a better understanding of stress, theorists have tried to classify the principal types of stress. None of their organizational schemes has turned out to be altogether satisfactory. It's virtually impossible to classify stressful events into nonintersecting categories. Although this problem presents conceptual headaches for researchers, it need not prevent us from describing four major types of stress: frustration, conflict, change, and pressure. As you read about each of these, you'll surely recognize four very familiar adversaries.

Frustration

"It has been very frustrating to watch the rapid deterioration of my parents' relationship. Over the last year or two they have argued constantly and have refused to seek any professional help. I have tried to talk to them, but they kind of shut me and my brother out of their problem. I feel very helpless and

Figure 3.1. Types of conflict.
Psychologists have identified three basic types of conflict. In approach-approach or avoidance-avoidance conflicts, the person is torn between two goals. In an approach-avoidance conflict there is only one goal under consideration, but it has both positive and negative aspects.

sometimes even very angry, not at them, but at the whole situation."

The scenario above illustrates frustration. As psychologists use the term, *frustration* **occurs in any situation in which the pursuit of some goal is thwarted.** In essence, you experience frustration when you want something and you can't have it. We all have to deal with frustration virtually every day. Traffic jams, for instance, are a routine source of frustration that can affect mood and blood pressure (Novaco, Stokols, Campbell, & Stokols, 1979). Fortunately, most of our frustrations are brief and insignificant. You may be quite upset when you go to a repair shop to pick up your ailing stereo and find that it hasn't been fixed as promised. However, a week later you'll probably have your precious stereo, and all will be forgotten.

Of course, some frustrations can be sources of significant stress. Failures and losses are two common kinds of frustration that are often very stressful. We all fail in at least some of our endeavors. Some of us make failure almost inevitable by setting unrealistic goals for ourselves. People tend to forget that for every newly appointed vice-president in the business world, there are dozens of middle-level executives who don't get promoted. Losses may be especially frustrating because we are deprived of something that we are accustomed to having. For example, there are few things that are more frustrating than losing a dearly loved boyfriend, girlfriend, or spouse.

Frustration may be self-imposed in that we frequently erect barriers to our own success. For instance, if you choose not to study adequately for an exam and then experience frustration when you flunk it, you have created your own frustration. Similarly, if your absenteeism at work prevents you from getting the promotion you

wanted, your frustration is your responsibility. Such self-defeating patterns of behavior are surprisingly common (Baumeister & Scher, 1988).

Conflict

"Should I or shouldn't I? I became engaged at Christmas. My fiancé surprised me with a ring. I knew if I refused the ring he would be terribly hurt and our relationship would suffer. However, I don't really know whether or not I want to marry him. On the other hand, I don't want to lose him either."

Like frustration, conflict is an unavoidable feature of everyday life. That perplexing question "Should I or shouldn't I?" comes up countless times in our lives. *Conflict* **occurs when two or more incompatible motivations or behavioral impulses compete for expression.** As we discussed in Chapter 2, Sigmund Freud proposed nearly a century ago that internal conflicts generate considerable psychological distress. This link between conflict and distress was measured with new precision in a recent study by Robert Emmons and Laura King (1988). They used an elaborate questionnaire to assess the overall amount of internal conflict experienced by 88 subjects in two studies. They found that higher levels of conflict were associated with higher levels of anxiety, depression, and physical symptoms.

Conflicts come in three types, which were originally described by Kurt Lewin (1935) and investigated extensively by Neal Miller (1944, 1959). The types of conflict are approach-approach, avoidance-avoidance, and approach-avoidance. They are diagrammed in Figure 3.1.

In an *approach-approach conflict* **a choice must be made between two attractive goals.** The problem, of course, is that you can choose just one of the two goals. For example, you have a free afternoon; should you play tennis or racquetball? You're out for a meal; do you want to order the pizza or the spa-

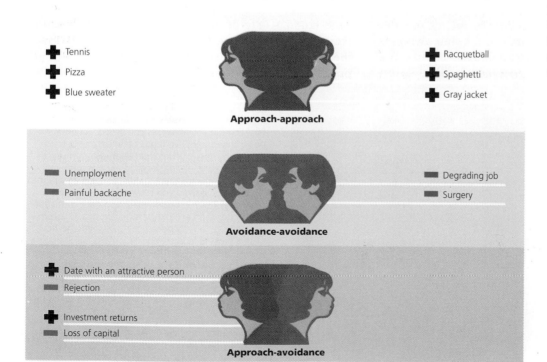

Tennis
Pizza
Blue sweater

Racquetball
Spaghetti
Gray jacket

Approach-approach

Unemployment
Painful backache

Degrading job
Surgery

Avoidance-avoidance

Date with an attractive person
Rejection

Investment returns
Loss of capital

Approach-avoidance

ghetti? You can't afford both; should you buy the blue sweater or the gray jacket?

Among the three kinds of conflict, the approach-approach type tends to be the least stressful. People usually don't stagger out of restaurants, exhausted by the stress of choosing which of several appealing entrées to eat. In approach-approach conflicts you typically have a reasonably happy ending, whichever way you decide to go. Nonetheless, approach-approach conflicts centering on important issues may sometimes be troublesome. If you are torn between two appealing college majors or two attractive boyfriends, you may find the decision-making process quite stressful.

In an *avoidance-avoidance conflict* **a choice must be made between two unattractive goals.** Forced to choose between two repelling alternatives, you are, as they say, "caught between the devil and the deep blue sea." For example, let's say you have very painful backaches. Should you submit to surgery that you dread, or should you continue to live with the pain?

Obviously, avoidance-avoidance conflicts are most unpleasant and very stressful. Typically, people keep delaying their decision as long as possible, hoping that they will somehow be able to escape the conflict situation. For example, you might delay the surgery to alleviate your backaches in the hope that the backaches will disappear on their own.

In an *approach-avoidance conflict* **a choice must be made about whether to pursue a single goal that has both attractive and unattractive aspects.** For instance, imagine that you're offered a career promotion that will mean a large increase in pay. The catch is that you will have to move to a city that you hate. Approach-avoidance conflicts are very common, and they can be very stressful. Any time you have to take a risk to pursue some desirable outcome, you are likely to find yourself in an approach-avoidance conflict. Should you risk rejection by asking out that attractive person in class? Should you risk your savings by investing in a new business that could fail?

Approach-avoidance conflicts often produce *vacilla-tion.* That is, we go back and forth, beset by indecision. We decide to go ahead, then we decide not to, then we decide to go ahead again. Humans are not unique in this respect. Many years ago, Neal Miller (1944) observed the same vacillation in his ground-breaking research with rats. Miller created approach-avoidance conflicts in hungry rats by alternately feeding and shocking them at one end of a runway apparatus. Eventually, these rats tended to hover near the center of the runway. They would alternately approach and retreat from the goal box at the end of the alley.

In a series of studies, Miller (1959) plotted out how an organism's tendency to approach a goal (the approach gradient in Figure 3.2a) and to retreat from a goal (the avoidance gradient in Figure 3.2a) increase as the organism nears the goal. He found that avoidance motivation increases more rapidly than approach motivation (as reflected by the avoidance gradient's steeper slope in Figure 3.2a). Based on this principle, Miller concluded that *in trying to resolve an approach-avoidance conflict, we should focus more on decreasing avoidance motivation than on increasing approach motivation.*

How would this insight apply to complex human dilemmas? Imagine that you are counseling a friend who is vacillating over whether to ask someone out on a date. Miller would assert that you should attempt to downplay the negative aspects of possible rejection (thus lowering the avoidance gradient) rather than dwelling on how much fun the date could be (thus raising the approach gradient). Figure 3.2b shows the effects of lowering the avoidance gradient. If it is lowered far enough, the person should reach the goal (make a decision and take action).

More recent research has revealed that avoidance tendencies do not *always* increase more rapidly than approach tendencies (Epstein, 1982). In light of this new finding, the best advice for resolving an approach-avoidance conflict may be to work on both aspects of the conflict. In other words, you may want to attempt to lower the avoidance tendency and at the same time raise the approach tendency.

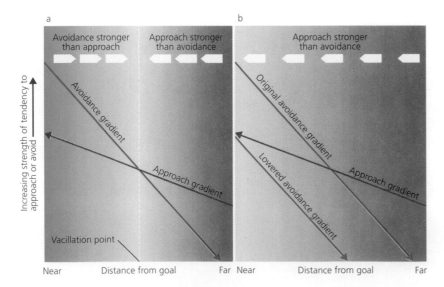

Figure 3.2. Approach-avoidance conflict.
(a) According to Miller, as you near a goal that has positive and negative features, avoidance motivation tends to rise faster than approach motivation (that's why the avoidance gradient has a steeper slope than the approach gradient), sending you into retreat. However, if you retreat far enough, you'll eventually reach a point where approach motivation is stronger than avoidance motivation, and you may decide to go ahead once again. The ebb and flow of this process leads to vacillation around the point where the two gradients intersect. (b) As the avoidance gradient is lowered, the person comes closer and closer to the goal. If the avoidance gradient can be lowered far enough, the person should be able to resolve the conflict and reach the goal.

Change

"After my divorce, I lived alone for four years. Six months ago, I married a wonderful woman who has two children from her previous marriage. My biggest stress is suddenly having to adapt to living with three people instead of by myself. I was pretty set in my ways. I had certain routines. Now everything is chaos. I love my wife and I'm fond of the kids, and they're not really doing anything wrong, but my house and my life just aren't the same and I am having trouble dealing with it all."

There is evidence that life changes may represent a key type of stress. *Life changes* **are any noticeable alterations in one's living circumstances that require readjustment.** Research on life change began when Thomas Holmes, Richard Rahe, and their colleagues set out to explore the relation between stressful life events and physical illness (Holmes & Rahe, 1967; Rahe & Arthur, 1978). They interviewed thousands of tuberculosis patients to find out what kinds of events preceded the onset of their disease. Surprisingly, the frequently cited events were not uni-

formly negative. There were plenty of aversive events, as expected, but there were also many seemingly positive events, such as getting married, having a baby, or getting promoted.

Why would positive events, such as moving to a nicer home, produce stress? According to Holmes and Rahe, it is because they produce *change*. Their thesis is that disruptions of our daily routines are stressful. According to their theory, changes in personal relationships, changes at work, changes in finances and so forth can be stressful even when the changes are welcomed.

Based on this analysis, Holmes and Rahe (1967) developed the Social Readjustment Rating Scale (SRRS) to measure life change as a form of stress. The scale assigns numerical values to 43 major life events that are supposed to reflect the magnitude of the readjustment required by each change (see Figure 3.3). In taking the scale, respondents are asked to indicate how often they experienced any of these 43 events during a certain time period (typically, the past year). The person then adds up the numbers associated with each event checked. This sum is an index of the amount of change-related stress the person has recently experienced.

The SRRS has been used in well over 1000 studies by researchers all over the world (Holmes, 1979). Overall, these studies have shown that people with higher scores on the SRRS tend to be more vulnerable to many kinds of physical illness and many types of psychological problems as well (Barrett, Rose, & Klerman, 1979; Elliott & Eisdorfer, 1982). These results have attracted a great deal of attention, and the SRRS has been reprinted in many newspapers and popular magazines. The attendant publicity has led to the widespread conclusion that life change is inherently stressful.

More recently, however, experts have criticized this research, citing problems with the methods used (Schroeder & Costa, 1984) and problems in interpreting the findings (Perkins, 1982). At this point, it is a key interpretive issue that concerns us. Many critics have argued that the SRRS does not measure *change* exclusively. The main

Social Readjustment Rating Scale	
Life event	**Mean value**
Death of spouse	100
Divorce	73
Marital separation	65
Jail term	63
Death of close family member	63
Personal injury or illness	53
Marriage	50
Fired at work	47
Marital reconciliation	45
Retirement	45
Change in health of family member	44
Pregnancy	40
Sex difficulties	39
Gain of a new family member	39
Business readjustment	39
Change in financial state	38
Death of a close friend	37
Change to a different line of work	36
Change in number of arguments with spouse	35
Mortgage or loan for major purchase (home, etc.)	31
Foreclosure of mortgage or loan	30
Change in responsibilities at work	29
Son or daughter leaving home	29
Trouble with in-laws	29
Outstanding personal achievement	28
Wife begins or stops work	26
Begin or end school	26
Change in living conditions	25
Revision of personal habits	24
Trouble with boss	23
Change in work hours or conditions	20
Change in residence	20
Change in school	20
Change in recreation	19
Change in church activities	19
Change in social activities	18
Mortgage or loan for lesser purchase (car, TV, etc.)	17
Change in sleeping habits	16
Change in number of family get-togethers	15
Change in eating habits	15
Vacation	13
Christmas	12
Minor violations of the law	11

Figure 3.3. Social Readjustment Rating Scale (SRRS). Devised by Holmes and Rahe (1967), this scale measures the change-related stress in one's life. The numbers on the right are supposed to reflect the average amount of stress (readjustment) produced by each event.

problem is that the list of life changes on the SRRS is dominated by events that are clearly negative or undesirable (death of a spouse, fired at work, and so on). These negative events probably generate great frustration. Although there are some positive events on the scale, it could be that frustration (generated by negative events), rather than change, creates most of the stress assessed by the scale.

To investigate this possibility, researchers began to take into account the desirability and undesirability of subjects' life changes. Subjects were asked to indicate the desirability of the events that they checked off on the SRRS and similar scales. The findings in these studies clearly indicated that life change is *not* the crucial dimension measured by the SRRS. Undesirable or negative life events cause most of the stress tapped by the SRRS (Perkins, 1982; Zeiss, 1980).

Should we discard the notion that change is stressful? Not entirely. Other lines of research, independent of work with the SRRS, support the hypothesis that change is an important form of stress. For instance, there is evidence linking geographic mobility to impaired mental and physical health (Brett, 1980). More research is needed, but it is quite plausible that change constitutes a major type of stress in our lives. However, at present, there is little reason to believe that change is *inherently* or *inevitably* stressful. Some life changes may be quite challenging, while others may be quite benign.

Pressure

"My father questioned me at dinner about some things I did not want to talk about. I know he doesn't want to hear my answers, at least not the truth. My father told me when I was little that I was his favorite because I was 'pretty near perfect' and I've spent my life trying to keep that up, even though it's obviously not true. Recently, he has begun to realize this and it's made our relationship very strained and painful."

At one time or another, most of us have probably remarked that we were "under pressure." What does this mean? *Pressure* **involves expectations or demands that one behave in a certain way.** Pressure can be divided into two subtypes: the pressure to *perform* and the pressure to *conform.* You are under pressure to perform when you are expected to execute tasks and responsibilities quickly, efficiently, and successfully. For example, salespeople usually are under pressure to move lots of merchandise. Professors at research institutions are often under pressure to publish in prestigious journals. Comedians are under pressure to be amusing. Secretaries are often under pressure to complete lots of clerical work in very little time. Pressures to conform to others' expectations are also common in our lives. Businessmen are expected to wear suits and ties. Suburban homeowners are expected to keep their lawns manicured. Teenagers are expected to adhere to their parents' values and rules. Young adults are expected to get themselves married by the time they're 30.

Although widely discussed by the general public, the concept of pressure has received scant attention from researchers. Recently, however, Weiten has devised a scale to measure pressure as a form of life stress (Weiten, 1988; Weiten & Dixon, 1984). The result is a 48-item self-report measure, called the Pressure Inventory, which is still undergoing development. In the first two studies with this scale, a strong relationship has been found between pressure and a variety of psychological symptoms and problems. In fact, pressure has turned out to be more strongly related to measures of mental health than the SRRS and other established measures of stress (see Figure 3.4). These findings suggest that pressure may be an important form of stress that merits more attention from researchers.

KEY FACTORS IN OUR APPRAISAL OF STRESS

We noted earlier that stress lies in the eye of the beholder. Quite a variety of factors influence our subjective apprais-

Figure 3.4. Pressure and psychological symptoms. A comparison of pressure and life change as sources of stress suggests that pressure may be more strongly related to mental health than change. In one study, Weiten (1988) found a correlation of .59 between scores on the Pressure Inventory (PI) and symptoms of psychological distress. In the same sample, correlation between SRRS scores and psychological symptoms was only .28. (Data from Weiten, 1988)

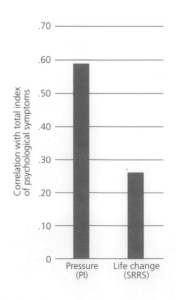

70

I: THE DYNAMICS OF ADJUSTMENT

als of potentially stressful events. Four that stand out are (1) our familiarity with the challenge, (2) the controllability of the events, (3) the predictability of the events, and (4) the imminence of the threat.

Familiarity

An important consideration in your appraisal of stress is your familiarity with the stressful demands. Generally, the more unfamiliar you are with a potentially stressful event, the more threatened you are likely to feel (McGrath, 1977). Hence, a person's first major job interview, or first appearance in a courtroom, or first purchase of a home tends to be more stressful than subsequent similar events. Familiarity with a challenge can make yesterday's crisis today's routine.

Controllability

Another factor that influences your appraisal of stress is your perception of how much control you can exert over the event in question. For example, if you are facing surgery and a lengthy rehabilitation period, your feelings might range from a sense of powerlessness to a firm belief that you will be able to speed up the recovery process. Stern, McCants, and Pettine (1982) found that when events are viewed as controllable, they tend to be less stressful.

In another study (Breier et al., 1987) subjects were exposed to equal amounts of controllable and uncontrollable loud noise as a form of stress. In the controllable condition, subjects could learn a sequence of button pushes that would temporarily stop the noise. When the noise was controllable, subjects reported less stress and less tension. Furthermore, objective indicators of physiological arousal showed that the subjects in the study experienced less arousal in the controllable noise condition (see Figure 3.5).

The finding that controllability reduces stress is fairly typical for this line of research, although it is not univer-

sal (Folkman, 1984). Jerry Burger (1989) has identified some situations in which greater control is associated with *increased* stress. Burger points out that control has negative as well as positive aspects. On the negative side, when events are controllable, people have to accept greater responsibility for their outcomes. *Hence, people who are very concerned about how others will evaluate them often find being in control quite stressful.* Nonetheless, the general trend is for people to view events over which they have more control as less stressful.

Predictability

If you experience a stressful event—for instance, being fired at work—is it more traumatic when the event comes out of nowhere (unpredictable stress) or when you can see the event coming for some time (predictable stress)? In general, it appears that we prefer predictable stress over surprise packages. When researchers expose subjects to the stress of predictable and unpredictable noise, they usually find that subjects are bothered more by the unpredictable noise (Matthews, Scheier, Brunson, & Carducci, 1989). Major stressors, such as the progression of an illness or job loss, seem to be less devastating when they can be anticipated over a period of time. We may prefer predictability because it allows us to engage in anticipatory coping to prepare for the stress.

However, the effects of predictability are complex. There are situations in which people prefer not to know about stress in advance (Burger, 1989). For instance, when understudy actors or rookie athletes are pressed into service as last-minute substitutes for more experienced performers, many comment, "It was better that way. I didn't have time to dwell on it and get nervous." The value of predictability probably depends on whether there's much that you can do to prepare for the stress. If preparation won't help (or if you already feel prepared), knowing about stress in advance may only allow you to dwell on the threatening event, which will usually make it all the more threatening.

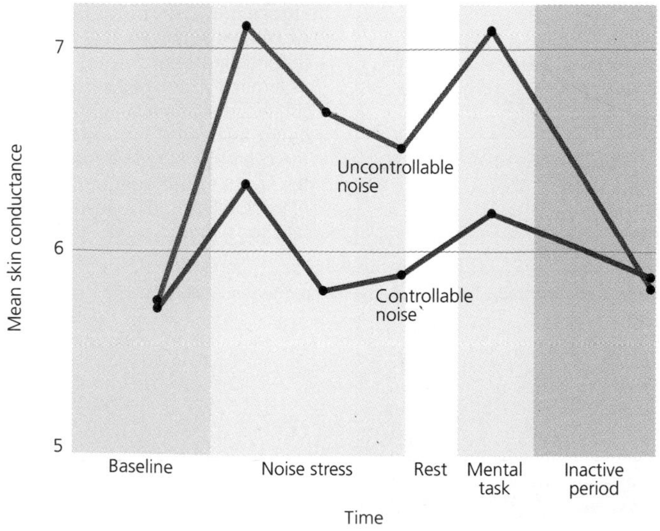

Figure 3.5. Controllability and physiological arousal. Skin conductance is an easily measured index of the physiological arousal that may be produced by stress. In the study by Breier et al. (1987), subjects experienced considerably higher physiological arousal when exposed to uncontrollable noise in comparison to controllable noise.

Imminence

If you *do* know about a threatening event in advance, your stress usually increases as the event becomes more imminent (comes closer in time). When a threat lies in the distant future, its stressfulness may be minimal. However, as the challenge looms near, concern and distress typically escalate (Lazarus & Folkman, 1984). Thus, as you approach the day on which you have to take a critical exam, or submit to serious surgery, or speak at a convention, you generally will find the stress increasing. In fact, your stress may peak during the period of anticipation, rather than with the event itself. For example, after a big exam, students often remark, "Taking it wasn't nearly as bad as anticipating it and worrying about it."

In summary, the appraisal of stress is a complicated process. Factors such as controllability and predictability have varied effects on our appraisal of stress, depending on the exact circumstances. However, research on this process is important because our stress appraisals make all the difference in the world to how we respond to stress, which is our next topic.

RESPONDING TO STRESS

Our response to stress is complex and multidimensional. Stress affects us at several levels. Consider again the chapter's opening scenario, in which you're driving home in heavy traffic, thinking about overdue papers, tuition increases, and parental pressures. Let's look at some of the reactions we mentioned. When you groan audibly in reaction to the traffic report, you're experiencing an *emotional response* to stress, in this case, annoyance and anger. When your pulse quickens and your stomach knots up, you're exhibiting *physiological responses* to stress. When you shout insults at another driver, your verbal aggression is a *behavioral response* to the stress at hand. Thus, we can analyze our reactions to stress at three levels: (1) our

emotional responses, (2) our physiological responses, and (3) our behavioral responses. Figure 3.6 depicts these three levels of response.

Emotional Responses

Emotion is an elusive concept. There is much debate about how to define emotion, and there are many conflicting theories that purport to explain emotion. However, we all have extensive personal experience with emotions. We all have a good idea of what it means to be anxious, elated, gloomy, jealous, disgusted, excited, guilty, or nervous. Rather than pursue the technical debates about emotion, we'll rely on your familiarity with the concept and simply note that *emotions* **are powerful, largely uncontrollable feelings, accompanied by physiological changes.** When we are under stress, we often react emotionally. More often than not, stress tends to elicit unpleasant emotions rather than pleasurable feelings.

The link between stress and emotion was apparent in a study of 96 women who filled out diaries about stresses and moods they experienced over 28 days (Caspi, Bolger, & Eckenrode, 1987). The investigators found that daily fluctuations in stress correlated with daily fluctuations in mood. As stress increased, mood tended to become more negative. As the researchers put it, "Some days everything seems to go wrong, and by day's end, minor difficulties find their outlet in rotten moods" (p. 184).

Emotions Commonly Elicited

There are no simple one-to-one connections between certain types of stress and particular emotions. Stressful events may evoke many different emotions, although some are certainly more likely than others. We'll use Plutchik's (1980) model of primary emotions to highlight the types of emotions that are especially common in response to stress. Figure 3.7 shows the eight primary emotions identified by Plutchik, including varying levels of intensity for some of the emotions. Although stress could elicit any of the emotions shown in Figure 3.7,

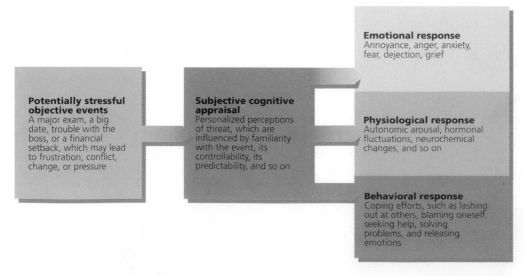

Figure 3.6. Our multidimensional response to stress. A potentially stressful event, such as a major exam, will elicit a subjective, cognitive appraisal of how threatening the event is. If the event is viewed with alarm, the stress may trigger emotional, physiological, and behavioral reactions. Our response to stress is multidimensional.

Potentially stressful objective events
A major exam, a big date, trouble with the boss, or a financial setback, which may lead to frustration, conflict, change, or pressure

Subjective cognitive appraisal
Personalized perceptions of threat, which are influenced by familiarity with the event, its controllability, its predictability, and so on

Emotional response
Annoyance, anger, anxiety, fear, dejection, grief

Physiological response
Autonomic arousal, hormonal fluctuations, neurochemical changes, and so on

Behavioral response
Coping efforts, such as lashing out at others, blaming oneself, seeking help, solving problems, and releasing emotions

© 1968 UNITED FEATURE SYNDICATE, INC. REPRINTED WITH PERMISSION.

Woolfolk and Richardson (1978) suggest that reactions along the following dimensions are particularly likely: (1) annoyance, anger, and rage; (2) apprehension, fear, and terror; and (3) pensiveness, sadness, and grief.

ANNOYANCE, ANGER, AND RAGE. Stress frequently produces feelings of anger ranging in intensity from mild annoyance to uncontrollable rage. Frustration is particularly likely to generate the emotion of anger. Some people become visibly angry in response to nearly every trivial setback. The pressure to conform also seems likely to elicit anger and resentment.

APPREHENSION, FEAR, AND TERROR. This dimension of emotion is probably evoked by stress more than any other. *Anxiety* falls along this dimension, somewhere between apprehension and fear. Psychologists have conducted thousands upon thousands of studies on anxiety since Freud pinpointed the link between conflict and anxiety many years ago. Although Freud emphasized how conflict causes anxiety, it is clear that apprehension, anxiety, and fear can be elicited by the pressure to perform, the threat of impending frustration, and the uncertainty associated with change. Thus, all of the major types of stress can evoke emotions in this category.

PENSIVENESS, SADNESS, AND GRIEF. Sometimes stress simply brings us down, evoking sadness and dejection. We all get depressed from time to time, especially in response to frustration. Sadness and depression are particularly likely when we feel powerless to do anything about the stress in our lives.

Effects of Emotional Arousal

Emotional responses are a natural and normal part of life. Even unpleasant emotions serve important purposes. Like physical pain, painful emotions can serve as warnings that we need to take action. However, it is important to note that strong emotional arousal can sometimes interfere with efforts to cope with stress.

The well-known problem of *test anxiety* illustrates how emotional arousal can hurt performance. Often, students who score poorly on an exam will nonetheless insist that they know the material. Many of them are probably telling the truth. Many researchers have found a negative correlation between test-related anxiety and exam performance. Students who display high test anxiety tend to score low on exams (Wine, 1982). Test anxiety can interfere with test taking in several ways, but the critical consideration appears to be the disruption of attention to the test (Sarason, 1984). Test-anxious students waste too much time worrying about how they are doing and wondering whether others are having similar problems. In other words, their minds wander too much from the task of taking the test.

Although emotional arousal may hurt coping efforts,

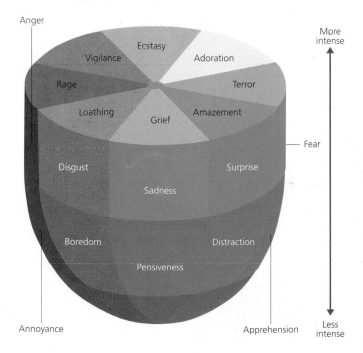

Figure 3.7. The dimensions of emotion. Plutchik's model of emotion provides a useful scheme for analyzing the emotional reactions evoked by stressful events. Plutchik identified eight primary emotions that vary in intensity. Stress can trigger a wide range of emotions, but reactions involving three of the eight primary emotions are especially common: anger, sadness, and fear.

3: STRESS AND ITS EFFECTS

73

this is not *necessarily* the case. Various theories of "optimal arousal" predict that performance on a task should improve with increased emotional arousal—up to a point where arousal becomes too high and is disruptive (Hebb, 1955; Malmo, 1975). The level of arousal at which performance peaks is called the *optimal level of arousal.*

This optimal level of arousal varies from one task to another. It appears to depend (in part) on the complexity of the task at hand. The conventional wisdom is that *as a task becomes more complex, the optimal level of arousal (for peak performance) tends to decrease.* Figure 3.8 shows this relationship. As you can see, a fairly high level of arousal should be optimal on simple tasks (for example, driving eight hours to help a friend in a crisis). However, performance should peak at a lower level of arousal on complex tasks (for example, making a complicated decision in which you have to weigh many factors).

Most of the research evidence on optimal levels of arousal comes from rather simple animal learning studies. Hence, it may be risky to generalize these principles to human coping efforts. Nonetheless, optimal-arousal theories provide a plausible model of how emotional arousal could have either beneficial or disruptive effects on coping.

Physiological Responses

As we just discussed, stress frequently elicits strong emotional responses. These emotional responses bring about important physiological changes. Even in cases of moder-

ate stress, you may notice that your heart has started beating faster, you have begun to breathe harder, and you are perspiring more than usual. How does all this (and much more) happen? Let's see.

The "Fight or Flight" Response

The *fight-or-flight response* **is a physiological reaction to threat that mobilizes an organism for attacking (fight) or fleeing (flight) an enemy.** First described by Walter Cannon (1932), the fight-or-flight response occurs in the body's autonomic nervous system. **The *autonomic nervous system (ANS)* is made up of the nerves that connect to the heart, blood vessels, smooth muscles, and glands.** As its name hints, the autonomic nervous system is somewhat *autonomous.* That is, it controls involuntary, visceral functions that we don't normally think about, such as heart rate, digestion, and perspiration.

The autonomic nervous system can be broken into two divisions (see Figure 3.9). The *parasympathetic division* of the ANS generally conserves bodily resources. For instance, it slows heart rate and promotes digestion to help the body save and store energy. The fight-or-flight response is mediated by the *sympathetic division* of the ANS, which mobilizes bodily resources for emergencies. In one experiment, Cannon studied the fight-or-flight response in cats by confronting them with dogs. Among other things, he noticed an immediate acceleration in breathing and heart rate and a reduction in digestive processes.

Elements of the fight-or-flight response are also seen in humans. Imagine your reaction if your car nearly spun

Figure 3.8. Arousal and performance. The effect of emotional arousal on task performance depends on the complexity of the task. On complicated tasks, a relatively low level of arousal tends to be optimal (results in the best performance). On simpler tasks, however, performance may peak at much higher levels of arousal.

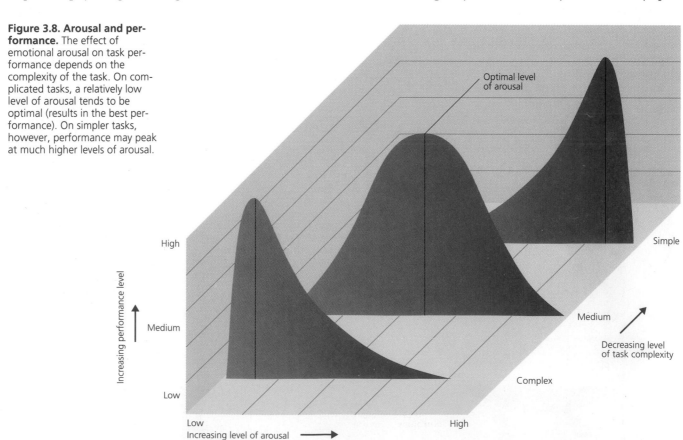

out of control on the highway. Your heart would race, and your blood pressure would surge. You might get "goose bumps" and experience a "knot in your stomach." These reflex responses are part of the fight-or-flight response.

In a sense, this automatic reaction is a leftover from our evolutionary past. It is clearly an adaptive response in the animal kingdom, where the threat of predators often requires a swift response of fighting or fleeing. But among humans, the fight-or-flight response appears less adaptive. Most of our stresses cannot be handled simply through fight or flight. Work pressures, marital problems, and financial difficulties require far more complex responses. Moreover, our stresses often continue for lengthy periods of time, so that our fight-or-flight response leaves us in a state of enduring physiological arousal. Concern about the effects of prolonged physical arousal was first voiced by Hans Selye, a Canadian scientist who conducted extensive research on stress.

The General Adaptation Syndrome

The concept of stress was added to our language by Hans Selye (1936, 1956, 1982). Selye was born in Vienna, but spent his entire professional career at McGill University in Montreal. Beginning in the 1930s, Selye exposed laboratory animals to a diverse array of both physical and psychological stressors (heat, cold, pain, mild shock, restraint, and so on). The patterns of physiological arousal seen in the animals were largely the same, regardless of the type of stress. Thus, Selye concluded that stress reactions are *nonspecific*. In other words, he maintained that they did not vary according to the specific type of stress encountered.

Initially, Selye wasn't sure what to call this nonspecific response to a variety of noxious agents. In the 1940s, he decided to call it *stress*, and the word has been part of our vocabulary ever since. In Selye's theory, stress referred to the body's *response* to threat. Ironically, late in his career, he admitted that it would have been better to use the word *strain* to refer to the body's response to noxious stimuli, while using the term *stress* to refer to the noxious stimulus events. But, as he explained, "My English was not yet good enough for me to distinguish between the words 'stress' and 'strain'" (Selye, 1976, p. 50). As the years passed, other theorists began to use the term stress to refer to troublesome stimulus events, creating some confusion. As we noted at the beginning of the chapter, most modern theorists sidestep this confusion by defining stress as neither a stimulus nor a response, but as a certain type of stimulus-response transaction.

In any case, Selye (1956, 1974) formulated an influential theory of stress reactions called the general adaptation syndrome. **The *general adaptation syndrome* is a model of the body's stress response, consisting of three stages: alarm, resistance, and exhaustion.** In the first stage of the general adaptation syndrome, an *alarm reaction* occurs when an organism recognizes the existence of a threat. Physiological arousal increases as the body musters its resources to combat the challenge. Selye's alarm reaction is essentially the fight-or-flight response originally described by Cannon.

However, Selye took his investigation of stress a couple of steps further by exposing laboratory animals to *prolonged* stress, similar to the chronic stress often endured by humans. If stress continues, the organism may progress to the second phase of the general adaptation syndrome, called the *stage of resistance*. During this phase, physiological changes stabilize as coping efforts get under way. Typically, physiological arousal continues to be higher than normal, although it may level off somewhat as the organism becomes accustomed to the threat.

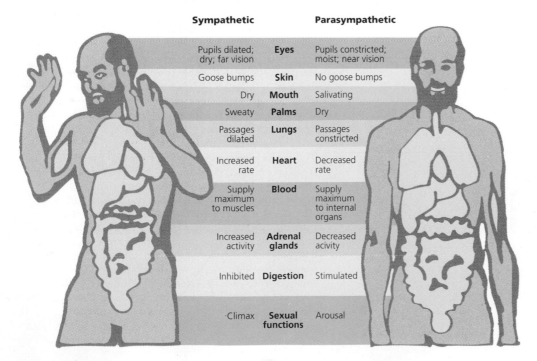

	Sympathetic		Parasympathetic
	Pupils dilated; dry; far vision	**Eyes**	Pupils constricted; moist; near vision
	Goose bumps	**Skin**	No goose bumps
	Dry	**Mouth**	Salivating
	Sweaty	**Palms**	Dry
	Passages dilated	**Lungs**	Passages constricted
	Increased rate	**Heart**	Decreased rate
	Supply maximum to muscles	**Blood**	Supply maximum to internal organs
	Increased activity	**Adrenal glands**	Decreased acivity
	Inhibited	**Digestion**	Stimulated
	Climax	**Sexual functions**	Arousal

Figure 3.9. The autonomic nervous system (ANS). The ANS is composed of the nerves that connect to the heart, blood vessels, smooth muscles, and glands. The ANS is subdivided into the sympathetic division, which mobilizes bodily resources in times of need, and the parasympathetic division, which conserves bodily resources. Some of the key functions controlled by each division of the ANS are summarized in the center of the diagram.

If the stress continues over a substantial period of time, the organism may enter the third stage, called the *stage of exhaustion*. According to Selye, the body's resources for fighting stress are limited. If the stress cannot be overcome, the body's resources may be depleted, and physiological arousal will decrease. Eventually, there may be a collapse from exhaustion. During this phase, the organism's resistance declines, as shown in Figure 3.10. This reduced resistance may lead to what Selye called "diseases of adaptation."

Selye's theory and research forged a link between stress and physical illness. He showed how prolonged physiological arousal that is meant to be adaptive could lead to diseases. Although his belief that stress reactions are nonspecific remains controversial (Mason, 1975), his model provided guidance for a generation of researchers who worked out the details of how stress reverberates throughout the body. Let's look at some of those details.

Brain-Body Pathways

When we experience stress, the brain sends signals to the endocrine system along two major pathways (Asterita, 1985). **The *endocrine system* consists of glands that secrete chemicals called hormones into the bloodstream.** The major endocrine glands, such as the pituitary, pineal, thyroid, and adrenal glands, are shown in Figure 3.11.

The hypothalamus, a small structure near the base of the brain, appears to initiate action along both of the pathways. The first pathway (shown on the right in Figure 3.12) is routed through the autonomic nervous system. The hypothalamus activates the sympathetic division of the ANS. A key part of this activation involves stimulating the central part of the adrenal glands (the adrenal medulla) to release large amounts of *catecholamines* into the bloodstream. These hormones radiate throughout your body, producing many important physiological changes. The net result of catecholamine elevation is that your body is mobilized for action. Heart rate and blood flow increase, pumping more blood to your brain and muscles. Respiration and oxygen consumption speed up, facilitat-

ing alertness. Digestive processes are inhibited to conserve your energy. The pupils of your eyes dilate, increasing visual sensitivity.

The second pathway (shown on the left in Figure 3.12) involves more direct communication between the brain and the endocrine system. The hypothalamus sends signals to the so-called master gland of the endocrine system, the pituitary gland. The pituitary secretes a hormone (ACTH) that stimulates the outer part of the adrenal glands (the adrenal cortex) to release another important set of hormones—*corticosteroids*. These hormones stimulate the release of more fats and proteins into circulation, thus helping to increase your energy. They also mobilize chemicals that help to inhibit tissue inflammation in case of injury.

Stress can also produce other physiological changes that we are just beginning to understand. The most critical changes occur in the immune system. Your immune system provides you with resistance to infections. However, mounting evidence indicates that stress can suppress the functioning of the immune system, making it less effective in repelling invasions by infectious agents

Hans Selye

Figure 3.10. The general adaptation syndrome. According to Selye, our physiological response to stress can be broken into three phases. During the first phase, the body mobilizes its resources for resistance after a brief initial shock. In the second phase, resistance levels off and eventually begins to decline. If the third phase of the general adaptation syndrome is reached, resistance is depleted, leading to health problems and exhaustion.

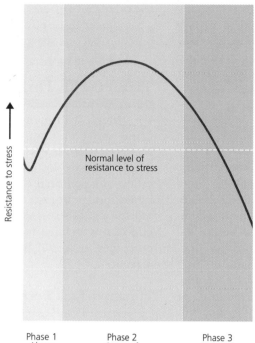

Normal level of resistance to stress

Resistance to stress

Phase 1
Alarm reaction

Phase 2
Stage of resistance

Phase 3
Stage of exhaustion

Time

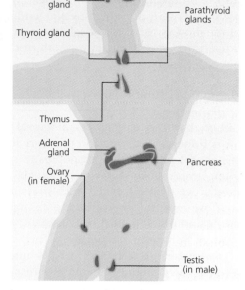

Figure 3.11. The endocrine system. The endocrine glands secrete hormones into the bloodstream. The locations of the principal endocrine glands are shown here. The hormones released by these glands regulate a variety of physical functions and play a key role in our response to stress.

Pituitary gland
Pineal gland
Parathyroid glands
Thyroid gland
Thymus
Adrenal gland
Pancreas
Ovary (in female)
Testis (in male)

Figure 3.12. Brain-body pathways in stress. In times of stress, the brain sends signals along two pathways. The pathway through the autonomic nervous system controls the release of catecholamine hormones that help mobilize the body for action. The pathway through the pituitary gland and the endocrine system controls the release of corticosteroid hormones that increase energy and ward off tissue inflammation.

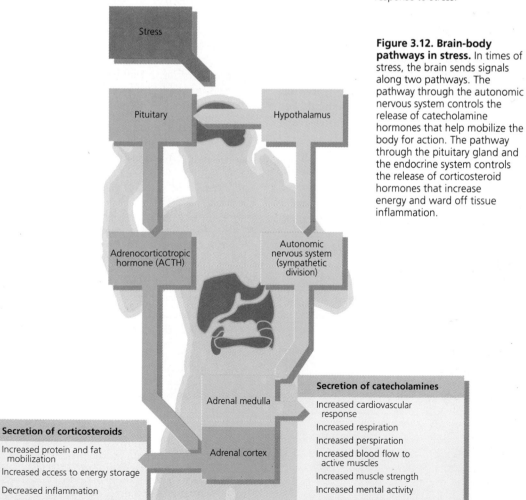

Stress

Pituitary

Hypothalamus

Adrenocorticotropic hormone (ACTH)

Autonomic nervous system (sympathetic division)

Adrenal medulla

Adrenal cortex

Secretion of corticosteroids

Increased protein and fat mobilization

Increased access to energy storage

Decreased inflammation

Secretion of catecholamines

Increased cardiovascular response

Increased respiration

Increased perspiration

Increased blood flow to active muscles

Increased muscle strength

Increased mental activity

(Solomon, Amkraut, & Rubin, 1985). The exact mechanisms underlying immunal suppression remain a mystery for the moment. It is becoming clear, however, that our physiological responses to stress extend into every corner of our bodies. As you will see, these physiological reactions can have an impact on both our mental and our physical health.

Behavioral Responses

Although we respond to stress at several levels, our behavior is the crucial dimension of our reactions. Our emotional and physiological responses to stress—which are often undesirable—tend to be largely automatic. However, if we deal effectively with stress at the behavioral level, we may shut down these potentially harmful emotional and physiological responses.

Most behavioral responses to stress involve coping. *Coping* **refers to active efforts to master, reduce, or tolerate the demands created by stress.** Notice that this definition is neutral as to whether coping efforts are healthy or maladaptive. The popular use of the term often implies that coping is inherently healthy. When we say that someone "coped with her problems," we imply that she handled them effectively.

In reality, coping responses may be either healthy or unhealthy. For example, if you were flunking a history course at midterm, you might cope with this stress in the following ways. (1) You could increase your study efforts. (2) You could seek special help from a tutor. (3) You might blame your professor for your poor grade. (4) Or you might give up on the class without really trying. Clearly, the first two coping responses would be healthier than the latter two. Thus, coping efforts may range from healthy to maladaptive.

People cope with stress in an endless variety of ways. Because of the complexity and importance of coping processes, we'll devote all of the next chapter to ways of coping. At this point, it is sufficient to note that our coping strategies help to determine whether stress has any positive or negative effects on us. In the next section, we'll see what some of those effects can be as we discuss the possible outcomes of our struggles with stress.

THE POTENTIAL EFFECTS OF STRESS

We struggle with many stresses every day. Most of them come and go without leaving any enduring imprint. However, when stress is severe or when demands pile up, stress may have lasting effects. These effects are often called "adaptational outcomes." They are relatively durable (though not necessarily permanent) consequences of exposure to stress. Although stress can have beneficial effects, research has focused mainly on possible negative outcomes, so you'll find our coverage slanted in that direction.

Impaired Task Performance

Frequently, stress takes its toll on our ability to perform effectively on the task at hand. For instance, Roy Baumeister's work shows how pressure can interfere with perfor-

RECOMMENDED READING

Comprehensive Stress Management
by Jerrold S. Greenberg (William C. Brown, 1990)

This is a very practical book that serves as a textbook in many of the courses on stress that are popping up in our colleges and universities. Although its principal focus is on stress *management*, which we cover in the next chapter, it contains more information on the nature and causes of stress than any comparable book. It is written in a highly personable manner and is also well illustrated.

In the first part of the book, Greenberg elaborates on the concept of stress, describes how stress affects physiological functioning, and discusses the connection between stress and a host of physical diseases. The final part includes unusual chapters on stress in specific populations. Greenberg looks at occupational stress, college stress, family stress, stress linked to sex roles, and stress among the elderly. In between the first and final parts of the book, Greenberg provides ten chapters on approaches to stress management, including meditation, biofeedback, relaxation techniques, and ways to change appraisals of stress.

> Women experience stressors, such as the one just described, that are based [on] sex-role stereotyping. Their work in the home is not valued, they earn less than they should earn when working outside the home, or they are expected to be "superwomen," that is, excellent lovers, wives, mothers, and employees. However, men, too, experience stress as a result of sex-role stereotyping. Do you think it's easy being ashamed to show fear? Men are supposed to be strong, and many consider fear a sign of weakness. Don't you think it stressful to have the responsibility of being the "breadwinner"? [p. 321]

mance. Baumeister's (1984) theory assumes that pressure to perform often makes us self-conscious and that this elevated self-consciousness disrupts our attention. He theorizes that attention may be distorted in two ways. First, elevated self-consciousness may divert attention from the demands of the task, creating distractions. Second, on well-learned tasks that should be executed almost automatically, the self-conscious person may focus *too much* attention on the task. Thus, the person thinks too much about what he or she is doing.

Baumeister (1984) found support for his theory in a series of laboratory experiments in which he manipulated the pressure to perform well on a simple perceptual-motor task. Even more impressive, his theory was supported in a study of the past performance of professional sports teams in championship contests (Baumeister & Steinhilber, 1984). According to Baumeister, when a championship series such as baseball's World Series goes to the final, decisive game, the home team is under greater pressure than the visiting team. Why? Because players desperately want to succeed in front of their hometown fans. As a result, they experience elevated self-consciousness. Conventional wisdom suggests that home teams have the advantage in sports. But Baumeister argues that the performance of the home team declines when pressure mounts in the final game of a championship series.

To test this hypothesis, Baumeister and Steinhilber (1984) analyzed past championships in professional baseball and basketball. These sports settle their championships with a series of games. Thus, the performance of the home teams in early games can be compared against their performance in the final game. As hypothesized, Baumeister and Steinhilber found that the winning percentage for home teams was significantly lower in final games than in early games in both sports (see Figure 3.13). Furthermore, statistics showed that the home team in baseball made more fielding errors in game 7 than in early games. In basketball, the home team's free-throw shooting percentage went down in the last game.

The most obvious explanation for these findings is that the home team frequently "chokes under pressure," as predicted by Baumeister's theory. Thus, stress can impair task performance—even in gifted professional athletes.

Disruption of Cognitive Functioning

An interesting experimental study suggests that Baumeister is on the right track in looking to *attention* to explain how stress impairs task performance. In a study of stress and decision making, Keinan (1987) was able to measure three specific aspects of subjects' attention under stressful and nonstressful conditions. Keinan placed subjects under stress by telling them that they might receive painful but harmless electric shocks while working on a decision-making task at a computer. No one was actually shocked, and subjects were given the option of quitting the study when they were told about the shock. Keinan found that stress disrupted two out of the three aspects of attention measured in the study. Stress increased subjects' tendency (1) to jump to a conclusion too quickly without considering all their options and (2) to do an unsystematic, poorly organized review of their available options.

Stress may disrupt other aspects of our cognitive processes besides attention. In some people, a high level of emotional and physiological arousal leads to reduced flexibility in thinking, poor concentration, and less effective memory storage (Mandler, 1982).

Furthermore, *severe* stress can leave people dazed and confused, in a state of shock (Horowitz, 1979). In these states, people report feeling emotionally numb, and they respond in a flat, apathetic fashion to events around them. They often stare off into space and have difficulty maintaining a coherent train of thought. Their behavior frequently has an automatic, rigid, stereotyped quality. Fortunately, this disorientation usually occurs only in extreme situations involving overwhelming stress. For instance, you will sometimes see shock among people who have just been through a major disaster, such as a fire, a flood, or a tornado.

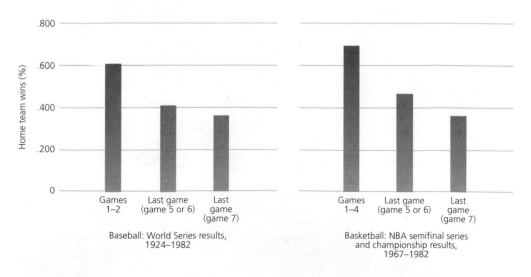

Figure 3.13. Choking under pressure. In early World Series and NBA championship contests that involve less pressure, the home team enjoys an advantage. But when it comes to the last game, the home team frequently chokes under pressure, as evidenced by the decreased winning percentages shown here. (Data from Baumeister & Steinhilber, 1984)

Burnout

Burnout is an overused buzzword that means different things to different people. Nonetheless, Ayala Pines and her colleagues have described burnout in a systematic way that has facilitated scientific study of the syndrome (Pines & Aronson, 1988; Pines, Aronson, & Kafry, 1981). **Burnout involves physical, mental, and emotional exhaustion that is attributable to work-related stress.** The physical exhaustion includes chronic fatigue, weakness, and low energy. The mental exhaustion is manifested in highly negative attitudes toward oneself, one's work, and life in general. The emotional exhaustion includes feeling hopeless, helpless, and trapped.

What causes burnout? According to Pines and her colleagues (1981), "it usually does not occur as the result of one or two traumatic events but sneaks up through a general erosion of the spirit" (p. 3). They view burnout as an emotional disturbance that is brought on gradually by heavy, chronic, job-related stress.

Initially, theorists thought that burnout was unique to the helping professions, such as social work, clinical psychology, and counseling. The high burnout rate in the helping professions was blamed on helpers' emotionally draining relations with their clients. However, it has gradually become clear that burnout is a potential problem in all occupations (Maslach, 1982). Indeed, work stress may not be the only cause of burnout. It's possible that chronic stress from other roles, such as parenting or being a student, may lead to burnout.

Delayed Effects: Posttraumatic Stress Disorders

The effects of stress are not necessarily apparent right away. There may be a time lag between the occurrence of stress and the appearance of its effects. **The *posttraumatic stress disorder* involves disturbed behavior attributed to a major stressful event that emerges after the stress is over.** Posttraumatic stress disorders have mostly been seen in veterans of the Vietnam war. Among Vietnam veterans, posttraumatic disorders typically begin to surface anywhere from 9 to 60 months after the soldier's discharge from military service (Shatan, 1978). There were, of course, immediate stress reactions among the soldiers as well—but these were expected. The delayed reactions were something of a surprise.

While posttraumatic stress disorders are widely associated with the experiences of Vietnam veterans, they have been seen in response to other cases of severe stress as well. A recent study of mental health by Helzer, Robins, and McEvoy (1987) suggests that posttraumatic stress disorders have been experienced by roughly 5 out of every 1000 men and 13 out of every 1000 women in the general population.

What types of stress besides combat are severe enough to produce posttraumatic disorders? Among females, the most common cause found by Helzer and his colleagues was a physical attack, such as a rape. Other causes among women included seeing someone die (or seeing someone seriously hurt), close brushes with death, serious accidents, and discovering a spouse's affair. Among men, all the posttraumatic disorders were due to combat experiences or to seeing someone die.

In the study by Helzer and his associates (1987), a long time lag between the severe stress and the onset of the

posttraumatic disorder was seen only in cases caused by war experiences. There may be something unique about how people cope with the stress of war. In all the other cases, the posttraumatic stress syndrome surfaced soon after the occurrence of the extremely stressful event.

What are the symptoms of posttraumatic stress disorders? Common symptoms seen in combat veterans have included nightmares, paranoia, emotional numbing, guilt about surviving, alienation, and problems in social relations (A. Blank, 1982). In the more diverse collection of cases identified by Helzer et al. (1987), the most common symptoms were nightmares, difficulties in sleeping, and feelings of jumpiness.

Psychological Problems and Disorders

Posttraumatic stress disorders are caused by a single episode of extreme stress. Of greater relevance to most of us are the effects of chronic, prolonged, everyday stress. On the basis of clinical impressions, psychologists have long suspected that chronic stress might contribute to many types of psychological problems and mental disorders. Since the late 1960s, advances in the measurement of stress have allowed researchers to verify these suspicions in empirical studies. In the domain of common psychological problems, studies indicate that stress may contribute to poor academic performance (Lloyd, Alexander, Rice, & Greenfield, 1980), insomnia (Hartmann, 1985), nightmares (Cernovsky, 1989), sexual difficulties (Malatesta & Adams, 1984), drug abuse (Krueger, 1981), and anxiety and dejection (Weiten, 1988).

Above and beyond these everyday problems, research reveals that stress often contributes to the onset of full-fledged psychological disorders, including depression (Hammen, Mayol, deMayo, & Marks, 1986), schizophrenia (Spring, 1989), neurotic disorders (McKeon, Roa, & Mann, 1989), and eating disorders (Strober, 1989). We'll discuss these relations between stress and mental disorders in detail in Chapter 15. Of course, stress is only one of many factors that may contribute to psychological

Beginning in September 1989, Hurricane Hugo caused devastating damage in the Caribbean and in the southeastern United States. Experiencing the horrors of natural disasters, such as tornadoes and earthquakes, can sometimes lead to posttraumatic stress disorder.

disorders. Nonetheless, it is sobering to realize that stress can have a dramatic impact on our mental health.

Physical Illness

It is just as sobering to realize that stress can also have a dramatic impact on our physical health. The idea that stress can contribute to physical diseases is not entirely new. Evidence that stress can cause physical illness began to accumulate back in the 1930s. By the 1950s, the concept of psychosomatic disease was widely accepted. *Psychosomatic diseases* **are genuine physical ailments caused in part by psychological factors, especially emotional distress.** The underlying assumption is that stress-induced autonomic arousal contributes to most psychosomatic diseases. Please note, these diseases are not *imagined* physical ailments. The term *psychosomatic* is often misused to refer to ailments that are "all in the head." This is an entirely different syndrome, which we'll discuss in Chapter 14.

Common psychosomatic diseases include high blood pressure, ulcers, asthma, skin disorders such as eczema and hives, and migraine and tension headaches (Kaplan, 1985). These diseases do not *necessarily* have a strong psychological component in every affected individual. There is a genetic predisposition to most psychosomatic diseases, and in some people these diseases are largely physiological in origin (Weiner, 1977). More often than not, however, psychological factors contribute to psychosomatic diseases. When they do, stress is the culprit at work.

Prior to the 1970s, it was thought that stress contributed to the development of only a few physical diseases (the psychosomatic diseases). In the 1970s, however, researchers began to uncover new links between stress and a great variety of diseases previously believed to be purely physiological in origin. Although there is room for debate on some specific diseases, stress may influence the onset and course of heart disease, stroke, tuberculosis, multiple sclerosis, arthritis, diabetes, leukemia, cancer, various types of infectious disease, and the common cold (Elliott & Eisdorfer, 1982; Miller, 1983). We'll take a more detailed look at the evidence linking stress to some of these diseases in Chapter 14.

Beneficial Effects

The beneficial effects of stress are more difficult to pinpoint than the harmful effects because they tend to be more subtle. Although research data are sparse, there are at least three ways in which stress can have positive effects.

First, stressful events help to satisfy our need for stimulation and challenge. Studies suggest that most people prefer an intermediate level of stimulation and challenge in their lives (Suedfeld, 1979). Although we think of stress in terms of stimulus overload, underload can be extremely unpleasant as well. Thus, most of us would experience a suffocating level of boredom if we lived a stress-free existence. In a sense, then, stress fulfills a basic need of the human organism.

Second, stress frequently promotes personal growth or self-improvement. Stressful events sometimes force us to develop new skills, learn new insights, and acquire new strengths. In other words, the adaptation process initiated by stress may lead to personal changes that are changes for the better. Confronting and conquering a stressful challenge may lead to improvements in specific coping abilities and to enhanced self-esteem. For example, a breakup with a boyfriend or a girlfriend frequently leads individuals to change aspects of their behavior that they find unsatisfactory. Moreover, even if we do not conquer stressors, we may be able to learn from our mistakes.

Third, today's stress can inoculate us so that we are less affected by tomorrow's stress. Some studies suggest that exposure to stress can increase our stress tolerance—as long as the stress isn't overwhelming (Epstein, 1983; Janis, 1983). Thus, a woman who has previously endured business setbacks may be much better prepared than most people to deal with a bank foreclosure on her home.

In light of the negative effects that stress can have, improved stress tolerance is a desirable goal. We'll look next at the factors that influence our ability to tolerate stress.

FACTORS INFLUENCING STRESS TOLERANCE

The effects of stress vary from one person to another. Some people seem to be able to withstand the ravages of stress better than others. Why? Because there are a number of *moderator variables* that moderate the impact of stress on our physical and mental health. To shed light on differences in how well people tolerate stress, we'll look at four key moderator variables: social support, hardiness, optimism, and sensation seeking. As you'll see, these factors influence our appraisals of potentially stressful events and our emotional, physical, and behavioral responses to stress. These complexities are diagrammed in Figure 3.14,

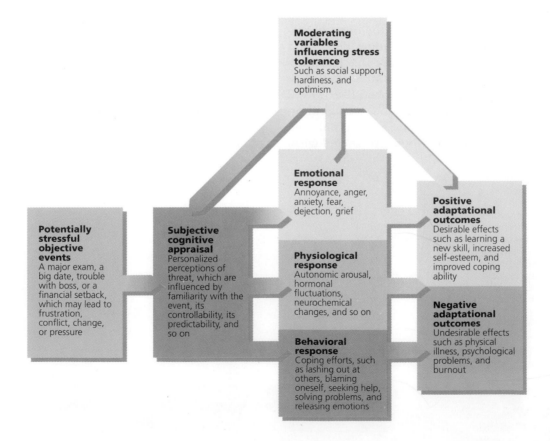

which builds on Figure 3.6 to provide a more complete overview of all the factors involved in our reactions to stress.

Social Support

Friends may be good for your health! This startling conclusion emerges from studies on social support as a moderator of stress. *Social support* **involves various types of aid and succor provided by members of one's social networks.** In one study of social support, Gore (1978) looked at the moderating role of support in 100 stably employed married men who were facing a very powerful form of stress: the loss of their jobs after a plant shutdown. Social support from wives, friends, and relatives was assessed. Gore found that those with relatively strong social support showed (1) less emotional response to the frustration and (2) fewer symptoms of physical illness.

In a more recent study, Jemmott and Magloire (1988) examined the effect of social support on immunal functioning in a group of students going through the stress of final exams. They found that students who reported stronger social support had higher levels of an antibody that plays a key role in warding off respiratory infections.

Many other studies have found evidence that social support is favorably related to physical health (Cohen, 1988). Social support seems to be good medicine for the mind as well as the body, as most studies find an association between social support and mental health (Leavy, 1983). It appears that social support serves as a protective buffer for us during times of high stress, reducing the negative impact of stressful events. Furthermore, social support has its own positive effects on health, which may be apparent even when we aren't under great stress (Cohen & Syme, 1985).

Researchers are trying to figure out just *how* social support promotes health and eases the impact of stressful events. House (1981) has proposed that social support serves four important functions.

Emotional support involves expressions of affection, interest, and concern that tell us we are appreciated. It includes behaviors like listening sympathetically to our problems. It presumably bolsters our self-esteem.

Appraisal support involves helping people to evaluate and make sense of their troubles and problems. It includes efforts to clarify the nature of the problem and provide feedback about its significance.

Informational support involves providing advice about how to actually handle the problem. This includes discussing possible solutions and the relative merits of alternative coping strategies.

Instrumental support involves providing material aid and services. This may include a wide range of activities, such as providing someone with a place to stay, lending money, going along to a social service agency, or helping to assume work or family responsibilities.

House's analysis raises the point that social *bonds* are not equivalent to social *support*. Some friends and family members may not provide the kinds of support House describes. Indeed, some people in our social circles may be a source of more *stress* than *support*. People close to us can put us under pressure, make us feel guilty, break promises, and otherwise compound our stress.

Pagel, Erdly, and Becker (1987) looked at both the good and bad sides of social relations in measuring subjects' satisfaction with their social networks. They found that the *helpfulness* of friends and family wasn't as important as whether friends and family *caused emotional distress*. Adapting a line from an old Beatles song, the investigators concluded that "We get by with *and in spite of* a little help from our friends." To some extent, then, people who report good social support may really mean that their friends and family aren't driving them crazy.

Hardiness

Suzanne Kobasa reasoned that if stress affects some people less than others, then some people must be *hardier* than others. She set out to determine whether personality factors might be the key to these differences in hardiness.

Figure 3.14. Overview of the stress process. This diagram builds on Figure 3.6 (our multidimensional response to stress) to provide a more complete overview of the factors involved in stress. This diagram adds the potential effects of stress (seen on the far right) by listing some of the positive and negative adaptational outcomes that may result from stress. It also completes the picture by showing that moderating variables (seen at the top) can intervene to influence the effects of stress.

Kobasa (1979) used a modified version of the Holmes and Rahe (1967) stress scale (SRRS) to measure the amount of stress experienced by a group of executives. As in most other studies, she found a modest correlation between stress and the incidence of physical illness. However, she carried her investigation one step further than previous studies. She compared the high-stress executives who exhibited the expected high incidence of illness against the high-stress executives who stayed healthy. She administered a battery of psychological tests, comparing the executives along 18 dimensions of personality. She found that the hardier executives "were more committed, felt more in control, and had bigger appetites for challenge" (Kobasa, 1984, p. 70). Thus, the personality traits found to be associated with hardiness include the following (Kobasa, Maddi, & Kahn, 1982).

Commitment. The hardy executives typically displayed a clear sense of values. They had well-defined goals and a commitment to their importance. In contrast, the less hardy executives were characterized as alienated (lacking direction and commitment to a value system).

Challenge. The stress-resistant executives tended to seek out and actively confront challenges. They viewed change, rather than stability, as the norm in life. They welcomed change instead of clinging to the past. In comparison, the less stress-resistant executives were more likely to view change as alarming.

Control. The hardy executives had a stronger belief in their ability to control their own destiny than the less stress-resistant executives, who were more likely to feel powerless. Hardy executives felt that their outcomes were governed mainly by their own actions and behavior, as opposed to fate and luck.

Thus, *hardiness* **is a personality syndrome marked by commitment, challenge, and control that is purportedly associated with strong stress resistance.** Currently there is an active debate about the key elements of hardiness and exactly how it affects our health (Funk & Houston, 1987; Hull, van Treuren, & Virnelli, 1987). Nonetheless, Kobasa's work has stimulated research on how personality affects our health and our tolerance of stress. Of particular interest is new work on optimism, a widely discussed trait that researchers have paid little attention to until recently.

Optimism

Defining *optimism* **as a general tendency to expect good outcomes,** Michael Scheier and Charles Carver (1985) found a correlation between optimism and relatively good physical health in a sample of college students. In a pair of subsequent studies, they found that optimists and pessimists cope with stress differently (Scheier, Weintraub, & Carver, 1986). Optimists are more likely to engage in action-oriented, problem-focused coping. They are more willing than pessimists to seek social support, and they are more likely to emphasize the positive in their appraisals of stressful events. In comparison, pessimists are more likely to deal with stress by giving up or engaging in denial.

In a related line of research, Christopher Peterson and Martin Seligman have studied how people explain bad events (personal setbacks, mishaps, disappointments, and such). They identified a pessimistic explanatory style whereby some people tend to blame setbacks on their personal shortcomings. In a retrospective study of men who graduated from Harvard back in the 1940s, they found an association between this pessimistic explanatory style and relatively poor health (Peterson, Seligman, & Vaillant, 1988). In their attempt to explain this association, they speculate that pessimism leads to passive coping efforts and poor health care practices.

Finally, a recent study suggests that an optimistic cognitive style may be a key factor underlying the hardiness syndrome described by Kobasa. Allred and Smith (1989) used the usual personality tests to identify male subjects who were high or low in hardiness. Then they studied the men's thought processes under conditions of low and high stress. They found that hardy individuals reported more positive thoughts under high stress than less hardy individuals.

High sensation seekers actively pursue stimulation and risk. They enjoy experiences such as mountain climbing that many of us would find stressful and unpleasant.

I: THE DYNAMICS OF ADJUSTMENT

There are only a few studies on the effects of optimism versus pessimism, but they all suggest that this aspect of personality influences the impact of stress. Future research on this dimension of personality should clarify its role in moderating the effects of stress.

Sensation Seeking

Sensation seeking is yet another personality trait that affects how we respond to stress. First described by Marvin Zuckerman (1971, 1979), *sensation seeking* **is a generalized preference for high or low levels of sensory stimulation.** People who are high in sensation seeking prefer, and perhaps even need, a high level of stimulation. They are easily bored, and they enjoy challenges. They like activities that may involve some physical risk, such as mountain climbing, white water rafting, and surfing. They satisfy their appetite for stimulation by experimenting with drugs, numerous sexual partners, and novel experiences (such as travel to unusual places). They relish gambling, spicy foods, provocative art, wild parties, and unusual friends.

Obviously, high sensation seekers actively pursue experiences that many people would find very stressful. However, now that you know how subjective stress is, it should come as no surprise that sensation seekers see these experiences as less threatening than other people would. Zuckerman believes that there is a biological predisposition toward high sensation seeking.

In regard to adjustment processes, Zuckerman makes a couple of intriguing points about sensation seeking. First, he suggests that in marriage and other intimate relationships, people very high and very low in sensation seeking may have difficulty understanding each other, not to mention finding mutually enjoyable activities. Thus, progress in romantic relationships may be easier when partners are compatible in sensation seeking. This hypothesis received some support in a study that showed that partners in intimate relationships *do* tend to be fairly similar in sensation seeking (Lesnick-Oberstein & Cohen, 1984). Second, Zuckerman suggests that it is important for high and low sensation seekers to select the "right" type of occupation. It seems likely that a high sensation seeker would be frustrated by routine, monotonous work, while a low sensation seeker might be overwhelmed easily by the stress of a high-pressure job.

SUMMARY

Stress involves transactions with the environment that are perceived as threatening. Stress is a common, everyday event, and even routine hassles can be problematic. To a large degree, stress lies in the eye of the beholder. Whether we feel threatened by events depends on how we appraise them. Much of our everyday stress is self-imposed.

Major types of stress include frustration, conflict, change, and pressure. Frustration occurs when an obstacle prevents us from attaining some goal. There are three principal types of conflict: approach-approach, avoidance-avoidance, and approach-avoidance. The latter is especially stressful. Vacillation is a common response to approach-avoidance conflict. A large number of studies with the SRRS suggest that change is stressful. Although this may be true, it is now clear that the SRRS is a measure of general stress rather than just change-related stress. Two kinds of pressure (to perform and conform) also appear to be stressful.

Our appraisals of potentially threatening events are highly subjective. Stressful events are usually viewed as less threatening when they are familiar, controllable, and predictable, and when they lie in the distant future. However, controllability and predictability have varied effects on the appraisal of stress.

Emotional reactions to stress typically involve anger, fear, or sadness. Emotional arousal may interfere with our coping. The optimal level of arousal on tasks varies, depending on the complexity of the task.

Our physiological arousal in response to stress was originally called the fight-or-flight response by Cannon. Selye's general adaptation syndrome describes three stages in our physiological reaction to stress: alarm, resistance, and exhaustion. Diseases of adaptation may appear during the stage of exhaustion. There are two major pathways along which the brain sends signals to the endocrine system in response to stress. Actions along these paths release two sets of hormones into the bloodstream, catecholamines and corticosteroids. Stress can also affect our immunal system.

Our behavioral response to stress involves coping. Coping efforts may be healthy or maladaptive. If we cope effectively with stress, we can short-circuit potentially harmful emotional and physical responses.

Although stress can have positive effects, research on the effects of stress has concentrated on negative outcomes. Common negative effects include impaired task performance, disruption of attention and other cognitive processes, pervasive exhaustion known as burnout, post-traumatic stress disorders, a host of everyday psychological problems, full-fledged psychological disorders, and varied types of damage to one's physical health. However, stress fulfills a basic human need for challenge and can lead to personal growth and self-improvement.

People differ in how much stress they can tolerate without experiencing ill effects. A person's social support is a key consideration. The personality factors associated with hardiness—commitment, challenge, and a sense of being in control—increase stress tolerance. People high in optimism and sensation seeking also have advantages in coping with stress.

In the upcoming Application, we'll discuss how you can monitor the amount of stress in your life. You'll get to see how you score on a widely used measure of life stress.

Monitoring Your Stress

Rank-order the following five events in terms of how stressful they would be for you (1 = the most stressful event, 5 = the least stressful event).

☐ **1.** Change in residence.

☐ **2.** Fired at work.

☐ **3.** Death of a close family member.

☐ **4.** Pregnancy.

☐ **5.** Personal injury or illness.

All five events appear on the Social Readjustment Rating Scale (SRRS), developed by Holmes and Rahe (1967), which we described earlier (see Figure 3.3). If you ranked them in the same order as Holmes and Rahe's subjects, the rankings would be 5, 3, 1, 4, and 2. If you didn't rank them in that order, don't worry about it. That merely shows that the perception of stress is very personal and subjective. Unfortunately, the SRRS fails to take this subjectivity into account. That is just one of a number of basic problems with the SRRS.

The SRRS and the research associated with it have received a great deal of publicity. The scale has been reprinted in many newspapers and magazines. In these popular articles, readers have been encouraged to attribute great significance to their scores. They have sometimes been told that they should reduce or minimize change in their lives if their scores are high (Cohen, 1979). Such bold advice could be counterproductive, and it needs to be qualified carefully. Therefore, in this application section we'll elaborate on some of the problems with the SRRS as a measurement scale, introduce you to a newer and much improved scale for measuring stress, and explain why your scores on any stress scale should be interpreted with caution.

PROBLEMS WITH THE SRRS

As you learned earlier in this chapter, the SRRS was developed in the early 1960s by Thomas Holmes and Richard Rahe (1967). They designed the scale to measure the amount of change-related stress that people experience. The scale assigns values to 43 life events that supposedly indicate how stressful those events are. You respond to the scale by checking off those events that have happened to you in a recent time period. Then you add up the values of the checked events to arrive at your score. In a host of studies, these scores have been found to be related to the likelihood of developing an intimidating array of physical illnesses and psychological problems (Barrett, Rose, & Klerman, 1979; Elliott & Eisdorfer, 1982).

Before we discuss the shortcomings of the SRRS, we should emphasize that Holmes and Rahe deserve enormous credit for having the imagination to tackle the difficult task of measuring life stress. Over two decades ago, they had the insight to recognize the potential importance of stress and the ingenuity to develop a scale that would permit its measurement. They pioneered a new area of research that has turned out to be extremely productive. However, their ground-breaking foray into the assessment of stress was not without its flaws, and their scale has been improved upon. So, borrowing from the analyses of a number of critics (notably, Cleary, 1980; Derogatis, 1982; Monroe, 1982; Rabkin & Streuning, 1976), let's look at some of the major problems with the SRRS. Although our list is not exhaustive, the key problems are as follows.

First, as already discussed, the assumption that the SRRS measures change exclusively has been shown to be inaccurate. We now have ample evidence that the desirability of the events experienced affects adaptational outcomes more than the amount of change that they require (Perkins, 1982). Thus, it seems prudent to view the SRRS as a measure of diverse forms of stress, rather than as a measure of change-related stress.

Second, the SRRS fails to take into account differences among people in their subjective perception of how stressful an event is. For instance, while divorce may deserve a stress value of 73 for *most* people, a particular person's divorce might generate much less stress and merit a value of only 25. Hurst, Jenkins, and Rose (1978) have suggested that it might be better to have respondents rate how personally stressful events were for them than to use the standardized, average weights. Research by Sarason, Johnson, and Siegel (1978) indicates that such an approach *can* provide better prediction. Thus, the normative weights assigned to events on the SRRS may not capture the true impact of an event on a particular person.

Third, many of the events listed on the SRRS are highly ambiguous. For instance, what qualifies as "trouble with boss"? Should you check that item because you're sick and tired of your supervisor? What constitutes a "change in living conditions"? Does your purchase of a great new stereo qualify? How should the "pregnancy" item be interpreted? Should a man who has a pregnant wife check that item? As you can see, the SRRS includes many "events" that are described inadequately, producing considerable ambiguity about how one should respond.

Fourth, the SRRS does not sample from the domain of stressful events very thoroughly. Could the 43 events listed on the SRRS exhaust all the major stresses that people typically experience? A study designed to explore that question found many significant omissions. The study led to the development of an expanded version of the SRRS that lists 102 life events (Dohrenwend, Krasnoff, Askenasy, & Dohrenwend, 1978).

THE LIFE EXPERIENCES SURVEY

In light of these problems, a number of researchers have attempted to develop improved versions of the SRRS (for instance, Dohrenwend et al., 1978; Paykel, 1974). The scale that seems to be gaining the greatest use is the Life Experiences Survey (LES), assembled by Irwin Sarason and colleagues (Sarason, Johnson, & Siegel, 1978). The LES revises and builds on the SRRS in a variety of ways that correct, at least in part, most of the problems just discussed.

Specifically, the LES has the following characteristics. It recognizes that stress involves more than mere change and asks respondents to indicate whether events had a positive or negative impact on them. This strategy permits researchers to compute scores for positive change, negative change, and total change. These scores help researchers gain much more insight into which facets of stress are most crucial.

The LES also takes into consideration differences among people in their appraisal of stress. It accomplishes this by dropping the normative weights and replacing them with personally assigned weightings of the impact of relevant events. Ambiguity in items is decreased by providing more elaborate descriptions of many items to clarify their meaning. There is still some ambiguity in the scale, but there is no complete solution for this problem.

The failure of the SRRS to sample the domain of stressful events fully is dealt with in several ways. First, some significant omissions from the SRRS were corrected in the LES. Second, the LES allows the respondent to write in personally important events that are not included on the scale. Third, the LES reprinted here (see Figure 3.15) has an extra section just for students. Sarason et al. (1978) suggest that a special, tailored section of this sort should be added for a specific population whenever it is useful.

We suggest that you respond to the LES in Figure 3.15. Although we have been critical of people overinterpreting SRRS scores, there is much to be said for making an estimate of how much stress you've been under recently. If you score high, you may want to think about ways to reduce some of the stress in your life.

Arriving at your scores on the LES is very simple. Just add up all the positive impact ratings on the right side of the zero. That sum is your positive change score. Your negative change score is the sum of all of the negative impact ratings that you made on the left (disregard the minus signs in adding the numbers). Adding these two values yields your total change score. Approximate norms for all three of these scores are listed in Figure 3.16 (on page 90) so that you can get some idea of what your score means.

Research to date suggests that your negative change score is the crucial one. Positive change has not been found to be a very good predictor of adaptational outcomes. In direct comparisons with the SRRS, the negative change score has turned out to be a better predictor of mental and physical health than SRRS scores (Sarason et al., 1978). Thus far, research has shown that negative change

Figure 3.15. The Life Experiences Survey (LES). Like the SRRS, the LES is designed to measure change-related stress. However, Sarason, Johnson, and Siegel (1978) corrected many of the problems apparent in the SRRS.

Listed below are a number of events that sometimes bring about change in the lives of those who experience them and that necessitate social readjustment. Please check those events you have experienced in the recent past and indicate the time period during which you have experienced each event. Be sure that all checkmarks are directly across from the items that they correspond to. Also, for each item checked below, please indicate the extent to which you viewed the event as having either a positive or a negative impact on your life at the time the event occured. That is, indicate the type and extent of impact that the event had. A rating of –3 would indicate an extremely negative impact. A rating of 0 suggests no impact, either positive or negative. A rating of +3 would indicate an extremely positive impact.

	0 to 6 mo	7 mo to 1 yr	Extremely negative	Moderately negative	Somewhat negative	No impact	Slightly positive	Moderately positive	Extremely positive
Section 1									
1. Marriage			–3	–2	–1	0	+1	+2	+3
2. Detention in jail or comparable institution			–3	–2	–1	0	+1	+2	+3
3. Death of spouse			–3	–2	–1	0	+1	+2	+3
4. Major change in sleeping habits (much more or much less sleep)			–3	–2	–1	0	+1	+2	+3
5. Death of a close family member:			–3	–2	–1	0	+1	+2	+3
a. mother			–3	–2	–1	0	+1	+2	+3
b. father			–3	–2	–1	0	+1	+2	+3
c. brother			–3	–2	–1	0	+1	+2	+3
d. sister			–3	–2	–1	0	+1	+2	+3
e. grandmother			–3	–2	–1	0	+1	+2	+3
f. grandfather			–3	–2	–1	0	+1	+2	+3
g. other (specify)			–3	–2	–1	0	+1	+2	+3
6. Major change in eating habits (much more or much less food intake)			–3	–2	–1	0	+1	+2	+3
7. Foreclosure on mortgage or loan			–3	–2	–1	0	+1	+2	+3
8. Death of close friend			–3	–2	–1	0	+1	+2	+3
9. Outstanding personal achievement			–3	–2	–1	0	+1	+2	+3
10. Minor law violations (traffic tickets, disturbing the peace, etc.)			–3	–2	–1	0	+1	+2	+3
11. *Male*: Wife/girlfriend's pregnancy			–3	–2	–1	0	+1	+2	+3
12. *Female*: Pregnancy			–3	–2	–1	0	+1	+2	+3
13. Changed work situation (different work responsibility, major change in working conditions, working hours, etc.)			–3	–2	–1	0	+1	+2	+3
14. New job			–3	–2	–1	0	+1	+2	+3
15. Serious illness or injury of close family member:			–3	–2	–1	0	+1	+2	+3
a. father			–3	–2	–1	0	+1	+2	+3
b. mother			–3	–2	–1	0	+1	+2	+3
c. sister			–3	–2	–1	0	+1	+2	+3
d. brother			–3	–2	–1	0	+1	+2	+3
e. grandfather			–3	–2	–1	0	+1	+2	+3
f. grandmother			–3	–2	–1	0	+1	+2	+3
g. spouse			–3	–2	–1	0	+1	+2	+3
h. other (specify)			–3	–2	–1	0	+1	+2	+3
16. Sexual difficulties			–3	–2	–1	0	+1	+2	+3
17. Trouble with employer (in danger of losing job, being suspended, being demoted, etc.)			–3	–2	–1	0	+1	+2	+3
18. Trouble with in-laws			–3	–2	–1	0	+1	+2	+3
19. Major change in financial status (a lot better off or a lot worse off)			–3	–2	–1	0	+1	+2	+3
20. Major change in closeness of family members (increased or decreased closeness)			–3	–2	–1	0	+1	+2	+3

	0 to 6 mo	7 mo to 1 yr	Extremely negative	Moderately negative	Somewhat negative	No impact	Slightly positive	Moderately positive	Extremely positive
21. Gaining a new family member (through birth, adoption, family member moving in, etc.)			−3	−2	−1	0	+1	+2	+3
22. Change of residence			−3	−2	−1	0	+1	+2	+3
23. Marital separation from mate (due to conflict)			−3	−2	−1	0	+1	+2	+3
24. Major change in church activities (increased or decreased attendance)			−3	−2	−1	0	+1	+2	+3
25. Marital reconciliation with mate			−3	−2	−1	0	+1	+2	+3
26. Major change in number of arguments with spouse (a lot more or a lot fewer arguments)			−3	−2	−1	0	+1	+2	+3
27. *Married male*: Change in wife's work outside the home (beginning work, ceasing work, changing to a new job, etc.)			−3	−2	−1	0	+1	+2	+3
28. *Married female*: Change in husband's work (loss of job, beginning new job, retirement, etc.)			−3	−2	−1	0	+1	+2	+3
29. Major change in usual type and/or amount of recreation			−3	−2	−1	0	+1	+2	+3
30. Borrowing for a major purchase (buying home, business, etc.)			−3	−2	−1	0	+1	+2	+3
31. Borrowing for smaller purchase (buying car or TV, getting school loan, etc.)			−3	−2	−1	0	+1	+2	+3
32. Being fired from job			−3	−2	−1	0	+1	+2	+3
33. *Male*: Wife/girlfriend having abortion			−3	−2	−1	0	+1	+2	+3
34. *Female*: Having abortion			−3	−2	−1	0	+1	+2	+3
35. Major personal illness or injury			−3	−2	−1	0	+1	+2	+3
36. Major change in social activities, e.g., parties, movies, visiting (increased or decreased participation)			−3	−2	−1	0	+1	+2	+3
37. Major change in living conditions of family (building new home, remodeling, deterioration of home or neighborhood, etc.)			−3	−2	−1	0	+1	+2	+3
38. Divorce			−3	−2	−1	0	+1	+2	+3
39. Serious injury or illness of close friend			−3	−2	−1	0	+1	+2	+3
40. Retirement from work			−3	−2	−1	0	+1	+2	+3
41. Son or daughter leaving home (due to marriage, college, etc.)			−3	−2	−1	0	+1	+2	+3
42. Ending of formal schooling			−3	−2	−1	0	+1	+2	+3
43. Separation from spouse (due to work, travel, etc.)			−3	−2	−1	0	+1	+2	+3
44. Engagement			−3	−2	−1	0	+1	+2	+3
45. Breaking up with boyfriend/girlfriend			−3	−2	−1	0	+1	+2	+3
46. Leaving home for the first time			−3	−2	−1	0	+1	+2	+3
47. Reconciliation with boyfriend/girlfriend			−3	−2	−1	0	+1	+2	+3

Other recent experiences that have had an impact on your life.
List and rate.

	0 to 6 mo	7 mo to 1 yr	Extremely negative	Moderately negative	Somewhat negative	No impact	Slightly positive	Moderately positive	Extremely positive
48. _____			−3	−2	−1	0	+1	+2	+3
49. _____			−3	−2	−1	0	+1	+2	+3
50. _____			−3	−2	−1	0	+1	+2	+3

Section 2. Students only

	0 to 6 mo	7 mo to 1 yr	Extremely negative	Moderately negative	Somewhat negative	No impact	Slightly positive	Moderately positive	Extremely positive
51. Beginning a new school experience at a higher academic level (college, graduate school, professional school, etc.)			−3	−2	−1	0	+1	+2	+3
52. Changing to a new school at same academic level (undergraduate, graduate, etc.)			−3	−2	−1	0	+1	+2	+3
53. Academic probation			−3	−2	−1	0	+1	+2	+3
54. Being dismissed from dormitory or other residence			−3	−2	−1	0	+1	+2	+3
55. Failing an important exam			−3	−2	−1	0	+1	+2	+3
56. Changing a major			−3	−2	−1	0	+1	+2	+3
57. Failing a course			−3	−2	−1	0	+1	+2	+3
58. Dropping a course			−3	−2	−1	0	+1	+2	+3
59. Joining a fraternity/sorority			−3	−2	−1	0	+1	+2	+3
60. Financial problems concerning school (in danger of not having sufficient money to continue)			−3	−2	−1	0	+1	+2	+3

Figure 3.16. Norms for the Life Experiences Survey (LES). Approximate norms for college students taking the LES are shown for negative, positive, and total change scores. These norms are based on 345 undergraduates studied by Sarason, Johnson, and Siegel (1978). Data for males and females were combined, as sex differences were negligible.

Score category	Norms for LES		
	Negative change	Positive change	Total change
High	14 and above	16 and above	28 and above
Medium	4–13	7–15	12–27
Low	0–3	0–6	0–11

scores are related to a variety of adaptational outcomes, including menstrual discomfort, nonconformity, job dissatisfaction, athletic injuries, vaginal infections, anxiety, psychological discomfort, depression, and coronary disease (Passer & Seese, 1983; Sarason, Levine, & Sarason, 1982; Williams & Deffenbacher, 1983).

A CAUTIONARY NOTE

While there is merit in getting an estimate of how much stress you have experienced lately, you should interpret scores on the LES or any measure of stress with caution. You need not panic if you add up your negative change score and find that it falls in the "high" category. Although it is clear that there is a connection between stress and a variety of undesirable adaptational outcomes, there are a couple of reasons why a high score shouldn't cause undue concern.

First, the strength of the association between stress and adaptational problems is modest. Most of the correlations observed between stress scores and illness have been relatively low, often less than .30 (Kobasa, 1979). For researchers and theorists, it is very interesting to find any relationship at all. However, the link between stress and adaptational problems is too weak to permit us to make confident predictions about individuals. Many people endure high levels of stress without developing significant problems.

Second, stress is only one of a multitude of variables that affect your susceptibility to various maladies. Stress interacts with many other factors, such as your lifestyle, coping skills, social support, hardiness, and genetic inheritance, in influencing your mental and physical health. It's important to remember that stress is only one actor on a crowed stage.

In light of these considerations, you should evaluate the potential meaning of SRRS or LES scores with caution. A high score should be food for thought, but not reason for alarm.

1. Define stress in terms of Lazarus's transactional model.

2. Summarize three general points about the nature of stress.

3. List four principal types of stress.

4. Describe three types of conflict and discuss our reactions to conflicts.

5. Summarize evidence on life change as a form of stress.

6. Explain how familiarity, controllability, predictability, and imminence influence our appraisal of stress.

7. List three dimensions of emotion commonly elicited by stress.

8. Discuss the effects of emotional arousal on coping efforts.

9. Describe the fight-or-flight response.

10. Describe the three stages of the general adaptation syndrome.

11. Describe the two major pathways along which the brain sends signals to the endocrine system in response to stress.

12. Discuss the effects of stress on task performance.

13. Describe burnout and posttraumatic stress disorders.

14. Discuss the potential impact of stress on mental and physical health.

15. Discuss three ways in which stress might lead to beneficial effects.

16. Discuss how social support affects stress tolerance.

17. Discuss how hardiness, optimism, and sensation seeking influence stress tolerance.

18. List four problems with the SRRS that were described in the application section.

19. Summarize how the LES corrects problems that are characteristic of the SRRS.

20. Explain why one should be cautious in interpreting scores on stress scales.

KEY TERMS

Approach-approach conflict
Approach-avoidance conflict
Autonomic nervous system (ANS)
Avoidance-avoidance conflict
Burnout
Conflict
Coping
Emotions
Endocrine system
Fight-or-flight response
Frustration
General adaptation syndrome
Hardiness
Life changes
Optimism
Posttraumatic stress disorder
Pressure
Primary appraisal
Psychosomatic diseases
Secondary appraisal
Sensation seeking
Social support
Stress
Type A personality

KEY PEOPLE

Thomas Holmes &
Richard Rahe
Suzanne Kobasa
Richard Lazarus
Neal Miller
Hans Selye
Marvin Zuckerman

Sensation-Seeking Scale

INSTRUCTIONS

Each of the items below contains two choices, A and B. Please indicate in the spaces provided on the left which of the choices most describes your likes or the way you feel. It is important that you respond to all items with only one choice, A or B. In some cases you may find that both choices describe your likes or the way you feel. Please choose the one that better describes your likes or feelings. In some cases you may not like either choice. In these cases mark the choice you dislike least. We are interested only in your likes or feelings, not in how others feel about these things or how one is supposed to feel. There are no right or wrong answers. Be frank and give your honest appraisal of yourself.

THE SCALE

_____ 1. A. I would like a job which would require a lot of traveling.

B. I would prefer a job in one location.

_____ 2. A. I am invigorated by a brisk, cold day.

B. I can't wait to get indoors on a cold day.

_____ 3. A. I find a certain pleasure in routine kinds of work.

B. Although it is sometimes necessary, I usually dislike routine kinds of work.

_____ 4. A. I often wish I could be a mountain climber.

B. I can't understand people who risk their necks climbing mountains.

_____ 5. A. I dislike all body odors.

B. I like some of the earthy body smells.

_____ 6. A. I get bored seeing the same old faces.

B. I like the comfortable familiarity of everyday friends.

_____ 7. A. I like to explore a strange city or section of town by myself, even if it means getting lost.

B. I prefer a guide when I am in a place I don't know well.

_____ 8. A. I find the quickest and easiest route to a place and stick to it.

B. I sometimes take different routes to a place I often go, just for variety's sake.

_____ 9. A. I would not like to try any drug that might produce strange and dangerous effects on me.

B. I would like to try some of the new drugs that produce hallucinations.

_____ 10. A. I would prefer living in an ideal society where everyone is safe, secure, and happy.

B. I would have preferred living in the unsettled days of our history.

_____ 11. A. I sometimes like to do things that are a little frightening.

B. A sensible person avoids activities that are dangerous.

_____ 12. A. I order dishes with which I am familiar, so as to avoid disappointment and unpleasantness.

B. I like to try new foods that I have never tasted before.

_____ 13. A. I can't stand riding with a person who likes to speed.

B. I sometimes like to drive very fast because I find it exciting.

_____ 14. A. If I were a salesperson, I would prefer a straight salary rather than the risk of making little or nothing on a commission basis.

B. If I were a salesperson, I would prefer working on a commission if I had a chance to make more money than I could on a salary.

_____ 15. A. I would like to take up the sport of water skiing.

B. I would not like to take up the sport of water skiing.

_____ 16. A. I don't like to argue with people whose beliefs are sharply divergent from mine, since such arguments are never resolved.

B. I find people who disagree with my beliefs more stimulating than people who agree with me.

_____ 17. A. When I go on a trip, I like to plan my route and timetable fairly carefully.

B. I would like to take off on a trip with no pre-planned or definite routes or timetables.

_____ 18. A. I enjoy the thrills of watching car races.

B. I find car races unpleasant.

_____ 19. A. Most people spend entirely too much money on life insurance.

B. Life insurance is something that no one can afford to be without.

_____ 20. A. I would like to learn to fly an airplane.

B. I would not like to learn to fly an airplane.

_____ 21. A. I would not like to be hypnotized.

B. I would like to have the experience of being hypnotized.

_____ 22. A. The most important goal of life is to live it to the fullest and experience as much of it as you can.

B. The most important goal of life is to find peace and happiness.

_____ 23. A. I would like to try parachute jumping.

B. I would never want to try jumping out of a plane, with or without a parachute.

_____ 24. A. I enter cold water gradually, giving myself time to get used to it.

B. I like to dive or jump right into the ocean or a cold pool.

25. A. I do not like the irregularity and discord of most modern music.

B. I like to listen to new and unusual kinds of music.

26. A. I prefer friends who are excitingly unpredictable.

B. I prefer friends who are reliable and predictable.

27. A. When I go on a vacation, I prefer the comfort of a good room and bed.

B. When I go on a vacation, I would prefer the change of camping out.

28. A. The essence of good art is in its clarity, symmetry of form, and harmony of colors.

B. I often find beauty in the "clashing" colors and irregular forms of modern paintings.

29. A. The worst social sin is to be rude.

B. The worst social sin is to be a bore.

30. A. I look forward to a good night of rest after a long day.

B. I wish I didn't have to waste so much of a day sleeping.

31. A. I prefer people who are emotionally expressive even if they are a bit unstable.

B. I prefer people who are calm and even-tempered.

32. A. A good painting should shock or jolt the senses.

B. A good painting should give one a feeling of peace and security.

33. A. When I feel discouraged, I recover by relaxing and having some soothing diversion.

B. When I feel discouraged, I recover by going out and doing something new and exciting.

34. A. People who ride motorcycles must have some kind of an unconscious need to hurt themselves.

B. I would like to drive or ride on a motorcycle.

SCORING THE SCALE

The scoring key is reproduced below. You should circle your response of A or B each time it corresponds to the keyed response below. Add up the number of responses you circle. This total is your score on the Sensation-Seeking Scale. Record your score below.

1. A	8. B	15. A	22. A	29. B
2. A	9. B	16. B	23. A	30. B
3. B	10. B	17. B	24. B	31. A
4. A	11. A	18. A	25. B	32. A
5. B	12. B	19. A	26. A	33. B
6. A	13. B	20. A	27. B	34. B
7. A	14. B	21. B	28. B	

MY SCORE _____

WHAT THE SCALE MEASURES

As its name implies, the Sensation-Seeking Scale (SSS) measures one's need for a high level of stimulation. Sensation seeking involves the active pursuit of experiences that many people would find very stressful. Marvin Zuckerman (1979) believes that this thirst for sensation is a general personality trait that leads people to seek thrills, adventures, and new experiences.

The scale you have just responded to is the second version of the SSS. Test-retest reliabilities are quite respectable and there is ample evidence to support the scale's validity. For example, studies show that high sensation seekers appraise hypothetical situations as less risky than low sensation seekers and are more willing to volunteer for an experiment in which they will be hypnotized. The scale also shows robust positive correlations with measures of change seeking, novelty seeking, extraversion, and impulsiveness. Interestingly, SSS scores tend to decline with age.

INTERPRETING YOUR SCORE

Our norms are based on percentiles reported by Zuckerman and colleagues for a sample of 62 undergraduates. Although males generally tend to score a bit higher than females on the SSS, the differences are small enough to report one set of (averaged) norms. Remember, sensation-seeking scores tend to decline with age. So, if you're not in the modal college student age range (17–23), these norms may be a bit high.

NORMS

High Score:	21–34
Intermediate Score:	11–20
Low Score:	0–10

CHAPTER 3
PERSONAL PROBE

Where's the Stress in Your Life?

As you learned in Chapter 3, it's a good idea to be aware of the stress in your life. For this exercise you should keep a stress awareness record for one week. Construct a record sheet like that shown below. About twice a day, fill in the information on any stressful events that have occurred. Under "Type of Stress" indicate whether the event involves frustration, conflict, pressure, change, or some combination.

Day	Time	Stressful Event	Type of Stress	Your Reaction

At the end of the week, answer the following questions.

1. Is there a particular type of stress that is most frequent in your life?

2. Is there a particular locale or set of responsibilities that produces a great deal of stress for you?

3. Are there certain reactions to stressful events that you display consistently?

4. Is there anything reasonable that you could do to reduce the amount of stress in your life?

4

Coping Processes

"I have begun to believe that I have intellectually and emotionally outgrown my husband. However, I'm not really sure what this means or what I should do. Maybe this feeling is normal and I should ignore it and continue my present relationship. This seems to be the safest route. Maybe I should seek a lover while continuing with my husband. Then again, maybe I should start anew and hope for a beautiful ending with or without a better mate."

The woman quoted above is in the throes of a thorny conflict. Although it is hard to tell just how much emotional turmoil she is experiencing, it's clear that she is under substantial stress. What should she do? Is it psychologically healthy to remain in an emotionally hollow marriage? Is seeking a secret lover a reasonable way to cope with this unfortunate situation? Should she just strike out on her own and let the chips fall where they may? There are no simple answers to these questions. As you'll soon see, decisions about how to cope with life's difficulties can be terribly complex.

This chapter focuses on how we cope with stress. In the previous chapter we discussed the nature of stress and its potential effects. We learned that stress can be a challenging, exciting stimulus to personal growth. However, we also saw that stress can prove damaging to our psychological and physical health because it often triggers emotional and physiological responses that may be harmful. These emotional and physiological responses to stress tend to be largely automatic. Controlling them depends on the coping responses that we make to stressful situations. Thus, our mental and physical health depend, in part, on our ability to cope effectively with stress.

Our plan of attack in the present chapter is as follows. We'll begin with a general discussion of the concept of coping. Then we will review some common coping patterns that tend to have relatively little value. After discussing these ill-advised coping techniques, we'll sketch an overview of what it means to engage in healthier, "constructive" coping. The remainder of the chapter will expand on the specifics of constructive coping. We hope our discussion will provide some new ideas about how to deal with the inevitable stresses of modern life.

THE CONCEPT OF COPING

In Chapter 3, we learned that *coping* refers to active efforts to master, reduce, or tolerate the demands created by stress. Let's take a closer look at this concept and discuss some general points about coping.

Types of Coping Strategies

Coping strategy	Example	Correlation with self-esteem	Correlation with anxiety
Active coping	I take additional action to try to get rid of the problem.	.27*	−.25*
Planning	I try to come up with a strategy about what to do.	.22*	−.15
Suppression of competing activities	I put aside other activities in order to concentrate on this.	.07	−.10
Restraint coping	I force myself to wait for the right time to do something.	−.03	−.19*
Seeking social support for instrumental reasons	I ask people who have had similar experiences what they did.	.12	.01
Seeking social support for emotional reasons	I talk to someone about how I feel.	.06	.14
Positive reinterpretation and growth	I look for something good in what is happening.	.16*	−.25*
Acceptance	I learn to live with it.	.12	−.15
Turning to religion	I seek God's help.	−.06	.11
Focus on and venting of emotions	I get upset and let my emotions out.	−.01	.36*
Denial	I refuse to believe that it has happened.	−.28*	.35*
Behavioral disengagement	I give up the attempt to get what I want.	−.31*	.37*
Mental disengagement	I turn to work or other substitute activities to take my mind off things.	−.08	.21*
Alcohol-drug disengagement	I drink alcohol or take drugs in order to think about it less.	−.11	.11

1. *We cope with stress in many different ways.* In recent years, a number of researchers have attempted to identify and classify the various coping techniques that people employ in dealing with stress. Their work reveals that we use quite a variety of coping strategies. For instance, in a study of how 255 adult subjects dealt with stress, McCrae (1984) identified 28 different coping techniques. In another study, Carver, Scheier, and Weintraub (1989) found that they could sort their subjects' coping tactics into 14 categories, which are listed in Figure 4.1. Thus, in grappling with stress, we select our coping tactics from a large and varied menu of options.

2. *We exhibit consistent styles of coping.* Although we have a large menu of coping tactics to choose from, most of us come to rely on some strategies more than others (Folkman, Lazarus, Gruen, & DeLongis, 1986). We do, of course, adapt our coping techniques to situational demands. For instance, you might suppress a general tendency to lash out sarcastically at others when dealing with your boss. Nonetheless, our coping strategies show some stability across situations. We each have our personal style of coping with life's difficulties. As we progress through this chapter, it may be fruitful for you to analyze your style of coping.

3. *Coping strategies vary in their adaptive value.* In everyday terms, when we say that someone "coped with his problems," we imply that he handled them effectively. In reality, however, coping processes may range from healthy to downright pathological. For example, if you coped with the disappointment of not getting a promotion by plotting to sabotage your company's computer system, there would be little argument that this was an unhealthy way of coping. Differences in the value of various coping strategies were apparent in the study that identified the 14 coping techniques listed in Figure 4.1. Charles Carver and his colleagues correlated subjects' reliance on each coping strategy with various personality measures, such as their self-esteem and anxiety. They found that some coping patterns (active coping, planning, positive reinterpretation) were associated with relatively high self-esteem and low anxiety. In contrast, other coping patterns were associated with lower self-esteem and higher anxiety (see Figure 4.1).

In light of findings such as these, we will distinguish between coping patterns that tend to be healthy and those that tend to be maladaptive. Bear in mind, however, that our generalizations about the adaptive value of various coping strategies are based on trends or tendencies. No coping strategy can ensure a successful outcome. Furthermore, the adaptive value of a coping technique depends on the exact nature of the situation. As you'll see in the next section, even ill-advised coping strategies may have adaptive value in some instances.

COMMON COPING PATTERNS OF LIMITED VALUE

"Recently, after an engagement of 22 months, my fiancée told me that she was in love with someone else, and that we were through. I've been a wreck ever since. I can't study because I keep thinking about her. I think constantly about what I did wrong in the relationship and why I wasn't good enough for her. Getting drunk is the only way I can get her off my mind. Lately, I've been getting plastered about five or six nights a week. My grades are really hurting, but I'm not sure that I care."

This young man is going through a very hard time and does not appear to be handling it very well. He's blaming himself for the breakup with his fiancée. He's turning to alcohol to dull the pain that he feels, and it sounds like he may be giving up on school. Given his situation, these coping responses aren't particularly unusual, but they're only going to make his problems worse.

In this section, we'll examine some relatively common coping patterns that tend to be less than optimal. Specifically, we'll discuss giving up, aggression, blaming yourself, indulging yourself, and defense mechanisms. Some of these coping tactics may be helpful in certain circumstances, but more often than not, they are counterproductive.

Figure 4.1. Classifying coping strategies. Carver, Scheier, and Weintraub (1989) sorted their subjects' coping responses into 14 categories. The categories are listed here (column 1) with a representative example from each category (column 2). Carver et al. correlated subjects' reliance on each coping category with their self-esteem (column 3) and their anxiety (column 4). Many of the observed correlations were statistically significant (those with the asterisks). Positive correlations with self-esteem and negative correlations with anxiety suggest that a coping strategy is relatively effective. As you can see, some coping strategies appear to be healthier than others.

Giving Up

When confronted with stress, sometimes we simply give up and withdraw from the battle. This response of apathy and inaction tends to be associated with the emotional reactions of sadness and dejection. Bruno Bettelheim (1943) observed this reaction among prisoners in the Nazi concentration camps of World War II. Some prisoners aggressed against their captors through acts of sabotage and worked valiantly to maintain their will to live. However, many others sank into apathy and made no effort to adapt and survive.

Martin Seligman (1974) has developed a model of this giving-up syndrome that appears to shed light on its causes. In Seligman's research, animals are subjected to electric shocks they cannot escape. The animals are then given an opportunity to learn a response that will allow them to escape the shock. However, many of the animals have become so apathetic and listless that they don't even try to learn the escape response. When researchers made similar manipulations with *human* subjects using inescapable noise (rather than shock) as the stressor, they observed parallel results (Hiroto & Seligman, 1975). This syndrome is referred to as learned helplessness. ***Learned helplessness* involves passive behavior produced by exposure to unavoidable aversive events.** Unfortunately, this tendency to give up may be transferred to situations in which we are not really helpless. Hence, some people routinely respond to stress with fatalism and resignation. They passively accept setbacks that might be dealt with effectively.

Seligman originally viewed learned helplessness as a product of conditioning. However, research with human subjects has led Seligman and his colleagues to revise their theory. The current model proposes that our *cognitive interpretation* of aversive events determines whether we develop learned helplessness. Specifically, helplessness seems to occur when we come to believe that events are beyond our control. This belief is particularly likely to emerge when we tend to attribute setbacks to personal

Coping tactics such as verbal aggression are almost always counterproductive.

inadequacies instead of situational factors (Abramson, Seligman, & Teasdale, 1978).

As you might guess, giving up is not a highly regarded method of coping. In the Carver et al. (1989) study of coping, the strategy of giving up (behavioral disengagement) showed some of the highest correlations with anxiety and poor self-esteem. Furthermore, many studies suggest that learned helplessness can contribute to depression (Peterson & Seligman, 1984).

However, giving up could be adaptive in some instances. For example, if you were thrown into a job that you were not equipped to handle, it might be better to quit rather than face constant pressure and diminishing self-esteem. There is something to be said for recognizing our limitations. There may also be occasions when we need to recognize that our goals are unrealistic. The highly competitive nature of American society leads many of us to push ourselves toward heights that are very difficult to achieve. Goals such as gaining admission to medical school, becoming a professional actress, or buying an expensive home may be better discarded if they are not realistic. The value of any coping response depends on the situation. Even a coping strategy such as giving up, which sounds terribly "un-American," may sometimes be adaptive. As you will see again and again, there are no

simple rules regarding the best ways to cope with life's challenges.

Striking Out at Others

A young man, aged 17, cautiously edged his car into traffic on the Corona Expressway in Los Angeles. His slow speed apparently aggravated the men in a pickup truck behind him. Unfortunately, he angered the wrong men—they shot him to death. During that same weekend in 1987 there were six other roadside shootings in the Los Angeles area. All of them were triggered by minor incidents or "fender benders." Frustated motorists are attacking each other more and more frequently, especially on the overburdened highways of Los Angeles.

These tragic incidents of highway violence vividly illustrate that people often respond to stressful events by striking out at others with aggressive behavior. **Aggression involves any behavior intended to hurt someone, either physically or verbally.** Snarls, curses, and insults are much more common than shootings or fistfights, but aggression of any kind can be problematic. Many years ago, a team of psychologists (Dollard et al., 1939) proposed the *frustration-aggression hypothesis*, which held that aggression is always due to frustration. Decades of research have

verified their proposal that there is a causal link between frustration and aggression.

However, this research has also shown that there isn't an inevitable, one-to-one correspondence between frustration and aggression. In a discussion of qualifications to the frustration-aggression hypothesis, Leonard Berkowitz (1969) concluded (1) that frustration does not *necessarily* lead to aggression, (2) that many factors in addition to frustration (such as one's personality) influence the likelihood of aggression, and (3) that frustration may produce responses other than aggression (for example, apathy). Although these are important qualifications, it is clear that frustration often leads to aggression.

Frequently, we lash out aggressively at others who had nothing to do with our frustration. Often we cannot vent our anger at the real source of our frustration. Thus, you'll probably suppress your anger rather than lash out verbally at a police officer who gives you a speeding ticket. Twenty minutes later, however, you might be downright brutal in rebuking a gas station attendant who is slow in servicing your car. As we discussed in Chapter 2, this diversion of anger to a substitute target was noticed long ago by Sigmund Freud, who called it *displacement.*

Freud theorized that behaving aggressively could get pent-up emotion out of your system and thus be adaptive. He coined the term **catharsis to refer to this release of emotional tension.** There is some experimental evidence to support Freud's theory of catharsis. In a widely cited study, Hokanson and Burgess (1962) found that the opportunity to aggress physically or verbally after frustration led to a smaller increase in subjects' blood pressure (see Figure 4.2). Given the potential negative effects of emotional arousal, this study suggests that expressing aggression may have some adaptive value.

However, after reviewing additional research by Hokanson and others, Carol Tavris (1982) concludes that aggressive behavior does not reliably lead to catharsis. She asserts, "Aggressive catharses are almost impossible to find in continuing relationships because parents, children, spouses and bosses usually feel obliged to aggress

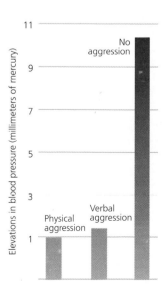

Figure 4.2. Aggression and blood pressure. After frustrating subjects, Hokanson and Burgess (1962) found that those who were allowed to engage in either physical or verbal aggression showed smaller increases in blood pressure than subjects who had no opportunity for aggression. These findings support the idea that aggressive behavior permits us to cathart (drain off) emotional tension. As the text notes, however, many other studies have failed to support the catharsis value of aggression.

back at you; and indirect, 'displaced' aggression does nothing but make you angrier and more upset" (p. 131). Thus, the adaptive value of aggressive behavior tends to be minimal. Hurting someone, especially an irrelevant someone, is not likely to alleviate frustration. Moreover, the interpersonal conflicts that often emerge from aggressive behavior may produce additional stress. If you pick a fight with your spouse after a terrible day at work, you may create new stress and lose valuable empathy and social support from your spouse.

Indulging Yourself

Stress sometimes leads to self-indulgence. When troubled by stress, many of us engage in excessive consummatory behavior. For instance, after an exceptionally stressful day, some people head for their refrigerator, a grocery store, or a restaurant in pursuit of something chocolate. In a similar vein, others cope with stress by making a beeline for the nearest shopping mall for a spending spree. Thus, excesses in consummatory behavior refer to injudicious patterns of eating, drinking, smoking, using drugs, spending money, and so forth.

In their classification of coping responses, Moos and Billings (1982) list *developing alternative rewards* as a common response to stress. It makes sense that when things are going poorly in one area of our lives, we may try to compensate by pursuing substitute forms of satisfaction. When this happens, consummatory responses probably rank high. They are relatively easy to execute, and they tend to be very pleasurable. Thus, it is not surprising that there is evidence relating stress to increases in eating (Slochower, 1976), smoking (Tomkins, 1966), consumption of alcohol (Marlatt & Rose, 1980), and some types of drug use (Krueger, 1981).

There is nothing inherently maladaptive about indulging oneself as a way of coping with life's stresses. The pursuit of alternative rewards is a readily available coping strategy that may have merit if kept under control. If a hot fudge sundae or some new clothes calm your nerves after

a major setback, who can argue? However, if a person consistently responds to stress with chronic and excessive consummatory behavior, obvious problems are likely to develop. Excesses in eating may produce obesity. Excesses in drinking can lead to alcoholism, drunk driving, and a host of other problems. Excesses in drug use may endanger one's health and result in drug dependence. Excesses in spending may create havoc in one's personal finances. Given the risks associated with self-indulgence, it has rather marginal adaptive value.

Blaming Yourself

In a postgame interview after a tough defeat, a prominent football coach was brutally critical of himself. He said that he was outcoached, that he had made poor decisions, and that his game plan was faulty. He almost eagerly assumed all the blame for the loss himself. In reality, he had taken some reasonable chances that didn't go his way and had suffered the effects of poor execution by his players. Looking at it objectively, the loss was attributable to the collective failures of 50 or so players and coaches. However, the coach's unrealistically negative self-evaluation was a fairly typical response to frustration. When confronted by stress (especially frustration and pressure), we often become highly self-critical.

Our tendency to engage in negative self-talk in response to stress has been noted by a number of influential theorists. Albert Ellis (1973, 1987) calls this phenomenon "catastrophic thinking" and focuses on how it is rooted in irrational assumptions. Aaron Beck (1976, 1987) analyzes negative self-talk into specific tendencies. Among other things, he asserts that people often (1) unreasonably attribute their failures to personal shortcomings, (2) focus on negative feedback from others while ignoring favorable feedback, and (3) make unduly pessimistic projections about the future. Thus, if you performed poorly on an exam, you might blame it on your woeful stupidity, dismiss a classmate's comment that the test was unfair, and hysterically predict that you will flunk out of school.

Although there is some value in recognizing our weaknesses, Ellis and Beck agree that negative self-talk tends to be counterproductive. According to Ellis, catastrophic thinking causes, aggravates, and perpetuates emotional reactions to stress that are often problematic. Along even more serious lines, Beck marshals evidence that negative self-talk can contribute to the development of depressive disorders. In general, it appears that self-blame and self-criticism are not very healthy ways to cope with stress.

Defensive Coping

Defensive coping is very common in response to stress. We noted in Chapter 2 that the concept of defense mechanisms was originally developed by Sigmund Freud. Though rooted in the psychoanalytic tradition, this concept has gained widespread acceptance from psychologists of most persuasions. Building on Freud's initial insights, modern psychologists have broadened the scope of the concept and added to Freud's list of defense mechanisms.

Defense mechanisms **are largely unconscious reactions that protect a person from unpleasant emotions such as anxiety and guilt.** There are many specific mechanisms of defense. For example, Laughlin (1979) lists 49 different defenses. In our discussion of Freud's theory in Chapter 2, we described repression, regression, rationalization, reaction formation, projection, displacement, and identification. At this point, we'll introduce some additional defense mechanisms and elaborate on the nature and value of defensive coping.

Additional Defense Mechanisms

In addition to the seven commonly used defense mechanisms discussed in Chapter 2, Figure 4.3 lists five more defenses that people frequently employ. *Denial* **involves refusing to perceive or face unpleasant realities.** Unlike repression, which involves unconscious blocking of distressing material, denial involves a *conscious* effort to suppress unpleasant thoughts. In denial, threatening thoughts surface, but you refuse to believe them. For example, in spite of substantial evidence, you might deny that your spouse appears to be having an extramarital affair. In contrast, *intellectualization* **involves suppressing unpleasant emotions while engaging in detached analyses of threatening problems.** For instance, if your spouse was having an affair, you might endlessly analyze the sad state of modern marriage instead of expressing your anger—thus turning your problem into an impersonal, intellectual puzzle.

Fantasy, overcompensation, and undoing are three other ways of coping with problems defensively. *Fantasy* **involves gratifying frustrated desires by thinking about imaginary achievements and satisfactions.** For example, in response to a string of financial setbacks, you might daydream frequently about making a killing in the stock market. We often express our hostile feelings in fantasy. Thus, you might daydream about gaining revenge on the people you hold responsible for your financial problems. *Overcompensation* **involves making up for frustration in one area by seeking overgratification in another area.** For instance, you might compensate for financial frustration by recklessly pursuing many sexual partners. If your sexual manipulations made you feel bad, you might engage in undoing, a defense that we use to cope with guilt. *Undoing* **involves rituals intended to atone for unacceptable desires or behaviors.** For example, you might atone for your sexual excesses by remaining abstinent for a certain number of days.

The Nature of Defense Mechanisms

Although widely discussed in the popular press, defense mechanisms are often misunderstood. We will use a question-answer format to elaborate on the nature of defense mechanisms in the hopes of clearing up any misconceptions.

WHAT DO DEFENSE MECHANISMS DEFEND AGAINST? Above all else, defense mechanisms shield us from the *emotional discomfort* elicited by stress. Their main purpose is to ward

Common Defense Mechanisms	
Mechanism	**Example**
Denial of reality. Protecting oneself from unpleasant reality by refusing to perceive or face it.	A smoker concludes that the evidence linking cigarette use to health problems is scientifically worthless.
Fantasy. Gratifying frustrated desires by imaginary achievements.	A socially inept and inhibited young man imagines himself chosen by a group of women to provide them with sexual satisfaction.
Intellectualization (isolation). Cutting off emotion from hurtful situations or separating incompatible attitudes by logic-tight compartments.	A prisoner on death row awaiting execution resists appeal on his behalf and coldly insists that the letter of the law be followed.
Undoing. Atoning for or trying to magically dispel unacceptable desires or acts.	A teenager who feels guilty about masturbation ritually touches door knobs a prescribed number of times following each occurrence of the act.
Overcompensation. Covering up felt weaknesses by emphasizing some desirable characteristic, or making up for frustration in one area by overgratification in another.	A dangerously overweight woman goes on eating binges when she feels neglected by her husband.

Figure 4.3. Additional defense mechanisms. Like the seven defense mechanisms described in our discussion of Freudian theory in Chapter 2 (see Figure 2.3), these five defenses are frequently used in our efforts to cope with stress.

off unwelcome emotions or to reduce their intensity. Foremost among the emotions guarded against is anxiety. We are especially protective when the anxiety is due to some threat to our self-esteem. We also use defenses to suppress dangerous feelings of anger so they do not explode into acts of aggression. Guilt and dejection are two other emotions that we often try to evade through defensive maneuvers.

HOW DO THEY WORK? Through *self-deception*. Defense mechanisms accomplish their goals by distorting reality so it does not appear so threatening. For example, let's say you're doing very poorly in school and you are in danger of flunking out. Initially, you might use denial to block awareness of the possibility that you could flunk out. This might temporarily fend off feelings of anxiety. If it becomes difficult to deny the obvious, you might resort to *fantasy*, daydreaming about how you will salvage adequate grades by getting spectacular scores on the upcoming final exams, when the objective fact is that you are hopelessly behind in your studies. Thus, defense mechanisms work their magic by bending reality in self-serving ways.

ARE THEY CONSCIOUS OR UNCONSCIOUS? Both. Freud originally assumed that our defenses operate entirely at an unconscious level. However, the concept of defense mechanisms has been broadened by other theorists to include maneuvers that we may be aware of. Thus, defense mechanisms operate at varying levels of awareness, although they are largely unconscious.

ARE THEY NORMAL? Definitely. We all use defense mechanisms on a fairly regular basis. They are entirely normal patterns of coping. The notion that only neurotic people use defense mechanisms is inaccurate.

Can Illusions Be Healthy?

The most critical question concerning defense mechanisms is *Are they healthy?* This is a complicated question. More often than not, the answer is no. Generally, defense mechanisms are poor ways of coping for a number of reasons. First, defensive coping is an avoidance strategy, and avoidance rarely provides a genuine solution to our problems. Holahan and Moos (1985) found that people who exhibit high resistance to stress use avoidance strategies less than people who are frequently troubled by stress. Second, defensive tactics use up energy that could be spent more wisely by tackling the problem. In other words, defensive pseudosolutions may prevent us from employing more constructive coping strategies. Third, defensive coping often leads us to delay facing up to a problem. This delay may allow the problem to fester and grow. For example, if you blocked out obvious warning signs of cancer or diabetes and failed to obtain needed medical care, your defensive behavior could be fatal.

The shortcomings of defensive coping were highlighted in a long-term study of men graduated from Harvard. Periodic interviews and tests allowed George Vaillant (1977) to distinguish between men who depended on "immature" defense mechanisms that involved radical distortions of reality and those who depended on "mature" defenses that involved much less distortion of reality. As Figure 4.4 shows, the men who used immature defenses experienced much poorer outcomes than the men who relied on more mature defenses. They exhibited less happiness, poorer adjustment, fewer harmonious marriages, more barren friendship networks, and a higher incidence of mental illness. Thus, when defenses lead to wholesale distortions of reality, they clearly are not healthy.

Although defensive behavior tends to be relatively unhealthy, it can sometimes be adaptive. For example, *overcompensation* for athletic failures could lead you to work extra hard in the classroom. Creative use of *fantasy*

Figure 4.4. A comparison between men who used mature and immature defenses. In a long-running study of Harvard graduates, Vaillant (1977) was able to compare the adjustment of men who depended on mature (reality-oriented) versus immature coping strategies. Only statistically significant differences are shown here. All of them favor the men who appeared to depend more on realistic coping mechanisms.

Defensive Coping and Adjustment		
Adjustment	**Predominant adaptive style (%)**	
	Mature (N = 25)	*Immature (N = 31)*
Overall		
Top third in adult adjustment	60	0
Bottom third in adult adjustment	4	61
Top third rating for "happiness"	68	16
Career and social		
High income	88	48
Rich friendship pattern	64	6
Marriage at least harmonious	61	28
Barren friendship pattern	4	52
Psychological		
10+ psychiatric visits	0	45
Ever diagnosed mentally ill	0	55

is sometimes the key to dealing effectively with temporary periods of frustration, such as a stint in the military service or a period of recovery in the hospital.

Most theorists used to regard accurate contact with reality as the hallmark of sound mental health (Jahoda, 1958; Jourard & Landsman, 1980). However, after studying *denial* and other defenses, Richard Lazarus acknowledges that sometimes "illusion and self-deception can have positive value in a person's psychological economy" (Goleman, 1979, p. 47). Consistent with this notion, Ward, Leventhal, and Love (1988) found that cancer patients who relied on repression experienced fewer treatment side effects than patients who carefully monitored the course of their disease.

Shelley Taylor and Jonathon Brown (1988) have reviewed several lines of evidence suggesting that "certain illusions may be adaptive for mental health and well-being" (p. 193). First, they note that "normal" people tend to have overly favorable self-images. In contrast, depressed subjects exhibit less favorable—but more realistic—self concepts. Second, normal subjects overestimate the degree to which they control chance events. In comparison, depressed subjects are less prone to this illusion of control. Third, normal individuals are more likely than depressed subjects to display unrealistic optimism in making projections about the future.

Thus, it is hard to make sweeping generalizations about the adaptive value of self-deception. Some of the personal illusions that we create through defensive coping may help us to deal with life's difficulties. Roy Baumeister (1989) theorizes that it's all a matter of degree and that there is an "optimal margin of illusion." According to Baumeister, extreme distortions of reality are maladaptive, but small illusions are often beneficial.

In summary, defensive coping and self-deception can be healthy or unhealthy, depending on the circumstances. As a rule, the more your defenses prevent you from engaging in constructive coping, the more unhealthy they probably are. To fully appreciate this point, we need to consider what it is that makes coping "constructive."

THE NATURE OF CONSTRUCTIVE COPING

Our discussion thus far has focused on coping strategies that usually are less than ideal. Of course, we also exhibit many healthy strategies for dealing with stress. We will use the term *constructive coping* **to refer to efforts to deal with stressful events that are judged to be relatively healthy.** No strategy of coping can *guarantee* a successful outcome. Even the healthiest coping responses may turn out to be ineffective in some cases. Thus, the concept of constructive coping is simply meant to convey a healthy, positive connotation, without promising success.

Constructive coping does *not* appear to depend particularly on one's intelligence—at least not the abstract, "academic" intelligence measured by conventional IQ tests. Seymour Epstein, a professor at the University of Massachusetts, has shown an interest in "why smart people think dumb." His interest was stimulated, in part, by a course that he teaches in which students keep daily records of their most positive and negative emotional experiences for class discussion. Commenting on these discussions, Epstein says, "One cannot help but be impressed, when observing students in such a situation, with the degree to which some otherwise bright people lead their lives in a manifestly unintelligent and self-defeating manner" (Epstein & Meier, 1989, p. 333).

To investigate this matter more systematically, Epstein and Petra Meier (1989) devised an elaborate scale to assess the degree to which people engage in constructive coping and thinking. They found that constructive thinking was favorably related to mental and physical health, and to measures of "success" in work, love, and social relationships. However, subjects' IQ scores were only very weakly related to their constructive coping scores.

What makes certain coping strategies constructive? Frankly, in labeling certain coping responses constructive or healthy, psychologists are making value judgments. It's a gray area in which opinions will vary to some extent. Nonetheless, there is some consensus among the experts

REPRINTED WITH SPECIAL PERMISSION OF NORTH AMERICAN SYNDICATE, INC.

that emerges from the burgeoning research on coping and stress management. Key themes in this literature include the following.

1. Constructive coping involves confronting problems directly. It is task-relevant and action-oriented. It involves a conscious effort to rationally evaluate your options in an effort to solve your problems.
2. Constructive coping is based on reasonably realistic appraisals of your stress and coping resources. A little self-deception may sometimes be adaptive, but excessive self-deception and highly unrealistic negative thinking are not.
3. Constructive coping involves learning to recognize, and in some cases inhibit, potentially disruptive emotional reactions to stress.
4. Constructive coping involves learning to exert some control over potentially harmful or destructive habitual behaviors. It requires the acquisition of some behavioral self-control.

The points just discussed should give you a general idea of what we mean by constructive coping. These assumptions will guide our discourse in the remainder of this chapter as we discuss how to cope more effectively with stress.

To organize our discussion, we will use a classification scheme proposed by Rudolph Moos and Andrew Billings (1982) to divide constructive coping techniques into three broad groups. These three types of coping strategies, which are classified according to their focus or goal, are the following.

• *Appraisal-focused coping* involves efforts to reevaluate the apparent demands or redefine the apparent meaning of stressful events.

Its goal is to alter your appraisal of the threat in the situation.
• *Problem-focused coping* involves efforts to circumvent, modify, remedy, or conquer the problem and its consequences. Its goal is to directly master the threat or problem itself.
• *Emotion-focused coping* involves efforts to control and usually reduce the emotional reactions aroused by stress. Its goal is to reestablish a healthy emotional equilibrium.

Of course, like most efforts to classify complex behavior, this scheme is not entirely satisfactory. There are coping tactics that are difficult to categorize because they have more than one goal. Nonetheless, this scheme gives us a framework for analyzing healthy approaches to coping.

APPRAISAL-FOCUSED CONSTRUCTIVE COPING

People often underestimate the importance of the appraisal phase in the stress process. They fail to appreciate the highly subjective feelings that color the perception of threat to one's well-being. One very useful way to deal with stress is to alter your appraisal of threatening events. In this section, we'll examine Albert Ellis's ideas about reappraisal and discuss the value of using humor and positive reinterpretation to cope with stress.

Figure 4.5. Albert Ellis's A-B-C model of emotional reactions. Most of us are prone to attribute our negative emotional reactions (C) directly to stressful events (A). However, Ellis argues that our emotional reactions are really caused by the way we think about these events (B).

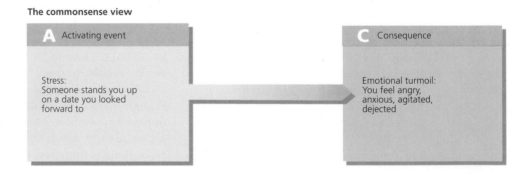

The commonsense view

| **A** Activating event | **C** Consequence |

Stress:
Someone stands you up on a date you looked forward to

Emotional turmoil:
You feel angry, anxious, agitated, dejected

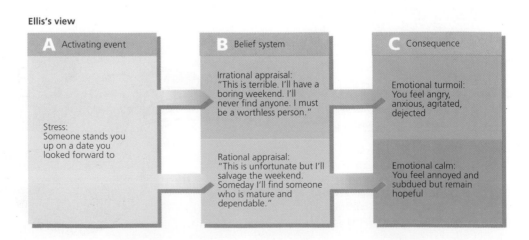

Ellis's view

| **A** Activating event | **B** Belief system | **C** Consequence |

Stress:
Someone stands you up on a date you looked forward to

Irrational appraisal:
"This is terrible. I'll have a boring weekend. I'll never find anyone. I must be a worthless person."

Rational appraisal:
"This is unfortunate but I'll salvage the weekend. Someday I'll find someone who is mature and dependable."

Emotional turmoil:
You feel angry, anxious, agitated, dejected

Emotional calm:
You feel annoyed and subdued but remain hopeful

Ellis's Rational Thinking

Albert Ellis (1977, 1985) is a prominent theorist who believes that we can short-circuit our emotional reactions to stress by altering our appraisals of stressful events. Ellis's insights about stress appraisal are the foundation for a widely used system of therapy that he devised. *Rational-emotive therapy* **is an approach to therapy that focuses on altering clients' patterns of irrational thinking to reduce maladaptive emotions and behavior.**

Ellis maintains that *you feel the way you think.* He argues that problematic emotional reactions are caused by negative self-talk, which he calls catastrophic thinking. *Catastrophic thinking* **involves unrealistic appraisals of stress that exaggerate the magnitude of one's problems.** Ellis uses a simple A-B-C sequence to explain his ideas (see Figure 4.5).

A: *Activating event.* The A in Ellis's system stands for the activating event that produces the stress. The activating event may be any potentially stressful transaction. Examples might include an automobile accident, the cancellation of a date, a delay while waiting in line at the bank, or a failure to get a promotion you were expecting.

RECOMMENDED READING

How to Stubbornly Refuse to Make Yourself Miserable About Anything — Yes, Anything!

by Albert Ellis (Carol Communications, 1988)

This is the most recent "popular" book by Albert Ellis, the world-renowned architect of rational-emotive therapy. At last count, Ellis had written 49 books, about evenly divided between popular books intended for a general audience and technical books intended for mental health professionals. This book doesn't break any new ground for Ellis, but it does bring his ideas together in one succinct, readable summary, complete with exercises.

Ellis is a bit prone to overstatement, asserting that his book "will help you achieve a profound philosophic change and a radically new outlook on life." Whether it does so or not, his ideas clearly can be helpful in coping with stress more effectively. If you're a victim of catastrophic thinking, this book is worth reading. The writing is casual and down-to-earth. For instance, the following passage comes from a chapter titled *Forget Your "Godawful" Past.*

> For several years I was a highly successful psychoanalyst and thought that I was greatly helping my clients by exploring the gory details of their early life and showing them how these experiences made them disturbed—and how they could now understand and remove these early influences.
>
> How wrong I was!
>
> After I honestly admitted that my psychoanalytic "cures" were hardly as good as I would have liked them to be, I began to see that helping people to understand their past was not only doing them little good but was actually blocking their dealing with their *present* problems. [p. 69]

B: *Belief system.* B stands for your belief about the event. This represents your appraisal of the stress. According to Ellis, we often view minor setbacks as disasters. Thus, we engage in catastrophic thinking: "How awful this is. I can't stand it! Things never turn out fairly for me. I'll be in this line forever. I'll never get promoted."

C: *Consequence.* C stands for the consequence of your negative thinking. When your appraisals of stressful events are terribly negative, the consequence tends to be emotional distress. Thus, we feel angry, or outraged, or anxious, or panic-stricken, or disgusted, or dejected.

Ellis asserts that most of us do not understand the importance of phase B in this three-stage sequence. We unwittingly believe that the activating event (A) *causes* the consequent emotional turmoil (C). However, Ellis maintains that A does not cause C. It only appears to do so. Instead, Ellis asserts that B causes C. Our emotional distress is actually caused by our catastrophic thinking in appraising stressful events.

According to Ellis, it is commonplace for people to turn inconvenience into disaster and make "mountains out of molehills." For instance, imagine that someone stands you up on a date that you were eagerly looking forward to. You might think "Oh, this is terrible. I'm going to have another rotten, boring weekend. People always mistreat me. I'll never find anyone to fall in love with. I must be a crummy, worthless person." Ellis would argue that such thoughts are terribly irrational. He would point out that it does not follow logically from being stood up that you (1) must have a lousy weekend, (2) will never fall in love, or (3) are a worthless person.

The Roots of Catastrophic Thinking

Ellis theorizes that unrealistic appraisals of stress are derived from irrational assumptions that we hold. He maintains that if you scrutinize your catastrophic thinking, you will find that your reasoning is based on an indefensibly unreasonable premise, such as "I must have approval from everyone" or "I must perform well in all endeavors." These faulty assumptions, which we often

Albert Ellis

hold unconsciously, generate our catastrophic thinking and our emotional turmoil. To facilitate emotional self-control, it is important to learn to spot irrational assumptions and the unhealthy patterns of thought that they generate. Let's look at five particularly common irrational assumptions. A lengthier list can be found in Figure 4.6.

1. *I must have love and affection from certain people.* We all want to be liked and loved. There is nothing wrong with that. However, many of us foolishly believe that we should be liked by everyone we come into contact with. If you stop to think about it, that's clearly unrealistic. Once we fall in love, we tend to believe that our future happiness depends absolutely on the continuation of that one, special relationship. We believe that if our current love relationship were to end, we would never again be able to achieve a comparable one. This is an unrealistic view of the future. Such views make us anxious during a relationship and severely depressed if it comes to an end.

2. *I must perform well in all endeavors.* We live in a highly competitive society. We are taught that victory brings happiness. Consequently, we feel that we must always win. For example, many sports enthusiasts are never satisfied unless they perform at their best level. However, by definition, their best level is not their typical level, and they set themselves up for inevitable frustration.

3. *Other people should always behave competently and be considerate of me.* We are often angered by others' stupidity and selfishness. For example, you may become outraged when a mechanic fails to fix your car properly or when a salesperson treats you rudely. It would be nice if people were always competent and considerate, but you know better—they are not! Yet many of us go through life unrealistically expecting others' efficiency and kindness.

4. *Everyone I identify with should have pleasant experiences.* Many of us extend our personal boundaries so that we become very upset when unfortunate events happen to others. When a friend's wife walks out on him, we become furious and depressed for him. The broader your personal boundaries are, the more you are likely to experience others' stress. Consider, for example, sports fans who go berserk when a referee or umpire makes a bad call that goes against their team. Such people are becoming stressed over events that have little direct bearing on their lives.

5. *Events should always go the way I like.* Some people simply won't tolerate any kind of setback. They assume that things should always go their way. For example, some commuters become very tense and angry each time they get stuck in a rush-hour traffic jam. They seem to believe that they are entitled to coast home easily every day, even though they know that rush hour rarely is a breeze. Such expectations are clearly unrealistic and doomed to be violated. Yet few people recognize the obvious irrationality of the assumption that underlies their anger unless it is pointed out to them.

Reducing Catastrophic Thinking

How can you reduce your unrealistic appraisals of stress? Ellis asserts that you must learn (1) how to detect catastrophic thinking and (2) how to dispute the irrational assumptions that cause it. Detection involves acquiring the ability to spot unrealistic pessimism and wild exaggeration in your thinking. Examine your self-talk closely.

Irrational Assumptions in Everyday Thinking

Irrational assumption	Rational alternative	Irrational assumption	Rational alternative
1 I must be loved or approved of by everyone for everything I do.	It's best to concentrate on my own self-respect, on winning approval for practical purposes, and on loving rather than being loved.	6 It's easier to avoid facing difficulties and responsibilities than to face them.	The "easy way out" is invariably the much harder alternative in the long run.
2 I must be thoroughly competent, adequate, and achieving in order to be worthwhile.	I'm an imperfect creature who has limitations and fallibilities like anyone else—and that's okay.	7 I'm dependent on others and need someone stronger than I am to rely on.	It's better to take the risk of relying on myself and thinking and acting independently.
3 It's horrible when things aren't the way I'd like them to be.	I can try to change or control the things that disturb me—or temporarily accept conditions I can't change.	8 There's always a precise and perfect solution to human problems, and it's catastrophic not to find it.	The world is full of probability and chance, and I can enjoy life even though there isn't always an ideal solution to a problem.
4 There isn't much I can do about my sorrows and disturbances, because unhappiness comes from what happens to you.	I feel how I think. Unhappiness comes mostly from how I look at things.	9 The world—especially other people—should be fair, and justice (mercy) must triumph.	I can work toward seeking fair behavior, realizing that there are few absolutes in life.
5 If something is dangerous or fearsome, I'm right to be terribly upset about it and to dwell on the possibility of its occurring.	I can frankly face what I fear and either render it nondangerous or accept the inevitable.	10 I must not question the beliefs held by society or respected authorities.	It's better to evaluate beliefs for myself—on their own merits, not on who happens to hold them.

I: THE DYNAMICS OF ADJUSTMENT

Ask yourself why you're getting upset. Force yourself to verbalize your concerns, covertly or out loud. Look for key words that often show up in catastrophic thinking, such as *should, ought, never,* and *must.*

Disputing your irrational assumptions requires subjecting your entire reasoning process to scrutiny. Try to root out the assumptions from which your conclusions are derived. We often are unaware of these assumptions. Once they are unearthed, their irrationality may be quite obvious. If your assumptions seem reasonable, ask yourself whether your conclusions follow logically. Try to replace your catastrophic thinking with more low-key, rational analyses. These strategies should help you to redefine stressful situations in ways that are less threatening. Strangely enough, another way to do this is to turn to humor.

Humor as a Stress Reducer

A few years ago, the Chicago area experienced its worst flooding in about a century. Thousands of people saw their homes wrecked when two rivers spilled over their banks. As the waters receded, the flood victims returning to their homes were subjected to the inevitable TV interviews. A remarkable number of victims, surrounded by the ruins of their homes, *joked* about their misfortune. When the going gets tough, it may pay to laugh about it. In a study of coping styles, McCrae (1984) found that 40% of his subjects reported using humor to deal with stress.

In analyzing the stress-reducing effects of humor, Dixon (1980) emphasizes its impact on the appraisal of stress. Finding a humorous aspect in a stressful situation redefines the situation in a less threatening way. Dixon notes that laughter can also discharge pent-up emotions. These dual functions of humor may make joking about life's difficulties a particularly useful coping strategy.

Some psychologists have long suspected that humor might be a worthwhile coping response. But empirical evidence to that effect has emerged only in recent years (Martin & Lefcourt, 1983; Nezu, Nezu, & Blissett, 1988).

For instance, Martin and Lefcourt (1983) found that a good sense of humor functioned as a buffer to lessen the negative impact of stress on mood. Some of their results are shown in Figure 4.7. It plots how mood disturbance increased as stress went up in two groups of subjects—those who were high or low in their use of humor. Notice how higher stress leads to a smaller increase in mood disturbance in the high humor group.

Positive Reinterpretation

When you are feeling overwhelmed by life's difficulties, there is merit in the common-sense strategy of recognizing that "things could be worse." No matter how terrible our problems seem, most of us know people who have even bigger troubles. That is not to say that you should derive satisfaction from others' misfortune. However, comparing your own plight with others' even tougher struggles can help you put your problems in perspective. Research by McCrae (1984) suggests that this strategy of making positive comparisons with others is a widely used coping mechanism. It seems to be a relatively healthy one, in that it can facilitate calming reappraisals of stress without the necessity of distorting reality.

Another way to engage in positive reinterpretation is to

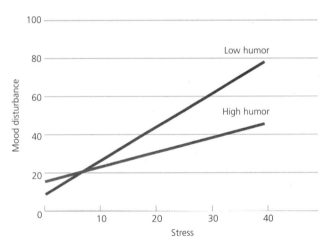

Figure 4.7. Humor and coping. Martin and Lefcourt (1983) related stress to mood disturbance in subjects who were either high or low in their use of humor. Increased stress led to smaller increases in mood disturbance in the high humor group, suggesting that humor has some value in efforts to cope with stress.

Figure 4.6. Irrational assumptions that can cause emotional disturbance. Irrational assumptions like those listed here are often held unconsciously. According to Ellis, constructive coping depends on detecting these assumptions and replacing them with more rational views, like the examples provided here. (Adapted by Basil Najjar from Ellis, 1977)

search for something good in a bad experience. Distressing though they may be, many of our setbacks have positive elements. After experiencing divorces, illnesses, firings, financial losses, and such, many people remark that "I came out of the experience better than I went in," or "I grew as a person." The positive aspects of a personal setback may be easy to see after the stressful event is behind you. The challenge is to recognize these positive aspects while you are still struggling with the setback, so that it becomes less stressful. Research suggests that positive reinterpretation is an effective coping method (Folkman et al., 1986).

PROBLEM-FOCUSED CONSTRUCTIVE COPING

Problem-focused coping involves efforts to remedy or conquer the stress-producing problem itself. In this category, we'll discuss systematic problem solving, the importance of seeking help, effective time management, and improving self-control.

Steps in Systematic Problem Solving

In dealing with life's problems, the most obvious course of action is to tackle the problems head-on. In the study of coping by Carver, Scheier, and Weintraub (1989), the two coping tactics that reflect this approach (active coping and planning) were favorably related to higher self-esteem and lower anxiety. Since there are an infinite number of personal problems that may arise, we can only sketch a very general outline of how to engage in systematic problem solving. The problem-solving plan to be described here is a synthesis of observations by various experts, especially Mahoney (1979) and Miller (1978). It involves four steps: (1) clarify the problem, (2) generate alternative courses of actions, (3) evaluate your alternatives and select a course of action, and (4) take action while maintaining flexibility.

Clarify the Problem

You can't tackle a problem head-on if you're not sure what the problem is. Therefore, the first step in any systematic problem-solving effort is to clarify the nature of the problem. Sometimes the problem will be all too obvious. At other times it may be quite difficult to pin down the source of trouble. In any case, you need to arrive at a specific and concrete definition of your problem.

Two common tendencies typically hinder our efforts to get a clear picture of our problems. First, we often describe our problems in vague generalities (for example, "My life isn't going anywhere" or "I never have enough time"). Second, we tend to focus too much on negative feelings. This tendency confuses the consequences of problems ("I'm so depressed all the time" or "I'm so nervous I can't concentrate") with the problems themselves.

To overcome these tendencies and develop a clear specification of your problem, it may be helpful to think in terms of the four types of stress discussed in Chapter 3. Most problems can be analyzed in terms of frustration, conflict, pressure, and change. In the case of frustration, you need to identify the motive being thwarted and the barrier preventing you from attaining your goal. In the case of pressure, it helps to pinpoint the source of the pressure. Once you start thinking in these terms, you may

RECOMMENDED READING

Stress, Sanity, and Survival
by R.L. Woolfolk & F.C. Richardson (Sovereign, 1978)

This is a low-key self-help book that, unlike most of its competitors, promises little but delivers a great deal. It is rich in anecdotal illustrations and is every bit as readable as the high-profile, best-selling self-help books. However, it is notable in that it does not offer a simple recipe for solving all your personal problems, it is devoid of psychobabble, and it presents fairly explicit directions on how to reshape your behavior. If this book is flawed in any way, it is simply that the authors tried to cover too much ground and occasionally sacrificed detail and depth for breadth. Perhaps its greatest strength is its analysis of everyday emotions. Borrowing liberally from Albert Ellis, the authors do an excellent job of explicating the sources of our emotional distress and describing how we can conquer our emotions by changing our mode of thinking.

Learn to recognize and accept both your personal shortcomings and your lack of control over much of what will ultimately happen to you. For some people it is the acceptance of the permanent uncertainty and ambiguity of life that finally cuts the knots of senseless striving, or allows them to give up the burden of pretending to be more "in the know" than anyone else. As a middle-aged client of ours, who had finally quit domineering his wife and children after many years, remarked, "It is very hard to be right all the time, especially when you usually don't know what you are talking about." [pp. 104–105]

be surprised how often your problem boils down to internal conflict. Whatever your troubles are, it is crucial that you dig beneath the superficial appearances to arrive at a specific and concrete definition of your problem.

Generate Alternative Courses of Action

The second step in systematic problem solving is to generate alternative courses of action. Notice that we did not call these alternative *solutions*. Many problems do not have a readily available solution that will completely resolve the problem. If you think in terms of searching for complete solutions, you may prevent yourself from considering many worthwhile courses of action. Instead, it is more realistic to search for alternatives that may produce some kind of improvement in your situation.

Besides avoiding the tendency to insist on solutions, you need to avoid the temptation to go with the first alternative that comes to mind. Many of us are a little trigger-happy. We thoughtlessly try to follow through on the first response that occurs to us. Various lines of evidence suggest that it is wiser to engage in brainstorming about a problem. *Brainstorming* **involves generating as many ideas as possible while withholding criticism and evaluation.** In other words, you generate alternatives without paying any attention to their apparent practicality. This approach facilitates creative expression of ideas.

Evaluate Your Alternatives and Select a Course of Action

Once you generate as many alternatives as you can, you need to start evaluating the possibilities. There are no simple criteria for judging the relative merits of your alternatives. However, there are three general issues you will probably want to address. First, ask yourself whether each alternative is a realistic plan. In other words, what is the probability that you can successfully execute the intended course of action? Try to think of any obstacles you may have failed to anticipate. In making this assessment, it is important to try to avoid both foolish optimism and unnecessary pessimism.

Second, consider any costs or risks associated with each alternative. The "solution" to a problem is sometimes worse than the problem itself. Assuming you can successfully implement your intended course of action, what are the possible negative consequences? Finally, compare the desirability of the probable outcomes of each alternative. After eliminating the unrealistic possibilities, list the probable consequences (both good and bad) associated with each alternative. Then review and compare the desirability of these potential outcomes. In making your decision, you have to ask yourself "What is important to me? Which outcomes do I value the most?"

Take Action While Maintaining Flexibility

Once you have chosen your course of action, you should follow through and try to implement your plan. In so doing, try to maintain flexibility. Do not get locked into a particular course of action. Few choices are truly irreversible. You need to monitor results closely and be willing to revise your strategy.

Being flexible does not mean that you should execute your plan halfheartedly. To be able to evaluate your plan accurately, you must enact it with vigor and confidence and give it time to succeed. In evaluating your course of action, try to avoid the simplistic success/failure dichotomy. You should simply look for any improvement of any kind. If your plan doesn't work out too well, consider whether it was undermined by any unforeseen circumstances that you could not have anticipated. Finally, remember that you can learn from your failures. Even if things did not work out, you may now have new information that will facilitate a new attack on the problem.

Seeking Help

In your efforts to solve problems systematically, keep in mind the value of seeking aid from friends, family, coworkers, and neighbors. Because of potential embarrassment, many people are reluctant to acknowledge their problems and seek help from others. What makes this reality so lamentable is that others can provide a great deal of help in many ways.

Two of the four types of social support discussed in Chapter 3, *informational support* and *instrumental support,* may aid problem-focused coping. As you proceed through the first three steps of systematic problem solving, informational support in the form of advice can be of immense value. It helps to be able to bounce ideas off someone as you try to clarify your problem, generate alternative strategies, and evaluate those alternatives. Once you decide on a course of action, instrumental support in the form of material aid may make all the difference in the world.

Social support can have an impact in other coping domains besides problem-solving efforts. According to House's (1981) analysis of social support (see Chapter 3), others may often provide *emotional support* in the form of affection. This type of support may aid emotion-focused coping. Our friends may also provide *appraisal support* by helping us to make sense out of life's difficulties. This type of social support may aid appraisal-focused coping. Thus, seeking help from others is a strategy that has enormous potential in that social support can facilitate all three types of coping.

Using Time More Effectively

Do you constantly feel like there's too much to do, and too little time to do it in? Do you feel overwhelmed by your responsibilities at work, at school, and at home? Do you feel like you're always rushing around, trying to meet an impossible schedule? If you answered yes to some of these questions, you're struggling with time pressure. You can estimate how well you manage time by responding to the brief questionnaire in Figure 4.8. If the results suggest that your time is out of your control, you may be able to make your life less stressful by learning sound time-management strategies.

R. Alec Mackenzie (1972), a prominent time-management researcher, points out that time is a unique resource. It can't be stockpiled like money, food, or other precious resources. Time is a nonrenewable resource:

Figure 4.8. Assessing your time management. The brief questionnaire shown here should allow you to estimate how well you manage your time. (From Le Boeuf, 1987)

you can't turn back the clock. Furthermore, everyone, whether rich or poor, gets an equal share of time—24 hours per day, 7 days a week. Whether it seems to fly by or to drag along, time actually flows at the same steady pace for everyone. Although time is the most equitably distributed resource we have, some of us spend it much more wisely than others. Let's look at some of the ways in which we let time slip through our fingers without accomplishing much.

The Causes of Wasted Time

When people complain about "wasted time," they're usually upset because they haven't accomplished what they really wanted to with their time. Wasted time is time

---

How Well Do You Manage Your Time?

Listed below are ten statements that reflect generally accepted principles of good time management. Answer these items by circling the response most characteristic of how you perform your job. Please be honest. No one will know your answers except you.

1. Each day I set aside a small amount of time for planning and thinking about my job.
   0. Almost never. 1. Sometimes. 2. Often. 3. Almost always.

2. I set specific, written goals and put deadlines on them.
   0. Almost never. 1. Sometimes. 2. Often. 3. Almost always.

3. I make a daily "to do list," arrange items in order of importance, and try to get the important items done as soon as possible.
   0. Almost never. 1. Sometimes. 2. Often. 3. Almost always.

4. I am aware of the 80-20 rule and use it in doing my job. (The 80-20 rule states that 80 percent of your effectiveness will generally come from achieving only 20 percent of your goals.)
   0. Almost never. 1. Sometimes. 2. Often. 3. Almost always.

5. I keep a loose schedule to allow for crises and the unexpected.
   0. Almost never. 1. Sometimes. 2. Often. 3. Almost always.

6. I delegate everything I can to others.
   0. Almost never. 1. Sometimes. 2. Often. 3. Almost always.

7. I try to handle each piece of paper only once.
   0. Almost never. 1. Sometimes. 2. Often. 3. Almost always.

8. I eat a light lunch so I don't get sleepy in the afternoon.
   0. Almost never. 1. Sometimes. 2. Often. 3. Almost always.

9. I make an active effort to keep common interruptions (visitors, meetings, telephone calls) from continually disrupting my work day.
   0. Almost never. 1. Sometimes. 2. Often. 3. Almost always.

10. I am able to say no to others' requests for my time that would prevent my completing important tasks.
    0. Almost never. 1. Sometimes. 2. Often. 3. Almost always.

To get your score, give yourself
    3 points for each "almost always"
    2 points for each "often"
    1 point for each "sometimes"
    0 points for each "almost never"
Add up your points to get your total score.

If you scored
    0–15 Better give some thought to managing your time.
    15–20 You're doing OK, but there's room for improvement.
    20–25 Very good.
    28–30 You cheated!

devoted to unnecessary, unimportant, or unenjoyable activities. Why do we waste our time on such activities? There are many reasons. Prominent among them are the following.

INABILITY TO SET PRIORITIES. Time consultant Alan Lakein (1973) emphasizes that it's often tempting to deal with routine, trivial tasks ahead of larger and more difficult tasks. Thus, students working on a major term paper often read their mail, do the dishes, fold the laundry, reorganize their desk, or dust the furniture instead of concentrating on the paper. Routine tasks are easy, and working on them allows us to rationalize our avoidance of more important tasks. Unfortunately, we often use up too much time on trivial pursuits, so that our more important tasks are left undone.

INABILITY TO SAY NO. Other people are constantly seeking our time. They want us to exchange gossip in the hallway, go out to dinner on Friday night, cover their hours at work, help with a project, listen to their sales pitch on the phone, join a committee, or coach Little League. Clearly, we can't do everything that everyone wants us to. However, some people just can't say no to others' requests for their time. Such people end up fulfilling others' priorities instead of their own. Thus, McDougle (1987) concludes, "Perhaps the most successful way to prevent yourself from wasting time is by saying *no*" (p. 112).

INABILITY TO DELEGATE RESPONSIBILITY. Some tasks should be delegated to others—secretaries, subordinates, fellow committee members, other coaches, spouses, children, and so on. However, many people have difficulty delegating work to others. Barriers to delegation include unwillingness to give up any control, lack of confidence in subordinates, fear of being disliked, the need to feel needed, and the attitude that "I can do it better myself" (Mitchell, 1987). The problem, of course, is that people who can't delegate waste a lot of time on trivial work or others' work.

INABILITY TO THROW THINGS AWAY. Some people are "pack rats" who can't throw anything into the wastebasket. Their desks are cluttered with piles of mail, newspapers, magazines, reports, and books. Their filing cabinets overflow with old class notes or ancient memos. At home, their kitchen drawers bulge with rarely used utensils, their closets bulge with old clothes that are never worn, and their attics bulge with discarded junk. Pack rats waste time in at least two ways. First, they lose time looking for things that are lost amongst all the chaos. Second, they end up reshuffling the same paper, rereading the same mail, re-sorting the same reports, and so on. They would be better off if they made more use of their wastebaskets. Indeed, Mackenzie (1972) notes that "The art of waste-basketry has been designated by at least one management consultant as the most critical skill in managing one's work" (p. 69).

INABILITY TO ACCEPT ANYTHING LESS THAN PERFECTION. High standards are admirable, but some people have difficulty finishing projects because they expect them to be flawless. They can't let go. They dwell on minor problems and keep making microscopic changes in their papers, projects, and proposals. They are caught in what Emanuel (1987) calls the "paralysis of perfection." They end up spinning their wheels, redoing the same work over and over. There's nothing inherently wrong with trying to improve the quality of your work. But it pays to recognize when you have reached a point of diminishing returns, where further changes result in imperceptible improvements—if they're improvements at all.

Time-Management Techniques

What's the key to better time management? Most people assume that it's increased *efficiency*—that is, learning to perform tasks more quickly. Improved efficiency may help a little, but time-management experts maintain that efficiency is overrated. They emphasize that the key to better time management is increased *effectiveness*—that is, learning to allocate time to your most important tasks. This distinction is captured by a widely quoted slogan in

Using modern technology, such as cellular car phones and portable computers, can improve one's efficiency, but these techniques don't guarantee effective performance.

the time-management literature: "Efficiency is doing the job right, while effectiveness is doing the right job." Let's look at the experts' suggestions about how to use time more effectively (based on Lakein, 1973; Lebov, 1980; Mackenzie, 1972).

1. *Monitor your use of time.* The first step toward better time management is to monitor your use of time to see where it all goes. This requires keeping a written record of your activities, similar to that shown in Figure 4.9. At the end of each week, you should analyze how your time was allocated. Based on your personal roles and responsibilities, create categories of time use such as studying, child care, housework, commuting, work at the office, work at home, eating, and sleeping. For each day, add up the hours allocated to each category. Record this information on a summary sheet like that in Figure 4.10. Two weeks of record keeping should allow you to draw some conclusions about where your time goes. Your records will help you to make informed decisions about reallocating your time. When you begin your time-management program, these records will also give you a baseline for comparison, so that you can see whether your program is working.

2. *Clarify your goals.* You can't wisely allocate your time unless you decide what you want to accomplish with your time. Lakein (1973) suggests

that you ask yourself "What are my lifetime goals?" Write down all the goals that you can think of, even relatively frivolous things like going deep-sea fishing or becoming a wine expert. Some of your goals will be in conflict. For instance, you can't become a vice-president at your company in Wichita and move to the West Coast. Thus, the tough part comes next. You have to wrestle with your goal conflicts. Figure out which goals are most important to you, and order them in terms of priority. These priorities should guide you as you plan your activities on a daily, weekly, and monthly basis.

3. *Plan your activities using a schedule.* People resist planning because it takes time, but in the long run it saves time. Thorough planning is essential to effective time

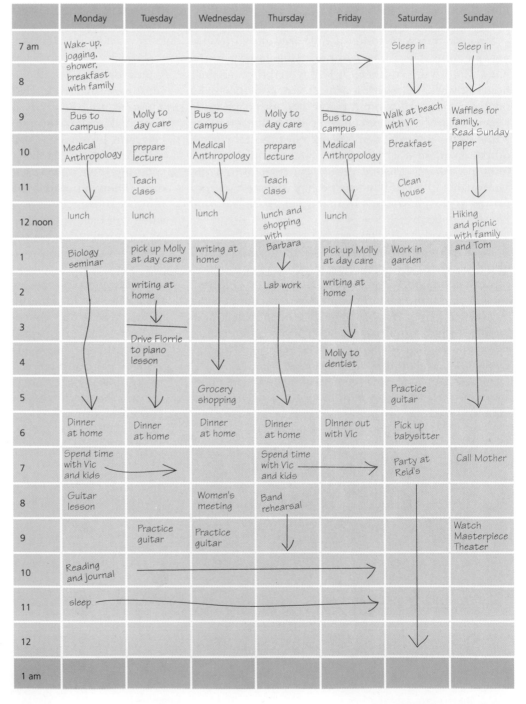

Figure 4.9. Example of a time log. Experts recommend keeping a detailed record of how you use your time to improve your time management. The example depicted here shows the kind of record keeping that should be done.

management. At the beginning of each week, you should make up a list of short-term goals. This list should be translated into daily "to do" lists of planned activities. To avoid the tendency to put off larger projects, break them into smaller, manageable components, and set deadlines for completing the components.

Your planned activities should be allocated to various time slots on a written schedule. In making your plans, beware of the tendency to overschedule. Be realistic about what you can accomplish. Since unexpected interruptions and problems are inevitable, don't schedule every minute of the day. Schedule your most important activities into the time periods when you tend to be most energetic and productive.

4. *Protect your prime time.* The best-laid plans can quickly go awry because of interruptions. There isn't any foolproof way to eliminate interruptions. But you may be able to shift most of them into certain time slots while protecting your most productive time. The trick is to announce to your family, friends, and co-workers that you're blocking off certain periods of "quiet time" when visitors and phone calls will be turned away. Of course, you also have to block off periods of "available time" when you're ready to deal with everyone's problems.

5. *Increase your efficiency.* Although efficiency is not the key to better time management, it's not irrelevant. Time-management experts do offer some suggestions for improving efficiency, including the following (Klassen, 1987; Schilit, 1987).

• *Handle paper once.* When memos, letters, reports, and such arrive on your desk, they should not be stashed away to be read again and again before you deal with them. Most paperwork can and should be dealt with immediately.

• *Tackle one task at a time.* Jumping from one problem to another is inefficient. Insofar as possible, stick with a task until it's done. In scheduling your activities, try to allow enough time to complete tasks.

• *Group similar tasks together.* It's a good idea to bunch up small tasks that are similar in nature. This strategy is useful when you're paying bills, replying to letters, returning phone calls, and so forth.

• *Make use of your downtime.* Most of us endure a lot of "downtime," waiting in doctors' offices, sitting in needless meetings, riding on buses and trains. In many of these situations, you may be able to get some of your easier work done—if you think ahead and bring it along.

Improving Self-Control

Self-discipline and self-control are the key to handling many of life's problems effectively. All four forms of stress described in Chapter 3 can create challenges to your self-control. Whether you're struggling with the *frustration* of poor grades in school, constant *conflicts* about your overeating, *pressure* to do well in sports, or downhill *changes* in finances that require readjustment, you will need reasonable self-control if you expect to make much progress.

For many of us, however, satisfactory self-control is difficult to achieve. Fortunately, the last several decades have produced major advances in the technology of self-control. These advances have emerged from research on *behavior modification*, an approach to controlling behavior that utilizes the principles of learning and conditioning. Because of its importance, we'll devote the entire Application at the end of this chapter to improving self-control through behavior modification.

EMOTION-FOCUSED CONSTRUCTIVE COPING

Let's be realistic: There are going to be occasions when appraisal-focused coping and problem-focused coping are not successful in warding off emotional turmoil. Some problems are too serious to be whittled down much by reappraisal, and others simply can't be "solved." Moreover, even well-executed coping strategies may take time to work before emotional tensions begin to subside.

Time Use Summary Form

Activity	Mon.	Tues.	Wed.	Thurs.	Fri.	Sat.	Sun.	Total	%
1. sleeping	8	6	8	6	8	7	9	52	31
2. eating	2	2	3	2	3	2	3	17	10
3. commuting	2	2	2	2	2	0	0	10	6
4. housework	0	1	0	3	0	0	2	6	4
5. in class	4	2	4	2	4	0	0	16	9
6. part-time job	0	5	0	5	0	3	0	13	8
7. studying	3	2	4	2	0	4	5	20	12
8. relaxing	5	4	3	2	7	8	5	34	20
9.									
10.									

Figure 4.10. Time use summary. To analyze where your time goes, you need to review your time log and create a weekly time use summary, like the one shown here. The exact categories to be listed on the left depend on your circumstances and responsibilities.

Hence, it is helpful to have some coping mechanisms that are useful in reducing emotional arousal. We'll discuss the merits of four such coping strategies in this section: releasing pent-up emotions, distracting yourself, meditation, and relaxation exercises.

Releasing Pent-Up Emotions

In view of the potential problematic physiological arousal that accompanies emotions, it's probably not a good idea to let strong emotions seethe within you for a long time. Hence, there may be some merit in Freud's notion that you should try to release emotions, or experience what he called *catharsis*. We noted earlier that aggressive behavior doesn't consistently produce catharsis of anger, but Freud believed that catharsis could also occur in other ways.

For example, verbalization may have some value in releasing anxiety. In other words, it could help to "talk it out." You may be able to discharge some of your anxiety by letting your secret fears, misgivings, and suspicions spill out in a candid conversation. Many approaches to psychotherapy depend on this principle. The key to doing this in a socially acceptable manner is to find someone who is really willing to listen. You shouldn't unload your problems on just anyone.

When you're dejected, it may be worthwhile to go ahead and "cry your heart out." We have a natural inclination to use this simple response. Unfortunately, many of us—especially men—are taught that crying is inappropriate behavior for an adult. However, there is nothing wrong with crying if the situation merits it.

Frankly, the evidence for catharsis effects is rather weak, coming mostly from clinical reports and anecdotal accounts. A recent experimental study did not support the idea that crying is cathartic (Kraemer & Hastrup, 1988). However, crying and talking it out don't create interpersonal complications the way aggressive behavior does. Thus, they may be reasonable, albeit unproven, coping strategies.

Distracting Yourself

Distraction involves diverting your attention from a problem by thinking about other things or engaging in other activities. Substantial reliance on this strategy was observed in a study of the coping efforts of 60 married couples (Stone & Neale, 1984). If your stomach is churning over a snafu at work, it may be a good idea to go out to a movie, take up your knitting, or head for the bowling alley. Activities that require focused attention are probably best when using this strategy.

The adaptive merits of distraction are open to debate. On the one hand, distracting yourself is probably inferior

RECOMMENDED READING
How to Get Control of Your Time and Your Life
by Alan Lakein (Wyden, 1973)

If you're locked in a perennial struggle with time—and if you're losing the battle—this may be the book for you. Alan Lakein is an expert on time management who has served as a consultant for numerous corporations. Although his book is slanted toward improving time use in the business world, its basic ideas can be useful to anyone. He emphasizes that he is not an "efficiency expert" who tries to reduce wasted motion. Instead, he sees himself as an "effectiveness expert" who has a system that can aid you in making the right decisions about how to allocate your time.

At the core of his system is the idea that you have to decide what is important to you. Lakein suggests that you closely examine your goals and make a list of both long-term and short-term priorities. Then, each day, review the tasks at hand and tackle those that will contribute the most to achieving your life goals. Lakein points out that many of us tend to tackle simple, routine tasks first, while saving the important tasks for later, when we supposedly will have more time. He mercilessly crucifies the logic underlying this tendency, citing the "80/20 rule" (see below) as a reason to concentrate on important tasks.

> The 80/20 rule says, "If all items are arranged in order of value, 80 percent of the value would come from only 20 percent of the items, while the remaining 20 percent of the value would come from 80 percent of the items." Sometimes it's a little more, sometimes a little less, but 80 percent of the time I think you will find the 80/20 rule is correct.

> 80 percent of sales comes from 20 percent of customers
> 80 percent of production is in 20 percent of the product line
> 80 percent of sick leave is taken by 20 percent of employees
> 80 percent of dinners repeat 20 percent of recipes
> 80 percent of TV time is spent on 20 percent of programs most popular with the family
> 80 percent of telephone calls come from 20 percent of all callers. [p. 71]

to problem-focused coping that might yield a longer-lasting solution. On the other hand, distracting yourself clearly is a better idea than self-indulgence, lashing out at others, or getting bogged down in negative self-talk. Thus, it appears to be a strategy that has modest, short-term value when more direct tactics have failed to produce progress.

Meditation

Recent years have seen an explosion of interest in meditation as a method for relieving stress. **Meditation refers to a family of mental exercises in which a conscious attempt is made to focus attention in a nonanalytical way.** There are many approaches to meditation. In the United States, the most widely practiced approaches are those associated with yoga, Zen, and transcendental meditation (TM). Although all three of these approaches are rooted in Eastern religions (Hinduism, Buddhism, and Taoism), most Americans who practice meditation have only vague ideas regarding its religious significance. Of interest to us is the idea that meditation can calm inner emotional turmoil.

Most meditative techniques look deceptively simple. For example, in TM a person is supposed to sit in a comfortable position with eyes closed and silently focus attention on a *mantra*, a specially assigned Sanskrit word that creates a resonant sound. This exercise in mental self-discipline is to be practiced twice daily for 20 minutes. The technique has been described as "diving from the active surface of the mind to its quiet depths" (Bloomfield & Kory, 1976, p. 49).

Advocates of TM claim that it can improve energy level, health, interpersonal relationships, and general happiness while reducing tension and anxiety caused by stress (Bloomfield & Kory, 1976; Schwartz, 1974). These are not exactly humble claims. Moreover, TM advocates assert that they can back up their claims with scientific evidence. Let's examine that evidence.

What are the *physical effects* of going into the meditative state? Some studies suggest that there are changes in the electrochemical activity of the brain. Most studies also find declines in subjects' heart rate, respiration rate, oxygen consumption, and carbon dioxide elimination (see Figure 4.11). Many researchers have also observed increases in skin resistance and decreases in blood lactate—physiological indicators associated with relaxation (Davidson, 1976; Woolfolk, 1975). Taken together, these bodily changes suggest that meditation can lead to a potentially beneficial physiological state characterized by relaxation and suppression of arousal.

These findings generated quite a bit of excitement in the 1970s. However, additional research employing better experimental controls soon dampened some of this enthusiasm. It turns out that these physical changes are not unique to meditation. A variety of systematic relaxation training procedures can produce similar results (Holmes, 1984).

The findings on the *psychological effects* of meditation are similar. There is some evidence that meditation can improve mood, lessen fatigue and reduce anxiety (Smith, 1975). However, meditation does not appear to be any more effective in achieving these goals than other systematic relaxation procedures that are practiced regularly and effectively (Shapiro, 1984).

Hence, if you are troubled by chronic emotional tension, learning to meditate may be an effective way to reduce your troublesome arousal. However, the benefits of meditation are not as spectacular as some proponents have claimed. Furthermore, you probably can attain the same benefits through less exotic relaxation techniques, such as the one we discuss next.

Relaxation Procedures

There is ample evidence that systematic relaxation procedures can soothe emotional turmoil and reduce problematic physiological arousal (Lehrer & Woolfolk, 1984).

Figure 4.11. Transcendental meditation (TM) and physiological arousal. The physiological changes shown on this graph (based on Wallace & Benson, 1972) are evidence of physical relaxation during the meditative state. However, such changes can also be produced by other systematic relaxation procedures.

There are a number of worthwhile approaches to achieving beneficial relaxation. The most prominent systems are Jacobson's (1938, 1970) *progressive relaxation*, Luthe's (1962) *autogenic training*, and Benson's (1975; Benson & Klipper, 1988) *relaxation response*. We'll discuss Benson's approach because it is a simple one that virtually anyone can learn to use.

After studying various approaches to meditation, Herbert Benson, a Harvard Medical School cardiologist, came to the same conclusions as most other researchers. He decided that elaborate religious rituals and beliefs are not necessary to profit from meditation. He also concluded that what makes meditation beneficial is the relaxation it induces. After "demystifying" meditation, Benson (1975) set out to devise a simple, nonreligious procedure that could provide similar benefits. He calls his procedure the "relaxation response."

After studying meditation and a variety of relaxation techniques, Benson concluded that the following four factors are critical to effective relaxation.

1. *A quiet environment.* It is easiest to induce the relaxation response in a distraction-free environment. After you become skilled at the relaxation response, you may be able to accomplish it in a crowded subway. Initially, however, you should practice it in a quiet, calm place.

2. *A mental device.* To shift attention inward and keep it there, you need to focus your attention on a constant stimulus, such as a sound or word that you recite over and over. You may also choose to gaze fixedly at a bland object, such as a vase. Whatever the case, you need to focus your attention on something.

3. *A passive attitude.* It is important not to get upset when your attention strays to distracting thoughts. You must realize that such distractions are inevitable. Whenever your mind wanders from your attentional focus, calmly redirect attention to your mental device.

4. *A comfortable position.* Reasonable body comfort is essential to avoid a major source of potential distraction. Simply sitting up straight works well for most people.

Some people can practice the relaxation response lying down, but for most people such a position is too conducive to sleep.

Benson's (1975, pp. 114–115) actual procedure for inducing the relaxation response is deceptively simple. For full benefit, it should be practiced daily.

1. Sit quietly in a comfortable position.
2. Close your eyes.
3. Deeply relax all your muscles, beginning at your feet and progressing up to your face. Keep them relaxed.
4. Breathe through your nose. Become aware of your breathing. As you breathe out, say the word "ONE" silently to yourself. For example, breathe IN . . . OUT, "ONE"; IN . . . OUT, "ONE"; etc. Breathe easily and naturally.
5. Continue for 10 to 20 minutes. You may open your eyes to check the time, but do not use an alarm. When you finish, sit quietly for several minutes, at first with your eyes closed and later with your eyes opened. Do not stand up for a few minutes.
6. Do not worry about whether you are successful in achieving a deep level of relaxation. Maintain a passive attitude and permit relaxation to occur at its own pace. When distracting thoughts occur, try to ignore them by not dwelling on them and return to repeating "ONE." With practice, the response should come with little effort. Practice the technique once or twice daily, but not within two hours after any meal, since the digestive processes seem to interfere with the elicitation of the relaxation response.

SUMMARY

Coping involves behavioral efforts to master, reduce, or tolerate the demands created by stress. We cope with stress in many different ways, but most of us have certain styles of coping. Coping strategies vary in their adaptive value.

Giving up, possibly best understood in terms of learned

One constructive means of coping with stress is daily meditation.

Herbert Benson

helplessness, is a common coping pattern that tends to be of limited value. Another is striking out at others with acts of aggression. Frequently caused by frustration, aggression tends to be counterproductive because it often creates new sources of stress. Blaming yourself with negative self-talk and indulging yourself are other relatively nonadaptive coping patterns. Particularly common is defensive coping, which may involve any of a number of defense mechanisms. Although the adaptive value of defensive coping tends to be less than optimal, it depends on the situation. Some of our illusions may be healthy.

Constructive coping is rational, realistic, and action-oriented. It also involves inhibiting troublesome emotions and learning self-control. Appraisal-focused constructive coping is facilitated by Ellis's suggestions on how to reduce catastrophic thinking by digging out the irrational assumptions that cause it. Other valuable strategies include using humor to deal with stress and looking for the positive aspects of setbacks and problems.

Problem-focused constructive coping can be facilitated by following a four-step process: (1) clarify the problem, (2) generate alternative courses of action, (3) evaluate your alternatives and select a course of action, and (4) take action while maintaining flexibility. Other coping tactics with potential value include seeking social support and acquiring strategies to improve self-control. Effective time management can also aid problem-focused coping. Better time management doesn't depend on increased efficiency as much as on setting priorities and allocating time wisely.

Our discussion of emotion-focused coping noted the possible value of releasing pent-up emotions and the occasional efficacy of distracting yourself. Meditation can be helpful in reducing emotional turmoil, but its benefits have been exaggerated. Although they are less exotic, systematic relaxation procedures, such as Benson's "relaxation response," can be very effective ways to cope with troublesome emotional arousal.

In our upcoming application section, we return to the issue of problem-focused coping and discuss how to improve self-control. We'll examine a step-by-step program for using behavioral techniques to enhance self-discipline.

Achieving Self-Control

Answer the following questions yes or no.

☐ **1.** Do you have a hard time passing up food, even when you're not hungry?

☐ **2.** Do you wish you studied more often?

☐ **3.** Would you like to reduce your smoking or drinking?

☐ **4.** Do you experience difficulty in getting yourself to exercise regularly?

☐ **5.** Do you wish you had more "will-power"?

If you answered yes to any of these questions, you have struggled with the challenge of self-control. This Application discusses how you can use the techniques of behavior modification to improve your self-control. If you stop to think about it, self-control—or, actually, a lack of it—underlies many of the personal problems that we struggle with in everyday life.

***Behavior modification* is a systematic approach to changing behavior through the application of the principles of conditioning.** Advocates of behavior modification assume that our behavior is a product of learning, conditioning, and environmental control. They further assume that *what is learned can be unlearned.* Thus, they set out to "recondition" people to produce more desirable patterns of behavior.

Behavior modification can be a powerful tool. Beginning in the 1960s, advocates of behavior modification fanned out across the country, applying their technology with great success in schools, businesses, hospitals, factories, child-care facilities, prisons, mental health centers, and drug-abuse programs (Goodall, 1972; Kazdin, 1982). The technology of behavior modification can also be very useful in efforts to improve self-control.

Our discussion will borrow liberally from an excellent book on self-modification by David Watson and Roland Tharp (1989). There are five steps in the process of self-modification. These steps are listed below and outlined in a flow-chart in Figure 4.12.

Step 1: Specify your target behavior.

Step 2: Gather baseline data.

Step 3: Design your program.

Step 4: Execute and evaluate your program.

Step 5: Bring your program to an end.

SPECIFYING YOUR TARGET BEHAVIOR

The first step in any systematic effort at self-modification is to specify the "target" behaviors. These are the behaviors that you will try to change in some way. This crucial step can be more complicated than it sounds.

A behavior modification program can be applied only to a clearly defined, overt behavioral response. However, many of us

Figure 4.12. Steps in a self-modification program. This flowchart provides an overview of the steps necessary to execute a self-modification program.

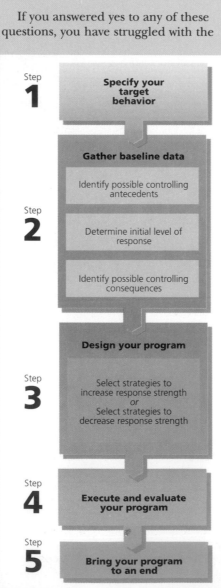

Step **1** **Specify your target behavior**

Step **2** **Gather baseline data**
- Identify possible controlling antecedents
- Determine initial level of response
- Identify possible controlling consequences

Step **3** **Design your program**
- Select strategies to increase response strength
  or
- Select strategies to decrease response strength

Step **4** **Execute and evaluate your program**

Step **5** **Bring your program to an end**

tend to be vague in describing our problems and identifying the exact nature of the behavior we want to change.

The basic problem is that we usually think in terms of negative personality *traits* rather than undesirable *behaviors*. For example, asked what behaviors he would like to change, a man might say, "I'm too irritable." That may well be accurate as far as it goes, but it is of little help in designing a self-modification program. To use a behavioral approach, we need to translate vague statements about traits into clear descriptions of the specific *behaviors* that lead us to think of ourselves as having those traits.

The best way to do this is to thoughtfully ponder past behavior or closely observe future behavior in order to list specific *examples* of responses that lead to the trait description. For instance, the man who characterizes himself as "too irritable" might translate this description into two overly frequent responses, such as arguing with his wife and snapping at his children. These are specific responses for which a self-modification program could be designed.

GATHERING BASELINE DATA

The second step in your behavior modification effort is to gather baseline data. **The *baseline period* is a span of time before you begin your program, during which you systematically observe your target behavior.** People are often tempted to skip this step and move ahead. It is imperative to resist this temptation because you need to know the original response level of your target behavior in order to evaluate your progress. You can't tell whether your program is working unless you have a baseline for comparison. In gathering your baseline data, you need to monitor three things: (1) the initial response level of the target behavior, (2) the typical antecedents of the target behavior, and (3) the typical consequences of the target behavior.

INITIAL RESPONSE LEVEL. In most cases, you simply need to keep track of how often the target response occurs in a certain time interval. Thus, you might count the daily frequency of snapping at your children, smoking cigarettes, biting your

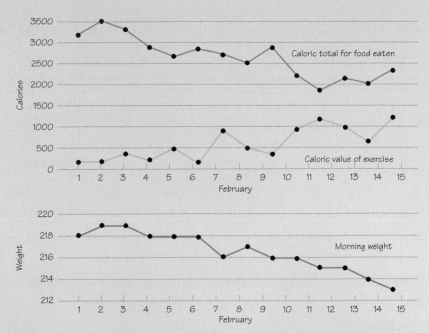

fingernails, or whatever the target behavior happens to be.

The appropriate unit of measurement depends on the nature of the target response. If studying is your target behavior, you will probably monitor *hours* of study. If you want to modify your eating habits, you will probably want to keep track of how many *calories* you consume. Whatever the unit of measurement, *it is crucial to gather accurate data.* You may need to carry some sort of portable device for recording your behavior, such as a hand-held counter or an index card on which you make notes. Keep permanent written records. It is usually best to portray these records graphically (see Figure 4.13). There are no simple guidelines for how long you should gather baseline data. Generally, you need to gather data until you can identify a *pattern* of responding.

ANTECEDENTS. **Antecedents are events that typically precede your target behavior.** Often these events play a major role in governing your target response. If classical conditioning controls the behavior, antecedents may literally trigger your target response. If operant conditioning controls the behavior, antecedents may serve as signals (discriminative stimuli) that affect the probability that you will emit the target response. In either case, recognizing links between antecedents

Figure 4.13. Example of record keeping in a self-modification program for losing weight. Graphic records are ideal for tracking progress in behavior modification efforts.

and target behaviors can be very helpful as you design your program. For example, if your target is overeating, you might discover that the bulk of your overeating occurs late in the evening after you've had a couple of beers. Once you pinpoint this kind of antecedent-response connection, you can design your program to circumvent it or to break it down.

CONSEQUENCES. Finally, you need to identify the reinforcement that is maintaining a target behavior or the punishment that is suppressing it. There are several things worth remembering in trying to identify reinforcers. First, sometimes the *response itself is the reinforcement.* Consummatory responses such as smoking or eating are intrinsically reinforcing. Second, remember that avoidance behavior is usually maintained by *negative reinforcement.* That is, the payoff for avoidance usually is the removal of something aversive, such as anxiety or a threat to self-esteem. Third, bear in mind that some responses only receive *intermittent reinforcement.* You can avoid unnecessary confusion in your search for reinforcers by being aware that a response may not be reinforced every time.

DESIGNING YOUR PROGRAM

Once you have selected a target behavior and gathered adequate baseline data, it is time to assemble your program. Generally, your program will be designed either to increase or to decrease the frequency of a target response. These are somewhat different tasks, so we'll discuss each type of program separately.

Increasing Response Strength

Efforts to increase the frequency of a target response depend largely on the use of positive reinforcement. In other words, you reward yourself for behaving properly. Although the basic strategy is quite simple, there are a number of considerations in doing it skillfully.

SELECTING A REINFORCER. If you intend to reward yourself for increasing a response, you need to find an effective reinforcer. Your choice will depend on your unique personality and situation. Reinforcement is subjective; something that is reinforcing for one person may not be reinforcing for another. Figure 4.14 lists questions that you can ask yourself in order to ascertain what your personal reinforcers are. Be sure to be realistic and choose a reinforcer that is *available* to you.

You don't have to come up with spectacular new reinforcers that you've never experienced before. *You can use reinforcers that you are already getting.* However, you have to restructure the contingencies so that you get them only if you behave appropriately. For example, let's assume that you usually buy a record or two each week. In designing a program to increase your studying, you could make your reinforcer the purchase of two records (or compact discs) each week. Of course, you would have to eliminate all other record purchases except those that you earn through your self-modification program. Thus, reinforcers that are already available to you can be made contingent upon your target behavior in order to strengthen that behavior.

ARRANGING THE CONTINGENCIES. Once you have chosen your reinforcer, you then have to set up reinforcement contingencies. Your reinforcement contingencies will describe the exact behavioral goals that must be met and the reinforcement that may then be awarded. For example, in a program to increase exercise, you might make spending $25 on clothes (the reinforcer) contingent upon jogging 15 miles during the week (the target behavior). In a program to increase study behavior, you might make listening to your stereo each night contingent upon studying three hours each day.

Try to set behavioral goals that are both challenging and realistic. You want your goals to be challenging so that they lead to improvement in your behavior. However, setting unrealistically high goals—a common mistake in self-modification—often leads to unnecessary discouragement.

You also need to be concerned about doling out too much reinforcement. If reinforcers are too easy to get, you may become *satiated*, and the reinforcer may lose its motivational power. For example, if you designed a program in which the reinforcer was the purchase of two rock albums each week, it might work fine for a while—until the albums you really wanted were salted away. Thus, reinforcement contingencies have to be set up so they don't lose their effectiveness.

THE TOKEN ECONOMY. One way to avoid the satiation problem is to put yourself on a token economy. **A *token economy* is a system for doling out symbolic reinforcers that are exchanged later for a variety of genuine reinforcers.** Thus, you might develop a "point system" for exercise behavior, accumulating points that can be spent on albums, movies, restaurant meals, and so forth (see Figure 4.15). You can also use a token economy to reinforce a *variety* of related target behaviors, as opposed to a single specific response. For example, the token economy in Figure 4.15 is set up to strengthen three different, although related, responses (jogging, tennis, and sit-ups).

Another advantage of the token economy is that it permits you to symbolically reinforce yourself *immediately* when you engage in appropriate behavior. Without the token economy you might have to wait until the end of the day or the week before you receive any reinforcement. Such delays make a reinforcer less effective.

What Are Your Reinforcers?

1. What will be the rewards of achieving your goal?
2. What kind of praise do you like to receive, from yourself and others?
3. What kinds of things do you like to have?
4. What are your major interests?
5. What are your hobbies?
6. What people do you like to be with?
7. What do you like to do with those people?
8. What do you do for fun?
9. What do you do to relax?
10. What do you do to get away from it all?
11. What makes you feel good?
12. What would be a nice present to receive?
13. What kinds of things are important to you?
14. What would you buy if you had an extra $20? $50? $100?
15. On what do you spend your money each week?
16. What behaviors do you perform every day? (Don't overlook the obvious or commonplace.)
17. Are there any behaviors you usually perform instead of the target behavior?
18. What would you hate to lose?
19. Of the things you do every day, which would you hate to give up?
20. What are your favorite daydreams and fantasies?
21. What are the most relaxing scenes you can imagine?

Figure 4.14. Selecting a reinforcer. The questions listed here may help you to identify your personal reinforcers. (From Watson & Tharp, 1989)

Responses Earning Tokens

Response	Amount	Number of tokens
Jogging	1/2 mile	4
Jogging	1 mile	8
Jogging	2 miles	16
Tennis	1 hour	4
Tennis	2 hours	8
Sit-ups	25	1
Sit-ups	50	2

Redemption Value of Tokens

Reinforcer	Tokens required
Purchase one record album of your choice	30
Go to movie	50
Go to nice restaurant	100
Take special weekend trip	500

Figure 4.15. Example of a token economy to reinforce exercise. This token economy was set up to strengthen three types of exercise behavior. The person can exchange tokens for four different types of reinforcers.

Generally, rapid reinforcement works better than delayed reinforcement. In fact, this is the heart of the problem when we struggle with self-discipline. For example, the reinforcement for overeating, your enjoyment of the food, is immediate. In contrast, the reinforcement for eating less (a slimmer, better-looking, healthier you) is typically several months away. It's not a fair contest. The more rapid reinforcement will win out most of the time. However, the rapid reinforcement provided in token economies can often neutralize this problem.

SHAPING. In some cases, you may want to reinforce yourself for a response that you are not presently capable of making, such as speaking in front of a large group, smoking no cigarettes whatsoever, or jogging five miles a day. This calls for using the technique of *shaping* to build gradually toward your ultimate behavioral goal. **Shaping is accomplished by reinforcing closer and closer approximations of a desired response.** Thus, you might initially reward yourself for jogging two miles a day and add a half-mile each week, until you reach your goal of five miles a day. In shaping yourself, you should set up a schedule spelling out how and when your target behaviors and reinforcement contingencies should change. It's a good idea to move forward very gradually.

Decreasing Response Strength

Let's turn now to the challenge of reducing the frequency of an undesirable response. You can go about this task in a number of ways. You might guess that *extinction* (terminating reinforcement) would be the obvious strategy for decreasing the strength of a response. This is often true when designing a program to modify someone else's behavior. However, self-modification programs often center on unwanted responses that are inherently reinforcing (smoking and eating, for example), making it impossible to cut off reinforcement for the response. In such cases, your principal options include the use of reinforcement, control of antecedents, and punishment.

REINFORCEMENT. Reinforcement can be used in an indirect way to decrease the frequency of a response. This may sound paradoxical since, by definition, reinforcement strengthens a response. The trick lies in how you define the target behavior. For example, in the case of overeating you might define your target behavior as eating more than 1600 calories a day (an excess response to be decreased) or eating less than 1600 calories a day (a deficit response to be increased). You can choose the latter definition and reinforce yourself whenever you eat less than 1600 calories in a day. Thus, you can reinforce yourself for not emitting a response, or for emitting it less, and thereby decrease a response through reinforcement.

CONTROL OF ANTECEDENTS. There are antecedents that increase the likelihood of many unwanted responses. A worthwhile strategy for decreasing the occurrence of an undesirable response is to identify these antecedents and avoid exposure to them. This strategy is especially useful when you are trying to decrease the frequency of a consummatory response, such as smoking or eating. In the case of overeating, for instance, the easiest way to resist temptation is to avoid having to face it. A good behavioral program to reduce overeating often depends on controlling exposure to antecedents that promote extravagant eating. Figure 4.16 lists a variety of suggestions for controlling antecedents to reduce overeating.

Control of antecedents can also be helpful in a program to increase studying. Although the core of such a program should involve the reinforcement of good study behavior, control of antecedents may be needed to reduce loafing, daydreaming, and socializing when you are supposed to be studying. For example, the key to increasing study behavior often lies in *where* you study. You can reduce excessive socializing by studying somewhere devoid of people. Similarly, you can reduce loafing by studying someplace where there is no TV, stereo, or phone to distract you.

PUNISHMENT. The strategy of decreasing unwanted behavior by punishing yourself for that behavior is an obvious option, and one that people overuse. The biggest problem with punishment in a self-modification effort is that it is difficult to follow through and punish yourself. Nonetheless, there may be situations in which your manipulations of reinforcers need to be bolstered by the threat of punishment.

If you're going to use punishment, keep two guidelines in mind. First, do not use punishment alone; use it in conjunction with positive reinforcement. If you set up a program in which you can *only* earn *negative* consequences, you probably won't stick to the program. Thus, make sure you can earn some positive outcomes. Second, use a relatively mild punishment so you will actually be able to administer it to yourself.

Nurnberger and Zimmerman (1970) have developed a creative method of self-punishment. They had subjects write out a check to an organization they hated (for instance, the campaign of a political candidate they despised). The check was held by a third party. If the subjects failed to meet their behavioral goals, the third party actually mailed the check. Such a punishment is relatively harmless but can serve as a strong source of motivation.

EXECUTING AND EVALUATING YOUR PROGRAM

Once you have designed your program, the next step is to put it to work by enforcing the contingencies that you have carefully planned. During your intervention period, continue to accurately record the frequency of your target behavior so you can evaluate your progress. The success of your program depends on your not "cheating." The most common form of cheating is to reward yourself when you have not actually earned it.

There are a couple of things that you can do to increase the likelihood that you will comply with your program. One is to

---

Controlling the Antecedents of Overeating

A. Shopping for food
1. Do not purchase problematic foods. These include
   a. very fattening, high-calorie foods
   b. your favorite foods, unless they have very low caloric values (you will be tempted to overconsume favorite foods)
   c. foods requiring little preparation (they make it too easy to eat)
2. To facilitate the above, you should
   a. use a shopping list from which you do not deviate
   b. shop just after eating (your willpower is reduced to jelly when you're hungry)
   c. carry only enough money to pay for items on your list

B. In your kitchen
1. Don't use your kitchen for anything other than food preparation and consumption. If you study or socialize there, you'll be tempted to eat.
2. Keep food stock stored out of sight.
3. If you have problematic foods in your kitchen (for other household members, of course) arrange cupboards and the refrigerator so that these foods are out of reach or in the rear.
4. Don't hover over cooking food. It will cook itself.
5. Prepare only enough food for immediate consumption.

C. While eating
1. Don't do anything besides eating. Watching TV or reading promotes mindless consumption.
2. Leave serving dishes on the kitchen counter or stove. Don't set them right in front of you.
3. Eat from a smaller dish. It will make a quantity of food appear greater.
4. Slow the pace of eating. Relax and enjoy your food.

D. After eating
1. Quickly put away or dispose of leftover foods.
2. Leave the kitchen as soon as you are through.

E. In regard to restaurants
1. Insofar as possible, do not patronize restaurants. Menus are written in a much too seductive style.
2. If social obligations require that you eat out, go to a restaurant that you don't particularly like.
3. When in restaurants, don't linger over the menu, and don't gawk at the food on other tables.
4. Avoid driving down streets and going to shopping centers that are loaded with alluring fast-food enterprises.

F. In general
1. Try to avoid boredom. Keep yourself busy.
2. Try to avoid excessive sleep loss and fatigue. Your self-control diminishes when you are tired.
3. Avoid excessive fasting. Skipping meals often leads to overeating later.

Figure 4.16. Control of antecedents. Controlling antecedents that trigger overeating is often a crucial part of behavioral programs for weight loss. The tips listed here have proven useful to many people.

Figure 4.17. Behavioral contract. Behavior modification experts recommend the use of a formal, written contract similar to that shown here.

I, _____ , do hereby agree to initiate my self-change strategy as of

(date) _____ and to continue it for a minimum period of

_____ weeks—that is, until (date) _____

My specific self-change strategy is to _____

_____

_____

_____

I will do my best to execute this strategy to my utmost ability and to evaluate its effectiveness only after it has been honestly tried for the specified period of time.

Optional Self-Reward Clause: For every _____ day(s) that I successfully comply with my self-change contract, I will reward myself with _____

_____

In addition, at the end of my minimum period of personal experimentation, I will reward myself for having persisted in my self-change efforts. My reward at that time will be _____

_____

I hereby request that the witnesses who have signed below support me in my self-change efforts and encourage my compliance with the specifics of this contract. Their cooperation and encouragement throughout the project will be appreciated.

Signed _____

Date _____

Witness:

Witness:

write up a *behavioral contract*—**a written agreement outlining a promise to adhere to the contingencies of a behavior modification program** (see Figure 4.17). The formality of signing such a contract in front of friends or family seems to make many people take their program more seriously. You can further reduce the likelihood of cheating by having someone other than yourself dole out the reinforcers and punishments. When a spouse, friend, or family member is monitoring your behavior, it is much harder to cheat.

When set into action, behavior modification programs often turn out to need some fine-tuning. So don't be surprised if you need to make a few adjustments. Several flaws are especially common in designing self-modification programs. Among the things you should look out for are (1) depending on a weak reinforcer, (2) permitting lengthy delays between appropriate behavior and the actual reinforcement, and (3) trying to do too much too quickly by setting unrealistic goals. Often, a small revision or two can turn a failing program around and make it a success.

ENDING YOUR PROGRAM

Generally, when you design your program you should spell out the conditions under which you will bring it to an end. This involves setting terminal goals such as reaching a certain weight, studying with a certain regularity, or going without cigarettes for a certain length of time. Often, it is a good idea to phase out your program by planning a gradual reduction in the frequency or potency of your reinforcement for appropriate behavior.

If your program is successful, it may fade away without a conscious decision on your part. Often, new and improved patterns of behavior become self-maintaining. Responses such as eating right, exercising regularly, or studying diligently may become habitual so that they no longer need to be supported by an elaborate program. Whether your program fades out intentionally or spontaneously, you should always be prepared to reinstitute the program if you find yourself slipping back to your old patterns of behavior.

1. Discuss three general points about coping.

2. Discuss the adaptive value of giving up as a response to stress.

3. Discuss the adaptive value of aggression.

4. Discuss the adaptive value of indulging yourself.

5. Discuss the adaptive value of negative self-talk.

6. Describe the five defense mechanisms introduced in the chapter and explain how defense mechanisms work.

7. Discuss the adaptive value of defense mechanisms, including recent work on healthy illusions.

8. Describe the nature of constructive coping and list the three categories of constructive coping tactics.

9. Describe Ellis's analysis of how catastrophic thinking causes maladaptive emotions.

10. Discuss the merits of positive reinterpretation and humor as coping strategies.

11. List and describe four steps in systematic problem solving.

12. Discuss the diverse benefits of seeking help as a coping strategy.

13. Explain five common causes of wasted time and summarize advice on managing time effectively.

14. Discuss the adaptive value of releasing pent-up emotions and distracting yourself.

15. Summarize the evidence on the effects of meditation.

16. Describe the requirements and procedure for Benson's relaxation response.

17. Explain why traits cannot be target behaviors in self-modification programs.

18. Discuss the three kinds of information you should pursue in gathering your baseline data.

19. Discuss how to use reinforcement to increase the strength of a response.

20. Discuss how to use reinforcement, control of antecedents, and punishment to decrease the strength of a response.

21. Discuss issues related to fine-tuning and ending a self-modification program.

KEY TERMS

Aggression
Antecedents
Baseline period
Behavioral contract
Behavior modification
Brainstorming
Catastrophic thinking
Catharsis
Constructive coping
Coping
Defense mechanisms

Denial
Fantasy
Intellectualization
Learned helplessness
Meditation
Overcompensation
Rational-emotive therapy
Shaping
Token economy
Undoing

KEY PEOPLE

Aaron Beck
Herbert Benson
Albert Ellis
Sigmund Freud
Martin Seligman

Self-Control Schedule

INSTRUCTIONS

Indicate how characteristic or descriptive each of the following statements is of you by using the code given below.

+3 very characteristic of me, extremely descriptive
+2 rather characteristic of me, quite descriptive
+1 somewhat characteristic of me, slightly descriptive
−1 somewhat uncharacteristic of me, slightly undescriptive
−2 rather uncharacteristic of me, quite undescriptive
−3 very uncharacteristic of me, extremely undescriptive

Record your responses in the spaces provided on the left.

THE SCALE

1. When I do a boring job, I think about the less boring parts of the job and the reward that I will receive once I am finished.

2. When I have to do something that is anxiety-arousing for me, I try to visualize how I will overcome my anxieties while doing it.

3. Often by changing my way of thinking I am able to change my feelings about almost everything.

4. I often find it difficult to overcome my feelings of nervousness and tension without any outside help.

5. When I am feeling depressed, I try to think about pleasant events.

6. I cannot avoid thinking about mistakes I have made in the past.

7. When I am faced with a difficult problem, I try to approach its solution in a systematic way.

8. I usually do my duties quicker when somebody is pressuring me.

9. When I am faced with a difficult decision, I prefer to postpone making a decision even if all the facts are at my disposal.

10. When I find that I have difficulties in concentrating on my reading, I look for ways to increase my concentration.

11. After I plan to work, I remove all the things that are not relevant to my work.

12. When I try to get rid of a bad habit, I first try to find out all the factors that maintain this habit.

13. When an unpleasant thought is bothering me, I try to think about something pleasant.

14. If I would smoke two packages of cigarettes a day, I probably would need outside help to stop smoking.

15. When I am in a low mood, I try to act cheerful so my mood will change.

16. If I had the pills with me, I would take a tranquilizer whenever I felt tense and nervous.

17. When I am depressed, I try to keep myself busy with things that I like.

18. I tend to postpone unpleasant duties even if I could perform them immediately.

19. I need outside help to get rid of some of my bad habits.

20. When I find it difficult to settle down and do a certain job, I look for ways to help me settle down.

21. Although it makes me feel bad, I cannot avoid thinking about all kinds of possible catastrophes in the future.

22. First of all I prefer to finish a job that I have to do and then start doing the things I really like.

23. When I feel pain in a certain part of my body, I try not to think about it.

24. My self-esteem increases once I am able to overcome a bad habit.

25. In order to overcome bad feelings that accompany failure, I often tell myself that it is not so catastrophic and that I can do something about it.

26. When I feel that I am too impulsive, I tell myself, "Stop and think before you do anything."

27. Even when I am terribly angry at somebody, I consider my actions very carefully.

28. Facing the need to make a decision, I usually find out all the possible alternatives instead of deciding quickly and spontaneously.

29. Usually, I do first the things I really like to do even if there are more urgent things to do.

30. When I realize that I cannot help but be late for an important meeting, I tell myself to keep calm.

31. When I feel pain in my body, I try to divert my thoughts from it.

32. I usually plan my work when faced with a number of things to do.

33. When I am short of money, I decide to record all my expenses in order to plan carefully for the future.

34. If I find it difficult to concentrate on a certain job, I divide the job into smaller segments.

35. Quite often I cannot overcome unpleasant thoughts that bother me.

36. Once I am hungry and unable to eat, I try to divert my thoughts away from my stomach or try to imagine that I am satisfied.

SCORING THE SCALE

The items listed below are reverse-scored items. Thus, for each of them you should go back and simply change the + or − sign in front of the number you recorded.

4	9	18	29
6	14	19	35
8	16	21	

After making your reversals, all you need to do is add up the numbers you recorded for each of the 36 items. Of course, it is important to pay close attention to the algebraic sign in front of each number. The total you arrive at is your score on the Self-Control Schedule (SCS). Record your score below.

MY SCORE _____

WHAT THE SCALE MEASURES

Developed by Michael Rosenbaum (1980), the Self-Control Schedule assesses your ability to employ self-management methods to solve common behavioral problems. Specifically, it measures your tendency to (1) use rational self-talk to modify emotional responses, (2) use systematic problem-solving strategies, and (3) delay immediate gratification when necessary. It also measures your perceptions regarding your self-control skills.

Rosenbaum (1980) administered the SCS to a diversified batch of six samples including both student and nonstudent populations, many of them from Israel (Rosenbaum is affiliated with the University of Haifa). Test-retest reliability (.86 for four weeks) was excellent. Support for the validity of the scale was derived from evidence that it correlates negatively with established measures of irrational thinking. Additional supportive evidence was garnered in an experimental study wherein high scorers on the SCS showed better self-control on a laboratory task than did low scorers.

INTERPRETING YOUR SCORE

Our norms are based on an American sample of 111 undergraduate students studied by Rosenbaum (1980). Although females tend to score a little higher on the scale than do males, the difference is not large enough to merit separate norms (so their means have been averaged).

NORMS

High score:	Above 48
Intermediate score:	6–47
Low score:	Below 6

Can You Detect Your Irrational Thinking?

You should begin this exercise by reviewing the theories of Albert Ellis. To briefly recapitulate, Ellis believes that unpleasant emotional reactions are caused not by events themselves, but by catastrophic interpretations of events derived from irrational assumptions. It is therefore important to detect and dispute these catastrophic modes of thinking. Over a period of a week or so, see if you can spot two examples of irrational thinking on your part. Describe these examples as requested below.

Example No. 1
Activating event:

Irrational self-talk:

Consequent emotional reaction:

Irrational assumption producing irrational thought:

More rational, alternative view:

Example No. 2
Activating event:

Irrational self-talk:

Consequent emotional reaction:

Irrational assumption producing irrational thought:

More rational, alternative view:

PART II
THE INTERPERSONAL REALM

5

Person Perception

It's Friday night, and you're bored. The menu of TV shows for the evening looks pretty dull. The thought of studying on a Friday night is positively revolting. You call a couple of friends to see whether they want to go out to a movie. Both friends tell you that they would "love" to go, but they have other commitments. One needs to study, and the other has to go grocery shopping. You feel that their reasons for not going out with you are rather flimsy. It seems that if they really wanted to go with you, they could have worked it in. To what do you attribute these "rejections"? Do the friends really have other commitments? Are they apathetic about going out? Are they being sincere when they say that they would love to go out with you? Is it possible that they really don't enjoy spending time with you? Could it be that they find you boring? Are you boring?

These questions illustrate a basic process we engage in constantly. That process is the interpretation of behavior. We have a fundamental need to understand both our own behavior and the behavior of others. In our effort to explain behavior, we create and rely on images, or pictures, of ourselves and other people. This chapter discusses how we develop these pictures and how they influence our social interactions.

BASIC PRINCIPLES OF SOCIAL PERCEPTION

We'll begin our discussion by examining some basic principles of social perception. In this section we'll take a look at the attribution process, our preference for consistency among our beliefs, and our penchant for selective perception.

The Attribution Process

Attributions **are inferences that people draw about the causes of events, others' behavior, and their own behavior.** For example, let's say that someone compliments you on your clothing. To what should you *attribute* this compliment? Was this person truly impressed by your dress? Or was the compliment merely part of everyday social routine? Could the compliment be part of an effort to butter you up? Or suppose that your boss bawls you out for doing a sloppy job on some insignificant project. To what do you *attribute* this tongue-lashing? Was your boss just in a grouchy mood? Is your boss under too much pressure? Was your work really that sloppy?

These two examples from everyday life illustrate the nature of the attribution process. We routinely make attributions to make sense out of our experiences. These attributions involve inferences that ultimately represent guesswork on our part.

Key Dimensions of Attributions

Fritz Heider (1958) was the first to describe the crucial dimension along which we make attributions. Heider asserted that we tend to locate the cause of behavior either *within a person*, attributing it to personal factors, or *outside of a person*, attributing it to environmental factors.

Elaborating on Heider's insight, various theorists have agreed that our explanations of behavior and events can be categorized as internal or external attributions (Jones & Davis, 1965; Kelley, 1967; Weiner, 1974). *Internal attri-* **butions ascribe the causes of behavior to personal dispositions, traits, abilities, and feelings.** *External attributions* **ascribe the causes of behavior to situational demands and environmental constraints.** For example, if a friend's business fails, you might attribute the failure to your friend's lack of business acumen (an internal, personal factor) or to negative trends in the economy (an external, situational explanation). Parents who find out that their teenage son just banged up the car may blame it on his carelessness (a personal disposition) or on slippery road conditions (a situational factor).

Whether our attributions are internal or external can have a tremendous impact on our everyday interactions. Blaming a friend's business failure on poor business acumen as opposed to a poor economy obviously affects

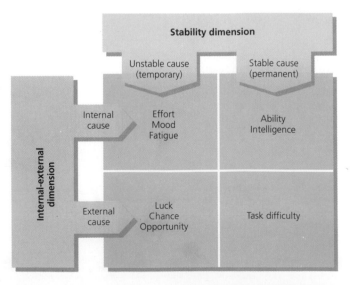

how you view your friend—not to mention whether you'll lend her money. Likewise, if parents attribute their son's automobile accident to slippery road conditions, they are likely to deal with it very differently than if they attribute it to his carelessness. Furthermore, as we'll discuss later (in Chapter 15), certain patterns of attribution may even contribute to serious depressive disorders. Studies suggest that people who attribute their setbacks to internal, personal causes while discounting external, situational explanations may be more prone to depression than people who display opposite tendencies (Alloy, Clements, & Kolden, 1985; Huesmann & Morikawa, 1985). There is also evidence that the attributions spouses make to explain each other's behavior can affect their marital satisfaction (Bradbury & Fincham, 1988).

Some psychologists have sought to discover additional dimensions of attributional thinking besides the internal-external dimension. After studying the attributions people make in explaining success and failure, Bernard Weiner and his colleagues concluded that we often focus on the *stability* of the causes underlying behavior (Weiner, 1974; Weiner et al., 1972). According to Weiner, the stable-unstable dimension in attribution cuts across the internal-external dimension, creating four types of attributions for success and failure, as shown in Figure 5.1.

Let's apply Weiner's model to a concrete event. Imagine that you are contemplating why you failed to get a job you wanted. You might attribute your setback to internal factors that are stable (lack of ability) or unstable (inadequate effort to put together an eye-catching résumé). Or you might attribute your setback to external factors that are stable (too much outstanding competition in your chosen field) or unstable (bad luck). If you got the job, the explanations that you might offer for your success would fall in the same four categories: internal-stable (your excellent ability), internal-unstable (your hard work to assemble a superb résumé), external-stable (lack of top-flight competition), and external-unstable (good luck).

More recently, Weiner (1986) has begun to explore a third factor in attributions: the controllability-uncontrollability of the causes underlying our actions. The addition of this factor to the model results in eight types of attributions.

Actor-Observer Differences

Attributions are only inferences. Our attributions may not be the correct explanations for events. Paradoxical as it may seem, we often arrive at inaccurate explanations even when we contemplate the causes of *our own* behavior. Ultimately, attributions represent *guesswork* about the causes of events. Interestingly, these guesses tend to be slanted in certain directions.

In particular, our view of our own behavior can be quite different from the view of someone else observing us. When an actor and an observer draw inferences about the causes of the actor's behavior, they often make different attributions. As an example, imagine that you've come to pick up your car at a garage where it is being serviced and you become angry and insulting when you're told that it's not ready as promised. Observers who overhear your harsh, sarcastic remarks are likely to make an internal attribution and infer that you are surly, rude, and obnoxious. They may be right, but if asked, *you* would probably attribute your anger to the frustrating situation. Perhaps you called just before you came to the garage and you were assured that your car was ready. Because observers often are unaware of such situational considerations, they tend to make internal attributions for another's behavior.

In comparison to observers, actors are more aware of the situational factors that have influenced their behavior. Hence, they are more prone than observers to locate the cause of their behavior in the situation. In general, then, *actors favor external attributions for their behavior, while observers are prone to explain the same behavior with internal attributions* (Jones & Nisbett, 1971).

Actor-observer differences in attribution become a bit more complicated when people are explaining success and failure (Whitley & Frieze, 1983, 1985). In explaining

Figure 5.1. Key dimensions of attributional thinking.
Weiner's model assumes that our explanations for success and failure emphasize internal versus external causes and stable versus unstable causes. For example, if you attribute an outcome to great effort or to lack of effort, you are citing internal causes that lie within the person. Since effort can vary over time, the causal factors at work are unstable. Other examples of causal factors that fit into each of the four cells in Weiner's model are shown in the diagram.

failure, the usual actor-observer biases are apparent. Actors tend to make external attributions, blaming their failures on unfavorable situational factors. Observers tend to attribute the same failures to the actors' personal shortcomings. Thus, if you fail an exam,

"I think you'll find my test results are a pretty good indication of your abilities as a teacher."

you may place the blame on the poorly constructed exam, lousy teaching, distractions in the hallway, or a bad week at work (all external attributions). However, an observer is more likely to attribute your failure to your lack of ability or to your lack of study (both of which are internal attributions).

In explaining *success*, however, the usual actor-observer differences are reversed to some degree. Thus, if you get a high exam score, you'll probably make an internal attribution and point to your ability or your hard work (Forsyth & McMillan, 1981). In comparison, an observer may be more likely to infer that the test was easy or that you were lucky (external attributions). In other words, actors like to take credit for their successes, while observers lean toward situational explanations for others' triumphs.

Because of such differences in the perspectives of actors and observers, we will discuss self-perception and perception of others separately. Although the two topics have much in common, the crucial issues are somewhat different.

The Premium on Consistency

In developing our pictures of ourselves and others, we strive for consistency. That is, we prefer that our attitudes and beliefs mesh together nicely. ***Cognitive dissonance exists when related cognitions are inconsistent—that is,*** **they contradict each other.** First described by Leon Festinger (1957), cognitive dissonance is assumed to create an unpleasant state of tension. This tension is supposed to motivate people to reduce their dissonance, usually by altering one or both of the clashing cognitions.

Consider a simple example. Let's say that you see yourself as a hardworking, reliable person. However, you are presently sitting at the ballpark taking in a baseball game after calling in sick at work. Obviously, the cognitions "I'm reliable" and "I'm skipping work" are inconsistent and thus create dissonance. Festinger's theory suggests that you will feel some need to modify one of the cognitions in order to reduce the disturbing feeling of dissonance. Thus, you may admit to yourself that you're not all that reliable. Or you may look for some way to rationalize skipping work so that it does not appear that you're being unreliable ("Even the best of us play hooky once in a while"). The first alternative would require modifying your self-concept, a threatening prospect for most people. Hence, you're more likely to choose the second, less drastic alternative. In either case, the crucial point is that we try to maintain consistency among our beliefs, even if we have to twist reality a little bit (or a lot).

Selectivity in Social Perception

There is an old saying that "people see what they expect to see." This commonsense notion that expectations influence perceptions has been confirmed repeatedly by social scientists. For example, in a classic study, Harold Kelley (1950) showed how a person is preceded by his or her reputation. Students in a class at the Massachusetts Institute of Technology (MIT) were told that a new lecturer would be speaking to them. Before the class, the students were given a short description of the incoming instructor, with one important variation. Half the students were led to expect a "warm" person, while the other half were led to expect a "cold" one (see Figure 5.2). All the subjects were exposed to exactly the same 20 minutes of lecture and interaction with the new instructor. How-

Leon Festinger

Mr. Blank is a graduate student in the Department of Economics and Social Science here at M.I.T. He has had three semesters of teaching experience in psychology at another college. This is his first semester teaching Ec. 70. He is 26 years old, a veteran, and married. People who know him consider him to be a rather cold person, industrious, critical, practical, and determined.

Mr. Blank is a graduate student in the Department of Economics and Social Science here at M.I.T. He has had three semesters of teaching experience in psychology at another college. This is his first semester teaching Ec. 70. He is 26 years old, a veteran, and married. People who know him consider him to be a very warm person, industrious, critical, practical, and determined.

ever, those who were led to expect a warm person rated the instructor as significantly more considerate, sociable, humorous, good-natured, informal, and humane than those who were led to expect a cold person!

If there's any ambiguity in someone's behavior, we're likely to interpret what we see in a way that is consistent with our expectations (Darley & Gross, 1983). Thus, after dealing with a pushy female customer, a salesman who believes in gender stereotypes might characterize the woman as "emotional." However, a pushy male who exhibits exactly the same behavior may be characterized as "aggressive."

In summary, the process of social perception is highly subjective. Our attributions are ultimately guesses about the causes of events, and these guesses are influenced by a variety of biases. We prefer consistency among our cognitions, even if we have to distort reality to achieve it. And we have a strong tendency to see what we expect to see in our interpersonal interactions. With these principles in mind, let's turn now to the matter of self-perception.

SELF-PERCEPTION

In a significant departure from the conventional wisdom that our attitudes determine our behavior, Daryl Bem (1972) suggested that the reasons for our behavior are not always readily apparent—even to ourselves. According to Bem's ***self-perception theory,*** **when we are unsure of our beliefs, we try to understand ourselves by inferring our attitudes from our behavior.** Typically, a person might explain his habits by saying, "I don't like plays; therefore, I don't go to them." However, Bem suggests that sometimes the reasoning proceeds in the opposite direction. Thus, a person may say, "Gee, I don't go to any plays. I guess I don't like them." When we are certain about how we feel, we're less likely to make inferences based on our behavior (Chaiken & Baldwin, 1981). Nonetheless, we are frequently involved in efforts to understand our own

Figure 5.2. Descriptions of the guest lecturer in Kelley's (1950) study. Only a single phrase is different in these two descriptions, but students perceived the same person quite differently depending on which description they heard prior to the lecture.

RECOMMENDED READING

Encounters with the Self

by Don E. Hamachek (Holt, Rinehart & Winston, 1987)

This book is all about the many aspects of the self-concept. It describes how the contours of the self-concept are molded by our interactions with others, how the self-concept continues to undergo metamorphosis throughout life, and how the self-concept is expressed in our everyday behavior. Though reasonably compact in size, the book is quite broad in scope, and Hamachek manages to cover a number of intriguing topics, including defense mechanisms, how we perceive others, the role of physical appearance in shaping self-concept, how child-rearing styles influence self-concept, how self-perceptions affect academic adjustment, feelings of inferiority, and how to pursue a more positive self-image.

This is one of those rare books that can provide satisfactory reading for both the layperson and the sophisticated professional. Academicians will appreciate the well-documented and thorough review of relevant research. Nonprofessional readers will find the book highly readable and brimming with practical insights and advice. Although the author disavows any intention of writing a "self-help" book, this volume is likely to be about as helpful to readers as any mere book can be.

> Some individuals avoid finding out more about themselves for fear of having to give up a self with which they have grown comfortable or "satisfied." Most people have an initial inclination to resist personal change anyway, but this resistance is even stronger for those who refuse to insert new or changed behavior into their current concept of self. For example, a shy, timid, submissive person may not want to know his strengths and assets for fear that he might have to be more assertive and socially aggressive. If shyness has become a way of life designed to protect him from the risks of social disapproval (in this case, nothing ventured, nothing lost—in terms of self-esteem), then it may be difficult indeed for him to give up being timid. Other individuals are reluctant to find out more about themselves because of the threat of having to become more personally mature. Maturity implies many things, among which are a certain degree of independence and autonomy, capacity for self-discipline, certainty about goals and values, and motivation toward some level of personal achievement. Most of all, greater maturity means greater responsibility, and for some this may be a frightening possibility. [p. 45]

behavior. In this section we focus on this process of self-perception and related issues.

Self-Concept

Through the processes of social perception you develop a self-concept. **A *self-concept* is a collection of beliefs about one's own nature, unique qualities, and typical behavior.** For example, your self-concept might include beliefs such as "I am tall," "I play the clarinet," "I am a good student," "I am lazy," and "I am friendly." As you can see from these examples, the self-concept includes many separate but interrelated aspects. Remember, too, that self-concepts are not necessarily accurate. Nonetheless, we all have concepts of our unique physical self, social self, emotional self, and intellectual self (Hamachek, 1987).

Cutting across all these components of the self, there is the crucial dimension of *self-evaluation*. We generally look at ourselves in an approving or disapproving manner. These favorable or unfavorable self-evaluations determine our self-esteem. As we shall see later, self-esteem is probably the most important aspect of our self-concept.

A person's self-concept is not set in concrete—but it is not easily changed, either. Once our self-concepts are established, we have a tendency to preserve and defend them. Therefore, our pictures of ourselves tend to be fairly stable. In the context of this stability, however, the self-concept has a certain dynamic quality. Although it rarely changes overnight, your self-concept may very well undergo gradual change over time.

Sidney Jourard argues that one's self-concept is both descriptive and prescriptive (Jourard & Landsman, 1980). Its *descriptive* nature is obvious in that it describes past patterns of behavior. Its *prescriptive* nature—that is, how it *influences* our *future* behavior—may be less apparent. Like Carl Rogers (1959), Jourard maintains that our self-concept regulates future behavior because we try to act in ways that are consistent with it. Jourard believes that we feel uncomfortable when we act out of character. Therefore, our personal perception of what we are like prescribes

how we should behave in the future. It's a two-way street: Our behavior influences our self-concept, and our self-concept influences our behavior.

Your self-concept is not merely an obscure abstraction of interest to psychologists. It governs your day-to-day behavior in significant ways. For instance, if you have been eyeing an attractive classmate recently, your self-esteem may be the crucial factor that determines whether you actually approach that person.

Factors Shaping Your Self-Concept

A variety of sources influence your self-concept. Chief among them are your own observations, feedback from others, and cultural values. Let's look at each of these.

Your Own Observations

Your own observations of your behavior are obviously a major source of information about what you are like. Early in childhood we begin observing our own behavior and drawing conclusions about ourselves. For example, young children will make statements about who is the tallest, who can run fastest, or who can swing the highest.

As these examples show, our observations of ourselves do not take place in a social vacuum. Even in early childhood they involve comparisons with other children. *Social comparison theory* **proposes that people need to**

Part of our self-concept comes from comparing ourselves to others in our reference group to see how we stack up.

compare themselves with others in order to gain insight into their own behavior (Festinger, 1954; Goethals & Darley, 1977). The potential impact of such social comparisons was dramatically demonstrated in an interesting study (Morse & Gergen, 1970). Subjects thought they were being interviewed for a job. Half the subjects met another applicant who appeared to be extremely impressive. The other half were exposed to a competitor who appeared to be a clod. All subjects filled out measures of self-esteem both before and after the bogus job interviews. The results indicated that subjects who encountered the impressive competitor showed a decrease in self-esteem after the interview. In contrast, those who met the unimpressive competitor showed increases in self-esteem. Thus, our comparisons with others can have immediate effects on our self-concept.

Of course, we do not choose just anyone for a point of comparison. **A *reference group* is a set of people against whom you compare yourself.** Reference groups are usually made up of people who are similar to us in certain key ways. The crucial dimensions of similarity depend on which aspects of our behavior we are trying to evaluate. If you want to judge the progress of your racquetball game, you will probably compare yourself against people who have been playing for a similar length of time. If you want to evaluate your career progress, you'll compare yourself with people of roughly the same age who are in the same general occupational area. Consistent with this hypothesis, one study found that when subjects were led to believe that performance on a task was influenced by gender, males wanted to know how other men did, while females sought information about the performance of other women (Zanna, Goethals, & Hill, 1975).

Our observations of our behavior are not entirely objective. As you may recall from our discussion of Carl Rogers's (1959) views on personality (see Chapter 2), we learn early in life about what is judged to be good and bad behavior. In order to feel worthy of others' affection, we tend to distort our perceptions of our behavior in ways that permit positive self-evaluations. This means that your self-concept may not be a particularly accurate reflection of your behavior.

The general tendency is to distort reality in a positive direction (see Figure 5.3). In other words, there is considerable evidence that most of us tend to evaluate ourselves in a more positive light than we really merit. The strength of this tendency was highlighted in a large survey conducted as part of the Scholastic Aptitude Test (SAT)—of some 829,000 high school seniors (Myers, 1980). In this survey, 70% of the students rated themselves above average in "leadership ability." Only 2% rated themselves below average. Obviously, by definition, 50% must be "above average" and 50% below. Nonetheless, in regard to "ability to get along with others," 100% of the subjects saw themselves as above average! Furthermore, 25% of the respondents thought that they belonged in the top 1%.

Although our general tendency is to distort reality in a positive direction, this is not a universal rule. A minority of people tend to do just the opposite. They constantly evaluate themselves in an unrealis-

As she sees herself: Unchanged since age 22. Sociable, scintillating, sexy.

As the husband sees her: Older than her years. Someone more suited to suburban domesticity and PTA.

As he sees himself: Stylish haircut, rakish moustache; benevolent, generous, powerful. A smooth operator.

As the wife sees him: Somewhat of a slob, moody, not very decisive or strong.

Figure 5.3. Distortions in our self-images. How we see ourselves may be very different from how others see us. These pictures and text illustrate the subjective quality of self-concept and our perception of others. Generally, our self-images tend to be distorted in a positive direction.

tically negative way. Moreover, most of us tend to make *both* negative and positive distortions, although positive ones are more common. For example, you might overrate your social skill, emotional stability, and intellectual ability while underrating your physical attractiveness. Thus, the tendency to see ourselves in an overly favorable light is strong but not universal.

Feedback from Others

Your self-concept is also shaped by the feedback that you get about your behavior from other people. It should be readily apparent that not everyone has equal influence in our lives. Early in life our parents and other family members play a dominant role in providing us with feedback. As we grow older, feedback from a much wider array of people becomes significant.

Parents give their children a great deal of direct feedback. They constantly express approval or disapproval, making statements such as "You're cute as the dickens" or "You're a lazy bum like your Uncle Patrick." Most of us, especially when young, take this sort of feedback to heart. Consequently, it comes as no surprise that studies find an association between parents' views of a child and the child's self-concept (Wylie, 1979). There is even stronger evidence for a correspondence between children's *perceptions* of their parents' attitudes toward them and their own self-perceptions (Wylie, 1979).

Parents and family are not the only source of feedback during childhood. Teachers, Little League coaches, Scout leaders, and others also provide significant feedback. In adolescence, as one's peer group becomes more influential, friends play an important role in the development of our self-concepts (Smollar & Youniss, 1985).

The feedback we receive from others has to filter through our social perception systems. As a consequence, it may be distorted just as our own self-

observations may be. As you would logically expect, most people tend to be more receptive to positive than to negative feedback (Eagly & Whitehead, 1972). Interestingly, there is evidence that people with low self-esteem react more positively to those who compliment them and more negatively to those who criticize them than do people with high self-esteem (Berscheid, 1985).

Cultural Guidelines

Your self-concept is also shaped, albeit indirectly, by cultural values. The society in which we are brought up defines what is good and bad in personality and behavior. For example, American culture tends to put a premium on competitive success, strength, skill, and individuality. These cultural values influence how we interpret our behavior. We are more likely to make distortions in areas that our culture considers important.

Our cultural background is also responsible for various stereotypes that may mold our self-perceptions. For instance, gender stereotypes influence males' and females' self-perceptions and behavior. One study found that college students' gender stereotypes predicted which activities they tried and how much they enjoyed them (Carter & Myerowitz, 1984). In a similar manner, racial, class, and religious stereotypes can influence our self-perceptions.

Self-Esteem

Self-esteem refers to your overall assessment of your worth as a person; it is the evaluative component of your self-concept. Self-esteem is a global evaluation that blends many specific evaluations about your adequacy as a student, as an athlete, as a worker, as a spouse, as a parent, or whatever is relevant to you. Figure 5.4 shows how specific elements of self-concept may

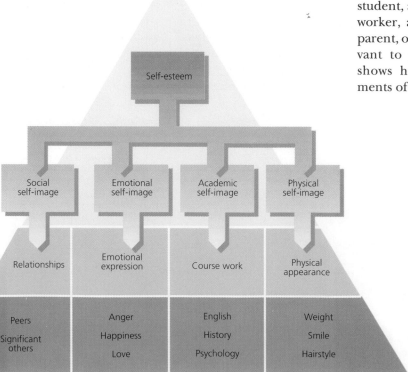

Figure 5.4. The structure of self-esteem. Our self-esteem is a global evaluation that combines assessments of different aspects of our self-concept, each of which is built up from many specific behaviors and experiences. (Adapted from Shavelson et al., 1976)

contribute to self-esteem. If you feel basically good about yourself, you would be said to have high self-esteem.

Self-esteem is a difficult concept to investigate, for two reasons. First, there is some doubt about the validity of many measures of self-esteem. The problem is that researchers tend to rely on self-reports from subjects, which obviously may be biased. For many people, the self-esteem they really feel and the level of self-esteem that they report on a questionnaire may be quite different (Wells & Marwell, 1976). Second, in probing self-esteem it is often quite difficult to separate cause from effect. A large volume of correlational data tells us that certain behavioral characteristics are associated with positive or negative self-esteem. However, it is hard to tell whether these behavioral tendencies are the cause or the effect of a particular level of self-esteem. This problem in pinpointing causation should be kept in mind as we look at the determinants and effects of self-esteem.

The Importance of Self-Esteem
The importance of adequate self-esteem can hardly be overestimated. To illustrate the potential influence of self-esteem, we will review some of the many problematic behavioral characteristics that often accompany low self-esteem.

People with unfavorable self-concepts tend to develop more emotional problems than people with high self-esteem (Fitts, 1972; Rosenberg, 1985; Wylie, 1979). Among other things, they are more likely to report that they are troubled by anxiety, depression, irritability, aggressiveness, feelings of resentment and alienation, unhappiness, insomnia, and psychosomatic symptoms.

There also is an association between low self-esteem and shyness (Cheek & Buss, 1981). People low in self-esteem often feel socially awkward, self-conscious, and especially vulnerable to rejection (Rosenberg, 1985). They have a particularly great need for acceptance from others, but they are often unable to take the initiative in seeking it out. Thus, they rarely join formal groups and do not participate very actively in social encounters. As a

result, they are also often lonely (Jones, Freeman, & Goswick, 1981).

People who have a negative self-concept are also less likely than most to authentically like other people (Baron, 1974; Wylie, 1979). They tend to look for flaws in others and "tear them down." Disparaging others allows them to feel a little better about themselves when they make their inevitable social comparisons. However, it also gives them a bias toward disliking others. They therefore tend to relate to others in negative ways—thereby courting rejection and compounding their problems.

Determinants of Self-Esteem
The foundations for high or low self-esteem appear to be laid very early in life. There is evidence that some children enter the first grade already possessing an unfavorable self-image (Wattenberg & Clifford, 1964).

Such an unfortunate circumstance so early in life would almost have to be attributable to parental feedback. Indeed, there is ample evidence that parents have a marked influence on their children's self-esteem. This became apparent in an extensive study of self-esteem in young boys conducted by Stanley Coopersmith (1967, 1975). He compared the child-rearing styles of parents of boys with high self-esteem and low self-esteem. Parents of boys with high self-esteem (1) expressed more affection to their children, (2) were more interested in their children's activities, (3) were more accepting of their children, (4) used sound, consistent disciplinary procedures, and (5) had relatively high self-esteem themselves (see Figure 5.5). In particular, it was parents' sincere interest in their children that seemed most strongly related to the development of a positive self-concept.

While parental feedback may be the crucial childhood determinant of self-esteem, it is clear that children (and adults) make their own judgments about themselves as well. Of course, an important basis for our self-judgments of success and failure is how well we "stack up" compared to others. Hence, schoolchildren whose academic performance is consistently and significantly lower than that

Figure 5.5. Self-esteem and parents' child-rearing techniques. Parents strongly influence youngsters' self-esteem. Coopersmith (1975) found interesting differences in child-rearing practices among the mothers of boys with high, medium, and low self-esteem.

of their peers are likely to have a negative self-image (Glasser, 1975). Yet seeing ourselves succeed in an endeavor as simple as learning to swim can lead to enhanced self-esteem (Koocher, 1971). Thus, our self-esteem may be augmented or diminished by our own observations of our successes and failures.

Of course, other people—especially parents and teachers—greatly influence our definitions of success and failure. Some overly demanding parents and teachers employ unrealistically high standards and are virtually never satisfied with children's performance. Sometimes these unrealistic standards are an unfortunate by-product of good intentions. The parents and teachers simply want to push the children to high levels of achievement. However, this push for excellence can backfire when it leads some children to apply unrealistically high standards to themselves. These unrealistic standards may cause the children to make largely unfavorable self-appraisals of their performance, thus lowering their self-esteem.

Perceptions of success and failure are also influenced by the nature of one's reference group. For example, one study found that preadolescents' self-esteem can be affected by the quality of competition they face in school (Marsh & Parker, 1984). In this study, children from schools in higher-socioeconomic-class areas with "high quality" competition were compared against children from schools in lower-class areas with "low quality" competition. In other words, children from a high-ability reference group were contrasted with children from a low-ability reference group. Interestingly, the children in the low-quality schools tended to display greater self-esteem than children of similar academic ability who were enrolled in the high-quality schools. The reason for this finding appears to be that students compare themselves to others in their own schools, not to a hypothetical reference group of, say, all bright students in the country (Rosenberg, 1979). Thus, it has been suggested that it may be beneficial to one's self-esteem to be "a large fish in a small pond" (Davis, 1966; Marsh & Parker, 1984). This finding that kids with similar talents vary in self-esteem,

depending on their reference group, demonstrates the immense importance of social comparison in the development of our self-concepts.

Public Selves

Whereas your self-concept involves how you see yourself, your public self involves how you want others to see you. A *public self* is an image or façade presented to others in social interactions. We rarely behave totally spontaneously. Let's face it: Most people see only an edited version of our behavior, which is usually calculated to present a certain image. This presentation of a public self may sound deceitful, but it is perfectly normal, and all of us do it (Alexander & Knight, 1971; Goffman, 1959, 1971). Actually, most of us are not limited to a single public self. Typically, we have a number of public selves that are tied to certain situations and certain people with whom we interact. For instance, you may have one public self for your parents and another for your siblings. You may have still others for your teachers, your same-sex friends, your other-sex friends, your spouse, your boss, your colleagues, your customers, and your neighbors.

Impression Management

Impression management refers to usually conscious efforts to present ourselves in socially desirable ways. Why do we engage in impression management? Basically, it's a matter of necessity. Erving Goffman (1959) argues that social norms virtually require us to engage in careful self-presentation. In other words, we are expected to portray ourselves in certain ways when interacting with our par-

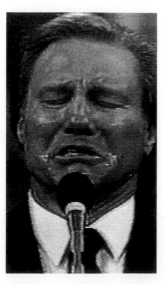

Popular TV evangelist Jimmy Swaggart was forced to resign his ministry in 1989 because of allegations of sexual misconduct. In his televised resignation speech (shown here), Swaggart said he was terribly ashamed and begged for forgiveness. Do you think Swaggart was truly remorseful, or were his tears part of a skillful impression-management effort?

RECOMMENDED READING

Why Am I Afraid to Tell You Who I Am?
by John Powell (Argus Communications, 1969)

This is a charming, easy to read, and nontechnical book that has proved very popular over the years. It focuses on self-awareness and interpersonal relationships. The central theme is: Why don't we open up to others instead of using roles as barriers to authentic communication? Powell points out that there are many reasons, which largely grow out of our insecurity. We are afraid that if we reveal our true selves, others might not like us. Powell conducts a fascinating review of a host of roles that people use as masks. He discusses "the body beautiful," "the braggart," "the clown," "the cynic," "the dreamer," "the flirt," "the hedonist," "the egghead," "the martyr," "the sex bomb," and "the predatory male," among others.

> None of us wants to be a fraud or to live a lie; none of us wants to be a sham, a phony, but the fears that we experience and the risks that honest self-communication would involve seem so intense to us that seeking refuge in our roles, masks, and games becomes an almost natural reflex action. [p. 13]

ents, peers, co-workers, and so forth. Goffman further points out that social norms also support others' acceptance of these efforts at impression management. Although people may be skeptical, they rarely challenge our self-presentations. Unless your self-presentation is clearly and extremely out of line with reality, people will keep their suspicions to themselves.

Impression management is necessary if we want people to like us, respect us, hire us, buy products from us, and so forth. This basic reality was illustrated in a study of behavior in job interviews (von Baeyer, Sherk, & Zanna, 1981). Female job applicants were led to believe that the man who would interview them held either very traditional, "chauvinistic" views of women or just the opposite. Applicants who expected a chauvinist presented themselves in a more "traditionally feminine" manner than subjects in the other condition. Their self-presentation efforts affected both their appearance (they wore more makeup) and their communication style (they talked less and gave more traditional answers to a question about marriage and children). The bottom line is this: Impression management is a normal feature of everyday social interactions. Although we certainly don't do it all the time, we probably do it a lot more than many of us realize.

Interestingly, our tendency to present ourselves in a favorable light is not just an act we put on to make ourselves look good to others. Studies have shown that subjects who publicly take credit for their successes and disavow responsibility for their failures actually perceive themselves this way (Greenberg, Pyszczynski, & Solomon, 1982; Reiss, Rosenfeld, Melburg, & Tedeschi, 1981). Hence, it is likely that we portray ourselves favorably not only for the purpose of impression management, but also because of our own needs to maintain self-esteem.

Self-Monitoring

According to Mark Snyder (1979, 1986), people vary in how aware they are of how they are being perceived by others. **Self-monitoring refers to the degree to which people attend to and control the impressions they make on others.** People who are high in self-monitoring are very sensitive to their impact on others. Those who are low in self-monitoring are less concerned about impression management and behave more spontaneously.

Compared to low self-monitors, high self-monitors display the following characteristics. They actively seek information about how they are expected to behave and try to tailor their actions accordingly (Snyder & Campbell, 1982). They are very sensitive to situational cues and relatively skilled at deciphering what others want to see. Moreover, they tend to act more in accordance with situational expectations than with their true feelings or attitudes (Zanna & Olson, 1982). Since high self-monitors control their emotions well and deliberately regulate nonverbal signals that are more spontaneous in others, they are relatively talented at self-presentation. In addition, they have been shown to be more accurate in judging other people's feelings (Geiser, Rarick, & Soldow, 1977). In contrast, low self-monitors are more likely to express their true beliefs, since they are more motivated to behave consistently with their internal feelings (McCann & Hancock, 1983).

Ingratiation

There are a number of strategies people use to make favorable impressions on others. We will look at a relatively common one—ingratiation—described by Edward Jones (1964; Jones & Pittman, 1982). **Ingratiation is a conscious and systematic effort to gain liking from another person.** Jones outlines four techniques that are commonly used in shrewd efforts to pursue others' affection.

Compliments. Good old-fashioned flattery is far from obsolete. The key is to make the compliments appear spontaneous and believable.

Conformity. Conforming to others' opinions tends to promote liking. As with compliments, it must be judiciously done in order to maintain credibility.

Mark Snyder

Favors. It doesn't hurt to do favors for those you want to like you. However, the favors shouldn't be too spectacular, or they may leave the target person with an irritating feeling of social indebtedness.

Presentation of a favorable self-image. If you expect to win another's liking, it certainly helps to portray yourself as likable. Depending on the situation, some false modesty may be useful.

In conclusion, however, we offer a word of caution. Most people are sensitive to sincerity in another person. And research indicates that when we doubt the sincerity of someone's flattering statements, we may like that person less (Kauffman & Steiner, 1968; Lowe & Goldstein, 1970).

Identity

A widely discussed concept related to self-perception is "ego identity." According to Erik Erikson (1968), a very influential psychoanalytic theorist (see Chapter 11), *identity* **refers to having a relatively clear and stable sense of who one is and what one stands for.** This means that although we have a multiplicity of thoughts and feelings and engage in many diverse activities, we remain "familiar" to ourselves in a fundamental way. In addition, our own sense of who we are must match pretty well with other people's views of us. This latter idea reflects Erikson's assertion that identity is rooted in both self and society.

According to James Marcia (1976), another authority on this subject, identity may be viewed from three perspectives. First, a sense of identity depends on your ability to integrate your own and your parents' expectations of you into a relatively congruent sense of self. Again, we see the emphasis on self and society (the latter, mediated through parental expectations). Although much of the process of identity formation is unconscious, the key point is that we create our identity. We do not just unquestioningly assume the roles and beliefs designated for us by our parents and society. Second, developing a

sense of identity gives individuals the ability to perceive themselves as ongoing entities—beings who have a past, present, and future, all of which feel connected. Finally, Marcia says that our unique identity will be reflected in our choices of careers, personal values, and beliefs.

Development of Identity

Obviously, your identity has its roots in childhood. Ideally, it continues to develop throughout adulthood. However, Erikson views adolescence as the most significant period for identity development, and research has supported his view. Studies show that identity concerns are particularly prominent among those in late adolescence (college-age individuals) (Archer, 1982; Marcia, 1980; Meilman, 1979). The fact that identity achievement is a concern during late adolescence probably reflects the conjunction of several developmental milestones during this time (Lloyd, 1985). That is, the achievement of a stable and familiar sense of self depends on physical and sexual maturity, competence in abstract thought, and a degree of emotional stability. In addition, identity achievement requires a certain amount of freedom from the constraining influences of parents and peers. As it happens, late adolescence is the period during which such conditions are first likely to exist.

Identity Statuses

According to Erikson, identity emerges out of crisis. Erikson uses the term "identity crisis" to refer to a normal developmental process. That is, for most people, an identity crisis is not a sudden or personally agonizing experience, but rather the gradual evolution of a sense of who one is (Coleman, 1978; Dusek & Flaherty, 1981).

The experience of an identity crisis usually results in a commitment to a specific career and personal ideology. According to Marcia, these two factors of *crisis* and *commitment* combine in various ways to produce four different identity statuses (see Figure 5.6). These are not stages that people pass through, but rather statuses that characterize a person's identity orientation at any particular time. That

		Crisis	
		Present	**Absent**
Commitment	**Present**	Identity achievement (successful achievement of a sense of identity)	Identity foreclosure (unquestioning adoption of parental or societal values)
	Absent	Identity moratorium (active struggling for a sense of identity)	Identity diffusion (absence of struggle for identity, with no obvious concern about this)

Figure 5.6. Marcia's four identity statuses. According to Marcia, the occurrence of an identity crisis and the development of personal commitments can combine into four possible identity statuses, as shown in this diagram.

is, it is possible that a person may never experience some of the statuses, including that of identity achievement. Let's examine the identity statuses described by Marcia.

IDENTITY FORECLOSURE. Some people do not exhibit a struggle for a unique, personal identity. Individuals in the foreclosure status have unquestioningly adopted the values and expectations of their parents rather than going through the process of developing their own beliefs and career choices. For example, an adolescent (or adult) who considers herself a Republican because her parents are Republicans would be classified in the foreclosure status. Although these individuals have made commitments—or, rather, adopted the commitments of others—without going through an identity crisis, they don't qualify as having achieved an independent identity.

MORATORIUM. Those individuals who are in the throes of struggling with a sense of identity are classified as being in the moratorium status. As part of the process of evolving a personally satisfying identity, adolescents are likely to engage in a variety of identity experiments, trying on different roles, beliefs, and behaviors. Most move on to the identity achievement status, but some drift into the status of identity diffusion.

IDENTITY DIFFUSION. Identity diffusion is characterized by a failure to achieve a stable and integrated sense of self. Individuals in this category experience considerable self-

doubt, but they don't appear to be concerned about doing anything to change their circumstances. Hence, they are different from those in the moratorium status, who are still struggling to resolve identity conflicts. People in the diffusion status are not presently experiencing an identity crisis; nor are they able to make commitments (see Figure 5.6). Identity diffusion is a serious problem for only a small number of adolescents, usually in cases where it is prolonged.

IDENTITY ACHIEVEMENT. The preferred identity status, of course, is that of identity achievement. In this case, a person has successfully passed through an identity crisis and is now able to make a commitment to a career objective and a set of personally meaningful beliefs.

To summarize, both identity achievement and identity foreclosure can be seen as resolutions of the identity crisis because a sense of commitment characterizes both statuses. Of course, in foreclosure, the commitment is not an independently developed one, as is desirable. Individuals in both the moratorium and diffusion statuses have only vague, or sometimes no, commitments. While those in identity diffusion have given up the search for identity, those in moratorium are still in pursuit of it.

To tie together our wide-ranging exploration of various aspects of self-perception (self-concept, self-esteem, public selves, and identity), we turn now to the issue of the "authentic" self.

The Search for the "Authentic" Self

Although we may be aware of the dubious accuracy of our self-presentations, Erving Goffman (1959) has argued that we sometimes come to believe our fabrications. In other words, if you present yourself in a certain way often enough, you may begin to actually see yourself in that way.

For example, if you are really quite conceited, but you incorporate false humility into many of your public selves, you might begin to view yourself as a humble person.

There is empirical evidence to support Goffman's assertion that our self-presentations may affect our actual self-concept (Jones, Rhodewalt, Berglas, & Skelton, 1981; Rhodewalt & Agustsdottir, 1986).

Although we all engage in some impression management, we vary greatly in how much we edit our behavior. As we have seen, some people are more concerned than others about portraying themselves appropriately for various audiences. Moreover, people differ in the degree of congruence or overlap among their various public selves (see Figure 5.7). Recall, here, Erikson's emphasis on the congruence between one's own sense of self and others' perceptions of us. In a similar fashion, Sidney Jourard (1971) maintained that constant misrepresentation for purposes of impression management may lead people to lose touch with their "authentic" selves. Jourard argued that this kind of confusion is very dangerous and that it may cause much psychological distress.

It is this identity-related confusion that leads many people to be concerned about "finding" themselves. This search for the real self became something of a fad in the 1970s, and many people used the concept to rationalize their "rudderless" lives. It has since become common to ridicule people who say they are "looking for the real me." However, this search for the authentic self may often be a genuine effort to come to grips with a self-concept and an identity that are in disarray.

Two practical points can be derived from this discussion. First, it is probably a good idea to avoid going overboard on self-presentation efforts. Taken to an excess, impression management may be harmful to one's sense of identity. Second, there is some merit in seeking knowledge about oneself. Accurate self-knowledge may facilitate development of a well-defined self-concept.

PERCEPTION OF OTHERS: SOURCES OF ERROR

We are now ready to shift gears and move from how we perceive ourselves to how we perceive others. Here, we are particularly interested in why we often see each other inaccurately. Mistakes in person perception appear to be quite common (Buckhout, 1980). We focus on this issue because accuracy in social perception can facilitate effective interpersonal relationships.

A multitude of factors contribute to inaccuracy in person perception. We have already mentioned the most obvious source of error—the pervasive tendency of people to create false impressions for each other. In this section, however, we will review some of our own perceptual tendencies that can lead us to form inaccurate impressions of others.

Stereotypes

Stereotypes **are widely held beliefs that people have certain characteristics simply because of their membership in a particular group.** For example, many people assume that Jews are shrewd and ambitious, that blacks have special athletic and musical ability, that Germans are methodical and efficient, that women are dependent and concerned

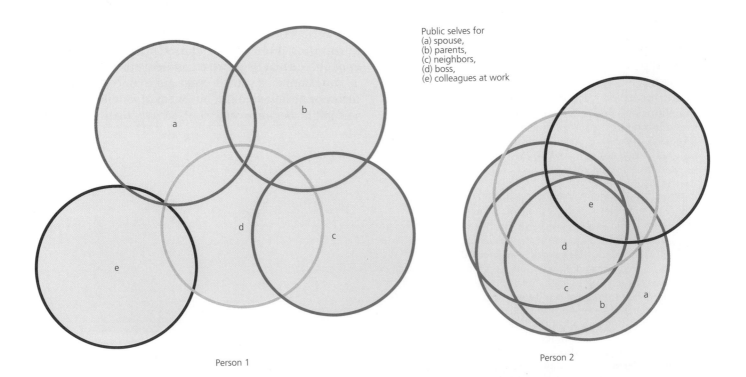

Public selves for
(a) spouse,
(b) parents,
(c) neighbors,
(d) boss,
(e) colleagues at work

Person 1

Person 2

about their appearance, and that men are unemotional and domineering.

The most prevalent kinds of sterotypes are those based on sex and race. Gender stereotypes, although in transition, remain pervasive. For example, in a study of gender stereotypes in 30 countries, males were typically characterized as adventurous, powerful, and independent, while females were characterized as sentimental, submissive, and superstitious (Williams & Best, 1982). Because of their great significance, we will focus on gender stereotypes in detail in our chapter on gender roles (Chapter 10). Ethnic and racial stereotypes have also undergone some changes but remain quite common (Dovidio & Gaertner, 1986; Jackman & Senter, 1981). We will look at the role of stereotyping in racial prejudice later in this chapter.

Although a kernel of truth may underlie some stereotypes, it should be readily apparent that not all Jews, Mexicans, lawyers, women, and so forth behave alike. There is enormous diversity in behavior within any group. Stereotyping involves a process of overgeneralizing that leads to a great deal of inaccuracy in social perception.

Stereotypes persist for several reasons. One has to do with the fact that stereotypes are functional. Because we are deluged with much more information than we can process, our tendency is to reduce complexity to simplicity. Unfortunately, there is a tradeoff for such sim-

plification, and that is inaccuracy, much of which we are unaware of.

A second reason that stereotypes persist is the selectivity in social perception discussed earlier. Because we tend to see what we expect to see, we twist and distort the behavior of others until it fits our stereotypes. For example, in one study, male students were asked to have a brief telephone conversation with a female student (Snyder, Tanke, & Berscheid, 1977). Half of the men were led to believe that the woman was physically attractive, while the other half were told that she was unattractive. In reality, there was no difference in the attractiveness of the female telephone partners. Prior to the actual telephone conversations, the men were asked to rate their partners-to-be on a variety of dimensions. Those men who believed that their partners were attractive judged that they would be poised, humorous, outgoing, and socially adept. Men with unattractive partners judged them to be awkward, serious, unsociable, and socially inept.

A third reason our stereotypes persist is that our beliefs about another person may actually elicit the expected behavior. For instance, in the study we were just describing (Snyder et al., 1977), after the men had completed their ratings of their partners, they spoke with the women for ten minutes on the telephone. Later, audio tapes of these conversations were analyzed by a judge who was "blind" to the nature of the study. Although there were no

Figure 5.7. Public selves and identity confusion. Person 1 has very divergent public selves with relatively little overlap among them. Person 1 is more likely to develop identity confusion than Person 2, whose public selves are more congruent with each other.

actual differences in attractiveness, independent judges rated the "attractive" women as more confident and animated than the "unattractive" women! In addition, the "attractive" women were judged to have displayed greater enjoyment of the conversations and greater liking for the men they spoke with than the "unattractive" women. These findings suggest that our expectations can actually alter others' behavior.

In conclusion, there are several ways in which we confirm and perpetuate our stereotypes. The unfortunate part of this process is that our stereotypes often lead to unfair treatment of others. In particular, women and certain ethnic groups are often victims of discrimination.

Excessive Focus on Physical Appearance

As just demonstrated, we often draw inferences about people's personality from their physical appearance. Yet there is little basis in fact for most of the conclusions we draw.

The most influential aspect of physical appearance is probably a person's overall attractiveness. There is plenty of evidence that physically attractive people are believed to possess many desirable personality traits. Thus, attractive people are more likely to be seen as interesting, poised, sociable, independent, exciting, and sexually warm than unattractive people (Brigham, 1980). We also believe that beautiful people are more intelligent (Clifford & Walster, 1973) and more pleasant (Adams & Huston, 1975) than others. Essays allegedly written by attractive women are rated higher than those supposedly written by unattractive women (Landy & Sigall, 1974). These findings suggest that we also see a link between good looks and competence. Furthermore, studies simulating jury trials have found that physically attractive defendants are better liked by the "juror" subjects and punished less severely than unattractive defendants (Cash, 1981; Efran, 1974).

On the other hand, if jurors believe that a defendant's attractiveness is a factor in a crime (a good-looking woman swindles a middle-aged bachelor out of money, for ex-

ample), they are not more lenient in sentencing (Sigall & Ostrove, 1975). Another drawback associated with attractiveness is the belief that attractive people are relatively vain and egotistical (Dermer & Thiel, 1975).

Nonetheless, our overall tendency is to see attractive people in a very favorable light (Dion, 1986; Patzer, 1985). As you may have inferred, all of these biases can also be reversed. Thus, we unjustifiably tend to see unattractive people in a very unfavorable light. We tend to perceive less attractive people as less sensitive, less interesting, less intelligent, less pleasant, and less competent than others. This prejudice against the plain and homely is clearly unfair.

Our social perceptions are also affected by other aspects of physical appearance. Tall people have been perceived, at various times, to be delicate, introverted, and intelligent, while short people have been viewed as passionate, petty, and negative (Roberts & Herman, 1986). Greater virility, confidence, maturity, and courage are attributed to bearded men rather than to clean-shaven men (Verinis & Roll, 1970). For women, the "dumb blond" stereotype is not entirely mythical. One study found that blond women were seen as more beautiful and feminine, but less intelligent and dependable, than other women (Lawson, 1971). We also judge people differently

when they wear eyeglasses. People with glasses are perceived as being relatively intelligent, industrious, and reliable (Argyle & McHenry, 1971; Boshier, 1975; Harris, Harris, & Bochner, 1982). On the other hand, they are not judged to be as attractive, outgoing, or athletic as those who don't wear glasses (Harris, Harris, & Bochner, 1982; Terry & Kroger, 1976).

Clothing is also a powerful determinant of our perceptions of others. For instance, one study found that female subjects were willing to draw conclusions about a person's shyness, snobbishness, and morality on the basis of the person's mode of dress (Gibbins, 1969). There is also evidence that people may be treated more honestly when they are well-dressed. In one clever study of this issue, a dime was left in an obvious place in a public phone booth (Bickman, 1971). When unsuspecting subjects pocketed the dime, an experimental confederate went into action. The confederate approached the subjects and asked whether they had found the dime that the confederate claimed to have forgotten in the booth. The confederate's mode of dress was varied to convey either high social status (suit and tie) or low status (work clothes, lunch pail). It was found that when the confederates were well-dressed, they got the dime back about twice as often as when they were more poorly dressed!

The Fundamental Attribution Error

As we saw in our earlier discussion of attribution, observers tend to attribute the behavior of others to dispositional tendencies while discounting the importance of situational factors. Although this tendency is not universal (Harvey, Town, & Yarkin, 1981), it is strong enough that Lee Ross (1977) called it the "fundamental attribution error." Thus, the *fundamental attribution error* **refers to observers' bias in favor of internal attributions in explaining others' behavior.** This bias leads us to leap to conclusions about others' personal qualities.

The fundamental attribution error is different from stereotyping or focusing on physical appearance in that

our inferences *are* based on actual behavior. However, those inferences may still be inaccurate. Because we underestimate the importance of situational factors, we often may attribute to people motives and traits that they do not actually have. For instance, imagine that you're at your bank and the person in line ahead of you flies into a rage over an error made in his account. You will probably infer that this person is temperamental or quarrelsome—and you *may* be right. However, this person may be an easygoing individual who is late for an appointment, has waited in line for 30 minutes, and just straightened out a similar error by the same bank last week. Thus, a person's behavior at a given time may or may not be reflective of his or her personality—but we tend to assume that it is.

Defensive Attribution

In attempting to explain the calamities and setbacks that befall other people, an observer's tendency to make internal attributions becomes even stronger than normal. Let's say that a friend is mugged and severely beaten. You may attribute the mugging to your friend's carelessness or stupidity ("He should have known better than to be in that neighborhood at that time") rather than to bad luck. Why? Because if you attribute your friend's misfortune to bad luck, you have to face the ugly reality that it could just as easily happen to you. To avoid disturbing thoughts such as these, we often attribute mishaps to victims' negligence (Thornton, 1984).

Defensive attribution **is a tendency to blame victims for their misfortune, so that we feel less likely to be victimized in a similar way.** Blaming victims for their calamities also helps us to maintain our belief that we live in a "just world" where people get what they deserve and deserve what they get (Lerner & Miller, 1976). Acknowledging to ourselves that the world is not just—that unfortunate events can happen as a result of chance factors—would mean having to admit the frightening possibility that the catastrophes that happen to others could also happen to

Television, movies, and magazines constantly brainwash us into placing great emphasis on physical beauty. Our culture emphasizes physical appearance to such an extent that it is a central factor in our perception and judgments of others.

us. By using defensive attribution, we can avoid such disturbing thoughts. Unfortunately, when we blame victims for their setbacks, we unfairly attribute undesirable traits to them, such as incompetence, foolishness, laziness, and greed. Thus, defensive attribution often leads us to derogate victims of misfortune.

Evidence suggests that this tendency to blame victims may be particularly strong when the victims are females, providing us with an example of gender stereotyping in action (Howard, 1984). For example, you often hear comments that rape victims "asked for it." Similarly, when a woman is killed by an abusive boyfriend or husband, people frequently blame the victim by remarking how stupid she was to stay with the man.

Implicit Theories of Personality

Implicit theories of personality **consist of our own personal assumptions about what personality traits go together.** For example, if you believe that warm people are usually cooperative, that uninhibited people are also irresponsible, or that socially smooth people are generally exploitive, you are using implicit theories of personality. Such theories are described as "implicit" because they aren't stated in formal terms and because most people are not conscious that they actually make such assumptions (Schneider, 1973).

While some implicit theories of personality are more commonly shared than others, such theories tend to be individualized. They are based on our unique experiences with people. Of interest to us is that these personal theories are typically based on very casual and inadequate observation. Hence, they frequently lead us to inaccurate conclusions about others' characteristics.

Illusory Correlation

Implicit theories of personality are created and supported by the illusory correlation effect (Hamilton & Gifford, 1976). **The** *illusory correlation effect* **occurs when**
we estimate that we have encountered more confirmations of an association between social traits than we have actually seen. Statements like "I've never met an honest lawyer" illustrate this effect. Thus we not only see what we expect to see, we also tend to overestimate how often we see it!

Memory distortions contribute to the illusory correlation effect. We may selectively recall facts that fit with our expectations about people. Evidence for such a tendency was found in a study by Cohen (1981). In this experiment, subjects watched a videotape of a woman who was described either as a waitress or as a librarian. The videotape showed the woman engaging in a variety of activities, including listening to classical music, drinking beer, and watching TV. When asked to recall what the woman did during the filmed sequence, subjects tended to remember activities consistent with their stereotypes of waitresses and librarians. For instance, subjects who thought the woman was a waitress tended to recall her beer drinking. In contrast, subjects who thought she was a librarian tended to recall her listening to classical music.

The Power of First Impressions

Although the evidence is not overwhelming, some studies suggest that first impressions have a powerful influence on our perceptions of others (Asch, 1946; Friedman, 1983; Hodges, 1974). **A** *primacy effect* **occurs when initial information carries more weight than subsequent information.** There are a couple of reasons why first impressions tend to be particularly potent. In part, this tendency is caused by the fact that people see what they expect to see. Once the initial impression creates a particular expectation, we may be equipped with a somewhat distorted perceptual set. Thereafter, we tend to see the person in light of our expectations. Moreover, our preference for consistency in social perception may lead us to discount later information that contradicts our initial impression. In either case, it is clear that primacy effects may undermine the accuracy of our impressions of other people.

Figure 5.8. Prejudice and discrimination. Prejudice and discrimination are highly correlated, but they don't necessarily go hand in hand. As the examples in the yellow cells show, there can be prejudice without discrimination and discrimination without prejudice.

Of course, it is possible to override a primacy effect. First impressions are not likely to last forever if most subsequent interactions contradict them. Interestingly, one study suggests that it may be easier to override positive first impressions than negative ones (Rothbart & Park, 1986). When the initial impression is negative, it may be especially difficult to change. Thus, "getting off on the wrong foot" may be particularly damaging to a person.

False Consensus and False Uniqueness

Often, we tend to assume that other people think and act in just the way we do (Ross, Greene, & House, 1977). **The *false consensus effect* involves our tendency to overestimate the degree to which others think and behave as we do.** This bias provides yet another source of error in social perception (Mullen et al., 1985). For example, let's say you know a man who "cheats" on his wife every chance he gets. When this person spots friends dining out with members of the other sex who are not their spouses, he is likely to assume that they, too, are engaging in marital infidelity, even though their socializing is probably entirely innocent. Essentially, he attributes his own behavioral tendencies to others.

Although quite common, this false-consensus assumption is not applied to all of our qualities. For instance, while we tend to overestimate the extent to which others share our opinions, we underestimate the likelihood that others possess talents or have abilities similar to ours (Marks, 1984). Thus, the *false uniqueness effect* **involves our tendency to underestimate the likelihood that others possess our admirable qualities.**

In summary, our perceptions of others are very subjective. Many of the tendencies that we exhibit in person perception contribute to inaccurate views of the people around us. Much of the time, these inaccurate perceptions are probably harmless. However, there clearly are occasions when these inaccuracies interfere with rewarding social relations. This is certainly true in the case of racial prejudice, which we consider next.

PERSON PERCEPTION AND RACIAL PREJUDICE

To further illustrate how inaccuracy in social perception develops and to show how it may affect our interpersonal behavior, let's briefly consider the social problem of racial and ethnic prejudice. Our main purpose is to show how distortions in the process of person perception contribute to prejudice.

First, we need to clarify a couple of terms that are frequently confused. *Prejudice* **is a negative attitude toward members of a group.** Whereas prejudice is a negative cognitive set, *discrimination* **involves behaving differently, usually unfairly, toward the members of a group.** Prejudice and discrimination do tend to go together, but there isn't a necessary correspondence between the two (see Figure 5.8). For example, a restaurant owner might be prejudiced against Chicanos and yet treat them like anyone else because he needs their business. This is an example of prejudice without discrimination. Although it is probably less common, discrimination without prejudice may also occur. For example, an executive who has favorable attitudes toward blacks may not hire them because his boss would be upset.

Inaccuracy in social perception is both a cause and an effect of racial prejudice. At least five of the sources of inaccuracy that we discussed in the previous section contribute to ethnic prejudice in important ways.

Stereotypes. Perhaps no factor plays a larger role in prejudice than stereotyping. Many people subscribe to derogatory stereotypes of various ethnic groups. Studies suggest that racial stereotypes have declined over the last 50 years, but they're not a thing of the past (Dovidio & Gaertner, 1986). Unfortunately, the *selectivity* of person perception makes it likely that people will see what they expect to see when they actually come into contact with minorities they view with prejudice. For example, Duncan (1976) had white subjects watch and evaluate an interaction on a TV monitor that was supposedly live (actually it was a video-

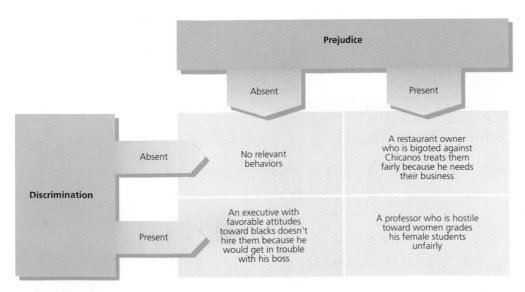

tape). Subjects saw two people get into an argument, during which one of them gave the other a slight shove. The race of the person giving the shove was varied across groups of subjects. The shove was coded as "violent behavior" by 73% of the white subjects when the actor was black, but by only 13% of the subjects when the actor was white. As we have noted before, our perceptions are highly subjective. Because of stereotypes, even "violence" may lie in the eye of the beholder.

Fundamental attribution error. Recall that the fundamental attribution error is a bias toward explaining events by pointing to the personal characteristics of the actors as causes (internal attributions). Pettigrew (1979) maintains that we are particularly prone to this error when evaluating targets of prejudice. Thus, when people take note of ethnic neighborhoods dominated by crime and poverty, they tend to blame these problems on the personal qualities of the residents. Other explanations emphasizing situational factors (job discrimination, poor police service, and so on) are downplayed or ignored. The old saying "They should be able to pull themselves up by their bootstraps" is a blanket dismissal of how situational factors may make it especially difficult for minorities to achieve upward mobility.

Defensive attribution. We have already seen that people sometimes unfairly blame victims of adversity to reassure themselves that they are unlikely to experience a similar fate. There is evidence that many of us engage in such defensive attribution when we encounter people who have been victimized by prejudice and discrimination. For example, it has been suggested that many Germans who lived through the Nazi persecutions of Jews somehow convinced themselves that those sent to concentration camps deserved their fate (Hallie, 1971).

Illusory correlation. The illusory correlation effect leads us to overestimate how often we confirm our expectations that certain people exhibit certain traits. For purposes of illustration, let's create an imaginary group of people called the Nerdians. Let us further assume that you have

One aspect of social perception that contributes to prejudice is the fundamental attribution error. For example, people tend to attribute the poor quality of life in impoverished areas to the characteristics of the residents, rather than to situational factors, such as job discrimination or poor public services.

always been led to believe that all Nerdians are loud-mouths. Over a period of years, you may work with ten Nerdians, only two of whom are actually loudmouths. However, evidence on illusory correlation suggests that there is an excellent chance that you will take note of those two and forget about the other eight. Thus, in spite of contradictory evidence, you may believe that your personal experience confirms what you were always told about Nerdians.

First impressions. Another problem emerges because of the power of first impressions. The problem is that many people's first impressions of minorities come not from actual interaction, but from disparaging remarks made by parents, neighbors, and others. Thus, many impressionable children develop unfavorable views of minority groups before they have any opportunity for rewarding interactions with members of these groups. Although these negative first impressions may eventually be overridden by contradictory experiences, primacy effects probably contribute to racial prejudice.

SUMMARY

Social perception involves the creation of images of ourselves and others. Patterns of attribution contribute to

these images, and these patterns can be slanted in a number of ways. Generally, we tend to attribute behavior either to internal dispositions or to external, situational factors. Stability is another key dimension of attributions. Observers tend to favor internal attributions in explaining an actor's behavior, while the actor is more likely to make an external attribution. These trends depend to some extent on whether attributions are being made about success or about failure. We usually try to maintain consistency among our beliefs because cognitive dissonance is unpleasant. Also, social perception is highly selective. Many lines of evidence demonstrate that we tend to see what we expect to see in our interpersonal interactions.

The self-concept is a set of ideas about what you are like. It is both descriptive and prescriptive. It is shaped by your own observations, which often involve social comparisons with others—usually similar others who make up your reference group. Of course, your observations may be distorted. Feedback from others is also influential in shaping your self-concept, but you may distort it as well. Finally, cultural guidelines can affect how we see ourselves.

Self-esteem is your global evaluation of your worth. Low self-esteem tends to be associated with emotional problems, difficulties in social interactions, and negative feelings toward others. Parents are especially important in determining our self-esteem. They provide direct feedback and influence the standards that we use to evaluate ourselves.

Public selves are the various images that we portray to others. A certain amount of impression management is expected, but some people edit their behavior more than others. People who are high in self-monitoring are especially sensitive to the impressions they make on others. They are very shrewd in adjusting their behavior to fit the situation.

Identity refers to having a relatively clear and stable sense of who you are and what you stand for. According to Erik Erikson, developing a sense of identity is a key challenge of adolescence. James Marcia has proposed that identity outcomes include foreclosure, moratorium, diffusion, and achievement. A number of theorists emphasize the importance of congruence between one's public selves and one's self-concept and sense of identity.

Many aspects of person perception lead us to see others inaccurately. We may be swayed by stereotypes or by excessive attention to physical attractiveness or other features of appearance. Misperceptions are also fostered by the fundamental attribution error and defensive attribution. Our implicit theories of personality may have little merit, but they are supported by the illusory correlation effect. Inaccuracy also occurs because first impressions can be difficult to overcome. Finally, the false consensus and false uniqueness effects can promote erroneous beliefs about others.

Racial prejudice provides a particularly unfortunate example of how we often view others inaccurately. Most of the usual sources of error in person perception contribute to prejudicial beliefs about minority groups.

Because of the enormous importance of self-esteem, the upcoming Application will discuss how to build a more positive self-concept. It will outline seven steps for promoting high self-esteem.

Building Self-Esteem

Answer the following yes or no.

☐ **1.** I am very sensitive to criticism.

☐ **2.** I tend to have a hard time accepting praise or flattery.

☐ **3.** I have very little confidence in my abilities.

☐ **4.** I often feel awkward in social situations and just don't know how to take charge.

☐ **5.** I tend to be highly critical of other people.

If you answered yes to most of the questions above, you may be suffering from what Alfred Adler called an *inferiority complex* (see Chapter 2). This syndrome, which is dominated by low self-esteem, is fairly common. It is also quite unfortunate. People with very low self-esteem tend to develop more emotional problems than others, set low goals for themselves, become socially invisible, conform against their better judgment, and court rejection by putting down others.

As you can see, self-esteem is a very important component of your self-concept. It appears that an overly negative self-image can contribute to many kinds of behavioral problems. An overly positive image can also cause problems, but people characterized by excessive conceit do not suffer in the same way that self-critical people do.

In this Application, we will describe seven guidelines for building higher self-esteem. These guidelines are based on our own distillation of the advice of many

"I don't suppose it's much compared with other inferiority complexes"

© 1976 PUNCH/ROTHCO.

theorists, including Rogers (1977), Ellis (1984), Jourard (Jourard & Landsman, 1980), Hamachek (1987), Mahoney (1979), and Zimbardo (1977).

1. Recognize That You Control Your Self-Image

The first thing you must do is recognize that *you* ultimately control how you see yourself. You *do* have the power to change your self-image. True, we have discussed at length how feedback from others influences your self-concept. Yes, social comparison theory suggests that we need such feedback and that it would be unwise to ignore it completely. However, the final choice about whether to accept or reject such feedback rests with you. Your self-image resides in your mind and is a product of your thinking. Although others may influence your self-concept, you are the final authority.

2. Don't Let Others Set Your Standards

A common trap that many of us fall into involves letting others set the standards by which we evaluate ourselves. People around us are constantly telling us that we should do this or we ought to do that. Thus, we hear that we "should study computer science" or "ought to lose weight" or "must move to a better neighborhood." Most of these people are well-intentioned, and many of them may have good ideas. Still, as you will recall from our discussion of identity, it is important that you make your *own* decisions about what you will do and what you will believe in. For example, consider a business executive in his early forties who sees himself in a negative light because he has not climbed very high in the corporate hierarchy. The crucial question is: Did he ever *really* want to make that arduous climb? It could be that he has misgivings about the value of such an effort. Perhaps he has gone through life thinking he should pursue that kind of success only because that standard was imposed on him by society. You should think about the source of and basis for your personal standards. Do they really represent goals and ideals that you value? Or do they represent goals and ideals you have passively accepted from others without thinking?

3. Recognize Unrealistic Goals

Even if you truly value certain ideals and sincerely want to achieve certain goals, another question remains. Are your goals realistic? Many people get in the habit of demanding too much of themselves. They always want to perform at their best, which is obviously impossible. For instance, you may have a burning desire to achieve international acclaim as an actress. However, the odds against such an achievement are enormous. It is important to recognize this reality so that you do not condemn yourself for failure. Some overly demanding people pervert the social comparison process by always comparing themselves against the *best* rather than against similar others. They assess their looks by comparing themselves with famous models, and they judge their finances by comparing themselves with the wealthiest people they know. Such comparisons are unrealistic and almost inevitably undermine self-esteem.

4. Modify Negative Self-Talk

The way you analyze your life influences how you see yourself (and vice versa). People who are low in self-esteem tend to engage in various counterproductive modes of thinking. For example, when they succeed, they may attribute their success to good luck, and when they fail, they may blame themselves. Quite to the contrary, you should take credit for your successes and consider the possibility that your failures may not be your fault. As discussed in Chapter 4, Albert Ellis has pointed out that we often think irrationally and draw unwarranted negative conclusions about ourselves. For example, if you apply for a job and are rejected, you might think, "They didn't hire me. I must be a worthless, inept person." The conclusion that you are a "worthless person" does *not* follow logically from the fact that you were not hired. Such irrational thinking and negative self-talk breed poor self-esteem. It is important to recognize the irrationality of negative self-talk and bring it to a halt.

5. Emphasize Your Strengths

This advice may seem trite, but it has some merit. People with low self-esteem often derive little satisfaction from their accomplishments and virtues. They dismiss compliments as foolish, unwarranted, or insincere. They pay little heed to their good qualities while talking constantly about their defeats and frailties. The fact is that we all have our strengths and weaknesses. You should accept those personal shortcomings that you are powerless to change and work on those that are changeable, without becoming obsessed about it. At the same time, you should take stock of your strengths and learn to appreciate them.

6. Work to Improve Yourself

As just mentioned, some personal shortcomings *can* be overcome. Although it is

---

RECOMMENDED READING

Like Yourself—and Others Will Too

by Abraham J. Twerski (Prentice-Hall, 1978)

We have emphasized repeatedly in this chapter that a negative self-concept can be a personal tragedy. Twerski explores this problem in much greater depth. Using numerous case studies, he shows how low self-esteem causes or contributes to a vast array of personal problems. Half the battle in reversing a negative self-image consists of recognizing the sources of negativity. Twerski's book can be very useful in helping you pinpoint these sources in your life.

Many faulty behavior patterns are the outcome of a negative self-image. The cases to be described are actual, true-life stories of persons treated or observed in the practice of psychiatry. These cases are only examples of maladaptation and by no means exhaust the legion of possible complications consequent to the negative self-image. Some of the cases cited depict a very intense behavioral consequence of the negative self-image. It is important to realize that, although very intense reactions are by no means infrequent, milder forms of such reactions are very common. To whatever extent a person reacts to a distorted self-concept, to that same extent he suffers the consequences of a maladaptation. [pp. 7–8]

Figure 5.9. The vicious circle of low self-esteem and rejection. A negative self-image can make expectations of rejection a self-fulfilling prophecy, because people with low self-esteem tend to approach others in negative, hurtful ways. Real or imagined rejections lower self-esteem still further, creating a vicious circle.

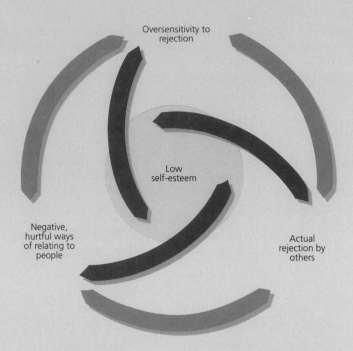

Oversensitivity to rejection

Low self-esteem

Negative, hurtful ways of relating to people

Actual rejection by others

important to reassess your goals and discard those that are unrealistic, this advice is not intended to provide a convenient rationalization for complacency. There is much to be said for setting out to conquer personal problems. In a sense, this entire text is based on a firm belief in the value of self-control and self-improvement. There is ample evidence that efforts at self-improvement can pay off by boosting self-esteem.

7. Approach Others with a Positive Outlook

People who are low in self-esteem often try to cut others down to their (subjective) size through constant criticism. As you can readily imagine, this faultfinding and generally negative approach to interpersonal transactions does not go over well with other people. Instead, it leads to tension, antagonism, and rejection. This rejection lowers self-esteem still further (see Figure 5.9). Efforts to build self-esteem can be facilitated by recognizing and reversing this self-defeating tendency. Approaching people with a positive, supportive outlook will promote rewarding interactions and help you earn their acceptance. There is probably nothing that enhances self-esteem more than acceptance and genuine affection from others.

KEY LEARNING OBJECTIVES

1. Describe the attribution process, including the key dimensions of attributions.

2. Describe how actors and observers are different in their attributional biases.

3. Use cognitive dissonance to explain why we strive for consistency in our beliefs.

4. Explain what is involved in selectivity in social perception.

5. Define self-concept and explain its prescriptive nature.

6. Summarize how various factors influence one's self-concept.

7. Define self-esteem and summarize evidence on the correlates of low self-esteem.

8. Discuss the determinants of self-esteem.

9. Explain public selves and why we engage in impression management.

10. Summarize how people who are high in self-monitoring tend to behave.

11. Describe ingratiation techniques.

12. Define identity and explain why it becomes a concern during late adolescence.

13. Describe Marcia's four identity statuses.

14. Explain why some people are involved in a search for their authentic self.

15. Explain how stereotypes contribute to inaccuracy in person perception.

16. Discuss how aspects of physical appearance influence our perception of others.

17. Describe the fundamental attribution error and defensive attribution.

18. Explain implicit theories of personality and illusory correlation.

19. Explain the primacy, false consensus, and false uniqueness effects.

20. List five sources of error in person perception that commonly contribute to racial prejudice.

21. Briefly describe seven steps for building higher self-esteem.

KEY TERMS

Attributions
Cognitive dissonance
Defensive attribution
Discrimination
External attributions
False consensus effect
False uniqueness effect
Fundamental attribution error
Identity
Illusory correlation effect
Implicit theories of personality
Impression management
Ingratiation

Internal attributions
Prejudice
Primacy effect
Public self
Reference group
Self-concept
Self-esteem
Self-monitoring
Self-perception theory
Social comparison theory
Stereotypes

KEY PEOPLE

Daryl Bem
Erik Erikson
Leon Festinger
Erving Goffman
Sidney Jourard
James Marcia
Mark Snyder

QUESTIONNAIRE
Self-Monitoring Scale

INSTRUCTIONS

The statements below concern your personal reactions to a number of situations. No two statements are exactly alike, so consider each statement carefully before answering. If a statement is true or mostly true as applied to you, mark T as your answer. If a statement is false or not usually true as applied to you, mark F as your answer. It is important that you answer as frankly and as honestly as you can. Record your responses in the spaces provided on the left.

THE SCALE

_____ 1. I find it hard to imitate the behavior of other people.

_____ 2. My behavior is usually an expression of my true inner feelings, attitudes, and beliefs.

_____ 3. At parties and social gatherings, I do not attempt to do or say things that others will like.

_____ 4. I can only argue for ideas I already believe.

_____ 5. I can make impromptu speeches even on topics about which I have almost no information.

_____ 6. I guess I put on a show to impress or entertain people.

_____ 7. When I am uncertain how to act in a social situation, I look to the behavior of others for cues.

_____ 8. I would probably make a good actor.

_____ 9. I rarely need the advice of my friends to choose movies, books, or music.

_____ 10. I sometimes appear to others to be experiencing deeper emotions than I actually am.

_____ 11. I laugh more when I watch a comedy with others than when alone.

_____ 12. In a group of people I am rarely the center of attention.

_____ 13. In different situations and with different people, I often act like very different persons.

_____ 14. I am not particularly good at making other people like me.

_____ 15. Even if I am not enjoying myself, I often pretend to be having a good time.

_____ 16. I'm not always the person I appear to be.

_____ 17. I would not change my opinions (or the way I do things) in order to please someone else or win their favor.

_____ 18. I have considered being an entertainer.

_____ 19. In order to get along and be liked, I tend to be what people expect me to be rather than anything else.

_____ 20. I have never been good at games like charades or improvisational acting.

_____ 21. I have trouble changing my behavior to suit different people and different situations.

_____ 22. At a party, I let others keep the jokes and stories going.

_____ 23. I feel a bit awkward in company and do not show up quite so well as I should.

_____ 24. I can look anyone in the eye and tell a lie with a straight face (if for a right end).

_____ 25. I may deceive people by being friendly when I really dislike them.

SCORING THE SCALE

The scoring key is reproduced below. You should circle your response of true or false each time it corresponds to the keyed response below. Add up the number of responses you circle. This total is your score on the Self-Monitoring Scale. Record your score below.

1. False	**6.** True	**11.** True	**16.** True	**21.** False
2. False	**7.** True	**12.** False	**17.** False	**22.** False
3. False	**8.** True	**13.** True	**18.** True	**23.** False
4. False	**9.** False	**14.** False	**19.** True	**24.** True
5. True	**10.** True	**15.** True	**20.** False	**25.** True

MY SCORE _____

WHAT THE SCALE MEASURES

Developed by Mark Snyder (1974), the Self-Monitoring (SM) Scale measures the extent to which you consciously employ impression management strategies in social interactions. Basically, the scale assesses the degree to which you manipulate the nonverbal signals that you send to others and the degree to which you adjust your behavior to situational demands. As we discussed, some people work harder at managing their public images than do others.

In his original study, Snyder (1974) reported very reasonable test-retest reliability (.83 for one month) and, for an initial study, provided ample evidence regarding the scale's validity. In assessing the validity of the scale, he found that in comparison to low SM subjects, high SM subjects were rated by peers as being better at emotional self-control and better at figuring out how to behave appropriately in new social situations. Furthermore, Snyder found that stage actors tended to score higher on the scale than undergraduates, as one would expect. Additionally, Ickes and Barnes (1977) summarize evidence that high SM people are (1) very sensitive to situational cues, (2) particularly skilled at detecting deception on the part of others, and (3) especially insightful about how to influence the emotions of others.

INTERPRETING YOUR SCORE

Our norms are based on guidelines provided by Ickes and Barnes (1977). The divisions are based on data from 207 undergraduate subjects.

NORMS

High score:	15–22
Intermediate score:	9–14
Low score:	0–8

How Does Your Self-Concept Compare to Your Self-Ideal?

Below you will find a list of 15 traits, each portrayed on a 9-point continuum. Mark with an X where you think you fall on each trait. Try to be candid and accurate; these marks will collectively describe a portion of your self-concept. When you are finished, go back and circle where you *wish* you could be on each dimension. These marks describe your self-ideal. Finally, in the spaces on the right, indicate the size of the discrepancy between self-concept and self-ideal for each trait.

1. Decisive   Indecisive ———
 9 8 7 6 5 4 3 2 1

2. Anxious   Relaxed ———
 9 8 7 6 5 4 3 2 1

3. Easily influenced   Independent thinker ———
 9 8 7 6 5 4 3 2 1

4. Very intelligent   Less intelligent ———
 9 8 7 6 5 4 3 2 1

5. In good physical shape   In poor physical shape ———
 9 8 7 6 5 4 3 2 1

6. Undependable   Dependable ———
 9 8 7 6 5 4 3 2 1

7. Deceitful   Honest ———
 9 8 7 6 5 4 3 2 1

8 A leader   A follower ———
 9 8 7 6 5 4 3 2 1

9. Unambitious   Ambitious ———
 9 8 7 6 5 4 3 2 1

10. Self-confident   Insecure ———
 9 8 7 6 5 4 3 2 1

11. Conservative   Adventurous ———
 9 8 7 6 5 4 3 2 1

12. Extraverted   Introverted ———
 9 8 7 6 5 4 3 2 1

13. Physically attractive   Physically unattractive ———
 9 8 7 6 5 4 3 2 1

14. Lazy   Hardworking ———
 9 8 7 6 5 4 3 2 1

15. Funny   Little sense of humor ———
 9 8 7 6 5 4 3 2 1

Overall, how would you describe the discrepancy between your self-concept and your self-ideal (large, moderate, small, large on a few dimensions)?

How do sizable gaps on any of the traits affect your self-esteem?

Do you feel that any of the gaps exist because you have had others' ideals imposed on you or because you have thoughtlessly accepted others' ideals?

6

Interpersonal Communi-

cation

Have you ever raced home, eager to tell someone about something that happened that day, only to find no one at home to listen to your story? It may not have been a spectacular or earthshaking tale; maybe you simply picked up an intriguing bit of gossip or met someone who was a little unusual. Still, it was something you wanted to share with others. Chances are you rehearsed your fascinating account all the way home. On finding no receptive ears for your story, do you remember how frustrated you felt? As this experience illustrates, people have a powerful need to share information about interesting or important events with others and, also, to hear their reactions.

Interpersonal communication is an integral part of human experience. Moreover, our interpersonal skills are highly relevant to adjustment, because they can be critical to our happiness and success in life. The purpose of this chapter is to help you become more aware of the bases for both effective and ineffective communication.

THE PROCESS OF INTERPERSONAL COMMUNICATION

Communication can be defined as the process of sending and receiving messages that have meaning. Our personal thoughts have meaning, of course, but when we "talk to ourselves," we are engaging in *intrapersonal* communication. In this chapter, we will focus on *interpersonal* communication—the face-to-face transmission of meaning between two or more people. We will define **interpersonal communication as an interactional process whereby one person sends a message to another.**

It is important to note several points about this definition. First, for a communication to qualify as *interpersonal*, at least two people must be involved. Second, interpersonal communication is a *process*. By this, we simply mean that it is usually composed of a series of actions: Mary talks/John listens, John responds/Mary

listens, and so on. Third, this process is *interactional*. Communication is generally not a one-way street: Both participants send as well as receive information when they're interacting. An important implication of this fact is that we need to pay attention to *both* our speaking *and* our listening skills if we want to improve the effectiveness of our communication.

Components of the Communication Process

To help you better understand the process of interpersonal communication, let's take a look at its essential components. As can be seen in Figure 6.1, David Berlo (1960) has divided the interpersonal communication process into four basic components: (1) the source of the message, (2) the message itself, (3) the channel in which the message is sent, and (4) the receiver of the message.

The *source* is the person who initiates, or sends, the message. In a typical two-way conversation, both people serve as sources (as well as receivers) of messages. Keep in mind that each source person brings a unique set of expectations and understandings to each communication situation. We will return to this important point shortly.

The *message* is the information or meaning that is transmitted from one person to another. The message is the content of the communication—that is, the ideas and feelings we convey to another person. Language is our primary means of sending messages, but we also communicate to others nonverbally. Nonverbal communication includes the facial expressions, gestures, and vocal inflections we use to supplement (and sometimes entirely change) the meaning of our verbal messages. For example, when you say, "Thanks a lot," your nonverbal communication can convey either sincere gratitude or sarcasm.

The *channel* refers to the medium through which the message reaches the receiver. We receive verbal messages, of course, by hearing them. We hear both the literal content of messages and the vocal inflections people use

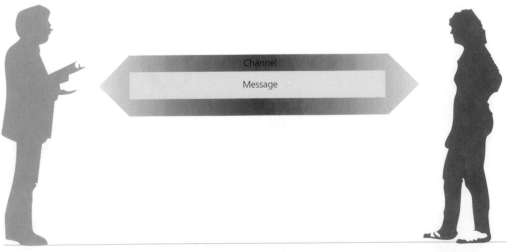

Source

Receiver

to communicate. Sometimes sound Is the only channel available for receiving information—for example, when you talk on the telephone. More often, however, we receive information from multiple channels simultaneously. We not only hear what people tell us, we also see the expressions on their faces, observe their gestures, experience eye contact with them, and, sometimes, feel their physical touch. The messages in the various channels may be consistent or inconsistent with each other, making our interpretation of them more or less difficult.

The *receiver* **is the person to whom the message is targeted.** As noted before, in a two-person interaction, each participant serves as both a source and a receiver. Each source/receiver has a unique history and set of beliefs and expectations that influence the communication process. Communication is more effective (and less problematic) when people have similar frames of reference (Clark, 1985).

Importance of Communication

Before we get into the details of interpersonal communication, let's take a moment to emphasize its significance. Communication with others—friends, lovers, parents, spouses, children, employers, employees—is such an essential and commonplace aspect of our lives that it's hard to overstate the importance of being able to communicate effectively. Moreover, many of life's satisfactions (and frustrations and heartaches, as well) hinge on our ability to communicate effectively with others. For example, research has shown that married couples who perceive themselves as effective communicators are more likely to be happily, rather than unhappily, married (Yelsma, 1984). Conversely, poor communication is reported to be the most common problem among couples who seek marriage counseling (Beck & Jones, 1973).

Most of our coverage in this chapter will be organized around the two basic channels for communication: (1) the verbal (linguistic) channel and (2) the nonverbal channel. We'll tackle the nonverbal channel first.

Figure 6.1. A model of interpersonal communication.
According to David Berlo (1960), interpersonal communication involves four elements: the source, the receiver, the message, and the channel through which the message is transmitted. In conversations, both participants function as source and receiver.

NONVERBAL COMMUNICATION

You're standing at the bar in your favorite lounge, gazing across a dark, smoky room filled with people drinking, dancing, and talking. You motion to thc bartender that you'd like another drink. Your companion comments on the loudness of the music, and you nod your head in agreement. You spot an attractive stranger across the bar; your eyes meet for a moment and you smile. In a matter of seconds, you have sent three messages without uttering a syllable. To put it another way, you have just sent three nonverbal messages.

Nonverbal communication **is the transmission of meaning from one person to another through means or symbols other than words.** Communication at the nonverbal level takes place through a variety of behaviors: facial expression, eye contact, body posture and movement, gestures, physical touch, interpersonal distance, and tone of voice. We will discuss each of these in this section.

Some experts maintain that most of the message transmissions in face-to-face interactions actually occur at the nonverbal level (Mehrabian, 1971; Philpott, 1983)! Clearly, a great deal of information is exchanged through nonverbal channels—perhaps more than most people realize. Thus, to enhance our effectiveness in communication, it's helpful to become more knowledgeable about the nature of nonverbal cues. Let's begin by examining some general principles of nonverbal communication. After reviewing these principles, we'll look at specific aspects of nonverbal communication, such as facial expression, eye contact, and so on.

General Principles

1. *Nonverbal communication is multichanneled.* Nonverbal communication typically involves simultaneous messages sent through a number of subchannels. For instance, information may be transmitted through gestures, facial expressions, eye contact, and vocal tone at the same time. In contrast, verbal communication is limited to a single

channel: speech. If you have ever tried to follow two people speaking at once, you are aware of how difficult it is to process multiple inputs of information. The multichanneled nature of nonverbal communication is one of the reasons many nonverbal transmissions sail by the receiver unnoticed.

2. *Nonverbal communication is relatively spontaneous.* In comparison with verbal communication, nonverbal transmissions tend to be more spontaneous (Verderber & Verderber, 1989). In other words, we often send nonverbal messages without thinking about them. Although it is certainly not unheard of for people to speak thoughtlessly, speech is usually under more conscious control than most nonverbal communication. It is this less guarded quality of nonverbal communication that often makes it a more accurate index of a person's true feelings.

3. *Nonverbal communication is relatively ambiguous.* Nonverbal messages tend to be less clear than spoken words. Although there is room for considerable ambiguity in speech, there usually is more consensus about the meaning of words than the meaning of nonverbal signs. A shrug or a raised eyebrow can mean different things to different people. Moreover, it is always difficult to know whether nonverbal messages are being sent intentionally. Although some popular books on body language imply otherwise, very few nonverbal signals carry universally accepted meanings (Swenson, 1973). Hence, they should be interpreted with caution.

4. *Nonverbal communication may contradict verbal messages.* We have all seen people who proclaim "I'm not angry" while their bodies clearly convey that they are positively furious. Thus, it is well known that verbal and nonverbal messages may be quite inconsistent. When confronted with such inconsistency, which message should you believe? Well, there are no absolute rules, but you're probably better off betting on the nonverbal signs because of their greater spontaneity. Indeed, there is evidence that deception by someone instructed to tell a lie is most readily detected in the nonverbal channel of communication (DePaulo, Lanier, & Davis, 1983).

5. *Nonverbal communication is very culture-bound.* Like language, nonverbal signals are different in different cultures (Hall, 1959). For instance, people of Northern European heritage tend to engage in less physical contact and keep a greater distance between themselves than people of Latin or Middle Eastern heritage. Thus, an Englishman might be quite upset when a well-meaning Brazilian "trespasses" on his personal space. Sometimes cultural differences can be quite dramatic. For example, in Tibet people greet their friends by sticking out their tongues (Ekman, 1975)!

Nonverbal signals can provide information about many things in interpersonal interactions. As we discuss specific forms of nonverbal communication, we will place special emphasis on information regarding social affiliation (or liking for another) and information about the status of the people who are interacting.

Facial Expression

Facial expressions convey emotions more than they convey anything else. In an extensive research program, Paul Ekman and his colleagues have identified seven primary emotions that have distinctive facial expressions. These seven emotions are anger, contempt, disgust, fear, happiness, sadness, and surprise (Ekman & Friesen, 1986). The facial expressions conveying these seven emotions appear to be universal. That is, individuals from a variety of cultures are able to identify them correctly (Ekman & Friesen, 1984, 1986). Typically, in such studies, subjects from a variety of cultures (Western and non-Western) are shown photographs depicting different emotions and are asked to match the photographs with the appropriate emotions. Some representative results from this research are depicted in Figure 6.2.

Although a small number of basic facial expresssions are universally recognizable, people in all cultures do not necessarily display the same emotions in the same ways. For example, if you stick out your tongue in China, this

Figure 6.2. Facial expressions and emotions. Ekman and Friesen (1984) found that people in highly disparate cultures showed fair agreement on the emotions portrayed in these photos. This consensus across cultures suggests that the facial expressions associated with certain emotions may have a biological basis.

Country	Fear	Disgust	Happiness	Anger
		Agreement in judging photos (%)		
United States	85	92	97	67
Brazil	67	97	95	90
Chile	68	92	95	94
Argentina	54	92	98	90
Japan	66	90	100	90
New Guinea	54	44	82	50

gesture conveys surprise (Klineberg, 1938). If you stick out your tongue in North America, you convey quite a different meaning! Further, sometimes it is not considered appropriate to express our feelings, so we try to hide them. The facial expression of emotion is regulated by a given society's norms. **Display rules are norms that govern the appropriate display of emotions.**

Sometimes we may not want to communicate all that we feel to someone else, or they to us. Is it possible to deliberately deceive others through facial expression? Yes! In fact, it appears that we are better at sending deceptive messages with our faces than with other areas of our bodies (Ekman et al., 1982). Recall the term "poker face," which is used to describe poker players who are skilled at carefully controlling their excitement about a good hand of cards (or their dismay about a bad one).

Eye Contact

Eye contact (also called mutual gaze) is another major channel of nonverbal communication. Above all else, it is the duration of eye contact between people that is most meaningful. A great deal of research has been done on communication through the eyes, and we will briefly summarize some of the more interesting findings (Kleinke, 1986).

People who engage in high levels of eye contact are likely to be judged as more attentive than those who maintain less eye contact. Speakers, interviewers, and experimenters receive higher ratings of competence when they maintain high rather than low eye contact with their audience. Similarly, those who engage in high levels of mutual gaze are likely to be perceived as having effective social skills and credibility. Gaze is also a means of communicating the intensity (but not the positivity or negativity) of feelings.

Some gender and racial differences have been found in patterns of eye contact. For example, women tend to gaze more at others in interactions than men do, as the research results in Figure 6.3 demonstrate (Giles & Street, 1985). Also, white listeners tend to gaze more when someone else is speaking than do black listeners (LaFrance & Mayo, 1976). Perhaps this is because eye contact is more likely to be considered rude or confrontational in black culture (Scheflen & Scheflen, 1972). Obviously, such differences in nonverbal communication can lead to misunderstandings if eye-gaze behaviors intended to convey interest and respect are interpreted as being disrespectful or dishonest.

If you gaze too steadily at another person, your eye contact becomes a stare. A stare causes most people to feel uncomfortable and to flee the situation (Ellsworth, Carlsmith, & Henson, 1972; Kleinke, 1986). Moreover, like threat displays among nonhuman primates such as baboons and rhesus monkeys, a stare can convey aggressive intent (Henley, 1986).

We can also communicate by reducing our eye contact with others. For example, eye contact usually is reduced when an interaction is unpleasant or embarrassing (Edelman & Hampson, 1981) or when people feel that their personal space is being invaded (Argyle & Dean, 1965; Kleinke, 1986). It is widely believed that a speaker trying to deceive a listener engages in relatively little eye

Figure 6.3. Gender differences in eye contact. In social interactions, women gaze at others more than men do. As shown by the results of this study (Exline, 1963), this difference occurs during both speaking and listening.

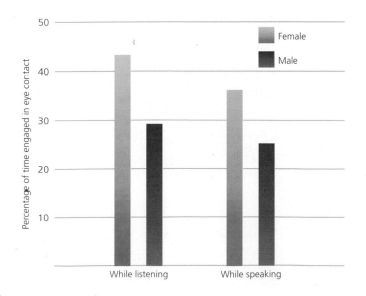

contact (Hemsley & Doob, 1978). Although we often interpret lack of eye contact as an indication of possible lying, studies suggest that liars are actually fairly skilled at maintaining normal eye contact (DePaulo, Stone, & Lassiter, 1985). Thus, eye contact is *not* a very reliable index of deceptive intent.

Research suggests that patterns of eye contact can reflect status differences in interactions. Generally, a lower-status individual gazes more at a higher-status partner when listening than vice versa (Berger, 1985). Status differences may underlie the frequently found sex differences in gazing behavior (Henley, 1977). For example, the finding that women look at men more often than men look at women parallels the finding that lower-status persons look more at higher-status partners. Similarly, women engage in staring (a dominant cue) less often than men and are more likely to avoid the gaze of another person (a subordinate cue) (Henley, 1986).

Eye contact is strongly related to feelings of interpersonal attraction (Kleinke, 1986). People who engage in high mutual gaze are judged by observers as liking each

other more than those who engage in relatively little eye contact. Maintaining eye contact with others generally causes them to like us, although people prefer a moderate amount of eye contact rather than constant (or no) mutual gaze. Also, couples who say they are in love spend more time gazing at each other than do other couples (Goldstein, Kilroy, & Van de Voort, 1976; Rubin, 1970).

Body Language

Body movements—those of the head, trunk, hands, legs, and feet—also provide nonverbal avenues of communication. *Kinesics* **is the study of communication through body movements.** What can body posture convey? For one thing, it provides information about the level of tension or relaxation that a person is experiencing. For example, leaning back with arms or legs arranged in an asymmetrical position (an "open" position) conveys a feeling of relaxation.

Body posture can also indicate a person's attitude toward you (Mehrabian, 1972). If someone leans toward you, this typically indicates interest and a positive attitude. When people angle their bodies away from you or cross their arms, their posture may indicate a negative attitude or defensiveness.

In addition, body posture can convey status differences. Generally, a higher-status person will look more relaxed. In contrast, a lower-status person will tend to exhibit a more rigid body posture, often sitting up straight with feet together, flat on the floor, and arms close to the body (a "closed" position) (Mehrabian, 1972). Erving Goffman (1956) noticed this disparity long ago in hospital staff meetings. The relatively high-status doctors tended to assume careless and comfortable positions, while lower-status personnel, such as nurses and social workers (who presumably would be more tense), tended to display less casual posture. Again, as we saw with eye contact, status and sex differences are frequently parallel. That is, men are more likely to exhibit the high-status "open" posture and women the lower-status "closed" posture (Hall, 1984).

Sustained eye contact can have very different meanings. It can signal intense hostility or mutual affection.

Hand Gestures

Hand gestures are used primarily to regulate conversations and to supplement speech (Scheflen & Scheflen, 1972). The *referencing gesture* is used to refer to an object or person who is the subject of conversation. For example, you might point at a car that you're commenting on. The *gesture of emphasis* is used to stress a point that is being made verbally. Thus, you might slam your fist onto a desk to emphasize the importance of your statement. *Demonstrative gestures* mimic what is being said. For example, in discussing a cutoff of someone's financial support, you might make chopping motions with your hand.

Touch

Touch takes many forms and can convey a variety of meanings. How do we interpret touching? Much, of course, depends on the nature of the relationship between two people and whether a touch is welcome. Research on touching is difficult to conduct and interpret, making generalizations risky.

Nonetheless, there is some research support for the following findings. First, females tend to engage in more same-sex touching than males. Second, same-sex pairs of people usually have higher levels of touching than cross-sex pairs (when the contact isn't intimate). Third, there does not appear to be an overall tendency for males to touch females more than vice versa (Eagly, 1987). Fourth, there are strong norms about *where* people are allowed to touch friends. These norms are quite different for same-sex as opposed to cross-sex interactions, as can be seen in Figure 6.4.

Like most aspects of nonverbal communication, touching can convey information about social status. Those who initiate a touch are generally assumed to have higher status than those who receive a touch. There also are gender differences in people's *responses* to touching (Henley & Freeman, 1981). Research indicates that women generally respond more favorably to touching than do men. This sex difference may depend on status differences. Support for this interpretation comes from the finding that both women and men react favorably to touching when the person initiating the touch is higher in status than the recipient (Major, 1981).

Personal Space

Proxemics is the study of people's use of interpersonal space. *Personal space* is a zone of space surrounding a person that is felt to "belong" to that person. This personal space that we consider "ours" is like an invisible bubble we carry around with us in our social interactions. As we will see, although the boundaries of our personal space are imaginary, this space may be marked off in tangible ways under some conditions. The size of this mobile zone is related to our cultural background, social status, personality, age, and sex. Interestingly, animals show a similar tendency, called *territoriality*—**the marking off and defending of certain areas as their own.**

As you might guess, the amount of distance people feel comfortable with between themselves and others depends on the nature of the social interaction. Based on his observations and analysis of social interactions in the United States, anthropologist Edward Hall (1966) has described four distance zones that are appropriate for

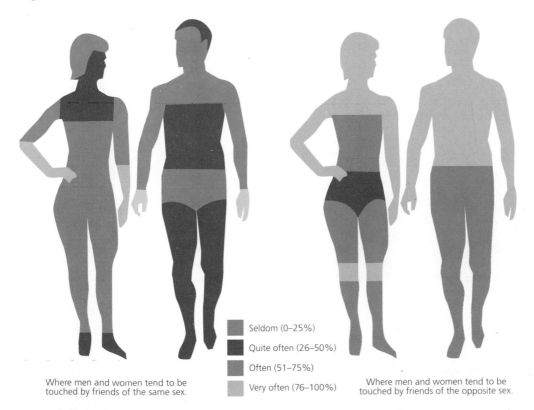

Figure 6.4. Where friends touch each other. Social norms govern where friends tend to touch each other. As these figures show, the patterns of touching are different in same-sex as opposed to cross-sex interactions. (Adapted from Marsh, 1988)

Seldom (0–25%)

Quite often (26–50%)

Often (51–75%)

Very often (76–100%)

Where men and women tend to be touched by friends of the same sex.

Where men and women tend to be touched by friends of the opposite sex.

particular kinds of encounters in American culture (see Figure 6.5).

- *Public distance (12 feet and beyond):* People often prefer to maintain this distance because it gives them the option of choosing to ignore someone without appearing rude. While interpersonal interactions can take place at distances beyond 12 feet, they tend to be quite impersonal.
- *Social distance (4–12 feet):* Most social interactions in the United States are transacted from this zone. It is a nice intermediate distance that makes most of us feel comfortable.
- *Personal distance (18 inches–4 feet):* This is the minimum distance maintained in most encounters between friends. In some situations, such as a cocktail party, strangers may venture into this zone.
- *Intimate distance (0–18 inches):* This obviously represents tight quarters and is appropriate only for very intimate relationships, such as those between parents and children or between lovers. Of course, there are obvious exceptions, such as in crowded subways and elevators, but these situations are often experienced as stressful.

Hall's analysis indicates that the appropriate distance between people is regulated by social norms and that these norms are determined in large part by the nature of the relationship and the situation. A large body of research supports his basic ideas (Darley & Gilbert, 1985). Like other aspects of nonverbal communication, personal distance can convey information about status. People of similar status tend to stand closer together than do people whose status is unequal. Moreover, it is the prerogative of the more powerful person in an interaction to set the "proper" interpersonal distance (Henley, 1977).

What happens when someone approaches us more closely than we feel is appropriate? Such invasions of personal space invariably result in feelings of discomfort and attempts to bring the interpersonal distance more in line with our expectations. To illustrate, let's say that you have parceled out some territory for yourself at a table in the library. Although there is space at other tables, a stranger sits down at "your" table and forces you to share it. How might you react? First, you will probably experience some tension, which could be betrayed by nonverbal signals such as body rigidity, a shuffling of position, or a lack of eye contact. Then you might express your disapproval nonverbally through a hostile stare or frown. You might decide to move to another table to reestablish a distance that feels comfortable to you. If moving away is not practical, you will probably reorient your body away from the intruder. Another common response to invasions of personal space is placing some barrier (for example, a stack of books) between you and the invader. Whatever response you choose, the point is that invasions of personal space rarely go unnoticed and they usually elicit a variety of reactions.

Paralanguage

The term *paralanguage* refers to *how* something is said rather than *what* is said. Thus, **paralanguage includes all vocal cues other than the content of the verbal message itself.** These cues may include how loudly or softly people

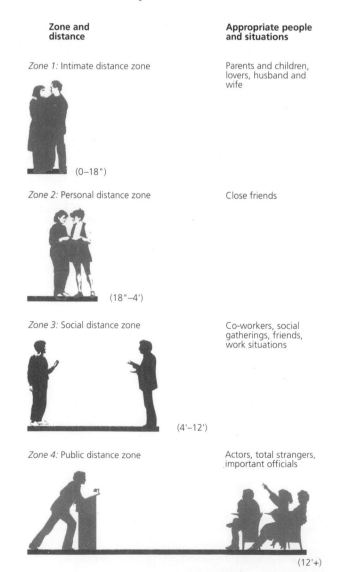

Zone and distance	Appropriate people and situations
Zone 1: Intimate distance zone	Parents and children, lovers, husband and wife
(0–18")	
Zone 2: Personal distance zone	Close friends
(18"–4')	
Zone 3: Social distance zone	Co-workers, social gatherings, friends, work situations
(4'–12')	
Zone 4: Public distance zone	Actors, total strangers, important officials
(12'+)	

Figure 6.5. Interpersonal distance zones. According to Edward Hall (1966), we like to keep a certain amount of distance between ourselves and others. The distance that makes us feel comfortable depends on whom we are interacting with and the nature of the situation. Generally, the zones depicted on the left are appropriate for the people and situations listed on the right.

speak, how fast they talk, and the rhythm and quality of their speech (Burgoon, 1985). Each of these aspects of vocalization can affect the message being transmitted.

Variations in vocal emphasis can give a particular string of words different meanings. Consider the sentence "I really enjoyed myself." If you vary the word that is accented, you can speak this sentence in three different ways, each resulting in a different meaning.

I really enjoyed myself.
(Even though others may not have had a good time, I did.)

I *really* enjoyed myself.
(My enjoyment was exceptional or greater than expected.)

I really *enjoyed* myself.
(Much to my surprise, I had a great time.)

As you can see from these examples, the way we say something can make a considerable difference in the meaning we convey. We can, in fact, actually reverse the literal meaning of a verbal message by how we say it. For example, the statement "That's just great!" can convey a feeling of genuine excitement or a sarcastic put-down. Thus, variations in vocal emphasis constitute a language within a language.

Aspects of vocalization can also communicate emotions. For example, rapid speech may mean that a person is happy, frightened, or nervous. Slower speech might be used when we are uncertain or when we want to emphasize a point. Loud vocalization is often indicative of anger. A relatively high pitch may indicate anxiety (Verderber & Verderber, 1989). Slow speech, low volume, and low pitch are often associated with sadness. Thus, vocal quality is another clue that you can use to discern someone's true feelings.

Keep in mind, however, that it is easy to assign meanings to voice quality that aren't valid. For example, it is quite common for people to stereotype certain vocal characteristics as indicative of specific personality traits

even though research doesn't support such associations (Heun & Heun, 1978). Examples of common vocal stereotypes include associating a deep voice with masculinity and maturity, and a high, breathy voice with femininity and youth.

Detecting Deception

As we have noted, the spontaneous nature of nonverbal communication often makes it a better index of a person's true feelings than what the person actually says. This reality raises an obvious question. Is it possible to detect deceit by monitoring nonverbal signals? Yes, but it isn't easy. The clues that suggest dishonesty don't necessarily correspond to popular stereotypes about how liars give themselves away.

Evidence on the nonverbal behaviors associated with deception is summarized in Figure 6.6 (based on DePaulo et al., 1985). The vocal and visual cues that have been studied are listed in the first column. The second column indicates whether these cues are really associated with

Figure 6.6. Detecting deception from nonverbal behaviors. This chart summarizes evidence on which nonverbal cues are *actually* associated with deception and which are *believed* to be a sign of deception, based on a research review by DePaulo, Stone, and Lassiter (1985).

Nonverbal Cues and Deception		
Kind of cue	Are cues associated with *actual* deception?	Are cues *believed* to be a sign of deception?
Vocal cues		
Speech hesitations	YES: Liars hesitate more.	YES
Voice pitch	YES: Liars speak with higher pitch.	YES
Speech errors (stutters, stammers)	YES: Liars make more errors.	YES
Speech latency (pause before starting to speak or answer)	NO	YES: People think liars pause more.
Speech rate	NO	YES: People think liars talk slower.
Response length	YES: Liars give shorter answers.	NO
Visual cues		
Pupil dilation	YES: Liars show more dilation	(No research data)
Adaptors (self-directed gestures)	YES: Liars touch themselves more.	NO
Blinking	YES: Liars blink more.	(No research data)
Postural shifts	NO	YES: People think liars shift more.
Smiling	NO	YES: People think liars smile less.
Gaze (eye contact)	NO	YES: People think liars engage in less eye contact.

deception. The third column indicates whether the same cues are widely believed to be associated with deception. As you can see, research does not support many stereotypical notions about lying. Contrary to popular belief, lying is *not* associated with slow talking, long pauses before speaking, excessive shifting of posture, reduced smiling, or lack of eye contact.

Nonetheless, there are some cues that do seem to be associated with dishonesty. Vocal cues include excessive hesitations and stammering, speaking with a higher pitch, and giving relatively short answers. Visual cues include excessive blinking and dilation of the pupils. Also, liars nervously touch themselves more than normal. It's also helpful to look for inconsistency between messages expressed via the face and those from the lower part of the body. For example, a friendly smile accompanied by a nervous shuffling of feet may be cause for concern. Another clue is whether there is any lack of spontaneity in the facial message compared to the verbal message. People tend to take more time to muster and send deceptive nonverbal signals than authentic ones. Because of this tendency, liars' verbal and facial expressions may be out of sync.

In conclusion, deception is potentially detectable, but detecting it is not a simple matter. The nonverbal behaviors that tend to accompany lying are subtle and can be difficult to spot.

Significance of Nonverbal Communication

Although we often are unaware of nonverbal communication, it clearly plays an important role in our lives. Various studies illustrate the significance of nonverbal communication. One of them examined the importance of nonverbal communication in marital relationships (Noller, 1980). Husbands and wives were instructed to send ambiguous messages to each other in the nonverbal channel. This enabled the experimenters to determine each couple's skill and success in nonverbal communication. These measures of couples' nonverbal skills were

then correlated with measures of their marital adjustment. A positive correlation between nonverbal skills and marital adjustment was found, suggesting that effective nonverbal communication may contribute to marital satisfaction.

Another study looked at differences between people in nonverbal expressive talent (Friedman, Prince, Riggio, & Di Matteo, 1980). Specifically, this study focused on individual differences in the ability to use facial expressions, gestures, body movements, and so forth to enhance the impact of verbal statements. The main conclusion of this study was that high expressiveness may be the key element of what we often vaguely label "charisma." Charisma usually refers to a special ability to lead, inspire, or captivate others. Thus, there is some reason to believe that nonverbal talent may be a crucial factor that helps make some people charismatic leaders. Of course, leaders also depend heavily on verbal communication, which we examine in the next section.

VERBAL COMMUNICATION

Let's turn now to communication in the verbal channel. First, we'll define effective communication. Then we'll consider some common problems that can act as barriers to effective communication. Finally, we will offer suggestions for achieving more effective communication.

Effective Communication: What Is It?

Communication is effective when the message we intend to convey is the message that is actually received. Therefore, it entails *both* the accurate transmission of a message *and* the accurate reception of a message. This means that there are at least two places for communication to break down.

Barriers to Effective Communication

A *communication barrier* is anything in the communication process that inhibits or blocks the accurate transmission and reception of messages. Barriers to effective communication can reside in the source, the receiver, or sometimes in both. Common barriers to effective communication include defensiveness, motivational distortion, carelessness, self-preoccupation, game playing, collusion, and instigation of unnecessary conflict.

Defensiveness

Perhaps the most basic barrier to effective communication is *defensiveness*—an excessive concern with protecting oneself from being hurt. We're prone to react defensively when we feel threatened (Gibb, 1961). For example, we tend to get defensive when we feel that others are going to evaluate us or when we believe that they are trying to control us. Defensiveness is also easily elicited when others attempt to communicate their superiority over us. Thus, people who overemphasize their status, wealth, brilliance, or power often put us on the defensive. Dogmatic people who convey "I'm always right" also tend to breed defensiveness.

It's important to note that a threat will elicit defensive behavior even if it is imagined rather than real. While we should try to cultivate a communication style that reduces the likelihood of arousing defensiveness in others, we need to remember that we don't have complete control over others' perceptions and reactions.

Motivational Distortion

In the previous chapter, we discussed at length how wishes, needs, and expectations can distort person perception. The same process commonly takes place in communication. That is, we often hear what we want to hear instead of what is actually being said.

Each of us has a unique frame of reference—certain attitudes, values, and expectations—that can influence what we hear. We also tend to experience emotional discomfort when we hear information that contradicts our views. One way of avoiding these unpleasant feelings is to engage in *selective attention*. That is, we actively choose to attend to information that supports our beliefs and to ignore information that contradicts them. Similarly, we may read meanings into statements that are not intended, and we may jump to erroneous conclusions. This tendency to distort information occurs most often in discussions of issues that we feel strongly about. Certain issues (politics, racism, abortion) are often highly charged for both the source and receiver. In these situations, misperceptions are especially likely to occur and to interfere with effective communication.

Carelessness

Simple carelessness is a common cause of communication problems. Carelessness on the part of the source of the communication usually involves saying the first thing that comes to mind. Virtually all of us can recall an instance in which we hurt someone's feelings unintentionally because we didn't stop to think before we spoke.

Probably even more common is the problem caused by a careless receiver, who fails to hear accurately the message being sent. Although we can process speech at up to about 600 words per minute, most people speak at a rate of only 100–140 words per minute (Adler & Towne, 1987). Thus, it is understandable that receivers can become bored, distracted, and inattentive. Effective listening, as we shall see, requires active effort.

Self-Preoccupation

We have all had the experience of trying to communicate with someone who is so self-focused as to make enjoyable two-way conversation impossible. Such people seem to talk for the sake of hearing themselves talk. Further, they rarely listen attentively. When another person is talking, they're wrapped up in rehearsing what they're going to say when they get a chance. These self-preoccupied people show little awareness of the negative effects they have on their listeners.

Charismatic speakers such as Jesse Jackson draw on both verbal and nonverbal communication skills to get across their message and motivate audiences.

People who are self-preoccupied can cause negative reactions in others for several reasons. First, the content of their remarks is usually so self-serving (seeking to impress, to gain unwarranted sympathy, and so on) that others find it offensive. Another problem is that these people consistently take up more than their fair share of conversation time. Some individuals do both—that is, they talk only about themselves *and* they do so at great length! After a "conversation" with someone like this, we typically feel that our need to communicate has been ignored. Usually, we try to avoid these people if we can. If not, we tend to respond only minimally so as to try to end the conversation as quickly as possible. Needless to say, people who fail to respect the social norm that conversations entail a mutual sharing of information risk alienating others.

Game Playing

"Game playing" is another barrier to effective communication. Game playing was first described by Eric Berne (1964), who originated transactional analysis. *Transactional analysis* **is a broad theory of personality and interpersonal relations that emphasizes patterns of communication.** In Berne's scheme, *games* **are manipulative interactions progressing toward a predictable outcome, in which people conceal their real motivations.** In its broadest sense, game playing can include the deliberate (or sometimes unintentional) use of ambiguous, indirect, or deceptive statements. Some game playing involves "verbal fencing" to avoid having to make clear one's meaning or intent. Particularly problematic are repetitive games that result in bad feelings and erode the trust and respect that are essential to good relationships. As such, games interfere with effective communication and are a destructive element in relationships. For a more complete discussion of games in intimate relationships, see the Chapter 9 Application.

Collusion

In contrast to the other barriers to effective communication, collusion requires at least two willing partners. These partners are usually involved in an intimate relationship. **In** *collusion,* **two people have an unspoken agreement to deny some problematic aspect of reality in order to sustain their relationship.** To accomplish this denial, the people suppress all discussion of the problem area. The classic example of collusion is the alcoholic partnership. In this case, the alcoholic requires the partner to join him or her in denying the existence of a drinking problem. To maintain the relationship, the partner goes along with the tacit agreement. The two people will then go to great lengths to avoid any comment about alcohol-related difficulties. Over time, the drinking usually gets worse and the relationship often deteriorates, thereby making it more difficult for the partner to continue the collusion. Since it is based on a mutual agreement to deny a specific aspect of reality, collusion obviously prevents effective communication.

Instigating Unnecessary Conflict

When a person consistently instigates unnecessary conflict with others, this contentiousness sets up barriers to effective communication. Such behavior comes in a variety of forms (Nye, 1973). Some people tend to deliberately annoy and provoke others to get a "rise" out of them. Problems also occur when people constantly engage in competition (attempts to gain something at the other's expense) or efforts at domination (attempts to control another person). Some people are also prone to blaming the other person when agreed-upon goals aren't achieved. These types of behaviors typically promote mistrust and resentment, as well as attempts to "get back" at the instigator—thereby making effective communication even less likely.

As we have seen, there are many problems that can interfere with effective communication. In upcoming pages, we will discuss suggestions that can help ensure that the message you intend to send is the message that is actually received. First, we'll describe a general attitude orientation that can promote a favorable climate for communication. Next, we'll list some guidelines for effec-

tive speaking. Finally, we'll offer some advice about effective listening.

Creating a Positive Interpersonal Climate

A positive interpersonal climate exists when people feel that they can be open rather than guarded or defensive in their communication. You can go a long way toward creating such a climate by putting the following suggestions into practive.

1. *Learn to feel and communicate empathy.* **Empathy involves adopting another's frame of reference so you can understand his or her point of view.** When you empathize with others, you are able to genuinely appreciate their feelings and understand their problems. Empathy includes being

RECOMMENDED READING

Contact: The First Four Minutes

by Leonard Zunin with Natalie Zunin (Ballantine Books, 1972; 2nd edition, 1988)

We talked in Chapter 5 about primacy effects, or the power of first impressions. The Zunins are convinced that when strangers encounter each other for the first time, the first four minutes are crucial to the impressions made. Actually, they offer little empirical evidence to support their assertion that four minutes (not, say, three or six) is the critical time interval. Nonetheless, they offer a great deal of worthwhile advice that might help you improve your interpersonal communication.

Despite the book's title, the Zunins discuss a wide range of topics besides how to handle initial encounters. Among other things, they offer insights on nonverbal communication, self-concept, and how to cope with rejection. The outstanding feature of the book, however, is its wealth of advice on how to make social overtures. In one chapter alone, there are 19 down-to-earth suggestions about conversational openers.

> Let us look in at a typical party. The hostess is introducing two strangers, after which she excuses herself to circulate. The two become locked in contact according to unwritten rules of social congeniality. They tend to respond to each other, perhaps automatically, guided by conditioned cultural traditions—but for a minimum period of time (again an average of four minutes). One of them may then say, "A pleasure meeting you. I'm going for a refill," and he walks away. He has been cordial enough and socially appropriate, but most probably the two have not made an effective or favorable contact.
>
> The average person shrugs off such a routine rejection and moves on to new contacts, which continue to range from three to five minutes, averaging four minutes. It is hardly an interval guaranteed to change your life, but what is communicated can determine whether or not strangers become acquaintances, friends, lovers, life-time mates—or remain strangers. [1972, p. 11]

sensitive to others' needs and accepting of their feelings. To clarify the meaning of empathy, it may be helpful to make a distinction between a person and his or her behavior. Being accepting and understanding toward a person does *not* necessarily mean that you must also condone or endorse the individual's behavior. For example, what if your roommate confides in you that he is worried about how much he drinks? In discussing the issue with him, you can come to understand the reasons for his excessive drinking without condoning this behavior. You can communicate your support for him, as a person, by continuing to be his friend—without encouraging him to continue drinking.

2. *Practice withholding judgment.* You can promote an open climate for communication by trying to be nonjudgmental. This doesn't mean that you give up your right to have opinions and make judgments. It merely means that you should strive to interact with people in ways that don't put them on the spot (forced to offer an opinion when they would rather not) or make them feel "put down" (or inadequate).

3. *Strive for honesty.* Mutual trust and respect thrive on authenticity and honesty. So-called hidden agendas often don't stay hidden very long. Even if others don't know exactly what your underlying motives are, they often can sense that you're not being entirely honest. Of course, striving for honesty does not mean that we are bound to communicate everything that we feel at any time to any person. While it is true that some interactions necessarily involve pain—for example, breaking up with a girlfriend or boyfriend—many unpleasant interactions can be avoided by being truthful without being needlessly hurtful.

4. *Approach others as equals.* You may know from personal experience that most of us don't like to be reminded of another's higher status or greater ability. You can improve the effectiveness of your communication if you try to disregard status differences in your conversations. Especially when you have the higher status, it is better to approach people on equal terms.

5. *Express your opinions tentatively.* Rather than giving the impression that you know all the answers, strive to communicate that your beliefs and attitudes are flexible and subject to revision. You can do this by using qualifying words or phrases. For instance, instead of saying, "This is how we should do it," you might say, "There are several possible approaches; the one that seems the best to me is . . . What do you think?"

Guidelines for Effective Speaking

Speaking effectively requires skills that are developed over a lifetime. Hence, we are realistic enough to know that a few paragraphs of advice won't produce dramatic changes in your speaking skills. Nonetheless, observing a few general guidelines can enhance the effectiveness of your communication. If you want more detailed information on this topic, we suggest that you consult Verderber and Verderber (1989), an excellent communications text.

1. *Consider the frame of reference of your listener or listeners.* In most situations, you are likely to have some knowledge about your listener(s). It is a good idea to consider your listeners' background, intelligence, attitudes, and so forth, so that you can put your message in terms that they can understand. In particular, try to avoid talking over the heads of your audience, and steer clear of jargon or special terminology that is foreign to them. Also, try to illustrate your ideas with examples that your listeners will be able to relate to from their own experience.
2. *Be specific and concrete.* Effective communication is hampered when you speak in vague generalities. If you do not communicate your ideas clearly, you usually leave listeners confused and frustrated. And don't confuse how long you talk with how clearly you communicate. You can speak for a long time without saying anything! Unless you're a politician, this is not something you want to do.
3. *Avoid "loaded" words.* Certain words are "loaded" in the sense that they tend to trigger negative emotional reac-

tions from listeners. In the interests of effective speech, it is usually best to avoid using words that are unnecessarily derogatory. For example, you can discuss politics without using terms such as "right-winger" and "knee-jerk liberal." Similarly, labels such as "male chauvinist pig" and "women's libber" need not come up in discussions of gender roles. You can remind children of chores left undone without calling them lazy. You can ask a sales clerk to correct an error without referring to it as a stupid mistake. And you can disagree with people who are older or younger than yourself without calling them senile or immature.
4. *Make your verbal and nonverbal messages congruent.* Now that you are aware of the great amount of information that is transmitted at the nonverbal level, you can appreciate the importance of consistency in your verbal and nonverbal messages. Inconsistency between the verbal and nonverbal channels can generate confusion and mistrust in your listeners. The relative spontaneity of nonverbal communication does make it somewhat difficult to control. Nonetheless, you can work at becoming more aware of your nonverbal signals. Furthermore, if you strive for honesty in your verbal communications, you will lessen the likelihood of incongruence in the nonverbal channel.

Guidelines for Effective Listening

As we have stressed, effective listening is a vital component of effective communication. What do we mean by "effective listening"? We are simply referring to the ability to receive the message that the sender intends. Listening is a vastly underappreciated skill. This is unfortunate, because we spend far more time listening than we do speaking.

Although you are not likely to experience a dramatic change in your speaking skills overnight, you *may* be able to substantially improve your listening fairly quickly. For one thing, most people probably are ineffective listeners because they are unaware of the elements of effective listening that we are about to discuss. Also, effective

listening hinges largely on your attitude. If you're willing to work at it, you can become a good listener.

The key to effective listening is to devote active effort to the task. We tend to think of listening as something we do with our ears, but to do it right, you have to use what lies between your ears! As you'll see in the guidelines that follow, successful listening requires that you actively attend to and process incoming information.

1. *Attend physically to the speaker.* The first step in active listening is to position yourself so that you can see and hear the speaker. Face the person squarely and maintain good eye contact. In so doing, you are also signalling your attentiveness to the speaker. In addition, if you adopt an "open" posture and lean forward, you will send a clear nonverbal message that you are interested in what the other person has to say (Egan, 1990).

2. *Actively attend to and process the verbal message.* We have already mentioned that a listener can receive information faster than a speaker can send it. This leaves extra time for the listener's attention to wander. The key to effective listening is to devote this extra time to the incoming stream of information rather than to irrelevant lines of thought. For example, you can review points already made, try to anticipate what the speaker will say next, and search for deeper meanings that may underlie the surface message (Huseman, Lahiff, & Hatfield, 1976).

3. *Pay attention to nonverbal signals.* You already know that much of information transmission takes place in the nonverbal channel. As we have noted, when verbal and nonverbal messages conflict with each other, people are more likely to rely on nonverbal cues. Furthermore, while we use verbal cues to get the "objective" meaning of a message, we depend on nonverbal cues for information about the emotional and interpersonal meanings of the message (Burgoon, 1985). Obviously, then, it is very important that you focus on nonverbal signals in order to achieve a full understanding of the message.

4. *Check your understanding of the message.* One of the most useful listening habits you can develop is to check

with the speaker from time to time to be sure that you have understood the message properly. There are a number of ways you can do this. The simplest way is to ask a direct question to clarify a point: "Do you mean that . . . ?" Another way is to summarize briefly what has just been said and see whether there are any objections or clarifications from the speaker: "Let's see, I believe I heard you say that . . . " If you think there was a deeper meaning underlying the words, a simple summary may not be sufficient. Instead, you may want to translate the ideas (including the underlying ones) into your own words to see whether the speaker agrees with your interpretation.

REVEALING OURSELVES TO OTHERS: SELF-DISCLOSURE

In our discussion of public selves in the preceding chapter, we noted that people don't always behave in a spontaneous and natural fashion. Rather, we all engage in *impression management.* That is, we carefully edit our behavior and monitor what we consciously reveal about ourselves to others. When we choose to reveal things about ourselves, we are engaging in self-disclosure.

Self-disclosure **is the voluntary act of verbally communicating private information about yourself to another person.** By "private," we mean information that would not otherwise be available to the other party. It doesn't have to be a deeply hidden secret, but it may be. In general terms, self-disclosure involves opening up about yourself to others. Conversations that include self-disclosure are experienced as deeper and more personally meaningful than our more routine, superficial interactions.

Self-disclosure is an important element in our lives. Why? Because self-disclosure is a key vehicle through which emotional intimacy develops (Taylor & Altman, 1987). And intimacy is the element that makes the difference between relationships we experience as meaningful and sustaining as opposed to those we experience as superficial and unsupportive.

Listening is more than just "receiving" a verbal message. It requires active attention and giving feedback to the speaker.

Intimate relationships in this sense may be platonic or sexual. Indeed, as you may have discovered, a sexually intimate relationship is not necessarily an emotionally intimate relationship. When we speak of intimacy, the important factor is not the presence of a sexual relationship, but rather the degree to which people are open and honest with each other.

One way of looking more closely at self-disclosure is to characterize it in terms of breadth and depth (Altman & Haythorn, 1965). *Breadth* refers to the number of different aspects of ourselves that we share with another person. *Depth* refers to the degree to which the information we disclose about ourselves is revealing. For example, you would probably feel quite comfortable chatting about your feelings about the weather and today's sports scores with strangers (not much breadth or depth). In contrast, your best friend probably knows a wide variety of information about you (greater breadth) and also how you feel about more private concerns, such as your jealousy toward your sister or your self-consciousness about your weight (greater depth). Figure 6.7 is a visual representation of breadth and depth in self-disclosure.

Self-disclosure can be risky. When we reveal important and private things about ourselves to others, we become more vulnerable to them. We often worry about self-disclosure. What if they don't respond to what we say, or what if they laugh at us? Because of our fears of being rejected or humiliated, we are often unsure about whether we should open up to others. How can you know whether it's safe to share personal information with someone else? In this section, we'll try to respond to this and related questions about self-disclosure.

Why Do We Engage in Self-Disclosure?

If self-disclosure is so scary—since it leaves us open to possible rejection—why do we take the gamble? Because the potential payoffs are so great. Self-disclosure serves many important functions in our personal and social lives, including the following (Derlega & Grezlak, 1979).

First, self-disclosure helps us express our feelings. As we saw in our discussion of coping in Chapter 4, expressing feelings to someone else can be helpful in reducing stress. For the most part, it's not a good idea to keep frustration and tension bottled up inside.

Second, self-disclosure helps us clarify our thoughts and feelings. We all get confused from time to time and feel overwhelmed by problems in our lives. Talking about these things can help us sort them out. Even thinking about talking to someone can help us to further analyze the problem and clarify our feelings.

Third, self-disclosure aids in social comparison and self-understanding. As we discussed in the previous chapter, social comparison theory suggests that we need to compare ourselves with others in order to gain a better understand of ourselves (Festinger, 1954). To obtain the comparative information we seek, we often need to engage in self-disclosure. For instance, if you wanted to know whether your anxieties about a particular class were realistic, you would probably have to divulge those anxieties to your fellow students to obtain the kind of feedback you needed.

Fourth, self-disclosure is crucial in developing deeper interpersonal relationships. If you would like to turn an acquaintanceship into a friendship, or if you want a friendship to be closer, self-disclosure may be the key. To get to know others better, you usually have to let them get to know you better. Your willingness to disclose to others is an important signal that you trust them. This is an important message to send to someone with whom you want to develop or deepen a relationship. We hasten to add, however, that simply "spilling your guts" indiscriminately is likely to have a negative effect.

Inappropriate Self-Disclosure

If you engage in little or no self-disclosure, your personal and social satisfactions are likely to be limited. On the other hand, telling everyone everything about you will land you in trouble fast. Self-disclosure, then, can be

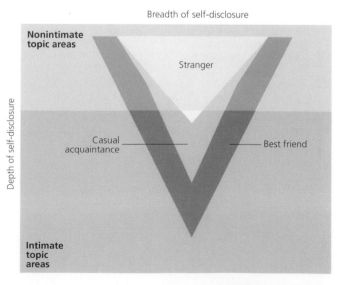

Figure 6.7. Breadth and depth of self-disclosure. Breadth of self-disclosure refers to how many things you open up about; depth refers to how far you go in revealing private information. Both the breadth and depth of our disclosures are greater with best friends as opposed to casual acquaintances or strangers. (Adapted from Altman & Taylor, 1973)

appropriate or inappropriate. Reaping its benefits requires that you know the difference.

When is self-disclosure inappropriate? One example is divulging personal information to almost anyone, regardless of the nature of your relationship. Perhaps you have been on the receiving end of this mistake. If so, you probably recall how awkward you felt when someone you barely knew told you his or her innermost secrets. Although we find our private business of great significance, it's important to remember that not everyone else is interested in it.

Another example of inappropriate self-disclosure is choosing the wrong person with whom to share private information. Here, the problem is making a mistake about a particular person—opening up to one who isn't interested in your concerns or who betrays your confidence. A final example of inappropriate self-disclosure is talking about private information in a place where you can be overheard by others you would rather *didn't* know the intimate details of your life.

Who Reveals What to Whom under What Circumstances?

As we have discussed, it is important to engage in self-disclosure in ways that work to your benefit, not your detriment. Before considering guidelines for appropriate self-disclosure, let's look at research findings on who tends to reveal what to whom under what circumstances.

Who?

Some people are more open and willing to engage in self-disclosure than others. However, this inclination to be open to others does not appear to be closely related to other personality traits. Research that has attempted to relate self-disclosure tendencies to personality factors has generally yielded weak and inconsistent results. These findings suggest that situational factors must also be taken into account (Archer, 1979).

There are some gender differences in self-disclosure,

but these, too, depend on the situation. In general, it has been found that females tend to be more openly self-disclosing than males (Gerdes, Gehling, & Rapp, 1981; Jourard, 1971). This disparity is typically attributed to differences in gender-role socialization. In our culture most men are taught to be unexpressive, particularly about tender emotions and feelings of vulnerability.

When males do engage in self-disclosure, it is more likely to be to a female than to another male (Komarovsky, 1976). Disclosing personal information is often interpreted as a sign of weakness, especially among males who hold traditional gender-role attitudes. Such men attempt to avoid showing any sign of perceived personal weakness for fear of appearing effeminate (Lombardo & Lavine, 1981). We might also point out that there is an inverse relationship between disclosure and power. To the extent that men have more power in a relationship, they need not disclose as much personal information (Henley & Freeman, 1981).

RECOMMENDED READING

The Transparent Self

by Sidney M. Jourard (Van Nostrand Reinhold, 1971)

This is a classic humanistic manifesto extolling the importance and value of self-disclosure. Jourard argues convincingly that many of us are troubled by an inability to open up to others. He explains the roots of this problem and discusses how self-disclosure can promote psychological health.

Jourard was a rare animal—an authentic humanist who backed up his ideas with hard-nosed research. Although he was research-oriented, the book is skillfully written in everyday language. Jourard discourses eloquently on how self-disclosure plays a key role in love, marriage, family, education, health care, and therapy.

Jourard was a pioneer researcher working in previously unexplored territory. Consequently, some of his ideas have turned out to be a bit oversimplified. Nonetheless, the book has some timeless advice about relationships and interpersonal communication.

> Now I think unhealthy personality has a similar root cause, one which is related to Selye's concept of stress. Every maladjusted person is a person who has not made himself known to another human being and in consequence does not know himself. Nor can he be himself. More than that, he struggles actively to avoid becoming known by another human being. He works at it ceaselessly, twenty-four hours daily, and it is work! In the effort to avoid becoming known, a person provides for himself a cancerous kind of stress which is subtle and unrecognized, but nonetheless effective in producing not only the assorted patterns of unhealthy personality which psychiatry talks about, but also the wide array of physical ills that have come to be recognized as the province of psychosomatic medicine. [pp. 32–33]

However, there is evidence suggesting that in some situations, at least, men may be more prone to self-disclosure than women. For example, in dealing with strangers (as opposed to friends), males tend to be more self-disclosing than females (Rosenfeld, Civikly, & Herron, 1979). Thus, it appears to be an oversimplification to say that women are more open than men.

What?

Obviously, it is easier for us to be open about some topics than others. We quickly give biographical information (for example, where we live, our age, or our education). But we are understandably reluctant to divulge inner fears, such as insecurities about our work. Also, we are generally willing to reveal socially desirable things about ourselves, such as our membership in the Jaycees. In contrast, we tend to be reticent about socially undesirable things, such as our convictions for tax evasion (Altman & Taylor, 1973).

To Whom?

A critical factor in self-disclosure is the target person who will receive the information. Usually, people are more likely to disclose personal information to females than to males. However, this trend is moderated by the exact nature of the topic (Cunningham, 1981). As you might expect, we tend to disclose more to people we like and to people we know relatively well (Derlega, Winstead, Wong, & Greenspan, 1987). The social status of the target person is also important (Slobin, Miller, & Porter, 1968). Self-disclosure is most common when people are of similar status. When there is a status discrepancy, we are more likely to reveal ourselves to people of higher status than to people of subordinate status.

As we move from adolescence toward adulthood, we tend to disclose less to our parents and same-sex friends and more to our other-sex friends. Generally speaking, we tend to disclose more to a spouse or partner than to anyone else (Jourard, 1971). Interestingly, research suggests that spouses who engage in a good deal of self-disclosure report relatively high levels of marital satisfaction (Hendrick, 1981). On the other hand, it has also been suggested that *equity* in self-disclosure, rather than high self-disclosure, may be the critical factor that helps couples avoid stress (Bowers, Metts, & Duncanson, 1985).

Some people are particularly skilled at getting others to open up and engage in self-disclosure. Sociability, self-esteem, empathy, and lack of shyness are associated with this ability to elicit self-disclosure from others (Miller, Berg, & Archer, 1983).

Under What Circumstances?

If you want to tell someone that you want to discontinue a relationship, you will normally wait for the appropriate time and place. You don't reveal this kind of information at the ballpark, as you're casually walking out the door, or as you wait in line to register for classes. Thus, there are appropriate situations for certain kinds of self-disclosure. Generally, we value privacy when we want to engage in significant self-disclosure.

While it is clear that the setting or circumstances have an enormous impact on self-disclosure, this issue has not been addressed adequately in self-disclosure research (Chelune, 1979). There is one situational variable that we know figures prominently in self-disclosure: *reciprocity*. A number of studies have shown that *we disclose more when people reciprocate by making disclosures to us.* Typically, a person returns a disclosure of approximately the same intimacy as that revealed by the first person in the pair (Archer, 1980). Thus, in a cyclical manner, self-disclosure breeds more self-disclosure.

The reciprocity norm governing self-disclosure appears to be most influential in the early stages of a relationship (Taylor & Altman, 1987). Hence, unless there are special circumstances operating, you can usually assume that if you engage in appropriate self-disclosure with a person to whom you'd like to feel closer, your listener will reciprocate. Being aware of this may alleviate some of your anxiety about opening up to others you do not know well.

Figure 6.8. Self-disclosure and psychological health.
According to Derlega and Chaikin (1975), both too much self-disclosure and too little are unhealthy. A moderate amount of disclosure appears to be optimal.

When Is Self-Disclosure Appropriate?

To disclose or not to disclose—that is the question. By now you should be able to appreciate the complexity of this question. The crucial issue in regard to self-disclosure is, when is it appropriate?

The answer is both simple and complex. We'll give you the simple part first. *Self-disclosure is appropriate when your listener is sincerely interested and willing to hear what you have to say.* But how do you know whether your target person is interested? This is where the answer gets complex. In trying to avoid inappropriate self-disclosure, it helps to go slowly and pay close attention to the other person's reaction. It's something like testing the water to see whether it's warm enough. Instead of jumping in all at once, you tentatively stick in a toe.

In assessing the other person's reaction, you need to pay close attention to both verbal and nonverbal cues. In the verbal channel, the positive signs to look for are empathy and reciprocity. In particular, if the other person reciprocates with self-disclosure, this generally indicates a willingness on his or her part to proceed to a more intimate level of communication. Of course, some people who aren't very comfortable engaging in self-disclosure themselves are sincerely willing to listen to you anyway. Hence, you cannot depend on reciprocity alone as an indicator of the other person's interest.

This is why tuning in to nonverbal signals is of crucial importance. Commonly, when people are uncomfortable with your self-disclosure, they will try to send you a nonverbal message to that effect, to avoid embarrassing you with a more obvious verbal warning. Often they will deliver this "stop" message by reducing eye contact and by displaying a puzzled, apprehensive, or pained facial expression. If seated, the other person may angle his or her body away from you; if the person is standing, he or she may increase the distance between the two of you or shuffle his or her feet impatiently. In contrast, if your target person faces you squarely, leans forward, appears relaxed, and maintains good eye contact, you can be fairly certain that he or she is willing to listen to your self-disclosure.

Interestingly, it has been suggested that there is a curvilinear relationship between self-disclosure and psychological adjustment (Archer, 1980; Derlega, & Chaikin, 1975). What this means can be seen in Figure 6.8. As the figure shows, either too little or too much self-disclosure may be associated with relatively poor adjustment. That is, an inability to be open is unhealthy, but so is being an "overdiscloser." According to this theory, the healthy personality engages in discriminating self-disclosure, revealing the appropriate thing to the appropriate person at the appropriate time.

AN EXAMPLE OF COMMUNICATION GONE AWRY: DATE RAPE

We conclude this chapter by considering a serious problem related to our theme of interpersonal communication: "date rape." Although date rape involves more than just communication gone awry, poor communication is a key factor surprisingly often. We have chosen to discuss this subject here, rather than in our chapter on sexuality, because the evidence indicates that rape is *not* really an expression of sexuality, but rather an act of aggression.

Since the vast majority of rapes are committed by men, our discussion will center on women as the victims of rape. *Acquaintance rape* occurs when a woman is forced to have unwanted intercourse with someone she knows. Acquaintance rape includes not only rapes committed on dates, but also those committed by nonromantic acquaintances (friends, co-workers, neighbors, relatives). *Date rape* is a more restrictive term that refers to forced and unwanted intercourse with someone in the context of dating.

The force involved in date rape typically is verbal or physical coercion, but it may sometimes involve the use of a weapon. Date rape can happen on a first date, with someone you've dated for a while, or with someone to whom you're engaged. Many people confuse date rape

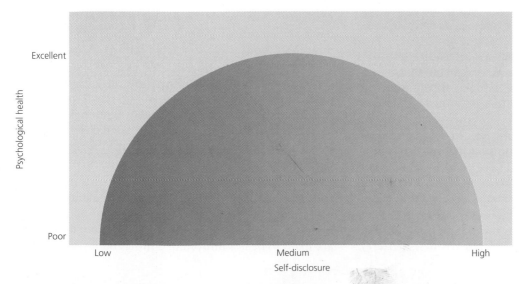

with seduction. The latter occurs when a woman is persuaded *and agrees* to have sex. Date rape often occurs when seduction fails and the man has sex with the woman without her consent.

All rape is traumatic, but it is particularly shattering when a woman is raped by someone she has liked and trusted. In addition, because most of us are not used to the idea that rape can occur with someone we know, it is particularly difficult for a victim of date or acquaintance rape to deal with her feelings of betrayal, rage, and shame. While there are differences in how women are affected by rape, most rape victims go through three stages: trauma, denial, and resolution.

Trauma. Many women experience a variety of emotional reactions to rape. Chief among them are fear of being alone, fear of men, fear of retaliation (especially if charges are filed), and fear of trusting subsequent dating partners. Feelings of depression, anger, helplessness, guilt, pain, shame, and anxiety are also common. Many rape victims show signs of stress-related physical problems. Emotional reactions can be exacerbated if the woman's family and friends are not supportive. Significant emotional difficulties are especially likely if family or friends blame the victim for the attack. As we saw in the previous chapter, it is common for people to blame victims of calamities (see the discussion of defensive attribution).

Denial. In this stage—which may last for months or years—rape victims try to put the trauma behind them and get on with life. During this period, women avoid talking about their rape as they try to deny that it took place. This strategy generally fails as a long-term solution because the powerful and painful emotions don't just go away.

Resolution. In order to move beyond the experience, a woman needs to deal with her feelings by talking with someone who is supportive and understanding: a friend, a counselor, or a member of the clergy. Once she has worked through her feelings and fears, she may be able to put the trauma in the past and begin to feel in control of her life again. Still, it is likely that she will always be haunted by the experience.

How Common Is Date Rape?

It is difficult to obtain accurate information about the prevalence of any form of rape. It is estimated that 90% of all rapes are never reported. It does appear that the problem of rape is growing, although it is unclear whether the increase is due to a growing number of rapes or to a higher percentage of rapes being reported. Only a minority of reported rapes are committed by strangers: about 60% of the victims say they knew their assailants. The majority of rape victims are between the ages of 15 and 25.

Research suggests that date rape is particularly common on college campuses. In a widely cited study, Mary Koss and her colleagues surveyed approximately 7,000 students at 32 colleges (Koss, Gidycz, & Wisniewski, 1987).

They found that about 1 in 7 women (15%) had been victims of rape. Moreover, 1 in 12 men admitted either to having forced a woman to have intercourse or to having tried to do so. However, *none* of these men identified himself as a rapist. Similarly, among the women who reported experiencing sexual aggression that met the definition of rape, 43% did not view themselves as victims of rape.

These results suggest that there is a lot of confusion and self-deception about what constitutes rape. It seems that many people believe that if a stranger leaps out of the bushes and sexually attacks you, it is rape. On the other hand, if someone you know coerces you into having sex, then it isn't rape. In fact, of the women in the college survey who reported experiences that met the definition of rape, only 11% had been raped by strangers. The vast majority had been raped by someone they knew: 30% by steady dates, 25% by nonromantic acquaintances, and 9% by husbands or other family members. The widespread reluctance to see date rape for what it is allows men to deny their responsibility and causes women who have been raped to question and doubt themselves. These patterns of thinking probably encourage the "blaming the victim" syndrome.

Factors Contributing to Date Rape

The phenomenon of date rape can be traced to a number of underlying factors. Communication problems are often critical, but before we focus on these, let's briefly examine other contributing factors.

The "double standard." Traditional norms of courtship suggest that males should initiate dates and sex, while females either consent or decline these advances. Also, society still encourages a double standard for males and females when it comes to sexual behavior. Men are encouraged to have sexual feelings and to act on them, while women are discouraged from being sexual unless they are "carried away" with emotion. The double standard promotes hidden norms that condone sexual aggression by men in dating relationships.

Changing sexual values. A variety of social trends have made sexual activity in the context of dating more common than it once was (see Chapter 13). Because sexual values remain in transition, however, we lack widely accepted standards about how people should behave. Up until the mid-1960s, there were campus curfews and other restrictions that functioned, among other things, to control and structure students' social and sexual behavior. For better or for worse, those controls no longer exist. Today's students are left to make their own rules without much guidance.

Alcohol and drugs. Drinking heavily or taking drugs on dates makes it likely that a person's judgment will be impaired. In these circumstances, both men and women are likely to be less inhibited. Unfortunately, alcohol and drugs make women more vulnerable to the use of force. For example, if a woman passes out, she is easy prey for anyone who is willing to take advantage of her.

Sexual violence in the media. Laboratory research on the effects of aggressive pornography (depicting rape and other sexual violence against women) suggests that such material elevates some men's tendency to behave aggressively toward women (Malamuth & Donnerstein, 1982). Furthermore, research has shown that exposure to such material can increase male viewers' acceptance of rape myths and their willingness to say that they would commit a rape, while decreasing their sensitivity to rape and the plight of rape victims (Donnerstein & Linz, 1984). Because sexual aggression is being displayed more frequently in films and on television, it is reasonable to speculate that media depictions are contributing to an increase in rape.

Miscommunication and Date Rape

Inadequate communication between dating partners often is a key factor contributing to date rape. Among dating couples, frank conversations about whether to engage in sexual activities, which behaviors are permissible, and what to do about birth control are, regrettably, the exception rather than the rule (Knox & Wilson, 1981). For one thing, most people (and young people, especially) are embarrassed to talk about sex. For another, many feel that talking about sex takes the mystery out of it. Also, many women apparently tell themselves that they'll wait until the occasion arises and then "decide" what to do. However, such an approach places women in a position where they are easily influenced by men and by situational forces.

Another problem is that dating partners often misunderstand what the other means. For instance, research shows that males are more likely than females to perceive friendly behavior as having sexual intent (Shotland, 1989). This means that a man can think a woman has communicated sexual interest (and act accordingly) when, in fact, she has not. If a man doesn't make an effort to clarify a woman's intentions, he can easily let himself feel that he has been "led on." He may then use his anger as an excuse to force the woman to have sex.

Misunderstandings also occur in dating relationships because social norms encourage game playing—manipulative interactions in which people conceal their true feelings. Thus, dating partners may not say what they mean or mean what they say. For example, some women say "no" (in words or in nonverbal behavior) to sexual activity when they actually mean "maybe" or "yes." So, men sometimes are genuinely confused about what a woman really means. The use of "token resistance" can lead men to ignore their partners' "misleading" verbal protests and watch for "true" nonverbal cues (Shotland, 1989). Since nonverbal cues are relatively ambiguous, it is likely that men will perceive sexual interest even when it's not there. Moreover, whether really confused or not,

many men have been taught to try to turn a woman's refusals into agreement. Hence, many young men and women learn to tease and manipulate each other without recognizing the potential hazards of such behavior.

In a study of token resistance among undergraduate women, 40% of the subjects reported that they had used this tactic (Muehlenhard & Hollabaugh, 1988). When only sexually experienced women were considered, this proportion rose to about 60%. The researchers were also interested in why the women engaged in token resistance. Subjects' responses were grouped into three categories: (1) *practical reasons* (fear of appearing promiscuous, fear of sexually transmitted diseases); (2) *inhibition-related reasons* (emotional, religious, and moral worries); and (3) *manipulative reasons* (getting the man more aroused, being in control). Obviously, when a woman engages in token resistance, the stage is set for miscommunication—and sometimes for tragedy. Because some men have learned to expect token resistance, women need to be especially firm in communicating their unwillingness to engage in sexual activity.

What can be done to reduce the incidence of date rape? We offer the following suggestions to people in dating relationships. (1) Recognize date rape for what it is: an act of sexual aggression. (2) Beware of excessive alcohol and drug use that may leave you out of control. (3) Think through your feelings, values, and intentions about sexual relations *before* the question of having sex arises. (4) Work on communicating your feelings and expectations about sex by engaging in appropriate self-disclosure. (5) Listen carefully to each other and respect each other's wishes.

Many of these suggestions involve striving to enhance interpersonal communication. Obviously, improved communication will not eliminate date rape, but it can go a long way toward reducing the problem.

SUMMARY

Interpersonal communication is the interactional process whereby one person sends a message to another. Communication takes place when a source sends a message to a receiver through either the verbal or nonverbal channels. Although we often take it for granted, communication plays an exceptionally important role in our lives.

Nonverbal communication tends to be more spontaneous than verbal communication, but it is also more ambiguous. Sometimes it contradicts what is communicated verbally. It is often multichanneled, and like language, it is culturally bound. Among other things, nonverbal communication provides information about social affiliation and about status. Elements of nonverbal communication include facial expression, eye contact, body language, hand gestures, touch, personal space, and paralanguage.

Facial expressions often convey emotional states. However, the face is relatively easy to use in efforts to send deceptive signals. The duration of eye contact is an important cue and is influenced by a variety of factors. Bodily posture may be indicative of a person's relaxation and attitude toward you. Hand gestures are used primarily to regulate and supplement speech. Touching can convey a variety of meanings.

Proxemics deals with the use of personal space. Hall has described how specific distances are maintained in certain kinds of social relationships. When these norms are violated and personal space is invaded, people tend to react negatively. Paralanguage is concerned with the use of vocal emphasis in speaking. Slight variations in vocal emphasis can reverse the literal meaning of a message.

There are nonverbal cues that are associated with deception, but many of these cues do not correspond to popular beliefs about how liars give themselves away. Discrepancies between facial expressions and other nonverbal signals may suggest dishonesty. However, the vocal and visual cues associated with lying are subtle, making the detection of deception difficult.

Communication is effective when the message the sender intends to convey is the message that is actually received. Effective communication may be blocked by barriers such as defensiveness, motivational distortion, carelessness, self-preoccupation, game playing, collusion, and instigation of unnecessary conflict. To promote a positive interpersonal climate, it helps to show empathy, treat people as equals, withhold judgment, strive for honesty, and express opinions tentatively. In speaking, it helps to consider your listener's frame of reference, be specific and concrete, avoid loaded words, and keep your verbal and nonverbal messages consistent. Effective listening depends on physically attending to the speaker, paying careful attention to both verbal and nonverbal signals, and checking your perceptions.

Self-disclosure involves revealing ourselves to others. We take the risk of opening up to others because self-disclosure serves many important functions, chief among them is developing emotional intimacy. Inappropriate self-disclosure, however, can cause interpersonal difficulties. Women tend to engage in more self-disclosure than men, but this disparity is not as consistent as once believed. The reciprocity norm is a key situational factor influencing self-disclosure. It appears that learning to engage in appropriate self-disclosure—revealing the appropriate thing to the appropriate person at the appropriate time—may be important to psychological health.

Poor communication often contributes to date rape, which involves forced intercourse in the context of dating. Date rape appears to be increasingly common, especially on college campuses, where most victims are raped by someone they know. Misunderstandings about sexual intentions are common in dating relationships because partners often fail to engage in adequate self-disclosure, misinterpret ambiguous nonverbal signals, and engage in game playing.

The application section of this chapter will discuss an important communication issue: interpersonal conflict. It will provide some guidelines about how to cope constructively with interpersonal discord.

Dealing with Conflict

Check those statements that apply to you. When I have a conflict with another person:

☐ **1.** I have to be the winner.

☐ **2.** I always begin by overstating my case.

☐ **3.** I play on the other party's weaknesses.

☐ **4.** I use threats to force the other person into submission.

☐ **5.** I will use deceit if necessary.

If you checked several of the items above, you take a very negative and short-sighted approach to dealing with interpersonal conflict. The characteristics listed above are associated with a strategy of domination. This strategy may pay off with victory, but it almost always leads to hard feelings.

Interpersonal conflict itself is inevitable, but hard feelings afterward are not. Conflict can be dealt with in positive ways and can produce positive outcomes for both parties. This application section will discuss how to deal with conflict constructively.

THE NATURE AND VALUE OF INTERPERSONAL CONFLICT

Conflict is an unavoidable feature of interpersonal interaction. People do not have to be enemies to be in conflict, and being in conflict does not make people enemies. *Interpersonal conflict* **exists whenever two or more people disagree.** By this definition, conflict will occur between friends and lovers, as well as between competitors and enemies. The discord may be a product of incompatible goals, values, attitudes, or beliefs.

Many people have the impression that conflict is inherently bad and that it should be suppressed if at all possible. In reality, conflict is neither inherently bad nor inherently good. Conflict is a natural phenomenon that may lead to either good or bad outcomes, depending on how people deal with it. Avoidance tends to be one of the worst ways of coping with conflict. Interpersonal discord that is suppressed usually affects a relationship in spite of the suppressive effort, and the effects tend to be negative.

When dealt with openly and constructively, interpersonal conflict can lead to a variety of valuable outcomes (Johnson & Johnson, 1975; Thomas, 1976). Among other things, constructive confrontation may (1) bring problems out into the open, where they can be solved, (2) put an end to chronic sources of discontent in a relationship, and (3) lead to new insights through the clashing of divergent views.

PERSONAL STYLES OF DEALING WITH CONFLICT

How do you react to conflict? Most people have a certain personal style in dealing with conflict (Sternberg & Soriano, 1984). We will describe five common styles in this section, so that you can see where you fit in (see Figure 6.9). These five modes of dealing with conflict—avoidance, accommodation, domination, compromise, and integration—are based on theoretical models pioneered by Blake and Mouton (1964) and Thomas (1976).

Avoidance

Some people simply don't like to face up to the existence of conflict. They operate under the unrealistic hope that if they ignore the problem, it will go away. When a conflict emerges, the avoider will change the subject, make a hasty exit, or pretend to be preoccupied with something else. This person finds conflict extremely unpleasant and distasteful and will go to great lengths to avoid being drawn into a confrontation. Of course, most problems will not go away while you pretend they don't exist. This style generally just delays the inevitable clash. Avoidance is not an adequate means of dealing with conflict.

Accommodation

Like the avoider, the accommodating person feels uncomfortable with conflict. However, instead of ignoring the disagreement, this person brings the conflict to a quick end by giving in easily. This style grows out of basic feelings of insecurity. People who are overly worried about acceptance and approval from others are likely to use this strategy of surrender. Accommodation is a poor way of dealing with conflict because it does not generate creative thinking and genuine solutions. Moreover, feelings of resentment (on both sides) may develop because the accommodating person often likes to play the role of a martyr.

Domination

The dominator turns every conflict into a black-and-white, win-or-lose situation. This person will do virtually anything to emerge victorious from the confrontation. The dominator tends to be aggressive and deceitful. This person rigidly adheres to one position and will use threats and coercion to force the other party to submit. Giving no quarter, the dominator will often get personal and "hit below the belt." This style is undesirable because,

like accommodation, it does not generate creative thinking aimed at mutual problem solving. Moreover, this approach is particularly likely to lead to postconflict tension, resentment, and hostility.

Compromise

Compromise is a pragmatic approach to conflict that acknowledges the divergent needs of both parties. A compromise approach involves negotiation and a willingness to "meet the other person halfway." While trying to be reasonable, the compromiser nonetheless works hard to maximize the satisfaction of his or her own needs. Thus, the compromise approach may involve some manipulation and misrepresentation. Compromise is a fairly constructive approach to conflict, but its manipulative aspects make it somewhat inferior to the final approach, that of integration.

Integration

While compromise simply entails "splitting the difference" between positions, integration involves a sincere effort to find a solution that will maximize the satisfaction of both parties. When this approach is used, the conflict is viewed as a mutual problem to be solved as effectively as possible. Integration thus encourages openness and honesty. Also, integration stresses the importance of criticizing the other person's *ideas* in a disagreement rather than the other *person*. Integration requires putting a lot of effort into clarifying differences and similarities in positions, so that you can build on the similarities. Generally, this is the most productive approach for dealing with conflict. Instead of resulting in a post-conflict residue of tension and resentment, integration tends to produce a climate of trust.

GUIDELINES FOR CONSTRUCTIVE CONFLICT RESOLUTION

In the preceding section, we emphasized the desirability of integration as an approach to conflict resolution. Here now are explicit guidelines on how to achieve an integrative style of dealing with interpersonal conflict (Johnson & Johnson, 1975).

Figure 6.9. Johnson's (1981) characterization of the five styles of dealing with interpersonal conflict. David Johnson has playfully used the stereotypic characteristics of five animals to capture the essence of the five basic styles of dealing with conflict.

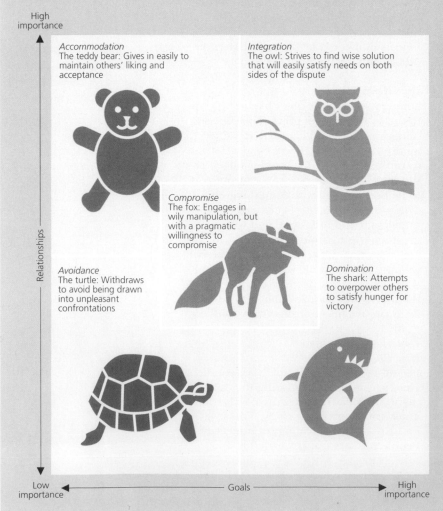

High importance

Relationships

Accommodation
The teddy bear: Gives in easily to maintain others' liking and acceptance

Integration
The owl: Strives to find wise solution that will easily satisfy needs on both sides of the dispute

Compromise
The fox: Engages in wily manipulation, but with a pragmatic willingness to compromise

Avoidance
The turtle: Withdraws to avoid being drawn into unpleasant confrontations

Domination
The shark: Attempts to overpower others to satisfy hunger for victory

Low importance

Goals

High importance

1. To begin with, acknowledge the existence of a conflict and the legitimacy of the other person's needs and goals.
2. Define the conflict as a mutual problem to be solved cooperatively, rather than as a win-lose proposition.
3. Choose a mutually acceptable time to sit down and work on resolving the conflict. It is not always best to tackle the conflict when and where it first arises.
4. Show respect for the other person's position. Try to empathize with, and fully understand, the other person's frame of reference.
5. Make communication honest and open. Don't withhold information or misrepresent your position. Avoid deceit and manipulation.
6. When conflicts surface, feel free to disagree with the other person's ideas without making disparaging remarks about the other person's stupidity or foolishness.
7. Approach the conflict as equals, with a balance of power between the two of you. If you have a higher status or more power (parent, supervisor), try to set this difference aside.
8. Put a great deal of effort into clarifying your respective positions. It is imperative that each of you understands the exact nature of your disagreements.
9. Communicate your flexibility and willingness to modify your position.
10. Emphasize the similarities in your positions rather than the differences. Try to use those similarities to build toward a mutually satisfactory solution.

RECOMMENDED READING

The Intimate Enemy:
How to Fight Fair in Love and Marriage
by George R. Bach & Peter Wyden (Morrow, 1969; paperback edition, Avon, 1981)

Few of us are fond of conflict. However, conflict has its value, and in any case it is a fact of life. In particular, some conflict is virtually inevitable in intimate relationships. In deference to this reality, Bach (a psychologist) and Wyden (a writer) have put together a guide about how to fight fairly and productively. A sampling of chapter titles conveys the content of the book. Among other things, Bach and Wyden cover "Why Intimates Must Fight," "Training Lovers to Be Fighters," "Male and Female Fight Styles," "Bad Fighters and How to Reform Them," "Fighting over Trivia," and "Fighting before, during, and after Sex."

The book is somewhat repetitive and rather lengthy, but its size is swelled by some interesting excerpts from actual fights. It is clearly written and quite provocative.

We have entered a psychological ice age. Except for occasional bursts of warmth, often fueled by sex after a few cocktails, truly intimate encounter has begun to disappear from civilized Western life. Closeness has become a paradox: longed for, but increasingly intolerable.

We believe that the inability to manage personal conflict is at the root of the crisis that threatens the structure of the American family. Communications between children and parents are breaking down. More and more young people are "tuning out" by escaping into the world of drugs and other short-lived emotional kicks. One out of every three marriages ends in divorce. [1969, p. 17]

1. List and describe the four components of the communication process.

2. List and discuss five general principles of nonverbal communication.

3. Discuss what can be discerned from facial cues.

4. Discuss characteristics associated with high levels of eye contact, including racial and gender differences.

5. Discuss how eye contact is related to social status and interpersonal attraction.

6. Discuss what can be discerned from body postures and hand gestures.

7. Discuss some of the research findings with regard to the communication meaning of touching.

8. Describe Hall's four interpersonal distance zones and how people respond to invasions of personal space.

9. Describe the role of paralanguage in communication.

10. Summarize evidence on detecting deception from nonverbal cues.

11. Discuss the significance of nonverbal messages in interpersonal relations.

12. List and discuss seven barriers to effective communication.

13. Describe five communication behaviors that tend to produce a positive interpersonal climate.

14. List four guidelines for effective speaking.

15. List four guidelines for effective listening.

16. Explain why we engage in self-disclosure and when it may be inappropriate.

17. Summarize evidence on who tends to disclose what to whom and under what circumstances.

18. Discuss when self-disclosure is appropriate and its relationship to adjustment.

19. Explain how poor communication and other factors contribute to date rape.

20. List and describe five personal styles of dealing with interpersonal conflict.

21. List ten guidelines for constructive conflict resolution.

KEY TERMS

Channel
Collusion
Communication barrier
Display rules
Empathy
Games
Interpersonal communication
Interpersonal conflict
Kinesics
Message

Nonverbal communication
Paralanguage
Personal space
Proxemics
Receiver
Self-disclosure
Source
Territoriality
Transactional analysis

KEY PEOPLE

Paul Ekman &
Wallace Friesen

Edward Hall

Sidney Jourard

QUESTIONNAIRE
Opener Scale

INSTRUCTIONS
For each statement, indicate your degree of agreement or disagreement, using the scale shown below. Record your responses in the spaces on the left.

4 = I strongly agree
3 = I slightly agree
2 = I am uncertain
1 = I slightly disagree
0 = I strongly disagree

THE SCALE

_____ 1. People frequently tell me about themselves.

_____ 2. I've been told that I'm a good listener.

_____ 3. I'm very accepting of others.

_____ 4. People trust me with their secrets.

_____ 5. I easily get people to "open up."

_____ 6. People feel relaxed around me.

_____ 7. I enjoy listening to people.

_____ 8. I'm sympathetic to people's problems.

_____ 9. I encourage people to tell me how they are feeling.

_____ 10. I can keep people talking about themselves.

SCORING THE SCALE
This scale is easy to score! Simply add up the numbers that you have recorded in the spaces on the left. This total is your score on the Opener Scale.

MY SCORE _____

WHAT THE SCALE MEASURES
Devised by Lynn Miller, John Berg, and Richard Archer (1983), the Opener Scale is intended to measure your perception of your ability to get others to "open up" around you. In other words, the scale assesses your tendency to elicit intimate self-disclosure from people. The items assess your perceptions of (a) others' reactions to you ("People feel relaxed around me"), (b) your interest in listening ("I enjoy listening to people"), and (c) your interpersonal skills ("I can keep people talking about themselves").

In spite of its brevity, the scale has reasonable test-retest reliability (.69 over a period of six weeks). Correlations with other personality measures were modest, but in the expected directions. For instance, scores on the Opener Scale correlate positively with a measure of empathy and negatively with a measure of shyness. Further evidence for the validity of the scale was obtained in a laboratory study of interactions between same-sex strangers. Subjects who scored high on the scale compared to those who scored low elicited more self-disclosure from people who weren't prone to engage in much disclosure.

INTERPRETING YOUR SCORE
Our norms are based on the original sample of 740 undergraduates studied by Miller, Berg, and Archer (1983). They found a small but statistically significant difference between males and females on the scale (females score a little higher). This gender difference is reflected in the norms shown below.

NORMS	Females	Males
High score:	35–40	33–40
Intermediate score:	26–34	23–32
Low score:	0–25	0–22

How Do You Feel about Self-Disclosure?

This exercise is intended to make you think about your self-disclosure behavior. Begin by finishing the incomplete sentences below (adapted from Egan, 1977). Go through the sentences fairly quickly; do not ponder your responses too long. There are no right or wrong answers.

1. I dislike people who . . .

2. Those who really know me . . .

3. When I let someone know something I don't like about myself . . .

4. When I'm in a group of strangers . . .

5. I envy . . .

6. I get hurt when . . .

7. I daydream about . . .

8. Few people know that I . . .

9. One thing I really dislike about myself is . . .

10. When I share my values with someone . . .

Based on your responses to the incomplete sentences, do you feel you engage in the right amount of self-disclosure? Too little? Too much?

In general, what prevents you from engaging in self-disclosure?

Are there particular topics on which you find it difficult to be self-disclosing?

Are you the recipient of much self-disclosure from others, or do people have difficulty opening up to you?

7

Group Dynamics and Social Influence

To a surprising extent, when an authority figure says "Jump!" many of us simply ask "How high?" Consider the following anecdote. In 1987, several suburbs just west of Chicago experienced a severe flood that required the mobilization of the National Guard and various emergency services. At the height of the crisis, a young man arrived at the scene of the flood, announced that he was from an obscure state agency in charge of emergency services, and proceeded to take control of the situation. City work crews, the fire department, local police, municipal officials, and the National Guard followed his orders with dispatch for several days, evacuating entire neighborhoods—until an official thought to check, and found out that the man was just someone who had walked in off the street. The impostor, who had small armies at his beck and call, had no training in flood control or emergency services, just a history of unemployment and psychological problems.

After news of the hoax spread, people criticized red-faced local officials for their unthinking compliance with the impostor's orders. However, many of the critics probably would have cooperated in much the same way if they had been in the officials' shoes. For most people, obedience to an authority figure is the rule, not the exception. And when we work together in groups, we often conform to the example of other group members without asking questions.

In this chapter, we will examine the phenomena of obedience and conformity and a host of other issues relating to group dynamics and social influence. Among other things, we'll address questions such as the following.

• Are individuals more productive when they work alone or when they work together in groups?
• Who leans toward more cautious decisions: individuals or groups?
• Is conformity more likely in a small group or a large group?
• Are leaders born or made?

• What type of leadership style is most effective?
• In persuasion efforts, is it wise to play on people's feelings of fear and guilt?
• What tactics do advertisers, salespeople, charlatans, and other influence artists employ to gain their ends?

We'll begin our coverage by discussing the nature of groups, group productivity, group decision making, and the dynamics of leadership. Then we'll shift to the subject of social influence and look at the principles of persuasion, conformity, and obedience to authority.

THE NATURE OF GROUPS

We may not think about it much, but most of us belong to a diverse array of groups that play a large role in our lives. We are members of clubs, classes, work crews, unions, sports teams, churches, fraternities, sororities, cliques, and committees. But what makes a collection of people a group?

What Is a Group?

Are the divorced fathers living in Baltimore a group? Are three strangers moving skyward in an elevator a group? What if the elevator gets stuck? How about four students from your psychology class who study together regularly? A jury deciding a trial? The Boston Celtics? The United States Congress? Some of these collections of people are groups and others aren't. Let's examine the concept of a group and find out which ones qualify.

In social psychologists' eyes, **a *group* consists of two or more individuals who interact and are interdependent.** The divorced fathers in Baltimore aren't likely to qualify on either count. Strangers sharing an elevator might interact briefly, but they're not interdependent. However, if the elevator got stuck and they had to deal with an emergency together, they could suddenly become a group. Your psychology classmates who study together are a

group, since they interact and depend on each other to achieve shared goals. So do the members of a jury, a sports team such as the Celtics, and a large organization such as the U.S. Congress.

Why Do We Join Groups?

We have little control over some of the groups that we belong to. You were born into your family, and you were assigned to classes in grade school and high school. If you take a certain job, you may be required to join a union. However, we voluntarily join most of the groups that we belong to. Why do we choose to seek membership in these groups? There are many reasons. Edgar Schein (1980), a prominent organizational theorist, suggests that we join groups to achieve the following goals.

To fulfill our need for affiliation. **The *affiliation motive* involves our need to associate with others and maintain social bonds.** Some animals (bears and bald eagles, for example) don't mind going it alone. Humans, however, react very badly to prolonged isolation. We need to spend time with others. Abraham Maslow called this motive the need for belongingness. He saw it as a very basic motive and placed it at the third level in his hierarchy of needs (see Chapter 2). Thus, we belong to groups to fulfill our needs for companionship, friendship, social support, and affection.

To enhance our sense of identity and self-esteem. When we belong to groups such as fraternities, sororities, country clubs, and cliques, the acceptance we receive from others can enhance our feelings of self-worth. Our memberships in some groups also help us to define who we are. For instance, a young boy might join a neighborhood gang to fortify his view of himself as a "tough guy." Similarly, a college professor might join the American Civil Liberties Union (ACLU) to enhance her vision of herself as a liberal intellectual.

To gain social comparison information. According to *social comparison theory* we need to compare ourselves with others to gain insight into our own feelings and behavior (see Chapter 6). In group interactions we can exchange information with others to check our perceptions of reality. As an example, Schein notes that when a group of workers agree that their boss is a slave driver, they are validating one another's feelings.

To increase mutual security and power. People often band together in groups to pursue common goals because there is power in numbers. One worker who complains about a slave driver boss probably won't get very far. However, if all six of the workers under this boss unite in their complaint, they may have some impact. The power of numbers is the key principle underlying the formation of labor unions, consumers' rights groups, and grass roots community organizations.

To get something accomplished. Obviously, an individual working alone cannot build a superhighway or a skyscraper. Many jobs of much smaller magnitude also require a team effort. Thus, we join groups to better accomplish an infinite variety of tasks.

Key Properties of Groups

When we join together in groups, we create social organisms with unique characteristics and dynamics that can take on a life of their own. Groups vary in many ways. Obviously, a study group, the Celtics, and the U.S. Congress are very different in terms of purpose, formality, the similarity of their members, and the diversity of their activities. Can anything meaningful be said about groups if they're so diverse? Yes. In spite of their immense variability, groups share certain properties that affect their functioning.

Among other things, most groups have *roles* that allocate special responsibilities to some members, *norms* about suitable behavior, a *communication structure* that reflects who talks to whom, and a *power structure* that determines which members wield the most influence (Forsyth, 1983). For example, a study group and the Celtics may appear to

At one time or another, people find themselves in many types of groups such as sports teams, unions, and juries. Groups vary in size, purpose, formality, activities, and other characteristics, but all have important effects on their members.

have little in common, but both might have a "harmonizer" whose role is to smooth over conflicts among members, a norm that "everyone pulls his or her own weight," and an unequal distribution of power among members. Other key properties of groups include their *size* and their *cohesiveness*. Let's examine each of these aspects of groups.

Roles and Norms

The members of a group are not necessarily interchangeable. In a small corporation, for instance, you wouldn't expect a computer programmer and a janitor to exchange responsibilities. In most groups, members develop specialized roles. This term is borrowed from the world of theater, where it refers to an actor's part in a play. **A *role* is a pattern of behavior expected of a person who has a certain position in a group.** For example, there are role expectations associated with your status as a student. You are expected to show up for classes, participate in discussion, ask questions, read assigned material, write papers, and take tests. The roles associated with being a student, a professor, a company president, a salesperson, or a secretary are examples of *institutionalized roles*. These are formal roles defined by institutions, such as businesses and schools. The expectations that go along with institutionalized roles usually are fairly explicit.

As groups evolve, informal roles that are less explicit may also emerge. These informal roles fall into two categories: task-related roles and socioemotional roles (Bales, 1958). **Task-related roles focus on moving the group toward completion of its mission.** Group members who fulfill task-related roles seek information, coordinate members' activities, refocus group discussion when necessary, and so forth. Their top priority is to get the job done. **Socioemotional roles focus on keeping interactions in the group friendly and supportive.** Members who perform socioemotional roles offer praise and encouragement, make jokes to relieve tension, highlight areas of agreement, and so forth. Their top priority is to maintain group harmony.

Figure 7.1. Examples of roles in groups. The roles we play in groups generally fall into two categories: task-related roles and socioemotional roles. Seven examples in each category are described here.

Some common task-related and socioemotional roles are listed in Figure 7.1. As you can see, people in groups occupy many different roles. An individual may fulfill several or more roles in a group. Some group members may fulfill both task-related and socioemotional roles, but most people specialize in one category or the other.

Our behavior in groups is influenced by norms as well as roles. ***Group norms* are rules regarding appropriate behavior.** For example, fraternities and sororities have norms about deference to senior members, adequate grades, and acceptable drinking. In the world of business, companies have norms about suitable attire, about going through appropriate channels to lodge complaints, and about how hard employees should work. Group norms usually are informal "unwritten laws," and they may differ dramatically from one group to another. For example, at one company, employees may be under intense pressure to work long hours. At another firm down the street, there may be pressure not to show up others by working hard. Thus, norms vary from one group to another, but all ongoing groups have normative expectations that shape members' behavior.

Task and Socioemotional Roles in Groups	
Role	**Function**
Task roles	
1. Information seeker	Emphasizes "getting the facts" by calling for background information from others
2. Opinion seeker	Asks for more qualitative types of data, such as attitudes, values, and feelings
3. Elaborator	Gives additional information— examples, rephrasing, implications—about points made by others
4. Coordinator	Shows the relevance of each idea and its relationship to the overall problem
5. Orienter	Refocuses discussion on the topic whenever necessary
6. Evaluator-critic	Appraises the quality of the group's efforts in terms of logic, practicality, or method
7. Energizer	Stimulates the group to continue working when discussion flags
Socioemotional roles	
1. Encourager	Rewards others through agreement, warmth, and praise
2. Harmonizer	Mediates conflicts among group members
3. Compromiser	Shifts his or her own position on an issue in order to reduce conflict in the group
4. Gatekeeper and expediter	Smooths communication by setting up procedures and ensuring equal participation from members
5. Standard setter	Expresses, or calls for discussion of, standards for evaluating the quality of the group process
6. Group observer and commentator	Informally points out the positive and negative aspects of the group's dynamics and calls for change if necessary
7. Follower	Accepts the ideas offered by others and serves as an audience for the group

Communication Structure

Perhaps the most important thing that we do in groups is to communicate with each other. As you may have noticed, some group members inevitably talk more than others. In one study of eight-person groups, the two most talkative members accounted for 60% of the group's discussion (Stephan & Mishler, 1952). In some groups, every member may be able to talk to every other member. However, many groups—for example, military units, corporations, and governmental bureaucracies—have prescriptions about appropriate channels of communication. **A *communication network* is a well-defined pattern of who talks to whom in a group.**

Social psychologists have studied many types of communication networks, such as the five-person networks diagrammed in Figure 7.2. A key feature of communication networks is how *centralized* they are. Communication is centralized when one person (or a small minority of members) can talk to the group at large while most members have limited exchanges with each other. For example, the kite and wheel are the most centralized networks shown in Figure 7.2.

Do centralized or decentralized networks solve problems more effectively? Which works faster? Which produces higher satisfaction among its members? Research on these issues has uncovered the following trends (McGrath, 1984). When dealing with simple problems, people in centralized networks solve problems faster and make fewer errors. However, when the problems are complex, decentralized networks are speedier and more effective. Group satisfaction is consistently higher in decentralized groups. We don't particularly like having our communication options heavily restricted.

Power Structure

Even more so than communication opportunities, power tends to be unevenly distributed in most groups. Power is a murky concept, but most theorists define *power* as the **potential to influence the group's decisions and individual members' behavior.** Power is often confused with high

status because they are associated, but they are *not* equivalent. For example, at colleges around the country, department chairpersons share a similar (high) status. However, the amount of power that they wield over their faculties varies enormously.

If status doesn't ensure power, what are the sources of social power? In a classic analysis, John R. P. French and Bertram Raven (1959) identified five key bases of power in groups, which are described in Figure 7.3. *Reward power* stems from a person's ability to control group members' reinforcers or payoffs. For example, a department chairperson who can control faculty members' promotions and pay raises (not all chairpersons can) has reward power. *Coercive power* is based on a person's ability or willingness to threaten and punish group members. In academia, a chairperson's coercive power is usually very limited because it is nearly impossible to fire a tenured faculty member, and there are no demotions. Coercive power tends to be greater in the business world, where many managers can easily demote or fire employees.

Expert power is derived from a person's special skills, abilities, or knowledge. For example, in designing a placement test, the members of an academic department might defer to a chairperson who has great expertise in testing theory. *Referent power* depends on how much a person is liked and respected by group members. Other things being equal, people who are well liked can exert more influence over a group than those who inspire disdain. Department chairpersons who have minimal reward, coercive, or expert power often carefully cultivate

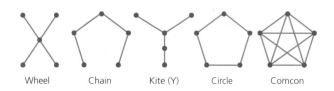

Wheel Chain Kite (Y) Circle Comcon

Figure 7.2 (above). Communication networks. Lines of communication in a group can be restricted in a variety of ways. These communication networks in five-person groups are among those that have been investigated frequently by social psychologists. Communication patterns can affect group productivity and morale.

Five Bases of Power	
Base	**Definition**
Reward power	Influence based on positive or negative reinforcers given or offered to the target
Coercive power	Influence based on punishment or threats directed toward the target
Expert power	Influence based on the target's belief that the powerholder possesses superior skills and abilities
Referent power	Influence based on the target's identification with, attraction to, or respect for the powerholder
Legitimate power	Influence based on the target's belief that the powerholder has a justifiable right to demand the performance of certain behaviors

Figure 7.3 (left). Sources of power. French and Raven (1959) identified five bases for power.

referent power. Finally, *legitimate power* stems from a person's recognized right to make certain demands. When group members defer out of a sense of duty or obligation, they are being swayed by legitimate power. Department chairs who are freely elected by their departments probably can rely on more legitimate power than chairpersons who are appointed by higher-echelon administrators.

Group Cohesiveness

The term *group cohesiveness* **refers to the strength of the liking relationships linking group members to each other and to the group itself.** Members of cohesive groups are close-knit, are committed, have "team spirit," and are very loyal to the group.

What makes a group cohesive? According to Ridgeway (1983), factors that foster high cohesiveness include similar attitudes among group members, personal liking for each other, and warm, pleasant group interactions. Groups also tend to become more cohesive when they are successful in attaining their goals. A threat from outside the group that unifies its members may also bolster cohesiveness.

The consequences of high cohesiveness are a mixed bag of positive and negative effects (Cartwright, 1968). On the positive side of the ledger, people in cohesive groups communicate with each other more and participate more in group activities. On the negative side, high cohesiveness increases the pressure on members to conform to the group's norms. Conformity is not inherently bad, but it can backfire if it suppresses critical thinking in a group. When members don't feel free to criticize their group's direction, poor decision making can result, as we'll see later in the chapter, when we discuss *groupthink*.

Group Size

Unlike cohesiveness, which is difficult to measure, size is a relatively unambiguous feature of groups. It is also an important feature. Variations in group size (the number of people in the group) can affect many aspects of the group experience. For instance, as groups increase in size, members' participation rates and the group's cohesiveness tend to decline (Shaw, 1981). As you'll see in upcoming sections of the chapter, group size can also influence conformity, the emergence of leadership, and group productivity, which we discuss next.

HELPING AND PRODUCTIVITY IN GROUPS

We noted earlier that people join groups because they need friendship and support, they see security and power in numbers, and they want to get jobs done more effectively. Given these goals, it makes sense that psychologists have shown an interest in helping behavior and productivity in groups. Let's look at some of their findings.

Helping Behavior and the Bystander Effect

Imagine that you have a precarious medical condition, and you have to go through life worrying about whether someone will leap forward to provide help if the need arises. Wouldn't you feel more secure when you are in larger groups? After all, there is "safety in numbers." Logically, as group size increases, the probability of having a good samaritan on the scene increases. Or does it? Apparently not. Many studies have uncovered a paradox called the *bystander effect:* **people in groups are less likely to provide needed help than when they are alone.**

Evidence that your probability of getting help *declines* as group size increases was first described by John Darley and Bibb Latané (1968). In their ground-breaking study, students in individual cubicles connected by an intercom participated in discussion groups of three sizes. The separate cubicles allowed the researchers to examine each individual's behavior in a group context, thus minimizing the problem of confounded variables in individual-group comparisons. Early in the discussion, a student who was an experimental accomplice hesitantly mentioned that he was prone to seizures. Later in the dis-

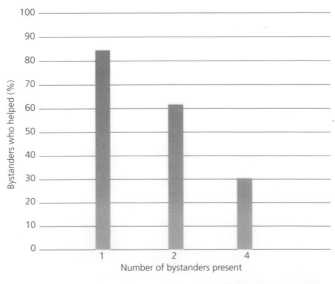

cussion, the same accomplice feigned a severe seizure and cried out for help. Although a majority of subjects sought assistance for the accomplice, Figure 7.4 shows that the tendency to seek help *declined* with increasing group size.

Similar trends have been seen in many other experiments. In these experiments, over 6,000 subjects have had opportunities to respond to apparent emergencies that have included fires, asthma attacks, faintings, crashes, and flat tires, as well as less pressing needs to answer a door or to pick up objects dropped by a stranger (Latané & Nida, 1981). Many of the experiments have been highly realistic studies conducted in subways, stores, and shopping malls. Many have compared individuals against groups in face-to-face interaction. Pooling the results of this research, Latané and Nida (1981) estimated that subjects who were alone provided help 75% of the time. In contrast, subjects in the presence of others provided help only 53% of the time. The only significant limiting condition on the bystander effect is that it is less likely to occur when the need for help is unambiguous.

What accounts for the bystander effect? A number of factors may be at work. Bystander effects are most likely in ambiguous situations because people look around to see if others think there's an emergency. If everyone hesitates, their inaction suggests that there's no real need for help. The *diffusion of responsibility* that occurs in a group is also important. If you're by yourself when you encounter someone in need of help, the responsibility to provide help rests squarely on your shoulders. However, if other people are present, the responsibility is divided among you, and everyone may say to themselves, "Someone else will help." A reduced sense of responsibility may contribute to other aspects of behavior in groups, as we'll see in our discussion of productivity.

Group Productivity and Social Loafing

Have you ever driven through a road construction project—at a snail's pace, of course—and become irritated because you see many workers, but they all seem to be standing around? Maybe the irony of the posted sign "Your tax dollars at work" made you imagine that they were all dawdling. And then again, perhaps not. Individuals' productivity often *does* decline in larger groups (Latané, Williams, & Harkins, 1979).

Two factors appear to contribute to reduced individual productivity in larger groups. One factor is reduced *efficiency* due to the *loss of coordination* among workers' efforts. As you put more people on a yearbook staff, for instance, you'll probably create more and more duplication of effort. You may also increase how often group members end up working at cross-purposes.

Reduced coordination among workers can show up on the simplest of tasks, as demonstrated years ago by an agricultural engineer named Max Ringelmann. He measured the amount of pressure exerted by individuals and groups who pulled on a rope as if they were playing tug-of-war. Ringelmann found that the amount of pressure produced per person declined steadily as he increased group size (Kravitz & Martin, 1986). He pointed out that even on this simple task, some group members pulled when others paused, so that lack of coordination undermined their efficiency.

The second factor contributing to low productivity in groups involves *effort* rather than efficiency. **Social loafing is a reduction in effort by individuals when they work in groups as compared to when they work by themselves.** To investigate social loafing, Latané et al. (1979) measured the sound output produced by subjects who were asked to cheer or clap as loud as they could. So they couldn't see or hear other group members, subjects were told that the study concerned the importance of sensory feedback and were asked to don blindfolds and put on headphones through which loud noise was played. This maneuver permitted a simple deception. Subjects were *led to believe* that they were working alone or in a group of two or six, when *individual* output was actually measured.

When subjects *thought* that they were working in larger groups (the pseudogroup condition), their individual output declined. Since lack of coordination could not

Figure 7.4. The bystander effect. As the number of apparent bystanders increased, the percentage of subjects who sought help for a victim of a (feigned) seizure declined. (Data from Darley & Latané, 1968)

affect individual output, the subjects' decreased sound production had to be due to reduced effort. Latané and his colleagues also had the same subjects clap and shout in genuine groups of 2 and 6 and found an additional decrease in production that was attributed to loss of coordination. Figure 7.5 shows how social loafing and loss of coordination combined to reduce productivity as group size increased.

According to Latané (1981), the bystander effect and social loafing share a common cause: diffusion of responsibility in groups. As group size increases, the responsibility for getting a job done is divided among more people, and many group members ease up because their individual contribution is less recognizable. Thus, social loafing occurs in situations where individuals can "hide in the crowd." Social loafing can be reduced by giving specific responsibilities to individuals in a group, so that their personal contributions remain recognizable (Weldon & Gargano, 1988).

In fairness to groups, although individual productivity usually declines, there may still be strength in numbers. The net productivity of twenty construction workers should dwarf that of one construction worker, barring inconceivable slacking off by the group. Obviously, there are many circumstances in which group performance is likely to exceed individual performance.

The nature of the task is a key determinant of whether groups or individuals tend to perform better (Steiner, 1976). Groups normally have an advantage on *additive tasks,* where the group's production is the sum of its members' efforts (for example, sandbagging a flooded river or stuffing envelopes). However, groups are less likely to excel on *conjunctive tasks,* where the group's production cannot exceed that of its weakest member (for example, climbing a mountain or running a relay).

Suggestions for Improving Group Productivity

When we work together in groups, productivity often is a crucial concern. Is there anything that we can do to in-crease the likelihood of productive interactions in groups? Research on group performance yields the following suggestions.

1. *Increase members' commitment to group goals.* Group members tend to work harder and are less prone to social loafing when they identify strongly with the group's goals (Zaccaro, 1984). Strong commitments to group goals are more likely when members feel that they've had reasonable input into the group's objectives (Latham & Yukl, 1975). Thus, it is wise to discuss and attempt to reach agreement on group goals to maximize motivation.

2. *Encourage open communication.* Groups that welcome open, candid interchanges among members tend to be more productive (Harper & Askling, 1980). A decentralized communication structure will usually work out best unless a group's tasks are very simple. It's especially important to avoid *defensiveness*—that is, excessive concern among members about being attacked and hurt (Gibb, 1973). As we discussed in Chapter 6, communication gets defensive when people are highly evaluative or controlling, when they act superior to others, and when they assume that they're always right. According to Osborn (1963), *brainstorming* is one way to reduce defensiveness. In brainstorming sessions, group members generate as many ideas as possible while temporarily withholding criticism and evaluation (see Chapter 4).

3. *Make use of process planning.* Process planning involves working out some ground rules about how the group will operate as it tackles a task. Process planning includes discussing matters such as the responsibilities of the chairperson, how frequently the group should meet, and

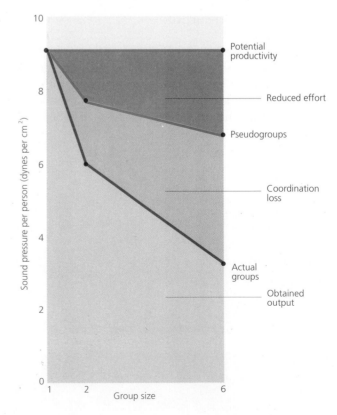

the criteria that should be used in making decisions. Forsyth (1983) points out that most groups plunge right into tasks and devote little or no thought to process planning. However, studies suggest that attention to process planning can increase a group's productivity and members' satisfaction with leadership (Hackman, Brousseau, & Weiss, 1976; Hirokawa, 1980).

4. *Try to keep cohesiveness high.* Groups high in cohesiveness tend to be more effective in achieving their goals (Shaw, 1981). Hence, it's usually a good idea to encourage members who assume socioemotional roles that promote harmonious relations in a group. However, bear in mind that high cohesiveness may create excessive conformity pressure. Also, Marvin Shaw (1981) notes that high cohesiveness can backfire in an organizational setting where a group's goals may be handed down from higher authorities. A group is more likely to rebel against leadership from outside the group (and thus undermine productivity) when its cohesiveness is high.

5. *Beware of overly large group size.* People organizing groups are often tempted to assemble a large group, working under the assumption that larger groups can get more accomplished. However, as we have already discussed, larger groups may yield diminishing returns because of social loafing and poor coordination of effort (Latane, Williams, & Harkins, 1979). The group size that will maximize productivity will vary widely depending on the nature of the group's task, but try to avoid assembling overly large, unwieldy groups.

DECISION MAKING IN GROUPS

Productivity is not the only issue of frequent concern to groups. When people join together in groups, they often have to make decisions about what the group will do and how it will use its resources. Whether it's your study group deciding what type of pizza to order, a jury deciding on a verdict, or Congress deciding whether to pass a bill, groups make decisions.

Figure 7.5. The effect of loss of coordination and social loafing on group productivity. The amount of sound produced per person declined noticeably when people worked in pairs or in a group of six (red line). This decrease in productivity reflects both loss of coordination and social loafing. Sound per person also declined when subjects merely *thought* they were working in pairs or a group of six ("pseudogroups"; green line). This smaller decrease in productivity is due to social loafing. (Data from Latané, Williams, & Harkins, 1979)

Evaluating decision making is often more complicated than evaluating productivity. In many cases, the "right" decision may not be readily apparent. Who can say whether your study group ordered the right pizza or whether Congress passed the right bills? Nonetheless, social psychologists have discovered some interesting tendencies in group decision making. We'll take a brief look at *group polarization* and then discuss *groupthink* in more detail.

Group Polarization

Who leans toward more cautious decisions: individuals or groups? Common sense suggests that groups will work out compromises that cancel out members' extreme views. Hence, the collective wisdom of the group should yield relatively conservative choices. Is common sense correct? Stoner (1961) investigated this question by asking individuals and groups to make decisions under conditions of uncertainty, like those seen in the following dilemma.

Mr. A., an electrical engineer who is married and has one child, has been working for a large electronics corporation since graduating from college five years ago. He is assured of a lifetime job with a modest, though adequate, salary and liberal pension benefits upon retirement. On the other hand, it is very unlikely that his salary will increase much before he retires. While attending a convention, Mr. A. is offered a job with a small, newly founded company which has a highly uncertain future. The new job would pay more to start and would offer the possibility of a share in the ownership if the company survived the competition of the larger firms.

Imagine that you are advising Mr. A. Listed below are several probabilities or odds of the new company proving financially sound. *Please check the lowest probability that you would consider acceptable to make it worthwhile for Mr. A. to take the new job.*

__ The chances are 1 in 10 that the company will prove financially sound.

__ The chances are 3 in 10 that the company will prove financially sound.

___ The chances are 5 in 10 that the company will prove financially sound.

___ The chances are 7 in 10 that the company will prove financially sound.

___ The chances are 9 in 10 that the company will prove financially sound.

___ Place a check here if you think Mr. A. should *not* take the new job no matter what the probabilities. [Kogan & Wallach, 1964]

Stoner had individual subjects give their recommendations and then asked the same subjects to engage in group discussion to arrive at a joint recommendation. Stoner then compared the average recommendation of a group's members against their group decision generated through discussion. He found that groups arrived at *riskier* decisions than individuals. Stoner's finding was replicated in other studies (Pruitt, 1971), and the phenomenon acquired the name *risky shift*.

However, investigators eventually determined that groups can shift either way, toward risk or caution, depending on which way the group is leaning to begin with (Myers & Lamm, 1976). It is a shift toward a more extreme position, an effect called *polarization*, that is the frequent result of group discussion. Thus, **group polarization occurs when group discussion strengthens a group's dominant point of view and produces a shift toward a more extreme decision in that direction** (see Figure 7.6). Group polarization does *not* involve widening the gap between factions in a group, as its name might suggest. In fact, group polarization can contribute to consensus in a group, as we'll see in our discussion of groupthink.

Groupthink

In contrast to group polarization, which is a normal process in group dynamics, groupthink is more like a disease that can infect decision making in groups. *Groupthink* **occurs when members of a cohesive group emphasize concurrence at the expense of critical thinking**

Figure 7.6. Group polarization. Two examples of group polarization are diagrammed here. In the first example (*top*) a group starts out mildly opposed to an idea, but after discussion there is stronger sentiment against the idea. In the second example (*bottom*), a group starts out with a favorable disposition toward an idea, and this disposition is strengthened by group discussion.

in arriving at a decision. As you might imagine, groupthink does not produce very effective decision making. Indeed, groupthink often leads to major blunders that may look incomprehensible after the fact.

Irving Janis (1972) first described groupthink in his effort to explain how President Kennedy and his advisers could miscalculate so badly in deciding to invade Cuba at the Bay of Pigs in 1961. The attempted invasion failed miserably and, in retrospect, seemed remarkably ill-conceived. As Janis put it, "I was puzzled: How could bright men like John F. Kennedy and his advisers be taken in by such a stupid, patchwork plan as the one presented to them by the C.I.A. representatives?" (1973, p. 16). Applying his many years of research and theory on group dynamics to the Bay of Pigs fiasco, Janis developed a model of groupthink, which is summarized in Figure 7.7.

Symptoms of Groupthink

When groups get caught up in groupthink, members suspend their critical judgment. The group starts censoring dissent as the pressure to conform increases. Soon, everyone begins to think alike. Moreover, "mind guards" try to shield the group from information that contradicts the group's view. For instance, at a critical meeting, President Kennedy did not give a key adviser who opposed the Cuban invasion an opportunity to speak.

If the group's view is challenged from outside, victims of groupthink tend to think in simplistic terms. They divide the world into the *in-group*, **the group they belong to and identify with, and the** *out-group*, **people who are not part of the in-group.** When groups shift into this "us versus them" thinking, members begin to overestimate the in-

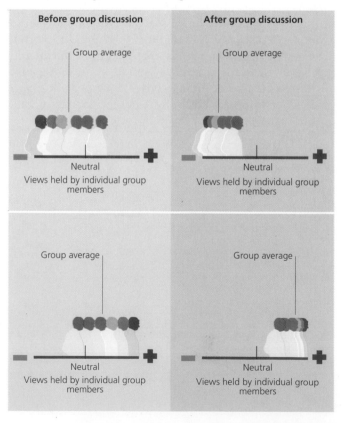

Before group discussion	After group discussion
Group average	Group average
Neutral	Neutral
Views held by individual group members	Views held by individual group members
Group average	Group average
Neutral	Neutral
Views held by individual group members	Views held by individual group members

group's unanimity, and they begin to view the out-group as the enemy. Groupthink also promotes incomplete gathering of information. The group's search for information is biased in favor of facts and opinions that support their decision.

After his description of groupthink, Janis and others reviewed other presidential blunders and found clear signs of groupthink underlying President Franklin Delano Roosevelt's lack of preparation for Japan's attack on Pearl Harbor. Janis also found evidence of groupthink in President Lyndon Johnson's continued escalation of the Vietnam War and in President Richard Nixon's cover-up of the Watergate break-in. Of course, groupthink is not limited to the highest levels of government. It may be even more prevalent in less public groups that make decisions every day in boardrooms, committee rooms, courtrooms, and back rooms all over the world.

Sources of Groupthink

What causes groupthink? Janis maintains that the danger of groupthink is greater when groups exhibit *high cohesiveness*. The pressure to go along with others can be very intense in cohesive groups. Members of cohesive groups are also more likely to adhere to group norms, such as "Don't rock the boat." Under these conditions, group discussions can easily lead to group polarization, strengthening the group's dominant view.

According to Janis, the probability of groupthink occurring depends on several other factors as well. For instance, groupthink is more likely when a group works in relative *isolation*, with little or no input from people outside the group. Groupthink is also promoted by *biased leadership*. When a group's power structure is dominated by a strong, directive leader who wants to push a particular decision through, the stage is set for groupthink. Finally, the likelihood of groupthink increases under *decisional stress*, when members feel pressured to make a very important decision. As we discussed in Chapter 3, stress can impair individuals' cognitive functioning. Under stress, people often do a poor job of reviewing their options and jump to conclusions too quickly (Keinan, 1987).

Preventing Groupthink

What can be done to reduce the likelihood of groupthink? Janis does not argue in favor of reducing group cohesiveness to prevent groupthink, because cohesiveness carries many benefits. Instead, he focuses on the other contributing factors—isolation, decisional stress, and biased leadership. To combat isolation, Janis suggests that groups should seek input from nonmembers. Thus, outsiders should occasionally be invited to meetings to provide a fresh perspective. To reduce decisional stress, Janis suggests that groups should allow themselves plenty of time in making decisions. Last, but not least, groups should take steps to avoid biased leadership. Leaders should strive to be impartial and encourage open discussion. Group members should speak up when their leaders appear to be stacking the deck in favor of a particular decision. The link between leadership and groupthink underscores the importance of leadership, which is the topic that we consider next.

LEADERSHIP IN GROUPS

Groups often need direction, which brings us to the matter of leadership. Leadership is terribly important because the actions of leaders can have far-reaching consequences. Would World War II have occurred without the demented leadership of Adolf Hitler? Would the

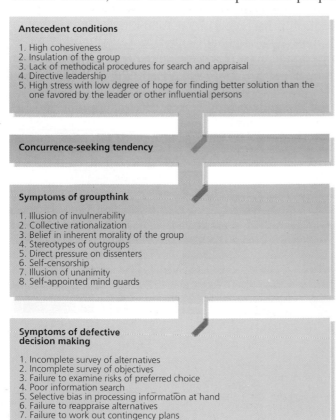

Figure 7.7. A model of groupthink. The antecedent conditions and symptoms of groupthink are outlined here, along with the effects on a group's decision making.

civil rights movement have progressed as it did in the 1960s without the inspirational leadership of Martin Luther King? Would the people of the Philippines have overthrown the corrupt regime of Ferdinand Marcos without the outstanding leadership of Corazon Aquino? It's hard to say for sure, but many scholars believe that these momentous events would not have occurred without the leadership of Hitler, King, and Aquino. In a similar vein, when people analyze the success or failure of corporations, colleges, unions, football squads, military units, work teams, clubs, and committees, they usually zero in on the issue of leadership.

What Is Leadership?

"A leader is a man who has the ability to get other people to do what they don't want to do, and like it." This tongue-in-cheek definition came from Harry S Truman, the 32nd president of the United States. Does it capture the essence of leadership? In some ways, yes. It recognizes that a leader tries to influence and motivate others. It also highlights the reciprocal, interactive nature of leadership. You can't have leaders without followers—people who are willing to be led. Incorporating these ideas into a formal definition, we arrive at the following. *Leadership* **is a reciprocal process in which certain people are permitted to motivate and influence others to facilitate the pursuit of group goals.** Does leadership always occur when people join together in groups? No. Let's look at some of the variables that influence the emergence of leadership.

When Do Leaders Emerge?

Leadership is not an inevitable outgrowth of group formation. In many simple situations leadership may be unnecessary. Three friends ordering a pizza may not need a leader. But some situations call for leadership. A key factor affecting the emergence of leadership is the *size of the group* (Hemphill, 1961). Small groups can get by without leaders, but as groups become larger, the need for

leadership grows. For instance, if a group ordering pizza contains eighteen people rather than three, some members will have to take charge and get things organized. Obviously, large organizations must have leaders to function effectively. Recognizing this reality, such organizations don't wait for leadership to emerge spontaneously. They appoint presidents, department heads, managers, and so forth.

The nature of a group's tasks or activities also influences the need for leadership (Argyle, 1969). A leader is more likely to emerge when a group tackles complex tasks, because it helps to have someone coordinating the group's efforts. Groups also show more willingness to follow leadership when they engage in more important activities. Available decision time is another key consideration. Leadership is more likely when a group has to reach a decision quickly. Thus, a variety of factors determine whether leaders emerge in group interactions.

Who Will Lead? Trait versus Situational Theories

If leadership is needed, who is likely to come to the forefront to provide it? Are certain types of people born to be leaders? Early investigations of leadership were guided by trait theories. *Trait theories* assume that leaders have certain personality traits that set them apart from their followers. Hundreds of studies were conducted, comparing leaders and followers, to identify these special leadership traits.

These studies uncovered a handful of modest associations between personality traits and the emergence of leadership. In comparison to followers, leaders tended to be more achievement-oriented, more responsible, more self-confident, more sociable, and more motivated to lead (Stogdill, 1974). However, the results of these studies were generally regarded as disappointing. The findings from one study to another were very inconsistent, and the correlations found between personality and leadership were terribly weak. Ultimately, investigators were forced

to conclude that there are no personality traits that reliably distinguish leaders from followers.

The failure of trait theories aroused interest in situational theories of leadership. *Situational theories* propose that different leaders emerge from a group in different situations. According to this approach, the key consideration is the fit between group members' abilities and the task at hand. For example, when the members of a school board discuss building proposals, someone with construction expertise may lead. When they discuss next year's budget, someone with accounting knowledge may lead. When they discuss educational innovations, someone with teaching experience may lead.

Like trait theories, situational theories of leadership proved to be too simplistic. Researchers failed to find a strong link between task demands and the selection of leaders. When groups work on a diverse array of tasks, the same people tend to assume leadership roles on task after task, even though situational demands have changed (Kenny & Zaccaro, 1983). Although they don't share highly similar personalities, some people apparently are cut out to be leaders.

Today, theorists recognize that who will lead depends on a variety of factors. Included among them are (1) situational and task demands, (2) the personality traits exhibited by potential leaders, and (3) the fit between these traits and followers' preferences (Hollander, 1985). Intricate interactions among these variables influence the selection of leaders. Thus, theories about the development of leadership have evolved from rather simple to very complex models.

What Do Leaders Do? Styles of Leadership

If you were the head of a department in a large corporation, how would you lead? Would you delegate authority readily, or would you closely supervise your workers? Would you welcome input from subordinates, or would you be a dictator? Would you motivate your staff with fear or with rewards? These are just a few of the questions that leaders face when they attempt to develop a personal leadership style.

Investigations of leadership style require assessments of what leaders do. In the decade following World War II, a team of psychologists at Ohio State University set out to develop a questionnaire to measure various aspects of leadership behavior (Halpin & Winer, 1952; Stogdill, 1963). They discovered that the activities of leaders sorted into two categories, representing two dimensions of lead-

---

RECOMMENDED READING

Improving Leadership Effectiveness: The Leader Match Concept
by Fred E. Fiedler & Martin M. Chemers (Wiley, 1984)

There are many books on enhancing leaders' effectiveness, but this one is different. Most books assume that the same general advice will apply equally well to all leaders and to all the situations they find themselves in. As we discuss in this chapter, Fred Fiedler's research suggests that this assumption is naive. The evidence indicates that different styles of leadership are optimal in different situations. Hence, Fiedler and Chemers maintain that leadership effectiveness depends on the match between the leader and the situation. They therefore devised their Leader Match training program, which has been used with considerable success in many organizational settings since 1976.

This book summarizes the essence of their training program. It begins by using Fiedler's least-preferred co-worker measure and other exercises to help readers determine their leadership style. The following five chapters help leaders evaluate the situational factors that exist in their organizations. Elaborate questionnaires allow the readers to assess the factors that are critical according to contingency theory: leader-member relations, position power, and task structure.

The following chapters provide advice on how to create a better match between one's leadership style and the situation. Fiedler and Chemers point out that it isn't easy to change individuals' leadership styles because their styles are deeply embedded in their personalites. Hence, they focus on how to modify leader-member relations, position power, and task structure in efforts to re-engineer situations to fit better with one's style of leadership.

It is even more difficult to change your basic leadership style. Practically speaking, it would be as difficult as suddenly trying to become a completely different person. If it were possible, everyone would be popular, lovable and effective. [p. 177]

It is much easier to change your leadership situation than your personality. Although you may find this hard to believe at first, your ability to control your immediate leadership environment is considerably greater than most people realize. This is true even of jobs that seem highly circumscribed and specific. Job engineering provides an important method for improving your own leadership performance and the effectiveness of your organization. [pp. 177–178]

ership: initiating structure and consideration. *Initiating structure* **is a dimension of leadership that reflects the degree to which a leader organizes, directs, and regulates the group's activities.** Leaders who are strong in initiating structure let members know what is expected of them. They emphasize deadlines, criticize poor work, enforce rules strictly, and push people to work hard. *Consideration* **is a dimension of leadership that reflects the degree to which a leader is warm, trusting, and supportive in interactions with group members.** Leaders who are high in consideration are friendly, approachable, and willing to listen. They explain their decisions, bend rules when necessary, and treat others as equals.

The Ohio State researchers who described initiating structure and consideration viewed them as independent, unrelated aspects of leadership. Thus, they believed that a leader could be strong on one dimension and weak on the other, strong on both dimensions, or weak on both dimensions.

However, subsequent researchers have argued that most leaders tend to be strong on one dimension or the other—but usually not both. In terms of leadership style, then, many theorists believe that leaders can be differentiated into two basic types: task-oriented leaders and relationship-oriented leaders (Forsyth, 1983). *Task-oriented leaders* score high in initiating structure. They focus on moving the group toward its goals and they emphasize performance and productivity. *Social-oriented leaders* score high in consideration. They try to keep everyone happy and they emphasize the group's cohesiveness and morale.

Which Leaders Will Be Most Effective? Fiedler's Theory

Given their emphasis on productivity, you might expect that task-oriented leaders would be more effective than social-oriented leaders. However, this is not necessarily true. In some situations, the domineering style of task-oriented leaders can undermine a group's morale and hurt productivity. Thus, the question of leadership effectiveness is more complex than it might first appear.

Fred Fiedler (1967, 1978) has developed a prominent theory of leadership effectiveness. His model is called a *contingency theory* because it proposes that the most effective style of leadership is contingent upon (depends on) various situational factors. Fiedler measures leadership style in an unusual way. He asks a leader to identify the most difficult person to work with in the group. The leader is then asked to rate this *least-preferred co-worker* on 18 bipolar scales (cold/warm, sincere/insincere, and so forth). Leaders who return relatively *high ratings* of their least-preferred co-worker are assumed to be warm, supportive, *relationship-oriented leaders.* Leaders who give relatively *low ratings* to their least-preferred co-worker are assumed to be hard-nosed, *task-oriented leaders.*

Fiedler's model analyzes three variables that are thought to influence the overall favorability of the leader's situation. *Leader-member relations* refers to whether the leader is liked, accepted, and trusted by the group. *Task structure* involves the degree to which the group's tasks are clearly defined. *Position power* represents the amount of power and authority the leader has over group members.

Figure 7.8. Fiedler's contingency model. The three situational factors that govern the overall favorability of a leader's situation are identified at the top of the diagram. These factors can combine into eight possible conditions, which are numbered in order of overall favorability (from I through VIII) on the right. The leadership style thought to be most effective for each condition is also identified on the right. The evidence suggests that task-oriented leaders are best when situational favorability is reasonably high or extremely low. Relationship-oriented leaders tend to excel when favorability is intermediate.

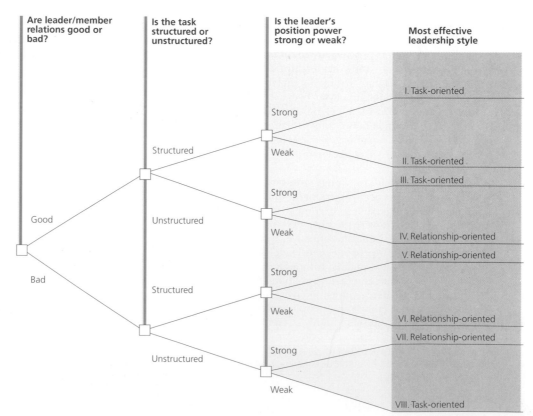

Figure 7.8 maps out how these three factors combine to create eight possible conditions of varied situational favorability.

Figure 7.8 also shows which types of leaders excel in which situations. As you can see, Fiedler's research suggests that task-oriented leaders are most effective when situational favorability is fairly high (conditions I–III) or when it is extremely low (condition VIII). At intermediate levels of favorability (conditions IV–VII), relationship-oriented leaders tend to work out better.

Many studies of leadership have yielded findings consistent with Fiedler's model (Strube & Garcia, 1981). However, the model is not without its critics. Some critics have expressed doubts about Fiedler's method for assessing whether leaders are task-oriented or relationship-oriented (Schriesheim & Kerr, 1977). They argue that leaders' ratings of their least-preferred co-worker could be influenced by many factors besides their leadership style. Other critics complain that Fiedler has failed to explain *why* relationship-oriented and task-oriented leaders excel in different situations (Ashour, 1973).

In recent years, Fiedler has expanded his theory, looking at additional variables in an effort to better understand why different types of leaders are effective in different situations (Fiedler & Garcia, 1987). In particular, Fiedler has examined the importance of leaders' intelligence and competence. According to Fiedler, leader intelligence is positively correlated with group productivity, but the strength of this correlation depends on a variety of factors. On one hand, this correlation is stronger when leaders are directive. On the other hand, this correlation is weaker when leaders are under a great deal of stress, because the stress diverts much of their attention from the task at hand. Additional research is needed to identify other variables that underlie the relationship between leadership style and leadership effectiveness.

Although Fiedler's theory is incomplete, its central thesis appears sound. A substantial body of evidence suggests that there is no one ideal or superior style of leadership. Thus, when it comes to leadership, we can conclude that "there's more than one way to skin a cat." We'll reach a similar conclusion in the next section, where we examine various approaches to persuasion.

PERSUASION: CHANGING OTHERS' ATTITUDES

Every day we are bombarded by efforts to alter our attitudes through persuasion. To illustrate, let's trace the events of an imaginary morning. You may not even be out of bed before you start hearing radio advertisements that are meant to persuade you to buy specific mouthwashes, computers, and tennis shoes. When you unfurl your newspaper, you find many quotes from government officials, all of which were carefully crafted to shape your opinions. On your way to school, you see billboards showing attractive models draped over automobiles and bottles of bourbon in the hopes that they'll affect your feelings about these products. When you arrive on campus, you find a group passing out leaflets that urge you to repent your sins and join the group in worship. In class, your economics professor champions the wisdom of free market in international trade. At lunch, the person you've been dating argues about the merits of an "open relationship." Your argument is interrupted by someone who wants both of you to sign a petition for nuclear disarmament. "Doesn't it ever let up?" you wonder.

When it comes to persuasion, the answer is no. As the survey data in Figure 7.9 show, a host of people are involved in efforts to persuade us. Indeed, the people closest to us (immediate family and close friends) are the ones who exert the most effort to mold our behavior through persuasion (Rule, Bisanz, & Kohn, 1985).

Persuasion **involves the communication of arguments and information intended to change another person's attitudes.** What are attitudes? William McGuire (1985) provides a succinct definition in *The Handbook of Social Psychology*: ***attitudes* locate objects of thought on dimensions of judgment.** "Objects of thought" may include

Fred E. Fiedler

"Who Tries to Persuade You?"	
Source	Percent
Immediate family	27
Extended family	7
Close friends	18
Circumstantial friends	7
Instructors	13
Salespeople	11
Other professionals	10
Trait-defined people (e.g., religious people)	5
Goal-defined people (e.g., people who are trying to impress me)	2

Figure 7.9. Sources of persuasion. When Rule et al. (1985) asked subjects "Who tries to persuade you?" they found that family and friends are our major sources of persuasive efforts.

social issues (capital punishment or gun control, for example), groups (liberals, farmers), institutions (the Lutheran church, the Supreme Court), consumer products (yogurt, computers), and people (the president, your next-door neighbor). "Dimensions of judgment" refers to the various ways in which we might evaluate the objects of our thoughts.

Like other forms of communication, the process of persuasion includes four basic elements, which were introduced in Chapter 6. The *source* is the person who sends a communication, and the *receiver* is the person to whom the message is sent. Thus, if you watched a presidential address on TV, the president would be the source. You and millions of other listeners would be the receivers in this persuasive effort. The *message* is the information transmitted by the source. The *channel* is the medium through which the message is sent. In examining communication channels, investigators have often compared face-to-face interaction against appeals sent via mass media (for example, television and radio). Although the research on communication channels is interesting, we'll confine our discussion to source, message, and receiver variables. Let's examine some of the factors that determine whether persuasion works.

Source Factors

Persuasion tends to be more successful when the source has high *credibility.* What gives a person credibility? Either expertise or trustworthiness. People try to convey their *expertise* by mentioning their degrees, their training, and their experience, or by showing an impressive grasp of the issue at hand (Hass, 1981).

Expertise is a plus, but *trustworthiness* is even more important (McGinnies & Ward, 1980). Whom would you believe if you were told that your state needs to reduce corporate taxes to stimulate its economy—the president of a huge corporation in your state or an economics professor from out of state? Probably the latter. Trustworthiness is undermined when a source, such as

the corporation president, appears to have something to gain. In contrast, trustworthiness is enhanced when people appear to argue against their own interests (Eagly, Wood, & Chaiken, 1978). This effect explains why salespeople often make remarks like "Frankly, my snowblower isn't the best and they have a better brand down the street, if you're willing to spend a bit more . . ."

Likability also increases the effectiveness of a persuasive source. Likability depends on a host of factors (see Chapter 8). A key consideration is a person's physical attractiveness. The favorable effect of physical attractiveness on persuasion was apparent in a study by Chaiken (1979). In this study, students were asked to obtain signatures for a petition. Chaiken found that the more attractive students were more successful. We also respond better to sources who are *similar* to us in ways that are relevant to the issue at hand (Berscheid, 1966).

The importance of source variables can be seen in advertising. Many companies spend a fortune to obtain an ideal spokesperson, like Bill Cosby, who combines trustworthiness, expertise (a doctorate in education), likability, and a knack for connecting with the average person. Companies quickly abandon a spokesperson who acquires any hint of scandal. For example, when tennis star Billy Jean King's lesbian affair surfaced a number of years ago, her endorsements dropped immediately. Thus, source variables are extremely important factors in persuasion.

Message Factors

Imagine that you are going to give a speech to a local community group advocating a reduction in state taxes on corporations. In preparing your speech, you would probably wrestle with a number of questions about how to structure your message. Should you look at both sides of the issue or just present your side? Should you deliver a low-key, logical speech, or should you try to strike fear into the hearts of your listeners? Should you spell out your conclusions for your listeners or use rhetorical questions

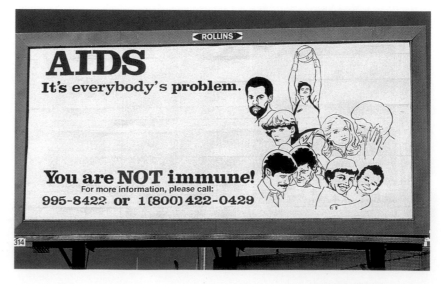

II: THE INTERPERSONAL REALM

to stimulate their thinking? Let's look at these message factors.

We'll assume that you're aware that there are two sides to the taxation issue. On the one hand, you are convinced that lower corporate taxes will bring new companies and factories to your state, stimulate economic growth, and increase jobs. On the other hand, you realize that reduced tax revenues may gradually hurt the quality of education and roads in your state. Nevertheless, you believe that the benefits of a lower rate will outweigh the costs. Should you present a *one-sided argument* that ignores the possible problems for education and road quality? Or should you present a *two-sided argument* that acknowledges concern about education and road quality, and then downplays the magnitude of these problems?

In general, two-sided arguments seem to be more effective. Just mentioning that there are two sides to an issue can increase your credibility with an audience (Jones & Brehm, 1970). One-sided messages work only when your audience is uneducated about the issue or when they are already very favorably disposed to your point of view (Lumsdaine & Janis, 1953).

Persuasive messages frequently attempt to arouse fear. Opponents of nuclear power scare us with visions of meltdowns. Antismoking campaigns emphasize the threat of cancer. Deodorant ads highlight the risk of embarassment. You could follow their lead and argue that if corporate taxes aren't reduced, your state will be headed toward massive unemployment and economic ruin. Does *fear arousal* work? Yes, studies involving a wide range of issues (nuclear policy, auto safety, and dental hygiene among others) have shown that the arousal of fear often increases persuasion. However, there are limiting conditions (Leventhal, 1970; Rogers, 1975).

The conditions under which fear arousal is likely to work are the following. Your listeners must view the dire consequences that you describe as exceedingly unpleasant, fairly probable if they don't take your advice, and avoidable if they do. In our hypothetical case, your listeners will surely agree that economic ruin is terrible. But you

Attitudes about social issues are common targets for persuasive messages. This public-service billboard uses a common persuasive strategy—arousal of fear.

may have trouble convincing them that your state is headed toward ruin or that reduced taxes are the way to avoid it. If you aren't confident about the weight of evidence on these points, you shouldn't arouse fear in your audience. A high level of fear may make them defensive, so that they tune you out.

What about *drawing conclusions* versus *asking rhetorical questions*? Should you clearly spell out your conclusions for your listeners, making remarks like "We must decrease corporate taxation to attract new business"? Or should you prod your listeners to draw their own conclusions (based on your arguments) by asking rhetorical questions like "Will any companies consider building in our state if our taxes remain too high?" Research by Richard Petty and John Cacioppo (1986) suggests that rhetorical questions are helpful when you are addressing a neutral audience and you have strong arguments in your favor. In most cases, especially if your arguments are weak, you had better try to draw your listeners' conclusions for them.

Receiver Factors

What about the receiver of the persuasive message? Are some people easier to persuade than others? Undoubtedly, but the personality traits that account for these differences interact with other considerations in complicated ways. Transient factors, such as forewarning the receiver about a persuasive effort and a receiver's initial position on an issue, seem to be more influential than a receiver's personality.

An old saying suggests that "to be forewarned is to be forearmed." The value of *forewarning* applies to targets of persuasive efforts (Freedman & Sears, 1965; McGuire, 1964). When you shop for a new TV, you *expect* salespeople to work at persuading you. To some extent this forewarning reduces the impact of their arguments.

The effect of a persuasive effort also depends on the discrepancy between a *receiver's initial position* on an issue and the position advocated by the source. Persuasion tends to work best when there is a moderate discrepancy between the two. Why? According to *social judgment theory*, people usually are willing to consider alternative views on an issue if the views aren't too different from their own (Sherif & Hovland, 1961; Upshaw, 1969). **A *latitude of acceptance* is a range of potentially acceptable positions on an issue centered around one's initial attitude position.** Persuasive messages that fall outside a receiver's latitude of acceptance usually fall on deaf ears. When a message falls within a receiver's latitude of acceptance, successful persuasion is much more likely (Atkins, Deaux, & Bieri, 1967).

Within the latitude of acceptance, however, a *larger* discrepancy between the receiver's initial position and the position advocated should produce greater attitude change than a smaller discrepancy. The reason is that people often "meet part way" to resolve disagreement. Figure 7.10 shows how this theory could apply to an audience member who heard your presentation advocating reduced corporate taxation.

Our review of source, message, and receiver variables has shown that persuasion involves a complex interplay of factors. Of course, persuasion is *not* the only method through which people influence each other. There are many other influence techniques that don't depend on the communication of arguments and information. We'll examine some of these in the Application.

CONFORMITY: YIELDING TO PRESSURE

If you keep a well-manicured lawn, or extol the talents of popular rock star Bruce Springsteen, are you exhibiting conformity? According to social psychologists, it depends on whether your behavior is the result of group pressure. ***Conformity* occurs when people yield to real or imagined social pressure.** For example, if you maintain a well-groomed lawn only to avoid complaints from your neigh-bors, you are yielding to social pressure. If you like Springsteen because you genuinely enjoy his records, that's *not* conformity. However, if you like Springsteen because it's "hip" and your friends would question your taste if you didn't, then you're conforming.

Asch's Studies

In the 1950s, Solomon Asch (1951, 1955, 1956) devised a clever procedure that minimized ambiguity about whether subjects were conforming, allowing him to investigate the variables that govern conformity. Let's recreate one of Asch's (1955) classic experiments. The subjects are male undergraduates recruited for a study of visual perception. A group of seven subjects are shown a large card with a vertical line on it. Then they are asked to indicate which of three lines on a second card matches the original "standard line" in length (see Figure 7.11). All seven subjects are given a turn at the task, and each announces his choice to the group. The subject in the sixth chair doesn't know it, but everyone else in the group is an accomplice of the experimenter. They're about to make him wonder whether he has taken leave of his senses.

The accomplices give accurate responses on the first two trials. On the third trial, line 2 clearly is the correct response, but the first five "subjects" all say that line 3 matches the standard line. The genuine subject can't believe his ears. Over the course of the experiment, the accomplices all give the same incorrect response on 12 out of 18 trials. Asch wants to see how the subject responds in these situations. The line judgments are easy and unambiguous. Working alone, people achieve better than 95% accuracy in matching the lines. So, if the subject consistently agrees with the accomplices, he isn't making honest mistakes—he is conforming. Will the subject stick to his guns and defy the group? Or will he go along with the group?

Averaging across 50 subjects, Asch (1955) found that the young men conformed on 37% of the trials. The subjects varied considerably in their tendency to con-

Figure 7.10. Latitude of acceptance and attitude change. A, B, and C are positions on the tax rate that one might advocate. A and B both fall within the receiver's latitude of acceptance, but position B should produce a larger attitude shift. Position C is outside the receiver's latitude of acceptance and should fall on deaf ears.

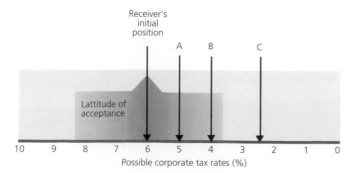

Figure 7.11. Stimuli used in Asch's conformity studies. Subjects were asked to match a standard line (*top*) with one of three other lines displayed on another card (*bottom*). The task was easy—until experimental accomplices started responding with obviously incorrect answers, creating a situation in which Asch evaluated subjects' conformity.

form, however. Out of the 50 subjects, 13 never caved in to the group, while 14 conformed on more than half the trials.

In subsequent studies, *group size* and *group unanimity* turned out to be key determinants of conformity (Asch, 1956). To examine group size, Asch repeated his procedure with groups that included 1 to 15 accomplices. Little conformity was seen when a subject was pitted against just one accomplice. Conformity increased rapidly as group size went from 2 to 4, peaked at a group size of 7, and then leveled off (see Figure 7.12). Thus, Asch concluded that as groups grow larger, conformity increases—up to a point.

Interestingly, group size made little difference if just one accomplice "broke" with the others, wrecking their unanimous agreement. The presence of another dissenter lowered conformity to about one-quarter of its peak, even when the dissenter made *inaccurate* judgments that happened to conflict with the majority view. Apparently, the subjects just needed to hear someone else question the accuracy of the group's perplexing responses.

Conformity versus Compliance

At first, Asch wasn't sure whether conforming subjects were really changing their beliefs in response to social pressure or just pretending to change them. When subjects were interviewed later, many reported that they had begun to doubt their eyesight and that they thought "the majority must be right." These interviews suggested that the subjects had actually changed their beliefs. However, critics asserted that the subjects may have been trying to rationalize their conformity after the fact.

A study that included a condition in which subjects made their responses anonymously, instead of publicly, settled the question. Conformity declined dramatically when subjects recorded their responses privately. This finding suggested that subjects in the Asch studies were not really changing their beliefs (Deutsch & Gerard, 1955).

Based on this evidence, theorists concluded that Asch's experiments evoked a particular type of conformity, called compliance. **Compliance occurs when people yield to social pressure in their public behavior, even though their private beliefs have not changed.** In the Asch studies, compliance resulted from subtle, implied pressure. However, compliance usually occurs in response to explicit rules, requests, and commands. For example, if you agree to wear formal clothes to a fancy restaurant that requires formal attire, even though you despise such rules, you're displaying compliance. Similarly, if you reluctantly follow a supervisor's suggestions at work, even though you think they're lousy ideas, you're complying with a superior's wishes. Compliance with an authority figure's directions is commonplace, as we see in our next section.

OBEDIENCE: YIELDING TO AUTHORITY

Obedience **is a form of compliance that occurs when people follow direct commands, usually from someone in a position of authority.** As we noted at the beginning of the chapter, when an authority figure says "Jump!" many of us simply ask "How high?" The extent to which many people will obey was made tragically apparent in the infamous "Jonestown massacre." As you may recall, Jim Jones was the charismatic leader of a religious cult called the People's Temple, which had set up a large encampment in the isolated wilderness of Guyana. Feeling pressured by a congressional investigation, Jones ordered all his followers to commit mass suicide by drinking cyanide-laced Kool-Aid. Although a small minority of Jones's followers refused to cooperate (a few escaped, a few were shot), most went along with his orders and took their own lives! How can we explain such extraordinary obedience? Was it due to the unique character of the people of Jonestown? Probably not. Both anecdotal and empirical evidence suggest that in the right circumstances most of us can be coaxed or coerced into doing virtually anything.

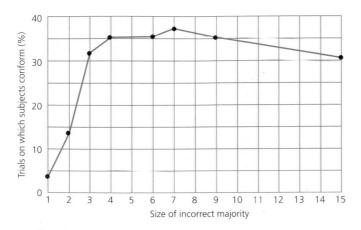

Figure 7.12. Conformity and group size. This graph shows the percentage of trials on which subjects conformed as a function of group size in Asch's research. Asch found that conformity became more frequent as group size increased, up to about 7 persons, and then leveled off. (Data from Asch, 1955)

Milgram's Studies

Stanley Milgram was a brilliantly creative social psychologist who set out to study this tendency to obey authority figures. Like many other people after World War II, he was troubled by how readily the citizens of Germany had followed the orders of dictator Adolf Hitler, even when the orders required morally repugnant actions, such as the slaughter of millions of Jews. Milgram, who had worked with Solomon Asch, set out to design a standard laboratory procedure for the study of obedience, much like Asch's procedure for studying conformity. The clever experiment that Milgram devised became one of the most famous and controversial studies in the annals of psychology. It has been hailed as a "monumental contribution" to science, and condemned as "dangerous, dehumanizing and unethical research" (Ross, 1988).

Milgram's (1963) subjects were a diverse collection of 40 men from the local community. They were told that the study was concerned with the effects of punishment on learning. When they arrived at the lab, they drew slips of paper from a hat to get their assignments. The drawing was rigged so that the subject always became the "teacher" and an experimental accomplice (a likable 47-year-old accountant) became the "learner."

The learner was strapped into an electrified chair through which a shock could be delivered whenever he made a mistake on the task. The subject was then taken to an adjoining room that housed the shock generator that he would control in his role as the teacher. Although the apparatus looked and sounded realistic, it was a fake and the learner was never shocked.

As the "learning experiment" proceeded, the accomplice made many mistakes that necessitated shocks. The teacher was instructed to increase the shock level after each wrong answer. At 300 volts, the learner began to pound on the wall between the two rooms in protest and soon stopped responding to the teacher's questions. From this point forward, subjects frequently turned to the experimenter for guidance. Whenever they did so, the experimenter firmly indicated that the teacher should continue to give stronger and stronger shocks to the now-silent learner. The dependent variable was the maximum shock the subject was willing to administer before refusing to cooperate.

As Figure 7.13 shows, 26 of the 40 subjects (65%) administered all 30 levels of shock. Although they tended to obey the experimenter, many subjects voiced and displayed considerable distress about harming the learner. The horrified subjects groaned, bit their lips, stuttered, trembled, and broke into a sweat—but they continued administering the shocks. Based on these findings, Milgram concluded that obedience to authority was even more common than he or others had anticipated.

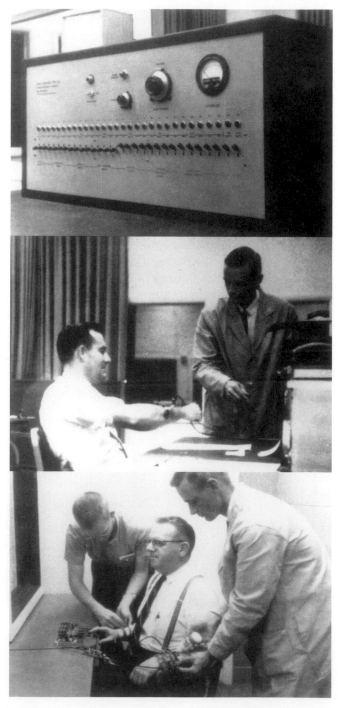

Figure 7.13. Milgram's (1963) experiment on obedience.
The photos show the fake shock generator, a subject being instructed in the use of the generator, and the "learner" being connected to the shock generator during an experimental session. The results of the study are summarized in the bar graph on page 205. The vast majority of subjects (65%) delivered the entire series of shocks to the learner.

In interpreting his results, Milgram argued that strong pressure from an authority figure can make decent people do terribly indecent things to others. Applying this insight to Nazi war crimes and other travesties, Milgram asserted that some sinister actions may not be due to actors' evil character so much as to situational pressures that can lead normal people to engage in acts of treachery and violence. Thus, he arrived at the disturbing conclusion that given the right circumstances, any of us might obey orders to inflict harm on innocent strangers.

If you're like most people, you're confident that you wouldn't follow an experimenter's demands to inflict harm on a helpless victim. But the empirical findings indicate that you're probably wrong. After many replications, the data are deplorable, but clear. Most of us can be coerced into engaging in actions that violate our morals and values.

After his initial demonstration, Milgram (1974) tried about 20 variations on his experimental procedure, looking for factors that influenced subjects' obedience. As a whole, Milgram was surprised at how stable subjects' obedience remained as he changed various aspects of his experiment.

The Ensuing Controversy

Milgram's study evoked an enduring controversy that continues today. Some critics argued that Milgram's results wouldn't generalize to the real world (Baumrind, 1964; Orne & Holland, 1968). They maintained that subjects who agree to participate in a scientific study *expect to obey* orders from an experimenter. Milgram (1964, 1968) replied by pointing out that so do soldiers and bureaucrats in the real world who are accused of villainous acts performed in obedience to authority. "I reject Baumrind's argument that the observed obedience doesn't count because it occurred where it is appropriate," said Milgram (1964). "That is precisely why it *does* count." Overall, the weight of evidence supports the generalizability of Milgram's results. The results were consistently replicated for many years, in diverse settings, with a variety of subjects and procedural variations (A. G. Miller, 1986).

Critics also questioned the ethics of Milgram's procedure (Baumrind, 1964). They noted that without prior consent, subjects were exposed to extensive deception that could undermine their trust in people and to severe stress that could leave emotional scars. Milgram's defenders argued that the brief distress experienced by his subjects was a small price to pay for the insights that emerged from his obedience studies. Looking back, however, many psychologists share the critics' concerns about the ethical implications of Milgram's work. His pro-

Level of shock (as labeled on Milgram's shock machine)

Volts	
450	65% of subjects
XXX 435	
405	
Danger: severe shock 375	
345	
Extreme-intensity shock 315	
285	
255	
Intense shock 225	
Very strong shock 195	
165	
Strong shock 135	
105	
Moderate shock 75	
45	
Slight shock 15	
0	

0 2 4 6 8 10 12 14 16 18 20 22 24 26 28
Number of subjects who stopped giving shock

Stanley Milgram

cedure is questionable by contemporary standards of research ethics. At most universities it would be difficult to obtain permission to replicate Milgram's study today—a bizarre epitaph for what may be psychology's best-known experiment.

SUMMARY

Groups consist of two or more individuals who interact and are interdependent. We join groups to fulfill our affiliation needs, to enhance our sense of identity, to engage in social comparison, to increase our mutual security, and to get jobs done efficiently. People in groups fulfill many different roles. Most people specialize in either task-related roles or socioemotional roles. Group norms, which are rules about appropriate behavior, also influence how we act in groups.

A communication network is a pattern of who talks to whom in a group. Centralized networks tend to work better when groups face simple problems, but decentralized networks are advantageous for more complex problems. There are five sources of power in groups: reward power, coercive power, expert power, referent power, and legitimate power. Cohesive groups are close-knit ones in which members like each other. Cohesiveness facilitates communication, but it can increase conformity. Cohesiveness tends to decline as groups increase in size.

The bystander effect refers to the curious finding that people who would help someone in need when alone are less likely to provide help when part of a group. Individuals' productivity often declines in larger groups because of loss of coordination and because of social loafing. Group productivity is enhanced by open communication, process planning, small size, cohesiveness, and agreement on group goals.

Group polarization occurs when discussion leads a group to shift toward a more extreme decision in the direction the group was already leaning. In groupthink, a cohesive group suspends critical judgment in a misguided effort to promote agreement in decision making. Unfortunately, poor decisions often result. Groupthink is promoted by high cohesiveness, working in isolation, biased leadership, and decisional stress.

The need for leadership is greater when a group is large, when its problems are complex, and when time is precious. Who will lead depends on situational demands, the personality traits of potential leaders, and the fit between these traits and group members' preferences. Leaders can be differentiated into two basic types: task-oriented leaders and social-oriented leaders. According to Fiedler's contingency theory, the most effective leadership style depends on a variety of situational factors.

The success of persuasive effects depends on several factors. A source of persuasion who is credible, expert, trustworthy, likable, physically attractive, and similar to the receiver tends to be relatively effective. Although there are some limitations, two-sided arguments, fear arousal, and drawing conclusions are effective elements in persuasive messages. Persuasion is undermined when a receiver is forewarned or when a receiver's initial position is very discrepant from the position advocated.

Asch found that subjects often conform to the group, even when the group reports inaccurate judgments. He found that conformity becomes more likely as group size increases, up to a group size of seven. Asch's experiments may have produced public compliance while subjects' private beliefs remained unchanged.

In Milgram's landmark study of obedience to authority, subjects showed a remarkable tendency to follow orders to shock an innocent stranger. Milgram concluded that situational pressures can make decent people do indecent things.

In the upcoming Application we continue to focus on social influence. We'll look at practical strategies that people use in interpersonal manipulations.

Seeing Through Social Influence Tactics

Which of the following is true?

☐ **1.** It's a good idea to ask for a small favor first before soliciting the larger favor that you're really after.

☐ **2.** It's a good idea to ask for a large favor first before soliciting the smaller favor that you're really after.

Would you believe that *both* of the statements above are true. Although the two approaches involve opposite strategies, both can be very effective ways to get people to do what you want. This paradox illustrates the complexity of social influence processes, which we'll examine from a practical standpoint in this Application.

We've already discussed the process of *persuasion*, which involves efforts to change others' attitudes through the communication of information. In this section, we'll focus on social influence tactics that depend more on *manipulation* than *information*. It pays to understand these strategies because advertisers, salespeople, and fund-raisers (not to mention friends and neighbors) use them frequently in efforts to influence our behavior. We'll begin by looking at the contradictory strategies described in our opening questions.

THE FOOT-IN-THE-DOOR TECHNIQUE

Door-to-door salespeople have long recognized the importance of gaining a little cooperation from sales targets (getting a "foot in the door") before hitting them with the real sales pitch. **The *foot-in-the-door technique* involves getting people to agree to a small request to increase the chances that they will agree to a larger request later** (see Figure 7.14). This technique is widely used in all walks of life. For example, groups seeking donations often ask people to simply sign a petition first. Salespeople routinely ask individuals to try a product with "no obligations" before they launch their hard sell. In a similar vein, a wife might ask her husband to get her a cup of coffee, and when he gets up to fetch it say, "While you're up, why don't you make me a grilled cheese?"

The foot-in-the-door technique was first investigated by Jonathon Freedman and his colleagues. In one study (Freedman & Fraser, 1966) the large request involved telephoning homemakers to ask whether a team of six men doing consumer research could come into their home to classify all their household products. Imagine six strangers tramping through your home, pulling everything out of your closets, cupboards, and drawers, and you can understand why only 22% of the

Figure 7.14. The foot-in-the-door and the door-in-the-face techniques. These two influence techniques are essentially the reverse of each other, but both can work. In the foot-in-the-door technique, you begin with a small request and work up to a larger one. In the door-in-the-face technique, you begin with a large request and work down to a smaller one.

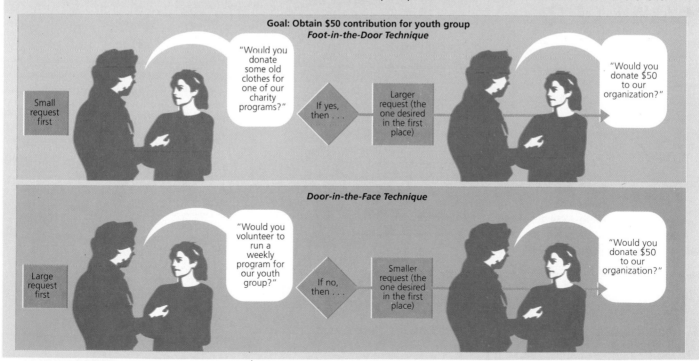

Goal: Obtain $50 contribution for youth group

Foot-in-the-Door Technique

Small request first → "Would you donate some old clothes for one of our charity programs?" If yes, then . . . → Larger request (the one desired in the first place) → "Would you donate $50 to our organization?"

Door-in-the-Face Technique

Large request first → "Would you volunteer to run a weekly program for our youth group?" If no, then . . . → Smaller request (the one desired in the first place) → "Would you donate $50 to our organization?"

subjects in the control group agreed to this outlandish request. Subjects who were given the foot-in-the-door treatment were contacted three days before the large request and asked to answer a few questions about the soaps used in their home. A remarkable 53% of these subjects subsequently agreed to the large request.

Many other studies have also shown that the foot-in-the-door technique is an effective strategy. Researchers aren't entirely sure *why* the technique is effective. Some believe that when people grant the initial favor they feel a sense of *commitment* to the person making the request. This feeling of commitment apparently makes them more willing to go along with a subsequent request from the same person. Of course, no strategy works all the time. The foot-in-the-door technique may be ineffective if the initial request is too small to create a sense of commitment or if the second request is so large it's unreasonable (Foss & Dempsey, 1979; Zuckerman, Lazzaro, & Waldgeir, 1979).

THE DOOR-IN-THE-FACE TECHNIQUE

The door-in-the-face technique reverses the sequence of requests employed with the foot-in-the-door technique. **The *door-in-the-face technique* involves making a very large request that is likely to be turned down to increase the chances that people will agree to a smaller request later** (see Figure 7.14). The name for this strategy is derived from the expectation that the initial request will be quickly rejected. For example, a husband who wants to coax his frugal wife into agreeing to buy an $18,000 sports car might begin by proposing that they purchase a $30,000 sports car. By the time she has talked her husband out of the $30,000 car, the $18,000 price tag may look quite reasonable to her.

The potential effectiveness of the door-in-the-face technique was demonstrated in a study by Robert Cialdini and his colleagues (Cialdini et al., 1975). Posing as representatives of a youth counseling program, they asked college students whether they would volunteer to spend two hours a week counseling juvenile delinquents for *two years.* All the subjects rejected this very large request. However, when the students subsequently were asked to chaperon a group of juvenile delinquents on a one-day trip to the zoo, 50% agreed to this much smaller request. Only 17% of the subjects in the control group agreed to this request when it was not preceded by the much larger request.

The door-in-the-face technique works for two reasons (Cialdini, 1988). First, everything is relative, and we are easily swayed by *contrast effects.* A 6'3" basketball player, who is really quite tall, can look downright small when surrounded by teammates who all are over 6'8". Similarly, an $18,000 car may seem cheap relative to a $30,000 car. Second, when people make concessions by reducing the size of their requests, most of us feel obliged to reciprocate by making concessions of our own. Hence, we agree to the smaller request.

The belief that we should reciprocate others' kindness is a powerful norm. Let's examine some of the other ways in which it is used in social influence efforts.

USING THE RECIPROCITY NORM

Perhaps you have walked through a large urban airport and been approached by a member of the Hare Krishna, an unconventional religious sect. If so, you may have been surprised when the Krishna member insisted on giving you a gift—usually a flower or a small book. What motivated this unexpected kindness? Calculated, cunning insight about how to manipulate people. The Krishnas are hoping that you'll feel obligated to repay their kindness when they ask you for a donation a moment later. Some people—especially those who have been approached before —aren't fooled by this strategem. But contributions *are* coaxed out of many people; indeed, the Krishnas have raised millions upon millions of dollars this way.

Most of us have been socialized to believe in the *reciprocity norm—***the rule**

that we should pay back in kind what we receive from others. Robert Cialdini (1988) has written extensively about how the reciprocity norm is used in social influence efforts. The Krishnas are hardly unique. Conventional charities also make use of the reciprocity principle. Groups seeking donations for the disabled, the homeless, and so forth routinely send address labels, key rings, and other small gifts with their pleas for donations.

Salespeople using the reciprocity principle distribute free samples to prospective customers. Cialdini (1988) describes the procedures used by the Amway Corporation, which sells such household products as detergent, floor wax, and insect spray. Amway's door-to-door salespeople give homemakers many bottles of their products for a "free trial." When they return a few days later, most of the homemakers feel obligated to buy some of the products.

The reciprocity rule is meant to promote fair exchanges in social interactions. However, when people manipulate the reciprocity rule, they usually give something of minimal value in the hopes of getting far more in return. For example, a person selling large computer systems may treat a potential customer at a nice restaurant in an effort to close a deal worth hundreds of thousands of dollars. According to Cialdini, the reciprocity norm is so powerful that it often works even when (1) the gift is uninvited, (2) the gift comes from someone you dislike, or (3) the gift results in an uneven exchange.

THE LOWBALL TECHNIQUE

Manipulations of the reciprocity rule can involve some wily trickery, but the lowball technique is even more deceptive. The name for this technique derives from a common practice in automobile sales, in which a customer is offered a terrific bargain on a car. The bargain price gets the customer to commit to buying the car. Soon after this commitment is made, the dealer starts revealing that there are some hidden costs. Typically, the customer learns that options apparently included in the original price are actually going to cost extra. Once they have committed to buying a car, most customers are unlikely to cancel the deal. Thus, **the *lowball***

Influence: Science and Practice
by Robert B. Cialdini (Scott, Foresman, 1988)

This is a brilliant book about the dynamics of social influence. Cialdini, a social psychologist, has conducted extensive empirical research on influence tactics such as the door-in-the-face technique and lowballing. As you might expect, Cialdini's book is based on his studies and his review of other scientific research on the topic. However, what makes his book unique is that he went far beyond laboratory research in his effort to better understand the ins and outs of social influence. For three years, he immersed himself in the real world of influence artists, becoming a "spy of sorts." As he puts it, "When I wanted to learn about the compliance tactics of encyclopedia (or vacuum cleaner, or portrait photography, or dance lessons) sales organizations, I would answer a newspaper ad for sales trainees and have them teach me their methods. Using similar but not identical approaches, I was able to penetrate advertising, public relations, and fund-raising agencies to examine their techniques" (from the preface). The result is an insightful book that bolsters scientific data with anecdotal accounts of how influence artists ply their trade. Familiarity with their strategies can help you to avoid being an easy mark or a "patsy."

> A few years ago, a university professor tried a little experiment. He sent Christmas cards to a sample of perfect strangers. Although he expected some reaction, the response he received was amazing— holiday cards addressed to him came pouring back from people who had never met nor heard of him. The great majority of those who returned cards never inquired into the identity of the unknown professor. . . .
>
> While small in scope, this study nicely shows the action of one of the most potent of the weapons of influence around us—the rule for reciprocation. The rule says that we should try to repay, in kind, what another person has provided us. [p. 21]

technique involves getting someone to commit to an attractive proposition before its hidden costs are revealed.

Car dealers aren't the only ones who use this technique. For instance, a friend might ask if you want to spend a week with him at his charming backwoods cabin. After you accept this seemingly generous proposition, he may add, "Of course there's some work for us to do. We need to repair the pier, paint the exterior, and . . ." Lowballing is very dishonest. You might guess that people would become angry and back out of a deal once its hidden costs are revealed. Although this certainly happens on occasion, lowballing is a surprisingly effective strategy (Burger & Petty, 1981).

REACTANCE AND FEIGNED SCARCITY
A number of years ago, Jack Brehm demonstrated that telling people they

can't have something only makes them want it more. This finding emerged in his research on reactance. **Reactance occurs when a person's freedom to behave in a certain way is impeded, thus leading to efforts to restore the threatened freedom.**

In one study of reactance (Brehm, 1966), subjects listened to four records and then were asked to rate how much they liked each one. As a reward for participating in the study, some subjects were told that they could have the record of their choice when they returned to make additional ratings on a second occasion. When subjects returned for the second session, they were told that one of the four records would not be available as their reward. The excluded record varied from subject to subject. It was always the record ranked third best by that individual in the first set of ratings. The subjects listened to the four records again and made their second set of ratings. Brehm found that the ratings of the excluded records increased significantly. In other words, the record that a subject could not have became all the more desirable!

This reactance effect helps to explain why companies often try to create the impression that their products are in scarce supply. Scarcity threatens your freedom to choose a product, thus creating reactance and an increased desire for the scarce product. Advertisers frequently feign scarcity to drive up the demand for products. Thus, we constantly see ads that scream "limited supply available," "for a limited time only," "while they last," and "time is running out."

The effect of scarcity was demonstrated dramatically in 1989 when Mazda introduced a new convertible called the Miata. Mazda chose to make a limited number of the new cars available for sale in the United States. The scarcity of the car sent consumers into a buying frenzy. The cars were snapped up so rapidly that dealers started charging up to $5000 *over* the list price!

THE SEVERE INITIATION EFFECT

Creating the illusion of scarcity is not the only way to increase people's attraction to something. Putting people through a "severe initiation" is another way to make something seem more desirable. In a classic study of this effect, Aronson and Mills (1959) put college women through a severe initiation before they could qualify to participate in what promised to be an interesting discussion of sexuality. In the screening test that represented the severe initiation, the women had to read obscene passages out loud to a male experimenter. After all that, the highly touted discussion of sexuality turned out to be a boring, taped lecture on reproduction in lower animals. Subjects in the severe initiation condition experienced a great deal of cognitive dissonance. **Cognitive dissonance exists when related thoughts are inconsistent—that is, they contradict each other.** In this case the women were thinking, "I went through a lot to get here" and "This discussion is terrible." How did they reduce their dissonance? Apparently by convincing themselves that the discussion was worthwhile, since they rated it more favorably than subjects in two control conditions (see Figure 7.15).

The severe initiation ruse is used in many facets of everyday life. A prominent example is the nightclubs that screen potential patrons and make them wait in lengthy lines. In many cases, these clubs have ample room inside. However, they make it hard to get in so that entry to the club seems like a precious opportunity. Restaurants that require reservations weeks in advance and country clubs that make it difficult for one to join are also taking advantage of the severe initiation effect. So, too, are fraternities and sororities that put potential members through elaborate screenings—not to mention "hell week," which may be the ultimate in severe initiations.

Figure 7.15. The severe-initiation effect. After going through a severe initiation, a mild initiation, or no initiation, subjects participated in a boring group discussion and then rated their liking of it. Subjects who had endured the severe initiation reported liking the discussion more—because they were trying to reduce their cognitive dissonance. (Data from Aronson & Mills, 1959)

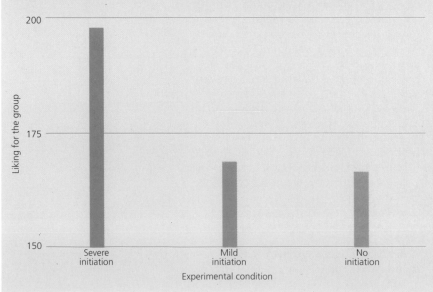

THE POWER OF MODELING

As we noted in Chapter 2, *observational learning* occurs when our behavior is swayed by our observations of others, who are called *models*. According to Albert Bandura (1986), much of our behavior is the product of imitation or modeling effects. These modeling effects are sometimes used in social influence efforts.

The power of modeling was demonstrated in an experiment designed to increase the contributions tossed into a Salvation Army kettle during the Christmas holiday (Bryan & Test, 1967). In this study, experimental accomplices posing as shoppers tossed money into a Salvation Army kettle as they walked by it. Thus, they modeled generous behavior for real shoppers who witnessed their contributions. As predicted, the shoppers exposed to these generous models made more contributions than the shoppers in a control condition, where the models were absent.

Potent modeling effects were also seen in a study in which the dependent variable was signing a petition (Helson, Blake, & Mouton, 1958). The subjects were students at the University of Texas, and the petition was not one that you would expect them to sign readily. It advocated the removal of all soft-drink machines from university buildings! Arrangements were made so that the subject was always walking with an experimental accomplice when the two of them were approached to sign the petition. When the accomplice refused to sign the petition, all the subjects also refused. However, when the accomplice agreed to sign the petition, the proportion of subjects who signed jumped from zero to one third.

Advertisers are well aware of our tendency to be influenced by what others do. That's why they run television ads in which both celebrities and "ordinary people" testify about how they use a particular detergent, deodorant, or gasoline. Modeling effects also explain why television producers use laugh tracks in their comedy shows. Research reveals that canned laughter leads audiences to laugh at jokes more frequently and longer (Fuller & Sheehy-Skeffington, 1974; Smyth & Fuller, 1972). People try to take advantage of modeling effects in many different situations. For instance, bartenders often slip a few dollar bills into their tip jars to fraudulently "model" healthy tipping from previous customers.

PLAYING ON GUILT

Another widely used influence technique is to make people feel guilty about something before advocating a response that should relieve some of their guilt. Charitable organizations seeking donations use this technique frequently, and studies suggest that it can be an effective strategy. In one study (Steele, 1975), some subjects contacted as part of a telephone poll were told that people in their area were generally unhelpful and unconcerned about the welfare of others. Control group subjects received a neutral phone call from the same poller. Two days later, the subjects were called by a local food cooperative seeking their assistance. The subjects who had previously been made to feel guilty about their lack of concern showed more willingness to help than the subjects in the control group.

In summary, people use a host of methods to coax compliance out of one another. Many of these influence techniques are more or less dishonest, but they're widely used anyway. There is no way to completely avoid being hoodwinked by influence strategies. However, an understanding of the strategies we have discussed is the first step toward reducing how often you are victimized by influence artists. As we noted in our discussion of persuasion, "to be forewarned is to be forearmed."

1. Explain the nature of groups and why we join them.

2. Describe the following properties of groups: roles, norms, communication structure, and power structure.

3. Describe group cohesiveness and summarize how it and group size influence group dynamics.

4. Explain the bystander effect and its causes.

5. Describe social loafing and summarize evidence on group productivity.

6. Explain group polarization.

7. Describe the sources and symptoms of groupthink and discuss how to prevent it.

8. Summarize information on the emergence of leadership, including trait and situational theories of leadership.

9. Describe Fiedler's contingency theory of leadership effectiveness.

10. Summarize evidence on source, message, and receiver factors that influence the process of persuasion.

11. Describe Asch's work on conformity.

12. Describe Milgram's classic study of obedience and the controversy it caused.

13. Describe the paradoxical foot-in-the-door and door-in-the-face strategies.

14. Explain how the reciprocity norm and lowballing are used in social influence.

15. Discuss how feigned scarcity and severe initiation can increase people's attraction to something.

16. Explain how modeling effects and guilt can be used in social influence.

KEY TERMS

Affiliation motive
Attitudes
Bystander effect
Cognitive dissonance
Communication network
Compliance
Conformity
Consideration
Door-in-the-face technique
Foot-in-the-door technique
Group
Group cohesiveness
Group norms
Group polarization
Groupthink

In-group
Initiating structure
Latitude of acceptance
Leadership
Lowball technique
Obedience
Out-group
Persuasion
Power
Reactance
Reciprocity norm
Role
Social loafing
Socioemotional roles
Task-related roles

KEY PEOPLE

Solomon Asch
Fred Fiedler
Irving Janis
Bibb Latané
Stanley Milgram

Argumentativeness Scale

INSTRUCTIONS

This questionnaire contains statements about arguing contro-versial issues. Indicate how often each statement is true for you personally by placing the appropriate number in the blank to the left of the statement:

1 = Almost never true
2 = Rarely true
3 = Occasionally true
4 = Often true
5 = Almost always true

THE SCALE

_____ 1. While in an argument, I worry that the person I am arguing with will form a negative impression of me.

_____ 2. Arguing over controversial issues improves my intelligence.

_____ 3. I enjoy avoiding arguments.

_____ 4. I am energetic and enthusiastic when I argue.

_____ 5. Once I finish an argument I promise myself that I will not get into another.

_____ 6. Arguing with a person creates more problems for me than it solves.

_____ 7. I have a pleasant, good feeling when I win a point in an argument.

_____ 8. When I finish arguing with someone I feel nervous and upset.

_____ 9. I enjoy a good argument over a controversial issue.

_____ 10. I get an unpleasant feeling when I realize I am about to get into an argument.

_____ 11. I enjoy defending my point of view on an issue.

_____ 12. I am happy when I keep an argument from happen-ing.

_____ 13. I do not like to miss the opportunity to argue a controversial issue.

_____ 14. I prefer being with people who rarely disagree with me.

_____ 15. I consider an argument an exciting intellectual challenge.

_____ 16. I find myself unable to think of effective points during an argument.

_____ 17. I feel refreshed and satisfied after an argument on a controversial issue.

_____ 18. I have the ability to do well in an argument.

_____ 19. I try to avoid getting into arguments.

_____ 20. I feel excitement when I expect that a conversation I am in is leading to an argument.

SCORING THE SCALE

Add up the numbers that you have recorded for items 1, 3, 5, 6, 8, 10, 12, 14, 16, and 19. This total reflects your tendency to *avoid* getting into arguments. Next, add up the numbers that you have recorded for items 2, 4, 7, 9, 11, 13, 15, 17, 18, and 20. This total reflects your tendency to *approach* argumen-tative situations. Record these subtotals in the spaces below. Subtract your avoidance score from your approach score to arrive at your overall score.

_____ – _____ = _____

Approach score   Avoidance score   Total score

WHAT THE SCALE MEASURES

This questionnaire measures an aspect of your social influence behavior. Specifically, it assesses your tendency to argue with others in persuasive efforts. Persons who score high on this scale are not bashful about tackling controversial issues, are willing to attack others verbally to make their points, and are less compliant than the average person. Developed by Infante and Rancer (1982), this scale has high test-retest reliability (.91 for a period of one week). Examinations of the scale's validity show that it correlates well with other measures of communi-cation tendencies and with friends' ratings of subjects' argumentativeness.

INTERPRETING YOUR SCORE

Our norms are based on the responses of over 800 under-graduate subjects studied by Infante and Rancer (1982).

NORMS

High score: 16 and above
Intermediate score: –6 to 15
Low score: –7 and below

What Types of Groups Do You Belong To?

Think of two groups that you belong to (preferably groups that you joined voluntarily, as opposed to your family, for example). Describe each of these groups in the spaces provided below.

Group 1 (indicate the name and nature of the group):

Group 2 (indicate the name and nature of the group):

Why did you join this group?

What are some norms that this group follows?

Do you play any special role(s) in this group?

Are there any constraints on who talks to whom in this group? Is communication centralized?

What is the power distribution in this group?

8
Friendship and Love

Bill was so keyed up, he hardly slept all night. Morning finally arrived and he was elated. Now it was less than two hours until he would see Susan for coffee. When he got to his first class, he found it practically impossible to keep his mind on the lecture. He was constantly distracted by thoughts and images of Susan. When class was finally over, he had to force himself not to walk too fast to the Student Union, where they had agreed to meet. Sound familiar? Chances are that you recognize Bill's behavior as that of someone falling in love.

Love and friendship play vital roles in our lives. They also play a large role in our psychological adjustment. Given their importance, it is ironic that psychologists didn't start studying these phenomena scientifically until the 1970s (Rubin, 1973). Research on romantic love got off to an especially late start. Why? In part, because many people don't believe that love is an appropriate topic for scientific study. For example, in 1975, United States Senator William Proxmire bestowed his infamous Golden Fleece Award (for waste of taxpayers' money) on two social psychologists who had had the audacity to study love. Ellen Berscheid and Elaine Hatfield (then Walster) had conducted pioneering research on love that was funded in part by a grant from the National Science Foundation. Their research was widely lauded in scientific circles. Senator Proxmire disagreed. "Americans want to leave some things in life a mystery," he asserted, "and right at the top of things we don't want to know is why a man falls in love with a woman and vice versa." Unfortunately, many people share Proxmire's view, and these attitudes have inhibited research on love and friendship.

Although it started late, the scientific study of interpersonal attraction is currently a very active area of research. Hence, we will be able to review a wealth of interesting findings in this chapter. First, we will look at some general theories about how close relationships develop and evolve. Next, we'll review some of the factors that are important in determining who is initially attracted to whom. Following that, we'll discuss what psychologists are discovering about friendships and love relationships, and we'll consider the problem of loneliness. In the application section, we'll focus on shyness.

THE NATURE OF CLOSE RELATIONSHIPS

Social psychologists define a **close relationship** as a **relatively long-lasting relationship in which two people interact frequently and engage in a variety of mutual activities, and in which the impact of their interactions is strong.** There are many different types of close relationships. Closeness may occur in friendships, work relationships, and family relationships, as well as in romantic relationships.

Development of Close Relationships

Close relationships usually take nurturing as well as time to develop. Levinger and Snoek (1972) have proposed a model that describes how interpersonal relationships evolve. This model, which is depicted in Figure 8.1, includes four stages.

Stage 0: Zero contact. At this point, two people are unaware of each other. This stage is labeled "0" and not "1" because there is no actual relationship at this point.

Stage 1: Unilateral awareness. You are aware of another person's existence, but you don't have any expectations of interacting. You have no idea whether the other person is aware of you. For example, you might recognize a person who is in one of your classes at school, but the two of you do not say hello in the hallway or interact in any way. This level of relatedness is facilitated by spatial and social proximity. It depends, in part, on how much interest you take in other people.

Stage 2: Bilateral surface contact. At this point, you are aware of each other and acknowledge that fact. However, inter-

Ellen Berscheid

actions tend to be brief and are governed by stereotyped role expectations. Communication is superficial, and maintenance of the relationship is not important to either of you. Ultimately, you know very little about each other. For example, you might exchange a casual hello and remarks about the weather with the attendant at the parking garage that you use regularly. This level of relatedness is facilitated by available time for verbal exchanges and your perception of the other person's social attractiveness and interest in you.

Stage 3: Mutuality. You respond to each other as unique individuals and share some real knowledge about each other. Communication may concern personal feelings, and maintenance of the relationship becomes important to both of you. For example, you might discuss difficulties you are having in school with a classmate who displays a genuine interest. This level of relatedness depends on your satisfaction with the other person's role-regulated behavior in the previous stage. Moving on to mutuality also depends on your perception of the person's potential likability. As shown in Figure 8.1, this stage actually includes a variety of relationships. These relationships fall on a continuum ranging from little interdependence (casual acquaintances) to great interdependence (marital partners, for example).

As you can see, chance factors such as enrollment in the same class or riding the same bus govern interactions in the early stages of a relationship. For relationships to develop further, however, different factors such as our intentions and the nature of previous interactions assume importance.

Social Exchange in Close Relationships

Once a close relationship has developed, what determines whether it continues? ***Social exchange theory*** **postulates that interpersonal relationships are governed by perceptions of the rewards and costs exchanged in interactions.** According to this model, interactions between acquaintances, friends, and lovers are likely to continue as long as the participants feel that the benefits they derive from the relationship are reasonable in comparison to the costs (Kelley & Thibaut, 1978; Thibaut & Kelley, 1959). Social exchange theory is based on B. F. Skinner's principle of reinforcement, which assumes that we try to maximize our rewards in life (see Chapter 2). Of course, it is important to note that what is considered a reward or a cost in a relationship is very subjective.

According to social exchange theory, we assess our current relationship outcomes against certain standards, which are also subjective. Your ***comparison level*** **is your standard of what constitutes an acceptable balance of rewards and costs in a relationship.** Your comparison level is based on the outcomes you have experienced in past relationships and the outcomes you have seen others experience in their relationships. It may also be influenced by your exposure to fictional relationships, such as those you have read about or seen on television. Another standard used in judging social exchanges is your *comparison level for alternatives.* In using this standard, you assess your relationship outcomes in comparison to the potential outcomes of other similar relationships that are actually available to you.

To illustrate, if both people in a romantic relationship feel that they are getting a lot out of the relationship (lots of strokes, high status) compared to its costs (a few arguments, occasionally giving up preferred activities), the relationship will probably be perceived as satisfactory and will be

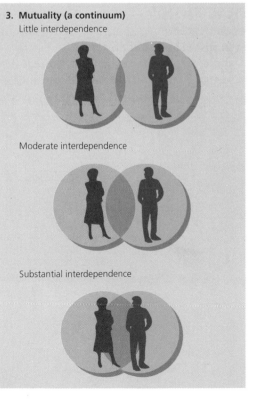

0. **Zero contact**

1. **Unilateral awareness**

2. **Bilateral surface contact**

3. **Mutuality (a continuum)**
Little interdependence

Moderate interdependence

Substantial interdependence

Figure 8.1. A model of relationship development. According to Levinger and Snoek (1972), relationships evolve through a series of stages. In each stage, the interaction between the two people increases. The mutuality stage includes a continuum of close relationships marked by increasing interdependence.

maintained. However, if either person begins to feel that the ratio of rewards to costs is falling below his or her comparison level, then dissatisfaction is likely to occur. This person may attempt to alter the balance of costs and rewards or try to ease out of the relationship. The likelihood of ending the relationship depends on whether the person believes that alternative relationships are available that could yield greater outcomes.

This theory of an "interpersonal marketplace" provides a useful model for analyzing many types of relationships. Nonetheless, many people resist the idea that close relationships operate according to an economic model. Much of this resistance probably stems from discomfort with the idea that self-interest plays such an important role in the maintenance of relationships. Some of this resistance may also be due to a feeling that the principles of social exchange theory don't apply well to close relationships. In fact, there is some empirical support for this position. Margaret Clark and Judson Mills (1979) assert that there is a distinction between *exchange relationships* (with strangers, acquaintances, co-workers) and *communal relationships* (with close friends, lovers, family members). Research suggests that in exchange relationships, the usual principles of social exchange dominate. In communal relationships, social exchange principles also operate, but we apply these principles differently. For example, in communal relationships, rewards sometimes are given freely, without any expectation of prompt reciprocation (Clark, 1984). When people close to us need us, we help them without stopping to calculate whether and when they will reward us in kind.

FACTORS INFLUENCING INTERPERSONAL ATTRACTION

"I just don't know what she sees in him. She could do so much better for herself." "Sure, she's an OK person, but he's too good for her." How many times have you heard remarks like these? Probably quite often. Such comments illustrate the great interest we have in analyzing the dynamics of attraction. *Interpersonal attraction* **refers to positive feelings toward another person.** Who is attracted to whom is an exceedingly complex topic. A multitude of factors influence your assessment of another person's attractiveness. Furthermore, attraction is a two-way street, so there are intricate interactions between factors.

Our review of research in this area will deal with both friendship and love. Although liking and loving represent two different types of relationships, the dynamics of initial attraction in each case are sufficiently similar to justify a unified discussion. In some cases, a particular factor, such as physical attractiveness, may play a more influential role in love than in friendship, or vice versa. However, all the factors to be discussed in this section appear to enter into both types of attraction.

To simplify this complex issue, we will divide our coverage into three segments. In the first part, we will review the characteristics of other people that tend to make them attractive to us. In the second, we'll discuss how our own characteristics influence our assessment of others' attractiveness. In the third segment, we will analyze interaction factors—those that don't reside in either person alone, but emerge out of a pair's particular relationship to each other.

Characteristics of the Other Person

Have you ever had a friend attempt to set you up for a blind date? If so, what kinds of questions did you ask about the person? Did you inquire about your prospective date's manners, attitudes, and moral character? Probably not. Chances are, you wanted to know about your date's looks, personality, and intelligence. Research suggests that these are the main characteristics of others that influence our attraction to them. Let's look at the evidence.

Physical Attractiveness
A number of old sayings warn us about putting too much emphasis on physical attractiveness. Statements such as

Figure 8.2. Perceptions of the ideal woman and ideal man.
Which traits should the ideal woman and ideal man possess? A survey (Tavris, 1977) that addressed this question obtained the results shown here.

"Beauty is only skin deep" and "You can't judge a book by its cover" imply that we should be cautious about being seduced by physical beauty. However, the evidence suggests that we don't pay much attention to this advice!

The importance of physical attractiveness was clearly demonstrated in a classic study by Walster, Aronson, Abrahams, and Rottman (1966). They invited male and female freshmen to a dance where their dates had supposedly been selected by a computer. In reality, the couples had been paired randomly. However, the computer cover story provided a good rationale for asking participants to rate the degree to which they would like to go out with their dates again. These ratings were then correlated with other data collected on the participants, including their physical attractiveness (as assessed by impartial judges), their intelligence, their social skill, and various personality characteristics.

Out of this host of variables, only one was predictive of subjects' desire to see their dates again. That single variable of significance was physical attractiveness. For both sexes, more attractive partners were rated as more desirable for future dates. Obviously, linking good looks to attraction is hardly an exciting discovery. However, the finding that physical appearance was the *only* significant determinant of attraction in this study certainly underscores the prominence of this factor.

"But wait," you might say, "maybe physical attractiveness is only a powerful variable in people's initial encounters." After all, what else is there to go on besides appearance when you've just met someone? Little research has been done on this question, but at least one study failed to support this explanation. In this study, college men and women agreed to complete five dates during the course of the experiment. Physical attractiveness increased in importance from the first to subsequent dates (Mathes, 1975).

"Well," you might respond, "maybe physical attractiveness is only important with younger subjects, such as college students." Once again, research is sparse, but it does not support this explanation. One relevant study recruited subjects in their 30s who were enrolled in a commercial dating service. Subjects were asked to screen prospective partners on the basis of a photo and background information about the person's interests, ideals, hobbies, and relationship goals (Green, Buchanan, & Heuer, 1984). They were asked to select five people they would like to date and five people they definitely would not date. The results indicated that physical attractiveness was a major factor in date selection for both sexes. Age was also found to be an important factor. Interestingly, most women preferred men who were older, while most men preferred women who were younger. These findings about physical attractiveness and age in the initial screening of prospective dates have been replicated in a study using a video dating service (Woll, 1986).

The premium that most people appear to place on physical attractiveness presents something of a problem. Obviously, we cannot all be beautiful. However, the emphasis on beauty may not be as great as the evidence reviewed thus far suggests. Figure 8.2 summarizes some of the results of a large-scale survey on people's perceptions of the ideal man and woman (Tavris, 1977). Many personal qualities, such as intelligence, confidence, and warmth, are rated by both sexes as essential to the ideal more often than physical attractiveness. These results are somewhat reassuring. Still, we have seen in earlier chap-

What We Look for in the Ideal Man and Ideal Woman

How important or unimportant is each of the following traits to your concept of the ideal man and the ideal woman?	Percentage saying trait is "very important" or "essential" to ideal			
	Ideal man		Ideal woman	
	Men	Women	Men	Women
Intelligent	71	84	70	83
Self-confident	86	86	76	87
Physically strong	19	21	4	7
Tall	7	11	4	2
Physically attractive	26	29	47	32
Successful at work	54	66	41	60
Competitive	38	27	18	22
Aggressive	30	28	16	21
Takes risks	34	25	21	26
Stands up for beliefs	87	92	82	90
Fights to protect family	77	72	72	70
Able to love	88	96	92	97
Warm	68	89	83	88
Gentle	64	86	79	86
Soft	28	48	63	62
Romantic	48	66	64	67
Able to cry	40	51	50	58
Skilled lover	38	48	41	44
Many sexual conquests	5	4	4	5
Sexually faithful	42	67	56	66

ters that verbal reports are not necessarily an accurate reflection of how people actually behave.

WHAT MAKES SOMEONE ATTRACTIVE? The advertising industry has fostered a rather narrow conception of physical attractiveness. In fact, research suggests that people differ in regard to what they find attractive. In one study subjects were asked, "When you first meet someone, which one or two things about physical appearance do you tend to notice first?" As can be seen in Figure 8.3, responses varied widely.

Furthermore, some popular beliefs about ideal physical characteristics don't seem to hold up under scrutiny. For example, a study of female preferences regarding male body types found that the supposed ideal of a tall and muscular fellow was not the most popular among women. Instead, it appears that females respond most favorably to males who are of medium height (Graziano, Brothen, & Berscheid, 1978) and to those who have small

buttocks and thin waists and legs (Beck, 1979; Horvath, 1979).

Some theorists have argued that analyzing attractiveness into specific components is hopeless because what is crucial is the total picture (Murstein, 1971). The key point, however, is that one does not have to match up perfectly with Hollywood stereotypes of good looks. The range of what we consider attractive is probably wider than commonly believed.

THE MATCHING HYPOTHESIS. A person does not have to be spectacularly good-looking in order to enjoy a rewarding social life. People apparently take into consideration their own level of attractiveness in the process of dating and mating. **The *matching hypothesis* proposes that people of similar levels of physical attractiveness gravitate toward each other.** The matching hypothesis is supported by evidence that both dating and married couples tend to be similar in physical attractiveness (Feingold, 1988).

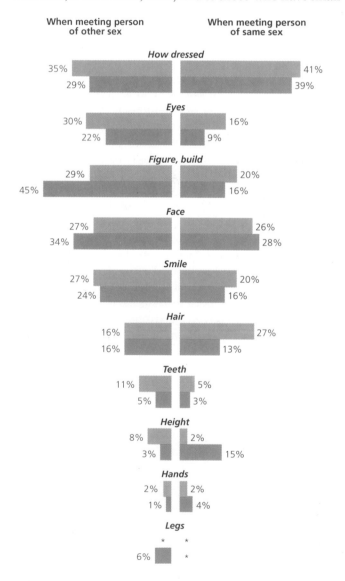

Figure 8.3 *(left)*. What men and women first notice about physical appearance. In a Roper Poll, people were asked, "When you first meet someone, which one or two things about physical appearance do you tend to notice first?" The subjects' responses depended to some extent on their gender and on whether they were meeting someone of the same sex or the other sex. Overall, the subjects' responses were highly varied.

According to the matching hypothesis, we tend to wind up with someone similar to ourselves in attractiveness.

What women notice first

What men notice first

*Less than .5%

However, there is some debate about whether we match up by our own choice (Aron, 1988; Kalick & Hamilton, 1986). Some theorists believe that we mostly pursue high attractiveness in partners and that our matching is the result of social forces beyond our control, such as rejection by more attractive others.

Most of the studies of physical beauty and attraction have focused on dating relationships; only a few have looked at friendship formation. However, the studies of friendship suggest that people prefer attractiveness in their friends as well as their dates (Lyman, Hatlelid, & Macurdy, 1981). Researchers have also found evidence for matching effects in same-sex friendships (McKillip & Riedel, 1983). Interestingly, this same-sex matching appears to occur among males, but not females (Feingold, 1988). The reasons for this gender difference are not readily apparent. Overall, additional research is needed on the matching hypothesis as it relates to friendship formation.

Desirable Personality Characteristics

Personality characteristics are another obvious factor influencing interpersonal attraction. Subjects rate a hypothetical person's likability much higher when the person is described as sincere, honest, and dependable rather than loudmouthed, deceitful, and obnoxious. Figure 8.4 displays some of the findings from Anderson's (1968) study on the likableness of 555 different personality-trait descriptions. These ratings give us some insight into what personal qualities we value in others.

The survey results on the ideal man and woman reported earlier also provide information on the personality characteristics we value. A glance back at Figure 8.2 will show that we look for qualities such as confidence, integrity, warmth, gentleness, and the ability to love. Other studies indicate that we like pleasant, agreeable people who express positive attitudes about things more than unpleasant, disagreeable people who express negative attitudes (Folkes & Sears, 1977; Kaplan & Anderson, 1973).

Intelligence and Competence

Generally, we prefer people who are bright and competent over those who are not. The survey data in Figure 8.2 support this idea. A high proportion of people reported that intelligence and success in work were essential features that they sought in their ideal mate. However, extremely competent people may sometimes be threatening to us, and we may occasionally dislike them.

Interestingly, under certain circumstances, highly competent people may be able to enhance their attractiveness by showing themselves to be fallible and, thus, more "human." In a study that tested this idea, male students listened to a tape recording of another male student who was supposedly being interviewed for an important position on campus. The interviewee was portrayed differently in four conditions: (1) unusually competent, (2) unusually competent and makes an embarrassing blunder (he spills coffee on himself), (3) somewhat inept, and (4) somewhat inept and makes the same embarrassing blunder (Aronson, Willerman, & Floyd, 1966). Which interviewee did the subjects like best? They preferred the highly competent student who committed the blunder. But, before you start making frequent blunders to enhance your likability, please note that the person the subjects liked least was the inept student who committed the blunder.

Moreover, a study by Kay Deaux (1972) suggests that our preference for competent people who make humanizing mistakes may be limited to individuals of the same sex. Deaux's experiment was basically the same as that conducted by Aronson et al., except that female subjects were included and both males and females played the role of the stimulus person. As before, male subjects liked the competent male more when he made a blunder. However, female subjects preferred the competent male who did *not* blunder. Similarly, male subjects rated the competent female who did not commit a blunder higher than the one who did. In explaining these perplexing findings, Deaux suggests that we may empathize more with people of our own sex and, hence, be more tolerant

Personality Traits People Like and Dislike		
Highly likable	**Slightly positive to slightly negative**	**Highly unlikable**
Sincere	Persistent	Ill-mannered
Honest	Conventional	Unfriendly
Understanding	Bold	Hostile
Loyal	Cautious	Loudmouthed
Truthful	Perfectionistic	Selfish
Trustworthy	Excitable	Narrow-minded
Intelligent	Quiet	Rude
Dependable	Impulsive	Conceited
Thoughtful	Aggressive	Greedy
Considerate	Shy	Insincere
Reliable	Unpredictable	Unkind
Warm	Emotional	Untrustworthy
Kind	Bashful	Malicious
Friendly	Naive	Obnoxious
Happy	Restless	Untruthful
Unselfish	Daydreamer	Dishonest
Humorous	Materialistic	Cruel
Responsible	Rebellious	Mean
Cheerful	Lonely	Phony
Trustful	Dependent	Liar

Figure 8.4. Likableness of personality traits. Norman Anderson (1968) asked subjects to rate the likableness of 555 personality trait descriptors. These data were collected to facilitate research on impression formation, but they provide us with some insight about the personality traits that we like and dislike in others.

of their blunders. She also suggests that our idealized images of the other sex may make it more difficult for us to accept their mistakes.

Social Status

Social status is another important determinant of a person's appeal. Several studies have shown that, in heterosexual dating, males "trade" occupational status for physical attractiveness in females, and vice versa (Deaux & Hanna, 1984). This trend was apparent in a study of personal ads in newspapers (Harrison & Saeed, 1977). This study found that females' ads were more likely to offer physical attractiveness and to seek financial security than males' ads. In contrast, men's ads were more likely to offer financial status and security, while providing more objective descriptions (height, hair color) of physical appearance. Moreover, several studies have shown that more attractive women are more likely to demand high status in their prospective dates than less attractive women (Harrison & Saeed, 1977). Of course, as women gain greater economic independence, males' social and financial status may have less impact on females' dating preferences.

Your Own Characteristics

Thus far, we have discussed how others' characteristics influence your attraction to them. Now we are ready to turn the spotlight on you, examining the role that self-esteem and self-perception processes play in attraction.

Self-Esteem

As we noted in Chapter 5, our self-esteem influences how we relate to others. For example, low self-esteem subjects select less attractive dates than high self-esteem subjects (Kiesler & Baral, 1970). Thus, people with a favorable self-concept may see themselves as having a wider range of dating choices than those with an unfavorable self-concept.

Self-esteem also affects our reactions to others' evalu-ations of us (Berscheid, 1985; Jones, 1973). Individuals with low self-esteem tend to react more positively to favorable evaluators and more negatively to unfavorable evaluators than people with high self-esteem. Thus, people may be more vulnerable to others' views of them—for better or for worse—if their self-esteem is low.

Self-Perception

Daryl Bem (1972) has theorized that we sometimes infer our attitudes from our overt responses and behavior (see Chapter 5). Various studies suggest that self-perception plays a key role in attraction. In one such study, male subjects were asked to view pictures of seminude females (Valins, 1966). A microphone was attached to the chest of each subject so that he could hear his heartbeat amplified. In reality, the experimenter controlled the auditory feedback of the heart rate. In this way, the men were led to believe that slides of certain women triggered a dramatic change in their heartbeat. Later the subjects were asked to rate their attraction to the women seen in the slides. The men were most attracted to the women who had apparently affected their heartbeat.

The Valins study illustrates our need to interpret our emotional states. Stanley Schachter's (1964) theory of emotion proposes that when we experience the physiological arousal that is usually associated with emotion (which was faked in this study by providing false feedback on heart rate), we try to explain our arousal by looking at the situation we are in. In the Valins study, the most plausible explanation the men had for their speeded-up heartbeat was that they were really "turned on" by the women they were viewing at the time.

Similar evidence has been found in a study in a naturalistic setting. The experimenters in this study arranged for young men crossing a footbridge to encounter a good-looking young woman who was actually a confederate of the experimenters (Dutton & Aron, 1974). The woman stopped the men on the bridge, asking them to complete a questionnaire for a class project she was doing. When the men returned the questionnaire, she offered to ex-

Self-perception theory sheds light on why being around someone we find appealing can trigger feelings that are difficult to interpret.

plain the research at some future time and gave them her phone number. The key to the experiment was that this procedure was enacted on two very different bridges. One was a long suspension bridge that swayed precariously over a 230-foot drop. The other bridge was a solid, safe structure a mere 10 feet above a small stream. The experimenters reasoned that men crossing the high suspension bridge would experience emotional arousal and that some of them might misinterpret their arousal as being caused by the woman rather than the bridge. If these men attributed their arousal to the woman, they would probably infer that they found her very attractive. The dependent variable in the study was the percentage of men who later called the woman to pursue a date. Consistent with the experimenters' hypothesis, those men who met the woman in an aroused state (on the precarious bridge) were more likely to ask her out than those who met her in a normal emotional state (on the safe bridge).

What does all this mean? These findings suggest that the self-perception processes described by Bem and Schachter may be particularly relevant to our efforts to understand the emotional turmoil triggered by romantic attraction. Many of us spend long hours musing about whether someone is "right" for us. Much of this thought involves self-perception efforts: "Wow, I just glow when I'm around Bill. I can't stop smiling. He must be the one." Or "Gee, I don't get very excited when Mary Ann calls to say she's coming over. I guess maybe I'm not all that crazy about her." Thus, it appears that interpersonal attraction may be influenced by the way we interpret our behavior and our feelings.

While highlighting the importance of self-perception, it's worth noting that our propensity to misinterpret emotional arousal may be the basis for the tendency to mistake lust for love. If artificial manipulations of physical arousal in experiments can be misinterpreted, it is easy to imagine how arousal genuinely elicited by another person might be misunderstood. Thus, the emotional arousal evoked by sexual attraction may often be mislabeled "love." Although sexual arousal is an important aspect of romantic love, love is more than mere lust. Nonetheless, research on self-perception shows just how easy it may be for people to mix up sexual arousal and more profound feelings of love.

Interaction Factors

Some factors in the dynamics of attraction lie neither in you nor in the other person. Instead, they emerge out of your unique relationship with each other. Hence, they are called interaction factors. These include proximity, similarity, and reciprocity.

Proximity

It would be difficult for you to develop a friendship with someone you never met. It happens occasionally (between pen pals, for instance), but attraction usually depends on people being in the same place at the same time, making proximity a major factor in attraction. **Proximity refers to geographic, residential, and other forms of spatial closeness.** Generally, we become acquainted with, and attracted to, people who live, work, shop, and play nearby.

The importance of proximity was apparent in a study of friendship patterns among married graduate students living in university housing projects (Festinger, Schachter, & Back, 1950). People whose doors were close together were most likely to become friends. Moreover, those whose homes faced the central court area had more than twice as many friends in the complex as those whose homes faced outward. Using the centralized court area

apparently increased the likelihood that people would meet and befriend others.

Proximity effects were also found in a study of Maryland state police trainees (Segal, 1974). At the training academy, both dormitory rooms and classroom seats were assigned on the basis of alphabetical order. Six months after their arrival, subjects were asked to name their closest three friends among the group of trainees. The trainees whose last names were closer together in the alphabet were much more likely to be friends than trainees whose names were widely separated in the alphabet.

Proximity effects may seem self-evident, but it is sobering to realize that our friendships and love interests are shaped by seating charts, desk arrangements in offices, and dormitory floor assignments. In spite of the increasing geographic mobility in modern society, people still tend to marry someone who grew up nearby (Ineichen, 1979).

Similarity

Is it true that "birds of a feather flock together," or do "opposites attract"? Research provides far more support for the former than the latter. Married and dating couples tend to be similar in age, race, religion, social class, education, intelligence, physical attractiveness, and attitudes (Brehm, 1985; Hendrick & Hendrick, 1983). Similarity is also seen among friends. For instance, adolescent best friends are similar in educational goals and performance, political and religious activities, and illicit drug use (Kandel, 1978).

The most obvious explanation for these correlations is that similarity causes attraction. Laboratory experiments on *attitude similarity* conducted by Donn Byrne and his colleagues, suggest that similarity does cause liking (Byrne, 1971; Byrne, Clore, & Smeaton, 1986). In these studies, subjects who have previously provided information on their own attitudes are led to believe that they will be meeting a stranger. They are given information about the stranger's views that has been manipulated to show various degrees of similarity to their own views. As attitude similarity increases, subjects' ratings of the likability of the stranger increase (see Figure 8.5). This evidence supports the notion that similarity promotes attraction. However, it's also consistent with a somewhat different explanation proposed by Rosenbaum (1986).

Rosenbaum has marshalled evidence suggesting that similarity effects occur in attraction, not because similarity fosters liking, but because *dissimilarity* leads us to *dislike* others. In one study of his hypothesis, Rosenbaum (1986) found that Democrats did not rate other Democrats (similar others) higher than controls as much as they rated Republicans (dissimilar others) lower than controls. Thus, Rosenbaum downplays the importance of attitude similarity, arguing instead that *dissimilarity causes disdain.* More recent evidence suggests that liking is influenced by *both* similarity and dissimilarity in attitudes (Smeaton, Byrne, & Murnen, 1989).

Reciprocity

In his best-selling book *How to Win Friends and Influence People,* Dale Carnegie (1936) suggested that people can gain others' liking by showering them with praise and flattery. However, we all have heard that "flattery will get you nowhere." Which advice is right?

The evidence suggests that flattery will get you somewhere, with some people, some of the time. In interpersonal attraction, **reciprocity involves liking those who show that they like us.** In general, it does appear that liking breeds liking and loving promotes loving (Byrne & Murnen, 1988).

But what if other people say nice things about us that are inconsistent with our self-perceptions? Do we still like them? Studies suggest that we like people more when they give us positive evaluations that match our self-concepts as opposed to positive evaluations that contradict our self-concepts (Berscheid, 1985; Shrauger, 1975). Why? Because when we have doubts about the sincerity of another's positive evaluation, we tend to like that person less

Figure 8.5. Attitude similarity and attraction. When asked to rate the likability of a hypothetical stranger, subjects give progressively higher ratings to people who share more attitudes with them. (Data from Gonzales et al., 1983)

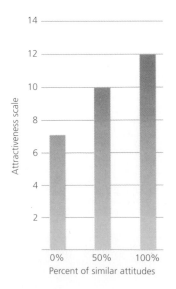

Figure 8.6 (right). Important qualities in a friend. The traits listed here are those that subjects cited most often when asked what makes a good friend. (Based on Parlee et al., 1979)

(Kauffman & Steiner, 1968; Lowe & Goldstein, 1970). Thus, flattery can sometimes have the opposite effect of that predicted by Carnegie.

You might expect that another qualification to the reciprocity principle would involve the widely discussed strategy of playing "hard to get." According to this strategy, showing relatively little interest in the social overtures of a person of the other sex (nonreciprocity) may make the other person even more eager to pursue the relationship. However, the empirical evidence suggests that playing hard to get may not be advisable. Research indicates that we prefer members of the other sex who appear hard for *others* to get but who eagerly accept us (Walster, Walster, Piliavin, & Schmidt, 1973).

Our review of the dynamics of attraction has shown that many factors influence the emergence of close relationships. In the next two sections we'll probe more deeply into the nature of friendship and romantic love.

FRIENDSHIP

Friends play a very significant role in our lives. They may provide help in times of need, advice in times of confusion, sympathy in times of failure, and praise in times of achievement. The importance of friends was underscored in a survey of 40,000 readers of *Psychology Today* magazine. In the survey, 51% of the respondents indicated that in a crisis they were more likely to turn to friends than to family for help (Parlee et al., 1979). In this section, we will discuss what makes a good friend and how gender and marital status affect patterns of friendship.

What Makes a Good Friend?

The most intriguing aspect of the *Psychology Today* survey was its investigation of what makes a "good friend." Figure 8.6 lists the most frequently endorsed qualities. The results suggest that loyalty is the heart and soul of friendship. As you can see, the top two qualities in Figure 8.6 are keeping confidences (an aspect of loyalty) and loyalty itself. As one might guess, the next most important ingredients of friendship are warmth/affection and supportiveness. The high ratings of candor (frankness) and a sense of humor are interesting and well worth keeping in mind.

These results generally coincide with those of another survey on friendship, although one other important factor emerged in this second survey (Block, 1980). That additional factor was a willingness to let friends be themselves. Block points out that we often put people under pressure to behave in ways that are consistent with our expectations. Such "conditional" expectations would appear to resemble those held by many parents for their children. As we discussed in Chapter 2, Carl Rogers believes that conditional affection contributes to distortions in our self-concepts, and for this reason he advocates unconditional acceptance in child rearing. Consistent with Rogers's theory, Block's respondents emphasized the importance of relatively unconditional acceptance from their friends.

A slightly different way of looking at what is important in friendship comes from a cross-cultural study. In this investigation, students in four countries (England, Italy, Japan, and Hong Kong) were interviewed (Argyle & Henderson, 1984). The authors wanted to see whether they could find enough agreement on how friends should conduct themselves to permit the formulation of some informal rules governing friendships. To qualify as a rule, subjects had to agree that the rule was important in a friendship, that failure to adhere to the rule could destroy the friendship, and that the rule could differentiate between current and former friends and between intimate and nonintimate friends. Based on the students' responses, the authors were able to identify six informal rules. As can be seen in Figure 8.7, the common thread running through these rules seems to be providing

The Rules of Friendship

1 Share news of success with a friend.

2 Show emotional support.

3 Volunteer help in time of need.

4 Strive to make a friend happy when in each other's company.

5 Trust and confide in each other.

6 Stand up for a friend in his or her absence.

Figure 8.7. Vital behaviors in friendship. A cross-cultural inquiry (Argyle & Henderson, 1984) into the behaviors that are vital to friendship identified the six rules of friendship listed here.

Quality

Keeps confidence
Loyalty
Warmth, affection
Supportiveness
Frankness
Sense of humor
Willingness to make time for me
Independence
Good conversationalist
Intelligence
Social conscience

0   10   20   30   40   50   60   70   80   90   100

Percentage of respondents who said quality was "important" or "very important" in friendship

emotional and social support to friends. Hence we can conclude that loyalty, emotional support, and letting us be ourselves appear to be the most important expectations that we have of our friends.

Gender Differences in Friendship

Men's and women's friendships have a lot in common, but there are some interesting differences. For one thing, women's friendships are more likely to focus on talking and emotional intimacy. In contrast, men's friendships tend to be based on shared interests and doing things together (Hays, 1985; Sherrod, 1989).

Men's and women's friendships can also be differentiated in terms of their topics of conversation. Women are far more likely than men to discuss personal problems,

feelings, and people (Caldwell & Peplau, 1982; Davidson & Duberman, 1982). There is one exception to this rule, involving males who do not adhere to traditional gender roles. These men appear to divulge as much to their best male friend as most women do to their best female friend (Lavine & Lombardo, 1984).

Friendships between men tend to be regulated by social roles. That is, men tend to relate to each other as business partners, as tennis rivals, or as baseball fans. Moreover, men generally rate their same-sex friendships as less intimate than do women. Men also perceive less emotional support to be available from their friends than most women do (Sherrod, 1989).

A recent study suggests that there are two possible reasons for these gender differences in friendships (Reis, Senchak, & Solomon, 1985). First, men and women appear to have different pathways to intimacy (shared activities versus self-disclosure, respectively). Second, men may have less need for intimacy than do women.

We noted in Chapter 3 that social support from friends (and others) reduces the impact of stress and is associated with better mental health. This finding raises an interesting question. Do women's same-sex friendships yield greater mental health benefits than men's because of their greater intimacy? Apparently not. The evidence suggests that same-sex friendships buffer stress and reduce depression in both males and females (Cohen, Sherrod, & Clark, 1986; Cohen & Wills, 1985).

Marital Status and Friendship Patterns

When a person marries, the freedom to develop friendships with members of the other sex is curtailed by social norms (Bell, 1981). For one thing, cross-sex friendships may be seen as a threat by the spouse. There is also a tendency for some people to assume that something must be missing in a marital relationship if either spouse is involved in a close cross-sex friendship. Because of these norms, married people tend to form their friendships with other *couples*. Some studies suggest that these friend-

Conversations about intimate topics are much more common in female friendships than in male friendships.

ships between couples tend to involve less intimacy than friendships between individuals (Bell, 1981).

In spite of these constraints, wives are more likely than husbands to depend on a close friend rather than on their spouse as their principal confidant (Blau, 1971). Among other things, this suggests that while most wives are expected to listen to their husbands' personal concerns, many husbands may be unwilling or unable to do the same for their wives. If so, this problem may be a major cause of strain in many marriages.

The social norms that limit the freedom of married people to pursue new friendships seem unfortunate. As we have already noted, friends are a valuable resource in times of stress. Moreover, with close-knit kinship networks becoming less common, it seems even more important for people to be free to develop worthwhile friendships outside their marriage. The increasing rate of divorce provides yet another reason for encouraging people to seek nonmarital companionships. In times of marital distress, it is especially important for a person to have friends to depend on for emotional support.

ROMANTIC LOVE

Wander through a bookstore and you'll see an endless array of titles such as *How to Be Loved, Love Can Be Found, Men Who Can't Love, Women Who Love Too Much*, and *How to Survive the Loss of a Love*. Turn up your radio and you'll hear the refrains of "Love Will Find a Way," "Prove Your Love," "Victim of Love," "All You Need Is Love," and "Love Has No Pride." Although there are other forms of love, such as parental love and platonic love, these books and songs are all about *romantic love*, a subject of consuming interest for most of us.

People have always been interested in love and romance. However, the scientific study of love has a short history that dates back only to the 1970s. Love has proven to be an elusive subject of study. It is difficult to define, difficult to measure, and frequently difficult to under-

stand. Nonetheless, psychologists have begun to make some progress in their study of love. Let's look at their theories and research. We'll begin by examining some myths about romantic love.

Myths about Love

Romantic love is a highly idealized concept in our culture. Some interesting as well as troublesome myths have been nurtured by this idealism—as well as by American television and movies. Accordingly, our first task is to take a realistic look at love and dispel some of these problematic notions. Most of our discussion will be based on the writings of Elaine Hatfield (formerly Walster) and Ellen Berscheid (Berscheid, 1988; Berscheid & Walster, 1978; Hatfield, 1988; Walster & Berscheid, 1974), who probably have conducted more research on love than anyone else. Although they're rigorous researchers who have made major contributions to the scientific study of love, Berscheid and Hatfield have also been willing to offer down-to-earth, practical insights about the nature of love.

Myth 1: When you fall in love, you'll know it. People often spend a great deal of time agonizing over whether they are experiencing true love or mere infatuation. When these people consult others, they are often told "If it were true love, you'd know it." This statement, which is tantamount to telling the person that he or she is not really in love, is simply not accurate. A minority of people may recognize love clearly and quickly. However, most of us have to struggle with some confusion. There is no "bolt out of the sky" that clearly marks the beginning of love. On the contrary, love usually grows gradually, and doubts are quite normal.

Myth 2: When love strikes, you have no control over your behavior. This myth suggests that love is so powerful that we are incapable of behaving wisely once we are under its spell. While it may be comforting to tell ourselves that we have no control in matters of the heart, this rationaliza-

Married people tend to form their friendships with other *couples* rather with *individuals*. Thus marriage puts social constraints on the kinds of friendships people form.

tion can lead to serious mistakes. A belief in this myth encourages people to avoid taking responsibility for actions that can significantly affect their lives. In the early stages of romantic relationships it is difficult to be clear about our feelings. However, because this is true, we need to proceed particularly cautiously in making important decisions about sexual involvements or long-term commitments.

Myth 3: Love is a purely positive experience. Our idealization of love sometimes creates unrealistic expectations that love should be an exclusively enjoyable experience. In reality, love may bring intense negative emotions and great pain. Ambivalent feelings in love are quite common. In part, this may be because we tend to expect and demand a lot from someone we love. Research indicates that we tend to be more critical and less tolerant of lovers and spouses than we are of friends (K. E. Davis, 1985). People often ask, "Can you love and hate someone at the same time?" This common question shows that many people find that love brings with it feelings of intense anger as well as sublime joy. The passionate quality of love is such that a lover is capable of taking us to emotional peaks in either direction.

Myth 4: True love lasts forever. Love may last forever, but unfortunately, you can't count on it. People perpetuate this myth in an interesting way. If they have a romantic relationship that eventually disintegrates, they conclude that it was never really love. Hence, they relegate the dissolved relationship to the inferior status of infatuation. This rationalization allows people to continue their search for the one, great, idealized lover who will supposedly bring complete happiness. It's more realistic to view love as a sometimes wonderful, sometimes frustrating experience that might be encountered on several occasions in one's life.

Myth 5: Love can conquer all problems. This myth is the basis for many unsuccessful marriages. Numerous couples, fully aware of problems in their relationship (for example, poor communication, disagreement about sex

roles) forge ahead into marriage anyway. They naively say to themselves, "As long as we love each other, we'll be able to work it out." While authentic love certainly helps in tackling marital problems, it is no guarantee of success. In fact, there is some provocative evidence that how much you *like* your lover may be more important than how much you *love* your lover. When researchers correlated a host of variables with a measure of the "successfulness" of romantic relationships, liking for one's partner was more highly correlated (.62) with relationship success than was love (.50) of one's partner (Sternberg & Grajek, 1984). A small difference such as this in just one study is hardly definitive. However, it raises the possibility that liking may conquer problems more effectively than love.

Gender Differences Regarding Love

The differences in how males and females are socialized in our society appear to affect their attitudes toward love. The traditional stereotype suggests that women are more romantic than men. However, much of the research evidence suggests the opposite—that men are more romantic than women! For example, one study reported that men score higher than women on romanticism scales and that men recognize love earlier than women do (Kanin, Davidson, & Scheck, 1970). The same study also found that females are more cautious and rational than males in selecting their mates. Other researchers report that men tend to fall in love more easily than women, while women fall out of love more easily than men (Hill, Rubin, & Peplau, 1976; Rubin, Peplau, & Hill, 1981). Furthermore, these researchers found that women seem to experience less emotional turmoil than men when romantic relationships break up.

As a whole, the evidence suggests that men are more romantic than women. However, we should note that women do seem more romantic with regard to *expressions* of love. That is, women are more willing to verbalize and display their affection (Balswick & Avertt, 1977). There is also evidence that women may be more sensitive than

Figure 8.8. Sternberg's triangular theory of love. According to Robert Sternberg (1986), love includes three components: intimacy, passion, and commitment. These components are portrayed here as points on a triangle. The absence of all three components is called nonlove, which is not shown in the diagram. The other possible combinations of these three components yield the seven different types of relationships mapped out here.

men to problems that occur in relationships (Hill et al., 1976).

What might account for the surprising finding that men appear to be more romantic than women? It may be a reflection of economic realities. Wives are still more economically dependent on their husbands than vice versa. Hence, women may assume that the decision about whom they will marry is a decision about the kind of lifestyle (status and income) they will have. According to this view, being romantic in the choice of a potential partner may be a luxury that men can afford more readily than women can.

Theories of Love

How are love relationships different from other types of close relationships? Can the experience of love be broken down into certain key elements? Are some of these elements more important than others? These are the kinds of questions addressed by new theories of love that have emerged from the recent explosion of research on romantic relationships. In this section we'll look at two particularly prominent theories of love.

Triangular Theory of Love
Robert Sternberg's (1986, 1988) *triangular theory of love* posits that all love experiences have three components: intimacy, passion, and commitment. Each of these components is represented as a point of a triangle, from which the theory derives its name (see Figure 8.8).

Intimacy refers to **warmth, closeness, and sharing in a relationship.** Signs of intimacy include giving and receiving emotional support, wanting to promote the welfare of the loved one, and sharing one's self and one's posses-

sions with the person. Self-disclosure is necessary to achieve and maintain feelings of intimacy in a relationship.

Passion refers to the intense feelings (both positive and negative) experienced in love relationships, including sexual desire. Sternberg suggests that while sexual needs may be dominant in many close relationships, other needs also figure in the experience of passion. Among them are our needs for affiliation, self-esteem, dominance, submission, and self-actualization.

Commitment involves the decision and intent to maintain a relationship in spite of the difficulties and costs that may arise. According to Sternberg, commitment has a short-term and a long-term aspect. The short-term one concerns our conscious decision that we love someone. The long-term aspect reflects our determination to make a relationship endure. Although the decision to love someone usually comes before commitment, some people make a commitment without consciously deciding that they love the other person.

Sternberg has described eight different types of relationships that can result from the presence or absence of each of the three components of love (see Figure 8.8). One of these relationship types, *nonlove*, is not pictured in the diagram because it is defined as the absence of any of the three components. According to Sternberg, most of our interpersonal relationships fall into this category.

Liking is found at the top of Sternberg's triangle. Liking involves the experience of only one component of love—intimacy. In liking relationships we feel warm and close to other people, but we don't experience passionate feelings for them or make long-term commitments to them.

Infatuation represents a second point on the triangle that involves only one component of love—in this case, passion. When people talk about "falling in love at

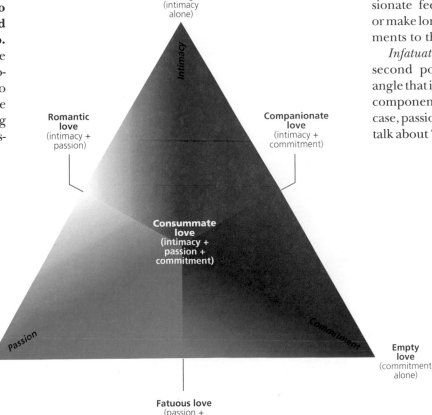

Liking
(intimacy alone)

Intimacy

Romantic love
(intimacy + passion)

Companionate love
(intimacy + commitment)

Consummate love
(intimacy + passion + commitment)

Passion

Commitment

Infatuation
(passion alone)

Empty love
(commitment alone)

Fatuous love
(passion + commitment)

first sight," they're experiencing infatuation. Sternberg mentions three problems typically associated with infatuation. First, the partner is loved only as an idealized object—a projection of the lover's needs—rather than as the person he or she really is. Second, infatuation tends

BLOOM COUNTY. © 1984 BY THE WASHINGTON POST WRITERS GROUP. REPRINTED WITH PREMISSION.

to be obsessive, consuming time and energy needed for other activities. Third, since infatuations are usually one-sided, they often cause feelings of distress. Because of the nature of infatuated relationships, they are likely to be troublesome.

Empty love, the third point on the triangle, refers to a relationship in which only commitment is currently present. In our culture, this type of relationship is most commonly found in the last stages of a long-term relationship. In other cultures where marriages are arranged by parents, this type of love typically exists in the initial stages of a marital relationship.

In Sternberg's model, there are four types of love that can result from combinations of the three components. The first is *fatuous love*, which is a combination of passion and commitment. This type of love often occurs in "whirlwind courtships." People meet, fall in love, and get married so quickly that the intimacy component has no time to develop. These relationships are quite likely to break up when the passion fades, because the usually shallow commitment has little intimacy to sustain it.

In Sternberg's scheme, the combination of intimacy and passion is called *romantic love*. This means that two people feel strongly drawn to each other and share highly personal information with each other. Still, with romantic love, there is no long-term commitment to maintain the relationship. It may be that the commitment component will be added to the relationship at a later time. Or it may never develop, as in a summer love affair. Romantic love can begin as infatuation (passion only) or liking (intimacy only). Each of these states can develop into romantic love with the addition of the other necessary component.

Companionate love involves the combination of intimacy and commitment. This type of love is seen in marriages in which passion has faded, or in lifelong, intimate friendships. According to Sternberg, most romantic love relationships eventually become companionate love relationships as passion subsides. For some couples, the relative lack of passion in their relationship is acceptable. Other couples (or one of the partners) may be motivated to seek passion in extramarital affairs. Or they may dissolve the companionate love relationship for the opportunity to develop a new romantic love—which will very likely change into companionate love eventually.

Last, *consummate love* results when all three components of love—intimacy, passion, and commitment—are present. Although many of us wish and strive for consummate love, attaining it can be difficult. As you might speculate, maintaining consummate love is even more difficult.

Romantic Love as Attachment

In a second ground-breaking theory of love, Cindy Hazan and Phillip Shaver (1987) have looked not at the components of love, but at similarities between romantic love and attachment relationships in infancy. **Infant attachment refers to the strong emotional bond that infants usually**

A consummate-love relationship is intimately passionate and committed.

develop with their caregivers during the first year of their lives. Hazan and Shaver suggest that infant attachments and romantic attachments share a number of features. These include intense fascination with the other person, distress at separation, and efforts to stay close and spend time together. They also make the provocative suggestion that our romantic relationships in adulthood follow the same form as our attachments in infancy.

What forms do attachments in infancy take? Research indicates that these early attachments vary in quality and that infants tend to fall into three groups (Ainsworth, Blehar, Waters, & Wall, 1978). Most infants develop a *secure attachment*. However, some are very anxious when separated from their caretaker, a syndrome called *anxious-ambivalent attachment*. A third group of infants, characterized by *avoidant attachment*, never connect very well with their caretaker.

According to Hazan and Shaver, we relive our early bonding with our parents in our adult romances. They theorize, for example, that an adult who had an anxious-ambivalent attachment in infancy will tend to have romantic relations marked by anxiety and ambivalence. Hazan and Shaver's (1987) initial survey study provided some support for their theory. They found that adults' love relationships could be sorted into groups that paralleled the patterns of attachment seen in infants. Specifically, they found that their subjects fell into the following three categories.

Secure adults (56% of subjects). People in this category reported that they found it easy to get close to others, that they trusted other people, and that they were comfortable with mutual dependence. Further, they rarely worried about being abandoned by their partner. Of the three groups of adults, these subjects were found to have the longest-lasting relationships and the fewest divorces. They described their parents as behaving warmly to them and to each other.

Avoidant adults (24% of subjects). These individuals indicated that they felt somewhat uncomfortable getting close to others and had difficulty trusting their partners completely. They reported experiencing jealousy, emotional highs and lows, and a fear of intimacy in their relationships. They described their parents as less warm than did secure adults and saw their mothers as cold and rejecting.

Anxious-ambivalent adults (20% of subjects). Subjects in this category reported that they found their partners unwilling to get as close as they would like and that they worried about their lovers leaving them. They also reported feelings of extreme sexual attraction and jealousy in their relationships. They described their relationship with their parents as less warm than did secure adults and felt that their parents had unhappy marriages.

Hazan and Shaver (1987) found that the percentage of adults falling into each category was roughly the same as the percentage of infants in each comparable category.

RECOMMENDED READING
A New Look at Love
by Elaine Hatfield & G. William Walster (University Press of America, 1985)

This book represents a fine effort at combining empirical research with practical advice. As you may have noticed from the references to studies in this chapter, Hatfield and Walster have conducted a great deal of research on the mysteries of love. Moreover, they have been among the more innovative and down-to-earth investigators in this area. Although their own work is highlighted in this book, their review of research is broad in scope. The book is smoothly written, with minimal dependence on technical jargon.

Unlike many psychologists from a research background, Hatfield and Walster are not timid about giving practical advice on ordinary questions. Drawing from scientific research, casual observation, and their own extensive thinking about the subject, they offer astute advice on how to deal with the intricacies of romantic relationships. The book is filled with fascinating case histories and intriguing questionnaires. Unfortunately, the second edition has not been revised or updated. Since the first edition was printed in 1978, some of the findings may be out of date. Even so, we think the book has a lot to offer.

Critics of Hatfield and Walster appear to have derived some amusement from the fact that this former husband-and-wife team was broken up by divorce soon after the publication of the first edition of this book. Although admittedly ironic, their parting of ways in no way undermines the quality of their contribution to the understanding of love. As they pointed out themselves, love is a beautiful but *fragile* flower.

> Passionate love is characterized by fragility. Every lover always hopes that *this* love will last forever. But the rest of us, looking on, know that that's unlikely. [p. 108]

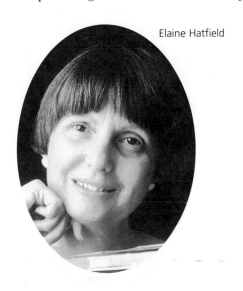

Elaine Hatfield

Also, subjects' recollections of their childhood relations with their parents were consistent with the idea that we relive our infant attachment experiences in adulthood.

The results of a single survey should always be regarded as tentative. Additional research is needed to further explore the link between attachment and romantic love. Nonetheless, Hazan and Shaver's ideas and results are thought-provoking, to say the least.

The Course of Romantic Love

Must passion fade? Regrettably, the answer to this question appears to be yes. Several theorists suggest that the intense attaction and arousal we feel for a lover seems destined to subside. For example, in his triangular theory of love, Sternberg (1986) hypothesizes that passion reaches its peak early and then declines in intensity. In contrast, both intimacy and commitment appear to increase as time progresses, although they develop at different rates (see Figure 8.9).

Based on their research, Ellen Berscheid and Elaine Hatfield also conclude that passionate love tends to peak early and then fights a difficult battle against the erosion of time. At first, love is "blind," so we usually develop a very idealized picture of our lover. However, as time passes, the intrusion of reality often undermines this idealized view.

Must the decline of passion lead to the demise of romantic love? Not necessarily. Some relationships do dissolve when passion fades. However, many others evolve into different, but still satisfying, phases. Let's examine the research on why some relationships endure while others expire.

Why Relationships Fail

Most people find being in love exhilarating and wish it could last forever. Indeed, when we're consumed by passionate love, it's hard to believe our feelings for the other person won't last forever. Unfortunately, while many relationships do withstand the test of time, many do not.

A longitudinal study of couples in the Boston area (Hill, Rubin, & Peplau, 1976) provides some interesting insights about what causes couples to break up. In this study, 200 couples (predominantly college students) were followed over a period of two years. To participate in the study, couples had to be "going steady" and believe that they were in love. At the end of the two-year period, it was found that almost half (45%) of the relationships had dissolved. The reasons the couples gave for going their separate ways are shown in Figure 8.10. Their reasons suggest two prominent factors that contribute to romantic breakups.

Premature commitment. Virtually all of the reasons for breakups involved things that could only be known after some sharing of personal information over time. Many people seem to make romantic commitments without taking the time to get to know who their partner really is. These people may find out later that they don't really like their partner. Or they may discover that they have little in common with their partner.

Ineffective conflict resolution. The vast majority of couples report having disagreements. For instance, one study of 1,000 engaged couples reported that 80% of them had arguments (Burgess & Wallin, 1953). Interestingly, research indicates that the likelihood of disagreements increases as couples learn more about each other and become more interdependent. For example, one study reported that disagreements among casually dating couples were significantly lower than among couples who were dating seriously (Braiker & Kelley, 1979). Unfortunately, as we discussed in Chapter 6, many people do not know how to deal with conflict constructively. This inability to wrestle effectively with conflicts appears to be a key factor in romantic breakups.

Helping Relationships Last

Is there anything we can do to increase the chances that our love relationships will last? The best advice is probably to engage in extensive self-disclosure and to take plenty of

Figure 8.9. The course of love over time. According to Sternberg (1986), the three components of love typically progress differently over time. He theorizes that passion peaks early in a relationship and then declines. In contrast, intimacy and commitment are thought to build gradually.

time to get to know the other person before you make a long-term commitment. Some recent research based on Sternberg's theory found that the best predictors of whether dating couples' relationships would continue were their levels of commitment and intimacy (Hendrick, Hendrick, & Adler, 1988). Hence, it appears that early attention to the intimacy foundations of a relationship and ongoing, mutual efforts to build a commitment can help foster more enduring love. In addition, it is important to develop effective conflict resolution skills to deal successfully with inevitable disagreements.

LONELINESS

We have emphasized throughout this chapter that friendship and love play important roles in our lives. We shall now discuss what happens when the fundamental need for these social relations is thwarted. **Loneliness occurs when a person has fewer interpersonal relationships than desired or when these relationships are not as satisfying as desired.** Loneliness is *not* the same as spending time alone. People can feel lonely even when surrounded by others (at a party or concert, for instance). Conversely, some people cherish solitude and are content with less social interaction than most of us prefer. Thus, loneliness is a highly subjective and personal feeling.

Three kinds of loneliness have been identified by Young (1982). *Chronic loneliness* is a condition that affects people who have been unable to develop a satisfactory interpersonal network over a period of years. *Transitional loneliness* occurs when people who have had satisfying social relationships in the past become lonely because of a specific disruption of their social network (examples include death of a loved one, divorce, and moving to a new locale). *Transient loneliness* involves brief and sporadic feelings of loneliness, which many people may experience even when their social life is reasonably adequate.

Loneliness may not occur in all areas of a person's life.

For instance, you might be highly satisfied with your friendship network but feel very dissatisfied about not having a suitable romantic relationship. Psychologists have been interested in identifying the specific areas of life in which people experience relationship deficits that produce feelings of loneliness. Research suggests that loneliness can be attributable to perceived deficits in four areas: (1) romantic/sexual relationships, (2) friendship relationships, (3) family relationships, and (4) community relationships (Schmidt & Sermat, 1983). Thus, in trying to better understand an individual's loneliness, it may be useful to pinpoint the exact nature of the social deficits that produce the feelings of loneliness.

Prevalence and Consequences of Loneliness

Survey studies designed to gain some insight into the prevalence of loneliness in our society have yielded notably disparate figures, depending on the nature of the sample interviewed and the shaping of the questions. For example, in a survey of some 400 Los Angeles workers, the statement "I often feel lonely" was endorsed by 10% of the respondents (Seeman, 1971). In contrast, in the previously mentioned *Psychology Today* survey on friendship, 67% of the respondents indicated that they felt lonely either "sometimes" or "often" (Parlee et al., 1979). In another study, 75% of new college students reported experiencing loneliness in their first few weeks on campus (Cutrona, 1982). Such startlingly high figures may reflect the nature of the samples studied. Or these figures may mean that most of us experience transient, everyday loneliness at one time or another.

The crucial question is how many people are chronically tormented by severe loneliness. We currently do not have sound data for a precise answer to this question. However, anecdotal evidence suggests that the number of people plagued by severe loneliness is substantial. For instance, telephone hotlines for troubled people report that complaints of loneliness dominate their calls.

The personal consequences of loneliness can be over-

What Causes Couples to Break Up?		
Factors	Women's reports (%)	Men's reports (%)
Interactive factors		
Becoming bored with relationship	77	77
Differences in interests	73	61
Differences in backgrounds	44	47
Differences in intelligence	20	10
Conflicting sexual attitudes	48	43
Conflicting marriage ideas	43	29
Noninteractive factors		
Woman's desire to be independent	74	50
Man's desire to be independent	47	61
Woman's interest in someone else	40	31
Man's interest in someone else	18	29
Living too far apart	28	41
Pressure from woman's parents	18	13
Pressure from man's parents	10	9

Figure 8.10. Factors contributing to romantic breakups. Couples who broke up after dating steadily were asked why by Hill, Rubin, and Peplau (1976). The factors commonly cited are listed here. The researchers distinguished between *interactive factors*, which consisted of problems that emerged out of the partners' ways of relating to each other, and *noninteractive factors*.

whelming. Painful thoughts of one's plight may come to dominate one's consciousness. As might be expected, studies have found a strong correlation between feelings of loneliness and feelings of depression (Rook, 1984; Young, 1982). Similarly, researchers have reported a relationship between loneliness and poor physical and psychological health (Rubenstein & Shaver, 1982). Thus, it is clear that the consequences of loneliness can be quite serious.

The Roots of Loneliness

A number of factors may contribute to feelings of loneliness. Since any event that ruptures the social fabric of a person's life may lead to loneliness, no one is immune. In this section, we will describe some social trends and personal qualities that are among the more prominent causes of loneliness.

Contributing social trends. A number of theorists have commented on various social trends that have undermined the sharing of intimacy in our culture (Flanders, 1982; Keyes, 1980; Packard, 1972). For instance, dramatic increases in residential mobility have played havoc with friendship networks. Families are becoming less effective sources of emotional security as divorce rates increase and the extended family becomes a relic of the past. While technology makes life easier in some respects, it can also have negative effects on our personal lives. For example, superficial social interactions become prevalent as we

order our meals at drive-up windows, do our banking at drive-through facilities, and so forth. Even worse, because of people's busy schedules, social interactions at home are reduced as family members eat on the run, on their own, or in front of the television. Moreover, the fact that people watch television so much tends to diminish meaningful family conversation. Finally, with the advent of personal computers, more and more people will spend time at terminals in their offices and homes, alone.

Low self-esteem. A key personal factor that promotes loneliness is low self-esteem (Cutrona, 1982; Hanson, Jones, & Carpenter, 1984). People who have unfavorable opinions of themselves often do not feel worthy of others' affection. They may make little effort to pursue close relationships. This lack of confidence probably has a spiraling effect, as low self-esteem begets loneliness and loneliness begets still lower self-esteem.

Poor social skills. Interpersonal skills, although not particularly difficult to develop, do have to be acquired. Poor social skills probably prevent many people from experiencing rewarding social interactions. Thus, one study found that lonely people tend to pay inadequate attention to their conversational partners (Jones, Hobbs, & Hockenbury, 1982). Another study of conversational style concluded that lonely people are relatively inhibited, speaking less than nonlonely people (Sloan & Solano, 1984). Anxiety about social skills also appears to contribute to loneliness (Solano & Koester, 1989).

Fear of intimacy. Some people with positive self-concepts

Figure 8.11. Patterns of thinking underlying loneliness. According to Young (1982), negative self-talk contributes to loneliness. Six clusters of irrational thoughts are illustrated here. Each cluster of cognitions leads to certain patterns of behavior (shown on the right) that promote loneliness.

and sound social skills seem overly wary of intimate interaction. They keep people at an emotional distance and (often unconsciously) limit their interactions to a relatively superficial level. Illustrative of this fear of intimacy is evidence that lonely people are relatively reluctant to take social risks (Schultz & Moore, 1984). The difficulty that lonely people tend to have in engaging in self-disclosure (Solano, Batten, & Parish, 1982) also demonstrates how this fear of intimacy undermines rewarding social interactions.

Negative self-talk. Ultimately, what underlies many of the factors just discussed is negative self-talk. Lonely people are prone to irrational thinking about their social skills, the probability of achieving intimacy, the likelihood of rejection, and so forth. For example, there is evidence that lonely people tend to reverse the normal attributional tendencies that people exhibit in explaining failures (see Chapter 5). Specifically, they attribute their interpersonal failures to basic personal defects in themselves instead of to situational factors (Anderson, Horowitz, & French, 1983). Young (1982) points out that lonely people engage in negative self-talk that prevents them from pursuing intimacy in an active and positive manner. He has identified some clusters of ideas that foster loneliness. Figure 8.11 shows examples of typical thoughts from six of these clusters of cognitions and the overt behaviors that result.

Coping with Loneliness

It is disheartening to report that there are no simple solutions for those who suffer from loneliness. A major reason that people have difficulty overcoming loneliness is that many of them tend to withdraw socially. For example, one study that asked people what they did when they felt lonely reported that the top responses were read and listen to music (Rubenstein & Shaver, 1982). Obviously, these activities are not going to help the lonely person acquire new friends. Thus, the key to overcoming loneliness may be to avoid the temptation to withdraw, to stay active socially, and to maintain an optimistic outlook. The importance of staying active socially cannot be overemphasized. As we learned earlier in this chapter, proximity is a powerful factor in the development of close relationships. You have to be around people in order to expand your network of friends.

It is difficult to offer more specific suggestions for overcoming loneliness because the remedy depends on the precise causes of the loneliness. Each of the loneliness-inducing clusters of cognitions and behaviors summarized in Figure 8.11 is discussed at some point in this text. Clusters A (poor self-concept, Chapter 5) and B (low self-disclosure, Chapter 6) have already been discussed. Clusters E and F represent the core of shyness and are addressed in the application section of this chapter. Cluster D (lack of assertiveness) is treated in Chapter 10, and cluster C (sexual anxiety) is discussed in Chapter 13. The fact that the problems relevant to loneliness are distributed across so many chapters should serve to demonstrate the complexity of this painful condition.

SUMMARY

The evolution of close relationships appears to involve four stages characterized by increasing levels of interdependence. According to social exchange theory, people remain in relationships as long as the costs are reasonable in comparison with the rewards. These perceptions of outcomes are evaluated relative to a person's comparison level.

The dynamics of attraction are similar for friendship and love. We tend to prefer physically attractive companions, but this preference is tempered to some extent by matching effects. Generally, we are attracted to people who are intelligent, competent, high in status, and equipped with a pleasant personality. Our own self-esteem and self-perception processes also figure importantly in our attraction to others. In addition, evidence

Clusters of Cognitions Typical of Lonely Clients		
Clusters	**Cognitions**	**Behaviors**
A	1. I'm undesirable.	Avoidance of friendship
	2. I'm dull and boring.	
B	1. I can't communicate with other people.	Low self-disclosure
	2. My thoughts and feelings are bottled up inside.	
C	1. I'm not a good lover in bed.	Avoidance of sexual relationships
	2. I can't relax, be spontaneous, and enjoy sex.	
D	1. I can't seem to get what I want from this relationship.	Lack of assertiveness in relationships
	2. I can't say how I feel, or he/she might leave me.	
E	1. I won't risk being hurt again.	Avoidance of potentially intimate relationships
	2. I'd screw up any relationship.	
F	1. I don't know how to act in this situation.	Avoidance of other people
	2. I'll make a fool of myself.	

indicates that proximity, similarity, and reciprocity promote attraction.

The key ingredients of friendship are loyalty, emotional support, and letting friends be themselves. Same-sex friendships among women tend to be characterized by more intimacy and self-disclosure than friendships among men. In some respects, social norms reduce friendship opportunities for married people.

A number of myths have grown around the concept of romantic love, including the idea that when you fall in love you'll know it, and the notion that you have no control over your behavior when love strikes. Other myths include the beliefs that love is purely positive, that it lasts forever, and that it can conquer all problems. Gender differences regarding love are interesting in that they do not support the traditional stereotype that women are more romantic than men.

Sternberg's triangular theory of love proposes that passion, intimacy, and commitment combine into different types of love. Hazan and Shaver theorize that our love relationships follow the form of our attachments in infancy. Initially, romantic love is usually characterized by passion, but strong passion appears to fade over time. In relationships that continue, passionate love evolves into a less intense, more mature form of love. Romantic relationships fail for many reasons. Chief among them are ineffective conflict resolution and the tendency to make premature commitments.

Loneliness involves discontent with the extent and quality of one's interpersonal network. Evidence suggests that a surprisingly large number of people in our society are troubled by loneliness. Although loneliness is promoted by a number of social trends, it appears to be due mainly to personal factors, such as low self-esteem, poor social skills, fear of intimacy, and negative self-talk. Coping with loneliness is difficult. The key appears to be staying involved socially rather than withdrawing.

The Application that follows will discuss shyness, a problem that intersects with loneliness to some degree. In this Application, we will discuss the prevalence and consequences of shyness and how to cope with this problem.

Understand-ing Shyness

Answer the following yes or no.

☐ **1.** When I am the focus of attention, I often become anxious.

☐ **2.** In interacting with people, I tend to be very self-conscious.

☐ **3.** I get embarrassed in social situations quite easily.

☐ **4.** I wish that I could be more assertive about pursuing social relation-ships.

☐ **5.** I am often concerned about being rejected by others.

If you answered yes to several of the questions above, you may be hampered in your social life by a very common prob-lem—shyness. Loneliness and shyness are intersecting problems. Although many lonely people are not shy, and many shy people are not lonely, it is nonetheless true that loneliness is a common conse-quence of shyness (Cheek & Busch, 1981).

Shyness **refers to discomfort, inhibition, and excessive caution in interpersonal relations**. Specifically, shy people tend (1) to be timid about expressing them-selves, (2) to be overly self-conscious about how others are reacting to them, (3) to embarrass easily, and (4) to experi-ence physiological symptoms of their anxiety, such as a racing pulse, blushing, or an upset stomach.

PREVALENCE AND CONSEQUENCES OF SHYNESS

Philip Zimbardo (1977, 1987) and his associates have done pioneering research on shyness. Their survey data indicate that shyness may be more common than previously realized. Over 80% of the respondents to their survey reported being shy during some stage of their lives. Moreover, 40% indicated that they were currently troubled by shyness. The personal implications of shyness are generally quite negative. Most shy people report that they do not like being shy. This is understandable in view of the common consequences of shyness. Shy people tend to have difficulty making friends, and they tend to be sexually

inhibited. They also are lonely and depressed more often than others.

SITUATIONAL NATURE OF SHYNESS

The traditional stereotype of the shy person as one who is timid all the time appears to be somewhat inaccurate. In Zimbardo's study, 60% of the shy people reported that their shyness was *situation-ally specific*. That is, they experienced shyness only in certain social contexts, such as asking someone for help or interacting with a large group of people. Figure 8.12 lists the situations that most commonly elicited shyness in Zimbardo's subjects.

The situational nature of shyness has led researchers to distinguish between state shyness and trait shyness (Asendorpf, 1989). *State shyness* involves a temporary

"What Makes You Shy?"

Other people	Percentage of shy students
Strangers	70
Opposite sex	64
Authorities by virtue of their knowledge	55
Authorities by virtue of their role	40
Relatives	21
Elderly people	12
Friends	11
Children	10
Parents	8

Situations	Percentage of shy students
Where I am focus of attention—large group (as when giving a speech)	73
Large groups	68
Of lower status	56
Social situations in general	55
New situations in general	55
Requiring assertiveness	54
Where I am being evaluated	53
Where I am focus of attention—small group	52
Small social groups	48
One-to-one different-sex interactions	48
Of vulnerability (need help)	48
Small task-oriented groups	28
One-to-one same-sex interactions	14

Figure 8.12. The situational determinants of shyness. Zimbardo (1977) asked subjects about the people and circum-stances that made them feel shy. The results of his survey showed that shyness depends to a large degree on situational factors.

Figure 8.13. Shyness as an approach-avoidance conflict. State shyness involves an approach-avoidance conflict in which a person both desires and fears social interaction. As we noted in Chapter 3, approach-avoidance conflicts can be highly stressful.

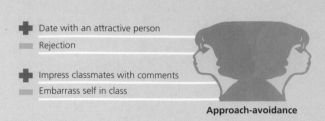

Date with an attractive person

Rejection

Impress classmates with comments

Embarrass self in class

Approach-avoidance

elevation in anxiety in reaction to certain social situations. According to Asendorpf (1986), the crux of the problem is that people experience an approach-avoidance conflict (see Figure 8.13). They are torn between their desire to interact with someone (approach motivation) and their fear of making a social blunder (avoidance motivation). What types of situations tend to elicit state shyness? According to Asendorpf, the most common triggers appear to be the presence of strangers and the anticipation of being evaluated by others.

Trait shyness is a consistent tendency to feel anxious and inhibited in a wide variety of social situations. People who are chronically tormented by discomfort in social interactions exhibit shyness as a stable personality trait (Jones, Briggs, & Smith, 1986). Some studies suggest that there is a genetic predisposition toward trait shyness (Daniels & Plomin, 1985).

COPING WITH SHYNESS

It would be naive to pretend that shyness can be overcome easily. However, it is important to emphasize that shyness *can* be overcome successfully! Think about it. In Zimbardo's survey, 40% of the respondents reported that they were *currently* shy, while 80% indicated that they *were* shy at some previous time. Obviously, half of the once-shy subjects felt that they had conquered their shyness.

Much of Zimbardo's (1977, 1987) book is devoted to how to deal with the problem of shyness. Basically, the three key steps in this process are (1) analyzing your shyness, (2) building your self-esteem, and (3) improving your social skills.

Analyzing Your Shyness

The first step is the easiest. You should analyze your shyness and try to pinpoint exactly what social situations tend to elicit your shy behavior. You should further try to ascertain what causes your shyness in the identified situations. To help identify the situations that trigger your shyness, you may want to use some of the techniques for gathering baseline data that we discussed in our coverage of behavior modification (see the Chapter 4 Application). You might also benefit from scanning Figure 8.12, which summarizes findings on which situations tend to generate shy behavior in others.

A number of reasons or combinations of reasons may account for trait shyness. Zimbardo enumerated eight common reasons: (1) concern about negative evaluation, (2) fear of rejection, (3) lack of self-confidence, (4) lack of specific social skills, (5) fear of intimacy, (6) preference for being alone, (7) emphasis on and enjoyment of nonsocial activities, and (8) personal inadequacy or handicap.

Building Your Self-Esteem

Poor self-esteem appears to be a key factor underlying trait shyness (Crozier, 1981). Hence, it is important for shy people to work on improving their self-confidence. In his book, Zimbardo spells out "fifteen steps to a more confident you." Many of these coincide with the suggestions made in the Chapter 5 Application on building self-esteem.

Improving Your Social Skills

The third step is the most difficult. As we have discussed repeatedly, it is not easy to change deeply ingrained habits. Zimbardo suggests using many of the behavior modification techniques that we covered in Chapter 4. Specifically, he recommends specifying certain target social responses to be increased and then setting up a reward system for engaging in these responses. He further emphasizes that one has to be realistic and work toward *gradual* improvement. For example, he suggests that people start with relatively simple and nonthreatening social behaviors, such as anonymous conversations. These are conversations with strangers in public places such as a theater line, a bank, or a stadium. Other simple social

responses that one might work on in the beginning include saying hello to strangers or giving compliments to others.

Zimbardo offers other suggestions for improving social skills that are too numerous to detail here. However, we can mention a few ideas to consider if you are troubled by shyness. First, it's a good idea to select a nonshy role model to watch closely. Identify someone in your personal sphere who is extraverted. It's probably a good idea to use a same-sex model. Observe how your role model handles various kinds of social situations. In particular, pay attention to how he or she acts in the situations that trigger your shyness. Second, develop "expertise" in some area so that you have something to contribute to conversations. In other words, become a movie buff or a sports buff or an amateur political analyst. Third, listen actively and attentively. People love to talk about themselves. Encourage them to do so. After going on and on about themselves, they'll probably compliment you on what an interesting and enjoyable "conversation" the two of you just had!

As you work on developing your social skills, bear in mind that your progress will probably be gradual. Social skills are honed over a lifetime. Although they *can* be improved with practice, it normally takes a good bit of time, and your progress may seem barely perceptible. However, if you stick with it, you *can* conquer shyness.

Philip Zimbardo

1. Describe Levinger and Snoek's model of relationship development.

2. Describe the principles of social exchange theory.

3. Summarize research on physical appearance as a factor in attraction.

4. Discuss how personality, competence, and social status influence interpersonal attraction.

5. Explain how self-esteem and self-perception may play a role in attraction.

6. Describe proximity, similarity, and reciprocity effects in attraction.

7. Summarize evidence on what makes a good friend.

8. Relate gender and marital status to patterns of friendship.

9. List five myths about love.

10. Discuss evidence on gender differences in romanticism.

11. Summarize Sternberg's triangular theory of love.

12. Explain Hazan and Shaver's view of romantic love as an attachment process.

13. Discuss why love relationships fail.

14. Describe three kinds of loneliness identified by Young.

15. Summarize evidence on the prevalence and consequences of loneliness.

16. List some social trends and personal factors that contribute to loneliness.

17. Summarize evidence on the prevalence and situational nature of shyness.

18. Discuss the steps suggested by Zimbardo for coping with shyness.

KEY TERMS

Close relationship
Commitment
Comparison level
Infant attachment
Interpersonal attraction
Intimacy

Loneliness
Matching hypothesis
Passion
Proximity
Reciprocity
Shyness
Social exchange theory

KEY PEOPLE

Ellen Berscheid
Elaine Hatfield (Walster)
Cindy Hazan & Philip Shaver
Robert Sternberg
Philip Zimbardo

NYU Loneliness Scale

INSTRUCTIONS
For each item below, circle the most appropriate answer. Try to respond as frankly and as honestly as you can.

THE SCALE
1. When I am completely alone, I feel lonely:
   - Almost never (10)
   - Occasionally (16)
   - About half the time (24)
   - Often (32)
   - Most of the time (40)

2. How often do you feel lonely?
   - Never, or almost never (10)
   - Rarely (11)
   - Occasionally (17)
   - About half the time (23)
   - Quite often (29)
   - Most of the time (34)
   - All the time, or almost all the time (40)

3. When you feel lonely, do you usually feel:
   - I never feel lonely (10)
   - Slightly lonely (13)
   - Somewhat lonely (20)
   - Fairly lonely (27)
   - Very lonely (33)
   - Extremely lonely (40)

4. Compared to people your own age, how lonely do you think you are?
   - Much less lonely (10)
   - Somewhat less lonely (16)
   - About average (24)
   - Somewhat lonelier (32)
   - Much lonelier (40)

5. I am a lonely person
   - Strongly disagree (10)
   - Disagree (20)
   - Agree (30)
   - Strongly agree (40)

6. I always was a lonely person
   - Strongly disagree (10)
   - Disagree (20)
   - Agree (30)
   - Strongly agree (40)

7. I always will be a lonely person
   - Strongly disagree (10)
   - Disagree (20)
   - Agree (30)
   - Strongly agree (40)

8. Other people think of me as a lonely person
   - Strongly disagree (10)
   - Disagree (20)
   - Agree (30)
   - Strongly agree (40)

SCORING THE SCALE
To score this scale, you simply add up the numbers on the right that correspond to the answers you chose. This sum, which should fall between 80 and 320, is your score on the NYU Loneliness Scale. Enter it below.

MY SCORE _____

WHAT THE SCALE MEASURES
As its name suggests, this scale is intended to measure the degree to which you feel lonely. It assesses loneliness in its broadest sense at a specific time. It does not attempt to distinguish between different types—chronic, transitional, or transient—of loneliness. Nor does It attempt to identify the specific kinds of social relations (friendships, intimate relations, and so on) that are lacking. Thus, it is a global measure of your current loneliness (which could change, of course, especially if it is largely transitional or transient loneliness).

Developed by Carin Rubenstein and Phillip Shaver (1982), this scale has been used in large surveys involving over 20,000 respondents. Internal reliability is excellent (correlations in the high .80s).

Using this scale, Rubenstein and Shaver (1982) found that lonely people tend to associate negative feelings (fear, anxiety, anger) with being alone. In comparison, those who don't feel very lonely associate more positive feelings (calm, relaxation, happiness) with solitude. People who score high on this scale report lower self-esteem and more symptoms of physical illness than those who score low.

INTERPRETING YOUR SCORE
Our norms are based on a diverse sample of people who responded to the scale when it was published in newspapers. The results of a newspaper survey may be affected by systematic bias in who chooses to fill out the survey. Nonetheless, a sample obtained in this way may be more representative than the small samples of undergraduates that are typically used in setting norms for many research scales. In any case, since there is modest evidence available on the validity of this scale, scores should be interpreted with extra caution.

NORMS

Most lonely:	207–320
More lonely than average:	171–206
Less lonely than average:	133–170
Least lonely:	80–132

*How Do You
Relate to
Friends?*

The following questions (adapted from Egan, 1977) are designed to help you think about how you deal with friendships.

1. Do you have many friends or very few?

2. Whether many or few, do you usually spend a lot of time with your friends?

3. What do you like in other people—that is, what makes you choose them as friends?

4. Are the people you go around with like you or different from you? Or are they in some ways like you and in other ways different? How?

5 .Do you like to control others, to get them to do things your way? Do you let others control you? Do you give in to others much of the time?

6. Are there ways in which your friendships are one-sided?

9

Marriage and Intimate Relationships

"**M**y hands are shaky. I want to call her again but I know it is no good. She'll only yell and scream. It makes me feel lousy. I have work to do but I can't do it. I can't concentrate. I want to call people up, go see them, but I'm afraid they'll see that I'm shaky. I just want to talk. I can't think about anything besides this trouble with Nina. I think I want to cry."

—A recently separated man quoted in *Marital Separation* [Weiss, 1975, p. 48]

The man quoted above is an emotional wreck. He is describing his feelings a few days after he and his wife broke up. He is still hoping for a reconciliation with his wife. In the meantime he feels overwhelmed by anxiety, remorse and depression. He feels very alone and very scared by the prospect of remaining alone. His emotional distress is so great that he can't think straight or work effectively.

This man's reaction to the loss of an intimate relationship is not all that unusual. Marital breakups are devastating for most people—a reality that illustrates the enormous importance of intimate relationships in our lives.

In this chapter we will take a look at marriage and other intimate relationships. We will discuss why people marry and how they progress toward the selection of a mate. To shed light on marital adjustment, we will describe the life cycle of the family, highlighting key vulnerable spots in marital relations. We will also address issues related to divorce, cohabitation, remaining single, and being gay. Finally, in the Application, we will examine the "games" that intimate couples play in their relationships. Let's begin by discussing recent challenges to our traditional concept of marriage.

CHALLENGES TO THE TRADITIONAL MODEL OF MARRIAGE

Marriage **is the legally and socially sanctioned union of sexually intimate adults.** Traditionally, the marital rela-tionship includes economic interdependence, common residence, sexual fidelity, and shared responsibility for children. Although the institution of marriage remains popular, it sometimes seems to be under assault from shifting social trends. This assault has prompted some experts (for example, Cherlin, 1981; Glenn & Weaver, 1988) to ask whether the institution of marriage is in trouble. It appears that marriage will weather the storm. But it's worth looking at some of the social trends that are shaking our traditional model of marriage.

Increased acceptance of singlehood. An increasing proportion of the adult population under age 35 is remaining single (Stein, 1989). In part, this trend reflects longer postponement of marriage than before. The median age at which people marry has been increasing gradually since the mid-1960s, as Figure 9.1 shows. Thus, remaining single is becoming a more viable lifestyle. Furthermore, the negative stereotype of people who remain single, which pictures them as lonely, frustrated, and unchosen, is gradually evaporating.

Increased acceptance of cohabitation. **Cohabitation refers to living together in a sexually intimate relationship without the legal bonds of marriage.** Negative attitudes toward couples "living together" appear to be declining, though many people continue to disapprove of the practice. It is difficult to get accurate information on the number of cohabiting couples. However, census data suggest that cohabitation has increased dramatically. One study of couples applying for marriage licenses in 1980 found that 53% already lived at the same address, as compared to just 13% in the same area in 1970 (Gwartney-Gibbs, 1986).

Reduced premium on permanence. Most people still view marriage as a permanent commitment, but many people are also strongly committed to their own personal growth (Morgan & Scanzoni, 1987). Marriage is often seen as just one context in which such growth can occur. Thus, an increasing number of people regard divorce as justifiable if their marriage fails to foster their interests as individu-

Figure 9.1. Median age at first marriage. The median age at which people marry for the first time has been creeping up for both males and females since the mid-1960s. This trend indicates that more people are postponing marriage.

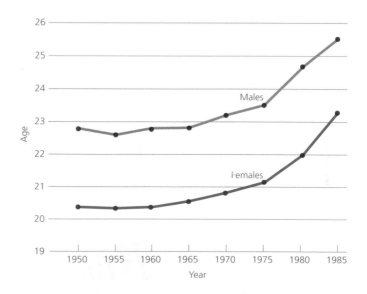

als. Accordingly, divorce rates have risen, and the social stigma associated with divorce has lessened. Some social critics (for example, Bernard, 1982) have even suggested that expectations of permanence in marriage are unrealistic in our turbulent modern society.

Transitions in gender roles. The women's movement and economic pressures have led to substantial changes in the expectations of many people entering marriage today. The traditional breadwinner and homemaker roles for the husband and wife are being discarded by many couples. Role expectations for husbands and wives are becoming more varied and flexible. Many people regard this trend as a step in the right direction (see Chapter 10). However, changing gender roles create new potential for conflict between marital partners.

Increased voluntary childlessness. An increasing number of married couples are choosing not to have children (Macklin, 1987). This trend is probably due to new career opportunities for women and the tendency to marry at a later age. Many people view married women who voluntarily remain childless as less well adjusted than those with children (Calhoun & Selby, 1980). However, this belief is not supported by the empirical evidence (Burman & de Anda, 1986).

In summary, the institution of marriage is in a period of transition, creating new adjustment challenges for modern couples. Support for the concept of monogamy remains strong, but changes in our society are altering our traditional model of marriage. The impact of these changes will be seen throughout this chapter as we discuss various facets of married life.

MOVING TOWARD MARRIAGE

"When you've been in love a few times, you start thinking of yourself as a used car. I started seeing a new man and I called him 'honey.' It was too soon and I saw him cringe when I did it. It made me feel so cheap. . . .

"I'm ashamed of being single, I have to admit it. I have grown to hate the word. The worst thing someone can say is, 'How come you're still not married?' It's like saying, 'What's wrong with you.' I look at women who are frumpy and physically undesirable and they're monochromatic and uninteresting and they don't seem unselfish and giving and I wonder, 'How did they become such an integral part of a man's life that he wanted to marry them and spend his life with them?' I'm envious. They're married and I date."

—A woman quoted in *Tales from the Front* [Kavesh & Lavin, 1988, p. 91]

The woman quoted above desperately wants to be married. The intensity of her motivation for marriage may be a bit unusual, but otherwise she is fairly typical. Like most of us, she has been socialized to believe that our lives aren't complete until we find a mate.

Although alternatives to marriage are more viable than ever, experts project that over 90% of us will marry at least once. Some of us will do it several times! But why? What motivates us to marry? And how do we choose our partners? We'll address these questions as we discuss the factors that influence our movement toward marriage.

The Motivation to Marry

A great variety of motivational factors propel people into marriage. Foremost among these is the desire to participate in a socially sanctioned, mutually rewarding, intimate relationship. Another key factor is the social pressure exerted on people to marry. Getting married is still the norm in our society. Our parents, relatives, and friends expect us to marry eventually, and they often make this abundantly clear with their comments and inquiries.

The popular view in our culture is that people marry because they have fallen in love. Although partially accurate, this view is terribly oversimplified. A multitude of motivational factors are involved in the decision to marry. Peter Stein (1975, 1976) interviewed single men and

women aged 22 to 45 who were judged to be neither unattractive nor socially inept. As you can see in Figure 9.2, he learned that there are many forces pushing and pulling us toward marriage or singlehood.

Although there are many good reasons for getting married, Stein's research reveals that people are often motivated by reasons that are less than ideal. For example, marriages motivated purely by physical attraction or the desire for a regular sexual outlet are likely to be fragile. Similarly, marriages motivated by the belief that one "should" be married by a particular age, or by the desire to escape an unsatisfactory home situation, have a weak base on which to build.

People vary greatly in the *strength* of their motivation to marry. Some people are eager to marry, while others are reluctant to assume the responsibility. Reiss (1980) has pointed out that marriage is a risky proposition. In deciding to get married, people make a long-range projection about the future of their relationship. Obviously, it is difficult to predict 50 years of commitment on the basis of one or two years of premarital interaction. There is no way to make this projection with absolute assurance of accuracy. Instead, marriage requires a leap of faith. Variability in the threshold for this leap of faith is probably a major determinant of when and why people marry. Yet we know very little about how this threshold is shaped or how it is related to personality.

Selecting a Mate

Modern Western cultures are somewhat unusual in permitting free choice of one's marital partner. Most societies rely on parental arrangements and severely restrict the range of acceptable partners along religious and class lines (Bumiller, 1989). Mate selection in American culture is a gradual process that begins with dating and moves on to sometimes lengthy periods

of courtship. In this section, we will look at the impact of endogamy, homogamy, and personal ideals on marital choice. We'll also discuss Bernard Murstein's S-V-R theory, which provides a good overview of the process of mate selection.

Endogamy

Endogamy **refers to the tendency of people to marry within their own social group.** Buss (1985) reviews extensive evidence indicating that we tend to marry people of the same race, religion, ethnic background, and social class. This endogamy is promoted by cultural norms and by the way proximity and similarity influence interpersonal attraction (see Chapter 8). Although endogamy appears to be gradually declining, it's likely to remain influential for the foreseeable future.

Homogamy

Homogamy **refers to the tendency of people to marry others who have similar personal characteristics.** Among other things, marital partners tend to be similar in age and education (Murstein, 1986). Census data from 1984 showed that the median age difference between people getting married was 2.4 years. These age differences are not symmetric, as husbands are usually older than their wives. As more people delay marriage until their thirties, the norm against women dating younger men may begin to pose problems. Without the freedom to date younger men, women will find their pool of potential partners dwindling more rapidly than men of similar age. In addition to age and education, there is evidence that married couples tend to be similar in physical attractiveness (Folkes, 1982) and in attitudes and values (Honeycutt, 1986).

Figure 9.2. The decision to marry. Stein (1975) interviewed single people between 22 and 45 to ascertain the motivational factors that influence the decision to marry. *Pushes toward marriage* involve deficits supposedly felt by single persons. *Pushes toward singlehood* involve deficits felt by married people. *Pulls* are positive factors associated with marriage or being single. The top boxes identify the factors favoring marriage, and the bottom boxes identify those favoring singlehood. Not everyone weighs all these factors, but this list illustrates the complexity of the decision to marry.

Pushes toward marriage	Pulls toward marriage
Economic security	Influence of parents
Influence from mass media	Desire for family
Pressure from parents	Example of peers
Need to leave home	Romanticization of marriage
Interpersonal and personal reasons	Love
Fear of independence	Physical attraction
Loneliness	Emotional attachment
Alternatives did not seem feasible	Security, social status, prestige
Cultural expectations, socialization	
Regular sex	
Guilt over singlehood	

Pushes toward singlehood	Pulls toward singlehood
Restrictions	Career opportunities
Suffocating one-to-one relationships, feeling trapped	Variety of experiences
Obstacles to self-development	Self-sufficiency
Boredom, unhappiness, anger	Sexual availability
Role playing and conformity to expectations	Exciting lifestyle
Poor communication with mate	Freedom to change and experiment
Sexual frustration	Mobility
Lack of friends, isolation, loneliness	Sustaining friendships
Limitations on mobility and available experience	Supportive groups
Influence of and participation in women's movement	Men's and women's groups
	Group living arrangements
	Specialized groups

Idealized Images

If you are not married, you can probably describe the kind of person you would eventually like to marry. Most of us develop a fairly clear picture of the man or woman we would like to have sweep us off our feet (Stiles, Gibbons, Hardardottir, & Schnellmann, 1987). Our idealized pictures influence our evaluation of potential mates. If a person does not compare favorably with our ideal, the discrepancy may undermine our attraction to the person. Some people create problems for themselves by holding highly unrealistic ideals of perfection that exclude virtually all potential partners.

Stimulus-Value-Role Theory

Bernard Murstein's (1976, 1986) *stimulus-value-role (S-V-R) theory* provides an insightful overview of the process of marital selection. Murstein theorizes that we generally proceed through three stages, named the stimulus, value, and role stages, as we progress toward marriage.

During the first stage, our attraction to members of the other sex depends mainly on their *stimulus value*. At this point, we focus on relatively superficial and easily identifiable characteristics of the other person. Foremost among these are the person's physical attractiveness, social status, occupational success, and reputation. Murstein borrows from *social exchange theory* (see Chapter 8) and argues that progress to the next stage depends on the pair's having relatively similar stimulus value, so as to produce an "even" exchange. The two persons may derive their stimulus value from different characteristics—one from wealth, say, and the other from beauty. However, progress to stage 2 is thought to depend on the couple's subjective perception that they possess similar stimulus value.

If a couple make it to the second stage, involving *value comparison*, the significance of stimulus variables may be reduced. Further progress now depends on compatibility in values. Typically, the pair will begin to explore each other's attitudes about religion, politics, sex, gender roles, leisure activities, and so forth. If fundamental in-

compatibilities are uncovered, the relationship may stall at stage 2, or it may come to an end. However, if the two persons discover similarity in values as they open up to each other, they are more likely to progress to stage 3.

In the *role stage*, people begin to think about marrying each other. Hence, they start evaluating whether the other person does a satisfactory job in the role of intimate companion. At this point, people focus on the distribution of power in their relationship, the reliability of emotional support, and the quality of their sexual liaison (if they have formed one). Although some people may marry after progressing through only the first two stages, Murstein maintains that marriage is generally delayed until couples are comfortable with role enactments in stage 3.

Predictors of Marital Success

Are there any factors that predict marital success? A great deal of research has been devoted to this question. This research has been plagued by one obvious problem: How do you measure "marital success"? Some researchers have simply compared divorced and intact couples in regard to premarital characteristics. Other researchers have used elaborate questionnaires to measure couples' marital satisfaction. However, these instruments appear to measure complacency and lack of conflict more than satisfaction. Although our measures of marital success are rather crude, some predictors of marital success have been found. These relations are all statistically weak, but they are intriguing nonetheless.

Family background. The marital adjustment of parents is correlated with the marital satisfaction of their children. People whose parents were unhappily married are more likely than others to have an unsatisfactory marriage. For a number of reasons, marital instability appears to run in families (Teachman, Polonko, & Scanzoni, 1987).

Age. The ages of the bride and groom are also related to the likelihood of success. Couples who marry young have

Similarity in interests and values is an important criterion in choosing a mate. Beyond the stage of initial attraction, the partners look for commonalities in their beliefs and desires, such as satisfaction with the simple things in life.

higher divorce rates (London & Wilson, 1988). Surprisingly, couples who marry late also have a higher propensity to divorce. Because they are selected from a smaller pool of potential mates, older newlyweds are more likely to differ in age, religion, social status, and education (Bitter, 1986). Such differences make marriage more challenging regardless of age.

Length of courtship. Longer periods of courtship are associated with a greater probability of marital success (Grover, Russell, Schumm, & Paff-Bergen, 1985). It is probably not the duration of courtship itself that is critical. Rather, this correlation may occur because people who are cautious about marriage have attitudes and values that promote marital stability.

Socioeconomic class. The frequency of divorce is higher in the working and lower classes than in the upper and middle classes (Raschke, 1987). There are probably many reasons, but a key one appears to be the greater financial stress in lower socioeconomic strata.

Personality. Generally, partners' personality traits are *not* predictive of marital success. However, the presence of serious psychological and emotional disorders in one or both partners is associated with marital problems (Raschke, 1987).

In summary, there are some thought-provoking correlations between couples' premarital characteristics and marital adjustment. However, there are no reliable predictors of marital success, as all these correlations are quite small. Researchers have found some stronger correlations when they have investigated the relationship between marital adjustment and the family life cycle. We'll examine this research next.

MARITAL ADJUSTMENT ACROSS THE FAMILY LIFE CYCLE

"Jennifer has taken a lot of time away from us, the time that we normally spend doing things together or talking. It seems like maybe on a weekend when we would normally like to sleep in, or just have lazy sex, Jennifer wakes up and needs to be fed. . . . But I'm sure that will pass as soon as Jennifer gets a little older. We're just going through a phase."

—A new mother quoted in *American Couples* [Blumstein & Schwartz, 1983, p. 205]

"We're just going through a phase." That statement highlights an important point: There are predictable

Figure 9.3. Stages of the family life cycle. The family life cycle can be divided into six stages, as shown here (based on Carter & McGoldrick, 1988). The family's key developmental task during each stage is identified in the second column. The third column lists additional developmental tasks at each stage.

The Family Life Cycle

Family life cycle stage	Emotional process of transition: Key developmental task	Additional changes in family status required to proceed developmentally
1. Between families: The unattached young adult	Accepting parent/offspring separation	a. Differentiation of self in relation to family of origin b. Development of intimate peer relationships c. Establishment of self in work
2. The joining of families through marriage: The newly married couple	Commitment to new system	a. Formation of marital system b. Realignment of relationships with extended families and friends to include spouse
3. The family with young children	Accepting new members into the system	a. Adjusting marital system to make space for child(ren) b. Taking on parenting roles c. Realignment of relationships with extended family to include parenting and grandparenting roles
4. The family with adolescents	Increasing flexibility of family boundaries to include children's independence	a. Shifting of parent-child relationships to permit adolescent to move in and out of system b. Refocus on midlife marital and career issues c. Beginning shift toward concerns for older generation
5. Launching children and moving on	Accepting a multitude of exits from and entries into the family system	a. Renegotiation of marital system as a dyad b. Development of adult-to-adult relationships between grown children and their parents c. Realignment of relationships to include in-laws and grandchildren d. Dealing with disabilities and death of parents (grandparents)
6. The family in later life	Accepting the shifting of generational roles	a. Maintaining own and/or couple functioning and interests in face of physiological decline; exploration of new familial and social role options b. Support for a more central role for middle generation c. Making room in the system for the wisdom and experience of the elderly; supporting the older generation without overfunctioning for them d. Dealing with loss of spouse, siblings, and other peers and preparation for own death; life review and integration

patterns of development for families, just as there are for individuals. These patterns make up the *family life cycle,* **an orderly sequence of developmental stages that families tend to progress through.** The institutions of marriage and family are inevitably intertwined. With the advent of marriage, two persons add a new member to their existing families and create an entirely new family. Typically, this new family forms the core of one's life as an adult.

The study of the family life cycle has primarily fallen within the province of *sociology,* **the scientific study of human society and its institutions.** Sociologists have proposed a number of models to describe family development (Mattessich & Hill, 1987). These models are basically similar. Our discussion will be organized around a six-stage model of family development outlined by Carter and McGoldrick (1988; McGoldrick & Carter, 1989). Figure 9.3 provides an overview of their model. It spells out the developmental tasks during each stage of the life cycle for families that eventually have children and remain intact. Carter and McGoldrick have described variations on this basic pattern that are associated with remaining childless or going through a divorce. However, we will focus on the most common pattern in this section.

Research suggests that the family life cycle is an important determinant of marital satisfaction. Rollins and Feldman (1970) measured spouses' overall satisfaction in different stages of the family life cycle. They found a U-shaped relationship (see Figure 9.4); that is, satisfaction was greatest at the beginning and at the end of the family life cycle, with a noticeable decline occurring in the middle. More recent studies have obtained similar results (Anderson, Russell, & Schumm, 1983). Obviously, marital adjustment is influenced by the nature of the challenges that couples confront at various points in the family life cycle. Let's look at these challenges.

Between Families: The Unattached Young Adult

As young adults become independent of their parents, they go through a transitional period during which they

are "between families" until they form a new family through marriage. What is interesting about this stage is that it is being prolonged by more and more people. The percentage of young adults who are postponing marriage until their late twenties or early thirties has risen dramatically (Sporakowski, 1988). The frequent extension of this stage is probably due to a number of factors. Chief among them are the availability of new career options for women, increased educational requirements in the world of work, and increased emphasis on personal autonomy.

Joining Together: The Newly Married Couple

In this phase, the newly married couple gradually settle into their roles as husband and wife. This phase *can* be quite troublesome, as the early years of marriage are often marred by numerous problems and disagreements (Johnson, White, Edwards, & Booth, 1986). Difficulties are especially likely if the spouses enter the marriage with different expectations about marital roles. *In general, however, this stage tends to be characterized by great happiness—the proverbial "marital bliss."* Spouses' satisfaction with their relationship tends to be relatively high early in marriage, before the arrival of the first child (Glenn & McLanahan, 1982).

This pre-children phase used to be rather short for most newly married couples, as they quickly went about the business of having their first child. Traditionally, couples simply *assumed* that they would proceed to have children. Remaining childless by choice was virtually unthinkable. However, in recent years more couples have found themselves struggling to *decide* whether to have children. Often, this decision occurs after numerous postponements, when the couple finally acknowledges that "the right time" is never going to arrive (Crane, 1985).

Couples who choose to remain childless cite the great costs incurred in raising children. In addition to the financial burdens, they mention costs such as giving up educational or career opportunities, loss of time for

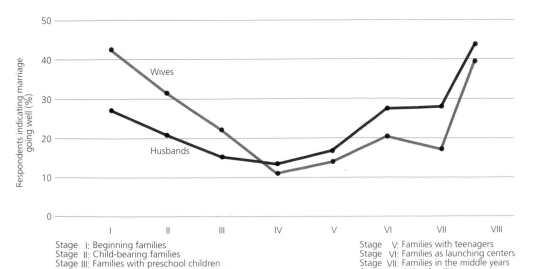

Figure 9.4. Marital satisfaction across the family life cycle. This graph depicts the percentage of husbands and wives who said their marriage was going well "all the time" at various stages of the family life cycle. Rollins and Feldman (1970) broke the family life cycle into eight stages instead of six. The U-shaped relationship shown here has been found in other studies as well.

Stage I: Beginning families
Stage II: Child-bearing families
Stage III: Families with preschool children
Stage IV: Families with school-aged children

Stage V: Families with teenagers
Stage VI: Families as launching centers
Stage VII: Families in the middle years
Stage VIII: Aging families

leisure activities and each other, loss of privacy and autonomy, and worry about the responsibility associated with child rearing (Bram, 1985; Burman & de Anda, 1986). These considerable costs probably explain why couples with children tend to report lower levels of marital satisfaction than voluntarily childless couples (Burman & de Anda, 1986).

Nonetheless, the vast majority of married couples continue to plan on having children, although many expect to delay having their first child until their late twenties (Roosa, 1988). In explaining their decision to have children, couples cite many reasons, including the responsibility to procreate, the joy of watching youngsters mature, the sense of purpose that children create, and the satisfaction associated with emotional nurturance and the challenge of child rearing (Goetting, 1986). In spite of the costs involved in raising children, most parents report no regret about their choice.

Family with Young Children

Although most parents are happy with their decision to have children, the arrival of the first child represents a major transition. The disruption of old routines can create a full-fledged crisis. The new mother, already physically exhausted by the birth process, is particularly prone to postpartum stress (Harriman, 1986). Wives are especially vulnerable when they have to shoulder the major burden of infant care.

Crisis during the transition to first parenthood is far from universal, however (Ruble, Fleming, Hackel, & Stangor, 1988). Couples who have high levels of intimacy, closeness, and commitment prior to the first child's birth are likely to maintain a high level of satisfaction after the child's birth (Lewis, 1988). They also tend to experience a smoother transition to parenthood, demonstrating greater warmth in their interactions with their infant (Lewis, Owen, & Cox, 1988).

The key to making this transition less stressful may be to have *realistic expectations* about parental responsibili-

ties. Belsky (1985) found that stress was greatest in new parents who had overestimated the benefits and underestimated the costs of their new role. This was especially true of the wives. Typically, it is the new mother who experiences the greatest lifestyle change after the birth of the first child. Therefore, she tends to suffer more when her overly optimistic expectations are violated. Prospective parents need to realize that although children can be unparalleled sources of joy and satisfaction, they also can be a gigantic headache.

Parenting is a very complex topic to which many entire books have been devoted. There are diverse styles of parenting that tend to yield different results (LeMasters, 1977). We will consider this topic in earnest in the application section of Chapter 11.

Family with Adolescent Children

As children move into adolescence, parents are often making a major transition themselves—into middle age. This can mean turbulent times for both generations. Parents tend to experience more intense midlife identity concerns if they have same-sex adolescent children (Steinberg & Silverberg, 1987). These parents are often prompted to reexamine their own values, accomplishments, and commitments as they watch their same-sex children struggle with similar issues.

As adolescent children seek to establish their own identities, parental influence over them tends to decline. Hence, conflicts between the children and their parents tend to escalate (Montemayor, 1986). Emotionally charged clashes over values are common, and power struggles frequently ensue. Conflict is particularly likely to surface between adolescents (of both sexes) and their mothers. Moreover, when conflict does occur, mothers are more

adversely affected by it than fathers (Steinberg & Silverberg, 1987). This may be because women's self-esteem has tended to be more closely tied than men's to the quality of their family relationships.

Launching Children into the Adult World

When a couple's children begin to reach their twenties, the family has to adapt to a multitude of exits and entries, as children leave and return, sometimes with their own spouses. During this period children have to progress from dependence to independence. Their progress is sometimes complicated when parents have difficulty letting go. Young adults can benefit from assistance and support, but some parents insist on continuing to take care of everything for them. They have difficulty relating to their children on an adult-to-adult basis. Generally, it is counterproductive when parents discourage young adults' movement toward independence.

When parents get all their children launched into the adult world, they find themselves faced with an "empty nest." This was formerly thought to be a difficult transition for many parents, especially mothers who were familiar only with the maternal role. Today, however, more women have experience with other roles outside the home, and most look forward to their "liberation" from child-rearing responsibilities (Reinke, Ellicott, Harris, & Hancock, 1985). In fact, as offspring strike out on their own, couples' marital satisfaction tends to start climbing to higher levels once again (Johnson, White, Edwards, & Booth, 1986).

The Family in Later Life

The postparental period often provides couples with new freedom to devote attention to each other. Many couples take advantage of this opportunity, traveling or developing new leisure interests. For many people this can be a period of increased intimacy and great satisfaction. Spouses do have to adapt to spending more time with

Parenting headaches add stress to the marital relationship. In fact, marital satisfaction tends to be lowest during the childrearing years.

each other, but most seem to make the adjustment without major problems (Treas, 1983). Of course, age-related considerations that are independent of the relationship, such as the increased likelihood of physical illness, can make the later years stressful. In general, however, the trend is for couples to report fairly high satisfaction until one of the spouses (usually the husband) dies.

VULNERABLE AREAS IN MARITAL ADJUSTMENT

"When we first got married, the first six months of conflicts were all about getting him to take account of what I had planned for him at home. . . . He would come waltzing in an hour and a half late for dinner, or cancel an evening with friends, because he had to close a deal. . . . We would argue and argue . . . not because I didn't want him to make a living . . . but because I thought he had to be more considerate."

—A wife quoted in *American Couples* [Blumstein & Schwartz, 1983, p. 174].

An unavoidable reality of marriage is that couples must confront a legion of problems together. During courtship, couples mostly focus on pleasurable activities. But when people marry, they must face many problems, such as arriving at acceptable role compromises, paying bills, and raising a family. There is no such thing as a problem-free marriage. Successful marriages depend on couples' ability to handle their problems. In this section we will analyze the major kinds of difficulties that are likely to emerge. We can't offer simple solutions for these problems. However, in navigating your way through life, it helps to know where the most perilous reefs are.

Unrealistic Expectations

Sabatelli (1988) notes that many people enter marriage with unrealistic expectations about how wonderful it's going to be. When expectations are too high, disappointment is likely. Part of the problem is the degree to which media portrayals romanticize love and marriage. Films and TV shows tend to focus on the excitement of falling in love rather than the sacrifice of caring for a sick spouse. Further, people who marry quickly tend to have an idealized picture of their new mate. This idealized picture often turns out to be inaccurate when they see their new mate in a wider variety of less pleasant situations. This kind of letdown can best be avoided by trying to be realistic about a prospective mate's qualities. Such realism is more likely if lovers are open with each other during the courtship period and disclose their frailties instead of hiding them.

Gaps in Role Expectations

When a couple marry, they assume new roles—those of husband and wife. With each role go certain expectations that the partners hold about how wives and husbands should behave. These expectations may vary greatly from one person to another. Gaps between partners in their role expectations can cause serious problems. Kitson and Sussman (1982) note that agreement about marital roles is a major determinant of marital stability. However, substantial differences in role expectations seem particularly likely in this era of transition in gender roles.

Our marital role expectations are shaped significantly by our exposure to our parents' relationship. The role expectations passed on by parents used to be fairly clear. A husband was supposed to act as the principal breadwinner, make the important decisions, and take care of certain household chores, such as car or yard maintenance. A wife was supposed to raise the children, cook, clean, and follow the leadership of her husband. Because each gender viewed the other as fundamentally different, couples didn't expect to "understand" each other, or to share many interests and activities. Spouses had different spheres of influence. The working world was the domain of the husband, the home the domain of the wife.

In recent years, however, the women's movement and other forces of social change have led to new expectations about marital roles. Young adults no longer blindly follow the model of their elders. Today, there are *options* from which to choose, so prospective mates can't assume that they share the same views on the appropriate responsibilities of spouses. Many people have changed their role conceptions, others cling to traditional views, and some are ambivalent. Still others claim to believe in equality in marriage and yet revert to traditional norms in their behavior. Thus, we live in a time of transition and consequent confusion.

Women may be especially vulnerable to ambivalence and confusion about marital roles. Recent surveys of college women (Baber & Monaghan, 1988; Machung, 1989) show that more women than ever are aspiring to demanding professional careers. At the same time, virtually all these women plan to marry, and most expect to become mothers. The majority say they would like two or three children. The typical college woman plans to complete her education first, then get married and establish herself in her career. Finally, she anticipates starting a family in her late twenties. She expects to marry a man who will assume equal responsibility for child rearing and domestic chores. Clearly, these women want to "have it all." Yet, some remnants of traditional thinking remain. When queried, the majority of women say their husband's career should take priority over their own (Machung, 1989). Most also say they should be the one to interrupt their career to raise young children, stay home when a child is sick, and arrange for child care.

And what about college men? Fewer males (49%) than females (69%) express a preference for an egalitarian marriage (Lewis, 1986). Males also tend to have more specific and better-informed career plans than their female counterparts (Machung, 1989). The vast majority of college men say their career should take priority over their wives' and that their wives should assume the major responsibility for child care. They are willing to "help out" with certain household chores (like washing the dishes) but not others (like cooking). In fact, males differ from

females in their view of what equality in marriage means. When the subjects in one survey (Machung, 1989) were asked to define an egalitarian marriage, half the men could not. The other half defined it in purely psychological terms, saying a marriage is "equal" if it is based on mutual understanding and trust. The women were considerably more concrete and task-oriented. They defined marital equality in terms of an equal sharing of chores and responsibilities. The evidence indicates that such equality is extremely rare. As Figure 9.5 shows, wives are still doing the bulk of the housework in America, even when they are employed outside the home. Obviously, women's and men's role expectations are at odds to some extent. These gaps in expectations create considerable potential for conflict.

Another way to analyze the marital role expectations of today's youth is to assess how realistic these expectations are, given current social policies and trends. Recall that the majority of college women plan to have several children, to interrupt their careers to care for them, and then to resume their careers where they left off (Baber & Monaghan, 1988). They apparently assume that they can leave their employment for long periods without loss of momentum or seniority and that they can live adequately for some time on their husband's income alone. These expectations seem somewhat naive given the increasing necessity for dual incomes, as well as organizational policies that make it difficult for wives or husbands to take more than several months' parental leave. As Hochschild (1989) points out, changes in social institutions and policies have not kept pace with peoples' changing aspirations.

In light of these realities, it is imperative that couples discuss role expectations in depth before marriage. If they discover that their views are very different, they need to take seriously the potential for problems. Many people casually dismiss gender-role disagreements, thinking they can "straighten out" their partner later on. But assumptions about marital roles, whether traditional or not, may be deeply held and not easily changed.

Work and Career Issues

The possible interactions between one's occupation and one's marriage are numerous and complex. Individuals' job satisfaction and involvement can affect their own marital satisfaction, their partners' marital satisfaction, and their children's development.

Husbands' Work and Marital Adjustment

Work has central importance in most men's lives. Hence, a host of studies have investigated the relationship between husbands' job satisfaction and their marital satisfaction. One could speculate that these two variables might be either positively or negatively related. On the one hand, if a husband is highly committed to a satisfying career, he may have less time and energy to devote to his marriage and family. On the other hand, the frustration and stress of an unsatisfying job might spill over to contaminate one's marriage.

In a review of the research on this question, Piotrkowski, Rapoport, and Rapoport (1987) suggest that both scenarios are realistic possibilities. Male executives and managers typically report high job satisfaction, but also a great deal of work/family conflict and low involvement with their wives and children. However, when husbands in a wide range of occupations are studied, most researchers find modest *positive* associations between the job satisfaction and marital satisfaction of husbands. That is, men who enjoy their work typically enjoy more satisfying marriages as well.

Wives' Work and Marital Adjustment

Relatively little research has been done on the relationship between *wives'* job satisfaction and their marital satisfaction. One recent study (Greenhaus, Bedeian, & Mossholder, 1987) found that high job performance by female (but not male) accountants was associated with *decreased* marital satisfaction. The authors speculated that these successful career women may have been experiencing role conflict and guilt over their strong work commit-

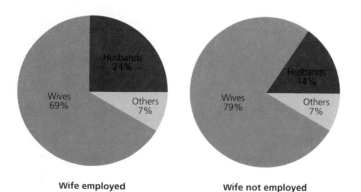

Wife employed　　　**Wife not employed**

Figure 9.5. Who does the housework? Berardo, Shehan, and Leslie (1987) studied the proportion of housework done by husbands, wives, and other family members. As these pie charts show, wives continue to do a highly disproportionate share of the housework, even if they are employed.

ment. These findings are interesting, but we need more research before we can draw conclusions about the effects of wives' work on their marital satisfaction.

Although few studies have looked at the impact of wives' work on their own marital satisfaction, many have examined the effect of wives' work on their husband's well-being or the couple's marital adjustment. This slant arises from traditional views that regard men's *lack* of employment, but women's *employment,* as departures from the norm (Bronfenbrenner & Crouter, 1982). Typically, these studies simply categorize women as working or nonworking and compare the husbands' (or couples') marital satisfaction.

Most of these studies find no consistent differences in the marital adjustment of male-breadwinner versus dual-career couples (Piotrkowski, Rapoport, & Rapoport, 1987). Recently, some investigators have begun to study the mediating influence of spouses' *attitudes* toward married women's employment, with enlightening results. It appears that marital satisfaction tends to be highest when partners share similar gender-role expectations and when the wife's employment status matches her own (and her husband's) preference about it (Spitze, 1988). In summary, although dual-career couples face special problems, their marriage need not be negatively affected.

Wives' Work and Children's Development

Another issue of great concern has been the potential impact of wives' employment on their children. Much of the research in this area has been guided by two implicit assumptions. The first assumption is that the more time mothers spend with their children, the better off the children are. The second assumption is that the full-time housewives of previous generations devoted more time to their children than today's employed wives. Both assumptions have been questioned (Hoffman, 1987). Extremely high levels of mother-child interaction can backfire, contributing to excessive dependency in children. Furthermore, yesterday's full-time mothers did not have modern, time-saving household conveniences, and they

There are innumerable books that attempt to tell couples how to make it all work. Aaron Beck's entry in this market appears to be superior to most of the others. Beck is the founder of cognitive therapy (see Chapter 16) and a renowned expert on the distorted thought patterns that promote anxiety and depression. He makes a compelling case that many married couples (especially those in distress) engage in the same errors of thinking as depressed and anxious people: namely, negativity, rigidity, and selectivity. If each spouse thinks about the other in such a distorted manner, then disillusionment, miscommunication, and frustration are inevitable.

Most of the chapters include one or more questionnaires that readers can use to probe their own relationships. In addition, Beck provides a great deal of practical advice about how to identify and change the distorted thought patterns that undermine the marital satisfaction of so many couples. A unique feature of Beck's book is its inclusion of many actual conversations of troubled couples, along with the unspoken thoughts that lie behind each line of dialogue.

The following interchange occurred when Marjorie wanted to hang a picture but had difficulty driving the nail into the wall:

KEN: [She's having a problem. I'd better help her.] Let me do it for you.

MARJORIE: [He has no confidence in my ability.] That's all right. I can do it myself [angrily].

KEN: What's the matter with you? I was only trying to help.

MARJORIE: That's all you ever do. You don't think I can do anything.

KEN: Well, you can't even drive a nail straight [laughs].

MARJORIE: There you go again—always putting me down.

KEN: I was just trying to help.

The spouses had completely different versions of Ken's intervention. Marjorie's goal of hanging the picture was to assure herself that she could handle manual tasks; in fact, she was looking forward to Ken's praise for her demonstration of competence and independence. His intrusion, though, brought her sense of incompetence to the surface. While each was correct in the belief that Ken lacked confidence in Marjorie's manual ability, Ken perceived himself as kind and considerate, while Marjorie viewed him as intrusive and patronizing. What started as an innocent gesture of helpfulness on his part led to hurt feelings and antagonism. [p. 59]

had more children. Thus, they may not have devoted any more time to each individual child than today's working mothers.

What does the research on maternal employment show? As a whole, the research indicates that maternal employment is not harmful to children (Etaugh, 1974). For instance, studies have found no link between mothers' employment status and the quality of infant-mother (or toddler-mother) emotional attachment (Chase-Lansdale, 1981; Easterbrooks & Goldberg, 1985). Clearly, a child *can* form a strong attachment to a working mother. Furthermore, the *attitudes* of both parents are important. Families in which both the wife and her husband are satisfied with the wife's role (whether she is employed or not) tend to have the most well-adjusted offspring (Easterbrooks & Goldberg, 1985). Not surprisingly, both spouses' degree of commitment to being effective parents is also critical. Fortunately, mothers' work generally does *not* occur at the expense of commitment to children (Greenberger & Goldberg, 1989).

In fact, there is evidence that maternal employment can have *positive* effects on children. Some studies have found that children of working mothers tend to be especially self-reliant and responsible (Hoffman, 1987). This advantage appears to be particularly pronounced for girls. Daughters of working mothers also tend to exhibit higher than average academic competence and career aspirations (Hoffman, 1987).

Financial Difficulties

How do couples' financial resources affect their marital adjustment? Neither financial stability nor wealth can ensure marital satisfaction. However, poverty can produce serious problems (Komarovsky, 1977). Without money, families live in constant dread of financial drains such as illness, layoffs, or broken appliances. Husbands tend to view themselves as poor providers, and their self-esteem may crumble as a result. This problem is sometimes aggravated by disappointed wives who criticize their husbands. Spontaneity in communication may be impaired by an understandable reluctance to talk about financial concerns. Thus, it is clear that poverty produces significant stress for married couples. Given this reality, it is important that prospective partners be realistic about their ability to finance a viable future.

Even when financial resources are plentiful, money can be a source of marital strain. Quarrels about how to spend money are common and potentially damaging at all income levels. Pittman and Lloyd (1988), for instance, found that perceived financial stress (regardless of a family's actual income) was associated with decreased marital satisfaction. Another study examined how happily married couples handled their money in comparison to couples that eventually divorced (Schaninger & Buss, 1986). In comparison to the divorced couples, the happy couples engaged in more joint decision making on finances. Thus, the best way to avoid troublesome battles over money is probably to engage in extensive planning of expenditures together.

Inadequate Communication

Effective communication is crucial to the success of a marriage. The damaging role that poor communication can play was clearly demonstrated in a study by Fowers and Olson (1989). They identified areas of marital functioning that differentiated between satisfied and dissatisfied couples. Of the three most important areas of functioning, two involved communication. These were spouses' comfort in sharing information with each other and their willingness to recognize and resolve conflicts between them. (The third area was the quality of their sexual relationship.) Similarly, in a study of couples who sought family counseling, nearly 87% of the couples reported communication difficulties (Beck & Jones, 1973). As Figure 9.6 shows, poor communication was the leading problem among these distressed couples.

A number of studies have compared communication patterns in happy and unhappy marriages. In a review of

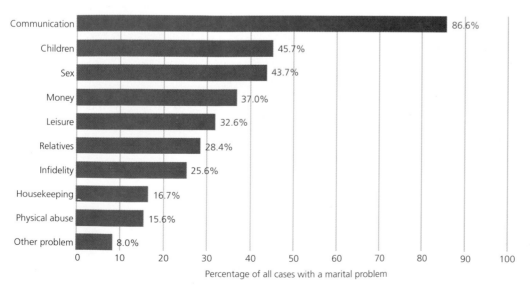

Figure 9.6. **Problems reported by couples seeking family counseling.** Beck and Jones (1973) found that communication was the most frequent problem identified by troubled couples. Rounding out the top five problems were disagreements about child rearing, sex, finances, and the use of leisure time.

Communication 86.6%
Children 45.7%
Sex 43.7%
Money 37.0%
Leisure 32.6%
Relatives 28.4%
Infidelity 25.6%
Housekeeping 16.7%
Physical abuse 15.6%
Other problem 8.0%

Percentage of all cases with a marital problem

this research, Noller and Gallois (1988) note that unhappily married spouses (1) find it difficult to convey positive messages, (2) misunderstand each other more often, (3) are less likely to recognize that they have been misunderstood, and (4) use more frequent, and more intense, negative messages. As already noted, self-disclosure is very important in marital communication. Partners who are similar in self-disclosure tend to be more satisfied than those who are dissimilar (that is, one partner prefers a great deal of self-disclosure and the other prefers less) (Davidson, Balswick, & Halverson, 1983).

As we discussed in Chapter 6, communication can be improved in many ways. Most of the advice offered in that chapter can be applied to marital communication. In particular, it is important to avoid defensiveness and to attempt to create a positive climate for communication. Developing constructive approaches to conflict resolution is also critical.

Problems with In-Laws

Research on in-law conflict has diminished in recent years. This may indicate that in-law trouble is less of a problem in our more mobile society. When intergenerational conflict does occur, it typically involves the wife and her mother-in-law. In fact, in-law trouble has been characterized as a "female problem," perhaps because women have traditionally shouldered the responsibility for maintaining kinship ties (Marotz-Baden & Cowan, 1987). Fischer (1983) found that wives tend to turn to their own mothers for help after giving birth. Yet they may regard their mother-in-law's concern over her new grandchild as "interference." In general, in-law strife tends to be greatest for couples who have not yet attained emotional or financial independence from their parents.

Sexual Problems

There is a strong link between couples' marital satisfaction and their perception of the quality of their sexual relationship (Fowers & Olson, 1989). Although this association is quite strong, it is difficult to discern which is the cause and which is the effect. The assertion that sexual problems cause marital distress, though true, would be an oversimplification, since marital distress also causes sexual problems (LoPiccolo & Daiss, 1987).

Sexual problems are often intertwined with other marital problems. For instance, disagreement about the appropriate frequency of sex may be due to differing role expectations. Communication problems may also be linked to sexual difficulties. While open sexual communication is associated with marital satisfaction, inhibited sexual communication is associated with marital distress (Banmen & Vogel, 1985). In addition, some couples depend too much on sexual intimacy to resolve nonsexual conflicts. This tendency may mask underlying relationship problems and interfere with more direct conflict resolution strategies (Maddock, 1989).

Jealousy

Romantic jealousy **has been defined as a complex of thoughts, emotions, and behaviors that result from the perception of a threat to one's intimate relationship.** To simplify, the "green-eyed monster" is aroused when you fear a loss of affection from a romantic partner. Although jealousy is a common and sometimes legitimate reaction, it is also a potentially destructive emotion in intimate relationships (Buunk & Bringle, 1987).

Some people are more prone to get jealous than others. It appears that this jealousy-prone disposition is primarily a function of poor self-esteem. Highly jealous persons tend to have a negative self-concept, to be relatively unhappy, and to feel insecure, inadequate, and dependent in their intimate relationship (Pines & Aronson, 1983; White, 1981). Furthermore, after experiencing a jealousy-provoking situation, people feel even more insecure, unattractive, and dependent, making future jealous reactions even more likely (Radecki-Bush, Bush, & Jennings, 1988).

The high divorce rate has led to some novel ways of dealing with its worrisome legal aspects. Attorney Robert Nordyke discovered that the drive-up window at his new office—a former savings and loan branch in Salem, Oregon—was perfect for serving legal papers on his clients' spouses.

Jealousy typically is triggered by a specific event. This event usually involves either being left out of some activity involving one's partner or something that suggests, even remotely, that the partner's affection could be lost. Salovey and Rodin (1986) studied over 50 jealousy-provoking circumstances. The situations that elicited the greatest romantic jealousy were as follows. (1) You find out your lover is having an affair. (2) Someone goes out with the person you like. (3) Someone gets closer to a person to whom you are attracted. (4) Your lover tells you how sexy an old boyfriend/girlfriend was. (5) Your lover visits a person he or she used to go out with.

Pathologically jealousy-prone persons may *imagine* a threat to their relationship where there is none. Such tendencies are likely to create unnecessary problems in marital relations. Pfeiffer and Wong (1989) point out that attempts to gain control over a partner through jealousy tend to be resented. Correcting this problem is not easy, since it is usually rooted in a deep-seated negative self-concept. Efforts to remedy the problem should focus on improving self-esteem and learning to think more rationally about one's relationship. People who are secure in a relationship are less likely to overreact when a spouse pays some attention to someone else. They are more likely to regard the event as normal and see the third person's interest in their spouse as an affirmation of their own good taste.

Growing in Different Directions

We have already mentioned the tendency for people to marry others similar to themselves (homogamy). However, it is always possible that partners will diverge in terms of their values and activity preferences. For instance, in the early years of a marriage, both members of a couple might enjoy a moderate amount of social entertaining with their friends. As the years wear on, one partner might find that activity tedious, while the other comes to enjoy it even more. Neither partner is wrong! They are simply evolving in different directions. However, this divergence can lead to bitter disagreements about how the couple should spend their time.

Although sometimes difficult, it is important that spouses allow each other room for personal growth. They should recognize that it is unrealistic to expect one's partner to remain exactly the same forever. In this era, with recreation playing an increasingly large role in our lives, more spouses may have to learn to engage in individual activities. At the same time, it is important to strive to maintain joint activities as well. Smith and his colleagues (Smith, Snyder, Trull, & Monsma, 1988) found a strong link between marital satisfaction and amount of joint leisure activity.

DIVORCE

"In the ten years that we were married I went from twenty-four to thirty-four and they were a very significant ten years. I started a career, started to succeed, bought my first house, had a child, you know, very significant years. And then all of a sudden, every goddamn thing, I'm back to zero. I have no house. I don't have a child. I don't have a wife. I don't have the same family. My economic position has been shattered. And nothing recoverable. All these goals which I had struggled for, every goddamn one of them, is gone."

—A recently divorced man quoted in *Marital Separation* [Weiss, 1975, p. 75]

The dissolution of a marriage tends to be a bone-jarring event for most people, as the bitter quote above illustrates. Any of the problems discussed in the previous section might lead a couple to consider divorce. However, people appear to vary in their threshold for divorce, just as they do in their threshold for marriage. Some couples will tolerate a great deal of disappointment and bickering without seriously considering divorce. Other couples are ready to call their attorney as soon as it becomes apparent that their expectations for marital bliss were somewhat unrealistic. Typically, however, divorce is the culmination of a gradual disintegration of the relationship brought about by an accumulation of many interrelated problems.

Increasing Rate of Divorce

Although relatively accurate statistics are available on divorce rates, it is still difficult to estimate the percentage of marriages ending in divorce. Crosby (1980) points out that the usually cited ratio of marriages in a year to divorces in the same year is highly misleading. It would be more instructive to follow people married in a particular year over a period of time, but little research of this nature has been done. In any case, it is clear that divorce rates have increased substantially in recent decades, as Figure 9.7 shows. Based on 1985 data, Norton and Moorman (1987) projected that 56% of women 35 to 39 years old in that year will end their first marriage in divorce. Slightly lower rates were projected for older and younger age groups. Most experts believe that divorce rates have stabilized. Some have even speculated that the fear of AIDS may result in longer-lasting marriages (Glick, 1988).

A wide variety of social trends have probably contributed to increasing divorce rates (Raschke, 1987). The stigma attached to divorce has gradually eroded. Many religious denominations are becoming more tolerant of divorce, and marriage has thus lost some of its sacred quality. The declining fertility rate and the consequent smaller families probably make divorce a more viable possibility. The entry of more women into the work force has made many wives less financially dependent on the continuation of their marriage. New attitudes emphasizing individual fulfillment seem to have counterbalanced older attitudes that encouraged dissatisfied spouses to suffer in silence. Reflecting all these trends, the legal barriers to divorce have also diminished.

Deciding on a Divorce

Divorces are often postponed repeatedly, and they are rarely executed without much forethought. It is difficult

to generalize about the relative merit of divorce as opposed to remaining in an unsatisfactory marriage. There is evidence that people who are currently divorced are significantly less happy than those who are currently married (Weingarten, 1985). Furthermore, divorce is often associated with great psychological distress in both spouses. Divorced men suffer primarily from a loss of emotional support and disrupted social ties to friends and relatives (traditionally, the wife's responsibility). In comparison, divorced women suffer more from reduced income (traditionally, the husband's responsibility) (Gerstel, Reissman, & Rosenfield, 1985). Thus, the distress of each spouse reflects the need to take over responsibilities that had been the province of the other spouse. This suggests the intriguing possibility that a divorce following an egalitarian marriage may tend to be less upsetting for both partners.

As painful as marital dissolution may be, remaining in an unhappy marriage is also potentially detrimental. A recent longitudinal study of wives (Schaefer & Burnett, 1987) found that marital quality was an even better predictor of a woman's psychological health three years later than her psychological health at the initial measurement! In particular, poor marital adjustment at Time 1 was predictive of significant depression and anxiety at Time 2. Other studies have shown that poor marital adjustment is also associated with depression in men (Ilfeld, 1977). These findings suggest that sticking it out in an unhappy marriage is counterproductive to one's adjustment.

Decisions about divorce must take into account the impact on a couple's children. There has been much debate about whether children benefit if parents persevere and keep an unhappy marriage intact. Children of divorce and children from homes characterized by persis-

Figure 9.7. Increasing divorce rates. The percentage of marriages ending in a divorce has been going up steadily for over 100 years. Today, experts estimate that over 50% of marriages will end in divorce. (Source: Cherlin, 1981)

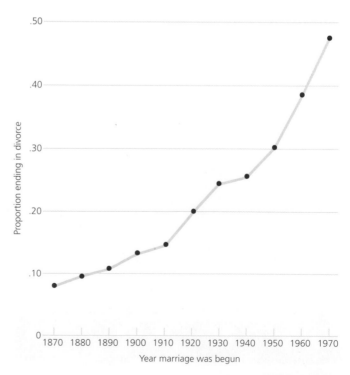

tent marital discord are *both* more prone to adjustment problems than children of happily married parents. But several studies (e.g., Slater & Haber, 1984) have shown that children's adjustment is affected more by the amount of conflict between their parents than by family structure (divorced or intact) as such. All in all, the weight of evidence suggests that in the long run it is less damaging to the children if unhappy parents divorce than if the children grow up in an intact but dissension-ridden home (Demo & Acock, 1988).

Nonetheless, one should not underestimate the trauma that most children go through when their parents divorce. Divorce may be especially tough on boys whose mothers have sole custody and who therefore are denied a stable male role model (Peterson & Zill, 1986). After a divorce, children may exhibit depression, anxiety, night-

mares, dependency, aggression, withdrawal, distractibility, lowered academic performance, and reduced physical health (Guidubaldi, Perry, & Nastasi, 1987). Fortunately, many of these effects are temporary. On the positive side, children of divorced parents may become more androgynous, mature, and independent (Demo & Acock, 1988). The children's recovery and subsequent adjustment seem to depend primarily on the quality of their relationship with the custodial parent and on how well the custodial parent is adjusting to the divorce (Stolberg, Camplair, Currier, & Wells, 1987).

Adjusting to Divorce

It is clear that divorce is an exceedingly stressful life event (Buehler & Langenbrunner, 1987). It often combines all four major sources of stress described in Chapter 3: frustration, conflict, pressure, and change. Although it can be devastating for either sex, generally divorce tends to be more stressful and disruptive for women than for men. Women are more likely to assume the responsibility of raising the children, while they are less likely to have adequate income on their own. According to Weitzman (1989), divorced women experience greater stress and feel more financially strapped than divorced men.

Obviously, newly divorced persons of either gender have numerous problems to confront. These problems include the following (Raschke, 1987).

The crisis of change. Is hard to think of events that produce more far-reaching change than divorce. The divorced person's lifestyle is usually altered radically. Furthermore, because people tend to define themselves in terms of being somebody's spouse, the divorced person must revise his or her very sense of identity. The emotional crisis may peak long before the actual divorce. Nonetheless, the difficulties of postdivorce transitions in socializing, child rearing, and so forth may seem overwhelming.

Emotional problems. A divorce may be preceded by much

RECOMMENDED READING

Second Chances: Men, Women, and Children a Decade after Divorce

by Judith S. Wallerstein & Sandra Blakeslee (Ticknor and Fields, 1990)

This book reports the findings of a large-scale longitudinal study of divorced couples and their children. Conventional wisdom holds that marital dissolution and its immediate aftermath creates a "crisis," after which each spouse has a "second chance" to find happiness. The children of divorce, too, are presumed to weather time-limited trauma and ultimately to adjust positively to their parents' newly stabilized lives. Wallerstein and Blakeslee present surprising evidence that calls both assumptions into question. Many of the couples they studied were still grappling with negative emotions from their failed marriage *ten years* after it ended. Their children appeared to be even more vulnerable, often harboring intense fears of betrayal and rejection that carried into their own intimate relationships in adolescence and early adulthood.

Despite the sometimes disturbing nature of their findings, however, Wallerstein and Blakeslee maintain an upbeat attitude throughout. By deftly interweaving empirical findings with relevant case material, they educate the reader about potential pitfalls faced by members of dissolving families. Further, they convey hope that such awareness will enable everyone involved to cope with these challenges successfully.

> Divorce is a different experience for children and adults because the children lose something that is fundamental to their development—the family structure. The family comprises the scaffolding upon which children mount successive developmental stages, from infancy into adolescence. It supports their psychological, physical, and emotional ascent into maturity. When that structure collapses, the children's world is temporarily without supports. And children, with a vastly compressed sense of time, do not know that the chaos is temporary. [p. 11]

quarreling and reciprocal derogation by the partners. The hurtful remarks, although they may have been flung thoughtlessly in anger, are often difficult to dismiss. One or both of the former spouses may experience feelings of failure and shame. Divorced people may also be plagued by perplexing feelings of ambivalence toward their former partner. Feelings of continued attachment may be jumbled with feelings of bitterness and anger. Recently divorced people often experience separation distress marked by feelings of loneliness and longing for the presence of the former spouse.

Practical problems. The emotional difficulties of divorce are usually accompanied by a variety of practical problems. If children are involved, arrangements for custody and support must be made. Both parents must adjust to a drastically different child-rearing situation. Patterns of socializing must be revamped. Old friendships with other couples are likely to decay, and new friendships must be forged. Although less prevalent than before, negative stereotypes of divorced people still exist. In particular, divorced women often are stereotyped as desperate for love and readily available for sex.

Rebuilding. Although divorce is difficult, the difficulties are *not* insurmountable. People do successfully retrench and rebuild. One should not feel reluctant about seeking professional therapy or soliciting support from relatives or friends. In view of the enormous stress associated with divorce, a need for professional assistance should not be seen as an indication of personal inadequacy. During the rebuilding period, there are four common syndromes that one should try to avoid (Cox, 1979).

1. *Retreat.* Some people retreat into a shell of self-pity. It is important to gradually edge back into interpersonal relationships.
2. *Rebound.* Some people jump back into the interpersonal marketplace too quickly and too eagerly. Obsessive pursuit of a new love may blind one's judgment and lead to another poor relationship.

3. *Return.* Some people are paralyzed by foolish and unrealistic yearning for the return of their former spouse. It is better to face up to reality and get on with life.
4. *Resentment.* Some people get bogged down by excessive resentment of their former spouse. This anger can have a very negative effect on children. It can also spill over and contaminate social relationships in general.

Remarriage

Evidence that courtship opportunities for the divorced are adequate is provided by the statistics on remarriage. Roughly three quarters of divorced women and five sixths of divorced men eventually remarry (Glick, 1984). About half of these remarriages occur within three years of the divorce. Among women, lesser education and lower income are associated with more rapid remarriage. In contrast, men who are better educated and financially well-off tend to remarry more quickly (Glick, 1980).

How successful are second marriages? The answer depends on your standard of comparison. Divorce rates *are* higher for second than for first marriages. However, this may simply indicate that this group of people sees divorce as a reasonable alternative to an unsatisfactory marriage. Nonetheless, studies of marital adjustment suggest that second marriages are somewhat less successful than first marriages (Cherlin, 1981; White & Booth, 1985). Of course, if you consider that in this pool of people *all* the first marriages ran into serious trouble, then the second marriages look rather good by comparison. In fact, in one study (Furstenberg & Spanier, 1984) the majority of remarried individuals reported that they had selected a spouse far more wisely the second time around.

It is more appropriate to evaluate remarriage by comparing divorced people who remarry against divorced people who do not. When Spanier and Furstenberg (1982) did this, they found that those who remarried were *not* any healthier or happier, on the average, than those who did not. However, they did find that the quality of

Figure 9.8. Cohabitation in the United States. The number of unmarried couples living together has been increasing rapidly since 1970 (based on U.S. Census data). This increase shows no signs of leveling off.

subjects' second marriage *was* related to their well-being. Thus, many divorced people do eventually find happiness in a subsequent marriage.

ALTERNATIVES TO MARRIAGE

We noted at the beginning of the chapter that the traditional model of marriage has been undermined by a variety of social trends. More and more people are choosing alternatives to marriage. We will examine some of these alternatives in this section. Specifically, we'll discuss cohabitation, remaining single, and gay relationships.

Cohabitation

As we saw earlier in the chapter, *cohabitation* refers to living together in a sexually intimate relationship outside of marriage. Recent years have witnessed a tremendous increase in the number of cohabiting couples. In 1988, there were approximately 2.6 million unmarried couples living together in the United States (see Figure 9.8). They represented about 5% of all couples (married and unmarried) sharing living quarters at that time. Despite the rapid increase in the number of couples living together, this practice has failed to attain widespread social acceptance. Cohabitants often report that their parents are not aware of their living arrangements and would not approve if they were. Those couples whose families know of their cohabitation typically experience a great deal of family pressure to marry (Jackson, 1989).

The principal motivations for cohabitation (as opposed to marriage) among the respondents in one study

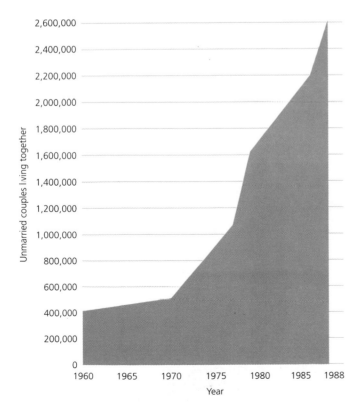

were more individualism, more freedom, no need to divorce, and lower taxes (Kotkin, 1985). Those who choose cohabitation tend to be relatively young, liberal in values, nonreligious, and pragmatic about intimate relationships (Macklin, 1983; Newcomb, 1983; Tanfer, 1987).

Although many people see cohabitation as a threat to the institution of marriage, some theorists see it as a new stage in the courtship process—a sort of trial marriage. Consistent with the latter view, researchers have found that the vast majority of cohabitants plan to marry eventually (Newcomb, 1986). Thus, it appears that cohabitation does not represent a repudiation of marriage.

In discussing the pros and cons of cohabitation, White (1987) points out that it may provide an opportunity for young people to experiment with marital-like responsibilities. As a prelude to marriage, it should reduce the likelihood of entering marriage with unrealistic expectations. Living together may also permit some couples to bail out of relationships that might otherwise have led to unsuccessful marriages. Although White's analyses seem plausible, the vast majority of studies have *not* found that premarital cohabitation increases the likelihood of subsequent marital success (Macklin, 1987). In fact, several studies have found an association between premarital cohabitation and higher divorce rates (Bennett, Blanc, & Bloom, 1988). Thus, although the vast majority of cohabitants speak favorably of their experience, there is presently little reason to believe that cohabitation improves couples' chances of marital success.

Remaining Single

There is substantial pressure to marry in our society. We are socialized to believe that we are not complete until we have found our "other half" and have entered into a partnership for life. We also refer to people's "failure" to marry. In spite of this pressure, an increasing proportion of young adults are remaining single, as Figure 9.9 shows (Stein, 1983).

Does the increased number of single adults mean that

people are turning away from the institution of marriage? For the most part, no (Cherlin, 1981). A variety of factors have contributed to the growth of the single population. Much of this growth is due to the increase in the median age at which people marry and the increased rate of divorce. More important, the vast majority of single, never married people *do* expect to marry eventually (Cargan & Melko, 1982).

Singlehood has been plagued by two very disparate stereotypes of the single life (Keith, 1986). On the one hand, single people are sometimes portrayed as carefree swingers who are too busy enjoying the fruits of promiscuity to shoulder marital responsibilities. On the other hand, they are seen as losers who did not succeed in snaring a mate. They may be portrayed as socially inept, unlucky, frustrated, lonely, and bitter. These stereotypes do a great injustice to the diversity that exists among those who are single.

The "swinging single" stereotype appears to be a media-manufactured illusion designed to lure singles' spending power into nightclubs and bars. In reality, the singles-bar circuit is frequently described as an experience in alienation and disappointment (Gordon, 1976). In comparison to married people, single people do have sex with more partners. However, they have sex less frequently, and they rate their sexual relations as less satisfying than their married counterparts (Cargan & Melko, 1982).

Generally, single people *do* rate themselves as less happy than married people. However, the reported happiness of married people has declined steadily since 1972. In the meantime, the reported happiness of singles has increased, thereby narrowing the gap considerably (Glenn & Weaver, 1988). Although earlier studies often found single women to be more satisfied with their lives than single men, recent data indicate that this difference is also decreasing (Glenn & Weaver, 1988).

Singles must often cope with some special challenges in addition to the problems confronted by most adults. Since adult social interaction tends to revolve around couples, there may be some extra difficulty in developing a satisfactory friendship network. The absence of a spouse to lean on makes an independent personality a virtual necessity. Single people trying to climb the corporate ladder have some bias working against them, as they are seen as less stable than their married counterparts. In addition, singles generally have lower lifetime earnings and may face discrimination in credit, insurance, and housing (Keith, 1986).

Although the increase in the single population does not reflect a widespread rejection of marriage, it is leading to more favorable attitudes toward singles. People used to assume that there was something wrong with an adult who remained single. Today, fewer people view singlehood as abnormal.

Gay Relationships

Up until this point, we have, for purposes of simplicity, focused our attention on *heterosexuals,* **those whose sexual desires and erotic behaviors are directed toward the opposite sex**. However, we have been ignoring a significant minority group: *homosexual (gay)* **men and women, whose sexual desires and erotic activities are directed toward the same sex**. It is difficult to estimate just how large this group is. Negative attitudes about homosexuality in our society continue to prevent many gays from "coming out of the closet." The best empirical data on the issue (which aren't very good) suggest that roughly 2% of women and 4-5% of men are *exclusively* homosexual (Van Wyk & Geist, 1984). Estimates by some gay-rights groups range as high as 10% for both sexes. Although these estimates are highly speculative, they may not be unreasonable if one's definition of homosexuality does not require an exclusive commitment to same-sex relationships (Paul &

Figure 9.9. The proportion of young people who remain single. This graph shows the percentage of single men and women, aged 20–24 or 25–29, in 1984 as compared to 1960 (based on U.S. Census data). The proportion of people remaining single has increased substantially for both sexes, in both age brackets. Single men continue to outnumber single women in these age brackets.

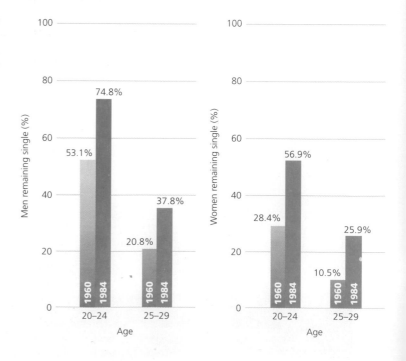

Weinrich, 1982). Thus, there may be as many as 25 million gay people in the United States.

Marking off a separate section on gay relationships may seem to imply that the dynamics of these relationships are different from those seen in heterosexual relationships. Actually, this is probably less true than most heterosexuals assume. It is clear that intimate relationships between gays must necessarily be somewhat different than the legally sanctioned marriages of heterosexuals. Nonetheless, recent studies (Duffy & Rusbult, 1985/1986; Leigh, 1989) have documented striking commonalities between heterosexuals and homosexuals in their intimate relationships. They are similar in terms of the forces that bring couples together, the factors that predict satisfaction with the relationship, and the problems couples face. Given these similarities, much of the material already covered in this chapter is relevant to gay couples.

Instead of providing special advice for gays, therefore, we will endeavor instead to review some of the research about the nature of gay relationships. At this point, we will focus on myths and realities regarding intimate relationships between gays.

There are a number of common and inaccurate stereotypes about gay relationships. First, many people assume that most gay couples adopt traditional masculine and feminine roles in their relationships, with one partner behaving in a cross-sexed manner. This appears to be true in only a small minority of cases. In fact, on the whole, gay couples appear to be more flexible about role expecta-

tions than heterosexuals (Harry, 1983; Zacks, Green, & Marrow, 1988).

Second, it is widely believed that gays are exceptionally promiscuous, engaging in casual sex with a spectacular number of partners. In reality, promiscuity has been relatively common among certain segments of the gay male population, but virtually nonexistent among lesbians (Tripp, 1987). Regardless of their sexual orientation (gay or straight), males tend to have somewhat different motivations than females for engaging in sex. Women are more likely to regard sexual activity as an expression of affection and commitment. Men tend to attach more importance to sexual pleasure and conquest (Leigh, 1989). Their socialization is more likely than women's to stress the desirability of varied and frequent sexual activity. The gay male, being free of the strictures of marriage and having his choice of like-minded partners, has simply been in a better position than his heterosexual counterpart to act on this masculine socialization (Blasband & Peplau, 1985). Since the advent of AIDS, however, homosexual males have faced unprecedented pressure, even within the gay community, to limit the number of their sexual partners (Kyle, 1989). Hence, promiscuity among gay men is clearly declining.

Third, popular stereotypes suggest that gays only rarely get involved in long-term intimate relationships. In reality, most homosexual men, and nearly all homosexual women, prefer stable, long-term relationships (Macklin, 1987; Tripp, 1987). Lesbian relationships are generally sexually exclusive. About half of committed male couples have "open" relationships, allowing for the possibility of sexual activity (but not affection) with outsiders. While intimate relationships among gays *are* less stable than marriages among straights, they may compare favorably with heterosexual cohabitation, which would be a more appropriate baseline for comparison. Both gays and heterosexual cohabitants may face opposition to their relationship from their families and from society in general, and neither enjoys the legal and social sanctions of marriage.

Despite the common stereotype that gays rarely form long-term relationships, the fact is that they are similar to heterosexuals in their attitudes and behaviors, and many enjoy long-term commitments in marriage-like arrangements.

Finally, an inevitable fate for any stereotyped group is that its members are lumped together and simplistically assumed to be identical. In reality, there is as much diversity among gays as there is among straights, dooming to failure any attempt to classify gays into "types" (Tripp, 1987). To identify an individual as "homosexual" is to say nothing more about that person's unique lifestyle, personality, or values than to describe someone as "heterosexual."

SUMMARY

The traditional model of marriage is being challenged by the increasing acceptability of singlehood, the increasing popularity of cohabitation, the reduced premium on permanence, changes in gender roles, and the increasing prevalence of voluntary childlessness. Nonetheless, marriage remains quite popular.

People vary in the strength of their motivation to marry. Many people are motivated by less-than-ideal reasons. Mate selection is influenced by endogamy, homogamy, and one's ideals. According to Murstein, the process of mate selection goes through three stages, which emphasize the stimulus value of the potential partner, value compatibility, and adequacy of role enactments.

Marital satisfaction and adjustment are influenced by the family life cycle. Newly married couples tend to be very happy before the arrival of children. Today more couples are struggling with the decision about whether to have children. The arrival of children is a major transition that is handled best by parents who have realistic expectations about the difficulties inherent in raising children. As children reach adolescence, parents should expect more conflict as their influence declines. They must learn to relate to their children as adults and help launch them into the adult world. Once the children have struck out on their own, marital satisfaction tends to rise once again.

Gaps in expectations about marital roles, or unrealistic expectations in general, may create marital stress. Occupational dissatisfaction and lack of money may also produce marital problems. Inadequate communication is a commonly reported marital problem, while in-law problems appear to be declining. Sexual difficulties, jealousy, and growing in different directions are other problems that are common in marital relationships.

Divorce is becoming increasingly common for a variety of reasons. Unpleasant as divorce may be, the evidence suggests that toughing it out in an unhappy marriage is often worse. Divorce can create problems for children, but so does a strife-ridden intact home. Divorce is quite stressful and may lead to a variety of emotional and practical problems associated with the crisis of change. In rebuilding, people should try to avoid four syndromes: retreat, rebound, return, and resentment. A substantial majority of divorced people remarry. These second marriages have a somewhat lower probability of success than first marriages.

The prevalence of cohabitation has increased dramatically. Nonetheless, it appears to be more of a prelude than an alternative to marriage. Single people are often stereotyped as losers or carefree swingers. Both pictures are largely inaccurate. Although singles generally have the same adjustment problems as married couples, evidence suggests that singles tend to be slightly less happy. Gay relationships are characterized by great diversity. It is not true that gays usually assume traditional masculine and feminine roles. Nor is it true that they rarely get involved in long-term intimate relationships. Popular beliefs about gay promiscuity appear to be inaccurate for women, though somewhat less so for men.

The upcoming Application will focus on the manipulative games that couples tend to play. It is hoped that your awareness of these game-playing tendencies might reduce your propensity to get locked into such counterproductive patterns.

Understanding the Games Couples Play

Answer the following yes or no.

☐ **1.** In intimate relationships, I sometimes catch myself being manipulative.

☐ **2.** In interacting with my partner, I sometimes notice that we get into subtle little battles to demonstrate our superiority.

☐ **3.** It often seems that people are operating with a "hidden agenda."

☐ **4.** Many people seem to derive some sort of perverse satisfaction from laying "guilt trips" on others.

☐ **5.** I sometimes think that life would be simpler if couples would tell each other what they were *really* thinking.

If you answered yes to several of the items above, you have noticed that people often tend to play "games" with each other. We all play games at least occasionally. This reality has been most insightfully analyzed by Eric Berne (1961, 1964, 1972). He developed *Transactional Analysis*, **a broad theory of personality and interpersonal relations that emphasizes patterns of communication.**

What are games in interpersonal relationships? In Berne's scheme, **games are manipulative interactions progressing toward a predictable outcome, in which people conceal their true motivations.** Games are not limited to intimate relationships. We may play games with co-workers, neighbors, and even strangers. However, games become particularly problematic in intimate relationships, where authentic communication is critical. Intimate couples are also vulnerable to games because there is more opportunity for *repetition* of destructive patterns. In this Application, we will introduce you to the basics of Transactional Analysis so that you can try to spot some of this game playing in your own intimate interactions.

EGO STATES IN TRANSACTIONAL ANALYSIS

In Transactional Analysis, **an *ego state* is a personality structure consisting of a coherent system of internal feelings.** Berne postulated the existence of three ego states: the Child, the Parent, and the Adult. (When these terms are capitalized, they refer to the ego state; otherwise they refer to the actual status of child, parent, or adult.) The theory states that we directly experience these ego states and that we shift in and out of them depending on the situation and our personal history. It is important to understand that there is no one-to-one correspondence between these ego states and a person's actual status. In other words, one does not have to be a child to experience the Child ego state or a parent to experience the Parent ego state.

Child

The Child ego state consists of "recordings" of childhood experiences that we retain throughout adulthood. In certain situations, we fall back into our childlike patterns of spontaneity and irresponsibility. For instance, when faced with frustration, a person who used to throw temper tantrums in childhood might revert to this strategy as an adult. In so doing, the person is operating from the Child ego state. Although this particular example is somewhat negative, operating from the Child ego state should not be equated with behaving immaturely. On the positive side, it is entry into the Child ego state that facilitates fresh and spontaneous enjoyment of recreational activities.

Parent

The Parent ego state also consists of recordings from childhood. However, these recordings largely involve assertions about right and wrong. They represent values and norms adopted from one's parents and other authority figures. For example, suppose that you suddenly realized that you were reading this text too lackadaisically, without really digesting the information. If you scolded yourself for your lethargic attitude, you would be operating from the Parent ego state. The Parent in us jumps in with criticism when we violate the morals instilled by our parents. The Parent is like a solemn judge, handing down decisions about the acceptability of our own behavior and the behavior of others.

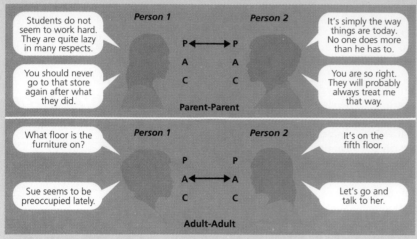

Figure 9.10. Type I complementary transactions. In Type I complementary transactions, two people address each other as equals.

Figure 9.11. Type II complementary transactions. In Type II complementary transactions, the receiver responds from the ego state addressed by the source, but the persons do not address each other as equals.

Adult

The Adult is more rational and less emotional than the Child or the Parent. We shift into the Adult ego state when we dispassionately weigh alternative courses of action, when we systematically endeavor to solve a problem, and so forth. The Adult is tuned into reality and attempts to maximize efficiency. Like the ego, as described by Freud, the Adult has "executive" responsibilities for making important decisions, which often involve mediating between the Child and the Parent.

TYPES OF TRANSACTIONS

The fundamental unit of social interaction in Transactional Analysis is the transaction. **A *transaction* consists of an initial statement by a communicating source and a response by the receiver.** There are several classes of transactions, depending on which ego states are communicating with each other.

In a *complementary transaction*, the receiver responds from the same ego state that was addressed by the source. Thus, the two persons communicate from *compatible* ego states. Two kinds of complementary transactions are possible. In Type I, the two persons are sending and receiving from the same ego state (see Figure 9.10). In other words, they communicate Adult-to-Adult, Child-to-Child, or Parent-to-Parent. In Type II, the two persons do *not* address each other as equals (see Figure 9.11). For example, the transaction might go Parent-to-Child and Child-to-Parent or Child-to-Adult and Adult-to-Child. In either kind of complementary transaction, people are cooperating in the communication effort.

In a *crossed transaction*, the receiver does not respond from the ego state addressed by the source. In a sense, the receiver refuses to cooperate with the source. Hence, the two persons communicate from *incompatible* ego states. For example, an Adult-to-Adult transmission might be answered with a Parent-to-Child response. There are a variety of possible combinations for crossed transactions, as you can see from the four examples in Figure 9.12. Crossed transactions tend to undermine effective communication and may create tension between the persons involved.

An *ulterior transaction* is a special type of complementary transaction that includes hidden messages intended to serve ulterior motives. These transactions are characterized by duplicity and pretense. They lie at the core of most games. In ulterior transactions *two* messages are sent and received. At the surface level there is the readily manifest message. Beneath the surface there occurs a latent but more meaningful exchange. Often, the manifest transmission is Adult-to-Adult for the sake of appearances. Beneath the surface, however, an altogether different sort of communication may be taking place.

GAMES IN INTIMATE RELATIONSHIPS

There are many kinds of games, including what Berne calls life games, party games, marital games, and sexual games. Our parents start shaping our preferences for certain games during our childhood. In adulthood, we may carry these game-

playing tendencies into our intimate relationships. A common problem for couples is that they tend to play the same destructive games over and over, often without recognizing it. In this section, we'll discuss some of the games that couples are especially likely to play.

If It Weren't for You

This game is commonly played by marital partners or other couples who have been together for a while. In it, one spouse charges the other with restricting her or his behavior. For example, a wife might casually bring up the fact that a friend will be receiving a graduate degree soon. Her husband might innocently respond, "That's great." This sets the stage for the wife to assert "If it weren't for you, I could have gone to graduate school." Thus, an old source of disharmony may be resurrected. There are a number of potential payoffs for the initiator of this game. Perhaps the wife didn't go to graduate school because she was afraid of the challenge. However, the self-deception in this game permits her to deny hidden insecurities and thereby maintain greater self-esteem. The guilt laid on her husband also provides a bargaining advantage in subsequent transactions.

Courtroom

"Courtroom" requires the availability of a third party who gets thrust (often with much discomfort) into the center of the game. In the presence of one's partner, a person says to the third party "Let me tell you what this clown (turkey, ogre, etc.) did yesterday." The "plaintiff" then

launches into a distorted account of the other partner's allegedly terrible behavior. The aim in this game is to make the "defendant" partner feel guilty so as to gain an advantage in future transactions. Part of the appeal of this game is that it's hard for the defendant not to play. Given the situation, the defendant has little choice but to mount a rebuttal.

Corner

In this game, one partner corners the other in a no-win situation. For example, the initiator, who normally handles a particular household chore—buying the groceries, say—asks the other partner to assume the responsibility today. If the second partner says no, he or she is condemned for failing to take on an adequate share of household duties. However, when the second partner agrees and does the grocery shopping, the initiator finds fault with the job, asserting that "the asparagus looks terrible, you got the wrong kind of paper towels," and so forth. Thus, the second partner can't win either way. Regardless of which way the second partner goes, the initiator garners more appreciation for the chore that he or she normally handles.

Threadbare

Spouses use this game to gain more control over family finances. In "Threadbare," a spouse makes an apparent sacrifice, going without something that would require some expenditure. The hidden agenda is to make it difficult for the other spouse to spend money guilt-

Figure 9.12. Crossed transactions. In crossed transactions, people communicate from incompatible ego states, as the receiver does not respond from the ego state addressed by the source. For example, in the exchanges in the upper left portion of the figure, the sender sends an Adult-to-Adult message, but the other person responds Parent-to-Child.

Games People Play
by Eric Berne (Grove Press, 1964)

It's hard to believe that this classic best-seller is over 25 years old. Reviewers have called it "disturbing" and "chilling" because of the way it cuts through our social façades to lay bare the guile, sham, and fraud that characterize so much of our interpersonal behavior. There is one shortcoming, in that some of Berne's analyses assume the existence of traditional gender roles, which are fading today. With the exception of this minor problem, Berne's descriptions of 120 games remain shrewd and discerning.

> Fortunately, the rewards of game-free intimacy, which is or should be the most perfect form of human living, are so great that even precariously balanced personalities can safely and joyfully relinquish their games if an appropriate partner can be found for the better relationship. [p. 62]

free. Let's say a husband continues to drive a shabby, old, beat-up car that he really could afford to replace. Driving the car appears to be a sacrifice and allows him to constantly harp about any money his wife spends. Often, the sacrifice only *appears* to be significant. The husband may not really care what kind of car he drives, but he will pretend that he does. If the car were important to him, he would probably find some other way to make his "sacrifice."

Why Don't You—Yes, But

This is a game of one-upmanship. One partner mentions a problem to the other, who innocently offers possible solutions—only to have them all rejected. Let's say a wife mentions some difficulty in correct-

ing a child's problem behavior. The husband responds sincerely with a series of ideas: "Why don't you . . . ?" However, the issue was brought up not to solicit suggestions but to *reject* them. The wife has already thought of all the obvious possibilities and rattles off a put-down for each one with "Yes, but . . ." This game allows the initiator to demonstrate his or her superiority while making the other party feel inadequate.

Sweetheart

This is a simple little gambit in which one partner tells a subtly derogatory story about the other partner, ending with, "Isn't that right, sweetheart?" The pseudo-affectionate ending makes it more difficult for the second spouse to issue a denial.

BEYOND GAMES

We have discussed only a small sampling of the games described by Berne. However, this sampling should clarify the problem with games: they are hollow, deceitful, manipulative patterns of interaction. Game playing sabotages genuine intimacy and promotes animosity and alienation in couples.

Can couples get away from game playing? According to Berne, the answer is yes. The key is to become aware of your counterproductive patterns of interaction. Berne felt that once couples gained insight into their games, they could choose not to play. Thus, by promoting this kind of insight, Transactional Analysis may aid people in achieving greater intimacy.

1. List five social trends that are undermining the traditional model of marriage.

2. Discuss several factors influencing the motivation to marry and the selection of a mate.

3. Summarize evidence on predictors of marital success.

4. Describe the family life cycle and its relationship to marital satisfaction.

5. Discuss changing attitudes about couples remaining childless.

6. Identify common problems that surface as a family's children reach adolescence and adulthood.

7. Discuss how unrealistic expectations and gaps in role expectations may affect marital adjustment.

8. Summarize how spouses' work affects their marital satisfaction and their children.

9. Discuss how financial issues and poor communication are related to marital adjustment.

10. Discuss how in-law problems and sexual problems are related to marital adjustment.

11. Discuss how the problems of jealousy and growing in different directions are related to marital adjustment.

12. Summarize evidence on divorce rates and the pros and cons of divorce.

13. List four sets of problems associated with divorce and four postdivorce syndromes to be avoided.

14. Summarize data on the frequency and success of remarriage.

15. Discuss the prevalence of cohabitation and whether it improves the probability of marital success.

16. Describe stereotypes of single life and summarize evidence on the adjustment of single people.

17. Describe three myths about homosexual couples.

18. Explain what games and ego states are in Berne's theory of Transactional Analysis.

19. Describe three types of transactions outlined by Berne.

20. Summarize the essence of the games described in the Application.

KEY TERMS

Cohabitation
Complementary transaction
Crossed transaction
Ego state
Endogamy
Family life cycle
Games
Gay

Heterosexual
Homogamy
Homosexual
Marriage
Romantic jealousy
Sociology
Transaction
Transactional Analysis
Ulterior transaction

KEY PEOPLE

Eric Berne
Bernard Murstein

Self-Report Jealousy Scale

INSTRUCTIONS

The following scale lists some situations in which you may have been involved, or in which you could be involved. Rate them with regard to how you would feel if you were confronted with the situation by circling a number that corresponds to one of the reactions shown on the right. Do not omit any items.

0 = Pleased
1 = Mildly upset
2 = Upset
3 = Very upset
4 = Extremely upset

THE SCALE

	0	1	2	3	4
1. Your partner expresses the desire that you both develop other romantic relationships.	0	1	2	3	4
2. Your partner spends increasingly more time at work with a co-employee you feel could be sexually attractive to your partner.	0	1	2	3	4
3. Your partner suddenly shows an interest in going to a party when he or she finds out that someone will be there with whom he or she has been romantically involved with previously.	0	1	2	3	4
4. At a party, your partner hugs someone other than you.	0	1	2	3	4
5. You notice your partner repeadedly looking at another.	0	1	2	3	4
6. Your partner spends increasingly more time in outside activities and hobbies in which you are not included.	0	1	2	3	4
7. At a party, your partner kisses someone you do not know.	0	1	2	3	4
8. Your boss, with whom you have had a good working relationship in the past, now seems to be more interested in the work of a co-worker.	0	1	2	3	4
9. Your partner goes to a bar several evenings without you.	0	1	2	3	4
10. Your partner recently received a promotion, and the new position requires a great deal of travel, business dinners, and parties, most of which you are not invited to attend.	0	1	2	3	4
11. At a party, your partner dances with someone you do not know.	0	1	2	3	4
12. You and a co-worker worked very hard on an extremely important project. However, your boss gave your co-worker full credit for it.	0	1	2	3	4
13. Someone flirts with your partner.	0	1	2	3	4
14. At a party, your partner repeatedly kisses someone you do not know.	0	1	2	3	4
15. Your partner has sexual relations with someone else.	0	1	2	3	4

16. Your brother or sister is given more freedom, such as staying up later, or driving the car.	0	1	2	3	4
17. Your partner comments to you on how attractive another person is.	0	1	2	3	4
18. While at a social gathering of a group of friends, your partner spends little time talking to you, but engages the others in animated conversation.	0	1	2	3	4
19. Grandparents visit your family, and they seem to devote most of their attention to a brother or sister instead of you.	0	1	2	3	4
20. Your partner flirts with someone else.	0	1	2	3	4
21. Your brother or sister seems to be receiving more affection and/or attention from your parents.	0	1	2	3	4
22. You have just discovered your partner is having an affair with someone at work.	0	1	2	3	4
23. The person who has been your assistant for a number of years at work decides to take a similar position with someone else.	0	1	2	3	4
24. The group to which you belong appears to be leaving you out of plans, activities, etc.	0	1	2	3	4
25. Your best friend suddenly shows interest in doing things with someone else .	0	1	2	3	4

SCORING THE SCALE

Give yourself 4 points for every item where your response was "extremely upset," 3 points for every item where your response was "very upset," 2 points for every item where your reponse was "upset," 1 point for every item where your response was "mildly upset," and 0 for every item where your response was "pleased." In other words, add up the numbers you circled. The total is your score on the Self-Report Jealousy Scale.

MY SCORE _____

WHAT THE SCALE MEASURES

As its name indicates, this scale measures your tendency to get jealous in a variety of situations. It does not measure *romantic jealousy* exclusively, as ten of the items relate to nonromantic jealousy. Hence, it assesses jealousy in a general way, with a heavy emphasis on romantic relationships.

This scale, which was developed by Bringle, Roach, Andler, and Evenbeck (1979), has adequate test-retest reliability. Correla-

tions with other personality traits have been examined in efforts to demonstrate its validity. People who score high on the scale tend to have low self-esteem, to be anxious, to see the world in negative terms, and to feel they have little control over their lives. These are interesting preliminary findings, although more research is needed to better validate this instrument.

INTERPRETING YOUR SCORE

Our norms are based on the sample of 162 college students studied by Bringle et al. (1979). They may be inappropriate for older, nontraditional college students.

NORMS

High score: 83–100
Intermediate score: 59–82
Low score: 0–58

How Do You Behave in Intimate Relationships?

The following questions (adapted from Corey & Corey, 1990) are intended to make you think about how you act in intimate relationships. They are designed for people in "couple-type" relationships, but if you are not currently involved in one, you can apply them to whatever relationship is most significant in your life (for instance, with your parents, children, or best friend).

1. What are some sources of conflict in your relationship? Check any of the following items that apply to you, and list any other areas of conflict in the space provided.

____Spending money

____Use of free time

____What to do about boredom

____Investment of energy in work

____Interest in others of the opposite sex

____Outside friendships

____Wanting children

____How to deal with children

____Differences in basic values

____In-laws

____Sexual needs and satisfaction

____Expression of caring and loving

____Power struggles

____Role conflicts

____Others (list below)

2. How do you generally cope with these conflicts in your relationship? Check the items that most apply to you.

____By open dialogue

____By avoidance

____By fighting and arguing

____By compromising

____By getting involved with other people or in projects

List other ways in which you deal with conflicts in your relationships.

3. List some ways in which you've changed during the period of your relationship. How have your changes affected the relationship?

4. How much do you need (and depend upon) the other person? Imagine that he or she is no longer in your life, and write down how your life might be different.

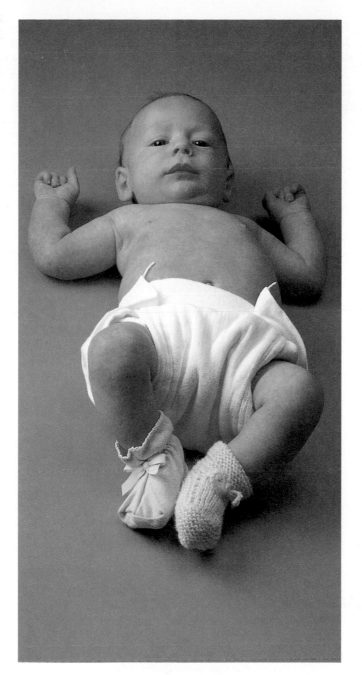

10
Gender and
Behavior

"I wanted to be a doctor, but I was told in direct and indirect ways that my ultimate ambition should be marrying a doctor and raising a family. I gave up my dream."

"For me the evidence of my mental competence was unavoidable, and I never had any trouble defending or voicing my opinion with men, because I beat them in all the tests. Consequently, none of them would come near me in my first seventeen years of life."

—Two women quoted in *Our Bodies, Ourselves* (Boston Women's Health Book Collective, 1973, p. 7)

"I could have made her feel better," said the young man, "if I'd told her that I had trouble speaking in class because I was very self-conscious. But instead of telling her (which would have helped me too), I didn't say anything. Trivial as it was, I couldn't bring myself to say that I, at twenty-one, a man who hoped to be a great writer, couldn't raise my hand in class."

"I play the reassuring, protective father. She is my faithful, dependent child. Her faith and dependency are a form of reassurance and support for me. But there are days when I would like to come to her, as she comes to me, as a child, to tell her that I was hurt when my roommate didn't think my seminar professor liked me anymore—but I could never bring myself to talk about such sentimental drivel even though I wanted to."

—Two men quoted in *Dilemmas of Masculinity* (Komarovsky, 1976, p. 165)

The women and men quoted above feel boxed in by gender roles. They all are struggling with limitations placed on their behavior by virtue of their sex. They are not unique or even unusual. No doubt you, too, have had occasions when you changed your behavior to bring it in line with society's concepts of masculinity and femininity.

Before proceeding further, we need to define some terms. In the context of this discussion, *sex* **refers to the biologically based categories of male and female.** In contrast, *gender* **refers to culturally constructed distinctions between masculinity and femininity** that don't necessarily correspond with one's biological sex (see Figure 10.1). For example, it is possible for males to be "feminine" and for females to be "masculine," although the opposite is more likely. Another way of making this distinction is this: We are *born* male or female (sex). On the other hand, we gradually *become* masculine or feminine (gender) through complex developmental processes that take years to unfold.

In this chapter, we will examine the role of gender in our lives. In particular, we will focus on how gender affects our interpersonal relationships and psychological adjustment. We will address a number of complex and controversial questions. Are there genuine behavioral differences between the sexes? If so, why do these differences exist? How do they develop? Are traditional gender roles healthy or unhealthy? Why are gender roles in our society changing, and what does the future hold? Let's begin by looking at gender stereotypes.

GENDER STEREOTYPES

Obviously, women and men are biologically different, both with regard to genitalia and other aspects of their anatomy and with regard to their physiological functioning. The readily apparent physical disparities between males and females lead us to expect behavioral differences as well. You may recall from Chapter 5 that *stereotypes* are widely held beliefs that people have certain characteristics simply because of their membership in a particular group. *Gender stereotypes* **are widely shared beliefs about males' and females' abilities, personality traits, and social behavior.** These stereotypes based on sex are very prevalent in our society. Research indicates that there is a great deal of consensus on supposed behavioral differences between men and women (Broverman et al., 1972; Smith & Midlarsky, 1985). People seem to subscribe to this consensus regardless of their age, sex, marital status, and educational background.

These gender stereotypes are too numerous to summarize here. Instead, you can examine Figure 10.2, which lists a number of behavioral characteristics thought to be

Figure 10.1. Terminology related to gender. The topic of gender involves many closely related ideas that are easy to confuse. The gender-related concepts introduced in this chapter are summarized here for easy comparison.

Gender-Related Concepts	
Sex	Biologically based categories of male and female, determined at birth
Gender	Culturally determined distinctions between masculinity and femininity
Gender stereotypes	Widely held and often inaccurate beliefs about males' and females' abilities, personality, and social behavior
Gender differences	Actual disparities between the sexes in behavior, based on research observations
Gender roles	Culturally defined expectations about appropriate behavior for males and females
Gender-role identity	A person's identification with the traits regarded as masculine or feminine (one's sense of being masculine or feminine)
Sexual orientation	A person's preference for sexual partners of the other sex (heterosexual), the same sex (homosexual), or either sex (bisexual)

associated with femininity and masculinity. This list is based on a study in which subjects were asked to indicate the extent to which various traits were characteristic of each sex (Broverman et al., 1972). Although this particular study was conducted in 1972, gender stereotypes in our society have largely remained stable (Martin, 1987; Ruble, 1983). The list may contain a few surprises, but you have probably encountered most of these stereotypes before. After all, we all know that women are more passive, dependent, emotional, irrational, submissive, persuasible, insecure, and talkative than men. Or do we? We'll examine the reality of the situation in a moment.

Before we review the actual evidence on gender differences in behavior, one other point should be emphasized. In gender-related stereotypes, women definitely get the short end of the stick. The traditional male stereotype is far more complimentary than the conventional female stereotype. The list in Figure 10.2 clearly suggests that men have cornered the market on competence and rationality. In contrast, the female stereotype is frequently negative and sometimes demeaning.

The fact that gender stereotypes favor males reflects an *androcentric bias*. That is, our society is organized in a way that favors "masculine" characteristics and modes of behavior ("andro" is from the Greek word for "man"). Research on the characteristics associated with good psychological adjustment illustrates how an androcentric bias permeates our culture. In one widely cited study, mental health professionals were assigned to three groups and asked to evaluate the same list of personality characteristics (Broverman et al., 1970). Subjects in one group were asked to select the characteristics that best described the "mature, healthy adult male." Subjects in the other groups were asked to do the same for the "mature, healthy adult female" or the "mature, healthy adult" (sex unspecified). The characteristics these mental health professionals chose to describe the healthy *adult* (independent, self-confident, logical) were basically the same as those they used to describe the healthy adult *male*. In contrast, the qualities they used to describe the "healthy" adult *female* (submissive, emotional, less objective) were quite different from those used to describe the healthy adult. In other words, while many masculine characteristics were associated with good psychological adjustment, not many feminine traits were.

Findings like these suggest that women face a dilemma that men do not. To oversimplify a bit, women must choose between being mentally healthy and masculine *or* mentally unhealthy and feminine. Furthermore, because many people regard masculine behavior in a female as unhealthy, women who struggle with this dilemma may be in a no-win situation. For the most part, our androcentric bias seems to favor masculine behavior only in males.

Now that we have set the stage by describing gender

Elements of Traditional Gender Stereotypes	
Feminine	**Masculine**
Not at all aggressive	Very aggressive
Not at all independent	Very independent
Very emotional	Not at all emotional
Very easily influenced	Not at all easily influenced
Very submissive	Very dominant
Very excitable in a minor crisis	Not at all excitable in a minor crisis
Very passive	Very active
Very illogical	Very logical
Very home-oriented	Very worldly
Easily hurt emotionally	Not easily hurt emotionally
Generally indecisive	Decisive
Very easily moved to tears	Never moved to tears
Very dependent	Not at all dependent
Very conceited about appearance	Never conceited about appearance
Very talkative	Not at all talkative
Very tactful	Very blunt
Very gentle	Very tough
Very aware of feelings of others	Not at all aware of feelings of others
Very interested in own appearance	Not at all interested in own appearance
Very desirous of security	Not very desirous of security

Figure 10.2. Traditional gender stereotypes. Broverman et al. (1972) identified a host of traits that are widely associated with masculinity and femininity. A partial list of these traits is shown here.

stereotypes and their andocentric slant, we can examine what the research actually shows about behavioral differences between the sexes. It should be stressed that we will be looking at gender differences in modern Western societies. The story can be quite different in other cultures.

RESEARCH ON GENDER DIFFERENCES AND SIMILARITIES

Gender differences are actual disparities between the sexes in their typical (average) behavior. The research on gender differences is not easy to summarize. A vast number of studies have been conducted, and many report conflicting findings. Moreover, new evidence is pouring in constantly. Nonetheless, we will try to give you an up-to-date overview of the empirical evidence on gender differences and similarities. We will examine research on supposed differences in cognitive abilities, personality traits, social behavior, and psychological health.

Cognitive Abilities

Perhaps we should first point out that no gender differences have been found in overall intelligence. This shouldn't be surprising, since intelligence tests are intentionally designed to minimize differences between the scores of males and females.

However, there may be some genuine differences between the sexes in specific cognitive skills. Three such disparities have shown up with some consistency in research. First, women tend to be superior to men in *verbal ability*. That is, females score somewhat higher than males on a variety of verbal tests, with the gap opening up during early adolescence (Hyde, 1981; Petersen, Crockett, & Tobin-Richards, 1982). Second, on tests of *mathematical ability*, males generally perform better than females (Benbow & Stanley, 1982; Hyde, 1981). This advantage first surfaces around the ages of 11 to 13. Third, males also tend to display better *visual-spatial ability* than females

(Linn & Petersen, 1986; Maccoby & Jacklin, 1974). This disparity usually emerges after the age of 8.

We hasten to emphasize that even these observed differences between males and females in mental abilities are *quite small.* Furthermore, an analysis of trends in research findings over the last 40 years suggests that gender differences in cognitive abilities are rapidly shrinking (Linn & Hyde, 1989). Indeed, after reviewing recent evidence on verbal talent, Janet Shibley Hyde and Marcia Linn (1988) concluded, "The difference is so small, that we argue that gender differences in verbal ability no longer exist."

Personality Traits

A number of personality traits have been examined in research on gender differences. We will discuss those that have attracted the most attention.

Emotionality

For the purposes of our discussion, we will define *emotionality* as "overreacting" to a stressful situation. Popular stereotypes suggest that women are typically more upset by stressful events than men. Supposedly, men are more likely to remain cool and calm. The empirical evidence on this issue is sparse, but the available data do *not* support the stereotype. In fact, there is evidence that in reacting to frustration, males are more emotionally volatile than females (Haviland & Malatesta, 1982; Maccoby & Jacklin, 1974). The belief in females' emotional reactivity may be due to their greater willingness to acknowledge certain emotions openly. Many men consider it "unmanly" to express emotions such as hurt and fear. However, this does not mean that women are more emotional than men. It merely means that most men are trained to hide some emotions that women typically do not.

In the area of emotionality, conventional wisdom also suggests that men vent their anger directly and often, while women either suppress their anger or express it

indirectly through sulking or nagging. Once again, the empirical evidence undermines the popular stereotypes. Research suggests that there are more similarities than differences between men and women in their expression of anger. The two sexes seem to experience anger equally often and for the same reasons—insults, condescending treatment, and so forth (Averill, 1982; Tavris, 1982). Also, both men and women report that they have trouble expresssing their angry feelings to those who have more power or status, such as parents, teachers, and employers. Both sexes tend to take their anger home and vent it at "safe" targets.

Nurturance

Nurturance is the provision of help, physical care, and emotional support to others. This term often is used in reference to caring for children. Because only women can bear children, it is widely assumed that women are predisposed to be more nurturant than men.

When self-reports are used or when individuals are observed by others, females *are* found to be more nurturing than males (Berman, 1976; Nash & Feldman, 1981). However, these gender differences disappear when subjects are observed indirectly (without their knowledge). Hence, it is likely that differences in nurturance reflect subjects' conformity with role expectations rather than actual gender differences. Moreover, the fact that some women opt not to have children rules out the existence of a maternal *instinct*. It is clear that women are assigned more responsibility for nurturance in our society. However, current research doesn't support the idea that women are by nature more nurturant than men.

Empathy

Empathy involves adopting another person's frame of reference to understand her or his point of view. When empathy is assessed by self-report measures, women describe themselves as more sensitive to the feelings of others than men do. However, this difference in empathy isn't seen when subjects don't know that their behavior is being observed (Eisenberg & Lennon, 1983). This finding suggests that role expectations are influencing women's self-descriptions. When researchers look at the ability to respond to people with problems, or to describe the feelings of characters in a story or picture, they don't find consistent differences between men and women (Eisenberg & Lennon, 1983; Maccoby & Jacklin, 1974). Thus, gender differences in empathy are elusive.

Social Behavior

Although gender differences in cognitive abilities and personality appear to be minimal, researchers have found some interesting disparities in social behavior.

Aggression

Aggression involves behavior that is intended to hurt someone, either physically or verbally (see Chapter 4). Research reveals that males tend to be more aggressive than females, although the size of this difference is modest (Eagly, 1987; Maccoby & Jacklin, 1974). Furthermore, when distinctions are made among different types of aggression, some researchers have found that girls tend to engage in more verbal and disobedient aggressive acts, while boys engage in more physical and destructive aggresssion (Barfield, 1976; Hyde, 1984). Recent research also suggests that the sexes may *think* differently about aggression (Eagly, 1987). For example, women report more guilt and anxiety after they have engaged in aggressive behavior and more awareness of the potential harmfulness of their aggression. These patterns of thinking probably help inhibit women's expression of aggression.

The disparity between the sexes in aggressive behavior shows up early in childhood. That it continues through adulthood is supported by the fact that men account for a grossly disproportionate share of violent crime (Kenrick, 1987). When we look at aggression outside the laboratory, we find wide differences between women and men in aggressive crimes such as assault, armed robbery, homicide, and rape (see Figure 10.3).

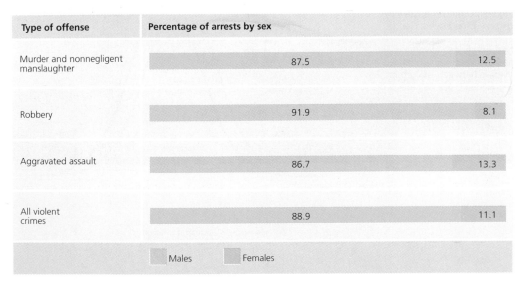

Type of offense	Percentage of arrests by sex	
Murder and nonnegligent manslaughter	87.5	12.5
Robbery	91.9	8.1
Aggravated assault	86.7	13.3
All violent crimes	88.9	11.1
	Males	Females

Figure 10.3. Gender differences in violent crimes. Males are arrested for violent crimes far more often than females, as these statistics show. These data support the findings of laboratory studies indicating that males tend to be more aggressive than females.

Assertiveness

Aggressiveness is often equated with assertiveness, but psychologists make important distinctions between these types of social behavior. **Assertiveness involves acting in your own best interests by expressing your feelings honestly and standing up for your legitimate rights** (rather than trying to hurt someone). It is widely believed that men are more assertive, while women are more passive, failing to speak up for themselves when they should. Although not entirely consistent, the empirical evidence appears to support this belief. For example, O'Leary (1977) cites various studies showing that in mixed-sex groups women talk less than men and are less likely to influence group processes or assume leadership roles. Similarly, after reviewing the evidence, Block (1976) concludes that males make more efforts at dominance than females.

Gender differences in assertiveness may reflect status differences and situational contraints. Males tend to have higher status than females, making it easier for them to be assertive. Furthermore, women may hesitate to be assertive because they fear social rejection for "unfeminine" behavior. Difficulties and dilemmas such as these have led to the increased popularity of assertiveness training for women. Many men can also benefit from assertiveness training, which is discussed in the application section at the end of this chapter.

Conformity

Conformity involves yielding to real or imagined social pressure. Traditional beliefs hold that females are more conforming than males, who are viewed as more independent-minded. Research has demonstrated that females *don't* conform to peer standards more than males unless there is group pressure to do so (Cooper, 1979; Eagly, 1978). However, when group pressure is present, females *are* more likely to conform than males—frequently because of their lower status within the group or because of their efforts to preserve social harmony (Eagly, 1983; Eagly & Carli, 1981; Eagly & Wood, 1982, 1985).

Figure 10.4. The nature of group differences. Gender differences are group differences that tell us little about individuals because there is great overlap between the groups. For a given trait, one sex may score higher on the average, but there is far more variation within each sex than between the sexes.

Nonverbal Communication

Researchers have also studied how the sexes compare in the realm of nonverbal communication. With regard to the *display* of nonverbal cues, the typical finding is that females display more submission and warmth cues, while males display more dominance and high-status cues (Frieze & Ramsey, 1976). It is quite likely that status differences between men and women play an important role in producing these behavioral differences (Henley, 1977; Mayo & Henley, 1981). There also is a gender difference in *sensitivity to nonverbal cues* in communication. A large body of studies indicate that women are more accurate than men in decoding nonverbal signals (Hall, 1984).

Psychological Health

With regard to mental health, the sexes are both similar and different. They are similar in that the overall incidence of mental disorders is roughly the same for both sexes. They are different in terms of what kinds of disorders they tend to develop.

Prior to the 1980s, research on the prevalence of mental illness suggested that about one out of every five people developed a disorder at some point in life and that mental disorders were more common in women than in men (Neugebauer, Dohrenwend, & Dohrenwend, 1980). However, most pre-1980 studies did not assess drug-related disorders or antisocial disorders adequately, because these disorders used to be defined vaguely. These happen to be disorders that are more common in men. More recent studies, which have counted these disorders more effectively, yield a different picture (Robins et al., 1984). Recent studies suggest that about one out of every three people will develop a psychological disorder at one time or another and that this is true for both males and females.

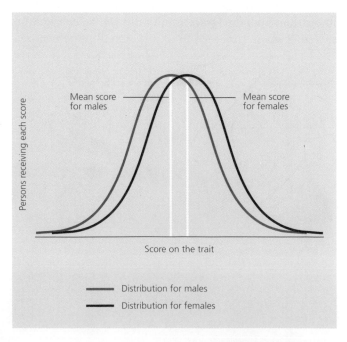

When researchers assess the prevalence of *specific* disorders, they *do* find differences between the sexes (H. S. Kaplan, 1983). As just noted, antisocial behavior, alcoholism, and other drug-related disorders are more prevalent among men. Women, on the other hand, are more likely than men to suffer from depresssion and anxiety disorders (phobias, for example). They also show higher rates of eating disorders (Rodin, Silberstein, & Striegel-Moore, 1985). In addition, women *attempt* suicide more often than men, but men *complete* suicides (actually kill themselves) more frequently than women (Cross & Hirschfeld, 1986).

Although the overall prevalence of psychological disorders is about the same for both sexes, there are substantially more females than males in psychotherapy (Al-Issa, 1982; Russo & Sobel, 1981). Why might this be? One reason is that women are more willing than men to acknowledge their emotional problems and seek professional help. Many men are reluctant to admit that they are struggling with anxiety or depression for fear of seeming "unmanly." Furthermore, people who exhibit antisocial or drug-related disorders often don't see themselves as having a problem. Thus, people are less likely to seek treatment for the disorders that are more common in men.

There may also be gender bias in the *diagnosis* of mental disorders that contributes to the disproportionate number of women in psychotherapy (Kaplan, 1983). Phyllis Chesler (1972) has argued that the male-dominated psychiatric establishment is overly eager to label women "crazy" or "neurotic." She views this alleged bias as a device to keep women in line by coercing them into adhering to traditional roles. The androcentric bias that allows women to be labeled mentally ill more readily than men may be even stronger in laypersons than in mental health professionals. Thus, many women may be propelled into therapy by their husbands' derogatory remarks about their "neurotic" qualities. While it is unlikely that gender bias alone accounts for the higher number of female patients, it probably contributes to this inequality.

Putting Gender Differences in Perspective

Although there are some genuine gender differences in behavior, bear in mind that they are *group* differences. That is, they tell us nothing about individuals. Essentially, we are comparing the "average man" with the "average woman." However, every individual is unique. The average female and male are ultimately figments of our imagination. Furthermore, even these group differences are relatively small. Figure 10.4 shows how scores on a trait might be distributed for men and women. Although the group averages are detectably different, you can see that there is great variability within each group (sex) and huge overlap between the two group distributions. Thus, a gender difference that shows up on the average does not by itself tell us anything about you or any other individual of either sex.

Another way to gauge the influence of gender on behavior is to estimate how much of the variation among people on a trait is accounted for by a person's sex. Estimates of these proportions can be made through meta-analysis, which is a special type of research review. **A *meta-analysis* combines the statistical results of many studies of the same question.** Janet Shibley Hyde (1981, 1984) has been a leading proponent of meta-analysis in the area of gender differences. Her reviews, which we have already cited many times, have helped to clarify research trends in gender differences. Figure 10.5 summarizes the findings of meta-analyses on gender effects by Hyde and others. These meta-analyses suggest that sex accounts for 1% or less of the variation among people in verbal ability, mathematics ability, and conformity (susceptibility to social influence). Furthermore, on the traits with the largest gender differences, sex accounts for only about 4–6% of the variation among individuals. Other factors besides sex, therefore, are far more important in accounting for the differences between individuals.

To summarize, the behavioral differences between males and females are fewer in number and smaller in size than popular stereotypes suggest. *Ultimately, the similarities*

Summary of Research on Gender Differences				
Characteristic	Researcher	Number of studies analyzed	Sex showing higher levels	Variance accounted for by sex (%)
Verbal abilities	Hyde & Linn (1988)	165	F better	<1
Mathematical abilities	Hyde (1981)	16	M better	1
Visual-spatial abilities	Hyde (1981)	10	M better	4.5
Aggression	Hyde (1984)	143	M greater	6
Decoding of nonverbal cues	Hall (1978)	75	F better	4
Susceptibility to social influence	Eagly & Carli (1981)	148	F more	1

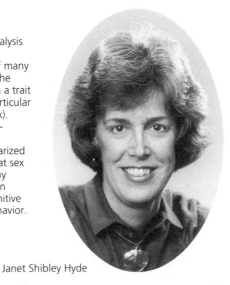

Figure 10.5. Meta-analyses of gender differences. Meta-analysis allows researchers to combine the results of many studies and estimate the amount of variation in a trait accounted for by a particular factor (in this case, sex). Some influential meta-analyses of gender differences are summarized here. They suggest that sex accounts for only a tiny portion of the variation among people in cognitive abilities and social behavior.

Janet Shibley Hyde

between women and men greatly outweigh the differences. For the most part, gender stereotypes bear little relation to reality. Instead, they promote errors in social perception, leading many of us to view ourselves and others inaccurately.

Although they are small, there are some genuine behavioral differences between the sexes that require explanation. In the next section, we begin to consider the origins of gender differences.

BIOLOGICAL ORIGINS OF GENDER DIFFERENCES

Are the gender differences that do exist acquired through learning, or are they biologically built in? Until now, we have deferred tackling this controversial question. Essentially, it represents the age-old issue of nature versus nurture. This issue pits heredity against the environment as the prime determinant of behavior. The "nature" theorists concentrate on how biological disparities between the sexes contribute to gender differences in behavior. "Nurture" theorists, on the other hand, emphasize the role of learning and the environment.

The idea that "anatomy is destiny" was widely accepted during the first half of the 20th century. Indeed, during the early part of the century, researchers simply *assumed* that gender differences were due largely to biological factors (Shields, 1975). The bias of the male-dominated scientific community was so strong that scholars managed to find "proof" that the frontal lobes of the brain, thought to be the seat of reason, were larger in men than in women. However, evidence later surfaced to suggest that the parietal lobes (rather than the frontal lobes) were crucial to complex cognition. Suddenly, scientists found that males had a size advantage in the parietal area instead (Shields, 1975). It is now clear that there are no meaningful size differences between male and female brains. This story simply illustrates how our culture's androcentric bias can contaminate research on gender differences.

In recent decades, biological explanations of gender differences have focused not on the brain's size, but on its organization and on the possible role of hormonal influences. We'll examine the evidence on brain organization first.

Brain Organization

Some theorists believe that male and female brains may be characterized by different organization. As you may know, the human brain is divided into two halves. **The** *cerebral hemispheres* **are the right and left halves of the cerebrum, which is the convoluted outer layer of the brain.** The largest and most complicated part of the human brain, the cerebrum is responsible for most complex mental activities.

There is evidence that the right and left cerebral hemispheres are specialized to handle different cognitive tasks (Sperry, 1982; Springer & Deutsch, 1984). For example, it appears that the *left hemisphere* is more actively involved in *verbal and mathematical processing*, while the *right hemisphere* is specialized to handle *visual-spatial and other nonverbal processing*. This pattern is generally seen in both right-handed and left-handed people. However, hemispheric specialization tends to be less consistent among those who are left-handed.

After these findings on hemispheric specialization surfaced, various theorists began to wonder whether there might be a connection between this division of labor in the brain and observed gender differences in verbal and spatial skills. Consequently, they began looking for disparities between males and females in brain organization.

They found some evidence that males exhibit more cerebral specialization than females (McGlone, 1980). In other words, there is a trend for males to depend more heavily than females on the left hemisphere in verbal processing and on the right hemisphere in spatial processing. Some theorists have argued that this difference in brain organization is responsible for gender differ-

Studies have shown that the brain's cerebral hemispheres, shown here, are somewhat specialized in the kinds of cognitive tasks they handle and that males exhibit more such specialization than females. Whether this difference bears any relation to gender differences in behavior is yet to be determined.

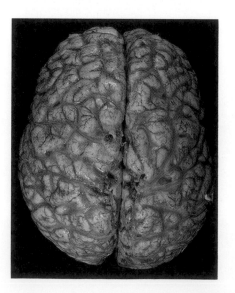

ences in verbal and spatial ability (Goleman, 1978). As a result of the interest aroused by these findings, the popular press has often touted the idea that there are "male brains" and "female brains," which are fundamentally different (Bleier, 1984).

This idea is intriguing, but we have a long way to go before we can explain gender differences in terms of right brain/left brain specialization. For one thing, studies have not been consistent in finding that males have more specialized brain organization than females (Fausto-Sterling, 1985; Harris, 1980; Kinsbourne, 1980). Moreover, even if men *do* show stronger cerebral specialization than women, no one is really sure just how that would account for the gender differences in cognitive abilities. It seems peculiar that strong specialization would produce an advantage for males on one kind of task (spatial) and a disadvantage on another kind of task (verbal). Furthermore, as we noted earlier, recent studies cast doubt on whether there are any real gender differences in verbal ability that need to be explained. Thus, the theory linking cerebral specialization to gender differences in mental abilities remains highly speculative.

Hormonal Influences

Biological explanations of gender differences have also focused on the possible role of hormones. **Hormones are chemical substances released into the bloodstream by the endocrine glands.** We know that hormones play a key role in sexual differentiation during prenatal development. Our biological sex is determined by our sex chromosomes. An XX pairing produces a female, and an XY pairing produces a male. However, both male and female embryos are essentially the same until about 8 to 12 weeks after conception. Around this time, male and female gonads (sex glands) begin to produce different hormonal secretions. The high level of *androgens* (the principal class of male hormones) in males and the low level of androgens in females leads to the differentiation of male and female genital organs.

The influence of prenatal hormones on sexual differentiation becomes apparent when something interferes with normal prenatal hormonal secretions. John Money and his colleagues have tracked the development of a small number of females who were exposed to high levels of androgens during their prenatal development. The girls were born to mothers who either had a hormonal malfunction during pregnancy or were given an androgen-like drug to prevent miscarriage. These *androgenized females* were born with genitalia that were partially male. The degree of masculinization of their genitals varied, depending on the extent of their prenatal hormonal imbalance. In some cases, the masculinization was so subtle that it went unnoticed for months and even years. Once noticed, most cases were treated with a combination of hormone therapy and surgical correction of the genitals.

Money and his colleagues wondered whether the prenatal dose of male hormones would affect the behavioral tendencies of these androgenized females. Sure enough, they found that the androgenized females showed "tomboyish" interests in vigorous outdoor activities. They also showed preferences for male playmates and "male" toys (Money & Ehrhardt, 1972).

The findings on androgenized females suggested to many theorists that prenatal hormones shape gender differences in humans. But there are—naturally—a few

---

RECOMMENDED READING

The New Our Bodies, Ourselves: A Book by and for Women

by The Boston Women's Health Book Collective (Simon & Schuster, 1984)

The New Our Bodies, Ourselves is a revised and greatly expanded version of a remarkably popular and worthwhile book. As its title suggests, it is primarily about the female body and how it works. However, it goes beyond this subject to talk about self-concept and interpersonal relationships with men and with women. The book grew spontaneously out of a women's discussion group that began meeting in Boston in 1969. Part of its charm lies in its unique mixture of information drawn from technical sources and information drawn from personal experiences. These two disparate sources of insight are interwoven nicely through the use of numerous quotations. The book is illustrated where necessary, and it provides many suggestions for additional reading. Rarest of all, it is exceptionally low-priced.

> Every society throughout history has had standards of beauty, but at no time before has there been such an intense media blitz telling us what we *should* look like. Magazine covers, films, TV shows, billboards surround us with images which fail to reflect the tremendous diversity among us. Never before have there been hundreds of profitable businesses set up to convince us we don't look good enough. [p. 5]

problems. First, it's always dangerous to draw conclusions about the general population based on a handful of subjects who have an abnormal condition. Second, most of the androgenized girls received drug treatments (cortisone) for their condition. These treatments could have influenced their activity levels. Third, the girls were born with male-looking genitals that often were not surgically corrected until age 2 or 3. Hence, their families may not have *raised* them in quite the same way as they would have raised "normal" girls. In light of these problems, research on androgenized females cannot conclusively demonstrate that prenatal hormones cause gender differences in behavior.

Researchers have also tried to link hormone levels in adults to gender differences. Once again, the findings are inconsistent and inconclusive. For example, even the seemingly plausible association between hormonal fluctuations and the premenstrual syndrome in women has been seriously questioned. **The *premenstrual syndrome* involves a negative shift in mood, thought to occur in the days preceding females' menstrual periods.** Although *some* women experience specific mood changes that are correlated with their menstrual cycle, there is little evidence to support the existence of a premenstrual syndrome defined as a specific *cluster of feelings* (Parlee, 1973). Some studies find no mood changes in female subjects as a function of their menstrual cycle (Golub & Harrington, 1981). In one study (Dan, 1976), husbands and wives kept daily records of their moods over a period of months. No significant mood differences between spouses were found, even though the wives were experiencing hormonal changes related to their menstrual cycles.

The purported link between hormones and the premenstrual syndrome has been further undermined by evidence that the syndrome is influenced by cultural expectations (Paige, 1973; Parlee, 1982). In one study, subjects filled out daily reports of physical and emotional symptoms. Women who were told that the study concerned *menstrual distress* reported more symptoms than their male counterparts. However, women who were led to believe that the study concerned their *general health* did not. Thus, the "menstrual blues" may be due more to social training than to hormonal fluctuations. As a whole, the evidence indicates that environmental events and social variables account for more of the variability in mood than do hormonal levels (Good & Smith, 1980; Landers, 1977).

In summary, researchers have made relatively little progress in their efforts to document the biological roots of gender differences in behavior. The idea that "anatomy is destiny" has proven difficult to demonstrate. Many theorists remain convinced that biological factors contribute to gender differences. However, the overall evidence, or rather, the lack of it, suggests that biology must play a relatively minor role. In contrast, efforts to link gender differences to disparities in the way males and females are socialized have proven more fruitful. In the next section we'll turn to a detailed analysis of gender-role socialization.

ENVIRONMENTAL ORIGINS OF GENDER DIFFERENCES

Let's begin this section with a riddle.

A boy and his father are in an automobile accident. The father is killed, and the boy is seriously injured. The boy is rushed to the hospital and taken into the operating room. A few minutes later, the surgeon comes out of the operating room and says, "I cannot operate on this boy; he is my son." Explain how this could be.

In view of the topic at hand (gender roles), you probably had little difficulty with our riddle. The answer is quite simple. The surgeon is the boy's mother. A surprisingly high number of people fail to recognize this when the riddle isn't placed in the middle of a chapter on gender roles. Many people have a hard time envisioning a woman in the role of surgeon. In their minds "it just doesn't compute."

Children learn behaviors appropriate to their gender roles very early in life. According to social learning theory, girls do the sorts of things their mothers do, while boys follow in Dad's footsteps.

As we noted in Chapter 7, a *role* is a pattern of behavior expected of a person based on her or his social position. There are role expectations that go along with being a student, a professor, a parent, a salesperson, a bartender, a lawyer, a neighbor, and so forth. *Gender roles* **are expectations about what is appropriate behavior for each sex**. For example, in our culture women have widely been expected to sew, do laundry, and cook meals. On the other hand, men have been expected to watch football, tinker with cars, and be the family breadwinner. In dating relationships, males have been expected to ask females out, open doors for them, drive the car, pick up the check, and so on. However, there is less ambiguity in our culture about gender-appropriate behavior for males than for females. Furthermore, the pressure for gender-appropriate behavior comes earlier for boys than for girls (Eme, 1979; Pleck, 1981).

Are gender roles in other cultures similar to those seen in our society? Generally, yes—but not necessarily. Despite a fair amount of cross-cultural consistency in gender roles, there is some dramatic variability as well (Munroe & Munroe, 1975). For instance, anthropologist Margaret Mead (1950) conducted a now-classic study of three tribes in New Guinea. She found one tribe in which *both* sexes followed our masculine role expectations (the Mundugumor). She found another tribe in which *both* sexes approximated our feminine role (the Arapesh). And she found one tribe in which the male and female roles were roughly the *reverse* of our own (the Tchambuli). Such remarkable discrepancies between cultures existing within 100 miles of one another demonstrate that gender roles are not a matter of biological destiny. Instead, like other roles, gender roles are acquired through socialization. *Socialization* **refers to the acquisition of the norms and roles expected of people in a particular society.** This process includes all the efforts made by a society to put its unique imprint on its members.

According to Alice Eagly (1987), gender differences arise largely because males and females are assigned different roles. For example, if women are usually given

the task of raising children, it's logical to expect them to become more nurturant. In contrast, if men are sent into the competitive world of work, they are likely to become more competitive. In other words, we adapt our behavior to our role assignments. Thus, Eagly's *social role theory* suggests that gender differences occur because males and females are guided by differing role expectations.

In this section, we'll explain the socialization of gender roles. Specifically, we will discuss how our society teaches children about gender roles and how these roles contribute to gender differences.

Processes in Gender-Role Socialization

How do we acquire our gender roles? Gender-role socialization takes place through several key learning processes. These include reinforcement and punishment, observational learning, and self-socialization.

Reinforcement and Punishment

The power of reinforcement and punishment was emphasized in our discussion of *operant conditioning* in Chapter 2. One important way that children learn gender roles is through being reinforced for "gender-appropriate" behaviors and punished for "gender-inappropriate" ones. Parents, siblings, teachers, and peers all utilize reinforcement and punishment to promote gender-appropriate behavior (Bandura, 1977; Mischel, 1970). For example, a young boy who has just hurt himself may be told by his dad that "big boys don't cry." If the child succeeds in inhibiting his crying, he may get a pat on the back, a warm smile, or even an ice cream cone—all potent reinforcers.

To demonstrate the effectiveness of reinforcement in modifying behavior, let's look at a representative experiment (Serbin, Connor, & Citron, 1978). For 20 minutes once a week, nursery school children were praised by their teachers whenever they engaged in two types of independent behavior (exploration and persisting on a task alone). During the same 20-minute period, teachers ignored two dependent behaviors (soliciting teacher

Alice Eagly

attention and seeking to be near the teacher). A second group of children were praised regardless of their behavior. After five weeks, the behavior of the two groups of children was compared. Both girls and boys in the first group showed more independent and less dependent behavior than the children in the second group—thanks to just 20 minutes of reinforcement per week.

The evidence suggests that parents use punishment more than reward in socializing gender roles (O'Leary, 1977). Many parents probably take gender-appropriate behavior for granted and don't go out of their way to reward it. But they may react very negatively to gender-inappropriate behavior. For instance, a 10-year-old boy who enjoys playing with dollhouses may elicit strong disapproval. Parents pay more attention to discouraging gender-inappropriate behavior in boys than in girls. Fathers are especially likely to punish gender-inappropriate behavior in their sons (Fagot, 1981; Langlois & Downs, 1980). This punishment usually involves verbal reprimands or ridicule rather than physical punishment.

Observational Learning

As explained in Chapter 2, *observational learning* occurs when a person's behavior is influenced by observations of others, who are called *models*. Parents serve as models for children, as do siblings, teachers, relatives, and other people who are important in children's lives. Note, too, that models are not limited to real people. For example, characters on television and in films also function as role models.

According to *social learning theory* (see Chapter 2), young children are more likely to imitate people who are nurturant, powerful, and similar to them (Mischel, 1970). Children imitate both sexes, but most children tend to imitate same-sex models more than other-sex models (Perry & Bussey, 1979). Thus, observational learning often leads young girls to play with dolls, toy stoves, and so forth. In contrast, young boys are more likely to tinker with toy trucks, miniature gas stations, and such. It's also likely that boys get more exposure to male models than

girls and that girls get more exposure to female models than boys. Thus, dad may take Johnny with him to the auto-parts store, while Mary goes grocery shopping with mom. Similarly, girls and boys spend more time with same-sex peers, who serve as each other's models.

Self-Socialization

Children are not merely passive recipients of gender-role socialization. There is evidence that children themselves are active agents in their own gender-role socialization. Several influential *cognitive theories* of gender-role development (Bem, 1981; Kohlberg, 1966; Martin & Halverson, 1981) emphasize such *self-socialization*.

Self-socialization entails three steps. First, children learn to classify themselves as male or female and to recognize their sex as a permanent quality (around ages 5 to 7). Second, this self-categorization motivates them to value those characteristics and behaviors that are associated with their sex. Third, they strive to bring their behavior in line with what is considered gender-appropriate in their culture. In other words, children get involved in their own socialization, working diligently to discover the rules that are supposed to govern their behavior.

Sandra Bem (1981) has theorized that children gradually learn to see the world through "gender-colored" glasses, which she calls *gender schemas* (*schemas* are cognitive structures that guide our information processing). To investigate this idea, she devised a questionnaire to assess **gender-role identity—a person's identification with the traits regarded as masculine or feminine.** Males who describe themselves in accordance with society's definition of masculinity and females who describe themselves in accordance with society's definition of femininity are said to have a *sex-typed* gender identity. Individuals who don't describe themselves in these ways—for example, people who see themselves as possessing *both* masculine and feminine characteristics—are said to have a *non-sex-typed* gender identity. (This second group includes several subgroups that we will describe later.)

According to Bem, sex-typed people spontaneously

Figure 10.6. Toy preferences and gender. This graph depicts the percentage of boys and girls asking for various types of toys in letters to Santa Claus (adapted from Richardson & Simpson, 1982). As you can see, boys and girls differ substantially in their toy preferences. These differences show the effects of gender-role socialization.

classify information on the basis of gender, even when other dimensions could serve equally well. Non-sex-typed individuals, on the other hand, are less likely to use gender to organize their perceptions. An interesting study appears to bear out this idea (Bem, 1981). Male and female undergraduates were classified as either sex-typed or non-sex-typed. Then, each subject looked at 60 different personality attributes (20 were "masculine," 20 were "feminine," and 20 were gender-neutral). As the 60 attributes were flashed on a projection screen, subjects pushed a "me" button or a "not me" button to indicate whether the attributes were descriptive of them.

Bem predicted that sex-typed subjects would tend to push the buttons *more quickly* because their gender schema would allow them to process gender-relevant information without much thought. Non-sex-typed people were expected to take longer to respond, because they would need time to think about whether an attribute was characteristic of them. As predicted, sex-typed individuals took less time than non-sex-typed individuals to push the buttons. Bem concluded that these results demonstrated the greater influence of gender schemas in sex-typed subjects.

Sources of Gender-Role Socialization

There are three *main* sources of gender-role socialization: families, schools, and the media. Of course, we are currently in an era of transition in gender roles. Hence, the generalizations that follow may say more about how you were socialized than about how your children will be.

Families
Obviously, a great deal of gender-role socialization occurs in the home (Huston, 1983). Most parents dress baby girls and boys in different colors and treat them differently from the very beginning. Parents have been observed playing more roughly with boy infants than with girl infants when the babies are a mere three weeks old (Moss, 1967). As children grow, their toy preferences also reflect

the influence of gender-role expectations (see Figure 10.6). When kids are old enough to help with household chores, their assignments often depend on their sex. Girls may do laundry and dishes while boys mow the lawn and sweep the garage. Likewise, the leisure activities that children are encouraged to engage in often vary by sex. For instance, Johnny may be shipped off to baseball practice while Mary gets ballet lessons.

In light of these patterns, it is not surprising that parents' attitudes about gender roles have been shown to influence the gender roles acquired by their children (Repetti, 1984). For example, one study found that only parents with nontraditional views seemed to encourage their daughters to be independent (Brooks-Gunn, 1986).

Schools
Schools also make a major contribution to the socialization of gender roles (Busch-Rossnagel & Vance, 1982; Etaugh & Harlow, 1975). Traditionally, many grade-school reading books in the early years have painted stereotypic pictures of the characteristics of males and females. One survey of 134 grade-school readers found that boy-centered stories outnumbered girl-centered stories 5 to 2 (Women on Words and Images, 1972). Moreover, in these stories, boys got to display cleverness 131 times, while girls were clever only 33 times. Girls were shown doing domestic chores more than three times as often as boys.

Many high school and college textbooks have also suffered from sex bias. For instance, a study of high school history texts reported that only when books discussed a specific woman or a topic obviously related to women (women's suffrage, for example) was the coverage judged to be balanced and objective. On most issues, there was no mention of women's contributions or their concerns (Kirby & Julian, 1981).

Complaints about gender bias in textbooks have led many publishers to reduce or eliminate their stereotypic portrayals of females and males. However, there are many other ways in which schools contribute to gender-role

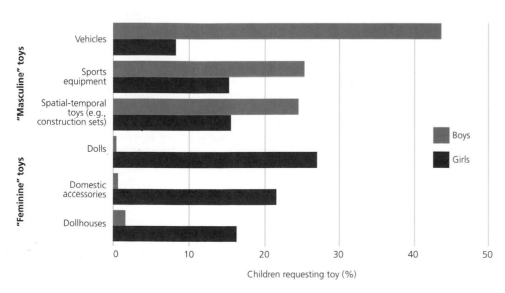

socialization. For one thing, most studies have shown that boys tend to get more attention from teachers than girls (Good, Sikes, & Brophy, 1973; Sadker & Sadker, 1985). Also, teachers seem to respond differently to specific behaviors of boys and girls. In one study of fourth- and fifth-graders, it was observed that teachers gave boys more positive feedback than girls for the intellectual quality of their work (Dweck, Davidson, Nelson, & Enna, 1978). The same study also found that teachers tended to attribute girls' failures to lack of ability while attributing boys' failures to lack of motivation.

As youngsters progress through the school system, they often are channeled in different directions based on their sex. Boys are encouraged to take science and mathematics, while girls are encouraged to take secretarial courses and home economics. In high schools, females continue to be underrepresented in math, physics, and chemistry courses (Linn & Hyde, 1989). Although it is less true than it used to be, many counselors still encourage male students to be physicians and engineers while guiding female students in the direction of nursing, teaching, and homemaking.

The Media

Television is yet another source of gender-role training (Morgan, 1982). Youngsters in the United States spend a lot of time watching TV—about 26 hours a week (Charren & Sandler, 1983). Television shows have traditionally depicted men and women in highly stereotypic ways (Basow, 1986). Women have typically been portrayed as loving mothers and dedicated homemakers, while men have been given dynamic, exciting roles as cool, competent leaders. When scriptwriters finally give a heroic role to a woman, they often have men come to her aid at the last minute. Even the commercials on TV contribute to gender-role socialization. Women are shown worrying about the ring around their husbands' collars, how shiny "their" dishes are, how white "their" laundry is, and how to use expensive cosmetics to "snare" a man.

Given these facts, it should come as no surprise that children who watch TV frequently have been found to hold more stereotyped beliefs about gender than children who watch less TV (McGhee & Frueh, 1980). In contrast, children who watch a great deal of educational TV tend to be less traditional about gender roles than other children (Repetti, 1984). This difference probably exists because many children's shows on educational TV systematically try to promote nontraditional gender roles. Thus, there appears to be a clear link between media content and the acquisition of gender roles.

CRITICISM OF TRADITIONAL GENDER ROLES

Stephanie is a bright and competent professional woman. She gets along well with others. Understandably, she wants her co-workers to see her as effective on the job. After all, she is not likely to win promotions or raises if others don't perceive her as capable. So, she works hard at impressing her colleagues. However, she notices that when she attempts to act like "one of the boys" (as the androcentric rules require for success), her behavior doesn't always have the positive effect she desires. She finds it especially annoying when she watches her male co-workers engage in the same behavior and have it pay off. Just the other day, she overheard one of them say, "John follows through and gets things done. But Stephanie is too aggressive. She doesn't know when to quit." What should she do? She senses that her current strategy is probably not going to earn her the promotion she wants. However, she knows that in her job adopting a more "feminine" style won't win her any points either.

Stephanie is caught in a double bind. In terms of acting "masculine," she is "damned if she does and damned if she doesn't." Her situation—which does not appear to be unusual—illustrates how conventional gender roles can be unnecessarily restrictive and prevent people from reaching their full potential.

Many psychologists believe that some unfortunate costs are associated with traditional gender roles, at least in our

modern society (for example, Bem, 1981; Lott, 1981). According to this perspective, traditional roles are too narrow. They constitute a kind of psychological strait-jacket, confining men and women alike. In this section, we'll discuss this viewpoint as we examine some problems that have been blamed on conventional gender roles.

Problems with the Female Role

Concerns about the limitations of women's roles have received the lion's share of attention. These concerns first became prominent with the advent of the feminist movement, which generated some compelling analyses of the problems associated with the traditional female role (for example, Friedan, 1964; Millett, 1970). Since then, research has shown that many of these concerns are justified. We'll discuss the problems of diminished aspirations, the "housewife syndrome," and ambivalence about sexuality.

Diminished Aspirations

Despite recent efforts to increase women's opportunities for achievement, young women continue to have lower aspirations than young men with comparable backgrounds and abilities. Higher intelligence and grades are generally associated with higher career aspirations, but this is less likely to hold true for girls than for boys (Danziger, 1983; Marini, 1978). Some obvious reasons for this finding arise from important differences between male and female gender roles. For one thing, there is some conflict between achievement and femininity built into the traditional female role. For instance, some women worry that they will be seen as unfeminine if they boldly strive for success (Horner, 1972).

There are other reasons why women experience more conflict about achievement than men. Traditionally, men are allowed to fill the roles of worker, spouse, and parent with relatively little competition among these roles. Males typically have major day-to-day responsibilities in only *one* role (worker), which is also a high-status role. Women, on the other hand, traditionally have day-to-day responsibilities as *both* spouse and parent. Furthermore, when women decide to work, they have major responsibilities in all *three* areas.

RECOMMENDED READING

Toward a New Psychology of Women

by Jean Baker Miller (Beacon Press, 1986)

Written by a well-known feminist psychiatrist and psychoanalyst, this book examines some of the effects of living in a sexist society on women (and men). Since Miller is a psychiatrist, it's not surprising that she focuses most of her attention on personality and its development. She explores the possibilities for positive changes in females' lives and personalities and how these changes might come about. The book was originally written in 1976; the 1986 edition reexamines the issues raised 10 years earlier, taking into account recent social changes and reflecting on the challenges still to be met.

> Anne had the great advantage of knowing at least what one of her important needs and desires was. Many psychological needs are much more difficult to grasp and define. One must have the chance to carry out this search in interaction with the world and the people in it. When women are not encouraged to undertake this pursuit, when they are in fact discouraged from doing so, they have much more difficulty learning about their needs and desires.
>
> There is, however, for women one seemingly easy way. One can divert oneself almost entirely from the difficult exploration of one's own needs and concentrate on serving others' needs. But when this happens, women often develop the belief—usually not explicitly articulated— that their own needs, even though unexamined, untested, and unexpressed, will somehow be fulfilled in return. To compound the situation, some women come to believe that others will love them (and become permanently devoted to them) because they are serving these others so much and so well. The tragedy here is that people do not usually love others for this reason. They may become dependent on their services, but that is different from real interest and love. In fact, if men and children become too dependent, they can come to feel trapped by their dependency and come to hate the person who is taking care of them so well. (This is one reason some men walk out on their super-wives and some children turn strongly against their super-mothers.) If women sense that they are not being loved, this reinforces their belief that others are concerned with them only because of the services they provide. They thus lose the sense that others are interested in them, in and of themselves, because of who they are. Although this is a terrible feeling, many women believe that they have to settle for it, especially after being married for some time. What alternatives have they had? [pp. 65–66]

Women typically select one of three lifestyle choices: marriage/family only, career only, or a combination of both. Each of these choices provides certain rewards, and each brings its own problems. Women who choose the traditional pattern may later regret not having been successful in a job. Women who opt for a career may feel some loss of status without a husband and children. Women who try to "have it all" will experience considerable conflict in meeting the often incompatible demands of multiple roles. If a woman is in an egalitarian marriage (one in which the husband assumes equal responsibility for child care and housework), combining a career and family becomes more feasible. Still, if a woman has a serious investment in her career, finding a supportive mate may be difficult. In trying to juggle these role incompatibilities, many women lower their aspirations or make unhappy compromises in ways that men can avoid.

The Housewife Syndrome

Women who don't work outside the home may experience a problem that Carol Tavris and Carole Wade (1984) have labeled the "housewife syndrome." The *housewife syndrome* refers to the frustration experienced by many (certainly not all) women whose sole identity is that of a housewife. There is evidence that full-time homemakers are less happy, more discouraged, and more self-doubting than single or married working women (Nickerson & Pitochelli, 1978). Furthermore, housewives tend to feel less in control of their environment than married career women do (Erdwins & Mellinger, 1984).

Why is staying at home hazardous to many women's health? Why isn't it beneficial to be out of the "rat race"? Two key aspects of the housewife role stand out as major contributing factors to the problem (Ferree, 1976). The first is the housewife's relative isolation from other supportive adults. Years ago, housewives were more likely to be part of a supportive social network consisting of other housewives and relatives living nearby. Today, in our more mobile society, fewer people live near their relatives or in close-knit neighborhoods. Also, there are fewer opportunities for companionship during the day because 56% of all wives work outside the home. Thus, many housewives spend their days in a social desert, yearning for adult conversation.

The second problem is the lack of status and recognition for child care and housework. "Women's work," especially that in the home, simply isn't highly valued (Porter, 1985). Because their work is taken for granted, housewives get relatively little overt appreciation. Moreover, child care and housework are tasks that are never really finished. Hence, it is difficult to experience a sense of accomplishment.

Ambivalence about Sexuality

Both women and men may have sexual problems that stem, in part, from their gender-role socialization. For many females, the problem is that they have difficulty enjoying sex. Why is this? Well, for one thing, rather than being encouraged to focus directly on getting sexual experience, as boys are, girls are encouraged to focus on romance (Simon & Gagnon, 1977). Also, compared to males, more females are brought up in ways that generate guilt, shame, and fears about sex. These negative emotions stem in part from the experience of menstruation (and its association with blood and pain) and fear of pregnancy. Females' concerns about sexual exploitation, rape, and incest can also contribute to the development of negative feelings about sex. Hence, many females approach sex with "emotional baggage" that men are less likely to carry. This means that many women are likely to have ambivalent feelings about sex instead of the largely positive feelings that most men have (Lott, 1987).

Problems with the Male Role

It is a common misconception that only women suffer from narrow gender roles. There are probably two reasons for this misconception. First, the negative aspects of traditional roles for women are more obvious than those associated with men's roles. Second, as we noted earlier, the women's movement stimulated concern about the costs of females' roles during the 1960s. Only more recently have similar concerns been raised about the costs of males' roles (Emerson, 1985; Fasteau, 1974; Goldberg, 1976; Pleck, 1981). We'll discuss males' difficulties with expectations regarding success, the expression of emotions, and sexuality.

Pressure to Succeed

Whereas many women are trained to be inhibited about pursuing success outside the home, most men are socialized to believe that job success is everything. They are encouraged to be highly competitive and are taught that a man's masculinity is measured by the size of his paycheck (Doyle, 1989; Gould, 1976). Small wonder, then, that so many men pursue success with a fervor that is sometimes dangerous to their health. The extent of this danger is illustrated by males' life expectancy, which is about eight years shorter than females' (of course, factors besides gender roles contribute to this difference).

RECOMMENDED READING

The Male Experience

by James A. Doyle (William C. Brown, 1989)

In this highly readable book, Doyle first provides a broad overview of the male experience from a variety of perspectives: historical, biological, anthropological, sociological, and psychological. Then he singles out three elements of the male role for examination: the antifeminine element, the sexual element, and the self-reliant element. There are also chapters on homosexuality and the role of power in male-female relationships. Finally, he looks at the question of whether real changes in traditional gender roles are possible in the near future. Doyle's book is well-researched, well-reasoned, and thought-provoking.

> The first and possibly the strongest element in the entire fabric of the male sex role is a negative or prohibitive injunction that states in its most basic form, "Boys, whatever you do, don't be like or do anything like a girl." Even before boys learn the other major lessons of their sex role, they are taught to avoid anything that even vaguely smacks of femininity.
>
> If the first lesson on the male sex role contained a simple statement to the effect that boys are different from girls by virtue that boys cannot do some things that girls can do (for example, "Johnny, when you grow up you can't have a baby; only girls like Mommy and your sister can have babies") that would be all right. But this first lesson does not end with a simple explanation of basic biological differences and some elementary sex education. No, it goes on to demean females. The first lesson of "don't be like a girl" is followed by several misogynist (hatred of women) postscripts. The first lesson goes something like this: "Don't be like a girl because . . . well, girls are bad, stupid, inferior, subordinate, and . . . well, girls are just plain icky! [p. 149]

The majority of men who have internalized this success ethic are unable to realize their dreams. How does this "failure" affect them? While many are able to adjust to it, many are not. The latter group is likely to suffer from poor self-esteem and a diminished sense of virility (Doyle, 1989). Males' obsession with success also creates problems for females. For instance, it contributes to economic discrimination against women. Many men want to "keep women in their place" because their self-esteem is threatened when a woman earns more than they do (Blumstein & Schwartz, 1983; Rubin, 1983). Men's emphasis on success also makes it more likely that they will spend long hours on the job, leaving them fewer hours to spend at home. This decreases the amount of time couples can spend together and increases the amount of time wives spend on housework and child care.

The Inexpressive Male

Most young boys are trained to believe that men should be strong, tough, cool, and detached. Males are socialized in a way that leads many of them to work overtime hiding their feelings. Public displays of tender emotions are especially taboo. A number of years ago, a presidential candidate, Edmund Muskie, made the mistake of shedding a few tears on the campaign trail. That incident—so antagonistic to the American male ideal—destroyed his campaign with an abruptness that was startling.

As noted earlier, there is little evidence that men are truly less emotional than women. The difference is that many men cover up their emotions. This is unfortunate on two counts. First, it makes it difficult for males to express feelings of affection for their loved ones. Many men can barely stutter through "I love you." Second, as we saw in Chapter 3, there are some risks inherent in bottling up emotions. Suppressed emotions contribute to many stress-related disorders.

Sexual Problems

Like women, men may experience sexual problems that derive partly from their gender-role socialization. For men, the problem is that they have a "macho" sexual image to live up to. Thus, there are few things that most men fear more than a sexual encounter in which they are unable to achieve an erection (Doyle, 1989). Unfortunately, these very fears often *cause* the impotence that men dread (see Chapter 13). The upshot is that males' obsession with sexual performance often produces anxiety that may interfere with their sexual responsiveness.

A related problem is the phenomenon of homophobia (Lehne, 1976). *Homophobia* **involves intense fear, hatred, and intolerance of homosexuality.** It manifests itself in abhorrence of any behavior that has homosexual overtones. For example, men have more difficulty touching each other in routine social interactions than women do. Homophobia is much more common in men than in women because there is more pressure on males to avoid any behavior characteristic of the other sex. Although they will tolerate "tomboyism" in girls, parents (especially fathers) are highly intolerant of any "sissy"

behavior exhibited by their sons. Unfortunately, males' homophobia leads to unnecessary derogation of homosexuals.

Sexism: A Special Problem for Women

Intimately intertwined with the topic of gender roles is the issue of sexism. *Sexism* **is discrimination against people on the basis of their sex.** Generally, the term is used to describe discrimination by men against women. However, it should be pointed out that sometimes *women* discriminate against other women. Also, *men* are occasionally the victims of sex-based discrimination.

In the broadest sense of the term, we have been discussing sexism throughout this chapter, in that we have talked extensively about how men and women are treated differently on the basis of their sex. In this section, we will focus on two specific issues: (1) economic discrimination against women and (2) the relegation of child care

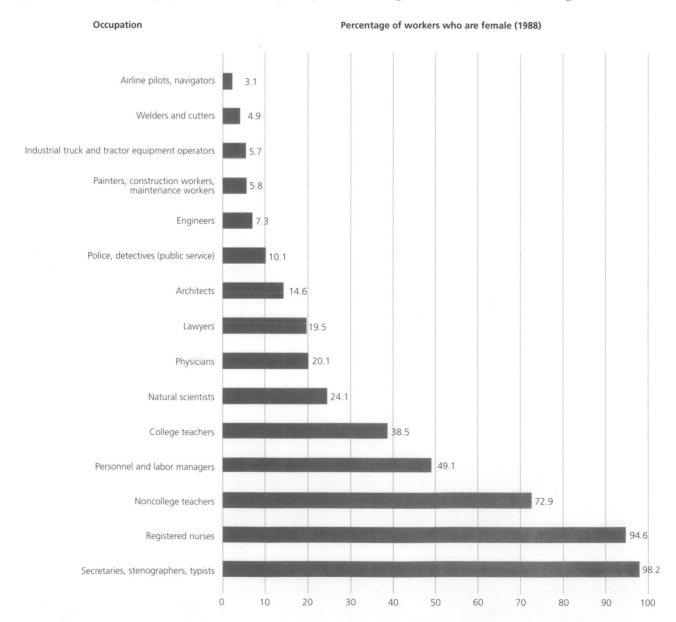

Occupation

Percentage of workers who are female (1988)

Occupation	Percentage
Airline pilots, navigators	3.1
Welders and cutters	4.9
Industrial truck and tractor equipment operators	5.7
Painters, construction workers, maintenance workers	5.8
Engineers	7.3
Police, detectives (public service)	10.1
Architects	14.6
Lawyers	19.5
Physicians	20.1
Natural scientists	24.1
College teachers	38.5
Personnel and labor managers	49.1
Noncollege teachers	72.9
Registered nurses	94.6
Secretaries, stenographers, typists	98.2

and housework to women even when they work full-time outside the home.

Let's consider the problem of economic discrimination first. Statistics show that more and more women are working. Yet, even as more women enter the work force, they continue to be the victims of discrimination. There are two aspects to this problem: (1) differential *access* to jobs and (2) differential *treatment* once on the job (Levitin, Quinn, & Staines, 1971).

With regard to *job access*, the problem is that women still don't have the same employment opportunities as men. For example, 40% of all employed women work in just ten traditionally female fields. Among these "pink ghetto" occupations are secretarial work, nursing, and preschool and kindergarten teaching (see Figure 10.7). Furthermore, such "women's" jobs are lower in status and in pay than "men's" jobs (Lemkau, 1979).

In one study of sex and job access, heads of psychology departments across the United States were asked to assess the quality of job applicants based on what were really fake résumés (Fidell, 1970). The only thing that varied on the résumés was the sex of the applicant (male or female names were substituted on the same résumés). Even though they had identical résumés, female applicants received lower ratings than the male applicants! A more recent study (Glick, Zion, & Nelson, 1988) confirms that sex bias in job access is still a problem. Women *are* gradually breaking into higher-status, male-dominated fields, but only very slowly (refer to Figure 10.7).

The second aspect of economic discrimination involves women being *treated differently at work*. One example of differential treatment of the sexes is salary. Women are usually paid less than men for the same work. For example, in 1985, the average woman earned 65 cents for every dollar earned by the average man in a comparable occupation. The size of this pay gap varies from one occupational area to another. However, the gap remains even when women break into higher-status occupations. For instance, female attorneys earn only 75 cents for every dollar earned by male attorneys (National Commission

on Working Women, 1983). Indeed, the average woman with five or more years of college education earns only slightly more than the average man with one to three years of high school (Mellor, 1984).

Another consequence of sexism is that women still do most of the child care and housework even when they work. You might expect that working women would be relieved of part of their responsibilities on the home front. Although men *are* spending more time on child rearing and household chores (Model, 1982; Robinson, 1980), the changes seem to be occurring very slowly. For example, one study reported that the typical American husband spends about 13 hours a week on household and child-care responsibilities whether or not his wife works (Pleck, 1983). In contrast, the typical employed wife spends 28 hours a week on these tasks (the unemployed wife spends 47 hours a week). This pattern holds true regardless of the wife's type of employment. For example, one study of married, full-time, practicing physicians found that female physicians spent more than twice as much time on domestic tasks as male physicians (Pyke & Kahill, 1983).

In summary, although there are costs associated with traditional sex roles for *both* sexes, sexism is a special and significant problem for women. In addition, when prejudice and discrimination prevent talented individuals from making contributions from which all could benefit, society as a whole suffers.

GENDER IN THE PAST AND FUTURE

Up until now, we have focused largely on *traditional* gender roles and some of the difficulties they tend to generate. In Western society, however, gender roles are in a state of transition (Dambrot, Papp, & Whitmore, 1984; Weeks & Gage, 1984). Sweeping changes have already occurred. It's hard to imagine today, but less than 100 years ago, women were not allowed to vote or manage their own finances. Only a few decades ago, it was virtually

Figure 10.7. Women in the world of work. The percentage of women who work outside the home has been increasing steadily over the past century. Nonetheless, women remain underrepresented in many traditionally masculine occupations and overrepresented in many traditionally feminine occupations. (Data from U.S. Department of Labor, *Handbook of Labor Statistics*, 1989)

unheard of for women to initiate dates, run corporations, or practice medicine. In this section, we'll discuss *why* gender roles are changing and what the future might hold.

Why Are Gender Roles Changing?

Many people are baffled about why gender roles are changing. They can't understand why age-old traditions are being flouted and discarded. There are a number of theories about why gender roles are in transition. Basically, they look at the past in order to explain the present and the future. A key consideration is that gender roles have always constituted a division of labor. In earlier, more "primitive" societies, the division of labor according to sex was a natural outgrowth of some simple realities. In most hunting-and-gathering societies, as well as most agricultural societies, an economic premium was put on *physical strength.* Generally, men tend to be stronger physically than women. Hence, men were better equipped to handle such jobs as hunting and farming. In most societies they got those assignments while the women were responsible for gathering, home maintenance, and child rearing (Nielsen, 1978). Another consideration was that women had to assume responsibility for nursing young children, since there were no baby bottles. In summary, although people might have worked out other ways of doing things (and some cultures did), there were some basic reasons for dividing labor according to sex in premodern societies.

Essentially, our traditional gender roles today are a carryover from our past. Once traditions are established, they have a way of perpetuating themselves. Moreover, males have had a vested interest in maintaining these traditions, since the arrangements made them something of a privileged class.

During the last century or so in Western society, these divisions of labor have become increasingly antiquated. Therein lies the prime reason for changes in gender roles, according to many theorists (Holter, 1975). *Tradi-*

A division of labor based on gender no longer makes economic sense in our society. Relatively few jobs require great physical strength; the rest call for skills possessed by both men and women.

tional gender roles no longer make economic sense! In our mechanized, industrial economy, physical strength has become less and less important in jobs. Moreover, as we move toward a service economy, physical strength will become even less relevant. Thus, the principal cause of shifts in gender roles appears to be economic change that has rendered the distinctions between these roles obsolete.

The future is likely to bring even more dramatic changes in gender roles. We can see the beginnings of some of these changes now. For example, although women still bear children, nursing responsibilities are now optional. Moreover, as women become more economically independent, they will have less need to get married for economic reasons. As artificial insemination becomes more common, more women may choose to be single parents. The possibility of developing a fetus outside the uterus may seem farfetched now, but some experts predict that it is only a matter of time. If so, this might mean that both men and women can choose to be "mothers"!

Traditional gender roles used to be taken for granted. They were considered a "God-given" fact of life. However, as we have seen, what appear to be obvious behaviorial differences between the sexes are often found to be stereotypes instead. Furthermore, the gender differences that do exist are most easily explained in terms of differences in socialization. Consequently, we have become more aware of the social and political bases for gender roles. This awareness has focused attention and public debate on the prejudices that underlie unequal treat-

ment of females (and, sometimes, males). This attention seems likely to add momentum to the movement toward nontraditional gender roles. It is safe to conclude that gender roles will remain in flux for some time to come.

Alternatives to Traditional Gender Roles

As people have become aware of the costs of traditional gender roles, there has been a lot of debate about moving beyond them. A big question in these discussions has been *what should we move toward?* To date, two ideas have received the most attention: (1) androgyny and (2) gender-role transcendence. Let's examine these concepts.

Androgyny

Androgyny is one type of gender-role identity. **Androgyny refers to the coexistence of both masculine and feminine personality traits in an individual.** In other words, an androgynous person is one who scores above average on measures of *both* masculinity and femininity.

To fully appreciate the nature of androgyny, we need to briefly review other kinds of gender identity (see Figure 10.8). As we noted earlier, males who score high on masculinity and low on femininity, and females who score high on femininity and low on masculinity, are said to be *sex-typed*. Males who score high on femininity but low on masculinity, and females who score high on masculinity but low on femininity, are said to be *cross-sex-typed*. Finally, males and females who score low on both masculinity and femininity are characterized as *sex-role undifferentiated*.

Keep in mind that we are referring here to behaviors traditionally associated with each sex. People sometimes confuse this kind of gender identity with sexual orientation. These are not the same thing. **Sexual orientation refers to a person's preference for a same-sex or other-sex partner in sexual relationships.** One can be homosexual, heterosexual, or bisexual (sexual preferences) and be androgynous, sex-typed, cross-sex-typed, or sex-role undifferentiated (gender-role identities).

It used to be assumed that males who scored high in masculinity and females who scored high in femininity were better adjusted than "masculine" women and "feminine" men. Sandra Bem (1975) challenged this prevailing view. She advanced the idea that androgynous people tend to be psychologically healthier than those who exhibit conventional sex-typing. She argued that traditionally masculine men and feminine women feel compelled to adhere to rigid and narrow gender roles that unnecessarily restrict their behavior. In contrast, androgynous individuals ought to be able to function more flexibly, and such flexibility should be adaptive. Finally, she suggested that parents should rear their children to be androgynous instead of sex-typed.

What about Bem's ideas? Are androgynous individuals psychologically healthier than people who are sex-typed? Since 1976, over a hundred studies have been conducted to answer this question (Bem, 1985; Cook, 1985). Some early studies *did* find a positive correlation between androgyny and mental health. Ultimately, however, the weight of the evidence did not support Bem's hypothesis that androgyny is especially healthy (Locksley & Colten, 1979; Pedhazur & Tetenbaum, 1979; Taylor & Hall, 1982). In fact, a comprehensive survey of the research reported that masculine traits (in either sex) were more strongly associated with psychological health than androgyny (Taylor & Hall, 1982).

These findings, as well as some problems with the concept of androgyny, have led Bem and other psychologists to take a different view of gender roles. We'll consider this new perspective next.

Gender-Role Transcendence

Some conceptual problems with androgyny caused theorists in this area to rethink their views. So that you can see the evolution of their ideas, we'll discuss several of these problems. One problem is that androgyny requires people to develop both masculine and feminine characteristics, rather than one or the other. While it can be argued that androgyny is less restrictive than traditional gender roles, it may also lead people to feel that they have two sources

Femininity score

Masculinity score

	High	Low
High	Androgynous	Masculine sex-typed (if male) or cross-sex-typed (if female)
Low	Feminine sex-typed (if female) or cross-sex-typed (if male)	Undifferentiated

Figure 10.8. Possible gender-role identities. This diagram summarizes the relations between subjects' scores on measures of masculinity and femininity and four possible gender identities.

of inadequacy to contend with, as opposed to only one (Bem, 1983).

Furthermore, the idea that people should have both masculine and feminine traits reinforces the assumption that gender is an integral part of human behavior (Bem, 1983; Lott, 1981). In other words, the androgyny perspective presupposes that masculine and feminine traits actually exist within us. However, many theorists maintain that masculinity and femininity are really only arbitrary labels that we have learned to impose on certain traits.

This assertion is the foundation for the *gender-role transcendence* perspective (Bem, 1983; Lott, 1981; Spence, 1983). This perspective suggests that to be fully human, we need to *transcend*, or go beyond, the restrictions of gender stereotypes and gender roles. This goal requires that we *not* simply divide human characteristics into masculine and feminine categories (and then combine them, as the androgyny perspective suggests). Rather, we should dispense with the artificially constructed gender categories and labels. Instead of the labels "masculine" and "feminine," we should use gender-neutral terms such as "instrumental" and "expressive" to describe personality traits and behaviors.

The advocates of gender-role transcendence argue that this practice would help us break our current habits of "projecting gender into situations irrelevant to genitalia" (Bem, 1985, p. 222) and hasten the advent of a gender-free society. They believe that if gender were eliminated (or even reduced) as a means of categorizing traits, each individual's unique capabilities and interests would assume greater importance. This would mean that individuals would be more free to develop their own unique potentials.

Although many social scientists find the concept of a gender-free society appealing, there are some who are concerned about the decline of traditional gender roles. For instance, Judith Bardwick (1973) has pointed out that the period of transition is apt to be quite stressful and that an egalitarian society might present some new problems. In a more polemical analysis, G. F. Gilder (1986) has argued that the demise of traditional gender roles could have disastrous consequences for our society. Gilder maintains that conventional gender roles provide a fundamental underpinning for our economic and social order. He asserts that changes in gender roles will damage intimate relationships between women and men and have a devastating impact on family life. Gilder argues that women are needed in the home in their traditional homemaker role to provide for the socialization of the next generation. Without this traditional socialization, Gilder predicts that our moral fabric will decay, leading to an increase in crime, violence, and drug abuse. Given these very different projections, it will prove most interesting to see what unfolds during the next few decades.

SUMMARY

There are many stereotypes about behavioral differences between the sexes. These stereotypes favor males, as our society is characterized by an androcentric bias.

Research generally does not support our stereotypes. While there are no gender differences in general intelligence, a few appear in specific cognitive abilities. Males appear to have a slight advantage in mathematical and visual-spatial ability, while women score higher in verbal ability. With regard to personality traits, research does not support the stereotypes of gender differences in emotionality, nurturance, or empathy. In the area of social behavior, more differences appear. For example, males do appear to be more aggressive and more assertive than females. Females seem to conform to group pressure a little more than males. Concerning sensitivity to nonverbal communication, women appear to have the advantage. The sexes are similar in overall mental health, but they differ in prevalence rates for specific psychological disorders. For a variety of reasons, more women than men receive psychotherapy. All in all, the gender differences that do exist are quite small. Moreover, they are group differences that tell us little about individuals.

Sandra Bem

Biological explanations of gender differences have focused on brain organization and hormonal influences. Some studies suggest that males exhibit more cerebral specialization than females. However, efforts to link this finding to gender differences in cognitive abilities are highly speculative. Efforts to link hormone levels to gender differences have also been troubled by interpretive problems. Thus, most experts still believe that socialization is more important than biology in producing behavioral disparities between the sexes.

The socialization of gender roles appears to take place through the processes of (1) reinforcement and punishment, (2) observational learning, and (3) self-socialization. These processes operate through many different social institutions, but families, schools, and the media appear to be the three primary sources of gender-role socialization.

Many theorists believe that traditional gender roles unnecessarily restrict people's behavior. Among the principal costs for women are (1) diminished aspirations, (2) frustration associated with the housewife role, and (3) ambivalence about sexuality. For males, the principal costs involve (1) excessive pressure to succeed, (2) inability to express emotions, and (3) sexual difficulties. In addition to these psychological problems, women face sexist hurdles in the economic domain and on the home front.

Gender roles have always represented a division of labor. They are changing today, and they seem likely to continue changing because they no longer mesh with economic reality. Consequently, an important question is how we might move beyond traditional gender roles. The perspectives of androgyny and gender-role transcendence provide two possible answers to this question.

In the upcoming Application, we'll talk about how to pursue a more assertive lifestyle. Assertiveness training has proved particularly popular among women, but it can be beneficial to members of either sex.

Learning to Be Assertive

Answer the following questions yes or no.

☐ **1.** When someone says something that you consider foolish, do you have difficulty voicing disagreement?

☐ **2.** When a salesperson pressures you to buy something you don't want, do you have a hard time expressing your lack of interest?

☐ **3.** When someone asks you for an unreasonable favor, do you have difficulty saying no?

☐ **4.** Do you feel timid about returning flawed merchandise?

☐ **5.** Do you have a hard time requesting even small favors from others?

☐ **6.** When you're in a group that is hotly debating an issue, are you shy about speaking up?

If you answered yes to several of the questions above, you may have difficulty being assertive. Many people of both sexes have a hard time being assertive. However, this problem is more common among females because they are socialized to be more passive and submissive than males. Consequently, assertiveness training has become especially popular among women. Men, too, find assertiveness training helpful, both because some males have been socialized to be passive and because some men need to learn to be less aggressive and more assertive. For most people, then, it is important to understand the differences between assertive, submissive, and aggressive behavior. In this Application, we will elaborate on those differences and discuss some procedures for increasing assertiveness.

THE NATURE OF ASSERTIVENESS

As we noted earlier, *assertiveness* involves acting in your own best interests by expressing your thoughts and feelings directly and honestly (Alberti & Emmons, 1986; Lange & Jakubowski, 1976). Essentially, assertiveness involves standing up for your rights when someone else is about to infringe on them. To be assertive is to speak out openly rather than pull your punches.

The nature of assertive behavior can best be clarified by contrasting it with submissive behavior and aggressive behavior. *Submissive behavior* involves consistently giving in to others on points of possible contention. Submissive people tend to let others take advantage of them. Typically, their biggest problem is that they cannot say no to unreasonable requests. They also have difficulty voicing disagreement with others and making requests themselves. In traditional trait terminology, they are timid. Although the roots of submissiveness have not been investigated fully, they appear to lie in excessive concern about gaining the social approval of others. However, the strategy of "not making waves" is more likely to garner others' contempt than their approval (Jakubowski-Spector, 1973).

It is sometimes difficult to differentiate between assertive behavior and aggressive behavior. In principle, the distinction is fairly simple. *Aggressive behavior* involves an intention to hurt or harm another. Assertive behavior includes no such intention to inflict harm, but it does involve defending your rights. The problem in real life is that assertive and aggressive behavior *may* overlap. When someone is about to infringe on their rights, people often lash out at the other party (aggression) while defending their rights (assertion). The challenge, then, is to learn to be firm and assertive without going a step too far and becoming aggressive.

Advocates of assertive behavior argue that it is much more adaptive than either submissive or aggressive behavior (Dawley & Wenrich, 1976). They maintain that submissive behavior leads to poor self-esteem, self-denial, emotional suppression, and strained interpersonal relationships. They assert that aggressive behavior tends to promote guilt, alienation, and disharmony. In contrast, assertive behavior is said to foster high self-esteem and satisfactory interpersonal relationships.

Of course, behaving assertively does *not* ensure that you will always get what you want! The essential point with assertiveness is that you are able to state what you want clearly and directly. Being able to do so makes you feel good about yourself and will usually make others feel good about you too. But, while being assertive will probably enhance your chances for getting what you want, it certainly won't guarantee it.

STEPS IN ASSERTIVENESS TRAINING

Numerous assertiveness training programs are available in book form or through seminars. Some recommendations about books appear in the Recommended Readings box in this section. Most of the programs are behavioral in nature and emphasize gradual improvement and reinforcement of appropriate behavior. Here we will summarize the key steps in assertiveness training.

Clarify the Nature of Assertive Behavior

Most programs begin, as we already have, by clarifying the nature of assertive behavior. In order to produce assertive behavior, you need to understand what it looks and sounds like. One way to accomplish this is to imagine situations calling for assertiveness and compare hypothetical submissive, assertive, and aggressive responses.

Let's consider one such comparison. In this example, a woman in assertiveness training is asking her partner, who is functioning as a "downer," to help plan a garden (excerpted from Bower & Bower, 1976, pp. 8, 9, 11).

The Passive Scene
SHE: Uh, excuse me but I wonder if you would be willing to take the time to decide about the garden?
DOWNER: (looking at paper) Not now, I'm busy.
SHE: Oh, okay.

The Aggressive Scene
SHE: Listen, I'm sick and tired of you putting off deciding about this damn garden. Are you going to help?
DOWNER: (looking at paper) Not now, I'm busy.
SHE: Why can't you look at me when you're turning me down? You don't give a damn about the garden or the house or me. I have to do everything around here myself!

The Assertive Scene
SHE: It's spring and time to make plans for our garden.
DOWNER: (looking at paper) Oh, c'mon—not now! It's only April.
SHE: I feel that the garden is more enjoyable if we've planned it carefully together in advance.
DOWNER: I'm not sure I'm going to have the time for that.
SHE: I've already drawn up and budgeted two alternative plans—will you look at them? I'd like to get your decisions about them, say, tonight after supper.

For people to whom assertive behavior is unfamiliar, this process of clarifying the nature of assertiveness can be critical. In such cases, it may be a good idea to read two or three books on assertiveness to get a good picture of assertive behavior. The differences between the three types of behavior may best be conceptualized in terms of how people deal with their own rights and the rights of others. Passive people sacrifice their own rights. Aggressive people tend to ignore the rights of others. Assertive people consider both their own rights *and* the rights of others.

Monitor Your Assertive Behavior

Most people vary in assertiveness from one situation to another. In other words, they may be assertive in some social contexts and timid in others. Consequently, once you understand the nature of assertive behavior, you should monitor yourself and identify when you are nonassertive. In particular, you should figure out *who* intimidates you, on *what topics*, and in *which situations*.

Observe a Model's Assertive Behavior

Once you have identified the situations in which you are nonassertive, think of someone who behaves assertively in those situations and observe that person's behavior closely. In other words, find someone to model yourself after. They should help you to learn how to behave assertively in situations crucial to you. Your observations should also allow you to see how rewarding assertive behavior can be, which should strengthen your assertive tendencies.

Practice Assertive Behavior

Ultimately, the key to achieving assertive behavior is to practice it and work toward gradual improvement. Your practice can take several forms. In *covert rehearsal,* you can imagine a situation requiring assertion and the dialogue that you would engage in. In *role playing,* you might get a therapist or friend to play the role of an antagonist. Then you act out your new assertive behaviors in this artificial situation.

Eventually, of course, you want to transfer your assertiveness skills to real-life situations. Most experts recommend that you use *shaping* to increase your assertive behavior gradually. As we discussed in the Chapter 4 Application, shaping involves rewarding yourself for making closer and closer approximations of a desired behavior. For example, in the early stages of your behavior-change program, your goal might be to make at least one assertive comment every day, while toward the end you might be striving to make at least eight such comments every day. Obviously, in designing a shaping program, it is important to set realistic goals for yourself.

Adopt an Assertive Attitude

Most assertiveness training programs employ a behavioral orientation and focus on specific responses for specific situations. However, some experts have pointed out that real-life situations are only rarely just like those portrayed in books (Shoemaker & Satterfield, 1977). Hence, they maintain that acquiring a repertoire of verbal responses for certain situations is not as important as developing a new attitude that you're not going to let people push you around (or let yourself push others around, if you're the aggressive type). Although most programs don't talk explicitly about attitudes, they do appear to instill a new attitude indirectly. A change in attitude is probably crucial to achieving flexible, assertive behavior.

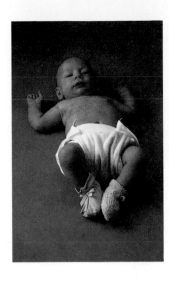

1. Explain the androcentric bias in gender stereotypes.

2. List three cognitive abilities on which males and females appear to differ.

3. Discuss gender differences in personality.

4. Summarize the evidence on gender differences in social behavior.

5. Discuss gender differences in mental health.

6. Discuss the size of gender differences and the nature of group differences.

7. Review the evidence relating gender differences in cognitive abilities to brain organization.

8. Review the evidence relating hormones to gender differences.

9. List and describe three processes in gender-role socialization.

10. Describe three sources of gender-role socialization.

11. Describe three common problems associated with traditional gender roles for women.

12. Describe three common problems associated with traditional gender roles for men.

13. Explain two ways in which women are victimized by sexism.

14. Explain why gender roles are currently in transition.

15. Describe the concepts of androgyny and gender-role transcendence.

16. Differentiate assertive behavior from passive and aggressive behavior.

17. Explain why assertive behavior is believed to be more adaptive than passive or aggressive behavior.

18. Describe five steps in increasing assertive behavior.

KEY TERMS

Aggression
Androgyny
Assertiveness
Cerebral hemispheres
Conformity
Empathy
Gender
Gender differences
Gender-role identity
Gender roles
Gender stereotypes

Homophobia
Hormones
Meta-analysis
Nurturance
Premenstrual syndrome
Sex
Sexism
Sexual orientation
Socialization

KEY PEOPLE

Sandra Bem
Alice Eagly
Janet Shibley Hyde
Margaret Mead
John Money

QUESTIONNAIRE

Self-Expression Scale

INSTRUCTIONS

The following inventory is designed to provide information about the way in which you express yourself. Please answer the questions by filling in the appropriate number from 0–4: Almost Always or Always, 0; Usually, 1; Sometimes, 2; Seldom, 3; Never or Rarely, 4. Your answer should reflect how you generally express yourself in the situation. If you find that the situation described is not presently applicable to you—for example, you do not have a roommate—answer it in terms of how you think you would be likely to react if you were in the situation. Please do not skip any questions.

THE SCALE

_____ 1. Do you ignore it when someone pushes in front of you in line?

_____ 2. When you decide that you no longer wish to date someone, do you have marked difficulty telling the person of your decision?

_____ 3. Would you exchange a purchase you discover to be faulty?

_____ 4. If you decided to change your major to a field which your parents will not approve, would you have difficulty telling them?

_____ 5. Are you inclined to be overapologetic?

_____ 6. If you were studying and if your roommate were making too much noise, would you ask him to stop?

_____ 7. Is it difficult for you to compliment and praise others?

_____ 8. If you are angry at your parents, can you tell them?

_____ 9. Do you insist that your roommate do his or her fair share of the cleaning?

_____ 10. If you find yourself becoming fond of someone you are dating, would you have difficulty expressing these feelings to that person?

_____ 11. If a friend who has borrowed $5.00 from you seems to have forgotten about it, would you remind this person?

_____ 12. Are you overly careful to avoid hurting other people's feelings?

_____ 13. If you have a close friend whom your parents dislike and constantly criticize, would you inform your parents that you disagree with them and tell them of your friend's assets?

_____ 14. Do you find it difficult to ask a friend to do a favor for you?

_____ 15. If food that is not to your satisfaction is served in a restaurant, would you complain about it to the waiter?

_____ 16. If your roommate without your permission eats food that he or she knows you have been saving, can you express your displeasure to your roommate?

_____ 17. If a salesperson has gone to considerable trouble to show you some merchandise which is not quite suitable, do you have difficulty saying no?

_____ 18. Do you keep your opinions to yourself?

_____ 19. If friends visit when you want to study, do you ask them to return at a more convenient time?

_____ 20. Are you able to express love and affection to people for whom you care?

_____ 21. If you were in a small seminar and the professor made a statement that you considered untrue, would you question it?

_____ 22. If a person of the opposite sex whom you have been wanting to meet smiles or directs attention to you at a party, would you take the initiative in beginning conversation?

_____ 23. If someone you respect expresses opinions with which you strongly disagree, would you venture to state your own point of view?

_____ 24. Do you go out of your way to avoid trouble with other people?

_____ 25. If a friend is wearing a new outfit that you like, do you tell that person so?

_____ 26. If after leaving a store you realize that you have been "shortchanged," do you go back and request the correct amount?

_____ 27. If a friend makes what you consider to be an unreasonable request, are you able to refuse?

_____ 28. If a close and respected relative were annoying you, would you hide your feelings rather than express your annoyance?

_____ 29. If your parents want you to come home for a weekend but you have made important plans, would you tell them of your preference?

_____ 30. Do you express anger or annoyance toward the opposite sex when it is justified?

_____ 31. If a friend does an errand for you, do you tell that person how much you appreciate it?

_____ 32. When a person is blatantly unfair, do you fail to say something about it to the person?

_____ 33. Do you avoid social contacts for fear of doing or saying the wrong thing?

_____ 34. If a friend betrays your confidence, would you hesitate to express annoyance to that person?

_____ 35. When a clerk in a store waits on someone who has come in after you, do you call the clerk's attention to the matter?

_____ 36. If you are particularly happy about someone's good fortune, can you express this to that person?

_____ 37. Would you be hesitant about asking a good friend to lend you a few dollars?

____38. If a person teases you to the point that it is no longer fun, do you have difficulty expressing your displeasure?

____39. If you arrive late for a meeting, would you rather stand than go to a front seat which could only be secured with a fair degree of conspicuousness?

____40. If your date calls on Saturday night 15 minutes before you are supposed to meet and says that she or he has to study for an important exam and cannot make it, would you express your annoyance?

____41. If someone keeps kicking the back of your chair in a movie, would you ask the person to stop?

____42. If someone interrupts you in the middle of an important conversation, do you request that the person wait until you have finished?

____43. Do you freely volunteer information or opinions in class discussions?

____44. Are you reluctant to speak to an attractive acquaintance of the opposite sex?

____45. If you lived in an apartment and the landlord failed to make certain necessary repairs after promising to do so, would you insist on it?

____46. If your parents want you home by a certain time which you feel is much too early and unreasonable, do you attempt to discuss or negotiate this with them?

____47. Do you find it difficult to stand up for your rights?

____48. If a friend unjustifiably criticizes you, do you express your resentment there and then?

____49. Do you express your feelings to others?

____50. Do you avoid asking questions in class for fear of feeling self-conscious?

SCORING THE SCALE

In order to score this scale, you must reverse the numbers you entered for 29 of the items. The items to be reversed are as follows: 3, 6, 8, 9, 11, 13, 15, 16, 19, 20, 21, 22, 23, 25, 26, 27, 29, 30, 31, 35, 36, 40, 41, 42, 43, 45, 46, 48, and 49.

For each of the 29 items just listed, make the following conversions: If you entered 0, change it to 4. If you entered 1, change it to 3. If you entered 2, leave it at 2. If you entered 3, change it to 1. If you entered 4, change it to 0.

Now add up the numbers for all 50 items, using the new numbers on the reversed items. This sum is your score on the College Self-Expression Scale. Enter it below.

MY SCORE _____

WHAT THE SCALE MEASURES

The College Self-Expression Scale (Galassi, Delo, Galassi, & Bastien,1974) is designed to measure assertiveness in college students. As we have discussed, assertiveness involves the degree to which people act in their own best interests by expressing their thoughts directly and honestly. Test-retest reliability over a two-week period is quite high (Galassi et al., 1974). Validity has been examined by correlating assertiveness scores with various scales from a widely used personality test called the Adjective Check List (Gough & Heilbrun, 1965). As predicted, assertiveness correlated positively with personality traits such as self-confidence, dominance, and autonomy while correlating negatively with traits such as abasement and deference (Galassi et al., 1974). Since it is important to distinguish between assertiveness and aggressiveness, the utility of the scale is enhanced by the fact that assertiveness scores do *not* correlate significantly with aggression scores on the Adjective Check List.

INTERPRETING YOUR SCORE

Our norms are based on a sizable sample, 1014 undergraduates at a major university. Although males scored a bit higher than females, the difference was not large enough to merit reporting separate norms by sex.

NORMS

Assertive Score: 146–200
Intermediate Score: 104–145
Nonassertive Score: 0–103

How Do You Feel about Gender Roles?

1. Can you recall any experiences that were particularly influential in shaping your attitudes about gender roles? If yes, give a couple of examples.

2. Have you ever engaged in cross-sex-typed behavior? Can you think of a couple of examples? How did people react?

3. Do you ever feel restricted by gender roles? If so, in what ways?

4. Have you ever been a victim of sex discrimination (sexism)? If so, describe the circumstances.

5. How do you think the transition in gender roles has affected you personally?

11
Development in Adolescence and Adulthood

"My mother always complains that I spend too much time on the telephone. She thinks that I'm just gossiping with my friends and feels that my time would be better spent studying. She can't seem to understand that my friends and I help each other through some pretty rough situations. She thinks that way because she doesn't believe that anything a teenager does besides homework is important. My Mom tells me to learn in school, but she doesn't realize that I'm actually trying to learn to survive school. Attending school is like a tryout for life. I know that it sounds silly to adults, but at times getting a date, being invited to a certain party, or being chosen to work on the school's newspaper can mean more than getting an A on a test."

—"Tracy," quoted in *Teenagers Talk about School* (Landau, 1988, p. 31)

Do Tracy's—or her mother's—complaints sound familiar? Have you ever been frustrated by your parents' or your child's inability to understand your point of view? Anyone who has participated in an adult-adolescent relationship is aware of differences between generations in attitudes, values, and social behavior. However, despite widespread publicity about the "generation gap," it is only since the 1970s that psychologists have given serious attention to development after adolescence. Until that time, it was widely assumed that developmental processes slowed to a crawl as people moved into adulthood. In recent years, however, social scientists have begun to realize that important developmental changes continue throughout adult life. They have started probing into these changes to identify crucial patterns and trends. In this chapter, we will examine some of the major developmental trends of adolescence and adulthood. We will also discuss some of the theories that attempt to explain these age-related changes.

KEY DEVELOPMENTAL CONCEPTS

The social scientists who study human development employ a variety of special concepts in their work. We need to examine some of these concepts before we begin to trace the patterns of development in adolescence and adulthood.

Development and Aging

Development **refers to the sequence of age-related changes that occur as a person progresses from conception to death.** Development is a reasonably orderly, cumulative process. It includes both the biological and the behavioral changes that take place as we grow older. An infant's newfound ability to grasp objects, a child's gradual mastery of grammar, and an adolescent's spurt in physical growth all represent development. So, too, do a young adult's increasing commitment to a vocation or a middle-aged person's struggle with a midlife crisis. All these transitions are predictable changes that are related to age.

There are many aspects to the process of human

development. We can focus on physical development, cognitive development, social development, and personality development, to name just a few key areas. The pacing of development in these different areas may be highly variable. Periods of rapid development may alternate with periods of stability called "plateaus." Further, during a particular time, development in one area (say, social relations) might be very rapid, while development in another area (say, cognitive abilities) might be very slow. Thus, development does not proceed at a constant pace or at the same rate across different areas.

While there are many common abilities in the ways individuals experience development, there are also differences across groups and individuals. Some developmental trends are universal across cultures and across historical periods. However, other trends may be unique to a particular culture or age cohort. **An *age cohort* is a group of people born in the same time period who develop in the same historical context**. People who belong to different age cohorts may be exposed to very different cultural experiences and expectations. For example, teenagers in the 1950s grew up in a different world than teenagers in the 1990s.

Although development is related to age, it is not the same as aging. *Aging* **refers to the biological process of growing older**. Aging is an inevitable, inexorable aspect of development. It takes place every minute of every day. It may or may not be accompanied by other developmental changes during a particular period. For instance, an individual's personality development might be negligible during a particular time, even though aging continues. Aging in the later years is the focus of *gerontology,* **a multidisciplinary field concerned with the study of old age and the elderly**.

Stages of Development

Most theories of development are stage theories. Such theories propose that people evolve through a series of stages in a predictable, orderly sequence. **A *stage* is a developmental period during which a person exhibits certain characteristic patterns of behavior and acquires specific capacities**. Stage theories focus on the *universals* in the developmental process across individuals and the *discontinuities* between the stages each individual experiences. We encountered an example of a stage theory in Chapter 2, when we discussed Sigmund Freud's notions about psychosexual development.

Stage theories are built on certain assumptions. First, they assume that people must progress through stages in a particular order because each stage builds on the previous stage. Second, they assume that progress through this orderly sequence is strongly related to age. In other words, they assume that we all go through the same stages at the same ages. Third, they assume that transitions from one stage to another involve fundamental changes or discontinuities in behavior.

There is considerable evidence that human developmental patterns often do *not* coincide with these assumptions (T. O. Blank, 1982; Troll, 1985). For instance, at any given time people often display a "mixed bag" of behaviors that are characteristic of several stages of development. This blending of stages violates the third assumption, that there are fundamental discontinuities between stages. The main problem with stage theories is that they don't account adequately for the *individual differences* that exist among people. Everyone does *not* develop in the same way or at the same pace. Troll (1982, 1985) reviews how various factors such as gender, social class, ethnic background, and personal experience promote variability in development. Thus, chronological age is only modestly related to developmental events in adolescence and adulthood.

These issues take on considerable importance in present-day society. Traditional barriers between childhood, adolescence, and adulthood may be breaking down. Today's children may be more knowledgeable than adults about such topics as drugs and computers. Some 16-year-olds are economically self-supporting, while some 30-year-olds remain financially dependent on their parents.

Members of the same age cohort tend to share similar cultural experiences and can perhaps relate better to one another than to people from an older or younger age cohort. This social group, for example, appears to be made up of men of about the same age.

Age ranges for specific life events are becoming increasingly wide (Neugarten & Neugarten, 1986). For instance, increasing numbers of first-time mothers may be found among 16-year-olds and also among 40-year-olds. College freshmen may be 18 or 60. Adults of all ages may be experiencing first marriage, remarriage, new parenthood, or career changes. In short, age distinctions are blurring. Traditional stage theories may lose validity as developmental patterns become more variable.

Although stage theories have their problems, most influential theories of human development continue to use the concept of stages. Stage theories do provide worthwhile descriptions of certain consistencies in human development. These descriptions can aid us in achieving a better understanding of the challenges we confront throughout life. However, when we describe various stage theories later in the chapter, you should bear in mind that *development is probably not as orderly, uniform, and predictable as these theories imply.* They are a bit too tidy to reflect the immense complexities of reality.

Age Roles and Social Clocks

You may recall that a *role* involves a pattern of behavior expected of a person in a particular social position. *Age roles* **are expectations about appropriate behavior that are based on one's chronological age.** The frequently used expression "They should act their age" captures the essence of age roles. Our society has widely accepted norms about how someone of a particular age should act, think, dress, and so forth. For instance, it is age roles that make it easy for someone in her 20s to live with mom and dad without attracting negative comment, while someone in her 30s will be criticized more frequently.

Like the gender roles discussed in Chapter 10, age roles often place *constraints* on people that prevent them from behaving in certain ways. Thus, some people decide they are too old to go back to school, too young to start their own business, or too feeble to take care of themselves. Often these limitations are self-imposed simply because a person accepts traditional age roles. Constraints may also be imposed *by others* who discriminate against people because of their age. *Ageism* **refers to discrimination against people on the basis of their age.** Such discrimination usually occurs when people are perceived as being too old, but occasionally people are treated unfairly because they are seen as too young. Like other forms of discrimination (such as sexism and racism), ageism often leads to economic subjugation.

Closely related to age roles is the concept of a social clock. **A** *social clock* **is a person's notion of a developmental schedule that specifies what the person should have accomplished by certain points in life.** For example, if you feel that you should be married by the time you're 30, that belief creates a marker on your social clock. While we each have our own individual social clocks, they are very much a product of our socialization. The members of a given age cohort tend to have similar social clocks (Helson, Mitchell, & Moane, 1984).

Social clocks can exert considerable influence over decisions concerning education, career moves, marriage, parenting, and other life choices. Social clocks also provide a basis for self-assessment. As people progress through adolescence and adulthood, they periodically ask themselves, "How am I doing for my age?" Adherence to a social clock based on prevalent age norms brings social approval and thus a way to evaluate one's own development. Social clocks may also influence the stressfulness of various life changes. Important events or transitions in life that come too early or too late according to one's social clock produce more stress than transitions that occur "on time" (Hogan, 1978). Indeed, it is easy to imagine how an early marriage, delayed career promotion, or premature retirement might be especially stressful. In particular, it appears that lagging behind one's personal schedule in regard to certain achievements produces chronic frustration and reduced self-esteem (Helson et al., 1984). Thus, many of us pay great heed to social clocks ticking in the background as we proceed through adolescence and adulthood.

Figure 11.1. Physical development at puberty. Hormonal changes during puberty lead not only to a growth spurt but also to the development of secondary sexual characteristics. The pituitary gland sends signals to the adrenal glands and gonads (ovaries and testes), which secrete hormones responsible for various physical changes that differentiate males and females.

THE TRANSITION OF ADOLESCENCE

Adolescence is a transitional period between childhood and adulthood. Its age boundaries are not exact, but in our society adolescence begins around age 13 and ends at about age 22. During this life period, physically mature individuals retain a childlike role in society (Goldhaber, 1986).

A period of adolescence is *not* universal across cultures. In many cultures young people move directly from childhood to adulthood. The period of adolescence is seen primarily in industrialized nations. In these societies, rapid technological progress has made lengthy education, and therefore prolonged economic dependence, the norm. Thus, in our own culture, junior high school, high school, and college students often have a "marginal" status. They are capable of reproduction and so are physiologically mature. Yet they have not achieved the emotional and economic independence from their parents that are the hallmarks of adulthood. Let's begin our discussion of adolescent development with its most visible aspect: the physiological changes that transform the body of a child into that of an adult.

Puberty and the Growth Spurt

Puberty **is the period of early adolescence marked by rapid physical growth and the development of reproductive capacity.** Puberty is brought on by hormonal changes that lead to accelerated growth and *sexual dimorphism—*

sex differences in appearance and build. The highlights of sexual differentiation are outlined in Figure 11.1.

Early adolescents of both sexes experience sudden increases in height and weight. However, males and females differ in patterns of skeletal and muscular growth and in the distribution of body fat. Males experience greater skeletal and muscle growth in the upper torso, leading to broader shoulders and enhanced upper body strength. Females experience a widening of the pelvic bones plus increased fat deposits in this area, resulting in wider hips (Chumlea, 1982). In both sexes, growth of the different parts of the body is uneven, resulting in temporary clumsiness in many adolescents.

The attainment of reproductive capacity typically occurs about midway through the growth spurt for both sexes (Schuster, 1986). Reproductive capacity is typically marked in females by *menarche—***the first occurrence of menstruation.** The comparable marker in males is the first *nocturnal emission.* For both sexes, however, these landmark events are often followed by some months of continued sterility. Coinciding with the development of reproductive capacity is the appearance of the *secondary sex characteristics—***physical features that are associated with one's sex but that are not directly involved in reproduction.** These include breast development in the female, facial hair and a deepening voice in the male, and pubic hair in both sexes.

On the average, puberty arrives about two years earlier in girls than in boys. Indeed, the major reason that adult males are taller than adult females is that males typically

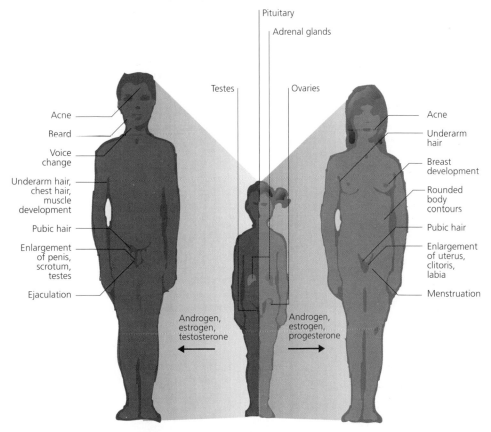

experience two additional years of prepuberty growth (Chumlea, 1982). Interestingly, there have been *generational* changes in the timing of puberty. Today's adolescents begin puberty earlier, and complete it more rapidly, than did their counterparts in ear-

lier generations. This trend apparently reflects improvements in nutrition and medical care.

Today, the average girl begins her growth spurt at about 11 years and experiences menarche at 12.7 years (Bullough, 1981). For boys, the onset of puberty is around age 13, with the first nocturnal emission occurring at about 14.5 years (Tanner, 1978). For both sexes, however, there is considerable individual variation. For instance, the "normal" age range for menarche is anywhere between 10 and 17 years (Bullough, 1981).

Although variation in the onset of puberty is normal, adolescents who mature unusually early or unusually late often feel uneasy about it. Puberty is a major transition requiring significant psychological adjustment. Those who perceive their development as "off time" may be particularly troubled. Girls who mature early and boys who mature late seem to feel especially awkward about their looks (Siegel, 1982). The early-maturing girl is taller and heavier than most of the girls and nearly all of the boys her age. The late-maturing boy is shorter and slighter than most of the boys and nearly all of the girls his age. To make matters worse, both groups have body types that are at odds with our cultural ideals of extreme slenderness for females and muscular physique for males. This disparity seems to be particularly upsetting for girls. Although adolescent girls in general wish to be thinner, early-maturing girls are especially dissatisfied with their body weight (Duke-Duncan et al., 1985). Thus, early-maturing girls and late-maturing boys may feel particularly anxious and self-consciousness about their changing bodies.

The consequences of maturing early or late may extend into adulthood. In one influential study, Mary Cover Jones (1965) found that males who matured late tended to display less leadership and have more feelings of inferiority than males who matured early—even after they reached their 30s. On a more positive note, the late-maturing males also tended to be more flexible, more perceptive about people, and more tolerant of ambiguity. In short, they were better able to cope with the complexities of adult life, perhaps because of the difficult adjustments they had to make in adolescence.

Cognitive Development

Cognitive development **refers to age-related transitions in patterns of thinking, including reasoning, remembering, and problem solving.** The investigation of cognitive development has been dominated in recent decades by the theory of Jean Piaget (1929, 1952, 1983), a Swiss scholar who devoted most of his life to the study of children's thinking.

Overview of Piaget's Theory

Piaget became interested in studying cognitive development while working with Theodore Simon, who had collaborated with Alfred Binet in devising the first useful intelligence test (Binet & Simon, 1905). In the process of administering IQ tests to many children, Piaget was intrigued to discover that children of the same age would often give similar *wrong* answers. This observation led

Jean Piaget

him to hypothesize that children of the same age think alike. According to Piaget, older children do not simply know *more* than younger ones. Rather, they use *different* reasoning processes as they actively attempt to make sense of the world around them. Eventually, Piaget proposed that children progress through four major stages, characterized by different ways of thinking, which are shown in Figure 11.2.

The First Three Stages during Childhood

The thought patterns of adolescence are built upon the accomplishments of earlier stages. Hence, we will begin our discussion by briefly describing the three stages of cognitive development during childhood.

The first stage lasts from birth to approximately age 2 and is called the *sensorimotor period*. During this stage, children progress from purely reflexive action to the beginnings of symbolic thought. The key to this transition is the young child's acquisition of the concept of object permanence. *Object permanence* **refers to the child's recognition that objects continue to exist even when they are no longer visible**. To a young infant, out of sight is literally out of mind. If you show an eye-catching toy to a 4-month-old child and then cover it with a pillow, the child will not attempt to search for the toy. The child does not realize that the toy continues to exist under the pillow. However, between the ages of 8 and 18 months, most babies gradually master object permanence as they become capable of picturing objects mentally. These mental images form the basis for symbolic thought.

During the *preoperational period*, which extends roughly from age 2 to age 7, children gradually improve in their use of mental images. In addition, they begin to use *words* as mental symbols, a feat that greatly expands their problem-solving capacity. Nonetheless, their thinking is still limited in important ways. For example, preoperational children are highly intuitive, relying on evidence from their senses to solve problems rather than using logical operations. They tend to focus on a single dimension of a problem while ignoring other relevant aspects.

Furthermore, preoperational children tend to be quite self-centered in their thinking. Piaget used the term *egocentrism* **to refer to this limited ability to share another person's point of view**.

Piaget asserted that these flaws in preoperational thinking account for the child's inability to grasp the concept of conservation. *Conservation* **is the awareness that physical quantities remain constant in spite of changes in their shape or appearance**. For instance, after seeing one of two identical balls of clay flattened into a pancake, most preoperational children will insist that the pancake now has more clay. They fail to understand that the amount of clay is conserved (remains the same) despite the change in shape.

Many of the weaknesses of preoperational thought are overcome during the *concrete operations period*. This stage usually lasts from about age 7 to age 11. During this stage, children gradually acquire the ability to solve problems logically rather than intuitively. They also learn to focus on more than one feature of a problem simultaneously and to mentally reverse, or "undo," an action. However, the child's new logical skills are typically restricted to *concrete* concepts. That is, the child can perform operations only on actual objects, or on mental images of actual objects. The ability to manipulate *abstract* concepts awaits the fourth and final stage, the stage of formal operations, to which we now turn.

Formal Operations Period

As children move into early adolescence, they gradually begin to apply the logical operations of the previous stage in a wider range of situations. In the *formal operations period*, youngsters' thinking is no longer constrained by physical reality or their personal experiences. Consider the following type of question that Piaget posed to children of various ages.

All Martians have blue hair.
I met a Martian today.
What color was his hair?

Plaget's Stages of Cognitive Development		
Approximate age range	**Stage**	**Major characteristics**
Birth to 2 years	Sensorimotor period	Coordination of sensory input and motor responses Development of object permanence Little or no capacity for symbolic representation
2 to 7 years	Preoperational period	Development of symbolic thought Irreversible, egocentric thinking
7 to 11 years	Concrete operations period	Mental operations applied to concrete objects and events Development of conservation, mastery of concept of reversibility
11 through adulthood	Formal operations period	Mental operations applied to abstractions Development of logical and systematic thinking

Figure 11.2. Overview of Piaget's stages. Piaget's theory of cognitive development identifies four stages through which youngsters evolve. The age norms and key characteristics of thought at each stage are summarized here.

Concrete operational children, having no experience of Martians, find this question silly and unanswerable. Most adolescents, however, recognize that these statements form a logical chain that demands the Martian's hair to be blue.

This ability to go beyond physical reality into the realm of hypothetical possibility is a hallmark of formal operational thought. Freed from the bounds of concrete reality, adolescents can now apply their logical skills to abstract concepts like love, justice, and truth. They may spend hours contemplating heady social and political issues that would never occur to a younger child.

Piaget viewed adolescents as "amateur scientists." Children in the concrete operations stage are action-oriented. They attack problems with a trial-and-error approach as they attempt to discover the underlying logic. In contrast, formal operational adolescents are thought-oriented. They conceive of the underlying logic first, and then set about testing their conceptions through experimentation. Piaget calls this kind of thinking *hypothetico-deductive reasoning*—**the ability to formulate specific hypotheses and test them systematically**.

Consider one of the problems devised by Piaget and his associate, Barbel Inhelder (Inhelder & Piaget, 1958). Children between the ages of 8 and 15 were given materials to construct a pendulum. Their task was to figure out which of four factors determine how fast the pendulum swings. They were told to consider the *weight* of the pendulum, the *height* from which it is released, the *length* of the string from which it dangles, and the *force* with which it is pushed. Most of the younger children simply tried various random combinations of the four factors. Those who had achieved formal operations, however, used a better approach. They began by generating all of the possible solutions. Then they systematically varied each factor while holding the others constant. Thus, they were able to eliminate hypothesized solutions one by one until only the correct one remained. In summary, formal operational thought is logical, abstract, reflective, and systematic.

Evaluating Piaget's Theory

In challenging the long-held assumption that children simply acquire increased knowledge with age, Piaget forced researchers to look at children's thinking in new ways. Piaget's theory has generated volumes of research, much of which supports his central propositions (Siegler, 1986). In such a far-reaching theory, though, there are bound to be a few weak spots.

In particular, Piaget's description of the formal operations period has been criticized on several grounds. There is some question regarding the universality of this stage. Many adults show little evidence of formal operational reasoning. Those who do reach formal operations generally do so at a later age than Piaget thought (Neimark, 1982). Piaget (1972) himself acknowledged this problem. While continuing to maintain that everyone achieves formal operations, he proposed that these reasoning skills might be demonstrated only in content areas for which an individual has particular aptitude or special training. For instance, an auto mechanic may evidence formal thought when diagnosing a car problem, but not when confronted with an unfamiliar physics problem. For many psychologists, however, this lack of generality of formal reasoning across content areas is damaging to the concept of formal operations as a distinct stage of development.

Other theorists have taken issue with Piaget's assertion that formal operational thought is the most mature form of reasoning (Basseches, 1984; Commons, Richards, & Kuhn, 1982). For example, Patricia Arlin (1975) views formal operations as a problem-solving stage that describes how individuals *answer* questions presented to them by others. She believes, however, that there are higher-level thinkers (like Piaget himself!) who have the ability to *ask* new questions. Arlin calls these exceptional thinkers "problem finders."

In spite of these criticisms, Piaget's work is a landmark achievement. Without his theory to stimulate and guide research, crucial questions about cognitive development might not have been confronted for decades.

Figure 11.3. Adolescent suicide. (a) The suicide rate for adolescents and young adults (ages 15–24) has increased in recent decades far more than the suicide rate for the population as a whole. (b) Nonetheless, the suicide rates for the 15–19 and 20–24 age groups remain lower than those for older adults. (Data from the National Center for Health Statistics)

Time of Turmoil? Adolescent Suicide

Is adolescence a period of disturbing emotional turmoil? G. Stanley Hall (1904), one of the first psychologists to study adolescence, thought so. Hall attributed this turmoil to adolescents' erratic physical changes and resultant confusion about self-image. Over the decades, a host of theorists have agreed with Hall's characterization of adolescence as a stormy period marked by emotional instability.

Recent years have seen a surge in *adolescent suicide,* a fact that would seem to support the idea that adolescence is a time of turmoil. However, the figures can be interpreted in different ways. On the one hand, suicide rates among adolescents *have* risen alarmingly in recent decades. This is apparent in Figure 11.3, which shows nearly a 140% increase in suicide among young people aged 15–24 between 1960 and 1982. On the other hand, even with this steep increase, the suicide rate for adolescents is low in comparison to the rates for older age groups. Figure 11.3 also plots suicide rates as a function of age. The figure reveals that the incidence of suicide in the 15–19 and 20–24 age groups is relatively low.

Actually, the suicide crisis among teenagers involves *attempted* suicide more than *completed* suicide. Experts estimate that when all age groups are lumped together, suicide attempts outnumber actual suicidal deaths by a ratio of about 8 to 1 (Cross & Hirschfeld, 1986). However, the ratio of attempted to completed suicides among adolescents may be 100 to 1 and possibly even higher—much higher than for any other age group (Sheras, 1983). According to David Curran (1987), suicide attempts by adolescents tend to be a "communicative gesture designed to elicit caring" (p. 12). To put it another way, they are desperate cries for attention, help, and support.

What drives an adolescent to such a dramatic but dangerous gesture? Research by Jacobs (1971) suggests that the "typical" suicidal adolescent has a long history of stress and personal problems extending back into childhood. Unfortunately, for some teenagers these problems—conflicts with parents, difficulties in school, loneliness—escalate during adolescence. As their efforts to cope with these problems fail, many teenagers rebel against parental authority, withdraw from social relations, and make dramatic gestures such as running away from home. These actions often lead to social isolation.

When an adolescent feels socially isolated, a pressing problem with great emotional impact may precipitate an attempted suicide. The precipitating problem—a lousy grade in school, not being allowed to go somewhere or buy something special—may appear trivial to an objective observer. But the seemingly trivial problem may serve as the final thread in a tapestry of frustration and distress.

Returning to our original question, does the evidence support the idea that adolescence is a period of emotional turbulence? Overall, the consensus of the experts appears to be *no.* The increase in adolescent suicide is a disturbing social tragedy that requires attention from parents, schools, and the helping professions (see the Chapter 15 Application for a discussion of suicide prevention). But even with the recent increases in suicidal behavior, fewer than 1% of adolescents attempt suicide.

What about the remaining 99% of the adolescent population? Research suggests that a majority of teenagers make it through adolescence without any more turmoil than one is likely to encounter in other periods of life. In one widely cited study of adolescent boys, a distinct minority (22%) went through a turbulent, crisis-dominated adolescence (Offer & Offer, 1975). Based on her extensive studies of adolescents, Anne Petersen (1987) concludes, "The adolescent's journey toward adulthood is inherently marked by change and upheaval but need not be fraught with chaos or deep pain" (p. 34).

Although turbulence and turmoil are not *universal* features of adolescence, this *is* a period during which challenging adaptations have to be made. In particular, most adolescents struggle to some extent in their effort to achieve a sound sense of identity.

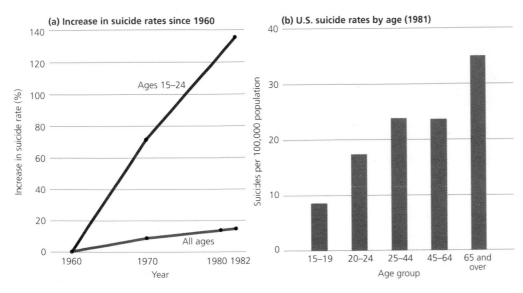

The Search for Identity

Erik Erikson (1963) has devised a theory of personality development that views adolescence as a period of pivotal importance. Building on earlier work by Sigmund Freud, Erikson partitioned the life span into eight stages. Each stage is assumed to bring a *psychosocial crisis* involving transitions in social relationships. According to Erikson, our personality is shaped by how we deal with these psychosocial crises.

Erikson viewed each crisis as a potential turning point that can yield different outcomes. He described the stages in terms of these alternative outcomes, which represent personality traits that people display over the remainder of their lives. All eight stages in Erikson's theory are charted in Figure 11.4.

Erikson was especially interested in personality development during adolescence, which is the fifth of the eight stages he describes. The psychosocial crisis during this stage pits *identity versus confusion* as potential outcomes. According to Erikson (1968), adolescents struggle with an "identity crisis." They work to establish a clear and stable sense of who they are, what they stand for, and how they fit into society. They look for an ideology, or system of values, that they can embrace as their own. They commit to a sexual orientation and to a vocational direction that expresses their newly articulated self-concept. As they formulate their identity, adolescents slowly achieve some psychological distance from their parents, becoming autonomous individuals with their own consciously chosen values and goals.

Although the struggle for a sense of identity neither begins nor ends in adolescence, it does tend to be especially intense during this period. Why? For many reasons. First, the physical changes of puberty force adolescents to revise their self-image and confront their sexuality. Second, the advent of formal operations promotes self-reflection. Third, faced with the end of mandatory schooling, adolescents must contemplate vocational directions and make decisions about their future.

Adolescents grapple with identity formation in a variety of ways. As we explained in Chapter 5, there are four types of identity status (Marcia, 1980), which represent different ways of dealing with one's identity crisis. *Foreclosure* involves a premature commitment to visions, values, and roles prescribed by one's parents. A *moratorium* involves delaying commitment for a while to experiment with alternative ideologies. *Identity diffusion* involves an unwillingness to confront the challenge of charting a life course and committing to an ideology. *Identity achievement* involves arriving at a sense of self and direction after some consideration of alternative possibilities. A sense of identity usually evolves gradually as a result of innumerable daily decisions: whether to date a particular person, take a particular course, use drugs, become sexually active, become politically involved, go to college, and so forth (Marcia, 1980).

Erikson and many other theorists believe that adequate identity formation is a cornerstone of sound psychological health. Identity confusion can interfere with important developmental transitions that should unfold during the adult years. In the remainder of the chapter, we will explore these transitions as we consider developmental trends across the expanse of adulthood.

PERSONALITY DEVELOPMENT IN ADULTHOOD

An article in the August 1989 issue of *Life* magazine featured "then-and-now" photographs and interviews of people who had attended the Woodstock Music Festival in 1969, an event that symbolized a youthful generation's rejection of the values of the majority culture. The interviews revealed that some of these music fans held on to the "counterculture" lifestyle of their youth. However, the vast majority went on to embrace the traditional values they had openly rejected two decades earlier. Is the "Woodstock generation" somehow unique in the extent of their personality change? How stable is personality over

Erikson's Stages of Psychosocial Development

Stages	Psychosocial crises	Significant social relationships	Favorable outcome
1. First year of life	Trust versus mistrust	Mother or mother substitute	Trust and optimisim
2. Second and third years	Autonomy versus doubt	Parents	A sense of self-control and adequacy
3. Fourth through sixth years	Initiative versus guilt	Basic family	Purpose and direction; ability to initiate one's own activities
4. Age 6 through puberty	Industry versus inferiority	Neighborhood; school	Competence in intellectual, social, and physical skills
5. Adolescence	Identity versus confusion	Peer groups and outgroups; models of leadership	An integrated image of oneself as a unique person
6. Early adulthood	Intimacy versus isolation	Partners in friendship and sex; competition, cooperation	An ability to form close and lasting relationships, to make career commitments
7. Middle adulthood	Generativity versus self-absorption	Divided labor, and shared household	Concern for family, society, and future generations
8. The aging years	Integrity versus despair	"Mankind"; "my kind"	A sense of fulfillment and satisfaction with one's life; willingness to face death

the life span? Are there discernible trends in the personality development of adults? Let's examine these questions.

The Stability Question

Does the shy 18-year-old become a shy 35-year-old and a shy 60-year-old? Psychologists have engaged in lively debate about whether personality remains stable in adulthood, and both sides have been able to cite supportive research.

On the one hand, a number of large-scale longitudinal studies provide evidence for long-term stability in personality (Finn, 1986; Stevens & Truss, 1985). Thus, Costa and McCrae (1986) note that the available evidence "points clearly to the conclusion that personality is generally stable in adulthood" (p. 407). On the other hand, some studies suggest that substantial personality changes continue to occur throughout the life span (Haan, Millsap, & Hartka, 1986; Helson & Moane, 1987). Based on their study that followed college-age women through their 40s, Helson and Moane (1987) conclude that "personality does change from youth to middle age in consistent and often predictable ways" (p. 185).

How can these seemingly incompatible conclusions be reconciled? Discrepant results from one study to the next may sometimes be due to incomparable subject samples, or to different data collection techniques. For instance, many of the studies utilize self-report measures, in which subjects rate their own personality characteristics. As Finn (1986) has pointed out, stability in self-report ratings may mean only that people's *views* of themselves remain stable over time, not that their actual personalities do.

Furthermore, certain aspects of personality seem to be more consistent than others. For instance, Conley (1985) found several traits that remain highly stable throughout adulthood. These include emotional stability, sociability, extraversion, assertiveness, responsibility, and dependability. Other traits appear to change systematically with age. Of these, perhaps the best documented is the tendency for people to become more androgynous. As we noted in Chapter 10, *androgyny* **refers to the coexistence of both masculine and feminine personality traits in an individual.** It seems that many males become more "feminine" and many females become more "masculine" as they grow older. In other words, people begin to discard the constraints imposed by traditional gender roles, with the result that men and women move toward greater similarity in personality.

In sum, adult personality is characterized by *both* stability and change. Although many aspects of personality are relatively stable over time, others are more likely to change.

Erikson's View of Adulthood

Insofar as personality changes, Erik Erikson's (1963) theory offers some clues about the nature of the changes we can expect. In his eight-stage model of development over the life span, the final three stages encompass adulthood. Like earlier stages, each adult stage is characterized by a psychosocial crisis that must be resolved.

Stage Six: Intimacy versus Isolation

During the sixth stage, encompassing young adulthood, the psychosocial crisis centers on whether a person can develop the capacity to share intimacy with others. Erikson is not concerned simply with the young adult's need to find a marriage partner. Rather, he is concerned with more subtle issues, such as whether one can learn to open up to others, truly commit to others, and give of oneself unselfishly. According to Erikson, these abilities depend on the individual's having successfully weathered the identity crisis of adolescence. The person who can experience genuine intimacy is thought to be more likely to develop a mature and successful marital relationship. Failure to resolve this psychosocial crisis favorably leads one to have difficulty relating to others in a genuine fashion. The resultant sense of isolation promotes manipulative relations with friends and troubled marriages.

A recent study found support for Erikson's hypotheses,

Figure 11.4. Overview of Erikson's stages. Erikson (1963) divides the life span into eight stages. Each stage involves a psychosocial crisis (column 2) that is played out in certain social relationships (column 3). If a crisis is handled effectively, a favorable outcome results (column 4).

Erik Erikson

with an interesting gender difference (Kahn, Zimmerman, Csikszentmihalyi, & Getzels, 1985). This study found that men who had not achieved a stable sense of identity tended to remain single. In contrast, women's likelihood of marrying was not affected by their identity status. However, women who lacked a strong sense of identity were more likely to experience marital breakups. Thus, rewarding intimate relationships appear to depend on whether the partners have first developed some sense of who they are as individuals.

Stage Seven: Generativity versus Stagnation

According to Erikson, developmental crises continue throughout adulthood. Next up, in middle adulthood, is the challenge of acquiring concern for the welfare of future generations, a concern Erikson called "generativity." Adults manifest generativity when they provide unselfish guidance to members of the next generation. The recipients of this guidance are often one's own children, but not necessarily. For a variety of reasons, some people bestow this altruistic direction on people other than their own offspring. For example, a 50-year-old female attorney might serve as a "mentor" for a younger woman in her law firm. Thus, generativity and its opposite, stagnation, do not hinge on whether one has children. Stagnation is characterized by self-absorption and self-indulgent preoccupation with satisfying one's own needs.

Stage Eight: Integrity versus Despair

In Erikson's last stage, during old age, the challenge is to achieve integrity, which involves finding meaning in one's life and looking back with a sense of satisfaction. Its opposite, despair, is the tendency to dwell on the mistakes of the past, bemoan paths not chosen, and bitterly contemplate one's imminent death. Rather than wallowing in regret and resentment, Erikson suggests that people should accept their fates in a dignified manner.

Erikson's theory paved the way for a flurry of research on phases of adult development in the 1970s. In the next section, we'll look at two newer theories that have also proven influential.

PHASES OF ADULT DEVELOPMENT: GOULD AND LEVINSON

Two independent studies of adult development attracted an enormous amount of attention during the 1970s. These two studies were summarized in a pair of widely read books: *Transformations,* by Roger Gould (1978), and *The Seasons of a Man's Life,* by Daniel Levinson and colleagues (1978). Both focused on the central years of adulthood, from the 20s through the 50s.

Gould (1972, 1978) based his model on case history and questionnaire data from two samples that included both men and women. Using this data base, Gould concluded that adult development could be broken into seven phases, which are summarized in Figure 11.5. *In each phase, the crucial issue is how the person wrestles with certain false assumptions about life that are left over from childhood.* For example, in Gould's first phase, young adults need to challenge and discard the assumption that "I'll always belong to my parents and believe in their world."

Levinson's theory was originally based on interviews with a small sample of male subjects (Levinson et al., 1974, 1978). More recently, Levinson and others have begun to apply his model to female subjects (Levinson, 1985, 1986; Roberts & Newton, 1987). Levinson has mapped out eight developmental phases in early and middle adulthood (refer to Figure 11.5). *He believes that phases of relative stability alternate with phases characterized by turmoil and transition.* In describing these phases, he traces changes in what he calls one's "life structure." A *life structure* encompasses the basic pattern or design of a person's life at a particular time, which is revealed through the choices the individual makes about marriage, career, child rearing, and so forth.

We will attempt to integrate Gould's and Levinson's

Figure 11.5. Overview of Gould's and Levinson's stages. Based on their research, Gould and Levinson arrived at different models of adult development. However, as this comparison shows, there are many similarities in their "ages and stages."

observations to provide an overview of adult development. Although their findings are not identical, their models are compatible. As you can see in Figure 11.5, the age ranges for their stages are often similar, and many congruent themes are apparent. Occasionally, we will mention the findings of other recent studies on adult development.

Leaving the Family and Becoming Independent (Early 20s)

Both Gould and Levinson emphasize that the key transition in the early 20s is the movement out from under the safe shelter of the family. This transition requires confronting insecurity about the future as the young adult attempts to establish independence. According to Gould, the false assumption that needs to be discarded is the idea that "I'll always belong to my parents and believe in their world." Levinson discusses how the young adult must scramble to achieve some financial independence while adapting to new roles, responsibilities, and living arrangements. Both theorists believe that this is a period characterized by considerable agitation and change.

According to Levinson, during this phase a young adult begins to shape a *Dream*—a vision of what she or he would like to become and accomplish as an adult. Initially, this Dream may be vague and unrealistic. Simplistic visions of becoming a baseball star, rising to the presidency, or finding a cure for cancer are common. Men's Dreams tend to center around occupational goals. Women are more likely to have "split Dreams" that include both career and family goals (Roberts & Newton, 1987). As young adults move through their 20s, they typically add definition, detail, and some realism to their vision of the future.

Entering the Adult World (Mid to Late 20s)

The remainder of the 20s is typically devoted to completing the transition into the adult world. This tends to be a relatively stable phase in comparison to the early 20s. Tentative decisions from the previous stage regarding marriage, family, and career are converted into deeper commitments that represent one's life structure.

The key conflict at this time centers on the contradictory urges to continue *exploring* various options and to make firm *commitments* to vocations, intimate relationships, and so forth. Thus, people in this phase find themselves struggling with doubts about whether they have committed themselves too quickly to an occupation or relationship, or delayed too long in making a decision. Gould emphasizes that the struggle to become fully independent of one's parents continues during this phase. Thus, young adults must work free of the false assumption "Doing things my parents' way, with willpower and perseverance, will bring results."

Levinson believes that a very special and important relationship is often formed during this phase. This is the

Two Stage Theories of Adult Development	
Gould's seven stages	**Levinson's eight stages**
1 Ages 16 to 18 People feel a strong desire to get away from parents, but autonomy is precarious	**1** Ages 17 to 22 Leave adolescence, make preliminary choices for adult life
2 Ages 18 to 22 Feel halfway out of family and worry about being reclaimed; peer group important ally in cutting family ties	**2** Ages 22 to 28 Initial choices in love, occupation, friendship, values, lifestyle
3 Ages 22 to 28 Feel established, autonomous, and separate from family; feel "now" is the time for living, growing, and building; peers still important, but self-reliance paramount	**3** Ages 28 to 33 Change in life structure; either a moderate change or, more often, a severe and stressful crisis
4 Ages 29 to 34 Begin to question what they are doing; feel weary of being what they are supposed to be, but continue	**4** Ages 33 to 40 Establish a niche in society, progress on a timetable, both in family and in career accomplishments
5 Ages 35 to 43 Feel that time seems to constrict for shaping the behavior of their adolescent children or "making it"; their own parents turn to them with muffled renewal of old conflicts	**5** Ages 40 to 45 Life structure comes into question, usually a time of crisis in the meaning, direction, and value of each person's life; neglected parts of the self (talents, desires, aspirations) seek expression
6 Ages 43 to 53 Feel "die is cast" and view life with bitterness; blame parents and find fault with children but seek sympathy from spouse	**6** Ages 45 to 50 Choices must be made, a new life structure formed; person must commit to new tasks
7 Ages 53 to 60 Feel less negative feelings than in the 40s; relationships with selves, parents, children, and friends become warmer and more mellow; marital happiness and contentment increase	**7** Ages 50 to 55 Further questioning and modification of the life structure; men who did not have a crisis at age 40 are likely to have one now
	8 Ages 55 to 60 Build a new life structure; can be time of great fulfillment

relationship with a *mentor*—an older, more experienced person who serves as a teacher, adviser, role model, and sponsor for the younger individual. Usually (but not always) the mentoring relationship emerges in a work setting with a senior colleague. Typically, the mentor is about a half-generation (8–15 years) older than the individual. The mentor's key function is to help define, support, and facilitate the younger person's Dream. The mentoring relationship is a transitional one, usually lasting from two to ten years.

Although Levinson found a great deal of mentoring among his male subjects, current evidence indicates that career women are less likely to enjoy the benefits of professional mentoring (Noe, 1988; Reinke, Ellicott, Harris, & Hancock, 1985). Presumably, this is because there are fewer older women available in work settings to serve as mentors for younger women. Also, the mentoring relationship tends to be emotionally intense. Consequently, it can be awkward for men to serve as mentors for younger women, since colleagues may misunderstand their relationship (Bowen, 1985). Interestingly, Reinke and her associates (1985) found that many of their female subjects had older friends or relatives whom they regarded as important role models. Perhaps women are more likely to find their "mentors" outside of the work setting.

Age 30 Transition: Doubts and Reevaluation

Around the age of 30, give or take a few years, both Gould and Levinson found signs of increased inner turmoil. Levinson found that the majority of his subjects experienced a crisis around this time. These crises centered on doubts about the commitments made in the previous stage. These doubts surface just as the person is feeling that choices are getting "locked in" to an extent that will make it difficult to alter her or his life path. Among married women, the age 30 transition often stimulates a reevaluation of how they have balanced career and family goals (Roberts & Newton, 1987). Many of these women

seek to renegotiate their marital roles with their husbands. Gould likewise sees this as a period of questioning one's decisions about marriage, family, and career. Thus, people struggle with the false assumption "Life is simple and controllable. There are no significant contradictory forces within me."

Settling Down and Becoming One's Own Person (30s)

According to Levinson, the vacillation found around age 30 is followed by a period of relative tranquility—for men, anyway. During this phase, men make a solid commitment to the life structure that was reformulated around age 30. They attempt to establish their niche in society and concentrate on climbing up their career ladders. Their pursuit of career advancement may necessitate that they challenge their mentors in order to advance more rapidly.

Studies that have applied Levinson's model to women have not found a distinct period of settling down in the 30s. Continued questioning and instability in life structure are more likely among women (Roberts & Newton, 1987). Gould has observed similar instability in both sexes. He concluded that the period of questioning around age 30 lasted until the mid-30s, at which time people begin to enter the midlife transition.

The Midlife Transition (Around Age 40)

A major landmark of adult development is the midlife transitional period, which Gould found to occur between

Individuals in their 20s and 30s can benefit from a mentoring relationship, especially at work. The mentor serves as an adviser and role model who shows the younger person the ropes of the business.

Passages
by Gail Sheehy (Bantam Books, 1976)

Based on her in-depth study of 115 men and women between the ages of 18 and 55, Gail Sheehy offers us an intriguing view of adult development. Like Levinson, Sheehy finds that phases of relative stability alternate with "passages": phases of turmoil and transition. The "Pulling Up Roots" passage of late adolescence, for instance, is followed by a relatively stable period during which people do what they think they "should" do as bona fide adults. With the approach of age 30 comes another tumultuous period in which people abandon the "shoulds" and strive instead for personal fulfillment, often discarding careers or mates in the process. The early 30s are again a time of settling down, only to be followed by a decade of upheaval—the midlife crisis—when people switch from counting the time they have already lived to counting the time they have left to live. If the midlife passage is negotiated successfully, previously suppressed aspects of the personality are integrated into a new and more authentic identity, making the succeeding years a time of renewal and growth.

In a later work, *Pathfinders* (1980), Sheehy extends her analysis of adult development from age 50 through the 80s. In both *Passages* and *Pathfinders*, Sheehy deftly interweaves theory with extensive interview data from her subjects. The result is two highly readable and immensely enjoyable books.

> Who's afraid of growing up? Who isn't? For if and when we do begin the process of reexamining all that we think and feel and stand for, in the effort to forge an identity that is authentically ours and ours alone, we run into our own resistance. There is a moment—an immense and precarious moment—of stark terror. And in that moment most of us want to retreat as fast as possible because to go forward means facing a truth we have suspected all along: We stand alone. [p. 359]

ages 35 and 45. Levinson found the modal age for this transition to be 40 to 45. Both theorists view this period as a potentially turbulent time of reappraisal and restructuring.

Levinson found that people subjected their life structure to tough scrutiny and reevaluation. Most found that they had not fulfilled their Dream. Dismayed by this reality, they worked to alter their expectations to be more realistic, or they increased their efforts to achieve their goals. Even those who *had* reached or exceeded their Dream experienced a crisis. Many found their success less satisfying than they had expected. All of them had to confront the fact that success and acclaim do not arrest the inexorable process of aging. In addition, Levinson found many of his subjects struggling to acknowledge previously suppressed aspects of their personalities. Both men and women sought to break down the rigid gender stereotypes by which they had structured their early adult lives. Women, freed from the responsibility of nurturing young children, began to express more independence, assertiveness, and competitiveness. Men, divesting themselves of their earlier assumption that career success would provide satisfaction, became more expressive and emotional. This movement toward convergence in gender roles during middle age has also been seen in studies that have measured masculinity/femininity directly (see Figure 11.6).

The confrontation with the aging process during the midlife transition is also emphasized by Gould. He notes that many people are forced to acknowledge their mortality as they witness the deaths of parents, colleagues, and friends. Thus, they wrestle with the false assumption "There is no evil or death in the world." Women also tend to struggle with the assumption that their husbands can serve effectively as "protectors." Those who succeed in outgrowing this assumption often become less dependent on their husbands. They tend to work harder on their own goals, concentrating less on helping their husbands to realize theirs. Gould also emphasizes that during this period people feel pressured by time. They

Figure 11.6. Age trends in masculinity and femininity. Levinson reports anecdotal evidence that men become less masculine and women less feminine as they move through adulthood. Other researchers have used scales to measure masculinity/femininity and observed a similar convergence. The graph shows the results of one such study (Monge, 1975).

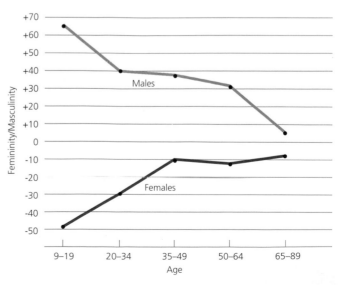

hear their social clocks ticking loudly as they frantically attempt to accomplish their goals.

In a study examining midlife transitions among career women, Lieblich (1986) found that over 80% experienced such a transition. Of these, about half moved in the direction of "masculinity," with increasing independence and career commitment and lessened family involvement (the same type of midlife transition Levinson found among his female subjects). The other half of Lieblich's sample, however, experienced a transition similar to that typically found in men: they moved in the direction of "femininity," focusing less on their careers and more on establishing close emotional ties.

Restabilization (Mid and Late 40s)

Both Gould and Levinson observed a period of relative calm after the instability frequently seen during the midlife transition. Although most people probably are not entirely satisfied with their lives, Gould notes that they feel that the die is cast. Hence, they begin to accept their fate with less resistance. Among his male subjects, Levinson found a tendency to shift some attention and energy away from career concerns in favor of family concerns. Levinson's female subjects showed a tendency to shift in the opposite direction, from family concerns to career concerns. Many of them entered or reentered the work force as their children left home. Although the "emptying of the nest" is widely believed to be a traumatic event for women, both Levinson (1985) and Reinke and her associates (1985) found that few women experienced it as such.

Culmination of Middle Adulthood (50s)

Information on developmental patterns after age 50 tapers off abruptly. Neither Gould nor Levinson has finished following his subjects through this decade. Although they lack concrete empirical data, both have made some theory-based projections. Gould suggests that

the 50s are a period of "mellowing" as people continue to become more tolerant and accepting of their past. The limited data available seem to support this idea (Lowenthal, 1975; Reinke et al., 1985). Levinson speculates that those people who do not have much of a midlife crisis around age 40 may experience a delayed transitional crisis near age 50. Otherwise, Levinson projects that the mid to late 50s may resemble the mid to late 30s, with people settling into the life structures that they have recently rearranged for themselves.

Late Adulthood (After Age 60): Disengagement?

A prominent theory about late adulthood suggests that a process of *disengagement* should ensue (Cumming, 1963, 1975). Disengagement theory suggests that older people gradually withdraw psychologically and socially from the world around them. Supposedly they reduce their emotional investment in current events and reduce their actual interactions with others as well. According to Cumming, successful disengagement should be associated with high morale, as older adults are freed from the necessity to behave in accordance with social norms.

There is some evidence supporting the idea that there is a trend toward disengagement during late adulthood (Havighurst, Neugarten, & Tobin, 1968; Mindel & Vaughan, 1978). For instance, the percentage of people who report having extensive social interactions declines significantly between age 50 and age 75, as can be seen in Figure 11.7.

However, disengagement theory is very controversial, and available evidence suggests that this process is not inevitable (Palmore, 1975). Some critics suggest that when disengagement does occur, it is imposed on older people by society rather than being a matter of choice. In other words, it is society that disengages from the elderly rather than the other way around. Moreover, some research (Lemon, Bengston, & Peterson, 1982; Palmore, 1975) suggests that those individuals who minimize disengagement tend to be the most satisfied and contented

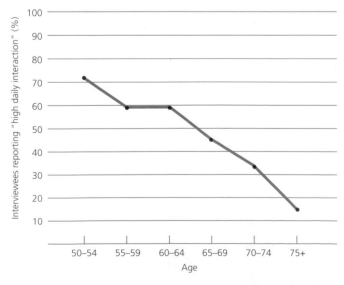

during late adulthood. How can we reconcile these contradictory findings? It may be that the developmental stream flows in the direction of disengagement, but a portion of older people with certain values and personality characteristics may resist this undercurrent successfully (Lemon et al., 1982).

Evaluating Gould and Levinson

The theories of Gould and Levinson have been highly influential in stimulating research on adult development, and they have achieved enormous popularity among the general public. Even so, the "ages and stages" approach of these theories has been criticized on several grounds. Two of the principal criticisms are as follows.

First, Gould and Levinson have mapped out the sequence of *typical* development, while saying little about *atypical* development. Like most stage theorists, they ignore the great individual differences among people. For instance, both imply that a midlife crisis is inevitable, but other studies show that *some* people sail through the midlife period with ease (Livson, 1976; McGill, 1980; Vaillant, 1977). Given the variability in both the timing and the sequence of events in adulthood, some theorists have questioned whether adult development should be viewed as an invariant, universal sequence of stages (Brim & Kagan, 1980).

Second, both theories describe the development of mainly middle- and upper-class people born in a particular historical period—just before or during the Great Depression of the 1930s. What these people went through may not be what their children will go through. Today's children are evolving in a very different world. In particular, developmental patterns for women seem likely to change given recent shifts in gender roles.

As an alternative to the ages-and-stages approach to adult development, many psychologists have simply set out to identify developmental trends across the expanse of adulthood. We'll summarize key trends in physical development in the next section.

Figure 11.7. Age trends in social interaction. In a test of disengagement theory, Cumming and Henry (1961) interviewed subjects of varying age about their social roles and networks. They found that the percentage of interviewees reporting "high daily interaction" with others declined steadily after age 50.

AGING AND PHYSICAL CHANGES

It is readily apparent that aging is accompanied by many changes in physical functioning. While some of the changes are quite obvious, others may be very subtle—but important. Except where otherwise noted, the following summary of trends in physical development is based on Whitbourne (1985).

Changes in Appearance

Height is rather stable in adulthood, although it does tend to decline by an inch or so after age 55, as the spinal column "settles." Weight is more variable and tends to increase in most adults up through the mid-50s, when a very gradual decline typically begins. Although weight often goes down late in life, the percentage of body weight that is fat tends to increase throughout adulthood, much to the chagrin of many people. The skin of the face and body tends to wrinkle and sag. The appearance of the face may change, as the nose and ears tend to become longer and wider, and the jaw appears to shrink. Hair tends to thin out and become gray in both sexes, and many males have to confront receding hairlines and baldness.

The net impact of these changes is that many older people view themselves as less attractive. This unfortunate reality is probably aggravated by the obsession of our society's media with youthful attractiveness. These changes in physical appearance may have a significant impact on older persons' self-concepts.

Neurological Changes

The nervous system is composed of *neurons*, **individual cells that receive, integrate, and transmit information.** The number of active neurons in the brain declines steadily during adulthood. As neurons die, the brain decreases in both weight and volume, especially after age 50. Although this progressive neuronal loss sounds alarming, it is a normal part of aging that may not have much functional significance. Our brains have billions of neurons, so these losses may be mere drops in a bucket. At present, there is little reason to suspect that this normal process contributes to the onset of *senile dementia,* **an abnormal and progressive decline in general cognitive functioning that is observed in a small minority of people over 65**.

Sensory Changes

The most important changes in sensory reception occur in the visual and auditory senses. Visual acuity is strongly related to age. The proportion of people with 20/20 vision declines steadily as age increases. From about age 30 to the mid-60s, the usual trend is toward becoming increasingly farsighted. After the mid-60s, the trend is toward greater nearsightedness. Difficulty adapting to darkness, sensitivity to glare, reduced peripheral vision, and a yellowing of color perception are common among older people. Depth perception begins to decline in the mid-40s. This loss may impair the older adult's ability to negotiate obstacles and barriers successfully.

Noticeable hearing losses usually do not show up until people reach their 50s. Whereas the vast majority of the elderly require corrective treatment for visual losses, only about one third of older adults suffer hearing losses that require corrective treatment. In addition, small sensory losses in touch, taste, and smell have been detected, usually after age 50. These losses generally have little impact on day-to-day functioning, although older people often complain that their food is somewhat tasteless. In contrast, visual and hearing losses often make interpersonal interaction more awkward and difficult, thus promoting social withdrawal in some older people.

Endocrine Changes

There are age-related changes in hormonal functioning, but their significance is not well understood. They do *not* appear to be the chief cause of declining sexual activity during the later years. Rather, this decline seems to be due to acceptance of social norms that older people don't have sexual desires and that sexual activity in the elderly is "inappropriate." For women, decreased sexual activity may simply reflect lack of opportunity, since the proportion of widows increases dramatically with age (Turner & Adams, 1988). The vast majority of older adults remain physically capable of engaging in rewarding sexual encounters right on through their 70s, although arousal tends to be somewhat slower and less intense.

Among women, menopause is a rather dramatic transition that typically occurs in the early 50s. *Menopause* **is the time when menstruation ceases.** Not so long ago, it was thought that menopause was almost universally accompanied by severe emotional strain. It is now clear that women are highly variable in their reactions to menopause and that the majority suffer little psychological distress (McKinlay, McKinlay, & Brambilla, 1987). Episodes of moderate physical discomfort during the transitional phase are fairly common. However, many women find this discomfort no more troublesome than that associated with menstruation itself. The loss of fertility that accompanies menopause is not necessarily traumatic, since it comes at an age when few women would realistically plan to have more children. When emotional distress does occur, it is more often a reaction to a perceived loss of physical attractiveness than to a loss of reproductive capacity.

Although there has been much discussion in recent years of "male menopause," there really is no equivalent experience among men. Significant endocrine changes do occur in males in their later years. However, these changes are very gradual and are largely unrelated to physical or psychological distress.

Changes in Health Status

Unfortunately, the quality of one's health does tend to diminish with increasing age (Siegler, Nowlin, & Blumenthal, 1980). There are many reasons for this trend. Vital

Figure 11.8. Age trends in health status. The data graphed here show that the percentage of people with a chronic health problem increases with age, as does the percentage of people whose activities are limited because of poor health. (Data from Wilder, 1971)

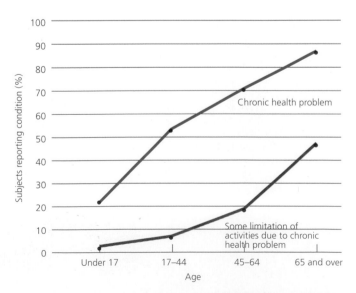

organ systems lose some of their functional capacity. Vulnerability to some diseases (such as heart disease) increases with age. For other diseases (such as pneumonia), the vulnerability may remain unchanged, but the effects of the condition, if contracted, may be more serious. In any case, there is a clear trend in the direction of declining health, as you can see in Figure 11.8. The proportion of people with a chronic health problem climbs steadily with age.

AGING AND COGNITIVE CHANGES

There are many widely held notions about intellectual decline during adulthood. It is commonly believed that intelligence drops during middle age and that memory lapses become more frequent in the later years. Are these common conceptions correct? Let's review the evidence on cognitive development during adulthood.

Intelligence

Researchers have long been interested in whether general intelligence, as measured by IQ tests, remains stable throughout the adult years. The early evidence on the stability of intelligence was rather disconcerting. Wechsler (1958) reported that intelligence peaked in the 20s and then declined across the remainder of the life span. We now understand that this finding was largely the product of methodological shortcomings associated with Wechsler's approach to data collection. More recent and better-designed studies have yielded a different picture (Hertzog & Schaie, 1988; Schaie, 1983). They suggest that IQ is fairly stable until about age 60, when a relatively small decline often begins. This post-60 decline appears to be associated with failing health (Field, Schaie, & Leino, 1988) and with problems in focusing attention (Stankov, 1988). These studies also indicate that there are large individual differences among people in IQ fluctuations. Although some people experience a modest decline during middle age, many others actually show an *increase* in IQ as late as their 50s. Overall, general intelligence seems to be stable throughout most of adulthood.

However, it does appear that people's IQ scores drop precipitously within the last several years before death (Berg, 1987). This phenomenon is referred to as "terminal drop." It probably reflects the effects of declining health in those who are approaching their death.

Memory

Many elderly people feel that their memory "isn't what it used to be." In support of this perception, numerous studies report declines in the proficiency of long-term memory in older adults (Howe & Hunter, 1986). However, most of these studies have asked subjects to memorize simple lists of words or paired associations. Older subjects may find such tasks meaningless and uninteresting. These artificial laboratory tasks bear little resemblance to the memory challenges that we encounter in everyday life. Thus, it's hard to say whether the memory losses seen in these studies have much practical significance.

Investigators have only recently begun to study age-related changes in memory for more meaningful, realistic content. There *do* seem to be some modest declines with age in memory for prose, television shows, conversations, past activities, and personal plans (Kausler, 1985). Such memory impairments could conceivably interfere with older adults' daily activities. However, the memory losses associated with aging are moderate in size and are *not* universal. Some older people, especially those who remain mentally active, suffer little memory impairment.

A popular misconception is that older people have very vivid recollections of events in the distant past while being very forgetful about recent events. In actuality, there is no evidence that the elderly have more numerous, or more vivid, early memories (Rabbitt & McGinnis, 1988). Their memories of events long ago may be loose reconstructions that are less accurate than people assume.

Age has not proved a barrier for many productive people in their 70s, 80s, and 90s. George Burns continues to perform well into his mid 90s. Artist Georgia O'Keeffe was still creating when she died at age 99.

Learning and Problem Solving

Although intelligence and memory may be more stable during adulthood than widely believed, there *are* some significant cognitive changes during the adult years. These changes show up most clearly when researchers look at specific aspects of learning and problem solving.

There is ample evidence that the ability to narrow one's focus of attention diminishes somewhat with increasing age, as does the ability to handle simultaneous multiple inputs (Plude & Hoyer, 1985; Stankov, 1988). These changes may be due to decreased efficiency in filtering out irrelevant stimuli. Most of the studies have simply compared extreme age groups (very young subjects against very old subjects). Hence, we're not sure about the age at which these changes tend to emerge.

In the cognitive domain, age seems to take its toll on *speed* first. Many studies indicate that one's speed in learning, solving problems, retrieving memories, and processing information tends to decline with age (Drachman, 1986). Although additional data are needed, some evidence suggests that this trend may be a gradual, lengthy one commencing in middle adulthood. The general nature of this trend (across differing tasks) suggests that it may be due to age-related changes in neurological functioning (Birren, Woods, & Williams, 1980). Alternatively, the slowing of cognitive processing with age could reflect increased cautiousness among older adults (Reese & Rodeheaver, 1985).

Overall *success* on laboratory problem-solving tasks also appears to decrease as people grow older (Charness, 1985). This decline is not as clear or as strong as that observed for speed of processing (Reese & Rodeheaver, 1985). For the most part, problem-solving ability is unimpaired if older people are given adequate time to compensate for their reduced speed in cognitive processing. Furthermore, many of the age-related decrements in cognitive functioning can be partly compensated for by increases in older adults' knowledge.

It should be emphasized that many people remain capable of great intellectual accomplishment well into their later years. This reality was verified in a study of scholarly, scientific, and artistic productivity that examined lifelong patterns of work among 738 men who lived at least through the age of 79 (Dennis, 1966). Figure 11.9 plots the percentage of professional works completed by these men in their 20s, 30s, 40s, 50s, 60s, and 70s. As you can see, in most professions the 40s decade was the most productive. However, in many areas productivity was remarkably stable through the 60s and even the 70s. Other researchers have focused on the *quality*, rather than the quantity, of output. They typically find that "masterpieces" occur at the same relative frequency among the works of creators of all ages (Simonton, 1988).

DEATH AND DYING

Dealing with the deaths of close friends and loved ones is an increasingly frequent adjustment problem as people move through adulthood. Moreover, the final challenge of life is to confront one's own death gracefully. In this section, we'll discuss research on death and dying.

Attitudes about Death

Research on death was relatively scarce until recently because death is a taboo topic in modern Western society. The most common strategy for dealing with death in our culture is *avoidance*. Evidence of our inability to confront death comfortably is plentiful. It is apparent in how we talk about death, using euphemisms such as "passed away" in order to avoid even the word itself. Our discomfort often leads us to unnecessarily quarantine the dying in hospitals and nursing homes in order to minimize our exposure to the specter of death. These are all manifestations of what Kastenbaum (1986) calls a *death system*—the **collection of rituals and procedures used by a culture to handle death**. Death systems vary from one culture to another. Ours happens to be rather negative and evasive.

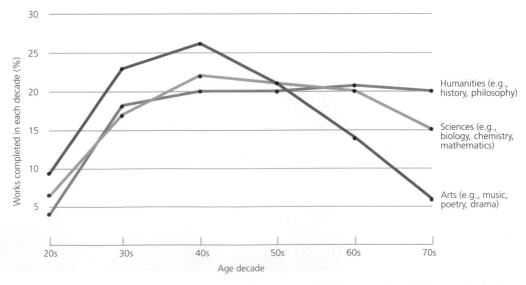

Negativism and avoidance are *not* universal features of all death systems. The Amish, for example, view death in a more calm and accepting fashion. They see death as a natural transition rather than as a dreaded adversary (Bryer, 1979). Thus, some cultures and subcultures display less fear of death than our majority culture.

Within our culture, individuals differ greatly in their attitudes about death. There are conflicting findings about whether *preoccupation* with thoughts about death peaks in middle or old age. However, the evidence is fairly clear that *fear* of death tends to decline after middle age (Kastenbaum, 1986). It may be that older people begin to feel they have lived a full life and that they gradually work through the meaning of death as they confront others' deaths more frequently. One's particular religious affiliation isn't especially influential in determining feelings about death, but a strong, deeply felt religious commitment (regardless of denomination) is associated with lower death anxiety. Ultimately, fear of death is an individual matter, greatly influenced by personality and family background (Rosenheim & Muchnik, 1984–1985).

The Process of Dying

Pioneering research on the experience of dying was conducted by Elisabeth Kübler-Ross (1969, 1970) during the 1960s. At first, her project met with immense resistance. Fellow physicians at the hospital where she worked were not inclined to cooperate with her requests to interview dying patients. Gradually, however, it became apparent that many such patients were enthusiastic about the discussions. They were frustrated by the "conspiracy of silence" that surrounds death and relieved to get things out in the open.

Eventually, Kübler-Ross interviewed over 200 terminally ill patients and developed a model of the process of dying. According to her model, people evolve through a series of five stages as they confront their own death. These "stages" often overlap and coexist. Hence, it may be more accurate to characterize them as typical *reactions*

that may or may not unfold sequentially. Huyck and Hoyer (1982, pp. 506–507) provide a succinct description of these reactions.

Stage 1: Denial. Denial, shock, and disbelief are the first reactions to being informed of a serious, life-terminating illness. According to Kübler-Ross, few patients maintain this stance to the end.

Stage 2: Anger. After denial, the patient often becomes nasty, demanding, difficult, and hostile. Asking and resolving the question "Why me?" can help the patient reduce resentment.

Stage 3: Bargaining. In this stage the patient wants more time and asks for favors to postpone death. The bargaining may be carried out with the physician or, more frequently, with God. Kübler-Ross gives the example of a dying woman who asked to be relieved of her severe pain just for one day so that she could attend her son's wedding. The woman promised that if she could just see her son married, she would then be able to die in peace. She was taught self-hypnosis to control the pain and was permitted to leave the hospital for one day. She did not want to return. "Dr. Ross," she said, "don't forget, I have another son."

Stage 4: Depression. Depression is a signal that the acceptance process has really begun. Kübler-Ross has referred to this stage as *preparatory grief*—the sadness of anticipating an impending loss.

Stage 5: Acceptance. The person who achieves acceptance has taken care of unfinished business. The patient has relinquished the unattainable and is now ready to die. He or she will want to be with close family members, usually a wife or husband and children; dying children want to be with their parents. Although patients desire the presence of someone warm, caring, and accepting at this time, verbal communication may be totally unnecessary.

Some doubts about the generality of Kübler-Ross's findings have been expressed (Kastenbaum, 1985). How-

Figure 11.9. Age trends in professional productivity.
Dennis (1966) compiled the percentage of professional works completed in each decade of life by 738 men who lived to at least age 79. Productivity peaked in the 40s decade, but professional output remained strong through the 60s decade, and even through the 70s decade for the humanities and sciences.

Elisabeth Kübler-Ross

ever, there is no question that she greatly improved our understanding of the process of dying and stimulated research that continues to add to our knowledge.

SUMMARY

Development refers to age-related changes that occur as a person progresses from conception to death. Most models of development are stage theories. Although such theories probably overestimate the uniformity of developmental patterns, they can be useful descriptive models.

Puberty, the period of physical growth leading to reproductive capacity, is a landmark event in adolescence. Boys who mature late and girls who mature early may find puberty particularly stressful. Piaget's theory of cognitive development describes age-related transitions in thinking. According to Piaget, adolescent thought is characterized by formal operations. Adolescents can apply logical operations to hypothetical possibilities and abstract concepts.

Many theorists have asserted that adolescence is a period of turmoil. The recent surge in attempted suicide by adolescents appears to support this notion. However, other sources of evidence suggest that adolescence is no more tumultuous than other periods of life. Erikson's psychoanalytic theory of development focuses on psychosocial crises in each of eight successive stages. These crises center on transitions in social relations. According to Erikson, the key challenge of adolescence is to progress toward a clear sense of identity.

In recent years, social scientists have extended the study of development to the adult years. The adult personality seems to be characterized by both stability and change. Successful progress through Erikson's three adult stages enables one to be capable of intimacy, to be concerned about future generations, and to face death with integrity.

Research by Gould and Levinson led to the emergence of two new theories of adult development. Gould's theory emphasizes false assumptions that must be discarded. Levinson's theory focuses on age-related changes in one's life structure. Although the models are far from identical, they share many congruent themes. Both propose that there are major life transitions around age 20, again around age 40, and probably around age 60.

Physical development during adulthood leads to many obvious changes in physical appearance and sensory acuity. After age 30 there is a steady loss of active brain cells. However, this loss has not been clearly related to reductions in cognitive functioning. Similarly, hormonal changes appear to be only modestly related to midlife distress or declining sexual activity. Unfortunately, health does tend to decline with increasing age for a variety of reasons.

Intelligence seems to remain fairly stable during most of adulthood. Memory processes probably deteriorate less than believed. Attentional capacity, speed of learning, and success in problem solving all tend to decline slightly during old age. However, most people remain capable of sound intellectual functioning in their later years.

Attitudes about death vary from one culture to another. Attitudes in our culture are characterized by negativism, avoidance, and fear. Research by Kübler-Ross suggests that dying individuals experience a variety of reactions ranging from denial to anger, bargaining, depression, and finally acceptance.

In our upcoming Application, we'll look at some of the ways parents can facilitate the development of their children by providing optimal combinations of affection and discipline.

Answer the following true or false.

☐ **1.** Historically, parents have always been deeply concerned about their children's development.

☐ **2.** Infant-mother emotional attachments are natural and are formed readily.

☐ **3.** Extensive use of punishment is the key to effective discipline.

☐ **4.** Parents shouldn't have to explain their reasons for punishing their children.

All the statements above are false. All represent popular myths about child rearing that we will encounter in our discussion of effective parenting.

We live in a child-centered society. Many of today's parents have an abiding interest in learning all they can about children's development. They search to find new and better ways to ensure optimal physical, emotional, and cognitive development in their children. Things haven't always been this way, however. Let's take a brief look at how the nature of parenting has changed (based on LeVine & White, 1987).

HISTORICAL CHANGES IN PARENT-CHILD RELATIONSHIPS

In preindustrial North America and Europe, young children worked along with their families in agriculture or craft production. Most families lived in rural areas, so formal schooling was available to few. Families typically had numerous children, some of whom were likely to die in infancy or childhood. Given this stark reality, parents used to be cautious about becoming deeply attached to any individual child.

Industrialization was accompanied by many changes in the structure of families. Many people migrated to urban areas to find jobs. Formal education thus became more accessible. It also became more necessary. For the first time, children were likely to make their eventual living through jobs that could not be taught to them by their parents. By the late 1800s, legislation mandated formal schooling for all children and limited their participation in the labor force. Collectively, these changes had the effect of setting aside childhood and (eventually) adolescence as developmental stages distinct from adulthood. No longer were children regarded as miniature adults. Instead, they were seen as unique individuals with their own personalities and needs. Moreover, families had fewer children, and more of them survived to adulthood. Hence, parents became more willing to allocate attention and affection to their children, a trend that has continued to the present.

MATERNAL BEHAVIOR AND INFANT-MOTHER ATTACHMENT

For the first few months of life, infants rely on built-in behaviors such as crying, cooing, and smiling to initiate and maintain contact with adult caregivers. Before long, infants start to recognize their most frequent caregiver (typically, the mother) and are more easily soothed by that person. By the age of 7 months or so, most babies develop a strong emotional attachment to a single, familiar caregiver (hereafter assumed to be the mother, to simplify our discussion). They often react with distress at separation from this attachment figure (Schaffer & Emerson, 1964).

However, contrary to popular belief, infants' attachment to their mothers is *not* automatic. Indeed, as we mentioned in Chapter 9, not all infants develop a secure attachment to their mothers. After extensive study of infant-mother attachments, Mary Ainsworth and her colleagues concluded that infants fell into three groups (Ainsworth, Blehar, Waters, & Wall, 1978). One group is described as *anxious and avoidant.* These babies tend to ignore their mothers. A second group is *anxious and ambivalent.* They seem to desire contact with the mother, yet they actively resist her when she comes near. Fortunately, the majority of infants are *securely attached.* A secure attachment to a caregiver during infancy is important, because it seems to provide a basis for successful social relationships later in life (Bretherton, 1985). In Erikson's terms, the securely attached baby has developed a sense of trust in the mother and toward the world at large.

Becoming an Effective Parent

The Hurried Child
by David Elkind (Addison-Wesley, 1988)

In this fascinating book, David Elkind shows how recent changes in the structure of family life have altered our views of children and their needs. Earlier generations saw children as needing adult protection and guidance, a view consistent with the "traditional" family structure, in which at least one parent was available to the children at all times. Today, in many step-, single-parent, and dual-earner families, such nurturing is impossible for parents to provide. Many of these parents have alleviated their anxiety about parenthood by adopting a new conception of children as "Superkids" who can take care of themselves.

This new view of children as "miniature adults" is mirrored in every facet of children's culture: education, television, movies, and music. Thus, society as a whole conspires with the parents to "hurry" children to outgrow their need for nurturance as quickly as possible.

According to Elkind, pressuring children to grow up fast can produce negative outcomes ranging from academic failure to psychosomatic illness to teenage suicide. Nevertheless, he maintains an attitude of optimism and hope that, with awareness of the pressures today's children face, parents can and will seek to alleviate their children's stress. Reading this book can help a concerned parent to do just that.

> The conception of children as competent to deal with, and indeed as benefitting from, everything and anything that life has to offer was an effective rationalization for parents who continue to love their children but who have neither the time, nor the energy, for childhood. . . .
>
> If child-rearing necessarily involves stress, then by hurrying children to grow up, or by treating them as adults, we hope to remove a portion of our burden of worry and anxiety and to enlist our children's aid in carrying life's load. We do not mean our children harm in acting thus—on the contrary, as a society we have come to imagine that it is good for young people to mature rapidly. Yet we do our children harm when we hurry them through childhood. [pp. xiii, 3]

Can a mother promote a secure attachment in her baby? Ainsworth and her associates reported that the mothers of securely attached infants enjoyed physical contact with the baby, were perceptive of the baby's needs, and had a good sense of timing (for instance, they knew when the baby wanted to be picked up or put down). The implication is that these are among the key attributes of effective parenting of infants.

DIMENSIONS OF CHILD REARING

As children move from infancy into toddlerhood, parents become more than mere caregivers. The manner in which parents react to a child's actions communicates their standards of appropriate and inappropriate behavior. Parents fulfill this role with varying degrees of conscious awareness.

It appears that two dimensions of parental behavior have important implications for children's development (Maccoby & Martin, 1983). The first involves how *demanding* parents are. A demanding parent sets high performance standards and expects increasingly mature behavior. An undemanding parent expects little of the child. The second dimension is the parents' degree of *responsiveness* to the child's needs. Responsive parents are sensitive to the child's changing desires and increasing competence. They modify their treatment of the child accordingly. Unresponsive parents fail to take the child's needs into account and do not adjust their child-rearing methods to match the child's level of development.

Relationships between parents' demandingness and responsiveness and their children's social and intellectual competence have been found in a series of studies by Diana Baumrind (Baumrind, 1967, 1971, 1978). In her initial study, Baumrind observed a sample of preschool children in a nursery school setting and at home. Each child was rated on several social and cognitive dimensions. During the home observations, the parents' behavior was also observed and rated. Additional data were obtained through interviews with the parents. Baumrind was able to identify three distinct "parenting styles": authoritarian, permissive, and authoritative.

Authoritarian parents are highly demanding, controlling, and power-assertive. They also tend to be somewhat emotionally distant. By virtue of their higher status, they issue commands that are to be obeyed without question ("Do it because I said so"). Such parents are also relatively unresponsive to their children, rigidly maintaining tight control even as their children mature.

Permissive parents make few or no demands of their children. They allow children free expression of impulses, setting few limits on appropriate behavior. Permissive parents may be responsive, warmly accepting and indulging children's desires. Or they may be unresponsive, indifferently ignoring their children much of the time.

Authoritative parents, like authoritarian parents, are demanding. They set high goals for their children. But authoritative parents are also responsive to their children's needs. They encourage verbal give-and-take, allowing children to question the parents' requests. They also provide age-appropriate explanations that emphasize the consequences of "good" and "bad" behavior. Authoritative parents maintain firm control but take into account each child's unique and changing needs. They are willing to negotiate with their children, setting new and less restrictive limits when appropriate, particularly as children mature.

EFFECTS OF PARENTING STYLES

Baumrind found that these parenting styles were associated with different clusters of traits in children, as summarized in Figure 11.10. The children of authoritarian parents tended to be moody, fearful, resentful, irritable, and unfriendly. Permissive parents tended to have children who were rebellious, undisciplined, impulsive, aggressive, and domineering. Authoritative parenting, in contrast, was associated with more positive outcomes. The children of authoritative parents tended to be self-reliant, self-disciplined, cooperative, friendly, and intellectually curious.

Of course, these data are correlational and they do *not* establish that the parenting style is the *cause* of the children's traits. The direction of influence probably goes both ways. For instance, parents may become increasingly authoritarian *in response to* their child's increasing resentment and irritability. Even so, Baumrind's results imply that authoritative parenting is most likely to foster social and cognitive competence in children.

What happened when these children got older? Baumrind made follow-up observations of her subjects when they were 8 to 9 years old. She found that the children of authoritative parents were still the highest in both social and cognitive competence. This was especially true for the girls.

Baumrind (1978) points out that authoritative parents make adjustments for a child's increasing age and maturity. As their children get older, authoritative parents set increasingly high standards of

Parenting Styles and Children's Traits	
Parenting style	**Children's behavioral profile**
Authoritative	*Energetic-friendly* Self-reliant Self-controlled Cheerful and friendly Copes well with stress Cooperative with adults Curious Purposive Achievement-oriented
Authoritarian	*Conflicted-irritable* Fearful, apprehensive Moody, unhappy Easily annoyed Passively hostile Vulnerable to stress Aimless Sulky, unfriendly
Permissive	*Impulsive-aggressive* Rebellious Low in self-reliance and self-control Impulsive Aggressive Domineering Aimless Low in achievement

Figure 11.10. Baumrind's findings on parenting style and children's traits. Diana Baumrind has studied three styles of parenting and their relations to children's social and intellectual competence. As you can see, authoritative parenting is associated with the most desirable outcomes. (Summary adapted from Schaffer, 1989)

behavior—high enough to encourage the child to "try," but not so high that the child is doomed to fail. The manner in which the parents explain and enforce these standards is also dependent on the child's age.

Another dimension of parenting that seems important is parental *warmth*. Although most parents are at least moderately affectionate toward their children, some are indifferent or even hostile and rejecting. Parental warmth appears to influence the degree to which children internalize the behavioral standards of their parents (Greenberger & Goldberg, 1989). Children whose parents hold them in high regard are likely to incorporate parental values into their own personalities. This should enable them to exercise self-control and to behave appropriately even when the parents are not present. In contrast, children whose parents show less warmth may fail to internalize their parents' values and tend to be less self-controlled. They may comply with parents' demands *in the parents' presence*

Discipline is more effective when the parent explains why the child is being punished.

(perhaps out of fear of punishment), but misbehave on their own.

ISSUES IN RAISING ADOLESCENTS

A widely held belief in our society is that adolescence is a time of rebellion, leading to chronic conflict between parents and their teenage children. Fortunately, however, most families with adolescents manage to forgo serious conflict and disorganization (Hill, 1987). Nevertheless, the rapid physical and cognitive development of adolescents does necessitate some parental adjustment. Adolescents' emerging cognitive abilities enable them to question parental values and to formulate a personal philosophy to guide their own behavior. Mundane conflicts between teens and their parents over such issues as curfews and choice of friends reflect adolescents' deeper concerns over issues of values, responsibilities, and roles (Powers, Hauser, & Kilner, 1989). The balance of power between parent and child is shifting during adolescence. Younger children accept their parents' power as a legitimate source of authority. The increasing autonomy of adolescents, however, requires a more equal parent-child relationship.

Authoritarian parents who are unwilling to relinquish their control promote hostility and rebellion in their adolescent children. Permissive parents, who never exercised control over their children, may find themselves faced with adolescents whose behavior is completely out of hand.

Authoritative parents who are willing to respond to their teenagers' input are most likely to avoid such turmoil (Baumrind, 1978). As Baumrind continues to follow her subjects, she expects to find that effective parenting of adolescents involves increasing parental responsiveness and decreasing parental demandingness (Baumrind, 1989).

USING PUNISHMENT EFFECTIVELY

Parents often wonder how punishment can be used more effectively in disciplinary efforts. The first suggestion from many psychologists would be that most parents should use punishment less. Why? Because punishment often has unintended side effects (Newsom, Favell, & Rincover, 1983; Van Houten, 1983). One of these side effects is the *general suppression of behavioral activity*. Some children who are punished heavily become withdrawn, inhibited, and less active than other children. It is also common for punishment to trigger *strong emotional responses*, including fear, anxiety, anger, and resentment. These emotional reactions can create a variety of problems, including hostility toward parents. Finally, studies show that *physical* punishment often leads to an increase in aggressive behavior. Children who are subjected to a lot of physical punishment tend to become more aggressive than the average youngster. The truckload of side effects associated with punishment make it less than ideal as a disciplinary procedure.

Although parents probably overuse punishment as a means of behavioral control, it does have a role to play in disciplinary efforts. The following guidelines summarize research evidence on how to make punishment effective while minimizing its side effects (Axelrod & Apsche, 1983; Parke, 1977; Walters & Grusec, 1977).

1. *Punishment should be swift.* A delay in delivering punishment undermines its impact. When mothers say, "Wait until your father gets home . . ." they are making a fundamental mistake in the use of punishment. Quick punishment highlights the connection between the prohibited behavior and its negative outcome.

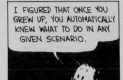

2. *Punishment should be just severe enough to be effective.* The intensity of punishment is a two-edged sword. Although more severe punishments tend to be more effective in suppressing unwanted behavior, they also increase the likelihood of undesirable side effects. Thus, it's best to use the least severe punishment that seems likely to have some impact.

3. *Punishment should be consistent.* If you want to eliminate an undesirable behavior, you should punish it each and every time it occurs. When parents are inconsistent about punishing a particular behavior, they only create confusion.

4. *Punishment should be explained.* When children are punished, the reason for their punishment should be explained as fully as possible, given the constraints of their age. The more children understand the reason why they were punished, the more effective the punishment tends to be.

5. *Make an alternative response available and reinforce it.* One shortcoming of punishment is that it only tells a child what *not* to do. Most undesirable behaviors have a purpose. If you can make another response available that serves the same purpose, doing so should hasten the weakening of the punished response. For example, many troublesome behaviors exhibited by children are primarily attention-seeking devices. Punishment of such attention-seeking responses will be more effective if children are provided with more acceptable ways to gain attention.

6. *Minimize dependence on physical punishment.* Modest physical punishment may be necessary when children are too young to understand a verbal reprimand or the withdrawal of privileges. A light slap on the hand or bottom should suffice. Otherwise, physical punishment should be avoided because it tends to increase aggressive behavior in children. Another consideration is that physical punishment often isn't as effective as most parents assume. Even a vigorous spanking isn't felt by a child an hour later. In contrast, withdrawing valued privileges can give children hours to contemplate the wisdom of changing their ways.

1. Explain the meaning of stages, age roles, and social clocks.

2. Describe the events of puberty and the effects of late or early maturation.

3. Provide an overview of Piaget's theory, including the major accomplishments of the first three stages.

4. Describe Piaget's formal operations period and controversies regarding it.

5. Discuss whether adolescence is a period of emotional turmoil.

6. Describe Erikson's theory of psychosocial development and his view of adolescence.

7. Summarize evidence on adult developmental trends in personality.

8. Describe stages 6 through 8 of Erikson's model of development.

9. Describe the key concepts and assumptions in Gould's and Levinson's theories of adult development.

10. Describe the phases of adult development identified by Levinson and Gould.

11. Describe disengagement theory and related evidence.

12. Summarize criticism of the "ages and stages" approach to adult development.

13. Summarize adult developmental trends in appearance, neurological functioning, and sensory acuity.

14. Discuss the significance of menopause and adult developmental trends in health status.

15. Summarize evidence on how cognitive functioning changes during the adult years.

16. Discuss cultural and individual attitudes about death.

17. Describe the five stages in the process of dying that were identified by Kübler-Ross.

18. Discuss the implications of Ainsworth's research on attachment.

19. Describe three parenting styles identified by Baumrind and their effects on children's development.

20. Discuss issues related to effective parenting of adolescents.

21. Summarize findings on how to use punishment effectively in disciplinary efforts.

KEY TERMS

Age cohort
Ageism
Age roles
Aging
Androgyny
Cognitive development
Conservation
Death system
Development
Egocentrism
Gerontology

Hypothetico-deductive
  reasoning
Menarche
Menopause
Neurons
Object permanence
Puberty
Secondary sex characteristics
Senile dementia
Sexual dimorphism
Social clock
Stage

KEY PEOPLE

Diana Baumrind

Erik Erikson

Roger Gould

Elisabeth Kübler-Ross

Daniel Levinson

Jean Piaget

QUESTIONNAIRE
Death Anxiety Scale

INSTRUCTIONS
If a statement is true or mostly true as applied to you, circle T.
If a statement is false or mostly false as applied to you, circle F.

THE SCALE

T F 1. I am very much afraid to die.

T F 2. The thought of death seldom enters my mind.

T F 3. It doesn't make me nervous when people talk about death.

T F 4. I dread to think about having to have an operation.

T F 5. I am not at all afraid to die.

T F 6. I am not particularly afraid of getting cancer.

T F 7. The thought of death never bothers me.

T F 8. I am often distressed by the way time flies so very rapidly.

T F 9. I fear dying a painful death.

T F 10. The subject of life after death troubles me greatly.

T F 11. I am really scared of having a heart attack.

T F 12. I often think about how short life really is.

T F 13. I shudder when I hear people talking about a World War III.

T F 14. The sight of a dead body is horrifying to me.

T F 15. I feel that the future holds nothing for me to fear.

SCORING THE SCALE
The scoring key is reproduced below. You should circle your response each time it corresponds to the keyed response below. Add up the number of responses that you circle. This total is your score on the Death Anxiety Scale.

1. True	**6.** False	**11.** True
2. False	**7.** False	**12.** True
3. False	**8.** True	**13.** True
4. True	**9.** True	**14.** True
5. False	**10.** True	**15.** False

MY SCORE _____

WHAT THE SCALE MEASURES
Virtually no one looks forward to death, but some of us fear death more than others. Some people are reasonably comfortable with their mortality, and others have difficulty confronting the idea that someday they will die. This scale measures the strength of your anxiety about death. When investigators do research on how age, sex, religion, health, and other variables are related to death anxiety, they use scales such as this one.

Developed by Lonetto and Templer (1983), the Death Anxiety Scale has excellent reliability. Demonstrating the validity of a scale that measures death anxiety is complex, but the scale does correlate with other measures of death anxiety. Scores also correlate positively with clinical judgments of subjects' death anxiety.

INTERPRETING YOUR SCORE
Our norms are based on a sample of 1271 adults (parents of adolescents) cited by Lonetto and Templer (1983). Although females tend to score a little higher than males on this scale, we have reported combined norms.

NORMS

High score: 9–15
Intermediate score: 4–8
Low score: 0–3

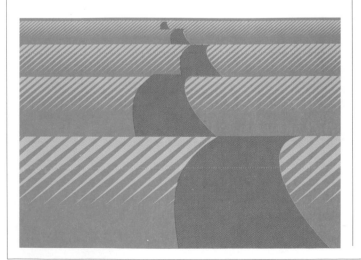

How Do You Feel about Age Roles?

1. Discuss how your behavior has been restricted by age roles. (For example, has anyone ever told you to "act your age?")

2. Have you ever been a victim of ageism? If so, describe.

3. Give an example of how a social clock has influenced your behavior.

4. List seven adjectives that you associate with being elderly.

5. Given the information reviewed in the chapter, do you feel that the adjectives you chose are accurate descriptions of the elderly? To what degree do they reflect stereotypes of the elderly?

12
Vocational Development and Work

"Piano tuning is not really business. It's a dedication. There's such a thing as piano tuning, piano rebuilding, and antique restoration. There's such a thing as scale designing and engineering, to produce the highest sound quality possible. I'm in all of this and I enjoy every second of it. . . . I don't see any possibility of separating my life from my work. . . . There seems something mystic about music, about piano tuning. There's so much beauty comes out of music. There's so much beauty comes out of piano tuning."

—A piano tuner quoted in *Working* (Terkel, 1974)

"The [telephone] dictates. This crummy little machine with buttons on it—you've just got to answer it . . . . Your job doesn't mean anything. Because *you're* just a little machine. A monkey could do what I do. . . .

"Until recently, I'd cry in the morning. I didn't want to get up. I'd dread Fridays because Monday was always looming over me. Another five days ahead of me. . . .

"I'll be at home and the telephone will ring and I get nervous. It reminds me of the telephone at work. . . ."

—A receptionist quoted in *Working* (Terkel, 1974)

The quotations above attest to the vast importance of work in adult life. They speak eloquently of the tremendous impact, either positive or negative, that our jobs may have on the quality of our lives. Perhaps this impact shouldn't be surprising, given that many people's sense of identity is determined by the nature of their work. When adults meet for the first time, their initial "How do you do?" is often followed by the more crucial question, "What do you do for a living?" The answer may convey information not only about one's occupation, but also about social status, lifestyle, personality, interests, and aptitudes.

A *vocation* is an urge or commitment to work in a particular occupational area. Research on vocational adjustment is concerned with such matters as how people arrive at vocational choices, the determinants of vocational success, factors relating to job satisfaction, and patterns of career development. Knowledge about these issues can help you make more informed career decisions, which in turn may enhance your occupational satisfaction with your work. Let's begin by looking at an overview of research on vocational development.

VOCATIONAL DEVELOPMENT ACROSS THE LIFE SPAN

The most influential theory of vocational development is that outlined by Donald Super (1957, 1985, 1988). He views vocational development as a process that unfolds gradually across most of the life span. This process begins in childhood and ends with retirement. Super asserts that one's self-concept is the critical factor that governs this developmental process. According to him, decisions about work and career commitments reflect people's attempts to express their changing views of themselves.

To map out these changes, Super breaks the vocational life cycle into five major stages and a variety of substages (see Figure 12.1). Although we will use Super's model to sketch an overview of vocational development, our discussion will incorporate insights from other theorists (Campbell & Heffernan, 1983; Ginzberg, 1972; Jordaan, 1974; Schein, 1978).

Stages of Vocational Development		
Stage	**Approximate ages**	**Key events and transitions**
Growth stage	0–14	A period of general physical and mental growth
Prevocational substage	0–3	No interest or concern with vocations
Fantasy substage	4–10	Fantasy is basis for vocational thinking
Interest substage	11–12	Vocational thought is based on individual's likes and dislikes
Capacity substage	13–14	Ability becomes the basis for vocational thought
Exploration stage	15–24	General exploration of work
Tentative substage	15–17	Needs, interests, capacities, values, and opportunities become bases for tentative occupational decisions
Transition substage	18–21	Reality increasingly becomes a basis for vocational thought and action
Trial substage	22–24	First trial job is entered after the individual has made an initial vocational commitment
Establishment stage	25–44	The individual seeks to enter a permanent occupation
Trial substage	25–30	A period of some occupational change due to unsatisfactory choices
Stabilization substage	31–44	A period of stable work in a given occupational field
Maintenance stage	45–65	Continuation in one's chosen occupation
Decline stage	65+	Adaptation to leaving work force
Deceleration substage	65–70	Period of declining vocational activity
Retirement substage	71+	A cessation of vocational activity

Growth Stage

The growth stage encompasses childhood, during which youngsters fantasize about exotic jobs they would find pleasurable. Generally, they imagine themselves as detectives, airplane pilots, and brain surgeons rather than plumbers, grocers, and bookkeepers. Until the very end of this period, youngsters are largely oblivious to realistic considerations such as the abilities or education required for various jobs. Instead, they base their fantasies on their likes and dislikes.

Exploration Stage

The pressure to develop a general career direction begins to intensify during high school. Pressure from parents, teachers, and peers leads high school students to identify a range of realistic career possibilities. By the end of high school, the individual is expected to have narrowed this general career direction into a specific one and to have taken preliminary steps to implement this vocational decision. These steps may involve going to work as an apprentice or trainee, or pursuing a particular major in college. Whether it's a matter of studying or working, the person tries to get a real taste of the projected occupation. Thus, the key transitions in the first part of this exploration stage involve (1) becoming more realistic about vocational opportunities and (2) beginning to test out various options.

During the latter part of this stage, people typically attempt to achieve full entry into the world of work. This usually involves finishing any remaining schooling and securing the crucial first job. Many challenges confront the new employee: making the transition from school to the workplace, learning to perform job tasks, and learning to get along with co-workers and supervisors. Many people in this phase are still only tentatively committed to their chosen occupational area. If their initial experiences are gratifying, their commitment will be strengthened. However, if their first experiences are not reward-

ing, they may shift to another occupational area, where they will continue the process of exploration.

Many young people find that their first job is a letdown. Two factors contribute to this disappointment. First, most professions and companies tend to intentionally distort the nature of work in their occupational area. In order to recruit talented people, they try to create a highly favorable picture, thus creating unrealistic expectations. Second, many entry-level jobs are not particularly challenging or interesting. Newly hired workers usually wield little influence in an organization. Worse, they often get stuck with the least rewarding tasks. In light of these realities and the tentative nature of vocational commitment at this point, it is not surprising that many young people experience doubts about their initial occupational choice.

Establishment Stage

"Big corporations turn me off. I didn't know it until I became a supervisor and I realized the games you have to play. . . . I won't be there forever. . . . Working in a bank, there's no thrill in that. . . . I'm still searching. . . . Maybe . . . my next job will be something where I can move around. Maybe a salesman."

—A bank supervisor quoted in *Working* (Terkel, 1974)

Vacillation continues to be moderately common during the first part of the establishment stage. For some people, like the young man quoted above, doubts begin to surface for the first time as they reappraise the match between their personal attributes and their current position. Others simply carry earlier doubts into this stage.

If a person's career choice turns out to be suitably gratifying, however, the person moves into the heart of the establishment stage. With the necessary skills and experience secured, the individual firmly commits to an occupational area. With few exceptions, future job moves will take place *within* this occupational area. Having made a commitment, the person's task is now to demonstrate the ability to function effectively in the chosen occupation. The individual must utilize previously acquired

Figure 12.1. Overview of Super's theory of vocational development. According to Donald Super, people go through five major stages (and a variety of substages) of vocational development over the life span. The approximate ages and key events for each stage are summarized here.

skills, learn new skills as necessary, and display flexibility in adapting to organizational changes.

Many people, particularly those in the professions, are guided and supported in their efforts during this stage by an older co-worker. **A *mentor* is someone with a senior position within an organization who serves as a role model, tutor, and adviser to a novice worker**. Mentoring relationships, like most social relationships, typically develop spontaneously. However, some large corporations (for example, AT&T and Federal Express) have implemented formal mentoring programs that match new employees with managers who can provide relevant training and advice (Zey, 1985). Workers who have a mentor benefit in numerous ways. They may acquire technical, managerial, social, and problem-solving skills. They may also develop increased self-confidence and greater understanding of the workings of their organization (Burke, 1984).

Maintenance Stage

As the years go by, opportunities for further career advancement and occupational mobility decline (see Figure 12.2). Around their mid-40s, many people cross into the maintenance stage, during which they worry more about *retaining* their achieved status than *improving* it. Rapidly changing technology may compel middle-aged employees to enhance and update their skills as they face competition from younger, more recently educated workers. The primary goal in this stage, however, is simply to protect the security, power, advantages, and "perks" that one has attained. With decreased emphasis on career advancement, many people shift energy and attention away from work concerns in favor of family concerns or leisure activities.

The realization that further career advancement is unlikely leads many people to take stock of what they have accomplished. This evaluation may lead to satisfaction or to disenchantment. Most of those who are disappointed learn to live with their frustration. Some, however, get bogged down in feeling sorry for themselves and may become depressed. This type of discontent often leads people to make career changes well into middle age (Kohen, 1975), even though organizational arrangements such as accumulated seniority and pension investments conspire to make such changes costly. For those in unskilled or semiskilled jobs, financial need is the prime motivator for such midlife transitions. Others may desire more personally satisfying work or may be seeking professional advancement (Arbeiter, Aslanian, Schmerbeck, & Brickell, 1978). It appears that it is people who are willing to take risks who tend to gamble on dramatic deviations from their original career paths (Krantz, 1977).

Decline Stage

Deceleration involves a decline in vocational activity during one's later years as retirement looms near. People redirect their energy and attention toward planning for this major transition. In his original formulation, which was based on research in the 1950s, Super projected that deceleration ought to begin around age 65. Since the 1970s, however, slowed economic growth and the entry of the large "baby boom" cohort into the work force have combined to create an oversupply of skilled labor and professional talent. This social change has created pressures that promote early retirement. Many large corporations have offered early retirement incentive programs in an attempt to trim unnecessary staff. In a 1982 survey of retiring workers, the majority retired at age 62. More than 75% exited the work force prior to age 65 (Bernstein & Bernstein, 1988).

However, projected economic and demographic changes may soon make early retirement a historical curiosity. Since 1935, when the Social Security Act arbitrarily set the retirement age at 65, life expectancies for both men and women have increased. Moreover, today's older persons enjoy better health than their counterparts of past generations. Even more significant is the immense size of the "baby boom" cohort, who will be facing retire-

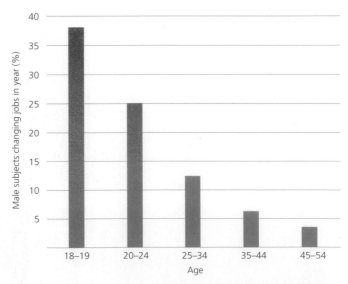

ment in the early decades of the 21st century. Because these baby boomers have had fewer children, a crisis may ensue as the smaller next generation of workers is faced with supporting a massive group of retirees. By the early years of the 21st century, it may become difficult for the United States to support its Social Security and pension programs (Kieffer, 1982). These financial pressures may lead to a restructuring of retirement programs so that early retirement becomes extremely expensive, if not impossible.

Retirement brings vocational activity to a halt. People approach this transition with highly varied attitudes. Many individuals look forward to it eagerly. Many others approach it with apprehension, unsure about how they will occupy themselves and worried about their financial viability. Mixed feelings are also common. Many people approach retirement with a combination of hopeful enthusiasm and anxious concern. Although concern about what lies ahead is not irrational, many studies have shown that retirement has no adverse effect on overall life satisfaction (Palmore, Fillenbaum, & George, 1984). Although retirement may mean less income, it can also mean having more time to spend on hobbies, household tasks, and friends (George, Fillenbaum, & Palmore, 1984).

Variations and Qualifications

As we mentioned in Chapter 11, stage theories tend to highlight general trends while ignoring the variability in developmental patterns. However, Super deserves credit for acknowledging that people follow different patterns in their vocational development. In fact, he identified several atypical patterns that do not coincide with the *conventional pattern* we have described.

Super described three atypical patterns for men. One of these is the *unstable pattern*. Men who follow this pattern alternate between trial jobs (exploratory, entry-level positions) and stable jobs throughout life. These men get beyond entry-level jobs and earn positions with potential,

but then forsake their progress and move on to another occupational area. In the *multiple-trial pattern*, men move quickly through an endless series of briefly held trial jobs. These men are occupational vagabonds who wander aimlessly from one career to another. Finally, men who follow a *stable pattern* enter a career immediately upon leaving school and remain in that career for their entire working lives.

For women, the variety of career patterns is even greater. In addition to the four patterns seen in men, Super describes three career patterns unique to women. Women who follow the *stable homemaking pattern* never work outside the home. Those who follow the *double-track pattern* attempt to combine homemaking and outside work throughout adulthood. The *interrupted pattern* is seen in women who temporarily leave the work force one or more times because of family responsibilities.

It is important to note that most of the research on vocational development has focused on *males'* careers. Until the mid-1970s, it was simply taken for granted that the theories and concepts used to explain men's vocational development would apply equally well to women. However, evidence suggests that men and women follow different patterns of vocational development (Fitzgerald & Betz, 1983). For example, a study of career progress among men and women (Larwood & Gattiker, 1984) uncovered some interesting gender differences. For the male subjects, it was possible to trace a clear, consistent path that led to vocational success. Among the female subjects, however, success was much less predictable and was characterized as nearly "random." Why was there no pattern for women? Women's vocational development may be less predictable because women are more likely than men to experience career interruptions as they leave the work force temporarily to concentrate on child rearing or family crises. Additionally, many women subordinate their career goals to their husbands' goals. To put these and other gender differences in perspective, let's look at women's participation in the work force.

Figure 12.2. Occupational mobility as related to age. Occupational mobility declines dramatically with increasing age, as these data from a study by Byrne (1975) clearly show. (From Arbeiter, 1979)

WOMEN IN THE WORKPLACE

For many years, popular wisdom held that "a woman's place is in the home." Today, however, well over half of all American women are either working or actively seeking employment (Rukeyser, Cooney, & Winslow, 1988). This more favorable work environment for women reflects dramatic economic and social changes that have occurred in recent decades. Accordingly, let's begin our discussion with a brief historical overview. Much of the material in the following section is drawn from an excellent history of American women in the labor force by Alice Kessler-Harris (1982).

Historical Overview

The influx of women into the ranks of wage earners is often attributed to economic conditions that developed during World War II. The United States entered a period of rapid industrial expansion at the same time that the armed forces were depleting the supply of male workers. As a result, women were offered opportunities to enter fields that had previously been denied them. Some companies hastily set up on-site child-care facilities, and a few even made available hot meals that women could take home to their families at the end of the workday. With such inducements, women entered the labor force in record numbers.

For the most part, however, the gains made by women during the war did not last. Once the soldiers came home, many women who had worked in low-paying industries quit their jobs. Women in higher-paying industries were more reluctant to quit, but they were often discharged to make openings available for returning servicemen. Nor did any permanent change take place in people's attitudes toward working women. In a 1946 survey by *Fortune* magazine, only a third of the men and two fifths of the women queried believed that a married woman without children, whose husband could support her, should be allowed to work if she wanted to (Kessler-Harris, 1982).

A more enduring trend toward change began in the 1950s. The postwar migration to the suburbs was accompanied by demands for a higher standard of living. The "good life" required not only a house and a car, but many expensive appliances as well. These lifestyle changes necessitated higher family incomes, and wives were the logical providers. Hence, by 1960, about 40% of adult women were employed (see Figure 12.3).

The inflationary pressures of the 1960s and 1970s forced even more married women to seek employment. During the same time period, several demographic trends helped to swell the ranks of women entering the work force. Among them were the increasing number of never-married women, divorced women, and married women who elected to remain childless. At the same time, changing attitudes about gender roles and improving occupational opportunities for females led more women into the world of work. By 1986, over 65% of adult women were in the labor force. In that same year, 54% of all married women with children under 6 were working at least part-time outside the home (Folbre, 1987).

Today's Workplace for Women

Is today's workplace essentially the same for women as it is for men? In most respects, the answer appears to be no. Although job discrimination on the basis of sex has been illegal for more than 25 years, women continue to face subtle obstacles to occupational success. Foremost among these is job segregation on the basis of gender. Certain jobs have historically been regarded as "masculine" or "feminine," and such stereotypes persist today (White, Kruczek, Brown, & White, 1989). Thus, as we noted in Chapter 10, a disproportionate number of women are employed in relatively low-paid "pink ghetto" occupations such as nurse, secretary, librarian, cashier, receptionist, maid, bank teller, and waitress. Employees in female-dominated fields typically earn less than employees in male-dominated fields even when the jobs require similar levels of training, skill, and responsibility (Ru-

Figure 12.3. Women in the work force. The percentage of adult women (aged 20–64) who work outside the home has been increasing throughout the century. The rate of increase began to escalate in the 1950s. Experts estimate that 80% of adult women will be in the work force by the year 2000. (From Matthews & Rodin, 1989)

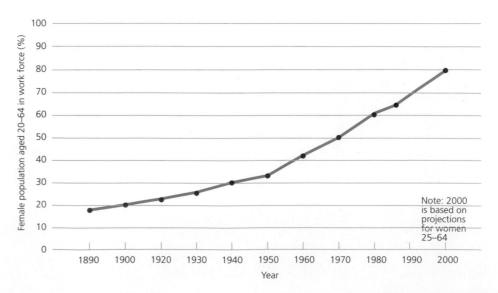

Note: 2000 is based on projections for women 25–64

keyser, Cooney, & Winslow, 1988). As a general rule, the greater the percentage of female workers within a field, the lower the average pay in that field (Folbre, 1987).

The world of work is also different for men and women because women have fewer opportunities to observe and emulate same-sex role models who occupy professional positions (Fitzgerald & Crites, 1980). As we noted in Chapter 11, females have a harder time finding a mentor in the workplace than do males. Furthermore, even though women have made great inroads in many sectors of the economy, they still face discrimination—especially when it comes to advancing to top management positions. Less than 2% of the corporate officers of Fortune 500 companies are female (Morrison & Von Glinow, 1990). There appears to be a "glass ceiling" that prevents most women from advancing beyond middle-management positions.

Sexual Harassment

Another problem for women is sexual harassment in the workplace. *Sexual harassment* **occurs when employees are subjected to unwanted sexually oriented behavior**. This broad definition includes behaviors ranging from suggestive comments or looks to unwanted touching or pressure for sexual favors, as well as sexual assault. Although males are occasionally subjected to sexual harassment, the vast majority of victims are female (Fitzgerald et al., 1988).

Sexual harassment is more widespread than most people realize. Recent surveys estimate that 50–75% of female workers in the United States have experienced at least one instance of sexual harassment (Fain & Anderton, 1987; Lafontaine & Tredeau, 1986). The typical victim is young and unmarried, has several years of technical training or college, and works in a male-dominated field. Women victimized by sexual harassment often develop physical and psychological symptoms of stress that may lead to decreased work motivation and productivity (Crull, 1979).

In recognition of the prevalence and the negative impact of sexual harassment, many organizations have taken steps to educate and protect their workers. These steps include programs designed to increase male employees' awareness of the problem, issuance of policies expressly forbidding harassment, and implementation of formal grievance procedures for handling allegations of harassment.

Although women face some special problems in the world of work, the vocational development of both sexes is also similar in some ways. For instance, male and female workers appear to be influenced by the same motivational forces. In the next section, we turn our attention to the needs that motivate people to become and remain members of the work force.

MOTIVATION TO WORK

Historically, workers have been motivated by two overriding considerations. The first, of course, is economic necessity. The income earned through employment is necessary to provide food, clothing, shelter, health care, and so on. Almost as important has been the so-called work ethic—the belief that a nonproductive lifestyle is morally unacceptable.

Today's workers, however, grew up in relative affluence, and many are inclined to take financial security almost for granted. Although earning money remains a necessity for most people, it is no longer enough to guarantee job satisfaction. Nor do today's workers unhesitatingly endorse the work ethic. The emphasis on personal fulfillment that emerged in the 1970s and 1980s has extended to the workplace. Contemporary workers have high expectations for their jobs. They want opportunities to learn, to fulfill their talents, and to accomplish something worthwhile (Hall, 1986).

With these historical trends in mind, let's examine three theories of work motivation. We will begin with the classic theories of Douglas McGregor and Frederick Herzberg. We will then discuss a more recent theory developed by Helen Astin.

Although more and more women can be found in the workplace, they tend to occupy lower- and middle-echelon jobs. Only a small percentage advance to executive levels.

McGregor's Theory X and Theory Y

McGregor (1960) postulates that managers base decisions on implicit assumptions about human nature. In other words, managerial policy reflects management's "theory" about what motivates workers. McGregor describes two basic theories of work motivation. *Theory X* assumes that people inherently dislike work and that they have little ambition. According to Theory X, workers need and prefer to be coerced, directed, and threatened to be productive.

In contrast, *Theory Y* assumes that people find work as natural and as satisfying as play or rest. According to Theory Y, workers can and will exercise self-direction and self-control when they are committed to achieving organizational objectives. According to McGregor, workers will be committed to attaining organizational goals to the extent that they can simultaneously fulfill their personal needs for autonomy, achievement, status, recognition, and self-fulfillment.

Whereas Theory X leads to direction and control through the exercise of authority, Theory Y suggests a profoundly different organizational structure. Theory Y implies that managers have the responsibility to create conditions in which workers can best attain their personal goals by working toward organizational goals. According to McGregor, if workers are unproductive, apathetic, or irresponsible, this is *not* a reflection of "human nature." Rather, it is a signal that management needs to revise its methods and policies.

Herzberg's Motivation-Hygiene Theory

Herzberg (1968) proposes that humans have two basic needs. The first is one we share with animals. It is the need to avoid unpleasant situations that lead to physical or psychological pain. In the context of work, these avoidance needs are met when working conditions are pleasant: a comfortable physical environment, good relationships with supervisors and co-workers, a fair salary, and job security. These factors deal not with the job itself, but rather with the context in which the job must be performed. Herzberg refers to these as *hygiene factors*. Their main effect is to *prevent* unhappiness and unproductivity on the job. Working conditions that fail to satisfy employees' need to avoid unpleasantness can produce dissatisfaction and poor job performance.

According to Herzberg, our second and more important need is uniquely human. It is our need for self-actualization, which was first described by Abraham Maslow (see Chapter 2). This motive reflects our need to fulfill our potential as creative, unique individuals. Workers meet this need through successful performance of job tasks, recognition and appreciation of this success, and opportunities for professional growth. These factors are associated with the job itself and are referred to as *motivators*, since they spur workers to greater effort. Opportunities for self-actualization on the job lead to higher worker satisfaction and enhanced job performance. Thus, for workers to be happy and productive, a pleasant working environment is not enough. Herzberg argues that jobs should also afford workers the opportunity for personal and professional growth.

Astin's Sociopsychological Model

Astin (1984) has proposed that contemporary men and women seek to fulfill three categories of needs through employment: survival, pleasure, and contribution. *Survival needs* include needs for food, shelter, clothing, medical care, and so on. These needs are met through the economic compensation we receive for our labor: salary, health insurance, pension funds, and the like. *Pleasure needs* consist of needs for enjoyment and gratification. These needs are met through the intrinsic satisfactions gained from work activities. Finally, Astin hypothesizes that we are motivated by a *need to contribute* to the welfare of others, including our family, our community, and our nation. This need is met by the appreciation and recognition we receive from others. Satisfying our need to con-

Work that some people find pleasurable may be boring or stressful to others. Thus, job satisfaction is in the "mind of the beholder."

tribute also helps us to derive a feeling of self-worth from our occupational endeavors.

Although McGregor, Herzberg, and Astin differ somewhat in their views of work motivation, they agree that work can fulfill a variety of human needs. Furthermore, all three theorists emphasize that the extent to which a job meets an individual's needs is closely related to the individual's degree of satisfaction with that job. There are, however, a number of factors affecting job satisfaction, as we discuss in the next section.

UNDERSTANDING JOB SATISFACTION

In making a vocational choice, in a sense we make a prediction about the future. We predict that the occupation we choose will lead to success and provide us with satisfaction. That is, we hope not only to do well in our chosen field, but to *enjoy* it as well. *Job satisfaction* **refers to one's happiness and contentment with a particular occupational position**. In making vocational decisions, it is useful to be aware of some of the determinants of job satisfaction.

Importance of Job Satisfaction

The significance of vocational satisfaction becomes apparent when we consider that it may have important implications not only for the employee, but also for the employer and even for society at large. From the employee's perspective, there are a number of reasons to be concerned about job satisfaction. Work-related problems are a significant source of stress. Hence, job dissatisfaction can have an adverse effect on an employee's physical health (Holt, 1982). The connection between job stress and disease may explain the dramatic finding that people who are satisfied with their work tend to live longer (Palmore, 1969). Furthermore, research suggests that job satisfaction is related to employees' overall adjustment and mental health (Warr, 1987).

The issue of job satisfaction is also an important one for employers. Although job satisfaction does not necessarily lead to increased productivity, job dissatisfaction can contribute to increased turnover, which is an expensive problem in most firms (Mobley, Horner, & Hollingsworth, 1978). Taking a broader perspective, job satisfaction can even have an impact on society at large. Considering the link between job stress and disease, excessive numbers of dissatisfied workers may tax our already overburdened health-care system. Furthermore, consumers may find themselves paying higher prices for goods and services if companies pass on the cost of high turnover rates. Thus, job satisfaction is an issue that concerns everyone.

Measuring Job Satisfaction

Before describing the factors associated with job satisfaction, we need to emphasize the complexity of this issue. First, job satisfaction is a multidimensional concept that is not easily measured. A job has many aspects. A person might be satisfied with one aspect, such as promotion opportunities, and dissatisfied with another, such as job security.

Second, job satisfaction is a highly personal matter that depends on more than just the nature of one's work. Two people working at the same job may exhibit very different levels of satisfaction. Your job satisfaction depends on your subjective *perception* of your working conditions. Imagine that your company institutes a new policy whereby each worker will now perform a greater variety of tasks. If you view this change as an opportunity to broaden your skills and alleviate boredom, your job satisfaction will be enhanced. But if you attribute this change to the company's desire to increase job duties without increasing pay, your job satisfaction will probably suffer.

To some extent, the tendency to feel satisfied with work may be a personality trait that transcends specific job characteristics. Staw and Ross (1985) measured the job satisfaction of 5000 men over a period of five years. Surprisingly, individuals' job satisfaction tended to re-

main very stable over this span of time, in spite of changes in their assignments, responsibilites, employers, and occupations.

As you can see, the assessment of job satisfaction is a complicated matter. Small wonder, then, that researchers have conducted well over 3000 studies on this issue (Locke, 1983). Although their findings are complex, they have isolated some factors that are related to job satisfaction for most people.

Ingredients of Job Satisfaction

Contrary to conventional wisdom, job satisfaction is not strongly related to job *level*. Many people assume that higher-status jobs lead to greater satisfaction. There may be a trend in that direction, but Seashore and Barnowe (1972) found that the "blue-collar blues" show up among plenty of high-status white-collar workers as well. Perhaps those in high-status positions use different standards to judge their satisfaction. Or perhaps those in low-status fields simply expect less from their jobs. In any case, job level is *not* the crucial factor determining job satisfaction.

What are the main ingredients of happiness at work? Quite a number of elements can contribute to job satisfaction. We will highlight some of the more important factors in this section. Although we will cite some individual studies, our discussion will be based primarily on three research reviews (Gruneberg, 1979; Hopkins, 1983; Locke, 1983).

Challenge

In their analysis of "blue-collar blues," Seashore and Barnowe (1972) found that people need challenge in their jobs. This makes sense in view of our earlier observation that people want to use their full potentials in their work. This point was underscored in a survey of over 23,000 *Psychology Today* readers conducted by Patricia Renwick and Edward Lawler (1978). When asked to rate the importance of various aspects of their jobs, the respondents ranked "chances to learn new things" and the

"opportunity to develop skills and abilities" third and fourth, respectively (see Figure 12.4).

The issue of challenging work has taken on new significance since the early 1970s. As we mentioned earlier, there has been an oversupply of professional talent since the sizable baby boom cohort began to enter the work force. The absorption of new workers into the labor force has been somewhat slower and more selective than it used to be. Many people have found that their college diplomas haven't won them the jobs they were trained for (Freeman, 1976), and many have found themselves underemployed. *Underemployment* **involves settling for a job that does not fully utilize one's skills, abilities, and training**. This problem declined during the 1980s, thanks to renewed economic expansion. Nonetheless, lack of challenge may contribute to job dissatisfaction among many people who continue to be underemployed.

Good Pay

When workers are asked to rate the importance of various job features, they generally rank pay surprisingly low. For instance, in the Renwick and Lawler (1978) survey, pay was ranked only 12th in importance out of 18 items. Their sample, however, was somewhat biased in that it contained a disproportionate number of affluent, well-educated, professional subjects. Good pay is typically ranked higher in importance by those in nonprofessional positions. Moreover, at all occupational levels, ratings of the importance of pay may be misleading. Although workers often rank pay low in importance, it tends to be a major source of complaints. This paradoxical finding suggests that people may be more concerned about pay than they would like to believe.

Pay, by the way, is one of those things that tend to be evaluated on a relative basis. People are very sensitive to what *others* earn. Workers tend to be satisfied with their pay to the extent that they perceive it as *fair*. For most of us, a fair salary is one that (1) compares favorably with that of other employees with similar training and seniority who work in the same field and (2) is commensurate with

What Is Most Important in People's Jobs?

1 Chances to do something that makes you feel good about yourself
2 Chances to accomplish something worthwhile
3 Chances to learn new things
4 Opportunity to develop your skills and abilities
5 The amount of freedom you have on your job
6 Chances you have to do things you do best
7 The resources you have to do your job
8 The respect you receive from people you work with
9 Amount of information you get about your job performance
10 Your chances for taking part in making decisions
11 The amount of job security you have
12 Amount of pay you get
13 The way you are treated by the people you work with
14 The friendliness of people you work with
15 Amount of praise you get for job well done
16 The amount of fringe benefits you get
17 Chances for getting a promotion
18 Physical surroundings of your job

the company's ability to pay (Levering, 1988). No matter how much we make, we may feel undercompensated if others are earning more or if our employers are making large profits that do not filter down to employees.

Security

"I used to joke at lunch. I'd say, 'If anybody hears that layoffs are comin', do me a favor. Send in my name.' Then a funny thing happened. I got laid off. I couldn't believe it. . . . I felt like a kid who wet his pants. I was afraid to go home and tell my wife. The rest of the day, nobody talked to me. They looked at me like I had cancer. I tried to smile, but I wanted to puke. The end of the day, I didn't want to leave. I even thought about just working through the next shift."

—A man quoted in *Psychology of Work Behavior* (Landy, 1989)

Being unemployed can have a devastating impact on one's psychological health. Job loss is related to the likelihood of psychological disorders (Banks & Jackson, 1982), substance abuse (Windshuttle, 1980), and marital separation (Liem & Rayman, 1982). Indeed, unemployment rates are a very significant predictor of suicide rates (Boor, 1980). Thus, it is not surprising that people value security in their jobs. Rankings of this factor vary with the strength of the economy. When economic times are good, security is sometimes ranked low in importance because employees begin to take it for granted. But job security becomes very important as soon as it is undermined, as the quotation above illustrates.

To enhance commitment and trust on the part of their employees, some large firms have adopted a no-layoff policy. This assurance of job security typically leads to increased job satisfaction (Levering, 1988). Of course, a no-layoff policy probably isn't feasible in many sectors of business and industry.

Meaningfulness

Meaningfulness as it relates to work is rather difficult to define. Generally, when people talk about their work being meaningful, they seem concerned about whether it makes a real contribution to society. In other words, they want their jobs to fulfill what Astin (1984) terms "contribution needs." This is an important issue for many people. In the Renwick and Lawler survey, respondents ranked "chances to accomplish something worthwhile" second in importance out of the 18 job characteristics studied.

Variety and Autonomy

Variety in a job is also an important consideration. People tend to find repetitive, assembly-line work boring and dissatisfying. A closely related consideration is job autonomy. Autonomy and variety tend to go hand in hand at work, and both are highly desired. Consequently, one way companies can increase employee satisfaction is by restructuring jobs so that each worker is allowed to perform a variety of what would otherwise be routine tasks. Another way is to utilize participative-management techniques in which workers at all levels are given maximum responsibility for how they do their jobs (Levering, 1988).

Friendship and Recognition

In Chapter 8 we discussed the prominent role that friendships play in our lives. For many people, friendship circles emerge largely out of interactions at work. Consequently, it is logical that the social aspects of a job are a prime determinant of job satisfaction. When interpersonal relationships at work are pleasant, people are more likely to be content with their jobs.

Whether it is provided through pay raises, promotions, or praise, people crave recognition for their work. Most of us need to have the value of our work validated by others, especially supervisors and co-workers. Many of us are quite willing to go beyond the minimum requirements of our jobs as long as our extra efforts are recognized and appreciated. In the absence of such feedback, we may feel undervalued and dissatisfied.

Role Clarity

A relatively obscure factor that turns out to be important to job satisfaction is role clarity. Workers like their job

Figure 12.4. Workers' evaluation of job characteristics. Renwick and Lawler (1978) asked subjects how important 18 aspects of their jobs were to them. These 18 job characteristics are ranked here from most important to least important, based on the averages of subjects' responses.

responsibilities to be clearly defined. When workers aren't sure what is expected of them, they tend to feel uncomfortable. Clear explanations of work requirements and performance criteria tend to promote job satisfaction.

Other Complexities

There are additional complexities in the job satisfaction equation. According to Peter Warr (1987), some of the job attributes that we value may be desirable only up to a certain point. He draws an analogy between the ingredients of job satisfaction and the vitamins our bodies need. Although we need our minimum requirements of various vitamins, high doses of some vitamins can be toxic. Similarly, although we may desire challenge, for instance, in our jobs, *too much* challenge may be harmful to our adjustment. Warr maintains that some desirable job attributes—such as good pay, job security, and recognition—have a consistent positive relationship to mental health (see Figure 12.5). However, he asserts that many other desirable job attributes—such as challenge, variety, autonomy, and decision-making input—have a curvilinear relationship to mental health. That is, these job characteristics have positive effects up to a point, but negative effects when they become excessive (see Figure 12.5). Why should some valued attributes of work have negative effects on our job satisfaction and adjustment? Because too much challenge or autonomy may produce a high level of job *stress*—a subject we explore in the next section.

STRESS IN THE WORKPLACE

We saw in Chapter 3 that stress can emerge from every corner of our lives. However, many theorists suspect that the workplace is the primary source of stress in modern society. In one study, the principal difference between patients suffering from heart disease and matched control subjects was that the heart patients had experienced more occupational stress (Russek & Russek, 1976). In this section, we'll discuss stress on the job and what employees and workers can do about it.

Sources of Stress on the Job

Some stress comes not from jobs themselves, but from the physical environment in which the jobs are performed. Examples of environmental stressors include extreme heat or cold, poor illumination, excessive noise, and air pollution. The effects of such stressors are more complex than we might expect. For instance, consider the effects of noise (Landy, 1989). Intense noise often impairs job performance, especially if it is intermittent, whereas low noise has little effect. Interestingly, *changes* in noise level often produce more distress and impaired performance than constant noise. Furthermore, some individuals are more sensitive than others to noise and suffer more from exposure to it.

Of course, the characteristics of jobs themselves may provide many sources of stress. Some jobs require workers to constantly do two or more things at once. For example, receptionists must frequently interrupt their typing to answer the telephone. Other jobs demand virtually perfect performance, since errors can have disastrous consequences. Consider, for example, the pressure under which surgeons or air traffic controllers must work. Still other jobs, like coal mining or fire fighting, require workers to face frequent threats to their physical safety. The list of potentially stressful job conditions is almost endless. Some of the more commonly experienced job stressors include prolonged physical labor, tedious work, work overload, long hours, unusual hours (such as rotating shifts), and the pressure of deadlines (Marshall & Cooper, 1981; Shostak, 1980). Another problem is "technostress" (Brod, 1988). This kind of stress is experienced by the increasing number of people who are having difficulty adapting to the new technology in the workplace, such as computers and automated offices.

Additional sources of stress can come from human relations problems within organizations. Workers may

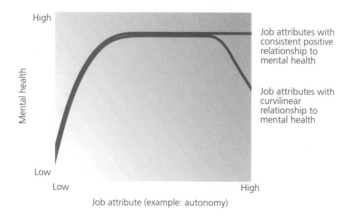

High

Mental health

Low

Low   High

Job attribute (example: autonomy)

Job attributes with consistent positive relationship to mental health

Job attributes with curvilinear relationship to mental health

Figure 12.5. Warr's theory relating job characteristics to mental health. According to Peter Warr (1987), desirable job characteristics that are related to mental health (and job satisfaction) fall into two categories. Some job attributes—such as good pay and job security—have a consistent positive relationship to mental health. Other job attributes—such as variety and autonomy—have a curvilinear relationship to mental health. In other words, too much of a good thing (for instance, challenge) can lead to negative effects.

struggle with role ambiguity if their job requirements are not clearly spelled out. They may be frustrated because they are denied input into decisions that will affect them. They may be underpromoted and underutilized. Conversely, they may find themselves overpromoted to positions for which they feel unprepared. Ultimately, many sources of occupational stress come from organizational factors, such as office politics, poor relations with supervisors, restrictions on communication, and the like (Blau, 1981).

Robert Karasek has proposed an intriguing model of occupational stress that emphasizes the importance of two factors (Karasek, 1979; Karasek & Theorell, 1990). These factors are (1) the *psychological demands* made upon a worker and (2) the *decision control* a worker has. Psychological demands are measured by asking employees questions such as: "Is there excessive work?" and "Must you work fast (or hard)?" Decision control is measured by asking employees questions such as "Do you have a lot of say in your job?" and "Do you have freedom to make decisions?" According to Karasek, *stress is greatest in jobs characterized by high psychological demands and low decision control.* Based on survey data obtained from workers, he has tentatively mapped out where various jobs fall on these two key dimensions of job stress, as shown in Figure 12.6. In this diagram, the jobs thought to be most stressful are those in the lower right area.

Of course, the personal characteristics of workers are a crucial consideration in understanding occupational stress. Stress lies in the eye of the beholder, and people vary widely in their ability to handle stress. Some of the personal qualities that may moderate the effects of job stress include physical stamina, tolerance for ambiguity, excellent job-related skills, and the ability to cope with change (French, Caplan, & Van Harrison, 1982; Matteson & Ivancevich, 1987). The impact of work stress may also be reduced by factors that moderate the effects of stress in general, such as social support, hardiness, and optimism (see Chapter 3).

In the final analysis, work stress arises out of the interaction of employ-

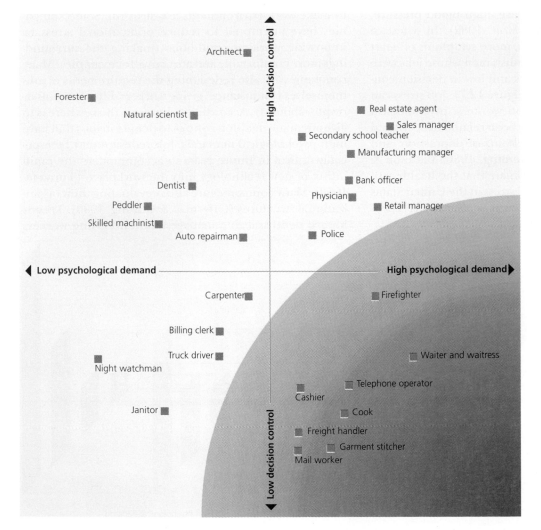

Figure 12.6. Karasek's model of occupational stress as related to specific jobs. Robert Karasek theorizes that occupational stress is greatest in jobs characterized by high psychological demands and low decision control. Based on survey data, this chart shows where various familiar jobs fall on these two dimensions. According to Karasek's model, the most stressful jobs are those shown in the shaded area on the lower right.

ees with their work environments. It is a matter of *person-environment fit.* When the worker and the job environment are compatible, stress will tend to be low. The greater the mismatch between the characteristics of the worker and the demands of the job, the greater the worker's stress is likely to be (French, Caplan, & Van Harrison, 1982). A good fit occurs when the person can provide the abilities needed to be successful at the job and when the job can adequately meet the employee's needs.

Effects of Job Stress

Like other forms of stress, occupational stress is associated with a host of negative effects. In the work arena itself, job stress has been linked to increases in industrial accidents (Levenson, Hirschfeld, Hirschfeld, & Dzubay, 1983), poor job performance (Jackson & Schuler, 1985), higher turnover rates (Powell, 1973), and increased absenteeism (Rosch & Pelletier, 1987). Experts estimate that stress-related reductions in workers' productivity may cost American industry about $300 billion per year (Karasek & Theorell, 1990).

Of course, the negative effects of occupational stress extend beyond the workplace. Foremost among these are adverse effects on employees' physical health (Wolf, 1986). Work stress has been related to a variety of physical maladies, including heart disease, high blood pressure, stroke, ulcers, and arthritis (Holt, 1982). In a test of Karasek's model of work stress, more symptoms of heart disease were found among Swedish men whose jobs were high in psychological demands and low in decision control (Karasek et al., 1981; see Figure 12.7). Job stress can also have a negative impact on workers' psychological health. Occupational stress has been related to decreased self-esteem, frequent anxiety, bouts of depression, and abuse of alcohol or drugs (Fleming, 1986; Matteson & Ivancevich, 1987). Experts estimate that the health care costs arising from occupational stress in the United States may run around $150 billion per year (Karasek & Theorell, 1990).

Dealing with Job Stress

There are essentially three avenues of attack for dealing with occupational stress (Ivancevich, Matteson, Freedman, & Phillips, 1990), as summarized in Figure 12.8. The first is to intervene at the *individual* level by modifying workers' ways of coping with job stress. The second is to intervene at the *organizational* level by redesigning the work environment itself. The third is to intervene at the *individual-organizational interface* by improving the fit between workers and their companies. Let's look at each approach in turn.

Interventions at the individual level are the most widely used strategy for managing work stress (Ivancevich et al., 1990). Many companies have instituted programs designed to improve their employees' coping skills. These programs usually focus on relaxation training, time management, cognitive approaches to reappraising stressful events, and other constructive coping strategies that we discussed in Chapter 4. Also popular are *wellness programs* that seek to improve employees' physical health (Gebhardt & Crump, 1990). These programs usually focus on exercise and fitness training, health screening, nutritional education, and the reduction of health-impairing habits, such as smoking and overeating.

Interventions at the organizational level are intended to make work environments less stressful. Some companies have attempted to reduce occupational stress by improving working conditions (making the surroundings more comfortable and attractive, for example). Many companies are also redesigning the requirements of jobs themselves (for instance, giving workers different tools or responsibilities). According to Karasek, the key here is to give adequate decision control to people in jobs that have high psychological demands. Job redesign may be especially critical in future years to accommodate the rapid influx of new technology into the workplace (Turnage, 1990). Many companies are also reevaluating their organizational structures (Offerman & Gowing, 1990). Trends toward decentralizing management and giving workers

Figure 12.7. Job characteristics in Karasek's model and heart disease prevalence.
Karasek et al. (1981) interviewed 1,621 Swedish men about their work and assessed their cardiovascular health. The vertical bars in this figure show the percentage of the men with symptoms of heart disease as a function of the characteristics of their jobs. The highest incidence of heart disease was found among men who had jobs high in psychological demands and low in decision control, just as Karasek's model of occupational stress would predict.

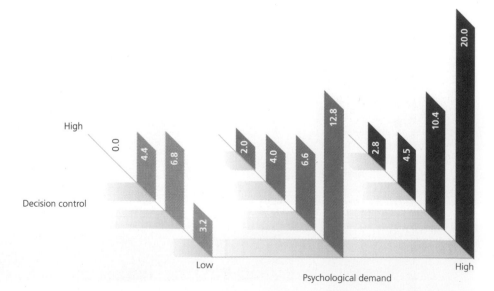

greater participation in decision making may help to reduce occupational stress.

Interventions at the individual-organizational interface can take many forms. In future years, the biggest challenge probably will be to accommodate the changing nature of the work force. The work force used to be dominated by married men who were the sole wage-earners in their homes. In recent years, however, dual-earner couples have come to represent 40% of the work force. Another 6% of workers are single parents (Friedman, 1987). These trends mean that people will be struggling more with role conflicts between their work responsibilities and their family responsibilities. To reduce this source of occupational stress, companies are slowly beginning to increase opportunities for parental leaves of absence, assistance with child care, and flexibility in work hours (Zedeck & Mosier, 1990). Of course, strain between work and family concerns is not entirely new, as we'll see in the next section, where we discuss workaholics.

REPRINTED BY PERMISSION. TRUBUNE MEDIA SERVICES.

CAN WORK BE ADDICTIVE? WORKAHOLICS

However stressful or satisfying their jobs might be, most people seek fulfillment in other areas of life as well. Most of us cherish our leisure activities and our relationships with our families and friends. However, a small minority of people devote nearly all their time and energy to their jobs. These people tend to avoid nonwork activities. They put in considerable overtime, take few vacations, regularly bring work home from the office, and think about work most of the time. They are energetic, intense, and overly ambitious. In short, they are "workaholics."

Psychologists are divided on the issue of whether workaholism is problematic. Should workaholics be praised for their dedication and encouraged in their single-minded pursuit of fulfillment through work? Or is workaholism a form of "addiction," a sign that an individual is driven by compulsions he or she cannot control?

In support of the former view, Machlowitz (1980) found that workaholics tend to be highly satisfied with their jobs and with their lives. They work hard simply because work is the most meaningful activity they know. Yet other evidence suggests that workaholics may have a pathological need to exercise rigid control over themselves and their environments (Schwartz, 1982).

How can these conflicting findings be reconciled? Naughton (1987) has suggested that there may be two different types of workaholics. One type, the job-involved workaholic, works for the pure joy of it. These people derive immense satisfaction from work and generally perform well in highly demanding jobs. The other type, the compulsive workaholic, is neither well-adjusted nor an asset to an employer. Compulsive workaholics are addicted to work. Their devotion to work reflects a rigid, overcontrolling personality. They approach their jobs in a ritualized manner and cannot deviate from their set routines. They often alienate their supervisors and co-workers with their rigidity. Interestingly, compulsive workaholics are not necessarily satisfied with their jobs, and they may be prone to develop *burnout*, which we described in Chapter 3. Thus, it appears that workaholism

Strategies for Managing Stress in the Workplace		
Individual	**Organizational**	**Individual-organizational interface**
Meditation	Organizational structure	Job demands/person style fit
Exercise	Job design	Participation preferences/practices
Relaxation techniques	Selection and placement programs	Autonomy preferences/practices
Cognitive approaches	Working conditions	Co-worker relationships
Goal setting	Training and development	
Time management		

Figure 12.8. Stress management interventions in the workplace. Ivancevich et al. (1990) distinguish between three types of programs to alleviate the effects of occupational stress. Interventions can occur at the individual (employee) level, at the organizational level, and at the individual-organizational interface.

may be either constructive or problematic, depending on the motivation underlying a person's dedication to work.

IMPORTANT CONSIDERATIONS IN VOCATIONAL CHOICE

One of your biggest decisions in life is choosing a vocation. The importance of this decision is enormous. It may determine whether you are successful or unsuccessful, employed or unemployed, happy or unhappy. Given our rapidly advancing technology and the increased training and education required to break into most fields, it is more important than ever to choose thoughtfully. We have already described some of the factors that tend to promote job satisfaction, and these should be taken into account in choosing an occupation. Additional information must be considered as well. To make an informed vocational choice, it is critical that you evaluate your personality, talents, and interests. It is also necessary to research the characteristics of the various job options available to you. The more you possess accurate information about your personal characteristics and about your job options, the better prepared you will be to choose a career that is suitable for you. To facilitate this end, we will discuss important considerations in vocational choice.

General Principles

As you explore your personal characteristics and investigate career opportunities, it will be helpful to keep the following generalizations in mind.

1. *There are limits on your career options.* Entry into a particular occupation is not simply a matter of choosing what you want to do. It's a two-way street. You get to make choices, but you also have to persuade schools and employers to choose you. Your career options will be limited to some extent by factors beyond your control, including fluctuations in the economy and the job market (Lock, 1988).
2. *You have the potential for success in a variety of occupations.* Vocational counselors stress that people have multiple potentials (Gilmer, 1975). There are over 20,000 different occupations to choose from! In light of the huge variety in occupational opportunities, it's foolish to believe that only one career would be right for you. If you expect to find one job that fits you perfectly, you may spend your entire lifetime searching for it.
3. *Chance may play a role in your vocational development.* Unplanned, accidental events can influence one's vocational evolution (Hart, Rayner, & Christensen, 1971). For example, your career plans might be changed by a particular college course that you took only because the class you really wanted was full. This reality does not mean that you should leave career development to fate. Rather, your challenge is to minimize the role of chance in your vocational development through thoughtful planning.
4. *Vocational choice is a developmental process that*

RECOMMENDED READING

Joyce Lain Kennedy's Career Book

by Joyce Lain Kennedy & Darryl Laramore (VGM Career Horizons, 1988)

Most vocational guidance books focus either on occupational choice *or* on job search skills. Kennedy and Laramore, however, manage to cover an extremely wide range of topics without sacrificing depth. They present a vast amount of information in a concise, fast-paced format. Although targeted at the 15-to-25 age bracket, this book is useful for first-time job seekers and career changers of all ages. This is because it focuses on occupational *strategies* and *processes* relevant to all stages of career development.

The various sections of the book cover topics as diverse as decision making, goal setting, information gathering, risk taking, self-awareness, demographic trends, jobs of the future, and lifelong career management. The sections can be read consecutively or "buffet style." Embedded in each section are numerous exercises and questionnaires designed to motivate the reader to apply the new information. The authors frequently direct the reader to additional sources of information as well. All in all, this is an extremely comprehensive and thorough work, and an invaluable reference.

> We can't be sure what lies beyond the calendar horizon of January 1, 2000, but it is customary for authors and commencement speakers to solemnly inform each new crop of graduates that the challenges they face are greater than any since the Ice Age. In your case, it's true. That's because of the technological speedup that is occurring as you read this page.
>
> You are going where no generation has gone before. But isn't that the same for everyone? Yes, but what's different for you, and why your challenge is greater than that of, say, your parents, is that your crystal ball is almost fogged over as a result of the *rate* of change: It's happening in fast-forward motion. [p. 389]

Figure 12.9. Overview of Holland's theory of vocational choice. According to John Holland, people can be divided into six personality types (personal orientations) that prefer different work environments. These connections between personality and vocational preferences are summarized here.

extends throughout life. Vocational choice involves not a single decision but a series of decisions. Although this process was once believed to extend only from prepuberty to one's early 20s, it is now recognized that the process often continues throughout life (Ginzberg, 1972). In fact, a major survey of adults in the United States (Arbeiter et al., 1978) found that 36%—over a third—were in a career transition, either actively seeking or considering a new career. However, many middle-aged people tend to underestimate the options available to them and therefore miss opportunities to make constructive changes. Hence, it is important to emphasize that vocational choices are not limited to one's youth.

5. *Some vocational decisions are not easily undone.* Although it's never too late to strike out in new vocational directions, it is important to recognize that many decisions are not readily reversed. One influential theory of occupational choice in the 1950s (Ginzberg, 1952) went so far as to propose that vocational decisions are characterized by *irreversibility.* That assertion has since been retracted as an overstatement (Ginzberg, 1972). But it is clear that once you invest time, money, and effort in moving along a particular career path, it may not be easy to change paths. This reality was illustrated by the Renwick & Lawler (1978) survey, in which nearly half (44%) of the respondents indicated that they felt "locked into" their current job. This potential problem highlights why it is important to devote systematic thought to your vocational choice.

6. *Vocational choice is an expression of one's personality.* Various influential theories of vocational choice focus on how this process is related to a person's ego functioning (Ginzberg, 1972), self-concept (Super, 1988), personal orientation (Holland, 1985), and psychological needs (Roe, 1977). Although these theories differ in their emphasis, they clearly agree that the choice of a career is an expression of one's personality.

Examining Your Personal Characteristics

Our discussion of vocational choice and job satisfaction points to the importance of self-knowledge in making career decisions. To select an occupation that you will find rewarding, you need to have a clear picture of yourself. In piecing together this picture, you will want to consider your personality, your abilities, and your interests (Shertzer, 1985).

Personality

Most vocational theorists agree that it is very important to choose an occupation that is compatible with your personality. In assessing your personality, you should try to identify your dominant traits, needs, and values. A particularly crucial characteristic to evaluate is how socially skilled you are. Some jobs require much more social dexterity than others.

John Holland (1985) has an interesting theory about how our personalities shape our careers. According to Holland, we have stereotypic views of the work environments associated with various occupations. He asserts that we search for a work environment that will fit our personality. Holland has identified six broad personality types, called *personal orientations.* Different types of work should be optimal for each of these personal orientations, which we will describe briefly (see Figure 12.9 for additional information).

Realistic. These people prefer tasks that require physical strength and coordination. They tend to avoid tasks that

---

Holland's Personal Orientations and Related Work Environments

Themes	Personal orientations	Work environments
Realistic	Values concrete and physical tasks. Perceives self as having mechanical skills and lacking social skills.	*Settings:* concrete, physical tasks requiring mechanical skills, persistence, and physical movement. *Careers:* machine operator, truck driver, draftsperson, barber.
Investigative	Wants to solve intellectual, scientific, and mathematical problems. Sees self as analytical, critical, curious, introspective, and methodical.	*Settings:* research laboratory, diagnostic medical case conference, work group of scientists. *Careers:* marine biologist, computer programmer, clinical psychologist, architect, dentist.
Artistic	Prefers unsystematic tasks or artistic projects: painting, writing, or drama. Perceives self as imaginative, expressive, and independent.	*Settings:* theater, concert hall, library, radio or TV studio. *Careers:* sculptor, actor, designer, musician, author, editor.
Social	Prefers educational, helping, and religious careers. Enjoys social involvement, church, music, reading, and dramatics. Is cooperative, friendly, helpful, insightful, persuasive, and responsible.	*Settings:* school and college classrooms, psychiatrist's office, religious meetings, mental institutions, recreational centers. *Careers:* counselor, nurse, teacher, social worker, judge, minister, sociologist.
Enterprising	Values political and economic achievements, supervision, and leadership. Enjoys leadership control, verbal expression, recognition, and power. Perceives self as extroverted, sociable, happy, assertive, popular, and self-confident.	*Settings:* courtroom, political rally, car sales room, real estate firm, advertising company. *Careers:* realtor, politician, attorney, salesperson, manager.
Conventional	Prefers orderly, systematic, concrete tasks with verbal and mathematical data. Sees self as conformist and having clerical and numerical skills.	*Settings:* bank, post office, file room, business office, Internal Revenue office. *Careers:* banker, accountant, timekeeper, financial counselor, typist, receptionist.

involve social skill, abstract thinking, subjectivity, or verbal skill. They prefer jobs in which tasks are physical or mechanical, and clearly defined, such as farming, auto mechanics, and engineering.

Investigative. Individuals in this category would rather work with ideas than with things or people. They enjoy abstract thinking and logical analysis, preferring understanding to acting. Investigative individuals can often be found working in research laboratories or libraries.

Artistic. People with this orientation dislike structured tasks, preferring instead to rely on their subjective impressions in dealing with the environment. They are impulsive and creative, and they tend to be socially aloof. They have a high need for emotional expression and often seek careers in art, music, or drama.

Social. These individuals prefer to interact with people, and they possess the necessary social skills to do so comfortably. They typically have greater verbal ability than mathematical ability. Social types are often found in the helping professions, such as teaching, nursing, and social work.

Enterprising. These people like to use their social skills to dominate or persuade others. They are confident, outgoing, and assertive. They prefer occupations like sales or supervision, positions in which they can express these characteristics.

Conventional. Those with a conventional orientation are conforming, systematic, and orderly. They typically have greater clerical and mathematical ability than verbal ability. Conventional people prefer working environments that are structured and predictable, and may be well suited to occupations in the business world.

Aptitudes and Abilities

It is important to realistically evaluate your aptitudes and abilities. Foremost among these is your general intelligence. Although intelligence does not necessarily predict occupational success, it does predict the likelihood of entering particular occupations. This is because intelligence is related to the academic success that is necessary to enter many fields. Certain professions, like law or medicine, are open only to those who can meet increasingly selective criteria as they move from high school to college to postgraduate training.

Other aptitudes and abilities are important as well. In many occupations, social skills or special talents are more important than general intelligence. Specific aptitudes that might make a person well suited for certain occupations include perceptual-motor coordination, creativity, artistic or musical talent, mechanical ability, clerical skill, mathematical ability, and persuasive talents.

Interests

As you meander through life, you acquire interests in different kinds of activities. Are you intrigued by the business world? The academic world? International affairs? Agriculture? The outdoors? Physical sciences? Arts and crafts? Music? Travel? Athletics? Human services? The list of potential interests is virtually infinite. Although interests may change, they tend to be relatively stable, and they definitely should be considered in the development of career plans.

Using Tests to Aid Career Planning

Numerous psychological tests are available that can be valuable in helping you arrive at a good picture of your personality, abilities, and interests. There are standardized tests of intellectual abilities, tests of spatial and mechanical skills, perceptual accuracy tests, tests of motor abilities, and personality and interest tests. If you are undecided about what kind of occupation might intrigue you, you might want to begin by taking a special kind of test. **Occupational interest inventories** measure your interests as they relate to various jobs or careers. There are many tests in this category. The most widely used are the Strong-Campbell Interest Inventory (SCII) and the Kuder Occupational Interest Survey (KOIS), both of which can be taken at most college counseling centers.

Figure 12.10. The Strong-Campbell Interest Inventory (SCII). The SCII estimates the similarity between the respondent's interests and the interests of people working in various occupations. The occupations are grouped into six categories that are based on the six types of work environments described by Holland. The first page of a two-page score report for W. B. is shown. It is normal to get high scores on many specific *occupational scales* (shown on the right side), and the test results should not be discounted if some of these seem far-fetched (for example, W. B. may be sure that she doesn't want to be a farmer, chef, or librarian). Broad patterns of interests captured by scores on the *general occupational themes* and *basic interest scales* (shown on the left side) often are more informative. For instance, W. B.'s high scores on science, mathematics, and nature may stimulate her to think about occupations that could satisfy all three of these interests.

Occupational interest inventories do not attempt to predict whether you would be successful in various occupations. They relate more to the likelihood of job *satisfaction* than job *success*. The tests are based on the assumption that if your interests are similar to the typical interests of people already in a particular occupation, then you might enjoy working in that occupational area.

Most occupational interest inventories share the following general strategy. The test developer begins by measuring the interests of people who are already established in various occupations and who report that they enjoy their work. Typical interest profiles are compiled for many occupational groups. When you take an occupational interest inventory, your interests are compared with these occupational profiles. You receive many scores indicating how similar your interests are to the typical interests of people in various occupations. If, for example, you receive a high score on the accountant scale of a test, your interests are similar to those of the average accountant. This correspondence in interests does not ensure that you would enjoy a career in accounting, but it is a moderately good predictor of job satisfaction (Swaney & Prediger, 1985).

The most recent revision of the Strong-Campbell Interest Inventory groups occupations into six broad categories that correspond to the six types of work environments identified by John Holland (1985). Holland's six prototype work environments are called *general occupational themes*. Scores on these general themes indicate whether you have a realistic, investigative, artistic, social, enterprising, or conventional personality, as described by Holland. As you can see in Figure 12.10, the SCII divides each theme into a few basic interest scales and then breaks basic interests down into specific occupational scores—162 in all.

Interest inventories like the SCII can provide worthwhile food for thought about possible careers. The results may confirm your subjective guesses about your interests and strengthen already existing vocational preferences. Aditionally, the test results may inspire you to investigate career possibilities that you had never thought of before. Unexpected results may stimulate you to rethink your vocational plans.

Although interest inventories can be helpful in

STRONG-CAMPBELL INTEREST INVENTORY OF THE
STRONG VOCATIONAL INTEREST BLANK

PAGE 1

PROFILE REPORT FOR: W B
ID: 1073484
AGE: SEX: F
DATE TESTED: 06/27/88
DATE SCORED: 06/27/88

SPECIAL SCALES: ACADEMIC COMFORT 57
INTROVERSION-EXTROVERSION 77
TOTAL RESPONSES: 322   INFREQUENT RESPONSES: 5

OCCUPATIONAL SCALES — STANDARD SCORES (F / M)

Similarity columns: Very Dissimilar / Dissimilar / Moderately Dissimilar / Mid-Range / Moderately Similar / Similar / Very Similar

REALISTIC

GENERAL OCCUPATIONAL THEME - R — Mod. High 52

BASIC INTEREST SCALES (STANDARD SCORE):
- AGRICULTURE — Average 46
- NATURE — Mod. High 60
- ADVENTURE — Very Low 30
- MILITARY ACTIVITIES — Very Low 40
- MECHANICAL ACTIVITIES — Mod. High 54

Occupation	F	M
Marine Corps enlisted personnel	(CRS)	22
Navy enlisted personnel	42	41
Army officer	31	28
Navy officer	41	26
Air Force officer	36	27
Air Force enlisted personnel		38
Police officer	14	10
Bus driver	43	40
Horticultural worker	57	51
Farmer	54	38
Vocational agriculture teacher	54	34
Forester	47	49
Veterinarian		38
Athletic trainer	28	
Emergency medical technician	35	31
Radiologic technologist	46	48
Carpenter	31	23
Electrician	32	35
Architect	37	(ARI)
Engineer	44	49

INVESTIGATIVE

GENERAL OCCUPATIONAL THEME - I — Average 49

BASIC INTEREST SCALES (STANDARD SCORE):
- SCIENCE — High 60
- MATHEMATICS — Very High 63
- MEDICAL SCIENCE — Average 45
- MEDICAL SERVICE — Average 48

Occupation	F	M
Computer programmer	60	59
Systems analyst	55	54
Medical technologist	59	49
R & D manager	47	36
Geologist	48	46
Biologist	58	
Chemist	55	54
Physicist	47	46
Veterinarian	48	
Science teacher	52	49
Physical therapist	48	28
Respiratory therapist	55	43
Medical technician	55	42
Pharmacist	55	27
Dietitian	49	
Nurse, RN		30
Chiropractor	41	18
Optometrist	58	47
Dentist	54	38
Physician	47	49
Biologist		55
Mathematician	50	56
Geographer	55	48
College professor	57	57
Psychologist	33	24
Sociologist	38	33

ARTISTIC

GENERAL OCCUPATIONAL THEME - A — Low 39

BASIC INTEREST SCALES (STANDARD SCORE):
- MUSIC/DRAMATICS — Low 40
- ART — Mod. Low 44
- WRITING — Low 41

Occupation	F	M
Medical illustrator	23	20
Art teacher	3	17
Artist, fine	21	28
Artist, commercial	-5	24
Interior decorator	4	22
Architect	(RIA)	30
Photographer	16	10
Musician	38	35
Chef	45	(EA)
Beautician		24
Flight attendant	5	16
Advertising executive	10	15
Broadcaster	5	16
Public relations director	-1	-1
Lawyer	10	12
Public administrator	11	14
Reporter	4	23
Librarian	51	46
English teacher	11	28
Foreign language teacher	(BA)	40

CONSULTING PSYCHOLOGISTS PRESS
577 COLLEGE AVENUE
PALO ALTO, CA 94306

working through career decisions, several cautions are worth noting. First, you may score high on some occupations that you're sure you would hate. Given the sheer number of occupational scales on the tests, this can easily happen by chance. However, you shouldn't dismiss the remainder of the test results just because you're sure that a few specific scores are "wrong." Second, don't let the test make career decisions for you. Some students naively believe that they should pursue whatever occupation yields their highest score. This is not how the tests are meant to be used. They merely provide information for you to consider. Ultimately, you have to think things out for yourself.

Third, you should be aware that there is a lingering sex bias on most occupational interest inventories. Many of these scales were originally developed 30 to 40 years ago, when outright discrimination or more subtle discouragement prevented women from entering many traditionally "male" occupations. Critics assert that interest inventories have helped to channel women into sex-typed careers, such as nursing and secretarial work, while guiding them away from more prestigious "male" occupations, such as medicine and engineering (Diamond, 1979). Undoubtedly, this was true in the past. Recently, progress has been made toward reducing sex bias in occupational tests, but it has not been eliminated yet. Thus, in interpreting interest inventory results, be wary of letting gender stereotypes limit your career options. A good career counselor should be able to help women—as well as men—sort through the effects of sex bias on their test results.

Researching Job Characteristics

In order to match yourself up with an occupation, you have to pursue information on jobs. As we have noted, there are over 20,000 occupations (Michelozzi, 1988). Their sheer number is overwhelming. Obviously, you have to narrow down the scope of your search before you can seek extensive information.

Once you have selected some jobs that might interest you, the next question is: Where do you get information on them? This is not a simple matter. The first step is usually to read some occupational literature. A very general reference is the *Occupational Outlook Handbook*, available in most libraries. Another good book is *Jobs! What They Are . . . Where They Are . . . What They Pay!* by Robert Snelling and Anne Snelling (1985). In addition to these very general books, you can often get more detailed information on particular occupations from government agencies, trade unions, and professional organizations. For example, if you were interested in a career in psychology, you could obtain a number of pamphlets or books from the American Psychological Association.

If you're still interested in an occupation after reading the available literature, it's often a good idea to talk to some people working in that area. Occupational literature tends to be a little one-sided and usually paints an overly positive picture. Talking to people in the field can provide you with more down-to-earth information. However, keep in mind that the people you talk to may not be a representative sample of those who work in that occupation. Don't make the mistake of rejecting a potentially satisfying career just because one person hates it.

In examining occupational literature and interviewing people, what kinds of information should you seek? To some extent, the answer depends on your unique values and needs. However, there are some general things that should be of concern to virtually anyone (Shertzer, 1985; Weinrach, 1979). The questions you can ask include the following.

- *The nature of the work*. What would your duties and responsibilities be on a day-to-day basis?
- *Working conditions*. Is the work environment pleasant or unpleasant, low-key or high-pressure?
- *Job entry requirements*. What education and training are required to break into this occupational area?
- *Potential earnings*. What are entry-level salaries, and how much can you hope to earn if you're exceptionally

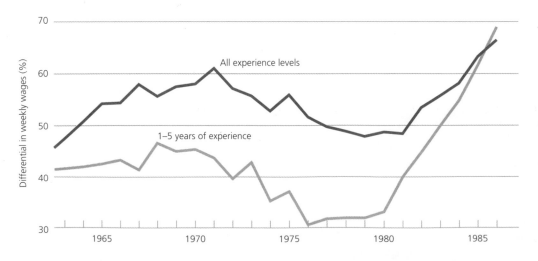

Figure 12.11. Trends in the wage gap between college and high school graduates. The graph shows the percent by which the weekly earnings of college graduates exceeded the earnings of high school graduates for workers with varying levels of experience on the job. Back in 1965, college graduates were earning about 40–55% more than high school graduates. This wage advantage grew some and then dipped during the 1970s. However, during the 1980s, the wage gap widened dramatically to over 60%. (Data from Murphy & Welch, 1989)

successful? What does the average person earn? What are the fringe benefits?

- *Potential status.* What is the social status associated with this occupation? Is it personally satisfactory for you?
- *Opportunities for advancement.* How do you "move up" in this field? Are there adequate opportunities for promotion and advancement?
- *Intrinsic job satisfaction.* Outside of money and formal fringe benefits, what can you derive in the way of personal satisfaction from this job? Will it allow you to have fun, to help people, to be creative, or to shoulder responsibility?
- *Future outlook.* How is supply and demand projected to shape up in the future for this occupational area?

By the way, if you're wondering whether your college education will be worth the effort in terms of dollars and cents, the answer generally is yes. The jobs that you can obtain with a college degree *do* tend to yield higher pay than those available to people with less education (Murphy & Welch, 1989). Indeed, college graduates' earnings advantage over high school graduates increased during the 1980s, especially in entry-level jobs, as shown in Figure 12.11).

SUMMARY

Vocational development encompasses the entire life span. According to Super, there are five stages in the occupational life cycle: growth, exploration, establishment, maintenance, and decline. Super asserts that vocational decisions are expressions of one's self-concept.

Since the 1950s, the participation of women in the work force has increased at all occupational levels. Even so, most women continue to be concentrated in the "pink ghetto" professions. Women's career development is often less orderly and predictable than that of men. This may be due to the necessity to juggle multiple roles, frequent career interruptions, limited availability of mentoring, and continuing discrimination.

People are motivated to work for a variety of reasons. Although financial necessity is a compelling factor for most, work may satisfy many other needs as well. Theorists like McGregor, Herzberg, and Astin agree that these include needs for achievement, recognition, and self-fulfillment. Job satisfaction appears to be related to mental and physical health, and even longevity. It is influenced by many variables, but certain factors are related to satisfaction with some consistency. These include challenge, good pay, meaningfulness, variety, autonomy, friendship, recognition, and role clarity.

Although stress is subjective, certain working conditions and job characteristics are especially likely to be stressful. These include a physically uncomfortable or hazardous working environment, having to perform two or more tasks at once, demands for perfect performance, long hours, tedious work, time pressure, and human relations problems. Occupational stress may be greatest when people work in jobs that have high psychological demands and low decision control.

The negative effects of stress include increased absenteeism, turnover, and accidents, along with lowered productivity. Job stress also can have adverse effects on workers' mental and physical health. Interventions to manage stress in the workplace can be made at the individual level, the organizational level, and at the individual-organizational interface.

Workaholics exhibit extreme dedication to their work, consistently giving more time and energy than the job demands. While many workaholics find great satisfaction and meaningfulness in their careers, others may be motivated by a pathological compulsion to control themselves and their environment.

In making vocational choices, certain guidelines should be kept in mind. One's vocational choice is not unlimited and may even be influenced by chance factors. Everyone has the potential for success in several occupations. Although the process of vocational development continues throughout life, some decisions are not easily reversed. Vocational choice is influenced by a vast array of factors, especially one's personality.

In making vocational decisions, one should consider how compatible one's personality, abilities, and interests are with the demands of various jobs. One's interests can be assessed through interest inventories, although the results should be considered only as food for thought. To accurately evaluate one's suitability for various jobs, it is advisable to seek information about the nature of the work, working conditions, entry requirements, potential earnings, potential status, opportunities for advancement, intrinsic satisfactions, and the future outlook for each occupational area being considered.

Armed with accurate information about oneself and about various job options, one is better equipped to narrow the list of possible careers to a select few. It is then time to proceed to obtaining some actual work experience by securing the all-important first job. In our upcoming Application, we will describe how to conduct an effective job search.

Getting Ahead in the Job Game

True or false? Choose one.

☐ **1.** The most common and effective job search method is answering classified ads.

☐ **2.** Your technical qualifications are the most important factor in determining the success of your job search.

☐ **3.** Employment agencies are a good source of leads to high-level professional jobs.

☐ **4.** You should make sure that your résumé is very thorough and includes everything you have ever done.

☐ **5.** It's a good idea to inject some humor into your job interviews. It will help both you and your interviewer relax.

There is no universally accepted approach to conducting an effective job search. However, most career counselors would agree that all of the statements above are generally false! Although there isn't a single "tried and true" method for obtaining desirable jobs, in this Application we'll summarize advice that can increase your chances of success.

Above all else, it is important to conduct a job search that is well-organized, thorough, and systematic. Sending out a hastily written résumé to a few randomly selected companies is a waste of effort. An effective job search requires lots of time and careful planning. People who are desperate for a job tend to behave in ways that cause prospective employers to see them as bad risks. Thus, it is crucial that you begin your search well in advance of the time when you will need a job. The best time to look for a job is when you don't need one. Then you can select an *employer*, rather than seeking an employer who will select *you*.

Of course, no amount of planning and effort will guarantee favorable results in a job search. Luck is definitely a part of the picture. Success may hinge on being in the right place, or meeting the right person, at the right time. Moreover, becoming a top candidate for a position will depend on factors other than your technical competence. This is not to say

that technical competence isn't necessary; it is. But given the realities of today's job market, employers are often inundated with applicants who possess all of the required training and experience. The one who is ultimately selected often is *not* the one with the best technical qualifications. Rather, hiring decisions are made on the basis of subjective impressions gleaned from résumés, telephone conversations, and face-to-face interviews (Lareau, 1985). These impressions will be based on perceptions of your personality, your appearance, your social skills, and your body language. Knowing this, you can practice certain strategies that may increase the odds in your favor.

No matter what type of job you are looking for, successful searches have certain elements in common. First, you must target specific companies or organizations you would like to work for. Then, you must inform these companies of your interest in such a way as to get them interested in *you*.

FINDING COMPANIES YOU WANT TO WORK FOR

Initially, you need to determine what general type of organization will best suit your needs. Do you want to work in a factory? A school? A hospital? A small business? A large corporation? A government agency? A human services agency? As discussed earlier in the chapter, to select an appropriate work environment, you need an accurate picture of your personal qualities and knowledge of various job categories and their characteristics.

Once you've decided on a setting, you need to target specific companies. That's easy; you simply look for companies that have advertised openings in your field, right? Not necessarily. If you restrict yourself to this approach, you may miss many valuable opportunities. Up to 80% of all vacancies, especially those above entry level, are never advertised at all (Bolles, 1987).

How should you proceed? Certainly, you should check the classified section in newspapers to identify the many positions that *are* advertised. If you are willing to relocate anywhere, a good source for business and professional jobs is the *National Business Employment Weekly*. You should also consult any trade or professional newspapers, magazines, or journals in your field.

There are two additional options to consider. You could go to an employment agency. However, keep in mind that these agencies generally handle only entry-level, hourly-wage jobs. In addition, they may charge up to 15% of the first year's gross earnings (Lareau, 1985). If you're interested in professional jobs, you might consider contacting executive recruiters, widely known as "headhunters." Executive recruiters work on commission for organizations that have vacancies to fill. They earn their livelihood by actively looking for people who have the qualifications being sought by the hiring organization. You can locate headhunters nationwide by consulting *The Directory of Executive Recruiters.*

What about the 80% of openings that are not advertised? Actually, this statistic is somewhat misleading. It includes a large number of vacancies that are filled by promotions within organizations (Lareau, 1985). Nonetheless, many companies do have openings that are not accessible through traditional channels. If you have targeted companies that haven't advertised any vacancies, you may want to initiate the contact yourself. In support of this approach, a survey by the Bureau of the Census indicated that "direct application to an employer" was both the most commonly used and the most effective job search method (Bolles, 1987). Bolles suggests the following strategy. First, identify a specific problem that the organization has, and develop a strategy to solve it. Then, find out who has the power to hire and fire (either through library research or a network of personal contacts). Finally, approach this person directly to convince him or her of your unique capability to help.

LANDING AN INTERVIEW

No one is going to hire you without "checking out the goods" first. This inspection process typically involves one or more formal interviews. How do you go about getting yourself invited in for an interview? If you are applying for an advertised vacancy, the traditional approach is to mail a résumé, and an accompanying cover letter, to the hiring organization. If your résumé stands out from the crowd, you may be invited for an interview.

If you are approaching an organization in the absence of a known position opening, your strategy may be somewhat different. You may still opt to send a résumé, along with a more detailed cover letter explaining why you have selected this particular company. Another option, suggested by Bolles (1987), is to introduce yourself (by phone or in person) directly to the person in charge of hiring and request an interview. You can increase your chances of success by using your network of personal contacts to identify some acquaintance that you and the person in charge have in common. Then, you can use this person's name to facilitate your approach. Once you do get in to see a potential employer, you should follow up with a thank-you note and a

---

RECOMMENDED READING

What Color Is Your Parachute? A Practical Manual for Job-Hunters and Career-Changers
by Richard Nelson Bolles (Ten Speed Press, 1990)

Richard Bolles is a clever, creative writer who has put together a landmark book on the process of hunting for a job. The book has been so successful that it's being updated yearly! Although Bolles devotes some attention to the matter of career choice, this book focuses mainly on the process of hunting for a job. Unlike many similar books, it does not assume that you're a recent college graduate seeking your first job. Instead, it devotes equal time to people shifting careers later in life.

Bolles's writing is humorous and very opinionated. However, his opinions have merit because he has done his homework; the book is thoroughly researched and documented. He destroys many of the myths about what does and does not work in seeking jobs. Bolles discusses a variety of practical topics, including where the jobs are, what will get you hired, how to get in to see the boss, whom to go see, and whom to avoid.

> So dream, dream, dream. Never mind "being realistic." According to the experts, 80% of the workers in this country are "underemployed." That's what comes of "being realistic." You don't want to end up in the same fix. But you will, if while you dream you corrupt your dream by keeping one eye fixed on what you think you know about the job market. . . .
>
> Only one job offer is tendered for every 1,470 resumes that the average company receives.
>
> Well, okay, so maybe they don't always work. But what's the harm in trying out a resume, just in case? Well, if you've got the money and the time, fine. But do keep in mind what we have discovered in the past: *that job-hunters who invest a lot of time on sending out their resume, often suffer tremendous damage to their self-esteem by having depended upon resumes.* [pp. 99, 152]

résumé that will jog the employer's memory about your training and talents.

PUTTING TOGETHER A RÉSUMÉ

No matter what your job search strategy, an excellent résumé is a critical ingredient. The purpose of a résumé is not to get you a job. Rather, it is to get you an interview. To do so effectively, it must communicate to the reader that you possess the minimum technical qualifications for the position, know the standard conventions of the business world, and are a person who is on the fast track to success. Furthermore, it must accomplish these goals without being flashy or gimmicky.

Your résumé will project the desired positive, yet conservative, image if you follow these guidelines (Lareau, 1985; Lipman, 1983):

1. Use white, ivory, or beige (*never* any other color) paper high in rag content.
2. Make sure there is not a single typographical error.
3. Use the best professional printing service available.
4. Keep it short. The normal maximum is two sides of an 8½" × 11" sheet of paper.
5. Don't write in full sentences, and avoid using the word "I." Instead, begin each statement with an "action" word that describes a specific achievement, as in: "Supervised a staff of fifteen" or "Handled all customer complaints."
6. Avoid giving any personal information that is superfluous to the job. It is an unnecessary distraction, and may give the reader cause to dislike you and therefore reject your application.

An effective résumé will generally contain the following information, laid out in an easy-to-read format (see Figure 12.12 for an example of an attractively prepared résumé).

- *Heading.* At the top of the page, give your name, address, and phone number. This is the only section of the résumé that is *not* given a label.
- *Objective.* State a precise career goal, remembering to use action words and to avoid the use of "I." An example might be "Challenging, creative position in the communication field requiring extensive background in newspaper, radio, and television."
- *Summary of qualifications.* Next comes a paragraph that sums up your unique qualifications for the position you described in your objective. Write this paragraph *after* you have completed the rest of your résumé.
- *Education.* List any degrees you possess, giving major field of study, date, and granting institution for each. If you received any academic honors or awards, these can be mentioned here.
- *Experience.* This section should be

Figure 12.12. Example of an attractively formatted résumé. The physical appearance of a résumé is very important. This example shows what a well-prepared résumé should look like.

TERESA M. MORGAN

Campus Address
1252 River St., Apt. 808
East Lansing, MI 48823
(517) 332-6086

Permanent Address
1111 W. Franklin
Jackson, MI 49203
(517) 782-0819

OBJECTIVE — To pursue a career in interior design, or a related field, in which I can utilize my design training. Willing to relocate after June 19____.

EDUCATION
Sept. 19____
June 19____ — **Michigan State University,** East Lansing, MI 48825. Bachelor of Arts—Interior Design, with emphasis in Design Communication and Human Shelter. Courses include Lighting, Computers, Public Relations and History of Art. (F.I.D.E.R. accredited) 3.0 GPA (4.0=A).

July 19____
Aug. 19____ — **Michigan State University overseas study,** England and France, Decorative Arts and Architecture. 4.0 GPA (4.0=A).

Sept. 19____
June 19____ — **Jackson Community College,** Jackson, MI 49201. Associate's degree. 3.5 GPA (4.0=A).

EMPLOYMENT
Sept. 19____
Present — **Food Service and Maintenance,** Owen Graduate Center, Michigan State University.
• Prepared and served food.
• Managed upkeep of adjacent Van Hoosen Residence Hall.

Dec. 19____
June 19____ — **Food Service and Maintenance,** McDonel Residence Hall.
• Served food and cleaned facility.
• General building maintenance.

June 19____
Dec. 19____ — **Waitress,** Charlie Wong's Restaurant, Jackson, MI.
• Served food, dealt with a variety of people on a personal level.
• Additional responsibilities: cashier, hostess, bartender, and employee trainer.

HONORS AND ACTIVITIES
• Community College Transfer scholarship from MSU.
• American Society of Interior Design Publicity Chairman; Executive board, MSU Chapter.
• Wharton Center of the Performing Arts (MSU), usher.
• MSU Student Foundation member.
• Sigma Chi Little Sisters.
• Independent European travel, summer 19____.
• Stage manager and performer in plays and musicals.
• Jackson High School Senior Class Treasurer.
• Jackson High School Yearbook Assistant Editor.

REFERENCES and **PORTFOLIO** available upon request.

---

organized chronologically, beginning with your most recent job and working backward. For each position held, describe your responsibilities and your achievements. Make these specific, and make sure your most recent position is the one with the greatest achievements. Never "pad" your résumé by listing trivial accomplishments.

If you are currently a student, or a recent graduate, your schooling will provide the basis for both your experience and your qualifications. In your summary of qualifications, emphasize the specific *skills* you have acquired through your education.

POLISHING YOUR INTERVIEW TECHNIQUE

The final, and most crucial, step in the process of securing a job is the face-to-face interview. If you've gotten this far, the employer already knows that you possess the requisite training and experience to do the job. Now your challenge is to convince the employer that you are the kind of person who would fit in well in the organization. Your interviewer will attempt to verify that you have the intangible qualities that will make you a good team player. Even more important, the interviewer will attempt to identify any "red flag" behaviors, attitudes, or traits that mark you as an unacceptable risk.

To create the right impression, you must appear to be confident, enthusiastic, and ambitious. Your demeanor should be somewhat formal and reserved, and you should avoid any attempts at humor—you never know what might offend your interviewer (Lareau, 1985). Above all, never give more information than the interviewer requests, especially negative information. If asked directly what your weaknesses are—a common ploy—respond with a "flaw" that is really a positive, as in "I tend to work too hard at times" (Lareau, 1985). Don't interrupt or contradict your interviewer. And don't ever blame or criticize anyone, especially previous employers (Lipman, 1983).

Developing an effective interview technique requires practice. Many experts suggest that you never turn down an interview, even if you know you don't want the job, simply to obtain the practice. Advance preparation is also crucial. Never go into an interview "cold." Find out all you can about the company before you go. Try to anticipate the questions that will be asked and have some answers ready. In general, you will not be asked simply to reiterate information from your résumé. Remember, it is your personal qualities that are being assessed now. A final word of advice: If possible, avoid any discussion of salary in an initial interview. The appropriate time for salary negotiation is *after* a firm offer of employment has been extended.

Careful preparation prior to a job interview will help you to be more confident and to put your best foot forward.

1. Summarize Super's five-stage model of vocational development.

2. Discuss variations and qualifications relative to Super's model of vocational development.

3. Summarize the history of women's participation in the work force.

4. Describe some problems for women in the workplace today.

5. Compare and contrast McGregor's, Herzberg's, and Astin's views on work motivation.

6. Explain how and why job satisfaction can be so important to one's adjustment.

7. List the ingredients that tend to contribute to job satisfaction.

8. Describe some of the sources of job stress.

9. Summarize the effects of job stress on physical and mental health.

10. Describe some things that organizations can do to reduce job stress.

11. Summarize current perspectives on "workaholism."

12. List six general principles to keep in mind in choosing a vocation.

13. Discuss the personal characteristics that one should consider in making vocational decisions.

14. Discuss the value of occupational interest inventories as they relate to career planning.

15. List some job characteristics that one should be concerned about in making vocational decisions.

16. Discuss strategies for targeting companies you would like to work for and landing job interviews.

17. Summarize guidelines for putting together an effective résumé.

18. List the dos and don'ts of interviewing for jobs.

KEY TERMS

Job satisfaction
Mentor
Occupational interest inventories
Sexual harassment
Underemployment
Vocation

KEY PEOPLE

Helen Astin
Frederick Herzberg
John Holland
Douglas McGregor
Donald Super

Assertive Job-Hunting Survey

INSTRUCTIONS

This inventory is designed to provide information about the way in which you look for a job. Picture yourself in each of these job-hunting situations and indicate how likely it is that you would respond in the described manner. If you have never job-hunted before, answer according to how you would try to find a job. Please record your responses in the spaces to the left of the items. Use the following key for your responses:

1 = Very unlikely   4 = Slightly likely

2 = Somewhat unlikely   5 = Somewhat likely

3 = Slightly unlikely   6 = Very likely

THE SCALE

____1. When asked to indicate my experiences for a position, I would mention only my paid work experience.

____2. If I heard someone talking about an interesting job opening, I'd be reluctant to ask for more information unless I knew the person.

____3. I would ask an employer who did not have an opening if he knew of other employers who might have job openings.

____4 I downplay my qualifications so that an employer won't think I'm more qualified than I really am.

____5. I would rather use an employment agency to find a job than apply to employers directly.

____6. Before an interview, I would contact an employee of the organization to learn more about that organization.

____7. I hesitate to ask questions when I'm being interviewed for a job.

____8. I avoid contacting potential employers by phone or in person because I feel they are too busy to talk with me.

____9. If an interviewer were very late for my interview, I would leave or arrange for another appointment.

____10. I believe an experienced employment counselor would have a better idea of what jobs I should apply for than I would have.

____11. If a secretary told me that a potential employer was too busy to see me, I would stop trying to contact that employer.

____12. Getting the job I want is largely a matter of luck.

____13. I'd directly contact the person for whom I would be working, rather than the personnel department of an organization.

____14. I am reluctant to ask professors or supervisors to write letters of recommendation for me.

____15. I would not apply for a job unless I had all the qualifications listed on the published job description.

____16. I would ask an employer for a second interview if I felt the first one went poorly.

____17. I am reluctant to contact an organization about employment unless I know there is a job opening.

____18. If I didn't get a job, I would call the employer and ask how I could improve my chances for a similar position.

____19. I feel uncomfortable asking friends for job leads.

____20. With the job market as tight as it is, I had better take whatever job I can get.

____21. If the personnel office refused to refer me for an interview, I would directly contact the person I wanted to work for, if I felt qualified for the position.

____22. I would rather interview with recruiters who come to the college campus than contact employers directly.

____23. If an interviewer says "I'll contact you if there are any openings," I figure there's nothing else I can do.

____24. I'd check out available job openings before deciding what kind of job I'd like to have.

____25. I am reluctant to contact someone I don't know for information about career fields in which I am interested.

SCORING THE SCALE

To score this scale, you have to begin by reversing your responses on 18 of the items. On these items, convert the response you entered as follows: 1 = 6, 2 = 5, 3 = 4, 4 = 3, 5 = 2, and 6 = 1. The items to be reversed are 1, 2, 4, 5, 7, 8, 10, 11, 12, 14, 15, 17, 19, 20, 22, 23, 24, and 25. After making your reversals, add up the numbers that you have recorded for the 25 items on the scale. This total is your score on the Assertive Job-Hunting Survey.

MY SCORE _____

WHAT THE SCALE MEASURES

Developed by Heather Becker, Susan Brown, Pat LaFitte, Mary Jo Magruder, Bob Murff, and Bill Phillips, this scale measures your job-seeking style (Becker, 1980). Some people conduct a job search in a relatively passive way—waiting for jobs to come to them. Others tend to seek jobs in a more vigorous, assertive manner. They act on their environment to procure needed information, obtain helpful contacts, and get their foot in the door at attractive companies. This scale measures your tendency to pursue jobs assertively.

Test-retest reliability for this scale is reasonable (.77 for an interval of two weeks). The scale's validity has been supported by demonstrations that subjects' scores increase as a result of training programs designed to enhance their job-hunting assertiveness. Also, those who have job-hunted before tend to score higher than those who have never job-hunted.

INTERPRETING YOUR SCORE

Our norms are based on a sample of college students who had applied to a university counseling center for career-planning assistance.

NORMS

High score: 117–150
Intermediate score: 95–116
Low score: 0–94

What Do You Know about the Career That Interests You?

Important vocational decisions require *information*. Your assignment in this exercise is to pick a vocation and research it. You should begin by reading some occupational literature. Then you should interview someone in the field. Use the outline below to summarize your findings.

1. *The nature of the work.* What are the duties and responsibilities on a day-to-day basis?

2. *Working conditions.* Is the working environment pleasant or unpleasant, low-key or high-pressure?

3. *Job entry requirements.* What kind of education and training are required to break into this occupational area?

4. *Potential earnings.* What are entry-level salaries, and how much can you hope to earn if you're exceptionally successful?

5. *Opportunities for advancement.* How do you "move up" in this field? Are there adequate opportunities for promotion and advancement?

6. *Intrinsic job satisfactions.* What can you derive in the way of personal satisfaction from this job?

7. *Future outlook.* How is supply and demand projected to shape up in the future for this occupational area?

13

Development and Expression of Sexuality

Sex. To some people it's a sport, to others an oppressive duty. For some it's recreation, for others it's business. Some people find it a source of great intimacy and pleasure. Others find it a source of extraordinary anxiety and frustration. Whatever the case, sexuality plays a central role in our lives.

In our culture, it sometimes seems that we are obsessed with sex. We joke and gossip about it constantly. Our magazines and novels are saturated with sex. The advertising business uses sex to sell us everything from toothpaste to automobiles. We have become voracious in our consumption of both pornography and books purporting to tell us how to improve our sex lives. In spite of all this, many lovers find it excruciatingly difficult to talk to each other about sex, and misconceptions about sexual functioning abound.

In this chapter we'll consider how we express our sexuality and how this affects our adjustment. Specifically, we'll look at the development of sexuality, the interpersonal dynamics of sexual relationships, the psychology and physiology of sexual arousal, patterns of sexual behavior, and problems related to sexuality. In the Application, we'll discuss some things that people can do to enhance their sexual relationships.

Let's begin with a cautionary note. Research on sexual behavior must be interpreted very carefully. Several problems, though not unique to sex research, are especially troublesome in this area of inquiry. For example, it is particularly difficult to get representative samples of subjects in sex research. Many people are understandably reluctant to discuss their sex lives. The crucial problem is that people who *are* willing to volunteer information about their sexual behavior appear to be more "liberal" and more sexually experienced than the general population (Wolchik, Braver, & Jensen, 1985).

Furthermore, given the difficulties in doing direct observation, sex researchers have depended mostly on interviews and questionnaires. Unfortunately, when questioned about their sexual behavior, people may be especially likely to provide inaccurate information because of shame, embarrassment, boasting, or wishful thinking (Bradburn & Sudman, 1979; Catania, McDermott, & Pollack, 1986). For these reasons, the results of sex research need to be evaluated with more than the usual cautionary skepticism.

BECOMING A SEXUAL PERSON

There is immense variety in how people express their sexuality. Some people barely express it at all. Rather, they work to suppress their sexual feelings and desires. At the other extreme, there are individuals who express their sexual urges with abandon, engaging in casual sex with great ease. Some people need to turn the lights out before they can have sex, while others would like to be on camera with spotlights shining. Some cannot even bring themselves to use sexual words without embarrassment, while others are eager to reveal the intimate details of their sex lives. To better understand this diversity, we need to examine developmental influences on human sexual behavior.

Key Features of Sexual Identity

As we noted earlier, *identity* refers to a stable sense of who one is and what one stands for (see Chapter 6). We'll use the term *sexual identity* **to refer to the complex of personal qualities, self-perceptions, attitudes, values, and preferences that guide one's sexual behavior.** In other words, your sexual identity consists of your sense of yourself as a sexual person. This conception of sexual identity includes four key features: your sexual orientation, body image, sexual values and ethics, and erotic preferences.

Sexual Orientation
In Chapter 10 we noted that sexual orientation refers to an individual's preference for sexual partners of one sex or the other. *Heterosexuals* **seek sexual relationships with**

Figure 13.1. Heterosexuality and homosexuality as end points on a continuum. Kinsey and other sex researchers view heterosexuality and homosexuality as a continuum rather than an all-or-none distinction. Kinsey created this seven-point scale (from 0 to 6) for describing one's sexual orientation. He used the term *ambisexual* to describe those falling in the middle of the scale, but the term *bisexual* is more widely used today.

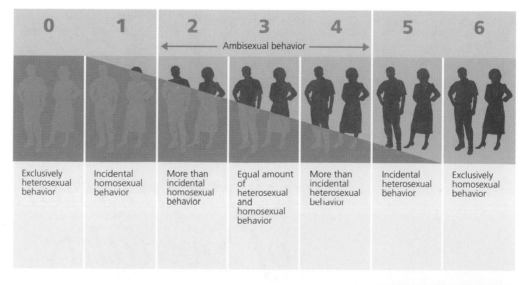

0	1	2	3	4	5	6

← Ambisexual behavior →

| Exclusively heterosexual behavior | Incidental homosexual behavior | More than incidental homosexual behavior | Equal amount of heterosexual and homosexual behavior | More than incidental heterosexual behavior | Incidental heterosexual behavior | Exclusively homosexual behavior |

members of the other sex. **Bisexuals** **seek sexual relationships with members of either sex.** **Homosexuals** **seek sexual relationships with members of the same sex.** In recent years, the terms *gay* and *straight* have become widely used to refer to homosexuals and heterosexuals, respectively. *Lesbian* is yet another term for homosexual women.

People tend to view heterosexuality and homosexuality as an all-or-none distinction. In other words, you're one or the other. However, in a large-scale survey of sexual behavior, Alfred Kinsey and his colleagues (1948, 1953) discovered that many people who define themselves as heterosexuals have had homosexual experiences—and vice versa. Thus, Kinsey and others have concluded that it is more accurate to view heterosexuality and homosexuality as end points on a continuum. Indeed, Kinsey devised a seven-point scale, shown in Figure 13.1, that can be used to characterize individuals' sexual orientation.

How are people distributed on this scale? No one knows for sure. It's hard to get accurate data. Furthermore, there's some debate about where to draw the lines between heterosexuality, bisexuality, and homosexuality on the Kinsey scale. The best estimates come from work by Van Wyk and Geist (1984). They cleaned up some sampling bias in the Kinsey survey data to arrive at the projections shown in Figure 13.2. As you can see, the vast majority (94–97%) of people are heterosexual. However, homosexual and bisexual orientations are probably more common than widely realized, accounting for perhaps 10 million people in the United States today.

Body Image
Your body image involves how you see yourself physically. Like other aspects of your self-concept, it may or may not be a very accurate reflection of reality. However, it definitely affects how you feel about yourself in the sexual domain. A positive body image is correlated with greater sexual activity and higher sexual satisfaction (Berscheid, Walster, & Bohrnstedt, 1973). The increasing use of plastic surgery for breast enhancements, face-lifts, and nose jobs is a testimonial to the importance of body image (Hamburger, 1988).

Sexual Values and Ethics
All cultures impose morality-based constraints on how people are expected to behave sexually (Davenport, 1977). Thus, we are trained to believe that certain expressions of sexuality are "right" while others are "wrong." The resulting attitudes about what is moral and immoral constitute our sexual values and ethics. These standards of appropriate conduct greatly influence our sexual behavior.

Erotic Preferences
Within the limits imposed by sexual orientation and values, there still are differences among people in what they find enjoyable (Blumstein & Schwartz, 1983). Erotic preferences involve one's personal tastes in sexual activities. Your erotic preferences encompass your attitudes about self-stimulation, styles of foreplay and intercourse, oral sex, and other possible sexual activities.

The years of childhood and adolescence are probably especially influential in molding one's sexual identity. This shaping process involves a complex interplay between physiological and psychosocial influences.

Physiological Influences

Obviously, your sexual identity is intimately tied to your biological sex. In particular, researchers have focused on the influence of hormones.

Hormones and Sexual Differentiation
Hormones clearly affect aspects of physical development that shape our sexual identity. For example, prior to birth, hormones direct the formation of the sexual organs in the developing fetus (Money & Ehrhardt, 1972). Around the third month of prenatal development, different hormonal secretions begin to be produced by male and female **gonads—the sex glands.** In males, the testes produce **androgens,** **the principal class of male sex**

Sexual orientation	Score on Kinsey scale	Estimated incidence (%)	
		Males	*Females*
Heterosexual	0–1	94.1	97.5
Bisexual	2–4	1.2	0.7
Homosexual	5–6	4.7	1.8

Figure 13.2. Estimated distribution of sexual orientations. The original Kinsey sample was not assembled to estimate the prevalence of sexual orientations. It had various types of sampling bias when used for this purpose. However, Van Wyk and Geist (1984) minimized this problem by systematically eliminating subjects who were sampled in a biased way (for instance, by asking for cooperation from a gay organization). The projections shown here, based on their reduced sample, are much better estimates than widely quoted figures taken from the original Kinsey data.

hormones. *Testosterone* is the most important of the androgens. In females, the ovaries produce *estrogens,* **the principal class of female sex hormones.** Actually, both classes of hormones are present in both sexes, but the relative balance is different. During prenatal development, the differentiation of the genitals depends primarily on the high versus low level of testosterone produced in males and females.

With the arrival of adolescence, hormones once again play a key role in sexual development (Dreyer, 1982). As we saw in Chapter 11, adolescents attain reproductive capacity as hormonal changes stimulate the maturation of the sexual organs. Hormonal changes also regulate the development of *secondary sex characteristics*—**physical features associated with sex, but not directly involved in reproduction.** Thus, in females, increased secretions of estrogens lead to breast development, widened hips, and more rounded body contours. In males, increased secretions of androgens lead to the development of facial hair, a deeper voice, and more angular body contours.

Hormones and Sexual Behavior

Although hormones unquestionably govern sexual anatomy and maturation, their influence on *sexual orientation* is less clear. Many theorists believe that there is a biological predisposition toward homosexuality (Doerr, Pirke, Kockott, & Dittmor, 1976; Dorner, 1988). These theorists maintain that hormonal differences between heterosexuals and homosexuals underlie a person's sexual orientation. This view is indirectly supported by evidence that most gays can trace their homosexual leanings back to the earliest years of childhood (Bell, Weinberg, & Hammersmith, 1981). However, studies comparing hormone levels in gays and straights have found only very small, inconsistent differences (Ricketts, 1984; Tourney, 1980). At present, there is no convincing evidence linking hormonal patterns to sexual preference, although this possibility can't be ruled out. If hormones shape sexual orientation, their effects must be complex and subtle.

Hormonal fluctuations clearly regulate sex *drive* in many species of animals (Feder, 1984). However, their influence on sexual desire in humans is much more modest. *Androgen* levels seem related to sexual motivation in *both* sexes. High levels of testosterone in female and male subjects correlate with higher rates of sexual activity (Knussmann, Christiansen, & Couwenbergs, 1986; Persky et al., 1978). Curiously, *estrogen* levels among women do *not* correlate well with sexual interest. There does appear to be an association between females' sex drive and their ovulation/menstruation cycles, but its hormonal basis is yet to be determined (Harvey, 1987; Stanislaw & Rice, 1988).

The correlations between hormone levels and sexual activity in humans are interesting, but they do *not* prove that hormonal surges *cause* sexual desire under normal circumstances. The correlations are relatively weak, and there is ambiguity about the *direction* of any causal relationships. Some evidence suggests that sexual arousal may cause hormonal surges rather than vice versa. Thus, there are doubts about whether normal hormonal swings have much impact on sexual desire (Persky, 1983).

In summary, physiological factors have important effects on sexual development. However, their influence on *anatomy* is much greater than their influence on sexual *activity*. To better understand the determinants of sexual behavior, we must look to psychosocial factors.

Psychosocial Influences

The principal psychosocial influences on sexual identity are essentially the same as the main sources of gender-role socialization discussed in Chapter 10. Sexual identity is shaped by families, schools and peers, and the media. We'll discuss each of these in turn.

Families

Parents and the home environment can affect the development of sexual identity throughout life, but they are especially influential in the early years. Children usually

Figure 13.3. Main sources of sexual information. When questioned about where they got their information about sex during childhood, Hunt's (1974) adult respondents cited friends and reading materials far more than their parents.

Where People Get Information about Sex during Childhood		
	Males (%)	Females (%)
Friends	59	46
Reading	20	22
Mother	3	16
Father	6	1
School program	3	5
Adults outside home	6	4
Brothers, sisters	4	6
Other, no answer	7	7

engage in some sex play and exploration before they reach school age (Martinson, 1980). Many experiment with self-stimulation of the genitals. Children also exhibit curiosity about sexual matters, asking questions such as "Where do babies come from?" Parental reactions to sexual exploration and curiosity can have a telling impact on a child's feelings about sex. Some parents respond to youngsters' sexual exploration with horror, dismay, and discouragement. Parents frequently punish innocent, exploratory sex play and squirm miserably when kids ask sexual questions. These sorts of reactions tend to convey to children that sex is "dirty." They may begin to feel guilty about their sexual urges and curiosity. Thus, parents who are uncomfortable with their sexuality can pass on that discomfort to their children at very early ages (Calderone & Ramey, 1982).

Open communication about sexual topics in the home correlates with better sexual adjustment among college students (Lewis & Janda, 1988). Furthermore, adolescents' attitudes about sexual conduct are more similar to their parents' attitudes when they are raised in families that encourage open sexual communication (Fisher, 1988). Ultimately, parents who make sex a taboo topic end up reducing their influence on their kids' evolving sexual identity. Their children turn elsewhere to seek information about sexuality. Thus, the "conspiracy of silence" about sex in the home often backfires by increasing the influence of peers, schools, and the media.

Schools and Peers

As you can see in Figure 13.3, friends are the principal source of sex information for both males and females (Hunt, 1974; Thornburg, 1981). Of course, friends may be ill-informed themselves. Hence, one's peer group can be a source of highly misleading information. Furthermore, peers are unlikely to instill the same kinds of sexual ethics that parents tend to champion. Spanier (1977) found that girls who learned the facts of life from their mothers were less sexually active than girls who got their information from peers and other sources.

Schools may influence sexual identity through sex education programs. Generally, these programs attempt to promote the more conservative sexual values that most parents would espouse (Spanier, 1977). Nonetheless, many parents try to extend the conspiracy of silence regarding sex into the classroom and campaign against such programs. Most of these parents are worried that sex education will lead to increased sexual experimentation. However, the evidence suggests that this concern is unfounded. Sex education programs lead to neither the experimentation that parents worry about nor the restraint that the programs advocate (Eisen & Zellman, 1987).

Media

As you may have noticed in Figure 13.3, reading materials are another major source of information on sex. Unfortunately, many popular books and magazines perpetuate myths about sex and miseducate their young readers. Although youngsters may pick up the facts of life from reading materials, music and video may have more impact on their sexual ethics. Sexual relationships are portrayed extensively on television. These portrayals are likely to influence young people's emerging sexual values (Strouse & Fabes, 1985). Lowry and Towles (1989) found that sexual content on TV soap operas increased during the 1980s. Furthermore, they concluded that TV soap operas portray sex "as a spur-of-the-moment activity pursued primarily by unmarried partners with little concern about either birth control or disease prevention" (p. 82).

The lyrics of rock music also contain extensive references to sexual behavior and norms of sexual conduct (Ray, Soares, & Tolchinsky, 1988). Rock videos, which have become extremely popular, may have even more sexual content. One study of music videos found that over 75% contained provocative depictions of sexuality (Sherman & Dominick, 1986). Rock videos routinely portray females as sex objects, and these portrayals appear to influence viewers' attitudes about sexual conduct (Hansen & Hansen, 1988).

Sex-charged music videos such as those starring Madonna appear to affect viewers' attitudes about sexual behavior.

The effects of erotic reading material, photographs, and films are the subject of considerable debate. Most people—although not all—find depictions of sexual activity arousing (Miller, Byrne, & Fisher, 1980). When physiological responses to erotic materials are measured in laboratory studies, men and women usually appear equally responsive (Heiman, 1977). But how much impact does sexually explicit material have on actual sexual behavior? Research suggests that exposure to erotic material elevates the likelihood of overt sexual activity for only a few hours (Cattell, Kawash, & DeYoung, 1972).

Although erotic materials do not appear to incite overpowering sexual urges, they may alter *attitudes* in ways that eventually influence sexual behavior. Zillmann and Bryant (1984) found that subjects exposed to a large dose of pornography developed more liberal attitudes about acceptable sexual practices. Furthermore, recent studies of *aggressive pornography* have raised concerns. Aggressive pornography typically depicts violence against women. Some studies indicate that this type of material increases male subjects' aggressive behavior toward women (Malamuth & Donnerstein, 1982). Exposure to aggressive pornography may also change males' attitudes about sexual aggression by perpetuating the myth that women enjoy being raped and ravaged (Malamuth, 1984).

In summary, our sexual identities are shaped by a host of intersecting influences. Given the multiplicity of factors at work, it is not surprising that people bring highly diverse expectations into their sexual relationships. This diversity can make sexual interactions exceedingly complicated, as we'll see in the next section.

INTERACTION IN SEXUAL RELATIONSHIPS

Because of their importance and their very emotional nature, sexual relationships tend to be highly charged sources of potential conflict. The fuse on this powder keg is often lit by the sparks that fly when incompatible expectations clash. In this section, we'll briefly discuss the interpersonal dynamics of sexual relationships.

Motives Underlying Sexual Interactions

Many different motives may lead people to enter into sexual relationships or to engage in sexual activities in an ongoing relationship. Consequently, two partners may *not* be motivated by the same desires or intentions. To date, there hasn't been much research on whether mismatched motives increase the likelihood of trouble in sexual interactions, but that's certainly a logical possibility.

What motivates us to engage in sexual encounters? Building on work by Neubeck (1972), Nass, Libby, and Fisher (1981, pp. 102–103) list a diverse array of motives underlying sexual interactions. Among these motives are the following.

- *Affection:* Longing for love, closeness, and physical and emotional union.
- *Lust:* Having passion for increasing and then gratifying sexual desires with a focus on sensual arousal, fantasies, and delight in touching and being touched.
- *Duty:* Feeling that it's our responsibility to have sex on schedule or to keep a partner from being uncomfortably frustrated. Typically a female feels that she can't leave a male unsatisfied, and the notion that he could masturbate or that she might feel equally uncomfortable if highly aroused but not satisfied is missing from traditional scripts.
- *Boredom:* Using sex to enhance a dull environment or routine activities.
- *Mending wounds:* Using sex as a way to make up after an argument or even to avoid dealing with a conflict.
- *Accomplishment:* Wanting to have sex as often as we think everyone else does, in every conceivable position, and perhaps break records with our "scores."
- *Recreation:* Having sex for fun and games or for the sake of creating pleasant sensations for each other.

Each person brings a sexual script, or set of expectations about sexual intentions, into a relationship. If these scripts differ—say, in each person's idea of who should initiate sexual activity—the couple can experience conflict.

• *Self-affirmation:* Acting out our perceived sexual identity so that the other will notice and approve of it.

A number of studies suggest that there are gender differences in the motives underlying sexual activity. In comparison to women, men appear to be motivated more by lust and the desire for physical gratification. In contrast, women are more likely to be motivated by their desire to express love and emotional commitment (Carroll, Volk, & Hyde, 1985). In one study of college students, Whitley (1988) asked subjects, "What was your most important reason for having sexual intercourse on the most recent occasion?" Lust and pleasure motives were cited by 51% of the men, but only 9% of the women. Love and emotional reasons were cited by 51% of the women, but only 24% of the men. Similar gender differences have been found in a community survey that looked at a broader sample of subjects than just college students (Leigh, 1989). Moreover, these gender differences appear to transcend sexual orientation, as they were observed in homosexuals as well as heterosexuals. The basis for these differences between men and women remain to be investigated. Some theorists speculate that these differences are due to gender-role socialization (Carroll et al., 1985). Other theorists believe that they are a product of biological influences (Knoth, Boyd, & Singer, 1988).

Sexual Scripts

In addition to differing in their motives for sex, people may be guided in their sexual relationships by very different scripts. *Scripts* are sets of expectations about how certain common activities should unfold. People have scripts for many activities, such as going grocery shopping or doing the laundry. Many of our scripts are ***social scripts—culturally programmed sets of expectations about how various social transactions should evolve.*** We have social scripts for events like going to a restaurant or visiting a doctor. Social scripts in life are similar to theatrical scripts for movies or plays. They spell out a sequence of events and how actors will interact. However, real-life scripts tend to be sketchier, allowing for more spontaneity, or "ad-libbing."

John Gagnon and William Simon have pointed out that we have social scripts for romantic relationships and sexual interactions (Gagnon & Simon, 1973; Simon & Gagnon, 1986). Our *sexual scripts* are a product of lifelong learning and socialization. These sexual scripts vary among people, depending on their social class, ethnic background, and religious upbringing. Although sexual scripts can be individualized, there are a handful of scripts that guide sexual conduct in most of us. Nass et al. (1981, pp. 23–24) describe five common sexual scripts in modern Western culture.

1. In the *traditional religious script*, sex is acceptable only within marriage. All other sexual activities are taboo, especially for women. Sex means reproduction, though it may also have something to do with affection.

2. In the *romantic script*, now the predominant one in our society, sex means love. According to this script, if we grow in love with someone, it's okay to "make love," either in or out of marriage. Without love, sex is a meaningless animal function. The eligible actors are two people who are in love, the ideal emotional state is uncontrollable loving passion, the words exchanged are assurances of affection, and all activities should appear to be spontaneous expressions of love.

3. In the *sexual friendship script*, people who are friends can also have an intimate sexual relationship. Although the association of the actors in this script is usually ongoing, typically it's not sexually exclusive.

4. In the *casual/mutual horniness script*, increasingly publicized by the mass media, sex is defined as recreational fun. The actors are casual acquaintances who are mutually sexually aroused. The qualities looked for in sexmaking may include joy, playfulness, abandon, variety, and increasingly, good technique.

5. In the *utilitarian-predatory script*, people have sex for some reason other than pleasure, reproduction, or love.

The reasons for sex might include economic gain (as in prostitution), career advancement, or power achievement. For example, to achieve power, some male groups see sex as "scoring" and believe they enhance their status within the group by boasting of their sexual exploits. Militant feminists, too, may define heterosexual activity as a power play rather than as a quest for love or pleasure.

The sexual scripts just described focus broadly on the *formation* of sexual liaisons. However, the day-to-day details of sexual interactions in established relationships are also guided by sexual scripts. People have expectations about which partner should initiate sexual encounters, where and when sex should take place, and the sequencing of sexual activities (Gagnon & Simon, 1987). For example, one person's sexual script might dictate that sex should occur only in the evening, progressing quickly from hugging and kissing to intercourse in a single position. Another person's sexual script might dictate that sex should occur whenever the urge strikes, progressing slowly from mutual fondling to oral contact to intercourse in several different positions. Obviously, if these two people became involved with each other, their differing sexual scripts could be a source of considerable conflict.

Only recently have researchers begun to study the sexual scripts that govern day-to-day interactions in ongoing relationships. For example, Byers and Heinlein (1989) examined patterns of initiating and refusing sexual overtures among married and cohabiting college students. They found that males initiated sexual encounters more often than females. However, both sexes responded favorably to initiations equally often. Only about one quarter of sexual initiations were turned away. This may mean that people learn to recognize when their partners will respond favorably to sexual overtures. Alternatively, it may mean that many people feel "duty-bound" not to refuse their partners. Hence, they have sex even when they are not really interested. Interestingly, Byers and Heinlein found that nonverbal signals—smiles, touch-ing, eye contact—played a key role in both sexual initiations and partners' responses.

Influence of Personality and Attitudes

Differences among people in sexual interest and erotic preferences are influenced to a large degree by personality and attitudes. In regard to *personality*, evidence suggests that *extraversion* is associated with greater sexual activity, with introverts being less active (Eysenck, 1976). Likewise, the personality trait of *sensation seeking*—preference for a high level of stimulation (see Chapter 3)—appears to be related to sexual behavior (Zuckerman, 1979). People who score high in sensation seeking engage in a wider range of sexual activities with a greater variety of partners. Correlations have also been found between sexuality and *self-monitoring*. This trait involves the degree to which people are aware of the impressions they make on others (see Chapter 5). High self-monitors are more willing than low self-monitors to have sexual relations in the absence of emotional closeness (Snyder, Simpson, & Gangestad, 1986).

RECOMMENDED READING

Understanding Human Sexuality
by Janet Shibley Hyde (McGraw-Hill, 1990)

College courses on sexuality are gradually appearing all over the country, and a host of new books to serve these courses are now available. If you can't enroll in a course on sexuality, you may want to read one of the better textbooks. If so, *Understanding Human Sexuality* by Janet Shibley Hyde is an outstanding candidate. Hyde's text is accurate, thorough, up-to-date, well organized, and written in an engaging, highly readable manner. What sets it apart from other texts is its clarity and sensitivity to readers' personal needs. It discusses the interpersonal aspects of sex without getting bogged down in physiology. Other excellent sexuality texts of similar quality include *Our Sexuality* by Robert Crooks and Karla Baur (Benjamin/Cummings, 1990) and *Understanding Sexuality* by Adelaide Haas and Kurt Haas (Times Mirror/Mosby, 1990). Any of these three books can provide you with an excellent introduction to the realities of human sexual expression.

> Throughout most of recorded history, at least until about 100 years ago, religion (and rumor) provided most of the information that people had about sexuality. . . . It was against this background of religious understandings of sexuality that the scientific study of sex began in the late nineteenth century, although, of course, religious notions continue to influence our ideas about sexuality to the present day. . . . The scientific study of sex has still not emerged as a separate, unified academic discipline like biology or psychology or sociology. Rather, it tends to be interdisciplinary—a joint effort by biologists, psychologists, sociologists, anthropologists, and physicians. [3rd edition, 1986, pp. 4, 8]

In regard to *attitudes*, studies have focused on people who experience a lot of guilt about sexual urges. People high in sex guilt have fewer sex partners, engage in sex less frequently, and employ a more limited range of sexual practices than others (Mosher, 1973). Among sexually active women, those with high sex guilt are less likely to use effective contraceptive methods than those with low sex guilt (Gerrard, 1987).

Some researchers have drawn a distinction between erotophobes and erotophiles. **Erotophobes are people who have very negative attitudes about sex. Erotophiles are people who have very favorable attitudes about sex.** Erotophobes tend to feel embarrassed when discussing sex and tend to condemn premarital sex. They dislike erotic materials and view sex as unimportant in their lives (Fisher, Byrne, White, & Kelley, 1988). In contrast, erotophiles are more comfortable discussing sex and more liberal about premarital sex. In comparison to erotophobes, they are more responsive to erotic materials and more likely to view sex as important in their lives. As you might anticipate, erotophiles are more sexually active than erotophobes.

Making Sexual Choices

We bring differing motives, scripts, personality traits, and attitudes into our sexual liaisons. Hence, it is not surprising that sexual interactions are a source of frequent conflict. Disagreements within couples about sex are commonplace (Blumstein & Schwartz, 1983; Levinger, 1970). Consider the following example:

"When we first married, my wife wanted intercourse morning, noon, and night. . . . I was so sore I couldn't walk. Even now, she would prefer making love at least twice a day seven days a week. She knows I can't that often, but I know she would like to." [Quoted in Rice, 1989, p. 336]

Variations among partners in sexual appetite are normal. The disagreements produced by these variations do not necessarily reflect lack of affection or declining sexual interest. However, they do mean that negotiation must be a key process in most sexual relationships.

You may not feel comfortable with the word *negotiation*. Its bartering connotations conflict with the religious and romantic sexual scripts that most of us embrace. Guided by these scripts, we often keep the negotiation process veiled in a shroud of ambiguity and subtlety. Nonetheless, intimate couples have to negotiate whether, how often, and when they will have sex, whether or not they acknowledge that they are negotiating. They also have to decide what kinds of erotic activities will take place, and what it all means to their relationship. This negotiation process may not be explicit—but it's there.

In the context of this process of negotiation, people have to make choices about their sexual behavior. However, it appears that many people let others make their sexual choices for them. Many of us take our sexual values, ethics, and scripts for granted, although this tendency is declining (Francoeur, 1987). Furthermore, some of us let our partners dictate the parameters of our sexual relationships. However, there is much to be said for thinking issues through on your own and taking full responsibility for your sexual choices. Many theorists assert that self-determination and autonomy are among the cornerstones of psychological health (for example, Maslow, 1970; Perls, 1969; Rogers, 1977).

In working out sexual choices, effective communication with one's partner is invaluable. However, a conspiracy of silence surrounds sex for many of us, as one woman's predicament illustrates.

"I know what I need in a sexual relationship, but how do I get this message across to my partner? I'm afraid that if I were to come right out and state my requests he would feel inadequate—like why didn't he think of it without me needing to tell him? But the truth of the matter is he usually doesn't come up with it on his own. So what do I do—keep my mouth shut and hope he will eventually figure it out or do I state specifically what I would like with the possibility of turning him off by being too demanding?

At this point in my life I generally opt for the former. Obviously, it is easier and less risky to say nothing." [Quoted in Crooks & Baur, 1983, pp. 237–238]

The difficulty we have in talking about sex is unfortunate. Studies show that open communication is associated with greater relationship satisfaction and greater sexual satisfaction (Markman, 1981; Zimmer, 1983). Most of the advice in Chapter 6 on how to improve verbal and nonverbal communication can be applied to sexual relationships. In particular, you may want to think about how constructive conflict-resolution strategies can be employed to keep the process of sexual negotiation healthy. With these thoughts about interpersonal aspects of sex in mind, let's turn our attention to physiological aspects of sexuality.

THE HUMAN SEXUAL RESPONSE

Assuming that partners are motivated to engage in sexual activity, what exactly happens physically? This may sound like a very simple question. However, very little was known about the physiology of the human sexual response before William Masters and Virginia Johnson conducted ground-breaking research in the 1960s. Although our society seems obsessed with sex, until relatively recently we did *not* encourage scientists to study sex. At first Masters and Johnson even had difficulty finding journals that were willing to publish their studies.

Masters and Johnson used physiological recording devices to monitor the bodily changes of volunteers engaging in sex. They even equipped an artificial penile device with a camera to study physiological reactions inside the vagina! Their observations and interviews with their subjects yielded a detailed description of the human sexual response that has won them widespread acclaim.

The Sexual Response Cycle

Masters and Johnson (1966, 1970) divide the sexual response cycle into four stages: excitement, plateau, orgasm, and resolution. With the exception of orgasm, the transitions from one stage to another are not clearly marked. Masters and Johnson's description of the sexual response cycle is a generalized one, outlining typical rather than inevitable patterns. You should keep in mind that there is considerable variability among people. Figure 13.4 shows how the intensity of sexual arousal changes as women and men progress through the phases of the sexual response cycle. Let's take a closer look at these phases.

Excitement Phase

During the initial phase of excitement, the level of arousal usually escalates rapidly. In both sexes, muscle tension, respiration rate, heart rate, and blood pressure increase quickly. In males *vasocongestion*—**engorgement of blood vessels**—produces penile erection and swollen testes. In females, vasocongestion leads to a swelling and harden-

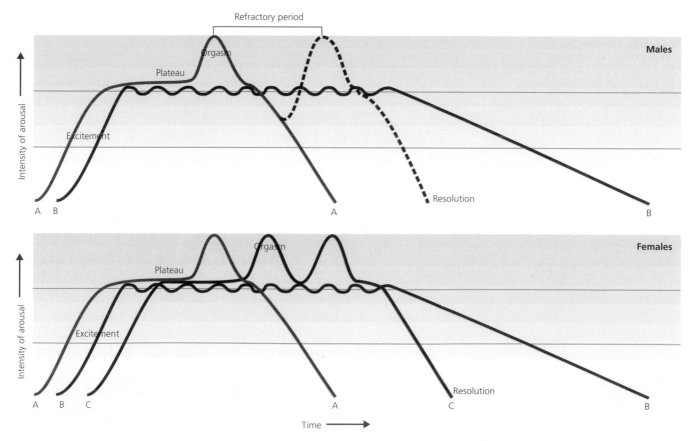

ing of the clitoris, expansion of the vaginal lips, and vaginal lubrication. Most women also experience nipple erection and a swelling of the breasts.

Plateau Phase

The name for this stage is misleading, as physiological arousal does not level off. Instead, during the plateau phase, physiological arousal usually continues to build, but at a much slower pace. In women, further vasocongestion produces a tightening of the vaginal entrance as the clitoris withdraws under the clitoral hood. Many men secrete a bit of fluid at the tip of the penis. This is not ejaculate, but it may contain sperm.

When foreplay is lengthy, it is normal for arousal to fluctuate in both sexes. This fluctuation is more apparent in men; erections may increase and decrease noticeably. In women, this fluctuation may be reflected in changes in vaginal lubrication.

Orgasm Phase

Orgasm occurs when sexual arousal reaches its peak intensity and is discharged in a series of muscular contractions that pulsate through the pelvic area. Heart rate, respiration rate, and blood pressure increase sharply as one experiences this exceedingly pleasant spasmodic response. In males, orgasm is usually accompanied by ejaculation of the seminal fluid.

The subjective experience of orgasm is very similar for men and women. Some investigators (Vance & Wagner, 1976; Wiest, 1977) have had subjects provide written descriptions of what their orgasms feel like without using specific words for genitals. Even psychologists and physicians could not tell which descriptions came from women and which came from men.

Resolution Phase

During the resolution phase, the physiological changes produced by sexual arousal subside. If one has not had an orgasm, the reduction in sexual tension may be relatively slow and sometimes unpleasant. After orgasm, men generally experience a *refractory period*, **a time following male orgasm during which males are largely unresponsive to further stimulation.** The refractory period varies from a few minutes to a few hours and increases with age.

Gender Differences in Patterns of Orgasm

As a whole, the sexual responses of women and men parallel each other fairly closely. The similarities clearly outweigh the differences. Nonetheless, there are some interesting differences between females and males in their patterns of experiencing orgasms. In the context of *intercourse*, women are somewhat less likely than men to reach orgasm (that is, they are more likely to follow pattern B in Figure 13.4). The gap between the sexes appears to have shrunk somewhat since Kinsey's data were collected. Nonetheless, Hunt (1974) still found that women achieve orgasm less consistently in intercourse than men.

There may be several reasons for this disparity and an understanding of these reasons may enhance sexual partners' interaction. First, although most women report that they enjoy intercourse, intercourse may not be the optimal mode of stimulation for women. Many women who only rarely or never reach orgasm in intercourse are able to climax regularly through self-stimulation (Hite, 1976). This may be because intercourse provides rather indirect stimulation to the clitoris, which appears to be the most sexually sensitive genital area in most women. Thus, approaches to arousal other than intercourse, such as manual or oral stimulation, may be more beneficial for many women. However, many couples are locked into a sexual script that prescribes that orgasms should be achieved through intercourse.

A second factor that may contribute to gender differences in orgasmic consistency is that more women than men are brought up to feel guilty about expressing their sexuality (Lott, 1987). Thus, guilt and ambivalence about sex may undermine sexual arousal in women more often than in men. A third contributing factor involves the

Figure 13.4. The human sexual response cycle. There are similarities and differences between men and women in patterns of sexual arousal. Pattern A, which culminates in orgasm and resolution, is the most typical sequence for both sexes. Pattern B, which involves sexual arousal without orgasm followed by a slow resolution, is also seen in both sexes, but it is more common among women. Pattern C, which involves multiple orgasms, is seen almost exclusively in women, as men go through a refractory period before they are capable of another orgasm. (Based on Masters & Johnson, 1966)

William Masters

Virginia Johnson

rapidity with which men and women reach a climax. Most men reach an orgasm more quickly than their female partners (Gebhard, 1966; Wolfe, 1981). Since women tend to require lengthier intercourse to achieve orgasm, they may have less orgasmic consistency because intercourse frequently is too brief. Consider one woman's experience:

"Sex for me is dull, boring, and uninspiring routine. My husband likes to 'make love' on Saturday night (he is too tired during the week). It's always the same way—a few kisses, some mechanical manipulation of my breasts, and presto, he is in and out and finished. I rarely am satisfied, but I don't even give a damn anymore. Actually I'm glad he finishes quickly. It's never fun to prolong boring things." [Quoted in Crooks & Baur, 1983, p. 218]

Is there any mystery about why this woman doesn't experience orgasms regularly? Obviously not. Intercourse with her husband is too brief, they have differing sexual scripts, and he is an inconsiderate sexual partner.

Since women reach orgasm through intercourse less consistently than men, they are more likely than men to fake an orgasm (Petersen et al., 1983). Surveys reveal that both sexes fake orgasms—women just do it more often. People appear to fake orgasms to make their partners feel better or to bring sexual activity to an end when they're fatigued. Generally, faking orgasms is probably not a good idea, as this practice undermines open communication about sex.

Although orgasmic consistency is lower in women than men, females are more likely than males to be *multiorgasmic*. A woman is said to be multiorgasmic if she experiences more than one climax in a very brief time (pattern C in Figure 13.4) with some regularity. Just how brief the time limitation should be is the source of some debate. Masters and Johnson originally thought that multiorgasmic women typically experienced a series of moderately intense orgasms, culminating in a very intense climax. However, a recent study suggests that multiorgasmic

women are more likely to experience two or more orgasms of roughly equal, full intensity (Amberson & Hoon, 1985).

In surveys, only about 10–15% of female respondents report reaching multiple orgasms with some regularity (Athanasiou, Shaver, & Tavris, 1970; Wolfe, 1981). Thus, women should certainly not feel inadequate if they are not multiorgasmic. Based on their research, Masters and Johnson concluded that multiorgasmic capacity is very rare in males. However, recent research suggests that multiple orgasms in men may be more common than previously believed (Dunn & Trost, 1989).

ACHIEVING SEXUAL AROUSAL

People engage in a wide variety of activities to elicit sexual arousal. *Erogenous zones* **are areas of the body that are sexually sensitive or responsive.** Areas such as the genitals and breasts usually come to mind when people think of erogenous zones. These *are* particularly sensitive areas for most people. But it's worth noting that many individuals fail to appreciate the potential that lies in other areas of the body. Virtually any area of the body can function as an erogenous zone.

Indeed, the ultimate erogenous zone may be the mind. By this we mean to convey that one's mental set is extremely important to sexual arousal. Vigorous and skillful genital stimulation by a partner may have absolutely no impact if a person is not in the mood for sex. Conversely, fantasy in the absence of any other stimulation can produce great arousal. In this section, we'll discuss techniques for achieving sexual arousal, starting with the use of fantasy.

Fantasy

Sexual fantasies are common and normal. Some of the more common themes in sexual fantasies are listed in Figure 13.5, based on research by Sue (1979). It should be

Figure 13.5. Common sexual fantasies. The percentage of men and women reporting various sexual fantasies during intercourse is shown here. Sue (1979) concludes that people fantasize about experiences they wouldn't seek out in real life.

Fantasies during Intercourse		
	Subjects reporting fantasy (%)	
Theme	*Males*	*Females*
A former lover	42.9	41.0
An imaginary lover	44.3	24.3
Oral–genital sex	61.2	51.4
Group sex	19.3	14.1
Being forced or overpowered into a sexual relationship	21.0	36.4
Others observing you engage in sexual intercourse	15.4	20.0
Others finding you sexually irresistible	55.2	52.8
Being rejected or sexually abused	10.5	13.2
Forcing others to have sexual relations with you	23.5	15.8
Others giving in to you after resisting you at first	36.8	24.3
Observing others engaging in sex	17.9	13.2
A member of the same sex	2.8	9.4
Animals	0.9	3.7

Note: For comparison, the responses of "frequently" and "sometimes" were combined for both males and females to obtain the percentages above. The number of respondents answering for a specific fantasy ranged from 103 to 106 for males and from 105 to 107 for females.

emphasized that if people fantasize about a particular kind of encounter, such as being forced to have sex, that does not necessarily mean that they would actually like to have such an encounter.

Fantasy often occurs in conjunction with other modes of sexual stimulation. For example, many people fantasize while engaging in masturbation, foreplay, or intercourse. Both men and women acknowledge that they fantasize during intercourse to increase their sexual arousal. Moreover, research suggests that fantasies *can* help people of both sexes to enhance their sexual excitement and achieve orgasm (Davidson, 1985).

Self-Stimulation

Stimulation of one's own genitals is commonly called masturbation. Because this term carries a decidedly negative connotation, many writers on sexuality prefer to use terms such as *self-stimulation* or *autoeroticism*. Because of its nonreproductive nature, autoeroticism has traditionally been condemned as immoral. In the 19th and early 20th centuries, it was widely assumed that self-stimulation was also harmful to one's physical and mental health. During this period, disapproval and suppression of masturbation were truly intense. Many antimasturbation devices were marketed to concerned parents. Children were forced to sleep in manacles, and some were fitted with genital cages (Karlen, 1971).

Given this heritage, it is not surprising that disapproval of masturbation continues to be widespread in our culture (Gagnon, 1985). Although Kinsey discovered over four decades ago that most people masturbate with no ill effects, guilt about self-stimulation is still prevalent.

In spite of these negative attitudes, self-stimulation is very common in our society. By adulthood, nine out of ten males and eight out of ten females report having masturbated at least once (Atwood & Gagnon, 1987). Self-stimulation remains common among adults even after marriage. Among younger married couples, 72% of the husbands and 68% of the wives reported engaging in self-stimulation (Hunt, 1974). Marital partners generally do not talk to each other about their masturbation. Most probably assume that their partner would view it as a sign of sexual discontent. However, the fact that self-stimulation is so widespread among married persons suggests that it probably is not a sign of dissatisfaction in most cases.

Experts on sexuality are gradually recognizing that self-stimulation is a normal, healthy, and sometimes important component of one's sexual behavior (Gadpaille, 1975). This route to sexual pleasure has obvious value when a sexual partner is unavailable. Moreover, many people are beginning to view self-stimulation as more than a poor substitute for "the real thing." Some people report that they derive more pleasure from self-stimulation than from intercourse (Hite, 1976).

Foreplay

Foreplay refers to the sexual activities that typically precede intercourse. Foreplay may include a wide range of sexual activities. Usually, it is initiated by kissing. This foreplay kissing may be extended to virtually any area of a partner's body. Mutual caressing is also an integral element of foreplay for most couples. Like kissing, this tactile stimulation may be applied to any area of the body. As in any phase of sex, specific techniques are not as important as good communication. Satisfying foreplay hinges on partners' communicating about what feels good to them.

The importance of foreplay is often underestimated, especially by men. Some people get so wrapped up in their anticipation of intercourse that they fail to appreciate the pleasure inherent in foreplay. This tendency may contribute to some sexual problems (Masters & Johnson, 1970).

Sexual partners often have differing expectations about the significance and appropriate length of foreplay. Among women, a common complaint about sex is that men are in too big a hurry (Denny, Field, & Quadagno,

"I think you're being silly. Would you like it better if I was thinking of you and sleeping with Robert Redford?"

1984). Ideally, these disparities should be brought out in the open and discussed. Partners who work to accommodate each other are more likely to have a satisfactory sexual liaison than those who ignore disagreements about foreplay.

Intercourse

Heterosexual intercourse, known more technically as *coitus*, **involves insertion of the penis into the vagina and (typically) pelvic thrusting.** It is the most widely endorsed and widely practiced sexual act in our society. Kinsey and his associates (1948, 1953) found that it accounted for 80–85% of the total sexual outlet for married couples. Insertion of the penis generally requires adequate vaginal lubrication, or it may be difficult and painful. In the absence of such lubrication, partners may choose to use artificial lubricants. The actual insertion is typically a cooperative act.

Partners may use any of a variety of positions in their intercourse. Many couples use more than one position in a single encounter. The man-above, or "missionary," position is the most common. When Kinsey's studies were done 40 years ago, many couples limited themselves to this position exclusively. Studies indicate that there is more variation today, as you can see if you examine the data in Figure 13.6. Hunt (1974) found that 75% of married couples reported using the female-above position. Furthermore, 50% of couples in his study reported using the side-by-side position and 40% the rear-entry position.

According to Masters and Johnson (1970), each position has its advantages and disadvantages. Although people tend to be fascinated by the relative merits of various positions, specific positions may not be as important as the tempo, depth, and angle of movements in intercourse. Most people appreciate variations in tempo, depth, and angle. As with other aspects of sexual relations, the crucial consideration is that partners talk to each other about their preferences.

Other Techniques

Among other techniques of sexual arousal, oral sex is the most common. *Cunnilingus* **refers to oral stimulation of the female genitals.** *Fellatio* **refers to oral stimulation of the penis.** Partners may stimulate each other simultaneously, or one partner may stimulate the other without immediate reciprocation. Oral-genital sex may be an element in foreplay, or it may constitute the main event in a sexual encounter. Oral sex is a major source of orgasms for many heterosexual couples. In homosexual relationships it plays a particularly central role.

As with masturbation, there is a residue of negative attitudes about oral sex. However, the prevalence of oral sex appears to have increased dramatically since the Kinsey studies of the late 1940s and early 1950s (Gagnon & Simon, 1987). Indeed, one study found that high school students today are slightly more likely to have had oral sex than intercourse (Newcomer & Udry, 1985). Among adults, about 90% report oral-genital contact (Blumstein & Schwartz, 1983; Wyatt, Peters, & Guthrie, 1988). Thus, it appears that oral sex is now a conventional component in most couples' sexual relationships.

Anal intercourse **involves insertion of the penis into a partner's anus and rectum.** Whereas oral and manual stimulation of the anal area are moderately common elements of foreplay, anal intercourse is less common. Still, when asked if they had ever had anal intercourse, 43% of the female respondents in a recent study said yes (Wyatt et al., 1988). Anal intercourse is more popular among homosexual male couples than among heterosexual couples (Bell & Weinberg, 1978). However, even among gay men it ranks behind oral sex and mutual masturbation in prevalence.

PATTERNS OF SEXUAL BEHAVIOR

In the previous section we focused on the sexual response itself. Our principal interests were physiology and tech-

Figure 13.6. Changes in the use of coital positions. About 20–25 years apart, Kinsey (1948, 1953) and Hunt (1974) asked their subjects about coital positions they used besides the man-above position. As you can see, Hunt's data indicate that by the 1970s couples were using a greater variety of positions for intercourse.

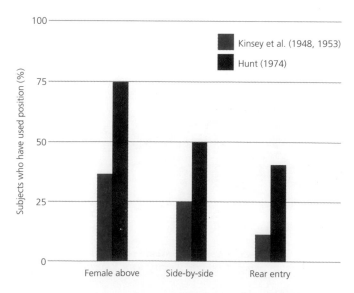

niques. In this section we'll discuss how variables such as age, sex, and marital status are related to patterns of sexual behavior. Let's begin by examining the so-called sexual revolution.

Has There Been a Sexual Revolution?

It is commonly suggested in the popular media that we have undergone a "sexual revolution." Just what would constitute a *revolution* in sexual behavior is unclear. Presumably, a revolution would involve sudden, radical, and widespread changes in the expression of our sexuality. But what would qualify as sudden, radical, or widespread is a matter of opinion.

Most sex researchers seem to feel that it would be more accurate to characterize the changes in our sexual behavior as *evolutionary* rather than *revolutionary*. To some extent, the sexual revolution has occurred more in our popular media than in our bedrooms. There *has* been radical change in the openness with which sex is discussed and portrayed in magazines, movies, and TV shows. However, a comparison of survey data across recent decades suggests that our actual behavior has changed gradually rather than suddenly.

The amount of change has probably been magnified by our tendency to talk more openly about sex. The extent of change may also be exaggerated because most people have difficulty envisioning their parents as sexual beings (Pocs & Godow, 1977). Hence, there is a curious tendency for people to underestimate the sexual activity of the previous generation. This is probably why a sexual revolution has been heralded in *every* decade of the 20th century! Undoubtedly, there *has* been substantial change in our sexual behavior, but it appears to have been less abrupt and less spectacular than widely believed.

Premarital Sex

The term *premarital sex* tends to conjure up images of furtive sex among teenagers. Of course, with more people delaying marriage, premarital sex increasingly involves relationships between mature adults. Obviously, the emotional implications of sex between a pair of 15-year-olds living with their parents and a pair of independent 30-year-olds are likely to be quite different.

Prevalence

It is clear that the prevalence of premarital sex has increased since the 1960s (Robinson & Jedlicka, 1982), as Figure 13.7 shows. Evidence suggests that by age 25, 97% of the men in our society and 67% of the women have engaged in premarital coitus (Hunt, 1974). Thus, people entering marriage as virgins have become a rather small minority group. Although the gap is shrinking, males are still more likely than females to engage in premarital sex. Some of the increase in premarital sex is attributable to later marriages, but premarital sex among teenagers *has* become more frequent as well (Dreyer, 1982).

Attitudes

People hold a number of viewpoints regarding premarital sex. Ira Reiss (1967) has identified four common attitudes.

- *Abstinence:* This point of view assumes that premarital sex is wrong under any circumstances and that one should abstain from all such activities.
- *Permissiveness with affection:* This attitude assumes that premarital sex is acceptable *if* it takes place in the context of a stable, loving relationship.
- *Permissiveness without affection:* This viewpoint endorses "casual" premarital sex between people who happen to be attracted to each other.
- *Double standard:* This is the notion that premarital intercourse is acceptable for men but not for women.

Most parents and most institutions (churches, schools, and so forth) in our society endorse the abstinence viewpoint. At the same time, considerable dismay has been voiced by people who believe that the viewpoint of

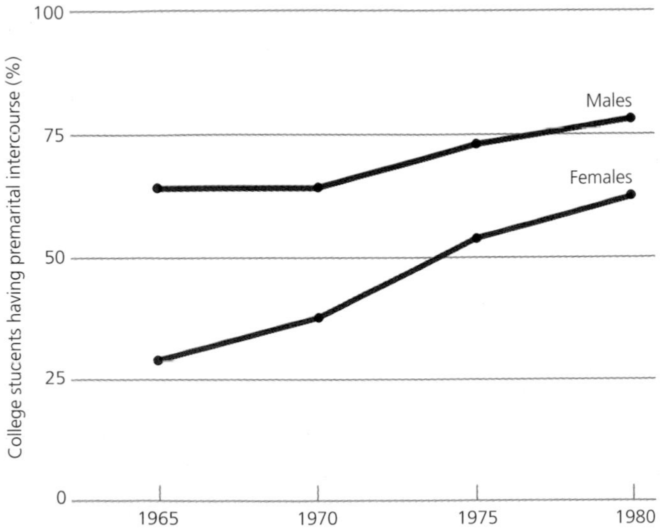

Figure 13.7. Increase in premarital sex among college students. The percentage of college students who report engaging in premarital intercourse has increased in recent decades. Males are still more likely to engage in premarital sex than females, but the gap has been closing. (Data from Robinson & Jedlicka, 1982)

permissiveness without affection has become the norm. What does the actual evidence indicate? Sprecher (1989) found no evidence of a double standard today. Instead, the data from several surveys (Earle & Perricone, 1986; Hunt, 1974; Zelnick & Kantner, 1977) suggest that permissiveness with affection is the dominant standard in our society. The casual "one-night stands" that get so much attention in the media appear to be less frequent than commonly believed. In a study of college students, only 33% of the males and 3% of the females endorsed premarital sex with a "casual acquaintance" (Earle & Perricone, 1986). Thus, concern about premarital promiscuity running rampant in our society may be overstated.

Marital Sex

Sex is a very important element in a marital union. There is ample evidence that couples' overall marital satisfaction is highly related to their satisfaction with their sexual interaction (Hunt, 1974; Tavris & Sadd, 1977). For example, Hunt found that spouses who characterized their marital relationship as "very close" were much more likely to rate their sex life as "very pleasurable" than those who characterized their marriage as "fairly close" or "not too close" (see Figure 13.8). Thus, good sex and a good marriage tend to go hand in hand. Of course, it is difficult to tell whether this is a matter of good sex promoting good marriages or good marriages promoting good sex. In all probability, it's a two-way street. It seems likely that marital closeness is conducive to sexual pleasure *and* that sexual satisfaction increases marital satisfaction.

Frequency and Practices

Married couples vary greatly in how often they have sex. *On the average*, couples in their 20s and 30s engage in sex about two or three times a week (Westoff, 1974). It appears that marital sex has increased in frequency since the Kinsey studies, but only slightly. As you can see in Figure 13.9, the frequency of sex among married couples tends to decrease as the years wear on (Trussell & Westoff,

1980). Couples report that this decline is due to increasing fatigue from work and child rearing and to growing familiarity with their sexual routine (Greenblat, 1983). As one man put it:

"In the beginning it was five times a week, three times in one day. But it changed because the early adrenaline wore off. Karin took a trip for a month and when she came back we were both too busy because we were working sixteen-hour days. So we sort of settled down to your typical boring existence." [Quoted in Blumstein & Schwartz, 1983, p. 199]

Although married couples' intercourse tends to become less frequent as time goes on, marital sex certainly does not have to be boring. A comparison of more recent surveys (Blumstein & Schwartz, 1983; Hunt, 1974; Tavris & Sadd, 1977) with the Kinsey data suggests that the sexual practices of married couples have become more diversified. The evidence suggests that couples today engage in lengthier foreplay and lengthier coitus. Married couples also use oral-genital techniques of arousal more often and use a greater variety of coital positions. Recent studies also suggest that husbands have become more concerned about their wives' sexual pleasure. This may be why wives are reaching orgasm with greater regularity than the wives of a couple of generations ago.

Effects of Aging

Married couples' level of sexual activity tends to decline during middle and late adulthood (Weizman & Hart, 1987; Wilson, 1975). In some people, this decline is due to decreased sexual desire and sexual capability (Kaplan, 1974). However, in many couples, the decline in sexual activity may be due to changing attitudes more than physiological factors. Our youth-oriented culture tends to discourage sexual expression in old age. People are led to believe that sexual activity among the elderly is inappropriate and even repugnant.

It *is* true that a person's sexual response changes with age (Diamond & Karlen, 1981). Arousal tends to build

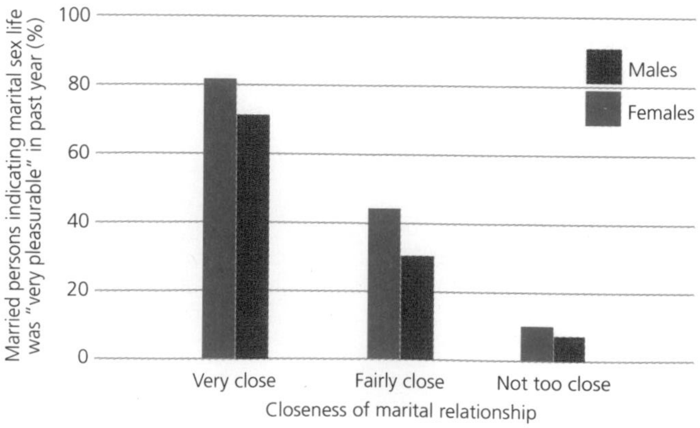

Figure 13.8. Sexual satisfaction and marital satisfaction. Hunt (1974) found that the better the subjects' marital relationship, the more likely they were to rate their sex life as very pleasurable. Thus, there is a correlation between good marriages and good sex.

more slowly in both sexes, and orgasms tend to diminish in frequency and intensity. Males' refractory periods lengthen, and females' vaginal lubrication and elasticity decrease.

In spite of these changes, however, people in their 60s, 70s, and 80s remain capable of rewarding sexual encounters. About 80% of couples over the age of 60 continue to engage in intercourse every week or two (Brecher, 1984). The married couples who remain sexually active in old age generally are those who had a relatively high level of sexual activity when they were younger (George & Weiler, 1981).

Extramarital Sex

Extramarital sex, known more negatively as "adultery" or "cheating," involves a married person engaging in erotic activity with someone other than his or her spouse. Clanton (1973) has differentiated among three types of extramarital liaisons. In *clandestine extramarital sex* the nonmarital sexual activity is successfully kept secret from one's spouse. In *consensual extramarital sex* the spouse is aware of the nonmarital activity. He or she accepts it and may even approve of it (as in "mate swapping" or "swinging," for instance). Finally, in *ambiguous extramarital sex* a spouse becomes aware of secretive nonmarital sexual activity, but chooses not to confront the participating spouse. Typically, the activity is tolerated, *without* approval, for the sake of avoiding marital strife or a clash that might lead to divorce. Surveys suggest that consensual extramarital sex remains relatively infrequent in our society (Davidson, 1988; Levin & Levin, 1975). Thus, most extramarital sex is of the clandestine or ambiguous variety. We'll limit our further discussion to these two types of extramarital activity.

Prevalence

The vast majority of people (about 75%) in our society express strong disapproval of extramarital sex (Reiss, Anderson, & Sponaugle, 1980). Nonetheless, a substan-

tial number of people get involved in extramarital activity. Roughly speaking, the data from various studies suggest that about 40–50% of husbands and about 25–35% of wives engage in extramarital activity at least once (Thompson, 1983). These figures may *not* mean that men are more likely than women to have an "affair." Much of the higher incidence of extramarital sex for males probably involves visits to prostitutes and one-time-only encounters. These kinds of activities are less frequent among women (Bell, Turner, & Rosen, 1975). Thus, if we define an "affair" as a repetitive encounter with someone other than a prostitute, the incidence of affairs may be similar for both sexes.

Motivations

Why do people pursue extramarital sexual encounters? There are many reasons. First, dissatisfaction with one's marriage is related to the likelihood of engaging in extramarital sex (Bell et al., 1975). People who are unhappy with their marriage may be seeking affection and emotional support that their marriage is not providing. Some may also be expressing anger toward their spouse. Second, there is evidence that dissatisfaction with just the *sexual* aspect of one's marriage may instigate interest in extramarital sex (Bell et al., 1975).

Third, even when the sexual component of a marriage is satisfactory, some people desire new and different sexual experiences (Buunk, 1980). Interestingly, the evidence suggests that this pursuit of variety and excitement may frequently lead to disappointment. Hunt (1974) found that extramarital sex involves less variety in arousal techniques and is less frequently viewed as "very pleasurable" than marital sex. Fourth, sometimes extramarital sexual activity occurs simply because two persons are attracted to each other. Erotic reactions to people other than one's spouse do not cease when one marries. Most people suppress these sexual desires because they disapprove of adultery. However, some people have a relatively tolerant attitude about extramarital sex (Atwater, 1982).

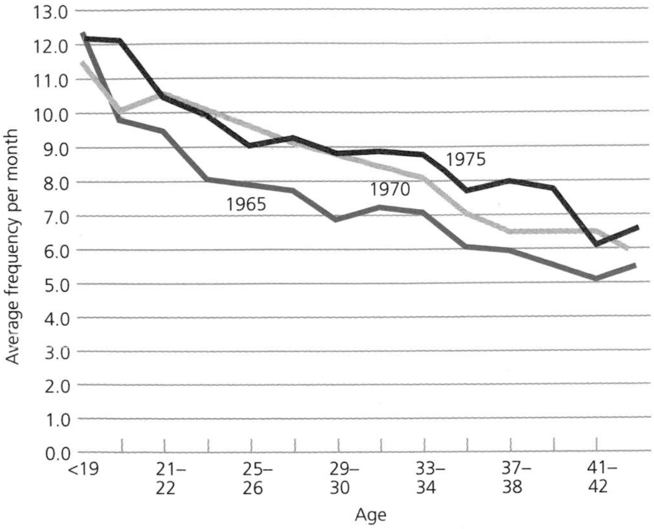

Figure 13.9. Age trends in the frequency of marital coitus. Data from three studies conducted at different times are summarized in this graph, based on responses from white married women. All three studies indicate a gradual decline in the frequency of intercourse among married couples as the years go by. (From Trussell & Westoff, 1980)

Impact

The impact of extramarital sexual activity on marriages has not been investigated extensively. The effects are likely to vary, depending on the nature of the activity and the nature of the marriage (Reiss & Furstenberg, 1981). Generally speaking, the deception and hypocrisy inherent in clandestine or ambiguous extramarital sex seem likely to undermine the trust and affection that are so important to a marriage. Of course, if one is motivated by marital dissatisfaction, there may be little trust or affection to undermine. Occasionally, extramarital affairs may have a positive effect on a marriage. Some participants inadvertently develop a new appreciation for the quality and importance of their marital union (Tavris & Sadd, 1977). Perhaps people who believe that "the grass is greener on the other side of the fence" learn that they actually have a "lush lawn."

PRACTICAL ISSUES IN SEXUAL ACTIVITY

Regardless of the context of sexual activity, two practical issues are often matters of concern: contraception and sexually transmitted diseases. These are complicated topics that fall in the province of medicine more than psychology. Nonetheless, we'll briefly discuss behavioral aspects of birth control and sex-related diseases.

Contraception

Most people desire to control whether and when they will conceive a child, and so they need reliable contraception. Despite the availability of effective contraceptive methods, however, many people fail to exercise much control.

Barriers to Effective Contraception

Effective contraception requires that intimate couples negotiate their way through a complex sequence of steps.

First, they must define themselves as sexually active. Second, they must have accurate knowledge about fertility and conception. Third, their chosen method of contraception must be readily accessible. Finally, they must possess the motivation and skill to use the method correctly and consistently. Failure to meet even one of these conditions can result in an unintended pregnancy.

Ineffective contraception is particularly prevalent among adolescents (Tanfer & Horn, 1985). Teens who are just beginning to experiment sexually often have ambivalent feelings about their behavior. Hence, they are especially prone to deny their need for contraception. Raised in a society in which intentional wrongdoing is regarded as more wrong than unintentional acts, many adolescents feel that sex is acceptable only if "we got carried away" (Cvetkovich, Grote, Bjorseth, & Sarkissian, 1975). Furthermore, misinformation about both fertility and contraception is rampant among adolescents. Many teens underestimate their own fertility ("I'm too young to get pregnant"; "I don't have sex often enough"). Many also overestimate the "costs" of birth control ("You can die from the pill"; "It takes away all the romance") (Luker, 1975). Further, effective family planning requires a level of abstract thinking that many adolescents have not yet attained. They need the ability to anticipate future consequences (possible pregnancy) that they have never experienced and can't even imagine experiencing, as well as the ability to plan for these consequences *not* to happen (Spain, 1985). Finally, ready access to contraceptive devices is often a problem for adolescents. Considering the combined impact of all these factors, contraceptive failure among teens is not surprising.

Even adults in stable relationships sometimes fail to practice birth control consistently. Use of contraception has no immediately experienced positive effects, but it can have immediate negative effects (for instance, the interruption of sexual activity to put on a condom). Many people therefore find it difficult to sustain their contraceptive efforts over the long haul.

Contraceptive failure is especially likely among those

© 1986, THE BOSTON GLOBE. REPRINTED BY PERMISSION OF THE LOS ANGELES TIMES SYNDICATE.

Figure 13.10. A comparison of widely used contraceptive techniques. Couples can choose from a variety of contraceptive methods. This chart summarizes the advantages and disadvantages of each method. Note that the actual failure rate is much higher than the ideal failure rate for all methods, because couples do not use contraceptive techniques consistently and correctly. (From Masters, Johnson, & Kolodny, 1988)

who experience guilt or anxiety about their sexuality. Gerrard (1987) has shown that women high in sex guilt tend to be less knowledgeable about contraception than others. They also select less reliable contraceptive methods, and they use their chosen method inconsistently. Additionally, they're more prone to defer to their male partner's wishes about sexual activities and may leave birth control up to him as well. This approach can backfire if the partner believes (as many men do) that contraception is the woman's responsibility.

Selecting a Contraceptive Method

Assuming that a couple is motivated to control their fertility, how should they go about selecting a technique? A rational choice requires accurate knowledge of the effectiveness, benefits, costs, and risks of the various methods. Figure 13.10 summarizes information on most of the methods currently available. The *ideal failure rate* estimates the probability of conception when the technique is used correctly and consistently. The *actual failure rate* is what occurs in the real world, when users' negligence is factored in. Let's look in more detail at the two most widely used birth control methods in the Western world: oral contraceptives and condoms (Calderone & Johnson, 1989).

Oral contraceptives are pills taken daily by mouth. They contain synthetic forms of two hormones—estrogen and/or progesterone. "The pill" actually refers to over 50 different oral contraceptive products that inhibit ovulation in women. Oral contraception is preferred by many couples because it is the only widely available method that is separated in time from the sex act itself. No other method (except for the intrauterine device, which is rarely prescribed today) permits a similar degree of sexual spontaneity.

Despite much worrisome publicity, use of oral contraceptives does not appear to increase one's overall risk for cancer (Eichhorst, 1988). In fact, the likelihood of certain forms of cancer (such as uterine cancer) is reduced in women who use low-dosage oral contraceptives. The pill *does* slightly increase the risk of certain cardiovascular disorders, such as heart disease and stroke. Thus, alternative methods of contraception should be considered by smokers over age 35 and those with any suspicion of cardiovascular disease (Eichhorst, 1988).

A *condom* is a sheath worn over the penis during intercourse to collect ejaculated semen. The condom is the only widely available contraceptive device for use by males. It can be purchased in any drugstore without a prescription. If used correctly, the condom is highly

Contraceptive Methods

Method	Effectiveness rating	Ideal failure rate (%)	Actual failure rate (%)	Advantages	Disadvantages
Birth control pills (combination)	Excellent	0.5	2–3	Highly reliable; coitus independent; has some health benefits	Side effects; daily use; continual cost
Minipill	Very good	1–2	5–10	Thought to have low risk of side effects; coitus independent	Breakthrough bleeding; daily use; continual cost
IUD	Excellent	1–3	5–6	No memory or motivation required for use; very reliable	Cramping, bleeding, expulsion; risk of pelvic inflammatory disease
Diaphragm and cream or jelly	Good–very good	3	15–20	No major health risks; inexpensive	Aesthetic objections
Condom	Very good	3	10	Protects against STDs; simple to use; male responsibility; no health risks; no prescriptions required	Unaesthetic to some; requires interruption of sexual activity
Sponge	Good–very good	3	15	24-hour protection; simple to use; no taste or odor; inexpensive; effective with several acts of intercourse	Aesthetic objections
Cervical cap	Good	3	10–20	Can wear for weeks at a time; coitus independent; no major health risks	May be difficult to insert; may irritate cervix
Spermicides	Good	3	18–22	No major health risks; no prescription required	Unaesthetic to some; must be properly inserted
Rhythm	Poor to fair	13	20–40	No cost; acceptable to Catholic church	Requires high motivation and periods of abstinence; unreliable
Withdrawal	Fair	9	20–25	No cost or health risks	Reduces sexual pleasure; unreliable
Douching	Poor	7	40+	Inexpensive	Extremely unreliable

effective in preventing pregnancy (Mishell, 1986). It must be placed over the penis after erection but before any contact with the vagina. Space must be left at the tip of the condom to collect the ejaculate. The man should withdraw before completely losing his erection, and hold the rim of the condom during withdrawal to prevent any semen from spilling into the vagina.

Condoms are generally made of latex rubber, but are occasionally made from animal membranes ("skin"). The use of rubber condoms can reduce the chances of contracting or passing on various sexually transmitted diseases. Skin condoms, however, do *not* offer protection against such diseases, which we will discuss in the next section.

Sexually Transmitted Diseases

A *sexually transmitted disease* (STD) is an illness that is transmitted primarily through sexual contacts. When people think of STDs they typically think of syphilis and gonorrhea, but these are only the tip of the iceberg. There are actually about 20 sexually transmitted diseases. Some of these diseases—for instance pubic lice—are

minor nuisances that can readily be treated. Some STDs, however, are severe afflictions that are difficult to treat. For instance, if it isn't detected early, syphilis can cause heart failure, blindness, and brain damage. The Acquired Immune Deficiency Syndrome (AIDS) is eventually fatal. We'll discuss AIDS in our upcoming chapter (Chapter 14) on health psychology. Here we will cover other common STDs.

Prevalence

No one is immune to sexually transmitted diseases. Even monogamous partners can develop some STDs (yeast infections, for instance). Sexually transmitted diseases occur more frequently than widely realized, and most STDs are increasing in prevalence. Health authorities estimate that there are about 10 million new cases in the United States each year. If you are between the ages of 15 and 55, you have about a one in four chance of developing a sexually transmitted disease during your lifetime (Gordon & Snyder, 1989). The highest incidence of STDs is seen in the adolescent age group (Krilov, 1988).

The principal types of sexually transmitted diseases are listed in Figure 13.11, along with their symptoms and

Sexually Transmitted Diseases (STDs)

STD	Transmission	Symptoms
Bacterial vaginosis	The most common causative agent, the *Gardnerella vaginalis* bacterium, is transmitted primarily by coitus.	In women, a fishy or musty-smelling thin discharge, like flour paste in consistency and usually gray. Most men are asymptomatic.
Candidiasis (yeast infection)	The *Candida albicans* fungus may accelerate growth when the chemical balance of the vagina is disturbed; it may also be transmitted through sexual interaction.	White, "cheesy" discharge; irritation of vaginal and vulvar tissue.
Trichomoniasis	The protozoan parasite *Trichomonas vaginalis* is passed through genital sexual contact or less frequently by towels, toilet seats, or bathtubs used by an infected person.	White or yellow vaginal discharge with an unpleasant odor; vulva is sore and irritated.
Chlamydial infection	The *Chlamydia trichomatis* bacterium is transmitted primarily through sexual contact. It may also be spread by fingers from one body site to another.	In men, chlamydial infection of the urethra may cause a discharge and burning during urination. *Chlamydia*-caused epidydimitis may produce a sense of heaviness in the affected testicle(s), inflammation of the scrotal skin, and painful swelling at the bottom of the testicle. In women, pelvic inflammatory disease caused by *Chlamydia* may include disrupted menstrual periods, abdominal pain, elevated temperature, nausea, vomiting, and a headache.
Gonorrhea ("clap")	The *Neisseria gonorrhoeae* bacterium ("gonococcus") is spread through genital, oral-genital, or genital-anal contact.	Most common symptoms in men are a cloudy discharge from the penis and burning sensations during urination. If disease is untreated, complications may include inflammation of the scrotal skin and swelling at base of the testicle. In women, some green or yellowish discharge is produced, but disease commonly remains undetected. At a later stage, pelvic inflammatory disease may develop.
Syphilis	The *Treponema pallidum* bacterium ("spirochete") is transmitted from open lesions during genital, oral-genital, or genital-anal contact.	*Primary stage:* A painless chancre appears at the site where the spirochetes entered the body. *Secondary stage:* The chancre disappears and a generalized skin rash develops. *Latent stage:* There may be no observable symptoms. *Tertiary stage:* Heart failure, blindness, mental disturbance, and many other symptoms may occur. Death may result.
Pubic lice ("crabs")	*Phthirus pubis*, the pubic louse, is spread easily through body contact or through shared clothing or bedding.	Persistent itching. Lice are visible and may often be located in pubic hair or other body hair.
Herpes	The genital herpes virus (HSV-2) appears to be transmitted primarily by vaginal, oral-genital, or anal sexual intercourse. The oral herpes virus (HSV-1) is transmitted primarily by kissing.	Small red, painful bumps (papules) appear in the region of the genitals (genital herpes) or mouth (oral herpes). The papules become painful blisters that eventually rupture to form wet, open sores.
Viral hepatitis	The hepatitis B virus may be transmitted by blood, semen, vaginal secretions, and saliva. Manual, oral, or penile stimulation of the anus is strongly associated with the spread of this virus. Hepatitis A seems to be primarily spread via the fecal-oral route. Oral-anal sexual contact is a common mode for sexual transmission of hepatitis A.	Vary from nonexistent to mild, flulike symptoms to an incapacitating illness characterized by high fever, vomiting, and severe abdominal pain.
Genital warts (venereal warts)	The virus is spread primarily through genital, anal, or oral-genital interaction.	Warts are hard and yellow-gray on dry skin areas; soft pinkish red and cauliflowerlike on moist areas.

Note: See Chapter 14 for a discussion of AIDS.

modes of transmission. As you can see, most of these are spread from one person to another through intercourse, oral-genital contact, or anal-genital contact. In regard to the transmission of STDs, three points are worth emphasizing. First, the risk of contracting STDs is clearly related to the number of sexual partners that one has. The more sexual partners you have, the higher your chances of exposure to a sexually transmitted disease. Second, people can often be carriers of sexually transmitted diseases without being aware of it. For instance, in its early stages gonorrhea may cause no readily apparent symptoms in women, who may unknowingly transmit the disease to their partners. Third, even when people know they have a sexually transmitted disease, they may not remain sexually abstinent or inform their partners. Due to guilt and embarrassment, many people ignore symptoms of sexually transmitted diseases and continue their normal sexual activities (Kramer, Aral, & Curran, 1980). Thus, you cannot assume that sexual partners will warn you that they may be contagious.

Prevention

Sexual abstinence is the best way to minimize the risk of acquiring sexually transmitted diseases. However, for most people this is not an appealing or realistic option. Short of abstinence, the best strategy is to engage in sexual activity only in the context of a long-term relationship, where you have an opportunity to know your partner reasonably well. Sexual interactions with casual acquaintances greatly increase your risk for STDs. In addition to being judicious about sexual relations, you might consider the following advice from Francoeur (1982, p. 321):

- Proper and consistent use of a condom and washing after sexual activity can reduce the risk when one is not monogamous or sexually exclusive.
- For a woman on the pill, a condom provides additional protection against the increased tendency to vaginal infections that comes with the effect of the hormonal pill on the vaginal environment.

Figure 13.11. Overview of common sexually transmitted diseases (STDs). This chart summarizes the symptoms and modes of transmission of ten common STDs. Note that intercourse is not required to transmit STDs. Many STDs can be contracted through oral-genital contact or other forms of physical intimacy. (Adapted from Crooks & Baur, 1990)

- Vaginal contraceptives, such as foams and creams, may provide some protection for men as well as for women.
- Watch for sores, rashes, or discharge around the vulva or penis, or elsewhere on the body, especially the mouth. Avoid kissing or oral sex with cold sores.
- Wash sexual organs with soap and warm water before and after contact.
- Urinate soon after intercourse.
- If sexually active with several partners in a year, have regular STD checkups. Most doctors and health clinics will not perform STD tests unless they are asked to. Too many doctors prefer to assume that "it would not happen to their patients, especially if they are married."
- If you have any reason to suspect an infection, find a good health clinic and have the appropriate test as soon as possible. If the test(s) are negative, you can stop worrying. If they are positive, getting the proper treatment is equally important. Don't delay because of embarrassment or fear. Don't mistake the spontaneous disappearance of symptoms as a sign that you really didn't have an STD. If you have a negative test, at least you know for sure you mistook the supposed symptoms. This knowledge is worth the small investment in a test.
- If the test(s) prove positive, notify your sexual partner(s) so they can be treated immediately. Avoid sexual intercourse and oral sex until both partners are fully treated and a physician or clinic says both are no longer infectious.

SUMMARY

Research on sexual behavior is particularly difficult to do because of problems in getting a representative sample and the dubious accuracy of self-report data. There is great variety among people in their sexual expression. One's sexual identity is made up of sexual orientation, body image, sexual values and ethics, and erotic preferences. Physiological factors such as hormonal fluctuations clearly shape sexual identity. However, hormone levels seem to influence sexual differentiation, maturation, and anatomy more than they do sexual activities. Psychosocial factors appear to have more impact on sexual behavior. Sources of socialization that shape sexual identity include families, schools and peers, and the media.

People frequently enter into sexual interactions with differing motivations. Men tend to be motivated more by physical gratification, whereas emotional motives tend to be more important for women. Sexual scripts regulate the formation and evolution of sexual relationships. Variations among people in erotic preferences are also shaped by their personality traits and their attitudes. Disparities between partners in sexual interest and erotic preferences understandably lead to conflicts that necessitate negotiation. Effective communication is the key to making this negotiation process a healthy one.

The physiology of the human sexual response was elucidated by Masters and Johnson. They analyzed the sexual response cycle into four phases: excitement, plateau, orgasm, and resolution. Men reach orgasm more consistently than women in intercourse. However, women have a greater capacity for multiple orgasms.

Sexual fantasies are normal and can play an important part in sexual arousal. Despite the strongly negative attitudes about masturbation that are traditional in our society, self-stimulation is quite common, even among married people. Foreplay may involve a wide range of erotic activities. Its importance is often underestimated, particularly by males. The key to satisfactory foreplay is good communication between the partners. Coitus is the most widely endorsed sexual act in our society. Four coital positions are commonly used. Although each has its advantages and disadvantages, positions by themselves are not a crucial determinant of sexual arousal. Oral-genital sex has become a common element in most couples' sexual repertoire. Anal sex continues to be a less common practice among heterosexuals.

The widely heralded sexual revolution appears to be exaggerated. However, the prevalence and acceptability of premarital sex have increased. The quality of one's sexual relationship is intimately tied to the quality of one's marriage. Younger married couples tend to have sex about two or three times a week. This frequency declines with advancing age. Consensual extramarital sex remains uncommon in our society. Clandestine and ambiguous extramarital sex are much more prevalent. Marital dissatisfaction, sexual discontent, curiosity, and chance attractions motivate people to get involved in extramarital sex.

Contraception and sexually transmitted diseases are two practical issues that concern many couples. For a variety of reasons, many people (especially adolescents) who do not want to conceive a child fail to use contraceptive procedures effectively, if at all. The contraceptive methods available differ in effectiveness and have various advantages and disadvantages. STDs are increasing in prevalence, especially among teenagers. STDs can be transmitted unknowingly, but some people continue sexual relations even when they realize they are contagious. The danger of STDs is higher among those who have had more sexual partners. Hence, one way to reduce one's risk is to avoid casual sex.

In our Application, we focus on issues that relate to enhancing sexual satisfaction. We'll discuss advances in the understanding and treatment of sexual problems.

Enhancing Sexual Relationships

Answer the following true or false.

☐ **1.** Sexual problems are very resistant to treatment.

☐ **2.** It's important to set very specific goals in sexual encounters.

☐ **3.** Sexual problems belong to couples rather than individuals.

☐ **4.** Most sexual problems have an organic basis.

☐ **5.** Sex therapists sometimes recommend masturbation as a treatment for certain types of problems.

The answers for the true-false questions above are (1) false, (2) false, (3) true, (4) false, and (5) true. If you answered several of the questions incorrectly, you have misconceptions about sexuality that may at some point affect your sexual relations. If so, you are not unusual. Although our society seems obsessed with sex, misconceptions about sexuality are commonplace. In this Application, we take a practical look at sexual problems and their possible solutions.

Sexual intercourse is really a pretty simple activity. Most animals execute the act with a minimum of difficulty. However, humans manage to make sexual relations terribly complicated, and many people suffer from sexual problems. Fortunately, recent advances in our understanding of sexual functioning have yielded many useful ideas on how to improve sexual relationships.

In the interests of simplicity, our advice is directed to heterosexual couples. Obviously, many readers may not be involved in a sexual relationship at present. But if you're not, we'll assume that someday you will be.

GENERAL SUGGESTIONS

Let's begin with some general ideas about how to enhance sexual relationships, drawn from several outstanding books on sexuality (Barbach, 1982; Crooks & Baur, 1990; Hyde, 1990). Even if you are satisfied with your sexual relations, these ideas may be useful as preventive medicine.

1. *Pursue adequate sex education.* A surprising number of people are ignorant about the realities of sexual functioning. In a book titled *Sexual Myths and Fallacies*, James McCary (1971) discusses over 80 common misconceptions about sexuality. So, the first step in promoting sexual satisfaction is to acquire accurate information about sex. The shelves of most bookstores are bulging with popular books on sex, but many of them are loaded with inaccuracies. Your best bet is to pick up a college textbook on human sexuality. Enrolling in a course on sexuality is also a good idea. More and more colleges are offering such courses today.

2. *Review your sexual value system.* Many sexual problems are derived from a negative sexual value system in which people associate sex with immorality and depravity. The guilt feelings caused by this orientation can interfere with sexual functioning. Given this possibility, experts on sexuality often encourage adults to examine the sources and implications of their sexual values.

3. *Communicate about sex.* As children, people often learn that they shouldn't talk about sex. Many people carry this feeling into adulthood and have great difficulty discussing sex, even with their partner. Good communication is extremely important in a sexual relationship. Figure 13.12 lists common problems in sexual relations reported by a sample of 100

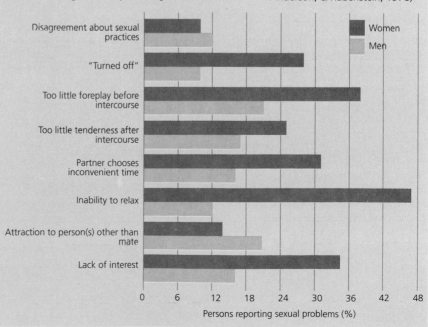

Figure 13.12. Common problems in sexual relations. The percentage of men and women reporting various types of problems in their sexual relationships is shown here, based on a sample of 100 couples. (Data from Frank, Anderson, & Rubenstein, 1978)

couples (Frank, Anderson, & Rubinstein, 1978). Many of the problems reported by the couples—such as choosing an inconvenient time, too little foreplay, and too little tenderness after sex—are largely due to poor communication. Your partner is not a mind reader. You have to share your thoughts and feelings to promote mutual satisfaction. Ask questions if you have doubts about your partner's preferences. Provide candid (but diplomatic) feedback when your partner asks about your reactions. Learn to make specific requests that effectively convey your erotic preferences.

4. *Avoid goal setting.* Sexual encounters are not tests—or races. Sexual relations usually work out best when people relax and enjoy themselves. However, some people get overly concerned about orgasms. A grim determination to climax typically makes it harder to do so. This mental set can lead to *spectatoring*—a stance in which a person is too busy monitoring what is going on to enjoy it. It's better to adopt the philosophy that getting there is at least half the fun.

5. *Enjoy your sexual fantasies.* As we noted earlier, the mind is the ultimate erogenous zone. Fantasizing during a sexual encounter is normal, and both sexes report that their sexual fantasies increase their excitement. Don't be afraid to use fantasy to enhance your sexual arousal. One woman's experience illustrates the potential value of both fantasy and open communication:

"I had this sexual fantasy that kept going through my mind. I would imagine coming home after a long, hard day of classes and being met by my partner, who would proceed to take me into the bedroom and remove all my clothes. He would then pick me up and carry me into the bathroom where a tub full of hot water and bubbles awaited. The fantasy would end with us making passionate love in the bathtub with bubbles popping off around us. Finally, I shared my fantasy with him. Guess what happened when I came home after the next long day? It was even better than I had imagined!" [Quoted in Crooks & Baur, 1983, p. 234]

6. *Be selective about sex.* Sexual encounters generally work out better when you have privacy and a relaxed atmosphere, when you are well rested, and when you are enthusiastic. If you consistently have sex in bad situations, your sexual relations may not be very rewarding. Realistically, you can't count on (or insist upon) having ideal situations all the time, but you should be aware of the value of being selective. If your heart isn't in it, it may be wise to wait. It also helps to remember that it is quite common for partners to disagree about when, where, and how often they should have sex. This sort of disagreement is normal. Hence, it should not be a source of resentment. Couples simply need to work toward reasonable compromises—through open communication.

UNDERSTANDING SEXUAL DYSFUNCTION

Many people struggle with *sexual dysfunctions*—impairments in sexual functioning that cause subjective distress. One study of patients coming to a family practice center for medical treatment found that 75% had sexual problems of some kind (Schein, Zyzanski, Levine, & Medalie, 1988). This estimate may be a little high for the population as a whole, since some of the sexual problems may have been spinoffs from the patients' medical problems. Nonetheless, it is clear that sexual problems are more common than widely appreciated. Figure 13.13 shows the percentage of subjects in another study reporting the dysfunctions that we will discuss (Frank et al., 1978). These data—

Figure 13.13. Sexual dysfunctions in normal couples. This graph shows the prevalence of various sexual dysfunctions in a sample of 100 "normal" couples, 80% of whom reported having happy or satisfying marriages. These data indicate that the most common dysfunctions are premature ejaculation in men and secondary orgasmic difficulties in women. (Data based on Frank, Anderson, & Rubenstein, 1978)

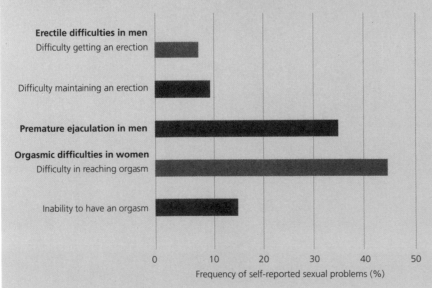

which are consistent with other estimates—suggest that roughly half of all couples are troubled by sexual problems to some degree.

Traditionally, people have assumed that a sexual problem lies in *one partner.* Although it is convenient to refer to a man's erectile difficulties or a woman's orgasmic difficulties, research indicates that most sexual problems emerge out of partners' unique ways of relating to each other. In other words, *sexual problems belong to couples rather than to individuals.*

Based on their research, Masters and Johnson concluded that a relatively small proportion of sexual dysfunctions have an organic basis. They maintain that most sexual problems are psychological in origin. In this section, we examine the symptoms and causes of three common sexual dysfunctions: erectile difficulties, premature ejaculation, and orgasmic difficulties (based on Levay, Weisberg, & Woods, 1981; Masters & Johnson, 1980).

Erectile difficulties **occur when a man is persistently unable to achieve or maintain an erection adequate for intercourse.** *Impotence* is the traditional name for this problem. However, sex therapists have discarded this term because of its demeaning connotation. A man who has never had an erection sufficient for intercourse is said to have *primary erectile difficulties.* A man who has had intercourse in the past but is currently having problems achieving erections is said to have *secondary erectile difficulties.* The latter problem is more common and easier to overcome.

The most common cause of erectile difficulties is anxiety about sexual performance, which can undermine sexual arousal. What leads to this troublesome anxiety? Its cause can range from a man's doubts about his virility to conflict about the morality of his sexual desires. Anxiety about sexual performance can also be caused by an overreaction to a specific incident in which a man cannot achieve sexual arousal. Many temporary conditions, such as fatigue, worry about work, an argument with his partner, a depressed mood, or too much alcohol can cause such incidents. If either partner turns the incident into a major catastrophe, the man may begin to get unduly concerned about his sexual response, and the seeds of anxiety may be sown.

Recent research suggests that physiological factors may contribute to erectile difficulties more often than Masters and Johnson's data suggested. A host of common diseases (such as diabetes) can produce erectile problems as a side effect (Melman & Leiter, 1983). Many of the medications used to treat physical illnesses can also cause erectile problems (Buffum et al., 1981). Thus, experts now estimate that organic factors may contribute to erectile dysfunction in as many as one quarter of the cases.

Premature ejaculation **occurs when sexual relations are impaired because a man consistently reaches orgasm too quickly.** What is "too quickly"? Any time requirement is hopelessly arbitrary. The critical consideration is the subjective feelings of the partners. If either partner feels that the ejaculation is persistently too fast for sexual gratification, there is a problem.

What causes premature ejaculation? Some men simply don't exert much effort to prolong intercourse. Most of these men do not view their ejaculations as premature, even if their partners do. Among men who *are* concerned about their

---

RECOMMENDED READING

Making Love: How to Be Your Own Sex Therapist
by Patricia Raley (Dial, 1976; Avon, 1980)

With the contemporary emphasis on achieving sexual satisfaction, more and more people are interested in reading books designed to help them cope with sexual problems or spice up their sex life. Many of the available books are of poor quality, but some are worthwhile. This is a very personal book that begins by having you take a look at your sexual history and attitudes. It is loaded with probing personal questions. The book devotes a good deal of attention to confronting sexual problems. It is nicely illustrated with many explicit and erotic photos. Furthermore, it does not assume that you are heterosexual.

Poets, doctors and lexicographers have all taken a turn at describing orgasm, but there is no universally accepted definition. That's probably because it depends on individual expectations and experience. . . . Take the description of an orgasm being like a sneeze, for instance. There is a tricky premonition that it is coming, a muscular spasm when it does come, and a sense of relief afterward. . . . Although you might use this description for someone who has never had an orgasm, you'd have to add that orgasms are not the same as sneezes. People just don't look forward to sneezing the way they do to having an orgasm. They don't count sneezes and they usually aren't very concerned about the sneezes of others. [1976, p. 125]

partners' satisfaction, problems may occur because their early sexual experiences emphasized the desirability of a rapid climax. Furtive sex in the back seat of a car, quick efforts at masturbation, and experiences with prostitutes are situations in which men typically attempt to achieve orgasm very quickly. A pattern of rapid ejaculation may be entrenched by these formative experiences.

Orgasmic difficulties **occur when people experience sexual arousal but have persistent problems in achieving orgasm.** When this problem occurs in men, it is often called *retarded ejaculation*. The traditional name for this problem in women, *frigidity*, is no longer used because of its derogatory implications. Since this problem is much more common among women, we'll limit our discussion to females. As with erectile difficulties, it is useful to distinguish between primary and secondary orgasmic difficulties. A woman who has never experienced an orgasm through any kind of stimulation is said to have *primary orgasmic difficulties*. Women who formerly experienced orgasms but are presently unable to do so are said to have *secondary orgasmic difficulties*. Women who seek treatment because they experience orgasm only through noncoital techniques (oral, manual, and self-stimulation) are put in the latter category. Although primary orgasmic difficulties would seem to be the more severe problem, they are actually more respon-

sive to treatment than secondary orgasmic difficulties.

Negative attitudes about sex are one of the leading causes of orgasmic difficulties among females. Women who have been taught that sex is dirty are likely to approach sex with ambivalent feelings that may be dominated by shame and guilt. These negative attitudes can inhibit sexual expression, undermine arousal, and impair orgasmic responsiveness.

A lack of authentic affection for one's partner seems to undermine sexual arousal in women more than in men. Thus, orgasmic difficulties in women sometimes occur when the emotional closeness in their relationship deteriorates. Females' arousal may also be inhibited by fear of pregnancy or excessive concern about achieving orgasm. Some women have orgasmic difficulties because intercourse tends to be too brief or because their male partners are unconcerned about their needs and preferences.

Another consideration is that intercourse provides less direct genital stimulation for women than it does for men. Thus, some women do not experience orgasms simply because they (and their partners) haven't explored sexual activities that they might find more rewarding than intercourse.

COPING WITH SPECIFIC PROBLEMS

With the advent of modern sex therapy, sexual problems no longer have to be chronic sources of shame and frustration. *Sex therapy* **involves the professional treatment of sexual dysfunctions.** With professional assistance, most sexual difficulties can be resolved (Arentewicz & Schmidt, 1983). Masters and Johnson have reported very high success rates for their treatments of specific problems, as shown in Figure 13.14. Some critics argue that the cure rates reported by Masters and Johnson are overly optimistic in comparison to those reported by other investigators (Zilbergeld & Evans, 1980). Nonetheless, there is a consensus that sexual dysfunctions can be conquered with encouraging regularity.

Of course, sex therapy isn't for everyone. It can be expensive and time-consuming. In some locations, it is

Figure 13.14. Success rates reported by Masters and Johnson in their treatment of sexual dysfunctions. This figure shows the success rates for cases treated between 1959 and 1985. Treatment was categorized as successful only if the change in sexual function was clear and enduring. The minimum follow-up period was two years, and in many cases it was five years. (Data from Masters, Johnson, & Kolodny, 1988)

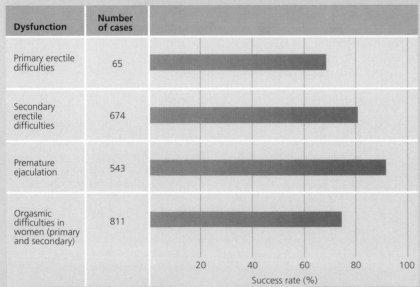

Dysfunction	Number of cases	Success rate (%)
Primary erectile difficulties	65	
Secondary erectile difficulties	674	
Premature ejaculation	543	
Orgasmic difficulties in women (primary and secondary)	811	

difficult to find. However, many people can benefit from ideas drawn from the professional practice of sex therapy (Hartman & Fithian, 1974; Kaplan, 1979, 1983; Masters & Johnson, 1980). In this section, we discuss experts' recommendations for dealing with erectile difficulties, premature ejaculation, and orgasmic difficulties.

Erectile Difficulties

The key to overcoming psychologically based erectile difficulties is to decrease the man's performance anxiety. It is a good idea for a couple to openly discuss the problem. The woman should be reassured that the difficulty is not due to the man's lack of affection. Obviously, it is crucial for her to be emotionally supportive rather than hostile and demanding.

Masters and Johnson use a procedure called *sensate focus* in the treatment of erectile difficulties and other dysfunctions. **Sensate focus is an exercise in which partners take turns pleasuring each other with guided verbal feedback while certain kinds of stimulation are temporarily forbidden.** One partner stimulates the other, who simply lies back and enjoys it while giving instructions and feedback about what feels good. Initially, the partners are not allowed to touch each other's genitals or to attempt intercourse. This prohibition should free the man from feelings of pressure to perform. Over a number of sessions, the couple gradually include genital stimulation in their sensate focus, but intercourse is still banned. With the pressure to perform removed, many men spontaneously get erections. Repeated arousals should begin to restore the man's confidence in his sexual response. As his confidence returns, the couple move on gradually to attempts at intercourse.

Premature Ejaculation

Men troubled by premature ejaculation range from those who climax almost instantly to those who cannot last the time that their partner requires. In the latter case, simply slowing down the tempo of intercourse may help. Sometimes the problem can be solved indirectly by discarding the traditional assumption that orgasms should come through intercourse. If the female partner enjoys oral or manual stimulation, these can be used to provide her with an orgasm either before or after intercourse. This strategy can reduce the performance pressure for the male partner, and couples may find that intercourse starts lasting longer.

The problem of instant ejaculation is more challenging to remedy. Sex therapists rely primarily on certain sensate focus exercises in which the man is repeatedly brought to the verge of orgasm. These sensate focus exercises can gradually help a man to recognize preorgasmic sensations and improve his control over his ejaculation response.

Orgasmic Difficulties

Since orgasmic difficulties among women are often due to negative attitudes about sex, a restructuring of values frequently is the key to conquering the problem. Thus, therapeutic discussions may be geared toward helping nonorgasmic women reduce their ambivalence about sexual expression. Sex therapists often suggest that women who have *never* had an orgasm try to have one through masturbation. Many women achieve orgasms in intercourse after an initial breakthrough with self-stimulation (LoPiccolo & Lobitz, 1972).

Treatments for orgasmic difficulties sometimes focus on couples' relationship problems more than on sexual functioning as such. In particular, efforts are often made to improve partners' communication skills. Thus, couples may discuss the complexities of initiating sexual overtures and the need to communicate openly about sexual turn-offs and turn-ons.

Some women are troubled by orgasmic difficulties only in the context of intercourse. If partners don't assume that orgasms must come through coitus, this need not be seen as a problem. However, many couples feel that it is important for the woman to experience orgasms during intercourse. Sensate focus exercises can be helpful in realizing this goal. The guided verbal feedback from the woman can greatly improve her partner's appreciation of her unique erotic preferences.

KEY LEARNING OBJECTIVES

1. List and describe four key aspects of sexual identity.

2. Discuss how hormones may influence sexuality.

3. Discuss how families, schools, peers, and the media shape sexual behavior.

4. Discuss how women and men may tend to differ in their sexual motives.

5. Describe five common sexual scripts in our culture and research on initiating and refusing sex.

6. Discuss how personality and attitudes influence sexuality.

7. Describe the four phases of the human sexual response cycle.

8. Discuss gender differences in patterns of orgasm.

9. Summarize evidence regarding the use of various techniques of sexual arousal.

10. Discuss whether there has been a sexual revolution.

11. Summarize evidence on patterns of premarital sex.

12. Summarize evidence on patterns of marital sex.

13. Summarize evidence on patterns of extramarital sex.

14. Describe common barriers to effective contraception and discuss the merits of condoms and the pill.

15. Describe various types of STDs and discuss their prevalence and prevention.

16. List six general suggestions for enhancing sexual relationships.

17. Discuss the nature, prevalence, and causes of sexual dysfunctions.

18. Discuss strategies for coping with various sexual problems.

KEY TERMS

Anal intercourse
Androgens
Bisexuals
Coitus
Cunnilingus
Erectile difficulties
Erogenous zones
Erotophiles
Erotophobes
Estrogens
Fellatio
Gonads
Heterosexuals
Homosexuals

Orgasm
Orgasmic difficulties
Premature ejaculation
Refractory period
Secondary sex characteristics
Sensate focus
Sex therapy
Sexual dysfunctions
Sexual identity
Sexually transmitted disease
    (STD)
Social scripts
Vasocongestion

KEY PEOPLE

Alfred Kinsey

William Masters &
Virginia Johnson

QUESTIONNAIRE

Sexuality Scale

INSTRUCTIONS

For the 30 items that follow, indicate the extent of your agreement or disagreement with each statement, using the key shown below. Record your responses in the spaces to the left of the items.

+2 = Agree

+1 = Slightly agree

 0 = Neither agree nor disagree

−1 = Slightly disagree

−2 = Disagree

THE SCALE

_____ 1. I am a good sexual partner.

_____ 2. I am depressed about the sexual aspects of my life.

_____ 3. I think about sex all the time.

_____ 4. I would rate my sexual skill quite highly.

_____ 5. I feel good about my sexuality.

_____ 6. I think about sex more than anything else.

_____ 7. I am better at sex than most other people.

_____ 8. I am disappointed about the quality of my sex life.

_____ 9. I don't daydream about sexual situations.

_____ 10. I sometimes have doubts about my sexual competence.

_____ 11. Thinking about sex makes me happy.

_____ 12. I tend to be preoccupied with sex.

_____ 13. I am not very confident in sexual encounters.

_____ 14. I derive pleasure and enjoyment from sex.

_____ 15. I'm constantly thinking about having sex.

_____ 16. I think of myself as a very good sexual partner.

_____ 17. I feel down about my sex life.

_____ 18. I think about sex a great deal of the time.

_____ 19. I would rate myself low as a sexual partner.

_____ 20. I feel unhappy about my sexual relationships.

_____ 21. I seldom think about sex.

_____ 22. I am confident about myself as a sexual partner.

_____ 23. I feel pleased with my sex life.

_____ 24. I hardly ever fantasize about having sex.

_____ 25. I am not very confident about myself as a sexual partner.

_____ 26. I feel sad when I think about my sexual experiences.

_____ 27. I probably think about sex less often than most people.

_____ 28. I sometimes doubt my sexual competence.

_____ 29. I am not discouraged about sex.

_____ 30. I don't think about sex very often.

SCORING THE SCALE

To arrive at your scores on the three subscales of this questionnaire, transfer your responses into the spaces provided below. If an item number has an R next to it, this item is reverse-scored, so you should change the + or – sign in front of the number you recorded. After recording your responses, add up the numbers in each column, taking into account the algebraic sign in front of each number. The totals for each column are your scores on the three subscales of the Sexuality Scale. Record your scores at the bottom of each column.

Sexual Esteem	Sexual Depression	Sexual Preoccupation
___ 1.	___ 2.	___ 3.
___ 4.	___ 5.R	___ 6.
___ 7.	___ 8.	___ 9.R
___ 10.R	___ 11.R	___ 12.
___ 13.R	___ 14.R	___ 15.
___ 16.	___ 17.	___ 18.
___ 19.R	___ 20.	___ 21.R
___ 22.	___ 23.R	___ 24.R
___ 25.R	___ 26.	___ 27.R
___ 28.R	___ 29.R	___ 30.R
___	___	___

WHAT THE SCALE MEASURES

Developed by William Snell and Dennis Papini (1989), the Sexuality Scale measures three aspects of your sexual identity. The Sexual Esteem subscale measures your tendency to evaluate yourself in a positive way in terms of your capacity to relate sexually to others. The Sexual Depression subscale measures your tendency to feel saddened and discouraged by your ability to relate sexually to others. The Sexual Preoccupation subscale measures your tendency to become absorbed in thoughts about sex on a persistent basis.

This is a relatively new scale that has not yet been the subject of extensive research. Internal reliability is excellent. Thus far, the scale's validity has been examined through factor analysis, which can be used to evaluate the extent of overlap among the subscales. The factor analysis showed that the three subscales do measure independent aspects of one's sexuality.

INTERPRETING YOUR SCORES

Our norms are based on Snell and Papini's (1989) sample of 296 college students drawn from a small university in the Midwest. Significant gender differences were found only on the Sexual Preoccupation subscale, so we report separate norms for males and females only for this subscale.

NORMS

Sexual Esteem	Sexual Depression	Sexual Preoccupation	
Both sexes	Both sexes	Males	Females
High score			
+14 to +20	+1 to +20	+8 to +20	−1 to +20
Intermediate score			
0 to +13	−12 to 0	−2 to +7	−10 to −2
Low score			
−20 to −1	−20 to −13	−20 to −3	−20 to −11

How Did You Acquire Your Attitudes about Sex?

1. Who do you feel was most important in shaping your attitudes regarding sexual behavior (parents, teachers, peers, early girlfriend or boyfriend, and so forth)?

2. What was the nature of their influence?

3. If the answer to the first question was *not* your parents, what kind of information did you get at home? Were your parents comfortable talking about sex?

4. In childhood, were you ever made to feel shameful, guilty, or fearful about sex? How?

5. Were your parents open or secretive about their own sex lives?

6. Do you feel comfortable with your sexuality today?

PART IV
MENTAL AND PHYSICAL HEALTH

14
Psychology and Physical Health

The patterns of illness found in a society tend to fluctuate over time, and there have been some interesting trends in our society during the last century or so. Before the 20th century, the principal threats to health were *contagious diseases* caused by an invasion of the body by a specific infectious agent. Because such diseases can be transmitted readily from one person to another, people used to live in fear of epidemics. The leading causes of death were diseases such as the plague, smallpox, typhoid fever, influenza, diphtheria, yellow fever, malaria, cholera, tuberculosis, polio, and scarlet fever. Today, the incidence of these diseases has declined to the point where none of them is among the leading killers in the United States (see Figure 14.1).

What neutralized these dreaded diseases? The general public tends to attribute the conquest of contagious diseases to advances in medical treatment. Although progress in medicine certainly played a role, Grob (1983) marshals evidence that the significance of such progress has been overrated. Of greater significance, according to Grob, were trends such as (1) improvements in nutrition, (2) improvements in public hygiene and sanitation (water filtration, treatment of sewage, and so forth), and (3) evolutionary changes in our immunal resistance to the diseases. Whatever the causes, infectious diseases are no longer the major threat to physical health in the industrialized nations of the world (many remain quite prevalent in Third World countries).

Unfortunately, the void left by contagious diseases has been filled all too quickly by various *chronic diseases*—illnesses that develop gradually over years (refer to Figure 14.1). Psychosocial factors, such as lifestyle and stress, play a much larger role in the development of chronic diseases than they do in contagious diseases. Today, the three leading chronic diseases (heart disease, cancer, and stroke) account for nearly two thirds of the deaths in the United States! Moreover, these mortality statistics reveal only the tip of the iceberg. Many other less serious illnesses (such as headaches, backaches, skin disorders, asthma, and ulcers) are also influenced by psychosocial factors.

In light of these dramatic trends, it is not surprising that the way we think about illness is changing. Traditionally, illness has been thought of as a purely biological phenomenon produced by an infectious agent or some internal physical breakdown. However, the shifting patterns of disease and new findings relating stress to physical illness have rocked the foundation of this biological model. In its place a new model is gradually emerging. **The *biopsychosocial model* holds that physical illness is caused by a complex interaction of biological, psychological, and sociocultural factors.** This new model does not suggest that biological factors are unimportant. Rather, it simply asserts that biological factors operate in a psychosocial context that can also be very influential.

The growing recognition that psychological factors influence our physical health has led to the emergence of

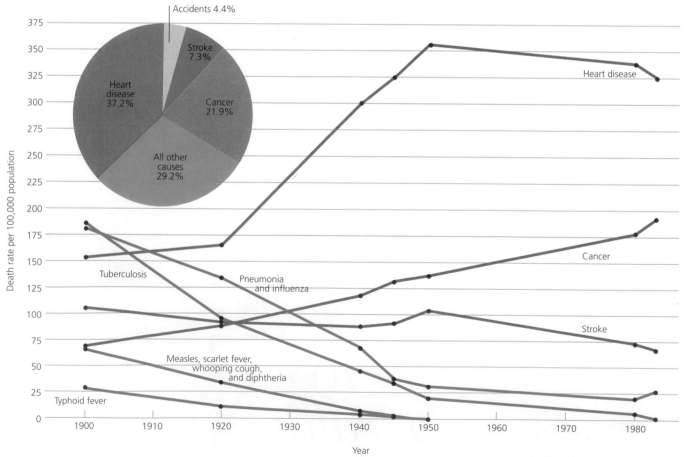

a new specialty within psychology. *Health psychology* **is concerned with how psychosocial factors relate to the promotion and maintenance of health, and with the causation, prevention, and treatment of illness.** This specialty is very youthful. The Health Psychology division of the American Psychological Association was founded only in 1978. Our focus in this chapter will be on this exciting new domain of health psychology.

There are three general ways in which psychological factors can influence our physical health (Krantz, Glass, Contrada, & Miller, 1981). These three methods of action are as follows.

1. *Direct effects of stress.* The most basic way in which psychological functioning can affect physical health is through the direct effects of stress on physiological processes. As we discussed in Chapter 3, stress tends to elicit wide-ranging physiological arousal, which can lead to bodily changes that may be damaging in the long run.
2. *Health-impairing habits.* There are many habitual patterns of behavior that can increase our vulnerability to various kinds of illnesses. For instance, there is ample evidence that the likelihood of developing heart disease is influenced by cigarette smoking, physical inactivity, poor diet, and other aspects of lifestyle.
3. *Reactions to illness.* Our behavioral response to symptoms of illness can have a decided impact on our health. Many people delay seeking needed medical consultation, thus increasing their risk of serious illness. Furthermore, a surprisingly great number of people ignore their doctors' advice or are unable to comply successfully with their doctors' instructions.

The three ways in which behavior can influence physical health will serve as our organizing scheme in this chapter. The chapter's first section analyzes the link between stress and illness. The second section examines common health-impairing habits, such as smoking and overeating. The third section discusses how our reactions to illness can affect our health. In the Application we will expand on a particular type of health-impairing habit—the use of "recreational drugs."

STRESS AND ILLNESS

As we noted in Chapter 3, during the 1970s researchers began to uncover new links between stress and a variety of diseases previously believed to be purely physiological in origin. In this section, we'll look at the evidence on the apparent link between stress and physical illness. We'll begin with heart disease, which is far and away the leading cause of death in North America.

Type A Behavior and Heart Disease

Heart disease accounts for nearly 40% of the deaths in the United States every year. *Coronary heart disease* **involves a reduction in blood flow from the coronary arteries, which supply the heart with blood.** This type of heart disease accounts for about 90% of heart-related deaths.

Atherosclerosis is the principal cause of coronary disease. *Atherosclerosis* **involves a gradual narrowing of the coronary arteries.** A buildup of fatty deposits and other debris on the inner walls of the arteries is the usual cause of this narrowing (see Figure 14.2). Atherosclerosis progresses slowly over periods of years. Narrowed coronary arteries may eventually lead to situations in which the heart is temporarily deprived of adequate blood flow, causing brief chest pain, a condition known as *angina pectoris.* If a coronary artery is blocked completely (by a blood clot, for instance), the abrupt interruption of blood flow can produce a full-fledged heart attack, known as a *myocardial infarction.*

In the 1960s and 1970s a pair of cardiologists, Meyer Friedman and Ray Rosenman (1974), were investigating the causes of coronary disease. Originally, Friedman and Rosenman were interested in the usual factors that were thought to produce a high risk of heart attack: smoking, obesity, physical inactivity, and so forth. Although they

Figure 14.1. Changing patterns of illness. Trends in the death rates for various diseases during the 20th century reveal that contagious diseases (shown in green) have declined as a threat to our health. However, the death rates for stress-related chronic diseases (shown in red) have either remained stable (as in the case of stroke) or increased dramatically (as in the case of cancer and heart disease). The pie chart (inset), which depicts the percentage of deaths caused by the leading killers today, shows the results of these trends: Three chronic diseases (heart disease, cancer, and stroke) account for 66% of all deaths.

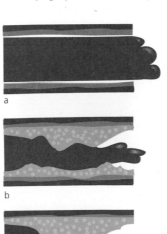

Figure 14.2. Atherosclerosis. (a) Blood flows through a normal artery. (b) Fatty deposits on the walls of the artery have narrowed the path for blood flow. (c) Advanced atherosclerosis. In this situation, a blood clot might suddenly block the flow of blood through the artery.

found that these factors were important, they eventually recognized that a piece of the puzzle was missing. Many people would smoke constantly, get little exercise, and be severely overweight, yet avoid the ravages of heart disease. At the same time, other people who seemed to be in much better shape in regard to these risk factors experienced the misfortune of a heart attack.

Gradually, Friedman and Rosenman unraveled the riddle. What was their explanation for these perplexing findings? Stress! Specifically, they found a connection between coronary risk and a pattern of behavior they called the *Type A personality*, which involves self-imposed stress and intense reactions to stress.

Elements of Type A Behavior

Friedman and Rosenman (1974) divided people into two basic types: Type A and Type B. **The *Type A personality* is marked by competitive, aggressive, impatient, hostile behavior.** Type A's are ambitious, hard-driving perfectionists who are exceedingly time-conscious. They routinely try to do several things at once. Thus, a Type A person may watch TV, talk on the phone, work on a report, and eat dinner all at the same time. Type A's are so impatient that they frequently finish others' sentences for them! They fidget frantically over the briefest delays. Often they are workaholics who drive themselves with many deadlines. They speak rapidly and emphatically. They are aggravated easily and get angry quickly.

In contrast, **the *Type B personality* is marked by relatively relaxed, patient, easygoing, amicable behavior.** Type B's are less hurried, less competitive, and less easily angered than Type A's.

The strength of one's Type A tendencies can be measured with either structured interviews or questionnaires. There is quite a bit of debate about the best method for assessing Type A behavior (Matthews, 1982). The checklist in Figure 14.3 lists some questions that are representative of those used in measurements of Type A behavior. The Type A personality is seen less frequently in women than men. When found among women, however, it appears to increase coronary risk about as much as in men (Haynes, Feinleib, & Eaker, 1983).

Evaluating the Risk

How strong is the link between Type A personality and coronary risk? Based on preliminary data, Friedman and his associates originally estimated that Type A's were *six* times as prone to heart attack as Type B's. At the other extreme, some studies have failed to find a clear association between Type A behavior and coronary risk (Ragland & Brand, 1988; Shekelle et al., 1985).

What can we make of these inconsistent findings? Some of the inconsistency may be due to problems in accurately classifying people as Type A or Type B (Dimsdale, 1988). However, the mixed findings also suggest that the relationship between Type A behavior and coronary risk is more modest than originally believed. The modest nature of this relationship probably means that Type A behavior increases coronary risk for only a portion of the population. Perhaps it makes a difference only among those who exhibit certain other risk factors (a genetic predisposition to heart disease, for example).

Which aspects of Type A behavior are most strongly related to increased coronary risk? Are need for control, job involvement, competitiveness, time urgency, and hostility equally important? These are questions of current interest in research on the Type A syndrome. Thus far, the research suggests that *quick-tempered anger* and *hard-driving competitiveness* may be more important for

Figure 14.3. The Type A personality. The ten questions shown here highlight some of the behavioral traits associated with the Type A personality.

Measuring the Type A Personality

You can use the checklist below to *estimate* the likelihood that you might be a Type A personality. However, the checklist should be regarded as providing only a rough estimate, because Friedman and Rosenman (1974) emphasize that *how* you answer certain questions in their interview is often more significant than the answers themselves. Nonetheless, if you answer "yes" to a majority of the items below, you may want to consider reading their book *Type A Behavior and Your Heart*.

_____ **1.** Do you find it difficult to restrain yourself from hurrying others' speech (finishing their sentences for them)?

_____ **2.** Do you often try to do more than one thing at a time (such as eat and read simultaneously)?

_____ **3.** Do you often feel guilty if you use extra time to relax?

_____ **4.** Do you tend to get involved in a great number of projects at once?

_____ **5.** Do you find yourself racing through yellow lights when you drive?

_____ **6.** Do you need to win in order to derive enjoyment from games and sports?

_____ **7.** Do you generally move, walk, and eat rapidly?

_____ **8.** Do you agree to take on too many responsibilities?

_____ **9.** Do you detest waiting in lines?

_____ **10.** Do you have an intense desire to better your position in life and impress others?

coronary risk than other elements of the Type A pattern (Booth-Kewley & Friedman, 1987).

There is evidence that the risk of a second heart attack in coronary patients can be reduced by therapeutic programs that decrease subjects' Type A behavior (Powell et al., 1984). Such programs train Type A persons to talk and move more slowly, to do only one thing at a time, to take life less seriously, to allow themselves to lose in competitive endeavors, to wait in lines patiently, and so forth.

Unfortunately, however, Type A patterns of behavior turn out to be quite resistant to modification (Rosenman & Chesney, 1982). Our competitive Western culture tends to value and reward Type A behavior. Type A habits that are developed over a lifetime are deeply entrenched and

---

RECOMMENDED READING

Is It Worth Dying For?

by Robert S. Eliot & Dennis L. Breo (Bantam Books, 1984, 1989)

Robert S. Eliot is a cardiologist whose recent work on "hot reactors" has been attracting attention. Eliot believes that some people are particularly vulnerable to heart attacks because they have an overly reactive cardiovascular response to stress. These hot reactors may or may not exhibit Type A behavior. Hot reacting involves a *physiological* tendency that is probably affected by one's genetic inheritance. Type A behavior involves *behavioral* tendencies that are presumably acquired through learning over a lifetime. A person might be a hot reactor only, a Type A personality only, or both (or neither). Those who are both a hot reactor and a Type A personality probably have a very elevated risk of coronary problems.

Eliot and Breo explain all this and much more in their highly readable book, which focuses on the connections between stress and coronary risk. In addition to explaining how stress, hot reacting, and Type A behavior influence the risk of heart attack, they discuss the significance of health-impairing habits such as physical inactivity, poor eating, and smoking. They construct a nice overview of how a diverse array of factors govern cardiac vulnerability and then offer a great deal of useful advice on how to minimize your susceptibilty to a heart attack.

> Jeff was a living demonstration of the difference between Type A behavior and hot reacting. He was psychologically intense most of the time, but he was not physiologically intense. His blood pressure rose a little under mental stress, as everyone's does, but it did not rise very much.
>
> Jeff was like a person driving without a muffler—the car may make plenty of noise, but that has nothing to do with how the engine is working. It could be in great shape or it could be burning up; you can't tell from the revved-up sound. At the same time, driving without a muffler isn't a good idea—the noise is a strain on everybody else, if not on the engine. Extreme Type A behavior is worth modifying for that reason alone. Jeff's psychological overreactions kept him in enough hot water to harm the overall quality of his life. [1984, p. 53]

---

are given up only very reluctantly, in spite of their dire consequences. Thus, getting Type A's to alter their behavior is a formidable challenge.

Cancer

If there is a single word that can strike terror into most of our hearts, it is probably cancer. We generally view cancer as the most sinister, tragic, loathsome, and unbearable of diseases. In reality, cancer is actually a *collection* of closely related diseases that vary in their characteristics and amenability to treatment.

***Cancer* refers to malignant cell growth, which may occur in many organ systems in the body.** The core problem in cancer is that cells begin to reproduce in a rapid, disorganized fashion. As this reproduction process lurches out of control, the teeming new cells clump together to form tumors. If this wild growth continues unabated, the spreading tumors create tissue damage and begin to interfere with normal functioning in the affected organ systems.

The causes of cancer are not well understood. Most experts believe that a modest genetic predisposition is involved. Deficiencies in immunal functioning are also thought to contribute. However, the evidence supporting these hypotheses is far from clear (Barofsky, 1981).

The research linking stress to cancer is thought-provoking but hardly definitive. Some studies *have* found a connection between high stress, as measured by the Social Readjustment Rating Scale (SRRS) and the onset of cancer (for example, Jacobs & Charles, 1980). Generally, however, the results in these kinds of investigations have been very inconsistent (Cooper, 1984). There is ample evidence that experimentally induced stress can affect the development of cancer in laboratory animals. But the relevance of such research to humans is difficult to judge (Sklar & Anisman, 1981).

Many studies have attempted to ascertain whether there is a *cancer-prone personality,* which might reflect unsuccessful patterns of coping with stress. These studies

©1987 MICHAEL TWOHY.

"While you've been learning to relax, Tom, I'm afraid a less enlightened 'Type A' personality got your job."

have yielded some intriguing threads of consistency, suggesting that lonely, depressed people who have difficulty expressing anger and hostility may have an elevated risk for cancer (Cox & Mackay, 1982; Dattore, Shontz, & Coyne, 1980; Greer, 1979; LeShan, 1966). However, these studies must be viewed with caution given the possibility that one's personality may change after the discovery that one has cancer. Furthermore, the personality traits tentatively linked to cancer vulnerability may not be specific to cancer. The same traits have been linked to an elevated risk for a variety of diseases, including coronary disease, asthma, and arthritis (Friedman & Booth-Kewley, 1987). Thus, there may be a *generic* disease-prone personality that predisposes people to a diverse array of health problems.

In conclusion, there is evidence linking stress, coping, and personality to cancer, but it is weak and ambiguous. This weakness may simply reflect our general inability to pin down the causes of this very complicated and mysterious ailment. Or it may mean that the contribution of psychological factors to the development of cancer is only a very small, marginal one. Future research should shed more light on this important question.

Other Diseases

The development of questionnaires to measure life stress has allowed researchers to look for correlations between stress and a variety of diseases. These researchers have uncovered many connections between stress and illness. For example, in a sample of female patients, Baker (1982) found an association between life stress and the onset of rheumatoid arthritis. Working with a sample of female students, Williams and Deffenbacher (1983) found that life stress was correlated with the number of vaginal (yeast) infections the women reported in the past year. In another study, investigators inoculated volunteers with cold viruses and found that those under high stress experienced more colds (Totman, Kiff, Reed, & Craig, 1980). Researchers have also found an association be-

tween high stress and hypertension (high blood pressure) in cultures as disparate as India (Lal, Ahuja, & Madhukar, 1982) and the United States (Egan, Kogan, Garber, & Jarrett, 1983).

These are just a handful of representative examples of studies relating stress to physical diseases. Figure 14.4 provides a longer list of health problems that have been linked to stress. Many of these stress/illness connections are based on very tentative or inconsistent findings, but the sheer length and diversity of the list is remarkable.

The studies described thus far have looked at relations between stress and *specific* diseases. Many studies have also looked at the relationship between stress and the occurrence of illness of any kind. Typically, these studies have found significant correlations between high stress and a high incidence of physical illness in general (Holmes & Masuda, 1974). Why should stress increase our risk for many kinds of illness? A partial answer may lie in our immunal functioning.

Figure 14.4. Stress and health problems. The onset or progress of the health problems listed here *may* be affected by stress. The evidence is fragmentary in many instances, but the number and diversity of problems on this list are alarming.

Health Problems That May Be Linked to Stress	
Health problem	**Representative evidence**
Common cold	Totman, Kiff, Reed, & Craig (1980)
Peptic ulcers	Cobb & Rose (1973)
Asthma	Plutchik, Williams, Jerrett, Karasu, & Kane (1978)
Headaches	Featherstone & Beitman (1984)
Menstrual discomfort	Siegel, Johnson, & Sarason (1979)
Vaginal infections	Williams & Deffenbacher (1983)
Genital herpes	VanderPlate, Aral, & Magder (1988)
Skin disorders	Brown (1972)
Rheumatoid arthritis	Baker (1982)
Chronic back pain	Holmes (1979)
Female reproductive problems	Fries, Nillius, & Petersson (1974)
Diabetes	Bradley (1979)
Complications of pregnancy	Georgas, Giakoumaki, Georgoulias, Koumandakis, & Kaskarelis (1984)
Hernias	Rahe & Holmes (1965)
Glaucoma	Cohen & Hajioff (1972)
Hyperthyroidism	Weiner (1979)
Hemophilia	Buxton, Arkel, Lagos, Deposito, Lowenthal, & Simring (1981)
Tuberculosis	Wolf & Goodell (1968)
Leukemia	Greene & Swisher (1969)
Stroke	Stevens, Turner, Rhodewalt, & Talbot (1984)
Appendicitis	Creed (1989)
Multiple sclerosis	Grant, McDonald, Patterson, & Trimble (1989)
Periodontal disease	Green, Tryon, Marks, & Huryn (1986)
Hypertension	Egan, Kogan, Garber, & Jarrett (1983)

Effects on Immunal Functioning

The apparent link between stress and illness raises the possibility that stress may undermine our immunal functioning. **The *immune response* involves the body's defensive reaction to invasion by bacteria, viral agents, or other foreign substances.** Our immune response works to protect us from many forms of disease. Immunal reactions are multifaceted, but they depend heavily on actions initiated by specialized white blood cells, called *lymphocytes*.

A wealth of studies indicate that experimentally induced stress can impair immunal functioning *in animals* (Ader & Cohen, 1984). Stressors such as crowding, shock, and restraint reduce various aspects of lymphocyte reactivity in laboratory animals.

Some studies have also related stress to suppressed immunal activity *in humans*. In one study, medical students provided researchers with blood samples so that their immunal response could be assessed (Kiecolt-Glaser et al., 1984). The students provided the baseline sample a month before final exams and contributed the "high-stress" sample on the first day of their finals. The subjects also responded to the SRRS as a measure of recent stress. Reduced levels of immune activity were found during the extremely stressful finals week. Reduced immunal activity was also correlated with higher scores on the SRRS. Thus, we are beginning to assemble some impressive evidence that stress can temporarily impair our immunal functioning. Suppression of our immune response may be the key to many of the links between stress and illness.

Accidents and Injuries

The role of stress in contributing to accidents has not attracted much publicity. However, research on this issue is remarkably consistent. Nearly all the studies find that high stress is associated with an increased incidence of personal accidents. Among other things, stress has been shown to be related to the likelihood of industrial accidents (Levenson, Hirschfeld, Hirschfeld, & Dzubay, 1983),

automobile accidents (Isherwood, Adam, & Hornblow, 1982) and football injuries (Passer & Seese, 1983).

The associations between stress and accidents have been modest in strength. However, the consistency of the evidence suggests that stress elevates the probability of an accident for at least a portion of the population. Our analysis of the effects of stress in Chapter 3 suggests some possible explanations for this relationship. The emotional arousal generated by stress may lead people to drive their cars aggressively (and dangerously), work too fast on the job, become reckless on the football field, and so forth. Emotional arousal can also impair cognitive functioning, leading to narrowed attention, distractibility, or poor judgment. Any of these effects could increase accident-proneness in a variety of settings. Also, when stress elicits either anger or dejection, people may simply become more careless.

Conclusions

In summary, a wealth of evidence shows that stress is related to our physical health. However, we have to put this intriguing finding in perspective. Virtually all of the relevant research is correlational in nature, so it cannot demonstrate conclusively that stress *causes* illness. The association between stress and illness could be due to a third variable. Perhaps some aspect of personality or some type of physiological predisposition makes people overly prone to experience stress *and* overly prone to experience illness (see Figure 14.5).

Moreover, critics of this research note that many of the studies employed research designs that may have inflated the apparent link between stress and illness (Schroeder & Costa, 1984). For example, researchers often have subjects make after-the-fact reports of how much stress and illness they endured during the last year or two. If some subjects have a tendency to recall more stress than others *and* to recall more illness than others, their better memories would artificially increase the correlation between stress and illness.

Figure 14.5. The stress/illness correlation. One or more aspects of personality, physiology, or memory might contribute to the correlation between high stress and high incidence of illness.

In spite of methodological problems favoring inflated correlations, the research in this area consistently indicates that the *strength* of the relationship between stress and health is modest. The correlations typically fall in the .20s and .30s. Clearly, stress is not an irresistible force that produces inevitable effects on our health. Actually, this should come as no surprise. As we saw in Chapter 3, some people handle stress better than others. Furthermore, stress is only one actor on a crowded stage. A complex network of biopsychosocial factors influence our health, including genetic endowment, exposure to infectious agents and environmental toxins, nutrition, exercise, alcohol and drug use, smoking, use of medical care, cooperation with medical advice, and current health status. In the next section we'll discuss some of these factors as we examine health-impairing habits and lifestyles.

HABITS, LIFESTYLES, AND HEALTH

Some people seem determined to dig an early grave for themselves. They do precisely those things they have been warned are particularly bad for their health. For example, some people drink heavily even though they know they're corroding their liver. Others eat all the wrong foods even though they know they're increasing their risk for a heart attack. Such downright self-destructive behavior is much more common than most people realize. In fact, research reveals that *chronic self-destructiveness* is a measurable personality trait that is related to a variety of potentially harmful behaviors, from driving recklessly (as reflected by traffic tickets) to postponing important medical tests (Kelley et al., 1984).

It may seem puzzling that people behave in self-destructive ways. Why do they do it? Several considerations are involved. First, many health-impairing habits creep up on people slowly. For instance, drug use may grow imperceptibly over years, or exercise habits may decline ever so gradually. Second, many health-impairing habits involve activities that are quite pleasant at the time. Actions such as eating favorite foods, smoking cigarettes, and getting "high" are potent reinforcing events. Third, the risks associated with most health-impairing habits are chronic diseases like cancer that usually lie 10, 20, or 30 years down the road. It is relatively easy to ignore risks that lie in the distant future. Fourth, it appears that *people have a tendency to underestimate the risks associated with their own health-impairing habits*, while viewing the risks associated with others' self-destructive behaviors much more accurately (Weinstein, 1984). In other words, most people are aware of the dangers associated with certain habits. However, they often engage in *denial* when it is time to apply this information to themselves.

In this section we'll discuss how health is affected by smoking, overeating and obesity, poor nutrition, lack of exercise, and poor sleep habits. We'll also look at lifestyle factors that relate to AIDS. The health risks of alcohol and drug use are covered in the Application.

Smoking

The smoking of tobacco is widespread in our culture, with current consumption running around 3300 cigarettes a year per adult in the United States. The percentage of

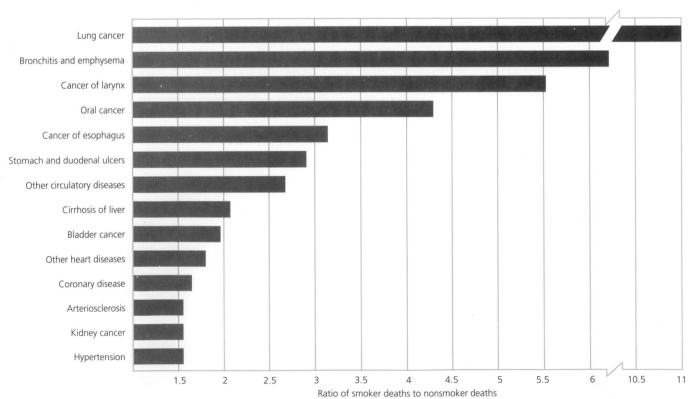

Ratio of smoker deaths to nonsmoker deaths

people who smoke has declined noticeably since the mid-1960s. Nonetheless, about 30% of adults in the United States continue to smoke regularly.

Health Effects

Suspicions about the health risks associated with tobacco use were voiced in some quarters throughout the 20th century. However, the risks of smoking were not widely appreciated until the mid-1960s. Since then, accumulating evidence has clearly shown that smokers face a much greater risk of premature death than nonsmokers (Hammond & Horn, 1984). For example, a 30-year-old male who smokes two packs a day has an estimated life expectancy that is *eight years shorter* than that of a similar nonsmoker. The overall risk is positively related to the number of cigarettes smoked and their tar and nicotine content. Cigar and pipe smoking are also associated with elevated health risks, although they are less hazardous than cigarette smoking.

Why are mortality rates higher for smokers? Smoking increases the likelihood of developing a surprisingly large range of diseases, many of which are highly lethal (see Figure 14.6). Lung cancer and heart disease are the two types of illness that kill the largest number of smokers (Fielding, 1985). However, smokers also have an elevated risk of other cancers, ulcers, bronchitis, emphysema, stroke, and cirrhosis of the liver.

The increased prevalence of diseases among smokers may not be due to their smoking alone. Some studies suggest that smokers are more likely than nonsmokers to exhibit a *variety* of health-impairing habits (Castro, Newcomb, McCreary, & Baezconde-Garbanati, 1989). For example, they may tend to consume more alcohol, more coffee, and more unhealthy foods than nonsmokers, while exercising less as well.

Why Do People Smoke?

A variety of factors influence whether people acquire the habit of smoking. *Social learning models* emphasize the importance of advertising and role models. Tobacco companies spend about $1.5 billion annually on sophisticated advertisements designed to convince us that smoking is glamorous and gratifying. Parents, friends, and co-workers provide an abundance of role models who smoke.

Psychological models emphasize that smoking can function as a coping device. In some people, smoking can reduce feelings of tension, anger, and anxiety. Furthermore, many people find the pharmacological effects of nicotine to be quite pleasant. Thus, the act of smoking is reinforced on a very regular basis.

Addiction models assert that tobacco use can lead to physical dependence in some individuals. The addiction model is supported by the finding that the relapse patterns for programs designed to help people quit smoking are very similar to the relapse patterns seen in the treatment of alcohol and heroin addiction (Hunt & Matarazzo, 1982). These striking parallels are apparent in Figure 14.7.

Giving Up Smoking

Studies show that if people can give up smoking, their health risks decline reasonably quickly. Five years after people stop smoking, their health risk is already noticeably lower than that of people who continue to smoke. The health risks of people who give up tobacco continue to decline until they reach a normal level after about 15 years (Rogot, 1974).

Unfortunately, for most smokers giving up smoking is very difficult. The long-term success rates for efforts to quit smoking are in the vicinity of only 25%. Discouragingly, people who enroll in formal smoking-cessation programs aren't any more successful than people who try to quit on their own (Cohen et al., 1989). However, light smokers (fewer than 20 cigarettes per day) are somewhat more successful at quitting than heavy smokers.

There isn't any single approach to quitting smoking that is most effective for everyone. However, if you attempt to give up smoking on your own (without professional consultation), you may want to consider the following advice.

Figure 14.6. Smoking and health. Smoking is associated with an increased risk for a diverse array of diseases. The magnitude of the elevated risk varies with the condition, ranging as high as 11 times normal in the case of lung cancer.

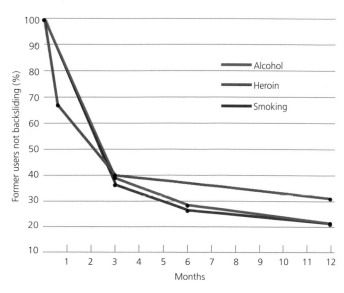

Figure 14.7 Relapse in efforts to quit smoking. It is quite difficult to give up smoking. As the graph shows, the relapse rates for returning to smoking within a year are similar to those for returning to alcohol and heroin use. (From Hunt & Matarazzo, 1982)

1. *Educate yourself thoroughly about the dangers of smoking.* Giving up smoking requires strong motivation. You can increase your motivation by becoming very familiar with the health problems caused by smoking. Programs that concentrate on education alone can be effective for some people (Windsor et al., 1985).

2. *Use self-modification techniques.* The self-modification techniques described in Chapter 4 can be invaluable in efforts to quit smoking. A good program should include careful monitoring of smoking habits, ample rewards for going without cigarettes, and control of antecedents to avoid situations that trigger smoking.

3. *Use nicotine substitutes.* Insofar as nicotine is addictive, it can be helpful to employ a substitute during your transitional period. Nicotine gum, which ironically requires a physician's prescription, has proved helpful in efforts to give up smoking (Oster, Huse, Delea, & Colditz, 1986).

Overeating

Obesity, **the condition of being overweight,** is a very common health problem, affecting as many as 70 million people in the United States. Obesity is similar to smoking in that it exerts a relatively subtle impact on health that is easy for many people to ignore. Though subtle, the long-range effects of obesity can be quite dangerous. According to Jeffrey and Lemnitzer (1981), overweight people have an increased risk of heart disease, hypertension, stroke, respiratory problems, arthritis, diabetes, gall bladder disease, and back problems (see Figure 14.8).

Determinants of Obesity

The traditional explanation of obesity is quite simple: Overweight people eat too much and exercise too little. This explanation is valid as far as it goes, but a variety of additional factors contribute to obesity.

Chief among these factors is *genetic predisposition.* In a recent study, adults raised by foster parents were compared with their biological and foster parents in regard to weight (Stunkard et al., 1986). The investigators found that the adoptees resembled their biological parents more than their adoptive parents. Thus, some people may inherit a genetic vulnerability to obesity. This genetic factor probably explains why some people can eat constantly without gaining weight, while other less fortunate people grow chubby eating far less.

What exactly is inherited by people who are prone to obesity? It may be a sluggish metabolism. Your **basal metabolic rate is your body's rate of energy output at rest, after a 12-hour fast.** People vary in their basal metabolic rate. This means that some of us burn off calories faster than others. Calories that are burned off won't be stored as fat.

There also is reason to believe that heredity affects the number of fat cells that we develop. Studies show that obese people have more fat cells than other people do (Knittle & Hirsch, 1968). Hence, some people may be predisposed to weight problems because they are genetically programmed to develop an excessive number of fat cells (Grinker, 1982). This intriguing notion brings us to *set-point theory,* which concerns how our bodies might regulate fat deposits.

People who lose weight on a diet have a rather strong (and depressing) tendency to gain back the weight they lose. The reverse is also true. People who have to work to put weight on often have trouble keeping it on. According to Richard Nisbett (1972), these observations suggest that your body may have a **set point, which represents its natural point of stability in body weight.** According to set-point theory, our bodies monitor fat-cell levels to keep them fairly stable (Keesey & Powley, 1975, 1986). Supposedly, when fat stores slip below a crucial set point, some mechanism increases our tendency to experience hunger. The location and nature of the cells that monitor fat stores are unknown.

The relevance of set-point theory to obesity should be readily apparent. Individuals with a high set point may find it terribly difficult to avoid weight problems. This does *not* mean that all obese people are doomed to remain obese forever. However, it may explain why most over-

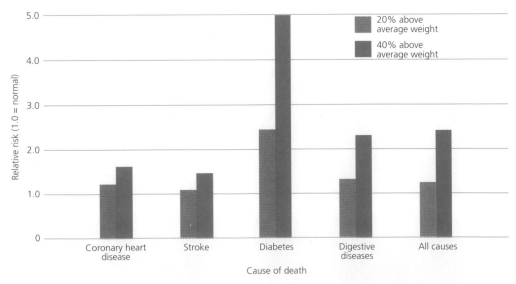

Figure 14.8. Obesity and mortality. This graph shows the increased mortality risks for men who are either 20% or 40% above average weight for their age and height. Clearly, obesity is a significant health risk. (Data from VanItallie, 1979)

weight people have to fight a lengthy, uphill battle to keep weight off.

While a variety of physiological factors may influence vulnerability to obesity, chronic overeating undeniably plays a very prominent role. Why is overeating such a routine habit for so many people? Stanley Schachter (1971) advanced the hypothesis that obese people are *overly sensitive to external cues* that affect their hunger and *relatively insensitive to internal physiological cues* that signal the true need for food. According to this notion, overweight people pay little attention to messages from their bodies but respond readily to external cues such as the availability of food, the attractiveness of the food, and the time of day. This formulation suggested that people overeat because they cannot ignore environmental cues that trigger hunger. For example, people who are not really hungry may be stimulated to pursue food simply by seeing a delectable commercial on TV.

Schachter's theory proved to be an incomplete explanation of obesity because it ignored the importance of the various physiological factors that we have discussed (Rodin, 1981). Nonetheless, Schachter deserves credit for showing how sensitivity to food cues can contribute to chronic overeating.

Losing Weight

Whether out of concern about their health or just old-fashioned vanity, an ever-increasing number of people are trying to lose weight. Unfortunately, our obsession with weight loss can sometimes become dangerous. According to medical and nutritional experts, many of the popular fad diets promising large, rapid weight reductions can be perilous to one's health. For instance, an article in the *Journal of the American Medical Association* (Wadden, Stunkard, Brownell, & VanItallie, 1983) revealed that by the end of 1982 the U.S. Food and Drug Administration had received 138 complaints of illness (including six deaths) from people using the Cambridge diet. Wadden et al. also mention that liquid-protein diets were thought to be associated with some 58 deaths before

they faded from view. Thus, it is important to understand that faddish, extreme nutritional programs are money-making ventures for their developers. They usually have little genuine merit and may even be dangerous. What, by the way, do Wadden et al. (1983) recommend to achieve safe, durable weight loss? They advocate "behavior modification, nutrition counseling and exercise" (p. 2834).

While there may be a number of causes of obesity, there is only one way to lose weight. You must change your ratio of energy intake (from food consumption) to energy output (from physical activities). To be quite specific, to lose one pound you need to burn up 3500 more calories than you consume. You have three options in trying to change your ratio of energy input to energy output. (1) You can sharply reduce your food consumption. (2) You can sharply increase your exercise output. (3) You can simultaneously decrease your food intake and step up your exercise output in more moderate ways. Most experts recommend the third option.

Although popular diet regimens promise rapid weight loss, experts agree that slow, gradual reductions in weight are more likely than rapid reductions to be maintained (Brownell, 1989). Self-modification techniques (see Chapter 4) can be very helpful in achieving gradual weight loss. Recent evidence also suggests that it is wise to monitor the *kinds* of calories that you consume as well as the *number* of calories. Foods with a high fat content are converted into body fat more readily than foods high in carbohydrates or protein (Gurin, 1989). Thus, people who want to "shape up" should consume low-fat diets. This point highlights the importance of nutritional patterns, which we consider in the next section.

Nutrition

Nutrition **is a collection of processes (mainly food consumption) through which an organism utilizes the materials (nutrients) required for survival and growth.** The term also refers to the *study* of these processes. Unfortunately, most of us don't study nutrition very much. Moreover, the

cunning mass marketing of nutritionally worthless foods makes it more and more difficult to maintain sound nutritional habits.

Nutrition and Health

Evidence is accumulating that patterns of nutrition influence susceptibility to a variety of diseases and health problems. Possible connections between eating patterns and health include the following.

1. Heavy consumption of foods that elevate serum cholesterol level (eggs, cheeses, butter, shellfish, sausage, and the like) appears to increase the risk of heart disease (Hegsted, 1984).
2. High salt intake has long been thought to be a contributing factor to the development of hypertension (Friedewald, 1982), although there is still some debate about its role.
3. Diets high in fats and low in fiber have been implicated as possible contributors to some forms of cancer (Hegsted, 1984).
4. Certain patterns of sugar consumption (not sugar itself) may hasten the onset of diabetes (Mayer, 1980).
5. Severe vitamin deficiencies can cause a variety of diseases, although these afflictions are not seen in North America as often as in "underdeveloped" countries (Whitney & Cataldo, 1987).

Of course, nutritional habits interact with other factors—genetics, exercise, environment, and so on— to determine whether one develops a particular disease. Nonetheless, the examples just described indicate that our eating habits *can* influence our physical health.

Many popular books and articles suggest that the link between nutrition and health can be taken one step further and that large doses of vitamins or heavy reliance on particular foods can raise immunal resistance to exceptionally high levels. A prime example of this line of thought is Pauling's (1970, 1980) assertion that vitamin C can prevent both cancer and the common cold. Rather extravagant claims have been made for the benefits of vitamin E, the B vitamins, high-fiber diets, and some minerals and vegetables. The last couple of decades have seen the emergence of a number of nutritional fads based on such claims.

What is the current thinking of nutritional experts on this issue? Can nutritional extremes provide super resistance to disease? According to Whitney and Cataldo (1987), probably not. In their excellent nutrition text, they review the evidence for many such claims. They conclude that the research findings contradict most of these claims and are inconclusive at best. Thus, there is little evidence that highly touted nutritional extremes can prevent disease. However, there is clear consensus that inadequate nutrition can have negative effects on health, making adequate nutrition a key part of a healthy lifestyle.

The Basis for Poor Nutrition

Nutritional deficiencies are more widespread in the United States than most people realize. However, these deficiencies are not particularly a function of low income or inability to afford appropriate foods. Instead, most malnutrition in America is attributable to lack of knowledge about nutrition and lack of effort to ensure good nutrition (Quillin, 1987).

In other words, our nutritional shortcomings are due to ignorance and poor motivation. Collectively, we are remarkably naive about the basic principles of nutrition. Our schools tend to provide very little education in this area. Most of us are not highly motivated to make sure our food consumption is nutritionally sound. Instead, we approach our eating very casually, guided not by nutritional needs but by convenience, palatability, and clever advertising.

For most people, then, the first steps toward improved nutrition involve changing attitudes and acquiring information. First and foremost, people need to recognize the importance of nutrition and commit themselves to making a real effort to regulate their eating patterns. Second,

Figure 14.9. The four basic food groups. The four key categories of food are described here, along with dietary recommendations.

people should try to acquire a basic education in regard to nutritional principles.

Nutritional Goals

The evidence indicates that the most healthful approach to nutrition is to follow well-moderated patterns of food consumption that ensure nutritional adequacy while limiting the intake of certain substances that can be counterproductive. Some general guidelines for achieving these goals include the following.

1. *Consume a balanced variety of foods.* Food is made up of a variety of components, six of which are essential to your physical well-being. These six *essential nutrients* are proteins, fats, carbohydrates, vitamins, minerals, and fiber. Proteins, fats, and carbohydrates supply the body with its energy. Vitamins and minerals help to release that energy and serve other important functions as well. Fiber provides roughage that facilitates digestion. It is probably a bit unrealistic to expect most people to keep track of which nutrients are found in which foods. However, it is fairly easy to promote adequate intake of all essential nutrients. All you have to do is to consume a balanced diet in terms of the *four basic food groups*, which are easy to remember: (1) milk and milk products, (2) meats or other protein sources, (3) fruits and vegetables, and (4) breads and cereals. Figure 14.9 includes some recommendations for balanced consumption of these four basic food groups.

2. *Avoid excessive consumption of fats, cholesterol, sugar, and salt.* These are all commodities that are overrepresented in the typical American diet. They are not inherently bad, but they can become problematic when consumed in excess. It is particularly prudent to limit the intake of saturated fats by eating less beef, pork, ham, hot dogs, sausage, lunch meats, nonskim milk, and fried foods. Consumption of many of the same foods also should be limited to reduce cholesterol intake, which influences vulnerability to heart disease. In particular, beef, pork, lamb, sausage, cheese, butter, and eggs are high in cholesterol. Refined (processed) sugar is believed to be grossly overconsumed. Hence, people should limit their dependence on soft drinks, chocolate, candies, pies, cakes, and jams. Finally, many people should cut down on their salt intake. This may require more than ignoring your salt shaker, as many prepackaged foods are loaded with salt.

3. *Increase consumption of complex carbohydrates, polyunsaturated fats, natural sugars, and foods with fiber.* If you're thinking that you have to avoid all the foods mentioned in the preceding paragraph, you may be wondering what's left to eat. Please note, however, that the experts suggest only that you reduce *excessive consumption* of those foods while increasing consumption in other areas. In particular, fruits, vegetables, and whole grains contain complex carbohydrates, natural sugars, and ample fiber. In order to substitute polyunsaturated fats for saturated ones, you can eat more fish, chicken, turkey, and veal. Additionally, you can trim meats of fat more thoroughly, use skim (nonfat) milk, and switch to vegetable oils that are high in polyunsaturated fats.

Four Basic Food Groups		
Food group	**Amount suggested and foods included**	**Nutrients provided**
1. Milk or milk products	Children: 3 or more glasses; smaller glasses for children under 9 Teenagers: 4 or more glasses (low-fat) Adults: 2 or more glasses (low-fat) 1 cup milk = 1 cup yogurt = 1 1/3 oz processed cheddar cheese = 1 1/2 cups cottage cheese = 2 cups ice cream	Protein, fat, carbohydrate Minerals: calcium, phosphorus, magnesium Vitamins: riboflavin, pyridoxine, D, and A (if fortified)
2. Meat	2 or more servings (1 serving = 2 to 3 oz cooked lean meat) Meat, poultry, fish, legumes	Protein, fat Minerals: iron, magnesium, phosphorus, zinc Vitamins: B vitamins (cobalamin, folic acid, niacin, pyridoxine, thiamine)
3. Fruits and vegetables	4 or more servings (1 serving = 1/2 cup raw or cooked) All fruits and vegetables (include one citrus fruit for vitamin C and one dark green or yellow vegetable for carotene)	Carbohydrate Minerals: calcium and iron (some greens) Vitamins: A (as carotene), B vitamins (folic acid, thiamine), C, E, K
4. Breads and cereals*	4 or more servings (1 serving = 1 slice fortified or whole grain bread = 1 oz fortified or whole grain dry cereal = 1 corn tortilla = 1/2–3/4 cup cooked fortified or whole grain cereal, rice, grits, macaroni, etc.)	Carbohydrate, protein Minerals: iron, magnesium, phosphorus, zinc Vitamins: B vitamins (niacin, pyridoxine, thiamine), E

*Bran, whole grain breads and cereals, and to a lesser degree, raw and dried fruits and raw vegetables will increase the amount of unabsorbable fiber in the diet.

Exercise

In 1984, James Fixx, the noted author of several books touting the benefits of running, died from a heart attack while out jogging. All over the country, people who rarely exercise probably nodded their heads knowingly and made comments about exercise having little real value. Despite such rationalizations, there is considerable evidence of a link between exercise and health.

The relationship between physical inactivity and increased risk of heart disease is well documented (Peters et al., 1983). Additionally, insofar as physical inactivity promotes obesity, it is related indirectly to increased risk for a variety of health problems, including diabetes, respiratory difficulties, hypertension, and stroke. In particular, though, lack of exercise is most strongly related to the very serious health problems that originate in the cardiovascular system (heart attack, hypertension, and stroke).

Benefits and Risks of Exercise

The potential benefits of regular exercise are substantial. First, regular exercise is associated with increased longevity (Paffenbarger, Hyde, Wing, & Hsieh, 1986). Moreover, a recent study showed that you don't have to be a dedicated athlete to benefit from exercise (Blair et al., 1989). Even a moderate amount of exercise reduces the risk of disease and is associated with lower mortality rates (see Figure 14.10). In particular, an appropriate exercise program can enhance cardiovascular fitness and thereby reduce your susceptibility to deadly cardiovascular problems. Second, exercise can serve as a buffer that reduces the potentially damaging physical effects of stress (Brown & Siegel, 1988). Third, a successful exercise program can produce desirable personality changes. A review of the research literature on the effects of exercise (Folkins & Sime, 1981) concludes that fitness training can lead to improvements in one's mood, self-concept, and work efficiency. Another study (McCann & Holmes, 1984) suggests that a systematic aerobic program can help to reduce feelings of depression.

It is important to note, however, that exercise programs have their own hazards. For example, jogging clearly elevates one's risk of muscular and skeletal injuries (it's especially hard on the knees) and can bring on heat stroke and possibly even a heart attack (Koplan et al., 1982). The fact that exercise can both improve cardiovascular health and cause a heart attack may seem paradoxical. However, this contradiction was explained in a study by Siscovick, Weiss, Fletcher, and Lasky (1984). They found that men who participated in *regular* habitual exercise activity lowered their cardiac risk. Vigorous exercise does temporarily (during the exercise) increase cardiac risk—but almost exclusively among those who do not exercise regularly. Although James Fixx's death appears inconsistent with the assertion that exercise decreases cardiac risk, Fixx took up jogging because he knew there was a history of heart problems in his family. In other words, he carried a hereditary vulnerability to heart attack that might have killed him 20 years earlier if it hadn't been for his regular exercise (his father had his first heart attack at age 35). In any case, an exercise program should be planned carefully to minimize the risks and maximize the benefits.

Devising an Exercise Program

Putting together a good exercise program is difficult for many people. Exercise is time-consuming, and if you're out of shape, your initial attempts may be painful, aversive, and discouraging. To circumvent these problems, it is wise to heed the following advice (Greenberg, 1990; Mirkin & Hoffman, 1978).

1. *Look for an activity that you will find enjoyable.* There are a great many physical activities to choose from (see Figure 14.11). Shop around for one that you find intrinsically enjoyable. This will make it much easier for you to follow through and exercise regularly.

2. *Increase your participation gradually.* Don't try to do too much too quickly. An overzealous approach can lead to frustration, not to mention injury. An exercise regimen

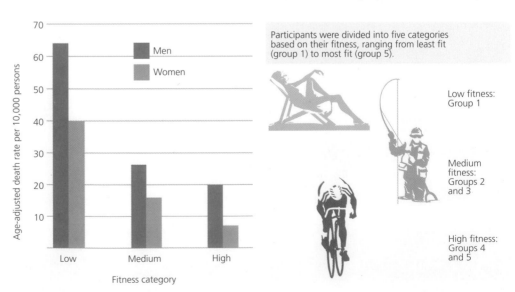

Figure 14.10. Physical fitness and mortality. Blair et al. (1989) studied death rates among men and women who exhibited low, medium, or high fitness. As you can see, fitness was associated with lower mortality rates in both sexes.

Participants were divided into five categories based on their fitness, ranging from least fit (group 1) to most fit (group 5).

Low fitness: Group 1

Medium fitness: Groups 2 and 3

High fitness: Groups 4 and 5

should be built up gradually. If you do experience injuries, avoid the common tendency to ignore them. Consult your physician to see whether continuing your exercise program is advisable.

3. *Exercise regularly without overdoing it.* Sporadic exercise will not improve your fitness. A widely cited rule of thumb is that you should plan on exercising vigorously for a minimum of 30 minutes three times a week, or you will gain little from your efforts. At the other extreme, don't try to become fit overnight by working out too vigorously and too frequently. Even highly trained athletes include days off in their schedules. These off days are necessary to allow muscles to recover from their hard work.

4. *Reinforce yourself for your participation.* To offset the inconvenience or pain that may be associated with exercise, it is a good idea to reinforce yourself for your participation. The behavior modification procedures discussed in Chapter 4 can be very helpful in shaping up a viable exercise program.

5. *Avoid the competition trap.* If you choose a competitive sport for your physical activity (for example, baseball, basketball, tennis), try to avoid becoming obsessed with victory. It is easy to get overly concerned with winning at games. When this happens, you put yourself under pressure. This is obviously self-defeating, in that it adds another source of stress to your life.

Sleep

It is easy to underestimate the importance of sleep in our lives. Adequate sleep is necessary for most of us to function effectively. Research has shown that even partial sleep deprivation can produce difficulty in concentration, fatigue, and poor performance on various kinds of tasks (Johnson, 1982). It is true that lack of sleep has only a modest link to health problems, because sleep deprivation tends to be self-limiting. Generally, people can go only two to three days without sleep, so massive sleep deprivation is relatively unusual. Nonetheless, there is evidence (Palmblad, 1981) that sleep deprivation can reduce the effectiveness of our immune response, making us more vulnerable to infections.

The sheer amount of sleep you get is not the only important consideration. The *kind* of sleep you get may also be relevant. Scientists have discovered that after we fall asleep, we evolve through a series of stages, during which the nature of our sleep changes. *REM sleep* **is a deep stage of sleep marked by rapid eye movements, dreaming, and brain wave activity like that seen when people are awake.** REM is an abbreviation for "rapid eye movement." The most noticeable sign of this stage of sleep is rapid, lateral eye movements that take place beneath the closed eyelids. Interestingly, it appears that most dreaming occurs during REM sleep. During the course of the night, most people go into the REM stage about four times (see Figure 14.12). As the

Sport	Jogging	Bicycling	Swimming	Skating (ice or roller)	Handball/Squash	Skiing—Nordic	Skiing—Alpine	Basketball	Tennis	Calisthenics	Walking	Golf	Softball	Bowling
Physical fitness														
Cardiorespiratory endurance (stamina)	21	19	21	18	19	19	16	19	16	10	13	8	6	5
Muscular endurance	20	18	20	17	18	19	18	17	16	13	14	8	8	5
Muscular strength	17	16	14	15	15	15	15	15	14	16	11	9	7	5
Flexibility	9	9	15	13	16	14	14	13	14	19	7	9	9	7
Balance	17	18	12	20	17	16	21	16	16	15	8	8	7	6
General well-being														
Weight control	21	20	15	17	19	17	15	19	16	12	13	6	7	5
Muscle definition	14	15	14	14	11	12	14	13	13	18	11	6	5	5
Digestion	13	12	13	11	13	12	9	10	12	11	11	7	8	7
Sleep	16	15	16	15	12	15	12	12	11	12	14	6	7	6
Total	148	142	140	140	140	139	134	134	128	126	102	67	64	51

How Beneficial Is Your Favorite Sport?

Figure 14.11. A scorecard on the benefits of 14 sports and exercises. Here is a summary of how seven experts rated the value of 14 sporting activities (the highest rating possible on any one item was 21). The ratings were based on vigorous participation four times per week.

night wears on, subsequent REM periods get progressively longer, so REM sleep dominates the later portion of a night's sleep.

Why is REM sleep significant? The evidence suggests that we need good-quality sleep, including a certain amount of REM sleep (Borbely, 1986). Most adults spend about 20% of their total sleep time in the REM stage (Webb & Agnew, 1968). Although this exact proportion is not essential for everyone, it is clear that the task of getting proper sleep is more complex than most people realize.

Maximizing the Quality of Your Sleep

Researchers who have studied the sleep process have uncovered some clues about how to maximize the beneficial effects of your sleep. Let's review some of their advice.

1. *Try to establish a regular pattern for sleeping.* Going to bed at about the same time each night promotes good sleep. Your body has a 24-hour rhythmic cycle involving consistent fluctuations in many physiological functions, such as body temperature and hormonal secretions. Highly irregular sleep patterns can disrupt this rhythm and lead to poor-quality sleep. Conversely, if you follow a regular pattern, your body may become primed for falling asleep quickly and easily at your usual bedtime.

2. *Try to get sustained sleep rather than naps.* Although some of us can profit from napping (Gillberg, 1984), most people benefit more from sustained sleep. For example, if you have a choice between (1) sleeping seven hours straight and (2) taking a two-hour catnap now and sleeping only five hours later, the seven consecutive hours of sleep will probably be more beneficial to you. The reason may be that as you sleep longer, you spend a greater proportion of time in the crucial REM stage.

3. *Avoid daytime habits that interfere with sleep.* You can improve your chances of getting satisfactory sleep by developing sensible daytime habits that won't disrupt your sleeping (Kales & Kales, 1984). For example, if

you've been having trouble sleeping at night, it's a good idea to avoid the temptation of daytime naps, so that you're *tired* when your bedtime arrives. Obviously, stimulant drugs such as cocaine and amphetamines make it difficult to sleep. It's also wise to minimize your consumption of less potent stimulants, such as coffee and cigarettes. Many foods and beverages contain more caffeine than people realize. Also, bear in mind that ill-advised eating habits can interfere with sleep. Try to avoid going to bed hungry, or uncomfortably stuffed, or soon after eating foods that disagree with you.

4. *Create a favorable environment for sleep.* This advice labors what should be obvious, but many people fail to heed it. Make sure that you have a good bed that is comfortable for you. Take steps to ensure that your bedroom is quiet enough and that the humidity and temperature are to your liking.

Battling Insomnia

Insomnia involves chronic problems in getting adequate sleep. There are three basic patterns of insomnia: (1) difficulty in falling asleep initially, (2) difficulty in remaining asleep, and (3) persistent early-morning awakening. As much as 30% of the adult population may have serious problems with insomnia (Hartmann, 1985). The following advice may be helpful if you suffer from insomnia.

1. *Don't initiate chemical warfare.* The most common approach to the treatment of insomnia is the prescription of sedative drugs, commonly known as sleeping pills. Unfortunately, this treatment is probably *too* common. According to sleep expert Ernest Hartmann (1978), sleeping pills are a poor long-range solution for insomnia for a number of reasons. For one thing, there is some danger of *overdose*. Apart from this risk, many people become *dependent* on sedatives to fall asleep. Moreover, with continued use, sedatives gradually lose their effectiveness, so people need to increase their dose to more dangerous levels, creating a vicious cycle of escalating dependency (see Figure 14.13). Ironically, sedatives also interfere with

Figure 14.12. The cycle of sleep. The graph maps out one subject's sleep cycle during the course of one night. REM stages are shown as thick bars. This cycle is very typical: There were four REM periods, and they tended to get longer as the night progressed.

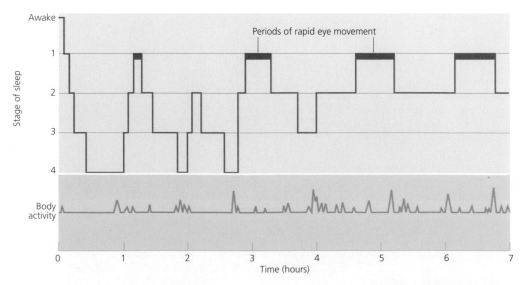

How to Sleep Like a Baby
by Dianne Hales (Ballantine, 1987)

This book is a lively, well-written analysis of practical issues related to sleep. It is intended primarily for people struggling with insomnia. However, it covers other sleep-related topics as well, including biological rhythms, daytime drowsiness, and dreaming. Although Hales is a professional writer (specializing in health issues) rather than a scientist, the information in the book is up-to-date and scientifically sound. Hales does an excellent job of explaining the many different reasons for sleep difficulties. She also provides an abundance of suggestions for improving the quality of your sleep. One highlight is her list of "101 ways to put yourself to sleep."

> Although you may not realize it, you live two lives—one in the waking world and one behind closed lids. In all, you spend a third of your life asleep, or more than 220,000 hours over the course of seventy years. You may think that during this time your sleeping body is like a car parked for the night: motionless, engine off, headlights dimmed. It is anything but.
>
> During sleep, muscles tense and relax. Pulse, temperature and blood pressure rise and fall. Chemicals crucial for well-being course through the bloodstream. The brain, like a Hollywood producer, conjures up fantastic stories, complete with cliffhanger plots and dazzling special effects. In fact, so much happens during sleep that it's astounding that we manage to sleep at all. [p. 7]

the normal cycle of sleep, reducing the proportion of time spent in the important REM stage. Sedatives may be a reasonable solution if your sleep is being disrupted by a short-term crisis. However, if you experience perennial sleep difficulties, you need to find some other solution.
2. *Don't panic.* If you run into a little trouble sleeping, don't panic. If you jump to the conclusion that you are becoming an insomniac, you may approach sleep with

anxiety that will aggravate the problem. An overreaction to sleep problems can begin a vicious cycle in which sleep difficulties lead to increased anxiety, which leads to increased sleep difficulties. Sleep problems are often temporary and they frequently clear up on their own.
3. *Try daydreaming yourself to sleep.* If you lie in bed thinking how terrible you'll feel tomorrow if you don't fall asleep, you'll just be more upset and less likely to drift off. The harder you work at falling asleep, the less successful you'll be. Instead, it's a good idea to launch yourself into a pleasant daydream. This is a normal presleep process that can take your mind off the fact that you're not sleeping.
4. *Bore yourself to sleep.* In her book *How to Sleep Like a Baby*, sleep expert Dianne Hales (1987) lists 101 suggestions for combatting insomnia. Many involve "boring yourself to sleep" by playing alphabet games, taking an imaginary stroll through your neighborhood, reciting poems, or listening to your clock. Another recommended strategy is to engage in some less-than-engaging activity. For instance, you might try reading your dullest textbook. It could turn out to be a superb sedative.
5. *Learn to relax.* In many people, insomnia is due to excessive tension. If you have persistent sleep problems, you may simply need to learn to relax more effectively. Anything that relaxes you—whether it's music, meditation, prayer, or a warm bath—can aid you in falling asleep. If necessary, try practicing Benson's (1975) relaxation response or some other relaxation exercise (see Chapter 4).

Lifestyle and AIDS

At present, the most problematic links between lifestyle and health may be those related to the Acquired Immune Deficiency Syndrome (AIDS). The number of AIDS cases is increasing at an alarming rate. The syndrome is caused by several related viruses that severely impair the body's immunal response to infections. Unless there is a major research breakthrough, AIDS will continue to be a fatal disease.

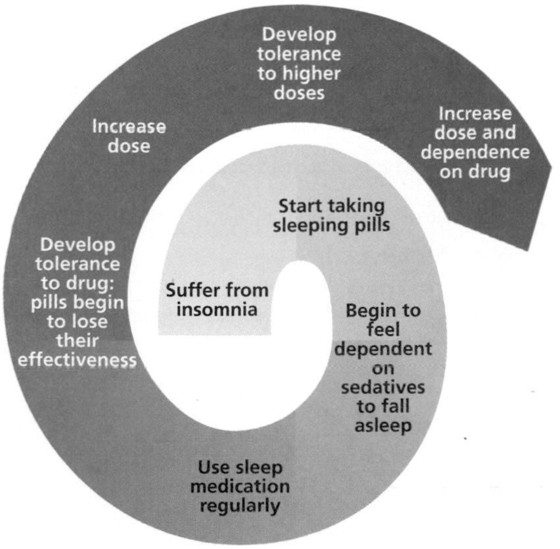

Figure 14.13. The vicious cycle of dependence on sleeping pills. Because of the body's ability to develop "tolerance" to drugs, regular use of sedatives can lead to escalating dependence as larger and larger doses are needed to fall asleep.

AIDS is transmitted through the exchange of bodily fluids, primarily semen and blood. To date, the two principal modes of transmission have been sexual contact among homosexual and bisexual men and the sharing of needles by intravenous drug users. These two modes of transmission have accounted for about 90% of all AIDS cases (Castro, Hardy, & Curran, 1986). However, the virus *can* be transmitted through heterosexual contact with an affected individual. Thus, the disease is slowly diffusing into the population at large, and it is *not* just a "homosexual problem." Among urban blacks, who have a higher rate of intravenous drug use than other groups, over one half of AIDS cases are already occurring in heterosexuals (Bakeman, Lumb, Jackson, & Smith, 1986).

Ironically, fear of AIDS is higher among low-risk groups that have relatively little knowledge about AIDS than among high-risk groups with more knowledge. Although San Francisco has the highest per capita incidence of AIDS in the United States, a sample of gay men and a sample of heterosexual persons drawn from San Francisco both reported less fear of AIDS than heterosexual samples drawn from New York and London (Temoshok, Sweet, & Zich, 1987). As the investigators in this study note, "Perhaps no medical phenomenon has been so feared or so misunderstood by the public." Although the myths persist, at present there is no evidence that AIDS can be transmitted through sneezing, shaking hands, sharing food, or other kinds of casual contact. Figure 14.14 contains a short quiz to test your knowledge of the facts about AIDS.

The lifestyle changes that minimize the risk of developing AIDS are fairly straightforward, although making the changes is often much easier said than done. In all groups, the more sexual partners a person has, the higher the risk that one will be exposed to AIDS. Thus, people can reduce their risk by having sexual contacts with fewer partners and by using condoms to control the exchange of semen. Among gay men, it is also important to curtail certain sexual practices (in particular, anal sex) that increase the probability of semen/blood mixing. Intrave-nous drug users could greatly reduce their risk by abandoning their drug use, but this is unlikely, since most are physically dependent on the drugs. Alternatively, they need to improve the sterilization of their needles and avoid sharing syringes with other users. (We'll review other dangers associated with drug use in the upcoming Application.)

REACTIONS TO ILLNESS

So far we have emphasized the psychosocial aspects of maintaining health and minimizing the risk of illness. Our health is also affected by how we *respond* to physical symptoms and illnesses. Some people engage in denial and ignore early warning signs of developing diseases. Others engage in active coping efforts to conquer their diseases. In this section, we discuss the perception of pain, the decision to seek medical treatment, the sick role, and compliance with medical advice.

The Perception of Pain

Pain signals are transmitted to the brain via two pathways. One is a *fast pathway* that registers localized pain and relays it directly to the cortex in a fraction of a second. This is the system that hits you with sharp pain when you first cut your finger. The second system uses a *slow pathway* routed through lower brain centers. Signals on this pathway lag a second or two behind those in the fast system. This system conveys the less localized, longer-lasting, aching pain that comes after the initial injury.

We tend to think of pain as a purely organic sensation resulting from some sort of tissue damage in the body. However, research in recent years has made it clear that the organic model of pain is much too simple. It fails to account for the host of psychological variables that can affect the experience of pain (Steger & Fordyce, 1982). These include the individual's expectations, anxiety or tension level, personality, and previous conditioning.

A Quiz on AIDS		
Answer the following "true" or "false."		
T	F	**1.** AIDS is caused by a virus.
T	F	**2.** AIDS is caused by inheriting a bad gene or genes.
T	F	**3.** AIDS is caused by a kind of bacteria.
T	F	**4.** A person can "carry" and pass on whatever causes AIDS without necessarily having AIDS or looking sick.
T	F	**5.** Whatever causes AIDS can be passed on through semen.
T	F	**6.** Whatever causes AIDS can be passed on through blood or blood products.
T	F	**7.** You can catch AIDS like you catch a cold because whatever causes AIDS can be carried in the air.
T	F	**8.** You can catch AIDS by being in the same room as someone with AIDS.
T	F	**9.** You can catch AIDS by shaking hands with someone who has AIDS.
T	F	**10.** Having a monogamous relationship decreases the risk of getting AIDS.
T	F	**11.** Using condoms reduces the risk of getting AIDS.
T	F	**12.** A vaccine for AIDS will be available within a year.

Answers: 1. T 2. F 3. F 4. T 5. T 6. T 7. F 8. F 9. F 10. T 11. T 12. F

The highly subjective nature of pain is easy to illustrate. Let's say you're working in your basement at home and you hit your thumb with a hammer. An hour later your thumb is still throbbing with excruciating pain when a family member screams from the kitchen that there's a fire in the oven. As you race to provide assistance with this emergency, the pain in your thumb will almost certainly dwindle dramatically. Your experience of pain will have been altered substantially, even though the organic basis for the pain has remained constant. If you still doubt the subjective basis of pain, just ask a nurse who routinely gives the same shots to many patients. You will surely be told that different patients display an exceptionally wide range of pain reactions to essentially the same stimulus. Moreover, these examples both involve *acute* pain from specific sources of tissue damage. The evidence indicates that *chronic,* long-lasting pain of unclear origin (such as lower back pain) is even more affected by psychological considerations.

The highly psychological nature of many chronic pain problems helps to account for the very modest success of medical treatment of chronic pain. Improvement rates for organic treatments typically range from 30% to 60% (Gatchel & Baum, 1988). The increasing recognition of the psychological basis of pain has led to the development of behavioral treatment programs for pain management. These new treatment regimens involve a variety of intervention procedures, including relaxation training, behavior modification, cognitive restructuring, hypnosis, and biofeedback.

The Decision to Seek Treatment

Have you ever experienced nausea, diarrhea, stiffness, headaches, cramps, chest pains, or sinus problems? Of course you have; we all experience some of these problems periodically. However, whether we view these sensations as *symptoms* is a matter of individual interpretation. When two persons experience the same unpleasant sensations, one may shrug them off as a nuisance while the

Figure 14.14. A quiz on knowledge of AIDS.
Misconceptions about AIDS abound, so it may be wise to take this brief quiz to test your knowledge of AIDS. (Adapted from Temoshok et al., 1987)

other may rush to a physician. Studies suggest that people who are relatively high in anxiety and low in self-esteem tend to report more symptoms of illness than others (Pennebaker, 1982). Variations in the perception of symptoms help to explain why there are great differences among people in their readiness to seek medical treatment.

The biggest problem in regard to treatment seeking, however, is the tendency of many people to delay the pursuit of needed professional consultation. This is important because early diagnosis can facilitate more effective treatment of many health problems.

A number of factors are associated with delays in seeking professional consultation. Gender is one of these: Males are more prone than females to put off seeking treatment (Mechanic, 1972). There is a weak tendency for lower education and socioeconomic status to be associated with greater delays (Rosenstock & Kirscht, 1979). This may be because it is more costly for people from the lower socioeconomic strata to seek care, as they often have less insurance, fewer sick days, and so forth. Understandably, people who are fearful of doctors and hospitals often delay seeking treatment. People who believe strongly in self-care also tend to wait before obtaining professional care (Krantz, Baum, & Wideman, 1980).

The Sick Role

Although many people tend to delay medical consultations, some people are positively eager to seek medical care. These people have learned that there are potential benefits to adopting the "sick role" (Parsons, 1979). For instance, fewer demands are placed on sick people, who often can selectively decide which demands to ignore. Sick people may also find themselves to be the center of attention from friends and relatives. This increase in attention from others can be very rewarding, especially to those who received little attention previously. Moreover, much of this attention is favorable, in that the sick person is showered with affection, concern, and sympathy.

Thus, some people grow to *like* the sick role, although they may not be aware of it. Such people readily seek professional care, but they tend to behave in subtle ways that prolong their illness (Kinsman, Dirks, & Jones, 1982). For example, they may only pretend to go along with medical advice, a common problem that we discuss next.

Compliance with Medical Advice

Many patients fail to follow the instructions they receive from physicians and other health care professionals. Noncompliance is not limited to people who have come to like the sick role, and it is a major problem in our medical care system.

It is difficult to precisely estimate the extent of noncompliance, since patients are not eager to admit their failure to comply with instructions. Nonetheless, studies suggest that noncompliance with medical advice may occur between one third and one half of the time (DiMatteo & Friedman, 1982). Although we saw that demographic variables (gender, social class, and education) are related to variations in treatment seeking, factors such as gender, social class, age, and education do *not* predict differences in compliance (Davidson, 1982).

Our discussion of compliance is not intended to suggest that you should passively accept all the professional advice you get from medical personnel. However, when you have doubts about a prescribed treatment, you should speak up and ask questions. Passive resistance can backfire. For instance, if a physician sees no improvement in a patient who falsely insists that he has been taking his medicine, the physician may abandon an accurate diagnosis in favor of an inaccurate one. The inaccurate diagnosis could lead to inappropriate treatments that might even be harmful to the patient.

Why don't people comply with the advice they have sought from highly regarded medical practi-

Training health practitioners to be courteous, friendly, and willing to explain problems in simple terms, as this physician is doing, will help improve patient compliance with medical advice.

tioners? Three reasons are especially prominent (DiMatteo & Friedman, 1982):

1. Frequently, noncompliance is due to a failure by the patient to understand the instructions as given. Highly trained professionals often forget that what seems obvious and simple to them may be obscure and complicated for many of their patients.
2. A key factor centers on how aversive or difficult the instructions are. If the prescribed regimen has unpleasant side effects, compliance will tend to decrease. The more that following instructions interferes with routine behavior, the less probable it is that the patient will cooperate successfully.
3. If a patient has a negative attitude toward a physician, this will increase the probability of noncompliance. When patients are unhappy with their interactions with the doctor, they are more likely to ignore the medical advice provided.

In response to the noncompliance problem, some health psychologists are exploring how to increase patients' adherence to medical advice. They have found that the communication process between the practitioner and the patient is of critical importance. Courtesy, warmth, patience, and a decreased reliance on medical jargon can improve compliance (DiNicola & DiMatteo, 1984). Thus, there is a new emphasis on enhancing health care professionals' communication skills.

SUMMARY

The biopsychosocial model holds that physical health is influenced by a complex network of biological, psycho-

logical, and sociocultural factors. Stress is one of the psychological factors that can affect our physical health. In particular, Type A behavior has been implicated as a contributing cause of coronary heart disease. This competitive, impatient, hostile pattern of behavior may double one's coronary risk. However, the evidence is contradictory, and more research is needed. The connection between stress and cancer is not well documented and appears to be very weak.

Researchers have found associations between stress and the onset of a variety of specific diseases. Stress may play a role in a host of diseases because it can temporarily suppress our immune reaction. While there's little doubt that stress can contribute to the development of physical illness, the link between stress and illness is modest in strength.

People frequently display health-impairing habits and lifestyles. These habits creep up on people slowly, and their risks are easy to ignore because the dangers often lie in the distant future. Smokers have much higher mortality rates than nonsmokers because they are more vulnerable to a host of diseases. Giving up smoking is difficult in part because nicotine is addictive. Obesity elevates one's risk for a great variety of health problems. Body weight is influenced by genetic endowment and other physiological factors, but overeating certainly contributes in most cases. Weight loss is best accomplished by decreasing caloric consumption while gradually increasing exercise.

Poor nutritional habits have been linked to heart disease, hypertension, cancer, and diabetes. Nutritional fads do not offer protection against disease. One's health can best be served by following balanced food consumption patterns while limiting the intake of certain substances that can be counterproductive. Lack of exercise elevates one's risk for cardiovascular diseases. Regular exercise can enhance cardiovascular fitness, buffer the effects of stress, and lead to desirable personality changes. Poor sleep habits have limited effects on health because of the self-limiting nature of sleep deprivation. Nonetheless, good sleep habits may make a small contribution to good health. Aspects of lifestyle are the key factors influencing one's risk of AIDS.

We all experience feelings of pain and physical symptoms, but some of us tend to ignore them. This may result in the delay of needed medical treatment. At the other extreme, a minority of people learn to like the sick role because it earns them attention and allows them to avoid stress. Noncompliance with medical advice is a major problem. The likelihood of noncompliance is greater when instructions are difficult to understand, when recommendations are difficult to follow, and when patients are unhappy with their doctor.

In the upcoming Application, we take a look at a health-impairing habit that is all too common in our society—drug abuse. We will examine the effects and risks of various recreational drugs.

Understanding the Effects of Drugs

Answer the following true or false.

☐ **1.** Smoking marijuana can make men impotent and sterile.

☐ **2.** Overdoses caused by cocaine are relatively rare.

☐ **3.** It is well documented that LSD causes chromosome damage.

☐ **4.** The most widely abused drug is marijuana.

As you will learn in this Application, all of the statements above are false. If you answered all of them accurately, you may already be well informed about drugs. If not, you should be. Intelligent decisions about drugs require an understanding of their effects and risks.

This Application focuses on the use of drugs for their pleasurable effects, commonly referred to as *drug abuse* or *recreational drug use*. Drug abuse is a very problematic health-impairing habit that reaches into every corner of our society. There were some small declines in the abuse of certain drugs during the 1980s (Johnston, O'Malley, & Bachman, 1987, 1988), but it appears that recreational drug use is here to stay for the foreseeable future.

Like other controversial social problems, recreational drug use often inspires more rhetoric than reason. For instance, a former president of the American Medical Association made headlines when he declared that marijuana "makes a man of 35 sexually like a man of 70." In reality, the research findings do not support this assertion. This influential physician later retracted his statement, admitting that he had made it simply to campaign against marijuana use (Leavitt, 1982). Unfortunately, such scare tactics can backfire by undermining the credibility of drug education efforts.

Recreational drug use involves personal, moral, political, and legal issues that are not matters for science to resolve. However, the more knowledgeable you are about drugs, the more informed your decisions and opinions about them will be. Accordingly, this Application is intended to provide you with nonjudg-mental, realistic coverage of issues related to recreational drug use. We'll begin by reviewing key drug-related concepts. Then we'll examine the effects and risks of six types of widely abused drugs: narcotics, sedatives, stimulants, hallucinogens, cannabis, and alcohol. We'll wrap up our coverage with a brief discussion of newer drugs that have become problematic in recent years.

DRUG-RELATED CONCEPTS

The drugs that people use recreationally are *psychoactive*. *Psychoactive drugs* **are chemical substances that modify a person's mental, emotional, or behavioral functioning.** Not all psychoactive drugs produce effects that lead to drug abuse. Generally, people prefer drugs that elevate one's mood or produce pleasant alterations in consciousness. The principal types of recreational drugs are described in Figure 14.15. This table lists representative drugs in each of six categories, how the drugs are taken, their principal medical uses, their desired effects, and their common side effects (based on Blum, 1984; Julien, 1988).

Most drugs produce tolerance effects. *Tolerance* **refers to a progressive decrease in a person's responsiveness to a drug with continued use.** Tolerance effects usually lead people to consume larger and larger doses of a drug to attain the effects they desire. As shown in Figure 14.16, tolerance builds more rapidly to some drugs than to others. The second column in the figure indicates whether the category of drugs tends to produce rapid or gradual tolerance.

In evaluating the potential problems associated with the use of a drug, a key consideration is the likelihood of either physical or psychological dependence. *Physical dependence* **(also called addiction) exists when a person must continue to take a drug to avoid withdrawal illness when drug use is terminated.** The symptoms of withdrawal illness vary depending on the drug. Withdrawal from heroin, barbiturates, and alcohol can produce fever, chills, tremors, convulsions, seizures, vomiting, cramps, diarrhea, and severe aches and pains. The agony of withdrawal from these drugs virtually

Comparison of Major Abused Drugs

Drugs	Methods of administration	Principal medical uses	Desired effects	Short–term side effects
Narcotics (opiates) Morphine Heroin	Injected, smoked, oral	Pain relief	Euphoria, relaxation, anxiety reduction, pain relief	Lethargy, drowsiness, nausea, impaired coordination, impaired mental functioning, constipation
Sedatives Barbiturates (e.g., Seconal) Nonbarbiturates (e.g., Quaalude)	Oral, injected	Sleeping pill, anticonvulsant	Euphoria, relaxation, anxiety reduction, reduced inhibitions	Lethargy, drowsiness, severely impaired coordination, impaired mental functioning, emotional swings, dejection
Stimulants Amphetamines Cocaine	Oral, sniffed, injected, freebased, smoked	Treatment of hyperactivity and narcolepsy, local anesthetic (cocaine only)	Elation, excitement, increased alertness, increased energy, reduced fatigue	Increased blood pressure and heart rate, increased talkativeness, restlessness, irritability, insomnia, reduced appetite, increased sweating and urination, anxiety, paranoia, increased aggressiveness, panic
Hallucinogens LSD Mescaline Psilocybin	Oral		Increased sensory awareness, euphoria, altered perceptions, hallucinations, insightful experiences	Dilated pupils, nausea, emotional swings, paranoia, jumbled thought processes, impaired judgment, anxiety, panic reaction
Cannabis Marijuana Hashish THC	Smoked, oral	Treament of glaucoma; other uses under study	Mild euphoria, relaxation, altered perceptions, enhanced awareness	Bloodshot eyes, dry mouth, reduced short-term memory, sluggish motor coordination, sluggish mental functioning, anxiety
Alcohol	Drinking		Mild euphoria, relaxation, anxiety reduction, reduced inhibitions	Severely impaired coordination, impaired mental functioning, increased urination, emotional swings, depression, quarrelsomeness, hangover

Note: The principal omission from this table is PCP (phencyclidine hydrochloride), which does not fit neatly into any of the listed categories. PCP has stimulant, hallucinogenic, and anesthetic effects. Its short-term side effects can be very dangerous. Common side effects include agitation, paranoia, confusion, and severe mental disorientation that has been linked to accidents and suicides.

Figure 14.15 *(above)*. **Major categories of abused drugs.** This chart summarizes the methods of ingestion, chief medical uses, and principal effects of the six major types of recreational drugs.

Figure 14.16. Specific risks for various categories of drugs. This chart shows estimates of the risk potential for tolerance, dependence, and overdose for the six major categories of drugs discussed in this Application.

Risks Associated with Abused Drugs

Drugs	Tolerance	Risk of physical dependence	Risk of psychological dependence	Fatal overdose potential
Narcotics (opiates)	Rapid	High	High	High
Sedatives	Rapid	High	High	High
Stimulants	Rapid	Moderate	High	Moderate to high
Hallucinogens	Gradual	None	Very low	Very low
Cannabis	Gradual	None	Low to moderate	Very low
Alcohol	Gradual	Moderate	Moderate	Low to high

RECOMMENDED READING

Drugs: A Factual Account

by Dorothy Dusek & Daniel A. Girdano (Addison-Wesley, 1980; McGraw-Hill, 1986)

Although slender in size, this book provides a thorough and well-documented introduction to the topic of recreational drug use. It is intended primarily for undergraduate students and is highly readable. A nice feature is that the authors place drugs in their social context. Historical and legal issues are discussed along with the effects of various drugs. The book begins with a discussion of why people use drugs. Then, after providing a brief introduction to physiology, the authors examine specific categories of drugs. The coverage includes legal as well as illegal drugs.

> Cocaine is one of the oldest drugs known with recorded use dating back hundreds of years. Coca's oldest use was in religious ceremonies as an inducer of meditative trance and as an aid for communicating with nature. The Incas reserved coca use for the nobility and priests, and those who were granted permission to use it were in extreme imperial favor. The leaves were offered in sacrifice to the gods, chewed during worship, and placed into the mouths of the dead to ensure a favorable welcome in the next life. For a while after the Spanish conquest of Peru, coca use was forbidden, until the Spanish discovered that the Indians could perform more work on less food while using the drug. A daily ration was then provided for the laborers. That practice became a habit that has never been relinquished. [1980, p. 127]

compels addicts to continue using them. Withdrawal from stimulant use leads to a different and somewhat milder syndrome dominated by fatigue, apathy, irritability, depression, and disorientation.

Psychological dependence exists when a person must continue to take a drug to satisfy intense mental and emotional craving for the drug. Psychological dependence is more subtle than physical dependence in that it is not marked by a clear withdrawal reaction. However, psychological dependence can create a powerful and even overwhelming need for a drug. Both types of dependence are established gradually with repeated use of a drug. Drugs differ greatly in their potential for creating either physical or psychological dependence. The third and fourth columns in Figure 14.16 provide estimates of the risk of each kind of dependence for the drugs covered in our discussion.

An *overdose* is an excessive dose of a drug that can seriously threaten one's life. Any drug can be fatal if a person takes enough of it, but some drugs involve more danger of overdose than others. The last column in Figure 14.16 estimates the risk

of accidentally consuming a lethal overdose of various drugs. Drugs that are central nervous system (CNS) depressants—narcotics, sedatives, and alcohol—carry the greatest risk of overdose. It's important to understand that the effects of these drugs are additive. Many overdoses involve lethal *combinations* of CNS depressants. What happens when people overdose on these drugs? Usually the respiratory system grinds to a halt, producing coma, brain damage, and death within a brief period. In contrast, fatal overdoses with CNS stimulants (cocaine and amphetamines) usually involve a heart attack, stroke, or cortical seizure.

Now that our basic vocabulary is spelled out, we can begin to examine the effects and risks of major recreational drugs. Our coverage is based largely on comprehensive books by Blum (1984), Julien (1988), and Segal (1988), but we'll cite additional sources when discussing specific studies or controversial points. Of course, we'll be describing the *typical* effects of each drug. Bear in mind that the effects of any drug depend on the user's age, body weight, physiology, personality, mood, expectations, and previous experience with the drug. The dose and potency of the drug, the method of administration, and the setting in which the drug is taken also influence its effects.

NARCOTICS

Narcotics **(or opiates) are drugs derived from opium that are capable of relieving pain.** In legal regulations, the term *narcotic* is used in a haphazard way to refer to a variety of drugs besides opiates. Our discussion will focus on heroin and morphine, but many of the points also apply to less potent opiates such as codeine, Demerol (meperidine), and methadone.

Effects

The most significant narcotics problem in modern Western society involves the use of heroin. Most users inject heroin intravenously with a hypodermic needle. The main effect of the drug is an overwhelming sense of euphoria. This euphoric effect has a "Who cares?" quality to it that makes the heroin high an attractive escape from reality. Common side effects include nausea, lethargy, drowsiness, constipation, and slowed respiration.

Risks

Narcotics carry a high risk for both *psychological dependence* and *physical dependence*. It is estimated that there are about a half-million heroin addicts in the United States (Jaffe, 1986). Although heroin withdrawal usually isn't life-threatening, it can be excruciatingly unpleasant, so that "junkies" have a desperate need to continue their drug use. Once dependence is entrenched, people tend to develop a *drug-centered lifestyle* that revolves around the need to procure more heroin. This happens because the drug is very expensive (up to $200 a day) and available only through highly undependable black market channels. Obviously it is difficult to lead a productive life if one's existence is dominated by a desperate need to "score" heroin. The inordinate cost of heroin forces many junkies to resort to criminal activities to support their habit.

Overdose is also a very real danger with heroin. Part of the problem is that it is difficult to judge the purity of heroin obtained through black market sources. More important, opiates are additive with other CNS depressants. Most narcotic overdoses occur in combination with the use of sedatives or alcohol. Junkies also risk the *contraction of infectious disease* because they usually are sloppy about sterilizing their hypodermic needles. The most common of these diseases used to be hepatitis. In recent years, the Acquired Immune Deficiency Syndrome (AIDS) has been transmitted at an alarming rate through the population of intravenous drug users.

SEDATIVES

Sedatives **are sleep-inducing drugs that tend to decrease central nervous system activation and behavioral activity.** In street jargon, these drugs are often called "downers." Over the years, the most widely abused sedatives have been the barbiturates, which are compounds derived from barbituric acid. Although distinctions are made between barbiturate and nonbarbiturate sedatives, the functional differences are minimal.

Effects

People abusing sedatives generally consume larger doses than are prescribed for medical purposes. These overly large doses have a euphoric effect similar to that produced by drinking large amounts of alcohol. Feelings of tension, anxiety, and depression are temporarily replaced by a very relaxed, pleasant state of intoxication, in which inhibitions may be loosened. Sedatives carry a truckload of problematic side effects. Motor coordination suffers badly, producing slurred speech and a staggering walk, among other things. Intellectual functioning also becomes sluggish, and judgment is impaired. The user's emotional tone may become unstable, with feelings of dejection often intruding on the intended euphoric mood.

Risks

Sedatives have the potential to produce both *psychological dependence and physical dependence*. Furthermore, they compete closely with narcotics as the leading cause of *overdoses* in the United States (O'Brien & Woody, 1986). This is because of their additive interactions with other CNS depressants (especially alcohol) and because of the degree to which they impair one's judgment. In their drug-induced haze, sedative abusers are prone to take doses that they would ordinarily recognize as dangerous. Also, with prolonged use, the dose of barbiturates needed to produce a high increases more rapidly than the dose the body can handle (see Figure 14.17). Thus, the margin of safety between an intoxicating dose and a

Figure 14.17. Complexities in tolerance to barbiturates. Because of tolerance effects, the dosage of barbiturates needed to get high increases gradually with continued use. However, the dosage that the body can handle (the lethal dose) increases more slowly. Hence, the margin of difference between an intoxicating dose and a lethal dose gets smaller and smaller. (Because of individual differences among people, dosages on the left are only approximate.)

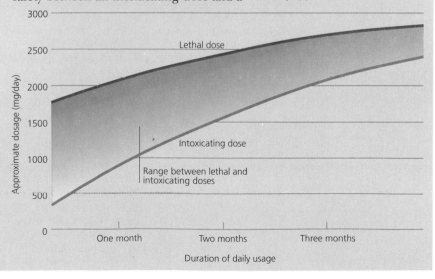

Recreational drug users come from all ages and all walks of life. Many people use drugs to spice up social activities.

lethal dose gradually narrows. Sedative users also elevate their risk for *accidental injuries* because these drugs can have drastic effects on motor coordination. Many users trip down stairs, fall off bar stools, get into automobile accidents, and so forth.

STIMULANTS

Stimulants **are drugs that tend to increase central nervous system activation and behavioral activity.** They range from mild, widely available stimulants, such as caffeine and nicotine, to stronger, carefully regulated stimulants, such as cocaine and amphetamines ("speed"). We'll focus on the latter two types of drugs.

Synthesized in a pharmaceutical laboratory, amphetamines are usually consumed orally. However, speed is also sold as a crystalline powder (called "crank") that may be snorted or injected intravenously. Recently, a smokable form of methamphetamine (called "ice") has been developed.

Cocaine is an organic substance extracted from the coca shrub, which grows most prominently in South America. It is usually consumed as a crystalline powder that is snorted through the nasal cavities. However, an increasing number of users are "freebasing" cocaine. Freebasing is chemical treatment that is

used to extract nearly pure cocaine concentrate from ordinary street cocaine. "Crack" is the most widely distributed by-product of this process, consisting of little chips of pure cocaine that are usually smoked. Because of its greater purity, smoking crack is far more dangerous than snorting cocaine powder. Also, smoking leads to a more rapid absorption of the drug into the bloodstream (Cregler & Mark, 1986).

Effects

Amphetamines and cocaine have fairly similar effects, except that cocaine produces a very brief high (20–30 minutes unless more is taken), while a speed high can last many hours. Stimulants produce a euphoria very different from that created by narcotics or sedatives. They produce a buoyant, elated, enthusiastic, energetic, "I can conquer the world!" feeling accompanied by increased alertness. Common side effects include increased blood pressure, muscle tension, sweating, and restlessness. Some users experience unpleasant feelings of irritability, anxiety, and paranoia.

Risks

Stimulants can cause *physical dependence*, but the physical distress caused by stimulant withdrawal is mild in comparison to that caused by narcotic or sedative withdrawal (Kleber & Gawin, 1986). *Psychological dependence* on stimulants is a much more common problem. Cocaine can create an exceptionally powerful psychological dependence that compels the user to pursue the drug with a fervor normally seen only with physical dependence. Both cocaine and amphetamines can suppress appetite and disrupt sleep. Thus, heavy use of stimulants may lead to poor eating, poor sleeping, and ultimately a *deterioration in physical health.* Some tentative evidence links heavy stimulant use to an increased risk of stroke, hypertension, and liver disease. Additionally, snorting cocaine through the nasal passages can produce serious nasal damage. Stimulant use occasionally leads to the onset of a severe *psychological disorder* that resembles paranoid schizophrenia (S. H. Snyder, 1979). This is a very debilitating disorder, dominated by paranoia, hallucinations, and poor contact with reality (see Chapter 15). All the risks associated with stimulant use increase greatly when more potent forms of the drugs (crack and ice) are used.

Overdoses on stimulants used to be relatively infrequent (Kalant & Kalant, 1979). However, in recent years, cocaine overdoses have increased sharply as more people have experimented with freebasing, smoking crack, and other more dangerous modes of ingestion (Mittleman & Wetli, 1984). The dangers of cocaine were underscored in a study of rats that were given unlimited access to heroin or cocaine (Bozarth & Wise, 1985). The rats "earned" drug injections delivered through implanted tubes by pressing a lever in an experimental chamber. The health of the rats on heroin deteriorated rapidly, and 36% of them died by the end of the 30-day study. The health of the rats on cocaine deteriorated even more rapidly, and by the end of the study 90% of them had died. Many of the rats on cocaine experienced severe seizures, but they would resume their lever pressing as soon as their convulsions subsided!

HALLUCINOGENS

Hallucinogens **are a diverse group of drugs that have powerful effects on mental and emotional functioning, marked most prominently by distortions in sensory and perceptual experience.** The principal hallucinogens are LSD, mescaline, and psilocybin,. These drugs have similar effects, although they vary in potency. Mescaline comes from the peyote plant, psilocybin from a particular type of mushroom. LSD is a synthetic drug.

Effects

Hallucinogens can intensify and distort perception in ways that are difficult to describe. They can produce awesome feelings of euphoria that sometimes include an almost mystical sense of "oneness" with the human race. This characteristic explains why they have been used in religious ceremonies in various cultures. Unfortunately, at the other end of the emotional spectrum, hallucinogens can also produce nightmarish feelings of anxiety, fear and paranoia, commonly called a "bad trip." Intellectual functioning is temporarily impaired as thought processes become meteoric but jumbled.

Risks

There is no potential for physical dependence on hallucinogens, and there are no known deaths attributable to overdose. Psychological dependence has been reported but appears to be very rare (Grinspoon & Bakalar, 1986). Research reports that LSD increases chromosome breakage were based on poor methodology (Dishotsky, Loughman, Mogar, & Lipscomb, 1971). However, like most drugs, hallucinogens may be harmful to a fetus if taken by a pregnant woman.

Although the dangers of hallucinogens have probably been exaggerated in the popular press, there are some significant risks. Emotion is highly volatile with these drugs, so that users can never be sure they won't experience *acute panic* from a terrifying bad trip. Generally, this disorientation subsides within a few hours, leaving no permanent emotional scars. However, in such a severe state of disorientation, *accidents and suicide* are possible. Users may experience *flashbacks*—vivid relivings of hallucinogenic experiences—months or even years after the original experience. Repetitious, frightening flashbacks can become very troublesome. A small minority of people who use hallucinogens subsequently develop a variety of *psychological disorders* that appear partially attributable to the drug (Hollister, 1978).

MARIJUANA

***Cannabis* is the hemp plant from which marijuana, hashish, and THC are derived.** Marijuana is a mixture of dried leaves, flowers, stems, and seeds taken from the plant. Hashish comes from the plant's resin. THC is the active chemical ingredient in cannabis that can be synthesized for research purposes (for example, to give to animals).

Effects

When smoked, cannabis has an almost immediate impact that may last several hours. The effects of the drug vary greatly, depending on the user's expectations and experience with the drug, the potency of the drug, and the amount smoked. The drug has subtle effects on emotion, perception, and cognition. Emotionally, the drug tends to create a mild, relaxed state of euphoria. Perceptually, it enhances the impact of incoming stimulation, thus making music sound better, food taste better, and so on. Cannabis tends to produce slight impairments in cognitive functioning (especially short-term memory) and perceptual-motor coordination while the user is high. However, there are huge variations among users (Jones, 1978).

Risks

Overdose and physical dependence are not problems, but like any other drug that produces pleasant feelings, marijuana has the potential to produce *psychological dependence*. There is no solid evidence that cannabis causes psychological disorders. However, marijuana can cause *transient problems with anxiety and depression* in some people. Some studies also suggest that cannabis may have a more *negative effect on driving* than widely believed. There is convincing evidence that marijuana use increases the chances for *respiratory and pulmonary diseases*, including lung cancer (Cohen, 1986).

The evidence on other widely publicized risks remains controversial. Here is a brief overview of the evidence on some of these controversies.

• *Does marijuana cause brain damage?* The handful of studies linking marijuana to brain damage have been shown to be methodologically unsound (Kuehnle, Mendelson, Davis, & New, 1977). Marijuana affects brain wave activity (Heath, 1976). However, there is no clear evidence that these changes in brain activity are permanent or pathological (Fried, 1977).

• *Does marijuana cause chromosome breakage?* There are inconsistent findings on this issue, but Cohen (1980) concludes that marijuana does not appear to elevate chromosomal breakage. High doses of THC have been shown to cause birth defects in animals. However, there is no evidence that marijuana causes birth defects in humans (Blum, 1984). Of course, caution dictates that pregnant women avoid using any drug.

• *Does marijuana reduce one's immunal response?* Cannabis may suppress the body's natural immune response slightly (Nahas, 1976). However, infectious diseases are no more common among marijuana smokers than nonsmokers. Hence, this effect apparently is too small to have any practical importance (Relman, 1982).

• *Does marijuana lead to impotence and sterility in men?* Cannabis appears to produce a small, reversible decline in sperm count among male smokers and may have temporary effects on hormone levels (Kolodny, Masters, Kolodner, & Toro, 1974). The popular media have frequently implied that marijuana therefore makes men sterile and impotent. In reality, there is no evidence that marijuana produces any lasting effects on male smokers' fertility or sexual functioning (Relman, 1982).

ALCOHOL

***Alcohol* encompasses a variety of beverages containing ethyl alcohol,** such as beers, wines, and distilled spirits. The concentration of alcohol in these drinks varies from about 4% in most beers up to 40% in 80-proof liquor (occasionally more in higher-proof liquors). Alcohol is the most widely used drug in our society. Because it is legal, many people use it very casually without even thinking of it as a drug.

Effects

The effects of alcohol are influenced by the user's experience, motivation, and mood, as well as by the presence of food in the stomach, the proof of the beverage, and the rate of drinking. Thus, there is great variability in how alcohol affects different people on different occasions. The central effect is a "Who cares?" brand of euphoria that temporarily boosts self-esteem as one's problems melt away. Negative emotions such as tension, worry, anxiety, and depression are dulled, and inhibitions may be loosened.

The side effects of alcohol are numerous. In substantial amounts, alcohol has a decidedly negative effect on intellectual functioning and perceptual-motor coordination. With their inhibitions released, some people become argumentative and prone to aggression. Finally, of course, there is that infamous source of regret, the "hangover," which may include headaches, dizziness, nausea, and vomiting.

Risks

Many people develop *psychological dependence* on alcohol, needing to drink constantly to alleviate anxiety or forget their problems. Eventually, *physical dependence* may be established. It's possible to *overdose* with alcohol alone, but a much more frequent problem is overdosing on combinations of alcohol and sedatives or narcotics. Estimates suggest that there are roughly 10 million alcoholics in the United States. *Drunk driving* is a major social problem. It has been estimated that alcohol contributes to 50% of all auto accidents.

Chronic, heavy alcohol consumption is associated with an elevated risk for a wide range of *serious health problems*. Included among these are liver disease, ulcers, pregnancy complications, malnutrition, heart disease, hypertension, stroke, some types of cancer, brain damage, and neurological disorders (Jones-Witters & Witters, 1983; Mello & Mendelson, 1978). Alcoholism can also produce severe *psychotic states*, characterized by delirium, disorientation, and hallucinations.

We have focused on the personal risks of drug abuse, but the enormous social costs of alcohol should be mentioned. Alcohol contributes to a substantial portion of drownings, fire fatalities, homicides, suicides, rapes, assaults, home accidents, and incidents of child abuse (see Figure 14.18). Alcohol-related absenteeism from work and reduced efficiency on the job cost American industry billions of dollars annually. It is hard to put a dollar value on the social costs of drug abuse, but one study (Harwood, Napolitano, Kristiansen, & Collins, 1984) estimated that alcohol cost the U.S. economy $89.5 billion in 1980. The comparable estimate for all other types of drugs *combined* was a little over half as much ($46.9 billion). In summary, the social costs of alcohol are staggering. Although it is legal (maybe *because* it is legal), alcohol is far and away the most problematic and costly of the recreational drugs.

OTHER DRUGS

Thus far, we have focused on the most commonly abused drugs in our culture. Most of these drugs have a history of abuse that goes back centuries, and even the newest have been around for many decades. In this section we'll briefly look at some newer, less widely abused drugs.

PCP

PCP (phencyclidine hydrochloride) is a perplexing drug that has gained some popularity in recent years. It is known on the street as "angel dust." PCP, which can

Alcohol misuse is blamed in . . .	
64% of murders in U.S.	50% of all road fatalities
41% of assaults	45% of fire deaths
34% of rapes	45% of drownings
29% of other sex crimes	22% of home accidents
30% of suicides	36% of pedestrian accidents
56% of fights or assaults in the home	55% of arrests
60% of child abuse	

Figure 14.18. The costs of alcohol. Although legal, alcohol is a very problematic drug, as the estimates shown here clearly demonstrate. All the estimates are based on U.S. statistics.

be synthesized easily by an illicit chemist, defies classification in that it has stimulant, hallucinogenic, and sedative effects (Vourakis & Bennett, 1979). This combination of effects produces a unique euphoria that often includes feelings of depersonalization.

Little is known about the long-term use of PCP, but the drug clearly carries many risks. Because of its sedative properties, overdose through respiratory depression is a problem. Although it is a less potent hallucinogen than LSD, PCP seems to produce a higher proportion of "bad trips," dominated by feelings of paranoia and agitation. PCP can produce a severe state of confusion and disorientation that has been linked to automobile accidents, drownings, and suicides. In fact, one study of 16 PCP-related deaths in the Los Angeles area (Noguchi & Nakamura, 1978) found that the majority were attributable to disordered behavior rather than to fatal doses of the drug.

Designer Drugs

Designer drugs **are illicitly manufactured variations on known recreational drugs.** Underground chemists typically make slight alterations in the chemical structure of opiates, amphetamines, or hallucinogens, assemble them into new combinations, or both. Designer drugs were originally invented to circumvent legal restrictions. Reasoning that authorities couldn't restrict drugs that didn't exist yet, enterprising drug dealers figured that they couldn't be prosecuted successfully for selling their new compounds. Flexible regulations that outlawed these new compounds were eventually developed. However, the market for designer drugs remains, and they continue to be manufactured.

The best-known designer drug is MDMA, which is sold on the street as "ecstasy" (Beck & Morgan, 1986). This compound is related to amphetamines and hallucinogens. It produces a short-lived high (about 90 minutes). Users feel warm, friendly, sensual, and serene, but alert. Problematic side effects include increased blood pressure, heart arrhythmias, and transient anxiety. Fentanyl is another designer drug that has gained a following among narcotics users (Stanford, 1987). Known on the street as "China white," this synthetic opiate is much more potent than heroin. It carries a very high risk of overdose.

The increasing popularity of designer drugs is especially alarming for two reasons. First, these drugs haven't been studied much yet, so their long-term risks are unknown. Second, these drugs are manufactured by "kitchen chemists" whose quality control varies enormously. Impurities, contaminants, and toxic by-products are often found in designer drugs because of inadvertent errors in the manufacturing process.

1. Explain how patterns of disease and conceptions of illness have changed in modern society.

2. List three ways in which psychological factors can influence health.

3. Describe the Type A behavior pattern and summarize the evidence linking it to coronary heart disease.

4. Summarize evidence linking stress to cancer and other diseases, immunal functioning, and accidents.

5. Give some reasons why people develop health-impairing habits.

6. Discuss the risks associated with smoking and the reasons people smoke.

7. Discuss the physiological and behavioral determinants of obesity.

8. Discuss fad diets and the key elements in effective weight loss.

9. Provide examples of links between nutrition and health and discuss the basis for poor nutrition.

10. List three general nutritional goals discussed in the text.

11. Summarize evidence on the benefits and risks of exercise.

12. List five guidelines for embarking on an effective exercise program.

13. List four guidelines for maximizing the quality of your sleep.

14. Discuss the text's suggestions for combatting insomnia.

15. Discuss the relationship between lifestyle factors and AIDS.

16. Discuss the subjective nature of pain.

17. Specify the crucial problem in treatment-seeking behavior and discuss correlates of treatment seeking.

18. Explain the appeal of the "sick role."

19. Discuss the prevalence of noncompliance with medical advice and its causes.

20. Explain various drug-related concepts discussed in the text.

21. Summarize the main effects and risks of narcotics, sedatives, stimulants, hallucinogens, marijuana, alcohol, PCP, and designer drugs.

KEY TERMS

Alcohol
Atherosclerosis
Basal metabolic rate
Biopsychosocial model
Cancer
Cannabis
Coronary heart disease
Designer drugs
Hallucinogens
Health psychology
Immune response
Insomnia
Narcotics
Nutrition

Obesity
Overdose
Physical dependence
Psychoactive drugs
Psychological dependence
REM sleep
Sedatives
Set point
Stimulants
Tolerance
Type A personality
Type B personality

KEY PEOPLE

Meyer Friedman &
Ray Rosenman

Stanley Schachter

Chronic Self-Destructiveness Scale

INSTRUCTIONS

For each of the following statements, indicate the degree to which the statement describes you. Record your responses in the spaces provided by writing in a letter from A to E, using the following scale: *A* expresses *strongest agreement*; *B* expresses *moderate agreement*; *C* indicates that you're *unsure* or *undecided*, or that it's a *toss-up*; *D* expresses *moderate disagreement*; *E* expresses *strongest disagreement*.

_____ 1. I like to listen to music with the volume turned up as loud as possible.

_____ 2. Life can be pretty boring.

_____ 3. When I was a kid, I was suspended from school.

_____ 4. I usually eat breakfast.

_____ 5. I do not stay late at school functions when I must get up early.

_____ 6. I use or have used street drugs.

_____ 7. I like to spend my free time "messing around."

_____ 8. As a rule, I do not put off doing chores.

_____ 9. Riding fast in a car is thrilling.

_____ 10. I tend to defy people in authority.

_____ 11. I have a complete physical examination once a year.

_____ 12. I have done dangerous things just for the thrill of it.

_____ 13. I am the kind of person who would stand up on a roller coaster.

_____ 14. I do not believe in gambling.

_____ 15. I find it necessary to plan my finances and keep a budget.

_____ 16. I let people take advantage of me.

_____ 17. I hate any kind of schedule or routine.

_____ 18. I usually meet deadlines with no trouble.

_____ 19. I am familiar with basic first-aid practices.

_____ 20. Even when I have to get up early, I like to stay up late.

_____ 21. I insist on traveling safely rather than quickly.

_____ 22. I have my car serviced regularly.

_____ 23. People tell me I am disorganized.

_____ 24. It is important to get revenge when someone does you wrong.

_____ 25. Sometimes I don't seem to care what happens to me.

_____ 26. I like to play poker for high stakes.

_____ 27. I smoke over a pack of cigarettes a day.

_____ 28. I have frequently fallen in love with the wrong person.

_____ 29. I just don't know where my money goes.

_____ 30. Wearing a helmet ruins the fun of a motorcycle ride.

_____ 31. I take care to eat a balanced diet.

_____ 32. Lots of laws seem made to be broken.

_____ 33. I am almost always on time.

_____ 34. I like jobs with an element of danger.

_____ 35. I often walk out in the middle of an argument.

_____ 36. Often I don't take very good care of myself.

_____ 37. I rarely put things off.

_____ 38. I speak my mind even when it's not in my best interest.

_____ 39. I usually follow through on projects.

_____ 40. I've made positive contributions to my community.

_____ 41. I make promises that I don't keep.

_____ 42. An occasional fight makes a guy more of a man.

_____ 43. I always do what my doctor or dentist recommends.

_____ 44. I know the various warning signs of cancer.

_____ 45 . I usually call a doctor when I'm sure I'm becoming ill.

_____ 46. I maintain an up-to-date address/phone book.

_____ 47. I sometimes forget important appointments I wanted to keep.

_____ 48. I drink two or fewer cups of coffee a day.

_____ 49. It's easy to get a raw deal from life.

_____ 50. I eat too much.

_____ 51. I often skip meals.

_____ 52. I don't usually lock my house or apartment door.

_____ 53. I know who to call in an emergency.

_____ 54. I can drink more alcohol than most of my friends.

_____ 55. The dangers from using contraceptives are greater than the dangers from not using them.

_____ 56. I seem to keep making the same mistakes.

_____ 57. I have my eyes examined at least once a year.

_____ 58. I lose often when I gamble for money.

_____ 59. I leave on an outdoor light when I know I'll be coming home late.

_____ 60. Using contraceptives is too much trouble.

_____ 61. I often use nonprescription medicines (aspirin, laxatives, etc.).

_____ 62. I do things I know will turn out badly.

_____ 63. When I was in high school, I was considered a good student.

_____ 64. I have trouble keeping up with bills and paperwork.

_____ 65. I rarely misplace even small sums of money.

_____ 66. I am frequently late for important things.

_____ 67. I frequently don't do boring things I'm supposed to do.

_____ 68. I feel really good when I'm drinking alcohol.

_____ 69. Sometimes when I don't have anything to drink, I think about how good some booze would taste.

_____ 70. It's really satisfying to inhale a cigarette.

_____ 71. I like to smoke.

_____ 72. I believe that saving money gives a person a real sense of accomplishment.

_____ 73. I like to exercise.

SCORING THE SCALE

The scoring instructions are different for males and females. The 73 items you just responded to actually represent two overlapping 52-item scales for each sex.

Females: Convert your letter responses to numbers from 1 to 5 (A = 1, B = 2, C = 3, D = 4, E = 5) for items 5, 8, 11, 15, 18, 19, 21, 22, 31, 33, 37, 39, 40, 43, 44, 45, 46, 53, and 63. Convert your responses in the opposite way (A = 5, B = 4, C = 3, D = 2, E = l) for items 1, 2, 6, 7, 9, 10, 12, 16, 17, 20, 23, 24, 25, 26, 28, 29, 30, 32, 36, 38, 41, 47, 49, 54, 56, 58, 60, 61, 62, 64, 66, 67, and 69. You should now have 52 items for which you have a number recorded instead of a letter. Add up these numbers, and the total is your score on the Chronic Self-Destructiveness Scale (CSDS) .

Males: Convert your letter responses to numbers from 1 to 5 (A = 1, B = 2, C = 3, D = 4, E = 5) for items 4, 14, 18, 21, 22, 39, 40, 45, 48, 53, 57, 59, 63, 65, 72, and 73. Convert your responses in the opposite way (A = 5, B = 4, C = 3, D = 2, E = l) for items 2, 3, 10, 12, 13, 17, 25, 26, 27, 28, 29, 30, 32, 34, 35, 36, 41, 42, 47, 49, 50, 51, 52, 54, 55, 56, 58, 60, 62, 64, 66, 67, 68, 69, 70, and 71. You should now have 52 items for which you have a number recorded instead of a letter. Add up these numbers, and the total is your score on the Chronic Self-Destructiveness Scale (CSDS).

MY SCORE _____

WHAT THE SCALE MEASURES

Developed by Kathryn Kelley and associates (Kelley et al., 1985), this scale measures your tendency to behave in a self-destructive manner. Kelley et al. (1985) define chronic self-destructiveness as a generalized tendency to engage in acts that increase the likelihood of future negative consequences and/or decrease the likelihood of future positive consequences. In other words, chronic self-destructiveness involves behavior that probably will be detrimental to one's well-being in the long run. This self-destructive quality is viewed as an aspect of personality that may underlie a diverse array of counterproductive, often health-impairing habits.

In their initial series of studies, Kelley et al. (1985) administered their scale to 12 groups of undergraduates, a group of business-women, and a group of hospital patients. In comparison to people with low scores, high scorers on the CSDS were more likely to (a) report having cheated in classes, (b) have violated traffic laws, (c) indulge in drug or alcohol abuse meriting treatment, (d) recall a rebellious stage in adolescence, and (e) postpone important medical tests.

INTERPRETING YOUR SCORE

Our norms are based on 234 female and 168 male undergraduates studied by Kelley et al. (1985). In light of the age trends mentioned above, these norms may not be appropriate for older students.

NORMS	Females	Males
High score	157–260	158–260
Intermediate score	105–156	97–157
Low score	52–104	52–96

How Do Your Health Habits Rate?

Eating habits	Almost always	Some-times	Almost never
1. I eat a variety of foods each day, such as fruits and vegetables, whole-grain breads and cereals, lean meats, dairy products, dry peas and beans, and nuts and seeds.	4	1	0
2. I limit the amount of fat, saturated fat, and cholesterol I eat (including fat on meats, eggs, butter, cream, shortenings, and organ meats such as liver).	2	1	0
3. I limit the amount of salt I eat by cooking with only small amounts, not adding salt at the table, and avoiding salty snacks.	2	1	0
4. I avoid eating too much sugar (especially frequent snacks of sticky candy or soft drinks).	2	1	0

Eating habits score: _____

Exercise/fitness	Almost always	Some-times	Almost never
1. I maintain a desired weight, avoiding overweight and underweight.	3	1	0
2. I do vigorous exercises for 15 to 30 minutes at least three times a week (examples include running, swimming, and brisk walking).	3	1	0
3. I do exercises that enhance my muscle tone for 15 to 30 minutes at least three times a week (examples include yoga and calisthenics).	2	1	0
4. I use part of my leisure time participating in individual, family, or team activities that increase my level of fitness (such as gardening, bowling, golf, and baseball).	2	1	0

Exercise/fitness score: _____

Alcohol and drugs	Almost always	Some-times	Almost never
1. I avoid drinking alcoholic beverages *or* I drink no more than one or two drinks a day.	4	1	0
2. I avoid using alcohol or other drugs (especially illegal drugs) as a way of handling stressful situations or the problems in my life.	2	1	0
3. I am careful not to drink alcohol when taking certain medicines (for example, medicine for sleeping, pain, colds, and allergies).	2	1	0
4 I read and follow the label directions when using prescribed and over-the-counter drugs.	2	1	0

Alcohol and drugs score: _____

What your scores mean:

9–10   Excellent

6–8   Good

3–5   Mediocre

0–2   Poor

Do any of your scores surprise you? Why?

Adapted from "Health Style: A Self-Test." Washington, D.C.: U.S. Department of Health and Human Services, Public Health Service, PHS 81-50155, 1981.

15
Psychological Disorders

"The government of the United States was overthrown more than a year ago! I'm the president of the United States of America and Bob Dylan is vice president!" So said Ed, the author of a prominent book on journalism, who was speaking to a college journalism class as a guest lecturer. Ed also informed the class that he had killed both John and Robert Kennedy, as well as Charles de Gaulle, the former premier of France. He went on to tell the class that all rock music songs were written about him, that he was the greatest karate expert in the universe, and that he had been fighting "space wars" for 2000 years. The students in the class were mystified by Ed's bizarre, disjointed "lecture," but they assumed that he was putting on a show that would eventually lead to a sensible conclusion. Their perplexed but expectant calm was shattered when Ed pulled a hatchet from the props he had brought with him and hurled the hatchet at the class! Fortunately, the hatchet sailed over the students' heads. At that point, the professor for the class realized that Ed's irrational behavior was not a pretense. The professor evacuated the class quickly while Ed continued to rant and rave about his presidential administration, space wars, vampires, his romances with female rock stars, and his personal harem of 38 'chicks.' " [Adapted from Pearce, 1974, pp. 40–41]

Clearly, Ed's behavior was abnormal. Even he recognized that when he agreed later to be admitted to a mental hospital, signing himself in as the "President of the United States of America." What causes such abnormal behavior? Does Ed have a mental illness, or does he just behave strangely? What is the basis for judging behavior as normal versus abnormal? Are people who have psychological disorders dangerous? How common are such disorders? Can they be cured? These are just a few of the questions that we will address in this chapter as we discuss psychological disorders and their complex causes.

ABNORMAL BEHAVIOR: MYTHS, REALITIES, AND CONTROVERSIES

Misconceptions about abnormal behavior are common. Hence, we need to clear up some preliminary issues before we describe the various types of disorders. In this section, we will discuss (1) the medical model of abnormal behavior, (2) the criteria of abnormal behavior, (3) stereotypes regarding psychological disorders, (4) the classification of psychological disorders, and (5) how common such disorders are.

The Medical Model Applied to Abnormal Behavior

In Ed's case, there's no question that his behavior was abnormal. But does it make sense to view his unusual and irrational behavior as a disease? This is a very controversial question. **The *medical model* proposes that it is useful to think of abnormal behavior as a disease.** This point of view is the basis for many of the terms that are used to refer to abnormal behavior, including mental *illness*, psychological *disorder*, and psycho*pathology* (*pathology* refers to manifestations of disease). The medical model gradually became the dominant way of thinking about abnormal behavior during the 18th and 19th centuries, and its influence remains strong today.

The medical model clearly represented progress over earlier models of abnormal behavior. Prior to the 18th century, most conceptions of abnormal behavior were based on superstition. People who behaved strangely were thought to be possessed by demons, witches in league with the devil, or victims of God's punishment. Their disorders were "treated" with chants, rituals, exorcisms, and such. If their behavior was seen as threatening, they were candidates for chains, dungeons, torture, and death (see Figure 15.1).

The rise of the medical model brought great improvements in the treatment of people who exhibited abnormal behavior. As victims of an illness, they were viewed

Figure 15.1. Historical conceptions of mental illness. Throughout most of history, psychological disorders were thought to be caused by demonic possession, and the mentally ill were candidates for chains and torture.

with sympathy rather than hatred and fear. Although living conditions in early asylums were often deplorable, there was gradual progress toward more humane care of the mentally ill. It took time, but ineffectual approaches to treatment eventually gave way to scientific investigation of the causes and cures of psychological disorders.

Problems with the Medical Model

In recent decades, however, critics have suggested that the medical model may have outlived its usefulness. A particularly vocal critic has been Thomas Szasz (1974). Szasz asserts that "strictly speaking, disease or illness can affect only the body; hence there can be no mental illness. . . . Minds can be 'sick' only in the sense that jokes are 'sick' or economies are 'sick'" (1974, p. 267). He further argues that abnormal behavior usually involves a deviation from social norms rather than an illness. He contends that such deviations are "problems in living" rather than medical problems. According to Szasz, the medical model's disease analogy converts moral and social questions about what is acceptable behavior into medical questions. Under the guise of "healing the sick," this conversion allegedly allows modern society to lock up deviant people and to enforce its norms of conformity.

The medical model has been criticized on other grounds, too. Three criticisms are especially prominent.

1. *Labeling.* Some critics are troubled because medical diagnoses of abnormal behavior pin potentially derogatory labels on people (Becker, 1973; Rothblum, Solomon, & Albee, 1986). Being labeled psychotic, schizophrenic, or mentally ill carries a social stigma that can be difficult to shake. Even after a full recovery, someone who has been labeled mentally ill may have difficulty finding a place to live, getting a job, or making friends. Deep-seated prejudice against people who have been labeled mentally ill is commonplace. The stigma of mental illness is not impossible to shed (Gove, 1975), but it undoubtedly creates additional difficulties for people who already have their share of problems.

Critics of the medical model also maintain that diagnostic labels such as *alcoholic* or *neurotic* can create unfortunate self-fulfilling prophecies (Scheff, 1975). Some people who are labeled alcoholic, for instance, seem to accept this designation as part of their identity. They proceed to live out the "alcoholic role" created for them instead of working to alter their behavior and conquer their problems.

2. *Pseudoexplanations.* Other critics of the medical model argue that the technical-sounding diagnoses that are part of the medical approach create an illusion that we understand more than we really do (Krasner & Ullmann, 1965). For instance, let's say that a fellow arrives at a psychiatric facility exhibiting a variety of symptoms that are characteristic of schizophrenic disorders. He says that he hears voices of nonexistent people, and he displays withdrawal, flat emotions, and disorganized, incoherent thinking. He is correctly diagnosed as having a schizophrenic disorder. Later, his bewildered family asks, "Doctor, why does he behave in these strange ways?" The doctor may often reply, "Because he is schizophrenic." That explanation may *sound* reasonable, but it's a pseudoexplanation involving circular reasoning. Saying that someone exhibits schizophrenic behavior because he is a schizophrenic is like saying that the reason a woman has red hair is that she is a redhead.

It is *not* accurate to say that a patient hears voices and is withdrawn, emotionally flat, and incoherent *because* he is schizophrenic. Quite the opposite is true. He is called "schizophrenic" because he hears voices and is withdrawn, emotionally flat, and incoherent. Schizophrenia and other diagnoses are only descriptive labels. They are not explanations of abnormal behavior.

3. *The patient role.* The medical model has also been criticized because it suggests that people with behavioral problems should adopt the passive role of medical patient (Korchin, 1976). In this passive role, mental patients are implicitly encouraged to wait for their therapists to do the work to effect a cure. Such passiveness can be problematic even when an illness is purely physical. In psychological

Thomas Szasz

disorders, this passiveness can seriously undermine the likelihood of improvement in the person's condition. In general, people with psychological problems need to be actively involved in their recovery efforts.

Putting the Medical Model in Perspective

So, what position should we take on the medical model? In this chapter, we will assume an intermediate position, neither entirely accepting the model nor entirely discarding it. There certainly are significant problems with the medical model, and the questions raised by its critics deserve serious attention. However, in its defense, the medical model *has* stimulated scientific research on abnormal behavior. Moreover, some of the problems that are blamed on the disease analogy are not unique to this conception of abnormality. People who displayed strange, irrational behavior were labeled and stigmatized long before the medical model came along. Pseudoexplanations of psychological disorders were even more common and more primitive before the advent of the medical model.

Hence, we'll take the position that the disease analogy *can* be useful as long as we remember that it is *only* an analogy. Medical concepts such as *diagnosis, etiology*, and *prognosis* have proven useful in the treatment and study of abnormality. *Diagnosis* **involves distinguishing one illness from another.** *Etiology* **refers to the apparent causation and developmental history of an illness. A** *prognosis* **is a forecast about the probable course of an illness.** These concepts have widely shared meanings that permit clinicians, researchers, and the public to communicate more effectively in their discussions of abnormal behavior.

So, flawed though it may be, we will employ the disease analogy and use terms such as *abnormal behavior, mental illness*, and *psychological disorders* interchangeably. Do keep in mind, however, that the medical model is only an analogy. Most psychological disorders are not genuine diseases. Medical labels do not explain abnormal behavior, and we need to be wary of the negative stereotypes associated with these labels. Remember, too, that the passive role of medical patient is not well suited to the treatment of psychological problems. With these thoughts in mind, let's discuss the criteria that are employed in judgments of mental health and mental illness.

Criteria of Abnormal Behavior

If your next-door neighbor scrubs his front porch twice every day and spends virtually all his time cleaning and recleaning his house, is he normal? If your sister-in-law goes to one physician after another to seek treatment for aches and pains that appear imaginary, is she psychologically healthy? How are we to judge what's normal and what's abnormal? More important, who is to judge?

These are complex questions. In a sense, we *all* make judgments about normality, in that we all express opinions about others' (and perhaps our own) mental health. Of course, formal diagnoses of psychological disorders are made by mental health professionals. In making these judgments, clinicians and laypeople generally apply the same criteria, albeit with highly varied levels of knowledge. Let's examine the criteria that are most frequently used in judgments of abnormality. Although two or three criteria may apply in a particular case, people are often viewed as disordered when only one criterion is met.

Deviance. As Szasz has pointed out, people often are said to have a disorder because their behavior deviates from what their society considers acceptable. Norms about normality vary somewhat from one culture to another, but all cultures have such norms. When people ignore these standards and expectations, they may be labeled mentally ill. Consider transvestites, for instance. *Transvestism* **is a sexual disorder in which a man achieves sexual arousal by dressing in women's clothing.** This behavior is regarded as disordered because a man who wears a dress, brassiere, and nylons is deviating from our culture's norms. The example of transvestism illustrates the arbi-

Figure 15.2. Normality and abnormality as a continuum. There isn't a sharp boundary between normal versus abnormal behavior. Behavior is normal or abnormal in degree, depending on the extent to which it is deviant, personally distressing, or maladaptive.

trary nature of cultural standards regarding normality. In our society, it is normal for women to dress in men's clothing, but not vice versa. Thus, exactly the same overt behavior (cross-sex dressing) is acceptable for one sex but deviant for the other!

Maladaptive behavior. In many cases, people are judged to have a psychological disorder because their everyday adaptive behavior is impaired. For example, this is the key criterion in the diagnosis of substance use (drug) disorders. In and of itself, recreational drug use is neither unusual nor necessarily deviant. However, when the use of cocaine, for instance, begins to interfere with a person's social or occupational functioning, a substance use disorder exists. In such cases, it is the maladaptive quality of the behavior that makes it disordered.

Personal distress. Frequently, the diagnosis of a psychological disorder is based on an individual's report of great personal distress. This is usually the criterion met by people who are troubled by depression or anxiety disorders. Depressed people, for instance, may or may not exhibit deviant or maladaptive behavior. Such people are usually labeled as having a disorder when they describe their subjective pain and suffering to friends, relatives, and mental health professionals.

Normality and Abnormality as a Continuum

Antonyms such as *normal* versus *abnormal* and *mental health* versus *mental illness* imply that people can be divided neatly into two distinct groups: those who are normal and those who are not. In reality, it is often difficult to draw a line that clearly separates normality from abnormality. On occasion, we all experience personal distress. We all act in deviant ways once in a while. And we all display some maladaptive behavior. People are judged to have psychological disorders only when their behavior becomes *extremely* deviant, maladaptive, or distressing. Thus, normality and abnormality exist on a continuum. It's a matter of degree, not an either-or proposition (see Figure 15.2).

The Cultural Bounds of Normality

Judgments of normality and abnormality are influenced by cultural norms and values. Behavior that is considered deviant or maladaptive in one society may be quite acceptable in another. For example, in modern Western society people who "hear voices" are assumed to be irrational and are routinely placed in mental hospitals. However, in some cultures, hearing voices is commonplace and hardly merits a raised eyebrow.

Cultural norms regarding acceptable behavior may change over time. For example, consider how views of homosexuality have changed in our society. Homosexuality used to be listed as a sexual disorder in the American Psychiatric Association's diagnostic system. However, in 1973 a committee appointed by the association voted to delete homosexuality from the official list of psychological disorders. This action occurred for several reasons. First, attitudes toward homosexuality in our society had become more accepting. Second, gay rights activists campaigned vigorously for the change. Third, research showed that gays and heterosexuals did not differ overall on measures of psychological health (Rothblum, Solomon, & Albee, 1986). As you might guess, this change stimulated a great deal of debate.

Gays are not the only group that has tried to influence the psychiatric diagnostic system. For example, in recent years, women's groups have lobbied against adding a new diagnosis called *masochistic personality disorder*, because they thought it would be applied in sexist ways to women who were victims of wife-battering (Kass, Spitzer, Williams, & Widiger, 1989).

The key point is that diagnoses of psychological disorders involve *value judgments* about what represents normal or abnormal behavior. The criteria of mental illness are not nearly as value-free as the criteria of physical illness. In evaluating physical diseases, people usually can agree that a weak heart or a bad kidney is pathological, regardless of their personal values. However, judgments about mental illness reflect prevailing cultural values,

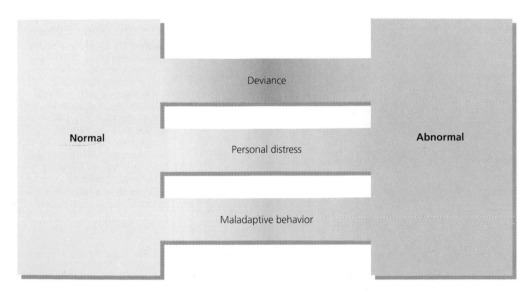

Normal

Abnormal

Deviance

Personal distress

Maladaptive behavior

social trends, and political forces as well as scientific knowledge.

Stereotypes of Psychological Disorders

We've seen that mental illnesses are not diseases in a strict sense and that judgments of mental health are not value-free. However, there are still other myths about abnormal behavior that need to be exposed as such. Let's examine four stereotypes about psychological disorders that are largely inaccurate.

1. *Psychological disorders are a sign of personal weakness.* Psychological disorders are often seen as a manifestation of personal weakness and thus are a source of shame. In reality, psychological disorders are a function of many factors—such as genetic predisposition, family background, and exposure to stress—over which we have little or no control. Mental illness can strike anyone. Mentally ill people are no more to blame for their troubles than people who develop leukemia or other physical illnesses.

2. *Psychological disorders are incurable.* Admittedly, there are mentally ill people for whom treatment is largely a failure. However, they are greatly outnumbered by people who *do* get better, either spontaneously or through formal treatment. The vast majority of people who are diagnosed as mentally ill eventually improve and lead normal, productive lives. Even the most severe psychological disorders can be treated successfully.

3. *People with psychological disorders are often violent and dangerous.* There appears to be little or no association between mental illness and violence-prone tendencies (Cockerham, 1981). This stereotype exists because incidents of violence involving the mentally ill tend to command media attention. For example, our opening case history, which described Ed's breakdown and the incident with the hatchet, was written up in a national newsmagazine. People such as John Hinckley, whose mental illness led him to attempt an assassination of President Reagan, receive extensive publicity. However, these indi-

viduals are not representative of the large number of people who have struggled with psychological disorders.

4. *People with psychological disorders behave in bizarre ways and are very different from normal people.* This is true only in a small minority of cases, usually involving relatively severe disorders. At first glance, people with psychological disorders usually are indistinguishable from those without disorders. A study by David Rosenhan (1973) showed that even mental health professionals may have difficulty distinguishing normality from abnormality. To study diagnostic accuracy, Rosenhan arranged for a number of normal people to seek admission to mental hospitals. These "pseudopatients" arrived at the hospitals complaining of one false symptom—hearing voices. Except for this single symptom, they acted as they normally would and gave accurate information when interviewed about their personal histories. *All* the pseudopatients were admitted, and the average length of their hospitalization was 19 days! Why is it so hard to distinguish normality from abnormality? The pseudopatients' observations about life on the psychiatric wards offer a clue. They noted that the real patients acted normal most of the time and only infrequently acted in a deviant manner.

As you might imagine, Rosenhan's study evoked quite a controversy about our diagnostic system for mental illness. Let's take a look at how this diagnostic system has evolved.

Psychodiagnosis: The Classification of Disorders

We can't lump all psychological disorders together without giving up hope of understanding them better. Hence, a great deal of effort has been invested in devising an elaborate system for classifying psychological disorders.

A modern landmark in this classification effort was established in 1952 when the American Psychiatric Association unveiled its *Diagnostic and Statistical Manual of Mental Disorders.* Known as DSM-I, this classification scheme described 60 disorders. Revisions intended to improve

David Rosenhan

Figure 15.3. Overview of the DSM-III-R system. DSM-III-R is the formal classification system used in the diagnosis of psychological disorders. It is a *multiaxial* system, which means that information is recorded on the five axes described here. (Adapted with permission from the *Diagnostic and Statistical Manual of Mental Disorders* [third edition, revised]. Copyright 1987, American Psychiatric Association.)

the system were completed in 1968 (DSM-II), 1980 (DSM-III), and 1987 (DSM-III-R). The next edition (DSM-IV) is due in 1993 (Frances, Widiger, & Pincus, 1989). Each revision of the DSM system has expanded the list of disorders covered. The current version, DSM-III-R, describes over 200 types of psychological disorders.

The Multiaxial System

The publication of DSM-III in 1980 introduced a new *multiaxial system* of classification. The multiaxial system asks for judgments about individuals on five separate dimensions, or "axes." Figure 15.3 provides an overview of the entire system and the five axes. The diagnoses of disorders are made on Axes I and II. Clinicians record any major disorders that are apparent on Axis I. They use Axis II to list any personality or developmental disorders, which often coexist with Axis I syndromes. People may receive diagnoses on both axes.

The remaining axes are used to record supplemental information. A patient's physical disorders are listed on

Axis I
Major Clinical Syndromes

1 *Disorders usually first evident in infancy, childhood, or adolescence*
This category includes disorders that arise before adolescence, such as attention deficit disorders, bulimia, anorexia, enuresis, and stuttering.

2 *Organic mental disorders*
These disorders are temporary or permanent dysfunctions of brain tissue caused by diseases or chemicals. Examples are delirium, dementia, and amnesia.

3 *Psychoactive substance-use disorders*
This category refers to the *maladaptive* use of drugs and alcohol. Mere consumption and recreational use of such substances are not disorders. This category requires an abnormal pattern of use, as with alcohol abuse and cocaine dependence.

4 *Schizophrenic disorders*
The schizophrenias are characterized by psychotic symptoms (for example, grossly disorganized behavior, delusions, and hallucinations) and by over 6 months of behavioral deterioration.

5 *Delusional disorders*
These disorders, of which paranoia is the most common, are characterized by persecutory delusions in the absence of other psychotic symptoms. In general, delusional patients are less impaired than schizophrenics.

6 *Mood disorders*
The cardinal feature is emotional disturbance. Patients may, or may not, have psychotic symptoms. These disorders include major depression, bipolar disorder, dysthymic disorder, and cyclothymic disorder.

7 *Anxiety disorders*
These disorders are characterized by physiological signs of anxiety (for example, palpitations) and subjective feelings of tension, apprehension, or fear. Anxiety may be acute and focused (panic disorder) or continual and diffuse (generalized anxiety disorder).

8 *Somatoform disorders*
These disorders are dominated by somatic symptoms that resemble physical illnesses. The symptoms cannot be accounted for by organic damage. There *must* also be strong evidence that these symptoms are produced by psychological factors or conflicts. This category includes somatization and conversion disorders and hypochondriasis.

9 *Dissociative disorders*
These disorders all feature a sudden, temporary alteration or dysfunction of memory, consciousness, identity, and behavior, as in depersonalization disorder, psychogenic amnesia, and multiple personality.

10 *Psychosexual disorders*
Psychological factors play major etiological roles in all of these disorders. There are 3 basic types: gender identity disorders (discomfort with identity as male or female), paraphilias (preference for unusual acts to achieve sexual arousal), and sexual dysfunctions (impairments in sexual functioning).

Axis II
Personality and Developmental Disorders

Personality disorders
These disorders are patterns of personality traits that are long standing, maladaptive, and inflexible and involve impaired functioning or subjective distress. Examples include borderline, schizoid, and passive-aggressive personality disorders.

Specific developmental disorders
These are disorders of specific developmental areas that are not due to another disorder. Examples include mental retardation, autism, and reading, writing, and arithmetic disorders.

Axis III
Physical Disorders and Conditions

Physical disorders or conditions are recorded on this axis. Examples include diabetes, arthritis, and hemophilia.

Axis IV
Severity of Psychosocial Stressors

Code	Term	Adult example
1	None	No relevant events
2	Mild	Starting or graduating from school
3	Moderate	Loss of job
4	Severe	Divorce
5	Extreme	Death of loved one
6	Catastrophic	Devastating natural disaster

Axis V
Global Assesment of Functioning (GAF) Scale

Code	Symptoms
90	Absent or minimal symptoms, good functioning in all areas.
80	Symptoms are transient and expectable reactions to psychosocial stressors.
70	Some mild symptoms or some difficulty in social, occupational, or school functioning, but generally functioning pretty well.
60	Moderate symptoms or difficulty in social, occupational, or school functioning.
50	Serious symptoms or impairment in social, occupational, or school functioning.
40	Some impairment in reality testing or communication, or major impairment in family relations, judgment, thinking, or mood.
30	Behavior is considerably influenced by delusions or hallucinations, serious impairment in communication or judgment, or inability to function in almost all areas.
20	Some danger of hurting self or others, occasional failure to maintain minimal personal hygiene, or gross impairment in communication.
10	Persistent danger of severely hurting self or others.

Axis III. On Axis IV, the clinician makes notations and ratings on the severity of stress experienced by the individual in the past year. On Axis V, estimates are made of the individual's current level of adaptive functioning (social and occupational behavior, viewed as a whole) and of the individual's highest level of functioning in the past year.

Most theorists agree that the multiaxial system is a step in the right direction because it recognizes the importance of several kinds of information besides a traditional diagnostic label. However, it appears that clinicians make little use of Axis III (Maricle, Leung, & Bloom, 1987). Furthermore, Axes IV and V are poorly defined and there is little evidence regarding their validity (Rey et al., 1988; Williams, 1985). Further research should lead to improvement of the supplementary axes in future editions of the DSM system.

Controversies over New Directions

You have undoubtedly heard people described as "neurotic." In the future, you will probably hear such descriptions less frequently. In a controversial move, DSM-III did away with a long-standing distinction between *neuroses* and *psychoses*, making both terms somewhat dated. Essentially, the accumulated evidence indicated that the disorders listed in each of these categories did not share enough in common to merit being grouped together. These disorders still exist, but they have been subdivided into smaller groups that have more in common.

Although neurosis and psychosis are not official diagnostic categories anymore, these concepts are still used informally as broad descriptive terms. **Neurotic refers to behavior marked by subjective distress (usually chronic anxiety) and reliance on avoidance coping.** People who are characterized as neurotic may be deeply troubled, but their reality contact and adaptive behavior are basically sound. In contrast, **psychotic refers to behavior marked by impaired reality contact and profound deterioration of adaptive functioning.** Generally, psychotic behavior is more obvious, more problematic for society, and more debilitating for the individual.

DSM-III also sparked controversy by adding everyday problems that are not traditionally thought of as mental illnesses to the diagnostic system. For example, DSM-III-R includes an academic underachievement disorder (not performing up to ability in school). It also includes a nicotine dependence disorder (distress derived from quitting smoking). Critics argue that everyday problems such as these should not be listed in the diagnostic structure because this listing casts the shadow of pathology on normal behavior (McReynolds, 1979). However, critics of the *old* system (DSM-II) complained because it omitted many common problems that were being treated by psychologists and psychiatrists.

Shifting definitions of normality and abnormality inevitably affect estimates regarding the number of people who suffer from psychological disorders. The changes made in DSM-III stimulated a flurry of research on the prevalence of specific mental disorders. Let's examine some of this research.

The Prevalence of Psychological Disorders

How common are psychological disorders? What percentage of the population is afflicted with mental illness? Is it 10%? Perhaps 25%? Could the figure range as high as 40% or 50%?

Such questions fall within the domain of **epidemiology, which is the study of the distribution of mental or physical disorders in a population.** In epidemiology, *prevalence* **refers to the percentage of people in a population who exhibit a disorder during a specified time period.** In the case of psychological disorders, the most interesting data are the estimates of *lifetime prevalence*, the percentage of people who endure a specific disorder at any time in their lives.

Estimates of lifetime prevalence suggest that psychological disorders are more common than most people realize. Prior to the advent of DSM-III, studies suggested that about *one fifth* of the population exhibited clear signs of mental illness at some time in their lives (Neugebauer,

Figure 15.4. Prevalence of common psychological disorders in the United States. The graph shows the estimated percentage of people who have ever suffered from each of four types of psychological disorders or from any kind of disorder (top bar). (Based on Robins et al., 1984)

Dohrenwend, & Dohrenwend, 1980). However, the older studies did not assess drug-related disorders very effectively, because these disorders were vaguely described in DSM-I and DSM-II. More recent studies, employing the explicit criteria for substance-use disorders in DSM-III, have found psychological disorders in roughly *one third* of the population! This increase in mental illness is more apparent than real, as it is mostly due to more effective tabulation of drug-related disorders. As Figure 15.4 shows, the most common disorders are (1) substance-use disorders, (2) anxiety disorders, and (3) mood disorders (Robins et al., 1984).

The raw numbers are more dramatic than the prevalence rates in Figure 15.4. Estimates based on these prevalence rates suggest that the United States contains nearly 4 million people who will be troubled at some time by schizophrenic disorders. Roughly 20 million people will experience depressive disorders. Approximately 40 million people will wrestle with anxiety disorders, and 42 million with substance-use disorders. If you're thinking that these estimates add up to more than one third of the population, you're right. The number of afflicted individuals is somewhat lower because some people have more than one disorder. Still, it's clear that psychological disorders are widespread. When psychologists note that mental illness can strike anyone, they mean it quite literally.

We are now ready to start examining the specific types of psychological disorders. Obviously, we cannot cover all 200 or so disorders listed in DSM-III. However, we will introduce most of the major categories of disorders to give you an overview of the many forms abnormal behavior takes. In discussing each set of disorders, we will begin with brief descriptions of the specific syndromes or subtypes that fall in the category. Then we'll focus on the *etiology* of the disorders in that category. Although there are many paths that may lead to specific disorders, some are more common than others. We'll highlight some of the common paths to enhance your understanding of the roots of abnormal behavior.

ANXIETY DISORDERS

We all experience anxiety from time to time. Anxiety is a natural and common reaction to many of life's difficulties. For some people, however, anxiety becomes a chronic problem. These people experience high levels of anxiety with disturbing regularity. **Anxiety disorders are a class of disorders marked by feelings of excessive apprehension and anxiety.** Studies suggest that anxiety disorders are fairly common, occurring in roughly 10%–15% of the population (Robins et al., 1984; Weissman, 1985). There are four principal types of anxiety disorders: generalized anxiety disorders, phobic disorders, panic disorders, and obsessive-compulsive disorders.

Generalized Anxiety Disorders

The *generalized anxiety disorder* is marked by a chronic, high level of anxiety that is not tied to any specific threat. This anxiety is sometimes called "free-floating anxiety" because of its nonspecific nature. People with this disorder worry constantly about yesterday's mistakes and tomorrow's problems. They often dread decisions and brood over them endlessly. Their anxiety is frequently accompanied by physical symptoms, such as trembling, muscle tension, diarrhea, dizziness, faintness, sweating, and heart palpitations.

Phobic Disorders

In a phobic disorder, an individual's troublesome anxiety has a specific focus. **A *phobic disorder* is marked by a persistent and irrational fear of an object or situation that presents no realistic danger.** The following case provides an example of a phobic disorder.

Hilda is 32 years of age and has a rather unusual fear. She is terrified of snow. She cannot go outside in the snow. She cannot even stand to see snow or hear about it on the weather report. Her phobia severely constricts her day-to-day behavior. Probing

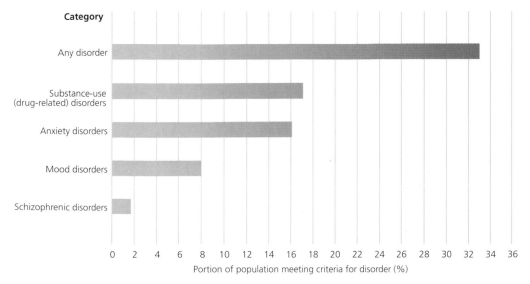

Category

Any disorder

Substance-use (drug-related) disorders

Anxiety disorders

Mood disorders

Schizophrenic disorders

0   2   4   6   8   10 12 14 16 18 20 22 24 26 28 30 32 34 36

Portion of population meeting criteria for disorder (%)

in therapy revealed that her phobia was caused by a traumatic experience at age 11. Playing at a ski lodge, she was buried briefly by a small avalanche of snow. She had no recollection of this experience until it was recovered in therapy. [Adapted from Laughlin, 1967, p. 227]

As Hilda's unusual snow phobia illustrates, people can develop phobic responses to virtually anything. Nonetheless, certain types of phobias are relatively common, including most of those listed in Figure 15.5. Particularly common are claustrophobia (fear of small, enclosed places), various animal phobias, and social phobias (fears of humiliation in interpersonal situations). Claustrophobia tends to develop before age 35, whereas animal phobias usually emerge during childhood and social phobias during adolescence (Ost, 1987). Many people troubled by phobias realize that their fears are irrational, but they still are unable to calm themselves when confronted by a phobic object.

Panic Disorders and Agoraphobia

A *panic disorder* **involves recurrent attacks of overwhelming anxiety that usually occur suddenly and unexpectedly.** These paralyzing attacks are accompanied by physical symptoms of anxiety. After a number of anxiety attacks, victims often become very apprehensive, wondering when their next panic will occur. Their concern about exhibiting panic in public may escalate to the point where they are afraid to leave home. This creates a condition called *agoraphobia*, which is a common complication of panic disorders.

Agoraphobia **is a fear of going out to public places** (its literal meaning is "fear of the marketplace or open places"). Because of this fear, some people become prisoners confined to their homes. As its name suggests, agoraphobia has traditionally been viewed as a phobic disorder. However, recent studies suggest that agoraphobia shares more kinship with panic disorders than phobic disorders (Turner, McCann, Beidel, & Mezzich, 1986). Most agora-

phobics are women, and the typical age of onset for the disorder is late adolescence or early adulthood (Barlow & Waddell, 1985).

Obsessive-Compulsive Disorders

Obsessions are *thoughts* that repeatedly intrude on one's consciousness in a distressing way. Compulsions are *actions* that one feels forced to carry out. Thus, **an obsessive-compulsive disorder is marked by persistent, uncontrollable intrusions of unwanted thoughts (obsessions) and urges to engage in senseless rituals (compulsions).** To illustrate, let's examine the bizarre behavior of a man once reputed to be the wealthiest person in the world.

The famous industrialist Howard Hughes was obsessed with the possibility of being contaminated by germs. This led him to devise extraordinary rituals to minimize the possibility of such contamination. He would spend hours methodically cleaning a single telephone. He once wrote a three-page memo instructing assistants on exactly how to open cans of fruit for him. The following is just a small portion of the instructions that Hughes provided for a driver who delivered films to his bungalow. "Get out of the car on the traffic side. Do not at any time be on the side of the car between the car and the curb. . . . Carry only one can of film at a time. Step over the gutter opposite the place where the sidewalk dead-ends into the curb from a point as far out into the center of the road as possible. Do not ever walk on the grass at all, also do not step into the gutter at all. Walk to the bungalow keeping as near to the center of the sidewalk as possible . . ." [Adapted from Barlett & Steele, 1979, pp. 227–237]

Obsessions often center on inflicting harm on others, personal failures, suicide, or sexual acts. People troubled by obsessions may feel that they have lost control of their minds. Compulsions usually involve stereotyped rituals that temporarily relieve anxiety. Common examples include constant handwashing, repetitive cleaning of things that are already clean, and endless rechecking of locks, faucets, and such. Unusual rituals intended to bring good luck are also a common form of compulsive behavior.

Figure 15.5. Common phobias. Frequently reported phobias are listed here, along with their typical age of onset and information on sex differences.

Common phobias	Approximate percent of all phobias	Sex difference	Typical age of onset
Agoraphobias (fear of places of assembly, crowds, open spaces)	10%–50%	Large majority are women	Early adulthood
Social phobias (fear of being observed doing something humiliating)	10%	Majority are women	Adolescence
Specific phobias Animals Cats (ailurophobia) Birds (avisophobia) Dogs (cynophobia) Horses (equinophobia) Insects (insectophobia) Snakes (ophidiophobia) Spiders (arachnophobia) Rodents (rodentophobia)	5%–15%	Vast majority are women	Childhood
Inanimate objects Dirt (mysophobia) Darkness (nyctophobia) Storms (brontophobia) Closed spaces Heights (acrophobia) (claustrophobia)	20%	None	Any age
Illness-injury (nosophobia) Death (thanatophobia) Cancer (cancerophobia) Venereal disease (venerophobia)	15%–25%	None	Middle age

Although many of us can be compulsive at times, full-fledged obsessive-compulsive disorders are relatively uncommon (Sturgis, 1984).

Etiology of Anxiety Disorders

Like most psychological disorders, anxiety disorders develop out of complicated interactions involving a variety of factors. Conditioning processes and aspects of child rearing appear especially important, but biological factors may also contribute to anxiety disorders.

Biological Factors

A handful of studies suggest that there may be a weak genetic predisposition to anxiety disorders (Noyes et al., 1987; Torgersen, 1983). These findings are consistent with a long-discussed theory that inherited differences in autonomic reactivity might make some people more vulnerable than others to anxiety disorders (Martin, 1971). According to this theory, people with high autonomic reactivity are especially likely to develop anxiety problems because their bodies overreact to the everyday stresses of life. Thought-provoking connections have also been found between anxiety disorders and a common heart defect, *mitral valve prolapse*. This anatomical defect, which makes people prone to heart palpitations, faintness, and chest pain, may predispose some people to problems with anxiety (Agras, 1985).

Conditioning

Many of our anxiety responses may be *acquired through classical conditioning* and *maintained through operant conditioning*. According to Mowrer (1947), an originally neutral stimulus (the snow in Hilda's case, for instance) may be paired with a frightening event (the avalanche) so that it becomes a conditioned stimulus eliciting anxiety (see Figure 15.6). This is classical conditioning, which we first described in Chapter 2.

Once a conditioned fear is acquired, a person may start avoiding the anxiety-producing stimulus. This avoidance response is negatively reinforced because it is followed by a reduction in unpleasant anxiety (see Figure 15.6). This involves operant conditioning (also explained in Chapter 2). Thus, separate conditioning processes may create and then sustain specific anxiety responses (McAllister, McAllister, Scoles, & Hampton, 1986).

Our tendency to develop phobias of certain types of objects and situations rather than others may be explained by Martin Seligman's (1971) concept of *preparedness*. Like many theorists, Seligman believes that classical conditioning creates most phobic responses. However, he theorizes that *we are biologically prepared by our evolutionary history to acquire some fears much more easily than others*. His theory would explain why we develop phobias of ancient sources of threat (for example, snakes and spiders) much more readily than modern sources of threat (for example, electrical outlets or hot irons). Thus far, laboratory studies have provided only modest support for Seligman's theory of preparedness (McNally, 1987).

The conditioning model of phobias is brought into question by evidence that many people with phobias cannot recall or identify a traumatic conditioning experience that led to their phobia (Marks, 1987). However, these failures to recall relevant conditioning experiences could reflect poor memory of childhood trauma. Or they could be due to unconscious repression, as in the case of Hilda's snow phobia. Although the details are still being worked out, there is ample evidence that conditioning frequently contributes to the development of anxiety disorders.

Child-Rearing Patterns

How we are reared as children may affect our vulnerability to anxiety disorders. Parents may unintentionally foster anxiety in their children in a variety of ways. In some cases, children may acquire fears and anxieties through *observational learning* (Bandura & Rosenthal, 1966). For example, if a father hides in a closet every time there's a thunderstorm, his children may acquire their father's fear of storms. Laboratory studies have shown that condi-

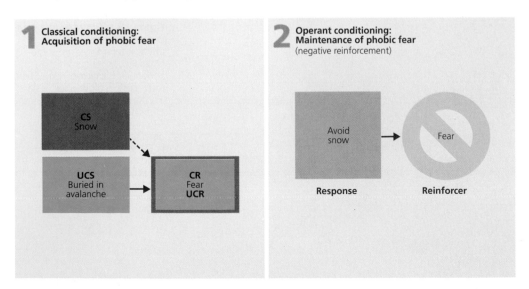

Figure 15.6. Conditioning as an explanation for phobias. Many phobias appear to be acquired through classical conditioning when a neutral stimulus is paired with an anxiety-arousing stimulus. Once acquired, a phobia may be maintained through operant conditioning because avoidance of the phobic stimulus leads to a reduction in anxiety, resulting in negative reinforcement.

tioned fears can be created in animals through observational learning (Mineka & Cook, 1986).

Associations have also been found between overprotection by parents and elevated anxiety in their children (Poznanski, 1973). Parents who are overprotective may make their children feel like the world is a dangerous place. This sense of threat could predispose the children to anxiety reactions later in life. Howard Hughes, for instance, was raised by an extremely overprotective mother. She worried constantly about his health and tried to shelter him from the real world throughout his childhood (Fowler, 1986). She may have planted the seeds for Howard's lifelong, chronic anxiety.

SOMATOFORM DISORDERS

Chances are, you have met people who always seem to be complaining about aches, pains, and physical maladies of doubtful authenticity. You may have thought to yourself, "It's all in his head" and concluded that the person exhibited a "psychosomatic" condition. However, as we discussed in Chapter 3, the term *psychosomatic* is widely misused. *Psychosomatic diseases* **are genuine physical ailments caused in part by psychological factors, especially emotional distress.** These diseases, which include maladies such as ulcers, asthma, and high blood pressure, have a genuine organic basis and are not imagined ailments. They are recorded on the DSM axis for physical problems (Axis III). When physical illness appears *entirely* psychological in origin, we are dealing with *somatoform disorders*, which are recorded on Axis I. *Somatoform disorders* **are physical ailments that have no authentic organic basis but are due instead to psychological factors.** Although their symptoms are more imaginary than real, victims of somatoform disorders are *not* simply faking illness. Their subjective distress is real. Deliberate feigning of illness for personal gain is another matter altogether, called *malingering*.

People with somatoform disorders typically seek treatment from physicians practicing neurology, internal medicine, and family medicine instead of psychologists or psychiatrists. Making accurate diagnoses of somatoform disorders can be difficult because the causes of physical ailments are sometimes hard to identify. In some cases, a diagnosis of somatoform disorder is wrongly made when a genuine organic cause for a person's physical symptoms goes undetected in spite of extensive medical examinations and tests (Rubin, Zorumski, & Guze, 1986).

Diagnostic difficulties make it hard to obtain sound data on the prevalence of somatoform disorders, but they appear to be fairly common. We will discuss three specific types of somatoform disorders: somatization disorders, conversion disorders, and hypochondriasis.

Somatization Disorders

Individuals with somatization disorders are often said to "cling to ill health." **A** *somatization disorder* **is marked by a history of diverse physical complaints that appear to be psychological in origin.** Somatization disorders occur mostly in women. Victims report an endless succession of minor physical ailments. They usually have a long and complicated history of medical treatment from many doctors. The distinguishing feature of this disorder is the diversity of victims' physical complaints. Over the years, they report a mixed bag of cardiovascular, gastrointestinal, pulmonary, neurological, and genitourinary symptoms. The unlikely nature of such a smorgasbord of symptoms often alerts a physician to the possible psychological basis for the patient's problems.

Conversion Disorders

Conversion disorders **involve a significant loss of physical function (with no apparent organic basis), usually in a single organ system.** Common symptoms include partial or complete loss of vision, partial or complete loss of hearing, partial paralysis, severe laryngitis or mutism, and

Figure 15.7. Glove anesthesia. In conversion disorders, the physical complaints are sometimes inconsistent with the known facts of physiology. Such is the case in glove anesthesia, in which the patient complains of losing feeling in a hand. Given the patterns of nerve distribution in the arm shown in (a), a loss of feeling in the hand exclusively (as shown in b) is a physical impossibility, indicating that the patient's problem is psychological in origin.

loss of feeling or function in limbs, such as that seen in the following case.

Mildred was a rancher's daughter who lost the use of both of her legs during adolescence. Mildred was at home alone one afternoon when a male relative attempted to assault her. She screamed for help, and her legs gave way as she slipped to the floor. She was found on the floor a few minutes later when her mother returned home. She could not get up, so she was carried to her bed. Her legs buckled when she made subsequent attempts to walk on her own. Due to her illness, she was waited on hand and foot by her family and friends. Neighbors brought her home-made things to eat or to wear. She became the center of attention in the household. [Adapted from Cameron, 1963, pp. 312–313]

People with conversion disorders are usually troubled by more severe ailments than people with somatization disorders. In some cases of conversion disorder, there are telltale clues about the psychological origins of the illness because the patient's symptoms are not consistent with medical knowledge about their apparent disease. For instance, the loss of feeling in one hand seen in "glove anesthesia" is inconsistent with the known facts of neurological organization (see Figure 15.7).

Hypochondriasis

Hypochondriacs constantly monitor their physical condition, looking for signs of illness. Any tiny alteration from their physical norm leads them to conclude that they have contracted a disease. *Hypochondriasis* **(more widely known as hypochondria) involves excessive preoccupation with health concerns and incessant worry about developing physical illnesses.** The following case illustrates the nature of hypochondria.

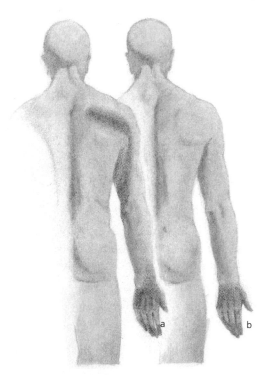

Jeff is a middle-aged man who works as a clerk in a drug store. He spends long hours describing his health problems to anyone who will listen. Jeff is an avid reader of popular magazine articles on medicine. He can tell you all about the latest medical discoveries. He takes all sorts of pills and vitamins to ward off possible illnesses. He's the first to try every new product on the market. Jeff is constantly afflicted by new symptoms of illness. His most recent problems were poor digestion and a heartbeat that he thought was irregular. He frequently goes to physicians who can find nothing wrong with him physically. They tell him that he is healthy. He thinks they use "backward techniques." He suspects that his illness is too rare to be diagnosed successfully. [Adapted from Suinn, 1984, p. 236]

When hypochondriacs are assured by their physicians that they do not have any real illness, they often are skeptical and disbelieving. As in Jeff's case, they frequently assume that the physician must be incompetent and they go shopping for another doctor. Hypochondriacs don't subjectively suffer from physical distress as much as they *overinterpret* every conceivable sign of illness. Hypochondria often appears alongside other psychological disorders, especially anxiety disorders and depression (Turner, Jacob, & Morrison, 1984). For example, Howard Hughes's obsessive-compulsive disorder was coupled with profound hypochondria.

Etiology of Somatoform Disorders

Inherited aspects of physiological functioning may predispose people to somatoform disorders (Jacob & Turner, 1984). However, available evidence suggests that these disorders are largely a function of personality and learning. Let's look at personality factors first.

Personality Factors
People with certain types of personality traits seem to be particularly prone to develop somatoform disorders. The prime candidates are people with *histrionic* personality characteristics (Nemiah, 1985). The histrionic personality tends to be self-centered, suggestible, excitable, highly

15: PSYCHOLOGICAL DISORDERS

437

emotional, and overly dramatic. Such people thrive on the attention they get when they become ill.

Learning: The Sick Role

As we discussed in the previous chapter, some people grow fond of the role associated with being sick (Pilowsky, 1978). Their complaints of physical symptoms may be reinforced by indirect benefits derived from their illness. What are the benefits commonly associated with physical illness? One payoff is that becoming ill is a superb way to avoid having to confront life's challenges. Many people with somatoform disorders are avoiding facing up to marital problems, career frustrations, family responsibilities, and the like. After all, when you're sick, others cannot place great demands upon you.

Attention from others is another payoff that may reinforce complaints of physical illness. When people become ill, they command the attention of family, friends, co-workers, neighbors, and doctors. The sympathy that illness often brings may strengthen a person's tendency to feel ill. This clearly occurred in Mildred's case of conversion disorder. Her illness paid handsome dividends in terms of attention, consolation, and kindhearted assistance from others.

DISSOCIATIVE DISORDERS

Dissociative disorders are among the more unusual syndromes that we will discuss. **Dissociative disorders are a class of disorders in which people lose contact with portions of their consciousness or memory, resulting in disruptions in their sense of identity.** We'll describe two dissociative syndromes, both of which are relatively uncommon.

Psychogenic Amnesia

Psychogenic amnesia **is a sudden loss of memory for important personal information that is too extensive to be due to normal forgetting.** Memory losses in psychogenic amnesia may cover anything from a few hours to an entire lifetime, although the latter is rare. In psychogenic amnesia, memory losses center on one's identity or on a specific, disturbing incident. When identity-related memory losses occur, people may forget their names, their families, where they live, and where they work. In spite of this wholesale forgetting, they remember matters unrelated to their identity, such as how to drive a car or the square root of 9. When memory losses center around a traumatic incident (such as an automobile accident or a fire), the person usually has a blank memory for the incident itself and for the next several hours to several days.

RECOMMENDED READING

You Are Not Alone: Understanding and Dealing with Mental Illness
by Clara C. Park & Leon N. Shapiro (Little, Brown, 1979)

Although psychological disorders are more common than widely realized, the topic of mental illness is shrouded in mystery. It is not a subject that we discuss casually or openly. It is very hard to find worthwhile practical advice for people suffering from psychological disorders and their friends and families. However, this book does a superb job of discussing practical considerations in dealing with mental illness.

Admittedly, this book looks like a ponderous, academic text that one would expect to be very dull. However, once you get past the Spartan appearance and the footnotes, you'll find interesting reading and a wealth of useful insights. Some of the topics are rarely discussed elsewhere. Among other things, the authors discuss the following:

- How to sift through the mental health services available in your community
- How to cope with your own distress about having a mentally ill friend or relative
- How to avoid having the family contribute to the problem rather than the solution
- How to explain mental illness to children
- What mental hospitals are like
- Insurance and financial considerations

This comprehensive book covers a wide range of disorders. Its practicality, realism, and willingness to tackle awkward issues are commendable.

> Perhaps it happens suddenly. The telephone call is from an unknown doctor; your son, who when you last heard from him had just got engaged to a lovely girl, is in the university hospital, hallucinating or incoherent. . . . However it comes, it throws up walls around you, as all your neighbors, it seems, go about their business of living with an ordinariness which suddenly seems enviable. There may be a hundred people with a similar experience of trouble living within a mile of you—indeed, if you live in a city, there certainly are—but the families of the mentally ill have a low visibility. Exhaustion and misery, if not shame and a conviction of guilt, may keep the knowledge of their plight even from their close friends. [p. 4]

Multiple-Personality Disorders

Multiple-personality disorders **involve the coexistence in one person of two or more largely complete, and usually very different, personalities.** In multiple-personality disorders, the divergences in behavior go far beyond those that people normally display in adapting to different roles in life. People with multiple personality feel that they have more than one identity. Each personality has its own name, memories, traits, and physical mannerisms. Although rare, this "Dr. Jekyl and Mr. Hyde" syndrome is frequently portrayed in novels, movies, and television shows. In popular media portrayals, the syndrome is often mistakenly called "schizophrenia." As you will see later, schizophrenic disorders are entirely different.

In a multiple-personality disorder, the original personality often is not aware of the alternate personalities. In contrast, the alternate personalities usually *are* aware of the original one and have varying amounts of awareness of each other. The alternate personalities frequently display traits that are quite foreign to the original personality. For instance, a shy, inhibited person might develop a flamboyant, extraverted alternate personality. Transitions between personalities often occur suddenly.

During the 1980s, there was a dramatic increase in the diagnosis of multiple-personality disorders (Braun, 1986). Some theorists believe that multiple-personality disorders used to be underdiagnosed; that is, they frequently went undetected (Kluft, 1987). Other skeptics argue that a handful of clinicians have begun overdiagnosing the condition (Thigpen & Cleckley, 1984). The debate about the reason for the sudden upsurge in multiple-personality diagnoses is far from settled. It probably won't be resolved without a great deal of additional research.

Etiology of Dissociative Disorders

Psychogenic amnesia is usually attributed to excessive stress. However, relatively little is known about why this extreme reaction to stress occurs in certain people but not others. The causes of multiple-personality disorders are equally obscure. Some skeptical theorists believe that people with multiple personalities are engaging in intentional role playing to use mental illness as a face-saving excuse for their personal failings (Spanos, Weekes, & Bertrand, 1985). Indeed, there is evidence that multiple-personality disorders are faked with some regularity.

However, various lines of evidence suggest to most theorists that at least some cases are authentic (Aalpoel & Lewis, 1984). Many of these cases seem to be rooted in severe emotional trauma occurring during childhood. A substantial portion of people with multiple-personality disorder have a history of disturbed home life, beatings and rejection from parents, sexual abuse, and forced repression of emotions (Aalpoel & Lewis, 1984). In the final analysis, however, we know very little about the causes of multiple-personality disorders.

MOOD DISORDERS

What did Abraham Lincoln, Marilyn Monroe, Ernest Hemingway, Winston Churchill, Janis Joplin, and Leo Tolstoy have in common? Yes, they all achieved great prominence, albeit in different ways at different times. But, more pertinent to our interest, they all suffered from severe mood disorders. Although mood disorders can be terribly debilitating, people with mood disorders may still achieve greatness, because such disorders tend to be *episodic*. In other words, emotional disorders often come and go. Thus, episodes of disturbance are interspersed among periods of normality.

Of course, we all have our ups and downs in terms of mood. Life would be dull indeed if our emotional tone was constant. All of us experience depression occasionally. Likewise, all of us have days that we sail through on an emotional high. Such emotional fluctuations are natural, but some people are prone to extreme distortions of mood. *Mood disorders* **are a class of disorders marked by**

Despite her great success and popularity, Marilyn Monroe suffered from periodic episodes of depression. It was at one of these low points that she took her own life.

emotional disturbances that may spill over to disrupt physical, perceptual, social, and thought processes.

There are two basic types of mood disorders: unipolar and bipolar (see Figure 15.8). People with *unipolar disorders* experience emotional extremes at just one end of the mood continuum—*depression*. People with *bipolar disorders* experience emotional extremes at both ends of the mood continuum, going through periods of both *depression and mania* (excitement and elation). The mood swings in bipolar disorders can be patterned in many different ways.

Recent studies suggest that periods of emotional disturbance may follow a seasonal pattern in some people. **In a *seasonal affective (mood) disorder* an individual's periods of depression or mania tend to occur repeatedly at about the same time of the year.** A seasonal pattern may be seen in either unipolar or bipolar disorders. The most common pattern appears to be recurrent depression in the fall and winter, alternating with normal or manic periods in the spring and summer (Rosenthal et al., 1986). Researchers suspect that seasonal patterns in mood disorders are tied to human biological rhythms. These rhythms are presumably affected by exposure to daylight, which varies according to the time of year (Wehr, Sack, Parry, & Rosenthal, 1986). Evidence on these hypothesized relations between biological rhythms and emotional disturbances is still fragmentary.

Depressive Disorders

The line between normal and abnormal depression can be very difficult to draw. Ultimately, a subjective judgment is required. Crucial considerations in this judgment include the duration of the depression and its disruptive effects. When a depression significantly impairs everyday adaptive behavior for more than a few weeks, there is reason for concern.

In *depressive disorders* people show persistent feelings of sadness and despair and a loss of interest in previous sources of pleasure. The most common symptoms of depressive disorders are summarized in Figure 15.9 and compared to the symptoms of mania. Negative emotions form the heart of the depressive syndrome, but many other symptoms may also appear. Depressed people often give up activities that they used to find enjoyable. For example, a depressed person might quit going bowling or give up a favorite hobby like photography. Reduced appetite and insomnia are common. People with depression often lack energy. They tend to move sluggishly and talk slowly. Anxiety, irritability, and brooding are frequently observed. Self-esteem tends to sink as the depressed person begins to feel worthless. Depression plunges people into feelings of hopelessness, dejection, and boundless guilt. The severity of abnormal depression varies considerably.

How common are depressive disorders? Very common. Recent studies using DSM-III diagnostic criteria suggest that about 6%–8% of the population endures a unipolar depressive disorder at some point in time (Robins et al., 1984). Unipolar disorders occur throughout the life span and are *not* strongly related to age (Lewinsohn, Duncan, Stanton, & Hautzinger, 1986).

Bipolar Mood Disorders

***Bipolar mood disorders* (formerly known as manic-depressive disorders) are marked by the experience of both depressed and manic periods.** The symptoms seen in manic periods generally are the opposite of those seen in depression (see Figure 15.9 for a comparison). In a manic episode, a person's mood becomes elevated to the point of euphoria. Self-esteem skyrockets as the person bubbles over with optimism, energy, and extravagant plans. People become hyperactive and may go for days without sleep. They talk rapidly and shift topics wildly as their minds race at breakneck speed. Judgment is often impaired. Some people in manic periods gamble impulsively, spend money frantically, or become sexually reckless. Like depressive disorders, bipolar disorders vary considerably in severity.

Figure 15.8. Episodic patterns in mood disorders. Episodes of emotional disturbance come and go unpredictably in mood disorders. People with unipolar disorders suffer from bouts of depression only, while people with bipolar disorders experience both manic and depressed episodes. The time between episodes of disturbance varies greatly.

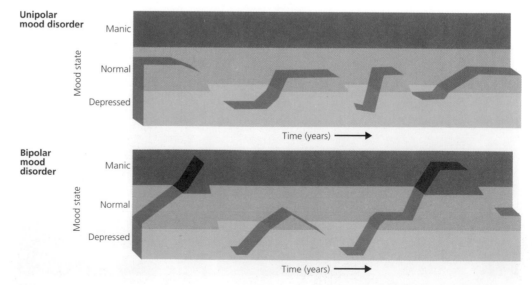

You may be thinking that the euphoria in manic episodes sounds appealing. If so, you are not entirely wrong. In their milder forms, manic states can seem attractive. The increases in energy, self-esteem, and optimism can be deceptively seductive. Because of the increase in energy, many bipolar patients report temporary surges of productivity and creativity (Jamison, Gerner, Hammen, & Padesky, 1980).

Although there may be some positive aspects to manic episodes, bipolar mood disorders ultimately prove to be very troublesome for most victims. Manic periods often have a paradoxical negative undertow of uneasiness and irritability. Moreover, mild manic episodes usually escalate to higher levels that become scary and disturbing. Impaired judgment leads many victims to do things that they greatly regret later, as you'll see in the following case.

Robert, a dentist, awoke one morning with the idea that he was the most gifted dental surgeon in his tri-state area. He decided that he should try to provide services to as many people as possible, so that more people could benefit from his talents. Thus, he decided to remodel his two-chair dental office, installing 20 booths so that he could simultaneously attend to 20 patients. That same day he drew up plans for this arrangement, telephoned a number of remodelers, and invited bids for the work. Later that day, impatient to get going on his remodeling, he rolled up his sleeves, got himself a sledgehammer, and began to knock down the walls in his office. Annoyed when that didn't go so well, he smashed his dental tools, washbasins, and X-ray equipment. Later, Robert's wife became concerned about his behavior and summoned two of her adult daughters for assistance. The daughters responded quickly, arriving at the family home with their husbands. In the ensuing discussion, Robert—after bragging about his sexual prowess—made advances toward his daughters. He had to be subdued by their husbands. [Adapted from Kleinmuntz, 1980, p. 309]

Although not rare, bipolar disorders are much less common than unipolar depression. Bipolar disorders affect a little under 1% of the population (Boyd & Weissman, 1986). The onset of bipolar disorders is age-related, with the peak of vulnerability occurring between the ages of 24 and 31 (Murphy, 1980).

Etiology of Mood Disorders

We know quite a bit about the etiology of mood disorders, although the puzzle hasn't been assembled completely. There appear to be a number of routes into these disorders involving intricate interactions between psychological and biological factors.

Genetic Vulnerability

The evidence strongly suggests that genetic factors influence the likelihood of developing major depression or a bipolar mood disorder. In studies that assess the impact of heredity on psychological disorders, investigators look at *concordance rates*. **A concordance rate indicates the percentage of twin pairs or other pairs of relatives that exhibit the same disorder.** If relatives who share more genetic similarity show higher concordance rates than relatives who share less genetic overlap, this finding supports the genetic hypothesis. Twin studies, which compare identical and fraternal twins (see Chapter 2), suggest that genetic factors *are* involved in mood disorders (Nurnberger & Gershon, 1982). Concordance rates average around 65% for identical twins but only 14% for fraternal twins, who share less genetic similarity.

In a widely heralded study, a research team linked a gene segment on a specific chromosome to bipolar mood disorder in a sample of Amish families (Egeland et al., 1987). Many experts felt that this study was a major breakthrough, but new data has not confirmed the original findings (Barinaga, 1989). It is not likely that a single gene leads to direct inheritance of bipolar disorders. Several sources of evidence, including the Egeland et al. study, suggest that people inherit a *heightened vulnerability* to this disorder, not the disorder itself. In the original Egeland et al. study, only 63% of the family members who were carriers of the implicated gene segment exhibited bipolar illness. Thus, heredity can create a *predisposition* to mood

Comparison of Manic and Depressive Symptoms

Characteristics	Manic episode	Depressive episode
Emotional	Elated, euphoric, very sociable, impatient at any hindrance	Gloomy, hopeless, socially withdrawn, irritable
Cognitive	Characterized by racing thoughts, flight of ideas, desire for action, and impulsive behavior; talkative, self-confident; experiencing delusions of grandeur	Characterized by slowness of thought processes, obsessive worrying, inability to make decisions, negative self-image, self-blame, and delusions of guilt and disease
Motor	Hyperactive, tireless, requiring less sleep than usual, showing increased sex drive and fluctuating appetite	Less active, tired, experiencing difficulty in sleeping, showing decreased sex drive and decreased appetite

Figure 15.9. Common symptoms in manic and depressive episodes. The emotional, cognitive, and motor symptoms exhibited in manic and depressive illnesses are largely the opposite of each other.

disorders. Environmental factors probably determine whether this predisposition is converted into an actual disorder.

Neurochemical Factors

Heredity may influence susceptibility to mood disorders by creating a predisposition toward certain types of neurochemical activity in the brain. **Neurotransmitters are chemicals that carry information from one neuron to another.** Correlations have been found between mood disorders and the levels of three neurotransmitters in the brain (norepinephrine, serotonin, and dopamine). *Norepinephrine* levels appear to be most critical, but investigators believe that mood disorders may be caused by intricate interactions between the three implicated neurotransmitters and perhaps other brain chemicals.

Although the details remain elusive, it seems clear that there is a neurochemical basis for at least some mood disorders. A variety of drug therapies are fairly effective in the treatment of severe mood disorders. Most of these drugs are known to affect the availability (in the brain) of the neurotransmitters that have been related to mood disorders (Zis & Goodwin, 1982). Since this effect is unlikely to be a coincidence, it bolsters the plausibility of the idea that neurochemical changes produce mood disturbances.

If alterations in neurotransmitter activity are the basis for many mood disorders, what causes the alterations in neurotransmitter activity? These neurochemical changes probably depend on our reactions to environmental events. Thus, a number of psychological factors have been implicated in the etiology of mood disorders. We'll examine evidence on patterns of thinking, interpersonal style, and stress.

Cognitive Factors

A variety of theories emphasize how cognitive factors contribute to depressive disorders (Abramson, Metalsky, & Alloy, 1988; Beck, 1976; Ellis, 1962; Seligman, 1983). In recent years, theories that focus on our patterns of *attribution* have generated a great deal of research on the cognitive roots of depression. As noted in Chapter 5, **attributions are inferences that people draw about the causes of events, others' behavior, and their own behavior.** We routinely make attributions because we want to *understand* our personal fates and the events that take place around us. For example, if your boss criticizes your work, you will probably ask yourself why. Was your work really that sloppy? Was your boss just in a grouchy mood? Was the criticism a manipulative effort to motivate you to work harder? Each of these potential explanations is an attribution.

Attributions can be analyzed along a number of dimensions. Three important dimensions are illustrated in Figure 15.10. The most prominent dimension is the degree to which we attribute events to *internal, personal factors versus external, situational factors.* For instance, if you performed poorly on a standardized mathematics test, you might attribute your poor showing to your lack of intelligence (an internal attribution) or to the horrible heat and humidity in the exam room (an external attribution).

Another key dimension is the degree to which we attribute events to factors that are *stable or unstable over time.* Thus, you might blame your poor test performance on exhaustion (an internal but unstable factor that could change next time) or on your low intelligence (an internal but stable factor). Some theories are also interested in the degree to which our attributions have *global versus specific implications.* Thus, you might attribute your low test score to your lack of intelligence (which has very general, global implications) or your poor math ability (the implications are specific to math). Figure 15.10 provides additional examples of attributions that might be made for poor test performance.

Theories that link attribution to depression are interested in the *attributional style* that people display, especially when they are trying to explain failures, setbacks, and other negative events. Studies show that *people who consistently tend to make internal, stable, and global attributions*

Figure 15.10. Attributional style and depression. Possible attributions for poor performance on a standardized math exam are shown here. Note how these explanations vary in terms of whether causes are seen as internal-external, stable-unstable, and specific-global. People who consistently explain their failures with attributions that are internal, stable, and global are particularly vulnerable to depression.

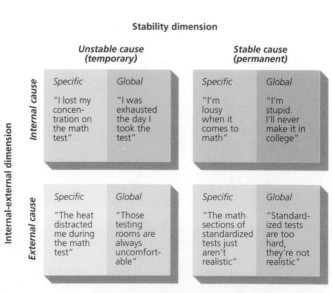

are more prone to depression than people who exhibit the opposite attributional styles (Robins, 1988; Sweeney, Anderson, & Bailey, 1986). Why? Because in making internal, stable, and global attributions, people blame their setbacks on personal inade-

REPRINTED WITH SPECIAL PERMISSION OF KING FEATURES SYNDICATE, INC

quacies (internal) they see as unchangeable (stable) and draw far-reaching (global) conclusions about their lack of worth as human beings. In other words, they draw depressing conclusions about themselves.

Thus, cognitive models of depression maintain that it is negative thinking that makes many people feel helpless, hopeless, and dejected. The principal problem with cognitive theories is their difficulty in separating cause from effect (see Figure 15.11). Does negative thinking cause depression? Or does depression cause negative thinking? Could both be caused by a third variable, such as neurochemical changes? Evidence can be mustered to support all three of these possibilities, suggesting that negative thinking, depression, and neurochemical alterations may feed off of each other as a depression deepens.

Ironically, depressed individuals' negative thinking may be more *realistic* than nondepressed individuals' more positive thinking. This unexpected possibility first surfaced in a study by Lauren Alloy and Lyn Abramson (1979). Depressed and nondepressed subjects worked on a laboratory task. The experimenters controlled how much the subjects' responses on the task (pressing or not pressing a button) influenced their outcomes (turning on a light, winning money). Afterward, subjects were asked to estimate how much their responses influenced their outcomes. As expected, the depressed subjects estimated that they had less control than the nondepressed subjects. However, this difference occurred because the nondepressed subjects *overestimated* their control. In comparison, the depressed subjects made fairly accurate

estimates. Since then, numerous studies have shown that depressed subjects' self-evaluations, recall of feedback from others, and predictions of future outcomes tend to be more realistic than those made by nondepressed subjects (Alloy & Abramson, 1988). Thus, depressed people may not be overly pessimistic so much as nondepressed people are overly optimistic.

Interpersonal Roots

Behavioral approaches to understanding depression emphasize how inadequate social skills put people on the road to depressive disorders (Lewinsohn, 1974). According to this notion, depression-prone people lack the social finesse needed to acquire many important kinds of reinforcers, such as good friends, top jobs, and desirable spouses. This paucity of reinforcers could understandably lead to negative emotions and depression. Consistent with this theory, researchers have found correlations between poor social skills and depression (Blechman, McEnroe, Carella, & Audette, 1986).

Another interpersonal factor is that depressed people tend to be depressing! Individuals suffering from depression often are irritable and pessimistic. They complain a lot, and they aren't very enjoyable companions. As a consequence, people tend to reject and avoid depressed individuals. Depressed people thus have fewer sources of social support than nondepressed people (Billings, Cronkite, & Moos, 1983). In turn, social rejection and lack of support may aggravate and deepen a person's depression (Klerman & Weissman, 1986).

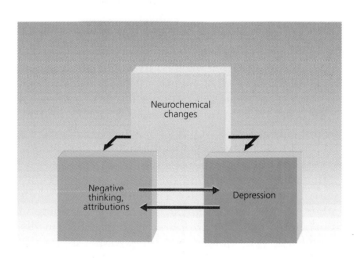

Figure 15.11. Interpreting the correlation between negative thinking and depression. Cognitive theories of depression assert that consistent patterns of negative thinking cause depression. Although these theories are highly plausible, depression could cause negative thoughts, or both could be caused by a third factor, such as neurochemical changes in the brain.

Precipitating Stress

Mood disorders sometimes appear mysteriously "out of nowhere" in people who are leading benign, nonstressful lives. For this reason, experts used to believe that mood disorders were not influenced much by stress. However, recent advances in the measurement of personal stress have altered this picture. The evidence available today suggests that there is a moderately strong link between stress and the onset of mood disorders (Ambelas, 1987; Hammen, Marks, Mayol, & deMayo, 1985). Some theorists believe that stress leads to disruptions of biological rhythms and sleep loss, which lead to neurochemical changes that cause mood disorders (Healy & Williams, 1988; Wehr, Sack, & Rosenthal, 1987).

Stress seems to act as a precipitating factor that triggers depression in some people. Of course, many people endure great stress without getting depressed. The impact of stress varies, in part because different people have different degrees of *vulnerability* to mood disorders. Variations in vulnerability appear to depend primarily on one's biological makeup. Similar interactions between stress and vulnerability probably influence the development of many kinds of disorders, including those that are next on our agenda—the schizophrenic disorders.

SCHIZOPHRENIC DISORDERS

Literally, *schizophrenia* means "split mind." However, when Eugen Bleuler coined the term in 1911, he was referring to the fragmenting of thought processes seen in the disorder—not to a "split personality." Unfortunately, writers in the popular media often assume that the split-mind notion refers to the rare syndrome in which a person manifests two or more personalities. As you have already learned, this syndrome is actually called *multiple-personality disorder*. Schizophrenia is a much more common, and altogether different, type of disorder.

Schizophrenic disorders **are a class of disorders marked by disturbances in thought that spill over to affect perceptual, social, and emotional processes.** How common is schizophrenia? Prevalence estimates suggest that about 0.5% to 1.5% of the population may suffer from schizophrenic disorders (Gottesman & Shields, 1982; Robins et al., 1984). That may not sound like much, but it means that in the United States alone there may be 3 or 4 million people troubled by schizophrenic disturbances.

General Symptoms

There are a number of distinct schizophrenic syndromes, but they share some general characteristics that we will examine before looking at the subtypes. Many of these characteristics are apparent in the following case history (adapted from Sheehan, 1982).

Sylvia was first diagnosed as schizophrenic at age 15. She has been in and out of many different types of psychiatric facilities since then. She has never been able to hold a job for any length of time. During severe flare-ups of her disorder her personal hygiene deteriorates. She rarely washes, wears clothes that neither fit nor match, smears makeup on heavily but randomly, and slops food all over herself. Sylvia occasionally hears voices talking to her. Sylvia tends to be argumentative, aggressive, and emotionally volatile. Over the years, she has been involved in innumerable fights with fellow patients, psychiatric staff members, and strangers. Her thoughts can be highly irrational, as is apparent from the following quotation:

"Mick Jagger wants to marry me. If I have Mick Jagger, I don't have to covet Geraldo Rivera. Mick Jagger is St. Nicholas and the Maharishi is Santa Claus. I want to form a gospel rock group called the Thorn Oil, but Geraldo wants me to be the music critic on *Eyewitness News*, so what can I do? Got to listen to my boyfriend. Teddy Kennedy cured me of my ugliness. I'm pregnant with the son of God. I'm going to marry David Berkowitz and get it over with. Creedmoor is the headquarters of the American Nazi Party. They're eating the patients here. Archie Bunker wants me to play his niece on his TV show. I work for Epic Records. I'm Joan of Arc. I'm Florence Nightingale. The door between the ward and the porch is the dividing line between New York and California. Divorce isn't a piece of paper, it's a feeling. Forget about Zip Codes. I need shock treatment. The body is run by electricity. My wiring is all faulty. A fly is a teen-age wasp. I'm marrying an accountant. I'm in the Pentecostal Church, but I'm considering switching my loyalty to the Charismatic Church." [Sheehan, 1982, pp.104–105]

Sylvia's case clearly shows that schizophrenic thinking can be bizarre and that schizophrenia can be a severe and debilitating disorder. Although no single symptom is inevitably present, the following symptoms are commonly seen in schizophrenia.

IRRATIONAL THOUGHT. Disturbed, irrational thought processes are the central feature of schizophrenic disorders. Various kinds of delusions are common. *Delusions* **are false beliefs that are maintained even though they clearly are out of touch with reality.** For example, affected persons frequently believe that their private thoughts are being broadcast to other people. They may also believe that thoughts are being injected into their mind against their will. In *delusions of grandeur*, people maintain that they are extremely famous or important. Sylvia expressed an endless array of grandiose delusions, such as thinking that Mick Jagger wanted to marry her, that she dictated the hobbit stories to Tolkien, and that she was going to win the Nobel Prize for medicine.

In addition to delusions, the schizophrenic person's train of thought deteriorates. Thinking becomes chaotic rather than logical and linear. There is a "loosening of associations" as the schizophrenic shifts topics in disjointed ways. The quotation from Sylvia illustrates this symptom dramatically. The entire passage involves a wild flight of ideas, but at one point (beginning with the sentence "Creedmoor is the headquarters...") she rattles off ten consecutive sentences that have no apparent connection to the preceding sentence.

DETERIORATION OF ADAPTIVE BEHAVIOR. Schizophrenia usually involves a noticeable deterioration in the quality of one's routine functioning in work, social relations, and personal care. Friends will often make remarks such as "Hal just isn't himself anymore." This deterioration is readily apparent in Sylvia's inability to get along with others or function in the work world. It's also apparent in her neglect of personal hygiene.

DISTORTED PERCEPTION. A variety of perceptual distortions may occur in schizophrenia, with the most common being auditory hallucinations. *Hallucinations* **are sensory perceptions that occur in the absence of a real, external stimulus or that represent gross distortions of perceptual input.** Schizophrenics frequently report that they hear voices of nonexistent or absent people talking to them. Sylvia, for instance, heard messages from former Beatle Paul McCartney. These voices often provide an insulting running commentary on the person's behavior ("You're an idiot for shaking his hand"). The voices may be argumentative ("You don't need a bath"), and they may issue commands ("Prepare your home for visitors from outer space").

DISTURBED EMOTION. Normal emotional tone can be disrupted in schizophrenia in a variety of ways. Some victims show a flattening of emotions. In other words, they show little emotional responsiveness. Others show inappropriate emotional responses that don't jell with the situation or with what they are saying. For instance, a schizophrenic patient might cry over a Smurfs cartoon and then laugh about a news story describing a child's tragic death. People with schizophrenia may also become emotionally volatile. This pattern was displayed by Sylvia, who often overreacted emotionally in erratic, unpredictable ways.

OTHER FEATURES. People with schizophrenic disorders may display a variety of other, less central symptoms. Many exhibit social withdrawal, interacting with others only very reluctantly. Some experience a *disturbed sense of self* or individuality. Also common is *poverty of speech,* which involves hesitant, uncommunicative verbal interactions. Sometimes, *abnormal motor behavior* is observed. A patient may rock back and forth constantly or become immobilized for great lengths of time.

Subtypes

Four subtypes of schizophrenic disorders are recognized, including a category for people who don't fit neatly into any of the first three categories.

PARANOID TYPE. As its name implies, *paranoid schizophrenia* **is dominated by delusions of persecution, along with delusions of grandeur.** In this common form of schizophrenia, people come to believe that they have many enemies who want to harass and oppress them. They may become suspicious of friends and relatives, or they may attribute the persecution to mysterious, unknown persons. They are convinced that they are being watched and manipulated in malicious ways. To make sense of this persecution, they often develop delusions of grandeur. They believe that they must be enormously important people, frequently seeing themselves as great inventors or as great religious or political leaders. For example, in the case described at the beginning of the chapter, Ed's belief that he was president of the United States was a delusion of grandeur.

CATATONIC TYPE. *Catatonic schizophrenia* **is marked by striking motor disturbances, ranging from muscular rigidity to random motor activity.** Some catatonics go into an extreme form of withdrawal known as a catatonic stupor. They may remain virtually motionless and seem oblivious to the environment around them for long periods of time. Others go into a state of catatonic excitement. They become hyperactive and incoherent. Some alternate between these dramatic extremes. The catatonic subtype is not particularly common, and its prevalence seems to be declining.

DISORGANIZED TYPE. In *disorganized schizophrenia,* **a particularly severe deterioration of adaptive behavior is seen.** Prominent symptoms include emotional indifference, frequent incoherence, and virtually complete social withdrawal. Aimless babbling and giggling are common. Delusions often center on bodily functions ("My brain is melting out my ears").

UNDIFFERENTIATED TYPE. People who are clearly schizophrenic but who cannot be placed into any of the three previous categories are said to have *undifferentiated schizophrenia,* **which is marked by idiosyncratic mixtures of schizophrenic symptoms.** The undifferentiated subtype is fairly common.

Some theorists are beginning to doubt the value of dividing schizophrenic disorders into the four subtypes just described (Pfohl & Andreasen, 1986). Critics note that the catatonic subtype is disappearing and that undifferentiated cases aren't a subtype as much as a hodgepodge of "leftovers." Critics also point out that the classic schizophrenic subtypes do not differ meaningfully in etiology, prognosis, or response to treatment. The absence of such differences casts doubt on the value of the current classification scheme.

Because of problems such as those just mentioned, Nancy Andreasen and others (Andreasen, 1982; Lewine, Fogg, & Meltzer, 1983) have proposed an alternative approach to subtyping. This new scheme divides schizophrenic disorders into just two categories based on the predominance of negative versus positive symptoms. *Negative symptoms* involve behavioral deficits, such as flattened emotions, social withdrawal, apathy, impaired attention, and poverty of speech. *Positive symptoms* involve behavioral excesses or peculiarities, such as hallucinations, delusions, bizarre behavior, and wild flights of ideas. Andreasen believes that researchers will find consistent differences between these two subtypes in etiology, prognosis, and response to treatment. Only time (and research) will tell whether the proposed subdivision based on positive versus negative symptoms will prove useful.

Course and Outcome

Schizophrenic disorders usually emerge during adolescence or early adulthood and only rarely after age 45 (Murphy & Helzer, 1986). The emergence of schizophrenia may be either very sudden or very gradual. Once it clearly emerges, the course of schizophrenia is variable (Ciompi, 1980), but patients tend to fall into three broad groups. Some patients, presumably those with milder disorders, are treated successfully and enjoy a full recovery. In other patients, treatment produces a partial recovery so that they can return to their normal life. However, they experience frequent relapses and are in and out of treatment facilities for much of the remainder of their lives. Finally, a third group of patients endure chronic illness that sometimes results in permanent hospitalization.

A number of factors are related to the likelihood of recovery from schizophrenic disorders (Lehmann & Cancro, 1985). A patient has a relatively *favorable prognosis* when (1) the onset of the disorder has been sudden rather than gradual, (2) the onset has occurred at a later age, (3) the patient's social and work adjustment were relatively good prior to the onset of the disorder, and (4) the patient has a relatively healthy, supportive family situation to return to. All of these predictors are con-

Nancy Andreasen

cerned with the etiology of schizophrenic illness, which is the matter we turn to next.

Etiology of Schizophrenia

Most of us can identify, at least to some extent, with people who suffer from mood disorders, somatoform disorders, and anxiety disorders. You probably can imagine events that might leave you struggling with depres-

---

RECOMMENDED READING

Surviving Schizophrenia: A Family Manual
by E. Fuller Torrey (Harper & Row, 1988)

E. Fuller Torrey is a very prominent psychiatrist who has specialized in the treatment and study of schizophrenia. He has conducted basic research and written technical articles on schizophrenia, as well as this practical book intended for the lay public. This book examines schizophrenia from every angle and offers plenty of down-to-earth advice on how to deal with this debilitating mental illness.

Torrey points out that there are many myths surrounding schizophrenia that have added to the anguish of families that have been victimized by this illness. He explains that schizophrenia is *not* caused by childhood trauma, domineering mothers, or passive fathers. He discusses how genetic vulnerability, flawed brain chemistry, and other factors contribute to the development of schizophrenic disorders.

Torrey discusses the treatment of schizophrenia at great length. He evaluates the utility of traditional psychotherapy, hospitalization, and medication. He also explains the various ways in which the disease can evolve. Some of the best material is found in chapters on what the patient needs and what the family needs.

Throughout the book, Torrey writes with clarity, eloquence, and conviction. He's not reluctant to express strong opinions. For instance, in an appendix he lists the ten worst readings on schizophrenia (along with the ten best), and his evaluations are brutal. He characterizes one book as "absurd drivel" and dismisses another by saying, "If a prize were to be given to the book which has produced the most confusion about schizophrenia over the past twenty years, this book would win going away." Scientists and academicians are usually reluctant to express such strong opinions, and Torrey's candor is remarkably refreshing.

Psychoanalysis is to schizophrenia as Laetrile is to cancer. Both have enjoyed surprising popularity considering the fact that they lack scientific basis, are completely ineffective, may make the patient worse if administered in toxic doses, and still attract patients who are willing to pay vast sums of money in desperation for a cure. Freud himself recognized that schizophrenic patients "are inaccessible to the influence of psychoanalysis and cannot be cured by our endeavors," but that observation has not stopped his followers from trying. [p. 220]

---

sion, or grappling with anxiety, or worrying about your physical health. But what could possibly have led Ed to believe that he had been fighting space wars and vampires? What could account for Sylvia thinking that she was Joan of Arc? Or that she dictated the hobbit novels to Tolkien? As mystifying as these delusions may seem, you'll see that the etiology of schizophrenic disorders is not all that different from the etiology of other disorders. We'll begin our discussion by examining the matter of genetic vulnerability.

Genetic Vulnerability

Evidence is plentiful that hereditary factors play a role in the development of schizophrenic disorders (Loehlin, Willerman, & Horn, 1988). For instance, in twin studies, concordance rates average around 45% for identical twins, in comparison to about 14% for fraternal twins (Gottesman & Shields, 1982). Studies also indicate that a child born to two schizophrenic parents has about a 46% probability of developing a schizophrenic disorder (as compared to the probability of about 1% for the population as a whole). These and other findings that demonstrate the genetic roots of schizophrenia are summarized in Figure 15.12. Overall, the picture is similar to that seen for mood disorders. Several converging lines of evidence indicate that people inherit a genetically transmitted *vulnerability* to schizophrenia.

Neurochemical Factors

Like mood disorders, schizophrenic disorders appear to be accompanied by changes in neurotransmitter activity in the brain (Karson, Kleinman, & Wyatt, 1986). *Dopamine* has been implicated as the critical neurotransmitter because most of the drugs that are useful in the treatment of schizophrenia are known to dampen dopamine activity in the brain. Admittedly, the evidence linking schizophrenia to neurotransmitter levels is riddled with interpretive problems (Davidson, Losonczy, & Davis, 1986). Nonetheless, investigators continue to search for the neurochemical bases of schizophrenia.

Structural Abnormalities in the Brain

Various studies have suggested that schizophrenic individuals have difficulty in focusing their attention (Mirsky & Duncan, 1986). Some theorists believe that many bizarre aspects of schizophrenic behavior may be due mainly to an inability to filter out unimportant stimuli. This lack of selectivity supposedly leaves victims of the disorder flooded with overwhelming, confusing sensory input.

These problems with attention suggest that schizophrenic disorders may be caused by neurological defects (Lehmann, 1985). Until recently, this theory was based more on speculation than on actual research. However, new advances in brain-imaging technology are beginning to yield some intriguing data. The findings suggest there is an association between enlarged brain ventricles (the hollow, fluid-filled cavities in the brain) and chronic schizophrenic disturbance (Andreasen, 1985).

The significance of enlarged ventricles in the brain is hotly debated, however. Enlarged ventricles have been found in only about 20%–25% of the schizophrenic persons tested (Weinberger, Wagner, & Wyatt, 1983). Moreover, enlarged ventricles are not unique to schizophrenia. They are a sign of many kinds of brain pathology. Furthermore, even if the association between enlarged ventricles and schizophrenia is replicated consistently, it will be difficult to sort out whether this brain abnormality is a cause or an effect of schizophrenia.

Communication Deviance

Over the years, hundreds of investigators have tried to relate patterns of family interaction to the development of schizophrenia. Popular theories have come and gone as empirical evidence has overturned once-plausible hypotheses (Goldstein, 1988). Vigorous research and debate in this area continue today. The current emphasis is on families' communication patterns and their expression of emotions.

Various theorists assert that vulnerability to schizophrenia is increased by exposure to defective interpersonal communication during childhood. Studies have

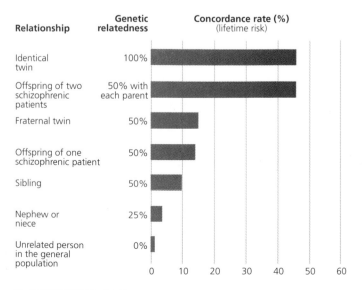

Figure 15.12. Genetic vulnerability to schizophrenic disorders. Relatives of schizophrenic patients have an elevated risk for schizophrenia. This risk is greater among closer relatives. Although environment also plays a role in the etiology of schizophrenia, the concordance rates shown here suggest that there must be a genetic vulnerability to the disorder. (Data from Nicol & Gottesman, 1983)

found a relationship between schizophrenia and *communication deviance* (Goldstein, 1984; Singer, Wynne, & Toohey, 1978). Communication deviance includes unintelligible speech, stories with no endings, heavy use of unusual words, extensive contradictions, and paying poor attention to children's communication efforts. The evidence suggests that schizophrenia is more likely to develop when youngsters grow up in homes characterized by vague, muddled, fragmented communication. Researchers speculate that communication deviance gradually undermines a child's sense of reality and encourages youngsters to withdraw into their own private worlds, setting the stage for schizophrenic thinking later in life.

Expressed Emotion

Studies of expressed emotion have primarily focused on how this element of family dynamics influences the *course* of schizophrenic illness after the onset of the disorder (Leff & Vaughn, 1985). *Expressed emotion* reflects the degree to which a relative of a schizophrenic patient displays highly critical or emotionally overinvolved attitudes toward the patient. Audiotaped interviews are used to assess relatives' expressed emotion. The interviews are carefully evaluated for critical comments, resentment toward the patient, and excessive emotional involvement (overprotective, overconcerned attitudes).

Studies show that a family's expressed emotion is a good predictor of the course of a schizophrenic patient's illness (Leff & Vaughn, 1981). After release from a hospital, schizophrenic patients who return to a family high in expressed emotion show relapse rates three or four times that of patients who return to a family low in expressed

emotion. Part of the problem for patients returning to homes high in expressed emotion is that their families probably are sources of more stress than social support. And like virtually all mental disorders, schizophrenia is influenced to some extent by life stress (Schwartz & Myers, 1977).

Precipitating Stress

Most theories of schizophrenia assume that stress plays a key role in triggering schizophrenic disorders (McGlashan, 1986; Zubin, 1986). According to this notion, various biological and psychological factors influence individuals' *vulnerability* to schizophrenia. High stress may then serve to precipitate a schizophrenic disorder in someone who is vulnerable. The stress-vulnerability model can integrate the diverse array of factors known to be involved in the etiology of schizophrenia.

Schizophrenia is the last of the major, Axis I diagnostic categories that we will consider. We'll complete our overview of different types of abnormal behavior with a brief look at the personality disorders. These disorders are recorded on Axis II in the DSM classification system.

PERSONALITY DISORDERS

We have seen repeatedly that it is often difficult to draw that imaginary line between healthy and disordered behavior. This is especially true in the case of personality disorders, which are relatively mild disturbances in comparison with most of the Axis I disorders. **Personality disorders are a class of disorders marked by extreme,**

Personality Disorders			
Cluster	Disorder	Description	% male
Anxious / fearful	Avoidant personality disorder	Excessively sensitive to potential rejection, humiliation, or shame; socially withdrawn in spite of desire for acceptance from others	50
	Dependent personality disorder	Excessively lacking in self-reliance and self-esteem; passively allowing others to make all decisions; constantly subordinating own needs to others' needs	31
	Passive-aggressive personality disorder	Indirectly resistant to demands for adequate social and occupational performance; tending to procrastinate, dawdle, and "forget"	54
	Obsessive-compulsive personality disorder	Preoccupied with organization, rules, schedules, lists, trivial details, extremely conventional, serious, and formal; unable to express warm emotions	50
Odd / eccentric	Schizoid personality disorder	Defective in capacity for forming social relationships, showing absence of warm, tender feelings for others	78
	Schizotypal personality disorder	Showing social deficits and oddities of thinking, perception, and communication that resemble schizophrenia	55
	Paranoid personality disorder	Showing pervasive and unwarranted suspiciousness and mistrust of people; overly sensitive; prone to jealousy	67
Dramatic / impulsive	Histrionic personality disorder	Overly dramatic; tending to exaggerated expressions of emotion; egocentric, seeking attention	15
	Narcissistic personality disorder	Grandiosely self-important; preoccupied with success fantasies; expecting special treatment; lacking interpersonal empathy	70
	Borderline personality disorder	Unstable in self-image, mood, and interpersonal relationships; impulsive and unpredictable	38
	Antisocial personality disorder	Chronically violating the rights of others; failing to accept social norms, to form attachments to others, or to sustain consistent work behavior; exploitive and reckless	82

inflexible personality traits that cause subjective distress or impaired social and occupational functioning. Essentially, people with these disorders display certain personality traits to an excessive degree and in rigid ways that undermine their adjustment. Personality disorders usually emerge in late childhood or adolescence and often continue throughout adulthood. It is difficult to estimate the prevalence of these subtle disorders, but it is clear that they are common (Merikangas & Weissman, 1986).

DSM-III-R lists 11 different personality disorders. All 11 disorders are described briefly in Figure 15.13. If you examine this table, you will find a diverse collection of maladaptive personality syndromes. You may also notice that some personality disorders essentially are mild versions of more severe Axis I disorders.

Clusters of Personality Disorders

As shown in Figure 15.13, the 11 personality disorders are grouped into three related clusters. The four disorders in the *anxious/fearful cluster* are marked by maladaptive efforts to control anxiety and fear about social rejection. People with the three disorders in the *odd/eccentric cluster* are distrustful, socially aloof, and unable to "connect" with others emotionally. The four personality disorders in the *dramatic/impulsive cluster* have less in common with each other than those grouped in the first two clusters. The histrionic and narcissistic personalities share a flair for overdramatizing everything. Impulsiveness is the common ground shared by the borderline and antisocial personality disorders.

Diagnostic Problems

Since the publication of DSM-III in 1980, many critics have argued that the personality disorders overlap too much with Axis I disorders and with each other (Frances & Widiger, 1986). The extent of this problem was documented in a study by Leslie Morey (1988). She reviewed the cases of 291 patients who had received a specific

Figure 15.13. Personality disorders. DSM-III-R describes 11 different personality disorders that fall into three clusters, as shown here. Some of these disorders are more common in men and some in women, as the figures in the far right column indicate. (Based on Millon, 1981)

personality disorder diagnosis to see how many of the patients could have met the criteria for any of the other ten personality disorders. Morey found massive overlap among the diagnoses. For example, among patients with a diagnosis of histrionic personality disorder, 56% also qualified for a borderline disorder, 54% for a narcissistic disorder, 32% for an avoidant disorder, 30% for a dependent disorder, and 29% for a paranoid disorder.

Clearly, there are fundamental problems with Axis II as a classification system, and revisions are sorely needed (Kiesler, 1986; Millon, 1986). The overlap among the personality disorders makes it virtually impossible to achieve consistent diagnoses. The poorly defined nature of personality disorders also hinders research. The only personality disorder that has a long history of extensive research is the antisocial personality disorder, which we examine next.

Antisocial Personality Disorder

The antisocial personality disorder has a misleading name. The antisocial designation does *not* mean that people with this disorder shun social interaction. Rather than shrinking from social interaction, many are sociable, friendly, and superficially charming. People with this disorder are *antisocial* in that they choose to *reject widely accepted social norms* regarding moral principles and behavior.

Description
The *antisocial personality disorder* is marked by impulsive, callous, manipulative, aggressive, and irresponsible behavior that reflects a failure to accept social norms. Antisocial personalities chronically violate the rights of others. They often use their social charm to cultivate others' liking or loyalty in order to exploit them. Since they haven't accepted the social norms they violate, antisocial personalities rarely feel guilty about their transgressions. Essentially, they lack an adequate conscience. The antisocial personality disorder occurs much more fre-

quently among males than females. Studies suggest that it is a moderately common disorder, seen in roughly 2%–3% of the population (Cadoret, 1986).

Many antisocial personalities get involved in illegal activities. Hare (1983) estimates that about 40% of convicted felons in prisons meet the criteria for an antisocial personality disorder. However, many antisocial personalities keep their exploitative, amoral behavior channeled within the boundaries of the law. Such people may even enjoy high status in our society (Sutker & Allain, 1983). In other words, the concept of the antisocial personality disorder applies to cutthroat business executives, scheming politicians, unprincipled lawyers, and money-hungry evangelists as well as to con artists, drug dealers, thugs, burglars, and petty thieves.

Antisocial personalities rarely experience genuine affection for others. However, they may be skilled at faking affection so they can exploit people. Sexually, they are predatory and promiscuous. They also tend to be irresponsible and impulsive. They can tolerate very little frustration, and they pursue immediate gratification. These characteristics make them unreliable employees, unfaithful spouses, inattentive parents, and undependable friends. Many antisocial personalities have a checkered history of divorce, child abuse, and job instability.

Etiology

Investigating the roots of antisocial personality disorders has proven difficult because people with these disorders generally do not voluntarily seek help from our mental health system. They usually don't see anything wrong with themselves. Many theorists believe that biological factors contribute to the development of antisocial personality disorders. Twin studies suggest that there is a genetic predisposition toward these disorders (Crowe, 1983).

Efforts to relate psychological factors to antisocial behavior have emphasized observational learning and inadequate socialization. Meyer (1980) reports that antisocial personalities tend to come from homes where discipline is inconsistent, ineffective, or nonexistent. Antisocial personalities are also more likely to emerge from homes where one or both parents exhibit antisocial traits (Robins, 1966). These parents presumably model exploitative, amoral behavior, which their children acquire through observational learning.

SUMMARY

The medical model assumes that it is useful to view abnormal behavior as a disease. There are serious problems with the medical model, but the disease analogy is useful if one remembers that it is only an analogy.

Three criteria are employed in deciding whether people suffer from psychological disorders: deviance, personal distress, and maladaptive behavior. Often, it is difficult to clearly draw a line between normality and abnormality. Contrary to popular stereotypes, people with psychologi-

cal disorders are not particularly bizarre or dangerous. Psychological disorders are not a manifestation of personal weakness, and even the most severe disorders are potentially curable.

DSM-III-R is the official psychodiagnostic classification system in the United States. This system describes over 200 disorders and asks for information about patients on five axes. It is clear that psychological disorders are more common than widely believed, affecting roughly one third of the population.

The anxiety disorders include the generalized anxiety disorder, phobic disorder, panic disorder, and obsessive-compulsive disorder. These disorders have been linked to a highly reactive autonomic nervous system, mitral valve prolapse, and child-rearing styles. Many anxiety responses, especially phobias, may be caused by classical conditioning and maintained by operant conditioning.

Somatoform disorders include somatization disorders, conversion disorder, and hypochondria. These disorders often emerge in people with highly suggestible, histrionic personalities. Somatoform disorders may be a learned avoidance strategy reinforced by attention and sympathy. Dissociative disorders include psychogenic amnesia and multiple personality. These disorders are uncommon, and their causes are not well understood.

The principal mood disorders are major (unipolar) depression and bipolar mood disorder. People vary in their genetic vulnerability to mood disorders, which are accompanied by changes in neurochemical activity in the brain. Cognitive models posit that an attributional style emphasizing internal, stable, and global attributions contributes to depression. Depression is often rooted in interpersonal inadequacies and sometimes is stress-related.

Schizophrenic disorders are characterized by deterioration of adaptive behavior, irrational thought, distorted perception, and disturbed mood. Schizophrenic disorders are classified as paranoid, catatonic, disorganized, or undifferentiated, although a new classification scheme is under study. Research has linked schizophrenia to a genetic vulnerability, changes in neurotransmitter activity, and structural abnormalities in the brain. Precipitating stress and unhealthy family dynamics, especially communication deviance and expressed emotion, may also contribute.

There are 11 personality disorders recorded on Axis II in DSM. Personality disorders can be grouped into three clusters: anxious/fearful, odd/eccentric, and dramatic/impulsive. However, specific personality disorders are poorly defined and there is excessive overlap among them. The antisocial personality disorder involves manipulative, impulsive, exploitative, aggressive behavior. Research on the etiology of this disorder has implicated genetic vulnerability, inadequate socialization, and observational learning.

In the upcoming Application, we take a look at a deadly problem: suicide. We'll describe some common myths about suicide and discuss suicide prevention.

Answer the following true or false.

☐ **1.** People who talk about suicide don't actually commit suicide.

☐ **2.** Suicides usually take place with little or no warning.

☐ **3.** People who attempt suicide are fully intent on dying.

☐ **4.** People who are suicidal remain so forever.

The four statements above are all false. They are myths about suicide that we will dispose of momentarily. First, however, let's discuss the magnitude of this tragic problem.

PREVALENCE OF SUICIDE

There are about 200,000 suicide attempts in the United States each year. Roughly one in eight of these attempts is "successful." This makes suicide the eighth leading cause of death in the United States. Worse yet, official statistics may underestimate the scope of the problem. Many suicides are disguised as accidents, either by the suicidal person or by the survivors who try to cover up afterward. Thus, experts estimate that there may be ten times more suicides than officially reported (Hirschfeld & Davidson, 1988).

WHO COMMITS SUICIDE?

Anyone can commit suicide. No segment of society is immune. Nonetheless, some groups are at higher risk than others (Cross & Hirschfeld, 1986). For instance, the prevalence of suicide varies according to *marital status*. Married people commit suicide less frequently than divorced, bereaved, or single people. In regard to occupational status, suicide rates are particularly high among people who are unemployed and among prestigious and pressured professionals, like doctors and lawyers.

Sex and *age* have complex relations to suicide rates. On the one hand, women *attempt* suicide more often than men. On the other hand, men are more likely to actually kill themselves in an attempt, so they *complete* more suicides than women. In regard to *age*, suicide attempts peak

between ages 24 and 44, but completed suicides are most frequent after age 55. However, age trends are different for men and women, as you can see in Figure 15.14.

Unfortunately, suicide rates have doubled among adolescents and young adults in the last couple of decades. *College students* are at higher risk than their noncollege peers. Academic pressures and setbacks do *not* appear to be the principal cause of this elevated suicide rate among collegians. Interpersonal problems and loneliness seem to be more important (see Figure 15.15).

Suicide is *not* committed only by people with severe mental illness, although elevated suicide rates are found for most categories of psychological disorders. As

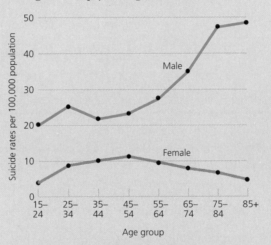

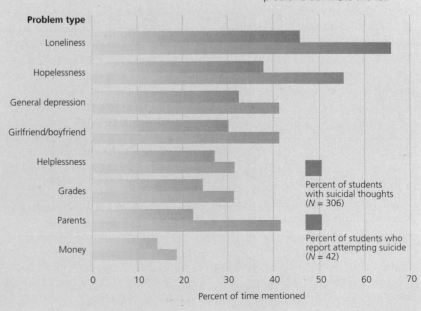

Percent of time mentioned

Under-standing and Preventing Suicide

Figure 15.14. Suicide rates in the United States by age and sex. At all ages, more men than women commit suicide, but the age patterns for the two sexes are noticeably different. The rate of male suicide peaks during the retirement years, whereas the rate of female suicide peaks in middle adulthood. (Data from Cross & Hirschfeld, 1986)

Figure 15.15. Personal problems reported by suicidal students. Westefeld and Furr (1987) gathered data on the problems mentioned by students who had attempted suicide or who reported suicidal thoughts. On the whole, interpersonal problems dominate this list.

Figure 15.16. The relationship between suicide and mood disorders. Two groups with elevated risk of suicide are people with mood disorders and people who have made previous suicide attempts. Between them, these groups account for a high percentage of suicides. (Adapted from Avery & Winokur, 1978)

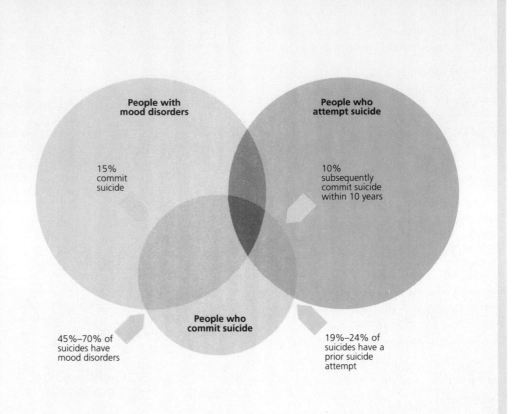

People with mood disorders

15% commit suicide

People who attempt suicide

10% subsequently commit suicide within 10 years

People who commit suicide

45%–70% of suicides have mood disorders

19%–24% of suicides have a prior suicide attempt

you might predict, suicide rates are highest for people with mood disorders, especially depression. Figure 15.16 shows how mood disorders and suicide attempts overlap.

MYTHS ABOUT SUICIDE

We began with four false statements about suicide. Let's examine these myths, which are discussed by Edwin Shneidman and his colleagues (Shneidman, 1985; Shneidman, Farberow, & Litman, 1970).

Myth 1: People who talk about suicide don't actually commit suicide. Undoubtedly, there are many people who threaten suicide without ever going through with it. Nonetheless, there is no group at higher risk for suicide than those who openly discuss the possibility. Many people who kill themselves have a history of earlier threats that they did not carry out.

Myth 2: Suicide usually takes place with little or no warning. It is estimated that eight out of ten suicide attempts are preceded by some kind of warning. These warnings may range from clear threats to vague statements. For example, at dinner with friends the night before he committed suicide, one prominent attorney cut up his American Express card, saying, "I'm not going to need this anymore." The probability of an actual suicide attempt is greatest when a threat is clear, when it includes a detailed plan, and when the plan involves a relatively deadly method.

Myth 3: People who attempt suicide are fully intent on dying. It appears that only about 3%–5% of those who attempt suicide definitely want to die. About 30% of the people who make an attempt seem ambivalent. They arrange things so that their fate is largely a matter of chance. The remaining two thirds of suicide attempts are made by people who appear to have no interest in dying! They only want to send out a very dramatic distress signal. Thus, they arrange their suicide so that a rescue is quite likely. These variations in intent probably explain why only about one eighth of suicide attempts end in death.

Myth 4: People who are suicidal remain so forever. Many people who become suicidal do so for a limited period of time. If they manage to ride through their crisis period, thoughts of suicide may disappear entirely. Apparently, time heals many wounds—if it is given the opportunity.

PREVENTING SUICIDE

There is no simple and dependable way to prevent someone from going ahead with a threatened suicide. One expert on suicide (Wekstein, 1979) makes the point that "perhaps nobody really knows *exactly* what to do when dealing with an imminent suicide" (p. 129). However, we will review some general advice that may be useful if you ever have to help someone through a suicidal crisis (Farberow, 1974; Shneidman et al., 1970).

1. *Provide empathy and social support.* First and foremost, you must show the suicidal person that you care. People often contemplate suicide because they see the world around them as indifferent and uncaring. Hence, you must demonstrate to the suicidal person that you are genuinely concerned. Even if you are thrust into a situation where you barely know the suicidal person, you need to provide empathy. Suicide threats are often a last-ditch cry for help. It is therefore imperative that you offer to help.

2. *Identify and clarify the crucial problem.* The suicidal person is often terribly confused and feels lost in a sea of frustration and problems. It is a good idea to try to help sort through this confusion. Encourage the person to try to identify the crucial problem. Once it is isolated, the crucial problem may not seem quite so overwhelming. It also may help to point out that the person's confusion is clouding his or her ability to rationally judge the seriousness of the problem.

3. *Suggest alternative courses of action.* People thinking about suicide often see it as the only solution to their problems. This is obviously an irrational view. Try to chip away at this premise by offering other possible solutions for the problem that has been identified as crucial. Suicidal people often are too distraught and disoriented to do this on their own. Therefore, it may help if you assist them.

4. *Capitalize on any doubts.* For most people, life is not easy to give up. They are racked by doubts about the wisdom of their decision. Many people will voice their unique reasons for doubting whether they should take the suicidal path. Zero in on these doubts. They may be your best arguments for life over death. For instance, if a person expresses concern about how her or his suicide will affect family members, capitalize on this source of doubt.

5. *Encourage professional consultation.* Most mental health professionals have at least some experience in dealing with suicidal crises. Many cities have suicide prevention centers with 24-hour hotlines. These centers are staffed with people who have been specially trained to deal with suicidal problems. It is important to try to get a suicidal person to seek professional assistance. The mere fact that you have talked a person out of attempting a threatened suicide does not mean that the crisis is over. The contemplation of suicide indicates that a person is experiencing great distress. Given this reality, professional intervention is crucial.

1. Describe and evaluate the medical model of abnormal behavior.

2. Explain the most commonly used critieria of abnormality and discuss two complexities in their application.

3. List four myths about psychological disorders.

4. Describe the five axes of DSM-III-R and discuss some controversial aspects of this system.

5. Discuss the prevalence of psychological disorders.

6. List four types of anxiety disorders and the symptoms of each disorder.

7. Discuss the contribution of biological factors, conditioning, and child rearing to the etiology of anxiety disorders.

8. Compare and contrast the three somato-form disorders and discuss their etiology.

9. Describe two dissociative disorders and discuss their etiology.

10. Describe the two major mood disorders: depression and bipolar mood disorder.

11. Explain how genetic and neurochemical factors may be related to the development of mood disorders.

12. Explain how cognitive factors, interpersonal factors, and stress may contribute to mood disorders.

13. Describe the general symptoms of schizophrenia.

14. Describe schizophrenic subtypes and discuss the course of schizophrenia.

15. Summarize how genetic vulnerability, neurochemical factors, and structural abnormalities in the brain may contribute to the etiology of schizophrenia.

16. Summarize evidence on how communication deviance, expressed emotion, and stress may contribute to schizophrenia.

17. Describe three broad clusters of personality disorders and diagnostic problems with these disorders.

18. Describe the antisocial personality disorder and discuss its etiology.

19. Summarize how age, sex, marital status, and occupation are related to the prevalence of suicide.

20. List four myths about suicidal behavior and summarize advice on preventing a suicide.

KEY TERMS

Agoraphobia
Antisocial personality disorder
Anxiety disorders
Attributions
Bipolar mood disorder
Catatonic schizophrenia
Concordance rate
Conversion disorders
Delusions
Depressive disorders
Diagnosis
Disorganized schizophrenia
Dissociative disorders
Epidemiology
Etiology
Generalized anxiety disorder
Hallucinations
Hypochondriasis
Medical model
Mood disorders
Multiple-personality disorders

Neurotic
Neurotransmitters
Obsessive-compulsive disorder
Panic disorder
Paranoid schizophrenia
Personality disorders
Phobic disorders
Prevalence
Prognosis
Psychogenic amnesia
Psychosomatic diseases
Psychotic
Schizophrenic disorders
Seasonal affective disorder
Somatization disorder
Somatoform disorders
Transvestism
Undifferentiated schizophrenia

KEY PEOPLE

Nancy Andreasen
David Rosenhan
Martin Seligman
Thomas Szasz

Manifest Anxiety Scale

INSTRUCTIONS

The statements below inquire about your behavior and emotions. Consider each statement carefully. Then indicate whether the statement is generally true or false for you. Record your responses (true or false) in the spaces provided.

THE SCALE

_____ 1. I do not tire quickly.

_____ 2. I believe I am no more nervous than most others.

_____ 3. I have very few headaches.

_____ 4. I work under a great deal of tension.

_____ 5. I frequently notice my hand shakes when I try to do something.

_____ 6. I blush no more often than others.

_____ 7. I have diarrhea once a month or more.

_____ 8. I worry quite a bit over possible misfortunes.

_____ 9. I practically never blush.

_____ 10. I am often afraid that I am going to blush.

_____ 11. My hands and feet are usually warm enough.

_____ 12. I sweat very easily even on cool days.

_____ 13. Sometimes when embarrassed, I break out in a sweat that annoys me greatly.

_____ 14. I hardly ever notice my heart pounding, and I am seldom short of breath.

_____ 15. I feel hungry almost all the time.

_____ 16. I am very seldom troubled by constipation.

_____ 17. I have a great deal of stomach trouble.

_____ 18. I have had periods in which I lost sleep over worry.

_____ 19. I am easily embarrassed.

_____ 20. I am more sensitive than most other people.

_____ 21. I frequently find myself worrying about something.

_____ 22. I wish I could be as happy as others seem to be.

_____ 23. I am usually calm and not easily upset.

_____ 24. I feel anxiety about something or someone almost all the time.

_____ 25. I am happy most of the time.

_____ 26. It makes me nervous to have to wait.

_____ 27. Sometimes I become so excited that I find it hard to get to sleep.

_____ 28. I have sometimes felt that difficulties were piling up so high that I could not overcome them.

_____ 29. I must admit that I have at times been worried beyond reason over something that really did not matter.

_____ 30. I have very few fears compared to my friends.

_____ 31. I certainly feel useless at times.

_____ 32. I find it hard to keep my mind on a task or job.

_____ 33. I am unusually self-conscious.

_____ 34. I am inclined to take things hard.

_____ 35. At times I think I am no good at all.

_____ 36. I am certainly lacking in self-confidence.

_____ 37. I sometimes feel that I am about to go to pieces.

_____ 38. I am entirely self-confident.

SCORING THE SCALE

The scoring key is reproduced below. You should circle each of your true or false responses that correspond to the keyed responses. Add up the number of responses you circle, and this total is your score on the Manifest Anxiety Scale.

1. False	9. False	17. True	25. False	33. True
2. False	10. True	18. True	26. True	34. True
3. False	11. False	19. True	27. True	35. True
4. True	12. True	20. True	28. True	36. True
5. True	13. True	21. True	29. True	37. True
6. False	14. False	22. True	30. False	38. False
7. True	15. True	23. False	31. True	
8. True	16. False	24. True	32. True	

MY SCORE _____

WHAT THE SCALE MEASURES

You just took a form of the Taylor Manifest Anxiety Scale (1953), as revised by Richard Suinn (1968). Suinn took the original 50-item scale and identified all items for which there was a social desirability bias (11) or a response set (1). He eliminated these 12 items and found that the scale's reliability and validity were not appreciably decreased. Essentially, the scale measures trait anxiety—that is, the tendency to experience anxiety in a wide variety of situations.

RESEARCH ON THE SCALE

Hundreds of studies have been done on the various versions of the Taylor Manifest Anxiety Scale. The validity of the scale has been supported by demonstrations that various groups of psychiatric patients score higher than unselected groups of "normals" and by demonstrations that the scale correlates well with other measures of anxiety. Although the Manifest Anxiety Scale is no longer a "state of the art" measure of anxiety, it is an old classic that is relatively easy to score.

INTERPRETING YOUR SCORE

Our norms are based on data collected by Suinn (1968) on 89 undergraduates who responded to the scale anonymously.

NORMS

High score:	16–38
Intermediate score:	6–15
Low score:	0–5

What Are Your Attitudes on Mental Illness?

1. List seven adjectives that you associate with people who are diagnosed as mentally ill.

Crazy, weird
queer, strange
eccentric, Deranged
Insane

2. If you meet someone who was once diagnosed as mentally ill, what are your immediate reactions?

guarded, careful

3. List some comments about people with psychological disorders that you heard when you were a child.

Stay away from

4. Have you had any actual interactions with "mentally ill" people that have supported or contradicted your expectations?

5. Do you agree with the idea that psychological disorders should be viewed as an illness or disease? Defend your position.

16
Psychotherapy

What do you picture when you hear the term *psychotherapy*? If you're like most people, you probably picture a troubled patient lying on a couch in a therapist's office, with the therapist asking penetrating questions and providing sage advice. Typically, people believe that psychotherapy is only for those who are "sick" and that therapists have special powers that allow them to "see through" their clients. It is also widely believed that therapy requires years of deep probing into a client's innermost secrets. Many people further assume that therapists routinely tell their patients how to lead their lives. Like most stereotypes, this picture of psychotherapy is a mixture of fact and fiction, as you'll see in the upcoming pages.

In this chapter, we'll take a down-to-earth look at the complex process of psychotherapy. We'll start by discussing some general questions about the provision of therapy. Who seeks therapy? What kinds of professionals provide therapy? How many different types of therapy are there? After we've considered these general issues, we'll examine some of the more widely used approaches to psychotherapy, analyzing their goals, techniques, and effectiveness. In the Application at the end of the chapter, we focus on practical issues in case you ever have to advise someone about seeking psychotherapy.

THE ELEMENTS OF PSYCHOTHERAPY: TREATMENTS, CLIENTS, AND THERAPISTS

Sigmund Freud, whom we discussed in Chapter 2, is widely credited with launching modern psychotherapy. Ironically, the landmark case that inspired Freud was actually treated by one of his colleagues, Josef Breuer. Around 1880, Breuer began to treat a young woman named Anna O. (a pseudonym). Anna exhibited a variety of physical maladies, including headaches, coughing, and a loss of feeling and movement in her right arm. Much to his surprise, Breuer discovered that Anna's physical symptoms cleared up when he encouraged her to talk about emotionally charged experiences from her past.

Breuer and Freud discussed the case, and they speculated that talking things through enabled Anna to drain off bottled-up emotions that had caused her symptoms. Breuer found the intense emotional exchange in this treatment not to his liking, so he didn't follow through on his discovery. However, Freud applied Breuer's insight to other patients, and his successes led him to develop a systematic treatment procedure, which he called *psychoanalysis*. Anna O. called her treatment "the talking cure." However, as you'll see, psychotherapy isn't always curative, and many modern therapies place little emphasis on talking.

Freud's breakthrough ushered in a century of progress for psychotherapy. Psychoanalysis spawned many offspring as Freud's followers developed their own systems of treatment. Since then, approaches to psychotherapy have steadily grown more numerous, more diverse, and more effective. Today, people can choose from a bewildering array of therapies.

The immense diversity of therapeutic treatments makes it terribly difficult to define the concept of *psychotherapy*. After organizing an unprecedented conference that brought together many of the world's leading authorities on psychotherapy, Jeffrey Zeig commented, "I do not believe there is any capsule definition of psychotherapy on which the 26 presenters could agree" (Zeig, 1987, p. xix). In lieu of a definition, we can identify a few basic elements that the various approaches to therapy have in common. All psychotherapies involve a helping relationship (the treatment) between a professional with special training (the therapist) and another person in need of help (the client). As we look at each of these elements—the treatment, the therapist, and the client—you'll see the diverse nature of modern psychotherapy.

Figure 16.1. Patterns of seeking treatment. Not everyone who has a psychological disorder receives professional treatment. This graph shows the percentage of people with specific disorders who obtained mental health treatment during a six-month period. Research suggests that only a minority of people with disorders receive treatment. (Data based on Shapiro et al., 1984)

Treatments: How Many Types Are There?

In their efforts to help people, psychotherapists employ many different methods of treatment. Included among them are discussion, emotional support, persuasion, conditioning procedures, relaxation training, role playing, prescription of drugs, biofeedback, and group therapy. Some therapists also use a variety of less conventional procedures, such as rebirthing, poetry therapy, and primal therapy. No one knows exactly how many approaches to treatment there are. One handbook (Herink, 1980) lists over 250 distinct types of psychotherapy!

Fortunately, we can impose some order on this chaos. As varied as therapists' procedures are, approaches to treatment can be classified into three major categories.

1. *Insight therapies.* Insight therapy is "talk therapy" in the tradition of Freud's psychoanalysis. This is probably the approach to treatment that you envision when you think of psychotherapy. In insight therapies, clients engage in complex, often lengthy verbal interactions with their therapists. The goal in these discussions is to pursue increased insight regarding the nature of the client's difficulties and to sort through possible solutions. Insight therapy can be conducted with an individual or with a group.

2. *Behavior therapies.* Behavior therapies are based on the principles of learning and conditioning, which were introduced in Chapter 2. Instead of emphasizing personal insights, behavior therapists make direct efforts to alter problematic responses (phobic behaviors, for instance) and maladaptive habits (drug use, for instance). Behavior therapists work on changing clients' overt behaviors. They employ different procedures for different kinds of problems. Most of their procedures involve either classical conditioning or operant conditioning.

3. *Biomedical therapies.* Biomedical approaches to therapy involve interventions into a person's biological functioning. The most widely used procedures are the prescription of drugs and electroconvulsive (shock) therapy. As the name bio*medical* therapies suggests, only physicians (usually psychiatrists) can provide these biological treatments.

We will examine approaches to therapy that fall into each of the three categories just described. Although we'll find very different methods in each category, the three major classes of treatment are not entirely incompatible. For example, a client might be seen in insight therapy and be given medication at the same time.

Clients: Who Seeks Therapy?

In the therapeutic triad (treatments, therapists, clients), the greatest diversity of all is seen among the clients. They bring to therapy the full range of human problems: anxiety, depression, unsatisfactory interpersonal relations, troublesome habits, poor self-control, low self-esteem, marital conflicts, self-doubt, a sense of emptiness, and feelings of personal stagnation. Therapy is sought by people who feel troubled, but the nature and severity of the trouble varies greatly from one person to another. The two most common presenting problems are excessive anxiety and depression (Lichtenstein, 1980).

A client in treatment does *not* necessarily have an identifiable psychological disorder. Some people seek professional help for everyday problems (career decisions, for instance) or vague feelings of discontent. Thus, therapy includes efforts to foster clients' personal growth as well as professional interventions for mental disorders.

People vary considerably in their willingness to seek psychotherapy. Men are less likely than women to enter therapy, and people from the lower socioeconomic classes are more reluctant to seek therapy than those from the upper classes (Lichtenstein, 1980). *Unfortunately, it appears that many people who need therapy don't receive it.* As Figure 16.1 shows, only a minority of people with actual disorders receive treatment (Shapiro et al., 1984). People

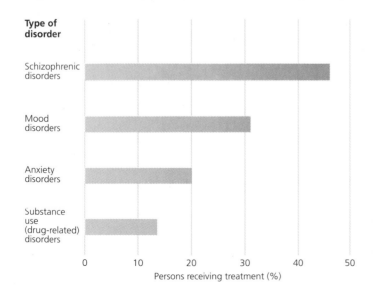

Type of disorder

Persons receiving treatment (%)

who could benefit from therapy do not seek it for a variety of reasons. Some are unaware of its availability, and some believe that it is always expensive. The biggest roadblock is that many people equate being in therapy with admitting personal weakness.

A small portion of clients are essentially forced into psychotherapy. In most cases, this coercion involves gentle pressure from a spouse, parent, friend, or employer. Sometimes, however, people are ordered into treatment by the courts, as in cases of involuntary commitment to a mental hospital.

Therapists: Who Provides Professional Treatment?

Friends and relatives may provide us with excellent advice about our personal problems, but their assistance does not qualify as therapy. Psychotherapy refers to *professional* treatment by someone with special training. A common source of confusion about psychotherapy is the variety of "helping professions" involved. Psychology and psychiatry are the principal professions involved in the provision of psychotherapy. However, therapy is also provided by psychiatric social workers, psychiatric nurses, and counselors, as outlined in Figure 16.2. Let's look at these mental health professions.

Psychologists

Two types of psychologists may provide therapy, although the distinction between them is more theoretical than real. *Clinical psychologists* **and** *counseling psychologists* **specialize in the diagnosis and treatment of psychological disorders and everyday behavioral problems.** In theory, the training of clinical psychologists emphasizes treatment of full-fledged disorders, whereas the training of counseling psychologists is slanted toward treatment of everyday adjustment problems in normal people. In practice, however, there is great overlap between clinical and counseling psychologists in training, in skills, and in the clientele they serve, so that they are virtually interchangeable.

Both types of psychologists must earn a doctoral degree (Ph.D., Psy.D., or Ed.D.). A doctorate in psychology requires five to seven years of training beyond a bachelor's degree. The process of gaining admission to a Ph.D. program in clinical psychology is highly competitive (about as competitive as for medical school). Psychologists receive most of their training on university campuses, although they serve a one- to two-year internship in a clinical setting, such as a hospital.

In providing therapy, psychologists use either insight or behavioral approaches. In comparison to psychiatrists, they are more likely to use behavioral techniques and less likely to use psychoanalytic methods. Clinical and counseling psychologists do psychological testing as well as psychotherapy, and many also conduct research.

Psychiatrists

Psychiatrists **are physicians who specialize in the treatment of psychological disorders.** Many psychiatrists also treat everyday behavioral problems. However, in comparison to psychologists, psychiatrists devote more time to relatively severe disorders (schizophrenia, mood disorders) and less time to everyday marital, family, job, and school problems.

Psychiatrists have an M.D. degree. Their graduate training requires four years of course work in medical school and a four-year apprenticeship in a residency at an approved hospital. Their psychotherapy training occurs during their residency, since the required course work in medical school is essentially the same for all students, whether they are going into surgery, pediatrics, or psychiatry.

In their provision of therapy, psychiatrists tend to emphasize biomedical treatments that nonmedical professionals cannot provide (drug therapy, for instance). Psychiatrists employ a variety of insight therapies, but psychoanalysis and its descendants remain dominant in psychiatry. In comparison to psychologists, psychiatrists are less likely to use group therapies or behavior therapies.

Different Types of Therapists

Title	Degree*	Years beyond bachelor's degree	Typical roles and activities
Clinical or counseling psychologist	Ph.D. Psy.D. Ed.D.	5–7	Diagnosis, psychological testing, insight and behavior therapy
Psychiatrist	M.D.	8	Diagnosis; insight, behavior, and biomedical therapy
Social worker	M.S.W.	2	Insight and behavior therapy, family therapy, helping patients return to the community
Psychiatric nurse	B.S., B.A., M.A.	0–2	Inpatient care, insight and behavior therapy
Counselor	M.A.	2	Insight and behavior therapy, working primarily with everyday adjustment problems and marital and career issues

*Ph.D = Doctor of Philosophy; Psy.D. = Doctor of Psychology; Ed.D. = Doctor of Education; M.D. = Medical Doctor; M.S.W. = Master of Social Work; B.S = Bachelor of Science; B.A. = Bachelor of Arts; M.A. = Master of Arts

Other Mental Health Professionals

Several other mental health professions provide psychotherapy services. In hospitals and other institutions, *psychiatric social workers* and *psychiatric nurses* often work as part of a treatment team with a psychologist or psychiatrist. Psychiatric nurses, who may have a bachelor's or master's degree in their field, play a large role in hospital inpatient treatment. Psychiatric social workers generally have a master's degree and typically work with patients and their families to ease the patient's integration back into the community.

Many kinds of *counselors* also provide therapeutic services. Counselors are usually found working in schools, colleges, and human service agencies (youth centers, geriatric centers, family planning centers, and so forth). Counselors typically have a master's degree. They often specialize in particular types of problems, such as vocational counseling, marital counseling, rehabilitation counseling, and drug counseling.

Although there are clear differences among the helping professions in education and training, their roles in the treatment process overlap considerably. In this chapter, we will refer to psychologists or psychiatrists as needed, but otherwise we'll use the terms *clinician*, *therapist*, and *mental health professional* to refer to psychotherapists of all kinds, regardless of their professional degree.

Now that we have discussed the basic elements in psychotherapy, we can examine specific approaches to treatment in terms of their goals, procedures, and effectiveness. We'll begin with a few representative insight therapies.

INSIGHT THERAPIES

There are many schools of thought about how to do insight therapy. Therapists with different theoretical orientations use different methods to pursue different kinds of insights. What these varied approaches have in common is that **insight therapies involve verbal inter-** **actions intended to enhance clients' self-knowledge and thus promote healthful changes in personality and behavior.**

There probably are around 200 different insight therapies, but the leading eight or ten approaches appear to account for the lion's share of treatment. In this section, we'll delve into psychoanalysis, related psychodynamic approaches, client-centered therapy, and cognitive therapy. We'll also discuss how insight therapy can be done with groups as well as individuals.

Psychoanalysis

After the case of Anna O., Sigmund Freud worked as a psychotherapist for almost 50 years in Vienna. Through a painstaking process of trial and error, he developed innovative techniques for the treatment of psychological disorders and distress. His system of *psychoanalysis* came to dominate psychiatry and remains extremely influential today (Greenley, Kepecs, & Henry, 1981).

Psychoanalysis **is an insight therapy that emphasizes the recovery of unconscious conflicts, motives, and defenses through techniques such as free association, dream analysis, and transference.** To appreciate the logic of psychoanalysis, we have to look at Freud's thinking about the roots of mental disorders.

Freud treated mostly anxiety-dominated disturbances, such as phobic, panic, obsessive-compulsive, and conversion disorders, which were then called *neuroses*. He believed that neurotic problems were caused by unconscious conflicts left over from early childhood. As explained in Chapter 2, he thought that these inner conflicts involved battles among the id, ego, and superego, usually over sexual and aggressive impulses. Freud theorized that people depend on defense mechanisms to avoid confronting these conflicts, which remain hidden in the depths of the unconscious. However, he noted that defensive maneuvers often lead to self-defeating behavior. Furthermore, he asserted that defenses usually are only partially successful in alleviating anxiety, guilt, and other

Figure 16.2. The principal mental health professions.
The majority of therapeutic services are provided by people trained in the five professions described here.

distressing emotions. With this model in mind, let's take a look at the therapeutic procedures employed in psychoanalysis.

Probing the Unconscious

Given Freud's assumptions, we can see that the logic of psychoanalysis is very simple. The analyst attempts to probe the murky depths of the unconscious to discover the unresolved conflicts causing the client's neurotic behavior. In a sense, the analyst functions as a psychological detective. In this effort to explore the unconscious, the therapist relies on two techniques: free association and dream analysis.

In *free association*, **clients spontaneously express their thoughts and feelings exactly as they occur, with as little censorship as possible.** Clients lie on a couch so they will be better able to let their minds drift freely. In free associating, clients expound on anything that comes to mind, regardless of how trivial, silly, or embarrassing it might be. Gradually, most clients begin to let everything pour out without conscious censorship. The analyst studies these free associations for clues about what is going on in the unconscious.

In *dream analysis*, **the therapist interprets the symbolic meaning of the client's dreams.** For Freud, dreams were the "royal road to the unconscious," the most direct means of access to patients' innermost conflicts, wishes, and impulses. Clients are encouraged and trained to remember their dreams, which they describe in therapy. The therapist then analyzes the symbolism in these dreams to interpret their meaning.

To better illustrate these matters, let's look at an actual case treated through psychoanalysis (adapted from Greenson, 1967, pp. 40–41). Mr. N. was troubled by an unsatisfactory marriage. He claimed to love his wife, but he pre-

ferred sexual relations with prostitutes. Mr. N. reported that his parents also endured lifelong marital difficulties. His childhood conflicts about their relationship appeared to be related to his problems. Both dream analysis and free association can be seen in the following description of a session in Mr. N.'s treatment.

Mr. N. reports a fragment of a dream. All that he can remember is that he is waiting for a red traffic light to change when he feels that someone has bumped into him from behind. . . . The associations led to Mr. N.'s love of cars, especially sports cars. He loved the sensation, in particular, of whizzing by those fat, old, expensive cars. . . . His father always hinted that he had been a great athlete, but he never substantiated it. . . . Mr. N. doubted whether his father could really perform. His father would flirt with a waitress in a cafe or make sexual remarks about women passing by, but he seemed to be showing off. If he were really sexual, he wouldn't resort to that.

As is characteristic of free association, Mr. N.'s train of thought meanders about with little direction. Nonetheless, clues about his unconscious conflicts are apparent. What did Mr. N.'s therapist extract from this session? The therapist saw sexual overtones in the dream fragment, where Mr. N. was bumped from behind. The therapist also inferred that Mr. N. had a competitive orientation toward his father, based on the free association about whizzing by fat, old, expensive cars. As you can see, analysts must *interpret* their clients' dreams and free associations. This is a critical process throughout psychoanalysis.

Interpretation

Interpretation involves the therapist's attempts to explain the inner significance of the client's thoughts, feelings, memories, and behaviors. Contrary to popular belief, analysts do not interpret everything, and they generally don't try to dazzle clients with startling revelations. Instead, analysts move forward inch by inch, offering interpretations that should be just out of the client's own reach. Mr. N.'s therapist eventually offered the following interpretations to his client.

I said to Mr. N. near the end of the hour that I felt he was struggling with his feelings about his father's sexual life. He seemed to be saying that his father was sexually not a very potent man. . . . He also recalls that he once found a packet of condoms under his father's pillow when he was an adolescent and he thought "My father must be going to prostitutes." I then intervened and pointed out that the condoms under his father's pillow seemed to indicate more obviously that his father used the condoms with his mother, who slept in the same bed. However, Mr. N. _wanted_ to believe his wish-fulfilling fantasy: mother doesn't want sex with father and father is not very potent. The patient was silent and the hour ended.

As you may already have guessed, the therapist has concluded that Mr. N.'s difficulties are rooted in an Oedipal complex (see Chapter 2). Mr. N. has unresolved sexual feelings toward his mother and hostile feelings about his father. These unconscious conflicts, which are rooted in his childhood, are distorting his intimate relations as an adult.

Resistance

How would you expect Mr. N. to respond to his therapist's suggestion that he was in competition with his father for the sexual attention of his mother? Obviously, most clients would have great difficulty accepting such an interpretation. Freud fully expected clients to display some resistance to therapeutic efforts. **_Resistance_ involves largely unconscious defensive maneuvers intended to hinder the progress of therapy.** Why do clients try to resist the helping process? Because they don't want to face up to the painful, disturbing conflicts that they have buried in their unconscious. Although they have sought help, they are reluctant to confront their real problems.

Resistance may take many forms. Patients may show up late for their sessions, merely pretend to engage in free association, or express hostility toward the therapist. For instance, Mr. N.'s therapist noted that after the session just described, "The next day he began by telling me that he was furious with me. . . ." Analysts use a variety of strategies to deal with their clients' resistance. Often, a key consideration is the handling of _transference_, which we consider next.

Transference

Transference occurs when clients start relating to their therapists in ways that mimic critical relationships in their lives. Thus, a client might start relating to a therapist as if the therapist were an overprotective mother, rejecting brother, or passive spouse. In a sense, the client _transfers_ conflicting feelings about important people onto the therapist. For instance, in his treatment, Mr. N. transferred some of the competitive hostility he felt toward his father onto his analyst.

Psychoanalysts often encourage transference so that clients begin to reenact relations with crucial people in the context of therapy. These reenactments can help bring repressed feelings and conflicts to the surface, allowing the client to work through them. The therapist's handling of transference is complicated and difficult because transference may arouse confusing, highly charged emotions in the client.

Undergoing psychoanalysis is not easy. It can be a slow, painful process of self-examination that routinely requires three to five years of hard work. Ultimately, if resistance and transference can be handled effectively, the therapist's interpretations should lead the client to profound insights. For instance, Mr. N. eventually admitted, "The old boy is probably right, it does tickle me to imagine that my mother preferred me and I could beat

In the psychoanalytic approach, the therapist encourages the client to reveal thoughts, feelings, and memories, which can then be interpreted in relation to the client's current problems.

out my father. Later, I wondered whether this had something to do with my own screwed-up sex life with my wife." According to Freud, once clients recognize the unconscious sources of their conflicts, they can resolve these conflicts and discard their neurotic defenses.

Modern Psychodynamic Therapies

Though still available, classical psychoanalysis as done by Freud is not widely practiced anymore. Freud's psychoanalytic method was geared to a particular kind of clientele that he was seeing in Vienna many years ago. As his followers fanned out across Europe and America, many found that it was necessary to adapt psychoanalysis to different cultures, changing times, and new kinds of patients. Thus, many variations on Freud's original approach to psychoanalysis have developed over the years. These descendants of psychoanalysis are collectively known as *psychodynamic approaches* to therapy.

Some of these adaptations, such as those by Carl Jung (1917) and Alfred Adler (1927), were sweeping revisions based on fundamental differences in theory. Other variations, such as those devised by Melanie Klein (1948) and Heinz Kohut (1971), involved more subtle changes in theory. Still other revisions (Alexander, 1954; Stekel, 1950) simply involved efforts to modernize and streamline psychoanalytic techniques (rather than theory), as outlined in Figure 16.3. Hence, today we have a rich diversity of psychodynamic approaches to therapy. Although these many variations are beyond the scope of our review, we will examine a few key trends seen in modern psychodynamic therapies, as highlighted by Kutash (1976) and Baker (1985).

First, many new approaches have tried to speed up the pace of psychodynamic therapy. Modern approaches are less likely to assume that it will take three to five years to make therapeutic gains.

Second, the goals of modern psychodynamic therapies usually go beyond the discovery of repressed conflicts and defenses. Modern analysts devote less attention to the workings of the unconscious and more attention to conscious processes.

Third, client-therapist interactions have become more direct. Modern analysts depend less on the gradual, rambling process of free association. Many analysts have abandoned the couch and free association in favor of face-to-face interaction that emphasizes candid communication.

Fourth, modern psychodynamic therapies no longer assume that neuroses grow out of conflicts centering on sex and aggression. Today, analysts put less emphasis on probing into these areas, especially clients' sexuality.

Fifth, there also is less emphasis on delving into a client's distant past to reconstruct early childhood experiences. Instead, there is increased interest in understanding the client's present problems and current social relations.

Psychodynamic therapies have continued to evolve since Freud's era. In recent decades, though, most of the major new innovations in insight therapy have emerged out of the humanistic tradition born in the 1950s. The most widely practiced humanistic therapy is Carl Rogers's *client-centered therapy*. Rogers's approach, which bears only slight resemblance to psychoanalysis, is next on our agenda.

Client-Centered Therapy

You may have heard of people going into therapy to "find themselves" or to "get in touch with their real feelings." These now-popular phrases emerged out of the human potential movement, which was stimulated in part by Carl Rogers's work (Rogers, 1951, 1986). Employing a humanistic perspective, Rogers devised *client-centered therapy* (also known as *person-centered therapy*) in the 1940s and 1950s.

Client-centered therapy is an insight therapy that emphasizes providing a supportive emotional climate for clients, who play a major role in determining the pace and direction of their therapy. You may wonder why the troubled, untrained client is put in charge of the pace and

Some Differences between Classical and Modern Psychoanalysis	
Classical psychoanalysis	**Modern psychoanalysis**
Frequency of treatment is usually four to five times per week.	Frequency of treatment is typically one to two times per week.
Patient is treated "on the couch."	Patient is typically seen "face to face."
Treatment goals emphasize character reconstruction.	Treatment emphasizes problem resolution, enhanced adaptation, and support of ego functions with limited character change.
Treatment approach emphasizes the neutrality and nonintrusion of the analyst.	Therapist assumes an active and direct stance.
Technique emphasizes "free association," uncovering, interpretation, and analysis of the transference and resistance.	A wide range of interventions are used, including interpretive, supportive, and educative techniques. Transference is typically kept less intense.

direction of the therapy. Rogers (1961) provides a compelling justification:

It is the client who knows what hurts, what directions to go, what problems are crucial, what experiences have been deeply buried. It began to occur to me that unless I had a need to demonstrate my own cleverness and learning, I would do better to rely upon the client for the direction of movement in the process. [pp. 11–12]

Rogers's theory about the principal causes of neurotic anxieties is quite different from the Freudian explanation. As discussed in Chapter 2, Rogers maintains that most personal distress is due to inconsistency, or "incongruence," between a person's self-concept and reality. According to his theory, incongruence makes people prone to feel threatened by realistic feedback about themselves from others. For example, if you inaccurately viewed yourself as a hardworking, dependable person, you would feel threatened by contradictory feedback from friends or co-workers. According to Rogers, anxiety about such feedback often leads to reliance on defense mechanisms, distortions of reality, and stifled personal growth. Excessive incongruence is thought to be rooted in clients' overdependence on others for approval and acceptance.

Given Rogers's theory, client-centered therapists stalk insights that are quite different from the repressed conflicts that psychoanalysts try to track down. Client-centered therapists help clients to realize that they do not have to worry constantly about pleasing others and winning acceptance. They encourage clients to respect their own feelings and values. They help people to restructure their self-concept to correspond better to reality. Ultimately, they try to foster self-acceptance and personal growth.

Therapeutic Climate

According to Rogers, the *process* of therapy is not as important as the emotional *climate* in which the therapy takes place. He believes that it is critical for the therapist to provide a warm, supportive, accepting climate. This creates a safe environment in which clients can confront their shortcomings without feeling threatened. The lack of threat should reduce clients' defensive tendencies and thus help them to open up. To create this atmosphere of emotional support, Rogers believes that client-centered therapists must provide three conditions.

1. *Genuineness.* The therapist must be genuine with the client, communicating in an honest and spontaneous manner. The therapist should not be phony or defensive.
2. *Unconditional positive regard.* The therapist must also show complete, nonjudgmental acceptance of the client as a person. The therapist should provide warmth and caring for the client with no strings attached. This does not mean that the therapist must approve of everything that the client says or does. A therapist can disapprove of a particular behavior while continuing to value the client as a human being.
3. *Empathy.* Finally, the therapist must provide accurate empathy for the client. This means that the therapist must understand the client's world from the client's point of view. Furthermore, the therapist must be articulate enough to communicate this understanding to the client.

Therapeutic Process

In client-centered therapy, the client and therapist work together as equals. The therapist provides relatively little guidance and keeps interpretation and advice to a minimum. So, just what does the client-centered therapist do, besides creating a supportive climate? Primarily, the therapist provides feedback to help clients sort out their feelings. The therapist's key task is *clarification*. Client-centered therapists try to function like a human mirror, reflecting statements back to their clients, but with enhanced clarity. They help clients to become more aware of their true feelings by highlighting themes that may be obscure in the clients' rambling discourse. The reflective nature of client-centered therapy can be seen in the following exchange between a client and therapist.

Figure 16.3. Comparing classical and modern psychoanalysis. Contemporary psychoanalytic therapists continue to practice in the tradition established by Freud, but there are a number of differences, as pointed out by Baker (1985). Baker divides contemporary psychodynamic therapies into three subgroups. "Modern psychoanalysis," profiled in the right column, refers to the group that has remained most loyal to Freud's ideas while modifying clinical techniques. (Adapted from Baker, 1985)

CLIENT: I really feel bad today . . . just terrible.

THERAPIST: You're feeling pretty bad.

CLIENT: Yeah, I'm angry and that's made me feel bad, especially when I can't do anything about it. I just have to live with it and shut up.

THERAPIST: You're very angry and feel like there's nothing you can safely do with your feelings.

CLIENT: Uh-huh. I mean . . . if I yell at my wife she gets hurt. If I don't say anything to her I feel tense.

THERAPIST: You're between a rock and a hard place—no matter what you do, you'll wind up feeling bad.

CLIENT: I mean she chews ice all day and all night. I feel stupid saying this. It's petty, I know. But when I sit there and try to concentrate, I hear all these slurping and crunching noises. I can't stand it . . . and I yell. She feels hurt—I feel bad—like I shouldn't have said anything.

THERAPIST: So when you finally say something you feel bad afterward.

CLIENT: Yeah, I can't say anything to her without getting mad and saying more than I should. And then I cause more trouble than it's worth. [Duke & Nowicki, 1979, p. 565]

By working with clients to clarify their feelings, client-centered therapists hope to gradually build toward more far-reaching insights. In particular, they try to help clients to become more aware of and comfortable about their genuine selves. Obviously, these are very ambitious goals. Client-centered therapy resembles psychoanalysis in that both seek to achieve a major reconstruction of a client's personality. We'll see more limited and specific goals in cognitive therapy, which we consider next.

Cognitive Therapy

In Chapter 3 we saw that our cognitive interpretations of events make all the difference in the world to how well we handle stress. In Chapter 15 we learned that cognitive factors play a key role in the development of depressive disorders. Citing the importance of findings such as these, Aaron Beck devised a treatment that focuses on clients' cognitive processes (Beck, 1987; Beck, Rush, Shaw, & Emery, 1979). **Cognitive therapy is an insight therapy that emphasizes recognizing and changing negative thoughts and maladaptive beliefs.** This approach resembles Albert Ellis's (1973, 1989) *rational-emotive therapy*. Since we covered Ellis's main ideas in our discussion of coping strategies (see Chapter 4), we'll focus on Beck's system here.

In recent years cognitive therapy has been applied fruitfully to a wide range of disorders (Hollon & Najavits, 1988), but it was originally devised as a treatment for depression. According to Beck, depression is caused by "errors" in thinking. He asserts that depression-prone people tend to do the following. (1) They blame their setbacks on personal inadequacies without considering circumstantial explanations. (2) They focus selectively on negative events while ignoring positive events. (3) They make unduly pessimistic projections about the future. (4) They draw negative conclusions about their worth as persons based on insignificant events. For instance, imagine that you earned a poor score on a minor quiz in a class. If you made the kinds of errors in thinking just described, you might blame the score on your woeful stupidity, dismiss comments from a classmate that it was an unfair test, hysterically predict that you will surely flunk the course, and conclude that you are not genuine college material.

Goals and Techniques

The goal of cognitive therapy is to change the way clients think. To begin, clients are taught to detect their automatic negative thoughts. These are self-defeating statements that people are prone to make when analyzing problems. Examples might include "I'm just not smart enough," "No one really likes me," and "It's all my fault." Clients are then trained to subject these automatic thoughts to reality testing. The therapist helps them to see how unrealistically negative the thoughts are.

The therapist's goal is not to promote unwarranted optimism, but rather to help the client to employ more

Aaron Beck

reasonable standards of evaluation. For example, a cognitive therapist might point out that a client's failure to get a desired promotion at work may be attributable to many factors and that this setback doesn't mean that the client is incompetent. Gradually, the therapist digs deeper, looking for the unrealistic assumptions that underlie clients' constant negative thinking. These, too, have to be changed.

Unlike client-centered therapists, cognitive therapists are actively involved in determining the pace and direction of treatment. They usually talk extensively in the therapy sessions. They may argue openly with clients as they try to persuade them to alter their patterns of thinking. The assertive nature of cognitive therapy is apparent in the following exchange between a patient and a therapist.

THERAPIST: What has your marriage been like?

PATIENT: It has been miserable from the very beginning . . . Raymond has always been unfaithful . . . I have hardly seen him in the past five years.

THERAPIST: You say you can't be happy without Raymond . . . Have you found yourself happy when you are with Raymond?

PATIENT: No, we fight all the time and I feel worse.

THERAPIST: Then why do you feel that Raymond is essential for your living?

PATIENT: I guess it's because without Raymond I am nothing.

THERAPIST: Would you please repeat that?

PATIENT: Without Raymond I am nothing.

THERAPIST: What do you think of that idea?

PATIENT: . . . Well, now that I think about it, I guess it's not completely true.

THERAPIST: You said you are "nothing" without Raymond. Before you met Raymond, did you feel you were "nothing"?

PATIENT: No, I felt I was somebody.

THERAPIST: Are you saying then that it's possible to be something without Raymond?

PATIENT: I guess that's true. I can be something without Raymond.

THERAPIST: If you were somebody before you knew Raymond, why do you need him to be somebody now?

PATIENT: (*puzzled*) Hmmm . . . Well, I just don't think that I can find anybody else like him.

THERAPIST: Did you have male friends before you knew Raymond?

PATIENT: I was pretty popular then.

THERAPIST: If I understand you correctly then, you were able to fall in love before with other men and other men have fallen in love with you.

PATIENT: Uh huh.

THERAPIST: Why do you think you will be unpopular without Raymond now?

PATIENT: Because I will not be able to attract any other man.

THERAPIST: Have any men shown an interest in you since you have been married?

PATIENT: A lot of men have made passes at me but I ignore them.

THERAPIST: If you were free of the marriage, do you think that men might be interested in you—knowing that you were available?

PATIENT: I guess that maybe they would be. [Beck et al., 1979, pp. 217-219]

Kinship with Behavior Therapy

Cognitive therapy borrows heavily from behavioral approaches to treatment, which we will discuss shortly. Specifically, cognitive therapists often use "homework assignments" that focus on changing clients' overt behaviors. Clients may be instructed to engage in overt responses on their own, outside of the clinician's office. For example, one shy, insecure young man in cognitive therapy was told to go to a singles bar and engage three different women in conversations for up to five minutes each (Rush, 1984). He was instructed to record his thoughts before and after each of the conversations. This assignment elicited various maladaptive patterns of thought that gave the young man and his therapist plenty to talk about in subsequent sessions. As this example illustrates, cognitive therapy is a creative blend of "talk

Despite the typical "patient on a couch" stereotype of psychotherapy, modern therapy sessions tend to be face-to-face conversations between therapist and client.

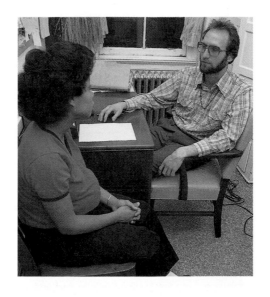

therapy" and behavior therapy, although it is primarily an insight therapy.

Cognitive therapy was originally designed as a treatment for individuals. However, it has recently been adapted for use with groups (Covi & Primakoff, 1988). Many insight therapies can be conducted on either an individual or group basis, so let's take a look at the dynamics of group therapy.

Group Therapy

Although it dates back to the early part of the 20th century, group therapy came of age during the 1950s and 1960s. During this period, the expanding demand for therapeutic services forced clinicians to use group techniques. *Group therapy* **involves the simultaneous treatment of several or more clients in a group.** Most major insight therapies have been adapted for use with groups. In fact, the ideas underlying Rogers's client-centered therapy spawned the much-publicized encounter group movement. Although group therapy can be conducted in a variety of ways, we can provide a general overview of the process as it usually unfolds (see Fuchs, 1984; Vinogradov & Yalom, 1988).

Participants' Roles

A therapy group typically consists of about five to ten participants. The therapist usually screens the participants. Most therapists exclude persons who seem likely to be disruptive. There is some debate about whether or not it is best to have a homogeneous group (people who are similar in age, sex, and presenting problem). Practical necessities usually dictate that groups are at least somewhat diversified.

The therapist plays a subtle role in group therapy. Therapists often stay in the background and focus mainly on promoting group cohesiveness. They model supportive behaviors for the participants and try to promote a healthy climate. The therapist always retains a special status, but the therapist and clients are on much more

equal footing in group therapy than in individual therapy. The leader in group therapy expresses emotions, shares feelings, and copes with challenges from group members. In other words, group therapists participate in the group's exchanges and "bare their own souls" to some extent.

In group therapy, participants essentially function as therapists for one another. Group members describe their problems, trade viewpoints, share experiences, and discuss coping strategies. Most importantly, they provide acceptance and emotional support for each other. In this supportive atmosphere, group members work at peeling away the social masks that cover their insecurities. Once their problems are exposed, members work at correcting

RECOMMENDED READING

The Psychotherapy Maze

by Otto Ehrenberg & Miriam Ehrenberg (Aronson, 1986)

This book is billed as a "consumer's guide to the ins and outs of therapy." The Ehrenbergs provide a frank and down-to-earth discussion of practical issues relating to psychotherapy. Most books on therapy are devoted to explaining different theoretical approaches to therapy. The Ehrenbergs go far beyond this in their book. They tackle practical issues such as how to select a therapist, how to help make therapy work for you, and how to judge whether therapy is doing you any good. They also discuss mundane but important details such as fees, insurance, missed sessions, and emergency phone calls. The Ehrenbergs' goal is to make therapy less intimidating and mysterious. They succeed handsomely in this endeavor.

> While everyone who is committed to therapy wants change, when therapy brings you to the point where the possibility of change becomes real, strong pulls emerge from within to keep you the way you are. Long-standing lifestyles cannot be given up, even if they have caused much suffering, without the anxiety of losing the familiar and the fear of confronting the unknown. Abandoning old patterns of existence when you are not sure that you can make it any other way is a frightening prospect. When therapy brings you to this point, you may want to run from it.
> Even without the cultural barriers, it's not easy to get started in psychotherapy. To begin with, there is the uncertainty about how to go about doing it: how do you pick a therapist, what do you say when you go to one, and what do you have to do once you're in therapy? If you are thinking of therapy for yourself, you probably feel anxious about starting off on a new experience in which a lot is a stake and the outcome is uncertain. You are not sure what is going to happen to you and how you are going to take to it. You might be worried about what other people are going to think of you. On top of all this, you have to overcome a certain amount of lethargy. Getting started means putting in time and effort, it means planning and committing yourself to a new routine, and it usually means having to make financial sacrifices. [p. 26]

them. As members come to value one another's opinions, they work hard to display healthy changes to win the group's approval.

Advantages of the Group Experience

Group therapies obviously save time and money, which can be critical in understaffed mental hospitals and other institutional settings. Therapists in private practice usually charge less for group than individual therapy, making therapy affordable for more people. However, group therapy is *not* just a less costly substitute for individual therapy. Group therapy has unique strengths of its own. Irwin Yalom (1975), who has studied group therapy extensively, has described some of these advantages.

1. *In group therapy, participants often come to realize that their misery is not unique.* Clients often enter therapy feeling very sorry for themselves. They think that they alone have a terribly burdensome cross to bear. In the group situation, they quickly see that they are not unique. They are reassured to learn that many other people have similar or even worse problems.

2. *Group therapy provides an opportunity for participants to work on their social skills in a safe environment.* Many personal problems essentially involve difficulties in relating effectively to people. Group therapy can provide a workshop for improving interpersonal skills that cannot be matched by individual therapy.

3. *Certain kinds of problems are especially well suited to group treatment.* There are specific types of problems and clients that respond especially well to the social support that group therapy can provide. Peer self-help groups illustrate this advantage. In peer self-help groups, people who have a problem in common get together regularly to help one another out. The original peer self-help group was Alcoholics Anonymous. Today, there are similar groups made up of former psychiatric patients, single parents, drug addicts, and so forth.

Whether therapy is conducted on a group basis or an individual basis, clients usually invest considerable time, effort, and money in insight therapies. Are they worth the investment? Let's examine the evidence on the effectiveness of insight therapy.

Evaluating Insight Therapies

In 1952, Hans Eysenck shocked mental health professionals by reporting that there was no sound evidence that insight therapy actually helped people. What was the basis for this startling claim? Eysenck (1952) reviewed numerous studies of therapeutic outcome for clients suffering from neurotic problems. He found that about two thirds of the clients recovered within two years. A two-thirds recovery rate sounds reasonable, except that Eysenck found the same recovery rate among *untreated* neurotics. As we noted in Chapter 15, psychological disorders sometimes clear up on their own. **A *spontaneous remission* is a recovery from a disorder that occurs without formal treatment.** Based on his estimate of the spontaneous remission rate for neurotic disorders, Eysenck concluded that "the therapeutic effects of (insight) psychotherapy are small or nonexistent."

In the ensuing years, critics pounced on Eysenck's (1952) article looking for flaws. They found a variety of shortcomings in his data. Eysenck made many arbitrary judgments about "recoveries" that were consistently unfavorable to the treated groups. Moreover, the untreated neurotics probably were not as severely disturbed as those who did pursue or require treatment. Ultimately, additional research indicated that Eysenck's estimate of the spontaneous remission rate was too high. More recent estimates suggest that the spontaneous remission rate for neurotic disorders is in the vicinity of 30%–40% (Bergin, 1971). Although Eysenck's conclusions were unduly pessimistic, he made an important contribution to the mental health field by sparking debate and research on the effectiveness of insight therapy.

Evaluating the effectiveness of any approach to psychotherapy is a complicated matter. This is especially true for insight therapies. If you were to undergo insight therapy, how would you judge its effectiveness? By how you felt? By looking at your behavior? By asking your therapist? By consulting your friends and family? What would you be looking for? People enter therapy with different problems and needs. Different schools of thought seek to realize entirely different goals. Thus, measures of therapeutic outcome are inevitably subjective.

A key problem is that both therapists and clients are biased strongly in the direction of evaluating therapy favorably (Rachman & Wilson, 1980). Why? Therapists want to see improvement because it reflects on their professional competence. Obviously, they hope to see clients getting better as a result of their work. Clients are slanted toward a favorable evaluation because they want to justify their effort, their heartache, their expense, and their time.

In spite of these difficulties, hundreds of therapy outcome studies have been conducted since Eysenck prodded researchers into action. These studies consistently indicate that insight therapy *is* superior to no treatment. Two major reviews of the literature (Luborsky, Singer, & Luborsky, 1975; Meltzoff & Kornreich, 1970) both conclude that therapy outshines no treatment in about 80% of the studies. In a comprehensive review, Smith, Glass, and Miller (1980) examined 475 studies and estimated that the average therapy client ends up better off than 80% of comparable, untreated controls.

Admittedly, this outcome research does not indicate that insight therapy leads to miraculous results. The superiority of therapy over no treatment is usually characterized as modest. In light of the price of therapy, there is room for debate about its cost-effectiveness. Overall, about 70%–80% of clients appear to benefit from insight therapy, while 20%–30% fail to show any clear improvement.

Some investigators have tried to figure out which clients are most likely to benefit from insight therapy. Schofield (1964) concluded that "YAVIS" clients are the best candidates for insight therapy. What's a YAVIS? The letters are an abbreviation for young, attractive, verbal, intelligent, and successful. However, a recent review of hundreds of studies on the prediction of therapeutic outcomes found little support for the first three of these factors (Luborsky, Crits-Christoph, Mintz, & Auerbach, 1988). This review *did* identify some other factors— besides being intelligent and successful—that are important. Luborsky and his colleagues found that insight therapy works out better for patients who are highly motivated and who have positive attitudes about therapy. They also found that less severely disturbed patients are more likely to benefit from insight therapy than patients with severe pathology.

Clients' personal characteristics tend to be considerably less important when behavioral treatments are employed. As you'll see in the next section, behavior therapies can be useful with a wide range of clients, including some who are severely disturbed.

BEHAVIOR THERAPIES

Behavior therapy is different from insight therapy in that behavior therapists make no attempt to help clients achieve grand insights about themselves. Why not? Because behavior therapists believe that such insights aren't necessary to produce constructive change. For example, consider a client troubled by compulsive gambling. The behavior therapist doesn't care whether this behavior is rooted in unconscious conflicts or parental rejection. What the client needs is to get rid of the maladaptive behavior. Consequently, the therapist simply designs a program to eliminate the compulsive gambling. Actually, behavior therapists may work with clients to attain very limited insights about how environmental factors evoke troublesome behaviors (Franks & Barbrack, 1983). This information can be helpful in designing a behavioral therapy program.

The crux of the difference between insight therapy and behavior therapy lies in how they view symptoms.

People who benefit most from insight therapy are those who expect it to help them, who are motivated to make it work, and who do not suffer from severe psychological disorders.

Insight therapists treat pathological symptoms as signs of an underlying problem. In contrast, behavior therapists think that the symptoms *are* the problem. Thus, **behavior therapies involve the application of the principles of learning to direct efforts to change clients' maladaptive behaviors.**

Behaviorism has been an influential school of thought in psychology since the 1920s. But behaviorists devoted little attention to clinical issues until Joseph Wolpe launched behavior therapy in 1958 with his description of *systematic desensitization*, which we will describe momentarily. Since then, there has been an explosion of interest in behavioral approaches to psychotherapy. Today, more and more psychologists are using behavioral approaches, especially those who work with children (O'Leary, 1984).

General Principles

Behavior therapies are based on certain assumptions (Lazarus & Fay, 1984). *First, it is assumed that behavior is a product of learning.* No matter how self-defeating or pathological a client's behavior might be, the behaviorist believes that it is the result of past conditioning. *Second, it is assumed that what has been learned can be unlearned.* The same learning principles that explain how the maladaptive behavior was acquired can be used to get rid of it. Thus, behavior therapists attempt to change clients' behavior by applying the principles of classical conditioning, operant conditioning, and observational learning.

Behavior therapies are close cousins of the self-modification procedures described in the Chapter 4 Application. Both employ the same principles of learning to alter behavior directly. In discussing *self-modification*, we examined some relatively simple procedures that people can apply to themselves to improve everyday self-control. In our discussion of *behavior therapy* we will examine more complex procedures used by mental health professionals in the treatment of more severe problems.

Like self-modification, behavior therapy requires that clients' vague complaints ("My life is filled with frustra-tion") be translated into specific, concrete behavioral goals ("I need to increase my use of assertive responses in dealing with colleagues"). Once the troublesome behaviors have been targeted, the therapist designs a program to alter these behaviors. The nature of the therapeutic program depends on the types of problems identified. Specific procedures are designed for specific types of problems, as you'll see in our discussion of systematic desensitization.

Systematic Desensitization

Devised by Joseph Wolpe (1958, 1987), systematic desensitization revolutionized the treatment of phobic disorders. **Systematic desensitization is a behavior therapy used to reduce clients' anxiety responses through counter-conditioning.** The treatment assumes that most anxiety responses are acquired through classical conditioning (as we discussed in Chapter 15). According to this model, a harmless stimulus (for instance, a bridge) may be paired with a frightening event (lightning strikes it), so it becomes a conditioned stimulus eliciting anxiety. The goal of systematic desensitization is to weaken the association between the conditioned stimulus (the bridge) and the conditioned response of anxiety. Systematic desensitization involves three steps.

First, the therapist helps the client to build an anxiety hierarchy. The hierarchy is a list of anxiety-arousing stimuli centering on the specific source of anxiety, such as flying, academic tests, or snakes. The client ranks the stimuli from the least anxiety-arousing to the most anxiety-arousing. This ordered list of related, anxiety-provoking stimuli is the anxiety hierarchy. An example of an anxiety hierarchy for one woman's fear of heights is shown in Figure 16.4.

The second step involves training the client in deep muscle relaxation. This second phase may begin during early sessions while the therapist and client are still constructing the anxiety hierarchy. Different therapists use different relaxation training procedures. Whatever procedures

Joseph Wolpe

are employed, the client must learn to engage in deep and thorough relaxation on command from the therapist.

In the third step, the client tries to work through the hierarchy, learning to remain relaxed while imagining each stimulus. Starting with the least anxiety-arousing stimulus, the client imagines the situation as vividly as possible while relaxing. If clients experience strong anxiety, they drop the imaginary scene and concentrate on relaxation. The clients keep repeating this process until they can imagine a scene with little or no anxiety. Once a particular scene is conquered, a client moves on to the next stimulus situation in the anxiety hierarchy. Gradually, over a number of therapy sessions, clients progress through the hierarchy, unlearning troublesome anxiety responses.

As clients conquer *imagined* phobic stimuli, they may be encouraged to confront the *real* stimuli. Desensitization to imagined stimuli *can* be effective by itself. However, many behavior therapists advocate following it up with planned exposures to the real anxiety-arousing stimuli (Lazarus & Wilson, 1976). The desensitization to imagined stimuli should reduce anxiety enough so that clients will be able to confront situations they used to avoid at all costs. Usually, these real-life confrontations prove harmless and the person's anxiety response declines further.

The principle at work in systematic desensitization is simple. Anxiety and relaxation are incompatible responses. The trick is to recondition people so that the conditioned stimulus elicits relaxation instead of anxiety. This is counterconditioning—an attempt to reverse the process of classical conditioning by associating the crucial stimulus with a new conditioned response. Although it seems deceptively simple, systematic desensitization can be very effective in eliminating specific anxieties (Leitenberg, 1976).

Aversion Therapy

Aversion therapy is far and away the most controversial of the behavior therapies. It's not something that you would sign up for unless you were pretty desperate. Psychologists usually suggest it only as a treatment of last resort, after other interventions have failed. What's so terrible about aversion therapy? The client has to endure decidedly unpleasant stimuli, such as shock or drug-induced nausea.

Aversion therapy **is a behavior therapy in which an aversive stimulus is paired with a stimulus that elicits an undesirable response.** For example, alcoholics have had drug-induced nausea paired with their favorite drinks during therapy sessions (Cannon, Baker, & Wehl, 1981). By pairing an *emetic drug* (one that causes vomiting) with alcohol, the therapist hopes to create a conditioned aversion to alcohol (see Figure 16.5).

Aversion therapy takes advantage of the automatic nature of responses produced through classical conditioning. Admittedly, alcoholics treated with aversion therapy know that

An Anxiety Hierarchy for Systematic Desensitization	
Degree of fear	Anxiety-arousing stimulus situations
5	I'm standing on the balcony on the top floor of an apartment tower.
10	I'm standing on a stepladder in the kitchen to change a light bulb.
15	I'm walking on a ridge. The edge is hidden by shrubs and treetops.
20	I'm sitting on the slope of a mountain, looking out over the horizon.
25	I'm crossing a bridge 6 feet above a creek. The bridge consists of an 18-inch-wide board with a handrail on one side
30	I'm riding a ski lift 8 feet above the ground.
35	I'm crossing a shallow, wide creek on an 18-inch-wide board, 3 feet above water level.
40	I'm climbing a ladder outside the house to reach a second-story window.
45	I'm pulling myself up a 30-degree wet, slippery slope on a steel cable.
50	I'm scrambling up a rock, 8 feet high.
55	I'm walking 10 feet on a resilient, 18-inch-wide board, which spans an 8-foot-deep gulch.
60	I'm walking on a wide plateau, 2 feet from the edge of a cliff.
65	I'm skiing an intermediate hill. The snow is packed.
70	I'm walking over a railway trestle.
75	I'm walking on the side of an embankment. The path slopes to the outside.
80	I'm riding a chairlift 15 feet above the ground.
85	I'm walking up a long, steep slope.
90	I'm walking up (or down) a 15-degree slope on a 3-foot-wide trail. On one side of the trail the terrain drops down sharply; on the other side is a steep upward slope.
95	I'm walking on a 3-foot-wide ridge. The slopes on both sides are long and more than 25 degrees steep.
100	I'm walking on a 3-foot-wide ridge. The trail slopes on one side. The drop on either side of the trail is more than 25 degrees.

Figure 16.4. Example of an anxiety hierarchy. Systematic desensitization requires the construction of an anxiety hierarchy like the one shown here, which was developed for a woman with a fear of heights who had a penchant for hiking in the mountains.

they won't be given an emetic outside of their therapy sessions. However, their reflex response to the stimulus of alcohol may be changed so that they respond to it with nausea and distaste. Obviously, this response should make it much easier to resist the urge to drink.

Troublesome behaviors treated successfully with aversion therapy include drug abuse, sexual deviance, gambling, shoplifting, stuttering, cigarette smoking, and overeating (Lazarus & Wilson, 1976; Sandler, 1975). Typically, aversion therapy is only one element in a larger treatment program. Of course, this procedure should only be used with willing clients when other options have failed (Rimm & Cunningham, 1985).

Social Skills Training

Many psychological problems grow out of interpersonal difficulties. Behavior therapists point out that we are not born with social finesse. We acquire our social skills through learning. Unfortunately, some people have not learned how to be friendly, how to make conversation, how to express anger appropriately, and so forth. Social ineptitude can contribute to anxiety, feelings of inferiority, and various kinds of disorders. In light of these findings, therapists are increasingly trying to devise treatments to improve patients' social abilities.

Social skills training **is a behavior therapy designed to improve interpersonal skills that emphasizes shaping, modeling, and behavioral rehearsal.** This type of behavior therapy can be conducted with individual clients or in groups. Social skills training depends on the principles of operant conditioning and observational learning. The therapist makes use of *modeling* by encouraging clients to watch socially skilled friends and colleagues, so that responses (eye contact, active listening, and so on) can be acquired through observation.

In *behavioral rehearsal*, the client tries to practice social techniques in structured role-playing exercises. The therapist provides corrective feedback and uses approval to reinforce progress. Eventually, clients try their newly acquired skills in real-world interactions. Usually, they are given specific homework assignments. *Shaping* is employed in that clients are gradually asked to handle more complicated and delicate social situations. For example, a nonassertive client may begin by working on making requests of friends. Only much later will the client be asked to tackle standing up to his or her boss.

Biofeedback

Biofeedback is another widely used therapy that has emerged from the behavioral tradition. **In *biofeedback* a bodily function (such as heart rate) is monitored, and information about it is fed back to a person to facilitate improved control of the physiological process.** Armed with precise information about internal bodily functions, people are able to exert far more control over some of them than previously thought possible. For example, many anxious people develop problematic high blood pressure. Obviously, it would be nice if these people could learn to control their blood pressure without depending on drugs that may have side effects. Evidence suggests that biofeedback *can* be used to train people to control their blood pressure (Shapiro, Schwartz, & Tursky, 1972).

To see how biofeedback works, let's look at *electromyograph* (EMG) feedback intended to enhance relaxation. An EMG is a device used to measure skeletal-muscular tension in the body. In a typical training session, a client is hooked up to an EMG, and its recordings are transformed into an auditory signal. Usually, the signal is a tone that increases and decreases in volume. The therapist explains that changes in the tone will reflect changes in the client's level of muscular tension. The client is instructed to raise or lower the tone.

Although people often have difficulty describing how they do it, most can learn to exert better control over their level of muscular tension. Essentially, EMG feedback helps them to improve their ability to engage in deep muscle relaxation. Promising results have been obtained

Figure 16.5. Aversion therapy. Aversion therapy uses classical conditioning to create an aversion to a stimulus that has elicited problematic behavior. For example, in the treatment of drinking problems, alcohol may be paired with a nausea-inducing drug to create a conditioned aversion to alcohol.

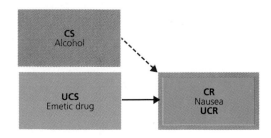

with EMG feedback in the treatment of anxiety (Raskin, Bali, & Peeke, 1981), tension headaches (Blanchard & Andrasik, 1982), and high blood pressure (Lustman & Sowa, 1983).

In some respects, biofeedback is a *biological* intervention, and it could be classified as a biomedical therapy. However, it is usually grouped with the behavior therapies because its use is not limited to physicians and the strategy emerged out of behavioral research. Studies have revealed that biofeedback can help people exert some control over brain wave activity, skin temperature, blood pressure, heart rate, and muscle tension (Adler & Adler, 1984). Early proponents of biofeedback may have gotten carried away in making extravagant claims about its benefits. Nonetheless, this unique intervention appears to have potential for treating many stress-related problems.

Evaluating Behavior Therapies

Behavior therapists have historically placed more emphasis than insight therapists have on the importance of measuring therapeutic outcomes. As a result, there is ample evidence attesting to the effectiveness of behavior therapy (Rachman & Wilson, 1980; Smith et al., 1980). How does the effectiveness of behavior therapy compare to that of insight therapy? In direct comparisons, the differences between the therapies are usually small (Smith et al., 1980). However, these modest differences tend to favor behavioral approaches (Kazdin & Wilson, 1978). Of course, behavior therapies are not well suited to the treatment of some types of problems (vague feelings of discontent, for instance). Furthermore, it's misleading to make global statements about the effectiveness of behavior therapies because they include many different procedures designed for different purposes. For example, the value of systematic desensitization for phobias has no bearing on the value of aversion therapy for sexual deviance.

For our purposes, it is sufficient to note that there is favorable evidence on the efficacy of most of the widely used behavioral interventions. Behavior therapies seem to be particularly effective in the treatment of anxiety problems, phobias, obsessive-compulsive disorders, sexual dysfunction, sexual deviance, drug-related problems, and obesity (Rachman & Wilson, 1980).

Only a few of these problems would be amenable to treatment with the biomedical therapies, which we consider next. To some extent, the three major approaches to treatment have different strengths. Let's see where the strengths of the biomedical therapies lie.

BIOMEDICAL THERAPIES

In the 1950s, a French surgeon was looking for a drug that would reduce patients' autonomic response to surgical stress. The surgeon noticed that chlorpromazine produced a mild sedation. Based on this observation, Delay and Deniker (1952) decided to give chlorpromazine to hospitalized schizophrenic patients. They wanted to see whether the drug would have calming effects on the patients. Their experiment was a dramatic success. Chlorpromazine became the first effective antipsychotic drug—and a revolution in psychiatry was begun. Hundreds of thousands of severely disturbed patients—patients who had appeared doomed to lead the remainder of their lives in mental hospitals—were gradually sent home thanks to the therapeutic effects of antipsychotic drugs (see Figure 16.6). Today, biomedical therapies, such as drug treatment, lie at the core of psychiatric practice.

***Biomedical therapies* involve physiological interventions intended to reduce symptoms associated with psychological disorders.** These therapies assume that psychological disorders are caused, at least in part, by biological malfunctions. As we discussed in the previous chapter, this assumption clearly has merit for many disorders, especially the more severe ones. We will discuss two biomedical approaches to psychotherapy: drug therapy and electroconvulsive (shock) therapy.

Figure 16.6. The declining inpatient population in mental hospitals. The number of inpatients in public mental hospitals has declined dramatically since the late 1950s. In part, this has been due to "deinstitutionalization"— a philosophy that emphasizes outpatient care whenever possible. However, above all else, this decline was made possible by the development of effective antipsychotic medications.

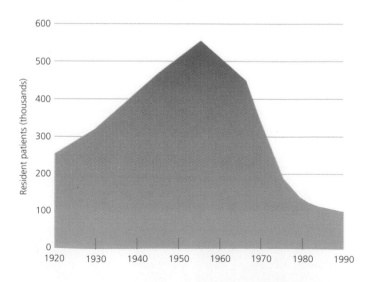

Treatment with Drugs

Psychopharmacotherapy involves the treatment of mental disorders with medication. We will refer to this kind of treatment more simply as *drug therapy*. Therapeutic drugs fall into three major groups: (1) antianxiety drugs, (2) antipsychotic drugs, and (3) antidepressant drugs. Another important drug that does not fit neatly into any of these categories is lithium, which is used in the treatment of bipolar mood disorders.

Antianxiety Drugs

Most of us know someone who pops pills to relieve anxiety. The drugs involved in this common coping strategy are *antianxiety drugs,* **which relieve tension, apprehension, and nervousness.** The most popular of these has been a drug known by its trade name, Valium. Trade names are the proprietary names that pharmaceutical companies use in marketing drugs. These names are often more widely known than the drugs' scientific or generic names. For example, the generic name for Valium is diazepam.

The drugs in the diazepam family are often called *tranquilizers.* They are routinely prescribed for people with anxiety disorders. They are also given to millions of people who simply suffer from chronic nervous tension. In the mid-1970s, pharmacists in the United States were filling nearly *100 million* prescriptions each year for Valium and similar antianxiety drugs. Many critics characterized this level of use as excessive (Lickey & Gordon, 1983).

Antianxiety drugs exert their effects almost immediately. They can be fairly effective in alleviating feelings of anxiety (Lader, 1984). However, their effects are measured in hours, so their impact is relatively short-lived. The principal side effects of antianxiety drugs are drowsiness and lethargy. There is some potential for abuse and dependency problems with these drugs. Some people get hooked on Valium and are unable to function without it (Lickey & Gordon, 1983). Problems with the abuse of tranquilizers led to a moderate decline in their use in the

1980s. Currently, researchers are studying the effects of a new antianxiety drug called Buspar (buspirone) that has less potential for abuse. Unlike Valium, Buspar is slow-acting, exerting its effects in seven to ten days, but with fewer sedative side effects (Newton, Marunycz, Alderdice, & Napoliello, 1986).

Antipsychotic Drugs

Antipsychotic drugs are used primarily in the treatment of schizophrenia. They also are given to people with severe mood disorders who become delusional. The trade names (and generic names) of some prominent drugs in this category are Thorazine (chlorpromazine), Mellaril (thioridazine), and Haldol (haloperidol). *Antipsychotic drugs* **are used to gradually reduce psychotic symptoms, including hyperactivity, mental confusion, hallucinations, and delusions.**

About two thirds of psychotic patients respond favorably to antipsychotic medication (Baldessarini, 1984). When antipsychotic drugs are effective, they work their magic gradually, as shown in Figure 16.7. Patients usually begin to respond within two days to a week. Further improvement may occur for several months. Many schizophrenic patients are placed on antipsychotics indefinitely because these drugs can reduce the likelihood of a relapse into an active schizophrenic episode.

Antipsychotic drugs undeniably make a major contribution to the treatment of severe mental disorders, but they are not without problems. They have many unpleasant side effects. Drowsiness, constipation, and cotton mouth are common. Patients may also experience tremors, muscular rigidity, and impaired coordination. After being released from a hospital, many schizophrenic patients, supposedly placed on antipsychotics indefinitely, discontinue their drug regimen because of the disagreeable side effects. Unfortunately, relapse into another schizophrenic episode often occurs within three to nine months after a patient stops taking antipsychotic medication (J. M. Davis, 1985).

In addition to minor side effects, antipsychotics may

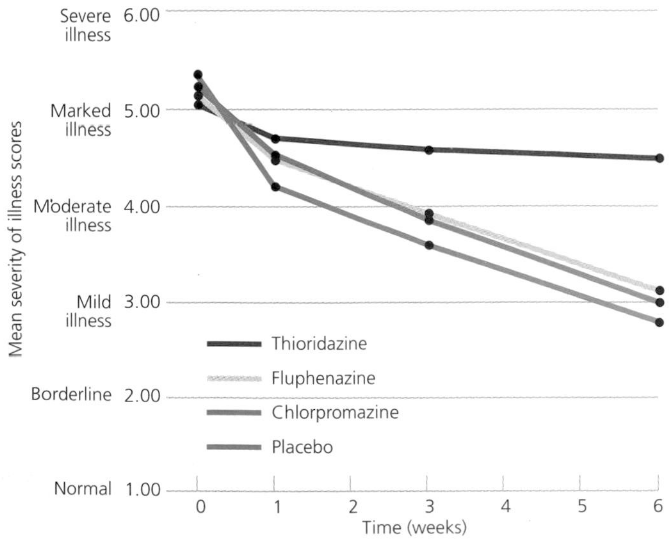

Figure 16.7. The time course of antipsychotic drug effects. Antipsychotic drugs reduce psychotic symptoms gradually, over a span of weeks, as graphed here. In contrast, patients given placebo pills show little improvement. (Data from Cole, Goldberg, & Davis, 1966; J. M. Davis, 1985)

cause a severe and lasting problem called *tardive dyskinesia*. **Tardive dyskinesia is a neurological disorder marked by chronic tremors and involuntary spastic movements.** This debilitating syndrome resembles Parkinson's disease, and there is no cure. There has been a heated debate about how often this serious side effect occurs as a result of antipsychotic drug therapy (Brown & Funk, 1986). It may occur in as many as 25% of patients who take antipsychotics over a prolonged period (Jeste & Wyatt, 1982). As the prevalence of this problem has come to be recognized, experts have urged psychiatrists to be more conservative about prescribing antipsychotics on a long-term basis.

Antidepressant Drugs

As their name suggests, **antidepressant drugs gradually elevate mood and help to bring people out of a depression.** There are two principal classes of antidepressants: *tricyclics* (such as Elavil) and *MAO inhibitors* (such as Nardil). These two sets of drugs appear to affect neurochemical activity in different ways and tend to work with different patients. The tricyclics are effective for a larger proportion of depressed patients (perhaps as many as 85%). They also have fewer problematic side effects than the MAO inhibitors (Glenn & Taska, 1984). Like antipsychotic drugs, antidepressants exert their effects gradually over a period of weeks. At present, psychiatrists are very enthusiastic about a new antidepressant, Prozac (fluoxetine), that appears to yield rapid therapeutic gains with relatively few side effects (Cole, 1988).

Lithium

Lithium is a chemical used to control mood swings in patients with bipolar mood disorders. Lithium has excellent value in preventing *future* episodes of both mania and depression in patients with bipolar illness. Lithium can also be used in efforts to bring patients with bipolar illness out of *current* manic or depressive episodes. However, antipsychotics and antidepressants are more frequently used for these purposes. On the negative side of the ledger, lithium does have some dangerous side effects if its use isn't managed skillfully (Georgotas, 1985). Lithium levels in the patient's blood must be monitored carefully because high concentrations of it can be highly toxic and even fatal. Kidney damage and cardiac complications are the major problems associated with lithium therapy.

Evaluating Drug Therapies

Drug therapies can produce clear therapeutic gains for many kinds of patients. What's especially impressive is that they can be effective in severe disorders that otherwise defy therapeutic endeavors. Nonetheless, drug therapies are controversial for two reasons.

First, some critics argue that drug therapies often produce superficial curative effects (Lickey & Gordon, 1983). For example, Valium does not really solve problems with anxiety. It merely provides temporary relief from an unpleasant symptom. Moreover, this temporary relief may lull patients into complacency about their problem and prevent them from working toward a more lasting solution. Thus, drug therapies may be more of a Band-Aid than a cure for psychological disorders.

Second, critics charge that many drugs are overprescribed and many patients overmedicated (Boutin, 1979; Leavitt, 1982). Drug interventions can be all too appealing as apparent "solutions" to psychiatrists and other hospital personnel. Writing out a prescription is much less challenging than conducting insight therapy or designing a behavior therapy program. Thus, many psychiatrists habitually hand out prescriptions without giving adequate consideration to more complicated interventions. This problem is compounded by the fact that drugs calm patients and make it easier for hospital staff to run their wards. Thus, critics argue that there is a tendency in some institutions to overmedicate patients to minimize disruptive behavior. This practice represents unethical "crowd control" more than therapy.

Obviously, drug therapies have stirred up some de-

Figure 16.8. One patient's experience with electroconvulsive therapy. Although some patients treated with electroconvulsive therapy (ECT) have much more favorable experiences, this moving memoir about ECT treatment paints a very unpleasant picture. (Quoted by permission from a former student)

bate. However, this controversy pales in comparison to the furious debates inspired by electroconvulsive (shock) therapy (ECT). ECT is so controversial that the residents of Berkeley, California, voted to outlaw ECT in their city. However, in subsequent lawsuits, the courts ruled that scientific questions cannot be settled through a vote, and they overturned the law. What makes ECT so controversial? You'll see in the next section.

Electroconvulsive Therapy (ECT)

In the 1930s, a Hungarian psychiatrist named Ladislas Meduna speculated that epilepsy and schizophrenia could not coexist in the same body. On the basis of this observation, which turned out to be inaccurate, Meduna theorized that it might be useful to induce epileptic-like seizures in schizophrenic patients. Initially, a drug was used to trigger these seizures. However, by 1938, a pair of Italian psychiatrists (Cerletti & Bini, 1938) demonstrated that it was safer to elicit the seizures with electric shock.

A Personal Experience with ECT

I'm not saying this is what all shock is about, or that it happens this way everywhere. I am saying that this is what happened to me in this particular institution.

Slang for shock in that institution was known as "gettin' Kentucky fried" and being taken to shock was known as "a visit to the Colonel." I was going for a visit.

Along the way, I always started making deals with God: "If you get me out of this one . . ." They never worked out. When the deals fell through, I started making every promise I knew I could keep, and just to be safe, a few I knew I couldn't. Looking back, it all seems kind of funny. At the time, I was sure they were trying to kill me.

The room where it was done was in the very center of the ward. This was not surprising. Almost all of our shock was done as a disciplinary measure, our very lives revolved around staff's ability to enforce discipline and order upon us. So to me, it was not too surprising that the Colonel set up shop where he did.

When the door opened, the intense whiteness of the fluorescent lights blinded me. Staff took advantage of this by leading me to the gurney where I was to lie down. By the time my eyes adjusted, I was on my back with several pairs of hands holding me down.

A mouthpiece was crammed rather indelicately into place, and the conductant was smeared on my temples. There was some technical talk and someone said "Now" (I wanted desperately to say wait a moment). And then there it was—one of the most excruciating pains I have ever felt. My back arched in an attempt to jump off the gurney, all the air squeezed out of my lungs, my legs flexed until they felt as if they would break, my head felt as if it would pop off. I was out of control; it was not me anymore.

I don't know how long it took but finally I passed out. When I opened my eyes again, I had the headache of headaches. I was confused, I couldn't connect two thoughts.

The next two or three days were a nightmare of confusion and awkward movements, always feeling like a thought was there, on the tip of your tongue, but not able to grab it. The more you grabbed at it, the more elusive it became, and the more frustrated you became.

Eventually, I returned to normal, but before that happened, I would go through a deep dark depression. I could fight the system, I could fight Staff, I could fight the drugs, the aides, and the other patients.

I could not fight this. I was beaten. My thoughts were exactly that, mine. Before shock they were untouched, now they had been reached and, worse still, disorganized externally. The depression then seemed to come from a sense of defeat, of being violated, and of being mentally raped.

How can I make you feel that?

Thus, modern electroconvulsive therapy was born, creating a peculiar tribute to the old advertising slogan "Better living through electricity."

***Electroconvulsive therapy (ECT)* is a biomedical treatment in which electric shock is used to produce a cortical seizure accompanied by convulsions.** In ECT, electrodes are attached to the skull over the temporal lobes of the brain (see the photo on page 478). A light anesthesia is induced and the patient is given a variety of drugs to minimize the likelihood of complications, such as spinal fractures. An electric current is then applied for about a second. The current should trigger a brief (5–20 seconds) convulsive seizure, during which the patient usually loses consciousness. Patients normally awaken in an hour or two. People typically receive between 6 and 20 treatments as inpatients at a hospital.

The clinical use of ECT peaked in the 1940s and 1950s, before effective drug therapies were widely available. ECT has long been controversial, and its use declined in the 1960s and 1970s. Nonetheless, ECT is *not* a rare form of therapy (Sackeim, 1985). Estimates suggest that about 60,000 to 100,000 people receive ECT treatments yearly in the United States, mainly for depression.

Controversy about ECT is fueled by patients' reports that the treatment is painful, dehumanizing, and terrifying. Concerns have also been raised by reports that staff members at some hospitals use the threat of ECT to keep patients "in line" (Breggin, 1979). Using ECT for disciplinary purposes is unethical, but the essay in Figure 16.8 suggests that it has happened in some institutions. This essay also provides a moving description of how aversive ECT can be for some patients.

Effectiveness of ECT

The effectiveness of ECT is hotly debated. There are ardent proponents who maintain that it is a remarkably effective treatment (Fink, 1988). However, equally ardent opponents argue that it is no more effective than a placebo (Friedberg, 1975). Reported improvement rates for ECT treatment range from negligible to very high (Friedberg, 1976; Small, Small, & Milstein, 1986). In part, these inconsistent findings are due to methodological weaknesses that are often found in ECT studies. Barton (1977) could find only *six* studies among hundreds on ECT that used appropriate control groups to assess therapeutic effects. Why are ECT studies so flawed? Probably because most investigators feel very strongly (pro or con) about ECT and their biases affect their research, both intentionally and inadvertently.

In light of these problems, conclusions about the value of ECT must be tentative. Although ECT was once considered appropriate for a wide range of disorders, even most proponents now recommend it only for mood disorders (especially depression). Overall, there seems to be enough favorable evidence to justify *conservative* use of ECT in treating severe mood disorders (Weiner & Coffey, 1988).

Curiously, insofar as ECT may be effective, no one is sure why. The discarded theories about how ECT works could fill several books. Until recently, it was widely accepted that the occurrence of a cortical seizure was critical to the treatment. However, this once-firm conclusion is now being questioned by many theorists (Sackeim, 1988). Today, many ECT advocates theorize that the treatment must affect neurotransmitter activity in the brain. However, the evidence supporting this theory is fragmentary and inconclusive (Frankel, 1984). ECT opponents have a radically different, albeit equally unproven, explanation for why ECT might appear to be effective. They maintain that some patients find ECT utterly terrifying and that these patients muster all their willpower to climb out of their depression to avoid further ECT treatments.

The debate about whether ECT works, and how it works, does *not* make ECT unique among approaches to psychotherapy. There are controversies regarding the effectiveness of many psychotherapies. However, this controversy is especially problematic in the case of ECT because the treatment may carry substantial risks.

Risks of ECT

Even ECT proponents acknowledge that memory losses, impaired attention, and other cognitive deficits are common short-term side effects of electroconvulsive therapy. However, proponents assert that these deficits are mild and usually last less than a month (Weeks, Freeman, & Kendell, 1981). In contrast, ECT critics maintain that these cognitive losses are significant and often permanent (Breggin, 1979). Complicating the issue considerably, recent studies using objective measures of patients' memory performance show that former ECT patients tend to overestimate their memory deficits (Sachs & Gelenberg, 1988).

So, what can we conclude about ECT and cognitive deficits? The truth probably lies somewhere in between the positions staked out by the proponents and opponents of ECT. In an unusually dispassionate review of the ECT controversy, Small et al. (1986) assert that "there is little doubt that ECT produces both short- and long-term intellectual impairment." However, they conclude that this impairment is not inevitable and that it is temporary in the vast majority of cases.

Most of the other risks once associated with ECT have been minimized by modern improvements in the procedure. Fractures and dislocations used to be a problem, but medications administered prior to the treatment have virtu-

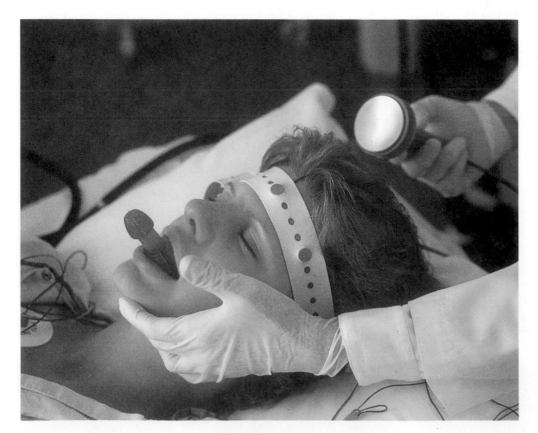

This patient is being prepared for electroconvulsive therapy. The band around the forehead contains electrodes. The mouthpiece keeps the patient from biting her tongue during the electrically induced seizures.

ally eliminated these complications (Kramer, 1985). In competent hands, ECT is a reasonably safe procedure with a mortality rate well under 1 in a 1000 (Weiner, 1985). The occasional deaths that occur are usually due to cardiac complications.

Because of the problems associated with ECT, there has been a trend toward more conservative use of the treatment (Weiner, 1984). More objective empirical research is needed to resolve some of the controversies swirling around ECT.

BLENDING APPROACHES TO PSYCHOTHERAPY

We have reviewed many different approaches to therapy, which are summarized and compared in Figure 16.9. However, there is no law that a client must be treated with just one approach. Often, a clinician will use several different approaches in working with a client. For example, a depressed person might receive cognitive therapy (an insight therapy), social skills training (a behavior therapy), and antidepressant medication (a biomedical therapy). Multiple approaches are particularly likely when a treatment *team* provides therapy.

Studies suggest that there is merit in combining multiple approaches to treatment (Klerman, 1978; Luborsky et al., 1975). One representative study compared the value of insight therapy alone, drug therapy alone, and a combination of insight and drug therapy for depression (Weissman et al., 1979). The subjects suffered from unipolar depression and were treated on an outpatient basis. The groups treated only with antidepressant medication or only with interpersonal therapy both responded well. However, the greatest improvement was found in the group treated with both. Interestingly, the two treatments complemented each other nicely. The drug therapy was particularly effective in relieving some symptoms, while the insight therapy was especially effective in relieving others. Thus, there is much to be said for combining approaches to treatment.

The value of multiple approaches may explain why a significant trend seems to have crept into the field of psychotherapy. There is a movement away from strong loyalty to individual schools of thought and a corresponding move toward integrating different approaches to therapy (Beitman, Goldfried, &

Major Approaches to Psychotherapy

Type of psychotherapy	Primary founders	Origin of disorder	Therapeutic goals	Therapeutic techniques
Psychoanalysis	Freud	Unconcious conflicts resulting from fixations in earlier development	Insights regarding unconscious conflicts and motives; personality reconstruction	Free association, dream analysis, interpretation, catharsis, transference
Client-centered therapy	Rogers	Incongruence between self-concept and actual experience; dependence on acceptance from others	Congruence between self-concept and experience; acceptance of genuine self; self-determination, personal growth	Genuineness, empathy, unconditional positive regard, clarification, reflecting back to client
Cognitive therapy	Beck Ellis	Irrational assumptions and negative, self-defeating thinking about events related to self	Detection of negative thinking; substitution of more realistic thinking	Thought stopping, recording automatic thoughts, refuting negative thinking, reattribution, homework assignments
Behavior therapy	Wolpe Bandura	Maladaptive patterns of behavior acquired through learning	Elimination of symptomatic, maladaptive behaviors; acquisition of more adaptive responses	Classical and operant conditioning, reinforcement, punishment, extinction, shaping, aversive conditioning, systematic desensitization, social skills, training, biofeedback
Biomedical therapies		Physiological malfunction, primarily abnormal neurotransmitter activity	Elimination of symptoms, prevention of relapse	Antipsychotic, antianxiety, and antidepressant drugs; lithium; electroconvulsive therapy (ECT)

Figure 16.9. Comparison of psychotherapy approaches. This chart compares behavior therapies, biomedical therapies, and three leading approaches to insight therapy.

Norcross, 1989). Most clinicians used to depend exclusively on one system of therapy while rejecting the utility of all others. This era of fragmentation may be drawing to a close. In two surveys in the 1980s of psychologists' theoretical orientations (Norcross & Prochaska, 1984; Smith, 1982), researchers were surprised to find that the greatest proportion of respondents described themselves as *eclectic* in approach (see Figure 16.10).

Theoretical eclecticism **involves selecting what appears to be best from a variety of theories or systems of therapy,** instead of committing to just one theoretical orientation. Eclectic therapists use ideas, insights, and techniques from a variety of sources. They adjust their strategy to the unique needs of each client. Eclecticism leads to a creative blending of different approaches to therapy. Some therapists, such as Arnold Lazarus (1989), have even developed systematic approaches to being eclectic.

SUMMARY

Psychotherapy involves three elements: treatment, clients and therapists. Approaches to treatment are diverse, but they can be grouped into three categories: insight therapies, behavior therapies, and biomedical therapies.

Insight therapies involve verbal interactions intended to enhance self-knowledge. In psychoanalysis, free association and dream analysis are used to explore the unconscious. When an analyst's probing hits sensitive areas, resistance can be expected. The transference relationship may be used to overcome this resistance. Classical psychoanalysis is not widely practiced anymore, but Freud's legacy lives on in a rich diversity of modern psychodynamic therapies.

The client-centered therapist tries to provide a supportive climate in which clients can restructure their self-concepts. The process of therapy emphasizes clarification of the client's feelings and self-acceptance. Cognitive therapy concentrates on changing the way clients think about events in their lives.

Most theoretical approaches to insight therapy have been adapted for use with groups. Group therapy has unique advantages in comparison to individual therapy.

Eysenck's work in the 1950s raised doubts about the effectiveness of insight therapy and stimulated research on its efficacy. The weight of the evidence suggests that insight therapies can be effective.

Behavior therapies use the principles of learning in direct efforts to change specific aspects of behavior. Systematic desensitization is a treatment for phobias. It involves the construction of an anxiety hierarchy, relaxation training, and step-by-step movement through the hierarchy. In aversion therapy, a stimulus associated with an unwanted response is paired with an unpleasant stimulus in an effort to eliminate the maladaptive response. Social skills training can improve clients' interpersonal skills through shaping, modeling, and behavioral rehearsal. Biofeedback involves providing information about bodily functions so that the client can attempt to exert some control over those physiological processes. There is ample evidence that behavior therapies are effective.

Biomedical therapies involve physiological interventions for psychological problems. Two examples of biomedical treatments are drug therapy and electroconvulsive therapy. A great variety of disorders are treated with drugs. The principal types of therapeutic drugs include antianxiety drugs, antipsychotic drugs, antidepressant drugs, and lithium. Drug therapies can be very effective, but they have their pitfalls. Many drugs produce problematic side effects.

Electroconvulsive therapy is used to trigger a cortical seizure that is believed to have therapeutic value for mood disorders, especially depression. There is contradictory evidence and heated debate about the effectiveness of ECT and about possible risks associated with its use.

Eclectic combinations of insight, behavioral, and biomedical therapies are often used fruitfully in the treatment of psychological disorders. In our upcoming Application, we'll sort through practical issues involved in selecting a therapist.

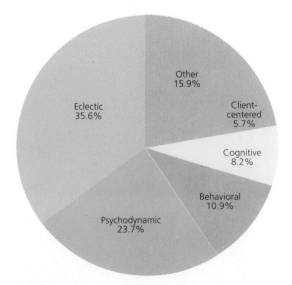

Figure 16.10. The leading approaches to therapy among psychologists. The pooled data from a survey of 415 clinical and counseling psychologists (Smith, 1982) and another survey of 479 clinical psychologists (Norcross & Prochaska, 1982) indicate that the most widely employed approaches to therapy are (in order) the eclectic, psychodynamic, behavioral, cognitive, and client-centered approaches.

Other
15.9%

Eclectic
35.6%

Client-
centered
5.7%

Cognitive
8.2%

Behavioral
10.9%

Psychodynamic
23.7%

Looking for a Therapist

Answer the following "true" or "false."

☐ **1.** Psychotherapy is an art as well as a science.

☐ **2.** The type of professional training a therapist has had is relatively unimportant.

☐ **3.** Psychotherapy can be harmful or damaging to a client.

☐ **4.** Psychotherapy does not have to be expensive.

☐ **5.** It is a good idea to shop around when choosing a therapist.

All of the statements above are true. Do any of them surprise you? If so, you're in good company. Many people know relatively little about the practicalities of selecting a therapist.

The task of finding an appropriate therapist is no less complex than shopping for any other major service. Should you see a psychologist or psychiatrist? Should you opt for individual therapy or group therapy? Should you see a client-centered therapist or a behavior therapist? The unfortunate part of this complexity is that people seeking psychotherapy often feel overwhelmed by personal problems. The last thing they need is to be confronted by yet another complex problem.

Nonetheless, the importance of finding a good therapist cannot be overestimated. Therapy can sometimes have harmful rather than helpful effects. We have already discussed how drug therapies and ECT can sometimes be damaging, but problems are not limited to these interventions. Talking about your problems with a therapist may sound harmless, but studies indicate that insight therapies can also backfire (Bergin & Lambert, 1978; Strupp, Hadley, & Gomes-Schwartz, 1977).

Although a great many talented therapists are available, psychotherapy, like any other profession, has incompetent practitioners as well. Therefore, you should shop for a skilled therapist, just as you would for a good attorney or a good mechanic. In this Application, we'll go over some information that should be helpful if you ever have to look for a therapist for yourself or for a friend or family member (based on Amada, 1985; Bruckner-Gordon, Gangi, & Wallman, 1988; Ehrenberg & Ehrenberg, 1986).

WHEN SHOULD YOU SEEK PROFESSIONAL TREATMENT?

There is no simple answer to this question. Obviously, people usually consider the possibility of professional treatment when they are psychologically distressed. However, there are other options besides psychotherapy. There is much to be said for seeking advice from family, friends, the clergy, and so forth. Insights about personal problems do not belong exclusively to people with professional degrees.

So, when should you turn to professionals for help? You should begin to think seriously about therapy (1) when you have no one to lean on, (2) when the people you lean on indicate that they're getting tired of it, (3) when you feel helpless and overwhelmed, or (4) when your life is seriously disrupted by your

---

RECOMMENDED READING

Making Therapy Work: Your Guide to Choosing, Using, and Ending Therapy

by Fredda Bruckner-Gordon, Barbara K. Gangi, & Geraldine U. Wallman (Harper & Row, 1988)

This book, written by three New York City therapists, follows in the highly practical tradition of the book by the Ehrenbergs that was recommended earlier. However, the two books have different strengths, and both are worthwhile reading for anyone who is in therapy or is considering therapy. A key strength of this book is its step-by-step approach to finding a therapist and making therapy work. The authors lead the uninitiated through a logical progression in which they discuss how to learn about therapy options, how to interview prospective therapists, how to establish an effective therapeutic alliance, how to analyze your reactions to therapy, and so forth. Another strength is that *Making Therapy Work* is loaded with self-analysis exercises to help readers probe their attitudes, feelings, and knowledge about therapy.

Talk about your thoughts, feelings and behavior as openly as possible. There is no magic in therapy, and no one can read your mind. Your therapist can know for sure only what you describe and demonstrate about yourself. Letting yourself be known can yield the good feelings attached to being understood and the likelihood that your therapist will be more engaged and better equipped to help you. . . .

You may be concerned about your therapist's reactions; perhaps you fear disapproval. There's no reason for you to trust automatically, but nothing will convince you like testing his or her responses. If you are having trouble revealing your thoughts and feelings, talk about this difficulty. [p. 83]

Principal Sources of Therapeutic Services

Source	Comments
Private practitioners	Self-employed therapists are listed in the Yellow Pages under their professional category, such as psychologists or psychiatrists. Private practitioners tend to be relatively expensive, but they also tend to be highly experienced therapists.
Community mental health centers	Community mental health centers have salaried psychologists, psychiatrists, and social workers on staff. The centers provide a variety of services and often have staff available on weekends and at night to deal with emergencies.
Hospitals	Several kinds of hospitals provide therapeutic services. There are both public and private mental hospitals that specialize in the care of people with psychological disorders. Many general hospitals have a psychiatric ward, and those that do not will usually have psychiatrists and psychologists on staff and on call. Although hospitals tend to concentrate on inpatient treatment, many provide outpatient therapy as well.
Human service agencies	Various social service agencies employ therapists to provide short-term counseling. Depending on your community, you may find agencies that deal with family problems, juvenile problems, drug problems, and so forth.
Schools and workplaces	Most high schools and colleges have counseling centers where students can get help with personal problems. Similarly, some large businesses offer in-house counseling to their employees.

Figure 16.11. Sources of therapeutic services.
Therapists work in a variety of organizational settings. Foremost among them are the five described here.

WHERE DO YOU FIND THERAPEUTIC SERVICES?

Psychotherapy can be found in a variety of settings. Contrary to general belief, most therapists are not in private practice. Many work in institutional settings such as community mental health centers, hospitals, and human service agencies. The principal sources of therapeutic services are described in Figure 16.11. The exact configuration of therapeutic services available will vary from one community to another. To find out what your community has to offer, you can consult your friends, the phone book, or a community or campus mental health center.

IS THE THERAPIST'S PROFESSION IMPORTANT?

Psychotherapists may be trained in psychology, psychiatry, social work, psychiatric nursing, or counseling. Many talented therapists can be found in all of these professions. Thus, the kind of degree that a therapist holds doesn't need to be a crucial consideration in your selection process. It *is* true that only a psychiatrist can prescribe drugs for disorders that merit drug therapy. However, some critics argue that many psychiatrists are too quick to try drugs to solve everything (Wiener, 1968). In any case, other types of therapists can refer you to a psychiatrist if they think that drug therapy would be helpful. If you have a health insurance policy that covers psychotherapy, you may want to check whether it carries any restrictions about the therapist's profession.

IS THE THERAPIST'S SEX IMPORTANT?

This depends on your attitude. If *you* feel that the therapist's sex is important, then for you it is. The therapeutic relationship must be characterized by trust and rapport. If you won't feel comfortable with a therapist of one sex or the other, this could inhibit the therapeutic process. Hence, you should feel free to look for a male or female therapist if you prefer to do so. This point is probably most relevant to female clients whose troubles may be related to the extensive sexism in our society. It is entirely reasonable for women to seek a therapist with a feminist perspective if that would make them feel more comfortable.

Speaking of sex, you should be aware that sexual exploitation is an occasional problem in the context of therapy. Studies indicate that a small minority of therapists take advantage of their clients sexually (Pope, Keith-Spiegel, & Tabachnick, 1986). These incidents almost always involve a male therapist making advances to a female client. There are absolutely no situations in which therapist-client sexual relations are an ethical therapeutic practice. If a therapist makes sexual advances, a client should terminate treatment.

problems. Of course, you do not have to be falling apart to justify therapy. You may want to seek professional advice simply because you want to get more out of life.

IS THERAPY ALWAYS EXPENSIVE?

Psychotherapy does not have to be prohibitively expensive. Private practitioners tend to be the most expensive, charging between $25 and $100 per (50-

minute) hour. These fees may seem high, but they are in line with those of similar professionals, such as dentists and attorneys. Community mental health centers and social service agencies are usually supported by tax dollars. Hence, they can charge lower fees than most therapists in private practice. Many of these organizations employ a sliding scale, so that clients are charged according to how much they can afford to pay. Thus, most communities have inexpensive opportunities for psychotherapy. Moreover, many health insurance plans provide at least partial reimbursement for the cost of psychotherapy.

IS THE THERAPIST'S THEORETICAL APPROACH IMPORTANT?

Logically, you might expect that the different approaches to therapy ought to vary in effectiveness. For the most part, however, this is *not* what researchers find. After reviewing the evidence, Luborsky et al. (1975) quote the dodo bird who has just judged a race in *Alice in Wonderland.* "Everyone has won and all must have prizes." Improvement rates for different theoretical orientations usually come out pretty close in most studies. In their massive review of outcome studies, Smith et al. (1980) estimated the effectiveness of many major approaches to therapy. As Figure 16.12 shows, the estimates cluster together closely.

These findings do not mean that all *therapists* are created equal. Some therapists unquestionably are more effective than others. However, these variations in effectiveness appear to depend on therapists' personal skills rather than differences in theoretical orientation. Good, bad, and mediocre therapists are found within each school of thought.

The key point is that effective therapy requires skill and creativity. Arnold Lazarus, who devised multimodal therapy (a form of eclectic therapy), emphasizes that therapists "straddle the fence between science and art." Therapy is scientific in that interventions are based on extensive theory and empirical research (Forsyth & Strong, 1986). Ultimately, though, each client is a unique human being, and the therapist has to creatively fashion a treatment program that will help that individual.

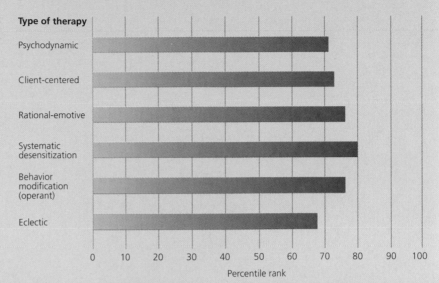

WHAT SHOULD YOU LOOK FOR IN A PROSPECTIVE THERAPIST?

Some clients are timid about asking prospective therapists questions about their training, approach, fees, and so forth. However, these are reasonable questions, and the vast majority of therapists will be most accommodating. Usually, you may ask your preliminary questions over the phone. If things seem promising, you may decide to make an appointment for an interview (you probably will have to pay for the interview). In this interview, the therapist will gather more information to determine the likelihood of helping you, given the therapist's training and approach to treatment. At the same time, you should be making a similar judgment about whether *you* believe the therapist could help you with your problems.

What should you look for? First, you should look for personal warmth and sincere concern. Try to judge whether you will be able to talk to this person in a candid, nondefensive way. Second, look for empathy and understanding. Is the person capable of appreciating your point of view? Third, look for self-confidence. Self-assured therapists will communicate a sense of competence without trying to intimidate you with jargon or boasting needlessly about what they can do for you. When all is said and done, you should *like* your therapist. Otherwise, it will be difficult to establish the needed rapport.

Figure 16.12. Efficacy of different approaches to therapy. Smith and Glass (1977) reviewed nearly 400 studies in which clients who were treated with a specific type of therapy were compared with a control group made up of people with similar problems who went untreated. The bars indicate the percentile rank (on outcome measures) attained by the average client treated with each type of therapy when compared to control subjects. The higher the percentile, the more effective the therapy was. As you can see, the different approaches were fairly close in their apparent effectiveness.

Figure 16.13. Signs of resistance. Resistance in therapy may be subtle, but Ehrenberg and Ehrenberg (1986) have identified some telltale signs to look for.

Signs of Resistance in Therapy

If you're dissatisfied with your progress in therapy, resistance may be the problem when:

1 You have nothing specific or concrete to complain about.

2 Your attitude about therapy changes suddenly just as you reach the truly sensitive issues.

3 You've had the same problem with other therapists in the past.

4 Your conflicts with the therapist resemble those that you have with other people.

5 You start hiding things from your therapist.

WHAT IF THERE ISN'T ANY PROGRESS?

If you feel that your therapy isn't going anywhere, you should probably discuss these feelings with your therapist. Don't be surprised, however, if the therapist suggests that it may be your own fault. Freud's concept of resistance has some validity. Some clients *do* have difficulty facing up to their problems. Thus, if your therapy isn't progressing, you may need to *consider* whether your resistance may be slowing progress. This self-examination isn't easy, as you are not an unbiased observer. Some common signs of resistance identified by Ehrenberg and Ehrenberg (1986) are listed in Figure 16.13.

Given the very real possibility that poor progress may be due to resistance, you should not be too quick to leave therapy when dissatisfied. However, it *is* possible that your therapist isn't sufficiently skilled or that the two of you are incompatible. Thus, after careful and deliberate consideration, you should feel free to terminate your therapy.

WHAT IS THERAPY LIKE?

It is important to have realistic expectations about therapy, or you may be unnecessarily disappointed. Some people expect miracles. They expect to turn their life around quickly with little effort. Others expect their therapists to run their lives for them. These are unrealistic expectations.

Therapy usually is a slow process. Your problems are not likely to melt away quickly. Moreover, therapy is hard work, and your therapist is only a facilitator. Ultimately, *you* have to confront the challenge of changing your behavior, your feelings, or your personality. This process may not be pleasant. You may have to face up to some painful truths about yourself. As Ehrenberg and Ehrenberg (1986) point out, "Psychotherapy takes time, effort and courage."

KEY LEARNING OBJECTIVES

1. Identify the three major categories of therapy and discuss why people do or do not seek psychotherapy.

2. Describe the various types of mental health professionals involved in the provision of therapy.

3. Explain the logic of psychoanalysis and describe the techniques used to probe the unconscious.

4. Discuss interpretation, resistance, and transference in psychoanalysis.

5. Summarize trends in modern psychodynamic approaches to therapy.

6. Describe therapeutic climate and process in client-centered therapy.

7. Discuss the logic, goals, and techniques of cognitive therapy.

8. Describe how group therapy is generally conducted and identify some advantages of group therapy.

9. Summarize evidence on the efficacy of insight therapies.

10. Summarize the general approach and principles of behavior therapies.

11. Describe systematic desensitization and aversion therapy.

12. Describe the use of social skills training and biofeedback.

13. Summarize evidence on the efficacy of behavior therapies.

14. Describe the principal drug therapies used in the treatment of psychological disorders.

15. Summarize evidence on the efficacy and problems of drug therapies.

16. Describe ECT and discuss its efficacy and its risks.

17. Discuss the merits of blending approaches to therapy.

18. Discuss when and where to seek therapy, and the potential importance of a therapist's sex, theoretical approach, and professional background.

19. Summarize what one should look for in a prospective therapist and what one should expect out of therapy.

KEY TERMS

Antianxiety drugs
Antidepressant drugs
Antipsychotic drugs
Aversion therapy
Behavior therapies
Biofeedback
Biomedical therapies
Client-centered therapy
Clinical psychologists
Cognitive therapy
Counseling psychologists
Dream analysis
Electroconvulsive therapy (ECT)
Free association
Group therapy

Insight therapies
Interpretation
Lithium
Psychiatrists
Psychoanalysis
Psychopharmacotherapy
Resistance
Social skills training
Spontaneous remission
Systematic desensitization
Tardive dyskinesia
Theoretical eclecticism
Transference

KEY PEOPLE

Aaron Beck
Hans Eysenck
Sigmund Freud
Carl Rogers
Joseph Wolpe

Attitudes Toward Seeking Professional Psychological Help

INSTRUCTIONS

Read each statement carefully and indicate your agreement or disagreement, using the scale below. Please express your frank opinion in responding to each statement, answering as you honestly feel or believe.

0 = Disagreement   1 = Probable disagreement

2 = Probable agreement   3 = Agreement

THE SCALE

_____ 1. Although there are clinics for people with mental troubles, I would not have much faith in them.

_____ 2. If a good friend asked my advice about a mental health problem, I might recommend that he see a psychiatrist.

_____ 3. I would feel uneasy going to a psychiatrist because of what some people would think.

_____ 4. A person with a strong character can get over mental conflicts by himself, and would have little need of a psychiatrist.

_____ 5. There are times when I have felt completely lost and would have welcomed professional advice for a personal or emotional problem.

_____ 6. Considering the time and expense involved in psychotherapy, it would have doubtful value for a person like me.

_____ 7. I would willingly confide intimate matters to an appropriate person if I thought it might help me or a member of my family.

_____ 8. I would rather live with certain mental conflicts than go through the ordeal of getting psychiatric treatment.

_____ 9. Emotional difficulties, like many things, tend to work out by themselves.

_____ 10. There are certain problems that should not be discussed outside of one's immediate family .

_____ 11. A person with a serious emotional disturbance would probably feel most secure in a good mental hospital.

_____ 12. If I believed I was having a mental breakdown, my first inclination would be to get professional attention.

_____ 13. Keeping one's mind on a job is a good solution for avoiding personal worries and concerns.

_____ 14. Having been a psychiatric patient is a blot on a person's life.

_____ 15. I would rather be advised by a close friend than by a psychologist, even for an emotional problem.

_____ 16. A person with an emotional problem is not likely to solve it alone; he or she _is_ likely to solve it with professional help.

_____ 17. I resent a person—professionally trained or not—who wants to know about my personal difficulties.

_____ 18. I would want to get psychiatric attention if I was worried or upset for a long period of time.

_____ 19. The idea of talking about problems with a psychologist strikes me as a poor way to get rid of emotional conflicts.

_____ 20. Having been mentally ill carries with it a burden of shame.

_____ 21. There are experiences in my life I would not discuss with anyone.

_____ 22. It is probably best not to know _everything_ about oneself.

_____ 23. If I were experiencing a serious emotional crisis at this point in my life, I would be confident that I could find relief in psychotherapy.

_____ 24. There is something admirable in the attitude of a person who is willing to cope with his conflicts and fears _without_ resorting to professional help.

_____ 25. At some future time I might want to have psychological counseling.

_____ 26. A person should work out his own problems; getting psychological counseling would be a last resort.

_____ 27. Had I received treatment in a mental hospital, I would not feel that it had to be "covered up."

_____ 28. If I thought I needed psychiatric help, I would get it no matter who knew about it.

_____ 29. It is difficult to talk about personal affairs with highly educated people such as doctors, teachers, and clergymen.

SCORING THE SCALE

Begin by reversing your response (0 = 3, 1 = 2, 2 = 1, 3 = 0) for items 1, 3, 4, 6, 8, 9, 10, 13, 14, 15, 17, 19, 20, 21, 22, 24, 26, and 29. Then add up the numbers for all 29 items on the scale. This total is your score. Record your score below.

MY SCORE _____

WHAT THE SCALE MEASURES

The scale assesses the degree to which you have favorable attitudes toward professional psychotherapy (Fischer & Turner, 1970). The higher your score, the more positive your attitudes about therapy. As we have discussed, there are many negative stereotypes about therapy, and many people are very reluctant to pursue therapy. This is unfortunate, because negative attitudes often prevent people from seeking therapy that could be beneficial to them.

NORMS

High score:	64–87
Medium score:	50–63
Low score:	0–49

What Are Your Feelings about Therapy?

The following questions (adapted from Corey & Corey, 1990) are intended to help you examine your attitudes regarding professional psychotherapy.

1. If you have had any experience with mental health professionals, describe what it was like.

2. Based on your experience, would you recommend professional counseling to a friend?

3. List any considerations that might prevent you from seeking some form of therapy even if you felt a need or desire to do so.

4. If you were looking for a therapist, what criteria would you employ in making your choice?

5. Briefly describe what you would expect to get out of professional therapy or counseling.

Glossary

adjustment The psychological processes through which people manage or cope with the demands and challenges of everyday life.

affiliation motive The need to associate with others and maintain social bonds.

age cohort A group of people born in the same time period who develop in the same historical context.

ageism Discrimination against people on the basis of their age.

age roles Expectations about appropriate behavior that are based on one's chronological age.

aggression Any behavior intended to hurt someone, either physically or verbally.

aging The biological process of growing older.

agoraphobia A fear of going out to public places.

alcohol Beverages containing ethyl alcohol.

anal intercourse Insertion of the penis into a sex partner's anus and rectum.

androgens The principal class of male sex hormones.

androgyny The coexistence of both masculine and feminine personality traits in an individual.

antecedents In behavior modification, events that typically precede a target behavior.

antianxiety drugs Drugs that relieve tension, apprehension, and nervousness.

antidepressant drugs Drugs that gradually elevate mood and help to bring people out of a depression.

antipsychotic drugs Drugs used to gradually reduce psychotic symptoms, including hyperactivity, mental confusion, hallucinations, and delusions.

antisocial personality disorder A type of personality disorder marked by impulsive, callous, manipulative, aggressive, and irresponsible behavior that reflects a failure to accept social norms.

anxiety disorders A class of disorders marked by feelings of excessive apprehension and anxiety.

approach-approach conflict A motivational conflict in which a choice must be made between two attractive goals.

approach-avoidance conflict A motivational conflict in which a choice must be made about whether to pursue a single goal that has both attractive and unattractive aspects.

assertiveness Acting in one's own best interests by expressing one's feelings honestly and standing up for one's legitimate rights.

atherosclerosis A disease characterized by gradual narrowing of the coronary arteries.

attitudes Conceptions that locate objects of thought on dimensions of judgment.

attributions Inferences that people draw about the causes of events, others' behavior, and their own behavior.

autonomic nervous system (ANS) That portion of the peripheral nervous system made up of the nerves that connect to the heart, blood vessels, smooth muscles, and glands.

aversion therapy A behavior therapy in which an aversive stimulus is paired with a stimulus that elicits an undesirable response.

avoidance-avoidance conflict A motivational conflict in which a choice must be made between two unattractive goals.

basal metabolic rate The body's rate of energy output at rest, after a 12-hour fast.

baseline period A span of time before beginning a behavior modification program, during which one systematically observes one's target behavior.

behavior Any overt (observable) response or activity by an organism.

behavioral contract A written agreement outlining a promise to adhere to the contingencies of a behavior modification program.

behaviorism A theoretical orientation based on the premise that scientific psychology should study observable behavior.

behavior modification A systematic approach to changing behavior through the application of the principles of conditioning.

behavior therapies The application of the principles of learning to direct efforts to change clients' maladaptive behaviors.

biofeedback A type of therapy in which a bodily function (such as heart rate) is monitored and information is fed back to a person to facilitate improved control of the physiological process.

biomedical therapies Physiological interventions intended to reduce symptoms associated with psychological disorders.

biopsychosocial model The idea that physical illness is caused by a complex interaction of biological, psychological, and sociocultural factors.

bipolar mood disorders Psychological disorders marked by the experiencing of both depressed and manic periods.

bisexuals People who seek sexual relationships with members of either sex.

brainstorming Generating as many ideas as possible while withholding criticism and evaluation.

burnout Physical, mental, and emotional exhaustion that is attributable to work-related stress.

bystander effect The phenomenon in which people in groups are less likely to provide needed help than when they are alone.

cancer Malignant cell growth, which may occur in many organ systems in the body.

cannabis The hemp plant from which marijuana, hashish, and THC are derived.

cardinal trait A dominant personality trait that permeates nearly all of a person's behavior.

case study An in-depth investigation of an individual subject.

catastrophic thinking Unrealistic appraisals of stress that exaggerate the magnitude of one's problems.

catatonic schizophrenia A type of schizophrenia marked by striking motor disturbances, ranging from muscular rigidity to random motor activity.

catharsis The release of emotional tension through behaving aggressively.

central traits Prominent, general personality dispositions.

cerebral hemispheres The right and left halves of the cerebrum, which is the convoluted outer layer of the brain.

channel The medium through which a message reaches the receiver.

classical conditioning A type of learning in which a neutral stimulus acquires the capacity to evoke a response that was originally evoked by another stimulus.

client-centered therapy An insight therapy that emphasizes providing a supportive emotional climate for clients, who play a major role in determining the pace and direction of their therapy.

clinical psychologists Psychologists who specialize in the diagnosis and treatment of psychological disorders and everyday behavioral problems.

clinical psychology The branch of psychology concerned with the diagnosis and treatment of psychological problems and disorders.

close relationship A relatively long-lasting relationship in which two people interact frequently and engage in a variety of mutual activities, and in which the impact of the interactions is strong.

cognition The thought processes involved in acquiring knowledge.

cognitive development Age-related transitions in patterns of thinking, including reasoning, remembering, and problem solving.

cognitive dissonance The psychological discomfort that occurs when related cognitions are inconsistent—that is, they contradict each other.

cognitive therapy An insight therapy that emphasizes recognizing and changing negative thoughts and maladaptive beliefs.

cohabitation Living together in a sexually intimate relationship without the legal bonds of marriage.

coitus Insertion of the penis into the vagina and (typically) pelvic thrusting.

collusion The situation that occurs when two people have an unspoken agreement to deny some problematic aspect of reality in order to sustain their relationship.

commitment The decision and intent to maintain a relationship in spite of the difficulties and costs that may arise.

communication barrier Anything in the communication process that inhibits or blocks the accurate transmission and reception of messages.

communication network A well-defined pattern of who talks to whom in a group.

comparison level One's standard of what constitutes an acceptable balance of rewards and costs in a relationship.

compensation A defense mechanism characterized by efforts to overcome imagined or real inferiorities by developing one's abilities.

complementary transaction A transaction in which the receiver responds from the same ego state that was addressed by the source.

compliance Yielding to social pressure in one's public behavior, even though one's private beliefs have not changed.

concordance rate A statistic indicating the percentage of twin pairs or other pairs of relatives that exhibit the same disorder.

conditioned response (CR) A learned reaction to a conditioned stimulus that occurs because of previous conditioning.

conditioned stimulus (CS) A previously neutral stimulus that has acquired the capacity to evoke a conditioned response through conditioning.

conflict The struggle that occurs when two or more incompatible motivations or behavioral impulses compete for expression.

conformity Yielding to real or imagined social pressure.

conscious According to Freud, whatever one is aware of at a particular point in time.

conservation The awareness that physical quantities remain constant in spite of changes in their shape or appearance.

consideration A dimension of leadership that reflects the degree to which a leader is warm, trusting, and supportive in interactions with group members.

constructive coping Efforts to deal with stressful events that are judged to be relatively healthy.

control group Similar subjects who do not receive the special treatment given to the experimental group.

conversion disorders Psychological disorders characterized by a significant loss of physical function (with no apparent organic basis), usually in a single organ system.

coping Active efforts to master, reduce, or tolerate the demands created by stress.

coronary heart disease A chronic disease characterized by a reduction in blood flow from the coronary arteries, which supply the heart with blood.

correlation The extent to which two variables are related to each another.

correlation coefficient A numerical index of the degree of relationship that exists between two variables.

counseling psychologists Psychologists who specialize in the diagnosis and treatment of psychological disorders and everyday behavioral problems.

crossed transaction A transaction in which the receiver does not respond from the ego state addressed by the source.

cunnilingus Oral stimulation of the female genitals.

death system The collection of rituals and procedures used by a culture to handle death.

defense mechanisms Unconscious reactions that protect a person from unpleasant emotions such as anxiety and guilt.

defensive attribution A tendency to blame victims for their misfortune, so that we feel less likely to be victimized in a similar way.

delusions False beliefs that are maintained even though they clearly are out of touch with reality.

denial Refusing to perceive or face unpleasant realities.

dependent variable The variable that is thought to be affected by manipulation of the independent variable.

depressive disorders Psychological disorders characterized by persistent feelings of sadness and despair and a loss of interest in previous sources of pleasure.

designer drugs Illicitly manufactured variations on known recreational drugs.

development The sequence of age-related changes that occur as a person progresses from conception to death.

diagnosis Distinguishing one illness from another.

discrimination Behaving differently, usually unfairly, toward the members of a group.

discriminative stimuli Cues that influence operant behavior by indicating the probable consequences of a response.

disorganized schizophrenia A type of schizophrenia characterized by a particularly severe deterioration of adaptive behavior.

displacement Diverting emotional feelings (usually anger) from their original source to a substitute target.

display rules Norms that govern the appropriate display of emotions.

dissociative disorders A class of psychological disorders in which people lose contact with portions of their consciousness or memory, resulting in disruptions in their sense of identity.

door-in-the-face technique Making a very large request that is likely to be turned down to increase the chances that people will agree to a smaller request later.

dream analysis A psychotherapeutic technique in which the therapist interprets the symbolic meaning of the client's dreams.

ego According to Freud, the decision-making component of personality that operates according to the reality principle.

egocentrism The preoperational child's limited ability to share another person's point of view.

ego state A personality structure consisting of a coherent system of internal feelings.

electroconvulsive therapy (ECT) A biomedical treatment in which electric shock is used to produce a cortical seizure accompanied by convulsions.

emotions Powerful, largely uncontrollable feelings, accompanied by physiological changes.

empathy Adopting another person's frame of reference to understand her or his point of view.

empiricism The premise that knowledge should be acquired through observation.

endocrine system Glands that secrete chemicals called hormones into the bloodstream.

endogamy The tendency of people to marry within their own social group.

epidemiology The study of the distribution of mental or physical disorders in a population.

erectile difficulties Male sexual dysfunction characterized by the persistent inability to achieve or maintain an erection adequate for intercourse.

erogenous zones Areas of the body that are sexually sensitive or responsive.

erotophiles People who have very favorable attitudes about sex.

erotophobes People who have very negative attitudes about sex.

estrogens The principal class of female sex hormones.

etiology The apparent causation and developmental history of an illness.

experiment A research method in which the investigator manipulates a variable (the independent variable) under carefully controlled conditions and observes any changes in a second (dependent) variable that result.

experimental group The subjects in an experiment who receive some special treatment in regard to the independent variable.

external attributions Ascribing the causes of behavior to situational demands and environmental constraints.

extinction The gradual weakening and disappearance of a conditioned response.

false consensus effect The tendency to overestimate the degree to which others think and behave as we do.

false uniqueness effect The tendency to underestimate the likelihood that others possess our admirable qualities.

family life cycle An orderly sequence of developmental stages that families tend to progress through.

fantasy Gratifying frustrated desires by thinking about imaginary achievements and satisfactions.

fellatio Oral stimulation of the penis.

fight-or-flight response A physiological reaction to threat that mobilizes an organism for attacking (fight) or fleeing (flight) an enemy.

fixation In Freud's view, a failure to move forward from one psychosexual stage to another as expected.

foot-in-the-door technique Getting people to agree to a small request to increase the chances that they will agree to a larger request later.

free association A psychotherapeutic technique in which clients spontaneously express their thoughts and feelings exactly as they occur, with as little censorship as possible.

frustration The feelings created when pursuit of some goal is thwarted.

fundamental attribution error Observers' bias in favor of internal attributions in explaining others' behavior.

games Manipulative interactions progressing toward a predictable outcome, in which people conceal their real motivations.

gay *See* homosexuals.

gender Culturally constructed distinctions between masculinity and femininity.

gender differences Actual disparities between the sexes in their typical (average) behavior.

gender-role identity A person's identification with the traits regarded as masculine or feminine.

gender roles Expectations about what is appropriate behavior for each sex.

gender stereotypes Widely shared beliefs about males' and females' abilities, personality traits, and social behavior.

general adaptation syndrome A model of the body's stress response, consisting of three stages: alarm, resistance, and exhaustion.

generalized anxiety disorder A psychological disorder marked by a chronic high level of anxiety that is not tied to any specific threat.

gerontology A multidisciplinary field concerned with the study of old age and the elderly.

gonads The sex glands.

group Two or more individuals who interact and are interdependent.

group cohesiveness The strength of the liking relationships linking group members to each other and to the group itself.

group norms Rules regarding appropriate behavior.

group polarization The phenomenon that occurs when group discussion strengthens a group's dominant point of view and produces a shift toward a more extreme decision in that direction.

group therapy The simultaneous treatment of several clients in a group.

groupthink The phenomenon that occurs when members of a cohesive group emphasize concurrence at the expense of critical thinking in arriving at a decision.

hallucinations Sensory perceptions that occur in the absence of a real, external stimulus or that represent gross distortions of perceptual input.

hallucinogens A diverse group of drugs that have powerful effects on mental and emotional functioning, marked most prominently by distortions in sensory and perceptual experience.

hardiness A personality syndrome marked by commitment, challenge, and control, that is purportedly associated with strong stress resistance.

health psychology The subfield of psychology concerned with how psychosocial factors relate to the promotion and maintenance of health, and with the causation, prevention, and treatment of illness.

heterosexuals People whose sexual desires and erotic behaviors are directed toward the opposite sex.

hierarchy of needs A systematic arrangement of needs, according to priority, in which basic needs must be met before less basic needs are aroused.

homogamy The tendency of people to marry others who have similar personal characteristics.

homophobia Intense fear, hatred, and intolerance of homosexuality.

homosexuals Men and women whose sexual desires and erotic activities are directed toward the same sex.

hormones Chemical substances released into the bloodstream by the endocrine glands.

humanism A theoretical orientation that emphasizes the unique qualities of humans, especially their free will and their potential for personal growth.

hypochondriasis (hypochondria) Excessive preoccupation with health concerns and incessant worry about developing physical illnesses.

hypothesis A tentative statement about the relationship between two or more variables.

hypothetico-deductive reasoning The ability to formulate specific hypotheses and test them systematically.

id In Freud's theory, the primitive, instinctive component of personality that operates according to the pleasure principle.

identification Bolstering self-esteem by forming an imaginary or real alliance with some person or group.

identity Having a relatively clear and stable sense of who one is and what one stands for.

illusory correlation effect The tendency to estimate that we have encountered more confirmations of an association between social traits than we have actually seen.

immune response The body's defensive reaction to invasion by bacteria, viral agents, or other foreign substances.

implicit theories of personality Our own personal assumptions about what personality traits go together.

impression management Usually conscious efforts to present oneself in socially desirable ways.

incongruence The disparity between one's self-concept and one's actual experience.

independent variable A condition or event that an experimenter varies in order to see its impact on another variable.

infant attachment The strong emotional bond that infants usually develop with their caregivers during the first year of their lives.

ingratiation A conscious and systematic effort to gain liking from another person.

in-group The group one belongs to and identifies with.

initiating structure A dimension of leadership that reflects the degree to which a leader organizes, directs, and regulates a group's activities.

insight therapies A group of psychotherapies in which verbal interactions are intended to enhance clients' self-knowledge and thus promote healthful changes in personality and behavior.

insomnia Chronic problems in getting adequate sleep.

intellectualization Suppressing unpleasant emotions while engaging in detached analyses of threatening problems.

interference Forgetting information because of competition from other learned material.

internal attributions Ascribing the causes of behavior to personal dispositions, traits, abilities, and feelings rather than to external events.

interpersonal attraction Positive feelings toward another person.

interpersonal communication An interactional process whereby one person sends a message to another.

interpersonal conflict Disagreement among two or more people..

interpretation A therapist's attempts to explain the inner significance of the client's thoughts, feelings, memories, and behaviors.

intimacy Warmth, closeness, and sharing in a relationship.

job satisfaction One's happiness and contentment with a particular occupational position.

kinesics The study of communication through body movements.

latitude of acceptance A range of potentially acceptable positions on an issue centered on one's initial attitude position.

leadership A reciprocal process in which certain people are permitted to motivate and influence others to facilitate the pursuit of group goals.

learned helplessness Passive behavior produced by exposure to unavoidable aversive events.

life changes Any noticeable alterations in one's living circumstances that require readjustment.

lithium A chemical used to control mood swings in patients with bipolar mood disorders.

loneliness The emotional state that occurs when a person has fewer interpersonal relationships than desired or when these relationships are not as satisfying as desired.

lowball technique Getting someone to commit to an attractive proposition before its hidden costs are revealed.

marriage The legally and socially sanctioned union of sexually intimate adults.

matching hypothesis The idea that people of similar levels of physical attractiveness gravitate toward each other.

mediation A family of mental exercises in which a conscious attempt is made to focus attention in a nonanalytical way.

medical model The idea that it is useful to think of abnormal behavior as a disease.

menarche The first occurrence of menstruation.

menopause The time when menstruation ceases.

mentor Someone with a senior position within an organization who serves as a role model, tutor, and adviser to a novice worker.

message The information or meaning that is transmitted from one person to another.

meta-analysis Statistical analysis that combines the results of many studies of the same question.

mnemonic devices Strategies for enhancing memory.

mood disorders A class of disorders marked by emotional disturbances that may spill over to disrupt physical, perceptual, social, and thought processes.

multiple-personality disorders Dissociative disorders involving the coexistence of two or more largely complete, and usually very different, personalities.

narcotics (opiates) Drugs derived from opium that are capable of relieving pain.

naturalistic observation An approach to research in which the researcher engages in careful observation of behavior without intervening directly with the subjects.

need for self-actualization The need to fulfill one's potential.

negative reinforcement Removing an unpleasant stimulus in order to strengthen (increase in frequency) a response.

neurons Individual cells that receive, integrate, and transmit information.

neurotic Referring to behavior marked by subjective distress (usually chronic anxiety) and reliance on avoidance coping.

neurotransmitters Chemicals that carry information from one neuron to another.

nonverbal communication The transmission of meaning from one person to another through means or symbols other than words.

nurturance The provision of help, physical care, and emotional support to others.

nutrition A collection of processes through which an organism utilizes the materials (nutrients) required for survival and growth.

obedience A form of compliance that occurs when people follow direct commands, usually from someone in a position of authority.

obesity The condition of being overweight.

object permanence The child's recognition that objects continue to exist even when they are no longer visible.

observational learning Learning that occurs when an organism's responding is influenced by the observation of others, who are called models.

obsessive-compulsive disorder A psychological disorder marked by persistent uncontrollable intrusions of unwanted thoughts (obsessions) and by urges to engage in senseless rituals (compulsions).

occupational interest inventories Tests that measure one's interests as they relate to various jobs or careers.

Oedipal complex According to Freud, the idea that children in the genital stage manifest erotically tinged desires for their opposite-sex parent, accompanied by feelings of hostility toward their same-sex parent.

operant conditioning A form of learning in which voluntary responses come to be controlled by their consequences.

operational definition In scientific research, a definition that describes the actions or operations that will be made to measure or control a variable.

optimism A general tendency to expect good outcomes.

orgasm The release that occurs when sexual arousal reaches its peak intensity and is discharged in a series of muscular contractions that pulsate through the pelvic area.

orgasmic difficulties Sexual disorders characterized by an ability to experience sexual arousal but persistent problems in achieving orgasm.

out-group People who are not part of the in-group.

overcompensation Making up for frustration in one area by seeking overgratification in another area.

overdose An excessive dose of a drug that can seriously threaten one's life.

overlearning Continued rehearsal of material after one first appears to have mastered it.

panic disorder Recurrent attacks of overwhelming anxiety that usually occur suddenly and unexpectedly.

paralanguage All vocal cues other than the content of the verbal message itself.

paranoid schizophrenia A type of schizophrenia dominated by delusions of persecution, along with delusions of grandeur.

passion The intense feelings (both positive and negative) experienced in love relationships, including sexual desire.

personality An individual's unique constellation of consistent behavioral traits.

personality disorders A class of disorders marked by extreme, inflexible personality traits that cause subjective distress or impaired social and occupational functioning.

personality trait A durable disposition to behave in a particular way in a variety of situations.

personal space A zone of space surrounding a person that is felt to "belong" to that person.

persuasion The communication of arguments and information intended to change another person's attitudes.

phobic disorders Anxiety disorders characterized by a persistent and irrational fear of an object or situation that presents no realistic danger.

physical dependence The need to continue to take a drug to avoid withdrawal illness.

placebo effects Experiencing some change from an empty, fake, or ineffectual treatment because of one's positive expectations about the treatment.

pleasure principle According to Freud, the principle upon which the id acts, demanding immediate gratification of its urges.

positive reinforcement Strengthening of a response through arrival of a pleasant stimulus.

posttraumatic stress disorder Disturbed behavior, attributed to a major stressful event, that emerges after the stress is over.

power The potential to influence a group's decisions and individual members' behavior.

preconscious According to Freud, material just beneath the surface of awareness that can be easily retrieved.

prejudice A negative attitude toward members of a group.

premature ejaculation Impaired sexual relations because a man consistently reaches orgasm too quickly.

premenstrual syndrome A negative shift in mood, thought to occur in the days preceding females' menstrual periods.

pressure Expectations or demands that one behave in a certain way.

prevalence The percentage of a population that exhibits a disorder during a specified time period.

primacy effect The fact that initial information tends to carry more weight than subsequent information.

primary appraisal An initial evaluation of whether an event is (1) irrelevant to one, (2) relevant, but not threatening, or (3) stressful.

prognosis A forecast about the probable course of an illness.

projection Attributing one's own thoughts, feelings, or motives to another.

proxemics The study of people's use of interpersonal space.

proximity Geographic, residential, and other forms of spatial closeness.

psychiatrists Physicians who specialize in the treatment of psychological disorders.

psychoactive drugs Chemical substances that modify a person's mental, emotional, or behavioral functioning.

psychoanalysis An insight therapy that emphasizes the recovery of unconscious conflicts, motives, and defenses through techniques such as free association, dream analysis, and transference.

psychodynamic theories All the diverse theories descended from the work of Sigmund Freud that focus on unconscious mental forces.

psychogenic amnesia A sudden loss of memory for important personal information that is too extensive to be due to normal forgetting.

psychological dependence The need to continue to take a drug to satisfy intense mental and emotional craving for it.

psychological test A standardized measure of a sample of a person's behavior.

psychology The science that studies behavior and the physiological and mental processes that underlie it and the profession that applies the accumulated knowledge of the science to practical problems.

psychopharmacotherapy The treatment of mental disorders with medication.

psychosexual stages In Freud's theory, developmental periods with a characteristic sexual focus that leave their mark on adult personality.

psychosomatic diseases Genuine physical ailments caused in part by psychological factors, especially emotional distress.

psychotic Referring to behavior marked by impaired reality contact and profound deterioration of adaptive functioning.

puberty The period of early adolescence marked by rapid physical growth and the development of reproductive capacity.

public self An image or façade presented to others in social interactions.

punishment The weakening (decrease in frequency) of a response because it is followed by the arrival of a (presumably) unpleasant stimulus.

rational-emotive therapy An approach to therapy that focuses on altering clients' patterns of irrational thinking to reduce maladaptive emotions and behavior.

rationalization Creating false but plausible excuses to justify unacceptable behavior.

reactance Efforts to restore a threatened freedom.

reaction formation Behaving in a way that is exactly the opposite of one's true feelings.

reality principle According to Freud, the principle by which the ego seeks to delay gratification of the id's urges until appropriate outlets and situations can be found.

receiver The person to whom a message is targeted.

reciprocity Liking those who show that they like us.

reciprocity norm The rule that we should pay back in kind what we receive from others.

reference group A set of people against whom you compare yourself.

refractory period A time following orgasm during which males are largely unresponsive to further stimulation.

regression A reversion to immature patterns of behavior.

reliability The measurement consistency of a test.

REM sleep A deep stage of sleep marked by rapid eye movements, dreaming, and brain wave activity like that seen when people are awake.

repression Keeping distressing thoughts and feelings buried in the unconscious.

resistance Largely unconscious defensive maneuvers intended to hinder the progress of therapy.

role A pattern of behavior expected of a person who has a certain position in a group.

romantic jealousy A complex of thoughts, emotions, and behaviors that result from the perception of a threat to one's intimate relationship.

schizophrenic disorders A class of disorders marked by disturbances in thought that spill over to affect perceptual, social, and emotional processes.

seasonal affective (mood) disorder A disorder characterized by periodic episodes of depression or mania that tend to occur at about the same time each year.

secondary appraisal An evaluation of one's coping resources and options for dealing with the stress.

secondary sex characteristics Physical features associated with sex but not directly involved in reproduction.

secondary traits Less consistent dispositions that surface in some situations but not others.

sedatives Sleep-inducing drugs that tend to decrease central nervous system activation and behavioral activity.

self-actualization *See* need for self-actualization.

self-concept A collection of beliefs about one's own nature, unique qualities, and typical behavior.

self-disclosure The voluntary act of verbally communicating private information about oneself to another person.

self-efficacy One's belief about one's ability to perform behaviors that should lead to expected outcomes.

self-esteem One's overall assessment of one's worth as a person.

self-monitoring The degree to which people attend to and control the impressions they make on others.

self-perception theory The idea that when people are unsure of their beliefs, they try to understand themselves by inferring their attitudes from their behavior.

senile dementia An abnormal and progressive decline in general cognitive functioning that is observed in a small minority of people over age 65.

sensate focus An exercise in which partners take turns pleasuring each other with guided verbal feedback while certain kinds of stimulation are temporarily forbidden.

sensation seeking A generalized preference for high or low levels of sensory stimulation.

set point A natural point of stability in body weight, thought to involve the monitoring of fat-cell levels.

sex The biologically based categories of male and female.

sexism Discrimination against people on the basis of their sex.

sex therapy The professional treatment of sexual dysfunctions.

sexual dimorphism Gender differences in appearance and build.

sexual dysfunctions Impairments in sexual functioning that cause subjective distress.

sexual harassment The subjection of employees to unwanted sexually oriented behavior.

sexual identity The complex of personal qualities, self-perceptions, attitudes, values, and preferences that guide one's sexual behavior.

sexually transmitted disease (STD) An illness that is transmitted primarily through sexual contacts

sexual orientation A person's preference for a same-sex or other-sex partner in sexual relationships.

shaping Acquisition of behavior through reinforcement of closer and closer approximations of a desired response.

shyness Discomfort, inhibition, and excessive caution in interpersonal relations.

social clock A person's notion of a developmental schedule that specifies what the person should have accomplished by certain points in life.

social comparison theory The idea that people need to compare themselves with others in order to gain insight into their own behavior.

social exchange theory The idea that interpersonal relationships are governed by perceptions of the rewards and costs exchanged in interactions.

socialization The acquisition of the norms and roles expected of people in a particular society.

social loafing A reduction in effort by individuals when they work in groups as compared to when they work by themselves.

social scripts Culturally programmed sets of expectations about how various social transactions should evolve.

social skills training A behavior therapy designed to improve interpersonal skills that emphasizes shaping, modeling, and behavioral rehearsal.

social support Aid and succor provided by members of one's social networks.

socioemotional roles Roles within a group that focus on keeping interactions in the group friendly and supportive.

sociology The scientific study of human society and its institutions.

somatization disorder A psychological disorder marked by a history of diverse physical complaints that appear to be psychological in origin.

somatoform disorders Physical ailments that have no authentic organic basis but are due instead to psychological factors.

source The person who initiates, or sends, a message.

spontaneous remission A recovery from a disorder that occurs without formal treatment.

SQ3R A study system designed to promote effective reading that includes five steps: survey, question, read, recite, and review.

stage A developmental period during which a person exhibits certain characteristic patterns of behavior and acquires specific capacities.

standardization The uniform procedures used in the administration and scoring of a test.

stereotypes Widely held beliefs that people have certain characteristics simply by virtue of their membership in a particular group.

stimulants Drugs that tend to increase central nervous system activation and behavioral activity.

stress Any circumstances that threaten or are perceived to threaten our well-being and thereby tax our coping abilities.

subjects The persons or animals whose behavior is systematically observed in a study.

superego The moral component of personality that incorporates social standards about what represents right and wrong.

surveys Structured questionnaires designed to solicit information about specific aspects of subjects' behavior.

systematic desensitization A behavior therapy used to reduce clients' anxiety responses through counterconditioning.

tardive dyskinesia A neurological disorder marked by chronic tremors and involuntary spastic movements.

task-related roles Roles within a group that focus on moving the group toward completion of its mission.

territoriality The marking off and defending of certain areas as one's own.

test norms Statistics that provide information about where a score on a psychological test ranks in relation to other scores on that test.

testwiseness The ability to use the characteristics and formats of an exam to maximize one's score.

theoretical eclecticism Selecting what appears to be best from a variety of theories or systems of therapy.

token economy A system for doling out symbolic reinforcers that are exchanged later for a variety of genuine reinforcers.

tolerance A progressive decrease in a person's responsiveness to a drug with continued use.

transaction An initial statement by a communicating source and a response by the receiver.

Transactional Analysis A broad theory of personality and interpersonal relations that emphasizes patterns of communication.

transference A phenomenon that occurs when clients start relating to their therapists in ways that mimic critical relationships in their lives.

transvestism A sexual disorder in which a man achieves sexual arousal by dressing in women's clothing.

twin studies Studies in which researchers assess hereditary influence by comparing the resemblance of identical twins and fraternal twins on a trait.

Type A personality A personality style marked by competitive, aggressive, impatient, hostile behavior.

Type B personality A personality style marked by relatively relaxed, patient, easygoing, amicable behavior.

ulterior transaction A special type of complementary transaction that includes hidden messages intended to serve ulterior motives.

unconditioned response (UCR) An unlearned reaction to an unconditioned stimulus that occurs without previous conditioning.

unconditioned stimulus (UCS) A stimulus that evokes an unconditioned response without previous conditioning.

unconscious According to Freud, thoughts, memories, and desires that are well below the surface of conscious awareness but that nonetheless exert great influence on our behavior.

underemployment Settling for a job that does not fully utilize one's skills, abilities, and training.

undifferentiated schizophrenia A type of schizophrenia marked by idiosyncratic mixtures of schizophrenic symptoms.

undoing Rituals intended to atone for unacceptable desires or behaviors.

validity The ability of a test to measure what it was designed to measure.

variables Any measurable conditions, events, characteristics, or behaviors that are controlled or observed in a study.

vasocongestion Engorgement of blood vessels.

vocation An urge or commitment to work in a particular occupational area.

References

Aalpoel, P. J., & Lewis, D. J. (1984). Dissociative disorders. In H. E. Adams & P. B. Sutker (Eds.), *Comprehensive handbook of psychopathology*. New York: Plenum Press.

Abramson, L. Y., Metalsky, G. I., & Alloy, L. B. (1988). The hopelessness theory of depression: Does the research test the theory? In L. Y. Abramson (Ed.), *Social cognition and clinical psychology: A synthesis*. New York: Guilford Press.

Abramson, L. Y., Seligman, M. E. P., & Teasdale, J. D. (1978). Learned helplessness in humans: Critique and reformulation. *Journal of Abnormal Psychology, 87*, 49–74.

Adams, G. R., & Huston, T. L. (1975). Social perception of middle-aged persons varying in physical attractiveness. *Developmental Psychology, 11*(5), 657–658.

Ader, R., & Cohen, N. (1984). Behavior and the immune system. In W. D. Gentry (Ed.), *Handbook of behavioral medicine*. New York: Guilford Press.

Adler, A. (1917). *Study of organ inferiority and its psychical compensation*. New York: Nervous and Mental Diseases Publishing Co.

Adler, A. (1927). *Practice and theory of individual psychology*. New York: Harcourt, Brace & World.

Adler, A. (1964). *Superiority and social interest: A collection of later writings* (H. L. Ansbacher & R. Ansbacher, Eds.). New York: Viking Press.

Adler, C. S., & Adler, S. M. (1984). Biofeedback. In T. B. Karasu (Ed.), *The psychiatric therapies*. Washington, DC: American Psychiatric Association.

Adler, R., & Towne, N. (1987). *Looking out/looking in*. New York: Holt, Rinehart & Winston.

Agras, W. S. (1985). Stress, panic and the cardiovascular system. In A. H. Tuma & J. Maser (Eds.), *Anxiety and the anxiety disorders*. Hillsdale, NJ: Erlbaum.

Ainsworth, M. D. S., Blehar, M. C., Waters, E., & Wall, S. (1978). *Patterns of attachment: A psychological study of the strange situation*. Hillsdale, NJ: Erlbaum.

Alberti, R. E., & Emmons, M. L. (1986). *Your perfect right: A guide to assertive behavior*. San Luis Obispo, CA: Impact.

Alexander, C. N., & Knight, G. W. (1971). Situated identities and social psychological experimentation. *Sociometry, 34*, 65–82.

Alexander, F. (1954). Psychoanalysis and psychotherapy. *Journal of the American Psychoanalytic Association, 2*, 722–733.

Al-Issa, I. (1982). Sex-differences in psychopathology. In I. Al-Issa (Ed.), *Culture and psychopathology*. Baltimore: University Park Press.

Alloy, L. B., & Abramson, L. Y. (1979). Judgment of contingency in depressed and nondepressed students: Sadder but wiser. *Journal of Experimental Psychology: General, 108*, 441–485.

Alloy, L. B., & Abramson, L. Y. (1988). Depressive realism: Four theoretical perspectives. In L. B. Alloy (Ed.), *Cognitive processes in depression*. New York: Guilford Press.

Alloy, L. B., Clements, C., & Kolden, G. (1985). The cognitive diathesis-stress theories of depression: Therapeutic implications. In S. Reiss & R. R. Bootzin (Eds.), *Theoretical issues in behavior therapy*. Orlando, FL: Academic Press.

Allport, G. W. (1937). *Personality: A psychological interpretation*. New York: Holt.

Allport, G. W. (1961). *Pattern and growth in personality*. New York: Holt, Rinehart & Winston.

Allred, K. D., & Smith, T. W. (1989). The hardy personality: Cognitive and physiological responses to evaluative threat. *Journal of Personality and Social Psychology, 56*(2), 257–266.

Altman, I., & Haythorn, W. W. (1965). Interpersonal exchange in socialization. *Sociometry, 23*, 411–426.

Altman, I., & Taylor, D. A. (1973). *Social penetration: The development of interpersonal relationships*. New York: Irvington.

Amada, G. (1985). *A guide to psychotherapy*. Lanham, MD: Madison Books.

Ambelas, A. (1987). Life events and mania: A special relationship? *British Journal of Psychiatry, 150*, 235–240.

Amberson, J. I., & Hoon, P. W. (1985). Hemodynamics of sequential orgasm. *Archives of Sexual Behavior, 14*(4), 351–360.

American Psychiatric Association. (1952). *Diagnostic and statistical manual of mental disorders* (1st ed.). Washington, DC: Author.

American Psychiatric Association. (1968). *Diagnostic and statistical manual of mental disorders* (2nd ed.). Washington, DC: Author.

American Psychiatric Association. (1980). *Diagnostic and statistical manual of mental disorders* (3rd ed.). Washington, DC: Author.

American Psychiatric Association. (1987). *Diagnostic and statistical manual of mental disorders* (3rd ed. rev.). Washington, DC: Author.

Anderson, C. A., Horowitz, L. M., & French, R. D. (1983). Attributional style of lonely and depressed people. *Journal of Personality and Social Psychology, 45*(1), 127–136.

Anderson, J. R. (1980). *Cognitive psychology and its implications*. New York: W. H. Freeman.

Anderson, N. H. (1968). Likableness ratings of 555 personality trait words. *Journal of Personality and Social Psychology, 9*, 272–279.

Anderson, S. A., Russell, C. S., & Schumm, W. R. (1983). Perceived marital quality and family life-cycle categories: A further analysis. *Journal of Marriage and the Family, 45*, 127–139.

Andreasen, N. C. (1982). Negative versus positive schizophrenia: Definition and validation. *Archives of General Psychiatry, 39*, 789–794.

Andreasen, N. C. (1985). Structural brain abnormalities in schizophrenia. In M. N.

Menuck & M. V. Seeman (Eds.), *New perspectives in schizophrenia*. New York: Macmillan.

Arbeiter, S. (1979). Mid-life career change. *AAHE Bulletin (American Association for Higher Education), 32*(2), 1, 11–12.

Arbeiter, S., Aslanian, C. B., Schmerbeck, F. A., & Brickell, H. M. (1978). *40 million Americans in career transition*. New York: College Entrance Examination Board.

Archer, R. L. (1979). Role of personality and the social situation. In G. J. Chelune & associates (Eds.), *Self-disclosure: Origins, patterns, and implications of openness in interpersonal relationships*. San Francisco: Jossey-Bass.

Archer, R. L. (1980). Self-disclosure. In D. M. Wegner & R. R. Vallacher (Eds.), *The self in social psychology*. New York: Oxford University Press.

Archer, S. L. (1982). The lower age boundaries of identity development. *Child Development, 53*, 1551–1556.

Arentewicz, G., & Schmidt, G. (Eds.). (1983). *The treatment of sexual disorders*. New York: Basic Books.

Argyle, M. (1969). *Social interaction*. New York: Aldine-Atherton.

Argyle, M., & Dean, J. (1965). Eye-contact, distance, and affiliation. *Sociometry, 28*, 289–304.

Argyle, M., & Henderson, M. (1984). The rules of friendship. *Journal of Social and Personal Relationships, 1*, 211–237.

Argyle, M., & McHenry, R. (1971). Do spectacles really affect judgments of intelligence? *British Journal of Social and Clinical Psychology, 10*, 27–29.

Arlin, P. K. (1975). Cognitive development in adulthood: A fifth stage? *Developmental Psychology, 11*, 602–606.

Aron, A. (1988). The matching hypothesis reconsidered again: Comment on Kalick and Hamilton. *Journal of Personality and Social Psychology, 54*(3), 441–446.

Aronson, E., & Mills, J. (1959). The effect of severity of initiation on liking for a group. *Journal of Abnormal and Social Psychology, 59*, 177–181.

Aronson, E., Willerman, B., & Floyd, J. (1966). The effect of a pratfall on increasing interpersonal attractiveness. *Psychonomic Science, 4*, 157–158.

Asch, S. E. (1946). Forming impressions of personality. *Journal of Abnormal and Social Psychology, 41*, 258–290.

Asch, S. E. (1951). Effects of group pressure on the modification and distortion of judgments. In H. Guetzkow (Ed.), *Groups, leadership and men*. Pittsburgh: Carnegie Press.

Asch, S. E. (1955). Opinions and social pressures. *Scientific American, 193*(5), 31–35.

Asch, S. E. (1956). Studies of independence and conformity: A minority of one against a unanimous majority. *Psychological Monographs, 70*(9, Whole No. 416).

Asendorpf, J. B. (1986). Shyness in middle and late childhood. In W. H. Jones, J. M. Cheek, & S. R. Briggs (Eds.), *Shyness: Perspectives on research and treatment.* New York: Plenum Press.

Asendorpf, J. B. (1989). Shyness as a final common pathway for two different kinds of inhibition. *Journal of Personality and Social Psychology, 57*(3), 481–492.

Ashour, A. S. (1973). The contingency model of leadership effectiveness: An evaluation. *Organizational Behavior and Human Performance, 9,* 339–355.

Asterita, M. F. (1985). *The physiology of stress.* New York: Human Sciences Press.

Astin, H. S. (1984). The meaning of work in women's lives: A sociopsychological model of career choice and work behavior. *Counseling Psychologist, 12*(4), 117–126.

Athanasiou, R., Shaver, P., & Tavris, C. (1970). Sex. *Psychology Today, 4*(2), 39–52.

Atkins, A., Deaux, K., & Bieri, J. (1967). Latitude of acceptance and attitude change: Empirical evidence for a reformulation. *Journal of Personality and Social Psychology, 6,* 47–54.

Atwater, L. (1982). *The extramarital connection: Sex, intimacy, and identity.* New York: Irvington.

Atwood, J. D., & Gagnon, J. H. (1987). Masturbatory behavior in college youth. *Journal of Sex Education and Therapy, 13*(2), 35–42.

Averill, J. R. (1982). *Anger and aggression: An essay on aggression.* New York: Springer-Verlag.

Avery, D., & Winokur, G. (1978). Suicide, attempted suicide, and relapse rates in depression. *Archives of General Psychiatry, 35,* 749–753.

Axelrod, S., & Apsche, J. (1983). *The effects of punishment on human behavior.* New York: Academic Press.

Baber, K. M., & Monaghan, P. (1988). College women's career and motherhood expectations: New options, old dilemmas. *Sex Roles, 19*(3/4), 189–203.

Bach, G. R., & Wyden, P. (1981). *The intimate enemy: How to fight fair in love and marriage.* New York: Avon.

Bakeman, R., Lumb, J. R., Jackson, R. E., & Smith, D. W. (1986). AIDS-risk group profiles in whites and members of minority groups. *New England Journal of Medicine, 315,* 191–192.

Baker, E. L. (1985). Psychoanalysis and psychoanalytic therapy. In S. J. Lynn & J. P. Garske (Eds.), *Contemporary psychotherapies: Models and methods.* Columbus, OH: Charles E. Merrill.

Baker, G. H. B. (1982). Life events before the onset of rheumatoid arthritis. *Psychotherapy and Psychosomatics, 38,* 173–177.

Baldessarini, R. J. (1984). Antipsychotic drugs. In T. B. Karasu (Ed.), *The psychiatric therapies.* Washington, DC: American Psychiatric Association.

Bales, R. F. (1958). Task roles and social roles in problem-solving groups. In E. E. Maccoby, T. M. Newcomb, & E. L. Hartley (Eds.), *Readings in social psychology.* New York: Holt, Rinehart & Winston.

Balswick, J., & Avertt, C. P. (1977). Differences in expressiveness: Gender, interpersonal orientation, and perceived expressiveness as contributing factors. *Journal of Marriage and the Family, 39,* 121–127.

Bandura, A. (1973). *Aggression: A social learning analysis.* Englewood Cliffs, NJ: Prentice-Hall.

Bandura, A. (1977). *Social learning theory.* Englewood Cliffs, NJ: Prentice-Hall.

Bandura, A. (1986). *Social foundations of thought and action: A social-cognitive theory.* Englewood Cliffs, NJ: Prentice-Hall.

Bandura, A., & Rosenthal, T. L. (1966). Vicarious classical conditioning as a function of arousal level. *Journal of Personality and Social Psychology, 3,* 54–62.

Bandura, A. Ross, D., & Ross, S. (1963). Vicarious reinforcement and imitative learning. *Journal of Abnormal and Social Psychology, 67*(6), 601–607.

Banks, M. H., & Jackson, P. R. (1982). Unemployment and the risk of minor psychiatric disorder in young people: Cross-sectional and longitudinal evidence. *Psychological Medicine, 12,* 789–798.

Banmen, J., & Vogel, N. A. (1985). The relationship between marital quality and interpersonal sexual communication. *Family Therapy, 12*(1), 45–58.

Barbach, L. G. (1982). *For each other: Sharing sexual intimacy.* Garden City, NY: Anchor.

Bardwick, J. M. (1973). Women's liberation: Nice idea, but it won't be easy. *Psychology Today, 6*(12), 26–33, 110–111.

Barfield, A. (1976). Biological influences on sex differences in behavior. In M. S. Teitelbaum (Ed.), *Sex differences: Social and biological perspectives.* New York: Anchor.

Barinaga, M. (1989). Manic depression gene put in limbo. *Science, 246,* 886–887.

Barlett, D. L., & Steele, J. B. (1979). *Empire: The life, legend and madness of Howard Hughes.* New York: Norton.

Barlow, D. H., & Waddell, M. T. (1985). Agoraphobia. In D. H. Barlow (Ed.), *Clinical handbook of psychological disorders.* New York: Guilford Press.

Barofsky, I. (1981). Issues and approaches to the assessment of the cancer patient. In C. K. Prokop & L. A. Bradley (Eds.), *Medical psychology: Contributions to behavioral medicine.* New York: Academic Press.

Baron, P. H. (1974). Self-esteem, ingratiation, and evaluation of unknown others. *Journal of Personality and Social Psychology, 30,* 104–109.

Barrett, J. E., Rose, R. M., & Klerman, G. L. (Eds.). (1979). *Stress and mental disorder.* New York: Raven.

Barton, J. L. (1977). ECT in depression: The evidence of controlled studies. *Biological Psychiatry, 12,* 687–695.

Basow, S. A. (1986). *Gender stereotypes: Traditions and alternatives.* Pacific Grove, CA: Brooks/Cole.

Basseches, M. (1984). *Dialectical thinking and adult development.* Norwood, NJ: Ablex.

Baumeister, R. F. (1984). Choking under pressure: Self-consciousness and paradoxical effects of incentives on skillful performance. *Journal of Personality and Social Psychology, 46*(3), 610–620.

Baumeister, R. F. (1989). The optimal margin of illusion. *Journal of Social and Clinical Psychology, 8*(2), 176–189.

Baumeister, R. F., & Scher, S. J. (1988). Self-defeating behavior patterns among normal individuals: Review and analysis of common self-destructive tendencies. *Psychological Bulletin, 104*(1), 3–22.

Baumeister, R. F., & Steinhilber, A. (1984). Paradoxical effects of supportive audiences on performance under pressure: The home field disadvantage in sports championships. *Journal of Personality and Social Psychology, 47*(1), 85–93.

Baumrind, D. (1964). Some thoughts on the ethics of reading Milgram's "Behavioral study of obedience." *American Psychologist, 19,* 421–423.

Baumrind, D. (1967). Child care practices anteceding three patterns of preschool behavior. *Genetic Psychology Monographs, 75,* 43–88.

Baumrind, D. (1971). Current patterns of parental authority. *Developmental Psychology Monographs, 4*(1, Pt. 2).

Baumrind, D. (1978). Parental disciplinary patterns and social competence in children. *Youth and Society, 9,* 239–276.

Baumrind, D. (1989). Rearing competent children. In W. Damon (Ed.), *Child development today and tomorrow.* San Francisco: Jossey-Bass.

Beattie, M. (1989). *Beyond codependency: And getting better all the time.* New York: Harper & Row.

Beck, A. T. (1976). *Cognitive therapy and the emotional disorders.* New York: International Universities Press.

Beck, A. T. (1987). Cognitive therapy. In J. K. Zeig (Ed.), *The evolution of psychotherapy.* New York: Brunner/Mazel.

Beck, A. T. (1988). *Love is never enough.* New York: Harper & Row.

Beck, A. T., Rush, A. J., Shaw, B. F., & Emery, G. (1979). *Cognitive therapy of depression.* New York: Guilford Press.

Beck, D. F., & Jones, M. A. (1973). *Progress on family problems: A nationwide study of clients' and counselors' views on family agency services.* New York: Family Service Association of America.

Beck, J., & Morgan, P. A. (1986). Designer drug confusion: A focus on MDMA. *Journal of Drug Education, 16*(3), 287–302.

Beck, S. B. (1979). Women's somatic preferences. In M. Cook & G. Wilson (Eds.), *Love and attraction.* New York: Pergamon Press.

Becker, H. A. (1980). The Assertive Job-Hunting Survey. *Measurement and Evaluation in Guidance, 13,* 43–48.

Becker, H. S. (1973). *Outsiders: Studies in the sociology of deviance.* New York: Free Press.

Beitman, B. D., Goldfried, M. R., & Norcross, J. C. (1989). The movement toward integrating the psychotherapies: An overview. *American Journal of Psychiatry, 146,* 138–147.

Bell, A. P., & Weinberg, M. S. (1978). *Homosexualities: A study of diversity among men and women.* New York: Simon & Schuster.

Bell, A. P., Weinberg, M. S., & Hammersmith, K. S. (1981). *Sexual preference—Its development in men and women.* Bloomington: Indiana University Press.

Bell, R. R. (1981). *Worlds of friendship.* Beverly Hills, CA: Sage Publications.

Bell, R. R., Turner, S., & Rosen, L. (1975). A multivariate analysis of female extramarital coitus. *Journal of Marriage and the Family, 37,* 375–383.

Belsky, J. (1985). Exploring differences in marital change across the transition to parenthood: The role of violated expectations. *Journal of Marriage and the Family, 47,* 1037–1044.

Bem, D. J. (1972). Self-perception theory. In L. Berkowitz (Ed.), *Advances in experimental social psychology* (Vol. 6). New York: Academic Press.

Bem, S. L. (1975). Androgyny vs. the tight little lives of fluffy women and chesty men. *Psychology Today, 9*(4), 58–62.

Bem, S. L. (1981). Gender schema theory: A cognitive account of sex typing. *Psychological Review, 88,* 354–364.

Bem, S. L. (1983). Gender schema theory and its implications for child development: Raising gender-aschematic children in a gender-schematic society. *Signs, 8,* 598–616.

Bem, S. L. (1985). Androgyny and gender schema theory: A conceptual and empirical integration. In T. B. Sonderegger (Ed.), *Nebraska symposium on motivation 1984: Psychology and gender* (Vol. 32). Lincoln: University of Nebraska Press.

Benbow, C. P., & Stanley, J. C. (1982). Consequences in high school and college of sex differences in mathematical reasoning ability: A longitudinal perspective. *American Educational Research Journal, 19,* 598–622.

Beneke, W. M., & Harris, M. B. (1972). Teaching self-control of study behavior. *Behavior Research and Therapy, 10,* 35–41.

Benjamin, L. T., Jr., Cavell, T. A., & Shallenberger, W. R., III. (1984). Staying with initial answers on objective tests: Is it a myth? *Teaching of Psychology, 11*(3), 133–141.

Bennett, N. G., Blanc, A. K., & Bloom, D. E. (1988). Commitment and the modern union: Assessing the link between premarital cohabitation and subsequent marital stability. *American Sociological Review, 53,* 127–138.

Benson, H. (1975). *The relaxation response* (1st ed.). New York: Morrow.

Benson, H., & Klipper, M. Z. (1988). *The relaxation response* (2nd ed.). New York: Avon.

Berardo, D. H., Shehan, C. L., & Leslie, G. R. (1987). A residue of tradition: Jobs, careers, and spouses' time in housework. *Journal of Marriage and the Family, 49,* 381–390.

Berg, S. (1987). Intelligence and terminal decline. In G. L. Maddox & E. W. Busse (Eds.), *Aging: The universal human experience.* New York: Springer.

Berger, C. R. (1985). Social power and interpersonal communication. In M. L. Knapp & G. R. Miller (Eds.), *Handbook of interpersonal communication.* Beverly Hills, CA: Sage Publications.

Bergin, A. E. (1971). The evaluation of therapeutic outcomes. In A. E. Bergin & S. L. Garfield (Eds.), *Handbook of psychotherapy and behavior change: An empirical analysis.* New York: Wiley.

Bergin, A. E., & Lambert, M. J. (1978). The evaluation of therapeutic outcomes. In S. L. Garfield & A. E. Bergin (Eds.), *Handbook of psychotherapy and behavior change: An empirical analysis.* New York: Wiley.

Berkowitz, L. (1969). The frustration-aggression hypothesis revisited. In L. Berkowitz (Ed.), *Roots of aggression: A re-examination of the frustration-aggression hypothesis.* New York: Atherton.

Berlo, D. K. (1960). *The process of communication: An introduction to theory and practice.* New York: Holt, Rinehart & Winston.

Berman, P. W. (1976). Social context as a determinant of sex differences in adults' attraction to infants. *Developmental Psychology, 12,* 365–366.

Bernard, J. (1982). *The future of marriage.* New Haven, CT: Yale University Press.

Berne, E. (1961). *Transactional analysis in psychotherapy.* New York: Ballantine.

Berne, E. (1964). *Games people play.* New York: Grove Press.

Berne, E. (1972). *What do you say after hello?* New York: Grove Press.

Bernstein, M. C., & Bernstein, J. B. (1988). *Social security: The system that works.* New York: Basic Books.

Berscheid, E. (1966). Opinion change and communicator-communicatee similarity and dissimilarity. *Journal of Personality and Social Psychology, 4,* 670–680.

Berscheid, E. (1985). Interpersonal attraction. In G. Lindzey & E. Aronson (Eds.), *The handbook of social psychology: Vol. 2. Special fields and applications.* New York: Random House.

Berscheid, E. (1988). Some comments on love's anatomy: Or, whatever happened to old-fashioned lust. In R. J. Sternberg & M. L. Barnes (Eds.), *The psychology of love.* New Haven, CT: Yale University Press.

Berscheid, E., & Walster, E. (1978). *Interpersonal attraction.* Reading, MA: Addison-Wesley.

Berscheid, E., Walster, E., & Bohrnstedt, G. (1973). The happy American body, a survey report. *Psychology Today, 7*(6), 119–131.

Bettelheim, B. (1943). Individual and mass behavior in extreme situations. *Journal of Abnormal and Social Psychology, 38,* 417–452.

Bickman, L. (1971). The effect of social status on the honesty of others. *Journal of Social Psychology, 85,* 87–92.

Billings, A. G., Cronkite, R. C., & Moos, R. H. (1983). Social-environment factors in unipolar depression. *Journal of Abnormal Psychology, 92,* 119–133.

Binet, A., & Simon, T. (1905). Methodes nouvelles pour le diagnostic du niveau intellectuel des anormaux. *L'Année Psychologique, 11,* 191–244.

Birren, J. E., Woods, A. M., & Williams, M. V. (1980). Behavioral slowing with age: Causes, organization, and consequences. In L. W. Poon (Ed.), *Aging in the 1980s: Psychological issues.* Washington, DC: American Psychological Association.

Bitter, R. G. (1986). Late marriage and marital instability: The effects of heterogeneity and inflexibility. *Journal of Marriage and the Family, 48,* 631–640.

Blair, S. N., Kohl, H. W., Paffenbarger, R. S., Clark, D. G., Cooper, K. H., & Gibbons, L. W. (1989). Physical fitness and all-cause mortality: A prospective study of healthy men and women. *Journal of the American Medical Association, 262,* 2395–2401.

Blake, R. R., & Mouton, J. S. (1964). *The managerial grid.* Houston: Gulf Publishing.

Blanchard, E. B., & Andrasik, F. (1982). Psychological assessment and treatment of the headache: Recent developments and emerging issues. *Journal of Consulting and Clinical Psychology, 50,* 859–879.

Blank, A. S., Jr. (1982). Stresses of war: The example of Viet Nam. In L. Goldberger & S. Breznitz (Eds.), *Handbook of stress: Theoretical and clinical aspects.* New York: Free Press.

Blank, T. O. (1982). *A social psychology of developing adults.* New York: Wiley.

Blasband, D., & Peplau, L. A. (1985). Sexual exclusivity versus openness in gay male couples. *Archives of Sexual Behavior, 14,* 395–412.

Blau, G. (1981). An empirical investigation of job stress, social support, service length, and job strain. *Organizational Behavior and Human Performance, 27,* 279–302.

Blau, Z. S. (1971). *Old age in a changing society.* New York: Van Nostrand.

Blechman, E. A., McEnroe, M. J., Carella, E. T., & Audette, D. P. (1986). Childhood competence and depression. *Journal of Abnormal Psychology, 95*(3), 223–227.

Bleier, R. (1984). *Science and gender: A critique of biology and its theories on women.* New York: Pergamon Press.

Block, J. D. (1980). *Friendship: How to give it; how to get it.* New York: Macmillan.

Block, J. H. (1976). Issues, problems, and pitfalls in assessing sex differences: A critical review of *The Psychology of Sex Differences. Merrill-Palmer Quarterly, 22,* 283–308.

Bloomfield, H. H., & Kory, R. B. (1976). *Happiness: The TM program, psychiatry, and enlightenment.* New York: Simon & Schuster.

Blum, K. (1984). *Handbook of abusable drugs.* New York: Gardner Press.

Blumstein, P., & Schwartz, P. (1983). *American couples: Money, work, sex.* New York: Morrow.

Bolles, R. N. (1987). *What color is your parachute? A practical manual for job-hunters and career-changers* (1st ed.). Berkeley, CA: Ten Speed Press.

Bolles, R. N. (1990). *What color is your parachute? A practical manual for job-hunters and career-changers* (2nd ed.). Berkeley, CA: Ten Speed Press.

Boor, M. (1980). Relationships between unemployment rates and suicide rates in eight countries, 1962–1976. *Psychological Reports, 60,* 562–564.

Booth-Kewley, S., & Friedman, H. S. (1987). Psychological predictors of heart disease: A quantitative review. *Psychological Bulletin, 101*(3), 343–362.

Borbely, A. (1986). *Secrets of sleep.* New York: Basic Books.

Boshier, R. (1975). A video-tape study on the relationship between wearing spectacles and judgments of intelligence. *Perceptual and Motor Skills, 40,* 69–70.

Boston Women's Health Book Collective. (1973). *Our bodies, ourselves: A book by and for women.* New York: Simon & Schuster.

Boston Women's Health Book Collective. (1984). *The new our bodies, ourselves: A book by and for women.* New York: Simon & Schuster.

Boutin, R. (1979). Psychoactive drugs: Effective use of low doses. *Psychosomatics, 20,* 403–405, 409.

Bowen, D. D. (1985). Were men meant to mentor women? *Training and Development Journal, 39*(2), 31–34.

Bower, G. H. (1970). Organizational factors in memory. *Cognitive Psychology, 1,* 18–46.

Bower, G. H., & Clark, M. C. (1969). Narrative stories as mediators of serial learning. *Psychonomic Science, 14,* 181–182.

Bower, S. A., & Bower, G. H. (1976). *Asserting yourself: A practical guide for positive change.* Reading, MA: Addison-Wesley.

Bowers, J. W., Metts, S. M., & Duncanson, W. T. (1985). Emotion and interpersonal communication. In M. L. Knapp & G. R. Miller (Eds.), *Handbook of interpersonal communication.* Beverly Hills, CA: Sage Publications.

Boyd, J. H., & Weissman, M. M. (1986). Epidemiology of major affective disorders. In J. H. Boyd & M. M. Weissman (Eds.), *Psychiatry: Vol. 5. Social, epidemiologic, and legal psychiatry.* New York: Basic Books.

Bozarth, M. A., & Wise, R. A. (1985). Toxicity associated with long-term intravenous heroin and cocaine self-administration in the rat. *Journal of the American Medical Association, 254*(1), 81–83.

Bradburn, N., & Sudman, S. (1979). *Improving interview method and questionnaire design.* Washington, DC: Jossey-Bass.

Bradbury, T. N., & Fincham, F. D. (1988). Individual difference variables in close relationships: A contextual model of marriage as an integrative framework. *Journal of Personality and Social Psychology, 54*(4), 713–721.

Braiker, H. B., & Kelley, H. H. (1979). Conflict in the development of close relationships. In R. L. Burgess & T. L. Huston (Eds.), *Social exchange in developing relationships.* New York: Academic Press.

Bram, S. (1985). Childlessness revisited: A longitudinal study of voluntarily childless couples, delayed parents, and parents. *Lifestyles: A Journal of Changing Patterns, 8*(1), 46–66.

Braun, B. G. (1986). Issues in the psychotherapy of multiple personality disorder. In B. G. Braun (Ed.), *Treatment of multiple personality disorder*. Washington, DC: American Psychiatric Press.

Brecher, E. M. (1984). *Love, sex, and aging*. Boston: Little, Brown.

Breggin, P. R. (1979). *Electroshock: Its brain disabling effects*. New York: Springer.

Brehm, J. W. (1966). *A theory of psychological reactance*. New York: Academic Press.

Brehm, S. S. (1985). *Intimate relationships*. New York: Random House.

Breier, A., Albus, M., Pickar, D., Zahn, T. P., Wolkowitz, O. M., & Paul, S. M. (1987). Controllable and uncontrollable stress in humans: Alterations in mood and neuroendocrine and psychophysiological function. *American Journal of Psychiatry, 144*(11), 1419–1425.

Bretherton, I. (1985). Attachment theory: Retrospect and prospect. In I. Bretherton & E. Waters (Eds.), Growing points of attachment theory and research. *Monographs of the Society for Research in Child Development, 50*(1 & 2, Serial No. 209).

Brett, J. M. (1980). The effect of job transfer on employees and their families. In C. L. Cooper & R. Payne (Eds.), *Current concerns in occupational stress*. New York: Wiley.

Brewer, M. (1975). Erhard Seminars Training: "We're gonna tear you down and put you back together." *Psychology Today, 9*(3), 35–40, 82, 88–89.

Brigham, J. C. (1980). Limiting conditions of the "physical attractiveness stereotype": Attributions about divorce. *Journal of Research on Personality, 14*, 365–375.

Brim, O. G., Jr., & Kagan, J. (1980). Constancy and change: A view of the issues. In O. G. Brim, Jr., & J. Kagan (Eds.), *Constancy and change in human development*. Cambridge, MA: Harvard University Press.

Bringle, R., Roach, S., Andler, C., & Evenbeck, S. (1979). Measuring the intensity of jealous reactions. *Catalogue of Selected Documents in Psychology, 9*, 23–24.

Brod, C. (1988). *Technostress: Human cost of the computer revolution*. Reading, MA: Addison-Wesley.

Bromage, B. K., & Mayer, R. E. (1986). Quantitative and qualitative effects of repetition on learning from technical text. *Journal of Educational Psychology, 78*(4), 271–278.

Bronfenbrenner, U., & Crouter, A. C. (1982). Work and family through time and space. In S. B. Kamerman & C. D. Hayes (Eds.), *Families that work: Children in a changing world*. Washington, DC: National Academy Press.

Brooks-Gunn, J. (1986). The relationship of maternal beliefs about sex typing to maternal and young children's behavior. *Sex Roles, 14*, 21–35.

Broverman, I. K., Vogel, S. R., Broverman, D. M., Clarkson, F. E., & Rosenkrantz, P. S. (1972). Sex-role stereotypes: A current appraisal. *Journal of Social Issues, 28*, 59–78.

Brown, J. D., & Siegel, J. M. (1988). Exercise as a buffer of life stress: A prospective study of adolescent health. *Health Psychology, 7*(4), 341–353.

Brown, P., & Funk, S. C. (1986). Tardive dyskinesia: Barriers to the professional recognition of an iatrogenic disease. *Journal of Health and Social Behavior, 27*, 116–132.

Brownell, K. D. (1989, June). When and how to diet. *Psychology Today*, 40–46.

Bruckner-Gordon, F., Gangi, B. K., & Wallman, G. U. (1988). *Making therapy work: Your guide to choosing, using, and ending therapy*. New York: Harper & Row.

Bry, A. (1976). *EST*. New York: Avon.

Bryan, J. H., & Test, M. A. (1967). Models and helping: Naturalistic studies in aiding behavior. *Journal of Personality and Social Psychology, 6*, 400–407.

Bryer, K. B. (1979). The Amish way of death: A study of family support systems. *American Psychologist, 34*, 255–261.

Buckhout, R. (1980). Nearly 2,000 witnesses can be wrong. *Bulletin of the Psychonomic Society, 16*, 307–310.

Buehler, C., & Langenbrunner, M. (1987). Divorce-related stressors: Occurrence, disruptiveness, and area of life change. *Journal of Divorce, 11*(1), 25–50.

Buffum, J., Pharm, D., Smith, D. E., Moser, C., Apter, M., Buxton, M., & Davison, J. (1981). Drugs and sexual function. In H. I. Lief (Ed.), *Sexual problems in medical practice*. Chicago: American Medical Association.

Bullough, V. L. (1981). Age at menarche. *Science, 213*, 365–366.

Bumiller, E. (1989). First comes marriage—Then, maybe, love. In J. M. Henslin (Ed.), *Marriage and family in a changing society* (3rd ed.). New York: Free Press.

Burg, B. (1974, November). Est: 60 hours to happiness. *Human Behavior*, 16–23.

Burger, J. M. (1989). Negative reactions to increases in perceived personal control. *Journal of Personality and Social Psychology, 56*(2), 246–256.

Burger, J. M., & Petty, R. E. (1981). The low-ball compliance technique: Task or person commitment? *Journal of Personality and Social Psychology, 40*, 492–500.

Burgess, E., & Wallin, P. (1953). *Engagement and marriage*. Philadelphia: Lippincott.

Burgoon, J. K. (1985). Nonverbal signals. In M. L. Knapp & G. R. Miller (Eds.), *Handbook of interpersonal communication*. Beverly Hills, CA: Sage Publications.

Burke, R. J. (1984). Mentors in organizations. *Group and Organization Studies, 9*, 353–372.

Burks, N., & Martin, B. (1985). Everyday problems and life change events: Ongoing versus acute sources of stress. *Journal of Human Stress, 11*(1), 27–35.

Burman, B., & de Anda, D. (1986). Parenthood or nonparenthood: A comparison of intentional families. *Lifestyles: A Journal of Changing Patterns, 8*(2), 69–84.

Buscaglia, L. (1982). *Living, loving & learning*. Thorofare, NJ: Charles B. Slack.

Busch-Rossnagel, N. A., & Vance, A. K. (1982). The impact of the schools on social and emotional development. In B. B. Wolman (Ed.), *Handbook of developmental psychology*. Englewood Cliffs, NJ: Prentice-Hall.

Buss, D. M. (1985). Human mate selection. *American Scientist, 73*, 47–51.

Bussey, K., & Bandura, A. (1984). Influence of gender constancy and social power on sex-linked modeling. *Journal of Personality and Social Psychology, 47*, 1292–1302.

Buunk, B. (1980). Extramarital sex in the Netherlands: Motivations in social and marital context. *Alternative Lifestyles, 3*(1), 11–39.

Buunk, B., & Bringle, R. G. (1987). Jealousy in love relationships. In D. Perlman & S. W. Duck (Eds.), *Intimate relationships: Development, dynamics, and deterioration*. Beverly Hills, CA: Sage Publications.

Byers, E. S., & Heinlein, L. (1989). Predicting initiations and refusals of sexual activities in married and cohabiting heterosexual couples. *Journal of Sex Research, 26*(2), 210–231.

Byrne, D. (1971). *The attraction paradigm*. New York: Academic Press.

Byrne, D., Clore, G. L., & Smeaton, G. (1986). The attraction hypothesis: Do similar attitudes affect anything? *Journal of Personality and Social Psychology, 51*(6), 1167–1170.

Byrne, D., & Murnen, S. K. (1988). Maintaining loving relationships. In R. J. Sternberg & M. L. Barnes (Eds.), *The psychology of love*. New Haven, CT: Yale University Press.

Byrne, J. D. (1975, February). Mobility rate of employed persons in new occupations. Bureau of Labor Statistics Manpower and Employment Special Labor Force Reports. *Monthly Labor Review*, 53–59.

Cadoret, R. J. (1986). Epidemiology of antisocial personality. In W. H. Reid, D. Dorr, J. I. Walker, & J. W. Bonner, III (Eds.), *Unmasking the psychopath: Antisocial personality and related syndromes*. New York: Norton.

Calderone, M. S., & Johnson, E. W. (1989). *The family book about sexuality*. New York: Harper & Row.

Calderone, M. S., & Ramey, J. (1982). *Talking with your child about sex*. New York: Random House.

Caldwell, M. A., & Peplau, L. A. (1982). Sex differences in same-sex friendship. *Sex Roles, 8*(7), 721–732.

Calhoun, L. G., & Selby, J. W. (1980). Voluntary childlessness, involuntary childlessness, and having children: A study of social perceptions. *Family Relations, 29*, 181–183.

Cameron, N. (1963). *Personality development and psychopathology*. Boston: Houghton Mifflin.

Campbell, R. E., & Heffernan, J. M. (1983). Adult vocational behavior. In W. B. Walsh & S. H. Osipow (Eds.), *Handbook of vocational psychology: Vol. 1. Foundations*. Hillsdale, NJ: Erlbaum.

Cannon, D. S., Baker, T. B., & Wehl, C. K. (1981). Emetic and electric shock alcohol aversion therapy: Six- and twelve-month follow-up. *Journal of Consulting and Clinical Psychology, 49*(3), 360–368.

Cannon, W. B. (1932). *The wisdom of the body*. New York: Norton.

Cargan, L., & Melko, M. (1982). *Singles: Myths and realities*. Beverly Hills, CA: Sage Publications.

Carnegie, D. (1936). *How to win friends and influence people*. New York: Simon & Schuster.

Carroll, J. L., Volk, K. D., & Hyde, J. S. (1985). Differences between males and females in motives for engaging in sexual intercourse. *Archives of Sexual Behavior, 14*(2), 131–139.

Carter, E. A., & McGoldrick, M. (1988). Overview: The changing family life cycle—A framework for family therapy. In E. A. Carter & M. McGoldrick (Eds.), *The changing family life cycle: A framework for family therapy* (2nd ed.). New York: Gardner Press.

Carter, R. J., & Myerowitz, B. E. (1984). Sex-role stereotypes: Self-reports of behavior. *Sex Roles, 10*, 293–306.

Cartwright, D. (1968). The nature of group cohesiveness. In D. Cartwright & A. Zander (Eds.), *Group dynamics: Research and theory* (3rd ed.). New York: Harper & Row.

Carver, C. S., Scheier, M. F., & Weintraub, J. K. (1989). Assessing coping strategies: A theoretically based approach. *Journal of Personality and Social Psychology, 56*(2), 267–283.

Cash, T. F. (1981). Physical attractiveness: An annotated bibliography of theory and research in the behavioral sciences (Manuscript 2370). *Catalog of Selected Documents in Psychology, 11*, 83.

Caspi, A., Bolger, N., & Eckenrode, J. (1987). Linking person and context in the daily stress process. *Journal of Personality and Social Psychology, 52*(1), 184–195.

Castro, K. G., Hardy, A. M., & Curran, J. W. (1986). The acquired immunodeficiency syndrome: Epidemiology and risk factors for transmission. In T. G. Cooney & T. T. Ward (Eds.), *Medical Clinics of North America* (Vol. 70). Philadelphia: Saunders.

Castro, K. G., Newcomb, M. D., McCreary, C., & Baezconde-Garbanati, L. (1989). Cigarette smokers do more than just smoke cigarettes. *Health Psychology, 8*(1), 107–129.

Catania, J. A., McDermott, L. J., & Pollack, L. M. (1986). Questionnaire response bias and face-to-face interview sample bias in sexuality research. *Journal of Sex Research, 22*(1), 52–72.

Cattell, R. B. (1950). *Personality: A systematic, theoretical and factual study.* New York: McGraw-Hill.

Cattell, R. B. (1966). *The scientific analysis of personality.* Chicago: Aldine.

Cattell, R. B., Eber, H. W., & Tatsuoka, M. M. (1970). *Handbook of the Sixteen Personality Factor Questionnaire (16PF).* Champaign, IL: Institute for Personality and Ability Testing.

Cattell, R. B., Kawash, G. F., & DeYoung, G. E. (1972). Validation of objective measures of ergic tension: Response of the sex erg to visual stimulation. *Journal of Experimental Research in Personality, 6,* 76–83.

Cerletti, U., & Bini, L. (1938). Un nuevo metodo di shockterapie "L'elettro-shock." *Boll. Acad. Med. Roma, 64,* 136–138.

Cernovsky, Z. Z. (1989). Life stress measures and reported frequency of sleep disorders. In T. W. Miller (Ed.), *Stressful life events.* Madison, CT: International Universities Press.

Chaiken, S. (1979). Communicator's physical attractiveness and persuasion. *Journal of Personality and Social Psychology, 37,* 1387–1397.

Chaiken, S., & Baldwin, M. W. (1981). Affective-cognitive consistency and the effect of salient behavioral information on self-perception of attitudes. *Journal of Personality and Social Psychology, 41,* 1–12.

Charness, N. (1985). Aging and problem-solving performance. In N. Charness (Ed.), *Aging and human performance.* Chichester, England: Wiley.

Charren, P., & Sandler, M. W. (1983). *Changing channels: Living (sensibly) with television.* Reading, MA: Addison-Wesley.

Chase-Lansdale, P. L. (1981). Maternal employment and quality of infant-mother and infant father attachment (Doctoral dissertation, University of Michigan, 1981). *Dissertation Abstracts International, 42,* 2562B.

Cheek, J. M., & Busch, C. M. (1981). The influence of shyness on loneliness in a new situation. *Personality and Social Psychology Bulletin, 7*(4), 572–577.

Cheek, J. M., & Buss, A. H. (1981). Shyness and sociability. *Journal of Personality and Social Psychology, 41,* 330–337.

Chelune, G. J. (1979). Measuring openness in interpersonal communication. In G. J. Chelune & associates (Eds.), *Self-disclosure: Origins, patterns, and implications of openness in interpersonal relationships.* San Francisco: Jossey-Bass.

Cherlin, A. J. (1981). *Marriage, divorce, remarriage.* Cambridge, MA: Harvard University Press.

Chesler, P. (1972). *Women and madness.* Garden City, NY: Doubleday.

Chumlea, W. C. (1982). Physical growth in adolescence. In B. B. Wolman (Ed.), *Handbook of developmental psychology.* Englewood Cliffs, NJ: Prentice Hall.

Cialdini, R. B. (1988). *Influence: Science and practice.* Glenview, IL: Scott, Foresman.

Cialdini, R. B., Vincent, J. E., Lewis, S. K., Catalan, J., Wheeler, D., & Darby, B. L. (1975). Reciprocal concessions procedure for inducing compliance: The door-in-the-face technique. *Journal of Personality and Social Psychology, 31,* 206–215.

Ciompi, L. (1980). Catamnestic long-term study on the course of life and aging in schizophrenics. *Schizophrenia Bulletin, 6,* 607–618.

Clanton, G. (1973). The contemporary experience of adultery: Bob and Carol and Updike and Rimmer. In R. W. Libby & R. N. Whitehurst (Eds.), *Renovating marriage.* Danville, CA: Concensus.

Clark, H. H. (1985). Language use and language users. In G. Lindzey & E. Aronson (Eds.), *The handbook of social psychology: Vol. 2. Special fields and applications.* New York: Random House.

Clark, M., & Mills, J. (1979). Interpersonal attraction in exchange and communal relationships. *Journal of Personality and Social Psychology, 37,* 12–24.

Clark, M. S. (1984). Record-keeping in two types of relationships. *Journal of Personality and Social Psychology, 47,* 549–557.

Cleary, P. J. (1980). A checklist for life event research. *Journal of Psychosomatic Research, 24,* 199–207.

Clifford, M. M., & Walster, E. H. (1973). The effect of physical attractiveness on teacher expectation. *Sociology of Education, 46,* 248–258.

Cockerham, W. C. (1981). *Sociology of mental disorder.* Englewood Cliffs, NJ: Prentice-Hall.

Cohen, C. E. (1981). Person categories and social perception: Testing some boundaries of the processing effects of prior knowledge. *Journal of Personality and Social Psychology, 40,* 441–452.

Cohen, F. (1979). Personality, stress and the development of physical illness. In G. C. Stone, F. Cohen, N. E. Adler, & associates (Eds.), *Health psychology—A handbook.* San Francisco: Jossey-Bass.

Cohen, S. (1980). *The substance abuse problem.* New York: Haworth Press.

Cohen, S. (1986). Marijuana. In A. J. Frances & R. E. Hales (Eds.), *Psychiatry Update: Annual Review* (Vol. 5). Washington, DC: American Psychiatric Press.

Cohen, S. (1988). Psychosocial models of the role of social support in the etiology of physical disease. *Health Psychology, 7*(3), 269–297.

Cohen, S., Lichtenstein, E., Prochaska, J. O., Rossi, J. S., Gritz, E. R., Carr, C. R., Orleans, C. T., Schoenbach, V. J., Biener, L., Abrams, D., DiClemente, C., Curry, S., Marlatt, G. A., Cummings, K. M., Emont, S. L., Giovino, A., & Ossip-Klein, D. (1989). Debunking myths about self-quitting: Evidence from 10 prospective studies of persons who attempt to quit smoking by themselves. *American Psychologist, 44*(11), 1355–1365.

Cohen, S., Sherrod, D., & Clark, M. (1986). Social skills and the stress-protective role of social support. *Journal of Personality and Social Psychology, 50,* 963–973.

Cohen, S., & Syme, S. L. (Eds.). (1985). *Social support and health.* New York: Academic Press.

Cohen, S., & Wills, T. A. (1985). Stress, social support, and the buffering hypothesis. *Psychological Bulletin, 98,* 310–357.

Cole, J. O. (1988). The drug treatment of anxiety and depression. *Medical Clinics of North America, 72*(4), 815–830.

Cole, J. O., Goldberg, S. C., & Davis, J. M. (1966). Drugs in the treatment of psychosis. In P. Solomon (Ed.), *Psychiatric drugs.* New York: Grune & Stratton.

Coleman, J. C. (1978). Current contradictions in adolescent theory. *Journal of Youth and Adolescence, 7,* 1–12.

Commons, M. L., Richards, F. A., & Kuhn, D. (1982). Systematic and metasystematic reasoning: A case for levels of reasoning beyond Piaget's stage of formal operations. *Child Development, 53,* 1058–1069.

Cook, E. P. (1985). *Psychological androgyny.* New York: Pergamon Press.

Cooper, C. L. (1984). The social-psychological precursors to cancer. *Journal of Human Stress, 10*(1), 4–11.

Cooper, H. M. (1979). Statistically combining independent studies: A meta-analysis of sex differences in conformity research. *Journal of Personality and Social Psychology, 37,* 131–146.

Coopersmith, S. (1967). *The antecedents of self-esteem.* San Francisco: W. H. Freeman.

Coopersmith, S. (1975). Studies in self-esteem. In R. C. Atkinson (Ed.), *Psychology in progress: Readings from Scientific American.* San Francisco: W. H. Freeman.

Corey, G., & Corey, M. S. (1990). *I never knew I had a choice.* Pacific Grove, CA: Brooks/Cole.

Costa, P. T., & McCrae, R. R. (1986). Personality stability and its implications for clinical psychology. *Clinical Psychology Review, 6,* 407–423.

Covi, L., & Primakoff, L. (1988). Cognitive group therapy. In A. J. Frances & R. E. Hales (Eds.), *Review of psychiatry* (Vol. 7). Washington, DC: American Psychiatric Association.

Cowan, C., & Kinder, M. (1987). *Women men love—women men leave.* New York: New American Library.

Cox, F. D. (1979). *Human intimacy: Marriage, the family, and its meaning.* St. Paul, MN: West.

Cox, T., & Mackay, C. (1982). Psychosocial factors and psychophysiological mechanisms in the etiology and development of cancer. *Social Science and Medicine, 16,* 381–396.

Crane, P. T. (1985). Voluntary childlessness: Some notes on the decision-making process. In D. B. Gutknecht & E. W. Butler (Eds.), *Family, self, and society: Emerging issues, alternatives, and interventions* (2nd ed.). New York: UPA.

Cregler, L. L., & Mark, H. (1986). Medical complications of cocaine abuse. *New England Journal of Medicine, 315*(23), 1495–1500.

Crooks, R., & Baur, K. (1983). *Our sexuality* (2nd ed.). Menlo Park, CA: Benjamin/Cummings.

Crooks, R., & Baur, K. (1990). *Our sexuality* (4th ed.). Menlo Park, CA: Benjamin/Cummings.

Crosby, P. (1980). A critique of divorce statistics and their interpretation. *Family Relations, 29,* 51–58.

Cross, C. K., & Hirschfeld, R. M. A. (1986). Epidemiology of disorders in adulthood: Suicide. In G. L. Klerman, M. M. Weissman, P. S. Appelbaum, & L. H. Roth (Eds.), *Psychiatry: Vol. 5. Social, epidemiologic, and legal psychiatry.* New York: Basic Books.

Crovitz, H. F. (1971). The capacity of memory loci in artificial memory. *Psychonomic Science, 24,* 187–188.

Crowe, R. (1983). Antisocial personality disorder. In R. Tarter (Ed.), *The child at psychiatric risk*. New York: Oxford University Press.

Crozier, W. R. (1981). Shyness and self-esteem. *British Journal of Social Psychology, 20*, 220–222.

Crull, P. (1979). *The impact of sexual harassment on the job: A profile of the experiences of 92 women*. Working Women's Research Series, Report No. 3.

Cumming, E. (1963). Further thoughts on the theory of disengagement. *International Social Science Journal, 15*, 377–393.

Cumming, E. (1975). Engagement with an old theory. *International Journal of Aging and Human Development, 15*, 187–191.

Cumming, E., & Henry, W. (1961). *Growing old: The process of disengagement*. New York: Basic Books.

Cunningham, J. D. (1981). Self-disclosure intimacy: Sex, sex of target, cross-national, and "generational" differences. *Personality and Social Psychology Bulletin, 7*(2), 314–319.

Curran, D. K. (1987). *Adolescent suicidal behavior*. Washington, DC: Hemisphere.

Cutrona, C. E. (1982). Transition to college: Loneliness and the process of social adjustment. In L. A. Peplau & D. Perlman (Eds.), *Loneliness: A sourcebook of current theory, research, and therapy*. New York: Wiley.

Cvetkovich, G., Grote, B., Bjorseth, A., & Sarkissian, J. (1975). On the psychology of adolescent use of contraception. *Journal of Sex Research, 11*, 256–270.

Dambrot, F. H., Papp, M. E., & Whitmore, C. (1984). The sex-role attitudes of three generations of women. *Personality and Social Psychology Bulletin, 10*(3), 469–473.

Dan, A. J. (1976). Patterns of behavioral and mood variation in men and women: Variability and the menstrual cycle. *Dissertation Abstracts International, 37*(6-B), 3145–3146.

Daniels, D., & Plomin, R. (1985). Origins of individual differences in infant shyness. *Developmental Psychology, 21*, 118–121.

Danziger, N. (1983). Sex-related differences in the aspirations of high school students. *Sex Roles, 9*, 683–695.

Darley, J. M., & Gilbert, D. T. (1985). Social psychological aspects of environmental psychology. In G. Lindzey & E. Aronson (Eds.), *The handbook of social psychology: Vol. 2. Special fields and applications*. New York: Random House.

Darley, J. M., & Gross, P. H. (1983). A hypothesis-confirming bias in labeling effects. *Journal of Personality and Social Psychology, 44*, 20–33.

Darley, J. M. & Latané, B. (1968). Bystander intervention in emergencies: Diffusion of responsibility. *Journal of Personality and Social Psychology, 8*, 377–383.

Dattore, P. J., Shontz, F. C., & Coyne, L. (1980). Premorbid personality differentiation of cancer and noncancer groups: A list of the hypotheses of cancer proneness. *Journal of Consulting and Clinical Psychology, 48*, 388–394.

Davenport, W. (1977). Sex in cross-cultural perspective. In F. A. Beach (Ed.), *Human sexuality in four perspectives*. Baltimore: Johns Hopkins University Press.

Davidson, B., Balswick, J., & Halverson, C. (1983). Affective self-disclosure and marital adjustment: A test of equity theory. *Journal of Marriage and the Family, 45*, 93–102.

Davidson, J. (1976). Physiology of meditation and mystical states of consciousness. *Perspectives in Biology and Medicine, 19*, 345–380.

Davidson, J. (1985). The utilization of sexual fantasies by sexually experienced university students. *Journal of American College Health, 34*(1), 24–32.

Davidson, J. (1988). *The agony of it all*. Los Angeles: J. P. Tarcher.

Davidson, L. R., & Duberman, L. (1982). Friendship: Communication and interactional patterns in same-sex dyads. *Sex Roles, 8*, 809–822.

Davidson, M. Losonczy, M. F., & Davis, K. L. (1986). Biological hypotheses of schizophrenia. In P. A. Berger & H. K. H. Brodie (Eds.), *American handbook of psychiatry: Vol. 8. Biological psychiatry* (2nd ed.). New York: Basic Books.

Davidson, P. O. (1982). Issues in patient compliance. In T. Millon, G. Green, & R. Meagher (Eds.), *Handbook of clinical health psychology*. New York: Plenum Press.

Davis, J. A. (1966). The campus as a frog pond. *American Journal of Sociology, 72*, 17–31.

Davis, J. M. (1985). Antipsychotic drugs. In H. I. Kaplan & B. J. Sadock (Eds.), *Comprehensive textbook of psychiatry/IV*. Baltimore: Williams & Wilkins.

Davis, K. E. (1985). Near and dear: Friendship and love compared. *Psychology Today, 19*(2), 22–30.

Dawley, H. H., Jr., & Wenrich, W. W. (1976). *Achieving assertive behavior: A guide to assertive training*. Pacific Grove, CA: Brooks/Cole.

Deaux, K. (1972). To err is humanizing: But sex makes a difference. *Representative Research in Social Psychology, 3*, 20–28.

Deaux, K., & Hanna, R. (1984). Courtship in the personals column: The influence of gender and sexual orientation. *Sex Roles, 11*, 363–375.

Delay, J., & Deniker, P. (1952). *Trente-huit cas de psychoses traitees par la cure prolongee et continue de 4560 RP*. Paris: Masson et Cie.

DeLongis, A., Folkman, S., & Lazarus, R. S. (1988). The impact of daily stress on health and mood: Psychological and social resources as mediators. *Journal of Personality and Social Psychology, 54*(3), 486–495.

Demo, D. H., & Acock, A. C. (1988). The impact of divorce on children. *Journal of Marriage and the Family, 50*, 619–648.

Dennis, W. (1966). Creative productivity between the ages of 20 and 80 years. *Journal of Gerontology, 21*, 1–8.

Denny, N., Field, J., & Quadagno, D. (1984). Sex differences in sexual needs and desires. *Archives of Sexual Behavior, 13*, 233–245.

DePaulo, B. M., Lanier, K., & Davis, T. (1983). Detecting the deceit of the motivated liar. *Journal of Personality and Social Psychology, 45*(5), 1096–1103.

DePaulo, B. M., Stone, J., & Lassiter, G. D. (1985). Deceiving and detecting deceit. In B. R. Schlenker (Ed.), *The self and social life*. New York: McGraw-Hill.

Derlega, V. J., & Chaikin, A. L. (1975). *Sharing intimacy: What we reveal to others and why*. Englewood Cliffs, NJ: Prentice-Hall.

Derlega, V. J., & Grzelak, J. (1979). Appropriateness of self-disclosure. In G. J. Chelune & associates (Eds.), *Self-disclosure: Origins, patterns, and implications of openness in interpersonal relationships*. San Francisco: Jossey-Bass.

Derlega, V. J., Winstead, B. A., Wong, P. T. P., & Greenspan, M. (1987). Self-disclosure and relationship development: An attributional analysis. In M. E. Roloff & G. R. Miller (Eds.), *Interpersonal processes: New directions in communication research*. Beverly Hills, CA: Sage Publications.

Dermer, M., & Thiel, D. (1975). When beauty may fail. *Journal of Personality and Social Psychology, 31*, 1168–1176.

Derogatis, L. R. (1982). Self-report measures of stress. In L. Goldberger & S. Breznitz (Eds.), *Handbook of stress: Theoretical and clinical aspects*. New York: Free Press.

Deutsch, M., & Gerard, H. B. (1955). A study of normative and informational social influences upon individual judgment. *Journal of Abnormal and Social Psychology, 51*, 629–636.

Diamond, E. E. (1979). Sex equality and measurement practices. *New Directions for Testing and Measurement, 3*, 61–78.

Diamond, M., & Karlen, A. (1981). The sexual response cycle. In H. I. Lief (Ed.), *Sexual problems in medical practice*. Chicago: American Medical Association.

DiMatteo, M. R., & Friedman, H. S. (1982). *Social psychology and medicine*. Cambridge, MA: Oelgeschlager, Gunn & Hain.

Dimsdale, J. E. (1988). A perspective on Type A behavior and coronary disease. *New England Journal of Medicine, 318*(2), 110–112.

DiNicola, D. D., & DiMatteo, M. R. (1984). Practitioners, patients, and compliance with medical regimens: A social psychological perspective. In A. Baum, S. E. Taylor, & J. E. Singer (Eds.), *Handbook of psychology and health: Vol. 4. Social psychological aspects of health*. Hillsdale, NJ: Erlbaum.

Dion, K. K. (1986). Stereotyping based on physical attractiveness: Issues and conceptual perspectives. In C. P. Herman, M. P. Zanna, & E. T. Higgins (Eds.), *Appearance, stigma and social behavior: The Ontario symposium on personality and social psychology* (Vol. 3). Hillsdale, NJ: Erlbaum.

Dishotzky, N. I., Loughman, W. D., Mogar, R. E., & Lipscomb, W. R. (1971). LSD and genetic damage: Is LSD chromosome damaging, carcinogenic, mutagenic, or teratogenic. *Science, 172*, 431–440.

Dixon, N. F. (1980). Humor: A cognitive alternative to stress? In I. G. Sarason & C. D. Spielberger (Eds.), *Stress and anxiety* (Vol. 7). Washington, DC: Hemisphere.

Doerr, P., Pirke, K. M., Kockott, G., & Dittmor, F. (1976). Further studies on sex hormones in male homosexuals. *Archives of General Psychiatry, 33*, 611–614.

Dohrenwend, B. S., Krasnoff, L., Askenasy, A. R., & Dohrenwend, B. P. (1978). Exemplification of a method for scaling life events: The PERI life events scale. *Journal of Health and Social Behavior, 19*, 205–229.

Dollard, J., Doob, L. W., Miller, N. E., Mowrer, O. H., & Sears, R. R. (1939). *Frustration and aggression*. New Haven, CT: Yale University Press.

Dollard, J., & Miller, N. E. (1950). *Personality and psychotherapy: An analysis in terms of learning, thinking and culture*. New York: McGraw-Hill.

Donnerstein, E., & Linz, D. (1984, January). Sexual violence in the media: A warning. *Psychology Today*, 14–15.

Dorner, G. (1988). Neuroendocrine response to estrogen and brain differentiation in heterosexuals, homosexuals, and transsexuals. *Archives of Sexual Behavior, 17*(1), 57–75.

Dovidio, J. F., & Gaertner, S. L. (Eds.). (1986). *Prejudice, discrimination, and racism*. New York: Academic Press.

Doyle, J. A. (1989). *The male experience*. Dubuque, IA: William C. Brown.

Drachman, D. A. (1986). Memory and cognitive function in normal aging. *Developmental Neuropsychology, 2,* 277–285.

Dreyer, P. H. (1982). Sexuality during adolescence. In B. B. Wolman (Ed.), *Handbook of developmental psychology.* Englewood Cliffs, NJ: Prentice-Hall.

Duck, S. (1983). *Friends for life: The psychology of close relationships.* New York: St. Martin's Press.

Duffy, S. M., & Rusbult, C. E. (1985/1986). Satisfaction and commitment in homosexual and heterosexual relationships. *Journal of Homosexuality, 12*(2), 1–23.

Duke, M., & Nowicki, S., Jr. (1979). *Abnormal psychology: Perspectives on being different.* Pacific Grove, CA: Brooks/Cole.

Duke-Duncan, P., Ritter, P. L., Dornbusch, S. M., Gross, R. T., & Carlsmith, J. M. (1985). The effects of pubertal timing on body image, school behavior, and deviance. *Journal of Youth and Adolescence, 14,* 227–235.

Duncan, B. L. (1976). Differential social perception and attribution of intergroup violence: Testing the lower limits of stereotyping of blacks. *Journal of Personality and Social Psychology, 34,* 590–598.

Dunn, M. E., & Trost, J. E. (1989). Male multiple orgasms: A descriptive study. *Archives of Sexual Behavior, 18*(5), 377–387.

Dusek, D., & Girdano, D. A. (1986). *Drugs: A factual account.* New York: McGraw-Hill.

Dusek, J. B., & Flaherty, J. F. (1981). The development of the self-concept during the adolescent years. *Monographs of the Society for Research in Child Development, 46*(4, Serial No. 191).

Dutton, D. G., & Aron, A. P. (1974). Some evidence for heightened sexual attraction under conditions of high anxiety. *Journal of Personality and Social Psychology, 30*(4), 510–517.

Dweck, C. S., Davidson, W., Nelson, S., & Enna, B. (1978). Sex differences in learned helplessness: II. The contingencies of evaluative feedback in the classroom, and III. An experimental analysis. *Developmental Psychology, 14,* 268–276.

Dyer, W. W. (1976). *Your erroneous zones.* New York: Thomas Y. Crowell.

Eagly, A. H. (1978). Sex differences in influenceability. *Psychological Bulletin, 85,* 86–116.

Eagly, A. H. (1983). Gender and social influence: A social-psychological analysis. *American Psychologist, 38,* 971–981.

Eagly, A. H. (1987). *Sex differences in social behavior: A social-role interpretation.* Hillsdale, NJ: Erlbaum.

Eagly, A. H., & Carli, L. L. (1981). Sex of researchers and sex-typed communications as determinants of sex differences in influenceability: A meta-analysis of social influence studies. *Psychological Bulletin, 90,* 1–20.

Eagly, A. H., & Whitehead, G. I. (1972). Effect of choice on receptivity to favorable and unfavorable evaluations of one's self. *Journal of Personality and Social Psychology, 22,* 223–230.

Eagly, A. H., & Wood, W. (1982). Inferred sex differences in status as a determinant of gender stereotypes about social influence. *Journal of Personality and Social Psychology, 43,* 915–928.

Eagly, A. H., & Wood, W. (1985). Gender and influenceability: Stereotype versus behavior. In V. O'Leary, R. Unger, & B. Wallston (Eds.), *Women, gender and social psychology.* Hillsdale, NJ: Erlbaum.

Eagly, A. H., Wood, W., & Chaiken, S. (1978). Causal inferences about communicators and their effect on opinion change. *Journal of Personality and Social Psychology, 36,* 424–435.

Earle, J. R., & Perricone, P. J. (1986). Premarital sexuality: A ten-year study of attitudes and behavior on a small university campus. *Journal of Sex Research, 22*(3), 304–310.

Easterbrooks, M. A., & Goldberg, W. A. (1985). Effects of early maternal employment on toddlers, mothers, and fathers. *Developmental Psychology, 21,* 774–783.

Edelman, R. J., & Hampson, S. E. (1981). Embarrassment in dyadic interaction. *Social Behavior and Personality, 9,* 171–177.

Efran, M. (1974). The effect of physical appearance on the judgment of guilt, interpersonal attraction, and severity of recommended punishment in a simulated jury task. *Journal of Research in Personality, 8,* 45–54.

Egan, G. (1977). *You and me: The skills of communicating and relating to others.* Pacific Grove, CA: Brooks/Cole.

Egan, G. (1990). *The skilled helper: Model, skills, and methods for effective helping.* Pacific Grove, CA: Brooks/Cole.

Egan, K. J., Kogan, H. N., Garber, A., & Jarrett, M. (1983). The impact of psychological distress on the control of hypertension. *Journal of Human Stress, 9*(4), 4–10.

Egeland, J. A., Gerhard, D. S., Pauls, D. L., Sussex, J. N., Kidd, K. K., Allen, C. R., Hostetter, A. M., & Housman, D. E. (1987). Bipolar affective disorders linked to DNA markers on chromosome 11. *Nature, 325,* 783–787.

Ehrenberg, O., & Ehrenberg, M. (1986). *The psychotherapy maze.* Northvale, NJ: Aronson.

Eichhorst, B. C. (1988). Contraception. *Primary Care, 15*(3), 437–459.

Eisen, M., & Zellman, G. L. (1987). Changes in incidence of sexual intercourse of unmarried teenagers following a community-based sex education program. *Journal of Sex Research, 23*(4), 527–544.

Eisenberg, N., & Lennon, R. (1983). Sex differences in empathy and related capacities. *Psychological Bulletin, 94,* 100–131.

Ekman, P. (1975). The universal smile: Face muscles talk every language. *Psychology Today, 9*(4), 35–39.

Ekman, P., & Friesen, W. V. (1984). *Unmasking the face.* Palo Alto, CA: Consulting Psychologists Press.

Ekman, P., & Friesen, W. V. (1986). A new pancultural facial expression of emotion. *Motivation and Emotion, 10*(2), 159–168.

Ekman, P. Friesen, W. V., & Ellsworth, P. (1982). What emotion categories or dimensions can observers judge from facial behavior? In P. Ekman (Ed.), *Emotion in the human face.* (2nd ed.). Cambridge, MA: Cambridge University Press.

Eliot, R. S., & Breo, D. L. (1989). *Is it worth dying for?* New York: Bantam Books.

Elkind, D. (1988). *The hurried child.* Reading, MA: Addison-Wesley.

Elliott, G. R., & Eisdorfer, C. (Eds.). (1982). *Stress and human health: Analysis and implications of research.* New York: Springer.

Ellis, A. (1962). *Reason and emotion in psychotherapy* (1st ed.). Seacaucus, NJ: Lyle Stuart.

Ellis, A. (1973). *Humanistic psychotherapy: The rational-emotive approach.* New York: Julian Press.

Ellis, A. (1977). *Reason and emotion in psychotherapy* (2nd ed.). Seacaucus, NJ: Lyle Stuart.

Ellis, A. (1984). *Reason and emotion in psychotherapy* (3rd ed.). Seacaucus, NJ: Lyle Stuart/Citadel Press.

Ellis, A. (1985). *How to live with and without anger.* New York: Citadel Press.

Ellis, A. (1987). The evolution of rational-emotive therapy (RET) and cognitive behavior therapy (CBT). In J. K. Zeig (Ed.), *The evolution of psychotherapy.* New York: Brunner/Mazel.

Ellis, A. (1988). *How to stubbornly refuse to make yourself miserable about anything—yes, anything!* Seacaucus, NJ. Lyle Stuart.

Ellis, A. (1989). Rational-emotive therapy. In R. J. Corsini & D. Wedding (Eds.), *Current Psychotherapies.* Itasca, IL: F. E. Peacock.

Ellsworth, P. C., Carlsmith, J. M., & Henson, A. (1972). The stare as a stimulus to flight in human subjects: A series of field experiments. *Journal of Personality and Social Psychology, 21,* 302–311.

Emanuel, H. M. (1987). Put time on your side. In A. D. Timpe (Ed.), *The management of time.* New York: Facts On File.

Eme, R. F. (1979). Sex differences in childhood psychopathology: A review. *Psychological Bulletin, 68,* 574–595.

Emerson, G. (1985). *Some American men.* New York: Simon & Schuster.

Emmons, R. A., & King, L. A. (1988). Conflict among personal strivings: Immediate and long-term implications for psychological and physical well-being. *Journal of Personality and Social Psychology, 54*(6), 1040–1048.

Epstein, S., & Meier, P. (1989). Constructive thinking: A broad coping variable with specific components. *Journal of Personality and Social Psychology, 57*(2), 332–350.

Epstein, S. P. (1982). Conflict and stress. In L. Goldberger & S. Breznitz (Eds.), *Handbook of stress: Theoretical and clinical aspects.* New York: Free Press.

Epstein, S. P. (1983). Natural healing processes of the mind: Graded stress inoculation as an inherent coping mechanism. In D. H. Meichenbaum & M. E. Jaremko (Eds.), *Stress reduction and prevention.* New York: Plenum Press.

Erdwins, C. J., & Mellinger, J. C. (1984). Midlife women: Relation of age and role to personality. *Journal of Personality and Social Psychology, 47,* 390–395.

Erikson, E. H. (1963). *Childhood and society.* New York: Norton.

Erikson, E. H. (1968). *Identity: Youth and crisis.* New York: Norton.

Etaugh, C. F. (1974). Effects of maternal employment on children: A review of recent research. *Merrill-Palmer Quarterly, 20,* 71–98.

Etaugh, C. F., & Harlow, H. (1975). Behaviors of male and female teachers as related to behaviors and attitudes of elementary school children. *Journal of Genetic Psychology, 127,* 163–170.

Exline, R. V. (1963). Explorations in the process of person perception: Visual interaction in relation to competition, sex, and the need for affiliation. *Journal of Personality, 31,* 1–20.

Eysenck, H. J. (1952). The effects of psychotherapy: An evaluation. *Journal of Consulting Psychology, 16,* 319–324.

Eysenck, H. J. (1967). *The biological basis of personality.* Springfield, IL: Charles C Thomas.

Eysenck, H. J. (1976). *Sex and personality.* London: Open Books.

Eysenck, H. J. (1982). *Personality, genetics and behavior: Selected papers.* New York: Praeger.

Eysenck, H. J., & Levey, A. (1972). Conditioning, introversion-extraversion and the strength of the nervous system. In V. D. Nebylitsyn & J. A. Gray (Eds.), *Biological bases of individual behavior*. New York: Academic Press.

Fagley, N. S. (1987). Positional response bias in multiple-choice tests of learning: Its relation to testwiseness and guessing strategy. *Journal of Educational Psychology, 79*(1), 95–97.

Fagot, B. I. (1981). Stereotypes versus behavioral judgments of sex differences in young children. *Sex Roles, 7,* 1093–1096.

Fain, T. C., & Anderton, D. L. (1987). Sexual harassment: Organizational context and diffuse status. *Sex Roles, 17,* 291–311.

Fancher, R. E. (1979). *Pioneers of psychology*. New York: Norton.

Farberow, N. L. (1974). *Suicide*. Morristown, NJ: General Learning Press.

Farina, A., Burns, G. L., Austad, C., Bugglin, C., & Fischer, E. H. (1986). The role of physical attractiveness in the readjustment of discharged psychiatric patients. *Journal of Abnormal Psychology, 95*(2), 139–143.

Fasteau, M. F. (1974). *The male machine*. New York: McGraw-Hill.

Fausto-Sterling, A. (1985). *Myths of gender: Biological theories about women and men*. New York: Basic Books.

Feder, H. H. (1984). Hormones and sexual behavior. In M. R. Rosenzweig & L. W. Porter (Eds.), *Annual review of psychology: 1984* (Vol. 35). Palo Alto, CA: Annual Reviews.

Feingold, A. (1988). Matching for attractiveness in romantic partners and same-sex friends: A meta-analysis and theoretical critique. *Psychological Bulletin, 104*(2), 226–235.

Ferree, M. M. (1976). The confused American housewife. *Psychology Today, 10*(4), 76–80.

Festinger, L. (1954). A theory of social comparison processes. *Human Relations, 7,* 117–140.

Festinger, L. (1957). *A theory of cognitive dissonance*. Stanford, CA: Stanford University Press.

Festinger, L., Schachter, S., & Back, K. (1950). *Social pressures in informal groups: A study of human factors in housing*. Stanford, CA: Stanford University Press.

Fidell, L. S. (1970). Empirical verification of sex discrimination in hiring practices in psychology. *American Psychologist, 25,* 1094–1098.

Fiedler, F. E. (1967). *A theory of leadership effectiveness*. New York: McGraw-Hill.

Fiedler, F. E. (1978). Recent developments in research on the contingency model. In L. Berkowitz (Ed.), *Group processes*. New York: Academic Press.

Fiedler, F. E., & Chemers, M. M. (1984). *Improving leadership effectiveness: The Leader Match Concept*. New York: Wiley.

Fiedler, F. E., & Garcia, J. E. (1987). *Leadership: Cognitive resources and performance*. New York: Wiley.

Field, D., Schaie, K. W., & Leino, E. V. (1988). Continuity in intellectual functioning: The role of self-reported health. *Psychology and Aging, 3,* 385–392.

Fielding, J. E. (1985). Smoking: Health effects and control. *New England Journal of Medicine, 313,* 491–498, 555–561.

Fink, M. (1988). Convulsive therapy: A manual of practice. In A. J. Frances & R. E. Hales (Eds.), *Review of psychiatry* (Vol. 7). Washington, DC: American Psychiatric Press.

Finn, S. E. (1986). Stability of personality self-ratings over 30 years: Evidence for an age/cohort interaction. *Journal of Personality and Social Psychology, 50,* 813–818.

Fischer, L. R. (1983). Mothers and mothers-in-law. *Journal of Marriage and the Family, 45,* 187–192.

Fisher, T. D. (1988). The relationship between parent-child communication about sexuality and college students' sexual behavior and attitudes as a function of parental proximity. *Journal of Sex Research, 24,* 305–311.

Fisher, W. A., Byrne, D., White, L. A., & Kelley, K. (1988). Erotophobia-erotophilia as a dimension of personality. *Journal of Sex Research, 25*(1), 123–151.

Fitts, W. (1972). *The self-concept and psychopathology*. Nashville, TN: Counselor Recording and Tests.

Fitzgerald, L. F., & Betz, N. E. (1983). Issues in the vocational psychology of women. In W. B. Walsh & S. H. Osipow (Eds.), *Handbook of vocational psychology: Vol. 1. Foundations*. Hillsdale, NJ: Erlbaum.

Fitzgerald, L. F., & Crites, J. O. (1980). Toward a career psychology of women: What do we know? What do we need to know? *Journal of Counseling Psychology, 27,* 44–62.

Fitzgerald, L. F., Shullman, S. L., Bailey, N., Richards, M., Swecker, J., Gold, Y., Ormerod, M., & Weitzman, L. (1988). The incidence and dimensions of sexual harassment in academia and the workplace. *Journal of Vocational Behavior, 32,* 152–175.

Flanders, J. P. (1982). A general systems approach to loneliness. In L. A. Peplau & D. Perlman (Eds.), *Loneliness: A sourcebook of current theory, research and therapy*. New York: Wiley.

Fleming, T. C. (1986). Alcohol and other mood-changing drugs. In S. Wolf & A. J. Finestone (Eds.), *Occupational stress: Health and performance at work*. Littleton, MA: PSG Publishing.

Folbre, N. (1987). *A field guide to the U.S. economy*. New York: Pantheon.

Folkes, V. S. (1982). Forming relationships and the matching hypothesis. *Personality and Social Psychology Bulletin, 8,* 631–636.

Folkes, V. S., & Sears, D. O. (1977). Does everybody like a liker? *Journal of Experimental Social Psychology, 13*(6), 505–519.

Folkins, C. H., & Sime, W. (1981). Physical fitness training and mental health. *American Psychologist, 36,* 373–389.

Folkman, S., Lazarus, R. S., Dunkel-Schetter, C., DeLongis, A., & Gruen, R. J. (1986). Dynamics of a stressful encounter: Cognitive appraisal, coping, and encounter outcomes. *Journal of Personality and Social Psychology, 50*(5), 992–1003.

Folkman, S., Lazarus, R. S., Gruen, R. J., & DeLongis, A. (1986). Appraisal, coping, health status, and psychological symptoms. *Journal of Personality and Social Psychology, 50*(3), 571–579.

Forsyth, D. R. (1983). *An introduction to group dynamics*. Pacific Grove, CA: Brooks/Cole.

Forsyth, D. R., & McMillan, J. H. (1981). Attributions, affect, and expectations: A test of Weiner's three-dimensional model. *Journal of Educational Psychology, 73,* 393–403.

Forsyth, D. R., & Strong, S. R. (1986). The scientific study of counseling and psychotherapy: A unificationist view. *American Psychologist, 41*(2), 113–119.

Foss, R. D., & Dempsey, C. B. (1979). Blood donation and the foot-in-the-door technique. *Journal of Personality and Social Psychology, 37,* 580–590.

Fowers, B. J., & Olson, D. H. (1989). ENRICH Marital Inventory: A discriminant validity and cross-validation assessment. *Journal of Marital and Family Therapy, 15*(1), 65–79.

Fowler, R. D. (1986). Howard Hughes: A psychological autopsy. *Psychology Today, 20*(5), 22–33.

Frances, A. J., & Widiger, T. (1986). The classification of personality disorders: An overview of problems and solutions. In A. J. Frances & R. E. Hales (Eds.), *Psychiatry Update: Annual Review* (Vol. 5). Washington, DC: American Psychiatric Press.

Frances, A. J., Widiger, T. A., & Pincus, H. A. (1989). The development of DSM-IV. *Archives of General Psychiatry, 46*(4), 373–375.

Francoeur, R. T. (1982). *Becoming a sexual person*. New York: Wiley.

Francoeur, R. T. (1987). Human sexuality. In M. B. Sussman & S. K. Steinmetz (Eds.), *Handbook of Marriage and the Family*. New York: Plenum Press.

Frank, E., Anderson, C., & Rubinstein, D. (1978). Frequency of sexual dysfunction in "normal" couples. *New England Journal of Medicine, 299,* 111–115.

Frankel, F. H. (1984). Electroconvulsive therapy. In T. B. Karasu (Ed.), *The psychiatric therapies*. Washington, DC: American Psychiatric Association.

Franks, C. M., & Barbrack, C. R. (1983). Behavior therapy with adults: An integrative perspective. In M. Hersen, A. E. Kazdin, & A. S. Bellack (Eds.), *The clinical psychology handbook*. New York: Pergamon Press.

Freedman, J., & Sears, D. (1965). Selective exposure. In L. Berkowitz (Ed.), *Advances in experimental social psychology* (Vol. 2). New York: Academic Press.

Freedman, J. L., & Fraser, S. C. (1966). Compliance without pressure: The foot-in-the-door technique. *Journal of Personality and Social Psychology, 4,* 195–202.

Freeman, R. B. (1976). *The over-educated American*. New York: Academic Press.

French, J. R. P., Jr., Caplan, R. D., & Van Harrison, R. (1982). *The mechanisms of job stress and strain*. New York: Wiley.

French, J. R. P., Jr., & Raven, B. (1959). The bases of social power. In D. Cartwright (Ed.), *Studies in social power*. Ann Arbor, MI: Institute for Social Research.

Freud, S. (1923). *The ego and the id. Standard Edition*, Vol. 19. London: Hogarth.

Freud, S. (1924). *A general introduction to psychoanalysis*. New York: Boni and Liveright. (Original work published 1920).

Freud, S. (1960). *The psychopathology of everyday life. Standard Edition*, Vol. 6. London: Hogarth. (Original work published 1901)

Fried, P. A. (1977). Behavioral and electroencephalographic correlates of the chronic use of marijuana—A review. *Behavioral Biology, 21,* 163–196.

Friedan, B. (1964). *The feminine mystique*. New York: Dell.

Friedberg, J. (1976). *Shock treatment is not good for your brain*. San Francisco: Glide Publications.

Friedewald, W. T. (1982). Current nutrition issues in hypertension. *Journal of the American Dietetic Association, 80,* 17.

Friedman, D. E. (1987). Work vs. family: War of the worlds. *Personnel Administrator, 32*(8), 36–39.

Friedman, H. S. (1983). Social perception and face-to-face interaction. In D. Perlman & D. C. Cozby (Eds.), *Social psychology*. New York: Holt, Rinehart & Winston.

Friedman, H. S., & Booth-Kewley, S. (1987). The "disease-prone personality": A meta-analytic view of the construct. *American Psychologist, 42*(6), 539–555.

Friedman, H. S., & Booth-Kewley, S. (1988). Validity of the Type A construct: A reprise. *Psychological Bulletin, 104*(3), 381–384.

Friedman, H. S., Prince, L. M., Riggio, R. E., & DiMatteo, M. R. (1980). Understanding and assessing nonverbal expressiveness: The affective communication test. *Journal of Personality and Social Psychology, 39*(2), 333–351.

Friedman, M., & Rosenman, R. F. (1974). *Type A behavior and your heart.* New York: Knopf.

Frieze, I. H., & Ramsey, S. J. (1976). Nonverbal maintenance of traditional sex roles. *Journal of Social Issues, 32*(3), 133–141.

Fromm, E. (1963). *Escape from freedom.* New York: Holt.

Fuchs, R. M. (1984). Group therapy. In T. B. Karasu (Ed.), *The psychiatric therapies.* Washington, DC: American Psychiatric Association.

Fuller, R. G. C., & Sheehy-Skeffington, A. (1974). Effects of group laughter on responses to humorous materials: A replication and extension. *Psychological Reports, 35,* 531–534.

Funk, S. C., & Houston, B. K. (1987). A critical analysis of the Hardiness Scale's validity and utility. *Journal of Personality and Social Psychology, 53*(3), 572–578.

Furstenberg, F. F., Jr., & Spanier, G. B. (1984). *Recycling the family: Remarriage after divorce.* Beverly Hills, CA: Sage Publications.

Gadpaille, W. J. (1975). *The cycles of sex.* New York: Scribner's.

Gagnon, J. H. (1985). Attitudes and responses of parents to pre-adolescent masturbation. *Archives of Sexual Behavior, 14*(5), 451–466.

Gagnon, J. H., & Simon, J. (1973). *Sexual conduct: The social origins of human sexuality.* Chicago: Aldine.

Gagnon, J. H., & Simon, W. (1987). The sexual scripting of oral genital contacts. *Archives of Sexual Behavior, 16*(1), 1–25.

Galassi, J. P., Delo, J. S., Galassi, M. D., & Bastien, S. (1974). The college self-expression scale: A measure of assertiveness. *Behavior Therapy, 5,* 165–171.

Gantt, W. H. (1975, April 25). Unpublished lecture, Ohio State University. Cited in D. Hothersall (1984), *History of psychology.* New York: Random House.

Gardner, J. N., & Jewler, A. J. (Eds.). (1989). *College is only the beginning: A student guide to higher education.* Belmont, CA: Wadsworth.

Gatchel, R. J., & Baum, A. (1988). *An introduction to health psychology.* New York: Random House.

Gebhard, P. H. (1966). Factors in marital orgasm. *Journal of Social Issues, 22,* 88–95.

Gebhard, P. H. (1972). Incidence of overt homosexuality in the United States and Western Europe. In J. Livengood (Ed.), *National Institute of Mental Health Task Force on Homosexuality: Final report and background papers.* Washington, DC: U.S. Government Printing Office.

Gebhardt, D. L., & Crump, C. E. (1990). Employee fitness and wellness programs in the workplace. *American Psychologist, 45*(2), 262–272.

Geiser, R. L., Rarick, D. L., & Soldow, G. F. (1977). Deception and judgment accuracy: A study in person perception. *Personality and Social Psychology Bulletin, 3,* 446–449.

George, L. K., Fillenbaum, G. G., & Palmore, E. (1984). Sex differences in the antecedents and consequences of retirement. *Journal of Gerontology, 39,* 364–371.

George, L. K., & Weiler, J. J. (1981). Sexuality in middle and later life. *Archives of General Psychiatry, 38,* 919–923.

Georgotas, A. (1985). Affective disorders: Pharmacotherapy. In H. I. Kaplan & B. J. Sadock (Eds.), *Comprehensive textbook of psychiatry/IV.* Baltimore: Williams & Wilkins.

Gerdes, E., Gehling, J., & Rapp, J. (1981). The effects of sex and sex-role concept on self-disclosure. *Sex Roles, 7,* 989–998.

Gerrard, M. (1987). Emotional and cognitive barriers to effective contraception: Are males and females really different? In K. Kelley (Ed.), *Females, males, and sexuality: Theories and research.* Albany: New York State University Press.

Gerstel, N., Reissman, C. K., & Rosenfield, S. (1985). Explaining the symptomatology of separated and divorced women and men: The role of material conditions and social network. *Social Forces, 64*(1), 84–101.

Gibb, B. (1964). *Test-wiseness as secondary cue response.* Unpublished doctoral dissertation, Stanford University, California.

Gibb, J. R. (1961). Defensive communication. *Journal of Communication, 1,* 141–148.

Gibb, J. R. (1973). Defensive communication. In W. G. Bennis, D. E. Berlew, E. H. Schein, & F. I. Steele (Eds.), *Interpersonal dynamics.* Homewood, IL: Dorsey Press.

Gibbins, K. (1969). Communication aspects of women's clothes and their relation to fashionability. *British Journal of Social and Clinical Psychology, 8,* 301–312.

Gibbs, N. (1989, June). Sick and tired. *Time,* 48–53.

Gilder, G. (1986). *Men and marriage.* New York: Pelican.

Giles, H., & Street, R. L., Jr. (1985). Communicator characteristics and behavior. In M. L. Knapp & G. R. Miller (Eds.), *Handbook of interpersonal communication.* Beverly Hills, CA: Sage Publications.

Gillberg, M. (1984). The effects of two alternative timings of a one-hour nap on early morning performance. *Biological Psychology, 19*(1), 45–54.

Gilmer, B. V. H. (1975). *Applied psychology: Adjustments in living and work.* New York: McGraw-Hill.

Ginzberg, E. (1952). Toward a theory of occupational choice. *Occupations, 30,* 491–494.

Ginzberg, E. (1972). Toward a theory of occupational choice: A restatement. *Vocational Guidance Quarterly, 20,* 169–176.

Glasser, W. (1975). *Schools without failure.* New York: Harper & Row.

Glenn, M., & Taska, R. J. (1984). Antidepressants and lithium. In T. B. Karasu (Ed.), *The psychiatric therapies.* Washington, DC: American Psychiatric Association.

Glenn, N. D., & McLanahan, S. (1982). Children and marital happiness: A further specification of the relationship. *Journal of Marriage and the Family, 44,* 63–72.

Glenn, N. D., & Weaver, C. N. (1988). The changing relationship of marital status to reported happiness. *Journal of Marriage and the Family, 50,* 317–324.

Glick, P., Zion, C., & Nelson, C. (1988). What mediates sex discrimination in hiring decisions? *Journal of Personality and Social Psychology, 55,* 178–186.

Glick, P. C. (1980). Remarriage: Some recent changes and variations. *Journal of Family Issues, 1,* 455–478.

Glick, P. C. (1984). Marriage, divorce, and living arrangements: Prospective changes. *Journal of Family Issues, 5,* 7–26.

Glick, P. C. (1988). Fifty years of family demography: A record of social change. *Journal of Marriage and the Family, 50,* 861–873.

Goethals, G. R., & Darley, J. M. (1977). Social comparison theory: An attributional approach. In J. M. Suls & R. L. Miller (Eds.), *Social comparison processes: Theoretical and empirical perspectives.* Washington, DC: Hemisphere/Halsted.

Goetting, A. (1986). Parental satisfaction: A review of research. *Journal of Family Issues, 7*(1), 83–109.

Goffman, E. (1956). The nature of deference and demeanor. *American Anthropologist, 58,* 473–502.

Goffman, E. (1959). *The presentation of self in everyday life.* Garden City, NY: Doubleday/Anchor.

Goffman, E. (1971). *Relations in public.* New York: Basic Books.

Gold, M. S. (1989). *The good news about panic, anxiety and phobias.* New York: Willard.

Goldberg, H. (1976). *The hazards of being male: Surviving the myth of masculine privilege.* New York: Nash.

Goldhaber, D. (1986). *Life-span human development.* New York: Harcourt Brace Jovanovich.

Goldstein, M. A., Kilroy, M. C., & Van de Voort, D. (1976). Gaze as a function of conversation and degree of love. *Journal of Psychology, 92,* 227–234.

Goldstein, M. J. (1984). *Family factors that antedate the onset of schizophrenia and related disorders: The results of a fifteen-year prospective longitudinal study.* Paper presented at the Regional Symposium of the World Psychiatric Association Meeting, Helsinki, Finland:

Goldstein, M. J. (1988). The family and psychopathology. In M. R. Rosenzweig & L. W. Porter (Eds.), *Annual review of psychology: 1988* (Vol. 39). Palo Alto, CA: Annual Reviews.

Goleman, D. (1978). Special abilities of the sexes: Do they begin in the brain? *Psychology Today, 12*(6), 48–59, 120.

Goleman, D. (1979). [Interview with Richard S. Lazarus, Positive denial: The case for not facing reality]. *Psychology Today, 13*(6), 44–60.

Golub, S., & Harrington, D. M. (1981). Premenstrual and menstrual mood changes in adolescent women. *Journal of Personality and Social Psychology, 41,* 961–965.

Gonzales, M. H., Davis, J. M., Loney, G. L., Lukens, C. K., & Junghans, C. H. (1983). Interactional approach to interpersonal attraction. *Journal of Personality and Social Psychology, 44,* 1192–1197.

Good, P. R., & Smith, B. D. (1980). Menstrual distress and sex-role attributes. *Psychology of Women Quarterly, 4,* 482–491.

Good, T. L., Sikes, J. N., & Brophy, J. E. (1973). Effects of teacher sex and student sex on classroom interaction. *Journal of Educational Psychology, 65,* 74–87.

Goodall, K. (1972). Field report: Shapers at work. *Psychology Today, 6*(6), 53–63, 132–138.

Gordon, S. (1976). *Lonely in America.* New York: Touchstone.

Gordon, S., & Snyder, C. W. (1989). *Personal issues in human sexuality: A guidebook for better sexual health.* Boston: Allyn & Bacon.

Gore, S. (1978). The effect of social support in moderating the health consequences of unemployment. *Journal of Health and Social Behavior, 19,* 157–165.

Gottesman, I. I., & Shields, J. (1982). *Schizophrenia: The epigenetic puzzle.* Cambridge, MA: Cambridge University Press.

Gough, W. C., & Heilbrun, A. B., Jr. (1965). *The adjective check list manual.* Palo Alto, CA: Consulting Psychologists Press.

Gould, R. L. (1972). The phases of adult life: A study in developmental psychology. *American Journal of Psychiatry, 129*, 521–531.

Gould, R. L. (1978). *Transformations: Growth and change in adult life.* New York: Simon & Schuster.

Gove, W. R. (1975). Labeling and mental illness: A critique. In W. R. Gove (Ed.), *The labeling of deviance: Evaluating a perspective.* New York: Halsted.

Graziano, W., Brothen, T., & Berscheid, E. (1978). Height and attraction: Do men and women see eye-to-eye? *Journal of Personality, 46*, 128–145.

Green, L. W., Tryon, W. W., Marks, B., & Huryn, J. (1986). Periodontal disease as a function of life events stress. *Journal of Human Stress, 12*(1), 32–36.

Green, S. K., Buchanan, D. R., & Heuer, S. K. (1984). Winners, losers, and choosers: A field investigation of dating initiation. *Personality and Social Psychology Bulletin, 10*, 502–511.

Greenberg, J., Pyszczynski, T., & Solomon, S. (1982). The self-serving attributional bias: Beyond self-presentation. *Journal of Experimental Social Psychology, 8*, 99–111.

Greenberg, J. S. (1990). *Comprehensive stress management.* Dubuque, IA: William C. Brown.

Greenberger, E., & Goldberg, W. A. (1989). Work, parenting, and the socialization of children. *Developmental Psychology, 25*, 22–35.

Greenblat, C. S. (1983). The salience of sexuality in the early years of marriage. *Journal of Marriage and the Family, 45*(2), 289–299.

Greenhaus, J. H., Bedeian, A. G., & Mossholder, K. W. (1987). Work experiences, job performance, and feelings of personal and family well-being. *Journal of Vocational Behavior, 31*, 200–215.

Greenley, J. R., Kepecs, J. G., & Henry, W. E. (1981). Trends in urban American psychiatry: Practice in Chicago in 1962 and 1973. *Social Psychiatry, 16*, 123–128.

Greenson, R. R. (1967). *The technique and practice of psychoanalysis* (Vol. 1). New York: International Universities Press.

Greenwald, J. (1973). *Be the person you were meant to be* (1st ed.). New York: Simon & Schuster.

Greenwald, J. (1982). *Be the person you were meant to be* (2nd ed.). New York: Dell.

Greer, S. (1979). Psychological inquiry: A contribution to cancer research. *Psychological Medicine, 9*, 81–89.

Grinker, J. A. (1982). Physiological and behavioral basis for human obesity. In D. W. Pfaff (Ed.), *The physiological mechanisms of motivation.* New York: Springer-Verlag.

Grinspoon, L., & Bakalar, J. B. (1986). Psychedelics and arylcyclohexylamines. In A. J. Frances & R. E. Hales (Eds.), *Psychiatric Update: Annual Review* (Vol. 5). Washington, DC: American Psychiatric Press.

Grob, G. N. (1983). Disease and environment in American history. In D. Mechanic (Ed.), *Handbook of health, health care, and the health professions.* New York: Free Press.

Grover, K. J., Russell, C. S., Schumm, W. R., & Paff-Bergen, L. A. (1985). Mate selection processes and marital satisfaction. *Family Relations, 34*, 383–386.

Gruneberg, M. M. (1979). *Understanding job satisfaction.* New York: Wiley.

Guidubaldi, J., Perry, J. D., & Nastasi, B. K. (1987). Growing up in a divorced family: Initial and long-term perspectives on children's adjustment. In S. Oskamp (Ed.), *Family processes and problems: Social psychologi-*

cal aspects (Vol. 7, *Applied Social Psychology Annual*). Newbury Park, CA: Sage Publications.

Gurin, J. (1989, June). Leaner, not lighter. *Psychology Today*, 32–36.

Gwartney-Gibbs, P. A. (1986). The institutionalization of premarital cohabitation: Estimates from marriage license applications, 1970 and 1980. *Journal of Marriage and the Family, 48*, 423–434.

Haan, N., Millsap, R., & Hartka, E. (1986). As time goes by: Change and stability in personality over 50 years. *Psychology and Aging, 1*, 220–232.

Haas, A., & Haas, K. (1990). *Understanding sexuality.* St. Louis: Times.Mirror/Mosby.

Hackman, J. R., Brousseau, K. R., & Weiss, J. A. (1976). The interaction of task design and group performance strategies in determining group effectiveness. *Organizational Behavior and Human Performance, 16*, 350–365.

Hales, D. (1987). *How to sleep like a baby.* New York: Balantine.

Hall, D. T. (1986). An overview of current career development theory, research, and practice. In D. Hall & associates (Eds.), *Career development in organizations.* San Francisco: Jossey-Bass.

Hall, E. T. (1959). *The silent language.* Garden City, NY: Doubleday.

Hall, E. T. (1966). *The hidden dimension.* Garden City, NY: Doubleday.

Hall, G. S. (1904). *Adolescence.* New York: Appleton.

Hall, J. A. (1984). *Nonverbal sex differences: Communication accuracy and expressive style.* Baltimore: Johns Hopkins University Press.

Hallie, P. P. (1971). Justification and rebellion. In N. Sanford & C. Comstock (Eds.), *Sanctions for evil.* San Francisco: Jossey-Bass.

Halpin, A. W., & Winer, B. J. (1952). *The leadership behavior of the airplane commander.* Columbus: Ohio State University Research Foundation.

Hamachek, D. E. (1987). *Encounters with the self.* New York: Holt, Rinehart & Winston.

Hamburger, A. C. (1988). Beauty quest. *Psychology Today, 22*(5), 28–32.

Hamilton, D. L., & Gifford, R. K. (1976). Illusory correlation in interpersonal perception: A cognitive basis of stereotypic judgments. *Journal of Experimental Social Psychology, 12*, 392–407.

Hammen, C., Marks, T., Mayol, A., & deMayo, R. (1985). Depressive self-schemas, life stress, and vulnerability to depression. *Journal of Abnormal Psychology, 94*(3), 308–319.

Hammen, C., Mayol, A., deMayo, R., & Marks, T. (1986). Initial symptom levels and the life-event-depression relationship. *Journal of Abnormal Psychology, 95*(2), 114–122.

Hammond, E. C., & Horn, D. (1984). Smoking and death rates—Report on 44 months of follow-up of 187,783 men. *Journal of the American Medical Association, 251*(21), 2840–2853.

Hansen, C. H., & Hansen, R. D. (1988). How rock music videos can change what is seen when boy meets girl: Priming stereotypic appraisal of social interactions. *Sex Roles, 19*(5–6), 287–316.

Hanson, R. O., Jones, W. H., & Carpenter, B. N. (1984). Relational competence and social support. In P. Shaver (Ed.), *Review of personality and social psychology* (Vol. 5). Beverly Hills, CA: Sage Publications.

Hare, R. D. (1983). Diagnosis of antisocial personality disorder in criminals. *American Journal of Psychiatry, 140*, 887–890.

Harper, N. L., & Askling, L. R. (1980). Group communication and quality of task solution in a media production organization. *Communication Monographs, 47*, 77–100.

Harriman, L. C. (1986). Marital adjustment as related to personal and marital changes accompanying parenthood. *Family Relations, 35*, 233–239.

Harris, L. J. (1980). Lateralized sex differences: Substrates and significance. *Behavioral and Brain Sciences, 3*, 236–237.

Harris, M. B., Harris, R. J., & Bochner, S. (1982). Fat, four-eyed, and female: Stereotypes of obesity, glasses, and gender. *Journal of Applied Social Psychology, 12*, 503–516.

Harris, T. (1967). *I'm OK—You're OK.* New York: Harper & Row.

Harrison, A. A., & Saeed, I. (1977). Let's make a deal: An analysis of revelations and stipulations in lonely heart advertisements. *Journal of Personality and Social Psychology, 35*, 257–264.

Harry, J. (1983). Gay male and lesbian relationships. In E. D. Macklin & R. H. Rubin (Eds.), *Contemporary families and alternative lifestyles: Handbook on research and theory.* Beverly Hills, CA: Sage Publications.

Hart, D. H., Rayner, F., & Christensen, E. R. (1971). Planning, preparation, and chance in occupational entry. *Journal of Vocational Behavior, 1*, 279–285.

Hartman, W. E., & Fithian, M. A. (1974). *Treatment of sexual dysfunction: A bio-psycho-social approach.* New York: Aronson.

Hartmann, E. (1978). *The sleeping pill.* New Haven, CT: Yale University Press.

Hartmann, E. L. (1985). Sleep disorders. In H. I. Kaplan & B. J. Sadock (Eds.), *Comprehensive textbook of psychiatry* (4th ed.). Baltimore: Williams & Wilkins.

Harvey, J. H., Town, J. P., & Yarkin, K. L. (1981). How fundamental is "the fundamental attribution error"? *Journal of Personality and Social Psychology, 40*(2), 346–349.

Harvey, S. M. (1987). Female sexual behavior: Fluctuations during the menstrual cycle. *Journal of Psychosomatic Research, 31*(1), 101–110.

Harwood, H., Napolitano, D., Kristiansen, P., & Collins, J. (1984). *Economic costs to society of alcohol and drug abuse and mental illness: 1980.* Research Triangle Park, NC: Research Triangle Institute.

Hass, R. G. (1981). Effects of source characteristics on cognitive responses and persuasion. In R. E. Petty, T. M. Ostrom, & T. C. Brock (Eds.), *Cognitive responses in persuasion.* Hillsdale, NJ: Erlbaum.

Hatfield, E. (1988). Passionate and companionate love. In R. J. Sternberg & M. L. Barnes (Eds.), *The psychology of love.* New Haven, CT: Yale University Press.

Hatfield, E., & Walster, G. W. (1985). *A new look at love.* Lanham, MD: University Press of America.

Havighurst, R. J., Neugarten, B., & Tobin, S. (1968). Disengagement and patterns of aging. In B. Neugarten (Ed.), *Middle age and aging.* Chicago: University of Chicago Press.

Haviland, J. J., & Malatesta, C. Z. (1982). The development of sex differences in nonverbal signals. In C. Mayo & N. Henley (Eds.), *Gender and nonverbal behavior.* New York: Springer-Verlag.

Haynes, S. G., Feinleib, M., & Eaker, E. D. (1983). Type A behavior and the ten-year incidence of coronary heart disease in the Framingham heart study. In R. H. Rosenman (Ed.), *Psychosomatic risk factors and coronary heart disease.* Bern, Switzerland: Huber.

Hays, R. B. (1985). A longitudinal study of friendship development. *Journal of Personality and Social Psychology, 48*, 909–924.

Hazan, C., & Shaver, P. (1987). Romantic love conceptualized as an attachment process. *Journal of Personality and Social Psychology, 52*, 511–524.

Healy, D., & Williams, J. M. G. (1988). Dysrhythmia, dysphoria, and depression: The interaction of learned helplessness and circadian dysrhythmia in the pathogenesis of depression. *Psychological Bulletin, 103*(2), 163–178.

Heath, R. G. (1976). Cannabis sativa derivatives: Effects on brain function of monkeys. In G. G. Nahas (Ed.), *Marijuana: Chemistry, biochemistry and cellular effects.* New York: Springer.

Hebb, D. D. (1955). Drives and the C.N.S. (conceptual nervous system). *Psychological Review, 62*, 243–254.

Hegsted, D. M. (1984). What is a healthful diet? In J. D. Matarazzo, S. M. Weiss, J. A. Herd, N. E. Miller, & S. M. Weiss (Eds.), *Behavioral health: A handbook of health enhancement and disease prevention.* New York: Wiley.

Heider, F. (1958). *The psychology of interpersonal relations.* New York: Wiley.

Heiman, J. R. (1977). A psychophysiological exploration of sexual arousal patterns in females and males. *Psychophysiology, 14*, 266–274.

Helson, H. Blake, R. R., & Mouton, J. S. (1958). Petition-signing as adjustment to situational and personal factors. *Journal of Social Psychology, 48*, 3–10.

Helson, R., Mitchell, V., & Moane, G. (1984). Personality and patterns of adherence and nonadherence to the social clock. *Journal of Personality and Social Psychology, 46*, 1079–1096.

Helson, R., & Moane, G. (1987). Personality change in women from college to midlife. *Journal of Personality and Social Psychology, 53*, 176–186.

Helzer, J. E., Robins, L. N., & McEvoy, L. (1987). Post-traumatic stress disorder in the general population: Findings of the epidemiologic catchment area survey. *New England Journal of Medicine, 317*(26), 1630–1634.

Hemphill, J. K. (1961). Why people attempt to lead. In L. Petrullo & B. M. Bass (Eds.), *Leadership and interpersonal behavior.* New York: Holt, Rinehart & Winston.

Hemsley, G. D., & Doob, A. N. (1978). The effect of looking behavior on perceptions of a communicator's credibility. *Journal of Applied Social Psychology, 8*, 136–144.

Hendrick, C., & Hendrick, S. (1983). *Liking, loving and relating.* Pacific Grove, CA: Brooks/Cole.

Hendrick, S. S. (1981). Self-disclosure and marital satisfaction. *Journal of Personality and Social Psychology, 40*, 1150–1159.

Hendrick, S. S., Hendrick, C., & Adler, N. L. (1988). Romantic relationships: Love, satisfaction, and staying together. *Journal of Personality and Social Psychology, 54*(6), 980–988.

Henley, N. M. (1977). *Body politics: Power, sex, and nonverbal communication* (1st ed.). Englewood Cliffs, NJ: Prentice-Hall.

Henley, N. M. (1986). *Body politics: Power, sex, and nonverbal communication* (2nd ed.). New York: Simon & Schuster.

Henley, N. M., & Freeman, J. (1981). The sexual politics of interpersonal behavior. In S. Cox (Ed.), *Female psychology: The emerging self.* New York: St. Martin's Press.

Herink, R. (Ed.). (1980). *The psychotherapy handbook.* New York: New American Library.

Hertzog, C., & Schaie, K. W. (1988). Stability and changes in adult intelligence: 2. Simultaneous analysis of longitudinal means and covariance structures. *Psychology and Aging, 3*, 122–130.

Herzberg, F. (1968). *Work and the nature of man.* London: Staples.

Heun, L. R., & Heun, R. E. (1978). *Developing skills for human interactions.* Columbus, OH: Charles E. Merrill.

Hill, C. T., Rubin, Z., & Peplau, L. A. (1976). Breakups before marriage: The end of 103 affairs. *Journal of Social Issues, 32*, 147–168.

Hill, J. P. (1987). Research on adolescents and their families: Past and prospect. In C. E. Irwin (Ed.), *Adolescent social behavior and health.* San Francisco: Jossey-Bass.

Hirokawa, R. Y. (1980). A comparative analysis of communication patterns within effective and ineffective decision-making groups. *Communication Monographs, 47*, 312–321.

Hiroto, D. S., & Seligman, M. E. P. (1975). Generality of learned helplessness in man. *Journal of Personality and Social Psychology, 31*, 311–327.

Hirschfeld, R. M. A., & Davidson, L. (1988). Risk factors for suicide. In A. J. Frances & R. E. Hales (Eds.), *Review of psychiatry* (Vol. 7). Washington, DC: American Psychiatric Press.

Hite, S. (1976). *The Hite report.* New York: Macmillan.

Hochschild, A. (1989). *The second shift: Working parents and the revolution at home.* New York: Viking Penguin.

Hodges, B. H. (1974). Effects of valence on relative weighting in impression formation. *Journal of Personality and Social Psychology, 30*, 378–381.

Hoffman, L. (1987). The effects on children of maternal and paternal employment. In N. Gerstel & H. Gross (Eds.), *Families and work.* Philadelphia: Temple University Press.

Hogan, D. P. (1978). The variable order of events in the life course. *American Sociological Review, 43*, 573–586.

Hokanson, J. E., & Burgess, M. (1962). The effects of three types of aggression on vascular processes. *Journal of Abnormal and Social Psychology, 65*, 446–449.

Holahan, C. J., & Moos, R. H. (1985). Life stress and health: Personality, coping, and family support in stress resistance. *Journal of Personality and Social Psychology, 49*(3), 739–747.

Holland, J. (1985). *Making vocational choices: A theory of vocational personalities and work environments.* Englewood Cliffs, NJ: Prentice-Hall.

Hollander, E. P. (1985). Leadership and power. In G. Lindzey & E. Aronson (Eds.), *Handbook of social psychology* (3rd ed.). New York: Random House.

Hollister, L. E. (1978). Psychotomimetic drugs in man. In L. L. Iversen, S. D. Iversen, & S. H. Snyder (Eds.), *Handbook of psychopharmacology.* New York: Plenum Press.

Hollon, S. D., & Najavits, L. (1988). Review of empirical studies on cognitive therapy. In A. J. Frances & R. E. Hales (Eds.), *Review of psychiatry* (Vol. 7). Washington, DC: American Psychiatric Press.

Holmes, D. S. (1984). Meditation and somatic arousal reduction: A review of the experimental evidence. *American Psychologist, 39*(1), 1–10.

Holmes, T. H. (1979). Development and application of a quantitative measure of life change magnitude. In J. E. Barrett, R. M. Rose, & G. L. Klerman (Eds.), *Stress and mental disorder.* New York: Raven.

Holmes, T. H., & Masuda, M. (1974). Life change and illness susceptibility. In B. S. Dohrenwend & B. P. Dohrenwend (Eds.), *Stressful life events: Their nature and effects.* New York: Wiley.

Holmes, T. H., & Rahe, R. H. (1967). The Social Readjustment Rating Scale. *Journal of Psychosomatic Research, 11*, 213–218.

Holroyd, K. A., & Lazarus, R. S. (1982). Stress, coping and somatic adaptation. In L. Goldberger & S. Breznitz (Eds.), *Handbook of stress: Theoretical and clinical aspects.* New York: Free Press.

Holt, R. R. (1982). Occupational stress. In L. Goldberger & S. Breznitz (Eds.), *Handbook of stress: Theoretical and clinical aspects.* New York: Free Press.

Holter, H. (1975). Sex roles and social change. In M. T. S. Mednick, S. S. Tangri, & L. W. Hoffman (Eds.), *Women and achievement: Social and motivational analyses.* Washington, DC: Hemisphere.

Honeycutt, J. M. (1986). A model of marital functioning based on an attraction paradigm and social-penetration dimensions. *Journal of Marriage and the Family, 48*, 651–667.

Hopkins, A. H. (1983). *Work and satisfaction in the public sector.* Totowa, NJ: Rowman & Allanheld.

Horner, M. J. (1972). Toward an understanding of achievement related conflicts in women. *Journal of Social Issues, 28*, 157–176.

Horowitz, M. J. (1979). Psychological response to serious life events. In V. Hamilton & D. M. Warburton (Eds.), *Human stress and cognition: An information processing approach.* New York: Wiley.

Horvath, T. (1979). Correlates of physical beauty in men and women. *Social Behavior and Personality, 7*, 145–151.

House, J. S. (1981). *Work stress and social support.* Reading, MA: Addison-Wesley.

Howard, J. A. (1984). Social influences on attribution: Blaming some victims more than others. *Journal of Personality and Social Psychology, 47*(3), 494–505.

Howe, M. L., & Hunter, M. A. (1986). Long-term memory in adulthood: An examination of the development of storage and retrieval processes at acquisition and retention. *Developmental Review, 6*, 334–364.

Hubbard, L. R. (1989). *Scientology: The fundamentals of thought.* Los Angeles, CA: Bridge.

Huesmann, L. R., & Morikawa, S. (1985). Learned helplessness and depression: Cognitive factors in treatment and inoculation. In S. Reiss & R. R. Bootzin (Eds.), *Theoretical issues in behavior therapy.* Orlando, FL: Academic Press.

Hull, J. G., Van Treuren, R. R., & Virnelli, S. (1987). Hardiness and health: A critique and alternative approach. *Journal of Personality and Social Psychology, 53*(3), 518–530.

Hunt, M. (1974). *Sexual behavior in the 1970s.* Chicago: Playboy Press.

Hunt, W. A., & Matarazzo, J. D. (1982). Changing smoking behavior: A critique. In R. J. Gatchel, A. Baum, & J. E. Singer (Eds.), *Handbook of psychology and health: Vol. 1. Clinical psychology and behavioral medicine, overlapping disciplines.* Hillsdale, NJ: Erlbaum.

Hurst, M. W., Jenkins, C. D., & Rose, R. M. (1978). The assessment of life change stress: A comparative and methodological inquiry. *Psychosomatic Medicine, 40*, 126–141.

Huseman, R. C., Lahiff, J. M., & Hatfield, J. D. (1976). *Interpersonal communication in organizations*. Boston: Holbrook Press.

Huston, A. C. (1983). Sex-typing. In P. H. Mussen (Ed.), *Handbook of child psychology* (Vol. 4, 4th ed.). New York: Wiley.

Huyck, M. H., & Hoyer, W. J. (1982). *Adult development and aging*. Belmont, CA: Wadsworth.

Hyde, J. S. (1981). How large are cognitive gender differences? *American Psychologist, 36,* 892–901.

Hyde, J. S. (1984). How large are gender differences in aggression? A developmental meta-analysis. *Developmental Psychology, 20,* 722–736.

Hyde, J. S. (1986). *Understanding human sexuality* (3rd ed.). New York: McGraw-Hill.

Hyde, J. S. (1990). *Understanding human sexuality* (4th ed.). New York: McGraw-Hill.

Hyde, J. S., & Linn, M. C. (1988). Gender differences in verbal ability: A meta-analysis. *Psychological Bulletin, 104,* 53–69.

Ickes, W., & Barnes, R. D. (1977). The role of sex and self-monitoring in unstructured dyadic interactions. *Journal of Personality and Social Psychology, 35,* 315–330.

Ilfeld, F. W. (1977). Current psychosocial stressors and symptoms of depression. *American Journal of Psychiatry, 134,* 161–166.

Ineichen, B. (1979). The social geography of marriage. In M. Cook & G. Wilson (Eds.), *Love and attraction*. New York: Pergamon Press.

Infante, D. A., & Rancer, A. S. (1982). A conceptualization and measure of argumentativeness. *Journal of Personality Assessment, 46,* 72–80.

Inhelder, B., & Piaget, J. (1958). *The growth of logical thinking from childhood to adolescence*. New York: Basic Books.

Isherwood, J., Adam, K. S., & Hornblow, A. R. (1982). Readjustment, desirability, expectedness, mastery and outcome dimensions of life stress suicide attempt and auto-accident. *Journal of Human Stress, 8*(1), 11–18.

Ivancevich, J. M., Matteson, M. T., Freedman, S. M., & Phillips, J. S. (1990). Worksite stress management interventions. *American Psychologist, 45*(2), 252–261.

Jackman, M. R., & Senter, M. S. (1981). Beliefs about race, gender, and social class: Different, therefore unequal. In D. J. Treiman & R. V. Robinson (Eds.), *Research in stratification and mobility* (Vol. 2). Greenwich, CT: JAI.

Jackson, P. G. (1989). Living together unmarried. In J. M. Henslin (Ed.), *Marriage and family in a changing society* (3rd ed.). New York: Free Press.

Jackson, S., & Schuler, R. (1985). A meta-analysis and conceptual critique of research on role ambiguity and role conflict in work settings. *Organizational Behavior and Human Decision Processes, 36,* 16–78.

Jacob, R. G., & Turner, S. M. (1984). Somatoform disorders. In S. M. Turner & M. Hersen (Eds.), *Adult psychopathology and diagnosis*. New York: Wiley.

Jacobs, J. (1971). *Adolescent suicide*. New York: Wiley Interscience.

Jacobs, T. J., & Charles, E. (1980). Life events and the occurrence of cancer in children. *Psychosomatic Medicine, 42*(1), 11–24.

Jacobson, E. (1938). *Progressive relaxation*. Chicago: University of Chicago Press.

Jacobson, E. (1970). *You must relax*. New York: McGraw-Hill.

Jaffe, J. H. (1986). Opioids. In A. J. Frances, & R. E. Hales (Eds.), *Psychiatric Update: Annual Review* (Vol. 5). Washington, DC: American Psychiatric Press.

Jahoda, M. (1958). *Current concepts of positive mental health*. New York: Basic Books.

Jakubowski-Spector, P. (1973). Facilitating the growth of women through assertive training. *Counseling Psychologist, 4,* 75–86.

Jamison, K. R., Gerner, R. H., Hammen, C., & Padesky, C. (1980). Clouds and silver linings: Positive experiences associated with the primary affective disorders. *American Journal of Psychiatry, 137*(2), 198–202.

Janis, I. L. (1958). *Psychological stress*. New York: Wiley.

Janis, I. L. (1972). *Victims of groupthink*. Boston: Houghton Mifflin.

Janis, I. L. (1973, January). Groupthink. *Yale Alumni Magazine,* 16–19.

Janis, I. L. (1983). Stress inoculation in health care. In D. H. Meichenbaum & M. E. Jaremko (Eds.), *Stress reduction and prevention*. New York: Plenum Press.

Jeffrey, D. B., & Lemnitzer, N. (1981). Diet, exercise, obesity and related health problems: A macroenvironmental analysis. In J. M. Ferguson & C. B. Taylor, *The comprehensive handbook of behavioral medicine: Vol. 2. Syndromes and special areas*. Jamaica, NY: Spectrum.

Jemmott, J. B., III, & Magloire, K. (1988). Academic stress, social support, and secretory Immunoglobin A. *Journal of Personality and Social Psychology, 55*(5), 803–810.

Jeste, D. V., & Wyatt, R. J. (1982). *Understanding and treating tardive dyskinesia*. New York: Guilford Press.

Johnson, D. R., White, L. K., Edwards, J. N., & Booth, A. (1986). Dimensions of marital quality: Toward methodological and conceptual refinement. *Journal of Family Issues, 7,* 31–49.

Johnson, D. W. (1981). *Reaching out: Interpersonal effectiveness and self-actualization*. Englewood Cliffs, NJ: Prentice-Hall.

Johnson, D. W., & Johnson, F. (1975). *Joining together*. Englewood Cliffs, NJ: Prentice-Hall.

Johnson, L. C. (1982). Sleep deprivation and performance. In W. B. Webb (Ed.), *Biological rhythms, sleep and performance*. New York: Wiley.

Johnston, L. D., O'Malley, P. M., & Bachman, J. G. (1987). *National trends in drug use and related factors among American high-school students and young adults, 1975–1986*. Washington, DC: National Institute on Drug Abuse.

Johnston, L. D., O'Malley, P. M., & Bachman, J. G. (1988). *Illicit drug use, smoking, and drinking by America's high-school students, college students, and young adults, 1975–1987*. Washington, DC: National Institute on Drug Abuse.

Jones, E. E. (1964). *Ingratiation*. New York: Appleton-Century-Crofts.

Jones, E. E., & Davis, K. (1965). From acts to dispositions: The attribution process in person perception. In L. Berkowitz (Ed.), *Advances in experimental social psychology* (Vol. 2). New York: Academic Press.

Jones, E. E., & Nisbett, R. E. (1971). *The actor and the observer: Divergent perceptions of the causes of behavior*. Morristown, NJ: General Learning Press.

Jones, E. E., & Pittman, T. S. (1982). Toward a general theory of strategic self-presentation. In J. Suls (Ed.), *Psychological perspectives on the self*. Hillsdale, NJ: Erlbaum.

Jones, E. E., Rhodewalt, F., Berglas, S., & Skelton, J. A. (1981). Effects of strategic self-presentation on subsequent self-esteem. *Journal of Personality and Social Psychology, 41,* 407–421.

Jones, M. C. (1965). Psychological correlates of somatic development. *Child Development, 36,* 899–911.

Jones, R. A., & Brehm, J. W. (1970). Persuasiveness of one- and two-sided communications as a function of awareness there are two sides. *Journal of Experimental Social Psychology, 6,* 47–56.

Jones, R. T. (1978). Marijuana: Human effects. In L. L. Iversen, S. D. Iversen, & S. H. Snyder, *Handbook of psychopharmacology* (Vol. 12). New York: Plenum Press.

Jones, S. C. (1973). Self- and interpersonal evaluations: Esteem theories versus consistency theories. *Psychological Bulletin, 79*(3), 185–199.

Jones, W. H., Briggs, S. R., & Smith, T. G. (1986). Shyness: Conceptualization and measurement. *Journal of Personality and Social Psychology, 51,* 629–639.

Jones, W. H., Freeman, J. A., & Goswick, R. A. (1981). The persistence of loneliness: Self and other determinants. *Journal of Personality, 49,* 27–48.

Jones, W. H., Hobbs, S. A., & Hockenbury, D. (1982). Loneliness and social skill deficits. *Journal of Personality and Social Psychology, 42*(4), 682–689.

Jones-Witters, P., & Witters, W. (1983). *Drugs and society: A biological perspective*. Monterey, CA: Wadsworth Health Sciences.

Jordaan, J. P. (1974). Life stages as organizing modes of career development. In E. L. Herr (Ed.), *Vocational guidance and human development*. Boston: Houghton Mifflin.

Jourard, S. M. (1971). *The transparent self*. New York: Van Nostrand Reinhold.

Jourard, S. M., & Landsman, T. (1980). *Healthy personality: An approach from the viewpoint of humanistic psychology*. New York: Macmillan.

Julien, R. M. (1988). *A primer of drug action*. New York: W. H. Freeman.

Jung, C. G. (1917). On the psychology of the unconscious. In *Collected works* (Vol. 7). Princeton, NJ: Princeton University Press.

Kahn, S., Zimmerman, G., Csikszentmihalyi, M., & Getzels, J. W. (1985). Relations between identity in young adulthood and intimacy at midlife. *Journal of Personality and Social Psychology, 49,* 1316–1322.

Kalant, H., & Kalant, O. J. (1979). Death in amphetamine users: Causes and rates. In D. E. Smith (Ed.), *Amphetamine use, misuse and abuse*. Boston: G. K. Hall.

Kales, A., & Kales, J. D. (1984). *Evaluation and treatment of insomnia*. New York: Oxford University Press.

Kalick, S. M., & Hamilton, T. E., III (1986). The matching hypothesis reexamined. *Journal of Personality and Social Psychology, 51*(4), 673–682.

Kandel, D. B. (1978). Similarity in real-life adolescent friendship pairs. *Journal of Personality and Social Psychology, 36,* 306–312.

Kanin, E. J., Davidson, K. R., & Scheck, S. R. (1970). A research note on male-female differentials in the experience of heterosexual love. *Journal of Sex Research, 6,* 64–72.

Kanner, A. D., Coyne, J. C., Schaefer, C., & Lazarus, R. S. (1981). Comparison of two modes of stress measurement: Daily hassles and uplifts versus major life events. *Journal of Behavioral Medicine, 4,* 1–39.

Kaplan, H. (1983). A woman's view of DSM-III. *American Psychologist, 38,* 786–792.

Kaplan, H. I. (1985). History of psychosomatic medicine. In H. I. Kaplan & B. J. Sadock (Eds.), *Comprehensive textbook of psychiatry/IV* (4th ed.). Baltimore: Williams & Wilkins.

Kaplan, H. S. (1974). *The new sex therapy.* New York: Brunner/Mazel.

Kaplan, H. S. (1979). *Disorders of sexual desire and other new concepts and techniques in sex therapy.* New York: Simon & Schuster.

Kaplan, H. S. (1983). *The evaluation of sexual disorders: Psychological and medical aspects.* New York: Brunner/Mazel.

Kaplan, M. F., & Anderson, N. H. (1973). Information integration theory and reinforcement theory as approaches to interpersonal attraction. *Journal of Personality and Social Psychology, 28,* 301–312.

Karasek, R. A., Jr. (1979). Job demands, job decision latitude, and mental strain: Implications for job redesign. *Administrative Science Quarterly, 24,* 285–308.

Karasek, R. A., Jr., Baker, D., Marxer, F., Ahlbom, A., & Theorell, T. (1981). Job decision latitude, job demands, and cardiovascular disease: A prospective study of Swedish men. *American Journal of Public Health, 71,* 694–705.

Karasek, R. A., Jr., & Theorell, T. (1990). *Healthy work: Stress, productivity, and the reconstruction of working life.* New York: Basic Books.

Karlen, A. (1971). *Sexuality and homosexuality.* New York: Norton.

Karson, C. N., Kleinman, J. E., & Wyatt, R. J. (1986). Biochemical concepts of schizophrenia. In T. Millon & G. L. Klerman (Eds.), *Contemporary directions in psychopathology.* New York: Guilford Press.

Kass, F., Spitzer, R. L., Williams, J. B. W., & Widiger, T. (1989). Self-defeating personality disorder and DSM-III-R: Development of the diagnostic criteria. *American Journal of Psychiatry, 146,* 1022–1026.

Kastenbaum, R. (1985). Dying and death: A life-span approach. In J. E. Birren & K. W. Schaie (Eds.), *Handbook of the psychology of aging* (2nd ed.). New York: Van Nostrand Reinhold.

Kastenbaum, R. (1986). *Death, dying, and human experience.* Columbus, OH: Charles E. Merrill.

Kauffman, D. R., & Steiner, I. D. (1968). Conformity as an ingratiation technique. *Journal of Experimental Social Psychology, 4,* 404–414.

Kausler, D. H. (1985). Episodic memory: Memorizing performance. In N. Charness (Ed.), *Aging and human performance.* Chichester, England: Wiley.

Kavesh, L., & Lavin, C. (1988). *Tales from the front.* New York: Doubleday.

Kazdin, A. E. (1982). History of behavior modification. In A. S. Bellack, M. Hersen, & A. E. Kazdin (Eds.), *International handbook of behavior modification and behavior therapy.* New York: Plenum Press.

Kazdin, A. E. & Wilson, G. T. (1978). *Evaluation of behavior therapy: Issues, evidence and research strategies.* Cambridge, MA: Ballinger.

Keesey, R. E., & Powley, T. L. (1975). Hypothalamic regulation of body weight. *American Scientist, 63,* 558–565.

Keesey, R. E., & Powley, T. L. (1986). The regulation of body weight. In M. R. Rosenzweig & L. W. Porter (Eds.), *Annual review of psychology: 1986* (Vol. 37). Palo Alto, CA: Annual Reviews.

Keinan, G. (1987). Decision making under stress: Scanning of alternatives under controllable and uncontrollable threats. *Journal of Personality and Social Psychology, 52*(3), 639–644.

Keith, P. M. (1986). The social context and resources of the unmarried in old age. *International Journal of Aging and Human Development, 23*(2), 81–96.

Kelley, H. H. (1950). The warm-cold dimension in first impressions of persons. *Journal of Personality, 18,* 431–439.

Kelley, H. H. (1967). Attribution theory in social psychology. In D. Levine (Ed.), *Nebraska Symposium on Motivation* (Vol. 15). Lincoln: University of Nebraska Press.

Kelley, H. H., & Thibaut, J. W. (1978). *Interpersonal relations: A theory of interdependence.* New York: Wiley-Interscience.

Kelley, K., Byrne, D., Przybyla, D. P. J., Eberly, C., Eberly, B., Greendlinger, V., Wan, C. K., & Gorsky, J. (1985). Chronic self-destructiveness: Conceptualization, measurement and initial validation of the construct. *Motivation and Emotion, 9*(2), 135–151.

Kennedy, J. L., & Laramore, D. (1988). *Joyce Lain Kennedy's career book.* Lincolnwood, IL: VGM Career Horizons.

Kenny, D. A., & Zaccaro, S. J. (1983). An estimate of variance due to traits in leadership. *Journal of Applied Psychology, 68,* 678–685.

Kenrick, D. T. (1987). Gender, genes, and the social environment. In P. C. Shaver & C. Hendrick (Eds.), *Review of Personality and Social Psychology* (Vol. 8). Beverly Hills, CA: Sage Publications.

Kessler-Harris, A. (1982). *Out to work: A history of wage-earning women in the United States.* New York: Oxford University Press.

Keyes, R. (1980). We, the lonely people. In J. Hartog, J. R. Audy, & Y. A. Cohen (Eds.), *The anatomy of loneliness.* New York: International Universities Press.

Kiecolt-Glaser, J. K., Garner, W., Speicher, C., Penn, G. M., Holliday, J., & Glaser, R. (1984). Psychosocial modifiers of immunocompetence in medical students. *Psychosomatic Medicine, 46*(1), 7–14.

Kieffer, J. A. (1982). So much for the great American dream of retiring early. *Generations, 6*(4), 7–9.

Kiesler, D. J. (1986). The 1982 interpersonal circle: An analysis of DSM-III personality disorders. In T. Millon & G. L. Klerman (Eds.), *Contemporary directions in psychopathology: Toward the DSM-IV.* New York: Guilford Press.

Kiesler, S. B., & Baral, R. L. (1970). The search for a romantic partner: The effects of self-esteem and physical attractiveness on romantic behavior. In K. J. Gergen & D. Marlowe (Eds.), *Personality and social behavior.* Reading, MA: Addison-Wesley.

Kinsbourne, M. (1980). If sex differences in brain lateralization exist, they have yet to be discovered. *Behavioral and Brain Sciences, 3,* 241–242.

Kinsey, A. C., Pomeroy, W. B., & Martin, C. E. (1948). *Sexual behavior in the human male.* Philadelphia: Saunders.

Kinsey, A. C., Pomeroy, W. B., Martin, C. E., & Gebhard, P. H. (1953). *Sexual behavior in the human female.* Philadelphia: Saunders.

Kinsman, R. A., Dirks, J. F., & Jones, N. F. (1982). Psychomaintenance of chronic physical illness: Clinical assessment of personal styles affecting medical management. In T. Millon, C. Green, & R. Meagher (Eds.), *Handbook of clinical health psychology.* New York: Plenum Press.

Kirby, D. F., & Julian, N. B. (1981). Treatment of women in high school history textbooks. *Social Studies, 72,* 203–207.

Kitson, G. C., & Sussman, M. B. (1982). Marital complaints, demographic characteristics, and symptoms of mental distress in divorce. *Journal of Marriage and the Family, 44,* 87–101.

Klassen, M. (1987). How to get the most out of your time. In A. D. Timpe (Ed.), *The management of time.* New York: Facts On File.

Kleber, H. D., & Gawin, F. H. (1986). Cocaine. In A. J. Frances & R. E. Hales (Eds.), *Psychiatric Update: Annual Review* (Vol. 5). Washington, DC: American Psychiatric Press.

Klein, M. (1948). *Contributions to psychoanalysis.* London: Hogarth.

Kleinke, C. L. (1986). Gaze and eye contact: A research review. *Psychological Bulletin, 100,* 78–100.

Kleinmuntz, B. (1980). *Essentials of abnormal psychology.* San Francisco: Harper & Row.

Klerman, G. L. (1978). Long-term treatment of affective disorders. In M. A. Lipton, A. DiMascio, & K. F. Killam (Eds.), *Psychopharmacology: A generation of progress.* New York: Raven.

Klerman, G. L., & Weissman, M. M. (1986). The interpersonal approach to understanding depression. In T. Millon & G. L. Klerman (Eds.), *Contemporary directions in psychopathology: Toward the DSM-IV.* New York: Guilford Press.

Klineberg, O. (1938). Emotional expression in Chinese literature. *Journal of Abnormal and Social Psychology, 33,* 517–520.

Kluft, R. P. (1987). Making the diagnosis of multiple personality disorder. In F. Flach (Ed.), *Diagnostics and psychopathology.* New York: Norton.

Knittle, J. L., & Hirsch, J. (1968). Effect of early nutrition on the development of rat epididymal fat pads: Cellularity and metabolism. *Journal of Clinical Investigation, 47,* 209.

Knoth, R., Boyd, K., & Singer, B. (1988). Empirical tests of sexual selection theory: Predictions of sex differences in onset, intensity, and time course of sexual arousal. *Journal of Sex Research, 24,* 73–89.

Knox, D., & Wilson, K. (1981). Dating behaviors of university students. *Family Relations, 30,* 255–258.

Knussman, R., Christiansen, K., & Couwenbergs, C. (1986). Relations between sex hormone levels and sexual behavior in men. *Archives of Sexual Behavior, 15*(5), 429–445.

Kobasa, S. C. (1979). Stressful life events, personality, and health: An inquiry into hardiness. *Journal of Personality and Social Psychology, 37,* 1–11.

Kobasa, S. C. (1984, September). How much stress can you survive? *American Health,* 64–77.

Kobasa, S. C., Maddi, S. R., & Kahn, S. (1982). Hardiness and health: A prospective study. *Journal of Personality and Social Psychology, 42*(1), 168–177.

Kogan, N., & Wallach, M. (1964). *Risk taking: A study in cognition and personality.* New York: Holt, Rinehart & Winston.

Kohen, A. I. (1975). Occupational mobility among middle-aged men. In U.S. Department of Labor, Manpower R&D, Monograph 15, *The preretirement years: Vol. 4. A longitudinal study of the labor market experience of men.* Washington, DC: U.S. Government Printing Office.

Kohlberg, L. (1966). A cognitive-developmental analysis of children's sex-role concepts and attitudes. In E. E. Maccoby (Ed.), *The development of sex differences.* Stanford, CA: Stanford University Press.

Kohut, H. (1971). *Analysis of the self.* New York: International Universities Press.

Kolodny, R. C., Masters, W. H., & Johnson, V. E. (1979). *Textbook of sexual medicine.* Boston: Little, Brown.

Kolodny, R. C., Masters, W. H., Kolodner, R. M., & Toro, G. (1974). Depression of plasma testosterone levels after chronic intensive marijuana use. *New England Journal of Medicine, 291,* 872–874.

Komarovsky, M. (1976). *Dilemmas of masculinity.* New York: Norton.

Komarovsky, M. (1977). The effects of poverty upon marriage. In J. E. DeBurger (Ed.), *Marriage today: Problems, issues, and alternatives.* Cambridge, MA: Schenkman.

Koocher, G. P. (1971). Swimming, social competence, and personality change. *Journal of Personality and Social Psychology, 18,* 275–278.

Koplan, J. P., Powell, K. E., Sikes, R. K., Shirley, R. W., & Campbell, C. C. (1982). An epidemiologic study of the benefits and risks of running. *Journal of the American Medical Association, 248*(23), 3118–3121.

Korchin, S. J. (1976). *Modern clinical psychology: Principles of intervention in the clinic and community.* New York: Basic Books.

Koss, M. P., Gidycz, C. A., & Wisniewski, N. (1987). The scope of rape: Incidence and prevalence of sexual aggression and victimization in a national sample of higher education students. *Journal of Consulting and Clinical Psychology, 55,* 162–170.

Kotkin, M. (1985). To marry or live together? *Lifestyles: A Journal of Changing Patterns, 7*(3), 156–170.

Kraemer, D. L., & Hastrup, J. L. (1988). Crying in adults: Self-control and autonomic correlates. *Journal of Social and Clinical Psychology, 6*(1), 53–68.

Kramer, B. A. (1985). Use of ECT in California, 1977–1983. *American Journal of Psychiatry, 142*(10), 1190–1192.

Kramer, M. A., Aral, S. O., & Curran, J. W. (1980). Self-reported behavior pattern of patients attending a sexually transmitted disease clinic. *American Journal of Public Health, 70,* 997–1000.

Krantz, D. L. (1977). The Santa Fe experience: In search of a new life—radical career change in a special place. In S. B. Sarason (Ed.), *Work, aging, and social change: Professionals and the one life—one career imperative.* New York: Free Press.

Krantz, D. S., Baum, A., & Wideman, M. V. (1980). Assessment of preferences for self-treatment and information in health care. *Journal of Personality and Social Psychology, 39,* 977–990.

Krantz, D. S., Glass, D. C., Contrada, R., & Miller, N. E. (1981). *Behavior and health: National Science Foundation's second five-year outlook on science and technology.* Washington, DC: U.S. Government Printing Office.

Krasner, L., & Ullmann, L. P. (Eds.). (1965). *Research in behavior modification.* New York: Holt, Rinehart & Winston.

Kravitz, D. A. & Martin, B. (1986). Ringelmann rediscovered: The original article. *Journal of Personality and Social Psychology, 50,* 936–941.

Krilov, L. R. (1988, March). Sexually transmitted diseases in adolescents. *Medical Aspects of Human Sexuality,* 67–77.

Krueger, D. W. (1981). Stressful life events and the return to heroin use. *Journal of Human Stress, 7*(2), 3–8.

Krueger, W. C. F. (1929). The effect of overlearning on retention. *Journal of Experimental Psychology, 12,* 71–78.

Kübler-Ross, E. (1969). *On death and dying.* New York: Macmillan.

Kübler-Ross, E. (1970). The dying patient's point of view. In O. G. Brim, Jr., H. E. Freeman, S. Levine, & N. A. Scotch (Eds.), *The dying patient.* New York: Russell Sage Foundation.

Kuehnle, J., Mendelson, J. H., Davis, K. R., & New, P. F. J. (1977). Computerized tomographic examination of heavy marijuana smokers. *Journal of the American Medical Association, 237,* 1231–1232.

Kutash, S. B. (1976). Modified psychoanalytic therapies. In B. B. Wolman (Ed.), *The therapist's handbook: Treatment methods of mental disorders.* New York: Van Nostrand Reinhold.

Kyle, G. R. (1989). Philosophos: AIDS and the new sexual order. *Journal of Sex Research, 26,* 276–278.

Lader, M. H. (1984). Antianxiety drugs. In T. B. Karasu (Ed.), *The psychiatric therapies.* Washington, DC: American Psychiatric Association.

Lafontaine, E., & Tredeau, L. (1986). The frequency, sources, and correlates of sexual harassment among women in traditional male occupations. *Sex Roles, 15,* 433–442.

LaFrance, M., & Mayo, C. (1976). Racial differences in gaze behavior during conversations: Two systematic observational studies. *Journal of Personality and Social Psychology, 33,* 547–552.

Lakein, A. (1973). *How to get control of your time and your life.* New York: Peter H. Wyden.

Lal, N. Ahuja, R. C., & Madhukar. (1982). Life events in hypertensive patients. *Journal of Psychosomatic Research, 26*(4), 441–445.

Landau, E. (1988). *Teenagers talk about school.* Englewood Cliffs, NJ: Julian Messner.

Landers, A. D. (1977). The menstrual experience. In E. Donelson & J. Gullahorn (Eds.), *Women: A psychological perspective.* New York: Wiley.

Landy, D., & Sigall, H. (1974). Beauty is talent. *Journal of Personality and Social Psychology, 29,* 299–304.

Landy, F. J. (1989). *Psychology of work behavior.* Pacific Grove, CA: Brooks/Cole.

Lange, A. J., & Jakubowski, P. (1976). *Responsible assertive behavior.* Champaign, IL: Research Press.

Langlois, J. H., & Downs, A. C. (1980). Mothers, fathers, and peers as socialization agents of sex-typed play behaviors in young children. *Child Development, 51,* 1237–1247.

Lareau, W. (1985). *Inside track: A successful job search strategy.* Piscataway, NJ: New Century.

Larwood, L., & Gattiker, U. (1984, August). *A comparison of the career paths used by successful men and women.* Paper presented at the meeting of the American Psychological Association, Toronto, Ontario.

Latané, B. (1981). The psychology of social impact. *American Psychologist, 36,* 343–356.

Latané, B., & Nida, S. A. (1981). Ten years of research on group size and helping. *Psychological Bulletin, 89,* 308–324.

Latané, B., Williams, K., & Harkins, S. (1979). Many hands make light the work: The causes and consequences of social loafing. *Journal of Personality and Social Psychology, 37,* 822–832.

Latham, G., & Yukl, G. (1975). Assigned vs. participative goal setting with educated and uneducated woods workers. *Journal of Applied Psychology, 60,* 299–302.

Laughlin, H. (1967). *The neuroses.* Washington, DC: Butterworth.

Laughlin, H. (1979). *The ego and its defenses.* New York: Aronson.

Lavine, L. O., & Lombardo, J. P. (1984). Self-disclosure: Intimate and non-intimate disclosures to parents and best friends as a function of Bem sex-role category. *Sex Roles, 11,* 735–744.

Lawson, E. D. (1971). Hair color, personality, and the observer. *Psychological Reports, 28,* 311–322.

Lazarus, A. A. (1989). Multimodal therapy. In R. J. Corsini & D. Wedding (Eds.), *Current psychotherapies.* Itasca, IL: F. E. Peacock.

Lazarus, A. A., & Fay, A. (1984). Behavior therapy. In T. B. Karasu (Ed.), *The psychiatric therapies.* Washington, DC: American Psychiatric Association.

Lazarus, A. A., & Wilson, G. T. (1976). Behavior modification: Clinical and experimental perspectives. In B. B. Wolman (Ed.), *The therapist's handbook: Treatment methods of mental disorders.* New York: Van Nostrand Reinhold.

Lazarus, R. S., & Folkman, S. (1984). *Stress, appraisal and coping.* New York: Springer.

Leavitt, F. (1982). *Drugs and behavior.* New York: Wiley.

Leavy, R. L. (1983). Social support and psychological disorder: A review. *Journal of Community Psychology, 11,* 3–21.

Lebov, M. (1980). *Practical tools & techniques for managing time.* Englewood Cliffs, NJ: Prentice-Hall.

Leff, J., & Vaughn, C. (1981). The role of maintenance therapy and relatives' expressed emotion in relapse of schizophrenia: A two-year follow-up. *British Journal of Psychiatry, 139,* 102–104.

Leff, J., & Vaughn, C. (1985). *Expressed emotion in families.* New York: Guilford Press.

Lehmann, H. E. (1985). Current perspectives on the biology of schizophrenia. In M. N. Menuck & M. V. Seeman (Eds.), *New perspectives in schizophrenia.* New York: Macmillan.

Lehmann, H. E., & Cancro, R. (1985). Schizophrenia: Clinical features. In H. I. Kaplan & B. J. Sadock (Eds.), *Comprehensive textbook of psychiatry/IV* (4th ed.). Baltimore: Williams & Wilkins.

Lehne, G. K. (1976). Homophobia among men. In D. S. David & R. Brannon (Eds.), *The forty-nine percent majority: The male sex role.* Reading, MA: Addison-Wesley.

Lehrer, P. M., & Woolfolk, R. L. (1984). Are stress reduction techniques interchangeable, or do they have specific effects? A review of the comparative empirical literature. In R. L. Woolfolk & P. M. Lehrer (Eds.), *Principles and practice of stress management.* New York: Guilford Press.

Leigh, B. C. (1989). Reasons for having and avoiding sex: Gender, sexual orientation, and relationship to sexual behavior. *Journal of Sex Research, 26*(2), 299–309.

Leitenberg, H. (1976). Behavioral approaches to the treatment of neuroses. In H. Leitenberg (Ed.), *Handbook of behavior modification and behavior therapy.* Englewood Cliffs, NJ: Prentice-Hall.

LeMasters, E. E. (1977). *Parents in modern America.* Homewood, IL: Dorsey Press.

Lemkau, J. P. (1979). Personality and background characteristics of women in male-dominated occupations: A review. *Psychology of Women Quarterly, 4,* 221–240.

Lemon, B. W., Bengston, V. L., & Peterson, J. A. (1982). An exploration of the activity theory of aging: Activity types and life satisfaction among inmovers to a retirement community. *Journal of Gerontology, 27,* 511–523.

Lerner, M. J., & Miller, D. T. (1976). Deserving and the emergence of forms of justice. In L.

Berkowitz (Ed.), *Advances in experimental social psychology* (Vol. 9). New York: Academic Press.

LeShan, L. (1966). An emotional life-history pattern associated with neoplastic disease. *Annals of the New York Academy of Sciences, 125,* 780–793.

Lesnik-Oberstein, M., & Cohen, L. (1984). Cognitive style, sensation seeking and assortative mating. *Journal of Personality and Social Psychology, 46*(1), 112–117.

Levay, A. N., Weissberg, J. H., & Woods, S. M. (1981). Intrapsychic factors in sexual dysfuctions. In H. I. Lief (Ed.), *Sexual problems in medical practice.* Chicago: American Medical Association.

Levenson, H., Hirschfeld, M. L., Hirschfeld, A., & Dzubay, B. (1983). Recent life events and accidents: The role of sex differences. *Journal of Human Stress, 9*(1), 4–11.

Leventhal, H. (1970). Findings and theory in the study of fear communications. In L. Berkowitz (Ed.), *Advances in experimental social psychology* (Vol. 5). New York: Academic Press.

Levering, R. (1988). *A great place to work.* New York: Random House.

Levin, R. J., & Levin, A. (1975, September). Sexual pleasure: The surprising preferences of 100,000 women. *Redbook, 145,* 51ff.

LeVine, R. A., & White, M. (1987). Parenthood in social transformation. In J. B. Lancaster, J. Altmann, A. S. Rossi, & L. R. Sherrod (Eds.), *Parenting across the life span: Biosocial dimensions.* New York: Aldine de Gruyter.

Levinger, G. (1970). Husbands' and wives' estimates of coital frequency. *Medical Aspects of Human Sexuality, 4,* 42–57.

Levinger, G., & Snoek, D. J. (1972). *Attraction in relationships: A new look at interpersonal attraction.* Morristown, NJ: General Learning Press.

Levinson, D. J. (1985). The life cycle. In H. I. Kaplan & B. J. Sadock (Eds.), *Comprehensive textbook of psychiatry/IV* (Vol. 1, 4th ed.). Baltimore: Williams & Wilkins.

Levinson, D. J. (1986). A conception of adult development. *American Psychologist, 41,* 3–13.

Levinson, D. J., Darrow, C. M., Klein, E. G., Levinson, M. H., & McKee, B. (1974). The psychosocial development of men in early adulthood and the midlife transition. In D. F. Ricks, A. Thomas, & M. Roff (Eds.), *Life history research in psychopathology* (Vol. 3). Minneapolis: University of Minnesota Press.

Levinson, D. J., Darrow, C. M., Klein, E. G., Levinson, M. H., & McKee, B. (1978). *The seasons of a man's life.* New York: Knopf.

Levitin, T., Quinn, R. P., & Staines, G. L. (1971). Sex discrimination against the American working woman. *American Behavioral Scientist, 15,* 237–254.

Lewin, K. (1935). *A dynamic theory of personality.* New York: McGraw-Hill.

Lewine, R. J., Fogg, L., & Meltzer, H. Y. (1983). Assessment of negative and positive symptoms in schizophrenia. *Schizophrenia Bulletin, 9,* 968–976.

Lewinsohn, P. M. (1974). A behavioral approach to depression. In R. J. Friedman & M. M. Katz (Eds.), *The psychology of depression: Contemporary theory and research.* New York: Halsted.

Lewinsohn, P. M., Duncan, E. M., Stanton, A. K., & Hautzinger, M. (1986). Age at first onset for nonbipolar depression. *Journal of Abnormal Psychology, 95*(4), 378–383.

Lewis, J. M. (1988). The transition to parenthood: II. Stability and change in marital structure. *Family Process, 27,* 273–283.

Lewis, J. M., Owen, M. T., & Cox, M. J. (1988). The transition to parenthood: III. Incorporation of the child into the family. *Family Process, 27,* 411–421.

Lewis, R. A. (1986). Men's changing roles in marriage and the family. *Marriage and Family Review, 9*(3/4), 1–10.

Lewis, R. J., & Janda, L. H. (1988). The relationship between adult sexual adjustment and childhood experiences regarding exposure to nudity, sleeping in the parental bed, and parental attitudes toward sexuality. *Archives of Sexual Behavior, 17*(4), 349–362.

Lichtenstein, E. (1980). *Psychotherapy: Approaches and applications.* Pacific Grove, CA: Brooks/Cole.

Lickey, M. E., & Gordon, B. (1983). *Drugs for mental illness: A revolution in psychiatry.* San Francisco: W. H. Freeman.

Lieblich, A. (1986). Successful career women at midlife: Crises and transitions. *International Journal of Aging and Human Development, 23,* 301–312.

Liem, R., & Rayman, P. (1982). Health and social costs of unemployment. *American Psychologist, 37,* 1116–1123.

Lindgren, H. C. (1969). *The psychology of college success: A dynamic approach.* New York: Wiley.

Linn, M. C., & Hyde, J. S. (1989). Gender, mathematics, and science. *Educational Researcher, 18*(8), 17–19, 22–27.

Linn, M. C., & Petersen, A. C. (1986). A meta-analysis of gender differences in spatial ability: Implications for mathematics and science achievement. In J. S. Hyde & M. C. Linn (Eds.), *The psychology of gender: Advances through meta-analysis.* Baltimore: Johns Hopkins University Press.

Lipman, B. E. (1983). *The personal job search program: How to market yourself.* New York: Wiley.

Litwack, M., & Resnick, M. R. (1984). *The art of self-fulfillment.* New York: Simon & Schuster.

Livson, F. B. (1976). Patterns of personality development in middle-aged women: A longitudinal study. *International Journal of Aging and Human Development, 7,* 107–115.

Lloyd, C., Alexander, A. A., Rice, D. G., & Greenfield, N. S. (1980). Life events as predictors of academic performance. *Journal of Human Stress, 6*(3), 15–26.

Lloyd, M. A. (1985). *Adolescence.* New York: Harper & Row.

Lock, R. D. (1988). *Taking charge of your career direction: Career planning guide, Book I.* Pacific Grove, CA: Brooks/Cole.

Locke, E. A. (1983). The nature and causes of job satisfaction. In M. D. Dunnette (Ed.), *Handbook of industrial and organizational psychology.* New York: Wiley.

Locksley, A., & Colten, M. E. (1979). Psychological androgyny: A case of mistaken identity? *Journal of Personality and Social Psychology, 37,* 1017–1031.

Loehlin, J. C., Willerman, L., & Horn, J. M. (1988). Human behavior genetics. In M. R. Rosenzweig & L. W. Porter (Eds.), *Annual Review of Psychology: 1988* (Vol. 39). Palo Alto, CA: Annual Reviews.

Lombardo, J., & Lavine, L. (1981). Sex-role stereotyping and patterns of self-disclosure. *Sex Roles, 7,* 403–411.

London, K. A., & Wilson, B. F. (1988). Divorce. *American Demographics, 10*(10), 22–26.

Lonetto, R., & Templer, D. I. (1983). The nature of death anxiety. In C. D. Spielberger & J. N. Butcher (Eds.), *Advances in personality assessment* (Vol. 3). Hillsdale, NJ: Erlbaum.

Longman, D. G., & Atkinson, R. H. (1988). *College learning and study skills.* New York: West.

LoPiccolo, J., & Daiss, S. (1987). Assessment of sexual dysfunction. In K. D. O'Leary (Ed.), *Assessment of marital discord: An integration for research and clinical practice.* Hillsdale, NJ: Erlbaum.

LoPiccolo, J., & Lobitz, C. (1972). The role of masturbation in the treatment of sexual dysfunction. *Archives of Sex Research, 2,* 163–171.

Lott, B. (1981). A feminist critique of androgyny: Toward the elimination of gender attributions for learned behavior. In C. Mayo & N. M. Henley (Eds.), *Gender and nonverbal behavior.* New York: Springer-Verlag.

Lott, B. (1987). *Women's lives.* Pacific Grove, CA: Brooks/Cole.

Lowe, C. A., & Goldstein, J. W. (1970). Reciprocal liking and attributions of ability: Mediating effects of perceived intent and personal involvement. *Journal of Personality and Social Psychology, 16,* 291–297.

Lowenthal, M. F. (1975). *Four stages of life: A comparative study of women and men facing transitions.* San Francisco: Josscy-Bass.

Lowry, D. T., & Towles, D. E. (1989). Soap opera portrayals of sex, contraception, and sexually transmitted diseases. *Journal of Communication, 39*(2), 76–83.

Luborsky, L., Crits-Christoph, P., Mintz, J., & Auerbach, A. (1988). *Who will benefit from psychotherapy?* New York: Basic Books.

Luborsky, L., Singer, B., & Luborsky, L. (1975). Comparative studies of psychotherapies: Is it true that everyone has won and all must have prizes? *Archives of General Psychiatry, 32,* 995–1008.

Luker, K. C. (1975). *Taking chances: Abortion and the decision not to contracept.* Berkeley: University of California Press.

Lumsdaine, A., & Janis, I. (1953). Resistance to counterpropaganda presentation. *Public Opinion Quarterly, 17,* 311–318.

Lustman, P. J., & Sowa, C. J. (1983). Comparative efficacy of biofeedback and stress inoculation for stress reduction. *Journal of Clinical Psychology, 31,* 191–197.

Luthe, W. (1962). Method, research and application of autogenic training. *American Journal of Clinical Hypnosis, 5,* 17–23.

Lyman, B., Hatlelid, D., & Macurdy, C. (1981). Stimulus-person cues in first-impression attraction. *Perceptual and Motor Skills, 52,* 59–66.

Maccoby, E. E., & Jacklin, C. N. (1974). *The psychology of sex differences.* Stanford, CA: Stanford University Press.

Maccoby, E. E., & Martin, J. A. (1983). Socialization in the context of the family: Parent-child interaction. In P. H. Mussen (Series Ed.) & E. M. Hetherington (Vol. Ed.), *Handbook of child psychology: Vol. 4. Socialization, personality, and social development.* New York: Wiley.

Machlowitz, M. M. (1980). *Workaholics: Living with them, working with them.* Reading, MA: Addison-Wesley.

Machung, A. (1989). Talking career, thinking job: Gender differences in career and family expectations of Berkeley seniors. *Family Studies, 15,* 35–58.

Mackenzie, R. A. (1972). *The time trap.* Amacom.

Macklin, E. D. (1983). Nonmarital heterosexual cohabitation: An overview. In E. D. Macklin & R. H. Rubin (Eds.), *Contemporary families and alternative lifestyles: Handbook on research and theory.* Beverly Hills, CA: Sage Publications.

Macklin, E. D. (1987). Nontraditional family forms. In M. B. Sussman & S. K. Steinmetz (Eds.), *Handbook of marriage and the family*. New York: Plenum Press.

Maddock, J. W. (1989). Healthy family sexuality: Positive principles for educators and clinicians. *Family Relations, 38*, 130–136.

Mahoney, M. J. (1979). *Self-change: Strategies for solving personal problems*. New York: Norton.

Major, B. (1981). Gender patterns in touching behavior. In C. Mayo & N. M. Henley (Eds.), *Gender and nonverbal behavior*. New York: Springer-Verlag.

Malamuth, N., & Donnerstein, E. (1982). The effects of aggressive-pornographic mass media stimuli. In L. Berkowitz (Ed.), *Advances in Experimental Social Psychology* (Vol. 15). New York: Academic Press.

Malamuth, N. M. (1984). Violence against women: Cultural and individual cases. In N. M. Malamuth & E. Donnerstein *Pornography and sexual aggression*. New York: Academic Press.

Malatesta, V. J., & Adams, H. E. (1984). The sexual dysfunctions. In H. E. Adams & P. B. Sutker (Eds.), *Comprehensive handbook of psychopathology*. New York: Plenum Press.

Malmo, R. B. (1975). *On emotions, needs and our archaic brain*. New York: Holt, Rinehart & Winston.

Mandler, G. (1982). Stress and thought processes. In L. Goldberger & S. Breznitz (Eds.), *Handbook of stress: Theoretical and clinical aspects*. New York: Free Press.

Marcia, J. E. (1976). *Studies in ego identity*. Unpublished monograph: Simon Fraser University, Burnaby, British Columbia.

Marcia, J. E. (1980). Identity in adolescence. In J. Adelson (Ed.), *Handbook of adolescent psychology*. New York: Wiley.

Maricle, R., Leung, P., & Bloom, J. D. (1987). The use of DSM-III axis III in recording physical illness in psychiatric patients. *American Journal of Psychiatry, 144*(11), 1484–1486.

Marini, M. M. (1978). Sex differences in the determination of adolescent aspirations: A review of research. *Sex Roles, 4*, 723–753.

Markman, H. J. (1981). Prediction of marital distress: A 5-year follow-up. *Journal of Consulting and Clinical Psychology, 49*, 760–762.

Marks, G. (1984). Thinking one's abilities are unique and one's opinions are common. *Personality and Social Psychology Bulletin, 10*(2), 203–208.

Marks, I. (1977). Phobias and obsessions: Clinical phenomena in search of laboratory models. In J. D. Maser & M. E. P. Seligman (Eds.), *Psychopathology: Experimental models*. San Francisco: W. H. Freeman.

Marks, I. M. (1987). *Fears, phobias, and rituals: Panic, anxiety, and their disorders*. New York: Oxford University Press.

Marlatt, G. A., & Rose, F. (1980). Addictive disorders. In A. E. Kazdin, A. S. Bellack, & M. Hersen (Eds.), *New perspectives in abnormal psychology*. New York: Oxford University Press.

Marotz-Baden, R., & Cowan, D. (1987). Mothers-in-law and daughters-in-law: The effects of proximity on conflict and stress. *Family Relations, 36*, 385–390.

Marsh, H. W., & Parker, J. W. (1984). Determinants of student self-concept: Is it better to be a relatively large fish in a small pond even if you don't learn to swim well? *Journal of Personality and Social Psychology, 47*(1), 213–231.

Marsh, P. (Ed.). (1988). *Eye to eye: How people interact*. Topsfield, MA: Salem House.

Marshall, J., & Cooper, C. L. (1981). The causes of managerial stress: A research note on methods and initial findings. In E. N. Corlett & J. Richardson (Eds.), *Stress, work, design, and productivity*. Chichester, England: Wiley.

Martin, B. (1971). *Anxiety and neurotic disorders*. New York: Wiley.

Martin, C. L. (1987). A ratio measure of sex stereotyping. *Journal of Personality and Social Psychology, 52*, 489–499.

Martin, C. L., & Halverson, C. F., Jr. (1981). A schematic processing model of sex typing and stereotyping in children. *Child Development, 52*, 1119–1134.

Martin, R. A., & Lefcourt, H. M. (1983). Sense of humor as a moderator of the relation between stressors and moods. *Journal of Personality and Social Psychology, 45*(6), 1313–1324.

Martinson, F. M. (1980). Childhood sexuality. In B. B. Wolman & J. Money (Eds.), *Handbook of human sexuality*. Englewood Cliffs, NJ: Prentice-Hall.

Maslach, C. (1982). Understanding burnout: Definitional issues in analyzing a complex phenomenon. In W. S. Paine (Ed.), *Job stress and burnout: Research, theory and intervention perspectives*. Beverly Hills, CA: Sage Publications.

Maslow, A. (1968). *Toward a psychology of being*. New York: Van Nostrand.

Maslow, A. (1970). *Motivation and personality*. New York: Harper & Row.

Mason, J. W. (1975). A historical view of the stress field, Part II. *Journal of Human Stress, 1*, 22–36.

Masters, W. H., & Johnson, V. E. (1966). *Human sexual response*. Boston: Little, Brown.

Masters, W. H., & Johnson, V. E. (1970). *Human sexual inadequacy* (1st ed.). Boston: Little, Brown.

Masters, W. H., & Johnson, V. E. (1980). *Human sexual inadequacy* (2nd ed.). New York: Bantam Books.

Masters, W. H., Johnson, V. E., & Kolodny, R. C. (1988). *Human sexuality*. Glenview, IL: Scott, Foresman.

Mathes, E. (1975). The effects of physical attractiveness and anxiety on heterosexual attraction over a series of five encounters. *Journal of Marriage and the Family, 37*, 769–774.

Matteson, M. T., & Ivancevich, J. M. (1987). *Controlling work stress: Effective human resource and management strategies*. San Francisco: Jossey-Bass.

Mattessich, P., & Hill, R. (1987). Life cycle and family development. In M. B. Sussman & S. K. Steinmetz (Eds.), *Handbook of marriage and the family*. New York: Plenum Press.

Matthews, K. A. (1982). Psychological perspectives on the Type-A behavior pattern. *Psychological Bulletin, 91*, 293–323.

Matthews, K. A., & Rodin, J. (1989). Women's changing work roles: Impact on health, family, and public policy. *American Psychologist, 44*(11), 1389–1393.

Matthews, K. A., Scheier, M. F., Brunson, B. I., & Carducci, B. (1989). Why do unpredictable events lead to reports of physical symptoms? In T. W. Miller (Ed.), *Stressful life events*. Madison, CT: International Universities Press.

Mayer, J. (1980). The bitter truth about sugar. In C. Borg (Ed.), *Annual editions: Readings in health*. Guilford, CN: Dushkin.

Mayo, C., & Henley, N. (1981). *Gender and nonverbal behavior*. New York: Springer-Verlag.

McAllister, W. R., McAllister, D. E., Scoles, M. T., & Hampton, S. R. (1986). Persistence of fear-reducing behavior: Relevance for the conditioning theory of neurosis. *Journal of Abnormal Psychology, 95*(4), 365–372.

McCann, C. D., & Hancock, R. D. (1983). Self-monitoring in communicative interactions: Social cognitive consequences of goal-directed message modification. *Journal of Experimental Social Psychology, 19*, 109–121.

McCann, I. L., & Holmes, D. S. (1984). Influence of aerobic exercise on depression. *Journal of Personality and Social Psychology, 46*(5), 1142–1147.

McCary, J. L. (1971). *Sexual myths and fallacies*. New York: Schocken Books.

McCrae, R. (1984). Situational determinants of coping responses: Loss, threat and challenge. *Journal of Personality and Social Psychology, 46*(4), 919–928.

McCrae, R., & Costa, P. T., Jr. (1985). Updating Norman's "adequate taxonomy": Intelligence and personality dimensions in natural language and in questionnaires. *Journal of Personality and Social Psychology, 49*, 710–721.

McCrae, R., & Costa, P. T., Jr. (1987). Validation of the five-factor model of personality across instruments and observers. *Journal of Personality and Social Psychology, 52*(1), 81–90.

McDaniel, M. A., & Einstein, G. O. (1986). Bizarre imagery as an effective memory aid: The importance of distinctiveness. *Journal of Experimental Psychology: Learning, Memory & Cognition, 12*, 54–65.

McDougle, L. G. (1987). Time management: Making every minute count. In A. D. Timpe (Ed.), *The management of time*. New York: Facts On File.

McGhee, P. E., & Frueh, T. (1980). Television viewing and the learning of sex-role stereotypes. *Sex Roles, 6*, 179–188.

McGill, M. E. (1980). *The 40 to 60 year old male*. New York: Simon & Schuster.

McGinnies, E., & Ward, C. D. (1980). Better liked than right: Trustworthiness and expertise as factors in credibility. *Personality and Social Psychology Bulletin, 6*, 467–472.

McGlashan, T. H. (1986). Schizophrenia: Psychosocial treatments and the role of psychosocial factors in its etiology and pathogenesis. In A. J. Frances & R. E. Hales (Eds.), *Psychiatry update: Annual review* (Vol. 5). Washington, DC: American Psychiatric Press.

McGlone, J. (1980). Sex differences in human brain asymmetry: A critical review. *Behavioral and Brain Sciences, 3*, 215–263.

McGoldrick, M., & Carter, E. A. (1989). The family life cycle—Its stages and dislocations. In J. M. Henslin (Ed.), *Marriage and family in a changing society*. New York: Free Press.

McGrath, J. E. (1977). Settings, measures and themes: An integrative review of some research on social-psychological factors in stress. In A. Monat & R. S. Lazarus (Eds.), *Stress and coping: An anthology*. New York: Columbia University Press.

McGrath, J. E. (1984). *Groups: Interaction and performance*. Englewood Cliffs, NJ: Prentice-Hall.

McGregor, D. (1960). *The human side of enterprise*. New York: McGraw-Hill.

McGuire, W. J. (1964). Inducing resistance to persuasion. In L. Berkowitz (Ed.), *Advances in Experimental Psychology* (Vol. 1). New York: Academic Press.

McGuire, W. J. (1985). Attitudes and attitude change. In G. Lindzey & E. Aronson (Eds.), *Handbook of social psychology* (Vol. 2, 3rd ed.). New York: Random House.

McKeon, J. Roa, B., & Mann, A. (1989). Life events and personality traits in obsessive-compulsive neurosis. In T. W. Miller (Ed.), *Stressful life events*. Madison, CT: International Universities Press.

McKillip, J., & Riedel, S. L. (1983). External validity of matching on physical attractiveness for same and opposite sex couples. *Journal of Applied Social Psychology, 13,* 328–337.

McKinlay, J. B., McKinlay, S. M., & Brambilla, D. (1987). The relative contributions of endocrine changes and social circumstances to depression in mid-aged women. *Journal of Health and Social Behavior, 28*(4), 345–363.

McNally, R. J. (1987). Preparedness and phobias: A review. *Psychological Bulletin, 101*(2), 283–303.

McReynolds, W. T. (1979). DSM-III and the future of applied social science. *Professional Psychology, 10,* 123–132.

Mead, M. (1950). *Sex and temperament in three primitive societies.* New York: Mentor Books.

Mechanic, D. (1972). Social psychologic factors affecting the presentation of bodily complaints. *New England Journal of Medicine, 286,* 1132–1139.

Mehrabian, A. (1971). *Silent messages.* Belmont, CA: Wadsworth.

Mehrabian, A. (1972). *Nonverbal communication.* Chicago: Aldine-Atherton.

Meilman, P. W. (1979). Cross-sectional age changes in ego identity status during adolescence. *Developmental Psychology, 15*(2), 230–232.

Mello, N. K., & Mendelson, J. H. (1978). Alcohol and human behavior. In L. L. Iversen, S. D. Iversen, & S. H. Snyder (Eds.), *Handbook of psychopharmacology* (Vol. 12). New York: Plenum Press.

Mellor, E. F. (1984, June). Investigating the differences in weekly earnings of women and men. *Monthly Labor Review, 107,* 17–28.

Melman, A., & Leiter, E. (1983). The urologic evaluation of impotence (male excitement phase disorder). In H. S. Kaplan (Ed.), *The evaluation of sexual disorders: Psychological and medical aspects.* New York: Brunner/Mazel.

Meltzoff, J., & Kornreich, M. (1970). *Research in psychotherapy.* New York: Atherton.

Mentzer, R. L. (1982). Response biases in multiple-choice test item files. *Educational and Psychological Measurement, 42,* 437–448.

Merikangas, K. R. & Weissman, M. M. (1986). Epidemiology of DSM-III axis II personality disorders. In A. J. Frances & R. E. Hales (Eds.), *Psychiatry Update: Annual Review* (Vol. 5). Washington, DC: American Psychiatric Press.

Meyer, R. (1980). The antisocial personality. In R. Woody (Ed.), *The encyclopedia of mental assessment.* San Francisco: Jossey-Bass.

Michelozzi, B. N. (1988). *Coming alive from nine to five: The career search handbook.* Palo Alto, CA: Mayfield.

Milgram, S. (1963). Behavioral study of obedience. *Journal of Abnormal and Social Psychology, 67,* 371–378.

Milgram, S. (1964). Issues in the study of obedience. *American Psychologist, 19,* 848–852.

Milgram, S. (1968). Reply to the critics. *International Journal of Psychiatry, 6,* 294–295.

Milgram, S. (1974). *Obedience to authority.* New York: Harper & Row.

Miller, A. G. (1986). *The obedience experiments: A case study of controversy in social science.* New York: Praeger.

Miller, C. T., Byrne, D., & Fisher, J. D. (1980). Order effects on sexual and affective responses to erotic stimuli by males and females. *Journal of Sex Research, 16,* 131–147.

Miller, G. P. (1978). *Life choices: How to make the critical decisions—about your education, career, marriage, family, life style.* New York: Thomas Y. Crowell.

Miller, G. T., Jr. (1985). *Living in the environment: An introduction to environmental science.* Belmont, CA: Wadsworth.

Miller, J. B. (1986). *Toward a new psychology of women.* Boston: Beacon Press.

Miller, L. C., Berg, J. H., & Archer, R. L. (1983). Openers: Individuals who elicit intimate self-disclosure. *Journal of Personality and Social Psychology, 44* (6), 1234–1244.

Miller, N. E. (1944). Experimental studies of conflict. In J. McV. Hunt (Ed.), *Personality and the behavior disorders* (Vol. 1). New York: Ronald.

Miller, N. E. (1959). Liberalization of basic S-R concepts: Extension to conflict behavior, motivation, and social learning. In S. Koch (Ed.), *Psychology: A study of a science* (Vol. 2). New York: McGraw-Hill.

Miller, N. E. (1983). Behavioral medicine: Symbiosis between laboratory and clinic. *Annual Review of Psychology, 34,* 1–31.

Millett, K. (1970). *Sexual politics.* Garden City, NY: Doubleday.

Millman, J., Bishop, C. H., & Ebel, R. (1965). An analysis of test-wiseness. *Educational and Psychological Measurement, 25,* 707–726.

Millman, J., & Pauk, W. (1969). *How to take tests.* New York: McGraw-Hill.

Millon, T. 1981. *Disorders of personality: DSM-III, Axis II.* New York: Wiley.

Millon, T. (1986). A theoretical derivation of pathological personalities. In T. Millon & G. L. Klerman (Eds.), *Contemporary directions in psychopathology: Toward the DSM-IV.* New York: Guilford Press.

Mindel, C. H., & Vaughan, C. E. (1978). A multidimensional approach to religiosity and disengagement. *Journal of Gerontology, 23,* 103–108.

Mineka, S., & Cook, M. (1986). Immunization against the observational conditioning of snake fear in rhesus monkeys. *Journal of Abnormal Psychology, 95*(4), 307–318.

Mirkin, G., & Hoffman, M. (1978). *The sports medicine book.* Boston: Little, Brown.

Mirsky, A. F., & Duncan, C. C. (1986). Etiology and expression of schizophrenia: Neurobiological and psychosocial factors. In M. R. Rosenzweig & L. W. Porter (Eds.), *Annual review of psychology: 1986.* Palo Alto, CA: Annual Reviews.

Mischel, W. (1970). Sex-typing and socialization. In P. H. Mussen (Ed.), *Carmichael's manual of child psychology* (Vol. 2). New York: Wiley.

Mischel, W. (1973). Toward a cognitive social learning conceptualization of personality. *Psychological Review, 80,* 252–283.

Mischel, W., & Mischel, H. N. (1976). A cognitive social learning approach to morality and self-regulation. In T. Lickona (Ed.), *Moral development and behavior: Theory, research and social issues.* New York: Holt, Rinehart & Winston.

Mishell, D. R. (1986). Contraceptive use and effectiveness. In D. R. Mishell & V. Davajan (Eds.), *Infertility, contraception, and reproductive endocrinology* (2nd ed.). Oradell, NJ: Medical Economics Books.

Mitchell, V. F. (1987). Rx for improving staff effectiveness. In A. D. Timpe (Ed.), *The management of time.* New York: Facts On File.

Mittleman, R. E., & Wetli, C. V. (1984). Death caused by recreational cocaine use. *Journal of the American Medical Association, 252*(14), 1889–1893.

Mobley, W. H., Horner, S. O., & Hollingsworth, A. T. (1978). An evaluation of precursors of hospital employee turnover. *Journal of Applied Psychology, 63,* 408–414.

Model, S. (1982). Housework by husbands: Determinants and implications. In J. Aldous (Ed.), *Two paychecks.* Beverly Hills, CA: Sage Publications.

Money, J., & Ehrhardt, A. A. (1972). *Man and woman, boy and girl: Differentiation and dimorphism of gender identity.* Baltimore: Johns Hopkins University Press.

Monge, R. (1975). Structure of the self-concept from adolescence through old age. *Experimental Aging Research, 1*(2), 281–291.

Monroe, S. M. (1982). Life events assessment: Current practices, emerging trends. *Clinical Psychology Review, 2*(4), 435–453.

Montemayor, R. (1986). Family variation in parent-adolescent storm and stress. *Journal of Adolescent Research, 1,* 15–31.

Moos, R. H., & Billings, A. G. (1982). Conceptualizing and measuring coping resources and processes. In L. Goldberger & S. Breznitz (Eds.), *Handbook of stress: Theoretical and clinical aspects.* New York: Free Press.

Morey, L. C. (1988). Personality disorders in DSM-III and DSM-III-R: Convergence, coverage, and internal consistency. *American Journal of Psychiatry, 145*(5), 573–577.

Morgan, M. (1982). Television and adolescents' sex-role stereotypes: A longitudinal study. *Journal of Personality and Social Psychology, 43,* 947–955.

Morgan, M. Y., & Scanzoni, J. (1987). Assessing variation in permanence/pragmatism orientations: Implications for marital stability. *Journal of Divorce, 11*(1), 1–24.

Morrison, A. M., & Von Glinow, M. A. (1990). Women and minorities in management. *American Psychologist, 45*(2), 200–208.

Morse, S., & Gergen, K. J. (1970). Social comparison, self-consistency, and the concept of self. *Journal of Personality and Social Psychology, 16,* 148–156.

Mosher, D. L. (1973). Sex differences, sex experience, sex guilt, and explicitly sexual films. *Journal of Social Issues, 29,* 95–112.

Moss, H. A. (1967). Sex, age, and state as determinants of mother-infant interaction. *Merrill-Palmer Quarterly, 13,* 19–36.

Mowrer, O. H. (1947). On the dual nature of learning: A reinterpretation of "conditioning" and "problem-solving." *Harvard Educational Review, 17,* 102–150.

Muehlenhard, C. L., & Hollabaugh, L. C. (1988). Do women sometimes say no when they mean yes? The prevalence and correlates of women's token resistance to sex. *Journal of Personality and Social Psychology, 54*(5), 872–879.

Mullen, B., Atkins, J. L., Champion, D. S., Edwards, C., Hardy, D., Storey, J. E., & Vanderklok, M. (1985). The false consensus effect: A meta-analysis of 115 hypothesis tests. *Journal of Experimental Social Psychology, 21,* 262–283.

Munroe, R. L., & Munroe, R. H. (1975). *Cross-cultural human development.* Pacific Grove, CA: Brooks/Cole.

Murphy, J. M. (1980). Continuities in community-based psychiatric epidemiology. *Archives of General Psychiatry, 37,* 1215–1223.

Murphy, J. M., & Helzer, J. E. (1986). Epidemiology of schizophrenia in adulthood. In G. L. Klerman, M. M. Weissman, P. S. Appelbaum, & L. H. Roth (Eds.), *Psychiatry: Vol. 5. Social, epidemiologic, and legal psychiatry.* New York: Basic Books.

Murphy, K., & Welch, F. (1989). Wage premiums for college graduates: Recent growth and possible explanations. *Educational Researcher, 18*(4), 17–26.

Murstein, B. I. (1971). Critique of models of dyadic attraction. In B. I. Murstein (Ed.), *Theories of attraction and love.* New York: Springer.

Murstein, B. I. (1976). *Who will marry whom? Theories and research in marital choice.* New York: Springer.

Murstein, B. I. (1986). *Paths to marriage.* Beverly Hills: Sage Publications.

Myers, D. G. (1980). *Inflated self: Human illusions and the biblical call to hope.* New York: Seabury Press.

Myers, D. G., & Lamm, H. (1976). The group polarization phenomenon. *Psychological Bulletin, 83*, 602–627.

Nahas, G. G. (1976). *Marijuana: Chemistry, biochemistry and cellular effects.* New York: Springer.

Nash, S. C., & Feldman, S. S. (1981). Sex-related differences in the relationship between sibling status and responsibility to babies. *Sex Roles, 7*, 1035–1042.

Nass, G. D., Libby, R. W., & Fisher, M. P. (1981). *Sexual choices: An introduction to human sexuality.* Monterey, CA: Wadsworth.

National Commission on Working Women. (1983). *Women's work: Undervalued, underpaid.* Washington, DC: Center for Women and Work.

Naughton, T. J. (1987). A conceptual view of workaholism and implications for career counseling and research. *Career Development Quarterly, 35*, 180–187.

Neimark, E. D. (1982). Adolescent thought: Transition to formal operations. In B. B. Wolman (Ed.), *Handbook of developmental psychology.* Englewood Cliffs, NJ: Prentice-Hall.

Nemiah, J. C. (1985). Somatoform disorders. In H. I. Kaplan & B. J. Sadock (Eds.), *Comprehensive textbook of psychiatry/IV.* Baltimore: Williams & Wilkins.

Neubeck, G. (1972). The myriad motives for sex. *Sexual Behavior, 2*(7), 51–56.

Neugarten, B. L., & Neugarten, D. A. (1986). Age in the aging society. *Daedalus, 115*(1), 31–49.

Neugebauer, R., Dohrenwend, B. P., & Dohrenwend, B. S. (1980). Formulation about hypotheses about the true prevalence of functional psychiatric disorders among adults in the United States. In B. P. Dohrenwend, B. S. Dohrenwend, M. S. Gould, B. Link, R. Neugebauer, & R. Wunsch-Hitzig (Eds.), *Mental illness in the United States: Epidemiological estimates.* New York: Praeger.

Newcomb, M. D. (1983). Relationship qualities of those who live together. *Alternative Lifestyles, 6*(2), 78–102.

Newcomb, M. D. (1986). Sexual behavior of cohabitors: A comparison of three independent samples. *Journal of Sex Research, 22*, 492–513.

Newcomer, S. F., & Udry, J. R. (1985). Oral sex in an adolescent population. *Archives of Sexual Behavior, 14*(1), 41–46.

Newman, M., & Berkowitz, B. (1976). *How to be awake and alive.* Westminster, MD: Ballantine.

Newsom, C., Favell, J. E., & Rincover, A. (1983). Side effects of punishment. In S. Axelrod & J. Apsche (Eds.), *The effects of punishment on human behavior.* New York: Academic Press.

Newton, R. E., Marunycz, J. D., Alderdice, M. T., & Napoliello, M. J. (1986). Review of the side-effect profile of Buspirone. *American Journal of Medicine, 80*(Supp. 3b), 17–21.

Nezu, A. M., Nezu, C. M., Blissett, S. E. (1988). Sense of humor as a moderator of the relation between stressful events and psychological distress: A prospective analysis. *Journal of Personality and Social Psychology, 54*(3), 520–525.

Nickerson, E. T., & Pitochelli, E. T. (1978, March). *Learned helplessness and depression in married women: Marriage as a depressing life style for women.* Paper presented at the meeting of the Eastern Psychological Association, Washington, DC.

Nicol, S. E., & Gottesman, I. I. (1983). Clues to the genetics and neurobiology of schizophrenia. *American Scientist, 71*, 398–404.

Nielsen, J. M. (1978). *Sex in society: Perspectives in stratification.* Belmont, CA: Wadsworth.

Nisbett, R. E. (1972). Hunger, obesity, and the ventromedial hypothalamus. *Psychological Review, 79*, 433–453.

Noe, R. A. (1988). Women and mentoring: A review and research agenda. *Academy of Management Review, 13*, 65–78.

Noguchi, T. T., & Nakamura, G. R. (1978). Phencyclidine-related deaths in Los Angeles County, 1976. *Journal of Forensic Science, 25*(3), 503–507.

Noller, P. (1980). Misunderstandings in marital communication: A study of couples' nonverbal communication. *Journal of Personality and Social Psychology, 39*(6), 1135–1148.

Noller, P., & Gallois, C. (1988). Understanding and misunderstanding in marriage: Sex and marital adjustment differences in structured and free interaction. In P. Noller & M. A. Fitzpatrick (Eds.), *Perspectives on marital interaction.* Clevedon, Avon, England: Multilingual Matters Ltd.

Norcross, J. C., & Prochaska, J. O. (1982). National survey of clinical psychologists: Affiliations and orientations. *Clinical Psychologist, 35*(3), 1, 4–6.

Norton, A. J., & Moorman, J. E. (1987). Current trends in marriage and divorce among American women. *Journal of Marriage and the Family, 49*, 3–14.

Novaco, R. W., Stokols, D., Campbell, J., & Stokols, J. (1979). Transportation, stress and community psychology. *American Journal of Community Psychology, 7*(4), 361–380.

Noyes, R., Jr., Clarkson, C., Crowe, R. R., Yates, W. R., & McChesney, C. M. (1987). A family study of generalized anxiety disorder. *American Journal of Psychiatry, 8*, 1019–1024.

Nurnberger, J. I., & Gershon, E. S. (1982). Genetics. In E. S. Paykel (Ed.), *Handbook of affective disorders.* New York: Guilford Press.

Nurnberger, J. I., & Zimmerman, J. (1970). Applied analysis of human behavior: An alternative to conventional motivational inferences and unconscious determination in therapeutic programming. *Behavior Therapy, 1*, 59–69.

Nye, R. D. (1973). *Conflict among humans.* New York: Springer.

O'Brien, C. P., & Woody, G. E. (1986). Sedative-hypnotics and antianxiety agents. In A. J. Frances & R. E. Hales (Eds.), *Psychiatric Update: Annual Review* (Vol. 5). Washington, DC: American Psychiatric Press.

Offer, D., & Offer, J. (1975). *From teenage to young manhood.* New York: Basic Books.

Offermann, L. R., & Gowing, M. K. (1990). Organizations of the future. *American Psychologist, 45*(2), 95–108.

O'Leary, K. D. (1984). The image of behavior therapy: It is time to take a stand. *Behavior Therapy, 15*, 219–233.

O'Leary, V. E. (1977). *Toward understanding women.* Pacific Grove, CA: Brooks/Cole.

Orne, M. T., & Holland, C. C. (1968). On the ecological validity of laboratory deceptions. *International Journal of Psychiatry, 6*, 282–293.

Osborn, A. F. (1963). *Applied imagination: Principles and procedures for creative problem solving* (3rd ed.). New York: Scribner's.

Ost, L. (1987). Age of onset in different phobias. *Journal of Abnormal Psychology, 96*(3), 223–229.

Oster, G., Huse, D. M., Delea, T. E., & Colditz, G. A. (1986). Cost-effectiveness of nicotine gum as an adjunct to physician's advice against cigarette smoking. *Journal of the American Medical Association, 256*, 1315–1318.

Packard, V. (1972). *A nation of strangers.* New York: David McKay.

Paffenbarger, R. S., Hyde, R. T., Wing, A. L., & Hsieh, C. (1986). Physial activity, all-cause mortality, and longevity of college alumni. *New England Journal of Medicine, 314*(10), 605–613.

Pagel, M. D., Erdly, W. W., & Becker, J. (1987). Social networks: We get by with (and in spite of) a little help from our friends. *Journal of Personality and Social Psychology, 53*(4), 793–804.

Paige, K. E. (1973). Women learn to sing the menstrual blues. *Psychology Today, 7*(4), 41–46.

Paivio, A. (1986). *Mental representations: A dual coding approach.* New York: Oxford University Press.

Palkovitz, R. J., & Lore, R. K. (1980). Note taking and note review: Why students fail questions based on lecture material. *Teaching of Psychology, 7*(3), 159–161.

Palmblad, J. (1981). Stress and immunologic competence: Studies in man. In R. Ader (Ed.), Psychoneuroimmunology. New York: Academic Press.

Palmore, E. (1969). Predicting longevity: A follow-up controlling for age. *Gerontologist, 9*, 247–250.

Palmore, E. (1975). *The honorable elders.* Durham, NC: Duke University Press.

Palmore, E., Fillenbaum, G. G., & George, L. K. (1984). Consequences of retirement. *Journal of Gerontology, 39*, 109–116.

Park, C. C., & Shapiro, L. N. (1979). *You are not alone: Understanding and dealing with mental illness.* Boston: Little, Brown.

Parke, R. D. (1977). Some effects of punishment on children's behavior—revisited. In E. M. Hetherington & R. D. Parke (Eds.), *Contemporary readings in child psychology.* New York: McGraw-Hill.

Parlee, M. B. (1973). The premenstrual syndrome. *Psychological Bulletin, 80*, 454–465.

Parlee, M. B. (1982). Changes in moods and activation levels during the menstrual cycle in experimentally naive subjects. *Psychology of Women Quarterly, 7*, 119–131.

Parlee, M. B., & the editors of *Psychology Today.* (1979). The friendship bond: PT's survey report on friendship in America. *Psychology Today, 13*(4), 43–54, 113.

Parsons, T. (1979). Definitions of health and illness in light of the American values and social structure. In E. G. Jaco (Ed.), *Patients, physicians and illness: A sourcebook in behavioral science and health.* New York: Free Press.

Passer, M. W., & Seese, M. (1983). Life stress and athletic injury: Examination of positive versus negative events and three moderator variables. *Journal of Human Stress, 9*, 11–16.

Patzer, G. L. (1985). *The physical attractiveness phenomena*. New York: Plenum Press.

Pauk, W. (1984). *How to study in college*. Boston: Houghton Mifflin.

Paul, W., & Weinrich, J. D. (1982). Whom and what we study: Definition and scope of sexual orientation. In W. Paul, J. D. Weinrich, J. C. Gonsiorek, & M. E. Hotvedt (Eds.), *Homosexuality: Social, psychological and biological issues*. Beverly Hills, CA: Sage Publications.

Pauling, L. C. (1970). *Vitamin C and the common cold*. San Francisco: W. H. Freeman.

Pauling, L. C. (1980). Vitamin C therapy of advanced cancer. *New England Journal of Medicine, 302*, 694.

Pavlov, I. P. (1906). The scientific investigation of psychical faculties or processes in the higher animals. *Science, 24*, 613–619.

Paykel, E. S. (1974). Life stress and psychiatric disorder. In B. S. Dohrenwend & B. P. Dohrenwend (Eds.), *Stressful life events: Their nature and effects*. New York: Wiley.

Pearce, L. (1974). Duck! It's the new journalism. *New Times, 2*(10), 40–41.

Pedhazur, E. J., & Tetenbaum, T. J. (1979). Bem sex-role inventory: A theoretical and methodological critique. *Journal of Personality and Social Psychology, 37*, 996–1016.

Pennebaker, J. W. (1982). *The psychology of physical symptoms*. New York: Springer-Verlag.

Perkins, D. V. (1982). The assessment of stress using life events scales. In L. Goldberger & S. Breznitz (Eds.), *Handbook of stress: Theoretical and clinical aspects*. New York: Free Press.

Perls, F. S. (1969). *Gestalt therapy verbatim*. Lafayette, CA: Real People Press.

Perry, D. G., & Bussey, K. (1979). The social learning theory of sex differences: Imitation is alive and well. *Journal of Personality and Social Psychology, 37*, 1699–1712.

Persky, H. (1983). Psychosexual effects of hormones. *Medical Aspects of Human Sexuality, 17*(9), 74–101.

Persky, H., Lief, H. I., Straus, D., Miller, W. R., & O'Brien, C. P. (1978). Plasma testosterone level and sexual behavior of couples. *Archives of Sexual Behavior, 7*, 157–173.

Peters, R. K., Cady, L. D., Jr., Bischoff, D. P., Bernstein, L., & Pile, M. C. (1983). Physical fitness and subsequent myocardial infarction in healthy workers. *Journal of the American Medical Association, 249*(22), 3052–3056.

Petersen, A. C. (1987). Those gangly years. *Psychology Today, 21*(9), 28–34.

Petersen, A. C., Crockett, L., & Tobin-Richards, M. H. (1982). Sex differences. In H. E. Mitzel (Ed.), *Encyclopedia of education research* (5th ed.). New York: Free Press.

Petersen, J. R., Kretchmer, A., Nellis, B., Lever, J., & Hertz, R. (1983, January and March). The *Playboy* readers' sex survey (Parts 1 and 2). *Playboy, 108*, 90.

Peterson, C., & Seligman, M. E. P. (1984). Causal explanations as a risk factor for depression: Theory and evidence. *Psychological Review, 91*, 347–374.

Peterson, C., Seligman, M. E. P., & Vaillant, G. E. (1988). Pessimistic explanatory style is a risk factor for physical illness: A thirty-five-year longitudinal study. *Journal of Personality and Social Psychology, 55*(1), 23–27.

Peterson, J. L., & Zill, N. (1986). Marital disruption, parent-child relationships, and behavior problems in children. *Journal of Marriage and the Family, 48*, 295–307.

Pettigrew, T. (1979). The ultimate attribution error: Extending Allport's cognitive analysis of prejudice. *Personality and Social Psychology Bulletin, 5*, 461–476.

Petty, R. E., & Cacioppo, J. T. (1986). The elaboration likelihood model of persuasion. In L. Berkowitz (Ed.), *Advances in experimental social psychology* (Vol. 19). New York: Academic Press.

Pfeiffer, S. M., & Wong, P. T. P. (1989). Multidimensional jealousy. *Journal of Social and Personal Relationships, 6*, 181–196.

Pfohl, B., & Andreasen, N. C. (1986). Schizophrenia: Diagnosis and classification. In A. J. Frances & R. E. Hales (Eds.), *Psychiatry Update: Annual Review* (Vol. 5). Washington, DC: American Psychiatric Press.

Phelps, S., & Austin, N. (1987). *The assertive woman*. San Luis Obispo, CA: Impact.

Philpott, J. S. (1983). *The relative contribution to meaning of verbal and nonverbal channels of communication: A meta-analysis*. Unpublished master's thesis, University of Nebraska, Omaha.

Piaget, J. (1929). *The child's conception of the world*. New York: Harcourt Brace.

Piaget, J. (1952). *The origins of intelligence in children*. New York: International Universities Press.

Piaget, J. (1972). Intellectual evolution from adolescence to adulthood. *Human Development, 15*, 1–12.

Piaget, J. (1983). Piaget's theory. In P. H. Mussen (Ed.), *Handbook of child psychology* (Vol. 1). New York: Wiley.

Pilowsky, I. (1978). A general classification of abnormal illness behaviors. *British Journal of Psychology, 51*, 131–137.

Pines, A., & Aronson, E. (1983). Antecedents, correlates, and consequences of sexual jealousy. *Journal of Personality, 51*, 108–136.

Pines, A. M., & Aronson, E. (1988). *Career burnout: Causes and cures*. New York: Free Press.

Pines, A. M., Aronson, E., & Kafry, D. (1981). *Burnout: From tedium to personal growth*. New York: Free Press.

Piotrkowski, C. S., Rapoport, R. N., & Rapoport, R. (1987). Families and work. In M. B. Sussman & S. K. Steinmetz (Eds.), *Handbook of marriage and the family*. New York: Plenum Press.

Pittman, J. F., & Lloyd, S. A. (1988). Quality of family life, social support, and stress. *Journal of Marriage and the Family, 50*, 53–67.

Pleck, J. H. (1981). *The myth of masculinity*. Cambridge, MA: MIT Press.

Pleck, J. H. (1983). Husbands' paid work and family roles: Current research issues. In H. Lopata & J. H. Pleck (Eds.), *Research in the interweave of social roles*. Greenwich, CT: JAI.

Plude, D. J., & Hoyer, W. J. (1985). Attention and performance: Identifying and localizing age deficits. In N. Charness (Ed.), *Aging and human performance*. Chichester, England: Wiley.

Plutchik, R. (1980). A language for the emotions. *Psychology Today, 13*(9), 68–78.

Pocs, O., & Godow, A. G. (1977). Can students view parents as sexual beings? *Family Coordinator, 26*, 31–36.

Pope, K. S., Keith-Spiegel, P., & Tabachnick, B. G. (1986). Sexual attraction to clients. *American Psychologist, 41*(2), 147–158.

Porter, S. A. (1985, August 23). What's a housewife worth? More than numbers show. *Providence Evening Bulletin*.

Powell, J. (1969). *Why am I afraid to tell you who I am?* Niles, IL: Argus Communications.

Powell, L. H., Friedman, M., Thoresen, C. E., Gill, J. J., & Ulmer, D. K. (1984). Can the Type A behavior pattern be altered after myocardial infarction? A second year report

from the recurrent coronary prevention project. *Psychosomatic Medicine, 46*(4), 293–313.

Powell, M. (1973). Age and occupational change among coal-miners. *Occupational Psychology, 47*, 37–49.

Powers, S. I., Hauser, S. T., & Kilner, L. A. (1989). Adolescent mental health. *American Psychologist, 44*, 200–208.

Poznanski, E. O. (1973). Children with excessive fears. *American Journal of Orthopsychiatry, 43*(3), 428–438.

Pruitt, D. G. (1971). Choice shifts in group discussion: An introductory review. *Journal of Personality and Social Psychology, 20*, 339–360.

Pyke, S. W., & Kahill, S. P. (1983). Sex differences in characteristics presumed relevant to professional productivity. *Psychology of Women Quarterly, 8*, 189–192.

Quillin, P. (1987). *Healing nutrients*. New York: Random House.

Rabbitt, P., & McGinnis, L. (1988). Do clever old people have earlier and richer first memories? *Psychology and Aging, 3*, 338–341.

Rabkin, J. G., & Streuning E. L. (1976). Life events, stress and illness. *Science, 194*, 1013–1020.

Rachman, S. J., & Wilson, G. T. (1980). *The effects of psychological therapy*. New York: Pergamon Press.

Radecki-Bush, C., Bush, J. P., & Jennings, J. (1988). Effects of jealousy threats on relationship perceptions and emotions. *Journal of Social and Personal Relationships, 5*, 285–303.

Ragland, D. R., & Brand, R. J. (1988). Type A behavior and mortality from coronary heart disease. *New England Journal of Medicine, 318*(2), 65–69.

Rahe, R. H., & Arthur, R. H. (1978). Life change and illness studies. *Journal of Human Stress, 4*(1), 3–15.

Raley, P. E. (1976). *Making love: How to be your own sex therapist*. New York: Dial Press.

Raley, P. E. (1980). *Making love: How to be your own sex therapist*. New York: Avon. (Paperback edition)

Raschke, H. J. (1987). Divorce. In M. B. Sussman & S. K. Steinmetz (Eds.), *Handbook of marriage and the family*. New York: Plenum Press.

Raskin, R., Bali, L. R., & Peeke, H. V. (1981). Muscle biofeedback and transcendental meditation: A controlled evaluation of efficacy in the treatment of chronic anxiety. In D. Shapiro, Jr., J. Stoyva, J. Kamiya, T. X. Barber, N. E. Miller, & G. E. Schwartz (Eds.), *Biofeedback and behavioral medicine 1979/80: Therapeutic applications and experimental foundations*. Chicago: Aldine.

Raugh, M. R., & Atkinson, R. C. (1975). A mnemonic method for learning a second-language vocabulary. *Journal of Educational Psychology, 67*, 1–16.

Ray, L., Soares, E. J., & Tolchinsky, B. (1988). Explicit lyrics: A content analysis of top 100 songs from the 50's to the 80's. *Speech Communication Annual, 2*, 43–56.

Reese, H. W., & Rodeheaver, D. (1985). Problem solving and complex decision making. In J. E. Birren & K. W. Schaie (Eds.), *Handbook of the psychology of aging* (2nd ed.). New York: Van Nostrand Reinhold.

Reinke, B. J., Ellicott, A. M., Harris, R. L., & Hancock, E. (1985). Timing of psychosocial changes in women's lives. *Human Development, 28*, 259–280.

Reis, H. T., Senchak, M., & Solomon, B. (1985). Sex differences in the intimacy of social interaction: Further examination of potential explanation. *Journal of Personality and Social Psychology, 48,* 1204–1217.

Reiss, I. I., & Furstenberg, F. F., Jr. (1981). Sociology and human sexuality. In H. I. Lief (Ed.), *Sexual problems in medical practice.* Chicago: American Medical Association.

Reiss, I. L. (1967). *The social context of premarital sexual permissiveness.* New York: Holt, Rinehart & Winston.

Reiss, I. L. (1980). *Family systems in America.* New York: Holt, Rinehart & Winston.

Reiss, I. L., Anderson, R. E., & Sponaugle, G. C. (1980). A multivariate model of the determinants of extramarital sexual permissiveness. *Journal of Marriage and the Family, 42,* 395–411.

Reiss, M., Rosenfeld, P., Melburg, V., & Tedeschi, J. T. (1981). Self-serving attributions: Biased private perceptions and distorted public descriptions. *Journal of Personality and Social Psychology, 41,* 224–231.

Relman, A. (1982). Marijuana and health. *New England Journal of Medicine, 306*(10), 603–604.

Renwick, P. A., & Lawler, E. E. (1978). What do you really want from your job? *Psychology Today, 11*(12), 53–65.

Repetti, R. L. (1984). Determinants of children's sex-stereotyping: Parental sex-role traits and television viewing. *Personality and Social Psychology Bulletin, 10*(3), 457–468.

Rey, J. M., Stewart, G. W., Plapp, J. M., Bashir, M. R., & Richards, I. N. (1988). DSM-III axis IV revisited. *American Journal of Psychiatry, 145,* 286–292.

Rhodewalt, F., & Agustsdottir, S. (1986). Effects of self-presentation on the phenomenal self. *Journal of Personality and Social Psychology, 50,* 47–55.

Rice, F. P. (1989). *Human sexuality.* Dubuque, IA: William C. Brown.

Richardson, J. G., & Simpson, C. H. (1982). Children, gender and social structure: An analysis of the contents of letters to Santa Claus. *Child Development, 53,* 429–436.

Ricketts, W. (1984). Biological research on homosexuality: Ansell's cow or Occam's razor? *Journal of Homosexuality, 10,* 65–93.

Ridgeway, C. L. (1983). *The dynamics of small groups.* New York: St. Martin's Press.

Rifkin, J. (1987). *Time wars: The primary conflict in human history.* New York: Simon & Schuster.

Rimm, D. C., & Cunningham, H. M. (1985). Behavior therapies. In S. J. Lynn & J. P. Garske (Eds.), *Contemporary psychotherapies: Models and methods.* Columbus, OH: Charles E. Merrill.

Ringer, R. J. (1978). *Winning through intimidation.* New York: Fawcett.

Roberts, J. V., & Herman, C. P. (1986). The psychology of height: An empirical review. In C. P. Herman, M. P. Zanna, & E. T. Higgins (Eds.), *Physical appearance, stigma, and social behavior: The Ontario symposium* (Vol. 3). Hillsdale, NJ: Erlbaum.

Roberts, P., & Newton, P. M. (1987). Levinsonian studies of women's adult development. *Psychology and Aging, 2*(2), 154–163.

Robins, C. J. (1988). Attributions and depression: Why is the literature so inconsistent? *Journal of Personality and Social Psychology, 54*(5), 880–889.

Robins, L. N. (1966). *Deviant children grow up.* Baltimore: Williams & Wilkins.

Robins, L. N., Helzer, J. E., Weissman, M. M., Orvaschel, H., Gruenberg, E., Burke, J. D., &

Regier, D. A. (1984). Lifetime prevalence of specific psychiatric disorders in three sites. *Archives of General Psychiatry, 41,* 949–958.

Robinson, F. P. (1970). *Effective study* (4th ed.). New York: Harper & Row.

Robinson, I. E., & Jedlicka, D. (1982). Change in sexual attitudes and behavior of college students from 1965 to 1980: A research note. *Journal of Marriage and the Family, 44*(1), 237–240.

Robinson, J. (1980). Housework technology and household work. In S. Berk (Ed.), *Women and household labor.* Beverly Hills, CA: Sage Publications.

Rodin, J. (1981). Current status of the internal-external hypothesis for obesity: What went wrong? *American Psychologist, 36*(4), 361–372.

Rodin, J., Silberstein, L., & Striegel-Moore, R. H. (1985). Women and weight: A normative discontent. In T. B. Sonderegger (Ed.), *Nebraska symposium on motivation 1984: Psychology and gender* (Vol. 32). Lincoln: University of Nebraska Press.

Roe, A. (1977). *The psychology of occupations.* New York: Wiley.

Rogers, C. R. (1951). *Client-centered therapy: Its current practice, implications, and theory.* Boston: Houghton Mifflin.

Rogers, C. R. (1959). A theory of therapy, personality, and interpersonal relationships, as developed in the client-centered framework. In S. Koch (Ed.), *Psychology: A study of a science* (Vol. 3). New York: McGraw-Hill.

Rogers, C. R. (1961). *On becoming a person: A therapist's view of psychotherapy.* Boston: Houghton Mifflin.

Rogers, C. R. (1977). *Carl Rogers on personal power.* New York: Delacorte.

Rogers, C. R. (1980). *A way of being.* Boston: Houghton Mifflin.

Rogers, C. R. (1986). Client-centered therapy. In I. L. Kutash & A. Wolf (Eds.), *Psychotherapist's casebook.* San Francisco: Jossey-Bass.

Rogers, R. W. (1975). A protection motivation theory of fear appeals and attitude change. *Journal of Psychology, 91,* 93–114.

Rogot, E. (1974). Smoking and mortality among U.S. veterans. *Journal of Chronic Diseases, 27,* 189–203.

Rollins, B., & Feldman, H. (1970). Marital satisfaction over the family life cycle. *Journal of Marriage and the Family, 32,* 20–28.

Rook, K. S. (1984). Research on social support, loneliness, and social isolation: Toward an integration. In P. Shaver (Ed.), *Review of personality and social psychology* (Vol. 5). Beverly Hills, CA: Sage Publications.

Roosa, M. W. (1988). The effect of age in the transition to parenthood: Are delayed childbearers a unique group? *Family Relations, 37,* 322–327.

Rosch, P. J., & Pelletier, K. R. (1987). Designing worksite stress management programs. In L. R. Murphy & T. F. Schoenborn (Eds.), *Stress management in work settings.* Washington, DC: National Institute for Occupational Safety and Health.

Rosen, G. M. (1987). Self-help treatment books and the commercialization of psychotherapy. *American Psychologist, 42*(1), 46–51.

Rosen, R. D. (1977). *Psychobabble.* New York: Atheneum.

Rosenbaum, M. (1980). A schedule for assessing self-control behaviors: Preliminary findings. *Behavior Therapy, 11,* 109–121.

Rosenbaum, M. E. (1986). The repulsion hypothesis: On the nondevelopment of relationships. *Journal of Personality and Social Psychology, 51*(6), 1156–1166.

Rosenberg, M. (1979). *Conceiving the self.* New York: Basic Books.

Rosenberg, M. (1985). Self-concept and psychological well-being in adolescence. In R. L. Leahy (Ed.), *The development of the self.* Orlando, FL: Academic Press.

Rosenfeld, L. B., Civikly, J. M., & Herron, J. R. (1979). Anatomical and psychological sex differences. In G. J. Chelune & associates (Eds.), *Self-disclosure: Origins, patterns, and implications of openness in interpersonal relationships.* San Francisco: Jossey-Bass.

Rosenhan, D. L. (1973). On being sane in insane places. *Science, 179,* 250–258.

Rosenheim, E., & Muchnik, B. (1984/1985). Death concerns in differential levels of consciousness as functions of defense strategy and religious beliefs. *Omega, Journal of Death and Dying, 155,* 15–24.

Rosenman, R. H., & Chesney, M. A. (1982). Stress, Type A behavior, and coronary disease. In L. Goldberger & S. Bresnitz (Eds.), *Handbook of stress: Theoretical and clinical aspects.* New York: Free Press.

Rosenstock, I. M., & Kirscht, J. P. (1979). Why people seek health care. In G. C. Stone, F. Cohen, N. E. Adler, & associates (Eds.), *Health psychology—A handbook.* San Francisco: Jossey-Bass.

Rosenthal, N. E., Carpenter, C. J., James, S. P., Parry, B. L., Rogers, S. L. B., & Wehr, T. A. (1986). Seasonal affective disorder in children and adolescents. *American Journal of Psychiatry, 143,* 356–358.

Ross, L. (1977). The intuitive psychologist and his shortcomings: Distortions in the attribution process. In L. Berkowitz (Ed.), *Advances in experimental social psychology* (Vol. 10). New York: Academic Press.

Ross, L., Greene, D., & House, P. (1977). The "false consensus effect": An egocentric bias in social perception and attribution processes. *Journal of Experimental Social Psychology, 13,* 279–301.

Ross, L. D. (1988). The obedience experiments: A case study of controversy. *Contemporary Psychology, 33*(2), 101–104.

Rothbart, M., & Park, B. (1986). On the confirmability and disconfirmability of trait concepts. *Journal of Personality and Social Psychology, 50,* 131–142.

Rothblum, E. D., Solomon, L. J., & Albee, G. W. (1986). A sociopolitical perspective of DSM-III. In T. Millon & G. L. Klerman (Eds.), *Contemporary directions in psychopathology: Toward the DSM-IV.* New York: Guilford Press.

Rotter, J. (1982). *The development and application of social learning theory.* New York: Praeger.

Rubenstein, C. M., & Shaver, P. (1982). The experience of loneliness. In L. A. Peplau & D. Perlman (Eds.), *Loneliness: A sourcebook of current theory, research and therapy.* New York: Wiley.

Rubin, E. H., Zorumski, C. F., & Guze, S. B. (1986). Somatoform disorders. In T. Millon & G. L. Klerman (Eds.), *Contemporary directions in psychopathology: Toward the DSM-IV.* New York: Guilford Press.

Rubin, Z. (1970). Measurement of romantic love. *Journal of Personality and Social Psychology, 16,* 265–273.

Rubin, Z. (1973). *Liking and loving: An introduction to social psychology.* New York: Holt, Rinehart & Winston.

Rubin, Z. (1983). *Intimate strangers: Men and women together.* New York: Harper & Row.

Rubin, Z., Peplau, L. A., & Hill, C. T. (1981). Loving and leaving: Sex differences in romantic attachments. *Sex Roles, 7*(8), 821–835.

Ruble, D. N., Fleming, A. S., Hackel, L. S., & Stangor, C. (1988). Changes in the marital relationship during the transition to first time motherhood: Effects of violated expectations concerning division of household labor. *Journal of Personality and Social Psychology, 55,* 78–87.

Ruble, T. L. (1983). Sex stereotypes: Issues of change in the 1970s. *Sex Roles, 9,* 397–402.

Rukeyser, L., Cooney, J., & Winslow, W. (1988). *Louis Rukeyser's business almanac.* New York: Simon & Schuster.

Rule, B. G., Bisanz, G. L., & Kohn, M. (1985). Anatomy of a persuasion schema: Targets, goals, and strategies. *Journal of Personality and Social Psychology, 48,* 1127–1140.

Rush, A. J. (1984). Cognitive therapy. In T. B. Karasu (Ed.), *The psychiatric therapies.* Washington, DC: American Psychiatric Association.

Rushton, J. P., Fulker, D. W., Neale, M. C., Nias, D. K. B., & Eysenck, H. J. (1986). Altruism and aggression: The heritability of individual differences. *Journal of Personality and Social Psychology, 50*(6), 1192–1198.

Russek, H. I., & Russek, L. G. (1976). Is emotional stress an etiological factor in coronary heart disease? *Psychosomatics, 17,* 63.

Russell, D. (1982). The measurement of loneliness. In L. A. Peplau & D. Perlman (Eds.), *Loneliness: A sourcebook of current theory, research and therapy.* New York: Wiley.

Russell, D., Peplau, L. A., & Cutrona, C. E. (1980). The revised UCLA Loneliness Scale: Concurrent and discriminant validity evidence. *Journal of Personality and Social Psychology, 39*(3), 472–480.

Russell, D., Peplau, L. A., & Ferguson, M. L. (1978). Developing a measure of loneliness. *Journal of Personality Assessment, 42,* 290–294.

Russo, N. F., & Sobel, S. B. (1981). Sex differences in the utilization of mental health facilities. *Professional Psychology, 12,* 7–19.

Sabatelli, R. M. (1988). Exploring relationship satisfaction: A social exchange perspective on the interdependence between theory, research, and practice. *Family Relations, 37,* 217–222.

Sachs, G. S., & Gelenberg, A. J. (1988). Adverse effects of electroconvulsive therapy. In A. J. Frances & R. E. Hales (Eds.), *Review of psychiatry* (Vol. 7). Washington, DC: American Psychiatric Press.

Sackeim, H. A. (1985). The case for ECT. *Psychology Today, 19*(6), 35–40.

Sackeim, H. A. (1988). Mechanisms of action of electroconvulsive therapy. In A. J. Frances & R. E. Hales (Eds.), *Annual review of psychiatry* (Vol. 7). Washington, DC: American Psychiatric Press.

Sadker, M., & Sadker, D. (1985, March). Sexism in the schoolroom of the '80s. *Psychology Today,* 54–57.

Salovey, P., & Rodin, J. (1986). The differentiation of social-comparison jealousy and romantic jealousy. *Journal of Personality and Social Psychology, 50,* 1100–1112.

Sandler, J. (1975). Aversion methods. In F. H. Kanfer & A. P. Goldstein (Eds.), *Helping people change: A textbook of methods.* New York: Pergamon Press.

Sarason, I. G. (1984). Stress, anxiety and cognitive interference: Reactions to stress. *Journal of Personality and Social Psychology, 46*(4), 929–938.

Sarason, I. G., Johnson, J. H., & Siegel, J. M. (1978). Assessing the impact of life changes: Development of the Life Experiences Survey. *Journal of Consulting and Clinical Psychology, 46,* 932–946.

Sarason, I. G., Levine, H. M., & Sarason, B. R. (1982). Assessing the impact of life changes. In T. Millon, C. Green, & R. Meagher (Eds.), *Handbook of clinical health psychology.* New York: Plenum Press.

Sarnacki, R. E. (1979). An examination of test-wiseness in the cognitive domain. *Review of Educational Research, 49,* 252–279.

Schachter, S. (1959). *The psychology of affiliation.* Stanford, CA: Stanford University Press.

Schachter, S. (1964). The interaction of cognitive and physiological determinants of emotional state. In L. Berkowitz (Ed.), *Advances in experimental social psychology* (Vol. 1). New York: Academic Press.

Schachter, S. (1971). *Emotion, obesity and crime.* New York: Academic Press.

Schaefer, E. S., & Burnett, C. K. (1987). Stability and predictability of quality of women's marital relationships and demoralization. *Journal of Personality and Social Psychology, 53,* 1129–1136.

Schaffer, D. R. (1989). *Developmental psychology: Childhood and adolescence.* Pacific Grove, CA: Brooks/Cole.

Schaffer, H. R., & Emerson, P. E. (1964). The development of social attachment in infancy. *Monographs of the Society for Research in Child Development, 29*(3, Serial No. 94).

Schaie, K. W. (1983). Age changes in adult intelligence. In D. S. Woodruff & J. E. Birren (Eds.), *Aging: Scientific perspectives and social issues.* Pacific Grove, CA: Brooks/Cole.

Schaninger, C. M., & Buss, W. C. (1986). A longitudinal comparison of consumption and finance handling between happily married and divorced couples. *Journal of Marriage and the Family, 48,* 129–136.

Scheff, T. (1975). *Labeling madness.* Englewood Cliffs, NJ: Prentice-Hall.

Scheflen, A. E., & Scheflen, A. (1972). *Body language and social order: Communication as behavioral control.* Englewood Cliffs, NJ: Prentice-Hall.

Scheier, M. F., & Carver, C. S. (1985). Optimism, coping and health: Assessment and implications of generalized expectancies. *Health Psychology, 4,* 219–247.

Scheier, M. F., Weintraub, J. K., & Carver, C. S. (1986). Coping with stress: Divergent strategies of optimists and pessimists. *Journal of Personality and Social Psychology, 51*(6), 1257–1264.

Schein, E. H. (1978). *Career dynamics: Matching individual and organizational needs.* Reading, MA: Addison-Wesley.

Schein, E. H. (1980). *Organizational Psychology.* Englewood Cliffs, NJ: Prentice-Hall.

Schein, M., Zyzanski, S. J., Levine, S., & Medalie, J. H. (1988). The frequency of sexual problems among family practice patients. *Family Practice Research Journal, 7*(3), 122–134.

Schilit, W. K. (1987). Thinking about managing your time. In A. D. Timpe (Ed.), *The management of time.* New York: Facts On File.

Schmidt, N., & Sermat, V. (1983). Measuring loneliness in different relationships. *Journal of Personality and Social Psychology, 44*(5), 1038–1047.

Schneider, D. (1973). Implicit personality theory: A review. *Psychological Bulletin, 79,* 294–309.

Schofield, W. (1964). *Psychotherapy: The purchase of friendship.* Englewood Cliffs, NJ: Prentice-Hall.

Schooler, C. (1972). Birth order effects: Not here, not now! *Psychological Bulletin, 78,* 161–175.

Schriesheim, C. A., & Kerr, S. (1977). Theories and measures of leadership: A critical appraisal of current and future directions. In J. G. Hunt & L. L. Larson (Eds.), *Leadership: The cutting edge.* Carbondale: Southern Illinois University Press.

Schroeder, D. H., & Costa, P. T., Jr. (1984). Influence of life events stress on physical illness: Substantive effects or methodological flaws? *Journal of Personality and Social Psychology, 46*(4), 853–863.

Schultz, N. R., Jr., & Moore, D. (1984). Loneliness: Correlates, attributions, and coping among older adults. *Personality and Social Psychology Bulletin, 10*(1), 67–77.

Schuster, C. S. (1986). *The process of human development: A holistic life-span approach* (2nd ed.). Boston: Little, Brown.

Schwartz, C. C., & Myers, J. K. (1977). Life events and schizophrenia: I. Comparison of schizophrenics with a community sample. *Archives of General Psychiatry, 34,* 1238–1241.

Schwartz, G. E. (1974). The facts on transcendental meditation, Part II: TM relaxes some people and makes them feel better. *Psychology Today, 7*(11), 39–44.

Schwartz, H. S. (1982). Job involvement as obsession. *Academy of Management Review, 7,* 429–432.

Seashore, S. E., & Barnowe, J. T. (1972). Collar color doesn't count. *Psychology Today, 6*(3), 53–54, 80–82.

Seeman, M. (1971). The urban alienations: From Marx to Marcuse. *Journal of Personality and Social Psychology, 19,* 135–143.

Segal, B. (1988). *Drugs and behavior.* New York: Gardner Press.

Segal, M. W. (1974). Alphabet and attraction: An unobtrusive measure of the effect of propinquity in a field setting. *Journal of Personality and Social Psychology, 30,* 654–657.

Seligman, M. E. P. (1971). Phobias and preparedness. *Behavior Therapy, 2,* 307–321.

Seligman, M. E. P. (1974). Depression and learned helplessness. In R. J. Friedman & M. M. Katz (Eds.), *The psychology of depression: Contemporary theory and research.* New York: Wiley.

Seligman, M. E. P. (1983). Learned helplessness. In E. Levitt, B. Rubin, & J. Brooks (Eds.), *Depression: Concepts, controversies and some new facts.* Hillsdale, NJ: Erlbaum.

Selye, H. (1936). A syndrome produced by diverse nocuous agents. *Nature, 138,* 32.

Selye, H. (1956). *The stress of life* (1st ed.). New York: McGraw-Hill.

Selye, H. (1974). *Stress without distress.* New York: Lippincott.

Selye, H. (1976). *The stress of life* (2nd ed.). New York: McGraw-Hill.

Selye, H. (1982). History and present status of the stress concept. In L. Goldberger & S. Breznitz (Eds.), *Handbook of stress: Theoretical and clinical aspects.* New York: Free Press.

Serbin, L. A., Connor, J. M., & Citron, C. C. (1978). Environmental control of independent and dependent behaviors in preschool girls and boys: A model for early independence training. *Sex Roles, 4,* 867–875.

Shapiro, D. H., Jr. (1984). Overview: Clinical and physiological comparison of meditation with other self-control strategies. In D. H. Shapiro & R. N. Walsh (Eds.), *Meditation: Classic and contemporary perspectives.* New York: Aldine.

Shapiro, D. H., Jr., Schwartz, G. E., & Tursky, B. (1972). Control of diastolic blood pressure in man by feedback and reinforcement. *Psychophysiology, 9,* 296–304.

Shapiro, S., Skinner, E. A., Kessler, L. G., Von Korff, M., German, P. S., Tischler, G. L., Leaf, P. J., Benham, L., Cottler, L., & Regier,

D. A. (1984). Utilization of health and mental health services. *Archives of General Psychiatry, 41*, 971–978.

Shatan, C. F. (1978). Stress disorders among Viet Nam veterans: The emotional content of combat continues. In C. R. Figley (Ed.), *Stress disorders among Viet Nam veterans: Theory, research and treatment.* New York: Brunner/Mazel.

Shavelson, R. J., Hubner, J. J., & Stanton, G. C. (1976). Self-concept: Validation of construct interpretations. *Review of Educational Research, 46*, 407–411.

Shaw, M. E. (1981). *Group dynamics: The psychology of small group behavior.* New York: McGraw-Hill.

Sheehan, S. (1982). *Is there no place on earth for me?* Boston: Houghton Mifflin.

Sheehy, G. (1976). *Passages.* Toronto: Bantam Books.

Sheehy, G. (1981). *Pathfinders.* New York: Morrow.

Shekelle, R. B., Hulley, S. B., Neaton, J. D., Billings, J. H., Borhani, N. O., Gerace, T. A., Jacobs, D. R., Lasser, N. L., Mittlemark, M. B., & Stamler, J. (1985). The MRFIT behavior pattern study: II. Type A behavior and incidence of coronary heart disease. *American Journal of Epidemiology, 122*, 559–570.

Sheras, P. L. (1983). Suicide in adolescence. In C. E. Walker & M. C. Roberts (Eds.), *Handbook of clinical child psychology.* New York: Wiley.

Sherif, M., & Hovland, C. I. (1961). *Social judgment: Assimilation and contrast effects in communication and attitude change.* New Haven, CT: Yale University Press.

Sherman, B. L., & Dominick, J. R. (1986). Violence and sex in music videos: TV and rock 'n' roll. *Journal of Communication, 36*(1), 79–93.

Sherrod, D. (1989). The influence of gender on same-sex friendships. In C. Hendrick (Ed.), *Review of personality and social psychology: Vol. 10. Close relationships.* Newbury Park, CA: Sage Publications.

Shertzer, B. (1985). *Career planning: Freedom to choose.* Boston: Houghton Mifflin.

Shields, S. A. (1975). Functionalism, Darwinism, and the psychology of women: A study in social myth. *American Psychologist, 30*, 739–754.

Shneidman, E. (1985). *At the point of no return.* New York: Wiley.

Shneidman, E. S., Farberow, N. L., & Litman, R. E. (Eds.). (1970). *The psychology of suicide.* New York: Science House.

Shoemaker, M. E., & Satterfield, D. O. (1977). Assertion training: An identity crisis that's coming on strong. In R. E. Alberti (Ed.), *Assertiveness: Innovations, applications, issues.* San Luis Obispo, CA: Impact.

Shostak, A. B. (1980). *Blue-collar stress.* Reading, MA: Addison-Wesley.

Shotland, R. L. (1989). A model of the causes of date rape in developing and close relationships. In C. Hendrick (Ed.), *Review of personality and social psychology: Vol. 10. Close relationships.* Newbury Park, CA: Sage Publications.

Shrauger, J. S. (1975). Responses to evaluation as a function of initial self-perception. *Psychological Bulletin, 82*(4), 581–596.

Siegel, O. (1982). Personality development in adolescence. In B. B. Wolman (Ed.), *Handbook of developmental psychology.* Englewood Cliffs, NJ: Prentice-Hall.

Siegler, I. C., Nowlin, J. B., & Blumenthal, J. A. (1980). Health and behavior: Methodological considerations for adult development

and aging. In L. W. Poon (Ed.), *Aging in the 1980s: Psychological issues.* Washington, DC: American Psychological Association.

Siegler, R. S. (1986). *Children's thinking.* Englewood Cliffs, NJ: Prentice-Hall.

Sigall, H., & Ostrove, N. (1975). Beautiful but dangerous: Effects of offender attractiveness and nature of the crime in juridic judgment. *Journal of Personality and Social Psychology, 31*, 410–414.

Silva, J., & Miele, P. (1977). *The Silva mind control method.* New York: Simon & Schuster.

Simon, W., & Gagnon, J. (1977). Psychosexual development. In D. Byrne & L. A. Byrne (Eds.), *Exploring human sexuality.* New York: Thomas Y. Crowell.

Simon, W., & Gagnon, J. (1986). Sexual scripts: Permanance and change. *Archives of Sexual Behavior, 15*(2), 97–120.

Simonton, D. K. (1988). Age and outstanding achievement: What do we know after a century of research? *Psychological Bulletin, 104*, 251–267.

Singer, M. T., Wynne, L. C., & Toohey, M. L. (1978). Communication disorders and the families of schizophrenics. In L. C. Wynne, R. L. Cromwell, & S. Matthysse (Eds.), *The nature of schizophrenia: New approaches to research and treatment.* New York: Wiley Medical.

Siscovick, D. S., Weiss, N. S., Fletcher, R. H., & Lasky, T. (1984). The incidence of primary cardiac arrest during vigorous exercise. *New England Journal of Medicine, 311*(14), 874–877.

Skinner, B. F. (1953). *Science and human behavior.* New York: Macmillan.

Skinner, B. F. (1974). *About behaviorism.* New York: Knopf.

Skinner, B. F. (1987). Whatever happened to psychology as the science of behavior? *American Psychologist, 42*(8), 780–786.

Sklar, L. S., & Anisman, H. (1981). Contributions of stress and coping to cancer development and growth. In K. Bammer & B. H. Newberry (Eds.), *Stress and cancer.* Toronto: C. J. Hogrefe.

Slater, E. J., & Haber, J. D. (1984). Adolescent adjustment following divorce as a function of familial conflict. *Journal of Consulting and Clinical Psychology, 52*, 920–921.

Sloan, W. W., Jr., & Solano, C. H. (1984). The conversational style of lonely males with strangers and roommates. *Personality and Social Psychology Bulletin, 10*(2), 293–301.

Slobin, D. I., Miller, S. H., & Porter, L. W. (1968). Forms of address and social relations in a business organization. *Journal of Personality and Social Psychology, 8*, 289–293.

Slochower, J. (1976). Emotional labelling of overeating in obese and normal weight individuals. *Psychosomatic Medicine, 38*, 131–139.

Small, I. F., Small, J. G., & Milstein, V. (1986). Electroconvulsive therapy. In P. A. Berger & H. K. H. Brodie (Eds.), *American handbook of psychiatry: Biological psychiatry* (Vol. 8, 2nd ed.). New York: Basic Books.

Smeaton, G., Byrne, D., & Murnen, S. K. (1989). The repulsion hypothesis revisited: Similarity irrelevance or dissimilarity bias. *Journal of Personality and Social Psychology, 56*(1), 54–59.

Smith, D. (1982). Trends in counseling and psychotherapy. *American Psychologist, 37*(3), 802–809.

Smith, G. T., Snyder, D. K., Trull, T. J., & Monsma, B. R. (1988). Predicting relationship satisfaction from couples' use of leisure time. *American Journal of Family Therapy, 16*, 3–13.

Smith, J. (1975). Meditation and psychotherapy: A review of the literature. *Psychological Bulletin, 32*, 553–564.

Smith, M. L., & Glass, G. V. (1977). Meta-analysis of psychotherapy outcome studies. *American Psychologist, 32*, 752–760.

Smith, M. L., Glass, G. V., & Miller, R. L. (1980). *The benefits of psychotherapy.* Baltimore: Johns Hopkins University Press.

Smith, P. A., & Midlarsky, E. (1985). Empirically derived conceptions of femaleness and maleness: A current view. *Sex Roles, 12*, 313–328.

Smollar, J., & Youniss, J. (1985). Adolescent self-concept development. In R. L. Leahy (Ed.), *The development of the self.* Orlando, FL: Academic Press.

Smyth, M. M., & Fuller, R. G. C. (1972). Effects of group laughter on responses to humorous materials. *Psychological Reports, 30*, 132–134.

Snell, W. E., Jr., & Papini, D. R. (1989). The sexuality scale: An instrument to measure sexual-esteem, sexual-depression, and sexual-preoccupation. *Journal of Sex Research, 26*(2), 256–263.

Snelling, R. O., & Snelling, A. M. (1985). *Jobs! What they are . . . Where they are . . . What they pay!* New York: Simon & Schuster.

Snyder, M. (1974). Self-monitoring of expressive behavior. *Journal of Personality and Social Psychology, 30*, 526–537.

Snyder, M. (1979). Self-monitoring processes. In L. Berkowitz (Ed.), *Advances in experimental social psychology* (Vol. 12). New York: Academic Press.

Snyder, M. (1986). *Public appearances/Private realities: The psychology of self-monitoring.* New York: W. H. Freeman.

Snyder, M., & Campbell, B. (1982). Self-monitoring: The self in action. In J. Suls (Ed.), *Psychological perspectives on the self.* Hillsdale, NJ: Erlbaum.

Snyder, M., Simpson, J. A., & Gangestad, S. (1986). Personality and sexual relations. *Journal of Personality and Social Psychology, 51*, 181–190.

Snyder, M., Tanke, E. D., & Berscheid, E. (1977). Social perception and interpersonal behavior: On the self-fulfilling nature of social stereotypes. *Journal of Personality and Social Psychology, 35*, 655–666.

Snyder, S. H. (1979). Amphetamine psychosis: A "model schizophrenia" mediated by catecholamines. In D. E. Smith (Ed.), *Amphetamine use, misuse, and abuse.* Boston: G. K. Hall.

Solano, C. H., Batten, P. G., & Parish, E. A. (1982). Loneliness and patterns of self-disclosure. *Journal of Personality and Social Psychology, 43*(3), 524–531.

Solano, C. H., & Koester, N. H. (1989). Loneliness and communication problems: Subjective anxiety or objective skills? *Personality and Social Psychology Bulletin, 15*(1), 126–133.

Solomon, G. F., Amkraut, A., & Rubin, R. T. (1985). Stress, hormones, neuroregulation and immunity. In S. R. Burchfield (Ed.), *Stress: Psychological and physiological interactions.* New York: Hemisphere.

Sotiriou, P. E. (1989). *Integrating college study skills: Reasoning in reading, listening and writing.* Belmont, CA: Wadsworth.

Spain, J. (1985). Counseling adolescents for contraceptive and sexual decisions. In P. B. Smith & D. M. Mumford (Eds.), *Adolescent reproductive health: Handbook for the health professional.* New York: Gardner Press.

Spanier, G. B. (1977). Sources of sex information and premarital sexual behavior. *Journal of Sex Research, 13*(2), 73–88.

Spanier, G. B., & Furstenberg, F. F., Jr. (1982). Remarriage after divorce: A longitudinal analysis of well-being. *Journal of Marriage and the Family, 44,* 709–720.

Spanos, N. P., Weekes, J. R., & Bertrand, L. D. (1985). Multiple personality: A social psychological perspective. *Journal of Abnormal Psychology, 94*(3), 362–376.

Spence, J. T. (1983). Comment on Lubinski, Tellegen, and Butcher's "Masculinity, femininity, and androgyny viewed and assessed as distinct concepts." *Journal of Personality and Social Psychology, 44,* 440–446.

Sperry, R. W. (1982). Some effects of disconnecting the cerebral hemispheres. *Science, 217,* 1223–1226, 1250.

Spitze, G. (1988). Women's employment and family relations: A review. *Journal of Marriage and the Family, 50,* 595–618.

Sporakowski, M. J. (1988). A therapist's views on the consequences of change for the contemporary family. *Family Relations, 37,* 373–378.

Sprecher, S. (1989). Premarital sexual standards for different categories of individuals. *Journal of Sex Research, 26*(2), 232–248.

Spring, B. (1989). Stress and schizophrenia: Some definitional issues. In T. W. Miller (Ed.), *Stressful life events.* Madison, CT: International Universities Press.

Springer, S. P., & Deutsch, G. (1984). *Left brain, right brain.* New York: W. H. Freeman.

Stanford, M. W. (1987). Designer drugs: Medical aspects and clinical management. *Alcoholism Treatment Quarterly, 4*(4), 97–125.

Stanislaw, H., & Rice, F. J. (1988). Correlation between sexual desire and menstrual cycle characteristics. *Archives of Sexual Behavior, 17*(6), 499–508.

Stankov, L. (1988). Aging, attention, and intelligence. *Psychology and Aging, 3,* 59–74.

Stark, E. (1989, June). Rx: 2 self-help books and call me in the morning. *Psychology Today, 26.*

Staw, B. M., & Ross, J. (1985). Stability in the midst of change: A dispositional approach to job attitudes. *Journal of Applied Psychology, 70*(3), 469–480.

Steele, C. M. (1975). Name-calling and compliance. *Journal of Personality and Social Psychology, 31,* 361–369.

Steger, J., & Fordyce, W. (1982). Behavioral health care in the management of chronic pain. In T. Millon, C. Green, & R. Meagher (Eds.), *Handbook of clinical health psychology.* New York: Plenum Press.

Stein, P. J. (1975). Singlehood: An alternative to marriage. *Family Coordinator, 24,* 489–503.

Stein, P. J. (1976). *Single.* Englewood Cliffs, NJ: Prentice-Hall.

Stein, P. J. (1983). Singlehood. In E. D. Macklin & R. H. Rubin (Eds.), *Contemporary families and alternative lifestyles.* Beverly Hills, CA: Sage Publications.

Stein, P. J. (1989). The diverse world of single adults. In J. M. Henslin (Ed.), *Marriage and family in a changing society* (3rd ed.). New York: Free Press.

Steinberg, L., & Silverberg, S. B. (1987). Influences on marital satisfaction during the middle stages of the family life cycle. *Journal of Marriage and the Family, 49,* 751–760.

Steiner, I. D. (1976). Task-performing groups. In J. W. Thibaut, J. T. Spence, & R. C. Carson (Eds.), *Contemporary topics in social psychology.* Morristown, NJ: General Learning Press.

Stekel, W. (1950). *Techniques of analytical psychotherapy.* New York: Liveright.

Stephan, F. F., & Mishler, E. G. (1952). The distribution of participation in small groups: An exponential approximation. *American Sociological Review, 17,* 598–608.

Stern, G. S., McCants, T. R., & Pettine, P. W. (1982). Stress and illness: Controllable and uncontrollable events' relative contributions. *Personality and Social Psychology Bulletin, 8*(1), 140–145.

Sternberg, R. J. (1986). A triangular theory of love. *Psychological Review, 93,* 119–135.

Sternberg, R. J. (1988). Triangulating love. In R. J. Sternberg & M. L. Barnes (Eds.), *The psychology of love.* New Haven, CT: Yale University Press.

Sternberg, R. J., & Grajek, S. (1984). The nature of love. *Journal of Personality and Social Psychology, 47,* 312–329.

Sternberg, R. J., & Soriano, L. J. (1984). Styles of conflict resolution. *Journal of Personality and Social Psychology 47*(1), 115–126.

Stevens, D. P., & Truss, C. V. (1985). Stability and change in adult personality over 12 and 20 years. *Developmental Psychology, 21,* 568–584.

Stiles, D. A., Gibbons, J. L., Hardardottir, S., & Schnellmann, J. (1987). The ideal man or woman as described by young adolescents in Iceland and the United States. *Sex Roles, 17,* 313–320.

Stoffer, G. R., Davis, K. E., & Brown, J. B., Jr. (1977). The consequences of changing initial answers on objective tests: A stable effect and a stable misconception. *Journal of Educational Research, 70,* 272–277.

Stogdill, R. M. (1963). *Manual for the Leader Behavior Description Questionnaire-Form XII.* Columbus: Bureau of Business Research, Ohio State University.

Stogdill, R. M. (1974). *Handbook of leadership: A survey of theory and research.* New York: Free Press.

Stolberg, A. L., Camplair, C., Currier, K., & Wells, M. J. (1987). Individual, familial and environmental determinants of children's post-divorce adjustment and maladjustment. *Journal of Divorce, 11,* 51–70.

Stone, A. A., & Neale, J. M. (1984). New measure of daily coping: Development and preliminary results. *Journal of Personality and Social Psychology, 46*(4), 892–906.

Stoner, J. A. F. (1961). *A comparison of individual and group decisions involving risk.* Unpublished master's thesis, Massachusetts Institute of Technology.

Strober, M. (1989). Stressful life events associated with bulimia in anorexia nervosa: Empirical findings and theoretical speculations. In T. W. Miller (Ed.), *Stressful life events.* Madison, CT: International Universities Press.

Strouse, J., & Fabes, R. A. (1985). Formal vs. informal sources of sex education: Competing forces in the sexual socialization of adolescents. *Adolescence, 78,* 251–263.

Strube, M. J., & Garcia, J. E. (1981). A meta-analytic investigation of Fiedler's contingency model of leadership effectiveness. *Psychological Bulletin, 90,* 307–321.

Strupp, H. H., Hadley, S. W., & Gomes-Schwartz, B. (1977). *Psychotherapy for better or worse: The problem of negative effects.* New York: Aronson.

Stunkard, A. J., Sorensen, T., Hanis, C., Teasdale, T. W., Chakraborty, R., Schull, W. J., & Schulsinger, F. (1986). An adoption study of human obesity. *New England Journal of Medicine, 314,* 193–198.

Sturgis, E. T. (1984). Obsessional and compulsive disorders. In H. E. Adams & P. B. Sutker (Eds.), *Comprehensive handbook of psychopatholgy.* New York: Plenum Press.

Sue, D. (1979). Erotic fantasies of college students during coitus. *Journal of Sex Research, 15,* 299–305.

Suedfeld, P. (1979). Stressful levels of environmental stimulation. In I. G. Sarason & C. D. Spielberger (Eds.), *Stress and anxiety* (Vol. 6). Washington, DC: Hemisphere.

Suinn, R. M. (1968). Removal of social desirability and response set items from the Manifest Anxiety Scale. *Educational and Psychological Measurement, 28,* 1189–1192.

Suinn, R. M. (1984). *Fundamentals of abnormal psychology.* Chicago: Nelson-Hall.

Super, D. E. (1957). *The psychology of careers.* New York: Harper & Row.

Super, D. E. (1985). Career and life development. In D. Brown & L. Brooks (Eds.), *Career choice and development.* San Francisco: Jossey-Bass.

Super, D. E. (1988). Vocational adjustment: Implementing a self-concept. *Career Development Quarterly, 36,* 351–357.

Sutker, P. B., & Allain, A. N. (1983). Behavior and personality assessment in men labeled adaptive sociopaths. *Journal of Behavioral Assessment, 5,* 65–79.

Swaney, K., & Prediger, D. (1985). The relationship between interest-occupation congruence and job satisfaction. *Journal of Vocational Behavior, 26,* 13–24.

Sweeney, P. D., Anderson, K., & Bailey, S. (1986). Attributional style in depression: A meta-analytic review. *Journal of Personality and Social Psychology, 50,* 974–991.

Swenson, C. H., Jr. (1973). *Introduction to interpersonal relations.* Glenview, IL: Scott, Foresman.

Szasz, T. S. (1974). *The myth of mental illness.* New York: Harper & Row.

Tanfer, K. (1987). Patterns of premarital cohabitation among never-married women in the United States. *Journal of Marriage and the Family, 49,* 483–497.

Tanfer, K., & Horn, M. C. (1985). *Family planning: Family planning perspectives.* New York: Alan Guttmacher Institute.

Tanner, J. M. (1978). *Fetus into man: Physical growth from conception to maturity.* Cambridge, MA: Harvard University Press.

Tavris, C. (1977). Men and women report their views on masculinity. *Psychology Today, 10*(8), 34–42, 82.

Tavris, C. (1982). *Anger: the misunderstood emotion* (1st ed.). New York: Simon & Schuster.

Tavris, C. (1989). *Anger: The misunderstood emotion* (2nd ed.). New York: Simon & Schuster.

Tavris, C., & Sadd, S. (1977). *The Redbook report on female sexuality.* New York: Delacorte.

Tavris, C., & Wade, C. (1984). *The longest war: Sex differences in perspective.* New York: Harcourt Brace Jovanovich.

Taylor, D. A., & Altman, I. (1987). Communication in interpersonal relationships: Social penetration processes. In M. E. Roloff & G. R. Miller (Eds.), *Interpersonal processes: New directions in communication research.* Beverly Hills, CA: Sage Publications.

Taylor, J. A. (1953). A personality scale of manifest anxiety. *Journal of Abnormal and Social Psychology, 48,* 285–290.

Taylor, M. C., & Hall, J. A. (1982). Psychological androgyny: Theories, methods, and conclusions. *Psychological Bulletin, 92,* 347–366.

Taylor, S. E., & Brown, J. D. (1988). Illusion and well-being: A social psychological perspective on mental health. *Psychological Bulletin, 103*(2), 193–210.

Teachman, J. D., Polonko, K. A., & Scanzoni, J. (1987). Demography of the family. In M. B. Sussman & S. K. Steinmetz (Eds.), *Handbook of marriage and the family*. New York: Plenum Press.

Tellegen, A., Lykken, D. T., Bouchard, T. J., Jr., Wilcox, K. J., Segal, N. L., & Rich, S. (1988). Personality similarity in twins reared apart and together. *Journal of Personality and Social Psychology, 54*(6), 1031–1039.

Temoshok, L., Sweet, D. M., & Zich, J. (1987). A three city comparison of the public's knowledge and attitudes about AIDS. *Psychology & Health, 1*(1), 43–60.

Terkel, S. (1974). *Working: People talk about what they do all day and how they feel about what they do*. New York: Pantheon.

Terry, R. L., & Kroger, D. L. (1976). Effects of eye correctives on ratings of attractiveness. *Perceptual and Motor Skills, 42*, 562.

Thibaut, J. W., & Kelley, H. H. (1959). *The social psychology of groups*. New York: Wiley.

Thigpen, C. H., & Cleckley, H. M. (1984). On the incidence of multiple personality disorder: A brief communication. *International Journal of Clinical and Experimental Hypnosis, 32*, 63–66.

Thomas, K. (1976). Conflict and conflict management. In M. D. Dunnette (Ed.), *Handbook of industrial and organizational psychology*. Chicago: Rand McNally.

Thompson, A. P. (1983). Extramarital sex: A review of the research literature. *Journal of Sex Research, 19*(1), 1–22.

Thornburg, H. (1981, April). Adolescent sources of information on sex. *Journal of School Health*, 274–277.

Thorndyke, P. W., & Hayes-Roth, B. (1979). The use of schemata in the acquisition and transfer of knowledge. *Cognitive Psychology, 11*, 83–106.

Thornton, B. (1984). Defensive attribution of responsibility: Evidence for an arousal-based motivational bias. *Journal of Personality and Social Psychology, 46*(4), 721–734.

Tomkins, S. S. (1966). Psychological model for smoking behavior. *American Journal of Public Health, 56*, 17–20.

Torgersen, S. (1983). Genetic factors in anxiety disorder. *Archives of General Psychiatry, 40*, 1085–1089.

Torrey, E. F. (1988). *Surviving schizophrenia: A family manual*. New York: Harper & Row.

Totman, R., Kiff, J., Reed, S. E., & Craig, J. W. (1980). Predicting experimental colds in volunteers from different measures of recent life stress. *Journal of Psychosomatic Research, 24*, 155–163.

Tourney, G. (1980). Hormones and homosexuality. In J. Marmor (Ed.), *Homosexual behavior*. New York: Basic Books.

Treas, J. (1983). Aging and the family. In D. S. Woodruff & J. E. Birren (Eds.), *Aging: Scientific perspectives and social issues*. Pacific Grove, CA: Brooks/Cole.

Tripp, C. A. (1987). *The homosexual matrix*. New York: Meridian.

Troll, L. E. (1982). *Continuations: Adult development and aging*. Pacific Grove, CA: Brooks/Cole.

Troll, L. E. (1985). *Early and middle adulthood: The best is yet to be*. Pacific Grove, CA: Brooks/Cole.

Trussell, J., & Westoff, C. F. (1980). Contraceptive practice and trends in coital frequency. *Family Planning Perspectives, 12*, 246–249.

Turnage, J. J. (1990). The challenge of new workplace technology for psychology. *American Psychologist, 45*(2), 171–178.

Turner, B. F., & Adams, C. G. (1988). Reported change in preferred sexual activity over the adult years. *Journal of Sex Research, 25*, 289–303.

Turner, S. M., Jacob, R. G., & Morrison, R. (1984). Somatoform and factitious disorders. In H. E. Adams & P. B. Sutker (Eds.), *Comprehensive handbook of psychopathology*. New York: Plenum Press.

Turner, S. M., McCann, B. S., Beidel, D. C., & Mezzich, J. E. (1986). DSM-III classification of the anxiety disorders: A psychometric study. *Journal of Abnormal Psychology, 95*(2), 168–172.

Twerski, A. J. (1978). *Like yourself—and others will too*. Englewood Cliffs, NJ: Prentice-Hall.

Underwood, B. J. (1970). A breakdown of the total-time law in free-recall learning. *Journal of Verbal Learning and Verbal Behavior, 9*, 573–580.

Upshaw, H. S. (1969). The personal reference scale: An approach to social judgment. In L. Berkowitz (Ed.), *Advances in experimental social psychology* (Vol. 4). New York: Academic Press.

Vaillant, G. E. (1977). *Adaptation to life*. Boston: Little, Brown.

Valins, S. (1966). Cognitive effects of false heart-rate feedback. *Journal of Personality and Social Psychology, 4*, 400–408.

Vance, E. B., & Wagner, N. N. (1976). Written descriptions of orgasm: A study of sex differences. *Archives of Sexual Behavior, 5*, 87–98.

Van Houten, R. (1983). Punishment: From the animal laboratory to the applied setting. In S. Axelrod & J. Apsche (Eds.), *The effects of punishment on human behavior*. New York: Academic Press.

VanItallie, T. B. (1979). Obesity: Adverse effects on health and longevity. *American Journal of Clinical Nutrition, 32*, 2727.

Van Wyk, P. H., & Geist, C. S. (1984). Psychosocial development of heterosexual, bisexual, and homosexual behavior. *Archives of Sexual Behavior, 13*(6), 505–544.

Verderber, K. S., & Verderber, R. F. (1989). *Inter-act: Using interpersonal communication skills* (2nd ed.). Belmont, CA: Wadsworth.

Verinis, J., & Roll, S. (1970). Primary and secondary male characteristics. *Psychological Reports, 26*, 123–126.

Vinogradov, S., & Yalom, I. D. (1988). Group therapy. In J. A. Talbott, R. E. Hales, & S. C. Yudofsky (Eds.), *The American Psychiatric Press textbook of psychiatry*. Washington, DC: American Psychiatric Press.

Von Baeyer, C. L., Sherk, D. L., & Zanna, M. P. (1981). Impression management in the job interview: When the female applicant meets the male (chauvinist) interviewer. *Personality and Social Psychology Bulletin, 7*(1), 45–51.

Vourakis, C., & Bennett, G. (1979). Angel dust: Not heaven sent. *American Journal of Nursing, 79*, 649–653.

Wachtel, P. L. (1989). *The poverty of affluence: A psychological portrait of the American way of life*. Philadelphia: New Society.

Wadden, T. A., Stunkard, A. J., Brownell, K. D., & VanItallie, T. B. (1983). The Cambridge diet. *Journal of the American Medical Association, 250*(20), 2833–2834.

Wallace, R. K., & Benson, H. (1972). The physiology of meditation. *Scientific American, 226*, 84–90.

Wallerstein, J. S., & Blakeslee, S. (1990). *Second chances: Men, women, and children a decade after divorce*. New York: Ticknor & Fields.

Walster, E., Aronson, E., Abrahams, D., & Rottman, L. (1966). Importance of physical attractiveness in dating behavior. *Journal of Personality and Social Psychology, 4*, 508–516.

Walster, E., & Berscheid, E. (1974). A little bit about love: A minor essay on a major topic. In T. L. Huston (Ed.), *Foundations of interpersonal attraction*. New York: Academic Press.

Walster, E., Walster, G. W., Piliavin, J., & Schmidt, L. (1973). Playing hard-to-get: Understanding an elusive phenomenon. *Journal of Personality and Social Psychology, 26*, 113–121.

Walters, C. C., & Grusec, J. E. (1977). *Punishment*. San Francisco: W. H. Freeman.

Ward, S. E., Leventhal, H., & Love, R. (1988). Repression revisited: Tactics used in coping with a severe health threat. *Personality and Social Psychology Bulletin, 14*(4), 735–746.

Warr, P. B. (1987). *Work, unemployment, and mental health*. Oxford: Clarendon.

Watson, A., & Boundy, D. (1989). *Willpower's not enough*. New York: Harper & Row.

Watson, D. L., & Friend, R. (1969). Measurement of social-evaluative anxiety. *Journal of Consulting and Clinical Psychology, 33*(4), 448–457.

Watson, D. L., & Tharp, R. G. (1989). *Self-directed behavior: Self-modification for personal adjustment*. Pacific Grove, CA: Brooks/Cole.

Watson, J. B. (1913). Psychology as the behaviorist views it. *Psychological Review, 20*, 158–177.

Wattenberg, W. W., & Clifford, C. (1964). Relation of self-concept to beginning achievement in reading. *Child Development, 35*, 461–467.

Webb, W. B., & Agnew, H. W., Jr. (1968). Measurement and characteristics of nocturnal sleep. In L. A. Abt & B. F. Riess (Eds.), *Progress in clinical psychology*. New York: Grune & Stratton.

Wechsler, D. (1958). *The measurement of adult intelligence*. Baltimore: Williams & Wilkins.

Weeks, D., Freeman, C. P. L., & Kendell, R. E. (1981). Does ECT produce enduring cognitive deficits? In R. L. Palmer (Ed.), *Electroconvulsive therapy: An appraisal*. Oxford: Oxford University Press.

Weeks, M. O., & Gage, B. A. (1984). A comparison of the marriage-role expectations of college women enrolled in a functional marriage course in 1961, 1972, and 1978. *Sex Roles, 11*, 377–388.

Wehr, T. A., Sack, D. A., Parry, B. L., & Rosenthal, N. E. (1986). The role of biological rhythms in the biology and treatment of insomnia and depression. In P. A. Berger & H. K. H. Brodie (Eds.), *American handbook of psychiatry: Biological psychiatry* (Vol. 8, 2nd ed.). New York: Basic Books.

Wehr, T. A., Sack, D. A., & Rosenthal. N. E. (1987). Sleep reduction as a final common pathway in the genesis of mania. *American Journal of Psychiatry, 144*, 201–204.

Weinberg, C. (1979). *Self creation*. New York: Avon.

Weinberger, D. R., Wagner, R. J., & Wyatt, R. J. (1983). Neuropathological studies of schizophrenia: A selective review. *Schizophrenia Bulletin, 9*, 198–212.

Weiner, B. (Ed.). (1974). *Achievement motivation and attribution theory*. Morristown, NJ: General Learning Press.

Weiner, B. (1986). An attribution theory of emotion and motivation. New York: Springer-Verlag.

Weiner, B., Frieze, I., Kukla, A., Reed, L., Rest, S., & Rosenbaum, R. M. (1972). Perceiving the causes of success and failure. In E. E. Jones, D. E. Kanouse, H. H. Kelley, R. E. Nisbett, S. Valins, & B. Weiner (Eds.), *Perceiving the causes of behavior*. Morristown, NJ: General Learning Press.

Weiner, H. (1977). *Psychobiology and human disease*. New York: Elsevier.

Weiner, H. (1978). Emotional factors. In S. C. Werner & S. H. Ingbar (Eds.), *The thyroid*. New York: Harper & Row.

Weiner, R. D. (1984). Does electroconvulsive therapy cause brain damage? *Behavioral and Brain Sciences, 7*, 1–53.

Weiner, R. D. (1985). Convulsive therapies. In H. I. Kaplan & B. J. Sadock (Eds.), *Comprehensive textbook of psychiatry/IV*. Baltimore: Williams & Wilkins.

Weiner, R. D. & Coffey, C. E. (1988). Indications for use of electroconvulsive therapy. In A. J. Frances & R. E. Hales (Eds.), *Review of psychiatry* (Vol. 7). Washington, DC: American Psychiatric Press.

Weingarten, H. R. (1985). Marital status and well-being: A national study comparing first-married, currently divorced, and remarried adults. *Journal of Marriage and the Family, 47*, 653–662.

Weinrach, S. G. (1979). *Career counseling: Theoretical and practical perspectives*. New York: McGraw-Hill.

Weinstein, N. D. (1984). Why it won't happen to me: Perceptions of risk factors and susceptibility. *Health Psychology, 3*(5), 431–458.

Weiss, R. S. (1975). *Marital separation*. New York: Basic Books.

Weissman, M. M. (1985). The epidemiology of anxiety disorders: Rates, risks and familial patterns. In A. H. Tuma & J. Maser (Eds.), *Anxiety and the anxiety disorders*. Hillsdale, NJ: Erlbaum.

Weissman, M. M., Prusoff, B. A., DiMascio, A., Neu, C., Goklaney, M., & Klerman, G. L. (1979). The efficacy of drugs and psychotherapy in the treatment of acute depressive episodes. *American Journal of Psychiatry, 136*, 555–558.

Weiten, W. (1984). Violation of selected item-construction principles in educational measurement. *Journal of Experimental Education, 51*, 46–50.

Weiten, W. (1988). Pressure as a form of stress and its relationship to psychological symptomatology. *Journal of Social and Clinical Psychology, 6*(1), 127–139.

Weiten, W., Clery, J., & Bowbin, G. (1980, September). *Test-wiseness: Its composition and significance in educational measurement*. Paper presented at the meeting of the American Psychological Association, Montreal, Quebec.

Weiten, W., & Dixon, J. (1984, August). *Measurement of pressure as a form of stress*. Paper presented at the meeting of the American Psychological Association, Toronto, Ontario.

Weitzman, L. J. (1989). The divorce revolution and the feminization of poverty. In J. M. Henslin (Ed.), *Marriage and the family in a changing society* (3rd ed.). New York: Free Press.

Weizman, R., & Hart, J. (1987). Sexual behavior in healthy married elderly men. *Archives of Sexual Behavior, 16*(1), 39–44.

Wekstein, L. (1979). *Handbook of suicidology*. New York: Brunner/Mazel.

Weldon, E., & Gargano, G. M. (1988). Cognitive loafing: The effects of accountability and shared responsibility on cognitive effort. *Personality and Social Psychology Bulletin, 14*(1), 159–171.

Wells, L. E., & Marwell, G. (1976). *Self-esteem: Its conceptualization and measurement*. Beverly Hills, CA: Sage Publications.

Wertheimer, M. (1970). *A brief history of psychology*. New York: Holt, Rinehart & Winston.

Westefeld, J. S., & Furr, S. R. (1987). Suicide and depression among college students. *Professional Psychology: Research and Practice, 18*, 119–123.

Westoff, C. (1974). Coital frequency and contraception. *Family Planning Perspectives, 6*, 136–141.

Whitbourne, S. K. (1985). *The aging body: Physiological changes and psychological consequences*. New York: Springer-Verlag.

White, G. L. (1981). Some correlates of romantic jealousy. *Journal of Personality and Social Psychology, 49*, 129–147.

White, J. M. (1987). Premarital cohabitation and marital stability in Canada. *Journal of Marriage and the Family, 49*, 641–647.

White, L. K., & Booth, A. (1985). Stepchildren in remarriages. *American Sociological Review, 50*, 689–698.

White, M. J., Kruczek, T. A., Brown, M. T., & White, G. B. (1989, May). *Occupational sex stereotypes among college students*. Paper presented at the meeting of the Midwestern Psychological Association, Chicago, Illinois.

Whitley, B. E., Jr. (1988). College students' reasons for sexual intercourse: A sex role perspective. *Paper presented at the 96th Annual Meeting of the American Psychological Association*, Atlanta, Georgia.

Whitley, B. E., Jr., & Frieze, I. H. (1983). *Expectancy confirmation and egotism as determinants of causal attributions: Two meta-analyses*. Manuscript submitted for publication.

Whitley, B. E., Jr., & Frieze, I. H. (1985). Children's causal attributions for success and failure in achievement settings: A meta-analysis. *Journal of Educational Psychology, 77*(5), 608–616.

Whitney, E. N., & Cataldo, C. B. (1987). *Understanding normal and clinical nutrition*. St. Paul, MN: West.

Wiener, D. N. (1968). *A practical guide to psychotherapy*. New York: Harper & Row.

Wiest, W. (1977). Semantic differential profiles of orgasm and other experiences among men and women. *Sex Roles, 3*, 399–403.

Wilder, C. S. (1971). Chronic conditions and limitations of activity and mobility: United States, July 1965 to June 1967. *U.S. Vital and Health Statistics, 10*(6), 334.

Williams, J. B. W. (1985). The multiaxial system of DSM-III, where did it come from and where should it go? II: Empirical studies, innovations, and recommendations. *Archives of General Psychiatry, 42*, 181–186.

Williams, J. E., & Best, D. L. (1982). *Measuring sex stereotypes: A thirty-nation study*. Beverly Hills, CA: Sage Publications.

Williams, N. A., & Deffenbacher, J. L. (1983). Life stress and chronic yeast infections. *Journal of Human Stress, 9*(1), 26–31.

Wilson, W. C. (1975). The distribution of selected sexual attitudes and behaviors among the adult population of the United States. *Journal of Sex Research, 11*, 46–64.

Windshuttle, K. (1980). *Unemployed*. Melbourne, Australia: Penguin.

Windsor, R. A., Cutter, G., Morris, J., Reese, Y., Manzella, B., Bartlett, E. E., Samuelson, C., & Spanos, D. (1985). The effectiveness of smoking cessation methods for smokers in public health maternity clinics: A randomized trial. *American Journal of Public Health, 75*, 1389–1392.

Wine, J. D. (1982). Evaluation anxiety: A cognitive-attentional construct. In H. W. Krohne & L. Laux (Eds.), *Achievement, stress and anxiety*. New York: Hemisphere.

Wolchik, S. A., Braver, S. L., & Jensen, K. (1985). Volunteer bias in erotica research: Effects of intrusiveness of measure and sexual background. *Archives of Sexual Behavior, 14*(2), 93–107.

Wolf, S. (1986). Common and grave disorders identified with occupational stress. In S. Wolf & A. J. Finestone (Eds.), *Occupational stress: Health and performance at work*. Littleton, MA: PSG Publishing.

Wolfe, L. (1981). *The Cosmo report*. New York: Arbor House.

Woll, S. (1986). So many to choose from: Decision strategies in videodating. *Journal of Social and Personal Relationships, 3*(1), 43–52.

Wolpe, J. (1958). *Psychotherapy by reciprocal inhibition*. Stanford, CA: Stanford University Press.

Wolpe, J. (1987). The promotion of scientific therapy: A long voyage. In J. K. Zeig (Ed.), *The evolution of psychotherapy*. New York: Brunner/Mazel.

Women on Words and Images. (1972). *Dick and Jane as victims: Sex stereotyping in children's readers*. Princeton, NJ: Author.

Woolfolk, R. L. (1975). Psychophysiological correlates of meditation. *Archives of General Psychiatry, 32*, 1326–1333.

Woolfolk, R. L., & Richardson, F. C. (1978). *Stress, sanity, and survival*. New York: Sovereign/Monarch.

Wurman, R. S. (1989). *Information anxiety*. New York: Doubleday.

Wyatt, G. E., Peters, S. D., & Guthrie, D. (1988). Kinsey revisited, Part I: Comparison of the sexual socialization and sexual behavior of white women over 33 years. *Archives of Sexual Behavior, 17*(3), 201–239.

Wyler, A. R., Masuda, M., & Holmes, T. H. (1971). Magnitude of life events and seriousness of illness. *Psychosomatic Medicine, 33*(2), 115–122.

Wylie, R. C. (1979). *The self-concept: Theory and research on selected topics*. Lincoln: University of Nebraska Press.

Yalom, I. D. (1975). *The theory and practice of group psychotherapy*. New York: Basic Books.

Yelsma, P. (1984). Marital communication, adjustment, and perceptual differences between "happy" and "counseling" couples. *American Journal of Family Therapy, 12*, 26–36.

Young, J. E. (1982). Loneliness, depression and cognitive therapy: Theory and application. In L. A. Peplau & D. Perlman (Eds.), *Loneliness: A sourcebook of current theory, research and therapy*. New York: Wiley.

Zaccaro, S. J. (1984). Social loafing: The role of task attractiveness. *Personality and Social Psychology Bulletin, 10*, 99–106.

Zacks, E. Green, R. J., & Marrow, J. (1988). Comparing lesbian and heterosexual couples on the Circumplex Model: An initial investigation. *Family Process, 27*, 471–484.

Zanna, M., Goethals, G. R., & Hill, J. (1975). Evaluating a sex-rated ability: Social comparison with similar others and standard setters. *Journal of Experimental Social Psychology, 11*, 86–93.

Zanna, M. P., & Olson, J. M. (1982). Individual differences in attitudinal relations. In M. P. Zanna, E. T. Higgins, & C. P. Herman (Eds.), *Consistency in social behavior: The Ontario symposium, Vol. 2*. Hillsdale, NJ: Erlbaum.

Zechmeister, E. B., & Nyberg, S. E. (1982). *Human memory: An introduction to research and theory*. Pacific Grove, CA: Brooks/Cole.

Zedeck, S., & Mosier, K. L. (1990). Work in the family and employing organization. *American Psychologist, 45*(2), 240–251.

Zeig, J. K. (1987). Introduction: The evolution of psychotherapy—Fundamental issues. In J. K. Zeig (Ed.), *The evolution of psychotherapy.* New York: Brunner/Mazel.

Zeiss, A. M. (1980). Aversiveness versus change in the assessment of life stress. *Journal of Psychosomatic Stress, 24*, 15–19.

Zelnick, M., & Kantner, J. F. (1977). Sexual and contraceptive experience of young unmarried women in the United States, 1976 and 1971. *Family Planning Perspectives, 9*, 55–71.

Zey, M. G. (1985). Mentor programs: Making the right moves. *Personnel Journal, 64*(2), 53–57.

Zilbergeld, B., & Evans, M. (1980). The inadequacy of Masters and Johnson. *Psychology Today, 14*(3), 28–34, 37–43.

Zillmann, D., & Bryant, J. (1984). Effects of massive exposure to pornography. In N. M. Malamuth & E. Donnerstein (Eds.), *Pornography and sexual aggression.* New York: Academic Press.

Zimbardo, P. G. (1977). *Shyness: What it is, what to do about it.* Reading, MA: Addison-Wesley.

Zimbardo, P. G. (1987). *Shyness.* New York: Jove.

Zimmer, D. (1983). Interaction patterns and communication skills in sexually distressed and normal couples: Two experimental studies. *Journal of Sex and Marital Therapy, 9*, 251–265.

Zis, A. P., & Goodwin, F. K. (1982). The amine hypothesis. In E. S. Paykel (Ed.), *Handbook of affective disorders.* New York: Guilford Press.

Zubin, J. (1986). Implications of the vulnerability model for DSM-IV with special reference to schizophrenia. In T. Millon & G. L. Klerman (Eds.), *Contemporary directions in psychopathology: Toward the DSM-IV.* New York: Guilford Press.

Zuckerman, M. (1971). Dimensions of sensation seeking. *Journal of Consulting and Clinical Psychology, 36*, 45–52.

Zuckerman, M. (1979). *Sensation Seeking: Beyond the optimal level of arousal.* Hillsdale, NJ: Erlbaum.

Zuckerman, M., Lazzaro, M. M., & Waldgeir, D. (1979). Undermining effects of the foot-in-the-door technique with extrinsic rewards. *Journal of Applied Social Psychology, 9*, 292–296.

Zunin, L., & Zunin, N. (1988). *Contact: The first four minutes.* New York: Ballantine.

Name Index

Hastrup, J. L., 114
Hatfield, Elaine, 216, 227, 231, 232
Hatfield, J. D., 171
Hatlelid, D., 221
Hauser, S. T., 328
Hautzinger, M., 440
Havighurst, R. J., 318
Haviland, J. J., 276
Hayes-Roth, B., 23
Haynes, S. G., 394
Hays, R. B., 226
Haythorn, W. W., 172
Hazan, Cindy, 230–231, 232
Healy, D., 444
Heath, R. G., 418
Hebb, D. O., 74
Heffernan, J. M., 334
Hegsted, D. M., 402
Heider, Fritz, 130
Heilbrun, A. B., Jr., 301
Heiman, J. R., 366
Heinlein, L., 368
Helson, H., 211
Helson, R., 306, 313
Helzer, J. E., 80, 81, 446
Hemphill, J. K., 196
Hemsley, G. D., 162
Henderson, M., 225
Hendrick, C., 224, 233
Hendrick, S. S., 174, 224, 233
Henley, N. M., 161, 162, 163, 164, 173, 278
Henry, W., 319, 361
Henson, A., 161
Herink, R., 459
Herman, C. P., 144
Herron, J. R., 174
Hertzog, C., 321
Heuer, S. K., 219
Heun, L. R., 165
Heun, R. E., 165
Hill, C. T., 228, 229, 232, 233
Hill, J. P., 135, 328
Hill, R., 249
Hirokawa, R. Y., 193
Hiroto, D. S., 98
Hirsch, J., 400
Hirschfeld, A., 346, 397
Hirschfeld, M. L., 346, 397
Hirschfeld, R. M. A., 279, 311, 451
Hite, S., 371, 373
Hobbs, S. A., 234
Hochschild, A., 253
Hockenbury, D., 234
Hodges, B. H., 146
Hoffman, L., 254, 255
Hoffman, M., 404
Hogan, D. P., 306
Hokanson, J. E., 99
Holahan, C. J., 102
Hollabaugh, L. C., 177
Holland, C. C., 205
Holland, John, 349–351
Hollingsworth, A. T., 341
Hollister, L. E., 418
Hollon, S. D., 466
Holmes, D. S., 115, 404
Holmes, Thomas H., 17, 64, 69, 83, 86, 396
Holroyd, K. A., 64
Holt, R. R., 341, 346
Holter, H., 292
Honeycutt, J. M., 246
Hoon, P. W., 372

Hopkins, A. H., 342
Horn, D., 399
Horn, J. M., 447
Horn, M. C., 378
Hornblow, A. R., 397
Horner, M. J., 287
Horner, S. O., 341
Horowitz, L. M., 235
Horowitz, M. J., 79
Horvath, T., 220
House, J. S., 83, 110
House, P., 147
Houston, B. K., 84
Hovland, C. I., 202
Howard, J. A., 146
Howe, M. L., 321
Hoyer, W. J., 322, 323
Hsieh, C., 404
Hubbard, L. Ron, 6
Huesmann, L. R., 131
Hull, J. G., 84
Hunt, Morton, 364, 365, 371, 373, 374, 375, 377
Hunt, W. A., 399
Hunter, M. A., 321
Hurst, M. W., 86
Huryn, J., 396
Huse, D. M., 400
Huseman, R. C., 171
Huston, A. C., 285
Huston, T. L., 144
Huyck, M. H., 323
Hyde, Janet Shibley, 276, 277, 279, 286, 367, 368, 383
Hyde, R. T., 404

Ickes, W., 155
Ilfeld, F. W., 258
Ineichen, B., 224
Infante, D. A., 213
Inhelder, Barbel, 310
Isherwood, J., 397
Ivancevich, J. M., 345, 346, 347

Jacklin, C. N., 276
Jackman, M. R., 143
Jackson, P. G., 261
Jackson, P. R., 343
Jackson, R. E., 408
Jacob, R. G., 437
Jacobs, J., 311
Jacobs, T. J., 395
Jacobson, E., 116
Jaffe, J. H., 415
Jahoda, M., 103
Jakubowski, P., 296
Jakubowski-Spector, P., 296
Jamison, K. R., 441
Janda, L. H., 365
Janis, Irving L., 66, 82, 194–195, 201
Jarrett, M., 396
Jedlicka, D., 375
Jeffrey, D. B., 400
Jemmott, J. B., III, 83
Jenkins, C. D., 86
Jennings, J., 256
Jensen, K., 362
Jerrett, I., 396
Jeste, D. V., 476
Jewler, A. Jerome, 20
Johnson, D. R., 249, 251
Johnson, David W., 179, 181
Johnson, E. W., 379

Johnson, F., 179, 181
Johnson, J. H., 87, 88, 89, 396
Johnson, L. C., 405
Johnson, Virginia, 370–371, 373, 374, 378, 385, 386, 387
Johnston, L. D., 412
Jones, E. E., 130, 131, 139, 142
Jones, M. A., 159, 255
Jones, Mary Cover, 308
Jones, N. F., 410
Jones, R. A., 201
Jones, R. T., 418
Jones, S. C., 222
Jones, W. H., 137, 234, 238
Jones-Witters, P., 419
Jordaan, J. P., 334
Jourard, Sidney M., 103, 134, 142, 150, 173, 174
Julian, N. B., 285
Julien, R. M., 412, 414
Jung, Carl, 464

K

Kafry, D., 80
Kagan, Jerome, 319
Kahill, S. P., 291
Kahn, S., 84, 314
Kalant, H., 417
Kalant, O. J., 417
Kales, A., 406
Kales, J. D., 406
Kalick, S. M., 221
Kandel, D. B., 224
Kane, C., 396
Kanner, A. D., 65
Kantner, J. F., 376
Kaplan, H. I., 81
Kaplan, H. S., 279, 376, 387
Kaplan, M. F., 221
Karasek, Robert, 345, 346
Karasu, T. B., 396
Karlen, A., 373, 376
Karson, C. N., 447
Kaskerelis, D., 396
Kass, F., 429
Kastenbaum, R., 322, 323
Kauffman, D. R., 140, 225
Kausler, D. H., 321
Kavesh, L., 245
Kawash, G. F., 366
Kazdin, A. E., 118, 474
Keesey, R. E., 400
Keinan, G., 195
Keith, P. M., 262
Keith-Spicgel, P., 482
Kelley, Harold H., 130, 132, 133, 217, 232
Kelley, K., 369, 398, 423
Kendall, R. E., 478
Kennedy, Joyce Lane, 348
Kenny, D. A., 197
Kenrick, D. T., 277
Kepecs, J. G., 461
Kerr, S., 199
Kessler-Harris, Alice, 338
Keyes, R., 234
Kiecolt-Glaser, J. K., 397
Kieffer, J. A., 337
Kiesler, D. J., 449
Kiesler, S. B., 222
Kiff, J., 396
Kilner, L. A., 328
Kilroy, M. C., 162
Kinder, M., 7
King, Laura, 67

Kinsbourne, M., 281
Kinsey, Alfred, 362, 363, 374, 376
Kinsman, R. A., 410
Kirby, D. F., 285
Kirscht, J. P., 409
Kitson, G. C., 252
Klassen, M., 113
Kleber, H. D., 417
Klein, Melanie, 464
Kleinke, C. L., 161, 162
Kleinman, J. E., 447
Kleinmuntz, B., 441
Klerman, G. L., 69, 86, 443, 479
Klineberg, O., 161
Klipper, Miriam Z., 10, 116
Kluft, R. P., 439
Knight, G. W., 138
Knittle, J. L., 400
Knoth, R., 367
Knox, D., 177
Knussmann, R., 364
Kobasa, Suzanne, 83–84, 90
Kockott, G., 364
Koester, N. H., 234
Kogan, H. N., 396
Kohen, A. I., 336
Kohlberg, Lawrence, 284
Kohn, M., 199
Kohut, Heinz, 464
Kolden, G., 131
Kolodner, R. M., 418
Kolodny, R. C., 378, 386, 418
Komarovsky, M., 173, 255, 274
Koocher, G. P., 138
Koplan, J. P., 404
Korchin, S. J., 427
Kornreich, M., 470
Kory, R. B., 115
Koss, M. P., 176
Kotkin, M., 261
Koumandakis, E., 396
Kraemer, D. L., 114
Kramer, B. A., 479
Kramer, M. A., 381
Krantz, D. L., 336
Krantz, D. S., 393, 409
Krasner, L., 427
Krasnoff, L., 87
Kravitz, D. A., 191
Krilov, L. R., 380
Kristiansen, P., 419
Kroger, D. L., 145
Kruczek, T. A., 338
Krueger, D. W., 81, 100
Krueger, W. C. F., 23
Kübler-Ross, Elisabeth, 10, 323
Kuehnle, J., 418
Kuhn, D., 310
Kutash, S. B., 464
Kyle, G. R., 263

L

Lader, M. H., 475
LaFitte, Pat, 359
Lafontaine, E., 339
LaFrance, M., 161
Lagos, J., 396
Lahiff, J. M., 171
Lakein, Alan, 20, 111, 112, 114
Lal, N., 396
Lambert, M. J., 481
Lamm, H., 194
Landau, E., 304
Landers, A. D., 282
Landsman, T., 103, 134, 150
Landy, D., 144

Landy, F. J., 33, 344
Lange, A. J., 296
Langenbrunner, M., 259
Langlois, J. H., 284
Lanier, K., 160
Laramore, Darril, 348
Lareau, W., 354, 355, 356, 357
Larwood, L., 337
Lasky, T., 404
Lassiter, G. D., 162, 165
Latané, Bibb, 190–191, 193
Latham, D., 192
Laughlin, H., 101, 434
Lavin, C., 245
Lavine, L., 173
Lawler, Edward, 342, 349
Lawson, E. D., 144, 145
Lazarus, Arnold A., 471, 472, 473, 480, 483
Lazarus, R. S., 64, 65, 66, 72, 97
Lazzarro, M. M., 208
Leavitt, F., 412, 476
Leavy, R. L., 83
Lebov, M., 112
Lecourt, H. M., 107
Leff, J., 448
Lehmann, H. E., 446, 447
Lehne, G. K., 290
Lehrer, P. M., 115
Leigh, B. C., 263, 367
Leino, E. V., 321
Leitenberg, H., 472
Leiter, E., 385
LeMasters, E. E., 250
Lemkau, J. P., 291
Lemnitzer, N., 400
Lemon, B. W., 318, 319
Lennon, R., 277
Leo, J., 52
Lerner, M. J., 145
LeShan, L., 396
Leslie, G. R., 253
Lesnick-Oberstein, M., 85
Leung, P., 432
Levay, A. N., 385
Levenson, H., 346, 397
Leventhal, H., 103, 201
Levering, R., 343
Levin, A., 377
Levin, R. J., 377
Levine, H. M., 90
LeVine, R. A., 325
Levine, S., 384
Levinger, G., 216–217, 369
Levinson, Daniel, 314, 315, 316, 318, 319
Levitin, T., 291
Lewin, Kurt, 67
Lewine, R. J., 445
Lewinsohn, P. M., 440, 443
Lewis, D. J., 439
Lewis, J. M., 250
Lewis, R. A., 252
Lewis, R. J., 365
Libby, R. W., 366
Lichtenstein, E., 459
Lickey, M. E., 475, 476
Lieblich, A., 318
Liem, R., 343
Lindgren, H. C., 22, 23
Linn, Marcia C., 276, 286
Linz, D., 177
Lipman, B. E., 356, 357
Lipscomb, W. R., 417
Litman, R. E., 452
Litwack, M., 7

Livson, F. B., 319
Lloyd, C., 81
Lloyd, M. A., 140
Lloyd, S. A., 255
Lobitz, C., 387
Lock, R. D., 348
Locke, E. A., 342
Locksley, A., 293
Loehlin, J. C., 447
Lombardo, J., 173
London, K. A., 248
Lonetto, R., 331
Longman, Debbie G., 20
LoPiccolo, J., 256, 387
Lore, R. K., 22
Losonczy, M. F., 447
Lott, B., 287, 288, 294, 371
Loughman, W. D., 417
Love, R., 103
Lowe, C. A., 140, 225
Lowenthal, F., 396
Lowenthal, M. F., 318
Lowry, D. T., 365
Luborsky, L., 470, 479, 483
Luker, K. C., 378
Lumb, J. R., 408
Lumsdaine, A., 201
Lustman, P. J., 474
Luthe, W., 116
Lyman, B., 221

M

Maccoby, Eleanor, 276, 277, 326
Machlowitz, M. M., 347
Machung, A., 252, 253
Mackay, C., 396
Mackenzie, R. Alec, 110, 111, 112
Macklin, E. D., 244, 245, 261, 263
Macurdy, C., 221
Maddi, S. R., 84
Maddock, J. W., 256
Madhukar, 396
Magder, L., 396
Magloire, K., 83
Magruder, Mary Jo, 359
Mahoney, M. J., 108, 150
Major, B., 163
Malamuth, N. M., 177, 366
Malatesta, C. Z., 276
Malatesta, V. J., 81
Malmo, R. B., 74
Mandler, G., 79
Mann, A., 81
Marcia, James, 140–141, 312
Maricle, R., 432
Marini, M. M., 287
Mark, H., 416
Markman, H. J., 370
Marks, B., 396
Marks, G., 147
Marks, I. M., 43, 435
Marks, T., 81, 444
Marlatt, G. A., 100
Marotz-Baden, R., 256
Marrow, J., 263
Marsh, H. W., 138
Marsh, P., 163
Marshall, J., 344
Martin, B., 65, 191, 435
Martin, C. L., 275, 284
Martin, J. A., 326
Martin, R. A., 107
Martinson, F. M., 365
Marunycz, J. D., 475
Marwell, G., 137
Maslach, C., 80

Maslow, Abraham, 50–51, 187, 369
Mason, J. W., 76
Masters, William, 370–371, 373, 374, 378, 385, 386, 387, 418
Masuda, M., 17, 396
Matarazzo, J. D., 399
Mathes, E., 219
Mathhews, K. A., 338
Matteson, M. T., 345, 346
Mattessich, P., 249
Matthews, K. A., 71, 394
Mayer, Jean, 402
Mayer, R. E., 23
Mayo, C., 161, 278
Mayol, A., 81, 444
McAllister, D. E., 435
McAllister, W. R., 435
McCann, B. S., 434
McCann, C. D., 139
McCann, I. L., 404
McCants, T. R., 71
McCary, James, 383
McCrea, Robert, 32, 33, 97, 107, 313
McCreary, C., 399
McDaniel, M. A., 25
McDermott, L. J., 362
McDonald, W. I., 396
McDougle, L. G., 111
McEnroe, M. J., 443
McEvoy, L., 80
McGhee, P. E., 286
McGill, M. E., 319
McGinnies, E., 200
McGinnis, L., 321
McGlashan, T. H., 448
McGlone, J., 280
McGoldrick, M., 248, 249
McGrath, J. E., 71, 189
McGregor, Douglas, 340
McGuire, William, 199, 201
McHenry, R., 145
McKeon, J., 81
McKillip, J., 221
McKinlay, J. B., 320
McKinlay, S. M., 320
McLanahan, S., 249
McMillan, J. H., 132
McNally, R. J., 435
McReynolds, W. T., 432
McWilliams, Peter, 10
Mcad, Margaret, 283
Mechanic, David, 409
Medalie, J. H., 384
Meduna, Ladislas, 477
Mehrabian, A., 159, 162
Meier, P., 103
Meilman, P. W., 140
Melburg, V., 139
Melko, M., 262
Mellinger, J. C., 288
Mello, N. K., 419
Mellor, E. F., 291
Melman, A., 385
Meltzer, H. Y., 445
Meltzoff, J., 470
Mendelson, J. H., 418, 419
Mentzer, R. L., 26
Merikangas, K. R., 449
Metalsky, G. I., 442
Metts, S. M., 174
Meyer, R., 450
Mezzich, J. E., 434
Michelozzi, B. N., 352
Midlarsky, E., 274

Miele, P., 6
Milgram, Stanley, 204–206
Miller, A. G., 205
Miller, C. T., 366
Miller, D. T., 145
Miller, G. P., 108
Miller, G. T., Jr., 3
Miller, Jean Baker, 287
Miller, Lynn, 183
Miller, N. E., 41, 67, 68, 82, 393
Miller, R. I., 470
Miller, S. H., 174
Millett, K., 287
Millman, Jason, 25
Millon, T., 449
Mills, Judson, 210, 218
Millsap, R., 313
Milstein, V., 478
Mindel, C. H., 318
Mineka, S., 436
Mintz, J., 470
Mirkin, G., 404
Mirsky, A. F., 447
Mischel, H. N., 46
Mischel, Walter, 46, 283, 284
Mishell, D. R., 380
Mishler, E. G., 189
Mitchell, V. F., 111, 306
Mittleman, R. E., 417
Moane, G., 306, 313
Mobley, W. H., 341
Model, S., 291
Mogar, R. E., 417
Monaghan, P., 252, 253
Money, John, 281, 363
Monge, R., 317
Monroe, S. M., 86
Monsma, B. R., 257
Montemayor, R., 250
Moore, D., 235
Moorman, J. E., 258
Moos, Rudolph H., 100, 102, 104, 443
Morey, Leslie, 449
Morgan, M., 286
Morgan, M. Y., 244
Morgan, P. A., 420
Morikawa, S., 131
Morrison, A. M., 339
Morrison, R., 437
Morse, S., 135
Mosher, D. L., 369
Mosier, K. L., 347
Moss, H. A., 285
Mossholder, K. W., 253
Mouton, J. S., 180, 211
Mowrer, O. H., 435
Muchnik, B., 323
Muehlenhard, C. L., 177
Mullen, B., 147
Muller, L. C., 174
Munroe, R. H., 283
Munroe, R. L., 283
Murff, Bob, 359
Murnen, S. K., 224
Murphy, J. M., 441, 446
Murphy, K., 352, 353
Murstein, Bernard, 220, 246, 247
Myerowitz, B. E., 136
Myers, D. G., 135, 194
Myers, J. K., 448

N

Nahas, G. G., 418
Najavits, L., 466

Subject Index

birth order, 40
bisexuals, 363
blaming, 132
    of victim, 145–146, 148, 176
blood pressure. *See* hypertension
"blue-collar blues," 342
body image, 363
body language, 160, 162
boredom, 82, 85
Boston Women's Health Book Collective, 281
brain, aging and, 319–320
brain abnormalities, 447
brain organization, gender and, 280–281
brainstorming, 109, 192
burnout, 80–81, 347
Buspar, 475
bystander effect, 190

C

caffeine, 416
calories, 401
Cambridge diet, 401
cancer, 392, 395–396, 399
candidiasis, 380
cannabis, 413, 418
carbohydrates, 403
cardinal traits, 33
career
    marriage and, 252, 253–255
    women and, 287–288
career advancement, 336
career change, 336, 349
career choice, 348–353, 360
career development, 335–337
career patterns, 337
carelessness, 167
case studies, 16–17, 51
catastrophic thinking, 100–101, 105–107, 128
catatonic schizophrenia, 445
catecholamines, 76, 77
catharsis, 99–100
cause and effect relationships, 14, 17
centralization, 189
central traits, 33
cerebral hemispheres, 280–281
cervical cap, 379
challenges, 84
change
    divorce as, 259
    reactions to, 84
    stress and, 69–70
channels, communication, 158–159, 200
charities, 209, 211
childhood, evolution of, 325
childlessness, 245, 249–250
child rearing, 326–329
    anxiety disorders and, 435–436
    self-esteem and, 137
children
    aggression in, 46–47
    divorce and, 258–259
    gender-role socialization of, 283–286
    job aspirations of, 335
    marriage and, 249–251
    sexuality of, 364–365
    working mother and, 254–255
"China white," 420
chlamydial infection, 380
chlorpromazine, 474, 475
choking under pressure, 79
cholesterol, 402, 403
chronic diseases, 4, 392
Chronic Self-Destructiveness Scale, 422
cigarette smoking, 398–400
clarification, 465

class attendance, grades and, 22
classical conditioning, 41–43, 53, 435, 471–472
classification system, for psychological disorders, 430–432
claustrophobia, 434
client-centered therapy, 464–466, 479
clinical psychologists, 460
clinical psychology, 11
clitoris, 371
close relationships, 216
    See also friendship; love; relationships
clothing, 145
cocaine, 413, 416–417
codeine, 414
coercive power, 189
cognition, 45, 46
cognitive development, 308–310
cognitive dissonance, 132, 210
cognitive skills
    aging and, 321
    gender and, 276
cognitive theory
    of gender-role socialization, 284–285
    of mood disorders, 442–443
cognitive therapy, 254, 466–468, 479
cohabitation, 244, 261, 263
cohesiveness, group, 190, 193, 194, 195
cohort, age, 305
coitus, 374, 376
colds, 396, 402
college education, value of, 352, 353
College Is Only the Beginning (Gardner & Jewler), 20
College Learning and Study Skills (Longman & Atkinson), 20
college students, suicide among, 451
collusion, 168
commitment, 140–141
    compliance and, 208
    in early adulthood, 315
    in groups, 192
    marriage and, 244
    to parenthood, 255
    in relationships, 229, 232, 233
    to values, 84
communal relationships, 218
communication, 3
    components of, 158–159
    defined, 158
    in groups, 189, 190, 192
    intimate, 171–175
    in marriage, 255–256
    nonverbal, 159–166
    persuasion as, 200
    in relationships, 217
    sexual, 365, 369–370, 373, 374, 383–384
    verbal, 166–171
    See also interpersonal communication
communication barriers, 167–169
communication deviance, 447–448
communication network, 189
community mental health centers, 483
companionate love, 230
comparison level, 217
comparisons, social, 107, 134–135, 172, 187
compensation, 39
competence, interpersonal attraction and, 221
competitiveness, 168, 394
complementary transactions, 266
compliance, 203
    with medical advice, 410
compliments, 139
Comprehensive Stress Management (Greenberg), 78

compromise, 180
compulsions, 434
concentration camps, 98, 148
concordance rates, 441, 447
concrete operations period, 309, 310
conditionability, 52
conditioned reflex, 42
conditioned response, 42, 43
conditioned stimulus, 42, 43, 471
conditioning
    of anxiety disorders, 435
    psychological disorders and, 471
    See also classical conditioning; operant conditioning
condoms, 379–380, 381, 408
conflict
    internal, 35–36, 109, 461–464
    interpersonal, 168, 179–181, 232
    in marriage, 251–257
    parent-adolescent, 328
    in sexual relationships, 369–370
    stress and, 67–68
conflict resolution, 181
conformity, 202–203
    gender and, 278, 279
    in groups, 190
    ingratiation and, 139
    pressure for, 70
congruence, 48–49, 142
conscious awareness, 35
conservation, 309
consideration, in leadership, 198
constructive coping, 103–116
    appraisal-focused, 104–108
    emotion-focused, 113–116
    problem-focused, 108–113
consummate love, 230
consummatory behavior, 100, 122
Contact: The First Four Minutes (Zunin & Zunin), 169
contagious diseases, 4, 392
contingencies, reinforcement, 120–121
contingency theory, 198–199
contraception, 378–380
contrast effects, 208
control
    lack of, 98
    over life, 84
control group, 14
controllability, 71
conversation. *See* communication; verbal communication
conversion disorders, 436–437
coordination, in groups, 191, 192
coping, 74, 84, 96–97, 346
    constructive, 103–116
    defensive, 101–103
    defined, 78
    maladaptive, 97–103
coronary heart disease, 393–394
correlation, 15, 17
correlational research, 14–17
correlation coefficient, 15–16
corticosteriods, 76, 77
Cosby, Bill, 200
counseling psychologists, 460
counselors, 461
counterconditioning, 472
courtship, 248
cover letter, 355
"crack," 416
cramming, for exams, 23
"crank," 416
credibility, 200, 201
crime, gender and, 277
crossed transactions, 266, 267

Freud's stages of, 37–39
Rogers's view of, 49
social learning view of, 46–47
personality disorders, 448–450
personality tests, 56–58
personality theories, 54
behavioral, 41–47
biological, 52–54
humanistic, 47–52
psychodynamic, 33–41
personality traits, 32–33, 58, 62, 146, 165
attractiveness and, 144
children's, and parenting style, 327
Eysenck's hierarchy of, 52
likable, 221
personal space, 163–164
person-centered therapy, 48
person perception, 130–133
inaccuracy in, 142–148
racial prejudice and, 147–148
persuasion, 199–202, 207
pessimism, 84–85
phallic stage, 38–39
phobias, 43, 434, 435, 471–472
phobic disorders, 433–434
physical attractiveness, 144–145, 219–221
persuasion and, 200
of psychiatric patients, 16
physical dependence, 415, 416, 419
physical fitness, 404–405
physical illness
aging and, 320–321
biopsychosocial model of, 392–393
drug abuse and, 416, 417, 418, 419
exercise and, 404
life changes and, 69–70
loneliness and, 234
nutrition and, 402
psychological factors in, 393, 436
psychosomatic, 436
reactions to, 408–410
social support and, 83
stress and, 7, 76, 81–82, 90, 346, 393–398
physiological arousal, 74–77, 79, 114
attraction and, 222–223
meditation and, 115
physiological needs, 50
physiological processes, as subject for
psychology, 11
"pink ghetto," 338
pituitary gland, 76, 77
placebo effects, 7
planning, 112–113, 192–193
playing hard to get, 225
pleasure needs, 340
pleasure principle, 34, 36
polarization, group, 193–194
pornography, 177, 366
positive reinforcement, 44
positive reinterpretation, 107–108
posttraumatic stress disorders, 80–81
posture, 162
poverty, 255
power, 187
in groups, 189–190
powerlessness, 71
practice, distributed, 23
preconscious, 35
predictability of events, 71
prejudice, 147–148
premarital sex, 375–376
premature ejaculation, 385–386, 387
premenstrual syndrome, 282
prenatal development, 363–364
prenatal hormones, 281–282
preoperational period, 309

preparatory grief, 323
preparedness, 435
pressure, 70
to conform, 202–203
to perform, 79
to succeed, 289
Pressure Inventory, 70
prevalence, of psychological disorders, 432–433
primacy effect, 146
primary appraisal, 66
primary process thinking, 34
problem solving
aging and, 322
systematic, 108–109
process planning, 192–193
productivity
aging and, 322
in groups, 191–193, 198, 199
stress and, 346
prognosis, 428
progress, paradox of, 2–5
progressive relaxation, 116
projection, 37
promiscuity, 263
proteins, 403
proxemics, 163
proximity, 223–224
Proxmire, William, 216
Prozac, 476
psilocybin, 417
psychiatric diagnosis system, 429, 430–432
psychiatric nurses, 461
psychiatric social workers, 461
psychiatrists, 460, 482
psychoactive drugs, 412–420
psychoanalysis, 34, 446, 458, 461–464, 479
modern, 464
psychoanalytic theory, 34–39, 40–41, 48
psychobabble, 8, 9
Psychobabble (Rosen), 9
psychodiagnosis, 430–432
psychodynamic therapies, 464
psychogenic amnesia, 438, 439
psychological dependence, 414, 415, 417, 418, 419
psychological disorders
Adler's view of, 39–40
attitudes toward, 456
classification of, 429, 430–432
drug abuse and, 417
Freud's view of, 39
gender and, 278–279
prevalence of, 432–433
recovery from, 469–470
self-disclosure and, 175
self-esteem and, 137
stereotypes of, 430
stress and, 81, 346
treatment for, 430, 459–460
See also abnormal behavior;
psychotherapy; *specific disorders*
psychological tests, 56–58, 350–352
psychologists, 460
psychology, 10–11
scientific method in, 12–17
theoretical diversity in, 54
Watson's view of, 41
psychopharmacotherapy, 475
psychosexual stages, 37–39
psychosis, 432
psychosocial crises, 312, 313–314
psychosomatic diseases, 81–82, 436
psychotherapists, 460–461
finding, 481–484
psychotherapy, 458

attitudes toward, 486, 487
behavioral approaches, 470–474
biomedical approaches, 474–479
eclectic approaches, 479–480
effectiveness of, 469–470, 474, 483
experience of, 484
gender and, 279
group, 468–469
insight approaches, 461–470
types of, 459
types of clients for, 459–460
Psychotherapy Maze, The (Ehrenberg &
Ehrenberg), 468
puberty, 307–308
pubic lice, 380
public self, 138–140, 142, 155
punishment, 45, 122–123, 283–284
as disciplinary measure, 328–329
physical, 328, 329

Q

quality of life, 2–5

R

race, eye contact and, 161
racial stereotypes, 143, 147–148
rage, 73
rape, 80, 146, 175–177
rational-emotive therapy, 105
rationalization, 37
rational thinking, 106–107
reactance, 210
reaction formation, 37
reading, as study skill, 20–21
reality principle, 34, 36
reasoning processes, 308–310
receiver, of communication, 159, 200, 201–202
reciprocity, in friendships, 224–225
reciprocity norm, 174, 175, 208–209
recreational drugs, 412–418
reference groups, 135, 138
reference power, 189
referencing gesture, 163
reflex, conditioned, 42
regression, 37
rehearsal, 23
reinforcement, 44–45, 120–123
in gender-role learning, 283–284
rejection, 152, 443
relationship-oriented leaders, 199
relationships
attraction and, 218–225
development of, 216–217
failure of, 232
friendship, 225–227
game playing in, 265–268
homosexual, 262–264
love, 227–233
quiz on, 272
romantic, 227–233, 367
sexual, 366–370, 383–387
social exchange in, 217–218
successful, 232–233
relaxation, 407
in systematic desensitization, 471–472
relaxation response, 116
relaxation techniques, 115–116
reliability, test, 57
religion, 4, 5, 323, 368
remarriage, 260–261
REM sleep, 405–406
repression, 37, 103
research, scientific, 12–17
resistance, 75, 76, 77, 463, 484

Credits

FIGURES

Chapter 1

3: *Figure 1.1:* From *Compendium of American Public Opinion*, by Dennis A Gilbert, p. 290. Copyright © 1987 by Dennis A. Gilbert. Reprinted with the permission of Facts on File, Inc., New York; **4:** *Figure 1.2:* Adapted from "Gallup Poll," January 16, 1986 in *Compendium of American Public Opinion*, by Dennis A Gilbert, p. 308. Copyright © 1987 by Dennis A. Gilbert. Reprinted with the permission of Facts on File, Inc., New York; **10:** *Figure 1.3:* From "Rx: 2 Self-Help Books and Call Me in the Morning," by E. Stark, *Psychology Today*, June 1989, p. 26. Reprinted by permission from *Psychology Today Magazine*. Copyright © 1989 (PT Partners, L. P.); **17:** *Figure 1.8:* Data from "The Consequences of Changing Initial Answers on Objective Tests: A Stable Effect and a Stable Misconception," by G. R. Stoffer, K. E. Davis, & J. B. Brown, Jr., 1977, *Journal of Education Research, 70,* 272–277. Reprinted by permission; **23:** *Figure 1.11:* Adapted from *The Psychology of College Success: A Dynamic Approach*, by permission of H. C. Lindgren, 1969. **24:** *Figure 1.12:* Adapted from "Narrative Stories as Mediators of Serial Learning," by G. H. Bower & M. C. Clark, 1969, *Psychonomic Science, 14,* 181–182. Copyright © 1969 by the Psychonomic Society. Adapted by permission of the Psychonomic Society; **25:** *Figure 1.13:* Adapted from "Analysis of a Mnemonic Device," by G. H. Bower, 1970, *American Scientist* (September–October) *58,* 496–499. Copyright © 1970 by American Scientist. Reprinted by permission.

Chapter 2

33: *Figure 2.1:* From "Validation of the Five-Factor Model of Personality across Instruments and Observers," by R. R. McCrae and P. T. Costa, Jr., 1987, *Journal of Personality and Social Psychology, 52*(1), 81–90. Reprinted by permission of the author; **51:** *Figure 2.13:* Adapted from *Personality: Theory, Research and Application*, by C. R. Potkay & B. P. Allen, p. 246, 1986. Copyright © 1986 by Wadsworth, Inc. Adapted by permission of Brooks/Cole Publishing Company; **52:** *Figure 2.14:* From H. J. Eysenck, *The Biological Basis of Personaltiy* (1st ed.), p. 36, 1967. Courtesy of Charles C Thomas, Publisher, Springfield, IL; **58:** *Figure 2.17:* From R. B. Cattell in *Psychology Today*, July 1973, 40–46. Reprinted with permission from *Psychology Today Magazine*. Copyright © 1973 (PT Partners, L. P.); **60:** *Questionnaire:* From "Measurement of Social-Evaluation Anxiety," by D. Watson & R. Friend, *Journal of Consulting and Clinical Psychology, 33*(4), 448–457. Copyright 1969 by the American Psychological Association. Reprinted by permisson.

Chapter 3

69: *Figure 3.3:* From "The Social Readjustment Rating Scale," by T. H. Holmes & R. H. Rahe, 1967, *Journal of Psychosomatic Research, 11,* 213–218. Copyright © 1967 by Pergamon Press, Inc. Adapted by permission; **71:** *Figure 3.5:* Adapted from "Controllable and Uncontrollable Stress in Humans: Alterations in Mood and Neuroendocrine and Psychophysiological Function," by Alan Breier, et al., 1987, *American Journal of Psychiatry, 144*(11), 1423. Copyright 1987, the American Psychiatric Association. Reprinted by permission; **73:** *Figure 3.7:* Based on art in "Language for Emotions," by R. Plutchik, 1980, *Psychology Today, 13*(9), 68–78. Reprinted with permission from *Psychology Today Magazine*. Copyright © 1980 (PT Partners, L. P.); **77:** *Figure 3.10:* Adapted from *The Stress of Life*, by Hans Selye, p. 121, 1956. Copyright © 1956 by McGraw-Hill, Inc. Adapted by permission; **79:** *Figure 3.13:* Based on "Paradoxical Effects of Supportive Audiences on Performance under Pressure: The Home Field Disadvantages in Sports Championships," by R. F. Baumeister and A. Steinhilber, 1984, *Journal of Personality and Social Psychology, 47*(1), 85–93. Copyright © 1984 by the American Psychological Association. Adapted by permission; **88–90:** *Figures 3.15 and 3.16:* From "Assessing the Impact of Life Changes," by I. G. Sarason, H. M. Levine, & B. R. Sarason. In T. Millon, C. Green, & R. Meagher (Eds.), *Handbook of Clinical Health Psychology*, pp. 366–400. Copyright 1982 by Plenum Publishing Corporation. Reprinted by permission; **92:** *Questionnaire:* Sensation-Seeking Scale, pp. 45–47, from *Sensation Seeking: Beyond the Optimal Level of Arousal*, by M. Zukerman (512-6). Copyright 1979 by Lawrence Erlbaum Associates, Inc. Reprinted by permission.

Chapter 4

96: *Figure 4.1:* From "Assessing Coping Strategies: A Theoretically Based Approach," by C. S. Carver, M. F. Scheier, & J. K. Weintraub, 1989, *Journal of Personality and Social Psychology, 56*(2), 267–283. Copyright 1989 by the American Psychological Association. Reprinted by permission; **99:** *Figure 4.2:* Adapted from "The Effects of Three Types of Aggression on Vascular Processes," by J. E. Hokanson & M. Burgess, 1962, *Journal of Abnormal and Social Psychology, 65,* 446–449. Copyright 1962 by the American Psychological Association. Adapted by permission; **101:** *Figure 4.3:* Adapted from *Abnormal Psychology and Modern Life* (8th ed.), by R. C. Carson, J. N. Butcher, & J. C. Coleman, pp. 64–65, 1988. Copyright © 1988 by Scott, Foresman and Company. Adapted by permission; **102:** *Figure 4.4:* Adapted from *Adaptation to Life*, by George E. Vaillant. Copyright © 1977 by George E. Vaillant. By permission of Little, Brown and Company; **107:** *Figure 4.7:* Adapted from "Sense of Humor as a Moderator of the Relation between Stressors and Moods," by R. A. Martin & H. M. Lefcourt, 1983, Journal of *Personality and Social Psychology, 45*(6), 1313–1324. Copyright 1983 by the American Psychological Association. Adapted by permission; **110:** *Figure 4.8:* LeBoeuf, "Managing Time Means Managing Yourself," Questionnaire, p. 45. Reprinted from *Business Horizons Magazine*, February 1980. Copyright 1980 by the Foundation for the School of Business at Indiana University. Used with permission; **115:** *Figure 4.11:* (Based on illustration on p. 86 by Lorelle A. Raboni of *Scientific American, 226,* 85–90, February 1972.) From "The Psychology of Meditation," by R. K. Wallace & H. Bensen. Copyright © 1972 by Scientific American, Inc. All rights reserved; **116:** *Quote:* From pp. 114–115 in *The Relaxation Response*, by Herbert Benson with Miriam Z. Klipper. Copyright © 1975 by William Morrow and Company, Inc. By permission of William Morrow and Company, Inc.; **121:** *Figure 4.14:* From *Self-Directed Behavior: Self-Modification for Personal Adjustment* (4th ed.), by D. L. Watson & R. L. Tharp, p. 182. Copyright © 1972, 1977, 1981, 1985 by Wadsworth, Inc. Reprinted by permission of Brooks/Cole Publishing Company; **126:** *Questionnaire:* Self-Control Schedule, pp. 63–65, from "A Schedule of Assessing Self-Control Behaviors: Preliminary Findings," by M. Rosenbaum, 1980, *Behavior Therapy, 11,* 109–121. Copyright 1980 Association for Advancement of Behavior Therapy. Reprinted by permission of the publisher and the author.

Chapter 5

130: *Figure 5.1:* From "Perceiving the Causes of Success and Failure," by B. Weiner, I. Frieze, A. Kukla, L. Reed, & R. M. Rosenbaum. In E. E. Jones, D. E. Kanuouse, H. H. Kelly, R. E. Nisbett, S. Valins, & B. Weiner (Eds.), *Perceiving Causes of Behavior*, 1972, General Learning Press. Reprinted by permission of the author; **136:** *Figure 5.4:* Based on "Self-Concept: Validation of Construct Interpretations," by R. J. Shavelson et al., 1976, *Review of Educational Research, 46,* 407–411. Copyright © 1976 by the American Educational Research Association. Adapted by permission of the publisher; **137:** *Figure 5.5:* Adapted from "Studies in Self-Esteem," by S. Coopersmith, *Scientific American*, February 1968, from illustration on p. 106. Adapted by permission; **140:** *Figure 5.6:* Adapted from "Identity in Adolescence," by J. E. Marcia, 1980. In J. Adelson (Ed.), *Handbook of Adolescent Psychology*, pp. 159–210. Copyright 1980 by John Wiley & Sons, Inc.; **154:** *Questionnaire:* From "Self-Monitoring of Excessive Behavior," by M. Snyder, 1974, *Journal of Personality and Social Psychology, 330,*

526–537. Copyright 1974 by the American Psychological Association. Reprinted by permission.

Chapter 6

160: *Figure 6.2:* From *Unmasking the Face,* by P. Ekman & W. V. Friesens, Consulting Psychologists Press. Copyright © 1984. Courtesy of Paul Ekman; **161:** *Figure 6.3:* Adapted from "Explorations in the Process of Person Perception: Visual Interaction in Relation to Competition, Sex, and Need for Affiliation," by R. Exline, 1963, *Journal of Personality, 31,* p. 11. Copyright 1963 by Duke University. Reprinted by permission of the author and the American Psychological Association; **163:** *Figure 6.4:* Adapted from *Eye to Eye: How People Interact,* by Peter Marsh, 1988, p. 89. Copyright Salem House Publishers, Topsfield, MA; **179:** *Figure 6.9:* Adapted from David W. Johnson, *Reaching Out: Interpersonal Effectiveness and Self-Actualization* (2nd ed.), © 1981, p. 204. Reprinted by permisson of Prentice-Hall, Englewood Cliffs, NJ; **183:** *Questionnaire:* From "Opener: Individuals Who Elicit Intimate Self-Disclosure," by L. C. Miller, J. H. Berg, & R. L. Archer, 1983, *Journal of Personality and Social Psychology, 6,* 123–124. Copyright 1983 by the American Psychological Association. Reprinted by permission.

Chapter 7

188: *Figure 7.1:* Adapted from "Functional Roles of Group Members," by K. D. Benne & P. Sheats, 1948, *Journal of Social Issues, 4*(2), 41–49; **189:** *Figure 7.3:* Adapted from "The Bases of Social Power," by J. R. P. French, Jr., & B. Raben, 1959. In D. Cartwright (Ed.), *Studies in Social Power,* Institute for Social Research; **190:** *Figure 7.4:* Adapted from "Bystander Intervention in Emergencies: Diffusion of Responsibility," by J. M. Darley & B. Latané, 1968, *Journal of Personality and Social Psychology, 8,* 377–383. Copyright © 1968 by the American Psychological Association. Adapted by permission; **192:** *Figure 7.5:* Adapted from "Many Hands Make Light the Work: The Causes and Consequences of Social Loafing," by B. Latané, K. Williams, & S. Harkins, 1979, *Journal of Personality and Social Psychology, 37,* 822–832. Copyright © 1979 by the American Psychological Association. Adapted by permission; **195:** *Figure 7.7:* Adapted with permission of The Free Press, a Division of Macmillan, Inc., from *Decision Making: A Psychological Analysis of Conflict, Choice and Commitment,* by Irving L. Janis & Leon Mann. Copyright © 1977 by The Free Press; **198:** *Figure 7.8:* From *Social Psychology,* by D. R. Forsyth, p. 506. Copyright © 1987 by Wadsworth, Inc., by permission of Brooks/Cole Publishing Company; **199:** *Figure 7.9:* Adapted from *Social Psychology,* by N. Deaux & L R. Wrightman, 1988, p. 186, based on data from B. G. Rule, G. L. Bisanz, & M. Kohn, 1985, *Journal of Personality and Social Psychology, 48,* 1127–1140; **202–203:** *Figures 7.11 and 7.12:* (Adapted from illustrations by Sarah Love on pp. 35 and 32, *Scientific American,* November 1955.) From "Opinion and Social Pressure," by Solomon Asch. Copyright © 1955 by Scientific American, Inc. All rights reserved; **204:** *Figure 7.13:* Copyright 1965 by Stanley Milgram, from the film *Obedience,* distributed by the New York University Film Division and the Pennsylvania State University, PCR. By permission of the Estate of Stanley Milgram; **210:** *Figure 7.15:*

Data from "The Effects of Severity on Initiation on Liking for a Group," by E. Aronson & J. Mills, 1959, *Journal of Abnormal and Social Psychology, 59,* 177–181; **213:** *Questionnaire:* From "A Conceptualization and Measure of Argumentiveness," by D. A. Infante & A. S. Rancer, 1982, *Journal of Personality Assessment, 46,* 72–80. Copyright © Lawrence Erlbaum Associates, Inc. Reprinted by permission.

Chapter 8

217: *Figure 8.1:* Adapted by permission from "A 3-Level Approach to Attraction: Toward an Understanding of Pair Relatedness," by G. Levinger, 1974. In T. L. Huston (Ed.), *Foundations of Interpersonal Attraction.* Copyright Academic Press; **218:** *Figure 8.2:* From "Men and Women Report Their Views on Masculinity," by Carol Tavris. *Psychology Today,* January 1977, p. 37. Reprinted with permission from *Psychology Today Magazine.* Copyright © 1977 (PT Partners, L. P.); **221:** *Figure 8.4:* From "Likableness Ratings of 555 Personality Trait Words," by N. H. Anderson, 1968, *Journal of Personality and Social Psychology, 9,* 272–279. Copyright 1968 by the American Psychological Association. Reprinted by permission; **224:** *Figure 8.5:* Adapted from "Interactional Approach to Interpersonal Attraction," by M. H. Gonzales, J. M. Davis, G. L. Loney, C. K. Lukens, & C. H. Junghans, 1983, *Journal of Personaltiy and Social Psychology, 44,* 1191–1197. Copyright 1983 by the American Psychological Association. Adapted by permission; **225:** *Figure 8.6:* From "The Friendship Bond," by Mary Brown Parlee and the Editors of *Psychology Today, 13*(4), 49. Reprinted with permission of *Psychology Today Magazine.* Copyright 1979 (PT Partners, L. P.); **225:** *Figure 8.7:* Adapted from "The Rules of Friendship," by M. Argyle & M. Henderson, 1984, *Journal of Social and Personal Relationships, 1,* 211–237; **229:** *Figure 8.8:* From "A Triangular Theory of Love," by R. J. Sternberg, 1986, *Psychological Review, 93,* 119–135. Copyright 1986 by the American Psychological Association. Reprinted by permission; **233:** *Figure 8.10:* Adapted from "Breakups before Marriage: The End of 103 Affairs," by C. T. Hill, Z. Rubin, & L. A. Peplau, 1976, *Journal of Social Issues, 32,* 147–168. Basic Books Publishing Co., Inc. Adapted by permission of the author. All rights reserved; **235:** *Figure 8.11:* From paper presented at the annual convention of the American Psychological Association, September 2, 1979. An expanded version of this paper appears in *New Directions in Cognitive Therapy,* edited by Emery, Hollon, & Bedrosian, Guilford Press, 1981, and in *Loneliness: A Sourcebook of Current Theory, Research and Therapy,* by L. A. Peplau and D. Perlman (Eds.). Copyright 1982 by John Wiley & Sons, Inc. Reprinted by permission of John Wiley & Sons, Inc., and Jeffrey Young; **237:** *Figure 8.12:* From P. Zimbardo, *Shyness.* Copyright © 1990 by Philip Zimbardo, Inc. Reprinted with permission of Addison-Wesley Publishing Co., Inc., Reading, MA; **241:** *Questionnaire:* From "The Experiencing of Loneliness," by Carin Rubenstein and Phillip Shafer, 1982. By permission of Dr. Carin Rubenstein.

Chapter 9

244: *Figure 9.1:* Data from U.S. Bureau of the Census, *Current Population Reports,* Series P-20, No. 412, "Households, Families, Marital Status

and Living Arrangements," March 1986 (Advance Report), Washington, DC: U.S. Government Printing Office, p. 4; **246:** *Figure 9.2:* Adapted from Peter J. Stein, "Singlehood: An Alternative to Marriage," *The Family Coordinator, 24*(4), 500. Copyright 1975 by the National Council on Family Relations, 3989 Central Ave., N.E., Suite 550, Minneapolis, MN 55421. Reprinted by permission; **249:** *Figure 9.4:* Based on "Marital Satisfaction over the Family Life Cycle," by Boyd C. Rollins and Harold Feldman. *Journal of Marriage and the Family, 32* (February 1970): 25. Copyright 1975 by the National Council on Family Relations, 3989 Central Ave., N.E., Suite 550, Minneapolis, MN 55421. Reprinted by permission; **253:** *Figure 9.5:* Adapted from "A Residue of Tradition: Jobs, Careers and Spouses' Time in Housework," by Donna H. Berardo, Constance L. Shehan, & Gerald R. Leslie. *Journal of Marriage and the Family, 49* (May 1987): 381–390. Copyright 1987 by the National Council on Family Relations, 3989 Central Ave., N.E., Suite 550, Minneapolis, MN 55421. Reprinted by permission; **255:** *Figure 9.6:* From *Progress on Family Problems: A Nationwide Study of Clients' and Counselors' Views on Family Agency Services,* by Dorothy Fahs Beck and Mary Ann Jones, by permission of the publisher. Copyright 1973 by Family Service America, New York; **258:** *Figure 9.7:* From Andrew Cherlin, 1981, *Marriage, Divorce, Remarriage.* Copyright 1981 by Harvard University Press. Reprinted by permission: **261:** *Figure 9.8:* Data from Glick & Norton, 1979. Population Reference Bureau, Washington, DC: U.S. Bureau of the Census; **262:** *Figure 9.9:* Data from the U.S. Bureau of the Census; **266–267:** *Figures 9.10, 9.11, and 9.12:* From (Figures 6.6, p. 241, 6.7, p. 242, and 6.8, p. 243) *Practical Applications of Psychology* (2nd ed.), by Anthony F. Grasha. Copyright © 1983 by Anthony Grasha. Reprinted by permission of HarperCollinsPublishers; **270:** *Questionnaire:* From "Measuring the Intensity of Jealous Relationships," by R. Bringle, S. Roach, C. Andler, & S. Evenbeck, 1979, *Catalogue of Selected Documents in Psycholoy, 9,* 23–24. Copyright 1979 by Select Press, San Rafael, CA. Reprinted by permission.

Chapter 10

275: *Figure 10.2:* Adapted from Table 1 of "Sex Role Stereotypes: A Current Appraisal," by I. K. Broverman, S. R. Vogel, D. M. Broverman, F. E. Clarkson, & P. S. Rosenkrantz, 1972, *Journal of Social Issues, 28,* 63. By permission of SPSSI and the author; **277:** *Figure 10.3:* Data from *1987 FBI Uniform Crime Reports*; **279:** *Figure 10.5:* From *Social Psychology,* by John C. Brigham, Table 10-4, p. 336. Copyright © 1986 by John C. Brigham. Reprinted by permission of HarperCollinsPublishers; **285:** *Figure 10.6:* Adapted from "Children, Gender and Social Structure: An Analysis of the Contents of Letters to Santa Claus," by J. G. Richardson & C. H. Simpson, 1982, *Child Development, 53,* 429–436. Copyright © 1982 by The Society for Research in Child Development, Inc. Adapted by permission; **290:** *Figure 10.7:* From U.S. Department of Labor, *Handbook of Labor Statistics,* 1989; **300:** *Questionnaire:* From "The College Self-Expression Scale: A Measure of Assertiveness," by J. P. Galassi, J. S. DeLo, M. D. Galassi, & S. Bastien, 1974, *Behavior Therapy, 5,* 165–171. Copyright 1974 by Academic Press. Reprinted by permission.

Chapter 11

312: *Figure 11.4:* Adapted from *Childhood and Society*, by Erik H. Erikson, by permission of W. W. Norton & Company, Inc. Copyright © 1950, © 1963 by W. W. Norton & Co., Inc. Copyright renewed by Erik H. Erikson; **317:** *Figure 11.6:* Adapted from "Structure of the Self-Concept from Adolescence through Old Age," by R. Monge, 1975, *Experimental Aging Research, 1*(2), 281–291. Copyright © Beech Hill Publishing Company (1975). Reprinted by permission; **318:** *Figure 11.7:* Adapted from *Growing Old*, by Elaine Cumming and William E. Henry. © 1961 by Basic Books, Inc., Publishing Company. Reprinted by permission of Basic Books, Inc., Publishers, New York; **320:** *Figure 11.8:* Data from "Chronic Conditions and Liminations of Activity and Mobility: United States, July 1965 to June 1967," by C. S. Wilder. In *U.S. Vital and Health Statistics, 1971, 10*(6); **322:** *Figure 11.9:* Based on data from "Creative Productivity between the Ages of 20 and 80 Years," by W. Dennis, 1966, *Journal of Gerontology, 21*(1), 1–8. Copyright © 1966 the Gerontological Society of America. Adapted by permission; **327:** *Figure 11.10:* Based on data from "Socialization Determinants of Personal Agency," a paper presented at the biennial meeting of the Society for Research in Child Development, New Orleans, 1977; **331:** *Questionnaire:* By permission of Donald I. Templer, California School of Professional Psychology.

Chapter 12

334: *Figure 12.1:* Adapted from *Theories of Occupational Choice and Vocational Development*, by J. Zaccaria, pp. 51–52. Copyright © 1970 by Time Share Corporation, New Hampshire; **336:** *Figure 12.2:* Data from "Occupational Mobility of Workers," by James J. Byrne, *The Monthly Labor Review*, February 1975, and adapted from "Mid-Life Career Change," by S. Arbeiter, 1979, *AAHE Bulletin, 32*(2), 11–12; **338:** *Figure 12.3:* Adapted from K. A. Matthews and J. Rodin, 1989, *American Psychologist, 44*(11), 1391. Copyright by the American Psychological Association. Adapted by permission; **342:** *Figure 12.4:* From "What You Really Want from Your Job," by P. A. Renwick & E. E. Lawler, 1978, *Psychology Today, 11*(12), 56. Reprinted with permission of *Psychology Today Magazine*. Copyright © 1978 (PT Partners, L. P.); **345:** *Figure 12.6:* Adapted from *Psychology of Work Behavior* (4th ed.), by F. J. Landy, p. 638. Copyright © 1989 by Wadsworth, Inc., by permission of Brooks/Cole Publishing Company; **346:** *Figure 12.7:* Redrawn from "Job Decision Latitude, Job Demands, and Cardiovascular Disease: A Prospective Study of Swedish Men," by R. A. Karasek, D. Baker, F. Marxer, A. Ahlbom, T. Theorell, 1981, *American Journal of Public Health, 71*, 694–705. Reprinted by permission; **347:** *Figure 12.8:* From "Worksite Stress Management Interventions," by J. M. Ivancevich, M. T. Matteson, S. M. Freeman, & J. S. Phillips, 1990, *American Psychologist, 45*(2), 252–261. Reprinted by permission; **349:** *Figure 12.9:* From John L. Holland, *Making Vocational Choices: A Theory of Vocational Personalities and Work Environments* (2nd ed.), © 1985, pp. 19–23, 36–40. Adapted by permission of Prentice-Hall, Inc., Englewood Cliffs, NJ; **351:** *Figure 12.10:* Reproduced by special permission of the distributor, Consulting Psychologists Press, Inc., Palo Alto, CA, for the publisher, Stanford University Press, from the Strong Interest Inventory, Form T325 of the Strong Vocational Interest Blank, by E. K. Strong, Jr., Jo-Ida C. Hansen, & David P. Campbell. Copyright 1974, 1981, & 1985 by the Board of Trustees of Leland Standord Junior University; **352:** *Figure 12.11:* From "Wage Premiums for College Graduates: Recent Growth and Possible Explanations," by K. Murphy & F. Welch, 1989, *Educational Researcher, 18*(4), 19. Copyright © by American Educational Research Association. Reprinted by permission of the publisher; **356:** *Figure 12.12:* From *Job Search: Career Planning Guidebook*, Book II, by R. D. Lock. Copyright © 1988 by Wadsworth, Inc.; **359:** *Questionnaire:* Assertive Job-Hunting Survey (1980) by Heather Becker, Susan Brown, Pat Lafitte, Mary Jo Magruder, Bob Murff, & Bill Phillips. Instrument reproduced with permission of Heather Becker.

Chapter 13

363: *Figure 13.2:* Data from "Psychosocial Development of Heterosexual, Bisexual, and Homosexual Behavior," by P. H. Van Wyk & C. S. Geist, 1984, *Archives of Sexual Behavior, 13*(6), 505–544. Copyright 1984 by Plenum Publishing Corp. Used with permission; **364:** *Figure 13.3:* Reprinted with permission of PEI Books, Inc., from *Sexual Behavior in the 1970s*, by Morton Hunt. Copyright 1974 by Morton Hunt; **372:** *Figure 13.5:* From "The Erotic Fantasies of College Students during Coitus," by David Sue, 1979, *The Journal of Sex Research, 15*, 303. Reprinted by permission; **375:** *Figure 13.7:* Data from "Change in Sexual Attitudes and Behavior of College Students from 1965 to 1980: A Research Note," by I. E. Robinson & D. Jedlicka, 1982, *Journal of Marriage and the Family, 44*(1), 237–240. Copyright 1982 by the National Council on Family Relations, 3989 Central Ave., N.E., Suite 550, Minneapolis, MN 55421. Reprinted by permission; **376:** *Figure 13.8:* Reprinted with permisson of PEI Books, Inc., from *Sexual Behavior in the 1970s*, by Morton Hunt. Copyright 1974 by Morton Hunt; **377:** *Figure 13.9:* From James Trussell & Charles Westoff, "Contraceptive Practice and Trends in Coital Frequency." *Family Planning Perspectives, 12*(5) (September/October 1980), 248. © The Alan Guttmacher Institute. Reprinted by permission; **379:** *Figure 13.10:* Adapted from Table 19-1, p. 527, *Human Sexuality* (3rd ed.), by William H. Masters, et al. Copyright © 1988 by William H. Masters, Virgiania E. Johnson, and Robert C. Kolodny. Reprinted by permission of HarperCollinsPublishers; **380:** *Figure 13.11:* Adapted from *Our Sexuality*, by R. Crooks & K. Baur, 1990, pp. 636–638. Benjamin/Cummings Publishing Company. Copyright 1990 Addison-Wesley Publishing Co. Adapted by permission; **383:** *Figure 13.12:* Adapted from "Frenquency of Sexual Dysfunction in 'Normal' Couples," by E. Frank, C. Anderson, & D. Rubenstein, 1978, *The New England Journal of Medicine, 299*, 1111–1115. Copyright 1978 by The New England Journal of Medicine. Reprinted by permission; **386:** *Figure 13.14:* Adapted from *Human Sexuality*, by W. H. Masters, V. E. Johnson, & R. C. Kolodny, 1988, p. 527. Copyright 1988 by Scott, Foresman and Company. Adapted by permission; **389:** *Questionnaire:* From "The Sexuality Scale: An Instrument to Measure Sexual-Esteem, Sexual-Depression, and Sexual-Preoccupation," by W. E. Snell & D. R. Papini, 1989, *Journal of Sex Research, 26*(2), 256–263. Society for Scientific Study of Sex. Reprinted by permission of the author.

Chapter 14

399: *Figure 14.7:* Adapted from "Associative Learning, Habit and Health Behavior," by W. A. Hunt, J. D. Matarazzo, S. M. Weiss, & W. D. Gentry, 1979, *Journal of Behavioral Medicine, 2*(2), 113. Copyright © 1979 by the Plenum Publishing Corp. Adapted by permission; **400:** *Figure 14.8:* Data from "Obesity: Adverse Effects on Health and Longevity," by T. B. Van Itallie, 1979, *American Journal of Clinical Nutrition, 32*, 2727; **404:** *Figure 14.10:* Based on data taken from "Physical Fitness and All-Cause Mortality," by S. N. Blair, H. W. Kohl, R. S. Paffenbarger, D. G. Clark, K. H. Cooper, & L. W. Gibbons, 1989, *Journal of American Medical Association, 262*, 2395–2401; **405:** *Figure 14.11:* Adapted from "How Different Sports Rate in Promoting Physical Fitness," by C. C. Conrad, *Medical Times*, May 1976, 4–5. Copyright 1976 by Romaine Pierson Publishers. Reprinted by permission; **408:** *Figure 14.14:* Adapted from "A Three-City Comparison of the Public's Knowledge and Attitudes about AIDS," by L. Temoshok, D. M. Sweet, & J. Zich, 1987, *Psychology & Health, 1*(1), 43–60. Copyright © 1987 by Harwood Academic Publishers GmbH. Adapted by permission; **415:** *Figure 14.17:* From *Barbiturates: Their Use, Misuse and Abuse*, by D. R. Wesson & D. E. Smith, 1977. Copyright 1977 by Human Sciences Press. Reprinted by permission; **422:** *Questionnaire:* From "Chronic Self-Destructiveness: Conceptualization, Measurement, and Initial Validation of the Construct," by K. Kelley, D. Bryne, D. P. J. Przybyla, C. Eberly, B. Eberly, V. Greendlinger, C. K. Wan, & J. Gorsky, 1985, *Motivation and Emotion, 9*(2). Copyright 1985 by Plenum Publishing Company. Reprinted by permission.

Chapter 15

431: *Figure 15.3:* Adapted and reprinted with permisson from the *Diagnostic and Statistical Manual of Mental Disorders*, Third Edition, Revised. Copyright © 1987 American Psychiatric Association; **434:** *Figure 15.5:* From *Fears & Phobias*, by I. M. Marks, 1969. Academic Press. Copyright 1969 by Isaac Marks. Reprinted by permission; **441:** *Figure 15.9:* From Sarason/Sarason, *Abnormal Psychology: The Problem of Maladaptive Behavior* (5th ed.), © 1987, p. 283. Reprinted by permission of Prentice-Hall, Inc., Englewood Cliffs, NJ; **447:** *Figure 15.12:* Adapted from "Clues to the Genetics and Neurobiology of Schizophrenia," by S. E. Nichol & I. I. Gottesman, 1983, *American Scientist, 71*, 398–404. Copyright © 1983 by Sigma Xi. Adapted by permission; **451:** *Figure 15.14:* Adapted from "Epidemiology of Disorders in Adulthood: Suicide," by C. K. Cross & R. M. A. Hirschfeld. In G. L. Klerman, M. M. Weissman, P. S. Appelbaum, & L. H. Roth (Eds.), *Psychiatry, Vol. 5, Social Epidemiologic and Legal Psychiatry*, 245–260, 1986, Basic Books. Adapted by permission of J. B. Lippincott Company, New York; **451:** *Figure 15.15:* Adapted from "Suicide and Depression among College Students," by J. S. Westefeld & S. R. Furr, 1987, *Professional Psychology: Research and Practice, 18*, 119–123. Copyright 1987 by the American Psychological Association. Adapted by permission; **452:** *Figure 15.16:* Adapted from "Suicide, Attempted Suicide and Relapse Rates in Depression," by D. Avery & G. Winokur, 1978, *Archives of General Psychiatry* (June), *35*, 749–753. Copyright 1978 by the American Medical Association. Adapted by permission; **455:** *Questionnaire:* From "A Personality Scale of Manifest Anxiety," by J. A. Taylor, 1953, *Journal of Abnormal and Social Psychology, 48*, 285–290.

Chapter 16

464: *Figure 16.3:* Adapted from "Psychoanalysis and Psychoanalytic Therapy," by E. L. Baker. In S. J. Lynn & J. P. Garske (Eds.), *Contemporary Psychotherapies: Models and Methods*, p. 52. Copyright © 1985 Merrill Publishing Co., Columbus, OH. Adapted by permission; **472:** *Figure 16.4:* From *Methods of Self-Change: An ABC Primer*, by K. E. Rudestam, pp. 42–43, 1980. Copyright © 1980 by Wadsworth, Inc. Reprinted by permission of Brooks/Cole Publishing Company; **475:** *Figure 16.7:* From data in NIMH-PSC Collaborative Study I and reported in "Drugs in the Treatment of Psychosis," by J. O. Cole, S. C. Goldberg, & J. M. Davis, 1966. In P. Solomon (Ed.), *Psychiatric Drugs*, Grune & Stratton. By permission of the author; **483:** *Figure 16.12:* Adapted from "Meta Analysis of Psychotherapy Outcome Series," by M. L. Smith & G. V. Glass, 1977, *American Psychologist, 32* (September), 752–760. Copyright © 1977 by the American Psychological Association. Adapted by permission; **486:** *Questionnaire:* From "Orientations to Seeking Professional Help: Development and Research Utility of an Attitude Scale," by E. H. Fisher & J. L. Turner, 1970, *Journal of Consulting and Clinical Psychology, 35*, 82–83. Copyright 1970 by the American Psychological Association. Reprinted by permission.

PHOTOGRAPHS

All chapter-opening photographs by Joan Vanderschuit, © 1990.

Chapter 1

2: © David R. Frazier/Photo Researchers, Inc.; **7:** © Craig McClain Photography.

Chapter 2

34: The Granger Collection; **39:** © 1990 Alan Carey/The Image Works; **42:** The Bettmann Archive; **45:** (left) Courtesy, B. F. Skinner, (right) © Sepp Seitz/Woodfin Camp & Associates. All rights reserved.

Chapter 3

64: Courtesy, Richard Lazarus; **76:** © Karsh/Ottowa/Woodfin Camp & Associates. All rights reserved; **80:** © Jim Stratford/Black Star; **84:** © Oli Tennent/TSW-Click/Chicago.

Chapter 4

98: © Larry Kolvoord/The Image Works; **105:** Courtesy, Albert Ellis; **111:** © Bill Bachmann/The Image Works; **116:** (left) © Gerd Ludwig/Woodfin Camp & Associates. All rights reserved, (right) By permission of Herbert Benson, photograph © 1990 Michael Lutch.

Chapter 5

132: Courtesy New School for Social Research, photo by Karen Zebulon © 1982; **134:** © Craig McClain Photography; **138:** © James Kamp 1988/Black Star; **139:** courtesy, Mark Snyder, photo by John Sheretz 1990; **144:** © Craig McClain Photography; **148:** © Richard Choy/Peter Arnold, Inc.

Chapter 6

162: (top) © Paul H. Henning 1987/Third Coast Stock Source, (bottom) © R. Drechsler/Third Coast Stock Source; **166:** © Lester Sloan 1988/Woodfin Camp & Associates; **170:** © Henley and Savage/TSW-Click/Chicago.

Chapter 7

186: (left) © Ch. Petit/Agence Vandystadt/Photo Researchers, Inc., (right) © Bob Daemmrich/Stock, Boston; **187:** © Jim Pickerell 1986/Black Star; **199:** Courtesy, Fred D. Fiedler; **200:** © Ray Pfortner/Peter Arnold, Inc.; **205:** (left) Courtesy, the Milgram Estate, (right) © Eric Kroll 1982, courtesy, the Milgram Estate.

Chapter 8

216: Courtesy, Ellen Berscheid; **220:** Jon Gray/TSW-Click/Chicago; **223:** © J. Villegier/Explorer/Photo Researchers, Inc.; **226:** © 1990 Jerry Howard/Positive Images; **227:** © EXROY/Explorer/Photo Researchers, Inc.; **230:** © Jon Feingersh 1988/Stock, Boston; **231:** Courtesy, Elaine Hatfield; **239:** Courtesy, Philip Zimbardo, photo © Sydney R. Goldstein.

Chapter 9

247: © Ken Fisher/TSW-Click/Chicago; **250:** © Erika Stone 1988; **257:** © Matthew McVay/SABA; **263:** © Eve Arnold/Magnum Photos.

Chapter 10

279: Courtesy, Janet Shibley Hyde; **280:** © A. Glauberman/Photo Researchers, Inc.; **282:** (left) © Jerry Howard/Stock, Boston, (right) © Rick Kopstein 1988/Monkmeyer Press Photo; **283:** Courtesy, Alice Eagly; **292:** © Jerry Howard/Positive Images; **294:** Courtesy, Sandra Bem.

Chapter 11

304: © William Strode/Woodfin Camp & Associates; **308:** © Yves DiBraine/Black Star; **313:** Harvard University News Office; **316:** © Chuck Keeler/TSW-Click/Chicago; **321:** (left) © Jacques M. Chenet/Woodfin Camp & Associates, (right) © Dan Budnik 1983/Woodfin Camp & Associates; **323:** AP/Wide World Photos; **328:** © Peter L. Chapman/Stock, Boston.

Chapter 12

339: © Robert McElroy 1985/Woodfin Camp & Associates; **341:** © Michael Abramson 1989/Woodfin Camp & Associates; **357:** © Julie Houck/TSW-Click/Chicago.

Chapter 13

365: AP/Wide World Photos; **367:** © 1990 Craig McClain Photography; **371:** AP/Wide World Photos.

Chapter 14

410: © 1986 Blair Seitz/Photo Researchers, Inc.; **416:** © Ken Gaghan/Jeroboam, Inc.

Chapter 15

426: Culver Pictures, Inc.; **427:** Courtesy, Thomas Szasz, photo by Joel Siegel/Varden; **430:** Courtesy, David Rosenhan; **439:** © Bruce Davidson/Magnum Photos; **446:** Courtesy, Nancy C. Andreasen.

Chapter 16

462: © Louis Fernandez/Black Star; **466:** Courtesy, Aaron T. Beck; **467, 470:** © Erika Stone; **471:** Courtesy, Joseph Wolpe; **478:** © Will McIntyre/Photo Researchers, Inc.

TO THE OWNER OF THIS BOOK:

We hope that you have found *Psychology Applied to Modern Life: Adjustment in the 90s, Third Edition,* useful. So that this book can be improved in a future edition, would you take the time to complete this sheet and return it? Thank you.

School and address: _____

Department: _____

Instructor's name: _____

1. What I like most about this book is: _____

_____

2. What I like least about this book is: _____

_____

3. My general reaction to this book is: _____

_____

4. The name of the course in which I used this book is: _____

_____

5. Were all of the chapters of the book assigned for you to read? _____

   If not, which ones weren't? _____

6. In the space below, or on a separate sheet of paper, please write specific suggestions for improving this book and anything else you'd care to share about your experience in using the book.

_____

_____

_____

_____

_____

_____

_____

_____

Optional:

Your name: _____   Date: _____

May Brooks/Cole quote you, either in promotion for *Psychology Applied to Modern Life: Adjustment in the 90s, Third Edition*, or in future publishing ventures?

Yes: _____   No: _____

Sincerely,

Wayne Weiten
Margaret A. Lloyd
Robin L. Lashley